#371   9.18

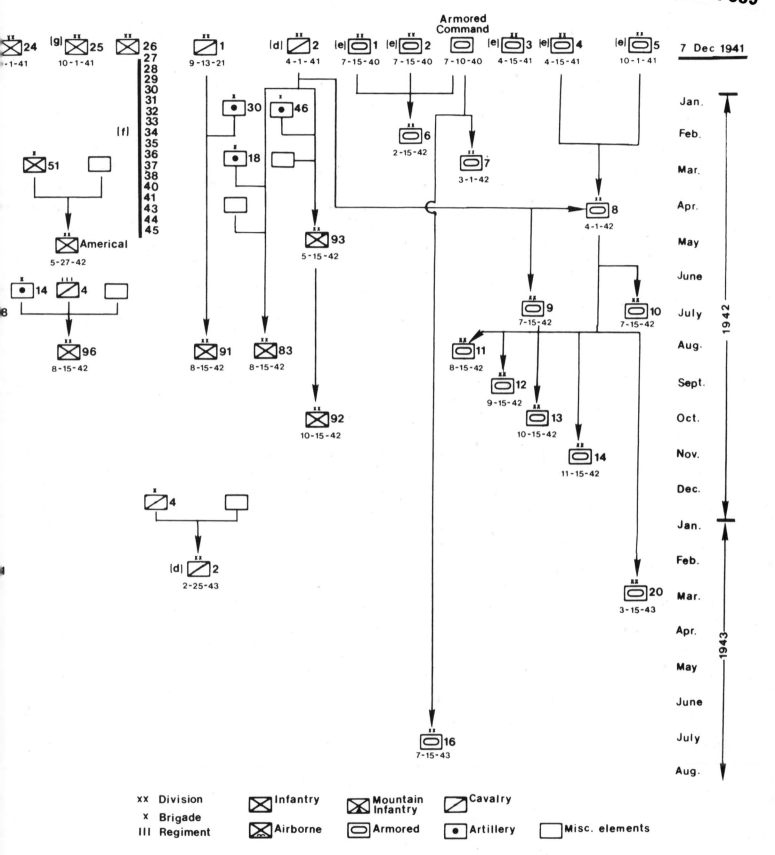

Armored Command

7 Dec 1941

xx	Division	
x	Brigade	
III	Regiment	

Infantry   Mountain Infantry   Cavalry

Airborne   Armored   Artillery   Misc. elements

Jan. Feb. Mar. Apr. May June July Aug. Sept. Oct. Nov. Dec.

1942

Jan. Feb. Mar. Apr. May June July Aug.

1943

ARMY DIVISIONS

1ST INFANTRY

2ND INFANTRY

3RD INFANTRY

5TH INFANTRY

4TH INFANTRY

6TH INFANTRY

7TH INFANTRY

8TH INFANTRY

9TH INFANTRY

10TH MOUNTAIN

11TH AIRBORNE

13TH AIRBORNE

17TH AIRBORNE

AMERICAL

24TH INFANTRY

25TH INFANTRY

26TH INFANTRY

ARMY DIVISIONS

27TH INFANTRY

28TH INFANTRY

29TH INFANTRY

30TH INFANTRY

31ST INFANTRY

32ND INFANTRY

33RD INFANTRY

34TH INFANTRY

35TH INFANTRY

36TH INFANTRY

37TH INFANTRY

38TH INFANTRY

39TH INFANTRY
(Not Active)

40TH INFANTRY

41ST INFANTRY

42ND INFANTRY

43RD INFANTRY

44TH INFANTRY

45TH INFANTRY

63RD INFANTRY

ARMY DIVISIONS

65TH DIVISION

66TH INFANTRY
(1st Design)

66TH INFANTRY

69TH INFANTRY

70TH INFANTRY

71ST INFANTRY

75TH INFANTRY

76TH INFANTRY

77TH INFANTRY

78TH INFANTRY

79TH INFANTRY

80TH INFANTRY

81ST INFANTRY

82ND AIRBORNE

83RD INFANTRY

84TH INFANTRY

85TH INFANTRY

86TH INFANTRY

87TH INFANTRY

88TH INFANTRY

ARMY DIVISIONS

89TH INFANTRY   90TH INFANTRY   91ST INFANTRY   92ND INFANTRY

93RD INFANTRY   94TH INFANTRY (Pre-War Design)   94TH INFANTRY   95TH INFANTRY (Pre-War Design)

95TH DIVISION   96TH INFANTRY   97TH INFANTRY   98TH INFANTRY

99TH INFANTRY   100TH INFANTRY   101ST AIRBORNE   102ND INFANTRY

103RD INFANTRY   104TH INFANTRY   106TH INFANTRY   PHILIPPINE DIVISION

ARMORED FORCE AND DIVISIONS

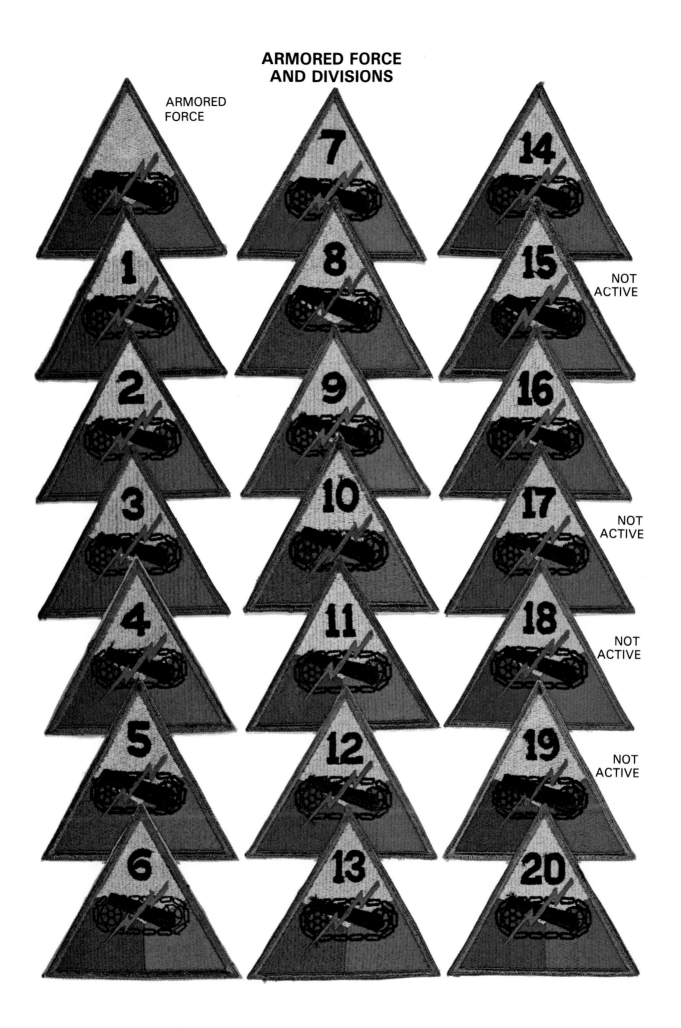

ARMORED FORCE

1

2

3

4

5

6

7

8

9

10

11

12

13

14

15 — NOT ACTIVE

16

17 — NOT ACTIVE

18 — NOT ACTIVE

19 — NOT ACTIVE

20

CAVALRY

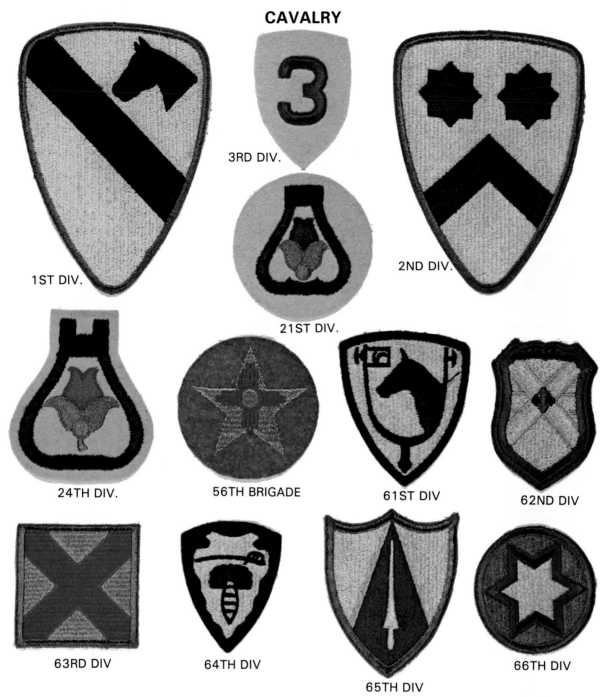

1ST DIV.

3RD DIV.

21ST DIV.

2ND DIV.

24TH DIV.

56TH BRIGADE

61ST DIV

62ND DIV

63RD DIV

64TH DIV

65TH DIV

66TH DIV

CHEMICAL MORTAR
BATTALIONS

2ND

83RD

93RD

96TH

81ST

84TH

91ST

INFANTRY UNITS

1ST SPECIAL SERVICE
FORCE

KACHIN RANGERS

JINGPAW RANGERS

2ND AIRBORNE
INFANTRY BRIGADE

99TH INFANTRY
BATTALION

158TH INFANTRY REGIMENT

442ND COMBAT TEAM
(1st Design)

(2nd Design)

474TH INFANTRY
REGIMENT

5307TH
COMPOSITE UNIT

501ST PARACHUTE
INFANTRY REGIMENT

503RD
RCT

1ST
RANGER
BATTALION

2ND

3RD

5TH

6TH

4TH

508TH
PARACHUTE
INFANTRY
REGIMENT

509TH PARACHUTE
INFANTRY BATTALION

RANGERS (Approved Design)

ARTILLERY AND ENGINEERS

1ST CA DISTRICT
(New England)

2ND
CA DISTRICT
(NY-Philadelphia)

3RD CA DISTRICT
(Chesapeake Bay)

4TH CA DISTRICT
(Southern)

9TH CA DISTRICT
(Pacific)

AA COMMAND,
CENTRAL

AA COMMAND,
EASTERN

AA COMMAND,
SOUTHERN

AA COMMAND,
WESTERN

HAWAIIAN CA BRIGADE

AA COMMAND

FA SCHOOL

14TH AA COMMAND

49TH AA BRIGADE

FIELD ARTILLERY
REPL TRAINING CENTER

AA ARTILLERY SCHOOL

98TH FIELD ARTILLERY
BATTALION

AMPHIBIOUS
TRAINING COMMAND

ENGINEER
AMPHIBIAN UNITS

36TH ENGINEER
COMBAT REGIMENT

Order of Battle
U.S. Army, World War II

WORLD WAR II ORDER OF BATTLE

Shelby L. Stanton
Captain, U.S. Army, Retired
Author of <u>Vietnam Order of Battle</u>

Foreword by Russell Weigley

Galahad Books · New York

Published in 1991 by

Galahad Books
A division of LDAP, Inc.
386 Park Avenue South
Suite 1913
New York, NY 10016

Galahad Books is a registered trademark of LDAP, Inc.

Published by arrangement with Presidio Press.

Library of Congress Catalog Card Number: 84-8299

ISBN: 0-88365-775-9

Printed in the United States of America.

Book design and layout by Shelby Stanton.

Color insignia plates courtesy Richard W. Smith, *Shoulder Sleeve
Insignia of the U.S. Armed Forces* 1941-1945*.

All photographs are official U.S. Army photographs except for those
on pages 39, 306, 433, 453, 477, 512, 515, 516, 534, 565, 566, and
594, which are from the author's collection.

Dedicated to the Honorable John D. Goodin

Raised in rural East Tennessee as the son of a Clinchfield Railroad conductor, John D. Goodin served as a tank platoon leader with the 2nd Battalion, 3rd Armored Regiment of the 3rd Armored Division in some of the hardest fighting of World War II from France through Germany. He was awarded the Bronze Star for Valor and the Purple Heart with Oak Leaf Cluster, twice being wounded in combat.

Returning to East Tennessee after the war, he became the first World War II national commander of the Military Order of the Purple Heart, opened a private law practice in 1951, and became the City Judge of Johnson City, Tennessee. He married the former Sara "Sally" Johnson of Shelbyville, Tennessee, whose first husband was shot down in the Pacific during World War II. Their three children are John, David, and Dee.

His patriotism and dedication to both community and nation is representative of the finest qualities and spirit of the American citizen-soldier who shouldered the terrible brunt of World War II, persevered to victory over two of the strongest armies ever fielded in world history, and secured the freedom which is our country's legacy.

Contents

Foreword

The United States Army is currently establishing a "New Manning System" intended to give overdue recognition to the importance of unit identities and traditions in fostering military efficiency. The NMS will constitute an American approximation of the British regimental system. The most historic combat-arms regiments of the American army are to be maintained on active duty in the peacetime army, and, as much as possible, soldiers will serve throughout their careers within a regiment. Regiments will have both overseas battalions and home battalions to permit interchanges of troops between the continental United States and garrisons abroad with minimal disruption of unit cohesion and unit spirit.

In the nineteenth- and early twentieth-century American army, soldiers identified themselves with their regiments, and the bonds of comradeship and tradition fostered by that identification did much to make the "old army" an effective fighting force, however small it was. Belatedly, the modern army has recognized that it ought to be possible to nourish the same kinds of bonds of comradeship and tradition notwithstanding the immense growth of even the peacetime army.

The current consciousness of unit identities and traditions makes the time propitious for the appearance of Shelby L. Stanton's second study of American orders of battle, the first having been his *Vietnam Order of Battle*. This survey is of World War II units of the United States Army. For the first time, detailed information on the service records of American World War II units, including those below the level of divisions, is made readily available. Here we can follow the World War II service of the combat-arms regiments, on which the New Manning System focuses, and a great variety of other nondivisional units. Captain Stanton's breadth and depth of coverage is extremely impressive, for, as his note on source materials indicates and as any researcher in World War II military history knows, to achieve his coverage required indefatigable research. The breadth and depth of coverage signifies, furthermore, that while the army's present concern with unit cohesion and lineage makes the appearance of the book timely, the value of this reference guide to World War II units goes well beyond the concerns of tracing and perpetuating unit lineages.

Historians cannot chronicle properly, and readers and students cannot understand properly, the American army's participation in World War II without being able to fit together the units comprising the army's order of battle. Identifying the units that were involved in any military operation may be only the first step toward following the operation, but it is a necessary step.

Living in Pennsylvania as I do, I have for years frequently taken visitors on tours of the battlefield of Gettysburg; for the visitors who do not know about such things, there is no escaping an explanation first of what an army corps, a division, a brigade, and a regiment were during the Civil War, and of how they fitted together, because the battle simply cannot be described except in terms of such organizations. The same holds true for discussing the campaigns of World War II, except that the task becomes more complicated because of the increasing variety of arms and services of the army and of their constituent parts. Until now, the task has also been complicated by the absence of a comprehensive and reliable guide to the units, below divisions as well as from divisions on up. Any reader of American World War II army history is henceforth likely to keep Captain Stanton's volume close at hand for quick reference and quick resolution of confusion, as will any researcher in the field. Writing a book about the American campaign in Europe from D day to VE day before Shelby Stanton's guide existed, I found that the most basic information about the army's order of battle was a prerequisite to telling my tale but often remarkably hard to disentangle from a maze of sources.

Ultimately, the historical uses of this book and the nurturing of unit traditions blend together. As a boy, I used to listen to my father's fellow veterans from his American Legion post retell their World War I experiences; they were old enough and the war was far enough in the past for them to enjoy the retelling. In their stories as in more carefully structured historical narratives, the unit identities were essential to following what went on. A veteran told how as a soldier of the 3rd Infantry Division in the Second Battle of Marne—when the division earned its sobriquet, "The Rock of the Marne"—he suffered the wounds that still sorely scarred and partially paralyzed him. For him, the otherwise nondescript 3rd Division shoulder patch with its three diagonal white stripes on a blue square became indelibly associated with the memory of the First World War, the horror of it but also the bravery it had called forth. (The diagonal white stripes are intended to signify the battles of the Marne, St. Mihiel, and the Meuse-Argonne. To the extent that patches can take on emotional connotations, they genuinely do so.)

The unit badges depicted in Stanton's guide to the World War II order of battle will, for many readers, also become freighted with significance far beyond any weight that such tiny objects would at first inspection seem capable of bearing. Together with the rest of the comprehensive data detailing all troop movements through the unit listings, this book becomes a rare and indispensable reference.

Russell F. Weigley
Professor of History
Temple University
Philadelphia, Pennsylvania

Acknowledgments

In researching and writing this book, the author used the actual unit records of the United States Army in World War II as his primary source because, to this date, no compilation of the army below division level has ever been assembled and published. Therefore, foremost acknowledgment must go to the thousands of unnamed army personnel who diligently compiled and submitted unit historical reports during that conflict. These materials are fully explained in this book's source credits.

In addition, the author was ably assisted by the efforts of the following individuals: Brigadier General Douglas Kinnard, Department of the Army Chief of Military History; Dr. John H. Hatcher, Archivist of the United States Army; Jack D. Kravitz, Acting Director of the Washington National Records Center; Frederick W. Pernell, Archivist-in-charge of the Research Room of the Washington National Records Center; Richard F. Myers, Chief, and Dr. George C. Chalou, Assistant Chief, of the Modern Military Field Branch; Steve Bern, Modern Military Field Branch; Wanda Radcliffe of the Army Declassification Branch; Dr. Robert K. Wright, Jr., John B. Wilson, and Dr. Charles D. Hendricks of the Army Organizational History Branch; Charles B. MacDonald; and Janice E. McKenney, Hannah M. Ziedlik, and Jefferson Powell of the Army Historical Services Division. Major General Robert M. Ives rendered encouragement and expert military insight. Guidance and advice were generously shared by James A. Sawicki, author of an excellent series of books on lineages of selected U.S. Army regiments and battalions; Steven Zaloga, armor expert and author; James W. Loop, insignia expert; and Sergeant First Class Gordon Rottman, one of the most knowledgeable and professional noncommissioned officers I have ever met.

Specific service was rendered by several noted scholars. Colonel Robert N. Waggoner provided many of the photographs, which he carefully selected to portray the combat soldier in action. Colonel James F. Greene, Jr., President of the American Society of Military Insignia Collectors, provided illustrations of unit distinctive insignia; and Richard W. Smith permitted use of several color plates from his book on World War II insignia. Helen V. Epperson did a superb job of typesetting the manuscript.

The dedicated staffs of the Historical Records Branch, Organizational History Branch, and Historical Reference Branch of the Army's Office of the Chief of Military History were most helpful and always ready to assist in tracing critical documentation. Finally, special thanks are due my father, Samuel Shelton Stanton, and my wife, Kathryn, who consistently demonstrated great understanding and support. I also wish to pay tribute to four outstanding Americans, Lois M. Jett, Charles K. Lucas III, Don R. McAdams, Jr., and Daniel Priest III.

The Author

Shelby L. Stanton, Attorney-at-Law, was born February 1, 1948, in Baton Rouge, Louisiana. He is the son of Samuel Shelton Stanton, a prominent professional engineer, and the grandson of Samuel Stanton (1888–1938), who was Captain of the SS *Tampa* of the Gulf & Southern Steamship Company.

Shelby L. Stanton received his Bachelor of Science from Louisiana State University and, as a Distinguished Military Graduate of the ROTC program, received his Regular Army commission as an infantry officer. During the Vietnam conflict he served six years on active duty as a combat rifle platoon leader in the 1st Battalion, 508th Infantry (Airborne) of the 3d Brigade, 82d Airborne Division, on a detachment in both 5th Special Forces Group (Airborne) and U.S. Army Special Forces Company, Thailand, as a ranger advisor to the Royal Thai Special Warfare Center at Lopburi, and as adjutant of the 20th Combat Engineer Brigade. He retired with the rank of Captain and returned to Louisiana State University, where he earned a Master's in Educational Administration and a Juris Doctor.

Shelby L. Stanton married Kathryn Rushnok in 1970 and they have four children; Diana Lee, David Shelton, Lucy Kah, and Samuel Curtis. He is the Chancellor of the Texas Society of the Sons of the American Revolution, and a past chapter president of the Military Order of the Purple Heart. He is also a member of the Sons of Union Veterans of the Civil War, tracing his ancestry to Curtis Stanton, a chief engineer of the monitor USS *Onandaga* which served on the James River in Virginia during 1864–1865.

Shelby L. Stanton is contributing editor to several military periodicals, and has award-winning research in a number of military simulation designs. He is also the author of *Vietnam Order of Battle*.

Explanatory Notes

Purpose and Scope

The purpose of *U.S. Army World War II Order of Battle* is to list and describe every major tactical unit of the army ground combat forces during that conflict from battalion through division in size. Within this framework are included all armored, cavalry, tank destroyer, coast artillery, antiaircraft artillery, field artillery, infantry, chemical mortar, and engineer units. Its scope basically includes all combat formations. Prior to the 1942 reorganization of the army, the Engineer Corps was designated a combat traditional arm rather than a service branch. During World War II, due to its larger logistical and construction responsibilities, the engineers were relabeled a technical service under the Army Service Forces. However, their combatant abilities, missions, and frequently direct infantry battlefield role reserved their place in this order of battle. Likewise, chemical mortar battalions functioned as frontline artillery and are included although the Chemical Warfare Service was also a technical service by definition. The difficult decision to limit this work was reached due to considerations of manageability, and this cut-off line is not meant to slight units of other army branches which sometimes also served in a frontline "rifleman" capacity.

Each unit contains a basic data base. This contains its full title, primary type or weapons composition, exact dates of service, locations in which formed and terminated, overseas wartime movements, campaign participation credit, and August 1945 locations at the end of World War II, if applicable. Units have been given different formats according to their size and hierarchy in the army chain of command. Divisions, being the most important standard combined-arms groupings, are given full wartime combat narratives and interior organizational details in addition to service paragraphs. Brigades, groups, and regiments are given brief service paragraphs, while battalions are granted linear summaries. Where authorized during World War II, line drawings of the appropriate distinctive insignia are illustrated for units of regimental or larger size.

Unit Title and Type

The unit title given is the final designation during its service within the book's time frame. One major factor affecting unit titles in this volume was the massed conversion of coast artillery into antiaircraft artillery. Such units are not separated in the text unless a numerical change resulted. The unit title reflects the unit's *final* status, and the exact date of branch transfer from coast artillery is noted, if applicable.

National Guard components are identified when inducted into federal service.

Unit type is given in parenthesis immediately following the title and refers most commonly to main weapons composition, mode of transport, and enlisted racial type. It reflects the unit's *final* structure during World War II. Changes in title or type during unit service are noted in the narrative, or parenthesized remarks in listings. As a result of army policy that all units be equipped, trained, and employed alike regardless of race, the identifying term "Colored" was usually dropped from the title on unit listings and orders after 1940, and this practice became official on 18 September 1942. Nevertheless, the racial type remained an integral part of the unit's full title and as such was retained in this book to fully identify the unit. The custom of using an asterisk and an accompanying footnote indicating race soon came to be the accepted means of identifying Negro units in station lists, orders, or in any list of units. Since asterisks were easily transposed to the wrong unit, or omitted entirely, the method became notoriously unreliable and caused mix-ups and "overall embarrassment" throughout the war, since separate billets and other facilities were required in advance of troop arrivals.

Unit Formation and Termination Dates

The time frame was chosen to cover both the army's World War II mobilization and demobilization as well as its actual wartime service, and as a result the period covered is 1 September 1939 through 31 December 1946. However, units are only tracked past August 1945 if already active during that month. Units raised or reactivated after September 1945 are not recorded since they properly belong to the postwar army. For example, the 611th Field Artillery Battalion was inactivated at Fort Riley, Kansas, on 6 February 1945 and reactivated 5 February 1946, but the latter is not picked up under the guidelines of this book. A single asterisk signifies that a unit is active through 1946 in the battalion listings. A unit already existing on active duty as of 1 September 1939 is identified as "Active," "Stationed," or "Serving" at the beginning of narratives, or with the designator "P" (Prior to 1 Sep 39) in battalion listings.

At this point it must be emphasized that this history is not a work of heraldry. The date chosen for formation purposes is the date that unit was actually raised and received personnel, and the date of termination is when the unit folded down. No attempt is made to distinguish whether it was activated or organized, or in the latter case inactivated or disbanded. National Guard units are considered as entering active federal service when inducted.

Unit Source

If a unit was derived primarily or entirely from one already on active service, as would occur in redesignations of organic regimental battalions to separately numbered battalions, then its source or "parent unit" is identified. This is fully explained in narratives, or placed in parentheses immediately following the date and location of the unit's formation in battalion listings. Sometimes a unit can transfer all of its equipment and personnel to a new unit and the army not consider that new unit a continuation of its predecessor. Therefore, the reader must be aware that unit sources do not necessarily imply unit redesignations, but may only refer to source of a majority of assets. While such distinctions have great lineage merit, they are not important in the historical frame of this volume.

Unit Service Narratives

Narrative paragraphs are reserved for essential unit data and a compressed movement log wherein frequent use of abbreviations and deletion of prepositions has been made to conserve space. In the interest of clarification, the following rules govern. All dates are those on which a unit actually *arrived* at the location given, even if the wording may sound ambiguous, such as, "sent to Ft Dix N.J. 13 Jan 44." When the dates that units entered countries of Europe are cited, only the *last* wartime entries into Germany and the *first* wartime entries into other countries are given to avoid the confusion of cross-border moves back and forth, which were especially prevalent during the German Ardennes Counteroffensive ("Battle of the Bulge"). However, division service paragraphs note all cross-border moves regardless.

Details of divisional infantry regiment battle records are found within the divisional narratives, which have been expanded to focus specifically on this aspect. Separate (nondivisional) infantry regiments contain combat history details within their own narratives. Regimental narratives also contain all detachments and attachments between divisions that affect them, and it is understood that a regiment returns to its parent division after such an attachment is remarked upon, unless otherwise indicated. Likewise, regimental narratives have not been burdened with redesignations of the divisions to which they were assigned, since these facts can be referenced in the division histories. In all cases the length of the service paragraph is contingent on the unit data base and not an indicator, by itself, of length of service or importance. For instance, due to more complicated command arrangements and frequent island movements, units serving in the Pacific usually require more space than their European counterparts.

Overseas Wartime Service

For purposes of this book, all stations outside the Zone of Interior (Continental United States) are "overseas." Overseas service is considered as commencing when a unit departed its Port of Embarkation or crossed overland into Canada. While all permanent Zone of Interior station changes are given for units larger than battalion, overseas relocations past the cessation of hostilities in that particular theater are not traced since, by definition, this is no longer considered overseas wartime service.

August 1945 Location

August 1945 locations are placed as close as possible to 14 August 1945, when Japan accepted the Allied surrender terms. Geographic spellings are those found in the army station lists from which this information was taken.

Criteria for Locational Dates

Dates used were derived, where possible, from the actual unit records and most often signify when the unit headquarters arrived. Thus, specific dates do not include earlier advance party or later rear detachment arrivals, or reflect the span of movement by echelon. Unit movement into an area could last days or weeks.

Battalion Listing Formats

Battalions have linear entries. The first line is used—in order—for the unit title and type; formation date and location; source of unit (in parentheses); a slash followed by termination date and location; and August 1945 location, if applicable. Single-line entries indicate that a unit never left the country cited in the formation space. The second line is used for overseas wartime locations and campaign key numbers in the following order: date unit *departed* Port of Embarkation or raised in overseas area, overseas wartime movements, a dash and campaign key codes arranged in numerical sequence, and arrival date when *returned* to Port of Embarkation in the United States, if applicable. Parenthesized notes and remarks are *italicized* and placed as space permits in view of the limited line allowance. Titles of units and weapons types are the final ones employed during World War II; changes are reflected by remarks.

Example

Unit Designation and type   Date Formed and Location (Source of Unit) / Inactivation and Location   August 1945 Location
Overseas Wartime Locations followed by - **Campaign Key Numbers** and PE return to United States, if applicable or space allows
 (notes and remarks)

104th Field Artillery Bn (105mm How Trk-D)   1 Sep 42 Ft Shafter Hawaii (2nd Bn 104th FA) / 31 Dec 45 Ft Lawton Wash   Okinawa
Hawaii: 1 Sep 42   Saipan: 17 Jun 44   Espiritu Santo: 4 Sep 44   Okinawa: 9 Apr 45 - **10, 19, 21**   SPE: 31 Dec 45 *(27th Inf Div)*

In this example the 104th Field Artillery Battalion was equipped with truck-drawn 105mm howitzers and organized at Fort Shafter, Hawaii, from the 2nd Battalion of the 104th Field Artillery on 1 September 1942. The reader may research the battalion's previous existence under the 104th Field Artillery Regiment in this book. The battalion went to Saipan 17 June 1944, to Espiritu Santo on 4 September 1944, and to Okinawa on 9 April 1945, where it was still stationed in August 1945. It is credited with the Eastern Mandates, Ryukyus, and Western Pacific campaigns. This information was derived by indexing the boldfaced campaign key numbers with Appendix I. Note these key number codes are in numerical sequence rather than chronological order, but since the appendix displays all campaign dates, they can be easily arranged by time sequence if desired. The battalion returned to the Seattle Port of Embarkation on 31 December 1945 and was inactivated that same day at Fort Lawton, Washington. Finally, it served under the 27th Infantry Division.

Terminology and Abbreviations

The military and ethnic terminology and abbreviations used in this Order of Battle have been deliberately conformed to World War II usage, and do not necessarily reflect modern parlance.

Part I

U.S. Army Organization in World War II

Chapter 1

U.S. Army Structure

The U.S. Army was organized into the Regular Army, known as the Army of the United States (AUS); the Organized Reserves; the National Guard; and the *Philippine Scouts* which were technically part of the Regular Army. All army ground units of World War II fell into one of the above categories.

The War Department had authorized a General Headquarters, United States Army (GHQ), in 1921, but this command was not activated until 26 July 1940. It was designed to facilitate mobilization by supervising the organization and training of the army field forces within the continental United States (the Zone of Interior). In October 1940 the command of corps areas was separated from the four armies which had been established in 1932. The United States was divided into four defense commands on 17 March 1941 which would become theaters of operation if invasion threatened. In addition to these training responsibilities, on 3 July 1941 GHQ was elevated to the command and planning for military operations in the Zone of Interior. As a prewar training headquarters, GHQ brought up to strength and trained the Regular and National Guard divisions which culminated in the large full-scale fall 1941 maneuvers in Louisiana and North/South Carolina. GHQ was superseded by the Army Ground Forces on 9 March 1942. The four defense commands and all theater of operations were placed under the War Department General Staff. Army units received their training under the Army Ground Forces or Services of Supply (which included engineer training) and then were sent to a theater of operations, overseas command, or stateside command.

Combat forces of the U.S. Army were classified according to the primary weapons and methods used in battle. These are discussed under their separate sections in this book. During World War II the army consisted of three army groups, several field armies, corps, and divisions. Combat units usually served under these formations.

The U.S. Army was based on uniform organization for standard units, each of which had a table of organization (T/O), or after 28 August 1943 a consolidated table of organization and equipment (T/O&E). These tables fixed the structure, strength, and equipment of these various unit types. Since they were designed to provide minimum essentials to standard organizations capable of performing their missions under general conditions, the actual field capacity of such units varied with their association with other units and provisions for support. In the field the strength of many units depended on specific assignments or local conditions. However, even in the greatest deviation from the tables, the basic pattern would still be clearly recognizable. During World War II these standardized units were combined as components of battalions, regiments, or divisions; or flexibly attached to groups, brigades, and higher commands. The principal function of corps and armies was to provide command, control, and the provision of additionally required support to those forces placed under them.

Divisions

Divisions were the largest units in the army having a prescribed organization, and functioned as the smallest formations including units of various arms and services. They were designed for normal operational self-sufficiency, which varied with division type. Since it was thought that the armored division might normally operate at a considerable distance from the mass of the forces, the motorized division somewhat less so, and the infantry division least so, maintenance, supply, and engineer support was distributed accordingly. All were held to a minimum since corps and armies were envisioned as containing pools of specialized units to render required support under unusual circumstances. Division types are discussed in more detail under their respective sections in this book.

The numbering of army divisions reflected the numerical heritage established in 1917. Regular Army divisions had been organized very rapidly within the assigned block 1–25, and this resulted in no numerical pattern. World War II also called upon numbers beyond this initial block. The National Guard division serial began with 26 and in World War I the numbers were geographically assigned with 26 in the New England area continuing to 41 in the Pacific Northwest. During the interwar period the National Guard added three new divisions, the 43rd, 44th, and 45th. The 26th became restricted to Massachusetts and the 43rd utilized to cover the rest of New England; the 44th added for New York and New Jersey; and the 45th was added for Oklahoma, Arizona, Colorado, and New Mexico. The 39th was not activated in World War II and the 42nd, created in World War I as a special National Guard division representing all states, was reconstituted in the Army of the United States on 5 February 1943 and activated as such in July 1943. National Army divisions were those formed in World War I from drafted personnel and started with the number 76. This component was the basis of the Organized Reserve divisions of World War II. However, the 82nd and 101st were both organized reserve divisions being ordered into active military service when the army decided to raise two airborne divisions. As a result they were redesignated and became Regular Army.

A total of 92 divisions served during World War II, and 89 were maintained. The Philippine Division was lost in action, and the 2nd Cavalry Division was partially inactivated in July 1942, fully reactivated in February 1943 and then inactivated again by May 1944 in North Africa. Since the Americal Division and both 24th and 25th Infantry Divisions were activated overseas, 87 divisions were prepared for combat and shipped to theaters by the Army Ground Forces.

Provisions for activating new divisions varied at different times during World War II. Between January and June 1942 each new infantry division organized was built around a cadre of 172 officers and 1,190 enlisted men from an already active unit. The cadre was selected two-three months prior to division activation and then given special training. The prospective division commander and his two principal subordinates were designated by the War Department no later than 78 days prior to the activation date, and key infantry and artillery officers selected by Army Ground Forces were brought to headquarters for a week of orientation. The commander and his staff then spent a month at the Command & General Staff School, and all other officers of the cadre simultaneously attended appropriate service schools; the assistant division commander attending the Infantry School at Fort Benning. Thirty-seven days before the activation date the commander and principal staff arrived at the division camp and were joined there one week later by the remainder of the officer cadre and the enlisted cadre. During the next few days the complement of 452 officers arrived from officer candidate schools, service schools, and other replacement facilities. On activation day the division was formally activated, with flags and music, and during the next 15 days received the enlisted "filler" of 13,425 selectees from reception centers. In the meantime, about 50 percent of the division's equipment had arrived and training could begin.

In May 1942 it was initially estimated 187 divisions were required. Between this and the close of hostilities an army of 89 divisions were finally made available for combat. This was because the overall strength of the army became fixed at a lower figure than had been expected and the requirements for service troops and overhead functions proved larger than foreseen. Economy in the tables of organizations of divisions in 1943 yielded 89 divisions active on 31 March 1945 with only 70,000 more men required over the 73½ divisions active on 31 December 1942. A higher proportion of infantry divisions to armored and mechanized divisions was constantly advised by the Army Ground Forces. The deletion of motorized divisions was gradually accepted, but recommendations to inactivate armored divisions and convert airborne divisions to light infantry divisions were not accepted. Plans for light divisions fluctuated widely and then were abandoned (Chart 1).

CHART 1.
The Projection and Raising of the U.S. Army Combat Formations in World War II—Divisions and Selected Battalions*

DIVISIONS	Active on 31 Dec 41	Active on 30 Jun 42	Active on 31 Dec 42	Active on 30 Jun 43	23 May 42 War Dept Estimated Troop Basis for 31 Dec 43	24 Nov 42 War Dept Approved Troop Basis for 31 Dec 43	15 Mar 43 War Dept Authorization Basis for 31 Dec 43	1 Jul 43 War Dept Approved Troop Basis for 31 Dec 43	Active on 31 Dec 43	Active on 30 Jun 44	15 Jan 44 War Dept Approved Troop Basis for 31 Dec 44	Active on 31 Dec 44	1 Jul 44 War Dept Approved Troop Basis for 30 Jun 45	1 Jan 45 War Dept Approved Troop Basis for 30 Jun 45	Active on 31 Mar 45
Infantry	29	33	52	63	59	62	71	64	64	66	64	66	66	66	66
Light Infantry	—	—	—	—	—	—	—	1	3	1	3	0	1	0	0
Cavalry	2	2	1½	2	1	2	2	2	2	1	2	1	1	1	1
Armored	5	8	14	15	46	20	20	16	16	16	16	16	16	16	16
Airborne	—	—	2	4	7	6	6	5	4	5	5	5	5	5	5
Motorized	—	4	4	0	23	10	1	0	0	0	0	0	0	0	0
Mountain or Jungle	—	—	—	—	4	0	0	0	0	0	0	1	0	1	1
BATTALIONS, NONDIVISIONAL															
Heavy Field Artillery	n	n	32	44	n	54	n	77	61	116	111	137	143	143	137
Medium Field Artillery	n	n	53	67	n	81	n	82	75	112	111	116	114	116	113
Light Field Artillery	n	n	57	101	n	105	n	107	95	87	91	93	80	88	76
Antiaircraft Artillery	n	n	391	547	n	781	n	720	557	479	526	347	460	345	331
Tank	n	n	26	41	n	38	n	73	65	64	60	65	63	65	60
Tank Destroyer	n	n	80	106	n	144	n	106	101	78	78	73	78	70	68

*Adopted from Robert Palmer, Ground Forces in the Army Dec 41-Apr 45 A Statistical Study, *The Organization of Ground Combat Troops*, Historical Division U.S. Army Wash D.C. 1947.

CHART 2.
Divisions Stripped in 1944 Prior to Embarkation

Effective 27 Apr 44 the following divisions were selected to bear the principal burden of providing enlisted men for overseas replacements and suffered the following losses accordingly between April-September 1944.

8th Armd Div	2,420	71st Inf Div	3,502
13th A/B Div	1,652	75th Inf Div*†	5,284
13th Armd Div	3,179	76th Inf Div*	7,071
16th Armd Div	2,947	78th Inf Div*††	5,523
20th Armd Div	2,846	86th Inf Div**	4,810
42nd Inf Div*	4,821	87th Inf Div**	4,610
63rd Inf Div*	4,185	89th Inf Div	3,060
65th Inf Div	5,581	97th Inf Div**	5,430
66th Inf Div**	4,882	100th Inf Div†	3,675
69th Inf Div†	5,299	103rd Inf Div†	2,550
70th Inf Div*	3,370	106th Inf Div**	5,050

*Previously stripped by draft of Feb 44, which had also affected the 10th Light, 84th Inf, and 92nd Inf Divs.

**Previously stripped by draft of Sep 43.

†Previously stripped by draft of Oct 43, which had also affected the 83rd Inf, 84th Inf, and 99th Inf Divs.

††Previously stripped by draft of Dec 43.

The aggregate of withdrawals for all purposes was tremendous. The 94th Inf Div, from activation to departure for port of embarkation, lost 8,890 enlisted men; the 65th Inf Div, 11,782; the 106th Inf Div, 12,442; the 100th Inf Div, 14,787; and the 69th Inf Div, 22,235. Additionally all suffered high officer losses, 1,336 in the 69th Inf Div, for example.

Source: Bell I. Wiley in *The Procurement and Training of Ground Combat Troops, The Army Ground Forces, United States Army in World War II*, Historical Division, Dept of the Army, Washington, D.C., 1948; 208, 472–74.

Divisions committed to battle soon began to suffer heavy and continuous losses. By May 1945 the five hardest-hit divisions (3rd, 4th, 9th, 36th, and 45th) had suffered 176 percent battle casualties in all components, and infantry divisions in sustained combat averaged 100 percent losses in infantry regiments every three months. To partially compensate for these losses, divisions not yet committed were ruthlessly stripped *(Chart 2)*. This negated much of the careful preparation and training programs used to prepare divisions, and many went into active theaters as formations hastily brought up to strength with a minimum of training as a result.

Armies and Corps

Through 1942 the army and corps were designed as command structures with their organic content determined in troop lists, and were known as the "type" army and the "type" corps. Their purpose, like that of the division, was to form up different elements into balanced combinations, but unlike divisions they were used chiefly as planning instruments to facilitate mobilization and training of balanced forces. It was understood that in actual operations armies and corps would consist of such forces as might be assigned or attached in the immediate situation.

The "type" army theoretically consisted of three corps; one antiaircraft artillery brigade; engineers to include three general service regiments, six separate battalions, two heavy ponton battalions, and a topographic, water supply, and camouflage battalion; three tank destroyer battalions; a signal construction and a signal operations battalion; and a host of companies and service units. During World War II the following armies were formed: First (1 Oct 33), Second (1 Oct 33), Third (1 Oct 33), Fourth (1 Oct 33), Fifth (5 Jan 43), Sixth (25 Jan 43), Seventh (10 Jul 43), Eighth (10 Jun 44), Ninth (15 Apr 44), Tenth (20 Jun 44), and Fifteenth (21 Aug 44). The First, Third, Fifth, Seventh, Ninth, and Fifteenth Armies served in Europe while the Sixth, Eighth, and Tenth served in the Pacific. The Fifth and Seventh were formed overseas in North Africa, and the Second and Fourth remained in the United States with training missions.

The army in combat was designed to be a command and administrative agency, allowing non-independent corps to concentrate on tactical operations and not be burdened with supply and maintenance considerations. Army also evacuated disabled or captured equipment, provided hospitals, and reinforced specialized or heavy-duty construction tasks. It controlled from two to three corps and attached supporting and service units according to mission and situation.

The "type" corps theoretically consisted of three infantry divisions, one antiaircraft regiment, one mechanized cavalry regiment, two engineer combat regiments, one field artillery brigade, one tank destroyer group, a signal battalion, and certain service units. Corps headquarters sizes were drastically reduced by the Army Ground Forces in 1943 as the corps concept evolved along flexible guidelines calling for separate combat battalions to be assigned or attached as needed. A corps became a variable combination of divisions and battalions, essentially consisting of a commander and a small staff to direct combat operations and operate the pool of nondivisional combat units placed under it. These included such elements as corps artillery, cavalry squadrons, and tank destroyer battalions. They were distributed to divisions, assembled for massed support action, or held in reserve. Since divisions had been streamlined, the corps became the key headquarters for the employment of combat elements in proper tactical combinations for the mission at hand. Except for independent corps, they were also relieved of service units which became more of an army responsibility under this concept. With all corps made flexible and the "type" corps abolished, the armored corps became an unnecessary special unit. The four in existence were accordingly converted to normal corps structures beginning in August 1943.

The army raised 26 corps in World War II, three being converted from armored corps *(Chart 3)*. A typical corps in combat operations in Europe consisted of one armored and two infantry divisions, a mechanized cavalry group, one–three engineer combat groups, two–three field artillery brigades, and one antiaircraft artillery brigade. It should be remembered that direct attachment at division level usually accounted for another three tank destroyer and three antiaircraft artillery battalions within the corps structure.

The 1943 Reorganization of the Army

The army adopted the flexible battalion/group system on 24 December 1942 which revolutionized army organization. While discussed in greater detail in the separate branch sections of this book, the system simply converted non-divisional fixed regiments in the antiaircraft artillery, field artillery, mechanized cavalry, and combat engineers to separate battalions and activated group headquarters at a ratio of one group to every four battalions. The group was a flexible tactical headquarters to which these independent battalions would be freely attached according to circumstances. To command these groups, brigades organically only consisting of a Headquarters & Headquarters Company were created and likewise units could be attached to them. This concept was implemented in 1943, but in practice

CHART 3.
Corps of the U.S. Army During World War II

Corps	Activation	Overseas	Inactivation
I	1 Nov 40 Columbia S.C.	24 Sep 42	28 Mar 50 Japan
Campaigns:	Papua, New Guinea, Luzon		
I Armored	15 Jul 40 Ft Knox Ky	N/A	11 Sep 42 Ft Knox Ky
I Armored	9 Jan 43 Casablanca, French Morocco	9 Jan 43	10 Jul 43 Sicily
Campaigns:	European Theater without inscription		
II	1 Aug 40 Ft Jay N.Y.	30 Jun 42	10 Oct 45 Austria
Campaigns:	Algeria–French Morocco, Tunisia, Sicily, Naples-Foggia, Rome-Arno, North Apennines, Po Valley		
II Armored	17 Jun 42 Cp Polk La	N/A	9 Oct 43 redes XVIII Corps
III	18 Dec 40 Presidio of Monterey Calif	5 Sep 44	10 Oct 46 Cp Polk La
Campaigns:	Northern France, Rhineland, Ardennes-Alsace, Central Europe		
III Armored	7 Jul 42 Cp Polk La	N/A	10 Oct 43 redes XIX Corps
IV	20 Oct 39 Ft Benning Ga	7 Mar 44	13 Oct 45 Cp Kilmer N.J.
Campaigns:	Rome-Arno, North Apennines, Po Valley		
IV Armored	5 Sep 42 Cp Young Calif	N/A	10 Oct 43 redes XX Corps
V	20 Oct 40 Cp Beauregard La	23 Jan 42	Returned to U.S. Jul 45
Campaigns:	Normandy, Northern France, Rhineland, Ardennes-Alsace, Central Europe		
VI	3 Aug 40 Ft Sheridan Ill	8 Feb 43	1 May 46 redes Constabulary
Campaigns:	Naples-Foggia, Anzio, Rome-Arno, Southern France, Ardennes-Alsace, Central Europe		
VII	25 Nov 40 Ft McClellan Ala	9 Oct 43	1 Mar 46 Presidio of S.F.
Campaigns:	Normandy, Northern France, Rhineland, Ardennes-Alsace, Central Europe		
VIII	14 Oct 40 Ft Sam Houston Tex	13 Dec 43	15 Dec 45 Cp Gruber Okla
Campaigns:	Normandy, Northern France, Rhineland, Ardennes-Alsace, Central Europe		
IX	24 Oct 40 Ft Lewis Wash	25 Sep 44	28 Mar 50 Japan
Campaigns:	Pacific Theater without inscription		
X	15 May 42 Cp Sherman Tex	14 Jul 44	27 Apr 55 Ft Riley Kans
Campaigns:	New Guinea, Southern Philippines, Leyte		
XI	15 Jun 42 Chicago Ill	16 Mar 44	11 Mar 46 Japan
Campaigns:	New Guinea, Southern Philippines		
XII	29 Aug 42 Columbia S.C.	10 Apr 44	15 Dec 45 Germany
Campaigns:	Northern France, Rhineland, Ardennes-Alsace, Central Europe		
XIII	7 Dec 42 Providence R.I.	15 Jul 44	25 Sep 45 Cp Cooke Calif
Campaigns:	Rhineland, Central Europe		
XIV	19 Dec 42 Brownwood Tex	25 Jan 43	31 Dec 45 Ft Lawton Wash
Campaigns:	Guadalcanal, Northern Solomons, Luzon		
XV	15 Feb 43 Cp Beauregard La	14 Dec 43	31 Mar 46 Germany
Campaigns:	Normandy, Northern France, Rhineland, Ardennes-Alsace, Central Europe		
XVI	7 Dec 43 Ft Riley Kans	20 Sep 44	7 Dec 45 Cp Kilmer N.J.
Campaigns:	Rhineland, Central Europe		
XVIII A/B*	9 Oct 43 redes from II Armored Corps	17 Aug 44	21 May 51 Ft Bragg N.C.
Campaigns:	Rhineland, Ardennes-Alsace, Central Europe		
XIX	10 Oct 43 redes from III Armored Corps	18 Jan 44	5 Sep 45 Germany
Campaigns:	Normandy, Northern France, Rhineland, Central Europe		
XX	10 Oct 43 redes from IV Armored Corps	11 Feb 44	1 Mar 46 Germany
Campaigns:	Normandy, Northern France, Rhineland, Ardennes-Alsace, Central Europe		
XXI	6 Dec 43 Cp Polk La	11 Sep 44	30 Sep 45 Germany
Campaigns:	Rhineland, Ardennes-Alsace, Central Europe		
XXII	15 Jan 44 Cp Campbell Ky	30 Dov 44	20 Jan 46 Germany
Campaigns:	Rhineland, Central Europe		
XXIII	15 Jan 44 Cp Bowie Tex	12 Oct 44	10 Feb 46 Germany
Campaigns:	European Theater without inscription		
XXIV	9 Apr 44 Ft Shafter Hawaii	9 Apr 44	25 Jan 49 Korea
Campaigns:	Leyte, Ryukyus		
XXXVI	10 Jul 44 Ft Riley Kans	N/A	25 Sep 45 Cp Callan Calif

*The XVIII Corps was redesignated XVIII (Airborne) Corps on 25 August 1944.

only antiaircraft, field artillery, and tank destroyers organized brigades and only the first mentioned were ever used in quantity.

At the same time revisions of mobilization planning based on theater experience reflected shifting requirements for nondivisional field artillery, combat engineer, antiaircraft, and tank destroyer units. Experience in the Italian campaign pointed up a pressing need for more heavy artillery, and both engineer combat and heavy ponton battalions were also increased. In other types of units the trend in activation during 1944 was sharply downward. All together, for instance, 258 antiaircraft artillery units were inactivated or disbanded by Army Ground Forces between 1 January 1944 and the end of the war in Europe. Tank destroyers had also been overestimated and between the same dates Army Ground Forces inactivated 26 of these battalions. A large portion of the personnel made available by inactivations of antiaircraft, coast artillery, tank destroyer, and other types of surplus units were utilized as fillers and replacement in infantry and other units for which the need increased. In many cases units that became surplus were converted en bloc, except for the field officers who were usually withdrawn prior to redesignation. Coast Artillery gun battalions were converted into heavy field artillery battalions; antiaircraft barrage balloon battalions into signal construction battalions; antiaircraft automatic weapons and/or gun battalions into field artillery rocket battalions; chemical mortar battalions into engineer combat battalions; and cavalry squadrons into signal information and monitoring companies. Negro units were converted primarily into service type units. Colored antiaircraft-type battalions became signal battalions; field artillery battalions became engineer combat and quartermaster truck units; and tank destroyer battalions became quartermaster truck, engineer fire-fighting, and port cargo units.

The Army Ground Forces

The Army Ground Forces was established on 9 March 1942 to succeed GHQ and given the mission to "provide ground force units properly organized, trained, and equipped for combat operations." In addition to armies and other units assigned for training, it contained the Antiaircraft Command, the Armored Force/Command, the Tank Destroyer Command/Center, the Airborne Command, the Amphibious Training Command/Center, the Desert Training Center, and the Replacement & School Command. The first mentioned are discussed within their respective sections, and the latter three are discussed here. The Amphibious Training Command was activated 20 May 1942 at Fort Edwards, Massachusetts, to train divisions for shore operations, moved to Carrabelle (later Fort Gordon Johnston), Florida in October 1942 where redesignated the Amphibious Training Center on 1 November 1942, and was disbanded on 10 June 1943. The Desert Training Center was activated 11 April 1942 at Indio, California, and it was redesignated as the California-Arizona Maneuver Area on 20 October 1943, which was closed 1 July 1944. It trained armored and mechanized units to operate and fight in the desert, tested equipment, and developed training methods and tactical doctrine. The Replacement & School Command was activated 27 March 1942 at Birmingham, Alabama, and disbanded on 1 November 1946. During World War II it controlled the conduct of training in the schools and replacement training centers of combat arms, while the Army Ground Forces retained direct control over training doctrine, methods, and literature.

Army Ground Forces activities evolved during the course of the war. The period March-October 1942 was characterized by incomplete authority which manifested itself in piecemeal modification of certain tables of organization. From October 1942–October 1943 Army Ground Forces assumed strong leadership in matters of organization, and this resulted in becoming the critical period during which the shape and structure of army forces in World War II were determined. From the end of 1943 until 1945 the organizational changes were put increasingly to the test of combat, and initiative in matters of tactical organization passed from the Army Ground Forces to the theater commanders. The role of Army Ground Forces changed to analyzing and recommending modifications in tables of organization based upon theater requests. After the cessation of hostilities in Europe, the Army Ground Forces became primarily concerned with organizational changes and problems incident to redeployment to finish the war against Japan in the Pacific.

Army Ground Forces established a Mountain Warfare Training Center at Camp Carson and a skiing center at Camp Hale in 1942. A few specially designated mountain units were assembled at the former. A cold weather training center was activated at Camp McCoy due to army operations in arctic conditions. Additionally, special installations had been created at the Desert Training Center, Airborne Command, and the Amphibious Training Command (latter responsibilities taken over by the Navy at San Diego). Each of these had the mission of testing equipment and formulating requirements within its area of concern and supervising the training of required specialized units. For example, formal training began at the parachute school at Fort Benning in the spring of 1941 and the school expanded until, at the height of the airborne effort, it was graduating 1,250 new paratroopers per week in addition to course completions from the rigger, demolitions, communications, and jumpmaster courses.

The final phase of training of ground units was bringing them up to a state of complete combat readiness and their delivery to staging areas prior to departing the various ports of embarkation. The Army Ground Forces shipped out over 2,000,000 men in prepackaged units. There were three peak periods of shipment: September 1942 when over 90,000 ground troops departed to train in Britain prior to the North African assault, January-March 1944 when over 315,000 ground combat troops were sent to Britain for the final buildup for the Normandy assault, and in August-October 1944 when 400,000 more were sent overseas for operations on the European front. In addition, large quantities of individual replacements were prepared for overseas movement at replacement training centers and deployed through replacement depots operated by the Army Service Forces.

Chapter 2

Infantry

The infantry was the fundamental basis of the army's combat capability in World War II, despite the large-scale advent of mechanization, armored warfare, and air power. Infantry was relied upon to destroy enemy land opposition and seize and hold ground in the offense, and on the defense to defeat the enemy attack. Other ground elements such as artillery, tanks, tank destroyers, and engineers were utilized on the battlefield to support the infantry in reaching and maintaining its objectives.

The most drastic change in infantry organization was the triangularization of the division as a result of interwar doctrinal and weapons experimentation culminating in the period 1937–39. The "square" four-regiment division designed to mass power under the static conditions of World War I was discarded as not mobile or flexible enough for modern conditions. On 1 January 1939 the new triangular infantry division emerged from concepts first field-tested in America by the 2nd Infantry Division in 1937. It reflected certain attributes of the German divisional structure and was premised on the association of all its elements, from squad to regiment, in three's. Ideally it was envisioned that a given element would fix the enemy while another maneuvered against him and the third acted as a reserve. The old interior brigade system was eliminated, but despite the reduction in manpower new weapons systems allowed the new division to deliver more firepower.

The army-wide process of change began during the winter of 1939–40 and was hastened by the success of German forces using the new combat team mode. However, as late as September 1940, the tables of organization for the triangular division were still not ready. In August preliminary charts were issued with directions that the 1st–9th Divisions conform by 1 October, with the rest of the regular army divisions slowly following. The eighteen National Guard divisions which were inducted in their square configuration were physically reorganized into the triangular pattern only during January and February of 1942. All army divisions raised in 1942 were formed under the triangular organization, which governed thereafter.

CHART 4.
Infantry Division

15 July 1943	Division Headquarters	Headquarters	Headquarters Company	Military Police Platoon	Ordnance Light Maintenance Company	Quartermaster Company	Signal Company	Infantry Regiment (3 each)	Division Artillery	Cavalry Reconnaissance Troop, Mecz	Engineer Battalion	Medical Battalion	Total Division (w/o attachments)*
Officers	38	2	4	3	9	10	7	139	130	6	27	34	687
Warrant Officers	8				1		4	5	9		3	2	42
Enlisted Men	103	7	106	70	137	183	215	2,974	2,021	149	617	429	12,959
Airplane, Liaison									10				10
Boats, Assault											14		14
Air Compressor, Trk											4		4
Tractor											3		3
Ambulance, 3/4-ton												30	30
M8 Armored Car										13			13
Sedan Car		1											1
Carbine, .30-cal	104	8	44	55	102	148	148	853	1,871	99	66		5,204
M3 Halftrack										5			5
Machinegun, .30-cal								42		13	18		157
Machinegun, .50-cal			3		5	13	6	35	89	3	12		236
Submachinegun, .45					12		32			30	16		90
57mm Gun			3					18					57
105mm Howitzer								6	36				54
155mm Howitzer									12				12
Rocket Launcher, AT			6		5	5	5	112	166	5	29		557
60mm Mortar								27		9			90
81mm Mortar								18					54
Pistol, .45-cal	17	1	16	1	2	2	1	275	289		3		1,157
Rifle, .30-cal	17		50	17	31	43	45	1,990		26	562		6,761
Truck, 1/4-ton		1	16	15	7	6	19	139	82	24	16	9	612
Truck, 3/4-ton		1	7	3	5	2	13	12	114		13	15	209
Truck, 1 1/2-ton			7				7	30				2	106
Truck, 2 1/2-ton					14	51	16	33	139	1	22	14	356
Truck, 2 1/2-ton Dump											27		27
Truck, 4-ton										15	3		18
Truck, Wrecker					3					1	1		5

*with attached medical, chaplain, and band strength total is 14,253

The Infantry Division

The standard infantry division of the U.S. Army in World War II was a general purpose fighting organization designed for "open warfare," which used motor transport and had a minimum of artillery and auxiliary elements intrinsically assigned. It was the fundamental combined-arms formation which had a permanent fixed structure. It relied on higher-echelon corps and army level units to provide specialized combat or logistical support required, such as engineer ponton units for bridging or transportation truck units to move all personnel and equipment simultaneously. During the war the infantry also formed several motorized and airborne divisions, a light (truck) division, a light (jungle) division, and a mountain division.

A critical shortage of shipping space and manpower limitations imposed by the War Department forced further streamlining of divisional organization beyond triangularization in 1942 and 1943. The approved strength of a division fell from 15,245 on 1 June 1941 to 14,253 on 15 July 1943, and finally to 14,037 on 24 January 1945. The 27 rifle companies, the "heart" of the division, retained their strength of 5,184 but headquarters and auxiliary troops were considerably pared. Inevitably this did affect rifle strength when infantrymen were tasked to perform the jobs previously done by the auxiliary personnel (such as military police duties concerning prisoners). Some of the reduction was offset by newer weapons, such as the introduction of hand-held rocket launchers while the number of antitank guns was decreased. By mid-1943 a 13 percent cut in personnel and 23 percent cut in vehicles, which were also reduced in size with more trailer utilization, saved 6,000 ship-tons in required equipment transport; a 15 percent reduction.

The army raised 66 infantry divisions during World War II, three overseas (the Americal in New Caledonia and both 24th and 25th in Hawaii). There is serious question whether this provided enough divisions in light of the sustained and costly campaigns of northern France and the German frontier in Europe, and New Guinea and the Philippines in the Pacific. It did result in infrequent unit rotation which tended to chew up and exhaust veteran units. Stateside divisions as well as those in England were often stripped and then sped into combat with inadequate preparation. Due to lack of troops several battlefield opportunities were missed and long frontages were not secured in areas which proved critical. After the German Ardennes Counteroffensive there was a final scramble for the few divisions remaining, which diverted the 86th and 97th at the last minute from their scheduled departures to the Pacific. The fact that Soviet offensives negated German ability to really profit from these circumstances does not erase the fact that manpower allocations weren't properly distributed, since the infantry division was the foundation of army means to achieve victory.

CHART 5.
Airborne Division

15 October 1942	Headquarters, Airborne Division	Headquarters Company	Military Police Platoon	Division Artillery	Infantry Parachute Regiment	Glider Infantry Regiment (2 each)	Engineer Battalion	Quartermaster Company	Signal Company	Medical Company	Airborne Antiaircraft Battalion	Ordnance Company	Division Total (w/o attachments)*
Officers	36	5	2	79	129	64	23	4	4	20	27	7	464
Warrant Officers	6			8	5	3	2				1	1	29
Enlisted Men	78	75	36	1,337	1,824	1,538	401	86	81	195	452	69	7,710
Parachute				431	1,753		139						2,323
Ambulance, light					2								2
Bicycle						29	10		9	4			81
Sedan Car		2			1								3
Carbine, .30-cal	82	62	35	1,391	495	635	377	57	84		353	46	4,252
37mm Gun				4		8	2				24		46
Machinegun, .30-cal					132	20	15						187
Machinegun, .50-cal		3		58		3					36	2	105
Submachinegun, .45-cal					154		33		1			15	203
75mm Pack Howitzer				36									36
Rocket Launcher, AT				177								5	182
60mm Mortar					27	24							75
81mm Mortar					12	12							36
Motorcycle, Solo			2										2
Pistol, .45-cal	29	1	3	33	1,753	136	15	1			2	1	2,110
Rifle, .30-cal		17			1,173	834	16	32			125	15	3,046
Truck, 1/4-ton		3	4	102	13	15	19	30	1	23	43	15	283
Truck, 3/4-ton		3		5	8	1					2		20
Truck, 2 1/2-ton		10	1	25	16	10	4					6	82
Handcart				20	76					7			179
Flamethrower							27						27

*Attached Medical and Chaplain brought division aggregate total to 8,505, added 1/4-ton × 16

Special Infantry Divisions

The motorized division was simply an infantry division equipped to move all of its elements simultaneously by motor. It was designed for employment alongside armored divisions at a ratio of one motorized to two armored divisions; the three to form a "type" armored corps. With an approved strength of 16,889 men they were more liberally provided with auxiliary elements to possess limited tactical independence. In April 1942 the 6th–9th Infantry Divisions were converted to the motorized configuration, and the 4th and 90th soon followed. However, in reality only the 4th Motorized Division was ever fully outfitted with the appropriate equipment and personnel and other special increases. Since it required as much shipping space as an armored division—without the same striking power—no theater commander requested it even though it was tagged for overseas shipment from August 1942 on. Since an infantry division could always be transported by the attachment of a troop transport battalion of six truck companies, the motorized division was eliminated beginning in March 1943 with the last, the 4th, being reconverted to infantry on 4 August 1943. Several infantry divisions were either wholly or partially motorized in the European theater, but instead of using truck companies which were fully employed in supply efforts, the needed motor transport was secured by immobilizing numerous antiaircraft artillery units.

The "airborne" division was first conceived by the army to be a task force formed for a particular mission by assigning air transportation to elements of a normal infantry division, reinforced by parachute troops. This concept was altered with the need for a more permanent organization in the early 1942 invasion plans against western Europe. In August 1942 the 82nd and 101st Airborne Divisions were formed from the assets of the former division with added parachute regiments, and on 15 October 1942 a table of organization was published for the airborne division. The army eventually raised five such divisions in World War II. The airborne division was initially a miniature infantry division with the same parts except that it added a small antiaircraft battalion and contained one parachute and two glider regiments. Light 75mm pack howitzers were substituted for the standard 105mm howitzers of an infantry division. Its total strength was 8,505, later raised to 9,115. However, the 82nd Airborne Division had its own special authorization level of 12 February 1943 and it and the 101st were considerably reinforced for combat operations by the wartime attachment of separate units up to regimental level in size. As a result of European experiences new airborne division "test" tables were rushed into use dated 16 December 1944, reconfiguring the division to one glider regiment and two parachute regiments and boosting its size to 13,906—about equal to a standard infantry division. The 13th, 17th, 82nd, and 101st Airborne Divisions—all in Europe—were converted accordingly by 1 March 1945. The 11th Airborne Division in the Southwest Pacific remained under the old tables of organization.

CHART 6.
Light Division (Truck)

21 January 1944	Division Headquarters	Headquarters Company	Military Police Platoon	Signal Platoon	Ordnance Light Maintenance Plat	Infantry Regiment (3 each)	Division Artillery	Engineer Battalion	Medical Battalion	Quartermaster Truck Company	Division Total (w/o attachments)
Officers	38	2	1	4	1	84	110	25	31	6	470
Warrant Officers	3			3		1	5	2			16
Enlisted Men	64	22	36	106	19	1,894	1,399	380	278	203	8,189
Airplane							8				8
Carbine, .30-cal	36	9	37	92	16	664	1,070	61		15	3,328
Cart, Hand		9		11	7	128	91		53		555
Machinegun, .30-cal						36					108
Machinegun, .50-cal							60			19	79
Submachinegun, .45-cal						81					243
75mm Pack Howitzer							48				48
Antitank rocket Launcher						6	56				74
60mm Mortar						27					81
81mm Mortar						6					18
Pistol, .45-cal	22	1				149	197	2			669
Rifle, .30-cal	36	14		21	4	1,247	247	344		194	4,601
Truck, 1/4-ton		2					116			149	267

The light division was planned as an all-purpose division usable in any conditions where relatively little equipment would be carried, the advantages being that it would save shipping space and avoid special refitting of standard infantry divisions. It was designed for mountain, jungle, airborne, or amphibious operations where it could rely on attached pack mules, native bearers, gliders, or landing craft, respectively. Its strength (in the light truck mode) totaled 8,984. Three light divisions were authorized in June 1943 and the 89th Light Division (Truck) was converted from the 89th Infantry Division; the 10th Light Division (Pack, Alpine) was activated from elements trained at the Mountain Training Center, primarily the 87th Mountain Infantry Regiment; and the 71st Light Division (Pack, Jungle) was raised built around the 5th and 14th Infantry Regiments which had already received jungle training in Panama. Actually all these remained experimental test divisions, and after organizational shortcomings were verified in February-April 1944 maneuvers, the 71st and 89th were converted to standard infantry divisions. Despite its jungle specialization the 71st was rushed to Europe as emergency reinforcement. The 10th was converted into a full-fledged mountain division in light of its high proportion of mountaineers and skiers in order to prevent waste of valuable

CHART 7.
Mountain Division

4 November 1944	Division Headquarters	Headquarters	Headquarters Company	Military Police Platoon	Ordnance Maintenance Company	Signal Company	Infantry Regiment (3 each)	Division Artillery	Cavalry Reconnaissance Troop	Engineer Battalion	Antitank Battalion	Medical Battalion	Quartermaster Battalion	Division Total
Officers	44	2	3	3	8	9	128	100	5	31	18	47	19	673
Warrant Officers	8				1	4	5	6		2	1	2	2	41
Enlisted Men	111	7	86	68	82	254	2,739	1,632	157	749	328	616	438	12,745
Airplane, Liaison								8						8
Air Compressor, Truck										2				2
20-ton Lowbed semi-										3				3
Tractor, Diesel										3				3
Carbine, .30-cal	111	8	60	53	65	204	887	1,682	28	111	100	117	356	5,556
Gun, 37mm							9							27
Gun, 57mm towed											18			18
Machinegun, .30-cal							60		6	18				204
Machinegun, .50-cal			3		2	2	7	30		7	6		14	85
Submachinegun, .45-cal			7	11			63	9		7				223
75mm Pack Howitzer								36						36
2.35" Rocket Launcher			6		3	5	60			26	18		25	263
60mm Mortar							27							81
81mm Mortar							18							54
Pistol, .45-cal	20	1		1	2	2	203	11		3	92	9	2	752
Rifle, .30-cal	20		29	17	17	50	1,845	45	134	687	155		101	6,790
Truck, ¼-ton		3	24	15	4	7	18	19		7	18	10	6	167
Truck, ¾-ton				3	3	4		3		4	4	19	3	43
Truck, 1½-ton Cargo											25			25
Truck, 2½-ton			6		8	7	16	1		8		23	57	158
Truck, 2½-ton Dump										12				12
Truck, 4-ton Wrecker					1						1			2
Truck, 4-/5-ton Tractor												3		3
Truck, 6-ton										3				3
Horse, Bell							9	3		3			12	45
Horse, Draft												18		18
Horse, Pack									27					27
Horse, Riding			32	4		21	48	206	155	21		33	15	631
Mule, Pack			50		30	64	725	1,057		417		75	651	4,519
Mule, Riding			22	4	5		128			90			216	721

training and assets otherwise. With a new 4 November 1944 table of organization authorization of 14,101 it was essentially an infantry division containing ski-mountain personnel and over 6,000 mules and horses substituting for normal motor transport (though vehicles were retained for heavy hauls). This division began arriving in Italy in December 1944, by which time the Fifth Army had been forced to employ standard infantry divisions for mountain fighting during almost the entire duration of the campaign there.

One special infantry division remains to be mentioned: the Philippine Division. It had been organized on 8 June 1921 for the security of that territory and was composed of a mix of American and *Philippine Scout* (Filipinos officered by Americans) units. It had been a square division until early 1941 scattered throughout the area, and was still in the process of triangular conversion when the United States entered the war and Japan invaded the Philippine Islands. As a result it was lacking essentials and required training, though in one limited instance this assisted its wartime establishment. Its former engineer regiment was ordered "triangularized" to a battalion, but the unit still retained the construction equipment authorized to it as a regiment. During the brief existence of this division it was fragmented in the defense of Bataan and forced to surrender there in April 1942. However, it was kept on the rolls of the army and reorganized and redesignated after the war as the 12th Infantry Division *(Philippine Scouts)* on 6 April 1946.

Infantry Regiments and Battalions

At the beginning of European hostilities the infantry remained emaciated from the drastic reductions of the interwar period, having suffered a 63 percent cut by 1932 with some 27 regiments inactivated. By 1938, of the 38 total remaining, 14 only had two battalions apiece. Beginning in 1940 some regular army regiments, inactive 18–19 years, were recalled to the colors at the same time 40 National Guard regiments were inducted, which were followed by 36 more of the latter category in 1941. The strength of the standard infantry regiment was raised from 2,542 in 1939 to 3,340 by 1 June 1941, and then trimmed to 3,118 by 15 July 1943 and to 3,068 by 24 January 1945. A cannon company (of self-propelled 75mm and 105mm howitzers, later towed) was added to the infantry regiment in April 1942, and a host of new weapons introduced which revolutionized regimental tactics. Infantry regiments also developed and increasingly employed the Regimental Combat Team concept during World War II. An RCT was a grouping of combat units, such as an artillery battalion, a company of engineers, a medical company, and a signal detachment, around an infantry regiment to accomplish a given mission. Additional elements required to perform specialized missions could be flexibly added. The RCT predecessors were the army's sublegions of 1792–96.

CHART NO. 8
Typical Infantry Regiments and Battalions of World War II

INFANTRY REGIMENT	T/O	Officers	Warrant Officers	Enlisted Men	105mm Howitzer	75mm Howitzer, Motor Carriage	57mm Gun	37mm Gun	Machinegun, .50-cal	Machinegun, .30-cal Heavy	Machinegun, .30-cal Light	Mortar, 81mm	Mortar, 60mm	Rocket Launcher, 2.36" Anti-Tank	Submachinegun, .45-cal	Carbine, .30-cal	Rifle, .30-cal	Pistol, .45-cal	Halftrack M3 Personnel or M21 81mm	Truck, 2½-ton	Truck, 1½-ton or 1-ton	Truck, ¾-ton	Truck, ¼-ton	Wrecker, Heavy	Tank Recovery Vehicle T5	Hand Utility Cart	Motor-scooter	Animals
Infantry	7-11 (26 Feb 44)	152	5	3100	6	—	18	—	35	24	18	18	37	112	—	836	1990	293	—	34	31	12	149	—	—	—	—	—
Glider Infantry	7-51 (5 Sep 42)	73	3	1602	—	—	—	8	3	8	12	12	24	—	—	635	834	136	—	10	—	1	18	—	—	76	—	—
Infantry, Glider	7-51 (1 Aug 44)	81	7	1540	—	—	—	8	3	8	12	12	24	81	36	814	731	9	—	10	—	3	24	—	—	96	29	—
Motorized Infantry	7-61 (1 Apr 42)	143	6	3423	2*	6*	—	24	34	24	18	18	27	—	—	1107	2107	213	—	138	—	114	82	—	—	—	—	—
Infantry, Mountain	7-131 (4 Nov 44)	143	5	2891	—	—	—	9	7	24	36	18	27	60	63	896	1846	205	—	16	—	—	18	—	—	—	—	953**
Infantry Parachute	7-31 (17 Feb 42)	140	5	1884	—	—	—	—	—	132	12	27	—	—	154	495	1173	1753	—	16	—	8	13	***	—	—	—	—
Infantry, Parachute	7-31 (1 Aug 44)	114	7	1951	—	—	—	—	4	132	12	27	73	54	1098	886	11	—	15	—	3	17	—	—	34	52	—	—
INFANTRY BATTALION																												
Armored Infantry	7-25 (15 Sep 43)	39	3	995	—	3	9	—	43	37	23	1	9	74	126	394	478	3	78	21	—	2	24	—	1	—	—	—
Infantry	7-15 (26 Feb 44)	35	—	836	—	—	3	—	6	8	6	6	9	29	—	219	571	81	—	—	4	2	34	—	—	—	—	—
Parachute	7-35 (1 Aug 44)	27	1	555	—	—	—	—	—	44	4	9	21	18	310	280	2	—	—	—	—	—	—	—	8	—	—	—
Ranger Infantry	7-85 (29 Feb 44)	27	—	489	—	—	—	—	24	6	18	14	****	56	338	198	—	—	—	—	6	9	—	—	—	—	—	—
Separate	7-95 (21 Jul 43)	41	1	899	—	—	3	—	8	8	6	6	9	27	—	237	588	76	—	8	4	1	37	—	—	—	—	—

*Self-Propelled
**Bell Horse × 9, Riding Horse × 51, Pack Mule × 765, Riding Mule × 128
***Plus Ambulance × 1, Sedan Car × 1
****Anti-Tank Rifle .55-cal × 3

The triangularization of the division demanded a price in historical heritage, as the process necessitated the loss of one regiment from every previously square division. Most of the regiments thus separated ended up orphaned and were used to provide filler personnel or training cadres before being inactivated stateside. For example, the National Guard 176th Infantry (the old 1st Virginia once commanded by George Washington) served as the capitol guard to Washington, D.C., before being inactivated at Fort Benning on 10 July 1944. The Regular Army's own 3rd Infantry *(Old Guard)* was dispatched to early overseas duty in Newfoundland and Greenland where bypassed by the mainstream of the war, sent back to Fort Benning, and then rushed to Europe in 1945 just in time to participate in the closing campaigns. However, several separate infantry regiments, such as the 156th Infantry (old *First Louisiana*) in France and the 158th Infantry ("Bushmasters," old *Arizona Volunteer Infantry*) in the Pacific, were well utilized as army-echelon fire brigades.

Armored infantry regiments were designed to provide the new armored divisions with their own necessary intrinsic infantry capability. Their real difference with ordinary infantry was their degree of mechanized shock value in lightly armored half-tracks and mobility on other vehicles. All but two were broken up into armored infantry battalions during the course of the war.

As a result of German practice, the army formed airborne regiments and battalions. Numbers above 500 were reserved for the designation of paratroop units while glider-borne infantry regiments were converted from standard ones with no numerical redesignation involved. This volunteer airborne infantry represented some of the most specialized, elite, well-trained, and aggressive troops fielded by the army in World War II. While their actual air assaults were spectacular exploits, some of their most valuable service was actually performed in a conventional ground role where they excelled as strategic reserves in hard-pressed circumstances.

Certain prewar regiments in the Regular Army were reserved for "nonwhite" races, in the terminology of the time. The 24th and 25th Infantry had contained only Negro enlisted men since 1866, the 65th was manned by Puerto Rican natives, and the 43rd, 45th, and 57th were *Philippine Scouts*. These were composed of Filipino enlisted and an outgrowth of a company of "Macabebe Scouts" organized on 1 September 1899 and part of the Regular Army establishment of the U.S. Army since 2 February 1901 under the designation *Philippine Scouts*. The formations were paid through direct U.S. Army funding which resulted in better quality, equipment, and pay than in the Philippine Army, though not equal to that of the United States Army. During the war the army raised other units representing different racial extractions, such as the 442nd Infantry Regiment and 100th Infantry Battalion, later absorbed into the former (both *Japanese-American Nisei*); the 99th Infantry Battalion *(Norwegian-American)*; the 101st Infantry Battalion *(Austrian-American)*; the 122nd Infantry Battalion *(Greek-American)*; and the 1st and 2nd Filipino Infantry Regiments.

Infantry Ranger Units and OSS Operational Groups

Several distinctive commando-oriented infantry types were raised by the army in response to particular requirements encountered in the global nature of World War II. The 1st Special Service Force, roughly a brigade in size, was a joint U.S.-Canada venture and a unique airborne unit composed of rugged volunteers expertly trained in amphibious, mountain, and winter commando warfare. The 474th Infantry absorbed most of its veterans in December 1944. The 5307th Composite Unit (Provisional) gained fame by its long-range jungle operations in northern Burma and was redesignated as the 475th Infantry in August 1944. The 1st-6th Ranger Battalions were formed as elite commando units designed for raiding and the accomplishment of the most difficult tasks. Other commando-type organizations included the Alaskan and Alamo Scouts.

Although the Office of Strategic Services (OSS) was an independent government agency, its larger military units were recruited from, manned by, and under the command of army personnel. Operational Groups were composed of foreign-language-qualified soldiers, primarily army and ideally parachutist-qualified, who were skilled in sabotage and guerrilla warfare, and were designed to be used in small groups to harass the enemy *behind* his lines. Their chief difference with army rangers was that the latter were supposed to be employed in *front* of enemy lines. The OG Branch was established on 4 May 1943 and was activated as a separate military unit within the OSS on 27 November 1944. The Operational Groups for Italy (later the 2677th OSS Regiment and 2671st Special Reconnaissance Battalion) arrived in theater August 1943 and March 1944. The OGs for France arrived in England January-March 1944; those for Yugoslavia arrived in theater October 1943–January 1944; and one German OG arrived in North Africa in July 1944. Greek OGs were provided by the bulk of the 122nd Infantry Battalion which was transformed into the Third Contingent, Unit B in Cairo, Egypt; and Norwegian OGs were gleaned from the 99th Infantry Battalion in December 1943. In addition, a large guerrilla force of native Kachin tribesmen was recruited and trained in northern Burma as the *Kachin Rangers* or *Jingpaw Rangers* under control of OSS Detachment 101.

Infantry School and Replacement Establishments

The Infantry School had been located at Fort Benning since October 1918 when the post was still under construction, and was rapidly expanded past September 1939. The curriculum was altered in August 1940 to overlap its 13-week regular course and by the spring of 1941, 26 classes were in continuous session. The Officer Candidate Course was initiated 1 July 1941 and by December 1942 classes were graduating almost daily. This enrollment was further substantially expanded beginning in October 1944. The Infantry School also provided training literature, advice, and films as well as resident instruction. The Infantry Board had been created by the War Department on 15 December 1939 at Fort Benning with the function of improving infantry weapons, training, and organization and continued in this capacity throughout World War II.

Four Infantry Replacement Training Centers began operating in March 1941. These were organized by regiment, battalion, and company, but this structure was used for instructional rather than any tactical functions. By 27 March 1942, when the Replacement and School Command was established and took control over all replacement training centers, four infantry RTCs were operating at Camp Croft, Camp Roberts, Camp Wheeler, and Camp Wolters. The Branch Immaterial RTCs at Fort McClellan and Camp Robinson were converted to Infantry in January 1943 and moved to Camp Fannin that September. Further Infantry Replacement Training Centers were activated at Camp Blanding on 4 August 1943, Camp Hood in March 1944, and Camp Rucker on 12 February 1945. Finally, Infantry Advanced Replacement Training Centers were activated at Camps Gordon and Maxey on 17 October 1944, Camp Howze on 18 October 1944, Camp Livingston on 13 November 1944, and Camp Shelby on 12 February 1945. Cadres for these were drawn from existing replacement training centers except at Camps Shelby and Rucker, where separate infantry regiments were reorganized to conform to standard tables of distribution applicable to replacement training centers.

The Airborne Command was activated 21 March 1942 at Fort Benning from the Provisional Parachute Group and transferred to Fort Bragg on 9 April 1942. It was concerned with the activation and preparation of airborne units and formed the Parachute School on 15 May 1942, which in turn was derived from the Parachute Section of the Infantry School first established in July 1941. On 28 February 1944 the Airborne Command was reorganized and became the Airborne Center on 1 March 1944. Finally, the Airborne Board was constituted on 17 November 1944 to continue airborne test and development functions at Camp Mackall, which traced its heritage to the original Parachute Test Platoon activated at Fort Benning in June 1940.

AUTHORIZED INFANTRY UNIT STRENGTHS — DIVISIONS, BRIGADES, REGIMENTS*

DIVISIONS	T/O	JUNE 1943	JUNE 1944	JUNE 1945
Airborne Division	71	8,505	8,596	8,556
Airborne Division (16 Dec 44 Test)	71T	—	—	12,979
Infantry Division	7	15,424	14,253	14,037
Light Division (Pack Alpine or Jungle)	72T	—	9,369	—
Light Division (Truck)	72T	—	8,988	—
Motorized Division	77	16,889	—	—
Mountain Division	70	14,965	14,965	14,102
BRIGADES				
HHC, Airborne Infantry Brigade (HHD in June 1943)	71-10-1S	54	76	74
REGIMENTS				
Armored Infantry Regiment	7-21	2,472	2,472	2,442
Glider Infantry Regiment	7-51	1,678	1,681	1,628
Glider Infantry Regiment (16 Dec 44 Test)	7-51T	—	—	3,114
Infantry Regiment	7-11	3,087	3,258	3,207
Light Infantry Regiment	7-71T	—	2,060	—
Motorized Infantry Regiment	7-61	3,572	—	—
Mountain Infantry Regiment	7-131	2,755	2,755	3,039
Parachute Infantry Regiment	7-31	2,029	2,025	2,122
Parachute Infantry Regiment (16 Dec 44 Test)	7-31T	—	—	2,532

*Basic Unit Table of Organization with current changes applicable to month listed. In cases of strength variation between divisional and nondivisional components of the same T/O, this chart reflects the latter.

AUTHORIZED INFANTRY UNIT STRENGTHS — BATTALIONS AND SPECIAL UNITS*

BATTALIONS	T/O	JUNE 1943	JUNE 1944	JUNE 1945
Armored Infantry Battalion	7-15	700	1,037	1,031
Chemical Battalion (Motorized/Chemical Mortar Bn)	3-25	1,010	622	672
Glider Infantry Battalion	7-55	643	644	658
Glider Infantry Battalion (16 Dec 44 Test)	7-55T	—	—	863
Infantry Battalion	7-15	850	871	860
Infantry Battalion (Separate)	7-95	916	941	929
Light Infantry Battalion	7-75T	—	624	—
Motorized Infantry Battalion	7-65	942	—	—
Mountain Infantry Battalion	7-135	744	744	851
Parachute Infantry Battalion	7-35	530	530	583
Parachute Infantry Battalion (16 Dec 44 Test)	7-35T	—	—	706
Ranger Infantry Battalion	7-85	511	516	516

SPECIAL

	T/O	JUNE 1943	JUNE 1944	JUNE 1945
Combined Intelligence Platoon (Alaskan Scouts)	7-157S	—	—	88
Cannon Company, 800th Infantry Regiment	23 Feb 43 Special	—	107	103

*Basic Unit Table of Organization with current changes applicable to month listed. In cases of strength variation between divisional and nondivisional components of the same T/O, this chart reflects the latter.

INFANTRY ACTIVITIES IN JUNE 1944

	OFFICERS	ENLISTED	TRAINEES
Infantry Board — Ft Bragg, N.C.	17	31	
Rocket Board — Ft Benning, Ga	8	8	
Infantry School — Ft Benning, Ga	883	4,113	
HHC, Airborne Center — Cp Mackall, N.C.	20	63	
Parachute School — Ft Benning, Ga	266	1,638	
Replacement Training Center — Cp Croft, S.C.	542	2,500	15,120
Replacement Training Center — Cp Fannin, Tex	671	2,889	16,000
Replacement Training Center — Cp Joseph T. Robinson, Ark	878	4,042	21,000
Replacement Training Center — Cp Hood, Tex	844	4,124	24,000
Replacement Training Center — Ft McClellan, Ga	992	4,548	23,700
Replacement Training Center — Cp Roberts, Calif	641	2,997	18,240
Replacement Training Center — Cp Wheeler, Ga	600	2,744	17,280
Replacement Training Center — Cp Wolters, Ga	578	2,749	16,080

Chapter 3

Armor

During the period following World War I there was much theoretical but little tangible progress in either tank production or tactics in the U.S. Army, a situation which was changed in 1938–40 in view of armored concepts the Germans perfected and then successfully employed in their Polish and French campaigns. An improvised armored division, formed with the mechanized 7th Cavalry Brigade from Fort Knox and the Provisional Tank Brigade from Fort Benning, dominated the 1940 Louisiana Maneuvers. In response the War Department created the Armored Force "for purposes of a service test" on 10 July 1940. The Armored Force was redesignated the Armored Command on 2 July 1943 and finally the Armored Center on 20 February 1944.

The Armored Division

The basic element of the Armored Force was the armored division. It was designed to provide high mobility, protected firepower, and shock potential enhanced by an independent ability to conduct sustained operations. The armored division of 15 November 1940 was structured as a complete, self-sufficient combined arms team capable of rapid offensive action to strike deep against vital rear area targets. This armored division had an armored brigade of 368 tanks organized into two light and one heavy armored regiment; a field artillery regiment; and division reconnaissance composed of a ground reconnaissance battalion and an attached aviation observation squadron. Division support boasted an armored infantry regiment and a field artillery battalion as well as an engineer battalion. Division service was provided with quartermaster, ordnance, and medical battalions and a signal company. Authorized division strength was placed at 12,697 personnel.

The reorganization of 1 March 1942 introduced what was to become known as the "heavy" armored division of World War II, and the 1st–3rd Armored Divisions went into combat under these 1942 tables. This division structure contained two armored regiments with two light and four medium tank battalions of three companies each. The armored

CHART 9.
Armored Division

15 September 1943

	Division Headquarters	Headquarters Company	CCA, CCB, CCR combined	Signal Company	Cavalry Rcn Sqdn, Mecz	Tank Battalion (3 each)	Armd Infantry Bn (3 each)	Division Artillery	Engineer Battalion	Div Trains HHC	Ordnance Maintenance Bn	Medical Battalion	Military Police Platoon	Division Total
Officers	42	5	27	7	42	37	36	101	32	7	40	33	3	558
Warrant Officers	8		2	3	3	3	3	6	3		6	2		51
Enlisted	114	133	163	292	890	689	962	1,516	658	96	716	382	88	10,001
Airplane, Liaison		2						6						8
Tractor, Crawler									3					3
M8 Armored Car		2			52									54
Carbine, .30-cal	134	83	123	239	574	257	394	1,254	153	56	592		67	5,228
75mm Howitzer Mtz					8		3							17
105mm Howitzer Mtz								54						54
M3 Halftrack		16	14	19	32	13	72	93	15	2	4	4	1	451
81mm Mortar Halftrack						3	3							18
Machinegun, .30-cal		10	6	13	68	18	60	66	38	2	28			465
Machinegun, .50-cal		8	8	13	29	26	43	78	20	2	38		1	404
Submachinegun, .45		45	56	62	238	449	126	348	103	38	165		23	2,803
57mm Gun	3						9							30
Rocket Launcher, AT		14	16	24	37	35	74	120	29	4	35		1	607
60mm Mortar					36		9							63
81mm Mortar					3	6	1	6						30
Pistol, .45-cal	18	1	13	1	3	3	3	21	3	3	5		1	87
Rifle, .30-cal		9			120	20	478		434	6				2,063
Light Tank		3	6		17	17								77
Medium Tank						53		9						168
Tank, 105mm How						6								18
Truck, ¼-ton		12	18	22	106	22	23	63	25	16	23	10	19	449
Truck, ¾-ton		2				2	2	9	7	10	19	15	3	77
Truck, 2½-ton Dump									18					18
Truck, 2½-ton Cargo		4	4	19	20	39	21	75	27	9	67	17		422
Truck, 2½-ton, Other				2							20			22
Truck, Treadway									6					6
Truck, 4-ton											3			3
Heavy Wrecker Trk					1	2	1	3	1		11			25
T5 Tank Recovery					3	6	1	6						30
Surgical Truck												6		6

brigade concept was eliminated and two combat command headquarters, popularly known as Combat Commands A and B, were added for mission flexibility. The artillery was reduced to three self-propelled 105mm field artillery battalions which remained standard throughout all subsequent division alterations. The 1942 "heavy" armored division had 390 tanks (232 medium and 158 light) and a personnel strength of 14,620. Changes through the end of the hostilities in Europe reduced this number to 14,488 for the 2nd and 3rd Armored Divisions, the only ones to retain this structure.

On 15 September 1943 the armored division was again reorganized, and all sixteen army armored divisions—except the 2nd and 3rd—eventually converted under these and later tables and became known as "light" armored divisions. The 1943 structure replaced the two armored regiments with three tank battalions, but each tank battalion was increased to three medium and one light tank company. The armored reconnaissance battalion was relabeled the cavalry reconnaissance battalion, and a reserve command (CCR) was added to CCA and CCB. Unfortunately the personnel authorizations for this new CCR were so skimpy that in Europe armored group headquarters & headquarters companies were usually attached to light armored divisions to correct this inadequacy. Tanks totaled only 263 (186 medium and 77 light) and personnel strength was reduced to 10,937. New tables published on 24 January 1945 added only nine more medium tanks and further reduced manpower to 10,670.

Armored Groups and Regiments

When the armored division was reorganized in 1943 to retain three tank battalions instead of its previous two armored regiments, the latter were duly broken up and two tank battalions became available as separate units in each case. Theoretically the reduction from six to three tank battalions should have released three in each, but the simultaneous enlargement of the battalions absorbed one battalion per division. Added to those already raised as separate, the army had 54 tank battalions in its armored divisions and 65 in the nondivisional pool by the end of 1943. Twenty armored groups were raised as controlling headquarters over these separate battalions. However the group lost its functions in theaters since these battalions were more or less permanently attached to infantry divisions. As a practical matter, most armored groups were integrated into armored divisions to shore up headquarters staffs. As previously discussed, the 32nd, 33rd, 63rd, and 67th Armored Regiments were not broken up since the 2nd and 3rd Armored Divisions remained under the 1942 "heavy" organization.

One unique armored regiment that existed during World War II was the Armored Force Demonstration Regiment activated at Fort Knox on 1 February 1942. It served as elite school troops and was organized as a miniature combined-arms replica of an armored division.

Tank Battalions

The 70th Tank Battalion (GHQ Reserve) was raised 15 July 1940 as a separate unit and was followed by the 191st–194th Tank Battalions organized December 1940–March 1941 from the 18 National Guard divisional tank companies already inducted. Both the 192nd and 194th were lost early in the campaign for the Philippine Islands. At first the separate tank battalion varied as being either heavy or light, but in 1943 it was reorganized to conform to the standard divisional tank battalion for ease of training and economy of supply and function. From 1943 the tank battalion was basically composed of 75mm M4 Sherman medium tanks and 37mm M5 light tanks, the latter being gradually replaced by M24 Chaffee light tanks commencing in late 1944. The 90mm M26 General Pershing heavy tank was used in some tank battalions of the 3rd and 9th Armored Divisions from February 1945 on.

The army had 65 separate tank battalions on 31 December 1944 as compared to 66 infantry divisions. It became standard practice in combat operations to attach a tank battalion to every front-line division, and the efficiency resulting from the long-standing relation encouraged such attachment on an almost permanent basis in many cases. Since tanks provided ideal infantry support in suppressing strongpoints and bunkers, rendering artillery fire support, as well as combating enemy vehicles, they began to be introduced as organic components of the division on 1 June 1945. After World War II the infantry division was reorganized to include its own intrinsic heavy tank battalion due to these factors.

CHART NO. 10
Typical Tank Battalions of World War II

TANK BATTALION	T/O	Officers	Warrant Officers	Enlisted Men	Medium Tank	Medium Tank w/105mm Howitzer	Medium Tank, Special	Light Tank	75mm Howitzer, motor carriage	75mm Pack Howitzer	Halftrack, 81mm Mortar M21	Rocket Launcher, 2.75" Anti-Tank	Machinegun, .50-cal	Machinegun, .30-cal	Submachinegun, .45-cal	Carbine, .30-cal*	Pistol, .45-cal	Halftrack, M3 Personnel	Halftrack, M3 Ambulance	Truck, 2½-ton	Truck, ¾-ton Command & Reconnaissance	Truck, ¾-ton Weapons Carrier	Truck, ¼-ton	Wrecker, Heavy	Tank Recovery Vehicle, T5	81mm Mortar
Tank Battalion	17-25 (15 Sep 43)	39	2	709	53	6	—	17	—	—	3	35	26	18	449	277	3	13	3	39	1	1	23	2	6	6
Medium, Special	17-45S (4 Dec 43)	32	2	669	18	—	54	—	—	—	—	27	20	16	439	240	3	9	3	39	2	1	24	2	5	5
Light Tank Battalion	17-15 (12 Nov 43)	34	2	513	—	—	—	59	3	—	3	22	17	9	293	237	3	12	2	23	1	1	21	2	—	—
Airborne Tank Battalion	17-55 (15 Jan 44)	27	3	356	—	—	—	56	—	3	—	8	23	22	211	159	3	—	—	—	—	13	41	—	—	—

*includes 15-20 Rifle, .30-cal

Specialized tank battalions were also formed. The army raised one flamethrower tank battalion, the 713th, which was so converted on 11 January 1945 and fought on Okinawa. The 743rd in Europe was partially organized in a flamethrowing role. Rollers, flails, and ploughs equipped mine-exploder and mine-excavator M4 tanks which formed the basis of several "special medium" tank battalions commencing in June 1943. The mine-clearing tank battalions that served in Europe were subordinated to the engineers, usually at a ratio of one company to combat engineer regiment requiring those services. The 28th Airborne Tank Battalion was raised on 6 December 1943 under a proposed organization published on 19 February 1944, and contained 37mm light airborne *Locust* tanks (M22), but never saw combat in that mode, being converted to a regular tank battalion in October of 1944. Six provisional Chinese-American tank battalions were raised at Ramgarh, India, in October 1943.

World War II also necessitated the creation of specialized amphibious tank and tractor battalions to fulfill assault landing and supply functions in the Pacific. The LVT (A) — Landing Vehicle, Tracked (Armored) — was developed for this purpose, and was used by both the army and the marines. The turretless LVT (A) without armament *(Water Buffalo)* was used for troop and cargo-carrier tasks, and the armor-plated versions with 37mm, later 75mm, turrets or machine guns provided fire support. Army amphibious tank and tractor battalions were equipped with these in 1944–45 (See Chart 13, page 26).

Armored Force School and Replacement Establishments

The Armored Force was constituted on 15 July 1940 at Fort Knox and assigned to the Army Ground Forces on 1 June 1942. It formulated tactical doctrine and supervised the training, organization, and direction of armored formations up to corps level. On 2 July 1943 it was redesignated the Armored Command and finally the Armored Center 16 February 1944, being discontinued on 30 October 1945.

The Armored Force School was approved 19 September 1940 and received its first students at Fort Knox on 4 November 1940. A Tank School had been established at Fort George G. Meade, but was moved to Fort Benning in 1932 where a year later it had been redesignated the Tank Section of the Infantry School. The Armored Force School began an officer candidate course in July 1941, and expanded rapidly until quotas were reduced and certain courses curtailed beginning in July 1943.

On 31 August 1931 the Tank Board, stationed at Fort George G. Meade, had been absorbed by the Infantry Board at Fort Benning, where it remained until transferred to Fort Knox in 1939. There the Armored Force Board was established on 15 July 1940 to carry on the development and testing of armored unit tactics, transportation, weapons, and equipment. The Landing Vehicle Board was established at Fort Ord on 11 April 1944 and operated there until its dissolution on 30 September 1945. The Board was initially under the Armored Board and was concerned with the development of amphibious tanks and tractors, but later it was transferred to the Cavalry Board since the latter coordinated all tracked vehicles other than tanks.

The Armored Force Replacement Training Center was originally envisioned as part of the Armored School, but in October 1940 the Replacement Center was made a separate installation. It finally became a part of the Replacement & School Command on 20 February 1944 and functioned at Fort Knox through the course of World War II.

ARMORED FORCE ACTIVITIES IN JUNE 1944	OFFICERS	ENLISTED	TRAINEES
Armored Board — Ft Knox, Ky	24	52	
Armored Force School — Ft Knox, Ky	426	3,111	
Landing Vehicle Board — Ft Ord, Calif	4	7	
HHC, Armored Center — Ft Knox, Ky	30	61	
Replacement Training Center — Ft Knox, Ky	491	2,427	11,712

Chapter 4

Cavalry

Prior to and during World War II there was little agreement on the proper employment and function of army cavalry on the armored/infantry battlefield, so the cavalry compromised between both. This then led to a postwar consensus that cavalry had either been misused altogether, or lacked enough combat striking power to properly fulfill its assigned reconnaissance roles. The basic problem was the demise of the horse in the scheme of modern warfare, upon which the prewar cavalry was largely reliant and very traditionally attached to. The final excuse given for the abandonment of horsed units was shipping space both for animals and for fodder, but this was not altogether true.

At the outset of the European war in 1939 the U.S. Army cavalry was already partially mechanized. The 1st and 13th Cavalry were already fully mechanized and combined into the technically advanced 7th Cavalry Brigade, a part of the Armored Forces. The 4th and 6th Cavalry were horse-mechanized; that is, their horses were transported about in large vans which could keep up with the rest of the motor vehicles, unload quickly and provide mounted action. Ten Regular Army all-horse regiments remained, but eight became concentrated in two horse cavalry divisions by late 1941. With the elimination of the Chief of Cavalry office in March 1942 the Army Ground Forces hastened to complete the mechanization process. The 2nd, 3rd, 11th, and 14th Cavalry transferred their personnel and equipment to new, identically numbered armored regiments in 1942, were inactivated, and reactivated as fully mechanized cavalry in 1943. The National Guard's four cavalry divisions and seventeen cavalry regiments were broken up prior to induction so that only seven partially mechanized regiments and a brigade of two horse cavalry regiments from Texas entered federal service. The latter two were dismounted and employed as foot infantry, and the others completely mechanized.

The last horse cavalry of the U.S. Army to fight mounted was the 26th Cavalry (Philippine Scouts) which was forced to destroy its horses upon withdrawal to Bataan in early 1942 to be defeated in normal infantry combat. Although

CHART 11.
Cavalry Division

1 August 1942	Div Headquarters	Headquarters Troop	Reconnaissance Sqdn	2 Cavalry Brigades (each)	Division Artillery	Signal Troop	Ordnance Company	Engineer Squadron	Medical Squadron	Quartermaster Sqdn	Total*
Officers	36	5	35	141	91	8	7	19	24	21	528
Warrant Officers	10		2	11	7	1	1	2		3	48
Enlisted Men	88	120	801	3,210	1,900	249	158	504	336	509	11,085
Air Compressor, Mtz			1					3			4
Raft, infantry support								6			6
Tractor w/angledozer								2			2
Armored Car, Light			38	13							64
M2 Halftrack + M3 Halftrack			1 + 2					7			8 + 2
Scout Car				8	3	7					26
Carbine, cal .30		40	238	178	1,724	196	106	97		301	3,058
Antitank Gun, 37mm				12	18			7			49
Machinegun, Heavy cal .30				16							32
Machinegun, cal .50		9	57	75	64						280
Machinegun, Light cal .30		9	60	106							281
Submachinegun, cal .45			83	21		54					179
Howitzer, field 75mm					24						24
Howitzer, 105mm field					12						12
Mortar, 81mm			9	8							25
Pistol, cal .45	119	58	268	2,976	202	1	23	31		2	6,656
Rifle, cal .30		32	249	1,864	72		37	397		230	4,745
Light Tank			17								17
Trucks, shop & repair, etc.						2	16				18
Ambulance, 3/4-ton									24		24
Horses, draft and pack				429	480				4		1,342
Horse, Riding + Horse, Bell		16		2,433	504			12	5 + 4		5,403 + 4
Mules									299		299
Truck, 1/4-ton		9	113	110	54	18	1	12	6	12	445
Truck, 3/4-ton		19	36	22	85	12	6	6	15	10	233
Truck, 1 1/2-ton									24		24
Truck, 2 1/2-ton (all types)		10	15	33	95	17	9	50		67	329
Truck-tractor, 4- and 5-ton		2					1	3	4	52	62
Truck, K53 and K54						5					5

*Without attachments; attached military police platoon, chaplain and medical brought officer total to 588 and enlisted total to 11,476 for a division aggregate of 12,112. It also added 50 carbines and 4 pistols and a small number of trucks.

animal transport was used by certain units in rugged areas of Burma, Sicily, India, and Italy, the traditional mounted cavalry vanished forever. Cavalry adopted new doctrines premised on light mechanized reconnaissance, converted into infantry, or perished.

The Cavalry Division

The horse cavalry division organization of 1 July 1939 contained two cavalry brigades (four regiments), one horse-drawn 75mm field howitzer artillery regiment, both a cavalry reconnaissance squadron and another cavalry reconnaissance troop, one engineer squadron, a quartermaster squadron, and a medical squadron, and Special Troops. It totaled 10,680 personnel on a wartime footing as well as 8,323 riding horses, 533 pack and draft horses, and 266 mules. The division also contained 18 light tanks, 611 trucks, and 140 motorcycles.

On 1 August 1942 the cavalry division was reorganized, but still contained the old "square" or brigade basis. However, the artillery was altered to consist of one 105mm and two 75mm howitzer battalions, and other components included a single reconnaissance squadron, signal troop, engineer squadron, ordnance company, medical squadron, and quartermaster squadron. Its strength was raised to 12,112 men but the total number of animals dropped to 7,298. Seventeen light tanks were retained and truck strength boosted to 1,182. A 30 September 1944 organization change reduced manpower to 11,216 and raised the animal strength slightly to 7,367. This latter reorganization was purely academic, however, as the single surviving cavalry division at the time had its own special organization and was fighting as infantry.

The army contained two cavalry divisions during World War II. The 1st Cavalry Division had been activated on 12 September 1921 at Fort Bliss where it transitioned from a horse mounted to dismounted infantry configuration 1 February–15 June 1943 prior to moving overseas. It arrived in Australia on 26 July 1943 where it was reorganized as the 1st Cavalry Division, Special, on 4 December 1943 partly under infantry and partly under cavalry tables of organization. Special allowances of heavy equipment and other components were supplied to tailor the division for combat in the Southwest Pacific. It contained, in addition to two brigades of four infantry type cavalry regiments, four 105mm artillery battalions, a tank company, and various normal combat support elements which brought its special authorized strength to 13,258—practically the same as an infantry division. It was reorganized wholly as infantry on 20 July 1945 in the Philippines, except that it retained its cavalry designations.

The 2nd Cavalry Division was activated 1 April 1941 at Fort Riley as a racially mixed formation; the 4th Brigade being Negro. It contained some of the oldest and proudest cavalry regiments of the Regular Army, but the lack of a requirement for horsed units led to its inactivation as a division on 15 July 1942 despite promising results in training maneuvers. The 4th Brigade remained active and formed the nucleus of the new 2nd Cavalry Division (Colored), reactivated 25 February 1943 at Fort Clark. The division arrived at Oran in North Africa during March of 1944 and was inactivated there on 10 May 1944. Its personnel were used to form service units in the theater.

Cavalry Brigades, Groups, and Squadrons

The cavalry mission of World War II was concentrated at squadron level, and all nondivisional mechanized cavalry regiments were broken up in late 1943 and early 1944 to form separate groups and squadrons. These were designed to perform reconnaissance missions employing infiltration tactics, fire, and maneuver, and engage in combat only to the extent necessary to accomplish their missions. Each cavalry group was composed of a Headquarters & Headquarters Troop and two or more attached mechanized cavalry reconnaissance squadrons. It was generally assigned to an army which attached it on a practically permanent basis to a specific corps, and the group was frequently further attached down to division level for operations. In addition to these separate mechanized cavalry reconnaissance squadrons in groups, each light armored division contained one (organized identically), each heavy armored division included a smaller armored reconnaissance battalion, and each infantry division had its own cavalry troop. In battle mechanized cavalry actually fought more often in an infantry mode.

Higher echelon cavalry brigades were intrinsic to the square concept of the cavalry division and brigade fates were tied to their divisions' survival. There were two exceptions. The separate 56th Cavalry Brigade from Texas, the only such National Guard unit inducted into federal service, operated over the two Texas National Guard regiments, the 112th and 124th Cavalry. However, after these were detached for overseas service, the brigade was no longer required and as a result it was redesignated as a separate cavalry reconnaissance troop which never left the States

CHART NO. 12
Cavalry Reconnaissance Squadron in World War II

CAVALRY RECONNAISSANCE SQUADRON	T/O 2-25	Officers	Warrant Officers	Enlisted Men	Armored Car, M8	75mm Howitzer on Carriage mot.	Light Tank	Halftrack, M3A1	Halftrack, Ambulance M3	Machinegun, .50-cal	Machinegun, .30-cal	81mm Mortar	60mm Mortar	Submachinegun, .45-cal	Carbine, .30-cal	Rifle, .30-cal	Pistol, .45-cal	Rocket Launcher, 2.36" Anti-Tank	Truck, 2½-ton	Wrecker, Heavy	Weapons Carrier, ¾-ton	Ambulance, ¾-ton	Truck, ¼-ton	Tank Recovery Vehicle, T5
Part of Armored Division	(15 Sep 43)	44	3	949	52	8	17	32	4	29	68	3	36	238	574	120	3	37	20	1	—	—	107	3
Part of Armored Division	(6 Jul 44)	44	3	861	52	8	17	32	4	29	68	3	36	235	536	120	3	37	20	1	1	1	110	3
Nondivisional	(15 Sep 43)	38	3	777	40	6	17	26	4	25	54	3	27	205	465	90	3	31	18	1	—	—	84	3
Nondivisional	(6 Jul 44)	38	3	702	40	6	17	26	4	25	54	3	27	202	434	90	3	31	18	1	1	1	87	3

and was inactivated at Camp Bowie on 9 November 1945. One separate Regular Army brigade existed on a provisional basis prior to the war for ceremonial and guard duty at Washington, D.C., and was appropriately known as the Washington Provisional Brigade. Since it was built around the 3rd Cavalry Regiment, it is listed in this book under cavalry. When the regiment was detached and moved to Georgia in February 1942, the brigade was discontinued soon afterward that May.

Cavalry regiments were either broken up into group and squadron components or remained organic to their respective divisions, as has already been discussed. Others were converted into armor and the 26th Cavalry was annihilated at Bataan. Two separate National Guard cavalry regiments, the 112th and 124th, from Texas remain to be mentioned. They were reorganized as special light infantry and performed such valuable service in the Asiatic-Pacific theater that their combat records earned them elite status.

Cavalry School and Replacement Establishments

The Cavalry School at Fort Riley had existed by that name since 1919 and continued through World War II, although its capacity was severely diminished past October 1943. A Cavalry Officer Candidate School was established there in July 1941 but was consolidated with the Armored School at Fort Knox by November 1944. The Cavalry Board coordinated all matter concerning tracked vehicles other than tanks. A Mechanized Cavalry Board had been formed at Fort Knox in November 1938 but was soon merged into the Armored Forces Board there. The single Cavalry Replacement Training Center began operations in March 1941 at Fort Riley where it remained.

CAVALRY ACTIVITIES IN JUNE 1944	OFFICERS	ENLISTED	TRAINEES
Cavalry Board — Ft Riley, Kans	5	3	
Cavalry School — Ft Riley, Kans	171	722	
Replacement Training Center — Ft Riley, Kans	271	1,254	6,720

Chapter 5

Tank Destroyers

During 1940–41 German armored employment in Europe forced the army to adopt strong antitank countermeasures which eventually led to a separate tank destroyer force. Provisional antitank battalions employing artillery usable against tanks (which was withdrawn from organic assignment to armies, corps, and divisions) were activated commencing 24 June 1941. These were not tested until the September maneuvers. On 3 December 1941 all antitank battalions were redesignated tank destroyer battalions to reflect their "offensive spirit," the old infantry antitank battalions were additionally renumbered, and all traditional association with their branch of origination (field artillery, etc.) was removed. This effectively created a new homogeneous tank destroyer force in the U.S. Army.

Tank Destroyer Brigades and Groups

In 1942 the army anticipated massed concentration of tank destroyer battalions against enemy armor which called for a tank destroyer brigade for each field army. Combat experience in 1943 negated these expectations. Even the group headquarters were scarcely used overseas, as tank destroyer battalions were commonly attached directly to divisions beginning in the African and Italian campaigns and operated independently in the Pacific. The War Department authorized only two brigades of which one was inactivated early in 1944, and the other was shipped to Europe where it saw limited employment in France.

Tank Destroyer Battalions

Initially three types of tank destroyer battalions existed: Light Towed, Light Self-Propelled, and Heavy Self-Propelled. It rapidly became obvious the 37mm antitank gun was too weak for its intended role, and the army converted all of its tank destroyer battalions during 1942 to one type—Heavy Self-Propelled with 24 75mm guns mounted on half-tracks. The high silhouette of this vehicular arrangement and unsatisfactory performance in North Africa prompted the army to return to the towed gun which could be dug in with only its muzzle protruding. An experimental battalion

CHART NO. 13
Typical Tank Destroyer, Amphibian Tank and Tractor Battalions of World War II

BATTALION	T/O	Officers	Warrant Officers	Enlisted Men	Landing Vehicle, Tracked (Combat)	Landing Vehicle, Tracked (Cargo)	76mm Gun on Motor Carriage	3" Gun, Anti-Tank, M1	81mm Mortar	Rocket Launcher, 2.36" Anti-Tank	Machinegun, .50-cal	Machinegun, .30-cal	Submachinegun, .45-cal	Rifle, .30-cal	Carbine, .30-cal	Pistol, .45-cal	M8 Armored Car	M10 Armored Car, Utility	Halftrack, M3 Personnel	Truck, 2½-ton	Truck, ¾-ton	Truck, 1½-ton	Truck, ¼-ton	Wrecker, Heavy	Tank Recovery Vehicle	Motorcycle
Tank Destroyer (S-P)	18-25 (15 Mar 44)	35	2	634	—	—	36	—	3	62	44	30	—	283	293	79	6	30	—	21	7	6	48	1	3	—
Tank Destroyer (Towed)	18-35 (7 May 43)	32	2	763	—	—	—	36	—	71	25	50	298	117	360	3	4	10	36	16	15	16	57	1	—	11
Amphibian Tank	17-115 (29 Jan 44)	33	4	740	75	12	—	—	—	16	12	—	519	—	221	15	—	—	—	16	3	—	14	1	—	—
Amphibian Tractor	17-125 (29 Apr 44)	20	2	500	119	—	—	—	—	10	238	238	138	—	363	9	—	—	—	12	1	—	9	1	—	—

with towed 3-inch guns was organized at the Tank Destroyer Center on 1 January 1943 and the self-propelled battalions in the United States were gradually converted to towed, but none used in combat during that year. In November 1943 the army decided that half the battalions would be self-propelled, equipped with the GMC Motor Carriage M10 with a 3-inch gun, and half would be towed with the M5 3-inch towed gun. In January 1944 the War Department alerted theater that a more mobile carriage, the M18 mounting a 76mm gun, was in production, and that an M36 model with a 90mm gun would be available as soon as production schedules permitted. Since all the self-propelled battalions were already equipped with the M10, it was decided by theater to refuse the M18 to simplify maintenance and supply and await the arrival of the heavier gunned M36.

Soon after the operations in France began, it was evident that the M10 was inadequate against certain German armor, and that the advantages of a self-propelled weapon greatly exceeded those of a towed weapon both on offense and defense. Action was initiated to speed up procurement of the 90mm M36 carriages, and early shipment of M18s was requested to Europe. The War Department was further requested to equip all M10 battalions scheduled for later arrival overseas in Europe with M36s preferably, or M18s, prior to embarkation. In August 1944 the first increments of M36s and M18s arrived in France and the self-propelled battalions began to re-equip with M36s and M18s accordingly, and as many towed battalions as possible were converted to self-propelled by being issued the replaced M10 equipment. By the cessation of hostilities in Europe the 12th Army Group, for instance, had 45 tank destroyer battalions of which 27 contained M36s, 13 had M18s, 6 were equipped with M10s, and only 4 were towed. The ratio of 50 percent towed battalions at the beginning of the European campaign had changed to 9 percent towed, a full 91 percent now being self-propelled. Because tank destroyer battalions were in general phased in faster than divisions, the ratio of tank destroyer battalions to divisions was usually better than one to one.

Tank destroyer battalions, especially on the mountainous Italian front which precluded massed armor, increasingly operated as reinforcing artillery. The decline of German armor during certain periods of the fighting in France and Germany also caused this role to prevail at intervals.

Initially as many as 222 tank destroyer battalions were envisioned by the army. In April 1943 the activation of new tank destroyer battalions was halted, and that October inactivations began in order to provide replacements to depleted divisions. Inactivations continued into 1944 until only 78 tank destroyer battalions were left. Tank destroyer battalions were among the most mechanized units in the army and were very powerful for their size. A single battalion carried thirty-six 3-inch or 76mm guns (towed or self-propelled), the same number of light field pieces as in the three light artillery battalions of a division. Of all the tank destroyers employed, the M36 proved the most successful, and was able to destroy the heaviest German Panther and Tiger tanks at long range. The M18 *Hellcat* was also a superb tank destroyer which was remarkably fast, enabling it to utilize hit-and-run tactics to destroy German armor while suffering little loss in return. The M10 was less successful.

Tank Destroyer Center and Replacement Establishments

The Tank Destroyer Tactical and Firing Center was activated at Fort Meade on 1 December 1941 and moved to Temple, Texas, 14 February 1942 where it was redesignated the Tank Destroyer Command on 2 March 1942. This was in turn designated the Tank Destroyer Center at Camp Hood 24 July 1942 and was discontinued after the war on 10 November 1945. The establishment of the Tank Destroyer School was directed in November 1941 but its classes did not begin until May 1942. On 24 July 1942 the school was transferred to the control of the Replacement & School Command. Until October 1942 new officers for tank destroyer units were detailed from other arms; then an officer candidate school was established at the Tank Destroyer School. In November 1944 the OCS was combined with the armored OCS at Fort Knox.

The Tank Destroyer Board, which tested and developed armament and equipment, was officially activated at Temple, Texas, on 9 March 1942, although it had informally existed earlier. It moved to Camp Hood on 18 September 1942 and was discontinued there on 22 September 1945. The Tank Destroyer Replacement Training Center at Camp Hood was activated 3 October 1942 and remained there throughout World War II.

TANK DESTROYER ACTIVITIES IN JUNE 1944	OFFICERS	ENLISTED	TRAINEES
Tank Destroyer Board — Cp Hood, Tex	14	25	
Tank Destroyer School — Cp Hood, Tex	122	329	
HHC, Tank Destroyer Center — Cp Hood, Tex	21	47	
Replacement Training Center — Cp Hood, Tex	323	1,475	6,608

Chapter 6

Field Artillery

Since 1901 army artillery had been divided into coast and field artillery branches, and remained separated during World War II. Field artillery had the mission of rendering close, continuous fire support to combat forces and providing long-range fires to restrict enemy movement and disrupt rear facilities, as well as serve in counterbattery capacities. Field artillery weapons are discussed in the field artillery battalion section where they came to be concentrated as a result of the battalion/group system employed by the U.S. Army in World War II.

Field Artillery Brigades and Corps Artillery

Prior to 1943 field artillery organization was fairly standard. Each army corps was supported by one independent field artillery brigade, composed of one 155mm gun and two 155mm howitzer regiments and one observation battalion. A field artillery brigade, consisting of one 155mm howitzer regiment and two 75mm howitzer regiments, was incorporated into each square division, but as these were triangularized their brigades were broken up. During 1943 the army adopted the battalion/group system which abolished the old fixed brigade and substituted a flexible brigade structure.

The new brigade intrinsically only contained a Headquarters & Headquarters Battery to which subordinated artillery units could be flexibly attached. During the middle of 1943 each corps was authorized its own corps artillery headquarters & headquarters battery. Since artillery groups were directly attached to corps artillery, field artillery brigades were no longer needed in quantity. At any rate, many of the field artillery brigades had to be redesignated during the latter part of 1943 to provide the newly required corps artillery headquarters batteries. A typical corps in World War II combat, based to ETO experience, controlled an average of 13 field artillery battalions, using intermediary group headquarters to assist in this control.

CHART NO. 14
Typical Heavy Artillery Battalions of World War II

FIELD ARTILLERY BATTALION TYPE	T/O	Officers	Warrant Officers	Enlisted Men	Airplane, Liaison	155mm Gun	8" Howitzer	240mm Howitzer or 8" Gun	Rocket Launcher, 2.36" Anti-tank	Machinegun, .50-cal HB	Carbine, .30-cal	Pistol, .45-cal	Cargo Carrier	Heavy Tractor	Heavy Wrecker Truck	Truck, 7½-ton Prime Mover	Truck, 2½-ton Cargo	Truck, ¾-ton Command & Reconnaissance	Truck, ¾-ton Weapons Carrier	Truck, ¼-ton Utility	Truck-mounted Crane
240mm Howitzer or 8" Gun (Tractor)	6-395 (18 Aug 43)	26	2	462	2	—	—	6	28	19	417	61	—	18	1	—	13	7	25	12	3
240mm Howitzer, M1918 (Truck-D)	6-95 (18 Aug 43)	26	2	457	2	—	—	6	28	19	412	61	—	—	1	18	13	7	25	12	3
8" Howitzer (Truck-D)	6-65 (2 Jul 43)	26	2	553	2	—	12	—	34	19	511	58	—	—	1	18	13	7	25	12	—
155mm Gun (Self-Propelled)	6-125 (29 Sep 43)	26	2	478	2	12	—	—	34	19	433	61	12	—	1	—	19	7	25	12	—
155mm Gun (Truck-D)	6-55 (31 Jul 43)	26	2	529	2	12	—	—	34	19	487	58	—	—	1	18	13	7	25	12	—

Field Artillery Regiments and Groups

The regiment was initially the basic foundation of the field artillery, but the demise of the square division concept and the implementation of the army flexible battalion/group system ended the regimental role. Triangularization terminated divisional field artillery regiments, and on 24 December 1942 the War Department granted permission to convert the nondivisional field artillery regiments into separate battalions. Group headquarters were to be activated in a ratio of one to each four battalions, and then serve as tactical headquarters to control a variable number of the battalions. During 1943 the old fixed field artillery regiments were converted accordingly under this concept, and their assets provided the nucleus for both group and battalion levels.

Field Artillery Battalions

As World War II progressed and the regiment diminished and finally disappeared from the field artillery scheme, the battalion/group system placed all field artillery weapons at the separate battalion or battery level. The army enjoyed a wide range of field artillery battalion types, each containing a particular weapon and mode of transport. These were divided into light artillery (75mm and 105mm howitzers), medium artillery (4.5-inch gun and 155mm howitzers), and heavy artillery (155mm gun, 8-inch gun or howitzer, and 240mm howitzers). There were also field artillery observation and late-war 4.5-inch rocket battalions. Due to critical U.S. artillery ammunition shortages in Europe, theater artillery even converted a few battalions and batteries to various German and French cannon to take advantage of captured ammunition stocks. All heavy field artillery was pooled at levels above division, along with considerable amounts of the medium and lighter pieces.

Light artillery provided the mainstay of divisional support-fire assets. The primary field piece was the excellent 105mm M2 and M3 howitzer, copied directly from its German counterpart. It was towed in both tractor and truck mode, much of the former going to the Pacific where muddy tropical conditions necessitated its use. Armored field artillery battalions were based on the 105mm howitzer motor carriage M7, later supplanted by the M37 past January 1945, which provided self-propelled artillery support for armored formations. The compact 75mm pack howitzer was employed by the lighter divisions and forces requiring a support weapon easily manhandled and capable of being transported by animal, airplane, glider, or dropped by parachute. The earlier horse-drawn field howitzer was phased out of army inventory by mechanization.

Medium field artillery primarily consisted of the 155mm howitzer M1, an accurate and versatile piece which was either towed by tractor or truck. The army also raised a number of tractor-drawn 4.5-inch gun battalions, but their performance fell below expectations in actual combat.

The army had urged considerable increases of heavy and medium artillery at intervals from September 1942 to March 1944. In 1942 the War Department did not accept this need, but partially relented in 1943. After the 1944 debacle at Cassino, Italy, which confirmed aerial bombardment could not substitute for heavy artillery, the War Department surpassed the highest proposals made by the Army Ground Forces at earlier dates. Increases were made

CHART NO. 15
Typical Light and Medium Artillery Battalions of World War II

FIELD ARTILLERY BATTALION	T/O	Officers	Warrant Officers	Enlisted Men	Airplane, Liaison	105mm Howitzer	4.5" Rocket Launcher	155mm Howitzer or 4.5" Gun	Machinegun, .50-cal	Machinegun, .30-cal	81mm Mortar	Submachinegun, .45-cal	Carbine, .30-cal	Rocket Launcher, 2.36" Anti-tank	Pistol, .45-cal	Tank, Medium	Halftrack, M3A1	Tank Recovery Vehicle, T5	Truck, 4-ton	Truck, 2½-ton	Tractor and Truck, 1½-ton Cargo	Truck, ¾-ton Command & Reconnaissance	Weapons Carrier, ¾-ton	Truck, ¼-ton	Trailer, 8-ton lowbed	Wrecker, Heavy
Armored	6-165 (15 Sep 43)	32	2	511	2	18*	—	—	26	22	2	116	413	40	5	3	32	2	—	25	—	2	1	22	—	1
105mm Howitzer (Truck-D)	6-25 (15 Jul 43)	31	2	488	2	12	—	—	21	—	—	—	443	40	66	—	—	—	—	37	—	8	19	22	—	—
155mm Howitzer or 4.5" Gun (Truck-D)	6-35 (15 Jul 43)	29	2	500	2	—	—	12	21	—	—	—	454	40	65	—	—	—	16	22	—	8	19	17	—	1
4.5" Rocket (Truck-D)	6-85 (10 Apr 45)	34	2	645	—	—	36	—	23	—	—	3	661	44	3	—	—	—	—	41	40	—	35	29	1	1
Observation	6-75 (9 Mar 44)	24	2	440	—	—	—	—	12	—	—	—	392	—	64	—	—	—	—	28	—	—	39	22	—	—

*on motor carriage

chiefly in 8-inch and 240mm howitzer battalions as a result of the April 1944 Lucas Review Board. Conversion of seacoast artillery and personnel from inactivated units provided easy formation, but the production of guns and ammunition proved more difficult. The army contained 137 heavy and 113 medium field artillery battalions on 1 April 1945, compared to 44 and 67 active respectively in June 1943.

The popular and effective *Long Tom* 155mm Gun battalions were either drawn by the 13-ton medium or 18-ton high-speed tractors, towed by trucks, or were self-propelled. The latter version was mounted on the M12 gun motor carriage, and past January 1945 on the superior M40 GMC carriage which first saw combat employment during the bombardment of Cologne, Germany. The most accurate artillery proved to be the 8-inch howitzer M2 which battalions were towed either by truck or tractor. In late 1944 the 576th Field Artillery Battalion was experimentally equipped with the self-propelled 8-inch howitzer variant on the M43 howitzer motor carriage. It did not see combat. The 8-inch gun was utilized for heavy bombardment operations and counterbattery fire and employed 18-ton high-speed tractors. The heaviest battalions contained the *Black Dragon* 240mm howitzer M1, which mobility due to combined 18-ton tractor power enabled them to be used in all major theaters.

Rocket artillery was first used in France by the 2nd Armored Division with tank-mounted T-34 launchers in August 1944. The 94th Infantry Division fired the T-27 8-tube ground mount extensively during September-October 1944 in the Lorient sector. However, rockets were never used extensively in Europe because their vast dispersion, relatively short range, and the fact that the Germans counterbatteried them both quickly and effectively were major drawbacks. However, they saw concentrated employment on Okinawa in 1945, where full battalions were outfitted with 60-tube, truck-mounted 4.5-inch rocket launchers.

Field Artillery School and Replacement Establishments

The Field Artillery School had been redesignated from the old School of Fire on 21 April 1919 to train battery-grade officers at Fort Sill. During World War II as many as 35 concurrent courses were running, ranging from a basic officers course to refresher courses for general officers and artillery staffs of new divisions, while enlisted specialist courses covered battery mechanics to radar operation. A Department of Motors was established in October 1940, a Department of Communications in December 1943, and the Department of Tactics became the Department of Combined Arms in April 1944. The Department of Animal Transport ceased to exist in September 1944. The Field Artillery Officer Candidate School opened on 1 July 1941 and was placed under the Replacement & School Command on 9 March 1942. With a course of three months, it continued to operate throughout the war but on reduced levels in 1944–45.

FIELD ARTILLERY TYPE	T/O	Officers	Warrant Officers	Enlisted Men	Airplane, Liaison	75mm Pack Howitzer	Machinegun, .50-cal	37mm Anti-tank Gun	Submachinegun, .45-cal	Rocket Launcher, 2.36" Anti-tank	Rifle, .30-cal Automatic	Carbine, .30-cal	Pistol, .45-cal	Truck, 2½-ton	Weapons Carrier, ¾-ton	Truck, ¼-ton	Motor-scooter	Handcart, utility	Riding Horse, bell mare	Riding Horse	Mule, Pack
75mm Pack Howitzer (Truck-D)	6-175 (28 Jul 43)	28	1	333	2	12	8	—	—	16	—	295	57	—	—	34	—	—	—	—	—
75mm Pack Howitzer (Mountain)	6-185*(4 Nov 44)	31	1	538	2	12	9	—	3	—	15	540	?	—	1	4	—	~	1	65	347
Parachute 75mm Pack Howitzer	6-215 (24 Feb 44)	39	2	542	2	12	23	4	—	70	—	556	12	15	1	18	12	12	—	—	—
Glider 75mm Pack Howitzer	6-225 (1 Aug 44)	24	3	345	2	12	9	—	—	50	—	305	?	4	3	43	17	6	—	—	—

CHART NO. 16
Typical Pack Artillery Battalions of World War II

*10th Mountain Division type

The Field Artillery Board had been established at Fort Riley in 1905, moved to Fort Sill in 1913, and to Fort Bragg in 1922. It was responsible for all the testing and development of non-tank or non-manpacked weapons and ammunition during World War II. In March 1941 three field artillery Replacement Training Centers began operations and were stationed at Forts Bragg and Sill, and Camp Roberts. These were placed under the Replacement & School Command on 9 March 1942.

FIELD ARTILLERY ACTIVITIES IN JUNE 1944

	OFFICERS	ENLISTED	TRAINEES
Field Artillery Board — Ft Bragg N.C.	18	27	
Field Artillery School — Ft Sill, Okla	855	2,366	
Replacement Training Center — Ft Bragg, N.C.	404	1,943	10,560
Replacement Training Center — Cp Roberts, Calif	251	1,071	5,760
Replacement Training Center — Ft Sill, Okla	343	1,709	8,640

AUTHORIZED FIELD ARTILLERY UNIT STRENGTHS*

	T/O	JUNE 1943	JUNE 1944	JUNE 1945
CORPS & BRIGADE ARTILLERY				
HHB, Corps Artillery (Motorized)	6-50-1	97	116	112
HHB, FA Brigade (Motorized)	6-20-1	111	103	107
FA Brigade	6-50	4,915	—	—
HHB, FA Group (Motorized)	6-12	—	99	99
HHD, Armored Artillery Group	6-12	95	—	—
DIVISION ARTILLERY				
Airborne Division Artillery	6-200	1,474	1,476	1,394
Armored Division Artillery	6-160	2,127	1,739	1,660
Cavalry Division (Horse) Artillery	6-110	2,095	2,097	1,777
Infantry Division Artillery**	6-10	2,004	2,230	2,170
Light Division Artillery	6-270T	—	1,943	—
Mountain Division Artillery	6-150	3,785	3,785	1,803
REGIMENTAL ARTILLERY				
FA Regiment (105mm Howitzer) (Truck-Drawn)	6-21	1,318	—	—
FA Regiment (155mm Howitzer) (Truck-Drawn)	6-31	1,380	—	—
FA Regiment (155mm Gun) (Motorized)	6-51	1,538	—	—
FA Regiment (240mm Howitzer) (Motorized)	6-141	1,494	—	—
18th FA Regiment (Composite) (Field Artillery School)	6-171	2,582	—	—
FIELD ARTILLERY OBSERVATION				
FA Observation Battalion	6-75	505	466	449

AUTHORIZED FIELD ARTILLERY UNIT STRENGTHS*

	T/O	JUNE 1943	JUNE 1944	JUNE 1945
LIGHT ARTILLERY				
FA Battalion (75mm Field Howitzer) (Horse)	6-115	678	678	585
FA Battalion (75mm Gun) (Horse-Drawn)	6-45	696	696	619
FA Battalion (75mm Howitzer) (Pack)	6-155	903	488	474
FA Battalion (75mm Pack Howitzer) (Truck-Drawn)	6-175	464	414	400
Glider FA Battalion (75mm Pack Howitzer)	6-225	384	396	366
Parachute FA Battalion (75mm Pack Howitzer)	6-215	573	583	538
FA Battalion (75mm Howitzer) (Mountain)	6-185	—	—	562
Armored FA Battalion	6-165	741	545	520
FA Battalion (105mm Howitzer) (Truck-Drawn)	6-25	471	521	482
FA Battalion (105mm Howitzer) (Tractor-Drawn)	6-325	—	512	490
MEDIUM ARTILLERY				
Rocket FA Battalion (4.5-inch Rocket) (Truck-Drawn)	6-85	—	—	681
FA Battalion (155mm Howitzer or 4.5-inch Gun) (Truck-Drawn)	6-35	627	531	507
FA Battalion (155mm Howitzer or 4.5-inch Gun) (Tractor-Drawn)	6-335	—	539	515
HEAVY ARTILLERY				
FA Battalion (155mm Gun) (Truck-Drawn	6-55	686	557	533
FA Battalion (155mm Gun) (Tractor-Drawn)	6-355	—	562	541
FA Battalion (155mm Gun) (Self-Propelled)	6-125	465	506	490
FA Battalion (8-inch Howitzer) (Truck-Drawn)	6-65	685	581	560
FA Battalion (8-inch Howitzer) (Tractor-Drawn)	6-365	—	586	568
FA Battalion (240mm Howitzer M1918) (Truck-Drawn)	6-145 or 6-95	664	485	464
FA Battalion (240mm Howitzer or 8-inch Gun) (Tractor-Drawn)	6-395	—	490	487

*Basic Unit Table of Organization with current changes applicable to month listed. Some T/O had minor personnel variation depending on whether unit was part of division or not, and in this chart nondivisional strengths are given in such cases.

**Includes Motorized Division Artillery for June 1943.

Chapter 7

Coast Artillery and Antiaircraft Artillery

Coast Artillery had existed as a distinct branch within the army since 1901 and as a combatant "line" arm past 4 June 1920. Its stated mission was to protect fleet bases, defeat naval and air attacks against cities and harbors, undertake beach defense while acting as army or theater reserve artillery, and provide a mine planter service. These broad requirements led to the unique character of army coast artillery in World War II, which ranged from anti-motor torpedo boat (AMTB) batteries within Harbor Defense units to railroad artillery, and directly led to its later major utilization as antiaircraft artillery.

The first army antiaircraft units had been formed on 10 October 1917. By September 1939 the large proportion of Coast Artillery available was antiaircraft in nature, and as the threat of enemy invasion faded coast artillery personnel and assets were increasingly transformed into Antiaircraft Artillery units. By the end of the war the seacoast defense role and consequently Coast Artillery had practically disappeared, and Antiaircraft Artillery prevailed. The World War II mission of Antiaircraft Artillery was the air defense of field forces and ground installations against all forms of enemy air attack by day or night.

While Coast Artillery barrage balloon, automatic weapons, antiaircraft gun, and searchlight battalions were being phased into the new Antiaircraft Artillery, one type of Coast Artillery battalion remained viable. This was the handful of 155mm *Long Tom* gun battalions used throughout World War II in the Pacific. These were mobile extensions of harbor defense artillery, but used as normal heavy artillery during the numerous island campaigns in which it participated. Coast Artillery still retained fixed fortifications artillery in numerous harbor forts, although by the end of World War II these were mostly in a maintenance or "caretaker" mode. At the close of World War II the Coast Artillery also had nine mine planter batteries and three junior mine-planter batteries based aboard Type 1, 2, and 3 army mine-planter cable vessels.

The Growth of Antiaircraft Artillery

The Antiaircraft Command was established 9 March 1942 at Washington, D.C., with the mission of instructing and training personnel for duty with antiaircraft artillery and barrage balloon units and organizing and training such units for combat duty. The headquarters was moved to Richmond, Virginia, 23 March 1942 and to Fort Bliss on 13 October 1944, and was discontinued there 30 October 1945.

In the three years following 31 December 1940 antiaircraft artillery increased over 1,750 percent, with a 2,400 percent increase projected by the 811 battalions the Army Ground Forces requested on 30 September 1942. Thereafter Army Ground Forces repeatedly advised reduction believing that provision for the Army Air Forces was sufficient to gain aerial supremacy, enabling antiaircraft strength to be placed into units of higher combat value as a result. The War Department hesitated to curtail the antiaircraft program until the Troop Basis of 4 October 1943, when the planned figure was reduced to 575 battalions. Even after this reduction antiaircraft artillery units active at the end of 1943 had an authorized strength nearly four times that of nondivisional field artillery. About 100 battalions were inactivated, until the total fell to 460 in 1944. By 1 April 1945, 331 antiaircraft artillery battalions of all types were in existence.

No other ground arm had to ship its units into combat as rapidly due to the heavy demand for antiaircraft protection early in World War II. This requirement extended from overseas bases to defense installations within the United States, and as a result units were shipped out with less than 12 weeks' training. Although poorly trained, they still took the best personnel and equipment which not only harmed the training and cadre base but led to undisciplined firing on friendly aircraft. The latter problem was only corrected by ordering withholding of fire in certain zones even when attacked by enemy airplanes, and the former problem largely corrected itself. By the end of 1943 equipment for training was more plentiful, the supply of antiaircraft units was coming into a more favorable ratio to overseas demand, and the number of new units to be trained declined. At the same time antiaircraft functions steadily increased and became more complex. For example, the role of antiaircraft artillery in a supplementary ground support role became a major doctrinal practice. As the antiaircraft artillery program was checked, and then slashed, other units such as infantry made up personnel shortages and large numbers of replacements were made available for overseas duty with depleted divisions. Many of the antiaircraft troops whose training caused such concern ended up in the infantry, and some regular antiaircraft units were also utilized in this capacity as well with the diminished enemy air threat in certain theaters.

Antiaircraft Artillery and Coast Artillery Brigades and Groups

Initially the Coast Artillery (Antiaircraft) Brigade was a fixed organization which contained 7,015 personnel. On 24 December 1942 permission was granted to reorganize antiaircraft units under the flexible army group/battalion system which abolished the old brigade structure and implemented tactical headquarters at brigade and group level to which subordinated battalions could be freely attached. Due to the large quantities of antiaircraft artillery the brigade headquarters became a widely used organization, usually assigned to army level and each controlling three like groups as well as several directly attached battalions.

Coast Artillery Brigades (Antiaircraft) were first activated or inducted into federal service during January-February 1941, and most were redesignated as Antiaircraft Artillery Brigades on 1 September 1943. These brigades declined in number as antiaircraft battalions were inactivated, and from October 1944 in Europe they normally controlled only two groups and a reduced number of independent battalions attached directly to brigade-level.

Beginning in August 1942 Coast Artillery Groups (Antiaircraft) were raised in quantity, and these were redesignated as Antiaircraft Artillery Groups during May-June 1943. These groups were primarily redesignations of former Coast Artillery Regiments being broken up under the guidelines of the group/battalion system. This continued through 1943 and into 1944. Additionally, the first Barrage Balloon Group was activated on 1 February 1942 and another followed on 1 May 1943, both being inactivated in September 1943.

Several types of Coast Artillery Groups were formed without antiaircraft roles. In August 1944 several Coast Artillery Groups (Harbor Defense) were redesignated from Coast Artillery Regiments in Hawaii, and in November 1944 another such conversion was made in Panama. Two Coast Artillery Training Groups, the 17th and 18th, existed at Camp Davis 10 March 1941–15 May 1942. Seven Coast Artillery Groups (155mm Gun) were activated, and three saw combat in the Pacific at New Guinea, Luzon, and Okinawa. The others were converted into field artillery groups or disbanded.

Coast Artillery Regiments and Harbor Defenses

Since the Antiaircraft Artillery was premised on the group/battalion system, only Coast Artillery contained fixed regiments, although of course most of these were antiaircraft Coast Artillery regiments. All regiments were broken up by the end of World War II with the exception of the 253rd (155mm Gun), which only had two batteries on active service in the Netherlands West Indies at the time. Six lost regiments defeated in the 1941 Philippine campaign remained on the books in a paper capacity only.

By far the most numerous were the Coast Artillery Regiments (Antiaircraft). These establishments averaged 2,304 if mobile and 2,155 if semimobile. Often their mobility status was freely altered depending on operational requirements, and the designation as one particular type in this book should not be taken as permanent. Many existed in the prewar Regular Army and more were activated through 1942, the National Guard regiments of this type being inducted beginning in September 1940. All were broken up in 1943; normally the regimental headquarters being redesignated as an antiaircraft artillery group headquarters, its 1st Battalion becoming a separate Antiaircraft Artillery Gun battalion, the 2nd Battalion becoming a separate Antiaircraft Artillery Automatic Weapons battalion, and the 3rd Battalion becoming a separate Searchlight battalion.

The Coast Artillery also had one 8-inch railway gun regiment of 2,040 men, a prewar organization broken up on 1 May 1943. Several 155mm Gun regiments (each 1,754 men) were raised or inducted commencing in 1940, and were broken up January-June 1944, with their battalions separated as independently numbered units. The Coast Artillery had numerous Harbor Defense regiments, most of them being of prewar vintage in reduced status at harbor forts. In September 1940 National Guard units of this type were inducted and positioned in harbor defenses of their home states. During March-October 1944 these regiments were either absorbed into their harbor defenses served, or broken up through inactivation and their battalions renumbered as separate entities. The Type C fixed harbor defense regiment contained 2,502 personnel; the Type A contained 1,943 personnel; the Type B contained 1,388 personnel; and the Type D contained only 655 personnel.

Harbor Defenses existed or were established at virtually every harbor facility in the United States and its territories, to include the Panama Canal Zone. These were organizations highly tailored to the specific conditions of defense necessary in each case, and were usually manned under individual tables of distribution and allowances. Harbor Defenses scattered their assets among nearby or controlling forts, camps, gun emplacements and positions, searchlight points, outposts, subposts, reservations, tactical positions, and battery sites.

Coast Artillery and Antiaircraft Artillery Battalions

With the introduction of the group/battalion system virtually all battalions became independent, and if previously part of a parent regiment received separate numbers and designations. These battalions were either attached to group or brigade level in varying quantities contingent on mission requirements, and some went directly to divisional attachment. As a standard allocation, a division usually rated a mobile or self-propelled antiaircraft automatic weapons battalion, and an antiaircraft artillery group had one antiaircraft artillery gun and two automatic weapons battalions, both mobile.

A wide variety of coast or antiaircraft artillery battalion types existed during World War II. These were equipped with 37mm M1A2 AA guns, multiple-mounted .50-caliber machine guns, twin 40mm gun motor carriages M19, *Bofors* 40mm automatic AA guns M1, 3-inch AA guns M3, 90mm AA guns M1 and M1A1, and 120mm AA guns M1. Battalions included a number of specialized types: Harbor Defense (with variable components), Composite (combined antiaircraft/seacoast weapons), 155mm *Long Tom* Gun, Antiaircraft Artillery Automatic Weapons, Antiaircraft Artillery Gun, Railway 8-inch Gun, Barrage Balloon (including low altitude and very low altitude variants), Airborne Antiaircraft Artillery (with flexible machine gun battery attachment, or fixed combination of automatic weapons and machine gun complements for airborne division use), Searchlight, Antiaircraft Artillery Machine Gun, and Seacoast Training Battalions.

Battalion mobility status in this book reflects that of the unit during the majority of its combat operations, or majority of service if not deployed overseas into a combat theater. Once battalions departed the United States their mobility designations rarely changed, even though many were stripped in theater by divisions and higher commands for their trucks and other vehicles.

Coast Artillery and Antiaircraft Artillery School and Replacement Establishments

Antiaircraft Artillery was separated from the seacoast artillery on 9 March 1942. The Coast Artillery Corps became

CHART NO. 17
Typical Coast Artillery Battalions of World War II

COAST ARTILLERY BATTALION	T/O	Officers	Warrant Officers	Enlisted Men	Searchlights	155mm Gun	Railway Gun	Anti-aircraft Gun, 37mm/40mm	Machinegun, .50-cal	Rifle, .30-cal	Carbine, .30-cal	Submachinegun, .45-cal	Pistol, .45-cal	Rocket Launcher, 2.36" Anti-tank	Tractor, 18-ton	Prime Mover, 6-ton	Wrecker, 4-ton	Truck, 2½-ton	Truck, 1½-ton	Truck, ¾-ton	Truck, ¾-ton Command & Reconnaissance	Truck, ¾-ton Weapons Carrier	Ambulance and Car, Sedan	Railway Train	Truck, ¼-ton
155mm Gun	4-155 (10 Dec 43)	25	1	512	8	8	—	—	24	427	56	31	3	22	4	—	—	15	—	10	—	—	—	—	3
AA Gun, Semimobile	4-175 (1 Apr 42)	31	2	722	—	—	—	16	16	660	—	—	75	—	—	6	1	20	—	1	5	5	1	—	8
AA Gun, Mobile	4-145 (1 Apr 42)	31	2	800	—	—	—	16	16	730	—	—	83	—	—	20	1	55	—	1	5	18	1	—	11
AA Auto-Wpns, Mobile	4-185 (1 Apr 42)	39	2	800	—	—	—	32	32	726	—	—	95	—	—	—	1	91	—	1	5	10	1	—	11
AA Auto-Wpns, Semimobile	4-195 (1 Apr 42)	39	2	748	—	—	—	32	32	682	—	—	87	—	—	—	—	25	—	1	5	5	1	—	11
Searchlight, Mobile	4-165 (1 Jan 42)	27	1	724	30	—	—	—	30	650	—	—	82	—	—	—	3	17	29	—	17	—	2	—	18
Airborne AA	4-275 (5 Sep 42)	29	1	475	—	—	—	24	36	125	353	—	2	—	—	—	—	—	—	—	—	2	—	—	45
Railway Artillery	4-45 (22 Mar 43)	20	3	582	4	—	8	4	2	514	52	27	2	—	—	—	—	13	—	—	1	7	—	*	6

*Railway Car × 5, Railway Locomotive × 1, Railway Tank Car × 3, **Railway Gondola Car × 8**, Railway Flat Car × 1, Railway Box Car × 5, Railway Kitchen Car × 3

CHART NO. 18
Typical Antiaircraft Artillery Battalions of World War II

ANTIAIRCRAFT ARTILLERY BATTALION	T/O	Officers	Warrant Officers	Enlisted Men	40mm AA Gun	90mm or 120mm AA Gun	37mm AA Gun	Multiple-Carriage, .50-cal MG	Machinegun, .50-cal HB	Machinegun, .30-cal	Submachinegun, .45-cal	Rifle, .30-cal	Carbine, .30-cal	Pistol, .45-cal	Rocket Launcher, 2.76" AT	Searchlight Unit	Tractor, 38-ton or 18-ton	Halftrack	Barrage Balloon	Truck, 4- or 5-ton	Truck, 2½-ton	Truck, ¾-ton	Truck, ¼-ton	Truck, 1-ton	Truck, K-56 and K-60	Heavy Wrecker	Hand Cart, Utility	Motor-scooter	Other
Gun (Mobile)	44-15 (22 Apr 44)	29	3	726	—	16*	—	16	39	—	105	546	87	3	8	—	20**	—	—	5	48	16	16	—	—	1	—	—	
Gun (Semimobile)	44-115 (26 Apr 44)	28	2	629	—	16	—	16	14	—	41	515	85	3	8	—	12	—	—	2	16	8	9	—	—	1	—	—	
Automatic Weapons (Mobile)	44-25 (22 Apr 44)	36	3	796	32	—	—	32	22	—	121	597	93	3	32	—	—	—	—	—	83	12	24	—	—	—	—	—	
Automatic Weapons (Semimobile)	44-125 (19 Apr 44)	37	2	774	32	—	—	32	5	—	41	658	91	3	32	—	—	—	—	—	23	7	12	—	—	—	—	—	
Automatic Weapons (Self-Propelled)	44-75 (19 Apr 44)	37	2	688	—	32	—	32	18	10	131	487	89	3	—	—	—	18	—	—	21	—	28	—	—	1	—	—	
Automatic Weapons (Air-Transportable)	44-225S (9 May 44)	37	2	764	32	—	—	32	5	—	53	637	90	3	32	—	—	—	—	—	18	—	37	—	—	—	34	—	
Airborne	44-275 (1 Aug 44)	31	2	478	—	—	24	—	36	—	48	—	438	3	—	—	—	—	—	—	2	2	46	—	—	—	42	15	
Searchlight	44-135 (23 May 44)	28	2	771	—	—	—	36	22	—	117	572	92	2	54	36	—	—	—	—	29	16	13	—	60	1	—	—	***
AA Balloon (Low Altitude)	44-315 (11 Jun 43)	36	1	931	—	—	—	—	16	—	—	751	115	6	—	—	—	—	81	—	19	9	15	—	—	—	—	—	
AA Balloon (Very Low Altitude)	44-325 (23 Jun 43)	30	1	851	—	—	—	—	5	—	42	750	70	5	—	—	—	—	405	—	14	14	15	—	—	—	—	—	

*90mm only
**18-ton only
***Ambulance × 1, Bicycle × 27
Note: In above Tables, only Type A given if several battalion types applicable.

a part of the Army Ground Forces, and the Coast Artillery School, organized in 1824 as the oldest army service school, was placed under the Replacement & School Command. Before this reorganization, seacoast and antiaircraft artillery instruction had been given at Camps Stewart and Davis and Forts Bragg and Monroe. Thereafter all seacoast instruction would be assigned to Fort Monroe, and all antiaircraft artillery instructors were sent to Camp Davis. Since the Coast Artillery Officer Candidate School had been established at Fort Monroe on 5 July 1941, overtaxed post facilities led to its movement to Camp Davis. It functioned to provide both seacoast and antiaircraft artillery officers, but as part of the above reorganization a seacoast division of the OCS was organized at Fort Monroe for the former in April 1942 and those instructors transferred. At the same time the Barrage Balloon School, Training Center, and Board was established at Camp Tyson. Antiaircraft Officer Candidate School classes were suspended on 12 January 1944..

The Antiaircraft Artillery School was activated at Camp Davis on 31 March 1942 and moved to Fort Bliss in October 1944, where the headquarters of the Antiaircraft Artillery School was already located. Antiaircraft artillery equipment was initially tested and developed at the Coast Artillery Board at Fort Monroe. On 9 March 1942 a separate Antiaircraft Artillery Board was established there, and moved to Camp Davis on 24 May 1942. Finally, on 28 August 1944, the board moved to Fort Bliss to join what became the center of army antiaircraft activities. The Coast Artillery Board had existed since 1907 at Fort Monroe and charged with review and development of harbor defense weapons which included mine planters, underwater detection devices, submarine mines and mine-control devices, and prior to March 1942 antiaircraft weapons.

Three Coast Artillery Replacement Centers began operation in March 1941. In March 1942 these were separated into antiaircraft artillery and seacoast establishments. The former were located at Fort Eustis (later Camp Stewart) and Camp Callan (later at Fort Bliss). The Camp McQuade, California, Coast Artillery Replacement Training Center — handling the seacoast establishment function — was activated 12 July 1942 under the Replacement and School Command and operated until December 1943.

ANTIAIRCRAFT ARTILLERY ACTIVITIES IN JUNE 1944	OFFICERS	ENLISTED	TRAINEES
HHB, Antiaircraft Artillery Command — Richmond, Va	18	107	
Antiaircraft Artillery Board — Cp Davis, N.C.	28	138	
Antiaircraft Artillery School — Cp Davis, N.C.	418	1,308	
Replacement Training Center — Ft Bliss, Tex (formerly Cp Callan)	282	1,253	6,990
Replacement Training Center — Cp Stewart, Ga (formerly Ft Eustis)	419	1,985	10,100

COAST ARTILLERY

	OFFICERS	ENLISTED	
Coast Artillery Board — Ft Monroe, Va	10	37	
Coast Artillery School — Ft Monroe, Va	181	459	
HHB, Barrage Balloon Training Center & Board — Cp Tyson, Tenn	11	57	

AUTHORIZED COAST AND ANTIAIRCRAFT ARTILLERY STRENGTHS*

HARBOR DEFENSE UNITS	T/O	JUNE 1943	JUNE 1944	JUNE 1945
HHB, Harbor Defense	4-260-1	44	**	**
CA Group (Harbor Defense)	4-62	—	**	**
CA Regiment (Harbor Defense) (Type A)	4-61	1,943	1,943	1,869
HHB, CA Regiment (Harbor Defense) (Type A)	4-62	135	135	131
CA Regiment (Harbor Defense) (Type B)	4-71	1,388	1,388	—
HHB, CA Regiment (Harbor Defense) (Type B)	4-72	123	123	—
CA Regiment (Harbor Defense) (Type C)	4-81	2,502	2,502	—
HHB, CA Regiment (Harbor Defense) (Type C)	4-82	153	153	—
CA Battalion (Harbor Defense)	4-65	527	527	514
HHB, CA Battalion (Harbor Defense)	4-66	44	44	—
CA Battalion (Harbor Defense) (Separate) (Type D)	4-95	655	655	—
HHB, CA Battalion (Harbor Defense) (Separate) (Type D)	4-96	147	147	

*Basic Unit Table of Organization with current changes applicable to month listed.

**Organization individually tailored under column headings to conform to unique harbor defense station forts and tactical positions and thus varied widely.

AUTHORIZED COAST AND ANTIAIRCRAFT ARTILLERY STRENGTHS*

	T/O	JUNE 1943	JUNE 1944	JUNE 1945
COAST ARTILLERY GUN & RAILWAY UNITS				
HHB, CA Group (155mm Gun)	4-152	—	—	73
CA Regiment (Railway Artillery)	4-41	2,040	—	—
CA Regiment (155mm Gun) (Mobile)	4-51	1,754	1,754	—
CA Battalion (Railway Artillery)	4-45	219	605	—
CA Battalion (155mm Gun) (Mobile)	4-55	479	479	—
CA Battalion (155mm Gun) — with two firing units	4-155	440	538	514
ANTIAIRCRAFT BRIGADES, GROUPS & REGIMENTS				
CA Brigade (AA) (Mobile)	4-10	7,015	—	—
HHB, CA Brigade (AA) (Mobile)	4-10-1	103	103	—
HHB, AAA Brigade	44-10-1	71	74	80
HHB, AAA Group	44-12	70	71	73
CA Regiment (AA) (Mobile)	4-11	2,304	—	—
CA Regiment (AA) (Semimobile)	4-111	2,155	2,155	2,041
COAST ARTILLERY ANTIAIRCRAFT BATTALIONS				
CA Battalion (AA) (Gun) (Separate) (Mobile)	4-145	833	—	—
CA Battalion (AA) (Gun) (Separate) (Semimobile)	4-175	755	755	—
CA Battalion (AA) (Gun) (Semimobile) 1st Bn, CA Regt (AA)	4-115	722	722	690
CA Battalion (AA) (Auto-Wpns) (Semimobile) 2nd Bn, CA Regt (AA)	4-125	755	755	727
CA Battalion (AA) (Searchlight) (Semimobile) 3rd Bn, CA Regt (AA)	4-135	486	486	467
ANTIAIRCRAFT ARTILLERY BATTALIONS				
Airborne AA Battalion	44-275	505	529	511
AAA Gun Battalion (Mobile)	44-15	743	758	726
AAA Gun Battalion (Semimobile)	44-115	645	644	631
AAA Auto-Wpns Battalion (Mobile)	44-25	774	835	801
AAA Auto-Wpns Battalion (Semimobile)	44-125	719	813	787
AAA Auto-Wpns Battalion (Self-Propelled)	44-75	709	727	702
AAA Auto-Wpns Battalion (Air-Transportable)	44-225S	—	803	780
AAA Machine-Gun Battalion	44-475T	—	312	—
AAA Searchlight Battalion (Semimobile)	44-135	853	847	807
BARRAGE BALLOON UNITS				
HHB, Barrage Balloon Group	4-312	106	58	—
CA Barrage Balloon Battalion (Separate)	4-315	1,144	—	—
AA Balloon Battalion (Low Altitude)	44-315	—	968	—
AA Balloon Battalion (Very Low Altitude)	44-325	—	882	846
SPECIAL				
130th CA Battalion (AA) (Gun) (Semimobile) (Separate)	4-175S	812	812	—

*Basic Unit Table of Organization with current changes applicable to month listed.

Chapter 8

Engineers

As a result of World War I engineer units were classified as general or special. General engineer units included divisional engineer components, the general service regiments, and the separate engineer battalions. Special engineer units were organized to perform particular functions and included heavy ponton battalions responsible for bridging, topographic units to supply maps, water supply battalions, and camouflage battalions to supervise camouflage and special materials. In September 1939 the Regular Army had only 12 active engineer units. Eight were combat regiments or parts of regiments down to a company, one was a squadron minus a troop and another was one troop of a squadron, and the remaining two were topographic battalions. Despite reorganizations and activations in response to the European war of 1940–41 the army engineers still remained unprepared upon the entry of the United States into World War II. The Corps of Engineers then restructured and refined its organization to meet the logistical and strategic engineering demands of the global conflict.

Initial Engineer Reorganizations

The combat engineer regiment of each square division and its squadron counterpart in the cavalry division were designed to fulfill only the most temporary front-line engineer work. The engineer squadron was mobile but incapable of tasks beyond hasty road repair and limited reconnaissance to assess requirements. As a result of the division triangularization process, the combat engineer regiment was terminated at division level and replaced by the engineer combat battalion. Refined during 1942 and 1943, the division engineer battalion was strengthened to become one of the division's most vital supporting assets. The armored engineer battalion was created to support the mechanized requirements of the new armored divisions.

The engineer general service regiment had been equipped with a variety of tools and specially trained soldiers for more permanent work required behind the front. By 1940 the separate engineer combat regiment and the engineer general service regiment were so similar that the only real difference occurred because the latter possessed the power shovel and a few more skilled men. In fact they were used interchangeably in the 1941 Louisiana and Carolina maneuvers. In 1942 this was gradually changed as construction machinery was eliminated from the engineer combat regiment, and the general service regimental organization was simplified. With the introduction of the army battalion/group system in late 1942, the engineers began the flexible grouping of independent battalions in 1943.

Engineer Brigades and Aviation Engineers

The Engineer Amphibian Brigade, later strengthened and redesignated the Engineer Special Brigade, was formed with the critical mission of transporting soldiers from a friendly near shore to a hostile far shore, the resupply of those troops after a beachhead was established, and the construction of shore facilities. With some naval reinforcement one brigade could transport and land the equivalent of one infantry division. Each was assigned a headquarters and headquarters company, three boat-and-shore regiments, a boat maintenance and a medical battalion, and a quartermaster, ordnance maintenance, and signal company. It totaled 7,340 men and contained 21 utility power boats, 32 command boats, 270 50-foot and 270 36-foot landing craft, and 51 patrol and fire & salvage boats. They performed crucial assault and ferrying functions in all theaters, but were particularly vital to army tactics throughout New Guinea and the Philippines where they became directly responsible for operational possibilities and successes.

Beginning in December 1943 the engineers in England expanded their organization to better control the profusion of engineer aviation troop units to be used in the upcoming European invasion. The IX Engineer Command was formed from the 902nd Engineer Air Force headquarters company and it organized the two provisional engineer aviation brigade headquarters to achieve flexibility behind the rapid allied advance in France. Each brigade of two regiments was designed to operate with one of the two tactical air commands then on the continent. As the Sixth Army Group linked up on the main front in September 1944, the 923rd Engineer Aviation Regiment was landed to assist. This regiment later formed the nucleus for the 3rd Engineer Aviation Brigade, created and charged with all maintenance and airfield development while the other two remained responsible for all construction work. It was reinforced by civilians and labor supervision units employing prisoners of war.

Engineer aviation units occupied an ambiguous position between the Corps of Engineers and the Army Air Forces throughout the war. Some theater commanders short of engineer troops used aviation engineers for any priority construction job, while others reserved them for air force projects only. During 1941 twelve engineer aviation battalions had been activated, hastily organized at scattered airbases and given crash training, and then rushed to Alaska, Hawaii, Panama, Puerto Rico, and the Philippines. The engineer aviation regiment was initially fixed with organic battalions, but observation in England soon verified one engineer aviation battalion was large enough to build one airfield in a reasonable time. By November 1942 battalions were being detached from regiments before being sent overseas. As a result regiments gradually took on functions of unit training centers in the United States, and overseas served as independent headquarters companies to control and coordinate separate engineer aviation battalions, which were assigned to them from general pools according to the situation.

Other specialized engineer aviation units were developed. Among these the topographic units produced air force target maps and camouflage battalions supervised and fabricated camouflage materials and decoys used at airbase installations. The engineer airborne aviation battalion was designed for rapid repair and maintenance of airdrome facilities seized by airborne forces, and was structured to perform this task either behind enemy lines or in close conjunction with front-line forces.

Engineer Groups

Two main types of engineer groups, combat and construction, emerged from the flexible grouping of engineer units begun in early 1943. Over 80 engineer combat groups were formed, some being redesignated by breaking up engineer combat and general service regiments, but most being activated as such. Twenty Engineer Construction Groups (including three aviation types organized in the Pacific in October 1944) were activated, many of these actually being redesignated from engineer combat groups in the Pacific theater commencing in May 1944. Engineer groups contained a headquarters to which a variable number of battalions were flexibly attached, usually two–four matching the group type being the norm in the field. Group integrity with the same subordinated battalions was not maintained in combat due to the claimed advantages of the group with regard to mission flexibility, and as a result the more permanent regiments were preferred by postwar consensus.

Twelve port construction-and-repair groups were activated from November 1942 through 1943. They were designed to supervise and control other engineer units engaged in building and repairing port facilities by furnishing technical personnel and special equipment. In practice they were not only used for port construction and maintenance, but also for clearance of inland waterways and heavy bridge building.

Fifteen base depot groups were activated to supervise the operation of engineer depot and maintenance units and coordinate their activities with engineer supply units at major engineer installations. These included base depots, intermediate depots, and advanced depots. Since the rapid advance of allied forces required more depots and dumps than originally foreseen, and rear depots were retained instead of being closed out, a shortage of depot troops forced engineer general service regiments to be permanently assigned this work in some instances. Often base equipment companies became entirely associated with depot operations to the detriment of their own functions as well. Theaters reacted by deactivating certain construction troop units and utilizing their personnel to form more base depot group headquarters and base depot companies.

Engineer Regiments

One of the largest and most critical engineer unit categories in World War II was the engineer general service regiment; over 100 serving with 82 still active at the war's conclusion. Their relative immunity from conversion under the army battalion/group system permitted regimental integrity, allowing cohesion both in training and operations which resulted in pride of accomplishment and high performance levels. Their purpose was to perform general construction work behind the front and in forward areas requiring a high percentage of skilled labor. They became responsible for general construction of hospitals, camps, depots, shops, and special plants; engaged in extensive railway construction and repair; conducted road construction which included some of the most grueling missions such as the Alaskan-Canadian Highway and the Burma Road; performed highway bridging involving timber trestle and permanent emplacements such as the Cologne Bridge (374th), the Mainz Crossing (1303rd), the spectacular Oppenheim Bridge (1301st), the Gernsheim Bridge (343rd), and the Ludwigshafen Bridge (344th)—all across the Rhine; port construction under specialized group direction; installation of bulk gasoline facilities and pipelaying and other construction in the POL distribution system; and operation of water supply equipment as water supply battalions and companies displaced forward.

Separate engineer battalions contained large pools of unskilled Negro labor troops, and these were converted to general service regiments as officers became available. A small number of Engineer Special Service Regiments were formed beginning in May 1942. These provided exceptionally skilled personnel familiar with heavy equipment to supervise quantities of civilian and/or military troops engaged in highly specialized construction tasks, which included rehabilitation of essential utilities, installation of special plants, and reconstruction of ports such as Cherbourg, France. The boat and shore regiments were assigned to engineer special brigades, aviation regiments are discussed under aviation engineers, and the combat regiments, of which over 30 were raised plus 18 in square National Guard divisions inducted, were dissolved into engineer combat groups and separate combat battalions.

Engineer Battalions and Organization for Combat

The army created a profusion of specialized engineer battalions, which are all listed in this book and several illustrated by the accompanying charts. Shortages of special types were typical. For example, engineer forestry units provided lumber and other products such as telephone poles and pilings, but often logging and milling were locally procured or performed by other engineer units and augmented by civilian and prisoner labor. In some cases units were not utilized in their assigned roles. In World War II engineer bridging troops consisted of treadway bridge companies with the assault bridge, replaced as soon as possible by the fixed or floating Bailey Bridge carried by light ponton companies. The heavy ponton battalions, however, were used almost exclusively as mobile engineer depots and dropped their organic heavy ponton bridges to carry other urgently needed engineer equipment instead. Theater construction requirements necessitated the employment of all types of battalions for general construction tasks, on which all military engineer units performed satisfactorily despite wide differences in training and equipment, the construction battalion being best equipped by nature.

At various times engineers were employed as infantry. Engineers as infantry frequently seized and held ground required for assigned engineering tasks. Many instances arose where extensive use of engineers as infantry was necessary to defend bridge sites and lines of communication from small infiltrating enemy groups after the regular infantry had moved forward. During the German Ardennes Counteroffensive both construction and combat engineers, as the only troops available, often held large portions of the front line under direct armored-infantry attack.

CHART NO. 19
Typical Combat-Type Engineer Battalions of World War II

ENGINEER BATTALION	T/O	Officers	Warrant Officers	Enlisted Men	37mm Gun M3 with M4 Carriage	Machinegun, .50-cal	Machinegun, .30-cal	Submachinegun, .45-cal	Rifle, .30-cal	Carbine, .30-cal	Pistol, .45-cal	Rocket Launcher, 2.36" Anti-tank	Halftrack, M2 or M3A1	Tractor, Diesel	Prime Mover, 6-ton	Truck or Wrecker, 4-ton	Truck, 2½-ton	Truck, 2½-ton Dump	Truck, 1½-ton	Truck, Air-Compressor	Weapons Carrier, ¾-ton	Truck, ¼-ton	Motorcycle or Motor-scooter	Prime Mover, Treadway	Shop, Motorized	Ambulance	Animals	Semitrailer, 20-ton	Other
Combat	5-15 (13 Mar 44)	29	3	634	—	12	18	16	565	65	3	29	—	4	3	1	22	27	1	4	13	16	—	—	1	—	—	3	*
Armored	5-215 (15 Sep 43)	35	3	670	—	20	18	103	434	153	3	29	17	3	—	1	27	18	—	4	8	26	—	6	—	—	—	—	—
Airborne	5-225 (1 Aug 44)	23	2	385	—	—	11	18	256	138	3	25	—	4	—	—	1	4	—	2**	—	19	25	—	—	—	—	—	—
Mountain	5-235 (4 Nov 44)	34	2	771	—	7	18	7	688	116	4	26	—	3	8	1	8	12	1	2	4	8	—	—	1	—	538***	3	—
Separate	5-35 (1 Apr 42)	33	1	1,084	5	—	—	—	915	134	39	—	5	—	1	8	8	16	—	5	—	14	2	—	—	1	—	—	****
Camouflage	5-95 (2 Aug 43)	28	2	356	—	5	—	8	—	368	2	25	—	—	—	—	—	8	—	—	1	38	8	—	—	—	—	—	—

*Assault Boat × 14
**On trailer only
***Bell Horse × 3, Riding Horse × 23, Pack Mule × 418, Riding Mule × 94
****Road Grader × 1, Powered Shovel × 1, Dozer-tractor × 8

Large-scale employment of combat engineers was also made during the siege of Aachen. General service regiments were used to maintain the defensive lines along the Meuse River farther to the rear during the Ardennes battle. Engineers saw continuous front-line duty in an infantry capacity during much of the fighting in the Pacific, where mopping up entrenched Japanese was conducted simultaneously with construction of airfields and other installations.

CHART NO. 20
Typical Special Engineer Battalions of World War II

ENGINEER BATTALION	T/O	Officers	Warrant Officers	Enlisted Men	Machinegun, .50-cal	Machinegun, .30-cal	Submachinegun, .45-cal	Rifle, .30-cal	Carbine, .30-cal	Pistol, .45-cal	Tractor, Diesel	Prime Mover, 6-ton	Truck, 2½-ton	Truck, 2½-ton Dump	Wrecker, 4-ton	Truck, 4- or 5-ton	Truck, 1½-ton	Truck, ¾-ton	Truck, ¼-ton	Motorized Air-Compressor	Road Grader	Motorized Shop	Powered Shovel, crawler-mounted	Road Scraper	Crane, Tractor- or Truck-	Concrete Mixer	20-ton lowbed Semitrailer	Other
Construction	5-75 (23 Dec 43)	29	2	913	20	8	—	812	117	3	10	—	27	13	1	—	15	1	27	8	4	4	2	6	3	2	12	Note 1.
Aviation	5-415 (15 May 44)	33	—	774	22	—	27	603	156	3	13	6	11	37	1	1	—	12	17	4	10	—	2	10	4	3	15	Note 2.
General Service	5-135 (27 Sep 44)	37	2	797	5	—	—	—	814	3	6	7	9	28	1	—	12	6	17	6	2	1	1	—	1	1	7	—
Heavy Ponton	5-275 (9 Jul 43)	17	3	376	12	8	—	—	386	2	4	64	15	—	2	8	—	12	3	1	—	1	—	—	2	—	—	Note 3.
Topographic, Army	5-55 (17 Nov 43)	19	3	423	5	—	11	—	424	2	—	—	25	—	1	2	4	5	11	—	—	—	—	—	—	—	—	Note 4.
Water Supply	5-65 (1 Apr 42)	25	2	472	—	—	—	—	448	36	—	—	32	—	1	21	—	15	5	1	—	—	—	—	—	—	—	Note 5.
Railway Operating	5-125 (1 Apr 42)	24	2	847	—	—	—	—	489	364	2	2	9	6	—	1	—	6	—	2	—	—	—	1	—	—	—	Note 6.
Boat Maintenance	5-555S (7 Apr 44)	20	6	387	30	—	—	80	331	2	6	3	11	—	1	—	2	6	12	—	—	33	—	—	6	—	3	Note 7.

Note 1. Skid-mounted Earth Auger × 1; 10-ton Road Roller × 2; 5-8-ton Road Roller × 3; Road Rooter × 2.
Note 2. Ditching Machine × 1; Tractor-drawn Mower × 1; Road Roller × 9; Rotary Sweeper × 1; Road Rooter × 1; M16 Multigun Carriage × 4; 60mm Mortar × 8; 4-ton Dumptruck × 14; Bituminous Distributor × 1; Asphalt Truck × 2.
Note 3. Ponton Bridge × 4; 25-ton Ponton lowbed semitrailer × 64; Stormboat × 20; Motorcycle × 6.
Note 4. Reproduction Equipments sections (camera, plate, press, etc) × 10; Rocket Launcher 2.36" AT × 15; 750-gal. 2½-ton Tank Truck × 1.
Note 5. Percussion Well-drilling machine × 1; Rotary Well-drilling machine × 1; 1,500-gal. water tank semitrailer × 21; Mobile Water Purification Unit × 9; Motorcycle × 3; 700-gal. 2½-ton Water Tank Truck × 60; Ambulance × 1.
Note 6. Ambulance × 1; Light Sedan Car × 1; Motorcycle × 1.
Note 7. Utility Power Boat × 6; Fire & Salvage Boat × 6.

AUTHORIZED ENGINEER UNIT STRENGTHS*

	T/O	JUNE 1943	JUNE 1944	JUNE 1945
CORPS ENGINEERS				
Hqs, Corps Engineers	5-100-1	20	—	—
BRIGADES				
Engr Amphibian Brigade / Engr Special Brigade	5-510	7,351	7,340	7,121
GROUPS				
HHC, Engr Combat Group	5-192	—	85	80
HHC, Engr Construction Group	5-72	—	97	94
HHC, Engr Port Construction & Repair Group	5-52	—	253	272
HHC, Engr Pipeline Group (Provisional)	5-1012T/D	—	—	66
REGIMENTS				
Engineers / Engr Special Service Regiment	5-251	1,324	1,324	1,290
Engr Combat Regiment	5-171	1,465	—	—
Engr General Service Regiment	5-21 or 5-121	1,321	1,321	1,795
Italian Engr General Service Regiment	5-21S-ISU	—	1,292	1,292
Engr Boat Regiment	5-511	3,667	—	—
Engr Shore Regiment	5-521	2,085	—	—
Engr Boat & Shore Regiment	5-511S	—	2,023	1,961
AVIATION ENGINEERS				
Engr Aviation Regiment	5-411	2,697	2,701	2,568
Engr Aviation Battalion	5-415	807	807	777
Airborne Engr Aviation Battalion	5-455	—	530	507
Engr Aviation Camouflage Battalion	5-465	—	600	575
Engr Aviation Topographic Battalion	5-400	—	**	**
GENERAL ENGINEER BATTALIONS				
Airborne Engr Battalion	5-225	436	440	410
Armored Engr Battalion	5-215	1,224	707	674
Engr Battalion (Separate)	5-35	1,117	1,117	1,074
Engr Boat Battalion	5-515	968	1,079	1,034
Engr Combat Battalion	5-15	768	666	637
Engr Construction Battalion	5-75	776	944	900
Engr Light Combat Battalion	5-475T	—	421	—
Engr Mountain Battalion	5-235	669	669	807
Engr Shore Battalion	5-525	622	704	689
Engr Squadron	5-115	539	539	446
SPECIAL ENGINEER BATTALIONS				
Engr Base Shop / Special Shop Battalion	5-535	1,055	936	896
HHC, Engr Base Topographic Battalion	5-186	—	—	81
Engr Boat Maintenance Battalion	5-555S	—	413	397
Engr Camouflage Battalion (Army)	5-95	476	386	369
Engr Composite Battalion / Engr Service Battalion	5-500	—	**	**
HHC, Engr Forestry Battalion	5-386	92	74	89
Engr General Service Battalion	5-135	—	—	836
Engr Heavy Ponton Battalion	5-275	530	396	381
Engr Oil Field Battalion***	5-665S	—	693	674
Engr Railway Operating Battalion****	5-125	872	872	816
Engr Refinery Battalion***	6-655S	—	743	709
Engr Topographic Battalion (Army)	5-55	530	445	426
Engr Topographic Battalion (GHQ)	5-185	1,000	1,000	—
Engr Water Supply Battalion	5-65	499	499	480

*Basic Unit Table of Organization with current changes applicable to month listed. Slash used to indicate change in title during the course of the war.

**Engineer Service Organization individually tailored under column headings with variable strength.

***Under Engineer Petroleum Production Depot.

****Units transferred to Transportation Corps under T/O 55-225 which is used if applicable.

Part II

Divisions of the U.S. Army in World War II

Chapter 9

Armored Divisions

Divisions:

1–14, 16, 20

1st Armored Division

No Distinctive Insignia Authorized

15 Jul 40 redesignated from 7th Cavalry Brigade at Ft Knox Ky and participated in VII Corps Arkansas Maneuvers 18–28 Aug 41; moved to Cp Polk La 1 Sep 41 as part of Second Army Louisiana Maneuvers; relocated to Ft Jackson S.C. area 30 Oct 41 to participate in the First Army Carolina Maneuvers; returned to Ft Knox Ky 7 Dec 41; staged at Ft Dix N.J. 11 Apr 42 until departed New York P/E 11 May 42; arrived North Ireland 16 May 42 and England 29 Oct 42; arrived North Africa 22 Dec 42 less elements which assaulted 8 Nov 42; arrived Italy 28 Oct 43; returned New York P/E 24 Apr 46 and inactivated at Cp Kilmer N.J. 25 Apr 46.

Campaigns: *Algeria–French Morocco, Tunisia, Naples-Foggia, Anzio, Rome-Arno, North Apennines, Po Valley*

Aug 45 Loc: Salzburg Austria

Typical Organization (1941):

1st Armored Brigade HHC
   1st Armored Regiment (Light)
   13th Armored Regiment (Light)
   69th Armored Regiment (Medium)
   68th Field Artillery Regiment (Armored)
   81st Reconnaissance Battalion (Armored)
27th Field Artillery Battalion (Armored)
 6th Infantry (Armored)

Headquarters
Hqs Company, 1st Armored Division
   16th Engineer Battalion (Armored)
   47th Medical Battalion (Armored)
141st Signal Company (Armored)
   19th Ordnance Battalion (Armored)
   13th Quartermaster Battalion (Armored)
   12th Observation Squadron *(attached)*

Typical Organization (1944/45):

 1st Tank Battalion
 4th Tank Battalion
13th Tank Battalion
 6th Armored Infantry Battalion
11th Armored Infantry Battalion
14th Armored Infantry Battalion
HHB Division Artillery
27th Armored Field Artillery Battalion
68th Armored Field Artillery Battalion
91st Armored Field Artillery Battalion
81st Cavalry Reconnaissance Squadron, Mecz

Headquarters
Hqs Company, 1st Armored Division
HHC, Combat Command A
HHC, Combat Command B
Hqs, Reserve Command
HHC, Division Trains:
   47th Medical Battalion, Armored
   123rd Armored Ordnance Maintenance Battalion
   Military Police Platoon
   16th Armored Engineer Battalion
141st Armored Signal Company
501st Counter Intelligence Corps Det

Overseas Wartime Assignments:

NATO - 22 Dec 42
British 5 Corps - Jan 43
II Corps - 11 Jan 43
NATO - May 43
II Corps - 28 Oct 43
VI Corps - Jan 44

Fifth Army - 8 Jun 44
IV Corps - 16 Jun 44
II Corps - 7 Oct 44
IV Corps - 19 Feb 45
II Corps - 1 Apr 45
IV Corps - 5 Apr 45

Commanders: MG Bruce Magruder: Jul 40
               MG Orlando Ward: Mar 42
               MG Ernest N. Harmon: Apr 43

MG Vernon E. Prichard: Jul 44
MG Roderick R. Allen: Sep 45

Killed in Action: 1,194   *Wounded in Action:* 5,168   *Died of Wounds:* 234

1st Armored Division Combat Narrative

CCB of the division landed east and west of Oran North Africa 8 Nov 42 and entered the city 10 Nov 42. On 24 Nov 42 CCB moved from Tafaroui Algeria to Bédja Tunisia and raided Djedeida Airfield the next day, reaching Djedeida 28 Nov 42. CCB moved southwest of Tebourba on 1 Dec 42, engaged German forces on El Guessa Heights 3 Dec 42, but its lines were pierced 6 Dec 42. CCB withdrew to Bédja with heavy equipment losses 10–11 Dec 42 and was placed in reserve. CCB next attacked 21 Jan 43 in the Ousseltia Valley and cleared that area until 29 Jan 43 when sent to Bou

Chebka, and arrived at Maktar 3 Feb 43. CCA fought at Faid Pass commencing 30 Jan 43 and advanced to Sidi Bou Zid where it was pushed back with heavy tank losses 14 Feb 43 and had elements isolated on Djebel Lessouda, Djebel Ksaira, and Garet Hadid. CCC, which had been constituted on 23 Jan 43 to raid Sened Station on 24 Jan 43, advanced toward Sbeita and counterattacked to support CCA in the Sidi Bou Zid area on 15 Feb 43, but was repulsed with heavy losses. The division withdrew from Sbeita 16 Feb 43 but by 21 Feb 43 CCB contained the German attack toward Tébessa. The German withdrawal allowed the division to recover Kasserine Pass 26 Feb 43 and assemble in reserve. The division moved northeast of Gafsa on 13 Mar 43 and attacked in heavy rains on 17 Mar 43 as CCA took Zannouch, but became immobilized by rain the next day. The division drove on Maknassy 20 Mar 43 and fought the Battle of Djebel Naemia 22–25 Mar 43 and then fought to break through positions barring the road to Gabès 29 Mar–1 Apr 43. It began to follow up the withdrawing German forces 6 Apr 43 and attacked toward Mateur with CCA on 27 Apr 43, which fell after hard fighting on Hills 315 and 299 on 3 May 43. The division fought the Battle for Djebel Achtel 5–11 May 43 and entered Ferryville 7 May 43. The German forces in Tunisia surrendered 9–13 May 43.

The division was reorganized in French Morocco and began arriving in Naples Italy on 28 Oct 43. Entering combat along the Rapido River in mid-Dec 43, the 6th Armd Inf took up positions on M.Lungo 31 Dec 43. A task force fought the Battle for M.Porchia 5–7 Jan 44 and suffered heavy losses. Less CCB, the division was landed at Anzio beginning 24 Jan 44 and attacked Colli Laziali 30 Jan–1 Feb 44 before going into defensive positions. It contained the German assault on the beachhead by counterattacking 19 Feb 44 after heavy air and artillery preparation. CCA and CCB opened the general offensive to breakout of the Anzio area 23 May 44 and cleared Campoleone Station with heavy tank losses on 29 May 44. Task Force Howze drove up Highway 6 against rear-guard resistance 3 Jun 44, and the division took Albano and entered Rome 4 Jun 44 as it pursued the retreating German forces up Highway 1. After Viterbo fell without opposition 9 Jun 44, the division was withdrawn for rehabilitation 10 Jun 44. It resumed the advance 21 Jun 44 and CCA, suffering heavy tank losses, fought the Battle for Casole d'Elsa 2–4 Jul 44. It then engaged in limited action until relieved on line 8 Jul 44. Elements with Task Force Ramey gained the heights along the Orlo River 20 Jul 44.

The division took over front-line positions 20 Aug 44 and crossed over the Arno River 1 Sep 44, CCA clearing M.Pisano by 3 Sep 44 and CCB taking the Altopascio road center by 4 Sep 44. The next day CCA took Lucca, and on 8 Sep 44 the division reverted to active patrolling before crossing the Serchio River on 10 Sep 44. CCB took Castelvecchio and M. Liguana 18 Sep 44, but CCA was delayed in the Ponte a Moriano area by heavy opposition. The division regrouped on 20 Sep 44 and CCA attacked the Monterumici Hillmass 8 Oct 44, where the division battled for most of October. The division relieved the 91st Inf Div on line on 22 Nov 44 and moved to Lucca on 26 Dec 44. The division made a limited attack and took Carviano 8 Mar 45 and fought for Salvaro 15–27 Mar 45, which fell after being evacuated. The division opened its offensive toward Suzzano 14 Apr 45 which it took the following day as it fought the Battle for Vergato 14–16 Apr 45. It moved rapidly forward astride the Samoggia River and CCB crossed the Panaro 22 Apr 45 as CCA bypassed Modena. CCA reached the Po River at Guastalla and Luzzaro the next day and crossed 25 Apr 45 to intercept retreating German forces west of Lake Garda. The division took up positions near Milan 29 Apr 45, which was already occupied by partisans, and then was relieved by the 34th Inf Div on the Ticino River northwest of Milan 1 May 45. Hostilities ceased in Italy 2 May 45.

2nd Armored Division

No Distinctive Insignia Authorized

15 Jul 40 activated at Ft Benning Ga and participated in the VII Corps Tennessee Maneuvers 2–28 Jun 41; moved to Ragley La 12 Aug 41 and participated in the Second-Third Army Louisiana Maneuvers; returned to Ft Benning Ga 29 Sep 41 and participated 2 Nov 41 in the First Army Carolina Maneuvers; returned to Ft Benning Ga 2 Dec 41; relocated to Monroe N.C. 10 Jul 42 for the II Armored Corps Carolina Maneuvers; transferred to Ft Bragg N.C. 15 Aug 42; staged at Ft Dix N.J. 3 Nov 42 until departed New York P/E 11 Dec 42; arrived North Africa 25 Dec 42 (less elements which invaded 8 Nov 42); assaulted Sicily 10 Jul 43 and departed 12 Nov 43; arrived England 25 Nov 43 and landed in France 7–9 Jun 44; crossed into Belgium 2 Sep 44 and into Holland 11 Sep 44; initially entered Germany 18 Sep 44; returned to Holland 22 Dec 44 and to Belgium same date; re-entered Germany 4 Feb 45; returned New York P/E 29 Jan 46 and arrived Cp Hood Tex 4 Feb 46 where active thru 1946.

Campaigns: *Algeria–French Morocco, Sicily, Normandy, Northern France, Rhineland, Ardennes-Alsace, Central Europe*

Aug 45 Loc: Drutte Germany

Typical Organization (1941):

2nd Armored Brigade HHC
  66th Armored Regiment (Light)
  67th Armored Regiment (Medium)
  68th Armored Regiment (Light)
  14th Field Artillery Regiment (Armored)
82nd Reconnaissance Battalion (Armored)
78th Field Artillery Battalion (Armored)
41st Infantry (Armored)

Headquarters
Hqs Company, 2nd Armored Division
17th Engineer Battalion (Armored)
48th Medical Battalion (Armored)
14th Quartermaster Battalion (Armored)
142nd Signal Company (Armored)
  16th Observation Squadron *(attached)*
  17th Ordnance Battalion (Armored)

Typical Organization (1944/45):

  66th Armored Regiment
  67th Armored Regiment
  82nd Armored Reconnaissance Battalion
  14th Armored Field Artillery Battalion
  78th Armored Field Artillery Battalion
  92nd Armored Field Artillery Battalion
  41st Armored Infantry Regiment
142nd Armored Signal Company
  17th Armored Engineer Battalion
738th Tank Battalion (Mine Clearing) *(elements attached 12 Jan 45–17 Jan 45)*
702nd Tank Destroyer Battalion *(11 Jun 44–21 Sep 44, 1 Oct 44–7 Feb 45, 27 Feb 45–9 May 45)*
195th AAA Auto-Wpns Battalion *(11 Jun 44–Past 9 May 45)*
  99th Infantry Battalion *(15 Aug 44–18 Sep 44)*

Headquarters
Hqs Company, 2nd Armored Division
Service Company, 2nd Armored Division
Division Trains:
  HHC
  Maintenance Battalion
  Supply Battalion
  48th Armored Medical Battalion
502nd Counter Intelligence Corps Det

Overseas Wartime Assignments (ETO):

First Army - 24 Nov 43
VII Corps - 27 Nov 43
XIX Corps - 8 Feb 44
V Corps - 12 Jun 44
VII Corps - 18 Jul 44
XIX Corps - 2 Aug 44
VII Corps - 7 Aug 44

XIX Corps - 13 Aug 44
V Corps - 18 Aug 44
XIX Corps - 19 Aug 44
XV Corps - 28 Aug 44
XIX Corps - 29 Aug 44
VII Corps - 22 Dec 44
XIX Corps - 16 Feb 45

Commanders: MG Charles L. Scott: Jul 40
        MG George S. Patton Jr: Jan 41
        MG Willis D. Crittenberger: Feb 42
        MG Ernest N. Harmon: Jul 42
        MG Hugh J. Gaffey: May 43

MG Edward H. Brooks: Apr 44
MG Ernest N. Harmon: Sep 44
MG Isaac D. White: Jan 45
BG John H. Collier: May 45
MG John M. Devine: Aug 45

Killed in Action: 981   *Wounded in Action:* 4,557   *Died of Wounds:* 202

2nd Armored Division Combat Narrative

Elements of the 66th and 67th Armd Inf landed at Mehdia and Fedala/Safi respectively on 8 Nov 42 in North Africa. CCB received the surrender of Mazagan on 11 Nov 42, and later some elements fought at Beja Tunisia. The division entered combat as a whole during the invasion of Sicily 10 Jul 43. CCA assaulted Licata while the rest of the division landed east of Gela. CCB mopped up the Niscemi area while CCA advanced, and on 15 Jul 43 the division assembled at Campobello and then followed the army advance to exploit breakthroughs. It was committed into action 22 Jul 43 and rapidly drove to the outskirts of Palermo. The division was then sent to England and trained for the invasion of Normandy France.

The division landed in Normandy France 9 Jun 44 and initially employed to strengthen the Auville-sur-le-Vey Bridgehead. It attacked 26 Jul 44 through 30th Inf Div and took St. Denis-le-Gast 28 Jul 44, being relieved in the Percy area 29 Jul 44. Tessy fell to CCA on 1 Aug 44 and on 7 Aug 44 the division was committed to stop the German drive on Avranches, and on 14 Aug 44 CCA overran Domfort. On 19 Aug 44 the division attacked west of Dreux to cut German forces off from the Seine between Paris and Elbeuf. It reached Le Neubourg 23 Aug 44 and resumed the advance 30 Aug 44, reaching positions northwest of Cambrai by 1 Sep 44. CCA crossed the Albert Canal on 13 Sep 44 and reached the Mass River the next day as the German defenders withdrew. CCB crossed the Albert at Meerseen 15 Sep

44, but its bridgehead was subjected to heavy fire the following day and CCA crossed at Valkenburg. The Germans were forced back to Sittard which was taken 18 Sep 44 as the division effected a breakthrough and drove to Gangelt, but a strong German counterattack restored their lines 19 Sep 44. The division then took up defensive positions near Geilenkirchen.

The division attacked 3 Oct 44 as it crossed the Wurm River at Marienburg to expand the 30th Inf Div Bridgehead. CCB attacked from Uebach the next day, suffering heavy tank losses, and CCA reinforced. CCB was stopped short of Geilenkirchen 6 Oct 44. The division fought through heavy combat at Baesweiler and Oidtweiler to attack Aachen Gap at Wuerselen starting 13 Oct 44. The division attacked 16 Nov 44 and took Puffendorf on the outer ring of the Juelich defenses with CCB, which was counterattacked the next day and CCA committed. Against strong opposition, CCB took Apweiler and held it against counterattack 18–19 Nov 44. The division renewed its attacks in heavy rain 20 Nov 44 and CCA fought the Battle for Merzenhausen 22–27 Nov 44. CCA then took Barmen and reached the Roer River on 28 Nov 44. The division then assumed defensive positions along the Roer until released as a result of the German Ardennes Counteroffensive, moving to the Durbuy-Marche area in Belgium 20–22 Dec 44.

CCA reached Buissonville 24 Dec 44 and CCB took Celles the next day and held it against counterattack. The division cleared Humain against strong opposition and then was relieved in the Havelange area by 83rd Inf Div, regrouping on 28 Dec 44. The division attacked toward Houffalize on 3 Jan 45 and fought the Battle for Odeigne 4–6 Jan 45, reached the Ourthe River 15 Jan 45, and occupied Houffalize 16 Jan 45. The division then was relieved by the 4th Cav Group 19 Jan 45 and withdrew for rehabilitation.

The division assembled across the Roer River on 27 Feb 45 and attacked 1 Mar 45 across the Cologne Plain as it assaulted over the Nord Canal. It concluded the offensive 4 Mar 45 as CCB took Verdingen on the Rhine. It crossed the Rhine River 27 Mar 45 and relieved the 17th A/B Div 29 Mar 45. CCB then drove to Lippstadt where it made contact with the advancing 3rd Armd Div 1 Apr 45. The division commenced the Battle for the Teutoburger Wald Passes 2 Apr 45 and by 5 Apr 45 CCA had reached and crossed the Weser River at Ohr and CCB at Grohnde. CCA advanced to take the bridge at Schulenberg over the Leine River intact the next day. After regrouping 7 Apr 45, the division renewed its offensive 10 Apr 45 as CCB took the Oker River bridge at Schladen. CCB then drove 57 miles to reach the Elbe River south of Magdeburg on 11 Apr 45. CCA assaulted Magdeburg with the 30th Inf Div 17–18 Apr 45. The division was moved to an occupation zone south of Braunschweig 20 Apr 45 and mopped up stragglers in Forst Konigslutter 21–22 Apr 45. Hostilities ended officially on 7 May 45.

3rd Armored Division

No Distinctive Insignia Authorized

15 Apr 41 activated at Cp Beauregard and moved to Cp Polk La 11 Jun 41; transferred to Cp Young Calif 26 Jul 42 for the Desert Training Center II Armored Corps California Maneuvers; moved to Cp Pickett Va 9 Nov 42 and arrived Indiantown Gap Mil Res Pa 21 Jan 43; staged at Cp Kilmer N.J. 26 Aug 43 until departed New York P/E 5 Sep 43; arrived England 18 Sep 43 and landed in France 23 Jun 44; crossed into Belgium 4 Sep 44 and entered Germany 15 Sep 44; returned to Belgium 20 Dec 44 and re-entered Germany 7 Feb 45 where inactivated on 10 Nov 45.

Campaigns: *Normandy, Northern France, Rhineland, Ardennes-Alsace, Central Europe*
Aug 45 Loc: Darmstadt Germany

Typical Organization (1941):

3rd Armored Brigade HHC
  32nd Armored Regiment (Light)
  33rd Armored Regiment (Light)
  40th Armored Regiment (Medium)
  67th Field Artillery Regiment (Armored)
83rd Reconnaissance Battalion (Armored)
54th Field Artillery Battalion (Armored)
36th Infantry (Armored)

Headquarters
Hqs Company, 3rd Armored Division
23rd Engineer Battalion (Armored)
45th Medical Battalion (Armored)
15th Quartermaster Battalion (Armored)
143rd Signal Company (Armored)
18th Ordnance Battalion (Armored)
22nd Observation Squadron *(attached)*

Typical Organization (1944/45):

32nd Armored Regiment
33rd Armored Regiment
36th Armored Infantry Regiment
54th Armored Field Artillery Battalion
67th Armored Field Artillery Battalion
391st Armored Field Artillery Battalion
143rd Armored Signal Company
23rd Armored Engineer Battalion
83rd Armored Reconnaissance Squadron

Headquarters
Hqs Company, 3rd Armored Division
Service Company, 3rd Armored Division
Division Trains:
 HHC
 Maintenance Battalion
 Supply Battalion
 45th Armored Medical Battalion
503rd Counter Intelligence Corps Det

643rd Tank Destroyer Battalion *(attached 22 Dec 44–26 Dec 44)*
703rd Tank Destroyer Battalion *(attached 25 Jun 44–17 Dec 44, 2 Jan 45–9 May 45)*
803rd Tank Destroyer Battalion *(attached 25 Jun 44–2 Jul 44)*
413rd AAA Gun Battalion *(attached 7 Jul 44–16 Jul 44)*
486th AAA Auto-Wpns Battalion *(attached 25 June 44–9 May 45)*

Overseas Wartime Assignments:

VII Corps - 20 Nov 43
XIX Corps - 8 Feb 44
VII Corps - 15 Jul 44

XVIII (A/B) Corps - 19 Dec 44
VII Corps - 23 Dec 44
XIX Corps - 1 May 45

Commanders: MG Alvin C. Gillem: Apr 41
MG Walton H. Walker: Jan 42
MG Leroy H. Watson: Aug 42
MG Maurice Rose: Aug 44

BG Doyle O. Hickey: Mar 45
BG Truman E. Boudinot: Jun 45
BG Frank A. Allen Jr: Jul 45
MG Robert W. Grow: Jul 45

Killed in Action: 1,810   *Wounded in Action:* 6,963   *Died of Wounds:* 316

3rd Armored Division Combat Narrative

The division arrived in Normandy France on 23 Jun 44 and entered combat against the Villiers-Fossard salient north-east of St Lô 29–30 Jun 44. CCB crossed into the Airel Bridgehead on 7 Jul 44 and the division reached the Haut-Vents crossroads after heavy combat by 11 Jul 44. CCB passed through the 1st Inf Div to seize Marigny 26 Jul 44, and CCA forced a crossing of the Sienne at Gavray on 30 Jul 44. It then secured a crossing of the Seé at Brécey 31 Jul 44 and on 1 Aug 44 CCB attacked toward St Pois. The division assembled 12 Aug 44 and the next day swung around Domfront toward the Vire-Argentan Road to close the Falaise Gap, capturing Ranes after heavy combat on 15 Aug 44. It fought through Fromenthal 16–17 Aug 44, and on 25 Aug 44 CCB crossed the Seine River below Paris at Tilly. The division crossed the Marne River in the Mieux area and continued to pursue against disorganized resistance, crossing the Aisne River east of Soissons on 29 Aug 44. Advancing east from Namur astride the Meuse, the division seized Huy 6 Sep 44, mopped up Liege 8 Sep 44, took Verviers against rear-guard resistance, and reached the *West Wall* at Schmidthof on 12 Sep 44.

The division breached *West Wall* fortifications between Roetgen and Rott with CCB on 13 Sep 44 as CCA pushed through antitank obstacles to Nutheim. CCB crossed the Vicht River southwest of Stolberg 14 Sep 44 as CCA reached Eilendorf, a suburb of Aachen. On 15 Sep 44 the division encountered the second belt of *West Wall* defenses where it suffered heavy tank losses in the Battle of Geisberg Hill which commenced that same day, as CCB took but was forced out of Mausbach. The next day CCA was halted in its advance on Stolberg, and CCB finally took Geisberg Hill 17 Sep 44 and then was forced off. The division then fought the Battle for Weissenberg Hill and Muensterbusch Hill 18–20 Sep 44. Stolberg finally fell 22 Sep 44, as the division postponed its *West Wall* offensive and used smoke screens to withdraw CCB task forces from Donnerberg. The division was next committed to clearing the Lousberg Heights and cutting the Aachen-Laurensberg Highway 18–28 Oct 44. The division attacked the Stolberg corridor on 16 Nov 44 and took heavy tank losses at Hastenrath and Scherpenseel which fell 18 Nov 44. The division took Huecheln after battling through a minefield on 24 Nov 44.

The division attacked to clear the west bank of the Roer River on 10 Dec 44 and took Geich the next day. As a result of the German Ardennes Counteroffensive, CCA went in defense of Eupen, CCB assisted 30th Inf Div, and the division assembled in the Hotton–Le Grand Pré area on 19 Dec 44. CCB attacked Stoumont and La Gleize 20 Dec 44 while the remainder of the division attacked to secure the Manhay-Houffalize Road. The division contained a German attack at Hotton, but lost a key road junction southeast of Manhay 23 Dec 44 and the following day its roadblock at Belle Haie was reduced. The division attacked to take Grandménil 25–26 Dec 44, and CCA recovered Sadzot after its temporary loss 28 Dec 44. After the 83rd Inf Div took over this zone at the end of the month, the division attacked toward Houffalize on 3 Jan 45. Fighting across Groumont Creek, the Bois de Groumont, and into Provedroux by 8 Jan 45, the 83rd Inf Div attacked through its lines the next day. The division then attacked into Bihain 12 Jan 45, reached the Ourthe River by 19 Jan 45, and seized Gouvy and Beho on 22 Jan 45.

The division attacked out of the Elle River bridgehead 26 Feb 45 and gained two bridgeheads at Glesch and Paffendorf the next day over the Erft River. After repulsing counterattacks, the division attacked out on 3 Mar 45 and took Stommeln with air support. It reached the Rhine River at Roggendorf and Worringen 4 Mar 45 and fought the Battle for Cologne 5–7 Mar 45 assisted by the 104th Inf Div. After maintaining defensive positions, it crossed the Rhine 23 Mar 45 and attacked again 25 Mar 45. It reached the Lahn River at Marburg 28 Mar 45 and then closed the Ruhr Pocket after the Battle of Paderborn 31 Mar–1 Apr 45. The division reached the Weser River on 7 Apr 45 and the Mulde River near Torten 15 Apr 45. It fought the Battle for Dessau 21–23 Apr 45 and was relieved along the Mulde 25 Apr 45. It withdrew to Sangerhausen for rehabilitation 26 Apr 45 and hostilities ended 7 May 45.

4th Armored Division

No Distinctive Insignia Authorized

15 Apr 41 activated at Pine Camp N.Y. and moved to Cp Forrest Tenn 2 Oct 42 for the I Corps Tennessee Maneuvers; arrived Cp Young Calif 17 Nov 42 where participated in the Desert Training Center No.1 California Maneuvers; transferred to Cp Bowie Tex 13 Jun 43; staged at Cp Myles Standish Mass 20 Dec 43 until departed Boston P/E 29 Dec 43; arrived England 11 Jan 44 and landed in France 13 Jul 44; crossed into Luxembourg 9 Feb 45 and entered Germany 9 Mar 45 where redesignated 1st Constabulary Brigade 1 May 46.

Campaigns: *Normandy, Northern France, Rhineland, Ardennes-Alsace, Central Europe*
Aug 45 Loc: Landshut Germany

Typical Organization (1941):

4th Armored Brigade HHC
  35th Armored Regiment (Light)
  37th Armored Regiment (Light)
  80th Armored Regiment (Medium)
  66th Field Artillery Regiment (Armored)
84th Reconnaissance Battalion (Armored)
22nd Field Artillery Battalion (Armored)
51st Infantry (Armored)

Headquarters
Hqs Company, 4th Armored Division
  24th Engineer Battalion (Armored)
  46th Medical Battalion (Armored)
144th Signal Company (Armored)
  20th Ordnance Battalion (Armored)
  18th Quartermaster Battalion (Armored)

Typical Organization (1944/45):

8th Tank Battalion
35th Tank Battalion
37th Tank Battalion
10th Armored Infantry Battalion
51st Armored Infantry Battalion
53rd Armored Infantry Battalion
  HHB Division Artillery
22nd Armored Field Artillery Battalion
66th Armored Field Artillery Battalion
94th Armored Field Artillery Battalion
25th Cavalry Reconnaissance Squadron, Mecz
504th Counter Intelligence Corps Det
704th Tank Destroyer Battalion *(attached 25 Apr 45–Past 9 May 45)*
811th Tank Destroyer Battalion *(attached 3 Mar 45–11 Mar 45)*
489th AAA Auto-Wpns Battalion *(attached 19 Jun 44–19 May 45)*

Headquarters
Hqs Company, 4th Armored Division
HHC, Combat Command A
HHC, Combat Command B
Hqs, Reserve Command
HHC, Division Trains:
  46th Medical Battalion, Armored
126th Armored Ordnance Maintenance Battalion
Military Police Platoon
24th Armored Engineer Battalion
144th Armored Signal Company

Overseas Wartime Assignments:

First Army - 18 Dec 43
VIII Corps - 22 Jan 44
XX Corps - 9 Mar 44
XV Corps - 20 Apr 44
VIII Corps - 15 Jul 44
XII Corps - 13 Aug 44
III Corps - 19 Dec 44

VIII Corps - 2 Jan 45
XII Corps - 12 Jan 45
VIII Corps - 4 Apr 45
X Corps - 9 Apr 45
VIII Corps - 17 Apr 45
XII Corps - 30 Apr 45

Commanders: MG Henry W. Baird: Apr 41
MG John S. Wood: May 42
MG Hugh J. Gaffey: Dec 44
MG William M. Hoge: Mar 45

BG B. L. Clarke: Jun 45
BG W. Lyn Roberts: Jul 45
MG Fay B. Prickett: Sep 45

Killed in Action: 1,143   *Wounded in Action:* 4,551   *Died of Wounds:* 213

4th Armored Division Combat Narrative

The division landed across Utah Beach France 13 Jul 44 and entered combat on 17 Jul 44, taking Coutances with CCB by 28 Jul 44. It took Avranches and captured the Seé River bridge 30 Jul 44 and then drove south to cut off the Brittany Peninsula as it reached Vannes 5 Aug 44. After investing Lorient on 7 Aug 44 it entered an evacuated Nantes 11 Aug 44 and took Orléans with CCA on 16 Aug 44. By 31 Aug 44 CCA had reached the Meuse River at Commercy and Pont-sur-Meuse and established bridgeheads. Relieved there by the 80th Inf Div on 2 Sep 44, the division crossed the Moselle River near Lorey against heavy opposition with CCB as CCA crossed into the Dieulouard Bridgehead stopping strong German counterattacks, all on 11–13 Sep 44. CCB forced the Marne-Rhine Canal at Crevic and Maixe against strong opposition 15 Sep 44 and CCR moved into Lunéville the next day. In a series of tank duels, the division mopped up the Arracourt region 19–22 Sep 44. A German attack overran CCA lines 25 Sep 44 and the division lost Vic-sur-Seille and Moncourt, then withdrew the next day from Juvelize and Coincourt. The Battle for Hill 318 was fought 27–28 Sep 44 with heavy losses, but on 29 Sep 44 the division finally defeated the German attempt to take Arracourt. The division then went over to the defensive on line from Chambrey to Xanrey to Henamenil until 11 Oct 44 and on 12 Oct 44 was relieved by the 26th Inf Div for rehabilitation.

The division attacked 9 Nov 44 and reached Fonteny which was taken by CCB 11 Nov 44. After suffering heavy tank losses to a German counterattack which retook Rodalbe on 12 Nov 44, the division advanced against strong opposition to capture Dieuze and recapture Rodalbe by 19 Nov 44. CCB crossed the Saare at Romelfing 24 Nov 44 and cleared Baerendorf in house-to-house fighting, checked a German counterattack there the next day, and took Wolfskirchen despite flooded streams 27 Nov 44. The division then cleared its zone of responsibility, and next opened the attack on Saare-Union 1 Dec 44, which was taken the following day by the 26th Inf Div. The division fought the Battle of Bining 5–6 Dec 44 and was relieved by the 12 Armd Div on 7 Dec 44.

In response to the German Ardennes Counteroffensive the division moved 150 miles as it assembled in the Arlon-Luxembourg area 20 Dec 44 while CCB reached the Bastogne area and contacted 10th Armd Div. On 22 Dec 44 the division took Martelange in the drive to relieve Bastogne, fought the Battle for Chaumont 23–25 Dec 44, and seized Bigonville in heavy combat 24 Dec 44. CCR pushed through Assenois to Bastogne on 26 Dec 44, and the next day vehicles from division entered the city and ended the siege. On 29 Dec 44 CCA opened the Arlon-Bastogne Highway. The division then held the corridor into Bastogne and gave fire-support to the 35th Inf Div, helping to clear Lutrebois 2 Jan 45. CCB attacked toward Noville 9 Jan 45 and the division attacked through 6th Armd Div toward Bourcy on 10 Jan 45. The division then maintained defensive positions, clearing Hosdorf on the Our River in a local attack 2 Feb 45.

CCB attacked through the 80th Inf Div at Geichlingen 22 Feb 45 and seized the bridge over the Pruem River at Sinspelt intact the next day. As CCA crossed the Pruem at Oberweiss 25 Feb 45, CCB established a bridgehead across the Nims at Rittersdorf. The following day it seized the high ground north of Bitburg but was unable to clear Erdorf on the Kyll River. On 27 Feb 45 CCA took Matzen and CCB captured Fliessen. The division assembled near Bitburg 3 Mar 45 and attacked through the 5th Inf Div on 5 Mar 45, reaching the Rhine River 8 Mar 45 where it regrouped and mopped up. The division then attacked out of the Moselle Bridgehead at Treis on 15 Mar 45 and reached the Nahe River at Bad Kreuznach on the following day. It moved to the Rhine River at Worms 20 Mar 45 and crossed 24 Mar 45, driving through the bridgehead there to reach the Main River near Hanau 25 Mar 45. It took an undefended Darmstadt the same day. On 28 Mar 45 the division attacked across the Main at Grossauheim and crossed the Werra River at Creuzburg on 1 Apr 45. The division took Gotha 4 Apr 45 and reached the Saale River south of Jena which it crossed on 12 Apr 45 to establish bridgeheads over the Zwick Mulde at Wolkenburg on 13 Apr 45. It withdrew to reserve on 19 Apr 45, and attacked again 6 May 45 through the Regen and Freyung Passes in Czechoslovakia. Forward elements were at Pisek when hostilities ended 7 May 45.

5th Armored Division

No Distinctive
Insignia Authorized

1 Oct 41 activated at Ft Knox Ky and transferred to Cp Cooke Calif 16 Feb 42; participated 14 Aug 42 in the Desert Training Center II Armored Corps Calif Maneuvers; returned to Cp Cooke Calif 19 Nov 42; moved 17 Mar 43 to the Second Army No.1 Tennessee Maneuvers; arrived at Pine Camp N.Y. 24 Jun 43 and at Indiantown Gap Mil Res Pa 8 Dec 43; staged at Cp Kilmer N.J. 4 Feb 44 until departed New York P/E 11 Feb 44; arrived England 24 Feb 44 and landed in France 25 Jul 44; crossed into Luxembourg 2 Sep 44 and into Belgium 5 Oct 44; initially entered Germany 1 Dec 44; returned to Belgium 24 Dec 44 and to Holland 5 Feb 45; re-entered Germany 25 Feb 45; returned New York P/E 10 Oct 45 and inactivated at Cp Kilmer N.J. 11 Oct 45.

Campaigns: *Normandy, Northern France, Rhineland, Ardennes-Alsace, Central Europe*
Aug 45 Loc: Muhlhausen Germany

Typical Organization (1941):

5th Armored Brigade HHC
  31st Armored Regiment (Light)
  34th Armored Regiment (Light)
  81st Armored Regiment (Medium)
  65th Field Artillery Regiment (Armored)
85th Armored Reconnaissance Battalion
58th Field Artillery Battalion (Armored)
46th Infantry (Armored)

Headquarters
Hqs Company, 5th Armored Division
  22nd Engineer Battalion (Armored)
  75th Medical Battalion (Armored)
145th Signal Company (Armored)
  21st Ordnance Battalion (Armored)
  19th Quartermaster Battalion (Armored)

Typical Organization (1944/45):

10th Tank Battalion
34th Tank Battalion
81st Tank Battalion
15th Armored Infantry Battalion
46th Armored Infantry Battalion
47th Armored Infantry Battalion
HHB Division Artillery
47th Armored Field Artillery Battalion
71st Armored Field Artillery Battalion
95th Armored Field Artillery Battalion
  85th Cavalry Reconnaissance Squadron, Mecz
505th Counter Intelligence Corps Det
628th Tank Destroyer Battalion *(attached 2 Aug 44–19 Dec 44, 28 Jan 45–9 May 45*
629th Tank Destroyer Battalion *(attached 29 Aug 44–14 Dec 44)*
771st Tank Destroyer Battalion *(attached 17 Apr 45–24 Apr 45)*
387th AAA Auto-Wpns Battalion *(attached 1 Aug 44–25 Mar 45, 28 Mar 45–9 May 45)*

Headquarters
Hqs Company, 5th Armored Division
HHC, Combat Command A
HHC, Combat Command B
Hqs, Reserve Command
HHC, Division Trains:
  75th Medical Battalion, Armored
  127th Armored Maintenance Battalion
  Military Police Platoon
22nd Armored Engineer Battalion
145th Armored Signal Company

Overseas Wartime Assignments:

Third Army - 3 Mar 44
XX Corps - 29 Mar 44
XII Corps - 17 Jun 44
Third Army - 31 Jul 44
XV Corps - 1 Aug 44
First Army (attached) - 24 Aug 44
XV Corps - 26 Aug 44

V Corps - 29 Aug 44
VII Corps - 29 Nov 44
V Corps - 23 Dec 44
XIX Corps - 27 Jan 45
XVI Corps - 29 Jan 45
XIII Corps - 1 Feb 45
XVIII (A/B) Corps - 4 May 45

Commanders: MG Jack W. Heard: Oct 41   BG Morrill Ross: Jul 45
       MG Lunsford E. Oliver: Mar 43   MG Holmes E. Dager: Sep 45

Killed in Action: 570   *Wounded in Action:* 2,442   *Died of Wounds:* 140

5th Armored Division Combat Narrative

The division arrived across Utah Beach France on 25 Jul 44 and concentrated between the Seé and Selune River to block German movement toward Avranches on 1 Aug 44. It drove south through Coutances, Avranches, and Vitre to cross the Mayenne River and take Le Mans 8 Aug 44. The next day the division swung north toward Alencon, and advanced to the edge of Argentan 12 Aug 44 which it then left to the 90th Inf Div. It advanced 60 miles to reach the Eure River at Dreux which fell 16 Aug 44. Advancing with the 79th Inf Div, the division reached the Seine River at Mantes-Gassicourt on 18 Aug 44 and started along the west bank toward Louviers the next day to cut off German retreat. By 22 Aug 44 it encountered strong opposition between the Seine and Eure Rivers and reached Houdebouville 24 Aug 44. The division moved through Paris 30 Aug 44 to spearhead the drive on Compiègne, and crossed the Oise River at Pont Ste Maxence with CCB on 31 Aug 44. It reached the Belgian border at Conde 2 Sep 44 and secured crossings over the Meuse River near Sedan on 5 Sep 44 with CCA at Bazeilles and CCR at Mohon, taking Sedan the next day. On 10 Sep 44 the city of Luxembourg fell to CCA without opposition. The 85th Rcn Sqdn entered Germany with a dismounted patrol near Stalzenburg on 11 Sep 44 and became the first allied unit to enter the Reich from the west. CCR crossed the Sauer River into Germany on 14 Sep 44 and cleared Wallendorf, driving through the *West Wall* to the edge of Bettingen the next day. The division then held the Wallendorf salient against counterattacks until 20 Sep 44, and then moved to defensive lines in the Monschau-Hofen sector.

CCR reinforced the 4th Inf Div in the Huertgen Forest on 16 Nov 44 and advanced in heavy combat. It was halted on 25 Nov 44 outside Grosshau by a large crater and mines, but by 29 Nov 44 seized Kleinhau. The division took Brandenburg with air support on 3 Dec 44 as CCR cleared a strongpoint at Vossenack 3–4 Dec 44. The division pushed into Bergstein the next day and by 16 Dec 44 had reached the Roer River in the Bilstein area. It resumed the attack toward the Roer on 20 Dec 44 and CCA fought the Battle for Schneidhausen 20–22 Dec 44, after which the division was relieved in line by the 8th and 83rd Inf Divs. It closed into Eupen on 24 Dec 44 and was placed in reserve.

CCA seized Eicherscheid on 30 Jan 45 and captured Colmar 2 Feb 45. CCR crossed the Roer River 25 Feb 45 and assembled south of Hottorf, attacking through mud which bogged division's CCB down outside Guenhoven 27 Feb 45. CCA crossed the Niers Canal on 1 Mar 45 and took both Anrath and Fischeln the next day. CCR mopped up the Orsoy area, which included the Battle of Repelen, 1–7 Mar 45, during which it reached the Rhine 5 Mar 45. CCA and CCB meanwhile assembled at Kempen. The division remained in the Kempen-Repelen area until 11 Mar 45, when relieved by the 75th Inf Div. The division then crossed the Rhine River at Wessel 30–31 Mar 45.

The division attacked 1 Apr 45 and bypassed Muenster to reach the Weser River on 3 Apr 45, where it was unable to secure the bridges intact at Minden and Rinteln. CCR crossed the Leine River south of Hannover on 9 Apr 45 and captured a bridge over the Oker River in the Ahnsen area the next day. The division reached the Elbe River on 12 Apr 45 with CCR at Wittenberge and CCA in the Tangermuende area. There the division mopped up until relieved 16 Apr 45 to clear the Forst Knesebeck. It attacked from the Daehre-Salzwedel line against strong opposition on 21 Apr 45 and took Dannenberg 23 Apr 45. It was relieved along the Elbe River 24 Apr 45 by the 29th Inf Div, after which it performed security functions until hostilities ended on 7 May 45.

6th Armored Division

No Distinctive Insignia Authorized

15 Feb 42 activated at Ft Knox Ky and moved to Cp Chaffee Ark 15 Mar 42; participated 25 Aug 42 in VIII Corps Louisiana Maneuvers; returned to Cp Chaffee Ark 21 Sep 42; moved to Cp Young Calif 10 Oct 42 to participate in Desert Training Center No.1 California Maneuvers; arrived Cp Cooke Calif 20 Mar 43; staged at Cp Shanks N.Y. 3 Feb 44 until departed New York P/E 11 Feb 44; arrived England 23 Feb 44 and landed in France 19 Jul 44; crossed into Luxembourg 29 Dec 44 and into Belgium 30 Dec 44; returned to France 12 Mar 45; entered Germany 20 Mar 45; returned to New York P/E 18 Sep 45 and inactivated same date at Cp Shanks N.Y.

Campaigns: *Normandy, Northern France, Rhineland, Ardennes-Alsace, Central Europe*
Aug 45 Loc: Apolda Germany

Typical Organization (1944/45):

15th Tank Battalion
68th Tank Battalion
69th Tank Battalion
9th Armored Infantry Battalion
44th Armored Infantry Battalion
50th Armored Infantry Battalion
HHB Division Artillery
128th Armored Field Artillery Battalion
212th Armored Field Artillery Battalion
231st Armored Field Artillery Battalion
86th Cavalry Reconnaissance Squadron, Mecz
506th Counter Intelligence Corps Det
737th Tank Battalion *(attached 22 Nov 44–3 Dec 44)*
603rd Tank Destroyer Battalion *(attached unknown–29 Jun 45)*
691st Tank Destroyer Battalion *(attached 15 Dec 44–23 Dec 44)*
777th AAA Auto-Wpns Battalion *(attached 22 Jul 44–29 Jun 45)*

Headquarters
Hqs Company, 6th Armored Division
HHC, Combat Command A
HHC, Combat Command B
Hqs, Reserve Command
HHC, Division Trains:
   76th Medical Battalion, Armored
   128th Armored Ordnance Maintenance Battalion
Military Police Platoon
25th Armored Engineer Battalion
146th Armored Signal Company

Overseas Wartime Assignments:

VIII Corps - 3 Mar 44
XX Corps - 9 Mar 44
VIII Corps *(attached)* - 25 Jul 44
VIII Corps - 1 Aug 44
Ninth Army - 5 Sep 44
Third Army - 16 Sep 44
XII Corps - 20 Sep 44
III Corps - 11 Dec 44
XII Corps - 18 Dec 44

XX Corps - 21 Dec 44
XII Corps - 25 Dec 44
III Corps - 28 Dec 44
VIII Corps - 11 Feb 45
XV Corps - 8 Mar 45
XX Corps - 23 Mar 45
XII Corps - 24 Mar 45
XX Corps - 28 Mar 45
VIII Corps - 17 Apr 45

Commanders: MG William H. H. Morris Jr: Feb 42
             MG Robert W. Grow: May 43
             BG George W. Read Jr: Jul 45

Killed in Action: 833   *Wounded in Action:* 3,666   *Died of Wounds:* 156

6th Armored Division Combat Narrative

The division landed across Utah Beach France on 19 Jul 44 and assembled at Le Mesnil on 25 Jul 44. It was committed through the 8th Inf Div to clear the heights near Le Bingard on 27 Jul 44 and CCA secured a bridgehead across the Sienne River near Pont de la Roche 29 Jul 44. On 31 Jul 44 CCR overran Granville and the division moved to Avranches where it relieved the 4th Armd Div and secured the area bridges. The division swung into Brittany on 1 Aug 44 and closed on Brest 7 Aug 44 while destroying a German force at Plouvien 8–9 Aug 44. While CCA invested Brest, CCB and CCR relieved the 4th Arm Div at Vannes and Lorient, respectively 12–15 Sep 44. The division then moved to relieve the 35th Inf Div of protecting the south flank between Orléans and Auxerre on 2 Sep 44. CCA was relieved in the Lorient sector by the 94th Inf Div on 13 Sep 44, and CCB relieved the 4th Armd Div at Lunéville on 19 Sep 44. The division attacked 8 Oct 44, crossed the Seille River 9 Nov 44 and mopped up the Nomeny area despite mud, mines, and congestion. The division established bridgeheads across the Nied Française River against strong opposition on 11 Nov 44 at Sanry, and CCA cleared Arraincourt on 13 Nov 44. The division reached Maderbach Creek at Remering with CCB by 25 Nov 44 after fierce fighting through mud, mines, and craters. CCA pushed through the Forêt de Puttlange but fell back on 26 Nov 44 and CCB was unable to get tanks through the mud along the Maderbach. The division was relieved in this area 2 Dec 44 and patrolled to the Saare River 5 Dec 44, taking Sarreguemines with the 35th Inf Div the next day. It then maintained defensive positions near Saarbruecken.

In response to the German Ardennes Counteroffensive, the division was given responsibility for the sector south of the Sauer River between Ettelbruck and Mostroff on 27 Dec 44. The division was heavily engaged in the Mageret-Wardin area east of Bastogne commencing 31 Dec 44, being forced to withdraw by German attacks until 8 Jan 45 when it counterattacked to recover lost ground in its sector. On 10 Jan 45 the 4th Armd Div attacked through its lines, and the next day the division took over the attack toward Bras. CCA captured Wardin 12 Jan 45 and CCB cleared Mageret 13–14 Jan 45. The division fought house-to-house in Oubourcy 15 Jan 45 and seized Moinet and Hill 510 on 20 Jan 45. Weiler fell 22 Jan 45 and Kalborn fell—after an unsuccessful previous attack—on 29 Jan 45. The division then took over a new zone west of the Our River on 4 Feb 45, and assembled at Kalborn 6 Feb 45.

The division attacked across the Our River at Kalborn and Dahnen on 7 Feb 45 and by 9 Feb 45 armor was crossed over the Bailey Bridge there. It relieved the 17th A/B Div 10–11 Feb 45 as CCB maintained the Our Bridgehead, and then renewed the offensive into the *West Wall* on 20 Feb 45. The penetration of the *West Wall* was marked as Ober Eisenach fell 22 Feb 45, and the final objective town of Muxerath was cleared 24 Feb 45. The division then moved to a new zone west of the Pruem River and relieved the 90th Inf Div 25 Feb 45. CCA established a small bridgehead at Manderscheid which was enlarged as CCB, after being initially forced back across, took Lunebach on 28 Feb 45. The division reached the Nims and crossed near Schoenecken on 3 Mar 45 and the following day assembled in reserve in the Arzfeld area.

The division attacked 20 Mar 45 at Homburg and CCA reached the Rhine River at Rhein-Durkheim the next day. The division crossed the Rhine River at Oppenheim on 25 Mar 45 and CCA reached the Main River, coming under heavy antiaircraft fire from Frankfurt. The division established bridgeheads across the Main and was relieved on 27 Mar 45, attacking north of Frankfurt on 30 Mar 45. By 2 Apr 45 it completed crossing the Fulda River at Malsfeld and encircled Mulhausen 4 Apr 45. After Langensalza fell 6 Apr 45 the division consolidated and then renewed its offensive 11 Apr 45 as it crossed the Saale River southwest of Naumberg. It reached the Zwick Mulde at Rochlitz on 14 Apr 45 and on 16 Apr 45 turned over its bridgehead there to the 76th Inf Div. The division maintained defensive positions along this river until hostilities ceased on 7 May 45.

7th Armored Division

No Distinctive Insignia Authorized

1 Mar 42 activated at Cp Polk La and moved 15 Sep 42 to the IV Corps Louisiana Maneuvers; returned to Cp Polk La 9 Nov 42; arrived 11 Mar 43 at the Desert Training Center No.2 California Maneuvers; transferred 12 Aug 43 to Ft Benning Ga; arrived at Cp Myles Standish Mass 22 Apr 44; staged at Cp Shanks N.Y. 2 May 44 until departed New York P/E 7 Jun 44; arrived in England 14 Jun 44 and landed in France 11 Aug 44; crossed into Belgium 26 Sep 44 and into Holland 8 Oct 44; returned to Belgium 28 Dec 44 and entered Germany 15 Mar 45; arrived Hampton Roads P/E 9 Oct 45 and inactivated at Cp Patrick Henry Va 9 Oct 45.

Campaigns: *Northern France, Rhineland, Ardennes-Alsace, Central Europe*
Aug 45 Loc: Delitzsch Germany

Typical Organization (1944/45):

17th Tank Battalion	Headquarters
31st Tank Battalion	Hqs Company, 7th Armored Division
40th Tank Battalion	HHC, Combat Command A
23rd Armored Infantry Battalion	HHC, Combat Command B
38th Armored Infantry Battalion	Hqs, Reserve Command
48th Armored Infantry Battalion	HHC, Division Trains:
434th Armored Field Artillery Battalion	77th Medical Battalion, Armored
440th Armored Field Artillery Battalion	129th Armored Ordnance Maintenance Battalion
489th Armored Field Artillery Battalion	Military Police Platoon
87th Cavalry Reconnaissance Squadron, Mecz	33rd Armored Engineer Battalion
HHB Division Artillery	147th Armored Signal Company
507th Counter Intelligence Corps Det	
814th Tank Destroyer Battalion *(attached 13 Aug 44–9 May 45)*	
820th Tank Destroyer Battalion *(attached 25 Dec 44–30 Dec 44)*	
203rd AAA Auto-Wpns Battalion *(attached 12 Aug 44–9 May 45)*	

Overseas Wartime Assignments:

First Army - 30 Jul 44	VIII Corps - 16 Dec 44
Third Army - 5 Aug 44	XVIII (A/B) Corps - 20 Dec 44
XX Corps - 10 Aug 44	V Corps - 29 Jan 45
XIX Corps - 25 Sep 44	III Corps - 7 Mar 45
Ninth Army - 8 Oct 44	V Corps - 19 Apr 45
XIII Corps - 9 Nov 44	XVIII (A/B) Corps - 30 Apr 45

Commanders: MG Lindsay McD. Silvester: Mar 42
MG Robert W. Hasbrouck: Nov 44
BG Truman E. Boudinot: Sep 45

Killed in Action: 898   *Wounded in Action:* 3,811   *Died of Wounds:* 200

7th Armored Division Combat Narrative

The division landed in Normandy France on 11 Aug 44 and drove through Nogent-le-Rotrou and fought the Battle of Chartres 15–17 Aug 44. The division attacked toward the Seine River 20 Aug 44 and gained a bridgehead across it at Melun on 24 Aug 44. It then drove rapidly to the Marne River which it crossed at Château-Thierry on 27 Aug 44, and CCA established a bridgehead across the Meuse at Verdun on 31 Aug 44. The division was halted short of Sedan as fuel was exhausted on 2 Sep 44. It attacked again 6 Sep 44 to force the Moselle which it reached the following day at Mondelange after heavy combat. The division contained the German Metz bridgehead, crossing elements over the Moselle under heavy fire 8 Sep 44 which had to be withdrawn 10–11 Sep 44. CCA battled the German lines west of Metz in fierce fighting while CCB crossed into the Arnaville Bridgehead 12 Sep 44 despite deep mud. It attacked the following day toward Mardigny but was quickly halted by heavy fire from Arry. CCR next attempted a breakout of the combined 5th Inf. Div–90th Inf Div–7th Armd Div bridgehead but failed. CCB and CCR advanced slowly toward the Seille River and the latter managed to get into Sillegny on 19 Sep 44 but was forced out with very heavy losses. CCA joined with CCB to reach the Seille and bypass Sillegny, but CCB was forced back from the river on 20 Sep 44. An attack across the river the next day was repulsed by intense fire. The division withdrew from Corny and Pournoy-la-Chétive on 24 Sep 44 and was relieved the next day by the 5th Inf Div.

The division then went to Holland and attacked from Oploo on 30 Sep 44 against heavy opposition to clear a corridor west of the Maas. CCB took Vortum 2 Oct 44 and the division fought the Battle of Peel Marshes and Overloon 2–6 Oct 44 before breaking off the attack. The division established a bridgehead across the Canal de Deurne on 16 Oct 44 as it defended along both this canal and Canal du Nord. German attacks penetrated the division lines west of Venlo on 27 Oct 44 and the division lost Liesel and gave ground south of Austen 29 Oct 44. It was then relieved in the sector and concentrated in the vicinity of Nederweert and Weert. CCA made a limited attack to clear German forces around the Meijel area in the Canal du Nord area 2–5 Nov 44, but this action was soon broken off.

The division was preparing to drive from Linnich Germany on the Roer River when elements were committed to the defense of St Vith 16 Dec 44. German attacks forced a withdrawal there on 21 Dec 44 and Manhay was lost 24 Dec 44, the latter being retaken 27 Dec 44. The division's zone was taken over by the 75th Inf Div 29 Dec 44. The division attacked through mines and deep snow toward St Vith on 20 Jan 45, and captured Born in house-to-house fighting the next day. CCA cleared Hunningen on 22 Jan 45, and then CCB attacked through CCA to clear St Vith itself 23 Jan 45. As CCB consolidated near St Vith, CCA seized Wallerode on 25 Jan 45. The offensive was concluded as CCB reduced the Bois de St Vith 27–28 Jan 45. CCR took Strauch and Steckenborn on 5 Feb 45 and the division took over the defense of the Hechelscheid sector on 6 Feb 45 as CCR mopped up toward Schmidt. The division then spent the remainder of February in rehabilitation.

On 7 Mar 45 the division assembled near Zulpich and then started clearing the zone west of the Rhine River between Bonn and Remagen. It placed cable across the Rhine on 14 Mar 45. The division assembled across the Rhine's eastern side 25 Mar 45 and attacked the next day, advancing to reach the Dill River between Herborn and Wetzlar on 27 Mar 45. The following day the division secured crossings between Marburg and Giessen over the Lahn River. It captured the Edersee Dam intact and secured crossings over the Eder River on 30 Mar 45. CCA attacked and took Niedersfeld 4 Apr 45 and began the reduction of the Ruhr Pocket against heavy opposition, CCB being heavily counterattacked at Gleidorf on 7 Apr 45. Frederburg fell after heavy combat on 8 Apr 45 and by 16 Apr 45 resistance in the Ruhr Pocket collapsed. The division assembled at Gottingen 18 Apr 45 and on 30 Apr 45 began the drive from the Elbe to the Baltic, which was unopposed and the latter reached west of Kluetz on 3 May 45. There the division made contact with advancing Soviet Army forces and was in that region when hostilities ended on 7 May 45.

8th Armored Division

No Distinctive
Insignia Authorized

1 Apr 42 activated at Ft Knox Ky and moved to Ft Campbell Ky 9 Jan 43; arrived at Cp Polk La 5 Mar 43 and sent to Fourth Army No.6 Louisiana Maneuvers 2 Feb 44; returned to Cp Polk La 26 Apr 44; staged at Cp Kilmer N.J. 2 Nov 44 until departed New York P/E 6 Nov 44; arrived England 19 Nov 44 and landed in France 5 Jan 45; crossed into Holland 5 Feb 45 and entered Germany 2 Mar 45; arrived Hampton Roads P/E 13 Nov 45 and inactivated same date at Cp Patrick Henry Va.

Campaigns: *Rhineland, Ardennes-Alsace, Central Europe*
Aug 45 Loc: Gottingen Germany

Typical Organization (1944/45)

18th Tank Battalion
36th Tank Battalion
80th Tank Battalion
  7th Armored Infantry Battalion
49th Armored Infantry Battalion
58th Armored Infantry Battalion
HHB Division Artillery
398th Armored Field Artillery Battalion
399th Armored Field Artillery Battalion
405th Armored Field Artillery Battalion
  88th Cavalry Reconnaissance Squadron, Mecz
508th Counter Intelligence Corps Det
691st Tank Battalion *(attached 6 Feb 45–5 Mar 45)*
809th Tank Destroyer Battalion *(attached 9 Feb 45–14 May 45)*
467th AAA Auto-Wpns Battalion *(attached 15 Jan 45–1 Feb 45)*
473rd AAA Auto-Wpns Battalion *(attached 6 Feb 45–6 May 45)*

Headquarters
Hqs Company, 8th Armored Division
HHC, Combat Command A
HHC, Combat Command B
Hqs, Reserve Command
HHC, Division Trains:
  78th Medical Battalion, Armored
  130th Armored Ordnance Maintenance Battalion
  Military Police Platoon
  53rd Armored Engineer Battalion
148th Armored Signal Company

Overseas Wartime Assignments:

Fifteenth Army - 8 Jan 45
Third Army *(attached)* - 12 Jan 45
XVI Corps - 1 Feb 45
XIX Corps - 1 Apr 45

XVI Corps - 9 Apr 45
Ninth Army - 12 Apr 45
XIX Corps - 15 Apr 45

Commanders: MG William M. Grimes: Apr 42
              MG John M. Devine: Oct 44
              BG Charles F. Colson: Aug 45

Killed in Action: 393   *Wounded in Action:* 1,572   *Died of Wounds:* 73

8th Armored Division Combat Narrative

The division landed in France on 5 Jan 45 and assembled near Bacqueville. The division moved to Pont-a-Mousson for further training, and CCA was detached to Koenigsmacker on 19 Jan 45 to participate in the drive against the Moselle-Saar salient with 94th Inf Div. CCA recaptured Nennig 23 Jan 45 and took Berg 25 Jan 45. The division moved to Simpelveld Holland, and then to Roermond Holland on 19 Feb 45 where it launched a diversionary attack pushing German forces north of the Heide Woods and east of the Roer River. The division crossed the Roer River at Hilfarthe on 27 Feb 45 and attacked toward Wegberg with CCA. As CCA overran Tetelrath CCB and CCR crossed the Roer the next day. The division sped north as CCA took Wachtendonk on 2 Mar 45 and the next day CCB captured Aldekerk as CCR crossed the Niers River at Muelhausen. The division was withdrawn, except for CCB which assisted the 35th Inf Div in the drive on Lintfort 4 Mar 45 which it captured along with Rheinberg on 5 Mar 45 after hard fighting. Task Force Murray (CCB) fought the Battle for Ossenberg 7–9 Mar 45.

The division crossed the Rhine River 26 Mar 45 and attacked Dorsten, which was captured after heavy fighting on 29 Mar 45, and continued east against scattered resistance. The division began the attack against the Ruhr Pocket 3 Apr 45 as CCA moved up the Paderborn-Soest Highway and CCR approached Elsen. The following day CCA reached the Mohne River and cleared Erwitte as CCR took Overhagen. On 6 Apr 45 CCB reached Ost Oennen, southwest of Soest. The division overran Werl 8 Apr 45 and took Unna on 11 Apr 45 and mopped up. It was relieved by the 95th Inf Div on 13 Apr 45 and passed into reserve in the Wolfenbuettel area where it mopped up resistance. On 18 Apr 45 CCB attacked in the woods south of Derenburg. The division attacked to clear the Blankenburg area at the east edge of the Harz Mountains on 20 Apr 45 and completed its operations there the following day as both Michaelstein and Cattenstedt were reached. The division was assigned security and occupation duty in the Harz Mountain region on 23 Apr 45, and was in that status when hostilities were declared ended on 7 May 45.

9th Armored Division

No Distinctive Insignia Authorized

15 Jul 42 activated at Ft Riley Kans and moved to Goff Calif 10 Jun 43 and Cp Ibis Calif 1 Aug 43 during the Desert Training Center No.3 California Maneuvers; moved to Cp Polk La 25 Oct 43 for the Third Army No.5 Louisiana Maneuvers; staged at Cp Kilmer N.J. 14 Aug 44 until departed New York P/E 18 Aug 44; arrived in England 1 Sep 44 and landed in France 3 Oct 44; crossed into Luxembourg 20 Oct 44 and into Belgium 18 Dec 44; returned to France 20 Dec 44 and to Belgium 21 Dec 44; returned to France 23 Dec 44 and to Belgium 22 Feb 45; entered Germany 2 Mar 45; arrived Hampton Roads P/E 13 Oct 45 and inactivated same date at Cp Patrick Henry Va.

Campaigns: *Rhineland, Ardennes-Alsace, Central Europe*
Aug 45 Loc: Bayreuth Germany

Typical Organization (1944/45):

2nd Tank Battalion
14th Tank Battalion
19th Tank Battalion
27th Armored Infantry Battalion
52nd Armored Infantry Battalion
60th Armored Infantry Battalion
HHB Division Artillery
  3rd Armored Field Artillery Battalion
16th Armored Field Artillery Battalion
73rd Armored Field Artillery Battalion
  89th Cavalry Reconnaissance Squadron, Mecz
509th Counter Intelligence Corps Det
656th Tank Destroyer Battalion *(attached 22 Feb 45–Past 9 May 45)*
811th Tank Destroyer Battalion *(attached 14 Nov 44–8 Jan 45)*
482nd AAA Auto-Wpns Battalion *(attached 2 Nov 44–9 Jan 45, 22 Feb 45–9 May 45)*

Headquarters
Hqs Company, 9th Armored Division
HHC, Combat Command A
HHC, Combat Command B
Hqs, Reserve Command
HHC, Division Trains:
  2nd Medical Battalion, Armored
  131st Armored Ordnance Maintenance Battalion
  Military Police Platoon
  9th Armored Engineer Battalion
149th Armored Signal Company

Overseas Wartime Assignments:

Ninth Army - 29 Jul 44
III Corps - 28 Aug 44
XIII Corps - 5 Sep 44
VIII Corps - 15 Oct 44
III Corps - 20 Dec 44
VIII Corps - 21 Dec 44
Supreme Headquarters, Allied
Expeditionary Forces (SHAEF) - 31 Dec 44

Fifteenth Army - 8 Jan 45
III Corps - 22 Feb 45
V Corps - 21 Mar 45
VII Corps - 28 Apr 45
VIII Corps - 30 Apr 45
V Corps - 4 May 45
Third Army - 6 May 45

Commanders: MG Geoffrey Keyes: Jul 42
             MG John W. Leonard: Oct 42

Killed in Action: 570   *Wounded in Action:* 2,280   *Died of Wounds:* 123

9th Armored Division Combat Narrative

The division landed in Normandy France on 3 Oct 44 and initially patrolled a quiet sector along the Luxembourg-German frontier. The German Ardennes Counteroffensive struck the division on 16 Dec 44, and CCB was ordered to St Vith as the division lost ground. CCR moved into positions along the Bastogne-Trois Vierges road 17 Dec 44 and the German drive breached the division's lines the following day. Fighting in widely scattered areas, CCA defended near Ermsdorf 20 Dec 44 and CCB withdrew from St Vith on 23 Dec 44. Meanwhile, remnants of CCR were employed in the defense of Bastogne under control of the 101st A/B Div. The remainder of the division was ordered to reserve at Sedan on 30 Dec 44.

The division rehabilitated in January 1945 and trained in February 1945. It attacked on 28 Feb 45 across the Roer River in the Soller region, CCA clearing strong opposition at Wollersheim and Langendorf on 2 Mar 45 as CCB reached the Roth River and established a bridgehead at Friesheim, and CCR captured Niederberg. The next day CCB reached the Erft River at Lommersum and was joined along the river by CCA and CCR in the Euskirchen vicinity on 4 Mar 45. The division then opened its offensive across the Erft River toward the junction of the Rhine and Ahr Rivers on 5 Mar 45. CCB overcame light resistance to seize the *Ludendorff* Railroad Bridge at Remagen, which was damaged and prepared for demolition but still standing intact on 7 Mar 45. It quickly crossed to establish a firm bridgehead across the Rhine and was joined there the next day by CCB as CCA defended the Ahr River Line. After consolidation the division attacked 22 Mar 45 to clear the region between Rhine and Wied Rivers and secured bridgeheads across the latter.

The division renewed its offensive on 26 Mar 45 and attacked through the 2nd Inf Div; CCA reached the Lahn River at Diez and CCB at Limburg. It assembled along the Lahn as CCR drove to contact the Third Army on the Cologne-Frankfurt Autobahn north of Idstein on 28 Mar 45. The division attacked again on 29 Mar 45 and by 31 Mar 45 had established a bridgehead across the Diemel River in the Warburg area which was then maintained against counterattacks.

The division started to an assembly area east of the Weser River 8 Aug 45, and attacked through the 2nd and 69th Inf Divs on 10 Apr 45 to spearhead the drive to the Saale River, which it reached 12 Apr 45. On 13 Apr 45 CCA reached the Weisse-Elster River near Pegau and consolidated. After heavy combat in the Borna area through factory districts at Deutzen, CCR reached the Mulde River and seized bridges in the Colditz-Lastau region on 15 Apr 45. The next day it crossed and cleared Colditz. The division then mopped up along the Mulde River until moved to the Borna-Taucha region in reserve on 21 Apr 45. It guarded utilities and factories at Rotha 22 Apr 45 until moved near Jena on 29 Apr 45. CCA was detached to the 1st Inf Div 3 May 45 for the drive on Karlsbad, and attacked 6 May 45 down the Cheb-Falknov Road. It was at Rudolec when hostilities were declared ended on 7 May 45.

10th Armored Division

No Distinctive Insignia Authorized

15 Jul 42 activated at Ft Benning Ga and moved 24 Jun 43 to the Second Army No.2 Tennessee Maneuvers; transferred to Cp Gordon Ga 5 Sep 43; staged at Cp Shanks N.Y. 1 Sep 44 until departed New York P/E 13 Sep 44; arrived France 23 Sep 44 and crossed into Luxembourg 17 Dec 44; returned to France 27 Dec 44; entered Germany 22 Feb 45; arrived Hampton Roads P/E 13 Oct 45 and inactivated same date at Cp Patrick Henry Va.

Campaigns: *Rhineland, Central Europe*
Aug 45 Loc: Garmisch-Partenkirchen Austria

Typical Organization (1944/45):

3rd Tank Battalion
11th Tank Battalion
21st Tank Battalion
20th Armored Infantry Battalion
54th Armored Infantry Battalion
61st Armored Infantry Battalion
HHB Division Artillery
419th Armored Field Artillery Battalion
420th Armored Field Artillery Battalion
423rd Armored Field Artillery Battalion
90th Cavalry Reconnaissance Squadron, Mecz
510th Counter Intelligence Corps Det
609th Tank Destroyer Battalion *(attached 16 Oct 44–9 May 45)*
638th Tank Destroyer Battalion *(attached unknown–15 Oct 44)*
796th AAA Auto-Wpns Battalion *(attached 16 Oct 44–9 May 45)*

Headquarters
Hqs Company, 10th Armored Division
HHC, Combat Command A
HHC, Combat Command B
Hqs, Reserve Command
HHC, Division Trains:
  80th Medical Battalion, Armored
132nd Armored Ordnance Maintenance Battalion
Military Police Platoon
55th Armored Engineer Battalion
150th Armored Signal Company

Overseas Wartime Assignments:

III Corps - 5 Sep 44
Third Army - 10 Oct 44
XX Corps - 23 Oct 44
VIII Corps *(attached)* - 17 Dec 44
III Corps - 20 Dec 44
XII Corps - 21 Dec 44

XX Corps - 26 Dec 44
XXI Corps *(attached)* - 17 Jan 45
XV Corps - 25 Jan 45
XX Corps - 10 Feb 45
XXI Corps *(attached)* - 23 Mar 45
VI Corps - 1 Apr 45

Commanders: MG Paul W. Newgarden: July 42
MG William H. H. Morris Jr: Jul 44
MG Fay B. Prickett: May 45

Killed in Action: 642   *Wounded in Action:* 3,109   *Died of Wounds:* 132

10th Armored Division Combat Narrative

The division landed at Cherbourg France on 23 Sep 44 and trained at Teurtheville France which it left 25 Oct 44. It entered the line in the Fort Driant sector to contain German forces there on 2 Nov 44. CCB crossed over the Bailey Bridge at Thionville and CCA crossed at Malling to screen in the Saar-Moselle Triangle on 14 Nov 44. Closely supported by aircraft, the division crossed CCA over the Nied River on 18 Nov 44 at a damaged bridge near Filstroff, but in order to speed the advance on the Saare River withdrew and destroyed the bridge there the next day. CCB meanwhile encountered heavy opposition as it neared Merzig on 19 Nov 44, and CCA was halted by obstacles of the Orscholz Switch Line the following day as CCB fell back under German counterattack. CCA advanced to Nennig and Tettingen on 22 Nov 44 but was forced out of both. As Tettingen was cleared on 25 Nov 44 the division broke off its advance toward Saarburg and repelled counterattacks against Borg. Finally, the division reached the Saare River opposite Merzig on 30 Nov 44 and overcame weak resistance in the Merzig area 1 Dec 44. The capture of Dreisbach the next day marked the completion of division clearing operations west of the Saare.

In response to the German Ardennes Counteroffensive the division was moved to Luxembourg City 17 Dec 44. CCB was engaged at Bastogne on 19 Dec 44 and CCA moved to positions near Echternacht, where it was relieved by the 4th Inf Div 20 Dec 44. The division formed CCX out of CCA, 9th Armd Div and CCR, 10th Armd Div 21 Dec 44 as CCA tried in vain to recover Waldbilling. The division fought at Bastogne, Noville, and Bras until relieved in Luxembourg on 26 Dec 44. The division was then moved east of the Saare to maintain defensive lines. CCB attacked toward Noville on 9 Jan 45 and captured Samrée the next day.

The division was moved to the Metz area on 10 Feb 45 and assembled in the Perl-Basch area 19 Feb 45. It renewed the offensive the next day to clear the Saar-Moselle Triangle as it attacked toward Kanzem and Wiltingen bridges and CCB drove northeast on Saarburg. Under heavy enemy fire which prevented bridging, armored-infantry was forced across the Saar near Ockfen 22-24 Feb 45. CCB crossed in the Taben area of 94th Inf Div the following day and on 26 Feb 45 the Ockfen and Serrig bridgeheads were joined and expanded to allow a heavy ponton bridge to be put in at Saarburg. That same day CCB reached Zerf. CCA attacked through CCB on 27 Feb 45 to enter Trier and take the Moselle River bridge intact 1-2 Mar 45. It then attacked across the Ruwer River near Eitelsbach against strong opposition 4 Mar 45 as CCB established a bridgehead under fire over the Kyll River near Ehrang. The Salm River was reached and a bridgehead thrown across in the Dorbach area on 9 Mar 45, and the following day Wittlich was captured. CCA completed the drive from the Alf River to the Moselle and was relieved by the 76th Inf Div at Bullay on 12 Mar 45, and the next day the division completed assembly at Trier for rehabilitation.

The division renewed its offensive 16 Mar 45 as it attacked through the 80th and 94th Inf Divs and reached the Prims River the day after. Bypassing Kaiserlautern, the division stormed Landau on 22 Mar 45. The division crossed the Rhine 28 Mar 45 and assembled in preparation for further attack the next day. It attacked across the Neckar River in the Wieblingen area and advanced against rear-guard resistance to effect a junction with the 100th Inf Div around Heilbronn 7 Apr 45. The division fought in Crailsheim Salient 8-10 Apr 45, when withdrawn for movement over the Kocher River in the 63rd Inf Div sector at Weissbach the following day. The division attacked 16 Apr 45 and helped clear Schwaebisch Hall 17-18 Apr 45. It achieved a complete breakthrough over the Rems River 19 Apr 45 and took Kirchheim the day after. The division consolidated and crossed the Danube at Ehingen 23-24 Apr 45, crossing the Austrian border near Fuessen on 28 Apr 45. The next day it attacked across the Lech River with CCA at Schongau and CCB at Fuessen. The division was at Klais and Garmisch Austria when it was halted to allow the passage of the 44th and 103rd Inf Divs through its lines 30 Apr 45. When hostilities were declared ended on 7 May 45 the division was at Innsbruck.

11th Armored Division

No Distinctive
Insignia Authorized

15 Aug 42 activated at Cp Polk La and moved 24 Jun 43 to the Third Army No.3 Louisiana Maneuvers; transferred to Cp Barkeley Tex 5 Sep 43; participated 29 Oct 43 in the Desert Training Center No.4 California Maneuvers; arrived Cp Cooke Calif 11 Feb 44; staged at Cp Kilmer N.J. 16 Sep 44 until departed New York P/E 29 Sep 44; arrived England 11 Oct 44 and landed in France 17 Dec 44; crossed into Belgium 29 Dec 44 and entered Germany 5 Mar 45 where inactivated 31 Aug 45.

Campaigns: *Rhineland, Ardennes-Alsace, Central Europe*
Aug 45 Loc: Urfahr Austria

Typical Organization (1944/45):

22nd Tank Battalion
41st Tank Battalion
42nd Tank Battalion
21st Armored Infantry Battalion
55th Armored Infantry Battalion
63rd Armored Infantry Battalion
HHB Division Artillery
490th Armored Field Artillery Battalion
491st Armored Field Artillery Battalion
492nd Armored Field Artillery Battalion
41st Cavalry Reconnaissance Squadron, Mecz
511th Counter Intelligence Corps Det
602nd Tank Destroyer Battalion *(attached 29 Dec 44–27 Jan 45, 4 Feb 45–24 Feb 45)*
705th Tank Destroyer Battalion *(attached 24 Feb 45–4 Jul 45)*
811th Tank Destroyer Battalion *(attached 27 Jan 45–4 Feb 45)*
575th AAA Auto-Wpns Battalion *(attached 23 Dec 44–24 May 45)*

Headquarters
Hqs Company, 11th Armored Division
HHC, Combat Command A
HHC, Combat Command B
Hqs, Reserve Command
HHC, Division Trains:
   81st Medical Battalion, Armored
   133rd Armored Ordnance Maintenance Battalion
   Military Police Platoon
   56th Armored Engineer Battalion
   151st Armored Signal Company

Overseas Wartime Assignments:

12th Army Group - 13 Dec 44
Ninth Army - 19 Dec 44
First Army - 20 Dec 44
VIII Corps - 23 Dec 44
XII Corps - 31 Dec 44

VIII Corps - 15 Jan 45
XX Corps - 12 Mar 45
XII Corps - 16 Mar 45
XX Corps - 24 Mar 45
XII Corps - 1 Apr 45

Commanders: MG Edward H. Brooks: Aug 42
MG Charles S. Kilburn: Mar 44
MG Holmes E. Dager: Mar 45

Killed in Action: 432   *Wounded in Action:* 2,394   *Died of Wounds:* 90

11th Armored Division Combat Narrative

The division landed in Normandy France on 17 Dec 44 and was immediately moved to defend the Givet-Sedan sector 23 Dec 44 as a mobile reserve in response to the German Ardennes Counteroffensive. The division moved to the vicininity of Neufchâteau 29 Dec 44 and attacked toward Houffalize against strong opposition on 30 Dec 44, suffering heavy losses. The next day CCB attacked Chenogne as CCR assaulted Acul. CCA attacked east of Rechrival 1 Jan 45 and the following day CCB captured Senonchamps. After defending the Bastogne Highway in fierce combat, the division attacked north on 13 Jan 45 and enveloped Bertogne before being stopped the next day by German defenses. CCA reached Velleroux 15 Jan 45 but fell back under counterattack and then stormed it successfully the following day. The division assumed responsibility for the Hardigny-Bourcy line 18 Jan 45 and began advancing in the wake of German withdrawals on 20 Jan 45, CCA crossing the Luxembourg border without opposition on 22 Jan 45. It then patrolled in the vicinity of Bois de Rouvroy. The division relieved the 90th Inf Div east of the Our River 4–5 Feb 45.

The division attacked into the *West Wall* on 6 Feb 45 as CCR seized Hill 568, but was unable to make further progress. A surprise assault, omitting artillery preparation, enabled the division to overrun numerous pillboxes on 18 Feb 45. By the next day CCR had captured Herzfeld and mopped up the Leidenborn area. Sengerich was cleared against decreasing resistance on 20 Feb 45, Roscheid fell next day, and its final objectives of Eschfeld and Reiff by 22 Feb 45. It then consolidated. CCA moved to Manderfeld and started relief of the 87th Inf Div 25 Feb 45 and this was completed the following day.

The division attacked with CCA on 1 Mar 45 to assist the 87th Inf Div reduce strongly defended pillboxes around Ormont. CCB crossed the Pruem River and attacked through the 4th Inf Div 3 Mar 45 toward the Kyll against light resistance, which it reached the next day near Lissigen under fire from the far shore. CCB then crossed at Ober 6 Mar 45 and established a small bridgehead against strong opposition. CCA attacked through the lines of the 90th Inf Div on 7 Mar 45 at Lissigen and took Kelberg after fierce combat. The division reached the Rhine River on 9 Mar 45 with CCA at Andernach and CCB near Brohl and then mopped up. The division then went into reserve. It passed through the Bullay bridgehead of 89th Inf Div 17 Mar 45 and began its second drive to the Rhine at Worms. It advanced rapidly against disorganized resistance and CCB took the airport south of the city and entered Worms on 21 Mar 45. The division assembled near Alzey and relieved the 4th Armd Div of the Oppenheim-Worms sector of the Rhine on 23 Mar 45 and assumed a defensive posture.

The division moved to the Main River at Hanau on 28 Mar 45 and attacked the next day through the lines of the 26th Inf Div toward Fulda. It battled past Gelnhausen which fell 30 Mar 45 and next attacked 1 Apr 45 near Schlitz. It pushed rapidly to the Werra River near Meiningen and established a bridgehead the next day. The division then cleared Thuringer Wald as CCA took Suhl in house-to-house fighting 3–4 Apr 45 and CCB captured Oberhof on the latter date. CCR took Meiningen on 5 Apr 45 and the division reassembled and cleared along the Schleusingen-Hildburghausen line 7–8 Apr 45. Supported by artillery and aircraft, the division attacked toward Coburg on 10 Apr 45 and the city surrendered the next day. It renewed its offensive on 12 Apr 45 and established bridgeheads over the Hasslach River at Kronach and Marktzeuln. After confusion with 14th Armd Div columns on the roads leading to Bayreuth, the city fell 14 Apr 45. The division relieved the 71st Inf Div along the Bayreuth-Gefrees line on 17 Apr 45 and attacked to take Grafenwohr 19 Apr 45. The division renewed the offensive 22 Apr 45 and reached the Naab River with CCB at Schwarzenfeld and then drove southeast from Cham along the Alpine Highway to clear Regen 24 Apr 45. Kreuzberg was captured the following day, and on 29 Apr 45 the division attacked south. CCA took Wegscheiden on the Austrian border after heavy combat 30 Apr 45, and the division advanced rapidly to take the Urfahr-Linz complex 5 May 45. The division met advancing Soviet forces at Amstetten 8 May 45.

12th Armored Division

No Distinctive Insignia Authorized

15 Sep 42 activated at Cp Campbell Ky and moved 6 Sep 43 to the Second Army No.3 Tennessee Maneuvers; arrived Cp Barkeley Tex 17 Nov 43 and relocated to Cp Bowie Tex 8 Jul 44; returned to Cp Barkeley Tex 16 Jul 44; staged at Cp Shanks N.Y. 8 Sep 44 until departed New York P/E 20 Sep 44; arrived England 2 Oct 44 and landed in France 9 Nov 44; entered Germany 21 Dec 44; returned New York P/E 1 Dec 45 and inactivated at Cp Kilmer N.J. 3 Dec 45.

Campaigns: *Rhineland, Ardennes-Alsace, Central Europe*
Aug 45 Loc: Heidenheim Germany

Typical Organization (1944/45):

23rd Tank Battalion
43rd Tank Battalion
714th Tank Battalion
17th Armored Infantry Battalion
56th Armored Infantry Battalion
66th Armored Infantry Battalion
HHB Division Artillery
493rd Armored Field Artillery Battalion
494th Armored Field Artillery Battalion
495th Armored Field Artillery Battalion
92nd Cavalry Reconnaissance Squadron, Mecz
512th Counter Intelligence Corps Det
827th Tank Destroyer Battalion (attached 19 Dec 44–13 Feb 45)
572nd AAA Auto-Wpns Battalion (attached 4 Dec 44–18 May 45)

Headquarters
Hqs Company, 12th Armored Division
HHC, Combat Command A
HHC, Combat Command B
Hqs, Reserve Command
HHC, Division Trains:
  82nd Medical Battalion, Armored
  134th Armored Ordnance Maintenance Battalion
  Military Police Platoon
119th Armored Engineer Battalion
152nd Armored Signal Company

Overseas Wartime Assignments:

Ninth Army - 13 Nov 44
XV Corps - 5 Dec 44
XXI Corps - 27 Dec 44
Seventh Army - 30 Dec 44
XV Corps - 3 Jan 45
VI Corps - 6 Jan 45
XXI Corps - 3 Feb 45

XV Corps - 11 Feb 45
XXI Corps - 28 Feb 45
XX Corps (attached) - 17 Mar 45
XXI Corps - 24 Mar 45
XV Corps - 26 Mar 45
XXI Corps - 31 Mar 45
Seventh Army - 4 May 45

Commanders: MG Carlos E. Brewer: Sep 42
MG Douglass T. Greene: Aug 44

MG Roderick R. Allen: Sep 44
BG Willard A. Holbrook Jr: Jul 45

Killed in Action: 616   *Wounded in Action:* 2,416   *Died of Wounds:* 109

12th Armored Division Combat Narrative

The division landed at Le Havre France on 9 Nov 44 and advance elements moved to the front at Weisslingen 5 Dec 44 and attacked toward the Maginot Line. The division relieved the 4th Armd Div 7 Dec 44 and CCA took Singling on 9 Dec 44. The next day CCA captured Rohrbach-lès-Bitche and the division reached Bettviller 12 Dec 44. The division reached Utweiler Germany by 21 Dec 44 and then withdrew for rehabilitation.

The division attacked the Rhine River strongpoint of Herrlisheim on 8 Jan 45 with CCB which seized part of the town the next day, but became surrounded on 10 Jan 45. After fierce fighting the division withdrew from Herrlisheim 11 Jan 45 and took up defensive positions west of the Zorn River. It next attacked to reduce the German Gambsheim Bridgehead on 16 Jan 45 but made little progress as CCB was held up at the river southeast of Rohrweiler. CCA managed to get into Herrlisheim on 17 Jan 45 but the 43rd Tank Battalion was wiped out there. CCA then abandoned the town the next day but suffered very heavy losses.

The division attacked through the 28th Inf Div at Colmar on 3 Feb 45 and CCB seized a bridgehead across the Ill River near Sundhoffen and Ste Croix en Plaine. CCA cleared Rouffach on 5 Feb 45 and effected junction with French forces which sealed the Colmar pocket in the Vosges Mountains. The division then withdrew to St Avold vicinity for rehabilitation, except that CCA assisted the 70th Inf Div near Forbach 2-8 Mar 45.

The division attacked through the lines of the 94th Inf Div on 18 Mar 45, bypassed Lauterecken, and reached the Rhine River north of Mannheim on 20 Mar 45. The division took Ludwigshafen on 21 Mar 45 and Speyer and Germersheim on 24 Mar 45, thus clearing the Saar Palatinate. The division crossed the Rhine at Worms 27-28 Mar 45 and advanced rapidly to take Wuerzburg against light resistance. It crossed the Main at Ochsenfurt 3 Apr 45 and CCA fought the Battle for Wuerzberg 4-5 Apr 45. The division assisted in the reduction of Schweinfurt by blocking the highway to Bamberg on 11 Apr 45, and the next day encircled the Uffenheim pocket with CCR. The division assaulted across the Aisch River at Ipsheim 14 Apr 45 and advanced with all three Combat Commands in the assault to capture Ansbach 18-19 Apr 45. After seizing Feuchtwagen on 20 Apr 45 the division sped toward the Danube River and CCA captured the bridge at Dillingen before it could be demolished on 22 Apr 45. The bridgehead was strengthened with the fall of Wertingen 24-25 Apr 45. The division then was relieved at the bridgehead by the 3rd Inf Div on 26 Apr 45 and crossed the Lech River at Landsberg 27-29 Apr 45. It cleared the area between the Ammer and Wurm on 30 Apr 45, and on 1 May 45 drove southeast from Starnberg across the Isar River to reach Inn. Elements crossed the Inn River on 3 May 45 into Austria, and the division was moving toward Innsbruck when placed in reserve the next day. It engaged in security duty until hostilities were declared ended on 7 May 45.

13th Armored Division

No Distinctive
Insignia Authorized

15 Oct 42 activated at Cp Beale Calif and participated in the IV Corps Oregon No.1 Maneuvers 15 Sep–8 Nov 43 after which it returned to Cp Beale; transferred to Cp Bowie Tex 18 Dec 43 and staged at Cp Kilmer N.J. 14 Jan 45 until departed New York P/E 17 Jan 45; arrived France 30 Jan 45 and entered Germany 3 Apr 45; arrived Newport News Va 23 Jul 45 and arrived Cp Cooke Calif 30 Jul 45 where inactivated 15 Nov 45.

Campaigns: *Rhineland, Central Europe*
Aug 45 Loc: Camp Cooke California

Typical Organization (1944/45):

24th Tank Battalion
45th Tank Battalion
46th Tank Battalion
16th Armored Infantry Battalion
59th Armored Infantry Battalion
67th Armored Infantry Battalion
HHB Division Artillery
496th Armored Field Artillery Battalion
497th Armored Field Artillery Battalion
498th Armored Field Artillery Battalion
93rd Cavalry Reconnaissance Squadron, Mecz
513th Counter Intelligence Corps Det
630th Tank Destroyer Battalion *(attached 10 Apr 45–12 Apr 45)*
801st Tank Destroyer Battalion *(attached 27 Apr 45–12 Jun 45)*
820th Tank Destroyer Battalion *(attached 10 Apr 45–12 Apr 45)*
574th AAA Auto-Wpns Battalion *(attached 19 Mar 45–13 May 45)*

Headquarters
Hqs Company, 13th Armored Division
HHC, Combat Command A
HHC, Combat Command B
Hqs, Reserve Command
HHC, Division Trains:
   83rd Medical Battalion, Armored
   135th Armored Ordnance Maintenance Battalion
   Military Police Platoon
124th Armored Engineer Battalion
153rd Armored Signal Battalion

Overseas Wartime Assignments:

12th Army Group - 18 Jan 45
Fifteenth Army - 21 Jan 45
Seventh Army *(attached)* - 23 Mar 45
12th Army Group - 31 Mar 45

Seventh Army *(attached)* - 8 Apr 45
XVIII (A/B) Corps *(attached)* - 10 Apr 45
Third Army - 21 Apr 45
XX Corps - 22 Apr 45

Commanders: MG John B. Wogan: Oct 42
                MG John Millikin: Apr 45

Killed in Action: 214   *Wounded in Action:* 912   *Died of Wounds:* 39

13th Armored Division Combat Narrative

The division landed at Le Havre France on 30 Jan 45 and was initially employed in occupation duty. It was deployed to Homberg near Kassel on 5 Apr 45 where it departed to participate in operations against the Ruhr Pocket on 8 Apr 45. The division attacked across the Sieg River in the Siegburg area and CCA reached the town of Siegburg as CCB established a bridgehead over the Agger River. CCB bypassed Troisdorf and reorganized in the Dunnwald area 11–12 Apr 45 as CCA cleared Lohmar and Altenrath. The division attacked north on 13 Apr 45 and advanced against strong opposition to the Wupper River in the Opladen area on 15 Apr 45, which it crossed the next day. CCB contacted the Ninth Army at Duisburg 17 Apr 45 and CCA pushed through Ratingen to the Rhine River on 18 Apr 45. There the division was relieved by the 8th Inf Div and assembled at Eschenau 20–22 Apr 45 and prepared for operations in Bavaria. It moved to Parsberg 26 Apr 45 and attacked the following day, advancing rapidly along the Danube River to the Isar River at Platting on 28 Apr 45. CCB, assisted by artillery fire and smoke, crossed there as a bridge was being constructed on 29 Apr 45, which CCR then also used due to its unsuccessful attempts to cross in the Landau area. CCB reached the Inn River in Eisenfelden region, but was unable to take the Marktl Bridge intact on 1 May 45. As the division closed along the Inn CAA received the surrender of Braunau the next day. The division then reassembled north of Inn 3 May 45 and was in that capacity when hostilities were declared ended on 7 May 45.

14th Armored Division

No Distinctive
Insignia Authorized

15 Nov 42 activated at Cp Chaffee Ark and moved 17 Nov 43 to the Second Army No.4 Tennessee Maneuvers; transferred to Cp Campbell Ky 19 Jan 44; staged at Cp Shanks N.Y. 6 Oct 44 until departed New York P/E 14 Oct 44; arrived in France 30 Oct 44 and entered Germany 19 Mar 45; arrived Hampton Roads P/E 16 Sep 45 and inactivated at Cp Patrick Henry Va 16 Sep 45.

Campaigns: *Rhineland, Ardennes-Alsace, Central Europe*
Aug 45 Loc: Wasserburg Germany

Typical Organization (1944/45):

25th Tank Battalion
47th Tank Battalion
48th Tank Battalion
19th Armored Infantry Battalion
62nd Armored Infantry Battalion
68th Armored Infantry Battalion
HHB Division Artillery
499th Armored Field Artillery Battalion
500th Armored Field Artillery Battalion
501st Armored Field Artillery Battalion
94th Cavalry Reconnaissance Squadron, Mecz
514th Counter Intelligence Corps Det
636th Tank Destroyer Battalion *(attached 28 Mar 45–23 Apr 45)*
398th AAA Auto-Wpns Battalion *(attached 15 Nov 44–12 May 45)*

Headquarters
Hqs Company, 14th Armored Division
HHC, Combat Command A
HHC, Combat Command B
Hqs, Reserve Command
HHC, Division Trains:
    84th Medical Battalion, Armored
    136th Armored Ordnance Maintenance Battalion
    Military Police Platoon
125th Armored Engineer Battalion
154th Armored Signal Company

Overseas Wartime Assignments:

6th Army Group *(attached)* - 1 Nov 44
Seventh Army - 10 Nov 44
XV Corps - 29 Nov 44

VI Corps - 5 Dec 44
XV Corps - 31 Mar 45
III Corps - 23 Apr 45

Commanders: MG Vernon E. Prichard: Nov 42
               MG Albert C. Smith: Jul 44

Killed in Action: 505   *Wounded in Action:* 1,955   *Died of Wounds:* 55

14th Armored Division Combat Narrative

The division landed at Marseille France 30 Oct 44 and sent elements to guard the Franco-Italian border 14 Nov 44. The division moved north to Rambervillers on 20 Nov 44 and the next day CCA attacked toward Schirmeck to cut German escape routes, contacting the 3rd Inf Div in that vicinity on 25 Nov 44. CCA then advanced through Obernai toward Barr on 27 Nov 44 to block exits from the Vosges Mountains and battled through Erstein to capture Barr after heavy combat on 29 Nov 44. The next day CCA cleared St. Pierre and the division then entered the Alsatian Plain.

The division attacked across the Lauter River on 12 Dec 44 and the next day CCA took Soultz-sous-Forêts. CCA captured Riedseltz on 15 Dec 44 as CCB seized both Salmbach and Schlerthal. It was then assigned defensive positions running south of Bitche near Neuhoffen and was hit by a strong German attack 1 Jan 45, which forced the division to withdraw. The division attacked from Kuhlendorf to break through to relieve the 79th Inf Div in Rittershoffen on 11 Jan 45, but CCA was halted in its first attempt. CCA cleared part of Rittershoffen the next day and on 13 Jan 45 the division took command of the Hatten-Rittershoffen sector where fierce fighting continued unabated. CCR lost ground at Hatten 16 Jan 45. CCB cleared Schweighausen and part of Bois de Ohlungen by 25 Jan 45. It then made a diversionary attack 1 Feb 45 east of Oberhoffen and withdrew, and the next day fought into Oberhoffen where it battled past 4 Feb 45. The division then assumed defensive posture and rehabilitated.

The division attacked across the Rothbach and Moder Rivers on 15 Mar 45 and moved forward to exploit breakthroughs. It crossed the Lauter River northeast of Schleithal on 19 Mar 45, and CCA attacked in the Wissembourg Gap the next day and reached the *West Wall*. It battled through strong opposition and fought the Battle for Steinfeld 20–22 Mar 45 with CCA and CCR. CCB captured Germersheim on the Rhine River 23 Mar 45 as CCA seized Schaidt. The division crossed the Rhine near Worms on 1 Apr 45 and attacked the next day through the lines of the 45th Inf Div toward Neustadt and Ostheim against diminishing resistance. CCB took Lohr from the retreating Germany forces

3 Apr 45 and captured Gemuenden on 5 Apr 45. In a rapid drive to Neustadt CCA took the town on 7 Apr 45 and then the division assembled. CCA and CCB assembled near Berg on 17 Apr 45 as CCR maintained its positions along the Creussen-Buchau line until relieved by the 71st Inf Div.

The division attacked 24 Apr 45 and reached the Altmuhl River at Beilngries and Gungolding and proceeded with bridging under heavy German fire. The division crossed 26 Apr 45 and reached the Danube the same day with CCA at Menning, CCB at Neustadt, and CCR at Mailing. It crossed the Danube River 28 Apr 45 and CCA advanced rapidly to reach the Isar River at Moosburg the following day. The division then crossed the Isar River at Moosburg 30 Apr 45 and fought into Landshut. CCB reached the Inn River near Aschau and took the bridge there intact on 2 May 45. The division was then utilized to process prisoners as hostilities were declared ended on 7 May 45.

16th Armored Division

No Distinctive
Insignia Authorized

15 Jul 43 activated at Cp Chaffee Ark and staged at Cp Shanks N.Y. 28 Jan 45 until departed New York P/E 5 Feb 45; arrived France 17 Feb 45; entered Germany 19 Apr 45 and Czechoslovakia 8 May 45; returned New York P/E 13 Oct 45 and inactivated at Cp Kilmer N.J. 15 Oct 45.

Campaigns: *Central Europe*
Aug 45 Loc: Stribro Czechoslovakia

Typical Organization (1944/45):

5th Tank Battalion
16th Tank Battalion
26th Tank Battalion
18th Armored Infantry Battalion
64th Armored Infantry Battalion
69th Armored Infantry Battalion
HHB Division Artillery
395th Armored Field Artillery Battalion
396th Armored Field Artillery Battalion
397th Armored Field Artillery Battalion
23rd Cavalry Reconnaissance Squadron, Mecz
516th Counter Intelligence Corps Det
633rd Tank Destroyer Battalion *(attached 1 May 45–14 Jun 45)*
571st AAA Auto-Wpns Battalion *(attached 20 Apr 45–19 May 45)*

Headquarters
Hqs Company, 16th Armored Division
HHC, Combat Command A
HHC, Combat Command B
Hqs, Reserve Command
HHC, Division Trains:
  216th Medical Battalion, Armored
  137th Armored Ordnance Maintenance Battalion
  Military Police Battalion
216th Armored Engineer Battalion
156th Armored Signal Company

Overseas Wartime Assignments:

Fifteenth Army - 29 Jan 45
Third Army - 17 Apr 45
V Corps - 6 May 45

Commanders: MG Douglass T. Greene: Jul 43
                 BG John L. Pierce: Sep 44

Killed in Action: 4   Wounded in Action: 28   Died of Wounds: 1

16th Armored Division Combat Narrative

The division arrived in France on 11–17 Feb 45 and moved to Nuremberg where it relieved the 71st Inf Div on 28 Apr 45. Its reconnaissance squadron participated in combat from the Isar to Wasserburg with the 86th Inf Div until 30 Apr 45. The division performed security duty at Nuremberg until 5 May 45 when it assembled in the Waidhaus area. The division attacked through the lines of the 97th Inf Div on 6 May 45 and CCB, making the main effort, advanced along the Bor-Pilsen Road to capture Pilsen and the Skoda Munitions Plant the same day. CCR advanced through Pilsen to assigned high ground east of the city. The division mopped up in that vicinity until hostilities were declared ended on 7 May 45.

20th Armored Division

No Distinctive
Insignia Authorized

15 Mar 43 activated at Cp Campbell Ky and staged at Cp Myles Standish Mass 21 Jan 45 until departed Boston P/E 6 Feb 45; arrived France 17 Feb 45 and entered Germany 3 Apr 45; arrived New York P/E 6 Aug 45 and arrived Cp Cook Calif 13 Aug 45; transferred to Cp Hood Tex 8 Mar 46 where inactivated 2 Apr 46.

Campaigns: *Central Europe*
Aug 45 Loc: Camp Cooke California

Typical Organization (1944/95):

9th Tank Battalion
20th Tank Battalion
27th Tank Battalion
8th Armored Infantry Battalion
65th Armored Infantry Battalion
70th Armored Infantry Battalion
HHB Division Artillery
412th Armored Field Artillery Battalion
413th Armored Field Artillery Battalion
414th Armored Field Artillery Battalion
33rd Cavalry Reconnaissance Squadron, Mecz
520th Counter Intelligence Corps Det
468th AAA Auto-Wpns Battalion *(attached 4 Apr 45–3 Jul 45)*

Headquarters
Hqs Company, 20th Armored Division
HHC, Combat Command A
HHC, Combat Command B
Hqs, Reserve Command
HHC, Division Trains:
 220th Medical Battalion, Armored
 138th Armored Ordnance Maintenance Battalion
 Military Police Platoon
220th Armored Engineer Battalion
160th Armored Signal Company

Overseas Wartime Assignments:

Fifteenth Army - 29 Jan 45
XXII Corps - 3 Apr 45
First Army *(attached)* - 7 Apr 45

First Army - 12 Apr 45
III Corps - 19 Apr 45
XV Corps - 23 Apr 45

Commanders: MG Stephen G. Henry: Feb 43
MG Roderick R. Allen: Oct 43

MG Orlando Ward: Sep 44
MG John W. Leonard: Aug 45

Killed in Action: 46   *Wounded in Action:* 134   *Died of Wounds:* 13

20th Armored Division Combat Narrative

The division landed at Le Havre France on 17 Feb 45 and moved to Buchy for training. It arrived at Langendernbach Germany on 10 Apr 45 and was sent to Wuerzburg 23 Apr 45. It was engaged at Dorf on 25 Apr 45, and then assembled near Deiningen. The division attacked through the 42nd and 45th Inf Div lines to open the drive on Munich 28 Apr 45 as it crossed the Danube. It advanced rapidly to Munich where it cleared strong opposition in certain sectors 29–30 Apr 45. It crossed the Inn River at Wasserburg on 3 May 45, entered Traunstein 4 May 45, and was enroute to Salzburg when hostilities were declared ended on 7 May 45.

Chapter 10

Cavalry Divisions

Divisions:

1 Special, 2, 2 (Colored)

Note on Color Insignia Plate: The shoulder patches of the 3, 21, 24, and 61–66 Cavalry Divisions are displayed for collecting purposes only. These divisions were never active during World War II.

1st Cavalry Division, Special

No Distinctive
Insignia Authorized

Stationed at Ft Bliss Tex as 1st Cavalry Division; moved to Toyahvale Tex 7–30 Oct 39 and returned to Ft Bliss Tex; moved to Cravens-Pitkin Louisiana Maneuver Area 13–24 Aug 40 and returned to Ft Bliss Tex; participated in Second-Third Army Louisiana Maneuvers 10 Aug–4 Oct 41 and returned to Ft Bliss Tex; participated in VIII Corps Louisiana Maneuvers near Mansfield La 27 Jul–21 Sep 42 and returned to Ft Bliss Tex; staged at Cp Stoneman Calif 21 Jul 43 until departed San Francisco P/E 26 Jun 43; arrived Australia 11 Jul 43 where redesignated as 1st Cavalry Division, Special on 4 Dec 43; departed Australia 18 Dec 43 and arrived New Guinea 20 Dec 43 by echelon, last contingent arriving 25 Feb 44; arrived Manus Island about 5–15 Mar 44; left Manus Island 12 Oct 44 and landed Leyte Philippines 20 Oct 44; departed Leyte 24 Jan 45 and landed on Luzon Philippines 26 Jan 45; arrived Japan 2 Sep 45 where active thru 1946.

Campaigns: *New Guinea, Bismarck Archipelago, Leyte, Luzon*
Aug 45 Loc: Lucena Batangas Philippine Islands

Typical Organization (1941):

1st Cavalry Brigade HHT:
  Weapons Troop
    5th Cavalry Regiment
    12th Cavalry Regiment
2nd Cavalry Brigade HHT:
Weapons Troop
    7th Cavalry Regiment
    12th Cavalry Regiment
HHB 1st Cavalry Division Artillery
  61st Field Artillery Battalion (75mm H-D)
  62nd Field Artillery Battalion (105mm Trk-D)
  82nd Field Artillery Battalion (75mm H-D)

Hqs & Hqs Troop, 1st Cavalry Division
    8th Engineer Squadron
    1st Medical Squadron
    16th Quartermaster Squadron
    91st Reconnaissance Squadron
    1st Antitank Troop
    1st Signal Troop
  27th Ordnance Medium Maintenance Company

Typical Organization (1944/45):

1st Cavalry Brigade HHT:
    5th Cavalry Regiment
    12th Cavalry Regiment
2nd Cavalry Brigade HHT:
    7th Cavalry Regiment
    8th Cavalry Regiment
HHB Division Artillery
  61st Field Artillery Battalion (105mm)
  82nd Field Artillery Battalion (105mm)
  99th Field Artillery Battalion (105mm)
  271st Field Artillery Battalion (105mm)

Headquarters Troop, 1st Cavalry Division
    8th Engineer Squadron
    1st Medical Squadron
    1st Signal Troop
  27th Ordnance Medium Maintenance Company
  16th Quartermaster Squadron
  302nd Reconnaissance Troop, Mecz*
  603rd Medium Tank Company**
  Military Police Platoon***
  801st Counter Intelligence Corps Det

*Replaced the 7th Reconnaissance Squadron which was assigned to division 16 Jan 42 and inactivated 4 Dec 43. Troop was mechanized commencing 30 Oct 44.
**Formerly Light Tank Company until 2 Dec 43.
***Assigned to division 30 Sep 44; previously attached.

Overseas Wartime Assignments:

Sixth Army - 26 Jul 43
X Corps - 1 Oct 44
Eighth Army - 26 Dec 44
Sixth Army - 27 Jan 45

XIV Corps - 31 Jan 45
XI Corps - 15 Jun 45
Eighth Army - 15 Aug 45

Commanders: MG Innis P. Swift: Apr 41
MG Verne D. Mudge: Aug 44

BG Hugh F. T. Hoffman: Feb 45
MG William C. Chase: Jul 45

Killed in Action: 734   *Wounded in Action:* 3,311   *Died of Wounds:* 236

1st Cavalry Division, Special, Combat Narrative

The division arrived in Australia on 26 Jul 43 and engaged in jungle and amphibious training at Toorbul Point and Port Stephens. The 2nd Cav Brigade departed Strathpine Australia 19 Dec 43 and arrived in Oro Bay New Guinea on 20 Dec 43. The division established its command post at Cap Sudest New Guinea 4 Jan 44, and by 25 Feb 44 the remainder of the division had arrived in Oro Bay from New Guinea. It then trained for operations in the Admiralty Islands.

A squadron of the 5th Cav landed on Los Negros Island 29 Feb 44 and after heavy combat occupied the Momote Airfield. It was reinforced by the 2nd Sqdn 7th Cav on 4 Mar 44, and on 6 Mar 44 the 12th Cav landed. The 2nd Cav Brigade arrived on 9 Mar 44 and employed the 8th Cav to assault Manus Island 15 Mar 44 which overran Lugos Mission, followed by the 7th Cav. By 18 Mar 44 Lorengau and its airfield had been captured, and the division mopped up both Los Negros and Manus and seized other nearby islands which secured the Admiralties by 18 May 44. The division then trained for Philippines operations until departure for the Philippines on 12 Oct 44.

The 5th, 7th, and 12th Cav assaulted Leyte Island on 20 Oct 44 and cleared San Jose, Tacloban Airfield, and Cataisan Peninsula. The 8th Cav landed at La Paz Samar Island and secured the San Juanico Strait on 24 Oct 44. The division regrouped on 28 Oct 44 as the 2nd Cav Brigade assembled at Barugo, converged on Carigara and contacted the 24th Inf Div 2 Nov 44. The 112th Cav was attached 15 Nov 44 and assumed responsibility for the Capocan-Carigara-Barugo area. The division cleared the Mt Badian–Hill 2348 region from 28 Nov–9 Dec 44 and the 112th Cav battled at the ridge south of Limon 30 Nov–10 Dec 44 when the 7th Cav relieved it and finally captured it on 14 Dec 44. The 12th Cav pushed into Lonoy on 19 Dec 44 and seized Kananga 21 Dec 44. The division attacked west toward the coast over swamps against scattered resistance on 23 Dec 44, and the 5th and 12th Cav reached the coast at Tibur on 28 Dec 44. The division then fought past Villaba to contact the 32nd Inf Div 30 Dec 44. The 8th Cav returned from patrolling on Samar Island 8 Jan 45 and the division prepared for movement to Luzon.

The division landed in the Mabilao area of Lingayen Gulf Luzon on 27 Jan 45, and the 112th Cav was relieved from attachment 31 Jan 45 as the division attacked with the 5th and 8th Cav from Guimba toward Manila. The division entered Manila 3 Feb 45 and fought through fierce opposition in the northern and eastern suburbs. The 12th Cav attacked into Rosario Heights 10 Feb 45, and the division overran Neilson Field to reach the shore of Manila Bay 12 Feb 45. The 7th Cav captured crossings over the Mariquina River in the Ugong-Rosario area 20 Feb 45. The 2nd Cav Brigade attacked from the Taytay area 23 Feb 45 toward the Shimbu Line but was checked 25 Feb 45 in the Antipolo area. The 5th Cav captured the Agriculture Building in Manila 1 Mar 45. The division began its drive against the Shimbu Line with four regiments abreast on 8 Mar 45 and stormed Bench Mark Hill 11, and seized the crest of Bench Mark Hill 9 on 10 Mar 45. It was relieved in the Antipolo area 12 Mar 45 and withdrew for rehabilitation.

The division began the drive on Lipa by taking Santo Tomas on 24 Mar 45 and Los Banos the following day. By 29 Mar 45 the 8th Cav had captured Lipa and established contact with the 11th A/B Div, and next opened the Batangas-Calamba supply road into Manila. The division then turned east and the 7th Cav seized Alaminos 1 Apr 45 while the 12th Cav fought the Battle for Imoc Hill 1–5 Apr 45. The 5th Cav had reached San Pablo on 2 Apr 45 and after heavy combat the division took Mauban on the east coast 10 Apr 45 and established contact with the 11th A/B Div at Lamon Bay the next day. The 1st Cav Brigade pushed into Bicol Peninsula 12 Apr 45 and the Japanese defenders had been pocketed north of Mt Matassana Bundoc by 16 Apr 45. This area was reduced by the 2nd Cav Brigade commencing 17 Apr 45. Beginning on 2 May 45 the 5th Cav probed Mt Isarong for the next two weeks. The division was relieved of its combat missions on 26 Jun 45 and engaged exclusively in training at Lucena, where it had been since 6 May 45. The division was in this capacity when hostilities ended.

2nd Cavalry Division (Horse)

No Distinctive
Insignia Authorized

1 Apr 41 activated at Ft Riley Kans and moved 26 Aug 41 to participate in the Second-Third Army Maneuvers; returned to Ft Riley Kans 4 Oct 41 where inactivated on 15 Jul 42.

Typical Organization (1941):

3rd Cavalry Brigade HHT:
  Weapons Troop
  2nd Cavalry Regiment
  14th Cavalry Regiment
4th Cavalry Brigade HHT (Cld):
  Weapons Troop (Cld)
  9th Cavalry Regiment (Cld)
  10th Cavalry Regiment (Cld)
HHB Division Artillery
  3rd Field Artillery Battalion (75mm)
  16th Field Artillery Battalion (75mm)

Hqs & Hqs Troop, 2nd Cavalry Division
  9th Engineer Squadron (Motorized)
  2nd Medical Squadron
  17th Quartermaster Squadron
  92nd Reconnaissance Squadron
  2nd Antitank Troop
  2nd Signal Troop
  24th Ordnance Medium Maintenance Company

Commanders: BG Terry de la Mesa Allen: Apr 41
              BG John Millikin: Jun 41
              BG John D. Coulter: May 42

2nd Cavalry Division (Horse) (Colored)

No Distinctive
Insignia Authorized

25 Feb 43 activated at Ft Clark Tex and staged at Cp Patrick Henry Va 4 Feb 44 until departed Hampton Roads P/E 28 Feb 44; arrived in North Africa 9 Mar 44 where inactivated 10 May 44 and assets utilized to create service and engineer units.

Campaigns: *European Theater without inscription*

Typical Organization (1943: with date of inactivation in North Africa):

4th Cavalry Brigade HHT (Cld):	23 Mar 44
9th Cavalry Regiment (Cld):	7 Mar 44
10th Cavalry Regiment (Cld):	10 Mar 44
5th Cavalry Brigade HHT (Cld):	12 Jun 44
27th Cavalry Regiment (Cld):	27 Mar 44
28th Cavalry Regiment (Cld):	31 Mar 44
HHB Division Artillery (Cld):	10 Mar 44
77th Field Artillery Battalion (75mm) (Cld):	26 Feb 44
79th Field Artillery Battalion (75mm) (Cld):	10 Mar 44
159th Field Artillery Battalion (105mm) (Cld):	*(Did not deploy to North Africa)*
Hqs & Hqs Troop, 2nd Cavalry Division (Cld):	10 May 44
162nd Engineer Squadron (Cld):	22 Mar 44
3rd Medical Squadron (Cld):	24 May 44
35th Cavalry Rcn Squadron, Mecz (Cld):	25 Mar 44
20th Cavalry Quartermaster Squadron (Cld):	23 Mar 44
114th Ordnance Medium Maintenance Company (Cld):	7 Mar 44
Military Police Platoon, 2nd Cavalry Div (Cld):	1 Jun 44

Commander: MG Harry H. Johnson: Feb 43

Killed in Action: None   *Wounded in Action:* None   *Died of Wounds:* None

Chapter 11

Airborne, Infantry, Light, Motorized, and Mountain Divisions

Airborne Divisions:

11 A/B, 13 A/B, 17 A/B, 82 A/B, 101 A/B, 1 A/B Task Force (Prov Seventh Army A/B Div)

Infantry Divisions*

1–9, 24–38, 40–45, 63, 66, 68, 69–71, 75–100, 102–104, 106, American, CAM, Philippine

Light Divisions:**

10, 71, 89

Motorized Divisions:**

4, 6, 7, 8, 90

Mountain Divisions:

10

*82nd Infantry Division included under 82nd Airborne Division
**Included under respective infantry or mountain divisions.

1st Infantry Division

Stationed at Ft Hamilton N.Y. as the 1st Division and moved to Ft Benning Ga 19 Nov 39 and to the Louisiana Maneuvers in the Sabine La area 11 May 40; returned to Ft Hamilton N.Y. 5 Jun 40 and moved to Ft Devens Mass 4 Feb 41; participated in both Carolina Maneuvers of Oct and Nov 41 and went to Samarcand N.C. 16 Oct 41; returned to Ft Devens Mass 6 Dec 41 and transferred to Cp Blanding Fla 21 Feb 42 where redesignated 1st Infantry Division 15 May 42; moved to Ft Benning Ga 22 May 42 and Indiantown Gap Mil Res Pa 21 Jun 42; departed New York P/E 1 Aug 42 and arrived in England 7 Aug 42; assaulted North Africa 8 Nov 42 and Sicily 10 Jul 43; returned to England 11 Nov 43 and assaulted Normandy France 6 Jun 44; crossed into Belgium 3 Sep 44 and entered Germany 15 Sep 44 where active thru 1946.

Campaigns: *Algeria–French Morocco, Tunisia, Sicily, Normandy, Northern France, Rhineland, Ardennes-Alsace, Central Europe*

Aug 45 Loc: Ansbach Germany

Typical Organization (1941):

16th Infantry Regiment
18th Infantry Regiment
26th Infantry Regiment
HHB Division Artillery
  5th Field Artillery Battalion (155mm)
  7th Field Artillery Battalion (105mm)
32nd Field Artillery Battalion (105mm)
33rd Field Artillery Battalion (105mm)

Headquarters, 1st Division
Headquarters & Military Police Company
Artillery Band
1st Engineer Battalion
1st Medical Battalion
1st Quartermaster Battalion
1st Reconnaissance Company
1st Signal Company

Typical Organization (1944/45):

16th Infantry Regiment
18th Infantry Regiment
26th Infantry Regiment
HHB Division Artillery
  5th Field Artillery Battalion (155mm)
  7th Field Artillery Battalion (105mm)
32nd Field Artillery Battalion (105mm)
33rd Field Artillery Battalion (105mm)
  1st Reconnaissance Troop, Mecz
745th Tank Battalion *(attached 6 Jun 44–8 May 45)*
634th Tank Destroyer Battalion *(attached 1 Aug 44–6 May 45)*
635th Tank Destroyer Battalion *(attached 7 Jun 44–30 Sep 44)*
703rd Tank Destroyer Battalion *(attached 18 Dec 44–31 Dec 44)*
103rd AAA Auto-Wpns Battalion *(attached 16 Jun 44–7 Feb 45, 24 Feb 45–8 May 45)*

1st Engineer Combat Battalion
1st Medical Battalion
1st Counter Intelligence Corps Det
Headquarters Special Troops
Hqs Company, 1st Infantry Division
Military Police Platoon
701st Ordnance Light Maintenance Company
1st Quartermaster Company
1st Signal Company

Overseas Wartime Assignments:

NATO - 8 Nov 42
II Corps - 1 Feb 43
First Army - 1 Nov 43
VII Corps - 6 Nov 43
V Corps - 2 Feb 44
First Army - 14 Jul 44
VII Corps - 1 Aug 44
V Corps - 16 Dec 44

XVIII (A/B) Corps - 26 Jan 45
III Corps - 12 Feb 45
VII Corps - 8 Mar 45
VIII Corps - 27 Apr 45
V Corps - 30 Apr 45
Third Army - 6 May 45
XV Corps - 30 Jun 45

Commanders: MG Donald Cubbison: Jul 41
               MG Terry de la Mesa Allen: Jun 42

MG Clarence R. Huebner: Jul 43
MG Clift Andrus: Dec 44

Killed in Action: 3,616   *Wounded in Action:* 15,208   *Died of Wounds:* 664

1st Infantry Division Combat Narrative

The division landed 8 Nov 42 in North Africa as the 16th and 18th Inf went ashore east of Oran and the 26th Inf landed at Les Andalouses, and entered Oran 10 Nov 42. The 18th Inf went into action at Djebel el Ahmera with the British, and the 26th Inf cleared the Ouseltia Valley by 25 Jan 43 and went into positions at Kasserine Pass 18 Feb 43. The division attacked as a concentrated whole for the first time on 16 Mar 43 east from El Guettar, and the 18th and 26th Inf contained two strong German counterattacks on 23 Mar 43. The 18th Inf was forced out of Djebel Berda on 25 Mar 43 and the attacks toward Gabes were checked by 28 Mar 43. The division took Sakket on 3 Apr 43 in an attempt to break this stalemate but further offensive movement down the Gabes road was stopped 5 Apr 43. The division then relieved the *British 4th Div* near Beja on 16 Apr 43 and attacked 22 Apr 43 along the Medjez el Bab-Tunis highway. After the 18th Inf cleared Hill 407 and the 26th Inf cleared Hill 575, the 26th Inf reached Djebel el Anz against strong German resistance of 28 Apr 43. The next day the 16th Inf began its attack on Hill 523, and the division was actively engaged in Tunisia until 9 May 43.

The division assaulted Gela Sicily 10 Jul 43. After fending off a German armored attack on 11 Jul 43 it pushed inland and took Mazzarino and Niscemi 14 Jul 43 and Barrafranca on 16 Jul 43. The division seized the Salso River crossings east of Caltanisseta and repelled a German counterattack at Gangi 25 Jul 43. It reached Troina 1 Aug 43 after a series of sharp battles over difficult terrain, but an all-out attack on the town failed 4 Aug 43. It was taken after the Germans withdrew during the night of 6 Aug 43. The division left Sicily 23 Oct 43 and landed in England to train for the invasion of northern France.

Reinforced by the 116th Inf, it assaulted Omaha Beach France in the face of fierce opposition. The 16th Inf, which led the division attack, reached the St Lô-Bayeux highway 10 Jun 44, and the 18th and 26th Inf seized Caumont 13 Jun 44. On 13 Jul 44 the division was relieved by the 5th Inf Div in line and withdrew to Colmbieres. It next attacked as part of the COBRA breakout effort on 26 Jul 44, took Marigny and secured the Sée River crossings 31 Jul 44. It sped south to Mortain where it was relieved by the 30th Inf Div 6 Aug 44, allowing it to then push forward to Mayenne with the 3rd Armd Div. The division assembled south of Paris on 25 Aug 44.

The 16th Inf mopped up the Belgian Mons Pocket 3 Sep 44, and the division crossed the Meuse River at Liege 9 Sep 44, reaching the German border against scattered rear-guard resistance. It laid siege to the fortress-city of Aachen and the battle was commenced with an attack on its municipal forest 12 Sep 44. As the division tried to encircle Aachen, the 16th Inf was halted at the *West Wall* 15 Sep 44. On 8 Oct 44 the division renewed its Aachen assault with the 18th Inf pushing through Verlautenheide, the 26th Inf attacking through the heart of the city, and the 16th Inf holding defensive positions near Eilendorf. By 12 Oct 44 the 26th Inf had gained most of the factory district between Aachen and Haaren and began an all-out central attack the next day. After severe fighting it had gained most of Observatory Hill but German counterattacks forced all further advances to a halt 15 Oct 44. The 16th Inf was forced to defend its area against strong German assaults as well. On 18 Oct 44 the division was reinforced for yet another attack on Aachen. The 26th Inf gained Observatory Hill and forced the Germans back into the western suburbs, and on 21 Oct 44 the city was finally taken by direct assault.

After being relieved by the 104th Inf Div, the division opened First Army's offensive to secure the Roer River crossings east of Aachen on 16 Nov 44. After 15 days of intense fighting in this sector the division had only gained four miles, which included the 26th Inf's capture of Laufenburg Castle 20 Nov 44, and on 29 Nov 44 the same regiment was hit hard by a strong German counterattack at Merode. The 9th Inf Div relieved the division 5 Dec 44 which then went to a rest area in the Luchem-Langerwehe-Juengersdorf-Merode region (less the 16th Inf attached to V Corps). As a result of the German Ardennes counteroffensive the division was sent to the Malmedy sector. It cleared the region south of Eupen, contained numerous German attacks in the Butgenbach-Faymonville region, and fought at Elsenborn Ridge 21–28 Dec 44. The division's lines were breached at Butgenbach 22 Dec 44 but shortly restored. It then attacked and took Steinbach 15 Jan 45, opening a passage for the 7th Armd Div drive toward St Vith. The division next ran into stiff resistance northeast of Schoppen as the 16th Inf cleared the Bambusch Woods. After blunting the German drive, the division advanced on the *West Wall* 28 Jan 45 and attacked through Buchholz Forest. It was relieved by the 99th Inf Div 5 Feb 45 and moved to assembly areas at Aywaille Belgium.

The division took over the 8th Inf Div zone and initiated the attack across the Roer River at Kreuznau with the 16th Inf on 25 Feb 45 against moderate opposition. The division took Burg 27 Feb 45 and the 16th Inf crossed the Neffel 1 Mar 45. The division reached Bonn 7 Mar 45 and captured it 9 Mar 45, ending German resistance west of the Rhine. On 15 Mar 45 the 16th Inf assaulted across the Rhine River and the division pressed its attack toward the Sieg in the face of strong German defenses. On 30 Mar 45 it attacked with three regiments in line to gain the heights dominating Seigen, and on 1 Apr 45 was relieved by the 8th Inf Div and trucked to blocking positions southwest of Paderborn to help seal the Ruhr Pocket. On 8 Apr 45 the division was called up to force the Weser River after the 3rd Armd Div had reached it only to find all the bridges blown. The 16th and 18th Inf expanded the bridgehead while the motorized 26th Inf attacked toward Einbeck. With the 4th Cav Gp attached the division was tasked with mopping up along the edge of the Harz Mountains. The bypassed German troops were encircled commencing 12 Apr 45 and organized resistance ended by 20 Apr 45.

The division next relieved the 97th Inf Div in place, and then was transferred to the Czechoslovakian border on 30 Apr 45. It made limited attacks 2 May 45 to improve its positions. On 6 May 45 the division opened its drive on Karlsbad. The 18th Inf had seized Sangerberg and Mnichov, the 16th Inf had taken Kynsperk, and the 26th Inf was in Schoenbach when hostilities were declared ended on 7 May 45.

2nd Infantry Division

No Distinctive Insignia Authorized

Stationed at Ft Sam Houston Tex as the 2nd Division and sent to maneuvers at Christine Tex 3–27 Jan 40, Horton Tex 26 Apr–28 May 40, and Cravens La 16–23 Aug 40; participated in the VIII Corps Brownwood Texas Maneuvers 1–14 Jun 41 at Comanche Tex and was sent to Mansfield La 11 Aug–2 Oct 41 for the Louisiana Maneuvers of Aug and Sep 41; transferred from Ft Sam Houston Tex to the VIII Corps Louisiana Maneuvers 27 Jul 42 where redesignated 2nd Infantry Division 1 Aug 42; returned to Ft Sam Houston Tex 22 Sep 42 and arrived Cp McCoy Wis 27 Nov 42; staged at Cp Shanks N.Y. 3 Oct 43 until departed New York P/E 8 Oct 43; arrived England 18 Oct 43 and landed in France 7 Jun 44; crossed into Belgium 29 Sep 44 and Germany 3 Oct 44 and entered Czechoslovakia 4 May 45; returned to New York P/E 20 Jul 45 and moved to Cp Swift Tex 22 Jul 45 and to Cp Stoneman Calif 28 Mar 46; arrived Ft Lewis Wash 15 Apr 46 where active thru 1946.

Campaigns: *Normandy, Northern France, Rhineland, Ardennes-Alsace, Central Europe*
Aug 45 Loc: Camp Swift Texas

Typical Organization (1941):

9th Infantry Regiment
23rd Infantry Regiment
38th Infantry Regiment
HHB Division Artillery
12th Field Artillery Battalion (155mm)
15th Field Artillery Battalion (105mm)
37th Field Artillery Battalion (105mm)
38th Field Artillery Battalion (105mm)

Headquarters, 2nd Division
Headquarters & Military Police Company
2nd Signal Company
2nd Engineer Battalion
2nd Medical Battalion
2nd Quartermaster Battalion
2nd Reconnaissance Troop

Typical Organization (1944/45):

9th Infantry Regiment
23rd Infantry Regiment
38th Infantry Regiment
HHB Division Artillery
12th Field Artillery Battalion (155mm)
15th Field Artillery Battalion (105mm)
37th Field Artillery Battalion (105mm)
38th Field Artillery Battalion (105mm)
2nd Reconnaissance Troop, Mecz

2nd Engineer Combat Battalion
2nd Medical Battalion
2nd Counter Intelligence Corps Det
Headquarters Special Troops
Hqs Company, 2nd Infantry Division
Military Police Platoon
702nd Ordnance Light Maintenance Company
2nd Quartermaster Company
2nd Signal Company

741st Tank Battalion *(attached 15 Jun 44–17 Aug 44, 3 Oct 44–8 May 45)*
759th Tank Battalion *(attached 18 Jun 44–28 Jun 44, 27 Jul 44–5 Aug 44)*
612th Tank Destroyer Battalion *(attached 14 Jun 44–9 May 45)*
629th Tank Destroyer Battalion *(attached 30 Oct 44–2 Dec 44)*
644th Tank Destroyer Battalion *(attached 12 Dec 44–27 Jan 45)*
462nd AAA Auto-Wpns Battalion *(attached 16 Jun 44–17 Aug 44, 3 Oct 44–8 May 45)*

Overseas Wartime Assignments:

First Army - 22 Oct 43

XV Corps - 24 Dec 43

V Corps - 14 Apr 44

XIX Corps - 17 Aug 44

VIII Corps - 18 Aug 44

V Corps - 20 Dec 44

VII Corps - 28 Apr 45

V Corps - 1 May 45

Third Army - 6 May 45

III Corps - 25 Jul 45

Commanders: MG John C. H. Lee: Nov 41

MG Walter M. Robertson: May 42

BG William K. Harrison: Jun 45

MG Edward M. Almond: Sep 45

Killed in Action: 3,031   *Wounded in Action:* 12,785   *Died of Wounds:* 457

2nd Infantry Division Combat Narrative

The division landed on the evening of 7 Jun 44 across Omaha Beach France and was committed in the Forêt de Cerisy and next attacked across the Elle and Aure Rivers. It assaulted the German strongpoint position on top of Hill 192 which commanded the approaches to St Lô on 12 Jun 44. Fierce fighting for Hill 192 continued through June and into July, and when the division finally took it on 11 Jul 44 it gained control of the St Lô highway also. After regrouping the division went on the offensive again 27 Jul 44 and took Notre Dame d'Elle as it exploited the St Lô breakthrough. It advanced to the Vire River by 4 Aug 44 and halted to allow XIX Corps to cross its front and take Vire itself. The division advanced across the Vire and took Tinchebray on 15 Aug 44. On 17 Aug 44 it moved west into Brittany and on 25 Aug 44 began the assault on the strong outer defenses of the German fortified city of Brest. By 2 Sep 44 it had seized Hill 105 which dominated the eastern approaches. The all-out attack on Brest commenced 8 Sep 44 and the division gained the old city wall by 17 Sep 44. The city surrendered after a 39-day battle.

On 26 Sep 44 the division moved by rail and motor and took up defensive positions at St Vith. The 106th Inf Div took over its positions in the Schnee Eifel 11 Dec 44, and the division shifted to begin its offensive for the Roer and Urft Dams 13 Dec 44. However, the German Ardennes counteroffensive forced the division to shift positions again to the Monschau Forest 16 Dec 44. Under heavy attack, the division withdrew to defensive positions along the Elsenborn Ridge until the German drive was halted. The 23rd Inf was attached to help 1st Inf Div clear Iveldingen and Rohrbusch on 15 Jan 45. The division itself began its attack to breach the *West Wall* 30 Jan 45 and captured Rocherath the following day. On 1 Feb 45 the division resumed the offensive for the Roer and Urft River dams. After gaining Scheuren on 5 Feb 45 it consolidated and switched sectors with the 9th Inf Div.

On 3 Mar 45 the division crossed the Roer River with the 38th Inf in the lead at Heimbach, while the 23rd Inf occupied Malsbenden. The 38th Inf took Gemund 4 Mar 45 after it overran stubborn pillbox nests along the Urft River's northern banks. Mounted on tanks and tank destroyers, soldiers of the 9th and 23rd Inf gained seven miles toward Ahr and cleared 25 towns, enabling the 23rd Inf to take the Kreuzbach Bridge intact on 7 Mar 45. Then the division moved south to take Breisig 11 Mar 45. It improved positions along the Rhine and guarded Remagen Bridge from 12–20 Mar 45. At 0400 on 21 Mar 45 the division crossed the Rhine River and the 38th Inf cleared the region between the Rhine and Wied Rivers, Datzeroth, and Segendorf. The 23rd Inf crossed the Rhine on 23 Mar 45 and the 38th Inf fought to expand its Wied Bridgehead while attached to the 9th Armd Div. With the 9th and 23rd Inf in the lead, the division took Ransbach and other towns 26 Mar 45 on the north flank of V Corps. By 27 Mar 45 it finished mopping up stragglers and clearing its zone. It next moved to Hadamar and Limburg to join the 9th Armd Div and moved rapidly forward on their tanks and vehicles, reaching positions just north of Ederstau See by the end of the month.

The division concentrated in the Sachsenhausen area, mopped up, and took responsibility for the Eder Bridges near Affoldern on 1 Apr 45. It went into the attack 5 Apr 45 to take the Weser River heights north of Hann Muenden. The 23rd Inf made the Weser River crossing at Veckerhagen, the division following on the tanks of the 9th Armd Div and making fast progress. On 14 Apr 45 the 9th and 23rd Inf established a bridgehead across the Saale using a damaged railroad bridge, cleared Merseburg 15 Apr 45, and captured Leipzig 19 Apr 45. It was then ordered to withdraw to the east bank of the Mulde 24 Apr 45. The division next moved 200 miles 1–3 May 45 to the German-Czech border near Schonsee and Waldmungen where it relieved the 97th and 99th Inf Divs. It was attacking Pilsen when hostilities ceased by order 7 May 45.

3rd Infantry Division

No Distinctive
Insignia Authorized

Stationed at Ft Lewis Wash as the 3rd Division and moved to Ft Ord Calif 22 Jan 40 and returned to Ft Lewis Wash 19 May 40; moved to Hunter-Liggett Mil Res Calif 25 May 41 for IX Corps California Maneuvers; returned to Ft Lewis Wash 1 Jul 41 and participated in Fourth Army Maneuvers there 15–30 Aug 41; transferred to Ft Ord Calif 1 May 42 and redesignated 3rd Infantry Division 1 Aug 42; arrived Cp Pickett Va 22 Sep 42 and staged at Cp Patrick Henry Va 27 Oct 42 and departed Hampton Roads P/E same date; assaulted Fedala North Africa 8 Nov 42 and assaulted Sicily 10 Jul 43; arrived Italy 18 Sep 43 and assaulted Anzio 22 Jan 44; assaulted southern France 15 Aug 44 and entered Germany 13 Mar 45; arrived New York P/E 4 Sep 46 and arrived Cp Campbell Ky 8 Sep 46 where active thru 1946.

Campaigns: *Algeria–French Morocco, Tunisia, Sicily, Naples-Foggia, Anzio, Rome-Arno, Southern France, Rhineland, Ardennes-Alsace, Central Europe*

Aug 45 Loc: Salzburg Austria

Typical Organization (1941):

7th Infantry Regiment
15th Infantry Regiment
30th Infantry Regiment
HHB Division Artillery
  9th Field Artillery Battalion (155mm)
10th Field Artillery Battalion (105mm)
39th Field Artillery Battalion (105mm)
41st Field Artillery Battalion (105mm)
3rd Antitank Battalion (Provisional)

Headquarters, 3rd Division
Headquarters & Military Police Company
Artillery Band
10th Engineer Battalion
  3rd Medical Battalion
  3rd Quartermaster Battalion
  3rd Reconnaissance Troop
  3rd Signal Company

Typical Organization (1944/45):

7th Infantry Regiment
15th Infantry Regiment
30th Infantry Regiment
HHB Division Artillery
  9th Field Artillery Battalion (155mm)
10th Field Artillery Battalion (105mm)
39th Field Artillery Battalion (105mm)
41st Field Artillery Battalion (105mm)
3rd Reconnaissance Troop, Mecz
756th Tank Battalion *(attached 13 Jul 44–1 Jul 45)*
601st Tank Destroyer Battalion *(attached 13 Jul 44–1 Jul 45)*
441st AAA Auto-Wpns Battalion *(attached 13 Jul 44–29 Jun 45)*

10th Engineer Combat Battalion
  3rd Medical Battalion
  3rd Counter Intelligence Corps Det
Headquarters Special Troops
Hqs Company, 3rd Infantry Division
Military Police Platoon
703rd Ordnance Light Maintenance Company
  3rd Quartermaster Company
  3rd Signal Company

Overseas Wartime Assignments:

NATO - 8 Nov 42
I Armored Corps - 1 Feb 43
Seventh Army Prov Corps - 15 Jul 43
II Corps - 31 Jul 43
VI Corps - 13 Aug 43
II Corps - 18 Nov 43
VI Corps - 27 Dec 43
II Corps - 29 May 44

Fifth Army - 5 Jun 44
VI Corps - 15 Jul 44
French II Corps (attached) - 15 Dec 44
XXI Corps - 28 Jan 45
French II Corps (attached) - 15 Feb 45
XV Corps - 12 Mar 45
XXI Corps - 23 Apr 45
XV Corps - 8 May 45

Commanders: MG Charles F. Thompson: Aug 40
BG Charles P. Hall: Aug 41
MG John P. Lucas: Sep 41
MG Jonathan W. Anderson: Mar 42

MG Lucian K. Truscott Jr: Apr 43
MG John W. O'Daniel: Feb 44
MG William R. Schmidt: Aug 45

Killed in Action: 4,922   *Wounded in Action:* 18,766   *Died of Wounds:* 636

80

3rd Infantry Division Combat Narrative

The division landed in North Africa northeast of Fedala 8 Nov 42 and entered Casablanca 11 Nov 42. Assigned the occupation of half of French Morocco, it arrived (less its 7th Inf) behind the 1st Inf Div for possible commitment on the Tunisian front 6 May 43. However, the division was soon pulled out to train for the pending operation against Sicily, which it assaulted 10 Jul 43. With the assistance of naval gunfire, the division took Agrigento 16–17 Jul 43 and reached Palermo ahead of armored columns on 22 Jul 43. On 1 Aug 43 it relieved the 45th Inf Div to drive east along the coastal highway. Despite mines and demolitions the 15th Inf, again assisted by naval gunfire, forced crossings over the Furiano River 4 Aug 43. The 7th Inf landed ahead of the general advance and a battalion of the 30th Inf repeated a coastal landing east of Agata on 7 Aug 43. This same battalion outflanked the retreating enemy by another successful landing at Capo d'Orlando 10 Aug 43. The division ended the Sicilian campaign by racing its 7th Inf into Messina, still under fire from the hostile Italian coast, on 16 Aug 43.

Nine days after the invasion of Italy the division landed at Salerno and started north into the mountains, driving through Battipaglia to take Acerno 22 Sep 43. It captured Avellino in a night assault 30 Sep 43 and crossed the Volturno River east of Capua on 13 Oct 43. It seized Cisterna 15 Oct 43 and then fought a furious ten-day battle for the Winter Line which commenced 5 Nov 43. Its 15th Inf on M.Lungo was relieved 31 Dec 43 by the 6th Armd Inf Regt. The division assaulted Anzio Italy 22 Jan 44 and was heavily engaged for the next four weeks. After being prevented from achieving its objectives by the overwhelming German opposition in the area, the division was regrouped 27 Jan 44. On 29 Jan 44 a German counterattack forced it back to the Mussolini Canal, but the division contained this threat. It defeated the final German attack on the Anzio perimeter in the Ponte Rotto sector on 3 Feb 44. It attacked out of the Anzio beachhead 23 Mar 44 and was designated at the garrison of Rome on 4 Jun 44, remaining in the latter city as Fifth Army Reserve.

The division landed in the Bay of Cavalaire and Pampelonne France 15 Aug 44 and cleared St Tropez by 17 Aug 44. The 15th and 30th Inf swept down Highway 7 toward Toulon, and on 24 Aug 44 the division reached the Rhône River at Arles. It cleared rearguard opposition from Montélimar, was relieved at the end of the month, and assembled at Voiron. On 6 Sep 44 it returned to attack and take Fort Fontain, opening the way to the outer defenses of Besançon, which fell to the division the following day. On 11 Sep 44 the division invested Vesoul and reached the Moselle, which it crossed over on a bridge found intact near Rupt at midnight 23 Sep 44. It then took over the St Amé area from the 36th Inf Div. Renewing the offensive on 4 Oct 44 the 7th Inf assaulted Vageny which fell 7 Oct 44 as the 15th Inf reduced a quarry strongpoint near Cleurie after a week-long battle. Advancing against formidable resistance toward St Dié, the division's 15th Inf seized Etival as German opposition crumbled on the Meurthe River. The 7th and 30th Inf crossed it in the Clairefontaine–St Michel area before dawn on 20 Nov 44 and spearheaded the drive on Strasbourg. The division emerged from Vosges onto the Alsatian Plain and entered Strasbourg 27 Nov 44 to relieve the *2eme Division Blindée* there.

On 5 Dec 44 the division began its attack toward the Maginot Line and cleared Bennwihr 24 Dec 44 after which it was relieved by the 28th Inf Div. The division renewed its offensive against the Colmar Pocket again on 26 Jan 45 and crossed the Canal de Colmar supported by the *5eme Division Blindee* on 29 Jan 44. At the end of the month it took Horbourg and the 7th Inf was at the outskirts of Colmar. It assaulted the *West Wall* Line 18 Mar 45, taking numerous pillboxes and bunkers, and the division seized the bridge at Zweibruecken intact on 20 Mar 45. After saturation bombing of the hostile shore, the division crossed the Rhine 26 Mar 45 and advanced rapidly to the Main which it crossed at Woerth on 30 Mar 45. In April the division moved into the Hohe Rhon Hills and opened its rapid advance on Nuremberg 11 Apr 45. The division entered the city 17 Apr 45 to take it block by block against determined resistance, finally clearing the heavily fortified city on 21 Apr 45. The division began the drive toward Augsburg 23 Apr 45 and relieved the 12th Armd Div at Dilligen Bridgehead. Augsburg was captured by the 7th and 15th Inf against light opposition 28 Apr 45, and the next day the division initiated its push toward Munich. On 4 May 45 the 7th Inf crossed into Austria through Salzburg to Berchtesgaden, where the division was located when hostilities ceased on 7 May 45.

4th Infantry Division

1 Jun 40 activated as the 4th Division at Ft Benning Ga and reorganized as 4th Division (Motorized) 1 Aug 40 and 4th Motorized Division 11 Jul 41; moved to Dry Prong La 1 Aug 41 for IV Corps Louisiana Maneuvers and returned to Ft Benning Ga 27 Aug 41; moved to Ft Jackson S.C. 30 Oct 41 for First Army Carolina Maneuvers and arrived back to Ft Benning Ga 3 Dec 41; arrived Cp Gordon Ga 29 Dec 41 and went to Carolina Maneuver Area 7 Jul 42; returned to Cp Gordon Ga 31 Aug 42 and moved to Ft Dix N.J. 12 Apr 43 where redesignated 4th Infantry Division 4 Aug 43; sent to Cp Gordon Johnston Fla 19 Sep 43 for III Corps Carrabelle Maneuvers; arrived Ft Jackson S.C. 1 Dec 43 and staged at Cp Kilmer N.J. 4 Jan 44 until departed New York P/E 18 Jan 44; arrived England 26 Jan 44 and assaulted Normandy France 6 Jun 44; crossed into Belgium 6 Sep 44 and into Germany 11 Sep 44; went to Luxembourg 12 Dec 44 and returned to Belgium 28 Jan 45 and to Germany 7 Feb 45; returned to France 10 Mar 45 and entered Germany again 29 Mar 45; returned New York P/E 10 Jul 45 and moved to Cp Butner N.C. 13 Jul 45 where inactivated 12 Mar 46.

No Distinctive Insignia Authorized

Campaigns: *Normandy, Northern France, Rhineland, Ardennes-Alsace, Central Europe*
Aug 45 Loc: Camp Butner North Carolina

Typical Organization (1941):

8th Infantry Regiment (Motorized)
12th Infantry Regiment (Motorized)*
22nd Infantry Regiment (Motorized)
HHB Division Artillery
20th Field Artillery Battalion (155mm)
29th Field Artillery Battalion (105mm)
42nd Field Artillery Battalion (105mm)
44th Field Artillery Battalion (105mm)

Headquarters, 4th Motorized Division
Headquarters & Military Police Company
4th Engineer Battalion
4th Medical Battalion
4th Quartermaster Battalion
4th Reconnaissance Troop
4th Signal Company

*Assigned 24 Oct 41.

Typical Organization (1944/45):

8th Infantry Regiment
12th Infantry Regiment
22nd Infantry Regiment
HHB Division Artillery
20th Field Artillery Battalion (155mm)
29th Field Artillery Battalion (105mm)
42nd Field Artillery Battalion (105mm)
44th Field Artillery Battalion (105mm)
4th Reconnaissance Troop, Mecz

4th Engineer Combat Battalion
4th Medical Battalion
4th Counter Intelligence Corps Det
Headquarters Special Troops
Hqs Company, 4th Infantry Division
Military Police Platoon
704th Ordnance Light Maintenance Company
4th Quartermaster Company
4th Signal Company

70th Tank Battalion *(attached 9 Jun 44–23 Mar 45, 23–27 Mar 45, 6 Apr–9 May 45)*
610th Tank Destroyer Battalion *(attached 25 Jan 45–10 Mar 45, 17 Mar 45–8 May 45)*
776th Tank Destroyer Battalion *(attached 9 Apr 45–18 Apr 45)*
801st Tank Destroyer Battalion *(attached 13 Jun 44–15 Oct 44, 30 Oct 44–8 Nov 44)*
802nd Tank Destroyer Battalion *(attached 9 Dec 44–27 Jan 45)*
803rd Tank Destroyer Battalion *(attached 9 Nov 44–25 Dec 44)*
893rd Tank Destroyer Battalion *(attached 23 Aug 44–29 Sep 44)*
377th AAA Auto Wpns Battalion *(attached 14 Jun 44–23 Mar 45, 23–27 Mar 45, 6 Apr–9 May 45)*

Overseas Wartime Assignments:

VII Corps - 2 Feb 44
VIII Corps - 16 Jul 44
VII Corps - 19 Jul 44
V Corps - 22 Aug 44
VII Corps - 8 Nov 44
VIII Corps - 7 Dec 44
III Corps - 20 Dec 44

XII Corps - 21 Dec 44
VIII Corps - 27 Jan 45
12th Army Group - 10 Mar 45
VI Corps - 20 Mar 45
XXI Corps - 25 Mar 45
Seventh Army - 8 Apr 45
Third Army - 2 May 45
III Corps - 6 May 45

Commanders: MG Walter E. Prosser: Jun 40   MG Fred C. Wallace: Jan 42
MG Lloyd R. Fredendall: Oct 40   MG Raymond O. Barton: Jul 42
MG Oscar W. Griswold: Aug 41   MG Harold W. Blakeley: Dec 44
MG Harold R. Bull: Oct 41   MG George P. Hays: Nov 45
MG Terry de la Mesa Allen: Dec 41

Killed in Action: 4,097   *Wounded in Action:* 17,371   *Died of Wounds:* 757

4th Infantry Division Combat Narrative

The division, reinforced by the 359th Inf of 90th Inf Div, assaulted Utah Beach France with the 8th Inf leading against light resistance 6 Jun 44. The 8th Inf relieved the isolated 82nd A/B Div at Ste Mere-Eglise and countered several German attacks 7 Jun 44. The following day the division began its drive on the Cotentin Peninsula toward Cherbourg, and the 22nd Inf took Azeville fort and Ozeville 9 Jun 44 with naval gunfire support. The division reached Cherbourg's main defenses by 21 Jun 44 and on 22 Jun 44 began its assault with the 12th Inf augmented by tank support. On 25 Jun 44 it breached the fortress-city and garrisoned it until relieved at the end of the month by the 101st A/B Div. The division then went south to participate in the general offensive in France.

On 6 Jul 44 it attacked toward Périers and participated in the COBRA breakout 25 Jul 44. The division sped south and took St Pois after a furious battle on 5 Aug 44, countered German attacks at Avranches and committed the 22nd Inf in the Le Teilleu area. The division entered Paris with French army units 25 Aug 44. On 1 Sep 44, riding on tanks of the 5th Armd Div's CCA, the division pushed to Chauny and assembled near Mézières, moving forward from the Meuse River 6 Sep 44. On 14 Sep 44 it penetrated the *West Wall* in the Schnee Eifel, but the 12th Inf was stopped after small gains over the next few days despite costly attacks. The 8th and 22nd Inf also failed to take Brandscheid and the offensive halted 17 Sep 44 in the face of German counterattacks. Making slow progress through October, the division moved into the Zweitfall area and relieved the 28th Inf Div on 6 Nov 44. Fighting in the Huertgen Forest, the 12th Inf was subjected to a strong German counterattack on 10 Nov 44 which cut off regimental elements until 15 Nov 44. The 8th and 22nd Inf had a gap wedged between them in forest fighting which stopped the offensive 19 Nov 44. During five costly days of combat in the Huertgen Forest the division had only gained 1½ miles. Attacks were renewed 22 Nov 44 and the 12th Inf finally closed the gap on 28 Nov 44. After severe fighting the 22nd Inf took Grossahau by frontal assault the following day. The 8th Inf reached the edge of Huertgen Forest 30 Nov 44 but failed in further advances, and on 3 Dec 44 the division was relieved by the 83rd Inf Div and moved to Luxembourg.

While in Luxembourg the division was subjected to the fury of the German Ardennes Counteroffensive on 16 Dec 44. Despite heavy losses and the loss of several isolated components, it managed to hold its lines at Dickweiler and Osweiler Reinforced by tanks, the 12th Inf made several unsuccessful efforts to rescue trapped elements near Echternach. On 22 Dec 44 the division renewed attacks there which finally took the town 27 Dec 44.

On 17 Jan 45 the 87th Div took over the division's zone along the Sauer from Echternach to Wasserbilling, releasing the division to seize the heights overlooking the Our and cross the river at Bettendorf 22 Jan 45. It resumed the offensive 29 Jan 45 and advanced into Germany 1 Feb 45, breaching the outer defenses of the *West Wall* along the Schnee Eifel River near Brandscheid on 4 Feb 45. On 9 Feb 45 the division crossed the Pruem River with the 8th Inf and stormed the town itself 12 Feb 45. It then went onto the defensive 11 Feb 44 defending the river from Olzheim to Watzerath against counterattacks. On 28 Feb 44 the division crossed the river in force but the 12th Inf was only able to make negligible gains. Gondelsheim was finally taken 4 Mar 45 and the division raced out of the Pruem bridgehead behind the 11th Armd Div to the Kyll 6 Mar 45. The 8th Inf reached the Honerath area by 8 Mar 45, and on 30 Mar 45 the division completed crossing the Rhine and followed behind 12th Armd Div, and was ferried across the Main at Ochenfuhrt 2 Apr 45. The 12th and 22nd Inf fought determined opposition up the wooded slopes in the Koenigshofen area, and the general offensive was resumed 10 Apr 45. The drive toward Rothenburg started 11 Apr 45 against strong German defenses and the city was taken by the 12th Inf on 17 Apr 45 as the 8th Inf reached Ansbach the same day.

The division then moved north toward the Danube, and forward elements crossed it on 25 Apr 45. The 8th Inf established a bridgehead across the Lech at Schwabstadl on 27 Apr 45, and by the end of the month the 12th and 22nd Inf had reached the Isar River bridges at Miesbach. The division was relieved by the 101st A/B Div in that sector on 2 May 45. On 4 May 45 it was moved to Neumarkt for occupation duty under Third Army.

5th Infantry Division

No Distinctive
Insignia Authorized

16 Oct 39 activated at Ft McClellan Ala as 5th Division and moved to Ft Benning Ga 9 Apr 40 and to Cp Beauregard La 11 May 40; arrived Ft Benjamin Harrison Ind 31 May 40 and Shamrock Wis 3 Aug 40; returned to Ft Benjamin Harrison Ind 4 Sep 40 and moved to Ft Custer Mich 13 Dec 40; sent to Cp Forrest Tenn 29 May 41 for VII Corps Tennessee Maneuvers; returned to Ft Custer Mich 1 Jul 41 and transferred to Cp Joseph T. Robinson Ark 25 Aug 41 where participated in VII Corps Arkansas Maneuvers and the Louisiana Maneuvers of Sep 41; returned to Ft Custer Mich 3 Oct 41; arrived New York P/E 22 Apr 42 and departed 30 Apr 42; arrived Iceland 11 May 42 and redesignated 5th Infantry Division 25 May 43; departed Iceland 5 Aug 43 and arrived Northern Ireland 9 Aug 43; landed in France 11 Jul 44 and entered Germany 8 Feb 45 and Czechoslovakia 1 May 45; arrived Boston P/E 19 Jul 45 and arrived at Cp Campbell Ky 22 Jul 45 where inactivated 20 Sep 46.

Campaigns: *Normandy, Northern France, Rhineland, Ardennes-Alsace, Central Europe*
Aug 45 Loc: Camp Campbell Kentucky

Typical Organization (1941):

2nd Infantry Regiment
10th Infantry Regiment
11th Infantry Regiment
HHB Division Artillery
19th Field Artillery Battalion (105mm)
21st Field Artillery Battalion (155mm)
50th Field Artillery Battalion (105mm)
46th Field Artillery Battalion (105mm)

Headquarters, 5th Division
Headquarters & Military Police Company
7th Engineer Battalion
5th Medical Battalion
5th Quartermaster Battalion
5th Reconnaissance Troop
5th Signal Company
5th Antitank Battalion (Provisional)

Typical Organization (1944/45):

2nd Infantry Regiment
10th Infantry Regiment
11th Infantry Regiment
HHB Division Artillery
19th Field Artillery Battalion (105mm)
21st Field Artillery Battalion (155mm)
46th Field Artillery Battalion (105mm)
50th Field Artillery Battalion (105mm)
5th Reconnaissance Troop, Mecz

7th Engineer Combat Battalion
5th Medical Battalion
5th Counter Intelligence Corps Det
Headquarters Special Troops
Hqs Company, 5th Infantry Division
Military Police Platoon
705th Ordnance Light Maintenance Company
5th Quartermaster Company
5th Signal Company

735th Tank Battalion *(attached 13 Jul 44–20 Oct 44, 1 Nov 44–20 Dec 44)*
737th Tank Battalion *(attached 23 Dec 44–11 Jun 45)*
654th Tank Destroyer Battalion *(attached 22 Dec 44–25 Dec 44)*
774th Tank Destroyer Battalion *(attached 14 Sep 44–24 Sep 44, 5 Nov 44–22 Nov 44)*
803rd Tank Destroyer Battalion *(attached 25 Dec 44–13 Jun 45)*
807th Tank Destroyer Battalion *(attached 17 Dec 44–21 Dec 44)*
818th Tank Destroyer Battalion *(attached 13 Jul 44–20 Dec 44)*
449th AAA Auto-Wpns Battalion *(attached 13 Jul 44–23 Nov 44, 29 Nov 44–31 Mar 45)*

Overseas Wartime Assignments:

First Army *(attached)* - 22 Oct 43
XV Corps - 24 Dec 43
V Corps - 13 Jul 44
Third Army - 1 Aug 44
XX Corps - 4 Aug 44

XII Corps - 21 Dec 44
XX Corps - 28 Mar 45
Third Army *(attached First Army)* - 7 Apr 45
XVI Corps *(attached)* - 22 Apr 45
III Corps - 25 Apr 45

Commanders: BG Campbell B. Hodges: Oct 39
MG Joseph M. Cummins: Sep 40
MG Charles H. Bonesteel: Jul 41

MG Cortlandt Parker: Aug 41
MG Stafford L. Irwin: Jun 43
MG Albert E. Brown: Apr 45

Killed in Action: 2,298   *Wounded in Action:* 9,549   *Died of Wounds:* 358

5th Infantry Division Combat Narrative

The division arrived at Utah Beach France 11 Jul 44 and assumed defensive positions from the 1st Inf Div near Caumont 13 Jul 44. On 26 Jul 44 it attacked to take Vidouville and made a limited advance to the Torigny-sur-Vire-Caumont Road, after which it was reassembled 1 Aug 44. On 8 Aug 44 the division opened its offensive toward Nantes, taking Angers 10 Aug 44, and with the assistance of the 7th Armd Div captured Chartes 18 Aug 44. Speeding eastward the division crossed the Seine at Montereau 24 Aug 44 and took Rheims 30 Aug 44 and established a bridgehead across the Meuse at Verdun at the month's end.

The division began the battle for Metz 7 Sep 44 as the 2nd Inf was stopped in the Amanviller-Verneville area and the 11th Inf pushed up the Meuse heights near Dornot. The 2nd Inf continued to batter the city's outer fortifications, and on 8 Sep 44 the division gained a precarious bridgehead over the Moselle which immediately came under heavy shell-fire and continuous counterattack. The 2nd Inf made repeated frontal assaults as engineers bridged the river for tanks on 12 Sep 44. But the Arnaville bridgehead effort was hampered by German shelling of the bridges, deep mud, and ammunition shortages. The 10th and 11th regrouped inside the perimeter and defended it against a strong German attack 17 Sep 44. The division attacked Fort Driant commencing 27 Sep 44, which guarded the northern approaches to Metz. The 11th Inf forced its way into the bastion's outer edges 3 Oct 44, but the Germans counter-attacked from tunnels after dark. The division committed itself entirely into this battle in very costly combat, but by 12 Oct 44 attempts to seize the fort were given up, and the division withdrew to rest. On 12 Nov 44 the division returned to the assault and was counterattacked at once as it entered the bridgehead of 6th Armd Div. Over the next few days the 2nd Inf took Ancerville; the 10th Inf reduced Fort Aisne, Boies de l'Hôspital, Marly, and Fort Queuleu; and the 11th Inf captured Prayelle Farm, Frescaty airfield, Fort Verdun, and Fort St Privat. On 18 Nov 44 the 10th and 11th Inf pushed into Metz itself, the division encircling the town completely the following day. Rearguard opposition inside Metz had been mopped up by 22 Nov 44, but the division kept infantry to contain the forts there while it relieved the 95th Inf Div and attacked across the Nied 25 Nov 44. The Ste Quentin fortifications surrendered to the division 6 Dec 44 as it was pulled back to assembly areas.

On 16 Dec 44 the German Ardennes counteroffensive began, and the division relieved the 95th Inf Div at the Saarlautern bridgehead, attacking out of it 18 Dec 44. After slow progress Waldbilling and Haller fell 25 Dec 44. Throughout January the division continued to reduce the southern flank of the German drive in conjunction with 4th Inf Div. On 4 Feb 45 it was relieved in line by the 6th Cav Gp and took up new positions. It attacked across the Sauer River near Echternach 7 Feb 45 despite strong currents and German shelling which prevented bridging. It expanded this bridgehead to the *West Wall* Line by 10 Feb 45, and by 19 Feb 45 cleared up to the west bank of the Pruem River. After regrouping, the 2nd and 10th Inf crossed it near Peffingen during the night of 24–25 Feb 45. The 11th Inf cut the Bitburg-Trier Highway on 27 Feb 45 and cleared to the west bank of the Kyll by the following day. The division opened its attack to establish the Kyll bridgehead between Erdorf and Philippsheim on 2 Mar 45. Progress was rapid as the division leapfrogged elements past numerous towns and reached the Moselle 10 Mar 45. The 2nd and 11th Inf crossed the river 14 Mar 45 after divisional regroupment and seized Treis, Lutz, and Eveshausen. Working closely with the 4th Armd Div, the division reached the Rhine with the 11th Inf at Oppenheim and Nierstein on 21 Mar 45. The next day the regiment crossed the river with little difficulty.

On 26 Mar 45 the 10th Inf captured the Rhine-Main airport as the division reached Frankfurt-am-Main. On 4 Apr 45 it completed clearing the city and secured it until 9 Apr 45 when it closed into the Olsenburg area. The 10th Inf attacked to take Arnsberg while the 2nd Inf reached the Rohr River 12 Apr 45. The 11th Inf rejoined the division from Frankfurt on 14 Apr 45, and the division then occupied Westphalian regions south of the Ruhr until relieved by the 75th Inf Div on 24 Apr 45. On 1 May 45 the division advanced across the Czechoslovakian border and into Austria behind armored units. On 5 May 45 the division attacked across the Tepla River and followed the 4th Armd Div through the Regen and Freyung Passes as the end of hostilities brought its offensive to a halt.

6th Infantry Division

No Distinctive Insignia Authorized

10 Oct 39 activated at Ft Lewis Wash as 6th Division and moved to Ft Jackson S.C. 9 Nov 39; relocated to Ft Benning Ga 12 Apr 40 and Alexandria La 8 May 40; relocated to Ft Snelling Minn 1 Jun 40 and sent to Lincoln Minn 17 Jul 40; returned to Ft Snelling Minn 18 Aug 40; participated in Arkansas Maneuvers of Aug 41 and Louisiana Maneuvers of Sep 41; arrived Ft Leonard Wood Mo 10 Oct 41 where redesignated 6th Motorized Division 9 Apr 42; moved to I Corps Tennessee Maneuvers 11 Sep 42 and returned to Ft Leonard Wood Mo 10 Nov 42; moved to Cp Young Calif 29 Nov 42 where participated in Desert Training Center No.1 IV Armored Corps Maneuvers until 22 Feb 43; arrived Cp San Luis Obispo Calif 28 Mar 43 where redesignated 6th Infantry Division 21 May 43; departed San Francisco P/E 21 Jul 43 and arrived Hawaii 29 Jul 43; left Hawaii 26 Jan 44 and arrived Milne Bay New Guinea 31 Jan 44; assaulted Sansapor New Guinea 30 Jul 44 and assaulted Lingayen Gulf Philippines 9 Jan 45; arrived Korea 18 Oct 45 where active thru 1946.

Campaigns: *New Guinea, Luzon*
Aug 45 Loc: Bagabag Philippine Islands

Typical Organization (1941):

1st Infantry Regiment
20th Infantry Regiment
63rd Infantry Regiment*
HHB Division Artillery
  1st Field Artillery Battalion (105mm)
  51st Field Artillery Battalion (105mm)
  53rd Field Artillery Battalion (105mm)
  80th Field Artillery Battalion (155mm)

*Assigned 1 Jun 41

Headquarters, 6th Division
Headquarters & Military Police Company
Artillery Band
6th Engineer Battalion
6th Medical Battalion
6th Quartermaster Battalion
6th Signal Company
6th Reconnaissance Troop

Typical Organization (1944/45):

1st Infantry Regiment
20th Infantry Regiment
63rd Infantry Regiment
HHB Division Artillery
  1st Field Artillery Battalion (105mm)
  51st Field Artillery Battalion (105mm)
  53rd Field Artillery Battalion (105mm)
  80th Field Artillery Battalion (155mm)
  6th Reconnaissance Troop, Mecz

6th Engineer Combat Battalion
6th Medical Battalion
6th Counter Intelligence Corps Det
Headquarters Special Troops
Hqs Company, 6th Infantry Division
Military Police Platoon
706th Ordnance Light Maintenance Company
6th Quartermaster Company
6th Signal Company

Overseas Wartime Assignments:

Hawaiian Dept - 29 Jul 43
Central Pacific Area Cmd - 14 Aug 43
Sixth Army** - 31 Jan 44
I Corps** - 25 Feb 44
Sixth Army** - 23 Mar 44
XI Corps** - 24 Apr 44
Sixth Army** - 26 May 44

**Attached ALAMO Force

Eighth Army - 12 Oct 44
I Corps - 20 Nov 44
Sixth Army - 14 Feb 45
XI Corps - 15 Mar 45
I Corps - 11 Jun 45
Eighth Army *(attached XIV Corps)* - 1 Jul 45

Commanders: BG Clement A. Trott: Oct 39
BG Frederick E. Uhl: Oct 40
MG Clarence S. Ridley: Jan 41
MG Durward S. Wilson: Sep 42

MG Franklin C. Sibert: Oct 42
MG Edwin D Patrick: Aug 44
MG Charles E. Hurdis: Mar 45

Killed in Action: 410 *Wounded in Action:* 1,957 *Died of Wounds:* 104

6th Infantry Division Combat Narrative

The division arrived at Milne Bay, New Guinea, on 31 Jan 44 and on 5 Jun 44 initial elements arrived at Toem in the Hollandia-Aitape area, followed by the 20th Inf on 11 Jun 44 and the 63rd Inf with rest of division 14 Jun 44. On 20 Jun 44 the 20th Inf began its attack toward Lone Tree Hill from Tirfoam River, but was slowed by heavy fire from a defile between it and Mt Saksin and was unable to gain the crest until 22 Jun 44, after which it was subjected to fierce Japanese counterattacks. The 1st Inf landed via sea just west of the hill to outflank the Japanese and forced a small beachhead which it was initially unable to expand. By 27 Jun 44 the 63rd Inf was able to mop up the Japanese forces in the Lone Tree Hill vicinity, and the division secured the Maffin Bay area by 12 Jul 44.

After the brief rest the 1st Inf assaulted Sansapor 30 Jul 44 in the Vogelkop Peninsula against no resistance, the preparatory bombardment being omitted to attain surprise. The 63rd Inf landed on undefended Middleburg and Amsterdam Islands. A battalion of the 1st Inf took the undefended plantation village at Cape Sansapor 31 Jul 44. The division secured the coast from Cape Waimak to the Mega River and garrisoned it until Dec 44.

On 9 Jan 45 the division landed at Lingayen Gulf onto Luzon Philippines and pursued the Japanese into the Cabaruan Hills and began holding actions on the Malisqui-Catablan-Torres line. Attacking in the 43rd Inf Div sector, the 63rd Inf gained Hill 363 on 14 Jan 45. The division attacked 17 Jan 45 as the 20th Inf pushed on the Cabaruan Hills and the 1st Inf drove toward Urdaneta. The 63rd Inf took Blue Ridge near Amlang after heavy fighting 21 Jan 45. The 1st Inf, assisted by air support, seized San Jose on 4 Feb 45 which was the Highway 5 gate to the Cagayan Valley. The 20th Inf took Munoz after a battle lasting several days, wiping out escaping Japanese columns there 7 Feb 45. The division then occupied positions along Luzon's eastern coast, bisecting Japanese forces on the island, and drove to Dinglan and Baler Bays to isolate Japanese on southern Luzon by 13 Feb 45. The 1st Inf operated on Bataan 14–21 Feb 45 and cut the peninsula from Abucay to Bagac.

The division shifted to confront the Shimbu Line northeast of Manila on 24 Feb 45. On that day the 63rd Inf seized Montalban and the 20th Inf reached the heights near Mataba. As Japanese resistance increased the 1st Inf was committed in the center toward Wawa Dam. After reaching the crest of Mt Pacawagan 26 Feb 45 the 63rd Inf was thrown off by the Japanese. Efforts by 1st Inf to take Mt Mataba were defeated and it withdrew 27 Feb 45 as the 63rd held the slope of Mt Pacawagan against assault. The division regrouped and renewed attacks by 1st Inf on 8 Mar 45 met unexpectedly light resistance. The 63rd Inf continued to hold its precarious positions in the Mt Pacawagan-Mataba sector. After hard fighting the 1st Inf seized Benchmark Hill on 11 Mar 45 and the 20th Inf was committed into the Shimbu Line assault. It shifted toward Mt Baytangan and reinforced by the 1st Inf, shifted its attack onto Mt Mataba under intense fire on 28 Mar 45. The entire division regrouped and renewed the offensive 2 Apr 45. The 20th and 63rd Inf switched sectors and the latter began the attack on Mt Mataba behind artillery fire 6 Apr 45. This attack was suspended until XI Corps artillery could saturate the Japanese positions, and then the 63rd Inf forced its way to the summit 10 Apr 45, but the hill was not cleared until 17 Apr 45.

On 16 Apr 45 the 1st Inf initiated its attack up Woodpecker Ridge near the junction of the Bosoboso and Mariquina Rivers. On 19 Apr 45 the division switched sectors with the 38th Inf Div and on 25 Apr 45 the 152nd Inf relieved the 1st Inf at the ridge. By 27 Apr 45 the attached 145th Inf finally gained the crest of Mt Pacawagen. The division then moved to the Kembu sector on 3 May 45 and took responsibility for Highway 5 south of Bayombong from the 37th Inf Div on 12 Jun 45. On 21 Jun 45 the 63rd Inf pushed to Kiangan and the 20th Inf took Bolog on 29 Jun 45. Though the Luzon campaign was officially declared over on 30 Jun 45, the division conducted mopping up operations in the Cagayan Valley and Cordilleras Mountains until the end of the war.

7th Infantry Division

No Distinctive Insignia Authorized

1 Jul 40 activated at Ft Ord Calif as 7th Division; moved to Longview Wash 19 Aug 41 for Fourth Army Maneuvers and returned to Ft Ord Calif 31 Aug 41; arrived San Jose Calif 11 Dec 41 where redesignated 7th Motorized Division 9 Apr 42 and transferred to Cp San Luis Obispo Calif 24 Apr 42; moved to Desert Training Center II Armored Corps Maneuvers 14 Aug 42 and returned Cp San Luis Obispo Calif 20 Oct 42 where redesignated 7th Infantry Division 1 Jan 43; arrived Ft Ord Calif 15 Jan 43 and departed San Francisco P/E 24 Apr 43; assaulted Attu Island Aleutians 11 May 43 and remained in Aleutians until arrived Hawaii 15 Sep 43; invaded Kwajalein Atoll 31 Jan 44 and arrived back in Hawaii 15 Feb 44; assaulted Leyte Philippines 20 Oct 44 and left 27 Mar 45; assaulted Okinawa 1 Apr 45; moved to Korea 8 Sep 45 where active thru 1946.

Campaigns: *Aleutian Islands, Eastern Mandates, Leyte, Ryukyus*
Aug 45 Loc: Okinawa

Typical Organization (1941):

17th Infantry Regiment	Headquarters, 7th Division
32nd Infantry Regiment	Headquarters & Military Police Company
53rd Infantry Regiment*	13th Engineer Battalion
HHB Division Artillery	7th Medical Battalion
31st Field Artillery Battalion (155mm)	7th Quartermaster Battalion
48th Field Artillery Battalion (105mm)	7th Reconnaissance Troop
49th Field Artillery Battalion (105mm)	7th Signal Company
57th Field Artillery Battalion (105mm)	

*Relieved from division 7 Nov 41; 159th Infantry Regt assigned division 29 Sep 41 and in turn relieved 23 Aug 43 when replaced by 184th Infantry Regt.

Typical Organization (1944/45):

17th Infantry Regiment	13th Engineer Combat Battalion
32nd Infantry Regiment	7th Medical Battalion
184th Infantry Regiment	7th Counter Intelligence Corps Det
HHB Division Artillery	Headquarters Special Troops
31st Field Artillery Battalion (155mm)	Hqs Company, 7th Infantry Division
48th Field Artillery Battalion (105mm)	Military Police Platoon
49th Field Artillery Battalion (105mm)	707th Ordnance Light Maintenance Company
57th Field Artillery Battalion (105mm)	7th Quartermaster Company
7th Reconnaissance Troop, Mecz	7th Signal Company

Overseas Wartime Assignments:

Amphibious Training Force #9 - 22 May 43	Tenth Army - 10 Feb 45
Central Pacific Area Cmd - 16 Sep 43	XXIV Corps - 22 Feb 45
V Amphibious Corps *(attached)* - 11 Dec 43	Tenth Army - 31 Jul 45
Central Pacific Base Cmd - 1 Jul 44	XXIV Corps - 15 Aug 45

Commanders: BG Joseph W. Stilwell: Jul 40
MG Charles H. White: Aug 41
MG Albert E. Brown: Oct 42

MG Charles H. Corlett: Apr 43
MG Archibald V. Arnold: Feb 44

Killed in Action: 1,948   *Wounded in Action:* 7,258   *Died of Wounds:* 386

7th Infantry Division Combat Narrative

Division elements departed San Francisco 24 Apr 43 to seize Attu Island in the Aleutians, and after several delays due to weather the 17th Inf landed in dense fog on 11 May 43 and attacked toward Jarmin Pass. The 32nd joined the assault 12 May 43 and the Japanese abandoned their positions there 17 May 43. The division took strongly defended Clevesy Pass 21 May 43 in attacks across frozen tundra and cleared Fish Hook Ridge by 27 May 43. Resistance collapsed on Attu at month's end, and the division trained on Adak Island. The 17th and 184th Inf landed on Kiska, which the Japanese had evacuated, 15 Aug 43. The division arrived in Hawaii 15 Sep 43 and engaged in intense jungle and amphibious training, after which it left 20–22 Jan 44 to assault the Marshall Islands.

The 17th Inf landed on Ennylabegan and Enubuj Islands 31 Jan 44, and the 32nd and 184th Inf assaulted heavily defended Kwajalein Atoll on 1 Feb 44. The 184th Inf was engaged in heavy combat against the blockhouse sector 3 Feb 44, and by 5 Feb 44 the division was mopping up the island. The 17th Inf took Ebeye Island 3 Feb 44 and other small islets until 6 Feb 44. On 8 Feb 44 the division left Kwajalein Atoll and engaged in rest and rehabilitation on Hawaii where it planned for the capture of Yap and the Palau Islands. It left Hawaii 15 Sep 44 and was concurrently given the mission of invading the Philippine Islands instead.

On 20 Oct 44 the division landed on Leyte Island's east coast and drove west from Dulag. The 32nd Inf seized contested Buri airstrip 27 Oct 44 and the 17th Inf battled for Dagami which fell 30 Oct 44. The division eliminated Japanese forces south of the Marabang River and captured Bambay, the 32nd Inf attacking toward Ormoc 14 Nov 44. The Battle of Shoestring Ridge began 23 Nov 44 as Japanese counterattacked the thinly spread 32nd Inf along the Palanas River. Reinforced by the 184th Inf, numerous Japanese attacks were repulsed in the bamboo thickets. The division was relieved in this sector 28 Nov 44 by the 11th A/B Division, which retained the 17th Inf temporarily. The division moved from San Pablo to Baybay 4 Dec 44. The 184th Inf attacked north from Damulaan 5 Dec 44 toward Ormoc, and advanced division soldiers overtook the 77th Inf Div, seizing Ipil 11 Dec 44 and dividing the Japanese forces on the island. The 32nd Inf attacked northeast 13 Dec 44 and joined forces with the 11th A/B Div moving west on 15 Dec 44. The division moved to Ormoc 24 Dec 44 and landed on undefended Ponson Island 15 Jan 45, Poro Island 19 Jan 45, and Pacijan Island 20 Jan 45. It left the Camotes Islands on 2 Feb 45 and returned to Tarragona on Leyte where it staged for the Ryukyus operations, its zone being turned over to the Americal Division on 10 Feb 45.

After much training and preparation the division departed Leyte 27 Mar 45 and assaulted Okinawa 1 Apr 45. The 17th Inf reached the east coast, severing the island and reaching the northern end of the Yonabaru airfield the following day. With the assistance of massed fires the 184th Inf took Tomb Hill 9 Apr 45, and after hard fighting the 17th Inf seized the military crest of Skyline Ridge and sealed the caves there by 23 Apr 45. The regiment took the Rocky Crags area but failed to force Kochi Ridge. The 184th Inf relieved the 32nd Inf in line on 1 May 45 despite Japanese infiltrators and attacked Gaja Ridge which it gained but lost to counterattack. The only major Japanese counteroffensive of the Ryukyus campaign hit the division 4–5 May 45 and brought the 17th Inf's efforts to take Kochi Ridge to another halt. By 9 May 45, as the 96th Inf Div relieved the 17th Inf, most of the Japanese had been cleared from their Kochi positions.

The division rehabilitated 12–21 May 45, patrolled rear areas, and trained replacements. On 22 May 45 it returned to the front, driving unopposed through the Yonabaru ruins to the hills beyond. On 26 May 45 the 32nd Inf ran into enemy strongpoints covering Shuri. The division had seized key positions by the end of the month in spite of this opposition and reached the southeast coast of Okinawa on 3 Jun 45. The battle for Hill 95 began 5 Jun 45 as the 17th and 32nd Inf used naval gunfire, corps artillery, and flamethrowing tanks. The 32nd Inf stormed and took it 11 Jun 45, and next captured Hill 89 near Mabuni, where the Japanese underground headquarters was located, on 21 Jun 45. The division mopped up rear areas and engaged in rehabilitation and training 21–30 Jun 45. On 5 Aug 45 it was given responsibility for the ground defense and internal security of the southern portion of Okinawa and continued this mission until the end of the war.

8th Infantry Division

No Distinctive Insignia Authorized

1 Jul 40 activated at Cp Jackson S.C. as 8th Division and redesignated there as 8th Infantry Division 31 Jul 41; moved to Carolina Maneuver Area 25 Sep 41; participated in both Oct and Nov 41 Carolina Maneuvers; arrived Ft Jackson S.C. 30 Nov 41 where redesignated 8th Motorized Division 9 Apr 42; participated in I Corps Tennessee Maneuvers Oct-Nov 42 and then moved to Cp Forrest Tenn 7 Nov 42; arrived Ft Leonard Wood Mo 29 Nov 42 and moved to Cp Young Calif 20 Mar 43 for IX Corps Desert Training Maneuvers No.2 where redesignated 8th Infantry Division 15 May 43; returned to Cp Forrest Tenn 15 Aug 43 and staged at Cp Kilmer N.J. 22 Nov 43 until departed New York P/E 5 Dec 43; arrived England 15 Dec 43 and arrived in France 3 Jul 44; crossed into Luxembourg 20 Nov 44 and into Germany on same date; arrived Hampton Roads P/E 10 Jul 45 and moved to Ft Leonard Wood Mo 13 Jul 45 where inactivated 20 Nov 45.

Campaigns: *Normandy, Northern France, Rhineland, Central Europe*
Aug 45 Loc: Fort Leonard Wood Missouri

Typical Organization (1941):

13th Infantry Regiment
28th Infantry Regiment
34th Infantry Regiment
HHB Division Artillery
28th Field Artillery Battalion (155mm)
43rd Field Artillery Battalion (105mm)
45th Field Artillery Battalion (105mm)
56th Field Artillery Battalion (105mm)

Headquarters, 8th Division
Headquarters & Military Police Company
12th Engineer Battalion
8th Medical Battalion
8th Quartermaster Battalion
8th Signal Company
8th Reconnaissance Troop

Typical Organization (1944/45):

13th Infantry Regiment
28th Infantry Regiment
121st Infantry Regiment*
HHB Division Artillery
28th Field Artillery Battalion (155mm)
43rd Field Artillery Battalion (105mm)
45th Field Artillery Battalion (105mm)
56th Field Artillery Battalion (105mm)
8th Reconnaissance Troop, Mecz
709th Tank Battalion *(attached 13 Jul 44–26 Jan 45)*
740th Tank Battalion *(attached 6 Feb 45–13 Mar 45, 6 Apr 45–12 May 45)*
644th Tank Destroyer Battalion *(attached 15 Jul 44–28 Apr 45)*
817th Tank Destroyer Battalion *(attached 9 Dec 44–8 Feb 45)*
893rd Tank Destroyer Battalion *(attached 19 Nov 44–10 Dec 44)*
445th AAA Auto-Wpns Battalion *(attached 11 Jul 44–12 May 45)*

12th Engineer Combat Battalion
8th Medical Battalion
8th Counter Intelligence Corps Det
Headquarters Special Troops
Hqs Company, 8th Infantry Division
Military Police Platoon
708th Ordnance Light Maintenance Company
8th Quartermaster Company
8th Signal Company

*Assigned 22 Nov 21 and replaced 34th Infantry Regt which was relieved 12 Jun 43.

Overseas Wartime Assignments:

First Army *(attached)* - 30 Nov 43
XV Corps - 24 Dec 43
VIII Corps - 1 Jul 44
V Corps - 19 Nov 44

VII Corps - 18 Dec 44
XIX Corps - 22 Dec 44
VII Corps - 3 Feb 45
XVIII (A/B) Corps - 26 Apr 45

Commanders: MG Philip B. Peyton: Jun 40
MG James P. Marley: Dec 40
MG William E. Shedd: Feb 41
MG Henry Terrell Jr: Mar 41
MG James P. Marley: Apr 41

MG Paul E. Peabody: Aug 42
MG William C. McMahon: Feb 43
MG Donald A. Stroh: Jul 44
MG William G. Weaver: Dec 44
MG Bryant E. Moore: Feb 45

Killed in Action: 2,532   *Wounded in Action:* 10,057   *Died of Wounds:* 288

8th Infantry Division Combat Narrative

The division landed across Utah Beach France 3 Jul 44 and was committed between the 79th and 90th Inf Divs, making attacks on 12 Jul 44 in the direction of Raids. It advanced slowly through the difficult and heavily defended hedgerow terrain and cut the Lessay-Périers road midway between the two towns on 26 Jul 44. The 13th Inf pushed through Rennes 8 Aug 44, while on 6 Aug 44 the 121st Inf was attached to the 83rd Inf Div for the attack on fortified Dinard west of St Malo. The entire division joined this attack 14 Aug 44 and Dinard finally fell 16 Aug 44. On 25 Aug 44 the division initiated the attack on the outer defenses of Brest after a preparatory bombardment, battled up Hill 80, and made the all-out assault on the fortress-city 8 Sep 44. The division shifted to clear the Crozon Peninsula 15 Sep 44 and took Crozon 19 Sep 44. The division then drove across France by rail and motor and relieved the 28th Inf Div in the Vossenack-Schmidt area on 19 Nov 44.

After artillery bombardment, the 121st Inf attacked into the Huertgen Forest 21 Nov 44 where the Germans had previously checked the 4th Inf Div. Assisted by tanks, in spite of heavy losses and continuous German counterattacks, the 13th and 121st Inf had the deep forest secured by 28 Nov 44. The 28th and 121st Inf next cleared Brandenberger Wald to provide a pathway for an armored drive down the Kleinhau-Brandenberg Highway 1 Dec 44. It spent the latter part of the month reducing a German pocket south of Obermaubach which was completed by 28 Dec 44. The division then pushed toward the Roer River.

Crossing with two regiments abreast near Dueren, the division went over the Roer on 23 Feb 45. The 13th Inf took the town and barracks at Dueren 25 Feb 45 as the 28th Inf cleared Stockheim and the 121st Inf captured Binsfeld. The division then followed the 3rd Armd Div, the 28th Div crossing the Erft Canal on 1 Mar 45. It took heavily defended Moedrath the following day, and the division drove to the Rhine River at Rodenkirchen on 7 Mar 45. It took over the zone of the 1st Inf Div there and maintained positions along the Rhine near Koln. In turn it was relieved from its defensive positions along the Rhine's west bank by the 86th Inf Div on 28 Mar 45. It completed movement over the river by the end of the month and cleared its portion of the Sieg River line with the capture of Siegen by the 13th Inf on 3 Apr 45.

The division attacked that portion of the Ruhr pocket between the Lenne and Ruhr Rivers after a long artillery barrage on 6 Apr 45. The 13th Inf took Seelbach Barracks, the 28th Inf reached Erndetebreuck and the 121st Inf seized both Eschenbach and Lutzel. Advancing rapidly, the division reached the Ruhr in the Wetter area and established contact with Ninth Army by 17 Apr 45. It released the 13th Armd Div and then relieved the 97th Inf Div on 20 Apr 45 and engaged in security operations. The division was then ordered to assemble for the final drive from the Elbe to the Baltic Sea, and it was placed under the operational control of the *British Second Army* 25 Apr 45. This necessitated its movement by rail and motor from the Ruhr and Cologne areas to the Elbe River. The 13th Inf was detached to assist the 82nd A/B Div establish a bridgehead across the Elbe in the Bleckede area on 28 Apr 45. It relieved the *British 5th Div* along the river and on 30 Apr 45 initiated the attack across the Elbe. The division attacked with the 121st Inf, followed by the 28th Inf, as it moved forward against light opposition and penetrated to Schwerin. The division was located there when hostilities were declared at an end 7 May 45.

9th Infantry Division

No Distinctive Insignia Authorized

1 Aug 40 activated at Ft Bragg N.C. as the 9th Division and participated in both Oct and Nov 41 Carolina Maneuvers and later amphibious training under the Atlantic Fleet Amphibious Corps; redesignated as 9th Infantry Division 1 Aug 42 and left Ft Bragg N.C. and arrived Ft Dix N.J. 25 Nov 42; departed New York P/E 11 Dec 42 and landed in North Africa 25 Dec 42 less elements which assaulted 8 Nov 42; arrived Palermo Sicily 31 Jul 43 and sent to England 25 Nov 43; landed in France 10 Jun 44 and crossed into Belgium 2 Sep 44; entered Germany 14 Sep 44 where active thru 1946.

Campaigns: *Algeria–French Morocco, Tunisia, Sicily, Normandy, Northern France, Rhineland, Ardennes-Alsace, Central Europe*
Aug 45 Loc: Bayreuth Germany

Typical Organization (1941):

39th Infantry Regiment
47th Infantry Regiment
60th Infantry Regiment
HHB Division Artillery
26th Field Artillery Battalion (105mm)
34th Field Artillery Battalion (155mm)
60th Field Artillery Battalion (105mm)
84th Field Artillery Battalion (105mm)

Headquarters, 9th Division
Headquarters & Military Police Company
Artillery Band
15th Engineer Battalion
9th Medical Battalion
9th Quartermaster Battalion
9th Reconnaissance Troop
9th Signal Company

Typical Organization (1944/45):

39th Infantry Regiment	15th Engineer Combat Battlion
47th Infantry Regiment	9th Medical Battalion
60th Infantry Regiment	9th Counter Intelligence Corps Det
HHB Division Artillery	Headquarters Special Troops
26th Field Artillery Battalion (105mm)	Hqs Company, 9th Infantry Division
34th Field Artillery Battalion (155mm)	Military Police Platoon
60th Field Artillery Battalion (105mm)	709th Ordnance Light Maintenance Company
84th Field Artillery Battalion (105mm)	9th Quartermaster Company
9th Reconnaissance Troop, Mecz	9th Signal Company

746th Tank Battalion *(attached 13 Jun 44–10 Jul 45)*
629 Tank Destroyer Battalion *(attached 16 Aug 44–25 Aug 44)*
899th Tank Destroyer Battalion *(attached 19 Jun 44–24 Jul 44)*
376th AAA Auto-Wpns Battalion *(attached 13 Jun 44–26 May 45)*
413th AAA Gun Battalion *(attached 20 Dec 44–3 Jan 45)*

Overseas Wartime Assignments:

First Army - 20 Nov 43	III Corps - 17 Feb 45
VII Corps - 25 Nov 43	VII Corps - 31 Mar 45
V Corps - 26 Oct 44	III Corps - 4 Apr 45
VII Corps - 6 Dec 44	VII Corps - 14 Apr 45
V Corps - 18 Dec 44	

Commanders: Col Charles B. Elliot: Aug 40   MG Manton S. Eddy: Aug 42
      BG Francis W. Honeycutt: Sep 40   MG Louis A. Craig: Aug 44
      MG Jacob L. Devers: Oct 40   MG Jesse A. Ladd: May 45
      MG Rene E. DeR. Hoyle: Aug 41

Killed in Action: 3,856   *Wounded in Action:* 17,416   *Died of Wounds:* 648

9th Infantry Division Combat Narrative

The division landed in North Africa on 8 Nov 42, the 39th Inf landing east of Algiers near Cap Matifou, the 47th Inf taking Safi, and the 60th Inf landing at Mehdia and encountering heavy resistance in its attempt to take Port-Lyautey airfield. Upon the sudden collapse of French opposition the division took its objectives 11 Nov 42 and then patrolled the Spanish-Moroccan border. It then returned to Tunisia in Feb 43, engaging in small defensive actions and patrols. On 12 Mar 43 it attached the 60th Inf to the 1st Armd Div which took Sened Station 21 Mar 43. The division entered action as a whole for the first time on 28 Mar 43 in southern Tunisia. The 47th attempted to attack from Djebel Berdi which had been abandoned by 1st Inf Div, to try to force a gap for the passage of 1st Armd Div, but the assault was repulsed with heavy losses. The division failed to take Hill 772 and on 11 Apr 43 was moved north and took over the *British 46th Div* sector. Reinforced by the *Corps France d'Afrique*, it attacked toward the Jefna positions 23 Apr 43, and the 60th Inf took Djebel Dardyss the next day. After sustained combat the 39th Inf seized Hill 382 north of Jefna at the end of the month, and the 60th Inf occupied Kef en Nsour 2 May 43 as the Germans withdrew to Bizerte. The 47th Inf cleared the hills north of Djebel Cheniti and on 8 May 43 entered Bizerte itself.

The 39th Inf was sent into Sicily 15 Jul 43 and the entire division arrived there at Palermo on 1 Aug 43. It assembled at Nicosia 4 Aug 43 and replaced 1st Inf Div on 7 Aug 43 and began the drive on Randazzo. Next it took part in the offensive toward Messina, and afterward moved to England 25 Nov 43 to prepare for the invasion of France.

The division landed across Utah Beach France 10 Jun 44 and the 39th Inf forced the Germans back to the Quinéville Ridge 12 Jun 44. On 14 Jun 44 the 60th Inf initiated its attack toward St Colombe and the following day the 47th Inf was committed to take high ground west of Orglandes. The division, reinforced with the 359th Inf, attacked with four regiments to establish a bridgehead across the Douve on 16 Jun 44. Advancing against disorganized opposition, the division reached the west coast of the Cotentin Peninsula and sealed it off 17 Jun 44, blocking German flight south and inflicting heavy losses. The division started the final assault on Cherbourg 19 Jun 44 with the 39th and 60th Inf, which attacked the semicircular fortification belt 21 Jun 44. The 39th Inf captured the German fortress commander and Octeville 26 Jun 44 while the 47th Inf cracked the arsenal the next day, ending resistance in the city. On 29 Jun 44 the 47th and 60th Inf attacked Cap de la Hague Peninsula and secured it quickly.

The division arrived in the Taute sector from Cherbourg on 9 Jul 44 and was hit by German armor which penetrated its lines in the Le Désert region 11 Jul 44. The division pushed slowly against determined opposition as it approached St Lô, reaching the Periers–St Lô road on 18 Jul 44. The 1st Inf Div then passed through its lines into the attack on Marigny 26 Jul 44. The division followed the 3rd Armd Div to occupy positions on the Fromental-Brouze area of highway links on 17 Aug 44 and helped close the Falaise Gap. On 21 Aug 44 it was committed in a defensive role at Mortagne. The division crossed the Marne in the Mieux area 27 Aug 44, and continued pursuit with the 3rd Armd Div east to the Namur-Dinant region. It crossed at Dinant against strong German opposition and established a bridgehead 6 Sep 44. The 47th Inf mopped up Liége while the division displaced to the Huy-Faimes vicinity on 8 Sep 44. The division assembled near Verviers in reserve 11 Sep 44, and on 14 Sep 44 the 47th Inf was sent to the Roetgen Forest while the 60th Inf drove north across Germany's border to secure Kalterherberg and the 39th Inf assaulted the *Scharnhorst* Line past Lammersdorf. By 17 Sep 44 the 47th Inf had battered through the second band of the *West Wall* and taken Vicht and Chevenhuette. The 60th Inf cleared Hoefen on the Hoefen-Alzen Ridge and the 39th Inf reduced a strongpoint after a three-day pitched battle.

The 60th Inf engaged in close-quarters fighting in the Huertgen Forest vicinity, and the 39th Inf took Hill 554 in the *West Wall* after heavy combat 29 Sep 44. Severe weather hampered continued fighting by the 60th Inf, which was reinforced by the 39th Inf, in the Huertgen area. Road Junction 471 in the forest was finally secured 14 Oct 44, but the division had been halted far short of its objective of Schmidt. The 28th Inf Div relieved it, but the 47th Inf — attached to the 1st Inf Div — pushed through the Huertgen Forest 16 Nov 44. On 7 Dec 44 the division relieved the 1st Inf Div in the Luchem-Langerwehe-Juengersdorf-Merode region. It returned to the offensive 10 Dec 44 with the 3rd Armd Div, and went forward to the Roer. When the German Ardennes Counteroffensive struck, the division contained attacks 16 Dec 44 toward Mariaweiler and Guerzenich. It next relieved the 2nd and 99th Inf Divs and defended the Monschau area, restoring the Monschau Forest line by 23 Dec 44. It held the defensive sector from Kalterherberg to Elsenborn through January 1945.

The division opened its next attack on the *West Wall* 30 Jan 45 and had reached Rohren and the edge of the Monschau Forest when it was sent to resume the Roer and Urft River dam offensive on 1 Feb 45. The 39th and 60th Inf reached the high ground southwest of Dreiborn while the 47th Inf cleared heights near Hammer. After house-to-house fighting through several towns, the 47th Inf seized Wollseifen and reached the Urft Lake and took Dam #5. On 7 Feb 45 the division consolidated and was reinforced by both the 309th and 311th Inf for the attack on Schwammenauel Dam which was captured by the former on 9 Feb 45 as the 60th Inf reached the Roer River's banks. The division then switched to the Huertgen Forest sector again and crossed the Roer near Boich on 26 Feb 45. The reinforced 39th Inf pushed toward Thum and Berg, followed by the 60th Inf. The 47th Inf crossed the Roer 28 Feb 45 and the division attacked toward the Rhine with the 9th Armd Div. On 7 Mar 45 the division reached Ramagen bridgehead where the latter had seized the *Ludendorf* Railroad Bridge intact, and took over the site's defense. The division then crossed the Rhine with the 60th Inf in the lead, and crossed the Wied River 22 Mar 45, moving rapidly behind the 9th Armd Div. It reached the Lahn River 28 Mar 45 and established defensive positions.

On 1 Apr 45 the division was moved to block German escape from the Ruhr pocket, and next attacked with the 39th Inf to clear the eastern portion of the Harz Mountains 14 Apr 45. On 18 Apr 45 the 60th Inf overran Maegdesprung and Friedrichsbrunn while the 47th Inf cleared Opperode and the motorized 39th Inf reached Quedlinburg. Organized German resistance in the division's sector ended 19 Apr 45. On 25 Apr 45 the division relieved the 3rd Armd Div along the Mulde River near Dessau and held that line until hostilities were declared ended on 7 May 45.

10th Mountain Division

No Distinctive
Insignia Authorized

15 Jul 43 activated at Cp Hale Colo as 10th Light Division (Pack, Alpine) and moved to Cp Swift Tex 22 Jun 44 where redesignated 10th Mountain Division 6 Nov 44; staged at Cp Patrick Henry Va 27 Dec 44 until departed Hampton Roads P/E 6 Jan 45; completely arrived in Italy 18 Jan 45; returned to Hampton Roads P/E 11 Aug 45 and moved to Cp Carson Colo 16 Aug 45 where inactivated 30 Nov 45.

Campaigns: *North Apennines, Po Valley*
Aug 45 Loc: Entrained from Camp Patrick Henry Virginia to Camp Carson Colorado

Typical Organization (1944/45):

85th Mountain Infantry Regiment
86th Mountain Infantry Regiment
87th Mountain Infantry Regiment*
HHB Division Artillery
604th Field Artillery Battalion (75mm)
605th Field Artillery Battalion (75mm)
616th Field Artillery Battalion (75mm)
10th Mountain Infantry Antitank Bn
1125th Armored Field Artillery Battalion (105mm) *(attached)*

10th Cavalry Reconnaissance Troop, Mecz
126th Mountain Engineer Battalion
10th Mountain Medical Battalion
Headquarters Special Troops
Hqs Company, 10th Mountain Division
Military Police Platoon
710th Ordnance Light Maintenance Company
110th Mountain Signal Company

*Assigned 22 Feb 44 and replaced 90th Infantry Regt which was relieved same date.

Overseas Wartime Assignments:

IV Corps - 15 Jan 45
Fifth Army - 28 Apr 45

Commanders: MG Lloyd E. Jones: Jul 42
MG George P. Hays: Nov 44

Killed in Action: 872   *Wounded in Action:* 3,134   *Died of Wounds:* 81

10th Mountain Division Combat Narrative

The 10th Mountain Division had been activated as the 10th Light Division (Pack, Alpine) at Cp Hale Colo 15 Jul 43 using several specially designated mountain units assembled at the Mountain Training Center which had trained at Lake Placid, Old Forge, and Mt Rainier. It had received intensive training in fighting across snow and mountainous terrain, and its mountaineer and ski personnel represented elite resources which led to the division being redesignated the 10th Mountain Division 6 Nov 44. Elements started leaving for Italy in December 1944, and among its ranks were famous American skiers, mountain climbers, forest rangers, and park and wildlife-service men.

After a brief training period the division entered combat in Italy 8 Jan 45 near Cutigliano and Orsigna. After preliminary defensive actions the division scaled the steep Sarasiccia-Campania cliff and took the German defenders by surprise during the night of 18–19 Feb 45. It made its main effort on the Belvedere-Gorgolesco Hillmass with the 85th and 87th Mtn Inf, omitting artillery preparation to gain surprise. Counterattacks against the Sarasiccia-Campania Ridge were defeated and the division gained the crests of both M.Belvedere and M.Gorgolesco on 20 Feb 45. It advanced against the crest of M.Torraccia in the face of strong German opposition, and reached its summit after heavy fighting on 24 Feb 45.

Next the division made a limited offensive to secure the heights west of Highway 64, which was opened by the 86th and 87th Mtn Inf on 3 Mar 45. The 87th Mtn Inf seized M.Terminale and M.Della Vedetta and blocked the Pietra Colora Road, and then advanced and took M.Acidola and adjacent mountaintops. The 86th Mtn Inf meanwhile cleared M.Grande d'Aiano. The 85th Mtn Inf was committed into the attack on 5 Mar 45 and pushed forward to M.Della Spe where it repulsed several German counterattacks. On 9 Mar 45 the division was able to improve its positions north of Castelnuovo with the unopposed seizures of both M.Valbura and M.Belvedere.

The final offensive was initiated on 14 Apr 45 as the division cleared the Pra del Bianco basin, securing Torre Iussi and Rocca di Roffeno. As the division spearheaded the drive, it took M.Pigna and M.Mantino 15 Apr 45 and went on to capture M.Ferra, S.Prospero, and M.Moscoso on 17 Apr 45. Emerging from the Apennines into the Po Valley, the division crossed Route 9 in the vicinity of Ponte Samoggia on 20 Apr 45. The Panaro River bridge at Bomporto was taken intact on 21 Apr 45 and the division crossed the Po River in assault boats 23 Apr 45, striking north toward the Villafranca Airport, southwest of Verona. After the 85th Mtn Inf made an amphibious crossing of Lake Garda which took Gargnano, the division secured Portio di Tremosine 30 Apr 45. German resistance in Italy formally ended on 2 May 45.

11th Airborne Division

No Distinctive
Insignia Authorized

25 Feb 43 activated at Cp Mackall N.C. as the 11th Airborne Division and participated in the Dec 43 Carolina Airborne-Troop Carrier Command Maneuvers moved to Cp Polk La 4 Jan 44 and staged at Cp Stoneman Calif 23 Apr 44 until departed San Francisco P/E 8 May 44; arrived New Guinea 25 May 44 and left 11 Nov 44; arrived Leyte Philippines 31 Jan 45; arrived Okinawa 12 Aug 45 and arrived Japan 30 Aug 45 where active thru 1946.

Campaigns: *New Guinea, Leyte, Luzon*
Aug 45 Loc: Okinawa

Typical Organization (1944):

187th Glider Infantry Regiment
188th Glider Infantry Regiment
511th Parachute Infantry Regiment
 HHB Division Artillery
457th Prcht Field Artillery Bn (75mm)
674th Glider Field Artillery Bn (75mm)
675th Glider Field Artillery Bn (75mm)
221st Airborne Medical Company

127th Airborne Engineer Battalion
152nd Airborne Antiaircraft Battalion
Headquarters Special Troops
Hqs Company, 11th Airborne Division
Military Police Platoon
711th Airborne Ordnance Maintenance Company
511th Airborne Signal Company
 11th Parachute Maintenance Company

Typical Organization (1945):

187th Glider Infantry Regiment
188th Parachute Infantry Regiment*
511th Parachute Infantry Regiment
 HHB Division Artillery
457th Prcht Field Artillery Bn (75mm)
472nd Glider Field Artillery Bn (75mm)**
674th Prcht Field Artillery Bn (75mm)*
675th Glider Field Artillery Bn (75mm)
221st Airborne Medical Company

127th Airborne Engineer Battalion
152nd Airborne Antiaircraft Battalion
Headquarters Special Troops
Hqs Company, 11th Airborne Division
Military Police Platoon
711th Airborne Ordnance Maintenance Company
511th Airborne Signal Company
408th Airborne Quartermaster Company
 11th Parachute Maintenance Company

 *Converted to Parachute status 20 Jul 45.
**Assigned to division 20 Jul 45.

Overseas Wartime Assignments:

Sixth Army - 25 May 44
X Corps - 24 Aug 44
Sixth Army - 28 Sep 44
Eighth Army - 26 Dec 44

Sixth Army - 9 Feb 45
XIV Corps - 10 Feb 45
Sixth Army - 15 Jun 45
Eighth Army - 15 Aug 45

Commander: MG Joseph M. Swing: Feb 43

Killed in Action: 494   *Wounded in Action:* 1,926   *Died of Wounds:* 120

11th Airborne Division Combat Narrative

The division arrived in New Guinea by echelon 25 May–11 Jun 44 and engaged in airborne training, practiced amphibious landings, and conducted jungle warfare maneuvers. The division departed New Guinea 11 Nov 44 and arrived at Leyte Island Philippines 18 Nov 44, landing on Bito Beach. The 511th Prcht Inf started the difficult march over the mountains from Burauen toward Mahonag 25 Nov 44, and the rest of the division relieved the 7th Inf Div in line in the Burauen–La Pez–Bugho sector 28 Nov 44. It battled Japanese parachutists who landed near the San Pablo airstrip 6 Dec 44 in a five-day engagement, and defended Bayug and Buri airfields. The division pushed west from Mahonag along the Talisayan River to the coastal plain of Ormoc Bay, elements of the 511th Prcht Inf making contact with the 7th Inf Div 15 Dec 44. Major operations on Leyte ended with the destruction of Japanese forces in the Anonang area. From 15–26 Jan 45 the division engaged in rehabilitation and prepared for operations on Luzon.

The division, less 511th Prcht Inf on Mindoro, assaulted the Nasugbu area of western Luzon on 31 Jan 45 and pushed inland toward Tagaytay Ridge with no initial opposition. The 188th Inf met delaying opposition and the 511th Prcht Inf was parachuted along Tagaytay Ridge 3 Feb 45, enabling the division to completely clear it. The 511th Prcht Inf then advanced toward Manila and seized the Paranaque River bridge at the south end of the city on 5 Feb 45. All three regiments were involved in fierce fighting to secure Nichols Field 7–13 Feb 45 and then flanked Fort McKinley 12–16 Feb 45 and captured it on 17 Feb 45. The division next conducted a combined overland, amphibious, and parachute assault to liberate prisoners at the Japanese internment camp at Los Banos 23 Feb 45.

The division commenced operations in southern Luzon 24 Feb 45 and opened Manila Harbor with the reduction of resistance in the Ternate area by 3 Mar 45. The division began operations to open Balayan and Batangas Bays on 5 Mar 45 and by 7 Mar 45 was engaged in reducing a strong ring of Japanese outposts between Lake Taal and Laguna de Bay. The 187th Glider Inf fought the Battle for Hill 660 8–11 Mar 45, and the 511th Inf fought the Battle for Mt Bijang 11–13 Mar 45 when it was forced off. After several days of air and artillery bombardment, the 511th Prcht Inf occupied it without opposition on 19 Mar 45. The 188th Glider Inf relieved the 158th Inf in Batangas 17 Mar 45 and on 24 Mar 45 started attacking north toward Lipa as the 187th Glider Inf opened the drive on Mt Macoled against strong opposition. The 188th Glider Inf secured Lipa Hill 27 Mar 45 and the 187th Glider Inf fought the Battle for Bukel Hill 31 Mar–1 Apr 45. By 4 Apr 45 Mt Malepunyo was isolated and the next day Talisay was captured by the 187th Glider Inf. The division began battling for the foothills south of Mt Malepunyo on 6 Apr 45 and took Atimonan on 10 Apr 45. The 511th Prcht Inf assumed responsibility for Mt Malepunyo 12 Apr 45 as the 187th Glider Inf returned to bypassed Mt Macoled. The 511th Prcht Inf fought the Battle for Mt Malepunyo 15–16 Apr 45 and the 187th Glider Inf fought the Battle for Mt Macoled 18–21 Apr 45. The division surrounded Mt Matassna Bundoc, the last Japanese strongpoint in southern Luzon, 17–26 Apr 45. The Battle for Mt Matassna Bundoc was fought by the 188th Glider Inf, 511th Prcht Inf, and attached 8th Cav 27–30 Apr 45, after which the division mopped up.

The final operation of the division was conducted by the 511th Prcht Inf which parachuted on Camalaniugan Airfield south of Aparri in northern Luzon to assist the 37th Inf Div on 23 Jun 45. It made contact with the 37th Inf Div between Alcala and Paret River on 26 Jun 45. The division staged at Lipa 1 Jul 45 and departed by air 14 Aug 45 to Okinawa where it assembled the next day as the war concluded.

13th Airborne Division

No Distinctive Insignia Authorized

13 Aug 43 activated at Ft Bragg N.C. and moved to Cp Mackall N.C. 17 Jan 44; staged at Cp Shanks N.Y. 20 Jan 45 until departed New York P/E 26 Jan 45 and arrived in France 6 Feb 45; returned to New York P/E 23 Aug 45 and moved to Ft Bragg N.C. 26 Aug 45 where inactivated 25 Feb 46.

Campaigns: *Central Europe*
Aug 45 Loc: Auxerre France

Typical Organization (1944):

88th Glider Infantry Regiment*
326th Glider Infantry Regiment
515th Parachute Infantry Regiment**
HHB Division Artillery
458th Prcht Field Artillery Bn (75mm)
676th Glider Field Artillery Bn (75mm)
677th Glider Field Artillery Bn (75mm)
409th Airborne Quartermaster Company

129th Airborne Engineer Battalion
153rd Airborne Antiaircraft Battalion
222nd Airborne Medical Company
13th Parachute Maintenance Company
Headquarters Special Troops
Hqs Company, 13th Airborne Division
Military Police Platoon
713th Airborne Ordnance Maintenance Company
513th Airborne Signal Company

*Disbanded 1 Mar 45.
**Assigned to division 10 Mar 44 and replaced 513th Prcht Inf Regt which was relieved same date. In 1943 the division contained the 189th and 190th Glider Inf Regts which were disbanded 4–8 Dec 43 and replaced by the 88th and 326th Glider Inf Regts.

Typical Organization (1945):

326th Glider Infantry Regiment
515th Parachute Infantry Regiment
517th Parachute Infantry Regiment***
HHB Division Artillery
458th Prcht Field Artillery Bn (75mm)
460th Prcht Field Artillery Bn (75mm)****
676th Glider Field Artillery Bn (75mm)
677th Glider Field Artillery Bn (75mm)
409th Airborne Quartermaster Company

129th Airborne Engineer Battalion
153rd Airborne Antiaircraft Battalion
222nd Airborne Medical Company
13th Parachute Maintenance Company
Headquarters Special Troops
Hqs Company, 13th Airborne Division
Military Police Platoon
713th Airborne Ordnance Maintenance Company
513th Airborne Signal Company

***Assigned 1 Mar 45.
****Assigned 22 Feb 45.

Overseas Wartime Assignments

XVIII (A/B) Corps - 6 Feb 45
First Allied (A/B) Army - 3 Apr 45

Commanders: MG George W. Griner: Aug 43
MG Elbridge G. Chapman Jr: Nov 45

Killed in Action: None   *Wounded in Action:* None   *Died of Wounds:* None

13th Airborne Division Combat Narrative

The division arrived in France on 6 Feb 45 and was never entered into combat; not being employed in Operation VARSITY, the airborne drop east of the Rhine River, because of insufficient airlift. It remained in France until 15 Aug 45.

17th Airborne Division

No Distinctive
Insignia Authorized

15 Apr 43 activated at Cp Mackall N.C. and participated in the Carolina Airborne-Troop Carrier Command Maneuvers of 6–10 Dec 43 and 5–10 Jan 44; moved to the Tennessee Maneuver Area 6 Feb 44 and took part in the Second Army No.5 Maneuvers; transferred to Cp Forrest Tenn 24 Mar 44 and staged at Cp Myles Standish Mass 12 Aug 44 until departed Boston P/E 20 Aug 44; arrived in England 25 Aug 44 and flown to Rheims France 24 Dec 44; crossed into Belgium 25 Dec 44 and returned to France 11 Feb 45; air-assaulted Wesel Germany 24 Mar 45; returned Boston P/E 15 Sep 45 and inactivated at Cp Myles Standish Mass 16 Sep 45.

Campaigns: *Rhineland, Ardennes-Alsace, Central Europe*
Aug 45 Loc: Essen Germany

Typical Organization (1944):

193rd Glider Infantry Regiment*
194th Glider Infantry Regiment
517th Parachute Infantry Regiment**
 HHB Division Artillery
466th Prcht Field Artillery Bn (75mm)
680th Glider Field Artillery Bn (75mm)
681st Glider Field Artillery Bn (75mm)
 17th Parachute Maintenance Company

139th Airborne Engineer Battalion
155th Airborne Antiaircraft Battalion
224th Airborne Medical Company
Headquarters Special Troops
Hqs Company, 17th Airborne Division
Military Police Platoon
717th Airborne Ordnance Maintenance Company
517th Airborne Signal Company
411th Airborne Quartermaster Company

 *Disbanded 1 Mar 45.
**Relieved from division 10 Mar 44 and replaced by 513th Parachute Infantry Regt.

Typical Organization (1945):

194th Glider Infantry Regiment
507th Parachute Infantry Regiment***
513th Parachute Infantry Regiment
 HHB Division Artillery
464th Prcht Field Artillery Bn (75mm)****
466th Prcht Field Artillery Bn (75mm)
680th Glider Field Artillery Bn (75mm)
681st Glider Field Artillery Bn (75mm)
 17th Parachute Maintenance Company
411th Airborne Quartermaster Company
761st Tank Battalion *(attached 15 Jan 45–27 Jan 45)*
811th Tank Destroyer Battalion *(attached 17 Jan 45–27 Jan 45)*

139th Airborne Engineer Battalion
155th Airborne Antiaircraft Battalion
224th Airborne Medical Company
Headquarters Special Troops
Hqs Company, 17th Airborne Division
Military Police Platoon
717th Airborne Ordnance Maintenance Company
517th Airborne Signal Company
 17th Counter Intelligence Corps Det
Reconnaissance Platoon

 ***Attached 27 Aug 44–1 Mar 45 and assigned to division 1 Mar 45.
****Assigned 4 Jun 45.

Overseas Wartime Assignments:

XVIII (A/B) Corps - 12 Aug 44
VIII Corps - 1 Jan 45
III Corps - 26 Jan 45
First Allied (A/B) Army - 6 Feb 45
XVIII (A/B) Corps - 15 Feb 45
12th Army Group (attached) - 24 Mar 45
Ninth Army (attached) - 30 Mar 45

XIII Corps - 31 Mar 45
First Allied (A/B) Army - 4 Apr 45
XVI Corps - 6 Apr 45
Ninth Army (attached to Fifteenth Army) - 25 Apr 45
XXII Corps - 27 Apr 45

Commander: MG William M. Miley: Apr 43

Killed in Action: 1,191   *Wounded in Action:* 4,904   *Died of Wounds:* 191

17th Airborne Division Combat Narrative

The division was flown to the Reims area of France 23–25 Dec 44 by emergency night flights and assembled at Mourmelon. The division defended the Meuse River from Givet to Verdun 27–31 Dec 45 and relieved the 28th Inf Div in the
Neufchâteau area 1 Jan 45. It attacked 3 Jan 45 five miles northwest of Bastogne and was strongly opposed at Dead
Man's Ridge, capturing Rechrival and Flamierge on 7 Jan 45. The division gained and then lost the high ground north
of Laval and was forced out of Flamierge by German counterattack on 8 Jan 45. On 11 Jan 45 the German forces commenced withdrawal and the division moved up to retake Flamierge the next day. Salle fell without opposition on
13 Jan 45, and the following day the 507th Prcht Inf secured Bertogne while the 194th Glider Inf took Givroulle and the
division reached the Ourthe River. It took over the Hardingny-Houffalize line on 18 Jan 45 and by 20 Jan 45 had
advanced beyond Tavigny. Steinbach and Limerle were occupied 22 Jan 45 and the division continued behind the
retreating Germans to take Espeler and Wattermal by 26 Jan 45, when it was relieved by the 87th Inf Div. The division
then began clearing operations and on 6 Feb 45 assaulted to the Our River which the 507th Prcht Inf crossed north of
Dasburg. The bridgehead came under heavy attack and the 6th Armd Div relieved the division on 10 Feb 45. It then
started to Châlons-sur-Marne for reserve duty.

The division made an airborne assault east of the Rhine River north of Wesel on 24 Mar 45 and took Diersfordt and
the high ground to the east, containing strong German counterattacks. The next day the 194th Glider Inf and 507th
Prcht Inf attacked across the Issel Canal. By 27 Mar 45 the 194th Glider Inf took positions near the Erle-Schermbeck
Road and the 513th Prcht Inf assisted the *British 6th Guards Armored Brigade* attack toward Dorsten. The following
day the 507th Prcht Inf overran Wulfen. The 194th Glider Inf was motored to Duelmen as the 2nd Armd Div began
passing through and relieved the division. The division crossed the Rhine River at Wesel on 31 Mar 45 and cleared
Muenster 2–3 Apr 45.

The division started to the Duisburg region on 5 Apr 45 and relieved the 79th Inf Div of defensive positions along the
Rhine-Herne Canal the next day. The 507th Prcht Inf attacked across the canal on 8 Apr 45 and cleared to the Berne
Canal by 9 Apr 45. The 507th Prcht Inf seized Essen without opposition on 10 Apr 45. The following day the division
cleared scattered resistance from the Mulheim-Duisburg sector of the Ruhr region, the 507th Prcht Inf gaining a
small bridgehead at Mulheim which it turned over to the 79th Inf Div. The division received the formal surrender of
Duisburg and began relief of the 79th Inf Div on 12 Apr 45. It then engaged in military government duties until hostilities were declared ended on 7 May 45.

24th Infantry Division

No Distinctive
Insignia Authorized

1 Oct 41 redesignated from the Hawaiian Division at Schofield Barracks Hawaii and moved to
Australia 8 Aug 43; arrived at Goodenough Island 15 Feb 44 and assaulted Tanahmerah Bay
New Guinea 22 Apr 44; assaulted Leyte Philippines 20 Oct 44 and landed on Mindoro 29 Jan 45
and arrived on Mindanao 17 Apr 45; departed Philippines 15 Oct 45 and arrived Japan 22 Oct
45 where active thru 1946.

Campaigns: *Central Pacific, New Guinea, Leyte, Southern Philippines, Luzon*
Aug 45 Loc: Davao Mindanao Philippine Islands

Typical Organization (1941):

19th Infantry Regiment
21st Infantry Regiment
299th Infantry Regiment*
HHB Division Artillery
11th Field Artillery Battalion (155mm)
13th Field Artillery Battalion (105mm)
52nd Field Artillery Battalion (105mm)
63rd Field Artillery Battalion (105mm)

Headquarters, 24th Infantry Division
Headquarters & Military Police Company
3rd Engineer Combat Battalion
24th Medical Battalion
24th Quartermaster Battalion
24th Signal Company
24th Reconnaissance Troop

*Inactivated 21 Jul 42

Typical Organization (1944/45):

19th Infantry Regiment
21st Infantry Regiment
34th Infantry Regiment**
HHB Division Artillery
11th Field Artillery Battalion (155mm)
13th Field Artillery Battalion (105mm)
52nd Field Artillery Battalion (105mm)
63rd Field Artillery Battalion (105mm)
24th Reconnaissance Troop, Mecz

3rd Engineer Combat Battalion
24th Medical Battalion
24th Counter Intelligence Corps Det
Headquarters Special Troops
Hqs Company, 24th Infantry Division
Military Police Platoon
724th Ordnance Light Maintenance Company
24th Quartermaster Company
24th Signal Company

**Assigned 12 Jun 43 and replaced the 298th Inf Regt which had been assigned to division 23 Jul 42–12 Jun 43 and attached 12–16 Jun 43.

Overseas Wartime Assignments:

Hawaiian Dept - 1 Oct 41
I Corps*** - 8 Aug 43
Sixth Army***-15 Jun 44
I Corps***-29 Jun 44

X Corps - 26 Sep 44
Eighth Army - 26 Dec 44
X Corps - 15 Aug 45

***Attached RECKLESS Task Force (redesig BEWITCH 17 Apr 44) from 23 Mar 44–25 Sep 44.

Commanders: MG Durward S. Wilson: Oct 41
MG Frederick A. Irving: Aug 42

MG Roscoe B. Woodruff: Nov 44
BG Kenneth F. Cramer: Nov 45

Killed in Action: 1,374   *Wounded in Action:* 5,621   *Died of Wounds:* 315

24th Infantry Division Combat Narrative

The division was stationed at Schofield Barracks Hawaii when Japanese planes attacked it 7 Dec 41 and directed as a result to build an elaborate system of coastal defenses on northern Oahu. In May 43 it was alerted to Australia and completed movement there by echelon 8 Sep 43, training at Cp Caves near Rockhampton. It staged and rehearsed at Goodenough Island 15 Feb 44, after which the 19th and 21st Inf landed at Tanahmerah Bay New Guinea 22 Apr 44 and the 34th Inf went ashore at Humboldt Bay. Despite torrential rains and marshy terrain the 21st Inf overran the Hollandia airdrome and linked up with the 41st Inf Div 26 Apr 44. The division engaged in extensive patrolling of its area until 6 Jun 44. On 15 Jun 44 the 34th Inf was detached to Biak Island where it seized both Boroke and Sorido airdromes 20 Jun 44 and then mopped up, rejoining the division 17 Jul 44.

After occupation duty at Hollandia, New Guinea, the division assaulted Leyte Philippines on 20 Oct 44, the 21st Inf landing in the Panaon Straight area and the rest of the division assaulting the Palo-Pawing area, seizing key Hill 522 in heavy combat. The 34th Inf was subjected to a fierce Japanese counterattack 21 Oct 44 while the 19th Inf took Palo and underwent counterattacks. The 34th Inf, supported by naval gunfire and air support, secured its Pawing area and both regiments pushed into the Leyte Valley 26 Oct 44 where they linked up with the 1st Cav Div converging on Carigara near the northern entrance of Ormoc Valley on 2 Nov 44. The 21st Inf relieved the 34th Inf at Breakneck Ridge west of Pinamopoan 5 Nov 44 and assaulted it despite a raging typhoon 8 Nov 44, gaining its crest finally on 12 Nov 44. The 32nd Inf Div relieved the division 17 Nov 44 and it moved to Jaro and Cavite, attaching the 19th Inf to Sixth Army 20 Nov 44 for operations on Mindoro as the major unit of the Western Visayan Task Force. The 34th Inf battled for Kilray Ridge until 2 Dec 44 under the 32nd Inf Div and then moved to Calubian and over water to beach defense at Pinamopoan with the division. The 19th Inf invaded Mindoro 15 Dec 44 between Caminawit Pt and San

Agustin, being joined by the 21st Inf which became part of the Western Visayan Task Force also 30 Dec 44. The division sent its remaining 34th Inf to clear the northwest part of Leyte, and it landed at Taglawigan 27 Dec 44 to accomplish its mission.

On 3 Jan 45 the 21st Inf landed on Marinduque Island and then returned to Mindoro, where the division arrived entirely 29 Jan 45. The 34th Inf landed at San Antonio and suffered heavy losses at the Battle of Zig Zag Pass. The 19th Inf was sent to Luzon 10 Feb 45 and attached to the 11th A/B Div to assist its drive from Nasugbu to Manila. The 19th Inf sent a battalion against Corregidor Island 16 Feb 43 to assist paratroopers air-assaulting the fortress. The division meanwhile landed the 19th Inf on Verde Island 23 Feb 45 and cleared several adjacent islands by 25 Mar 45 which included Lubang, Ambil, Cabra, Golo, Romblon, and Simara; the 34th Inf joining these operations 28 Feb 45 and the 19th Inf joining the offensive 7 Mar 45.

The division landed the 21st Inf at Baras and the 19th Inf at Parang on Mindanao on 17 Apr 45. Filipino forces were already in possession of Malabang, and the division drove overland along Highway 1 with the 19th Inf as the 21st Inf made amphibious drives up two branches of the Mindanao River. On 19 Apr 45 the 34th Inf in reserve was landed at Parang to reinforce, and moved by water to occupy undefended Fort Pikit and seized the junction of Highway 1 and the Sayre Highway the following day. On 24 Apr 45 the 34th Inf led the division push onto Digos on Davao Gulf. Despite demolitions and delaying obstacles the 19th Inf bypassed and contained Hill 550 commanding the Davao approaches on 1 May 45, and stormed the city 3 May 45. The 34th Inf reduced a Japanese pocket in the Guma sector and the 21st Inf, supported by massed artillery fires, attacked along the Talamo River 12 May 43. The 19th Inf and 34th Inf tackled Hill 550, which fell to the latter after a battle of several days on 21 May 45. As the division continued to clear the Talamo River Valley the 19th Inf captured Mandog 9 Jun 45. The end of organized Japanese resistance on Mindanao was declared 30 Jun 45, but the division continued operations in the Kibangay area. The 21st Inf landed at Sarangani Bay and secured the area 12 Jul 45. The division continued mopping up, patrolling, and performing security on Mindanao until the end of the war.

25th Infantry Division

No Distinctive Insignia Authorized

1 Oct 41 activated at Schofield Barracks Hawaii; relieved of Oahu defensive missions 2 Nov 42 and underwent jungle and amphibious warfare training; arrived Guadalcanal 23 Dec 42 and moved to Sasavele Island 1 Aug 43 en route to New Georgia Island 2 Aug 43; returned to Guadalcanal 25 Oct 43 and arrived New Zealand 9 Nov 43; went to New Caledonia 8 Feb 44 and back to Guadalcanal 21 Dec 44; arrived Tulagi Island 23 Dec 44 and Manus Island 29 Dec 44 enroute to Philippines where landed San Fabian Luzon 11 Jan 45; arrived Japan 28 Oct 45 where active thru 1946.

Campaigns: *Central Pacific, Northern Solomons, Guadalcanal, Luzon*
Aug 45 Loc: Bambam Philippine Islands

Typical Organization (1941):

27th Infantry Regiment
35th Infantry Regiment
298th Infantry Regiment
HHB Division Artillery
 8th Field Artillery Battalion (105mm)
64th Field Artillery Battalion (105mm)
89th Field Artillery Battalion (105mm)
90th Field Artillery Battalion (155mm)

Headquarters, 25th Infantry Division
Headquarters & Military Police Company
65th Engineer Battalion
25th Medical Battalion
25th Quartermaster Battalion
25th Signal Company
25th Reconnaissance Troop

Typical Organization (1944/45):

27th Infantry Regiment
35th Infantry Regiment
161st Infantry Regiment*
HHB Division Artillery
 8th Field Artillery Battalion (105mm)
64th Field Artillery Battalion (105mm)
89th Field Artillery Battalion (105mm)
90th Field Artillery Battalion (155mm)
25th Reconnaissance Troop, Mecz

65th Engineer Combat Battalion
25th Medical Battalion
25th Counter Intelligence Corps Det
Headquarters Special Troops
Hqs Company, 25th Infantry Division
Military Police Platoon
725th Ordnance Light Maintenance Company
25th Quartermaster Company
25th Signal Company

*Assigned 23 Jul 42 and replaced 298th Infantry Regt which was relieved same date.

100

Overseas Wartime Assignments:

Hawaiian Dept - Oct 41   Sixth Army - 17 Dec 44
XIV Corps - 2 Jan 43   I Corps (attached) - 16 Jan 45

Commanders: MG Maxwell Murray: Oct 41
MG J. Lawton Collins: May 42
MG Charles L. Mullins Jr: Jan 44

Killed in Action: 1,235   *Wounded in Action:* 4,190   *Died of Wounds:* 262

25th Infantry Division Combat Narrative

The division first saw combat during the Japanese 7 Dec 41 attack on Pearl Harbor, and was moved to beach positions to defend Honolulu and Ewa Plains against possible invasion. On 2 Nov 42 it was relieved of this defensive mission and given intensive training in jungle and amphibious warfare. The division began moving from Hawaii 25 Nov 42 and landed on Guadalcanal with the 35th Inf 17 Dec 42, the 27th Inf on 1 Jan 43, and the 161st Inf on 4 Jan 43.

The 35th Inf attacked Mt Austen 7 Jan 43 where some of the fiercest fighting in the Pacific was destined to take place, and on 10 Jan 43 the 27th Inf attacked Galloping Horse hillmass as the 35th Inf pushed up Seahorse Hill. After a temporary withdrawal due to the threat of large Japanese counterattacks, the division resumed the advance on Cape Esperance, the 161st Inf crossing the Umasani River 7 Feb 43 and reaching Bunina Pt. It linked up with the Americal Division at Tenero Village 9 Feb 43 and a period of garrison duty for the division on Guadalcanal followed.

The 161st Inf landed on New Georgia Island 22 Jul 43 and reinforced the 37th Inf Div, running into tenacious resistance as it tried to reach its lines of departure for the Munda attack. It assaulted contested Bartley Ridge which it cleared 31 Jul 43 with the help of the 145th Inf. The 27th Inf landed on Sasavele Island 1 Aug 43 and the following day the division landed on New Georgia. Munda fell 5 Aug 43 and the division was given the mission of pushing to Bairoko and Zieta and finishing off remaining opposition. The 27th Inf made a difficult cross-jungle-swamp trek to reach Piru Plantation and take Zieta 15 Aug 43. The 27th Inf, assisted by the 145th Inf, occupied Bairoko Harbor 25 Aug 43 and New Georgia was declared secured. The 35th Inf landed on Vella LaVella Island in the meantime on 15 Aug 43, and pushed east along the coast to attack Kokolope Bay 14 Sep 43. After month-long combat the island was secured 15 Sep 43. The 27th Inf was sent to Arundel to assist the 43rd Inf Div, and attacked 17 Sep 43 toward Stima Peninsula which the Japanese abandoned 21 Sep 43. The 27th Inf next made unopposed landings on Kolombangara 6 Oct 43 and brought the Central Solomons campaign to a close.

The division went to New Zealand 5 Dec 43 and engaged in rehabilitation and training. Its projected operation against Kavieng New Britain was cancelled 1 Jun 44 and the division landed in the San Fabian area of Luzon 11 Jan 45. On 16 Jan 45 it began operations on the central Luzon Plain of the Philippines, the 161st Inf securing San Manuel after heavy fighting which started 24 Jan 45. The 27th Inf took Umingan 2 Feb 45 and the 161st Inf seized San Isidro 4 Feb 45, cutting Japanese forces on Luzon in two. The 35th Inf finally captured Lupao after a pitched battle on 8 Feb 45 which cleared the central plain. The division redeployed to La Paz and prepared to assault the Caraballo Mountains. The offensive was initiated 21 Feb 45 as the division drove up Highway 5 toward Balete Pass. The 161st Inf captured Bryant Hill northwest of Puncan 25 Feb 45 and the 35th Inf captured Puncan 2 Mar 45 and opened the road as far as Digdig by 5 Mar 45. The division's 27th and 161st Inf pushed forward along Highway 5 while the 35th Inf moved up Old Spanish Trail. All encountered determined opposition and strong counterattacks. On 15 Mar 45 the division began the battle for Norton's Knob where entrenched Japanese repulsed attacks for the next ten days. Putlan fell 18 Mar 45, but Kapintalan was not captured until 19 Apr 45 following the Battle for Fishhook Ridge (35th Inf, 2 Apr 45), Crump Hill (161st Inf, 8–13 Apr 45), and Mt Myoko (27th Inf, 9–19 Apr 45). The 35th Inf was the first to enter that city as it secured Mt Myoko.

The division made a contested three-pronged drive on Balete Pass next. The 161st Inf took Lone Tree Hill on 25 Apr 45. The division was reinforced by the 148th and 126th Inf but the pass itself was not taken until 13 May 45 after a fierce battle for Kapintalan Ridge involving both the 27th and 35th Inf which had to seal over 200 caves. The division regrouped and the 27th Inf captured Santa Fe on 27 May 45, following which the division conducted mopping-up operations along Skyline Ridge and maintained a block on Old Spanish Trail. It relieved the 37th Inf Div south of Aritao 10 Jun 45 and secured Highway 5, and all Japanese bypassed by earlier operations, until relieved by the 32nd Inf Div 30 Jun 45. It then moved south of Tarlac for rehabilitation where it was when the war ended.

26th Infantry Division — Massachusetts National Guard

16 Jan 41 inducted into federal service at Boston Mass as the 26th Division and moved to Cp Edwards Mass 21 Jan 41; went to Ft Jackson-Bragg area 1 Oct 41 for the Oct and Nov 41 Carolina Maneuvers; returned Cp Edwards Mass 6 Dec 41 where redesignated 26th Infantry Division 12 Feb 42; moved to A.P. Hill Mil Res Va 9 Jul 42 and to Ft Dupont Del 9 Oct 42; arrived Ft Jackson S.C. 27 Jan 43 and Cp Gordon Ga 18 Apr 43; moved to Cp Campbell Ky 1 Sep 43 and to the Tenn Maneuver Area 24 Jan 44 for the Second Army No.5 Tennessee Maneuvers; returned to Ft Jackson S.C. 30 Mar 44 and staged at Cp Shanks N.Y. 20 Aug 44 until departed New York P/E 27 Aug 44; landed in France 7 Sep 44 and crossed into Luxembourg 19 Dec 44; returned to France 28 Jan 45 and entered Germany 7 Mar 45 and Austria 2 May 45 and Czechoslovakia 6 May 45; inactivated in Germany 29 Dec 45.

Campaigns: *Northern France, Rhineland, Ardennes-Alsace, Central Europe*
Aug 45 Loc: Passau Germany

Typical Organization (1941):

51st Infantry Brigade HHC
  101st Infantry Regiment
  182nd Infantry Regiment*
52nd Infantry Brigade HHC
  104th Infantry Regiment
  181st Infantry Regiment
51st Field Artillery Brigade HHB
  101st Field Artillery Regiment (75mm)
  102nd Field Artillery Regiment (75mm)
  180th Field Artillery Regiment (155mm)

Headquarters, 26th Division
Hqs and Hqs Det
Medical Det
Headquarters Company
  26th Military Police Company
  26th Signal Company
101st Ordnance Company
101st Engineers (Combat)
101st Medical Regiment
101st Quartermaster Regiment

*Relieved from division 14 Jan 42.

Typical Organization (1944/45):

101st Infantry Regiment
104th Infantry Regiment
328th Infantry Regiment**
 HHB Division Artillery
101st Field Artillery Battalion (105mm)
180th Field Artillery Battalion (155mm)
263rd Field Artillery Battalion (105mm)
102nd Field Artillery Battalion (105mm)
  26th Reconnaissance Troop, Mecz
735th Tank Battalion *(attached 21 Dec 44–25 Jan 45)*
761st Tank Battalion *(attached 29 Oct 44–12 Dec 44)*
778th Tank Battalion *(attached 29 Jan 45–16 Feb 45, 19 Mar 45–20 Jul 45)*
602nd Tank Destroyer Battalion *(attached 23 Oct 44–12 Dec 44)*
610th Tank Destroyer Battalion *(attached 12 Nov 44–12 Dec 44)*
691st Tank Destroyer Battalion *(attached 15 Oct 44–7 Dec 44)*
704th Tank Destroyer Battalion *(attached 14 Oct 44–16 Oct 44)*
818th Tank Destroyer Battalion *(attached 21 Dec 44–20 Jul 45)*
390th AAA Auto-Wpns Battalion *(attached 14 Oct 44–25 May 45)*

101st Engineer Combat Battalion
114th Medical Battalion
  26th Counter Intelligence Corps Det
Headquarters Special Troops
Hqs Company, 26th Infantry Division
Military Police Platoon
726th Ordnance Light Maintenance Company
  26th Quartermaster Company
  39th Signal Company

**Assigned 12 Feb 43 and replaced 181st Inf Regt which was relieved 27 Jan 43.

Overseas Wartime Assignments:

Ninth Army - 28 Aug 44
III Corps - 5 Sep 44
Third Army - 28 Sep 44
XII Corps - 1 Oct 44

III Corps - 12 Dec 44
XX Corps - 28 Jan 45
XII Corps - 23 Mar 45

Commanders: MG Roger W. Eckfeldt: Jan 41
    MG Willard S. Paul: Aug 43
    MG Harlan N. Hartness: Jun 45

MG Stanley E. Reinhart: Jul 45
MG Robert W. Grow: Nov 45

Killed in Action: 1,850   *Wounded in Action:* 7,886   *Died of Wounds:* 262

26th Infantry Division Combat Narrative

The division arrived at Cherbourg and Utah Beach France 7 Sep 44, relieved the 4th Armd Div 7 Oct 44, and maintained defensive positions in the Salonnes-Moncourt area. Its 328th Inf saw action with the 80th Inf Div in early Oct 44 during the drive on the Seille River. The division made a limited attack 22 Oct 44 west of Moncourt, and on 8 Nov 44 went on the offensive with three regiments abreast, seizing Vic-sur-Seille and its bridges intact. The 101st Inf battled up Hill 310 which it took 11 Nov 44 as the 104th Inf pushed to Rodalbe, and the 328th Inf stormed Berange Farm strongpoint the following day and entered Koecking Ridge Forest. The division kept advancing against strong German opposition but was forced to a halt on the Diéuze-Benestroff line 19 Nov 44. As the Germans withdrew,the 104th Inf took Marimont and the 328th Inf occupied Diéuze on 20 Nov 44, assisted by the 4th Armd Div. The division advanced rapidly behind the retreating Germans, but on 21 Nov 44 several elements of the 104th Inf were isolated at Albestroff. Flooding, mines, and German fire compounded the difficulty in enveloping the important crossroads town, and the 328th Inf was sent into the attack to assist the 101st Inf. Albestroff was finally taken again 23 Nov 44, but skillful rearguard actions kept the 328th Inf out of Honskirch until 27 Nov 44. The 101st Inf participated in 4th Armd Div's drive east of the Sarre. Both the 101st and 104th Inf took Sarre-Union in house-to-house fighting which lasted until 4 Dec 44.

The division regrouped after reaching the Maginot fortifications 7 Dec 44, and the 328th Inf attacked Fort Wittring at dawn 9 Dec 44 as Réderching fell to the 104th Inf the following day. The division was training replacements at Metz when the German Ardennes Counteroffensive struck 16 Dec 44, and the division was moved north to Luxembourg 20 Dec 44. On 22 Dec 44 it attacked in the Rambrouch-Grosbous vicinity and cleared Arsdorf after heavy fighting on 25 Dec 44 and pushed on to the Wiltz River. Its attacks there were repulsed and the division again regrouped 5-8 Jan 45, forcing a small bridgehead near Oberwampach across the Wiltz with the 328th Inf 20 Jan 45. Wiltz itself was captured on 22 Jan 45 and the division reached the Clerf River and took Clerf with the 101st Inf on 25 Jan 45. The division then maintained defensive positions in the Saarlautern area until 6 Mar 45.

It attacked toward the Rhine 13 Mar 45 with the 104th and 328th Inf in the lead, the former seizing the Prims River bridge at Huettersdorf 17 Mar 45 as the 328th Inf cleared Merzig and Haustadt. The Rhine was reached 21 Mar 45 and the division assembled at Alzey, and crossed the river at Oppenheim 26 Mar 45, moving into the Hanau bridgehead. The 101st and 328th Inf, reinforced by tanks of the 4th Armd Div, cleared the town in house-to-house fighting which lasted until 28 Mar 45. The 11th Armd Div then pushed through the division's bridgehead toward Fulda, and the division followed in its wake. Now well to the rear of the rapidly advancing American armor, the 101st Inf took Fulda 2 Apr 45 and on 4 Apr 45 the division crossed the Werra River in the Schmalkalden-Wasungen region. The division relieved the 11th Armd Div on 6 Apr 45 and established outposts near Themar.

The division reached the Nahe River 8 Apr 45 from Schmiedefeld to Rappelsdorf where link-up with the 11th Armd Div was again effected. The division entered the difficult Thuringer Wald 10 Apr 45 and reached the restraining line from Hof to Gefrees on 15 Apr 45. Continuing southeast along the Danube, the division closed the Ilz River 30 Apr 45 as the 104th Inf took positions beyond Hauzenberg without opposition, and the 328th Inf established a bridgehead across the river at Strasskirchen. The division crossed the Austrian border 1 May 45 with the 101st Inf screening behind the leading 104th and 328th Inf, all of which were trailing the 11th Armd Div. The division assisted in the capture of Linz 4 May 45. As hostilities came to a declared close on 7 May 45, the division was driving to the Vlatava River line southeast of Volary in Czechoslovakia.

27th Infantry Division   New York National Guard

15 Oct 40 inducted into federal service at New York N.Y. as the 27th Division and moved to Ft McClellan Ala 25 Oct 40; moved to Cp Forrest Tenn 21 May 41 and participated in the VII Corps Tennessee Maneuvers; returned to Ft McClellan Ala 29 Jun 41 and went to the Sabine Area Ark 6 Aug 41 for the VII Corps Arkansas Maneuvers and the Sep 41 Louisiana Maneuvers; returned Ft McClellan Ala 3 Oct 41 and moved to Riverside Calif 21 Dec 41; arrived San Francisco P/E 28 Feb 42 and departed 10 Mar 42; arrived Hawaii 20 Mar 42 where redesignated 27th Infantry Division 1 Sep 42; began combat training program 13 Aug 43 when relieved of island defense; left Hawaii 31 May 44 and landed on Saipan 17 Jun 44; arrived Espiritu Santo 18 Aug 44 and left 25 Mar 45; landed on Okinawa 9 Apr 45; went to Japan 7 Sep 45 and arrived Seattle P/E 24 Dec 45 and inactivated at Ft Lawton Wash 31 Dec 45.

Campaigns: *Central Pacific, Western Pacific, Ryukyus*
Aug 45 Loc: Okinawa

Typical Organization (1941):

53rd Infantry Brigade HHC
  105th Infantry Regiment
  106th Infantry Regiment
54th Infantry Brigade HHC
  108th Infantry Regiment*
  165th Infantry Regiment*
52nd Field Artillery Brigade HHB
  104th Field Artillery Regiment (75mm)
  105th Field Artillery Regiment (75mm)
  106th Field Artillery Regiment (155mm)

Headquarters, 27th Division
Hqs and Hqs Det
Medical Det
Headquarters Company
  27th Military Police Company
  27th Signal Company
102nd Ordnance Company
102nd Engineers (Combat)
102nd Medical Regiment
102nd Quartermaster Regiment

*Relieved from division 1 Sep 42. During the period 1 Sep 42–30 Oct 42 the division exchanged the 160th Infantry Regt for the 165th Infantry Regt.

Typical Organization (1944/45):

105th Infantry Regiment
106th Infantry Regiment
165th Infantry Regiment
 HHB Division Artillery
104th Field Artillery Battalion (105mm)
105th Field Artillery Battalion (105mm)
106th Field Artillery Battalion (155mm)
249th Field Artillery Battalion (105mm)
  27th Reconnaissance Troop, Mecz

102nd Engineer Combat Battalion
102nd Medical Battalion
  27th Counter Intelligence Corps Det
Headquarters Special Troops
Hqs Company, 27th Infantry Division
Military Police Platoon
727th Ordnance Light Maintenance Company
  27th Quartermaster Company
  27th Signal Company

Overseas Wartime Assignments:

Hawaiian Dept - 10 Mar 42
Central Pacific Area Cmd - 14 Aug 43
V Amphibious Corps *(attached)* - 13 Sep 43
XXIV Corps - 13 Apr 44
V Amphibious Corps - 15 Apr 44
Central Pacific Base Cmd - 1 Jul 44

Army Garrison Force Saipan - 30 Jul 44
South Pacific Base Cmd - 7 Sep 44
Tenth Army - 26 Nov 44
XXIV Corps - 9 Apr 45
Okinawa Island Cmd *(attached)* - 2 May 45
Army Garrison Force APO 331 - 19 Jul 45
Tenth Army - 30 Jul 45

Commanders: MG William N. Haskell: Oct 40
             BG Ralph McT. Pennell: Nov 41

MG Ralph C. Smith: Nov 42
MG George W. Griner Jr: Jun 44

Killed in Action: 1,512   *Wounded in Action:* 4,980   *Died of Wounds:* 332

27th Infantry Division Combat Narrative

The division moved to Hawaii in echelon 28 Feb–29 Mar 42 and there was assigned the defense of the outer islands until 2 Nov 42 when it was relieved of this mission, and moved to Oahu to assume the defense of Hawaii's south sector combined with training. A division task force based on the 165th Inf and 3rd Bn 105th Inf left Hawaii 10 Nov 43 for operations in the Marshalls, and invaded Butaritari Island Makin Atoll 20 Nov 43, the Japanese being defeated by 23 Nov 43. This task force returned to Hawaii on 2 Dec 43. The 106th Inf left Hawaii 23 Jan 44 for the Marshalls and assaulted Majuro 1 Feb 44 and the lagoon shore of Eniwetok Island 19 Feb 44. It garrisoned that island until returned to Hawaii 13 Apr 44.

The division began preparation for the Marianas operation 15 Mar 44 and departed Hawaii by echelon 25 May–1 Jun 44. On the night of 16 Jun 44 the 165th Inf was landed on Saipan to support the heavily engaged 4th Marine Div, and the 105th Inf was landed on the island the day following. The 165th Inf was supported by artillery and naval gunfire as it cleared Aslito Airfield and the surrounding heights 18 Jun 44. The 105th and 165th Inf then moved over rugged terrain and attacked Nafutan Point, and the 106th Inf was landed on Saipan 20 Jun 44. On 23 Jun 44 the division was committed in the cave-studded heights as the 106th Inf assaulted Death Valley and the 165th Inf fought on Purple Heart Ridge. The 106th In began reducing Hell's Pocket 28 Jun 44 and had cleared both Death Valley and Purple Heart Ridge by 30 Jun 44. Attacking with all three regiments, the division gained positions commanding Tanapag Plain, and on 4 Jul 44 the 106th Inf reached the seaplane base at Flores Pt. A Japanese counterattack smashed the 105th Inf 7 Jul 44, and the 165th Inf moved to block it. Isolated division troops had to be pulled off the island by water. The 165th Inf then cleared Harakiri Gulch and Saipan was declared secure 9 Jul 44, although the division continued to mop up in the mountains and cliffs of the island throughout August.

The division moved to Espiritu Santo 7 Aug–4 Oct 44 for rehabilitation and initiated specialized training for the upcoming Ryukyus operations. It left Espiritu Santo on 25 Mar 45 and arrived off Ulithi 3 Apr 45 where it was directed to Okinawa and the 105th Inf detached to operate against Kerama Retto. The division landed across the Hagushi Beaches on Okinawa 9 Apr 45 and established its command post at Kadena Airfield. The following day the 105th Inf assaulted Tsugen Shima and captured it by 11 Apr 45, after which it rejoined the division on Okinawa 13 Apr 45. The division participated in the 19 Apr 45 general assault against the outer belt of the Shuri defenses after heavy naval and air preparation which proved to have little effect on the well-organized system of Japanese cave and tunnel positions. The 106th Inf was halted at the Urasoe-Mura Escarpment which was only secured after the defeat of several Japanese counterattacks and a fierce battle which ended 23 Apr 45. The 105th Inf battled up Kakazu Ridge in a costly attack which also claimed 22 tanks, and a gap developed between it and the 96th Inf Div. The 165th Inf was committed 20 Apr 45 and became engaged in the Battle for Item Pocket which lasted until 27 Apr 45. The division made limited efforts to improve its positions, and captured contested Machinato Airfield 28 Apr 45, and on 1 May 45 was relieved by the 1st Marine Div and moved to Nago for rest.

On 3 May 45 the division detached a battalion from the 106th Inf for garrison duty on Ie Shima Island, and on 12 May 45 division elements landed unopposed and secured Tora Shima. The division then attacked from the south end of Ishikawa Isthmus to sweep the northern portion of Okinawa. The Battle for Onnatake Hill was fought 23 May–2 Jun 45, and the division finally reached the northern tip of Okinawa on 4 Aug 45. It returned to Onna to resume garrison duty 8 Aug 45 where it was located when the war ended.

28th Infantry Division   Pennsylvania National Guard

17 Feb 41 inducted into federal service at Philadelphia Pa as the 28th Division and moved to Indiantown Gap Mil Res Pa 21 Feb 41; went to A.P. Hill Mil Res Va 26 Aug 41 and returned Indiantown Gap 14 Sep 41; moved to Ft Jackson–Ft Bragg area 29 Sep 41 for the Oct and Nov 41 Carolina Maneuvers; returned Indiantown Gap Pa 9 Dec 41 and moved to Cp Livingston La 19 Jan 42 where redesignated 28th Infantry Division 17 Feb 42; moved to La Maneuver Area 18 Sep 42 and participated in IV Corps Louisiana Maneuvers and returned to Cp Livingston La 10 Nov 42; transferred to Cp Gordon Johnston Fla 27 Jan 43; arrived Cp Pickett Va 6 Jun 43 and participated in the XIII Corps West Virginia–Norfolk Maneuvers 2 Aug 30–30 Sep 43; departed Boston P/E 8 Oct 43 and arrived in England 18 Oct 43; landed in France 22 Jul 44 and crossed into Belgium 7 Sep 44 and into Luxembourg 8 Sep 44; first entered Germany 11 Sep 44; returned to Luxembourg 18 Dec 44 and to France 2 Jan 45; moved into Belgium 19 Feb 45 and re-entered Germany 21 Feb 45; returned Boston P/E 2 Aug 45 and moved to Cp Shelby Miss 7 Aug 45 where inactivated 13 Dec 45.

Campaigns: *Normandy, Northern France, Rhineland, Ardennes-Alsace, Central Europe*
Aug 45 Loc: Kaiserslautern Germany

Typical Organization (1941):

55th Infantry Brigade HHC	Headquarters, 28th Division
109th Infantry Regiment	Hqs and Hqs Det
110th Infantry Regiment	Medical Det
56th Infantry Brigade HHC	Headquarters Company
111th Infantry Regiment*	28th Military Police Company
112th Infantry Regiment	28th Signal Company
53rd Field Artillery Brigade HHB	103rd Ordnance Company
107th Field Artillery Regiment (75mm)	103rd Engineers (Combat)
108th Field Artillery Regiment (155mm)	103rd Medical Regiment
109th Field Artillery Regiment (75mm)	103rd Quartermaster Regiment

*Relieved from division 17 Feb 42.

Typical Organization (1944/45):

109th Infantry Regiment
110th Infantry Regiment
112th Infantry Regiment
 HHB Division Artillery
107th Field Artillery Battalion (105mm)
108th Field Artillery Battalion (155mm)
109th Field Artillery Battalion (105mm)
229th Field Artillery Battalion (105mm)
 28th Reconnaissance Troop, Mecz
707th Tank Battalion *(attached 6 Oct 44–8 Jan 45)*
744th Tank Battalion *(attached 30 Jul 44–27 Aug 44)*
777th Tank Battalion *(attached 28 Feb 45–26 Mar 45)*
602nd Tank Destroyer Battalion *(attached 24 Dec 44–31 Dec 44)*
629th Tank Destroyer Battalion *(attached 16 Sep 44–30 Sep 44)*
630th Tank Destroyer Battalion *(attached 20 Jul 44–30 Sep 44, 19 Jan 45–13 Mar 45, 3 Apr 45–8 Apr 45,*
 24 Apr 45–4 Jul 45)
741st Tank Destroyer Battalion *(attached 19 Sep 44–30 Sep 44)*
893rd Tank Destroyer Battalion *(attached 29 Oct 44–19 Nov 44)*
446th AAA Auto-Wpns Battalion *(attached 18 Apr 45–22 Apr 45)*
447th AAA Auto-Wpns Battalion *(attached 27 Jul 44–30 Jul 44, 26 Aug 44–30 Sep 44, 19 Jan 45–4 Jul 45)*

103rd Engineer Combat Battalion
103rd Medical Battalion
 28th Counter Intelligence Corps Det
Headquarters Special Troops
Hqs Company, 28th Infantry Division
Military Police Platoon
728th Ordnance Light Maintenance Company
 28th Quartermaster Company
 28th Signal Company

Overseas Wartime Assignments:

V Corps - 22 Oct 43
XX Corps - 14 Apr 44
Third Army - 24 Apr 44
XIX Corps - 26 Jul 44
V Corps - 28 Aug 44
VIII Corps - 19 Nov 44
Third Army - 8 Jan 45
Fifteenth Army - 9 Jan 45
French II Corps - 20 Jan 45
XXI Corps - 28 Jan 45

Fifteenth Army - 14 Feb 45
12th Army Group - 19 Feb 45
V Corps - 21 Feb 45
VIII Corps - 16 Mar 45
V Corps - 22 Mar 45
III Corps - 28 Mar 45
First Army - 7 Apr 45
Fifteenth Army - 10 Apr 45
XXII Corps - 13 Apr 45
XXIII Corps 26 Apr 45

Commanders: MG Edward Martin: Feb 41
    MG J. Garesche Ord: Jan 42
    MG Omar N. Bradley: Jun 42

MG Lloyd D. Brown: Jan 43
BG James E. Wharton: Aug 44
MG Norman D. Cota: Aug 44

Killed in Action: 2,316   Wounded in Action: 9,609   Died of Wounds: 367

28th Infantry Division Combat Narrative

The division landed in Normandy France on 22 Jul 44 and entered the hedgerow struggle north and west of St Lô. Advancing slowly against determined German defenders, it took Percy 1 Aug 44 and overran Gathemo with 2nd Armd Div assistance on 10 Aug 44. The division drove rapidly southward but its commander was killed 12 Aug 44. The division went into reserve except for the 109th Inf which pushed toward the Forêt de Mortain. The division assembled in the Mortagne area and was moved up to clear Verneuil 22 Aug 44. It then followed in the wake of the 2nd Armd Div and paraded through Paris 29 Aug 44 on its way to assigned attack positions northeast of the French capital. The division crossed the Oise River at Pont Ste Maxence in the Chantilly-Compiègne area 31 Aug 44. It continued across France and passed through Belgium east of Sedan, and crossed into Germany from Luxembourg near Binsfeld 11 Sep 44, capturing the Our River bridge intact.

The 110th Inf began hammering the *West Wall* west of Grosskampenberg 12 Sep 44, and both the 109th and 110th Inf breached it after overcoming heavy opposition two days later. The 110th Inf, assisted by engineers, seized key Hill 553 near Kresfeld 15 Sep 44. The 109th Inf battled several days for Roscheid and the 110th Inf seized Losenseifen Hill 16 Sep 44, but German resistance then ground the advance to a halt. The 112th Inf with the 5th Armd Div defeated strong German counterattacks against the Wallendorf Bridgehead on 19 Sep 44. The division then moved north to Elsenborn on 1 Oct 44 and returned to renew its attack on the *West Wall* 8 Oct 44, also detaching a battalion of the 110th Inf 18 Oct 44 to fight at Aachen. On 25 Oct 44 the division relieved the 9th Inf Div and attacked toward Schmidt 2 Nov 44 after heavy artillery preparation. The division pushed into the Huertgen Forest and over the next few days heavy fighting caused Vossenack and Schmidt to change hands several times. The division had to pull out the 112th Inf on 14 Nov 44 and on 17 Nov 44 withdrew the 110th Inf. The 8th Inf Div relieved it 19 Nov 44 in the Vossenack-Schmidt sector, and the division moved to the Our River in Luxembourg to hold a 25-mile front and rest.

The German Ardennes Counteroffensive hit the division all along its front 16 Dec 44. The division was pushed out of Wiltz 19 Dec 44, and disorganized division elements were forced in many instances to infiltrate back to friendly lines. The remnants of the 110th Inf blocked the Neufchâteau-Bastogne Highway on 20 Dec 44 but this gave way under German assault 22 Dec 44. The 112th Inf abandoned St Vith 23 Dec 44. The 17th A/B Div relieved the division in the Neufchâteau area 1 Jan 45, and the division then moved to defensive positions from Givet to Verdun along the Meuse River.

It relieved the 3rd Inf Div on 18 Feb 45 and took command of the sector from the Sigolsheim to Le Valtin in preparation for offensive action against the Colmar Pocket. On 1 Feb 45 it attacked and reached Colmar the day following, but tanks of the 5th Armd Div swept past it to enter the city first. After mopping up Colmar which was completed 3 Feb 45, the division joined French armor blocking the Vosges in the region southwest of Colmar along the Ill and Fecht Rivers. The division passed through the *12e Division Blindée* and crossed the Rhine-Rhone Canal 6 Feb 45, and relieved the 2nd Inf Div in line on 20 Feb 45. It seized Schleiden 4 Mar 45 and began its push toward the Ahr River 6 Mar 45 as the 110th Inf reached Zingsheim and the 112th Inf reached Goldbach on the first day of the offensive. It reached the Ahr at Blankenheim 7 Mar 45 and assembled in the Nieder Mendig sector for rehabilitation and the holding of defensive positions along the Rhine. On 13 Apr 45 it assumed occupation duty at Jelich, and on 24 Apr 45 relieved the 36th Inf Div at Regierungsbezirk Saarland. It then took over responsibility for the military government of Saarland and Hessen west of the Rhine as well as Pfalz. The division was in this mode when hostilities were declared ended on 7 May 45.

29th Infantry Division

Virginia, Maryland, Pennsylvania
District of Columbia National Guard

3 Feb 41 inducted into federal service at Washington D.C. as the 29th Division and moved immediately to Ft George G. Meade Md; relocated to A.P. Hill Mil Res Va 14 Sep 41 and to the Carolina Maneuver Area 29 Sep 41 where participated in both the Oct and Nov 41 Carolina Maneuvers; returned to Ft George G. Meade Md 9 Dec 41 where redesignated 29th Infantry Division 12 Mar 42; transferred to A.P. Hill Mil Res Va 22 Apr 42 and to the VI Corps Carolina Maneuvers 9 Jul 42; arrived Cp Blanding Fla 15 Aug 42 and staged at Cp Kilmer N.J. 20 Sep 42 until departed New York P/E 5 Oct 42; arrived England 11 Oct 42 and assaulted Normandy France 6 Jun 44; crossed into Holland 27 Sep 44 and into Germany 6 Oct 44; returned Holland 30 Oct 44 and Germany 10 Nov 44; returned New York P/E 16 Jan 46 and inactivated at Cp Kilmer N.J. 17 Jan 46.

Campaigns: *Normandy, Northern France, Rhineland, Central Europe*
Aug 45 Loc: Warendorf Germany

Typical Organization (1941):

58th Infantry Brigade HHC	Headquarters, 29th Division
115th Infantry Regiment	Hqs and Hqs Det
175th Infantry Regiment	Med Det
88th Infantry Brigade HHC	Headquarters Company
116th Infantry Regiment	29th Military Police Company
176th Infantry Regiment*	29th Signal Company
54th Field Artillery Brigade HHB	104th Ordnance Company
110th Field Artillery Regiment (75mm)	121st Engineers (Combat)
111th Field Artillery Regiment (75mm)	104th Medical Regiment
176th Field Artillery Regiment (155mm)	104th Quartermaster Regiment

*Relieved from division 11 Mar 42

Typical Organization (1944/45):

115th Infantry Regiment
116th Infantry Regiment
175th Infantry Regiment
 HHB Division Artillery
110th Field Artillery Battalion (105mm)
111th Field Artillery Battalion (105mm)
224th Field Artillery Battalion (105mm)
227th Field Artillery Battalion (155mm)
 29th Reconnaissance Troop, Mecz
743rd Tank Battalion *(attached 17 May 44–14 Jun 44)*
744th Tank Battalion *(attached 30 Sep 44–3 Nov 44)*
747th Tank Battalion *(attached 17 May 44–17 Aug 44, 28 Sep 44–6 Mar 45, 29 Mar 45–23 Jul 45)*
635th Tank Destroyer Battalion *(attached 17 May 44–7 Jun 44)*
803rd Tank Destroyer Battalion *(attached 30 Jun 44–1 Jul 44, 28 Jul 44–30 Jul 44)*
821st Tank Destroyer Battalion *(attached 28 Jun 44–13 Jul 44)*
823rd Tank Destroyer Battalion *(attached 26 Jun 44–3 Jul 44)*
459th AAA Auto-Wpns Battalion *(attached 9 Jun 44–17 Aug 44, 28 Sep 44–29 Oct 44)*
554th AAA Auto-Wpns Battalion *(attached 6 Nov 44–15 Aug 45)*

121st Engineer Combat Battalion
104th Medical Battalion
 29th Counter Intelligence Corps Det
Headquarters Special Troops
Hqs Company, 29th Infantry Division
Military Police Platoon
729th Ordnance Light Maintenance Company
 29th Quartermaster Company
 29th Signal Company

Overseas Wartime Assignments:

V Corps - 22 Oct 43
XIX Corps - 14 Jun 44
V Corps - 12 Aug 44
First Army - 19 Aug 44
VIII Corps - 5 Sep 44
XIX Corps - 21 Sep 44
XIII Corps - 23 Dec 44

XIX Corps - 4 Feb 45
XVI Corps - 29 Mar 45
Ninth Army - 5 Apr 45
XVI Corps - 12 Apr 45
XIII Corps - 17 Apr 45
XVI Corps - 4 May 45

Commanders: MG Milton A. Reckord: Feb 41
MG Leonard T. Gerow: Feb 42
MG Charles H. Gerhardt: Jul 43

Killed in Action: 3,887   *Wounded in Action:* 15,541   *Died of Wounds:* 899

29th Infantry Division Combat Narrative

On 6 Jun 44 the 116th Inf, attached temporarily to the 1st Inf Div, stormed Omaha Beach France and suffered heavy losses under adverse surf conditions and concentrated fire from the high bluffs. The 115th Inf followed onto the beach the same date as well as the remainder of the 29th Inf Div. The 116th Inf relieved the 2nd Ranger Bn at Pointe du Hoe on 8 Jun 44 while the 175th Inf took Isigny, an initial D-Day objective, and the 115th Inf reached the Aure at Longue-ville. The 115th Inf continued across the Vire but was forced to withdraw from the Montmartin-en-Graignes area on 13 Jun 44. The division opened the push on St Lô 16 Jun 44 as the 175th Inf battled up Hills 90 and 97, the 116th Inf pushed on Martinville Ridge, and the 115th Inf assisted the latter. The Germans drove a salient between the 116th and 175th Inf in the Villiers-Fossard area, and the 3rd Armd Div was committed to reduce it 29 Jun 44. On 12 Jul 44 the 116th Inf was halted on Martinville Ridge after penetrating German lines in front of St Lô, and the 175th Inf attacked the next day in an attempt to force the ridge. Parts of the 116th Inf were isolated astride the Bayeaux–St Lô Road 15–17 Jul 44. The division took St Lô 18 Jul 44 and it was relieved there by the 35th Inf Div on 20 Jul 44.

On 29 Jul 44 it attacked east of Percy and captured contested Vire 7 Aug 44. The division was moved west by motor into Brittany to positions outside the fortress of Brest, which it began attacking 25 Aug 44. The 116th and 175th Inf assaulted the Le Conquet Peninsula containing the formidable *Batterie Graf Spee*, and on 29 Aug 44 the division seized the crest of key Hill 103 but the battle for this commanding feature took several more days. The all-out assault on the city was made 8 Sep 44 and German resistance collapsed there on 18 Sep 44.

The division relieved the 2nd Armd Div in the Gangelt-Teveren area of Holland 29 Sep 44. The 116th Inf was detached and participated in the Uebach Bridgehead Battle 5 Oct 44, the Aachen Gap fighting 13 Oct 44, and frontally assaulted Wuerselen. The division began the offensive for the Roer 16 Nov 44 with the 115th and 175th Inf leading. Setterich was taken by the 116th Inf after heavy combat 19 Nov 44, enabling the 2nd Armd Div to push through. The 175th Inf took and lost Bourheim and then recaptured it and held it in the face of strong German counterattacks 23 Nov 44. On

1 Dec 44 the 116th Inf began the battle for two well-defended strongpoints west of the Roer opposite of Jeulich; the Hsenfeld Gut building-maze and the Juelich Sportplatz. It was forced to withdraw 7 Dec 44, and the 115th continued the battle and destroyed both with armored support 8 Dec 44. From 8 Dec 44–23 Feb 45 the division held defensive positions along the Roer and on the last day crossed the river in the Broich-Juelich sector. Supported by flame-throwing tanks, the 175th Inf captured Juelich and The Citadel on 24 Feb 45. The 116th and 175th Inf combined to seize Munchen-Gladbach on 1 Mar 45 and the division then consolidated, going into reserve 3 Mar 45.

On 1 Apr 45 the division assembled east of the Rhine and moved to the Sendenhorst-Ahlen region southeast of Muenster on 6 Apr 45. The division took responsibility for a large rear area extending from the Rhine to Dortmund-Ems Canal and extended it eastward. It then moved up to the front 17 Apr 45 to assist the attacking 5th Armd Div, and the 115th and 116th Inf moved rapidly forward encountering only light resistance. The division reached the Elbe River 24 Apr 45 and there relieved the 5th Armd Div. Late on 2 May 45 division patrols established contact with the advancing Soviet Army, and the division was then moved to Bremen 6 May 45 for continued military government duty. It was located near Bremen when hostilities were declared ended the next day.

30th Infantry Division

North Carolina, South Carolina, Georgia, Tennessee National Guard

16 Sep 40 inducted into federal service at Ft Jackson S.C. as the 30th Division and moved to Cp Forrest Tenn 27 May 41 for the VII Corps Tennessee Maneuvers; returned to Ft Jackson S.C. 1 Jul 41 and moved to Chester S.C. 27 Sep 41 for both Oct and Nov 41 Carolina Maneuvers; returned to Ft Jackson S.C. 29 Nov 41 where redesignated 30th Infantry Division 16 Feb 42; arrived Cp Blanding Fla 6 Oct 42 and Cp Forrest Tenn 30 May 43; relocated to Murfreesboro Tenn 4 Sep 43 and participated in the Second Army No.3 Tennessee Maneuvers; arrived Cp Atterbury Ind 10 Nov 43 and staged at Cp Myles Standish Mass 31 Jan 44 until departed Boston P/E 11 Feb 44; arrived England 23 Feb 44 and landed in France 10 Jun 44; crossed into Belgium 2 Sep 44 and into Holland 13 Sep 44 and into Germany 17 Sep 44; returned Belgium 17 Dec 44 and re-entered Germany 3 Feb 45; arrived Holland 6 Mar 45 and went back into Germany 19 Mar 45; arrived New York P/E 21 Aug 45 and moved to Ft Jackson S.C. 24 Aug 45 where inactivated 25 Nov 45.

Campaigns: *Normandy, Northern France, Rhineland, Ardennes-Alsace, Central Europe*
Aug 45 Loc: Wolmarstadt Germany

Typical Organization (1941):

59th Infantry Brigade HHC
  118th Infantry Regiment*
  121st Infantry Regiment**
60th Infantry Brigade HHC
  117th Infantry Regiment
  120th Infantry Regiment
55th Field Artillery Brigade HHB
  113th Field Artillery Regiment (155mm)
  115th Field Artillery Regiment (75mm)
  118th Field Artillery Regiment (75mm)

  *Relieved from division 24 Aug 42.
 **Relieved from division 22 Nov 41.

Headquarters, 30th Division
Hqs and Hqs Det
Med Det
Headquarters Company
  30th Military Police Company
  30th Signal Company
105th Ordnance Company
105th Engineers (Combat)
105th Medical Regiment
105th Quartermaster Regiment

Typical Organization (1944/45):

117th Infantry Regiment
119th Infantry Regiment***
120th Infantry Regiment
 HHB Division Artillery
113th Field Artillery Battalion (155mm)
118th Field Artillery Battalion (105mm)
197th Field Artillery Battalion (105mm)
230th Field Artillery Battalion (105mm)
 30th Reconnaissance Troop, Mecz
740th Tank Battalion *(attached 19 Dec 44–28 Dec 44)*
743rd Tank Battalion *(attached 1 Mar 44–23 Jun 45)*
744th Tank Battalion *(attached 7 Feb 45–28 Feb 45)*
801st Tank Destroyer Battalion *(attached 25 Feb 45–28 Feb 45, 1 Apr 45–5 Apr 45)*
807th Tank Destroyer Battalion *(attached 18 Mar 45–27 Mar 45)*
823rd Tank Destroyer Battalion *(attached 24 Jun 44–27 Jun 44, 3 Jul 44–24 Jul 45)*
116th AAA Gun Battalion *(attached 20 Jul 44–3 Aug 44)*
448th AAA Auto-Wpns Battalion *(attached 9 Jul 44–26 Apr 45, 3 May 45–9 May 45)*
459th AAA Auto-Wpns Battalion *(attached 19 Jul 44–27 Jul 44)*

105th Engineer Combat Battalion
105th Medical Battalion
 30th Counter Intelligence Corps Det
Headquarters Special Troops
Hqs Company, 30th Infantry Division
Military Police Platoon
730th Ordnance Light Maintenance Company
 30th Quartermaster Company
 30th Signal Company

***Assigned to division 1 Sep 42.

Overseas Wartime Assignments:

XIX Corps - 18 Feb 44
VII Corps - 15 Jul 44
XIX Corps - 28 Jul 44
V Corps - 4 Aug 44
VII Corps - 5 Aug 44
XIX Corps - 13 Aug 44
XV Corps - 26 Aug 44
XIX Corps - 29 Aug 44

Ninth Army - 22 Oct 44
V Corps *(attached)* - 17 Dec 44
XVIII (A/B) Corps - 21 Dec 44
XIX Corps - 3 Feb 45
XVI Corps - 6 Mar 45
XIX Corps - 30 Mar 45
XIII Corps - 8 May 45

Commanders: MG Henry D. Russell: Sep 40
    MG William H. Simpson: May 42

MG Leland S. Hobbs: Sep 42
MG Albert C. Cowper: Sep 45

Killed in Action: 3,003   *Wounded in Action:* 13,376   *Died of Wounds:* 513

30th Infantry Division Combat Narrative

The division landed across Omaha Beach France on 10 Jun 44. The 120th Inf captured Montmartin-en-Graignes the following day and then defended the Vire-Taute Canal line. The 117th Inf attacked across the Vire and the 120th Inf assaulted across the Vire-Taute Canal on 7 Jul 44, establishing a bridgehead at St Jean-de-Day which the 3rd Armd Div exploited. As the division advanced on St Lô it checked a German counterattack along the main Hauts-Vents Highway 11 Jul 44 and Pont Hébert fell after protracted fighting 14 Jul 44. Patrols reached the Periers–St Lô Road 18 Jul 44 and the division attacked across it 25 Jul 44 to drive beyond St Lô during Operation COBRA. The division took well-defended Troisgots 31 Jul 44 and relieved the 1st Inf Div near Mortain 6 Aug 44. It was subjected to a strong German counterattack which ruptured its lines in the area on the following day during the Battle for Avranches. The division went over to the offensive again 11 Aug 44 and forced back German gains to Mortain.

The division then pushed east behind the 2nd Armd Div, taking Nonancourt 21 Aug 44. It crossed into Belgium 2 Sep 44, and advanced over the Meuse River at Vise and Liege 11 Sep 44. The 120th Inf occupied Lanaye Holland and captured the locks intact the same day, and on 14 Sep 44 the 117th and 119th Inf advanced into Maastricht. The 119th and 120th Inf attacked toward the *West Wall* north of Aachen and the former reached positions commanding the Wurm River 18 Sep 44. The division attacked across the river between Aachen and Geilenkirchen 2 Oct 44 against strong German opposition, and the following day the 117th Inf seized Uebach after house-to-house fighting as the 119th Inf finally captured Rimburg Castle. The division was assisted by the 2nd Armd Div as it continued slow progress in the *West Wall*, but was checked by a German counterattack on 9 Oct 44 which isolated the 119th Inf at North Wuerselen. The encirclement of Aachen was completed regardless on 16 Oct 44 when the division made contact with the 1st Inf Div.

The division then rested and next attacked south in the Wuerselen area 16 Nov 44. It won the Battle for Warden 18 Nov 44 and the 120th Inf captured Lohn 23 Nov 44 and then held it against two German counterattacks. The division reached the Inde River 28 Nov 44 with the capture of Altkirch, and cleared most of the region between the Inde and Roer Rivers by 14 Dec 44. In response to the German Ardennes Counteroffensive the division was rushed to the Malmédy-Stavelot sector on 17 Dec 44. It held at Stavelot as engineers destroyed the Amblève River bridge there, but lost Stoumont 19 Dec 44, and after heavy fighting regained it 22 Dec 44. The division then cleared the region north of the Amblève between Stavelot and Trois Ponts. On 13 Jan 45 it launched its offensive toward Malmédy which included the Battle for the Recht-Born and Malmédy–St Vith Roads 17–19 Jan 45. The division was within two miles of St Vith 26 Jan 45 when it pulled out and reassembled near Lierneux, and later Aachen, in preparation for the Roer River Offensive. The division took over the defense of the Roer's west bank from Kirchberg to Merken on 7 Feb 45.

The 119th and 120th Inf assaulted across the Roer 23 Feb 45 near Schophoven, and as the division took Hambach 24 Feb 45 the 117th Inf crossed over and attacked toward Steinstrass. The 2nd Armd Div then pushed forward and the division turned to mopping up west of the Erft Canal 1 Mar 45 before being withdrawn for rehabilitation. The division assaulted across the Rhine with three regiments abreast 24 Mar 45 in the Buderich-Wallach-Rheinberg vicinity after heavy artillery shelling of German positions. It made contact with the *British 1st Commando Bde* the next day and pushed through heavily defended wooded terrain. The 8th Armd Div attacked through its positions toward Dorstein 28 Mar 45 and the division was assembled in the Drensteinfuhrt region 1 Apr 45. The division relieved the 2nd Armd Div in the Teutoburger Wald 3 Apr 45 and followed its advance on 6 Apr 45. The division sped east past the Weser River and seized Hamelin the following day. After Braunschweig fell to the 117th Inf on 11 Apr 45, the division reached the Elbe 13 Apr 45 and regrouped. After it concluded the Battle for Magdeburg with the 2nd Armd Div on 18 Apr 45, it relieved the latter on 20 Apr 45 and took over the security of the Magdeburg sector west of the Elbe. The division made contact with the advancing Soviet Army on 5 May 45 and was still in an occupational mode when the end of hostilities was declared 7 May 45.

31st Infantry Division

Louisiana, Mississippi, Alabama, Florida National Guard

25 Nov 40 inducted into federal service at Birmingham Ala as the 31st Division and moved to Cp Blanding Fla 22 Dec 40; moved to La Maneuver Area 4 Aug 41 where participated in the Aug 41 IV Corps Louisiana Maneuvers and the Sep 41 Louisiana Maneuvers; returned to Cp Blanding Fla 9 Oct 41 and on 28 Oct 41 participated in the First Army Carolina Maneuvers; returned Cp Blanding Fla 2 Dec 41 and transferred to Cp Bowie Tex 23 Feb 42 where redesignated 31st Infantry Division 27 Feb 42; went to La Maneuver Area 28 Jul 42 and took part in VIII Corps Louisiana Maneuvers; moved to Cp Shelby Miss 22 Sep 42 and on 26 Jun 43 took part in the Third Army No.3 Louisiana Maneuvers; arrived Cp Pickett Va 28 Aug 43 and participated in the XIII Corps West Virginia–Norfolk Maneuvers of 9 Sep–16 Nov 43; staged at Cp Patrick Henry Va 5 Mar 44 until departed Hampton Roads P/E 13 Mar 44; arrived Dobodura New Guinea 24 Apr 44 and moved to the Maffin Bay area New Guinea in Jul 44; assaulted Morotai Island 15 Sep 44 and landed on Mindanao Philippines 22 Apr 45; arrived San Francisco P/E 19 Dec 45 and was inactivated at Cp Stoneman Calif 21 Dec 45.

Campaigns: *New Guinea, Southern Philippines*
Aug 45 Loc: Valencia Mindanao Philippine Islands

Typical Organization (1941):

61st Infantry Brigade HHC	Headquarters, 31st Division
155th Infantry Regiment	Hqs and Hqs Det
156th Infantry Regiment*	Med Det
62nd Infantry Brigade HHC	Headquarters Company
124th Infantry Regiment**	31st Military Police Company
167th Infantry Regiment	31st Signal Company
56th Field Artillery Brigade HHB	106th Ordnance Company
114th Field Artillery Regiment (155mm)	106th Engineers (Combat)
116th Field Artillery Regiment (75mm)	106th Medical Regiment
117th Field Artillery Regiment (75mm)	106th Quartermaster Regiment

*Relieved from division 14 Jul 42.
**Relieved from division 15 Dec 41 and replaced by 154th Infantry Regt which in turn was disbanded 5 Apr 44 and 124th Infantry Regt raised from its assets and reassigned.

Typical Organization (1944/45):

124th Infantry Regiment
155th Infantry Regiment
167th Infantry Regiment
 HHB Division Artillery
114th Field Artillery Battalion (155mm)
116th Field Artillery Battalion (105mm)
117th Field Artillery Battalion (105mm)
149th Field Artillery Battalion (105mm)
 31st Reconnaissance Troop, Mecz

106th Engineer Combat Battalion
106th Medical Battalion
 31st Counter Intelligence Corps Det
Headquarters Special Troops
Hqs Company, 31st Infantry Division
Military Police Platoon
731st Ordnance Light Maintenance Company
 31st Quartermaster Company
 31st Signal Company

Overseas Wartime Assignments:

Sixth Army - 23 Mar 44
XI Corps - 24 Apr 44
Sixth Army - 25 Jun 44
XI Corps - 1 Sep 44

Eighth Army - 12 Oct 44
XI Corps *(attached)* - 12 Oct 44
Eighth Army Area Cmd *(attached)* - 20 Jan 45
X Corps *(attached)* - 10 Apr 45

Commanders: MG John C. Persons: Nov 40
                MG Clarence A. Martin: Sep 44

Killed in Action: 340   *Wounded in Action:* 1,392   *Died of Wounds:* 74

31st Infantry Division Combat Narrative

The advance echelon of the division reached Dobodura New Guinea 17 Mar 44 and by 24 Apr 44 the entire division was assembled there for amphibious and jungle warfare training. The 124th Inf was alerted for movement to Aitape New Guinea on 25 Jun 44 and landed there as the reserve for Task Force PERSECUTION 5 Jul 44. The rest of the division moved to Maffin Bay and relieved the 6th Inf Div. The 167th Inf arrived at Toem New Guinea 14 Jul 44 and the rest of the division completed landing in the Sarmi-Wadke Island vicinity 18 Jul 44. There it built bridges, roads and docks, and patrolled the area but limited engagements to avoid provoking large-scale Japanese reaction. The 124th Inf was also detached and went into action in the Aitape area 13 Jul 44 in the Battle for the Drinumor River. On 11 Sep 44 it returned to the division at Maffin Bay where it was staging for the invasion of Morotai Island.

The division assaulted Morotai against slight opposition on 15 Sep 44 and had expanded its perimeter beyond Pitoe Dome by the following day. The division then expanded the beachhead, patrolled the interior of the island, and occupied other small islands off its coast. Elements of the 167th Inf took Mapia Island by 17 Sep 44 and a company from the 124th Inf seized Asia Island by 20 Sep 44, both of which had been evacuated. The division continued its dual mission of defense and security at Morotai and Sansapor until 24 Mar 45 when it was directed to prepare for operation in the Philippines. It was relieved by the 93rd Inf Div on 12 Apr 45 and departed for Mindanao.

The division landed 22 Apr 45 in the previously secured Parang area of Mindanao in the Philippines and relieved the 24th Inf Div. The division began its push north up the Sayre Highway 27 Apr 45 against strong Japanese opposition in which fighting was waged in knee-deep mud, torrential rains, and in spite of obstacles and determined resistance. The 155th Inf defeated the Japanese in a firefight at Misinsman 1 May 45 and on 3 May 45 both the 124th and 167th Inf joined the division from Morotai, overrunning Kibawe Airstrip and securing the junction of Sayre Highway and the Kibawe-Talamo Trail. The division then continued its slow drive along the Sayre Highway and fought the Battle for Colgan Woods 5–12 May 45. Advance along the Talamo Trail was checked 16 May 45 but then continued by the 167th Inf throughout June, the regiment finally reaching Pinamola 26 Jun 45. The 155th Inf took the Japanese supply base at Malaybalay 21 May 45 and Kalasungay the next day, establishing a bridgehead across the Pulang River near Sanipon 27 May 45. By the end of June this division had forced the Japanese to withdraw into the interior of Mindanao and blocked off any threats toward Davao City.

The division continued mopping up operations in the Agusan River sector along both the Kibawe-Talamo Trail and the Sayre Highway from Malaybalay to Valencia until the end of the war. Following the Japanese surrender the division concentrated on accepting their capitulation on Mindanao.

32nd Infantry Division   **Michigan and Wisconsin National Guard**

15 Oct 40 inducted into federal service at Lansing Mich as the 32nd Division and moved to Cp Beauregard La 21 Oct 40; went to Cp Livingston La 15 Feb 41 and participated in the V Corps Louisiana Maneuvers 16–27 Jun 41; on 10 Aug 41 moved to the La Maneuver Area and participated in both the Aug and Sep 41 Louisiana Maneuvers; arrived Cp Livingston La 29 Sep 41 where redesignated 32nd Infantry Division 1 Feb 42; staged at Ft Devens Mass 2 Mar 42 until departed San Francisco P/E 22 Apr 42; arrived Australia 14 May 42 and elements fought in New Guinea Sep 42 and the division arrived there 19 Nov 42 and served until 21 Feb 43 when it returned to Australia; remained in Australia until 23 Oct 43 and landed on Goodenough Island 28 Oct 43; arrived Saidor New Guinea 7 Jan 44 and relocated to Hollandia New Guinea 1 Oct 44; landed on Leyte Philippines 14 Nov 44 and arrived on Luzon Philippines 27 Jan 45; moved to Japan 14 Oct 45 and inactivated there 28 Feb 46.

Campaigns: *New Guinea, Southern Philippines, Luzon*
Aug 45 Loc: Anabat Philippine Islands

Typical Organization (1941):

63rd Infantry Brigade HHC
  125th Infantry Regiment*
  126th Infantry Regiment
64th Infantry Brigade HHC
  127th Infantry Regiment
  128th Infantry Regiment
57th Field Artillery Brigade HHB
  120th Field Artillery Regiment (75mm)
  121st Field Artillery Regiment (155mm)
  126th Field Artillery Regiment (75mm)

*Relieved from division 8 Dec 41.

Headquarters, 32nd Division
Hqs and Hqs Det
Med Det
Headquarters Company
  32nd Military Police Company
  32nd Signal Company
107th Ordnance Company
107th Engineers (Combat)
107th Medical Regiment
107th Quartermaster Regiment

Typical Organization (1944/45):

126th Infantry Regiment
127th Infantry Regiment
128th Infantry Regiment
 HHB Division Artillery
120th Field Artillery Battalion (105mm)
121st Field Artillery Battalion (155mm)
126th Field Artillery Battalion (105mm)
129th Field Artillery Battalion (105mm)
  32nd Reconnaissance Troop, Mecz

114th Engineer Combat Battalion
107th Medical Battalion
  32nd Counter Intelligence Corps Det
Headquarters Special Troops
Hqs Company, 32nd Infantry Division
Military Police Platoon
732nd Ordnance Light Maintenance Company
  32nd Quartermaster Company
  32nd Signal Company

Overseas Wartime Assignments:

Army Forces Australia - 14 May 42
I Corps - 8 Sep 42
2nd Australian Corps (attached) - 9 Sep 42
Sixth Army - 6 Nov 43
ALAMO Force *(attached)* - 18 Feb 44
I Corps - 4 May 44
XI Corps - 27 Jun 44
Sixth Army - 2 Oct 44

X Corps - 14 Nov 44
Eighth Army - 26 Dec 44
Sixth Army - 27 Jan 45
I Corps *(attached)* - 30 Jan 45
I Corps - 15 Feb 45
XIV Corps *(attached)* - 30 Jun 45
Eighth Army - 1 Jul 45
XIV Corps *(attached)* - 1 Jul 45

Commanders: MG Irving A. Fish: Oct 40
           MG Edwin F. Harding: Mar 42
           MG William H. Gill: Feb 43

Killed in Action: 1,613   *Wounded in Action:* 5,627   *Died of Wounds:* 372

32nd Infantry Division Combat Narrative

The division arrived in Australia 14 May 42 and engaged in jungle warfare training at Cp Cable near Brisbane. The 126th and the 128th Inf moved to Port Moresby New Guinea 15–28 Sep 42 to attack east with a wide envelopment against Buna-Sanananda. The 128th Inf blocked the Japanese advance down Kokoda Trail, and a battalion of the regiment made a cross-country advance over the Owen Standley Mtns to reach Jaure 25 Oct 42. The 128th Inf was flown to Wanigela 14 Oct 42 and went by motor launch to Pongani 11 Nov 42 and consolidated in the Oro Bay area as the 126th Inf assembled at Natunga 14 Nov 42. The 127th Inf arrived at Port Moresby 27 Nov 42 and battalions from all three regiments participated in the Battle of the Buna-Gona beachhead commencing 19 Nov 42. The Duropa Plantation was assaulted 26 Nov 42, the 127th Inf moved up to Dobodura 4 Dec 42, and it seized evacuated Buna Village on 14 Dec 42 after heavy combat in the plantation and Simemi Creek bunker area. The Battle for Buna Mission was fought 24 Dec 42–1 Jan 43 and Government Plantation near Giropa Point fell the same day. The 127th Inf then pushed along the coast and overran Tarakena 8 Jan 43. The division fought in the Sanananda vicinity 16–23 Jan 43 until link-up with Australians ended the Buna-Sanananda campaign. The division left New Guinea by echelon 21 Jan–21 Feb 43 and returned to Cp Cable Australia.

The division arrived at Goodenough Island by echelon 23 Oct 43 and from there the 126th Inf assaulted Saidor New Guinea 2 Jan 44 and was joined by the 128th Inf 19 Jan 44. Junction with advancing Australian forces was effected 10 Feb 44 and the 128th Inf began a drive west to destroy retreating Japanese elements assisted by the 126th Inf, which landed at Yalau Plantation 5 Mar 44. Patrols contacted advancing Australian units on 21 Mar 44. The 127th Inf landed at Aitape New Guinea 23 Apr 44 as well as Tumleo and the Seleo Islands, and was reinforced by the arrival of the 126th Inf 4 May 44. Slight initial resistance in this area gave way to sustained Japanese action along the Drinumor River and the 127th Inf took the ridge north of Afua 5 Jun 44. The 126th Inf attacked to drive the Japanese back across the Drindarai 31 May 44, and the division was committed to regain lost positions along the Drinumor 12 Jul 44. Mopping up in the area tied down the division from 25 Aug–25 Sep 44. Elements reinforced the Wakde-Sarmi area of New Guinea 15 Aug 44 and the 126th Inf was detached to land at Gila Peninsula on Morotai Island 16 Sep 44. The remainder of the division left Aitape for Hollandia New Guinea 1 Oct 44 and staged for the Philippine campaign.

The division landed on Leyte Island Philippines 14 Nov 44 and relieved the 24th Inf Div. Attacking toward Ormoc 16 Nov 44, the division battled on Corkscrew Ridge and Breakneck Ridge and took Limon 22 Nov 44, bypassing pockets of resistance which were eliminated by mid-December. As the Limon Battles raged through December, the division fought the Battle of Kilay Ridge 29 Nov–5 Dec 44 and was counterattacked along Highway 2 during the night of 13–14 Dec 44. The 127th Inf linked up with the 1st Cav Div at Lonoy on 22 Dec 44 and the division gained the west coast of Leyte near Villaba 29 Dec 44.

The division was landed in Lingayen Gulf on Luzon 27 Jan 45 and began the final phase of the push on Manila, seizing San Nicolas 1 Feb 45. The Battle for Villa Verde Trail was fought 6–22 Feb 45 which included numerous Japanese counterattacks, and the division fought battles at Salacsac Pass and along the Arboredo and Ambayang Valleys in March. The 128th Inf relieved the 127th Inf continuing the drive up Villa Verde Trail 25 Mar 45, and captured Hill 159 despite torrential rains 6 Apr 45. Salacsac Pass finally fell to the 128th Inf 10 Apr 45 and clearing operations commenced along the Villa Verde Trail, Imugan falling 28 May 45, and contact being made with the 25th Inf Div near Santa Fe which secured vital Balete Pass. The division rehabilitated 4 Jun–8 Jul 45 and mopped up in the Bauang-Naguilian-Caba-Aringay area. It relieved the 25th Inf Div and then advanced from Anabat to reduce Japanese defenses in the Sierra Madre Mtns of northern Luzon, securing the Agno River Valley and opening Highway 11 in the Baguio area. The division was engaged in clearing operations there when the war ended.

33rd Infantry Division   Illinois National Guard

5 Mar 41 inducted into federal service at Chicago Ill as the 33rd Division and moved to Cp Forrest Tenn 12 Mar 41; went to Arkadelphia Ark 16 Aug 41 and participated in the VII Corps Arkansas and Sep 41 Louisiana Maneuvers; returned to Cp Forrest Tenn 7 Oct 41 where redesignated 33rd Infantry Division 21 Feb 42; arrived Ft Lewis Wash 13 Sep 42 and went to Cp Young Calif 13 Apr 43 for the IX Corps Desert Training Center No.8 California Maneuvers; staged at Cp Stoneman Calif 24 Jun 43 until departed San Francisco P/E 7 Jul 43; arrived Hawaii 12 Jul 43 and left 30 Apr 44; arrived at Finschhafen New Guinea 11 May 44 and Morotai Island 18 Dec 44; landed on Luzon Philippines 10 Feb 45 and arrived in Japan 25 Sep 45 where inactivated 5 Feb 46.

Campaigns: *New Guinea, Luzon*
Aug 45 Loc: Baguio Philippine Islands

Typical Organization (1941):

65th Infantry Brigade HHC
  129th Infantry Regiment*
  130th Infantry Regiment
66th Infantry Brigade HHC
  131st Infantry Regiment**
  132nd Infantry Regiment***
58th Field Artillery Brigade HHB
  122nd Field Artillery Regiment (75mm)
  123rd Field Artillery Regiment (155mm)
  124th Field Artillery Regiment (75mm)

   *Relieved from division 31 Jul 43.
  **Relieved from division 21 Feb 42.
***Relieved from division 14 Jan 42.

Headquarters, 33rd Division
Hqs and Hqs Det
Med Det
Headquarters Company
  33rd Military Police Company
  33rd Signal Company
108th Ordnance Company
108th Engineers (Combat)
108th Medical Regiment
108th Quartermaster Regiment

Typical Organization (1944/45):

123rd Infantry Regiment****
130th Infantry Regiment
136th Infantry Regiment*****
 HHB Division Artillery
122nd Field Artillery Battalion (105mm)
123rd Field Artillery Battalion (155mm)
124th Field Artillery Battalion (105mm)
210th Field Artillery Battalion (105mm)
 33rd Reconnaissance Troop, Mecz

   ****Assigned to division 28 Sep 42.
*****Assigned to division 1 Apr 42.

108th Engineer Combat Battalion
108th Medical Battalion
  33rd Counter Intelligence Corps Det
Headquarters Special Troops
Hqs Company, 33rd Infantry Division
Military Police Platoon
733rd Ordnance Light Maintenance Company
  33rd Quartermaster Company
  33rd Signal Company

Overseas Wartime Assignments:

Hawaiian Dept - 12 Jul 43
XI Corps - 11 May 44
Sixth Army - 20 Aug 44
Eighth Army - 28 Sep 44

XI Corps *(attached)* - 21 Dec 44
Sixth Army - 10 Feb 45
I Corps - 12 Feb 45

Commanders: MG Samuel T. Lawton: Mar 41
               MG Frank C. Mahin: May 42
               MG John Millikin: Aug 42

MG Percy W. Clarkson: Oct 43
BG Winfred G. Skelton: Nov 45

Killed in Action: 396   *Wounded in Action:* 2,024   *Died of Wounds:* 128

33rd Infantry Division Combat Narrative

The division arrived in Hawaii 12 Jul 43 and was assigned to defend the outer islands 18 Jul 43 in conjunction with jungle warfare training. It moved to Finschhafen New Guinea 11 May 44 and engaged in additional jungle and amphibious training, detaching the 123rd Inf to Maffin Bay New Guinea on 1 Sep 44 where it relieved the 31st Inf Div and patrolled the Wakde airdrome and Toem-Sarmi sector until 26 Jan 45.

The remainder of the division moved to Morotai Island 18 Dec 44 and landed on its west coast without opposition. From 22 Dec 44–29 Jan 45 it relieved 31st Inf Div forces garrisoning Race Island and Wajaboela as well as reducing Japanese forces at the headwaters of the Pilowo River on Morotai. It then staged for operations in the Philippines.

The division arrived in Lingayen Gulf and landed on Luzon 10 Feb 45, relieved the 43rd Inf Div in the Damortis-Rosario-Pozzorrubio area 15 Feb 45, and took over its zone of action. On 19 Feb 45 the division began its drive into the Caraballo Mountains toward its objective of Baguio, the summer capital of the Philippines and the Japanese headquarters. The division seized Questionmark and Benchmark Hills after heavy fighting 22 Feb 45, and after battling entrenched Japanese in the hills, the 130th Inf took Aringay and its bridge 7 Mar 45 without opposition and went on to capture Mt Magabang the following day. The 136th Inf maintained pressure as it advanced along Kennon Road and the 123rd Inf patrolled northeast of Pugo. A division task force composed of a battalion from the 130th Inf linked up with Filipino guerrillas of northern Luzon in the vicinity of San Fernando on 21 Mar 45, but the Japanese had already withdrawn. The attached 129th Inf (from 37th Inf Div) pushed up Highway 9 toward Baguio and encountered very heavy fighting in the Salat area 23 Mar–10 Apr 45. The 123rd Inf took Mt Calugong on 8 Apr 45 and pushed beyond Galiano on the Pugo-Baguio Trail.

The 130th Inf captured Asin on 12 Apr 45 but further advance halted by a Japanese tunnel complex nearby. Ground assault of the Asin Tunnels was suspended 15 Apr 45 while artillery bombardment was employed to soften up the strongpoint. The 130th Inf renewed its attacks 21 Apr 45 and resorted to reducing the tunnel lines one after the other in close combat. In the meantime the 123rd Inf pushed slowly up the Puga-Tuba Trail and arrived in Tuba on 25 Apr 45. On the same day the 130th Inf, trucked into positions, began the assault on the hills surrounding Baguio and took Mt Mirador. The Battle for Baguio ended 27 Apr 45 as both 33rd and 37th Inf Div columns converged and overran the city.

The division then relieved the 37th Inf Div on 4 May 45 and was given the mission of clearing northward from Baguio to break up remaining pockets of resistance. With the capture completed of the San Nicolas–Tebbo–Itogon route on 12 May 45, organized opposition collapsed. Forces advancing on Highway 11 occupied Tabio and Ambuclac on 13 Jun 45, and the area was secured after the fall of Bokod 17 Jun 45. The Daklan area was secured after Daklan Air-strip was captured by the division on 22 Jun 45. The division was relieved in the Baguio general area by the 32nd Inf Div on 30 Jun 45, and moved to Bauang for rehabilitation. The division was engaged in amphibious training in the Philippines when the war ended.

34th Infantry Division

North Dakota, South Dakota, Iowa, Minnesota National Guard

10 Feb 41 inducted into federal service at Council Bluffs Iowa as the 34th Division and moved to Cp Claiborne La 20 Feb 41; participated in the V Corps Louisiana Maneuvers 16–27 Jun 41 and arrived Bon Ami La 12 Aug 41 and was part of the Aug and Sep 41 Louisiana Maneuvers; returned to Cp Claiborne La 30 Sep 41 and staged at Ft Dix N.J. 8 Jan 42 until departed New York P/E 14 Jan 42; arrived Northern Ireland 31 Jan 42 where redesignated 34th Infantry Division 1 Feb 42; arrived in North Africa 3 Jan 43 less elements which assaulted 8 Nov 42 and landed in Italy 21 Sep 43; landed across Anzio Italy 25 Mar 44; arrived Hampton Roads P/E 3 Nov 45 and inactivated at Cp Patrick Henry Va the same date.

Campaigns: *Tunisia, Naples-Foggia, Anzio, Rome-Arno, North Apennines, Po Valley*
Aug 45 Loc: Iseo Italy

Typical Organization (1941):

67th Infantry Brigade HHC	Headquarters, 34th Division
133rd Infantry Regiment	Hqs and Hqs Det
168th Infantry Regiment	Med Det
68th Infantry Brigade HHC	Headquarters Company
135th Infantry Regiment	34th Military Police Company
164th Infantry Regiment*	34th Signal Company
59th Field Artillery Brigade HHB	109th Ordnance Company
125th Field Artillery Regiment (75mm)	109th Engineers (Combat)
151st Field Artillery Regiment (75mm)	136th Medical Regiment
185th Field Artillery Regiment (155mm)	109th Quartermaster Regiment

*Relieved from division 8 Dec 41.

Typical Organization (1944/45):

133rd Infantry Regiment	34th Reconnaissance Troop, Mecz
135th Infantry Regiment	109th Engineer Combat Battalion
168th Infantry Regiment	109th Medical Battalion
HHB Division Artillery	Headquarters Special Troops
125th Field Artillery Battalion (105mm)	Hqs Company, 34th Infantry Division
151st Field Artillery Battalion (105mm)	Military Police Platoon
175th Field Artillery Battalion (105mm)	734th Ordnance Light Maintenance Company
185th Field Artillery Battalion (155mm)	34th Quartermaster Company
	34th Signal Company

Overseas Wartime Assignments:

NATO - 1 Jan 43
French XIX Corps (attached) - 6 Feb 43
II Corps - 26 Feb 43
British 9 Corps (attached) - 4 Apr 43
II Corps - 21 Apr 43
VI Corps - 13 Aug 43

II Corps - 30 Dec 43
VI Corps - 22 Feb 44
IV Corps - 26 Jun 44
Fifth Army - 24 Jul 44
II Corps - 9 Sep 44
IV Corps - 23 Apr 45

Commanders: MG Ellard A. Walsh: Feb 41
                MG Russell P. Hartle: Aug 41

MG Charles W. Ryder: May 42
MG Charles L. Bolte: Jul 44

Killed in Action: 2,866   *Wounded in Action:* 11,545 *Died of Wounds:* 484

34th Infantry Division Combat Narrative

The division's 168th Inf landed west of Algiers 8 Nov 42, seized both the port and outlying airfields, and the rest of the division landed in North Africa 3 Jan 43. The 135th Inf moved into the Pichon–Maison des Eaux area 11 Feb 43 and the 168th Inf, with the 1st Armd Div, became isolated on Djebel-Lessouda 14 Feb 43 and was forced to infiltrate out at night. The division entered its first action as a whole as the 135th and 168th Inf drove toward Fondouk Gap 27 Mar 43; the 133rd Inf defending Sbeita with a battalion at Algiers. The division was forced to give up this offensive 31 Mar 43 and renewed attacks on the Fondouk Pass heights 8 Apr 43. After training near Maktar the division moved up by night march to relieve 1st Inf Div 22 Apr 43. The 135th Inf stormed Hill 490 28 Apr 43 and held it against counterattack. After the division took Hill 609 on 1 May 43 it drove through Chouigui Pass to Tebourba and Ferryville, and trained for further operations in Italy.

The division lent the 151st FA Bn to the assault at Salerno Italy 9 Sep 43 and followed ashore 21–25 Sep 43. The 133rd Inf landed at Paestum and took Benevento on 3 Oct 43 and established a bridgehead across the Calore River. The division fought through strong opposition and heavy rains to cross the Volturno River 13 Oct 43; the 133rd Inf crossing the river a second time farther up 18 Oct 43, and the 168th Inf entered evacuated Dragoni the following day. On 20 Oct 43 the division began the push on Capriati al Volturno and made its third Volturno crossing near Roccaravindo 3 Nov 43. It began the ten-day Battle for the Winter Line 5 Nov 43 as the 168th Inf stormed Mt Pantano and defeated German attempts to reclaim it, being relieved by the 135th Inf on the mountain 4 Dec 43. On 9 Dec 43 the division withdrew for rehabilitation.

The division returned to attack the Gustav Line 30 Dec 43 and relieved the 36th Inf Div in line. On 5 Jan 44 the 135th Inf assaulted S.Vittore, the 168th Inf moved to outflank La Chiala, and the 133rd Inf (attached to 1st Special Service Force) attacked Mt Majo. The 168th Inf cleared the heights overlooking the Rapido River 13 Jan 44 and the 135th Inf finally won Mt Trocchio on 15 Jan 44. The 133rd Inf crossed the Rapido north of Cassino 25 Jan 44 and the 168th Inf attacked through the bridgehead and took Hills 56 and 213 after hard fighting which included the repulse of a strong German counterattack 30 Jan 44. The next day the 133rd Inf attempted to clear the barracks north of Cassino but was repulsed despite armored reinforcement on 3 Feb 44. The farthest advance was made 5 Feb 44 when the 133rd Inf reached the Cassino Abbey walls before it was withdrawn. The 168th Inf next attacked in alternate rain and snow storms beginning 8 Feb 44, but its efforts up Monastery Hill were abandoned by 13 Feb 44. The division was then withdrawn for rehabilitation.

On 25 Mar 44 it landed at the Anzio perimeter and maintained defensive positions until 23 May 44 when the 133rd Inf led its attack toward M.Arrestino. After the junction of U.S. forces outside the beachhead 25 May 44 it followed the 1st Armd Div and saw heavy combat at Lanuvio. Crossings over the Albano at Rome were secured 4 Jun 44, and the 168th Inf reached the port of Civitavecchia 7 Jun 44. The 133rd Inf overran Tarquinia on Highway 1 9 Jun 44 and then the division took over the coastal advance from 36th Inf Div 26 Jun 44. The 135th Inf established a bridgehead across the Cecina River and the 133rd Inf fought the Battle of Cecina town 30 Jun–2 Jul 44, the 135th Inf next winning the Battle of Rosignano 3–7 Jul 44, and the 168th Inf taking Castellina 6 Jul 44. The 135th Inf finally entered Livorno and the division reached Arno River 22 Jul 44 and regrouped. It relieved the 88th Inf Div west of Highway 65 on 6 Sep 44 and began its attack on the Gothic Line 10 Sep 44, the 168th Inf capturing M.Frassino 15 Sep 44. The 133rd Inf finished the Battle for Torricella Hill 13–21 Sep 44 and went on to capture Montepiano 23 Sep 44 which marked the end of the Gothic Line barrier. After a hard battle M.Bastione fell to the 135th Inf on 28 Sep 44, and the Battle of M.Belmonte fought 16–23 Oct 44 which saw the employment of searchlights and "artificial moonlight."

The offensive against Bologna was initiated 15 Apr 45 and the division fought past Gorgognano Ridge, the Sevizzano Heights, and Drei Mori Hill to seize the city with the 133rd Inf on 21 Apr 45. The division was then placed under army command to garrison the city. On 23 Apr 45 it was moved to screen along Highway 9, taking Reggio and relieving the 1st Armd Div. After a brief delay south of Piacenza the division was sent to the Brescia area to mop up on 28 Apr 45. The pursuit there ended on 2 May 45 as German forces in Italy surrendered, with the division on the Ticino River northwest of Milan.

35th Infantry Division
Kansas, Missouri, Nebraska National Guard

23 Dec 40 inducted into federal service at Lincoln Nebr as the 35th Division and moved to Cp Joseph T. Robinson Ark 29 Dec 40; arrived for VII Corps Arkansas Maneuvers 12 Aug 41 and the Sep 41 Louisiana Maneuvers; returned to Cp Joseph T. Robinson Ark 5 Oct 41 and transferred to Ft Ord Calif 23 Oct 41; arrived Cp San Luis Obispo Calif 17 Jan 42 where redesignated 35th Infantry Division 1 Mar 42; went to Los Angeles Calif 21 Apr 42 and Pasadena Calif 2 Jun 42; returned to Cp San Luis Obispo Calif 18 Jan 43 and moved to Cp Rucker Ala 27 Mar 43; arrived Tenn Maneuver Area 17 Nov 43 to participate in the Second Army No.4 Tennessee Maneuvers and went to Cp Butner N.C. 21 Jan 44; there participated in the West Virginia Mountain Training Maneuvers 21 Feb 44–28 Mar 44; staged at Cp Kilmer N.J. 2 May 44 until departed New York P/E 12 May 44; arrived in England 26 May 44 and landed in France 6 Jul 44; crossed into Belgium 26 Dec 44 and into Luxembourg 27 Dec 44; returned to Belgium 8 Jan 45 and to France 19 Jan 45; entered Holland 31 Jan 45 and Germany 4 Feb 45; returned to Holland 3 Mar 45 and re-entered Germany 4 Mar 45; returned New York P/E 10 Sep 45 and moved to Cp Breckinridge Ky 13 Sep 45 where inactivated 7 Dec 45.

Campaigns: *Normandy, Northern France, Rhineland, Ardennes-Alsace, Central Europe*
Aug 45 Loc: Hamborn Germany

Typical Organization (1941):

69th Infantry Brigade HHC	Headquarters, 35th Division
134th Infantry Regiment	Hqs and Hqs Det
137th Infantry Regiment	Med Det
70th Infantry Brigade HHC	Headquarters Company
138th Infantry Regiment*	35th Military Police Company
140th Infantry Regiment**	35th Signal Company
60th Field Artillery Brigade HHB	110th Ordnance Company
127th Field Artillery Regiment (155mm)	110th Engineers (Combat)
130th Field Artillery Regiment (75mm)	110th Medical Regiment
161st Field Artillery Regiment (75mm)	110th Quartermaster Regiment

*Relieved from division 3 Feb 42.
**Relieved from division 27 Jan 43 and replaced by 320th Infantry Regt assigned 26 Jan 43.

Typical Organization (1944/45):

134th Infantry Regiment	60th Engineer Combat Battalion
137th Infantry Regiment	110th Medical Battalion
320th Infantry Regiment	35th Counter Intelligence Corps Det
HHB Division Artillery	Headquarters Special Troops
127th Field Artillery Battalion (155mm)	Hqs Company, 35th Infantry Division
161st Field Artillery Battalion (105mm)	Military Police Platoon
216th Field Artillery Battalion (105mm)	735th Ordnance Light Maintenance Company
219th Field Artillery Battalion (105mm)	35th Quartermaster Company
35th Reconnaissance Troop, Mecz	35th Signal Company

737th Tank Battalion *(attached 9 Jul 44–28 Aug 44, 11 Sep 44–22 Nov 44, 27 Nov 44–22 Dec 44)*
784th Tank Battalion *(attached 3 Feb 45–28 Feb 45, 10 Mar 45–9 May 45)*
654th Tank Destroyer Battalion *(attached 9 Jul 44–22 Dec 44, 26 Dec 44–12 Jan 45, 17 Jan 45–15 Mar 45,*
                                   25 Mar 45–26 Apr 45, 3 May 45–9 May 45)
691st Tank Destroyer Battalion *(attached 5 Sep 44–9 Sep 44)*
807th Tank Destroyer Battalion *(attached 3 Mar 45–10 Mar 45)*
821st Tank Destroyer Battalion *(attached 19 Jul 44–27 Jul 44)*
116th AAA Gun Battalion *(attached 20 Jul 44–3 Aug 44)*
448th AAA Auto-Wpns Battalion *(attached 9 Jul 44–26 Apr 45, 3 May 45–9 May 45)*
459th AAA Auto-Wpns Battalion *(attached 19 Jul 44–27 Jul 44)*

Overseas Wartime Assignments:

XV Corps - 5 May 44

Third Army *(attached to XIX Corps)* - 8 Jul 44

V Corps - 27 Jul 44

Third Army *(attached to V Corps)* - 1 Aug 44

Third Army - 5 Aug 44

XX Corps - 6 Aug 44

Third Army *(attached to VII Corps)* - 9 Aug 44

XII Corps - 13 Aug 44

Third Army - 23 Dec 44

XX Corps - 24 Dec 44

III Corps - 26 Dec 44

XX Corps - 18 Jan 45

XV Corps - 23 Jan 45

XVI Corps - 30 Jan 45

XIX Corps - 13 Apr 45

XIII Corps - 16 Apr 45

Commanders: MG R. E. Truman: Dec 40

MG William H. Simpson: Oct 41

MG Maxwell Murray: May 42

MG Paul W. Baade: Jan 43

Killed in Action: 2,485   *Wounded in Action:* 11,526   *Died of Wounds:* 462

35th Infantry Division Combat Narrative

The division arrived over Omaha Beach France 5–8 Jul 44 and the 137th Inf attacked along the Vire 11 Jul 44 but was halted at St Gilles, and the 320th Inf held to small gains north of St Lô. On 14 Jul 44 the division was able to reach the Pont Hébert–St Lô Highway and pushed toward the city through well-defended hedgerow terrain with heavy air and artillery support, gaining Hill 122 with the 134th Inf 15 Jul 44 and entering St Lô 18 Jul 44 after the defeat of twelve German counterattacks at Emelie. It then cleared high ground to the south and west and crossed the Vire River on 2 Aug 44.

The division was diverted to the Mortain-Avranches corridor while enroute to assembly areas as a result of the German counteroffensive there, and fought in that vicinity until 13 Aug 44 which included the rescue of a trapped battalion of the 30th Inf Div. Next the division drove east behind the 4th Armd Div, seized Orléans 18 Aug 44, took Montargis 23 Aug 44, and forced the Moselle at Crevechamps with the 137th Inf on 11 Sep 44. The 134th Inf entered the Lorey Bridgehead near Nancy 15 Sep 44 and recovered Agincourt in hard fighting 21 Sep 44. The division cleared the Bois de Faulx and defended the Forêt de Grémecey against strong German counterattacks which punctured its lines 30 Sep 44 and were only restored with the assistance of the 6th Armd Div. With the capture of Chambrey 1 Oct 44 the Forêt de Grémecey was secured. The division then closed the Seille River and took and held Fossieux 8–9 Oct 44, after which its front became quiet into November, permitting the division to regroup and train.

On 8 Nov 44 the 137th Inf attacked across the Seille and fought battles at the Bois d'Amélécourt with the 320th Inf, the Forêt de Château-Salins 10–11 Nov 44 with both 134th and later 320th Inf, and Vivièrs which was taken 10 Nov 44 by 137th Inf. The division stormed Morhange and captured it after heavy combat 15 Nov 44. The 137th Inf was hit by a German counterattack which forced it out of Hilsprich 23 Nov 44, and the 134th Inf finally took the town with tanks and massive artillery fire on 24 Nov 44. The division pushed into Sarreguemines 6 Dec 44 and as it fought for the town, the 134th and 320th Inf assaulted across the Saar River the next day and defended their bridgehead against strong German attacks with liberal air and artillery support. Sarreguemines was reduced after house-to-house combat 11 Dec 44, and the division attacked across the Blies 12 Dec 44 where the 134th Inf was subjected to fierce German counterattacks at Habkirchen, which was finally secured 15 Dec 44. The 137th Inf was driven out of Breiterwald the same day, and on 19 Dec 44 the division halted its offensive and moved to Metz for rehabilitation.

On 26 Dec 44 the division was moved to Arlon Belgium to help relieve Bastogne. After a 13-day battle in which the division faced four German divisional assaults, the 137th Inf took Villers-la-Bonne-Eau by assault on 10 Jan 45. The division advanced into the Lutrebois-Lutremagne area where the 320th Inf took Oubourcy in house-to-house combat 15 Jan 45 and the town of Lutrebois fell after a 5-day engagement. The division returned to Metz for rehabilitation on 18 Jan 45 and assembled near Maastricht Holland 3 Feb 45, relieved the *British 52nd Div* and held defensive positions along the Roer 6–22 Feb 45.

On 25 Feb 45 the division attacked across the Roer at Linnich and the 320th Inf advanced rapidly against moderate opposition to take Venlo Holland 1 Mar 45. On 6 Mar 45 the division reached the Rhine and mopped up Rheinberg, and then pushed through heavy resistance to the Wesel River where the 134th Inf seized Fort Blucher on 11 Mar 45. The division was sent to the rear for rehabilitation 12 Mar 45. The 134th Inf crossed the Rhine east of Rheinberg during the night of 25–26 Mar 45, followed by the division which was engaged at Kirchhellen until the end of the month. The 134th Inf reached the Zweig Canal at Meckinghoven 2 Apr 45 and then joined the rest of the division defending the Rhein-Herne Canal sector. After regrouping, the division attacked across the Rhein-Herne Canal to positions beyond Gelsenkirchen 9 Apr 45 and closed to the Ruhr River west of Witten 11 Apr 45. The division was then posted to the west bank of the Elbe from Tangermuende to Grieben, and with the return of the 134th Inf from corps, to the Colbitz Forest. The division then moved to Hannover for occupation duty on 26 Apr 45 and was in that capacity when hostilities were declared ended on 7 May 45.

36th Infantry Division   Texas National Guard

No Distinctive
Insignia Authorized

25 Nov 40 inducted into federal service at San Antonio Tex as the 36th Division and moved to Cp Bowie Tex 14 Dec 40; participated in the VIII Corps Brownwood Texas Maneuvers 1–13 Jun 41 and returned to Cp Bowie; moved to Mansfield La and took part in both Aug and Sep 41 Louisiana Maneuvers; arrived back at Cp Bowie Tex 2 Oct 41 where redesignated 36th Infantry Division 1 Feb 42; transferred to Cp Blanding Fla 19 Feb 42 and participated in the Carolina Maneuvers 9 Jul–15 Aug 42; stationed at Cp Edwards Mass 17 Aug 43 and departed New York P/E 2 Apr 43; arrived in North Africa 13 Apr 43 and assaulted Salerno Italy 9 Sep 43; assaulted southern France 15 Aug 44; entered Germany 23 Mar 45 and Austria 7 May 45; arrived Hampton Roads P/E 15 Dec 45 and inactivated at Cp Patrick Henry Va same date.

Campaigns: *Naples-Foggia, Anzio, Rome-Arno, Southern France, Rhineland, Ardennes-Alsace, Central Europe*

Aug 45 Loc: Kufstein Austria

Typical Organization (1941):

71st Infantry Brigade HHC
  141st Infantry Regiment*
  142nd Infantry Regiment
72nd Infantry Brigade HHC
  143rd Infantry Regiment
  144th Infantry Regiment
61st Field Artillery Brigade HHB
  131st Field Artillery Regiment (75mm)
  132nd Field Artillery Regiment (75mm)
  133rd Field Artillery Regiment (155mm)

*Relieved from division 1 Feb 42.

Headquarters, 36th Division
Hqs and Hqs Det
Med Det
Headquarters Company
  36th Military Police Platoon
  36th Signal Company
111th Ordnance Company
111th Engineers (Combat)
111th Medical Regiment
111th Quartermaster Regiment

Typical Organization (1944/45):

141st Infantry Regiment
142nd Infantry Regiment
143rd Infantry Regiment
 HHB Division Artillery
131st Field Artillery Battalion (105mm)
132nd Field Artillery Battalion (105mm)
133rd Field Artillery Battalion (105mm)
155th Field Artillery Battalion (155mm)
 36th Reconnaissance Troop, Mecz
191st Tank Battalion *(attached 26 Aug 44–31 Aug 44)*
753rd Tank Battalion *(attached 15 Aug 44–26 Dec 44, 4 Mar 45–29 Mar 45, 29 Apr 45–13 Jun 45)*
636th Tank Destroyer Battalion *(attached 15 Aug 44–29 Mar 45, 29 Apr 45–13 Jun 45)*
822nd Tank Destroyer Battalion *(attached 29 Apr 45–1 May 45)*
443rd AAA Auto-Wpns Battalion *(attached 7 Dec 44–13 Jan 45)*

111th Engineer Combat Battalion
111th Medical Battalion
 36th Counter Intelligence Corps Det
Headquarters Special Troops
Hqs Company, 36th Infantry Division
Military Police Platoon
736th Ordnance Light Maintenance Company
 36th Quartermaster Company
 36th Signal Company

Overseas Wartime Assignments:

VI Corps - April 43
II Corps - 18 Nov 43
Fifth Army - 26 Feb 44
VI Corps - 22 May 44
IV Corps - 11 Jun 44
VI Corps - 13 Jul 44
French First Army (attached) - 5 Dec 44

VI Corps - 15 Dec 44
XXI Corps - 27 Dec 44
Seventh Army - 30 Dec 44
XV Corps - 3 Jan 45
VI Corps - 18 Jan 45
Seventh Army - 29 Mar 45
XXI Corps - 27 Apr 45

Commanders: MG Claude V. Birkhead: Nov 40
          MG Fred L. Walker: Sep 41

MG John E. Dahlquist: Jul 44
BG Robert I. Stack: Nov 45

Killed in Action: 3,131   *Wounded in Action:* 13,191   *Died of Wounds:* 506

36th Infantry Division Combat Narrative

The division landed in North Africa on 13 Apr 43 and trained at Arzew and Rabat. The 141st and 142nd Inf led the division's invasion of Italy 9 Sep 43 in the Paestum area on the Gulf of Salerno. It repulsed four strong German counterattacks and advanced slowly against prepared positions, the 142nd Inf taking Altavilla 11 Sep 43 but being forced out the next day. After the division had secured the Salerno Plain from Agropoli to Altavilla it moved into reserve 20 Sep 43.

The division moved to the Mignano Gap 16 Nov 43 and relieved the 3rd Inf Div. Despite severe winter weather and strong opposition the division captured M.Maggiore 3 Dec 43. The 143rd Inf took part of M.Sammurco 7 Dec 43 and held it against counterattack, and the 142nd Inf renewed its assault up key M.Lungo 15 Dec 43 as the 143rd Inf attacked San Pietro. After heavy fighting M.Sammurco's southern and western slopes were cleared 26 Dec 43, and on 30 Dec 43 the division moved into reserve. On 20 Jan 44 the 141st and 143rd Inf attacked across the Rapido River in front of Cassino, but the bridgehead was defeated 22 Jan 44. The 142nd Inf overran Manna Farm 31 Jan 44 while attached to 34th Inf Div, and the 141st and 142nd Inf suffered heavy losses in close combat trying to storm Albaneta Farm 11 Feb 44. The division was relieved on M.Castellone 28 Feb 44, and after assisting the 34th Inf Div in further attacks on Cassino, was withdrawn for rehabilitation 12 Mar 44.

The division landed in the Anzio Perimeter 22 May 44 and engaged in holding actions except for the 141st Inf which took Velletri after heavy fighting 1 Jun 44. The division then entered Rome 4 Jun 44 and advanced up Highway 1 to take Magliano and then Piombino 26 Jun 44. It was then moved back to Paestum for rehabilitation and training for the invasion of southern France.

The division assaulted the Raphael-Fréjus area of southern France on 15 Aug 44 with all three regiments, and linked up with the 1st A/B Task Force near Le Muy on 17 Aug 44. The division then pushed up the Rhône River Valley commencing on 21 Aug 44 and the 141st Inf initiated the fierce battle for Montélimar 23 Aug 44 during which a German counterattack on 25 Aug 44 temporarily separated the 141st and 142nd Inf along the Roubion, and this gap at Bonlieu was not restored until 27 Aug 44. The next day the 142nd Inf surrounded Livron and blocked Highway 7, but the majority of German forces had already escaped the Montélimar trap, the town itself falling the same day. The division captured much equipment and large numbers of prisoners as the 143rd Inf reached the junction of the Drôme and Rhône Rivers 30 Aug 44 and ended the battle. On 2 Sep 44 the division halted to permit the French II Corps to enter Lyon, and the 143rd Inf forced the Doubs River at Avanne and the division invested Vesoul on 11 Sep 44. It surrendered 13 Sep 44 and the division pursued to the Moselle at Remiremont which the 141st Inf crossed on 21 Sep 44, the 142nd Inf capturing the town 23 Sep 44. This brought the division to the Vosges foothills.

The division fought the Battle for Bruyères 15–18 Oct 44, after which a battalion of the 141st Inf became cut off in the Forêt Domaniale de Champ on 23 Oct 44 and was rescued by the attached 442nd Inf (Nisei) after heavy combat 30 Oct 44. The forest was finally cleared 10 Nov 44 and the division reached the Meurthe River which it crossed at St Leonard and Clefcy 21 Nov 44. After encountering strong opposition the division breached the Ste Marie Pass to the Alsatian Plains on 25 Nov 44. It cleared Sélestat 4 Dec 44 with the 103rd Inf Div and then began its drive on the Colmar Pocket. The advance was halted 13 Dec 44 and resumed on 20 Dec 44. The division then assembled at Montbronn 1 Jan 45 and took up defensive positions in the Rohrweiler-Weyersheim region with the 143rd Inf 19 Jan 45. The 142nd Inf fought the Battle of Oberhoffen 1–12 Feb 45, and on 23 Feb 45 the division relieved the 101st A/B Div. It took Bitschhoffen 15 Mar 45 and penetrated German lines along the Moder River.

On 16 Mar 45, following a massed artillery barrage, the 142nd Inf crossed the Zintzel at Mertzwiller while the 141st Inf pushed through the Haguenau Forest against determined German resistance, and the motorized 143rd Inf was stopped below Eberbach. Crossing over the Bieberbach River, the division seized Dieffenbach 18 Mar 45 and fought through the Wissembourg Gap the following day. The division continued mopping up pillboxes west of the Rhine and reached the Rhine River at Leimersheim 24 Mar 45. It then maintained defensive positions until it turned over its sector to the 3ème Division d'Infanterie Algérienne.

On 24 Apr 45 the division was relieved in Regierungsbezirk Saarland and the division moved to relieve the 63rd Inf Div along the Danube. The 141st and 142nd Inf led the division's attack across the Lecht River 29 Apr 45, after which the division followed in the wake of the 10th Armd Div from the Landsberg area to take Bad Toelz 1 May 45 with the 141st Inf. The division then crossed the Isar River on 2 May 45 and had reached the Kufstein area of Austria when hostilities were declared ended 7 May 45.

37th Infantry Division   **Ohio National Guard**

15 Oct 40 inducted into federal service at Columbus Ohio as the 37th Division and moved to Cp Shelby Miss 20 Oct 40; participated in the V Corps Louisiana Maneuvers 16–27 Jun 41 and went to Evans La where was part of both Aug and Sep 41 Louisiana Maneuvers; returned to Cp Shelby Miss 3 Oct 41 where redesignated 37th Infantry Division 1 Feb 42; arrived Indian-town Gap Mil Res Pa 18 Feb 42 and moved to San Francisco P/E 11 May 42 and departed 26 May 42; arrived Fiji Islands 11 Jun 42 and Guadalcanal 5 Apr 43; landed on Kokorana Island Solomons 21 Jul 43 and New Georgia Island 22 Jul 43; returned to Guadalcanal 9 Sep 43 and went to Bougainville 8 Nov 43; landed Huon Gulf New Guinea 18 Dec 44 and Manus Island 22 Dec 44 enroute to Philippines where assaulted Lingayen Gulf Luzon 9 Jan 45; arrived Los Angeles P/E 18 Dec 45 and inactivated at Cp Anza Calif same date.

Campaigns: *Northern Solomons, Luzon*
Aug 45 Loc: San Jose Philippine Islands

Typical Organization (1941):

73rd Infantry Brigade HHC
  145th Infantry Regiment
  148th Infantry Regiment
74th Infantry Brigade HHC
  147th Infantry Regiment*
  166th Infantry Regiment**
62nd Field Artillery Brigade HHB
  134th Field Artillery Regiment (75mm)
  135th Field Artillery Regiment (75mm)
  136th Field Artillery Regiment (155mm)

Headquarters, 37th Division
Hqs and Hqs Det
Med Det
Headquarters Company
  37th Military Police Company
  37th Signal Company
112th Ordnance Company
112th Engineers (Combat)
112th Medical Regiment
112th Quartermaster Regiment

*Relieved from division in Apr 42 enroute to Tonga Island and replaced by 129th Infantry Regt which was assigned 31 Jul 43.
**Relieved from division 16 Jan 42.

Typical Organization (1944/45):

129th Infantry Regiment
145th Infantry Regiment
148th Infantry Regiment
  HHB Division Artillery
  6th Field Artillery Battalion (105mm)
135th Field Artillery Battalion (105mm)
136th Field Artillery Battalion (155mm)
140th Field Artillery Battalion (105mm)
37th Reconnaissance Troop, Mecz

117th Engineer Combat Battalion
112th Medical Battalion
  37th Counter Intelligence Corps Det
Headquarters Special Troops
Hqs Company, 37th Infantry Division
737th Ordnance Light Maintenance Company
  37th Quartermaster Company
  37th Signal Company
Military Police Platoon

Overseas Wartime Assignments:

South Pacific Area Cmd - 28 Sep 42
XIV Corps - 6 Apr 43
Island Command APO 709 - 11 Jul 43
Navy Task Force 31 - 22 Sep 43
I Marine Amphibious Corps - 1 Oct 43
South Pacific Area Command - 15 Dec 43
  (attached XIV Corps)

XIV Corps - 15 Jun 44
Sixth Army *(attached XIV Corps)* - 20 Nov 44
XIV Corps - 25 Jan 45
Sixth Army - 5 Mar 45
I Corps *(attached)* 11 Apr 45
Eighth Army *(attached XIV Corps)* - 1 Jul 45

Commander: MG Robert S. Beightler: Oct 40

Killed in Action: 1,094   *Wounded in Action:* 4,861   *Died of Wounds:* 250

37th Infantry Division Combat Narrative

The division arrived at Viti Levu in the Fiji Islands on 11 Jun 42 with the mission of both fortifying the islands and conducting intensive training. On 5 Apr 43 it moved to Guadalcanal where it continued training. The 148th Inf was detached and landed on Banika Island in the Russell Islands Group 7 Jun 43, and a battalion from it and the 145th Inf were attached to the 1st Marine Raider Regt for operations on New Georgia Island. The remainder of the 145th and 148th Inf arrived at Rendova New Georgia 7 Jul 43 and engaged in heavy fighting for Munda Airfield under the 43rd Inf Div. The 148th Inf attacked Bartley Ridge and then shifted its assault to Horseshoe Hill where it was surrounded 26 Jul–1 Aug 43 until the Japanese evacuated their positions. The 145th Inf finished clearing Bartley Ridge 31 Jul 43. The rest of the division had arrived on New Georgia in the meantime on 22 Jul 43 and all elements reverted to its control, and Munda Airfield was finally seized 5 Aug 43. The division pushed across the island and conducted combat patrolling until returned to Guadalcanal 2–22 Sep 43. The newly assigned 129th Inf, formerly the Espiritu Santo garrison force, moved up to join it as the division moved to Bougainville 5 Nov 43–12 Jan 44.

The 148th Inf landed first on Bougainville 8 Nov 43 and was followed by the 129th Inf on 13 Nov 43 and the 145th Inf which landed 19 Nov 43. Relieving the Marines there, the division took over the area perimeter defense, constructed roads and bridges, conducted patrols, and repulsed eight Japanese divisional attacks during March 1944. These included the 8 Mar 44 counterattack on Hill 700 which drove a salient in the lines of 145th Inf which wasn't reduced until 13 Mar 44 after heavy combat; the main counterattack of 11 Mar 44 toward Piva Airfield which hit the 129th Inf; and the 23 Mar 44 general counterattack which penetrated the lines of 129th Inf before it was defeated. The latter marked the last Japanese offensive activity in the Solomons and the division cleared the Laruma Valley during April 1944. The division remained on Bougainville until 14 Dec 44, conducting construction and combat activity up to 11 Oct 44 when it began training for operations in the Philippine Islands.

The division moved to the Philippines via Huon Gulf New Guinea and Manus Island, and landed against slight resistance at Lingayen Gulf Luzon 9 Jan 45. The 148th Inf took San Carlos 10 Jan 45 and the division assembled, and then advanced against strong Japanese opposition toward Clark Field and Fort Stotsenberg. The 145th and 148th Inf reached the Culayo-Magalang line and the runways of Clark Field 26 Jan 45 and captured their objectives with the 129th Inf on 31 Jan 45. The division then turned south toward Manila and the 148th Inf reached it 4 Feb 45. After crossing the Pasig River the division began the house-to-house combat which slowly reduced the city, and on 23 Feb 45 the assault was begun on Intramuros after heavy artillery preparation. The 145th stormed the Quezon and Parian Gates while the 129th Inf crossed the Pasig River in assault boats and stormed the Mint Building. The 148th Inf cleared the Legislative Building and by 3 Mar 45 the division had secured Manila. The division then garrisoned it until 26 Mar 45 and conducted mopping up activity.

The 129th Inf was detached to Bauang and attached to the 33rd Inf Div 26 Mar–10 Apr 45. The 145th Inf remained in Manila when the division moved to northwest Luzon for the offensive against Baguio and did not rejoin it until 2 Jun 45. The division commenced its drive 10 Apr 45 as the 129th and 148th Inf attacked up Highway 9 and took Three Peaks on 11 Apr 45. Following the Battle for Hairpin Hill the 148th Inf reached the Irisan River 17 Apr 45, but the ridges there were not cleared until 21 Apr 45 when the advance resumed. Mt Mirador fell after heavy combat to the 129th Inf on 26 Apr 45 and Baguio was overrun by the combined action of 33rd and 37th Inf Divs the following day. The division was relieved by the 33rd Inf Div and moved to San Jose 4 May 45 where it rested until 29 May 45. It then moved into the Balete Pass–Santa Fe area and attacked north on Highway 5 31 May 45, the 129th Inf capturing Aritao 5 Jun 45. Bagabag fell to the 145th Inf 9 Jun 45, and the division pushed across the Cagayen Valley and took Cauayan 16 Jun 45 and Ilagan 19 Jun 45. Although the Luzon campaign was officially closed 30 Jun 45 the division continued to mop up and secure its area, and was collecting and processing Japanese prisoners when the war ended.

38th Infantry Division   **Indiana, Kentucky, West Virginia National Guard**

17 Jan 41 inducted into federal service at Indianapolis Ind as the 38th Division and moved to Cp Shelby Miss 26 Jan 41; participated in V Corps Louisiana Maneuvers 16–27 Jun 41 and moved to Cooper La 7 Aug 41 and participated in both Aug and Sep 41 Louisiana Maneuvers; returned to Cp Shelby Miss 4 Oct 41 where redesignated 38th Infantry Division 1 Mar 42; moved to Louisiana Maneuver Area 20 Sep 42 for IV Corps Maneuvers; arrived Cp Carabelle Fla 23 Nov 42 and Cp Livingston La 28 Jan 43; left New Orleans P/E by echelon 31 Dec 43 and arrived completely in Hawaii by 21 Jan 44; left Hawaii 11 Jul 43 and landed Oro Bay New Guinea 23 Jul 44; departed New Guinea 30 Nov 44 and arrived Leyte Philippines 16 Dec 44; landed on Luzon 29 Jan 45 and assaulted El Fraile Island 13 Apr 45 and Caballo Island 27 Mar 45; returned Los Angeles P/E 9 Nov 45 and inactivated at Cp Anza Calif same date.

Campaigns: *New Guinea, Southern Philippines, Luzon*
Aug 45 Loc: Manila Philippine Islands

Typical Organization (1941):

75th Infantry Brigade HHC
  149th Infantry Regiment
  150th Infantry Regiment*
76th Infantry Brigade HHC
  151st Infantry Regiment
  152nd Infantry Regiment
63rd Field Artillery Brigade HHB
  138th Field Artillery Regiment (75mm)
  139th Field Artillery Regiment (75mm)
  150th Field Artillery Regiment (155mm)

*Relieved from division 10 Feb 42.

Headquarters, 38th Division
Hqs and Hqs Det
Med Det
Headquarters Company
  38th Military Police Company
  38th Signal Company
113th Ordnance Company
113th Engineers (Combat)
113th Medical Regiment
113th Quartermaster Regiment

Typical Organization (1944/45):

149th Infantry Regiment
151st Infantry Regiment
152nd Infantry Regiment
 HHB Division Artillery
138th Field Artillery Battalion (105mm)
139th Field Artillery Battalion (105mm)
150th Field Artillery Battalion (155mm)
163rd Field Artillery Battalion (105mm)
  38th Reconnaissance Troop, Mecz

113th Engineer Combat Battalion
113th Medical Battalion
  38th Counter Intelligence Corps Det
Headquarters Special Troops
Hqs Company, 38th Infantry Division
Military Police Platoon
738th Ordnance Light Maintenance Company
  38th Quartermaster Company
  38th Signal Company

Overseas Wartime Assignments:

Central Pacific Area Cmd - 17 Jan 44
Sixth Army - 23 Jul 44
X Corps - 24 Aug 44

Eighth Army - 28 Sep 44
XI Corps - 30 Jan 45
Eighth Army *(attached XIV Corps)* - 1 Jul 45

Commanders: MG Robert H. Tyndall: Jan 41
             MG Daniel I. Sultan: Apr 41
             MG Henry L. C. Jones: Apr 42

MG William C. Chase: Feb 45
MG Frederick A. Irving: Aug 45

Killed in Action: 645   *Wounded in Action:* 2,814   *Died of Wounds:* 139

38th Infantry Division Combat Narrative

The advance detachment of the division arrived in Hawaii 21 Dec 43 from San Francisco, followed by the bulk of the division which sailed from New Orleans and arrived in Hawaii completely by 21 Jan 44. There it relieved the 6th Inf Div of ground defense of Oahu until 11 Jul 44 when departed Hawaii for Oro Bay New Guinea, where it trained until 29 Nov 44 for operations in the Philippines.

The division left Oro Bay New Guinea on 30 Nov 44 and reached Leyte Philippines on 16 Dec 44. The 149th Inf assisted in reducing the Japanese paratroopers which had assaulted Buri, Bayung, and San Pablo airstrips 6 Dec 44, and cleared Buri Airfield after heavy combat by 10 Dec 44 in conjunction with the 11th A/B Div. A battalion of the 152nd Inf moved to Agojo Point on Samar under direct Sixth Army control, and the 151st Inf performed security operations in the Culasian Point–Barugo area under 24th Inf Div. The division was reassembled by 4 Jan 45 and landed in the San Narcisco area of Luzon on 29 Jan 45 without opposition.

Subic Bay was gained with the capture of Grande Island by a battalion of the 151st Inf as the port facilities at Olongapo fell 30 Jan 45. The division then commenced the drive to clear Highway 7, all three regiments participating in the fierce Battle of Zig Zag Pass 1–14 Feb 45 and Dinalupihan fell to the 149th Inf on 5 Feb 45. The reinforced 151st Inf landed at Mariveles Bataan 15 Feb 45 and defeated a major Japanese counterattack that night. The division pushed down the east coast road to Pilar and across the peninsula to Bagac, securing most of Bataan Peninsula by 21 Feb 45. A battalion of the 151st Inf was detached to relieve the 503rd Parachute Inf on Corregidor 24 Feb 45 and assigned to garrison the island 8 Mar 45. The division moved to Fort Stotsenburg on 10 Mar 45 and relieved the 43rd Inf Div there. It then pushed west to destroy entrenched Japanese forces between the fort and Mt Pinatubo. Battalion-sized landings were conducted in the meantime by the 151st Inf at Caballo Island and Fort Drum El Fraile Island on 27 Mar 45, and Carabao Island on 16 Apr 45.

The division relieved the 6th Inf Div in the Montalban sector on 25 Apr 45 after Mt Pinatubo fell to the 149th and 151st Inf on 15 Apr 45. The exchange of sectors between the two divisions was completed by 30 Apr 45. After intensive artillery bombardment the 152nd Inf attacked Woodpecker Ridge 2 May 45 but its advance was suspended until 4 May 45, when it attacked again and again was brought to a halt. In the meantime the 145th Inf attacked the Shimbu Line 4 May 45 as the division approached the Wawa Dam, and gained the top of Sugar Loaf Hill after heavy fighting on 6 May 45. The following day the 152nd Inf reattacked Woodpecker Ridge. The 145th Inf finally took Mt Binicayan on 9 May 45 after several assaults, and on 16 May 45 the 152nd Inf renewed its attempts to force Woodpecker Ridge. The 149th Inf relieved the 145th Inf on Mt Pacawagan and continued the drive on Wawa Dam which was met with strong opposition. The 152nd Inf tried to storm Woodpecker Ridge again on 18 May 45 and the attack, assisted by flamethrowing tanks, was resumed 21 May 45. On 22 May 45 Woodpecker Ridge fell and on 28 May 45 the Japanese abandoned Wawa Dam.

The division then moved to Bayanbayanan in preparation for new operations in southern Luzon on 23 Jun 45. The Luzon campaign was declared ended as of 30 Jun 45, but the division continued to mop up Japanese forces in the Marikana area of eastern Luzon until the war ended.

40th Infantry Division

California, Nevada, Utah National Guard

3 Mar 41 inducted into federal service at Los Angeles Calif as the 40th Division and moved to Cp San Luis Obispo Calif 10 Mar 41; went to Ft Lewis Wash 22 Aug 41 for the Fourth Army Maneuvers there; returned to Cp San Luis Obispo Calif 5 Sep 41 and moved to Los Angeles Calif 9 Dec 41 where redesignated the 40th Infantry Division 18 Feb 42; arrived Ft Lewis Wash 1 May 42 and staged at Cp Stoneman Calif 14 Aug 42 until departed San Francisco P/E 23 Aug 42; arrived Hawaii 1 Sep 42 where commenced jungle and amphibious training 17 Oct 43 after being relieved of defense duties; left Hawaii 25 Dec 43 and arrived Guadalcanal 31 Dec 43; arrived at Cape Gloucester New Britain 23 Apr 44 and moved to New Guinea 18 Dec 44 and Manus Island 20 Dec 44 enroute to the Philippines; landed on Luzon 9 Jan 45 and landed on Panay Island 15 Mar 45 and on Los Negros Island 29 Mar 45; arrived in Korea 22 Sep 45 and returned to San Francisco P/E 6 Apr 46 and was inactivated at Cp Mason Calif 7 Apr 46.

Campaigns: *Bismarck Archipelago, Southern Philippines, Luzon*
Aug 45 Loc: Negros Philippine Islands

Typical Organization (1941):

79th Infantry Brigade HHC
  159th Infantry Regiment*
  184th Infantry Regiment**
80th Infantry Brigade HHC
  160th Infantry Regiment***
  185th Infantry Regiment
65th Field Artillery Brigade HHB
  143rd Field Artillery Regiment (75mm)
  145th Field Artillery Regiment (75mm)
  222nd Field Artillery Regiment (155mm)

Headquarters, 40th Division
Hqs and Hqs Det
Med Det
Headquarters Company
  40th Military Police Company
  40th Signal Company
115th Ordnance Company
115th Engineers (Combat)
115th Medical Regiment
115th Quartermaster Regiment

*Relieved from division 29 Sep 41.
**Relieved from division 16 Jun 42.
***Relieved from division 1 Sep 42 but reassigned to division 25 Dec 43; during its absence the 165th Infantry Regt
    was assigned.

Typical Organization (1944/45):

108th Infantry Regiment****
160th Infantry Regiment
185th Infantry Regiment
HHB Division Artillery
143rd Field Artillery Battalion (105mm)
164th Field Artillery Battalion (105mm)
213th Field Artillery Battalion (105mm)
222nd Field Artillery Battalion (155mm)
  40th Reconnaissance Troop, Mecz

115th Engineer Combat Battalion
115th Medical Battalion
  40th Counter Intelligence Corps Det
Headquarters Special Troops
Hqs Company, 40th Infantry Division
Military Police Platoon
740th Ordnance Light Maintenance Company
  40th Quartermaster Company
  40th Signal Company

****Assigned to division 1 Sep 42.

Overseas Wartime Assignments:

Hawaiian Dept - 1 Sep 42
South Pacific Area Cmd - 31 Dec 43
Army Forces in the Far East - 18 Apr 44
Sixth Army - 23 Apr 44
Eighth Army - 28 Sep 44

XIV Corps - 20 Nov 44
Sixth Army - 21 Feb 45 *(attached to XI Corps)*
Eighth Army - 15 Mar 45
Sixth Army - 1 Jul 45
XXIV Corps - 15 Aug 45

Commanders: MG Walter P. Story: Mar 41
              BG Ernest J. Dawley: Sep 41

MG Rapp Brush: Apr 42
BG Donald J. Myers: Jul 45

Killed in Action: 614   *Wounded in Action:* 2,407   *Died of Wounds:* 134

40th Infantry Division Combat Narrative

The division arrived in Hawaii 1 Sep 42 and defended the outer islands until 16 Jan 43. It then assumed defense responsibility for northern Oahu, and intensified training after being relieved of this defensive mission 17 Oct 43. The division moved to Guadalcanal 20–31 Dec 43 and trained as well as engaged in limited combat patrolling. After the cancellation of projected operations against Lossuk Bay New Ireland on 12 Mar 44, the division was directed to relieve the 1st Marine Div in western New Britain Island, the 185th Inf arriving at Cape Gloucester on 23 Apr 44 and rest of the division following on 28 Apr 44. Cape Hoskins airdrome was occupied without opposition 7 May 44, elements sent to relieve the 112th Cav Regt at Arawe, and general security operations continued on New Britain until 27 Nov 44 when the division was relieved by the *Australian 5th Div.* The division assembled at Borgen Bay New Britain 28 Nov 44 and moved via Huon Gulf New Guinea and Manus Island to the Philippines.

The 160th and 185th Inf landed in the Baybay-Lingayen area of Luzon Philippine Islands on 9 Jan 45 and seized Lingayen Airfield virtually unopposed. After consolidating in the Dulig-Labrador-Uyong area, the 160th Inf began pushing down Route 13 and took Tarlac without resistance on 21 Jan 45. It forced a bridgehead at Bamban 23 Jan 45 and then encountered the main Japanese lines in the Bamban Hills, the 108th Inf being sent in to assist the advance. The 160th Inf moved up Storm King Mountain against strong opposition and supported by air and tank fire 6 Feb 45, the 185th Inf attacked Snake Hill and gained Hill 1500 on 15 Feb 45, and after several attempts the 108th Inf captured Hill 7 on 16 Feb 45. After the 160th Inf captured contested Object Hill 19 Feb 45 the division rested while air strikes softened up the Zambales Mountains. On 23 Feb 45 the 108th and 185th Inf renewed the offensive, taking Sacobia Ridge, and with the fall of Hill 1700 to the 185th Inf on 25 Feb 45 the division was relieved by the 43rd Inf Div on 2 Mar 45. It then assembled in the San Fabian–San Jacinto–Manaoag area for rehabilitation.

The 108th Inf was detached to Eighth Army Area Command and arrived on Leyte Island 13 Mar 45 where it was engaged in destroying Japanese remnants and reconnoitering Masbate Island and other islands off its coast. The 108th Inf next landed at Macajalar Bay in Mindanao and assisted in the clearing of Sayre highway, returning to division control 28 Jun 45.

The rest of the division left Luzon on 15 Mar 45 and the 185th Inf landed unopposed on southern Panay Island 18 Mar 45. It advanced rapidly and took Iloilo 20 Mar 45. The 160th Inf arrived on Panay Island 26 Mar 45, and leaving elements behind to complete mopping up, the division next landed on Los Negros Island 29 Mar 45. 185th Inf soldiers took the Bago River Bridge intact after landing at Patik, and the regiment landed unopposed near Pulupandan, securing Bacolod easily on 30 Mar 45 as the 160th Inf came ashore. On 2 Apr 45 Talisay was occupied and the division regrouped 8 Apr 45 in preparation for the attack on the Japanese defenses in the Negritos-Patog area. The 503rd Prcht Inf was attached, and the division attacked with three regiments on 9 Apr 45. Fighting was intense as the division cleared ridges and ravines in spite of sharp Japanese counterattacks and torrential rainstorms. The drive was stopped as air and artillery support was called in, and then resumed 17 Apr 45. The 160th Inf gained the military crest of Hill 3155 on 18 Apr 45 but lost it to a Japanese assault, and the position switched hands until finally won by the regiment 23 May 45. The 185th Inf stormed Virgine Ridge 2 May 45 and pushed toward the final Japanese strongpoint on Negros Occidental; Hill 4055. The Japanese withdrew from this mountain 31 May 45 and pulled back into the island interior, ending organized resistance. The division returned to Panay Island 13–27 Jun 45 where it was rejoined by the 108th Inf on 29 Jun 45. The division assembled in the Oton–Santa Barbara–Tigauan area for rehabilitation and training. It was in this mode when the war ended.

41st Infantry Division

Washington, Oregon, Idaho, Montana National Guard

16 Sep 40 inducted into federal service at Portland Oreg as the 41st Division and moved to Cp Murray Wash 20 Sep 40 and to Ft Lewis Wash 20 Mar 41; participated in IX Corps Maneuvers at Hunter-Liggett Mil Res Calif 5 Jun–2 Jul 41; returned to Ft Lewis Wash 4 Jul 41 and participated in the Fourth Army Maneuvers there 15–30 Aug 41; redesignated as the 41st Infantry Division 17 Feb 42 and departed San Francisco P/E 19 Mar 42; arrived in Australia 13 May 42 and landed Dobodura New Guinea 25 Jan 43; returned to Australia 29 Jul 43 and arrived Finschhafen New Guinea 20 Mar 44; assaulted Hollandia New Guinea 22 Apr 44 and Biak Island 27 May 44; departed Biak Island by echelon 29 Jan–1 Feb 45 and arrived Mindoro Philippines 9 Jan 45; assaulted Zamboanga Mindanao 10 Mar 45 and divisional elements fought on Palawan Island and the Sulu Archipelago; arrived Japan 6 Oct 45 where inactivated 31 Dec 45.

Campaigns: *New Guinea, Luzon, Southern Philippines*
Aug 45 Loc: Zamboanga Mindanao Philippine Islands

Typical Organization (1941):

81st Infantry Brigade HHC	Headquarters, 41st Division
161st Infantry Regiment*	Hqs and Hqs Det
163rd Infantry Regiment	Med Det
82nd Infantry Brigade HHC	Headquarters Company
162nd Infantry Regiment	41st Military Police Company
186th Infantry Regiment	41st Signal Company
66th Field Artillery Brigade HHB	116th Ordnance Company
146th Field Artillery Regiment (75mm)	116th Engineers (Combat)
148th Field Artillery Regiment (75mm)	116th Medical Regiment
218th Field Artillery Regiment (155mm)	116th Quartermaster Regiment

*Relieved from division 3 Aug 42.

Typical Organization (1944/45):

162nd Infantry Regiment
163rd Infantry Regiment
186th Infantry Regiment
HHB Division Artillery
146th Field Artillery Battalion (105mm)
167th Field Artillery Battalion (105mm)
205th Field Artillery Battalion (105mm)
218th Field Artillery Battalion (155mm)
41st Reconnaissance Troop, Mecz

116th Engineer Combat Battalion
116th Medical Battalion
41st Counter Intelligence Corps Det
Headquarters Special Troops
Hqs Company, 41st Infantry Division
Military Police Platoon
741st Ordnance Light Maintenance Company
41st Quartermaster Company
41st Signal Company

Overseas Wartime Assignments:

Army Forces in Australia - 6 Apr 42
I Corps - 8 Sep 42
Sixth Army - 24 Feb 44
I Corps - 23 Mar 44
Sixth Army - 6 May 44

I Corps - 15 Jun 44
Sixth Army - 29 Jun 44
Eighth Army - 9 Oct 44
I Corps - 1 Jul 45
X Corps - 15 Aug 45

Note: Attached to RECKLESS Task Force 23 Mar 44–17 Apr 44; to BEWITCH Task Force 17 Apr 44–6 May 44; and to HURRICANE Task Force 10 May 44–25 Sep 44.

Commanders: MG George A. White: Sep 40
BG Carlos A. Pennington: Nov 41

MG Horace H. Fuller: Dec 41
MG Jens A. Doe: Jun 44

Killed in Action: 743   *Wounded in Action:* 3,504   *Died of Wounds:* 217

41st Infantry Division Combat Narrative

The division moved by echelon to Australia, the 162nd Inf departing New York and arriving at Melbourne on 9 Apr 42, the 163rd Inf and division headquarters leaving San Francisco and arriving 6 Apr 42, and the 186th Inf and division artillery leaving San Francisco and reaching Australia 13 May 42. After training at Cp Seymour it moved to Rockhampton for intensive training on 19 Jul 42.

The 163rd Inf was sent to New Guinea and arrived 27 Dec 42, sent on to Dobodura 2 Jan 43, and began an attack to clear the road to Sanananda 8 Jan 43 which it accomplished by 22 Jan 43, ending the Papuan campaign. Meanwhile the rest of the division closed into Dobodura on 25 Jan 43 as the 186th Inf was flown to New Guinea to relieve the 32nd Inf Div in the Buna-Gona area. The 162nd Inf sailed from Australia 8 Feb 43 and was committed at Port Moresby and Oro Bay, and engaged in clearing the northern coast of New Guinea, reaching Mile Bay on 27 Feb 43. It made an unopposed landing at Nassau Bay 30 Jun 43 and started pushing toward Salamaua in conjunction with Australian forces 17 Jul 43. The 163rd Inf fought to the Kumisi River during February and then engaged in patrolling until returned to Australia from New Guinea 16 Jul 43. It was followed by the 186th Inf, but the 162nd Inf continued operations in the Sanananda-Killerton-Gona vicinity and stormed Roosevelt Ridge 14 Aug 43. After the Battle of Scout Ridge in Dot Inlet 9 Sep 43 the 162nd Inf arrived in Australia on 3 Oct 43.

After rehabilitation in Australia the division relocated to Finschhafen New Guinea on 20 Mar 44 and its regiments parceled out again on different tasks. The 163rd Inf landed at Wapil 22 Apr 44 to clear Aitape as the major unit of Task Force PERSECUTION, and the 162nd and 186th Inf as Task Force RECKLESS landed at Humboldt Bay 22 Apr 44. The two regiments captured both Hollandia and Sentani airdromes and after being relieved by the 24th Inf Div on 6 May 44, the division moved to Hollekang for rehabilitation. The 163rd Inf meanwhile secured Aitape and Rohn Point 24 Apr 44, overran Kamti Village, and landed against slight resistance at Arara New Guinea on 17 May 44. It secured the Arara and Toem area opposite Wakde Island which was stormed and taken despite caves and pillboxes 18–20 May 44. The 163rd Inf next made unopposed landings on Liki and Niroemoar Islands and defended the Tor River line on New Guinea until relieved 23 May 44 and sent to Biak to reinforce the division.

The 186th Inf landed against slight resistance on Biak Island 27 May 44, but 162nd Inf was forced from its positions west of Parai 29 May 44 and forced to withdraw by land and water to a small perimeter near Idbi. The 163rd Inf landed 31 May 44 and the 186th Inf pushed into the island plateau on 1 Jun 44 as the 162nd Inf regrouped and pushed through the Parai Defile which was not cleared until the entire division was committed on 12 Jun 44. The 186th Inf had seized Mokmar Airfield 7 Jun 44 and the caves were cleared by 4 Jul 44. With the destruction of Idbi Pocket on 22 Jul 44 the division mopped up the island until 20 Aug 44. The division departed Biak Island by echelon 29 Jan–1 Feb 45 and disembarked at Mindoro Philippine Islands 8–9 Feb 45.

The 186th Inf assaulted Palawan Island 28 Feb 45, took Puerto Princesa and its airfields, seized Hill 1445 on 8 Mar 45, and eliminated Japanese mountain positions until returned to division control at Zamboanga Mindanao on 27 Mar 45. The division had landed on Zamboanga Peninsula on Mindanao 10 Mar 45 and captured Zamboanga city and Caldera Point quickly, but Mt Capisan was not taken by the 162nd Inf until 24 Mar 45. When the 163rd Inf gained the heights near Mt Pulungbatu 29 Mar 45 organized resistance ended, but mopping up operations continued. Numerous islands were attacked, notably Sanga-Sanga by 162nd Inf elements on 2 Apr 45; Jolo Island by the 163rd Inf on 9 Apr 45; and Busuanga Island by the 186th Inf the same day. Fighting continued on Palawan, Jolo Island, Mindanao, and Zamboanga, and on 4 May 45 the 162nd Inf landed at Parang Mindanao to reinforce the 31st and later 24th Inf Divs until 6 Jul 45. The 163rd Inf fought the Battle for Mt Daho 16–22 Apr 45 which marked the end of organized Japanese opposition on Jolo Island. The division continued to mop up until the war ended.

42nd Infantry Division

No Distinctive Insignia Authorized

14 Jul 43 activated at Cp Gruber Okla and trained under X and XVI Corps; staged at Cp Kilmer N.J. 23 Dec 44 until departed New York P/E 6 Jan 45; arrived France 18 Jan 45 and entered Germany 18 Mar 45 and Austria 5 May 45; inactivated in Austria 29 Jun 46.

Campaigns: *Rhineland, Central Europe*
Aug 45 Loc: Wertheim Germany

Typical Organization (1944/45):

222nd Infantry Regiment
232nd Infantry Regiment
242nd Infantry Regiment
 HHB Division Artillery
232nd Field Artillery Battalion (105mm)
392nd Field Artillery Battalion (105mm)
402nd Field Artillery Battalion (105mm)
542nd Field Artillery Battalion (155mm)
 42nd Reconnaissance Troop, Mecz
191st Tank Battalion *(attached 17 Feb 45–4 Mar 45)*
749th Tank Battalion *(attached 26 Mar 45–28 Mar 45)*
510th Tank Destroyer Battalion *(attached 12 Mar 45–16 Mar 45)*
645th Tank Destroyer Battalion *(attached 17 Feb 45–4 Mar 45)*
692nd Tank Destroyer Battalion *(attached 15 Mar 45–29 Mar 45, 31 Mar 45–12 Jul 45)*
431st AAA Auto-Wpns Bn *(attached 16 Mar 45–27 Mar 45, 22 Apr 45–5 Jul 45)*

142nd Engineer Combat Battalion
122nd Medical Battalion
 42nd Counter Intelligence Corps Det
Headquarters Special Troops
Hqs Company, 42nd Infantry Division
 Military Police Platoon
 742nd Ordnance Light Maintenance Company
 42nd Quartermaster Company
132nd Signal Company

Overseas Wartime Assignments:

Seventh Army - 10 Dec 44
Third Army - 15 Dec 44
VI Corps - 24 Dec 44

XXI Corps - 25 Mar 45
XV Corps - 19 Apr 45

Commander: MG Harry J. Collins: Jul 43

Killed in Action: 553 *Wounded in Action:* 2,212 *Died of Wounds:* 85

42nd Infantry Division Combat Narrative

The division arrived at Marseille France 8–9 Dec 44 with an advance headquarters detachment and was organized into Task Force Linden, commanded by the assistant division commander. It entered combat near Strasbourg along the Rhine River 24 Dec 44 as it relieved the 36th Inf Div and defended the 31-mile front. There it was hit by several strong German counterattacks, one of which took Hatten from the 242nd Inf on 9 Jan 45. Task Force positions at Sessenheim and Bois de Sessenheim were overrun 18 Jan 45, but the 242nd Inf repulsed a German attack across the Moder against the Kaltenhouse area on 25 Jan 45. Task Force Linden closed in to Château Salins on 27 Jan 45 and reverted to army reserve.

The division first entered combat as a whole on 14 Feb 45 and took up defensive positions near Haguenau in the Hardt Mountains as it relieved the 45th Inf Div. Following a month of extensive patrolling and active defense, the division attacked the *West Wall* on 15 Mar 45 at Baerenthal and advanced rapidly. It crossed into Germany 18 Mar 45 and was halted by strong opposition in the *West Wall*. However, by 22 Mar 45 the Germans abandoned their positions and the division took Dahn easily. It then mopped up the region as bridgeheads were expanded beyond the Rhine.

The division moved across the Rhine 31 Mar 45 and pushed toward the Wuerzburg region behind the 12th Armd Div, seizing Wertheim 1 Apr 45. The 232nd Inf battled in the Wertheim-Marktheidenfeld area as it cleared that region west of the Main and forced a crossing at Homburg. The 242nd Inf drove along the Main to positions beyond the Bronn River 2 Apr 45, while the 222nd Inf secured Marienburg opposite Wuerzburg. At dawn the following day the 222nd Inf crossed the Main at Wuerzburg in a frontal assault, with the 232nd Inf following 4 Apr 45 under smoke screens. By 5 Apr 45 the German defense was overcome, and the division moved against Schweinfurt, reinforced by the 12th Armd Div. The battle for the city lasted 8–12 Apr 45 and was liberally supported by air bombardment. The division then moved southeast to prepare for the assault on Fuerth, west of Nuremberg. The 222nd and 232nd Inf reached the Aisch River in the Neustadt area on 15 Apr 45, and the division pushed rapidly on to Fuerth. There the division fought house-to-house and reduced it 18–19 Apr 45, and went on to attack Nuremberg in conjunction with the 3rd and 45th Inf Divs. The city fell on 20 Apr 45.

After being relieved of responsibility in the Fuerth sector 21 Apr 45, the division drove south toward the Danube and cleared routes of advance for the 12th Armd Div. It reached the river and took Donauwoerth on 25 Apr 45, and on the following day both 232nd and 242nd Inf attacked across the river to establish bridgeheads at Schaefstall and Altisheim. The division began the drive on Munich in the wake of the 20th Armd Div on 28 Apr 45 and passed through the city 30 Apr 45. The division then cut across the Austrian border north of Salzburg on 5 May 45 where it was located when hostilities were declared ended 7 May 45.

43rd Infantry Division

Maine, Vermont, Connecticut, Rhode Island National Guard

24 Feb 41 inducted into federal service at Hartford Conn as the 43rd Division and moved to Cp Blanding Fla 13 Mar 41; arrived Dry Prong La for the Aug and Sep 41 Louisiana Maneuvers on 5 Aug 41; returned Cp Blanding Fla 9 Oct 41 and transferred to Ft Jackson–Ft Bragg area 4 Nov 41 for the First Army Carolina Maneuvers; returned Cp Blanding Fla 1 Dec 41 and moved to Cp Shelby Miss 14 Feb 42 where redesignated 43rd Infantry Division 19 Feb 42; staged at Ft Ord Calif 6 Sep 42 until departed San Francisco P/E 1 Oct 42; arrived New Zealand 30 Oct 42 and New Caledonia 28 Nov 42; arrived Guadalcanal 28 Feb 43 and moved to Russell Islands 12 Mar 43; landed on New Georgia Island 22 Jun 43 and returned to Guadalcanal 28 Jan 44; moved to New Zealand 17 Feb 44 and Aitape New Guinea 22 Jul 44; departed New Guinea 28 Dec 44 and assaulted Lingayen Gulf Luzon Philippines 9 Jan 45; arrived Japan 13 Sep 45 and returned to San Francisco P/E 9 Oct 45 and inactivated at Cp Stoneman Calif 1 Nov 45.

Campaigns: *Guadalcanal, Northern Solomons, New Guinea, Luzon*
Aug 45 Loc: Cabanatuan Philippine Islands

Typical Organization (1941):

85th Infantry Brigade HHC
  102nd Infantry Regiment*
  169th Infantry Regiment
86th Infantry Brigade HHC
  103rd Infantry Regiment
  172nd Infantry Regiment
68th Field Artillery Brigade HHB
  103rd Field Artillery Regiment (75mm)
  152nd Field Artillery Regiment (75mm)
  192nd Field Artillery Regiment (155mm)

Headquarters, 43rd Division
Hqs and Hqs Det
Med Det
Headquarters Company
  43rd Military Police Company
  43rd Signal Company
118th Ordnance Company
118th Engineers (Combat)
118th Medical Regiment
118th Quartermaster Regiment

*Relieved from division 19 Feb 42.

Typical Organization (1944/45):

103rd Infantry Regiment
169th Infantry Regiment
172nd Infantry Regiment
 HHB Division Artillery
103rd Field Artillery Battalion (105mm)
152nd Field Artillery Battalion (105mm)
169th Field Artillery Battalion (105mm)
192nd Field Artillery Battalion (155mm)
 43rd Reconnaissance Troop, Mecz

118th Engineer Combat Battalion
118th Medical Battalion
 43rd Counter Intelligence Corps Det
Headquarters Special Troops
Hqs Company, 43rd Infantry Division
Military Police Platoon
743rd Ordnance Light Maintenance Company
 43rd Quartermaster Company
 43rd Signal Company

Overseas Wartime Assignments:

South Pacific Area Cmd - 22 Oct 42
XIV Corps - 18 Apr 43
South Pacific Area Cmd - 17 Feb 44
XI Corps - 14 Jul 44
Sixth Army - 20 Aug 44

Eighth Army - 2 Oct 44
I Corps - 20 Nov 44
Sixth Army - 17 Feb 45
Eighth Army - 15 Aug 45

Commanders: MG Morris B. Payne: Feb 41
 MG John H. Hester: Aug 41
 MG Leonard F. Wing: Aug 43

Killed in Action: 1,128   *Wounded in Action:* 4,887   *Died of Wounds:* 278

43rd Infantry Division Combat Narrative

The division, less 172nd Inf, arrived in New Zealand on 22 Oct 42. The 172nd Inf was sent to Espiritu Santo where it arrived 26 Oct 42 and upon entering the harbor lost its transport USS *President Coolidge* to a mine, but suffered only one fatality. The 172nd Inf was attached to the Espiritu Island Base Command until 21 Mar 43 and then went to Guadalcanal 23 Mar 43, and did not rejoin division until 29 Jun 43. The rest of the division moved from New Zealand to New Caledonia 2 Nov–30 Dec 42 and staged to Guadalcanal by echelon 17–28 Feb 43. The 103rd Inf landed on the Russell Islands without opposition 21 Feb 43 and the division engaged in construction and training there, detaching the 103rd Inf to Segi Point New Georgia 22 Jun 43.

The 169th Inf seized Onaiavisi Entrance to Rovianna lagoon and the 172nd Inf landed unopposed on Rendova Island 30 Jun 43. The 103rd Inf joined it 4 Jul 43, and the division moved to New Georgia 3–6 Jul 43. It attacked Munda Trail 6 Jul 43 but the 169th Inf was halted at the trail junction 10 Jul 43 with acute supply problems. The 172nd Inf, without food or water, reached the coast at Laiana by 13 Jul 43 and expanded its perimeter with the assistance of Marine tanks. The division was reinforced with the 145th and 148th Inf 15–23 Jul 43, and the division withstood a strong Japanese counterattack 17 Jul 43. The main assault on Munda came to another halt on 25 Jul 43, but the 103rd Inf took Ilangana and reached the coast at Kia the next day. The 103rd and 169th Inf reached the outer taxiways of Munda Airfield 1 Aug 43 and by 5 Aug 43 the objective fell after heavy fighting. Island combat continued unabated, the 169th Inf having a company isolated after landing at Baanga 12–15 Aug 43. The 172nd Inf seized Baanga Island 16–20 Aug 43.

The 172nd Inf landed on Arundel Island 27 Aug 43 and met determined opposition. It was reinforced as it assaulted by water and across the mainland, clearing Bobmoe Peninsula by 20 Sep 43 and forcing the Japanese to evacuate the following day. The division reassembled on New Georgia 22 Sep 43–22 Jan 44 and garrisoned Munda Airfield and Vila Airdrome on Kolobangara Island as well as Vella LaVella. It moved by echelon to New Zealand 23 Jan–26 Mar 44, except for the 172nd Inf which remained as a garrison on New Georgia until 15 Feb 44. After rehabilitation on New Zealand the division moved to Aitape New Guinea which was completed 4 Aug 44. Assuming defensive positions there, the 103rd and 169th Inf patrolled along the Drinumor River and at Tadji commencing 25 Jul 44. Reinforced by the 112th Cav Regt, the division took over responsibility for the river line 15 Aug 44. The only organized Japanese resistance was encountered at the mouth of the Dandriwad 25 Aug 44. Patrolling of the Aitape area continued until 10 Oct 44 when it was relieved by the *Australian 6th Div* to prepare for Philippine operations. The division departed New Guinea on 28 Dec 44.

It assaulted the San Fabian area of Luzon Philippine Islands with all three regiments 9 Jan 45 and the 103rd Inf took San Jacinto the following day. After heavy fighting the 169th Inf took Hill 318 and the 172nd Inf took Hill 580 on 13 Jan 45, and the 103rd Inf seized the crest of Hill 600 21 Jan 45. The attached 63rd and 158th Inf completed the Battle for

Blue Ridge on that same day. The 169th Inf next fought the Battle for Hill 355 15–24 Jan 45 while the 172nd Inf seized Hill 900 and secured Rosario 26 Jan 45. The 158th and 172nd Inf linked up at Cataguintingan 27 Jan 45, opening the Damortis-Rosario Road, and the division consolidated and went into reserve 17 Feb 45. The division then attacked outside Fort Stotsenburg 28 Feb 45 and relieved the 40th Inf Div in the Zambales Mtns by 2 Mar 45. On 14 Mar 45 the division attacked the Shimbu Line as the 172nd Inf battled up Sugar Loaf Mountain. The 103rd Inf seized Bench Mark 7, the last Japanese strongpoint west of the Morong River Valley on 16 Mar 45. A Japanese counterattack hit the 172nd Inf on Mt Caymayuman 21 Mar 45 which ended Japanese offensives in that region. With the fall of Hill 1200 to the 172nd Inf 1 Apr 45 the Shimbu Line was turned, allowing the 103rd Inf to secure the Santa Maria Valley. The division regrouped and attacked toward Ipo 6 May 45 and after heavy combat seized Ipo Dam intact 14–17 May 45. Mopping up in the Ipo sector lasted until 2 Jun 45 and the division was then moved to fight in the Wawa Wawa–Mt Haponang vicinity 26–30 Jun 45. On 1 Jul 45 the division was moved to Cabanatuan and trained there until the end of the war.

44th Infantry Division   New York and New Jersey National Guard

16 Sep 40 inducted into federal service at Trenton N.J. as the 44th Division and moved to Ft Dix N.J. 23 Sep 40; relocated to A.P.Hill Mil Res Va 5 Jun 41 and returned Ft Dix N.J. 5 Aug 41; arrived in the Ft Jackson–Ft Bragg area 30 Sep 41 for the First Army Carolina Maneuvers; returned to Ft Dix N.J. 9 Dec 41 and transferred to Cp Claiborne La 16 Jan 42 and redesignated 44th Infantry Division same date; arrived Ft Lewis Wash 27 Feb 42 and moved to Cp Polk La 25 Jan 44 where participated in the Fourth Army No.6 Louisiana Maneuvers; located to Cp Phillips Kans 8 Apr 44 and staged at Cp Myles Standish Mass 24 Aug 44 until departed Boston P/E 5 Sep 44; arrived in France 15 Sep 44 and entered Germany 25 Mar 45 and Austria 30 Apr 45; arrived New York P/E 20 Jul 45 and moved to Cp Chaffee Ark 24 Jul 45 where inactivated 30 Nov 45.

Campaigns: *Northern France, Rhineland, Central Europe*
Aug 45 Loc: Camp Chaffee Arkansas

Typical Organization (1941):

57th Infantry Brigade HHC	Headquarters, 44th Division
113th Infantry Regiment*	Hqs and Hqs Det
114th Infantry Regiment	Med Det
87th Infantry Brigade HHC	Headquarters Company
71st Infantry Regiment	44th Military Police Company
174th Infantry Regiment**	44th Signal Company
69th Field Artillery Brigade HHB	119th Ordnance Company
156th Field Artillery Regiment (75mm)	104th Engineers (Combat)
157th Field Artillery Regiment (155mm)	119th Medical Regiment
165th Field Artillery Regiment (75mm)	119th Quartermaster Regiment

*Relieved from division 16 Feb 42.
**Relieved from division 27 Jan 43 and replaced by 324th Infantry Regt assigned 1 Feb 43.

Typical Organization (1944/45):

71st Infantry Regiment	63rd Engineer Combat Battalion
114th Infantry Regiment	119th Medical Battalion
324th Infantry Regiment	44th Counter Intelligence Corps Det
HHB Division Artillery	Headquarters Special Forces
156th Field Artillery Battalion (105mm)	Hqs Company, 44th Infantry Division
157th Field Artillery Battalion (155mm)	Military Police Platoon
217th Field Artillery Battalion (105mm)	744th Ordnance Light Maintenance Company
220th Field Artillery Battalion (105mm)	44th Quartermaster Company
44th Reconnaissance Troop, Mecz	44th Signal Company

749th Tank Battalion *(attached 23 Oct 44–15 Feb 45)*
772nd Tank Battalion *(attached 26 Mar 45–9 May 45)*
776th Tank Destroyer Battalion *(attached 31 Oct 44–21 Nov 44, 25 Nov 44–9 May 45)*
813th Tank Destroyer Battalion *(attached 23 Oct 44–31 Oct 44)*
398th AAA Auto-Wpns Battalion *(attached 22 Oct 44–22 Nov 44)*
895th AAA Auto-Wpns Battalion *(attached 25 Nov 44–18 Apr 45)*

Overseas Wartime Assignments:

Ninth Army - 30 Aug 44

III Corps - 5 Sep 44

Ninth Army - 10 Oct 44

XV Corps - 14 Oct 44

Seventh Army - 8 Apr 45

XXI Corps - 15 Apr 45

VI Corps - 17 Apr 45

Commanders: MG Clifford R. Powell: Sep 40

MG James I. Muir: Aug 41

MG Robert L. Spragins: Aug 44

MG Williamn F. Dean: Jan 45

BG William A. Beiderlinden: Nov 45

BG Robert L. Dulaney: Nov 45

Killed in Action: 1,038   *Wounded in Action:* 4,209   *Died of Wounds:* 168

44th Infantry Division Combat Narrative

The division landed at Cherbourg France on 15 Sep 44 and trained for a month before beginning the relief of the 79th Inf Div on 18 Oct 44 at Forêt de Parroy, in the vicinity of Lunnéville France. The 71st Inf went into the line 23 Oct 44 followed by the 324th Inf the next day. The division was subjected to a strong German counterattack 25–26 Oct 44 and then continued active defense of its area. The 71st and 324th Inf attacked from Leintray to force a passage through the Vosges Mountains on 13 Nov 44, and took Avricourt 17 Nov 44 after heavy combat, pushing on to capture Sarrebourg 21 Nov 44. The division was on the west side of the Saverne Gap when the German forces counterattacked and forced it to make slight withdrawals, but the division checked the German advance at Schalbach 25 Nov 44 with the assistance of the 106th Cav Group. The 100th Inf Div then relieved it in the Sarrebourg sector 27 Nov 44. The division regrouped while its 114th Inf took Tieffenbach 29 Nov 44, and the entire division resumed its offensive 5 Dec 44 against the Maginot Line and took Ratzwiller. After Encherberg was taken 8 Dec 44 the division fought the Battle for Fort Simershof, near Hottviller, 13–19 Dec 44. The division then displaced to defensive positions east of Sarreguemines 21–23 Dec 44.

The German NORDWIND Counteroffensive struck the division there on 1 Jan 45 and drove it back to the Rimling vicinity, the German forces retaking Gros Réderching and re-entering Aachen on 3 Jan 45 before their advance was halted. The division's efforts to regain ground were stopped on line extending along the Boies de Blies Brucken to just north of Gros Réderching. Throughout January the division was reinforced by the 253rd and later 255th Inf of 63rd Inf Div. The division attacked to eliminate the German salient in the Gros Réderching area with the 324th Inf on 15 Feb 45 which forced the Buschenbusch Woods despite strong opposition. The division then held defensive lines in the Sarreguemines vicinity through most of March 1945.

The division crossed the Rhine at Worms 26–27 Mar 45 and relieved the 3rd Inf Div at Sandhofen. It then turned south along the Rhine and crossed the Neckar River to take evacuated Heidelberg on 29 Mar 45. The division was then relieved by the 63rd Inf Div and held in reserve. The division shifted to the west bank of the Main River and crossed at Gross Auheim in early April. It detached the 324th Inf which saw action at Crailsheim with the 10th Armd Div and drove on Rothenberg with the 4th Inf Div. The rest of the division engaged in training and was rejoined by the 324th Inf 19 Apr 45 for the combined attack behind 10th Armd Div. The division took responsibility for the Rems and Fils crossings the next day and placed the 114th Inf into blocking positions at Schwaebisch Gmuend, while the rest of the division continued in the wake of the 10th Armd Div. The 324th Inf crossed the Danube at Ehingen on 23 Apr 45 and pushed rapidly until being halted by blown bridges at the Iller River/Canal. The 114th Inf was moved up but failed to make contact with German forces retreating from Muensingen toward Ehingen. On 25 Apr 45 the 324th Inf crossed the Danube and cleared New Ulm and the 71st Inf crossed the Iller at Dietenheim and cleared Voehringen, while the 114th Inf assembled at Laupheim. The division then followed the 10th Armd Div and cleared Fuessen and Wertach on 28 Apr 45 as the 114th Inf crossed into Austria near Steinbach. The division rushed through the Fern Pass and entered the Inn Valley. The 324th Inf moved through the Wertach-Jungholz Pass and took Jungholz 30 Apr 45 and the 71st Inf completed clearing Fern Pass on 2 May 45. The 324th Inf seized Imst 4 May 45 and took Landeck without opposition on 5 May 45 as hostilities in that area ceased with the surrender of the German Nineteenth Army at Innsbruck.

45th Infantry Division

Arizona, Colorado, New Mexico,
Oklahoma National Guard

16 Feb 40 inducted into federal service at Oklahoma City Okla as the 45th Division and moved to Ft Sill Okla 23 Sep 40; arrived Cp Barkeley Tex 28 Feb 41 and went to Brownwood Tex 1 Jun 41 to participate in the VIII Corps Corps Texas Maneuvers there; returned to Cp Barkeley Tex 13 Jun 41 and moved to Mansfield La 4 Aug 41 where participated in both Aug and Sep 41 Louisiana Maneuvers; returned to Cp Barkeley Tex 4 Oct 41 where redesignated the 45th Infantry Division 23 Feb 42; arrived Ft Devens Mass 22 Apr 42 and Pine Camp N.Y. 8 Nov 42; transferred to Cp Pickett Va 27 Jan 43 and staged at Cp Patrick Henry Va 26 May 43 until departed Hampton Roads P/E 3 Jun 43; arrived in North Africa 22 Jun 43 and assaulted Scoglitti Sicily 10 Jul 43 and Salerno Italy 10 Sep 43; assaulted Anzio 22 Jan 44 and southern France 15 Aug 44; entered Germany 17 Mar 45 and arrived Boston P/E 10 Sep 45 and moved to Cp Bowie Tex 17 Sep 45 where inactivated 7 Dec 45.

Campaigns: *Sicily, Naples-Foggia, Anzio, Rome-Arno, Southern France, Rhineland, Ardennes-Alsace, Central Europe*

Aug 45 Loc: Munich Germany

Typical Organization (1941):

89th Infantry Brigade HHC
  157th Infantry Regiment
  158th Infantry Regiment*
90th Infantry Brigade HHC
  179th Infantry Regiment
  180th Infantry Regiment
70th Field Artillery Brigade HHB
  158th Field Artillery Regiment (75mm)
  160th Field Artillery Regiment (75mm)
  189th Field Artillery Regiment (155mm)

Headquarters, 45th Division
Hqs and Hqs Det
Med Det
Headquarters Company
  45th Military Police Company
  45th Signal Company
120th Ordnance Company
120th Engineers (Combat)
120th Medical Regiment
120th Quartermaster Regiment

*Relieved from division 11 Feb 42.

Typical Organization (1944/45):

157th Infantry Regiment
179th Infantry Regiment
180th Infantry Regiment
  HHB Division Artillery
158th Field Artillery Battalion (105mm)
160th Field Artillery Battalion (105mm)
171st Field Artillery Battalion (105mm)
189th Field Artillery Battalion (155mm)
  45th Reconnaissance Troop, Mecz

120th Engineer Combat Battalion
120th Medical Battalion
  45th Counter Intelligence Corps Det
Headquarters Special Troops
Hqs Company, 45th Infantry Division
Military Police Platoon
700th Ordnance Light Maintenance Company
  45th Quartermaster Company
  45th Signal Company

101st Tank Battalion *(attached 15 Aug 44–25 Aug 44, 30 Aug 44–9 Nov 44, 24 Nov 44–14 Feb 45, 5 Mar 45–15 Mar 45, 20 Mar 45–22 Mar 45)*
191st Tank Battalion *(attached 15 Aug 44–28 Nov 44, 29 Nov 44–16 Feb 45, 4 Mar 45–9 May 45)*
636th Tank Destroyer Battalion *(attached 6 Oct 44–27 Oct 44)*
645th Tank Destroyer Battalion *(attached 15 Aug 44–30 Sep 44, 6 Oct 44–26 Oct 44, 1 Nov 44–10 Nov 44, 1 Dec 44–14 Feb 45, 5 Mar 45–22 Mar 45, 1 Apr 45–10 May 45)*
106th AAA Auto-Wpns Battalion *(attached 15 Aug 44–10 Nov 44, 23 Nov 44–15 Mar 45, 20 Mar 45–25 Mar 45, 11 Apr 45–10 May 45)*

Overseas Wartime Assignments:

II Corps - Jun 43
Seventh Army Prov Corps - 1 Aug 43
VI Corps - 13 Aug 43
Seventh Army - 1 Nov 44

XV Corps - 22 Nov 44
VI Corps - 31 Dec 44
XV Corps - 15 Mar 45
Seventh Army - 6 May 45

Commanders: MG William S. Key: Sep 40   MG Robert T. Frederick: Dec 44
MG Troy H. Middleton: Oct 42   BG Henry J. D. Meyer: Sep 45
MG William W. Eagles: Dec 43

Killed in Action: 3,547   *Wounded in Action:* 14,441   *Died of Wounds:* 533

45th Infantry Division Combat Narrative

The division landed in North Africa on 22 Jun 43 and trained at Arzew. It assaulted Scoglitti Sicily 10 Jul 43, taking Comiso and Ragusa Airport and repulsing several German counterattacks to contact the *Canadian 1st Div* 12 Jul 43. It moved forward through Licodia and Monterosso the next day, crossed the Salso River at Caltanisetta 18 Jul 43 and clashed with Italian delaying forces in the Vallelunga area 20 Jul 43. The 157th Inf cut the north coastal Highway 113 on 22 Jul 43 and the division fought the Battle of Motta Hill 26–30 Jul 43, allowing the 179th Inf to reach S.Mauro. The 180th Inf reached Tusa 27 Jul 43 but failed in its first attempt to force the river. The division was engaged in combat approaching San Stefano by 29 Jul 43, and was relieved 1 Aug 43. It then moved to guard western Sicily, detaching the 157th Inf to make a landing near Barcellona in an attempt to block German-Italian withdrawals.

The division assaulted Salerno Italy 10 Sep 43 and the 179th Inf and 157th Inf engaged in heavy fighting at Ponte Sele and the Tobacco Factory. The 180th Inf was landed on 14 Sep 43 and held in reserve. The division seized the heights overlooking Eboli on 19 Sep 43 and pushed along Highway 91 into the mountains, taking Oliveto 22 Sep 43, and pushed to the Calore River 27 Sep 43 despite rains and German demolitions. It took over the 34th Inf Div's Calore River Bridgehead 3 Oct 43 and mopped up Titerno Creek, contacting the 34th Inf Div across the Volturno River 15 Oct 43. After Piedmonte d'Alife fell 20 Oct 43, the division was withdrawn to reserve. On 3 Nov 43 it resumed the offensive by crossing the Volturno below Sesto Campano and battled through the Hitler Line in a ten-day engagement, and next wrested key mountain heights from German defenders beginning 29 Nov 43. Hill 769 fell to the 179th Inf 6 Dec 43 and Mt la Posta to the 180th Inf 17 Dec 43. The 180th Inf attempted to clear the hills north of Cassino astride the S.Elia road, but on 9 Jan 44 the division was withdrawn.

The division assaulted Anzio Italy 22 Jan 44 and was engaged defending the beachhead for the next four months. On 11 Feb 44 the 179th Inf made a vain effort to recover the factory area and the 157th Inf was isolated west of the Albano Road by counterattacks. On 18 Feb 44 the division was subjected to a main German counterattack which was contained only after the 179th Inf was pushed back to the final beachhead lines. On 22 Feb 44 the British relieved the division and it engaged in holding actions until resuming the offensive during the breakout from Anzio on 23 May 44. The 179th and 180th Inf attacked up Albano Road 29 May 44 and by 4 Jun 44 the division secured crossings north of Rome. On 16 Jun 44 the division was withdrawn for rehabilitation.

The division assaulted Ste Maxime, southern France on 15 Aug 44. The 179th Inf took contested Barjols 18–19 Aug 44, and the 157th Inf crossed over the Durance River the next day using a partially destroyed bridge near St Paul. The division crossed the Rhône and Ain Rivers northeast of Lyon 30 Aug 44 and the 179th Inf saw heavy combat at Meximieux 1–2 Sep 44. In heavy fighting Villersexel was seized 13 Sep 44 and it crossed the Moselle in the secured Châtel area 21–22 Sep 44. The 180th Inf battled for Epinal 22–25 Sep 44 as the 157th Inf finally took Girmont 24 Sep 44, and the division entered the western foothills of the Vosges. After severe fighting Bruyères fell 19 Oct 44 and after several attempts the 180th Inf managed a bridgehead across the Mortagne near Fremifontaine 22–23 Oct 44. As the division was pushing slowly toward Raon-l'Etape west of the Meurthe, it was relieved 1–9 Nov 44 and moved to a rest area.

The division moved up to the Saverne Gap on 23 Nov 44 and captured the forts north of Mutzig in the Maginot Line 25 Nov 44 and moved up to the Moder when it took Mertzwiller in heavy combat on 5 Dec 44. Fighting across the Lauter into Budenthal on 18 Dec 44, the division engaged in fighting which isolated several elements, but the division contained the Germans along the Philippsbourg-Neuhoffen-Obersteinbach line by 1 Jan 45. The division battled in the Bitchie Pocket and captured Wingen 7 Jan 45, but was forced out of Althorn by counterattacks 11 Jan 45, and a battalion of the 157th Inf was decimated northeast of Reipertsweiler 18 Jan 45. The division was forced back to defensive positions along the Rothbach Rau–Moder River line 20 Jan 45 and lost Saegmuhl 24 Jan 45. On 17 Feb 45 it was relieved in line and withdrawn for rehabilitation.

The division was moved north to the Sarreguemines area 15 Mar 45 and reached the *West Wall* in the Zweibruecken region 17 Mar 45. Homburg fell 20 Mar 45 and the 176th Inf followed the 6th Armd Div to the Rhine 21 Mar 45, followed by the rest of the division. After saturation bombing the 179th and 180th Inf attacked across the river near Hamm 26 Mar 45. With three regiments abreast the division sped to the Main and established a bridgehead at Obernau on 28 Mar 45. The division fought the Battle for Aschaffenburg 28 Mar–3 Apr 45 which fell to the 157th Inf after house-to-house fighting. After attacking the Hohe Rohn Hills the division opened the drive on Nuremberg 11 Apr 45.

The Battle for Nuremberg was fought 16–20 Apr 45, and then the division moved south to the Danube to prepare a path for the 20th Armd Div toward Munich. The division attacked across the Danube with all three regiments abreast at Merxheim and Bergoldsheim on 26 Apr 45. It then followed in the wake of the 20th Armd Div to reach Munich 29 Apr 45, and remained in occupation of the area until hostilities were declared ended on 7 May 45.

63rd Infantry Division

No Distinctive
Insignia Authorized

15 Jun 43 activated at Cp Blanding Fla and trained under VII and III Corps; moved 22 Aug 43 to Cp Van Dorn Miss and trained under IX and XXI Corps; staged at Cp Shanks N.Y. 28 Dec 44 until departed New York P/E 5 Jan 45; arrived in France 14 Jan 45 and entered Germany 20 Mar 45; arrived Boston P/E 26 Sep 45 and inactivated at Cp Myles Standish Mass 27 Sep 45.

Campaigns: *Rhineland, Central Europe*
Aug 45 Loc: Bad Mergentheim Germany

Typical Organization (1944/45):

253rd Infantry Regiment	263rd Engineer Combat Battalion
254th Infantry Regiment	363rd Medical Battalion
255th Infantry Regiment	63rd Counter Intelligence Corps Det
HHB Division Artillery	Headquarters Special Troops
718th Field Artillery Battalion (155mm)	Hqs Company, 63rd Infantry Division
861st Field Artillery Battalion (105mm)	Military Police Platoon
862nd Field Artillery Battalion (105mm)	763rd Ordnance Light Maintenance Company
863rd Field Artillery Battalion (105mm)	63rd Quartermaster Company
63rd Reconnaissance Troop, Mecz	563rd Signal Company
70th Tank Battalion *(attached 12 Mar 45–18 Mar 45)*	
740th Tank Battalion *(attached 17 Mar 45–28 Mar 45)*	
753rd Tank Battalion *(attached 31 Mar 45–28 May 45)*	
692nd Tank Destroyer Battalion *(attached 30 Mar 45–31 Mar 45)*	
776th Tank Destroyer Battalion *(attached 16 Mar 45–21 Mar 45)*	
822nd Tank Destroyer Battalion *(attached 6 Feb 45–17 Mar 45, 21 Mar 45–28 May 45)*	
436th AAA Auto-Wpns Battalion *(attached 11 Feb 45–1 May 45)*	

Overseas Wartime Assignments:

Seventh Army - 10 Dec 44	XXI Corps - 26 Mar 45
XV Corps - 1 Feb 45	VI Corps - 1 Apr 45
XXI Corps - 22 Feb 45	XXI Corps - 19 Apr 45
XV Corps - 21 Mar 45	Seventh Army - 30 Apr 45

Commanders: MG Louis E. Hibbs: Jun 43
BG Frederick M. Harris: Aug 45

Killed in Action: 861   *Wounded in Action:* 3,326   *Died of Wounds:* 113

63rd Infantry Division Combat Narrative

Advanced elements of the division arrived in Marseille France on 8 Dec 44, trained at Haguenau, and organized as Task Force Harris to protect the east flank of the drive on the Rhine. It defended the Vosges and Maginot Line area 22–30 Dec 44 and battled the German offensive south of Bitche 1–19 Jan 45. The rest of the division closed in Marseille France 14 Jan 45 and the division assembled at Willerwald on 2 Feb 45 as Task Force Harris was discontinued. The division conducted patrolling activity until 15 Feb 45 when the 255th Inf attacked the Bois de Blies Brucken and the 253rd Inf fought the Battle for Auersmacher 17–19 Feb 45. The division completed the reduction of the Welferding salient with the capture of Buebingen and Bliesransbach 24 Feb 45.

The division renewed its attacks 3 Mar 45 as the 253rd Inf battled through heavily defended forest to Hahnsbusch 3–5 Mar 45. The division attacked the *West Wall* near Saarbruecken on 15 Mar 45 and took Fechingen, Eschringen, and Ensheim. After heavy combat the division breached a gap in the *West Wall* north of the latter town on 18 Mar 45. With the fall of St Ingbert and Hassel to 255th Inf on 20 Mar 45, the *West Wall* was pierced. After a brief rest, the division crossed the Rhine at Neuschloss on 28 Mar 45 and relieved the 44th Inf Div, crossing the Neckar in the Wieblingen area 30 Mar 45 and reaching Heidelberg. The division continued to advance behind the 10th Armd Div and fought through the region north of the Jagst River 3 Apr 45. The 253rd forced the river in the Griesheim-Herbolzheim region on 4 Apr 45 and fought house-to-house in Moeckmuehl. After frontal assaults against Hardenhauser Forest failed, the division enveloped the woods by 7 Apr 45. The 255th Inf reached the Kocher River and established a bridgehead at Weissbach 9 Apr 45.

The Kocher River bridgehead was expanded against strong German opposition and the 10th Armd Div attacked out of it 11 Apr 45. The division mopped up in that area and consolidated 14 Apr 45, returning to the attack the next day as it took Schwaebisch Hall with armored support by 18 Apr 45. The division seized the Rems Bridge at Unt Boebingen on 22 Apr 45 and leapfrogged battalions to reach the Danube River 25 Apr 45. The 254th Inf crossed the river on a damaged bridge in Riedheim and repulsed a German armored counterattack. The division was relieved 28 Apr 45 and withdrawn from the line. It was assigned security duty from the Rhine to Darmstadt and Wurzburg on a line to Stuttgart and Speyer, and was in this mode when hostilities were declared ended on 7 May 45.

65th Infantry Division

No Distinctive
Insignia Authorized

16 Aug 43 activated at Cp Shelby Miss and trained under XV and IX Corps; staged at Cp Shanks N.Y. 31 Dec 44 until departed New York P/E 10 Jan 45; arrived in France 21 Jan 45 and entered Germany 20 Mar 45; reached Austria 4 May 45 where disbanded 31 Aug 45.

Campaigns: *Rhineland, Central Europe*
Aug 45 Loc: Linz Austria

Typical Organization (1944/45):

259th Infantry Regiment
260th Infantry Regiment
261st Infantry Regiment
 HHB Division Artillery
720th Field Artillery Battalion (155mm)
867th Field Artillery Battalion (105mm)
868th Field Artillery Battalion (105mm)
869th Field Artillery Battalion (105mm)
 65th Reconnaissance Troop, Mecz
707th Tank Battalion *(attached 6 Apr 45 only)*
748th Tank Battalion *(attached 7 Apr 45–past 9 May 45)*
749th Tank Battalion *(attached 29 Mar 45–6 Apr 45)*
691st Tank Destroyer Battalion *(attached 4 Mar 45–6 Apr 45)*
808th Tank Destroyer Battalion *(attached 5 Apr 45–past 9 May 45)*
546th AAA Auto-Wpns Battalion *(attached 4 Mar 45–past 9 May 45)*

265th Engineer Combat Battalion
365th Medical Battalion
 65th Counter Intelligence Corps Det
Headquarters Special Troops
Hqs Company, 65th Infantry Division
Military Police Platoon
765th Ordnance Light Maintenance Company
 65th Quartermaster Company
565th Signal Company

Overseas Wartime Assignments:

Fifteenth Army - 25 Jan 45
XX Corps - 1 Mar 45

VIII Corps - 4 Apr 45
XX Corps - 17 Apr 45

Commanders: MG Stanley E. Reinhart: Aug 43
                         BG John E. Copeland: Aug 45

Killed in Action: 233   *Wounded in Action:* 927   *Died of Wounds:* 27

65th Infantry Division Combat Narrative

The division arrived at Le Havre France on 21 Jan 45 and trained until 1 Mar 45. It assembled in the Ennery area and relieved the 26th Inf Div 9 Mar 45, defending the Saarlautern Bridgehead from Orscholz to Wadgassen. After diversionary attacks commencing 13 Mar 45, the 261st Inf crossed the Saar near Menningen on 17 Mar 45, cleared the heights south of Merzig, and took Dillingen the following day. The rest of the division fought its way out of the bridgehead as the 259th Inf captured Fraulautern and the 260th Inf seized Saarlautern on 19 Mar 45. The division fought its way through the *West Wall* with the capture of Neunkirchen 21 Mar 45. It then assembled near Ottweiler for rehabilitation. Closing into the Schwabenheim area the division crossed the Rhine with both 260th and 261st Inf during the night of 29–30 Mar 45. It attacked across the Fulda 2 Apr 45 in the wake of the 6th Armd Div, and the 260th Inf reached the Reichensachen-Langenhain line 3 Apr 45 where it rested as armor with road priority passed it. The same day the 259th Inf crossed the Werra, and continued to the Greuzberg area 4 Apr 45. The division assaulted Langensalza which fell 6 Apr 45, but a German counterattack overran a battalion of the 261st Inf at Struth on 7 Apr 45. The division restored the situation with air support and went into reserve 8 Apr 45, moving to Berka 10 Apr 45.

The division moved to Waltershausen 11 Apr 45 and then mopped up stragglers at Arnstadt. On 17 Apr 45 it assembled in Bamberg and attacked toward Altdorf with the 259th and 260th Inf the next day. Neumarkt was taken after a sharp fight on 23 Apr 45 and the division drove to the Rhine against crumbling German resistance. The division forced the Danube southwest of Regensburg despite strong opposition, especially against the 261st Inf, on 26 Apr 45. The bridgehead was expanded and the 260th Inf took Regensburg 27 Apr 45 as the 13th Armd Div passed through its sector. The division followed the armor and crossed the Isar River at Platting 1 May 45. The 261st Inf reached the Inn River at Passau on 2 May 45 and assaulted across it at Neuhaus. Passau fell the next day and the 261st pushed toward Linz as the 260th Inf mopped up in local woods between Sandbach and Passau. The Inn River crossings were completed by 4 May 45 and on the following day the 260th Inf relieved forces in Linz as the 261st Inf reached the Enns River and overran Enns. The 260th Inf remained to garrison Linz and the division closed the Enns River 6 May 45, and made contact with the advancing Soviet Army in the vicinity of Strengberg on 8 May 45 as hostilities ceased.

66th Infantry Division

No Distinctive
Insignia Authorized

15 Apr 43 activated at Cp Blanding Fla and trained under VII Corps; moved to Cp Joseph T. Robinson Ark 17 Aug 43 and trained under IX Corps; arrived Cp Rucker Ala 7 Apr 44; staged at Cp Shanks N.Y. 23 Nov 44 until departed New York P/E 1 Dec 44; arrived England 12 Dec 44 and arrived France 25 Dec 44 where designated the 12th Army Group Coastal Sector responsible for containing the German fortress garrisons at St Nazaire and Lorient; returned New York P/E 6 Nov 45 and inactivated at Cp Kilmer N.J. 8 Nov 45.

Campaigns: *Northern France*
Aug 45 Loc: Chateaubriant France

Typical Organization (1944/45):

262nd Infantry Regiment
263rd Infantry Regiment
264th Infantry Regiment
 HHB Division Artillery
721st Field Artillery Battalion (155mm)
870th Field Artillery Battalion (105mm)
871st Field Artillery Battalion (105mm)
872nd Field Artillery Battalion (105mm)
 66th Reconnaissance Troop, Mecz

266th Engineer Combat Battalion
366th Medical Battalion
 66th Counter Intelligence Corps Det
Headquarters Special Troops
Hqs Company, 66th Infantry Division
Military Police Platoon
766th Ordnance Light Maintenance Company
 66th Quartermaster Company
566th Signal Company

19th French Régiment d'infanterie (attached 1 Jan 45–23 May 45)
21st French Régiment d'infanterie (attached 1 Jan 45–23 May 45)
32nd French Régiment d'infanterie (attached 1 Jan 45–23 May 45)
41st French Régiment d'infanterie (attached 1 Jan 45–23 May 45)
63rd French Régiment d'infanterie (attached 1 Jan 45–23 May 45)
65th French Régiment d'infanterie (attached 1 Jan 45–23 May 45)
67th French Régiment d'infanterie (attached 1 Jan 45–23 May 45)
71st French Régiment d'infanterie (attached 1 Jan 45–23 May 45)
93rd French Régiment d'infanterie (attached 1 Jan 45–23 May 45)
118th French Régiment d'infanterie (attached 1 Jan 45–23 May 45)
125th French Régiment d'infanterie (attached 1 Jan 45–23 May 45)
125th French AAA Group Forces Terrestres Anti-Aeriennes (attached 1 Jan 45–23 May 45)

Note: 422nd and 423rd Infantry Regt (from 106th Infantry Division) attached to division 15 Apr 45–15 May 45.

Overseas Wartime Assignments:

12th Army Group - 27 Dec 44
Fifteenth Army - 31 Mar 45

Commanders: MG Herman F. Kramer: Apr 43
MG Walter E. Lauer: Aug 45

Killed in Action: 795   *Wounded in Action:* 636   *Died of Wounds:* 5

66th Infantry Division Combat Narrative

The division arrived in Cherbourg France on 25 Dec 44 after being torpedoed in the English Channel with the loss of 14 officers and 748 enlisted men. The division was then attached to the 12th Army Group and became designated as the 12th Army Group Coastal Sector with operational control of all French forces in the area. It relieved the 94th Inf Div in the Brittany-Loire area on 29 Dec 44 and assumed the mission of containing the German St Nazaire and Lorient Pockets. This was achieved by the conduct of daily reconnaissance patrols, limited objective attacks, and the maintenance of harassing and interdictory fires on German installations. On 31 Mar 45 the division was placed under the Fifteenth Army which took command of the coastal sector of France. A heavy German counterattack near La Croix was repulsed on 16 Apr 45, as the 422nd and 423rd of the 106th Inf Div were attached to the division for training purposes. Several German strongpoints were captured in operations extending from 19–29 Apr 45. The German defenders of both Lorient and St Nazaire Pockets surrendered to the division 8 May 45, and the division was moved to the Koblenz area of Germany for occupation duty 20 May 45.

69th Infantry Division

No Distinctive
Insignia Authorized

15 May 43 activated at Cp Shelby Miss and trained under VII and IX Corps; staged at Cp Kilmer N.J. 23 Nov 44 until departed New York P/E 1 Dec 44; arrived England 12 Dec 44 and landed in France 24 Jan 45; crossed into Belgium 9 Feb 45 and entered Germany 8 Mar 45; returned to New York P/E 16 Sep 45 and inactivated at Cp Kilmer N.J. 18 Sep 45.

Campaigns: *Rhineland, Central Europe*
Aug 45 Loc: Naumhof Germany

Typical Organization (1944/45):

271st Infantry Regiment
272nd Infantry Regiment
273rd Infantry Regiment
 HHB Division Artillery
724th Field Artillery Battalion (155mm)
879th Field Artillery Battalion (105mm)
880th Field Artillery Battalion (105mm)
881st Field Artillery Battalion (105mm)
 69th Reconnaissance Troop, Mecz
777th Tank Battalion *(attached 29 Mar 45–15 Jun 45)*
661st Tank Destroyer Battalion *(attached 7 Feb 45–16 Jun 45)*
461st AAA Auto-Wpns Battalion *(attached 11 Mar 45–30 Jun 45)*

269th Engineer Combat Battalion
369th Medical Battalion
 69th Counter Intelligence Corps Det
Headquarters Special Troops
Hqs Company, 69th Infantry Division
Military Police Platoon
769th Ordnance Light Maintenance Company
 69th Quartermaster Company
569th Signal Company

Overseas Wartime Assignments:

12th Army Group - 18 Jan 45
Fifteenth Army - 7 Feb 45

V Corps - 7 Feb 45
VII Corps - 28 Apr 45

Commanders: MG Charles L. Bolte: May 43
MG Emil F. Reinhardt: Sep 44
BG Robert V. Maraist: Aug 45

Killed in Action: 341   *Wounded in Action:* 1,146   *Died of Wounds:* 42

69th Infantry Division Combat Narrative

The division landed at Le Havre France on 24 Jan 45 and advance elements moved to Montenau Belgium 6 Feb 45 to relieve the 99th Inf Div in line on 11 Feb 45. The division then held defensive positions in the *West Wall*, making a limited attack on the ridge east of the Prether River to ensure the safety of the Hellenthal-Hollerath Highway on 27 Feb 45. The heights were secured from Honningen to Reschied by 3 Mar 45 as the 271st Inf took the last high ground position.

The division attacked with three regiments abreast on 6 Mar 45 and pushed rapidly to take Schmidtheim and Dahlem which fell the next day. The division then mopped up, sent the 272nd Inf to take Waldorf and Hungersdorf south of the Ahr on 8 Mar 45, and patrolled and trained in its zone. On 21 Mar 45 the division moved to the Rhine and relieved the 2nd Inf Div. The 272nd Inf crossed the Rhine 26 Mar 45 and captured the Luftwaffe Citadel and the Lahn River towns of Bad Ems and Nassau the next day. The entire division followed across 28 Mar 45 and mopped up rear stragglers, and then began movement to a new zone near Weilburg 30 Mar 45. It relieved the 9th Armd Div at Naumburg on 3 Apr 45. After relieving the 80th Inf Div in the Kassel area it attacked 5 Apr 45, less the 272nd Inf which was guarding installations. On 7 Apr 45 the division reached the Werra River from Hann Muenden to Witzehausen and the 273rd and 272nd Inf crossed at both localities respectively. Following in the wake of the 9th Armd Div the division continued to drive forward, the 271st Inf battling through Weissenfels 14 Apr 45 and the 272nd Inf reaching the Weisse River at Luetzkewitz. The division ran into the outer defenses of Leipzig at Zwenkau on 16 Apr 45 and captured the city of Leipzig after house-to-house fighting by 19 Apr 45. It then relieved the 9th Armd Div in line along the Mulde River 21 Apr 45.

The 271st Inf secured the east bank of the Mulde after the Battle for Eilenburg on 23 Apr 45 and Wurzen surrendered to the 273rd Inf the following day. The division made patrol contact with the advancing Soviet Army near Riesa and Torgau on 25 Apr 45. The division then patrolled and policed its area until hostilities were declared officially ended 7 May 45.

70th Infantry Division

No Distinctive Insignia Authorized

15 Jun 43 activated at Cp Adair Oreg and trained under IV Corps; moved to Ft Leonard Wood Mo 25 Jul 44 and staged at Cp Myles Standish Mass 21 Dec 44 until departed Boston P/E 8 Jan 45; arrived in France 18 Jan 45 and entered Germany 27 Mar 45; arrived New York P/E 9 Oct 45 and inactivated at Cp Kilmer N.J. 11 Oct 45.

Campaigns: *Rhineland, Central Europe*
Aug 45 Loc: Frankfurt Germany

Typical Organization (1944/45):

274th Infantry Regiment
275th Infantry Regiment
276th Infantry Regiment
 HHB Division Artillery
725th Field Artillery Battalion (155mm)
882nd Field Artillery Battalion (105mm)
883rd Field Artillery Battalion (105mm)
884th Field Artillery Battalion (105mm)
 70th Reconnaissance Troop, Mecz
740th Tank Battalion *(attached 15 Mar 45–16 Mar 45)*
749th Tank Battalion *(attached 16 Feb 45–9 Mar 45)*
772nd Tank Battalion *(attached 22 Mar 45–24 Mar 45)*
781st Tank Battalion *(attached 3 Jan 45–16 Jan 45)*
648th Tank Destroyer Battalion *(attached 20 Feb 45–31 Mar 45)*
433rd AAA Auto-Wpns Battalion *(attached 12 Feb 45–20 Jul 45)*

270th Engineer Combat Battalion
370th Medical Battalion
 70th Counter Intelligence Corps Det
Headquarters Special Troops
Hqs Company, 70th Infantry Division
Military Police Platoon
770th Ordnance Light Maintenance Company
 70th Quartermaster Company
570th Signal Company

Overseas Wartime Assignments:

Seventh Army - 20 Dec 44
VI Corps - 28 Dec 44
XV Corps - 3 Feb 45
XXI Corps - 25 Feb 45

Seventh Army - 22 Mar 45
12th Army Group - 31 Mar 45
Third Army - 8 Apr 45

Commanders: MG John E. Dahlquist: Jun 43
 MG Allison J. Barnett: Jul 44
 BG Thomas W. Herren: Jul 45

Killed in Action: 755 *Wounded in Action:* 2,713 *Died of Wounds:* 79

70th Infantry Division Combat Narrative

The three regiments of the division arrived at Marseille France 10–15 Dec 44 in advance of the rest of the division, and were formed into Task Force Herren which assumed defensive positions along the west bank of the Rhine near Bischweiler on 28 Dec 44. As the German offensive advanced in the Bitche Salient, Task Force Herren was sent to assist the 45th Inf Div. The 276th Inf took up switch-positions in the Wingen-Wimmenau-Rosteig area on 3 Jan 45, and on 8 Jan 45 Task Force Herren was given the task of protecting the east flank of 45th Inf Div during the drive against the salient. On 17 Jan 45 the task force relieved the 103rd Inf Div south of Saarbruecken where it improved defensive positions. The rest of the division arrived in France 18 Jan 45 and Task Force Herren was dissolved 3 Feb 45.

The 276th Inf was attacked 8 Feb 45, and on 17 Feb 45 the regiment made a limited offensive against the heights south-west of Saarbruecken and fought the Battle for Forbach the following day and next the Battle for Oeting which involved house-to-house fighting 23 Feb 45. The 274th and 275th Inf cleared the heights commanding both Saar-bruecken and Stiring Wendel by 24 Feb 45. The division attacked beyond the Forbach-Saarbruecken Road on 3 Mar 45, supported by the 12th Armd Div. The 274th Inf finally captured Stiring Wendel on 5 Mar 45 after heavy combat and divisional patrols reached the outposts of the *West Wall* on 6 Mar 45. The German forces withdrew 13 Mar 45 and the division began pursuit operations immediately, driving north to the Saar and crossing into Germany 14 Mar 45. Saarbruecken was attacked on 15 Mar and 19 Mar 45, the town being occupied without opposition the next day. On 21 Mar 45 the division was withdrawn to army reserve.

The division was relieved of security in the Koblenz and Pfalz areas on 19 Apr 45, and it then participated in the reduction of the Saar Basin. It was operating in this capacity when hostilities were declared ended 7 May 45.

71st Infantry Division

No Distinctive Insignia Authorized

15 Jul 43 activated at Cp Carson Colo as the 71st Light Division (Pack, Jungle) and participated in the III Corps Hunter-Liggett Calif Maneuvers 11 Feb–15 May 44; moved to Ft Benning Ga 19 May 44 where redesignated the 71st Infantry Division on 26 May 44; staged at Cp Kilmer N.J. 14 Jan 45 until departed New York P/E 26 Jan 45; arrived in France 6 Feb 45 and entered Germany 24 Mar 45 and Austria 4 May 45; returned to New York P/E 10 Mar 46 where inactivated at Cp Kilmer N.J. on 11 Mar 46.

Campaigns: *Rhineland, Central Europe*
Aug 45 Loc: Wels Austria

Typical Organization (1943):

5th Infantry Regiment
14th Infantry Regiment
66th Infantry Regiment
HHB Division Artilery
607th Field Artillery Battalion (75mm)
608th Field Artillery Battalion (75mm)
609th Field Artillery Battalion (75mm)
581st Field Artillery Antitank Battery

271st Engineer Combat Battalion
371st Medical Battalion
731st Antiaircraft Artillery Machine Gun Bn
Division Headquarters
Hqs Company, 71st Light Division
Military Police Platoon
Ordnance Light Maintenance Platoon
Signal Platoon
Quartermaster Truck Company

Typical Organization (1944/45):

5th Infantry Regiment
14th Infantry Regiment
66th Infantry Regiment
HHB Division Artilery
564th Field Artillery Battalion (155mm)
607th Field Artillery Battalion (105mm)
608th Field Artillery Battalion (105mm)
609th Field Artillery Battalion (105mm)
71st Reconnaissance Troop, Mecz
749th Tank Battalion *(attached 15 Mar 45–28 Mar 45)*
761st Tank Battalion *(attached 28 Mar 45–10 May 45)*
635th Tank Destroyer Battalion *(attached 14 Mar 45–10 May 45)*
530th AAA Auto-Wpns Battalion *(attached 15 Mar 45–10 May 45)*

271st Engineer Combat Battalion
371st Medical Battalion
71st Counter Intelligence Corps Det
Headquarters, Special Troops
Hqs Company, 71st Infantry Division
Military Police Platoon
771st Ordnance Light Maintenance Company
251st Quartermaster Company
571st Signal Company

Overseas Wartime Assignments:

Fifteenth Army - 21 Jan 45

Seventh Army - 2 Mar 45

XV Corps - 9 Mar 45

XXI Corps - 22 Mar 45

VI Corps - 25 Mar 45

12th Army Group - 29 Mar 45

Third Army - 8 Apr 45

XII Corps - 11 Apr 45

XX Corps - 20 Apr 45

Commanders: BG Robert L. Spragins: Jul 43

MG Eugene M. Landrum: Oct 44

MG Willard G. Wyman: Nov 44

BG Onslow S. Rolfe: Aug 45

MG Arthur A. White: Oct 45

Killed in Action: 243   *Wounded in Action:* 843   *Died of Wounds:* 35

71st Infantry Division Combat Narrative

The division arrived at Le Havre France on 6 Feb 45 and moved to Limesay. It relieved the 100th Inf Div at Ratzwiller 11 Mar 45, and then pushed through the *West Wall* and captured Piermasens 21 Mar 45. It was relieved along the Rhine 29 Mar 45 and crossed the river the next day at Oppenheim and then assembled at Housenstamm near Frankfurt. The division then went into reserve where it intercepted a bypassed German force north of Hanau on 2 Apr 45. The Germans overran Waldensberg and the 5th and 14th Inf moved to force the Germans east into Budingen Wald while the 66th Inf blocked the forest's eastern exits. Assisted by the 5th Inf Div and part of the 2nd Cav Group, the division eliminated this pocket on 4 Apr 45. The division moved to the Fulda area beginning 5 Apr 45, and cleared to the Meiningen-Marisfeld-Juchsen line by 8 Apr 45. The division followed in the wake of the 11th Armd Div in a rapid drive to Coburg 10 Apr 45 and cut the Munich-Berlin Highway on 13 Apr 45. The division fought the Battle for Bayreuth 14–16 Apr 45 in heavy combat.

The division moved south and relieved the 14th Armd Div, eliminated German resistance in the Haag area 20 Apr 45, and cut the Sulzbach-Nuremberg Highway/railroad 21 Apr 45. The next day the 5th Inf overran Sulzbach-Rosenberg and the 14th Inf cleared Amberg with tank support. Bypassing German strongpoints, the division sped south and the 14th Inf crossed the Naab at Regenstauf 24 Apr 45 as the 5th Inf reached Regen. The 5th Inf went on to reach the Danube at Frengkofen as the 66th Inf reached the river and attacked Regensburg 25 Apr 45. On 26 Apr 45 the 5th Inf crossed the Danube at Frengkofen and the 14th Inf crossed in the Donaustauf-Sulzbach vicinity, each regiment being reinforced by a battalion of the 66th Inf. Regensburg surrendered to the division on 27 Apr 45. The division then followed behind the 13th Armd Div against crumbling resistance, and the 14th and 66th Inf assaulted across the Isar River using smoke and stormboats under direct German fire from positions on the far heights on 30 Apr 45. The bridgehead was expanded southeast of Landau to Eichendorf the next day. The 5th and 66th Inf seized the Inn River Dams and entered Austria 2 May 45. The 5th Inf advanced unopposed to Steyr on the Enns by 5 May 45, and the next day the 66th Inf reached the river and relieved the 80th Inf Div there. The 5th Inf moved forward and secured Ernsthofen Dam across the Enns River 6 May 45. The division contacted advancing Soviet Army forces east of Linz on 8 May 45 as hostilities ceased.

75th Infantry Division

No Distinctive
Insignia Authorized

15 Apr 43 activated at Ft Leonard Wood Mo and moved to La Maneuver Area 24 Jan 44 where participated in the Fourth Army No.6 Louisiana Maneuvers; transferred to Cp Breckinridge Ky 7 Apr 44 and staged at Cp Shanks N.Y. 7 Nov 44 until departed New York P/E 14 Nov 44; arrived England 22 Nov 44 and landed in France 13 Dec 44; crossed into Holland 18 Dec 44 and into Belgium 19 Dec 44; returned to France 27 Jan 45 and to Belgium 17 Feb 45; recrossed into Holland 18 Feb 45 and entered Germany 10 Mar 45; arrived Hampton Roads P/E 14 Nov 45 and inactivated at Cp Patrick Henry Va same date.

Campaigns: *Rhineland, Ardennes-Alsace, Central Europe*

Aug 45 Loc: Werdohl Germany

Typical Organization (1944/45):

289th Infantry Regiment
290th Infantry Regiment
291st Infantry Regiment
 HHB Division Artillery
730th Field Artillery Battalion (155mm)
897th Field Artillery Battalion (105mm)
898th Field Artillery Battalion (105mm)
899th Field Artillery Battalion (105mm)
 75th Reconnaissance Troop, Mecz
701st Tank Battalion *(attached 18 Mar 45–2 Apr 45)*
709th Tank Battalion *(attached 31 Jan 45–11 Feb 45)*
717th Tank Battalion *(attached 17 Apr 45–18 Apr 45)*
744th Tank Battalion *(attached 30 Mar 45–4 Jun 45)*
750th Tank Battalion *(attached 22 Dec 44–26 Jan 45)*
628th Tank Destroyer Battalion *(attached 10 Jan 45–15 Jan 45)*
629th Tank Destroyer Battalion *(attached 24 Dec 44–1 Jan 45)*
654th Tank Destroyer Battalion *(attached 24 Mar 45–25 Mar 45)*
772nd Tank Destroyer Battalion *(attached 22 Dec 44–4 Jun 45)*
807th Tank Destroyer Battalion *(attached 25 Mar 45–29 Mar 45)*
814th Tank Destroyer Battalion *(attached 30 Dec 44–5 Jan 45)*
440th AAA Auto-Wpns Battalion *(attached 22 Dec 44–26 Jan 45)*

275th Engineer Combat Battalion
375th Medical Battalion
 75th Counter Intelligence Corps Det
Headquarters Special Troops
Hqs Company, 75th Infantry Division
Military Police Platoon
775th Ordnance Light Maintenance Company
 75th Quartermaster Company
575th Signal Company

Overseas Wartime Assignments:

12th Army Group - 9 Dec 44
Ninth Army - 9 Dec 44
XVI Corps - 11 Dec 44
VII Corps - 22 Dec 44
XVIII (A/B) Corps - 29 Dec 44
VII Corps - 2 Jan 45
XVIII (A/B) Corps - 7 Jan 45

6th Army Group - 25 Jan 45
XXI Corps - 30 Jan 45
Seventh Army - 11 Feb 45
12th Army Group - 14 Feb 45
Ninth Army *(attached to British 8 Corps)* - 17 Feb 45
XVI Corps - 1 Mar 45

Commanders: MG Willard S. Paul: Apr 43
          MG Fay B. Prickett: Aug 43
          MG Ray E. Porter: Jan 45

MG Arthur A. White: Jun 45
BG Charles R. Doran: Oct 45

Killed in Action: 817   *Wounded in Action:* 3,314   *Died of Wounds:* 111

75th Infantry Division Combat Narrative

The division landed at Le Havre and Rouen France 13 Dec 44 and moved to Yvetot. The German Ardennes Counter-offensive of 16 Dec 44 caused it to be rushed to the front where it entered defensive positions along the Ourthe River on 23 Dec 44. After heavy combat around Sadzot the division moved to Aisne River at Grandmenil 5 Jan 45. On 8 Jan 45 it relieved the 82nd A/B Div along the Salm River and attacked across it 15 Jan 45 at Sâlmchateau and Bech. The division cleared the Grand Bois 22 Jan 45 and captured Aldringen 24 Jan 45, concluding its offensive.

The division moved to Ribeauville in Alsace-Lorraine on 28 Jan 45 and crossed the Colmar Canal 1 Feb 45 with two regiments abreast at Andolsheim. Fighting through the Forêt Domaniale, it reached the Rhine-Rhône Canal south of Neuf-Brisach on 6 Feb 45. The division entered Colmar and reached the Rhine River 7 Feb 45 and was withdrawn for rehabilitation at Luneville 11 Feb 45. It relieved the *British 6th A/B Div* along the Maas River near Roermond Holland on 21 Feb 45. The 291st Inf fought the Battle of Ossenberg 7–9 Mar 45, and the division relieved the 35th Inf Div along the Rhine from Wesel to Homburg 12 Mar 45. The 290th Inf crossed the Rhine 24 Mar 45 in the wake of the 30th and 79th Inf Divs, followed by the rest of the division on 30 Mar 45. The 289th and 290th Inf attacked through the pinned 8th Armd Div and reached the Dortmund-Ems Canal near Datteln 1 Apr 45.

The division attacked across the canal at Waltrop on 4 Apr 45 and began clearing the approaches to Dortmund. The division was reinforced by the 320th Inf and reached the Ruhr at Witten with four regiments, taking two bridges intact on 11 Apr 45. The division accepted the surrender of Herdecke on 14 Apr 45 and was withdrawn to Brambauer for rehabilitation.

The division relieved the 8th Inf Div in the Ruhr sector 22 Apr 45 and then relieved the 5th Inf Div south of the Ruhr on 23 Apr 45. The division was next assigned military government duties in Westphalia, and was serving in this capacity when hostilities were declared ended 7 May 45.

76th Infantry Division

No Distinctive Insignia Authorized

15 Jun 42 activated at Ft George G. Meade Md as the 76th Division and redesignated there as the 76th Infantry Division 1 Aug 42; designated Replacement Pool Division 2 Oct 42–1 Mar 43; moved to A.P. Hill Mil Res Va 28 Jul 43 and to Cp McCoy Wis 23 Sep 43; participated in Winter Maneuvers 17 Feb 44 at Watersmeet Mich and returned to Cp McCoy Wis 16 Mar 44; staged at Cp Myles Standish Mass 30 Nov 44 until departed Boston P/E 10 Dec 44; arrived England 20 Dec 44 and moved to France 12 Jan 45; crossed into Belgium 23 Jan 45 and into Luxembourg 25 Jan 45; entered Germany 1 Mar 45 where disbanded 31 Aug 45.

Campaigns: *Rhineland, Ardennes-Alsace, Central Europe*
Aug 45 Loc: Limbach Germany

Typical Organization (1944/45):

304th Infantry Regiment
385th Infantry Regiment
417th Infantry Regiment
 HHB Division Artillery
302nd Field Artillery Battalion (105mm)
355th Field Artillery Battalion (105mm)
364th Field Artillery Battalion (155mm)
901st Field Artillery Battalion (105mm)
 76th Reconnaissance Troop, Mecz
702nd Tank Battalion *(attached 26 Feb 45–11 Mar 45)*
707th Tank Battalion *(attached 2 Apr 45–4 Apr 45)*
749th Tank Battalion *(attached 4 Apr 45–9 May 45)*
691st Tank Destroyer Battalion *(attached 26 Jan 45–22 Feb 45, 2 Apr 45–9 May 45)*
808th Tank Destroyer Battalion *(attached 22 Feb 45–3 Apr 45)*
778th AAA Auto-Wpns Battalion *(attached 21 Jan 45–9 May 45)*

301st Engineer Combat Battalion
301st Medical Battalion
 76th Counter Intelligence Corps Det
Headquarters Special Troops
Hqs Company, 76th Infantry Division
Military Police Platoon
776th Ordnance Light Maintenance Company
 76th Quartermaster Company
 76th Signal Company

Overseas Wartime Assignments:

12th Army Group - 9 Jan 45
Fifteenth Army - 14 Jan 45
VIII Corps - 19 Jan 45

XII Corps - 25 Jan 45
XX Corps - 3 Apr 45
VIII Corps - 8 Apr 45

Commanders: MG Emil F. Reinhardt: Jun 42
MG William R. Schmidt: Dec 42
BG Henry C. Evans: Aug 45

Killed in Action: 433   *Wounded in Action:* 1,811   *Died of Wounds:* 90

76th Infantry Division Combat Narrative

The division landed at Le Havre France 12 Jan 45, assembled in the Limesy area, and moved to Champlon Belgium 23 Jan 45. It relieved the 87th Inf Div along the Sauer and Moselle Rivers near Echternach Luxembourg on 25 Jan 45. The 417th Inf attacked across the Sauer in the Weiterbach-Echternach area on 7 Feb 45 and battled through Echternacherbruck and the pillboxes of the *West Wall*, taking Ernzen by 14 Feb 45 with the 5th Inf Div. The rest of the division cleared the high ground north of Minden and mopped up west of the Pruem as it secured the bridgehead. The division crossed the Pruem River 24–25 Feb 45 and regrouped as the 304th Inf crossed the Nims at Wolsfeld the next day. The division renewed the offensive toward Trier on 27 Feb 45 and the 417th Inf reached the Kyll and the 304th Inf captured Olk on 1 Mar 45. The 385th Inf was reinforced and designated Task Force Onaway as it crossed the Kyll on 3 Mar 45 and drove on Herforst. It was disbanded 9 Mar 45 and the 385th Inf captured Grosslittgen as the 304th Inf took Musweiler. The 417th Inf helped the 10th Armd Div defend its Ruwer River bridgehead until 11 Mar 45. The division reached the Klein Kyll-Lieser Rivers from Karl to Wittlich, and had cleared most resistance by 14 Mar 45 as the 304th Inf crossed the Moselle near Mulheim.

On 21 Mar 45 the division relieved the 2nd Cavalry Group along the Rhine from Boppard to Bingen. The 385th and 417th Inf crossed the Rhine 26–27 Mar 45 at Boppard, battled through house-to-house fighting at Kamberg and were stopped by opposition from German officer-candidate forces until 1 Apr 45. The division reassembled at Homberg 3 Apr 45 and mopped up rearguard resistance as the 304th Inf reached the Wehre River and took the bridge at Niederhone on 5 Apr 45. The division advanced closely behind 6th Armd Div and reached the Buttstaedt area 11 Apr 45. The 304th Inf sped on to attack across the Wisse-Elster and attacked Zeitz 13 Apr 45, and the 417th Inf took over the assault on the town the next day to allow the 304th Inf to move on to Altenburg. Zeitz finally fell 15 Apr 45 and the division raced up to take over the 6th Armd Div bridgehead across the Mulde. The Zwick-Mulde Bridgehead was defended by the division near Chemnitz until hostilities were declared ended on 7 May 45.

77th Infantry Division

25 Mar 42 activated at Ft Jackson S.C. as the 77th Division and redesignated 77th Infantry Division 20 May 42; moved to La Maneuver Area 25 Jan 43 for the Third Army No.1 Louisiana Maneuvers; moved to Cp Young Calif 19 Apr 43 and participated in the Desert Training Center No.2 California Maneuvers; transferred to A.P. Hill Mil Res Va 1 Oct 43 and went to Cp Pickett Va 9 Oct 43 where participated in the XIII Corps West Virginia–Norfolk Maneuvers 15 Oct 43–2 Jan 44; staged at Cp Stoneman Calif 19 Mar 44 until departed San Francisco P/E 24 Mar 44; arrived on Hawaii 30 Mar 44 and arrived Eniwetok Island 17 Jul 44 enroute to Guam where it landed 22 Jul 44; departed Guam 3 Nov 44 and arrived Manus Island 15 Nov 44 enroute to Philippines where landed on Leyte 23 Nov 44; left the Philippines and sailed to the Ryukyus where assaulted Yakabi Shima and Zamami Shima 26 Mar 45 and Ie Shima 16 Apr 45; landed on Okinawa 27 Apr 45; arrived Cebu Island about 11 Jul 45 and Japan 5 Oct 45 where inactivated 15 Mar 46.

Campaigns: *Western Pacific, Leyte, Ryukyus*
Aug 45 Loc: *Cebu Philippine Islands*

Typical Organization (1944/45):

305th Infantry Regiment	302nd Engineer Combat Battalion
306th Infantry Regiment	302nd Medical Battalion
307th Infantry Regiment	77th Counter Intelligence Corps Det
HHB Division Artillery	Headquarters Special Troops
304th Field Artillery Battalion (105mm)	Hqs Company, 77th Infantry Division
305th Field Artillery Battalion (105mm)	Military Police Platoon
306th Field Artillery Battalion (155mm)	777th Ordnance Light Maintenance Company
902nd Field Artillery Battalion (105mm)	77th Quartermaster Company
77th Reconnaissance Troop, Mecz	77th Signal Company

Overseas Wartime Assignments:

Central Pacific Area Cmd - 1 Apr 44	South Pacific Base Cmd - 1 Nov 44
XXIV Corps - 13 Apr 44	Tenth Army - 10 Feb 45
Central Pacific Area Cmd - 18 Jun 44	XXIV Corps - 22 Feb 45
V Amphibious Corps (attached) - 22 Jun 44	Sixth Army - 8 Jul 45
Central Pacific Base Cmd - 1 Jul 44	IX Corps - 15 Jul 45
III Amphibious Corps (attached) - 9 Jul 44	Eighth Army - 15 Aug 45

Commanders: MG Robert L. Eichelberger: Mar 42
MG Roscoe B. Woodruff: Jun 42
MG Andrew D. Bruce: May 43

Killed in Action: 1,449   *Wounded in Action:* 5,935   *Died of Wounds:* 401

77th Infantry Division Combat Narrative

The division arrived in Hawaii 30 Mar 44 and moved to Ft Hase on Oahu, and engaged in jungle warfare and amphibious training. The 305th Inf arrived at Eniwetok 9 Jul 44 where it remained afloat until joined by the rest of the division 17 Jul 44, which then proceeded to Guam. The 305th Inf landed there 21 Jul 44 and assisted the 1st Provisional Marine Bde take Mt Alifan the following day. The 306th Inf landed at Agat Bay 23 Jul 44 and on 28 Jul 44 the 305th Inf gained the summit of Mt Tenjo. The division attacked out of its beachhead perimeter and took Barrigade Village, overrunning Mt Barrigada 4 Aug 44. The 305th Inf repulsed a strong Japanese counterattack 8 Aug 44 and the division attacked with three regiments abreast following naval and air bombardment on 7 Aug 44 to clear the northern third of the island. The division mopped up on Guam until it departed 3 Nov 44.

The division sailed to Leyte Island Philippines where it arrived 23 Nov 44. The division conducted an unopposed landing at Depositio below Ormoc 7 Dec 44 and the 306th and 307th Inf took Ormoc 10 Dec 44. The 305th Inf led the offensive from Ormoc and reduced a blockhouse strongpoint at Cogon by 14 Dec 44. The 307th Inf had a battalion detached to duty on Samar since 30 Nov 44 which rejoined it in time to take Valencia and its airfield 16–17 Dec 44, and went on to capture Libongao after heavy combat on 20 Dec 44. The 305th Inf repulsed Japanese counterattacks 23–24 Dec 44 and finished clearing up to Palompon Road by 31 Dec 44. The division relieved the 1st Cav Div and mopped up the northern and western portions of Leyte until 9 Feb 45 when it moved to Tarragona for rehabilitation.

The division left Leyte 18–24 Mar 45 for the Ryukyus Islands, where the 305th Inf assaulted Aka Island, the 306th Inf assaulted Geruma and Hokaji Islands, and the 307th Inf landed on Yakabit Island 26 Mar 45. On 27 Mar 45 the 306th Inf landed on Tokashiki Island. The 31 Mar 45 landing on Keise Shima marked the last landing in Kerama Retto preparatory to the Okinawa campaign. The division re-embarked at sea 2–10 Apr 45 and then landed the 305th and 306th Inf on Ie Shima Island 16 Apr 45. The 307th Inf landed the next day and the division fought past Government House Hill and Iegusugu Mountain to clear the island by 21 Apr 45. The 305th Inf remained on Ie Shima as a garrison force until 7 May 45, and the rest of the division landed over the secured Hagushi Beaches on Okinawa 27 Apr 45. There the division relieved the 96th Inf Div on 30 Apr 45.

The 307th Inf used cargo nets and ladders in the Battle for Maeda Escarpment 1–3 May 45, but then came under heavy Japanese fire from the reverse slope. The 306th Inf was subjected to a strong Japanese counterattack the next day, and the 307th Inf gained the reverse slope of the escarpment and held in against counterattack 5–6 May 45. The division pressed slowly southward to Shuri and Yonabaru, and as the 305th Inf pushed up heavily defended Route 5, the 306th and 307th Inf fought the Battle of Chocolate Drop Hill 11–20 May 45 which fell the same day as The Flattop. On 30 May 45 the division took three hills east of Shuri, battled past Hundred-Meter Hill, and pushed into the ruins of Shuri 31 May 45. The division then covered the rear of the 96th Inf Div and mopped up in the Shuri region. The 305th Inf advanced to plug the gap between XXIV Corps and the III Amphibious Corps, and during June the division covered the right flank of the former and sealed Japanese cave positions. The division moved to bivouac positions north of Shuri on 24 Jun 45 and engaged in outposting and patrols.

The 307th Inf departed Okinawa for Cebu Island, Philippines on 27 Jun 45, followed by the remainder of the division. From 11 Jul 45 until the end of the war the division engaged in construction and rehabilitation near Danao on the eastern coast of Cebu Island.

78th Infantry Division

No Distinctive Insignia Authorized

15 Aug 42 activated at Cp Butner N.C.; designated Replacement Pool Division 2 Oct 42–1 Mar 43; moved to the Carolina Maneuver Area 15 Nov 43; returned to Cp Butner N.C. 7 Dec 43 and went to the Tenn Maneuver Area 25 Jan 44 where participated in the Second Army No.5 Tennessee Maneuvers; arrived Cp Pickett Va 27 Mar 44 and staged at Cp Kilmer N.J. 4 Oct 44 until departed New York P/E 14 Oct 44; arrived England 25 Oct 44 and landed in France 22 Nov 44; entered Belgium 27 Nov 44 and Germany 7 Dec 44 where inactivated 22 May 46.

Campaigns: *Rhineland, Ardennes-Alsace, Central Europe*
Aug 45 Loc: Dillenberg Germany

Typical Organization (1944/45):

309th Infantry Regiment
310th Infantry Regiment
311th Infantry Regiment
 HHB Division Artillery
307th Field Artillery Battalion (105mm)
308th Field Artillery Battalion (105mm)
309th Field Artillery Battalion (155mm)
903rd Field Artillery Battalion (105mm)
 78th Reconnaissance Troop, Mecz
709th Tank Battalion *(attached 10 Dec 44–25 Jan 45)*
736th Tank Battalion *(attached 25 Jan 45–1 Feb 45)*
774th Tank Battalion *(attached 3 Feb 45–24 Feb 45)*
628th Tank Destroyer Battalion *(attached 19 Dec 44–23 Dec 44)*
817th Tank Destroyer Battalion *(attached 1 Dec 44–6 Dec 44)*
893rd Tank Destroyer Battalion *(attached 11 Dec 44–past 9 May 45)*
552nd AAA Auto-Wpns Battalion *(attached 20 Dec 44–past 9 May 45)*

303rd Engineer Combat Battalion
303rd Medical Battalion
 78th Counter Intelligence Corps Det
Headquarters Special Troops
Hqs Company, 78th Infantry Division
Military Police Platoon
778th Ordnance Light Maintenance Company
 78th Quartermaster Company
 78th Signal Company

Overseas Wartime Assignments:

Ninth Army - 9 Nov 44
XIX Corps - 28 Nov 44
V Corps - 5 Dec 44
VII Corps - 18 Dec 42
XIX Corps - 22 Dec 44
V Corps - 2 Feb 45

XVIII (A/B) Corps - 3 Feb 45
III Corps - 12 Feb 45
VII Corps - 16 Mar 45
XVIII (A/B) Corps - 2 Apr 45
First Army - 19 Apr 45

Commanders: MG Edwin P. Parker Jr: Aug 42
MG Ray W. Barker: Sep 45

Killed in Action: 1,427   *Wounded in Action:* 6,103   *Died of Wounds:* 198

78th Infantry Division Combat Narrative

The division landed in France on 22 Nov 44, moved to Tongres Belgium, and then to Roetgen Germany. It relieved the 1st Inf Div in line near Entenpfuhl 1–12 Dec 44, and detached the 311th Inf to fight under 8th Inf Div in the Battle of Huertgen Forest. The division attacked toward the Roer and Urft Dams on 12 Dec 44 and began the battle for Kesternich which finally fell to the 311th Inf on 31 Jan 45. Meanwhile, the division blocked the road junction near Monschau on 18 Dec 44 in response to the German Ardennes Counteroffensive, and cleared hill positions over the Kall River by 11 Jan 45. It attacked on 30 Jan 45 to contact the First Army at Widdau. After the division mopped up the Imgenbroich-Kesternich area, the 311th Inf crossed the flooded Roer River on 3 Feb 45. The drive on Schwammenauel Dam with three regiments abreast was halted soon after initiation, and resumed after heavy artillery bombardment on 7 Feb 45. Kommerscheidt fell to the 309th Inf, the 310th Inf cleared high ground leading to Schmidt, and the 311th Inf battled into the outer parts of the city. The 309th and 311th Inf were attached to the 9th Inf Div which took Schmidt after heavy combat and seized the dam 8–9 Feb 45.

The division entered Blens 13 Feb 45 and then consolidated and patrolled the west bank of the Roer. On 28 Feb 45 the 311th Inf crossed and drove south to Blens to join the rest of the division which crossed there 2 Mar 45 as the regiment took Heimbach in the bridgehead sector. The division then advanced to the Rhine and the 309th and 311th Inf crossed the river at Remagan attached to the 9th Inf Div which had responsibility for the bridgehead. The 310th Inf forced a bridgehead across the Ahr at Loehndorf. The division regrouped and attacked toward the Cologne-Frankfurt Autobahn on 11 Mar 45, and withstood counterattacks at Honnef the following day. The 309th Inf seized Hovel and cut the autobahn 16 Mar 45 as the 310th and 311th Inf took Konigswinter. The division regrouped again and drove along the east bank of the Rhine and secured the heights dominating the Konigswinter bridgesite on 18 Mar 45. The 311th Inf reached the Sieg River at Meindorf 21 Mar 45 as the 310th Inf captured Menden and cleared strongpoints around it 24 Mar 45. The 309th Inf eliminated a strongpoint near Hennef the next day, and the division then relieved the 1st Inf Div along the Sieg River.

The division was relieved along the south bank of the Sieg, and on 6 Apr 45 the 309th and 310th Inf attacked across it to reduce the Ruhr Pocket. The division battled through well-defended Waldbrol, Lichtenberg, and Freudenberg on 8 Apr 45. Advancing with the 13th Armd Div it seized Wipperfuerth on 13 Apr 45 and overran both Elberfeld and Wuppertal 16 Apr 45, which concluded its drive. The division was assigned the mission of guarding the rear of First Army and moved to Dillenburg 19 Apr 45. It was stationed near Marburg when hostilities were declared ended on 7 May 45.

79th Infantry Division

No Distinctive Insignia Authorized

15 Jun 42 activated at Cp Pickett Va as the 79th Division and redesignated there as 79th Infantry Division 1 Aug 42 and moved to Cp Blanding Fla 1 Sep 42; moved to Tenn Maneuvers Area 3 Mar 43 where participated in the Second Army No.1 Tennessee Maneuvers; transferred to Cp Forrest Tenn 19 Jul 43 and moved to Cp Young Calif 17 Aug 43 for the Desert Training Center No.3 California Maneuvers; arrived Cp Phillips Kans 4 Dec 43 and staged at Cp Myles Standish Mass 31 Mar 44 until departed Boston P/E 7Apr 44; arrived England 16 Apr 44 and landed in France 14 Jun 44; crossed into Belgium 17 Feb 45 and into Holland 22 Feb 45; entered Germany 3 Mar 45; arrived New York P/E 10 Dec 45 and inactivated at Cp Kilmer N.J. 11 Dec 45.

Campaigns: *Normandy, Northern France, Rhineland, Ardennes-Alsace, Central Europe*
Aug 45 Loc: Neheim Germany

Typical Organization (1944/45):

313th Infantry Regiment	304th Engineer Combat Battalion
314th Infantry Regiment	304th Medical Battalion
315th Infantry Regiment	79th Counter Intelligence Corps Det
HHB Division Artillery	Headquarters Special Troops
310th Field Artillery Battalion (105mm)	Hqs Company, 79th Infantry Division
311th Field Artillery Battalion (105mm)	Military Police Platoon
312th Field Artillery Battalion (155mm)	779th Ordnance Light Maintenance Company
904th Field Artillery Battalion (105mm)	79th Quartermaster Company
79th Reconnaissance Troop, Mecz	79th Signal Company
191st Tank Battalion *(attached 1 Dec 44–22 Dec 44)*	
717th Tank Battalion *(attached 8 Mar 45–20 Apr 45)*	
744th Tank Battalion *(attached 17 Apr 45–18 Apr 45)*	
749th Tank Battalion *(attached 1 Jul 44–24 Jul 44)*	
761st Tank Battalion *(attached 20 Feb 45–1 Mar 45)*	
781st Tank Battalion *(attached 22 Dec 44–3 Jan 45)*	
605th Tank Destroyer Battalion *(attached 22 Apr 45–30 Apr 45)*	
773rd Tank Destroyer Battalion *(attached 9 Sep 44–12 Oct 44)*	
809th Tank Destroyer Battalion *(attached 20 Mar 45–26 Mar 45)*	
813th Tank Destroyer Battalion *(attached 1 Jul 44–9 Sep 44, 12 Oct 44–21 Apr 45)*	
463rd AAA Auto-Wpns Battalion *(attached 1 Jul 44–9 Jul 45)*	

Overseas Wartime Assignments:

VII Corps - 18 Apr 44	XV Corps - 25 Nov 44
Third Army - 29 May 44	VI Corps - 5 Dec 44
VIII Corps - 1 Jul 44	Seventh Army - 6 Feb 45
XV Corps - 3 Aug 44	XVI Corps *(attached)* - 17 Feb 45
XII Corps - 29 Aug 44	XIII Corps - 1 Mar 45
XV Corps - 7 Sep 44	XVI Corps - 7 Mar 45
Third Army - 29 Sep 44	

Commanders: MG Ira T. Wyche: Jun 42   MG Anthony C. McAuliffe: Jul 45
                BG LeRoy H. Watson: May 45   BG LeRoy H. Watson: Aug 45

Killed in Action: 2,476   *Wounded in Action:* 10,971   *Died of Wounds:* 467

79th Infantry Division Combat Narrative

The division landed across Utah Beach France on 14 Jun 44, attacked toward Cherbourg with the 313th and 315th Inf on 19 Jun 44, and reached the outer fortifications of the fortress-city the following day. The division began its main assault 22 Jun 44 as the 313th Inf drove against the strongpoint at La Mare à Canards. The 314th Inf finally captured Fort du Roule 26 Jun 44. The division left Cherbourg and moved south to hold defensive lines along the Ollonde River until 2 Jul 44. The division then pushed down the west coast of the Cotentin Peninsula in driving rain and took La Haye-du-Puits after repelling German counterattacks on 8 Jul 44. It crossed the Ay River behind 8th Inf Div on 26 Jul 44 and took Lassey the next day, capturing Laval on 6 Aug 44. It sped past Le Mans on 8 Aug 44 and established a bridgehead near Mantes-Gassicourt over the Seine River 20 Aug 44, which it held against German counterattacks 22–27 Aug 44. It moved forward with the 2nd Armd Div and crossed the Therain River at the end of the month. The division then concentrated in the Joinville area on 10 Sep 44, and the 314th Inf battled through Charmes 12 Sep 44 and forded the Moselle as the 313th Inf captured Poussay and the 315th Inf seized Neufchâteau 13 Sep 44. After heavy combat as the division cleared its sector, the offensive was resumed on 18 Sep 44. On 20 Sep 44 the 314th Inf encountered German fire as it reached the Meurthe River near Lunéville attempting to turn the German flank. A battalion crossed the river near St Clement the next day but had to be withdrawn. The division moved forward despite intense attacks from the Forêt de Parroy, the 315th Inf losing and then recovering part of Lunéville 22 Sep 44 as the 314th Inf was delayed by counterattacks at Moncel. The 314th Inf frontally assaulted Forêt de Monden the following day in heavy combat and the division entered the Forêt de Parroy. The 315th Inf was temporarily isolated in fighting at the main road junction there on 5 Oct 44 and the division was forced on the defensive. An all-out divisional assault forced a German withdrawal from the forest with the final capture of the main road junction 9 Oct 44. The division next took Emberménil 3 Oct 44 and battled for the high ground east of the town 15–22 Oct 44. It was relieved in this area 24 Oct 44.

It rested at Lunéville and returned to the attack 13 Nov 44 with the 314th and 315th Inf out of the Montigny area which carried it across the Vezouse with the capture of Fremonville 19 Nov 44. It consolidated north of Strasbourg 25 Nov 44 and fought the Battle of Haguenau 9–11 Dec 44. The division reached the Lauter River at Schiebenhardt on 15 Dec 44 and held defensive lines at Wissembourg until 2 Jan 45. It then moved to the southern portion of the Rhine River held by Task Force Linden (42nd Inf Div). The Germans established a bridgehead at Gambsheim and by 6 Jan 45 the division had battled through Stattmatten to relieve encircled elements of the task force. German attacks forced the 315th Inf out of Hatten and Rittershoffen and defeated 314th Inf efforts to take Drusenheim, and by 12 Jan 45 both 14th Armd Div and 103rd Inf Div units were committed to the battle. The division lost Sessenheim 19 Jan 45 and by 21 Jan 45 division lines had been forced back to the Moder River. German assaults across the river at Neubourg and Schweighausen 24–25 Jan 45 punched through division positions which were restored the next day. The division remained on the defensive along the Moder River until 6 Feb 45.

It went into reserve and detached the 314th Inf to forward positions overlooking the Roer as a diversion for Operation GRENADE 23 Feb 45. The division crossed the Rhine with the 313th and 315th Inf after intensive artillery preparation on 24 Mar 45. It reached the Rhine-Herne Canal against strong opposition 29 Mar 45. The following day its 314th Inf concluded the drive to Emser Canal and the division established defensive positions there until 6 Apr 45. The division then relieved the 35th Inf Div west of Gelsenkirchen and attacked across the Emser and Rhine-Herne Canals with the 313th and 315th Inf on 7 Apr 45. It reached the Ruhr on 9 Apr 45 and moved against scattered resistance east along the Ruhr, establishing a small bridgehead at Kettwig 11 Apr 45. It was relieved the following day and reverted to security duty in the Dortmund area where it was posted when hostilities were declared ended on 7 May 45.

80th Infantry Division

No Distinctive
Insignia Authorized

15 Jul 42 activated at Cp Forrest Tenn as the 80th Division and redesignated there as the 80th Infantry Division 1 Aug 42; moved to the Tenn Maneuver Area 23 Jun 43 where participated in the Second Army No.2 Tennessee Maneuvers; arrived Cp Phillips Kans 8 Sep 43 and went to the Desert Training Center No.4 California Maneuvers 9 Dec 43; moved to Ft Dix N.J. 20 Mar 44 and staged at Cp Kilmer N.J. 23 Jun 44 until departed New York P/E 1 Jul 44; landed in England 7 Jul 44 and France 3 Aug 44; crossed into Luxembourg 20 Dec 44 and entered Germany 18 Feb 45 and Austria 5 May 45; returned New York P/E 3 Jan 46 and inactivated at Cp Kilmer N.J. 4 Jan 46.

Campaigns: *Northern France, Rhineland, Ardennes-Alsace, Central Europe*
Aug 45 Loc: Pichlwany Austria

Typical Organization (1944/45):

317th Infantry Regiment
318th Infantry Regiment
319th Infantry Regiment
  HHB Division Artillery
313th Field Artillery Battalion (105mm)
314th Field Artillery Battalion (105mm)
315th Field Artillery Battalion (155mm)
905th Field Artillery Battalion (105mm)
  80th Reconnaissance Troop, Mecz
702nd Tank Battalion *(attached 8 Aug 44–27 Feb 45, 11 Mar 45–past 9 May 45)*
610th Tank Destroyer Battalion *(attached 9 Aug 44–2 Sep 44, 23 Nov 44–6 Dec 44, 21 Dec 44–28 Jan 45)*
691st Tank Destroyer Battalion *(attached 16 Sep 44–18 Sep 44)*
802nd Tank Destroyer Battalion *(attached 28 Jan 45–4 Feb 45)*
808th Tank Destroyer Battalion *(attached 25 Sep 44–21 Dec 44)*
811th Tank Destroyer Battalion *(attached 3 Feb 45–4 Jul 45)*
633rd AAA Auto-Wpns Battalion *(attached 9 Aug 44–13 May 45)*

305th Engineer Combat Battalion
305th Medical Battalion
  80th Counter Intelligence Corps Det
Headquarters Special Forces
Hqs Company, 80th Infantry Division
Military Police Platoon
780th Ordnance Light Maintenance Company
  80th Quartermaster Company
  80th Signal Company

Overseas Wartime Assignments:

XII Corps - 1 Aug 44
XX Corps - 7 Aug 44
XV Corps - 8 Aug 44
XX Corps - 10 Aug 44
V Corps *(attached)* - 17 Aug 44

Third Army - 23 Aug 44
XII Corps - 26 Aug 44
III Corps - 19 Dec 44
XII Corps - 26 Dec 44
XX Corps - 10 Mar 45

Commanders: MG Joseph D. Patch: Jul 42
MG Horace L. McBride: Mar 43
MG Walter E. Lauer: Oct 45

Killed in Action: 3,038   *Wounded in Action:* 12,484   *Died of Wounds:* 442

80th Infantry Division Combat Narrative

The division landed across Utah Beach France on 3 Aug 44 and assembled near St Jores 7 Aug 44. After mopping up in the Le Mans area it assisted in the Battle for Falaise Gap, storming Le Bourg–St Léonard 17 Aug 44 and capturing Argentan on 20 Aug 44. It then followed in the wake of the 4th Armd Div to cross the Meuse River at Commercy 1 Sep 44. The division met strong opposition in efforts to force the Moselle at Toul as the 317th Inf was repulsed 6 Sep 44 and the 318th Inf fought for Fort de Villey-le-Sec 5–10 Sep 44. The division crossed on 12 Sep 44 and defended the bridgehead against counterattacks. The 319th Inf advanced into Toul as German forces struck the Dieulouard bridge-head again 15–16 Sep 44. The division fought for Bois de la Rumont 20–24 Sep 44. It fought pitched battles as it approached the Seille at a farm strongpoint taken by the 319th Inf 2 Oct 44, at Serrières with the 318th Inf, and at Sivry. There the 319th Inf lost elements to a German counterattack 3–4 Oct 44. The division attacked across the Seille River 8 Nov 44 with three regiments abreast. It advanced despite mud, mines, and highway congestion to seize a bridge at Faulquemont over the Nied Allemande River on 20 Nov 44. It took evacuated St Avold 27 Nov 44 and the 318th Inf fought the Battle of Farbersviller 3–4 Dec 44. On 7 Dec 44 the division was withdrawn for rehabilitation.

The division assembled in the Arlon Luxembourg area 20 Dec 44 and took Merzig after heavy combat on 23 Dec 44. It contained numerous German attacks at Heiderscheid and Ettelbruck and advanced to the Sauer with the 319th Inf on 24 Dec 44. The division checked German assaults near Ringel and blocked roads around Ettelbruck and Mostroff 27–28 Dec 44. On 6 Jan 45 the 319th Inf attacked across the Sure River near Heiderscheidergrund and the division advanced to capture Nocher by 18 Jan 45. It secured Burden on 20 Jan 45 but the 317th Inf was defeated in attempts to force the Wiltz River 21 Jan 45. The 319th Inf crossed at Merkols and Kautenbach on 23 Jan 45. The division pushed a bridgehead over the Clerf River and the 317th Inf cleared the heights beyond Hosingen 27 Jan 45. The next day the division took over the 4th Inf Div zone along the Our River.

After massive artillery preparation the division attacked across the Our and Sauer on 7 Feb 45 with the 319th Inf at Wallendorf and the 318th Inf near Dillingen. The heavy fire from the *West Wall* positions and swift current combined to prevent any bridging. As the *West Wall* fortifications and pillboxes were slowly reduced the bridgehead was expanded, and the 317th Inf crossed to clear the Bollendorf area on 14 Feb 45. Leaving the 319th Inf to contain remaining German forces, the division attacked out 18 Feb 45. The 318th Inf captured Mettendorf 21–22 Feb 45 as the

319th Inf completed the elimination of the *West Wall* positions between the Our and Gay Rivers with the capture of Roth. The division took Ober Geckler 23 Feb 45 and the 317th Inf crossed the Pruem River near Wissmannsdorf 27 Feb 45. It relieved the 4th Armd Div 3 Mar 45, and transferred to the Saar sector opposite Saarlautern on 11 Mar 45. The division attacked Wadern Forest on 13 Mar 45 and fought the Battle of Weiskirchen, where a battalion of the 318th was isolated, 14–15 Mar 45. The division established a bridgehead across the Prims in the Krettnich-Nunkirchen area 17 Mar 45, and followed the 10th Armd Div to take Kaiserlautern with the 319th Inf on 20 Mar 45.

The 319th Inf crossed the Rhine at Oppenheim 27 Mar 45, and the following morning the division made a simultaneous assault across both Rhine and Main Rivers as the 317th Inf crossed the Rhine at Mainz and the 319th Inf crossed the Main near Bischofsheim. The Mainz bridgehead was quickly expanded, and the division then followed the 6th Armd Div to take Kassel in house-to-house fighting 2–4 Apr 45. It moved to Gotha on 7 Apr 45 and drove on Erfurt which fell to the 317th and 318th Inf on 12 Apr 45 as Weimar surrendered to the 319th Inf. Jena was cleared 13 Apr 45 and the division took over the Zwick Mulde Bridgehead from the 4th Armd Div 16 Apr 45. The division was withdrawn for rehabilitation on 18 Apr 45 and stationed at Nuremberg 20–28 Apr 45. On 29 Apr 45 it crossed the Danube, and on 30 Apr 45 the 318th Inf crossed the Isar River over the railroad bridge at Mamming. The division reached the Inn River in the vicinity of Branau on 2 May 45, and overtook the 13th Armd Div to cross the river at Braunau 3 May 45. The division was at the Enns River near Kirchdorf when hostilities ceased 7 May 45.

81st Infantry Division

No Distinctive
Insignia Authorized

15 Jun 42 activated at Cp Rucker Ala as the 81st Division and redesignated as the 81st Infantry Division there 1 Aug 42; moved to Tenn Maneuver Area 20 Apr 43 where participated in the Second Army No.1 Tennessee Maneuvers; arrived 17 Jul 43 to take part in the Desert Training Center No.3 California Maneuvers; moved to Cp San Luis Obispo 20 Nov 43 and underwent Army Ground Forces Amphibious Training Maneuvers; transferred to Cp Beale Calif 19 Apr 44 where completed the exercise 1 May 44; staged at Cp Stoneman Calif 24 Jun 44 until departed San Francisco P/E 3 Jul 44; arrived Hawaii and located to Schofield Barracks 6 Jul 44 and left 12 Aug 44; arrived on Guadalcanal 24 Aug 44 and left 7 Sep 44; landed on Angaur Island in the Palau Islands 17 Sep 44 and on Peleliu 19 Oct 44; arrived in New Caledonia 14 Jan 45 and left 3 May 45; div detachment assaulted Iwo Jima 19 Feb 45; division arrived Manus Island 9–10 May 45 enroute to Philippines where landed on Leyte 16 May 45 and rehearsed for invasion of Japan; arrived in Japan 23 Sep 45 where inactivated 20 Jan 46.

Campaigns: *Western Pacific, Leyte*
Aug 45 Loc: Leyte Philippine Islands

Typical Organization (1944/45):

321st Infantry Regiment	306th Engineer Combat Battalion
322nd Infantry Regiment	306th Medical Battalion
323rd Infantry Regiment	81st Counter Intelligence Corps Det
HHB Division Artillery	Headquarters Special Troops
316th Field Artillery Battalion (105mm)	Hqs Company, 81st Infantry Division
317th Field Artillery Battalion (105mm)	Military Police Platoon
318th Field Artillery Battalion (155mm)	781st Ordnance Light Maintenance Company
906th Field Artillery Battalion (105mm)	81st Quartermaster Company
81st Reconnaissance Troop, Mecz	81st Signal Company

Overseas Wartime Assignments:

Central Pacific Base Cmd - 1 Jul 44	Sixth Army - 1 Jul 45
Tenth Army - 14 Jan 45	IX Corps - 15 Jul 45
Eighth Army - 3 May 45	Eighth Army - 15 Aug 45

Commanders: MG Gustave H. Franke: Jun 42
MG Paul J. Mueller: Aug 42

Killed in Action: 366   *Wounded in Action:* 1,942   *Died of Wounds:* 149

81st Infantry Division Combat Narrative

The division moved by echelon to Schofield Barracks Hawaii 4–16 Jul 44 and began preliminary rehearsals for Palau Island operations on 30 Jul 44. The division left Hawaii 11 Aug 44 and arrived on Guadalcanal 24 Aug 44 where conducted final rehearsals 30 Aug 44. The division arrived off Angaur Island in the Palaus and on 17 Sep 44 the 321st Inf assaulted and secured a beachhead from Cape Nagariois to Rocky Point as the 322nd Inf took the northern beaches, and the 323rd Inf feinted a landing off Angaur's western shore. The 321st Inf fought to Green Beach and the 322nd Inf reached the Phosphate Plant — where it was mistakenly bombed — on 18 Sep 44. The main effort of clearing southern Angaur began the following day and the 321st Inf drove to the south end of the island on 20 Sep 44. The island was declared secure and airbase development began, but the 322nd Inf moved to mop up Japanese entrenched in the Lake Salome Bowl depression in the northwest part of the island. After heavy artillery and air bombardment it attacked 21 Sep 44, but was forced to withdraw that night and pushed in the area again the next day. With positions untenable another night retreat was made both 22 and 23 Sep 44 and then the positions saturated with more artillery fire. Renewing the assault from another direction, the 322nd Inf gained a foothold in its northern portion and cleared positions along the southeastern rim 26 Sep 44. The next day the 322nd Inf had the Lake Salome Bowl encircled, gained positions inside it and ensued methodical elimination of the Japanese defenders, but suffered its highest losses in a single day of combat on 28 Sep 44. After the Japanese were pushed out into the northwest pocket on Angaur the area was subjected to close-in fire and the 322nd Inf feinted an attack on 6 Oct 44 to lure the defenders into exposed positions, then began its final assault 13 Oct 44. With the exception of stragglers, Japanese opposition was terminated 21 Oct 44.

The 323rd Inf had left the Palau Islands still afloat on 21 Sep 44 and occupied Ulithi Atoll, which was to become a key Pacific Fleet base, without opposition 22–24 Sep 44.

The 321st Inf departed Angaur on 22 Sep 44 and arrived on Peleliu 23 Sep 44 where it was attached to the 1st Marine Division until 20 Oct 44. The regiment advanced along the western coast and attacked the central high ground commencing 23 Sep 44. After air, naval, and artillery bombardment it pushed through Garekoru and was counterattacked the next day which caused a temporary loss of ground. The 321st Inf cleared the trail cutting off Japanese forces in the Umurbrogol Mtns 26 Sep 44 and began the assault there 27 Sep 44 which was continued until the 7th Marines took responsibility for the area 29 Sep 44. It then relieved the 6th Marines on Ngesbus and Kongauro Islands as well as finishing the battle of Amiangal Mountain 2 Oct 44. The 321st Inf seized Garakayo Island 9 Oct 44 and took over the final destruction of Umurbrogol Pocket at Peleliu from the Marines on 16 Oct 44, the same day the 323rd Inf took Ngulu Atoll between Yap and the Palaus. The 321st Inf renewed the assault there 18 Oct 44 and the division opened its headquarters on Peleliu 19 Oct 44, the 323rd Inf taking over the Umurbrogol reduction 26 Oct 44. Deep salients had been forced into the strongpoint but bad weather delayed a renewed offensive until 2 Nov 44 which, after heavy combat, destroyed remaining Japanese positions by 27 Nov 44. In the meantime the 81st Cav Rcn Troop took Grokottan Island 11 Nov 44, Nereregong Island 15 Nov 44, and Kayangel Atoll 30 Nov 44. The 321st Inf took Fais Island 1–4 Jan 45.

The division left for New Caledonia 3 Jan–19 Feb 45 and rehabilitated in the Oua Tom-Bouloupari area. The division was designated as area reserve for the Ryukyus Operation 6 Jan 45 but was relieved from this assignment on 18 Apr 45. The advance party arrived on Leyte Island Philippines 28 Apr 45, the division departing New Caledonia 3 May 45 and landing on Leyte 16 May 45. There the division engaged in construction and amphibious training 30 Jun–23 Jul 45, and mopped up in the northwestern portion of the island from 21 Jul–12 Aug 45.

82nd Airborne Division

No Distinctive
Insignia Authorized

25 Mar 42 activated at Cp Claiborne La as the 82nd Division and redesignated there as the 82nd Infantry Division 24 May 42; redesignated 82nd Airborne Division 15 Aug 42 and moved to Ft Bragg N.C. 3 Oct 42; staged at Cp Edwards Mass 18 Apr 43 until departed New York P/E 28 Apr 43; arrived North Africa 10 May 43 and air-assaulted Sicily 9 Jul 43 and returned to North Africa 19 Aug 43; moved back to Sicily 4 Sep 43 and landed in Italy 13 Sep 43; departed Italy 19 Nov 43 and returned to North Africa 22 Nov 43 and left 30 Nov 43; arrived Northern Ireland 9 Dec 43 and arrived England 14 Feb 44; air-assaulted Normandy France 6 Jun 44 and returned to England 13 Jul 44; air-assaulted Nijmegen-Arnhem Holland 17 Sep 44 and moved to France 14 Nov 44; crossed into Belgium 18 Dec 44 and into Germany 30 Jan 45; returned to France 19 Feb 45 and re-entered Germany 2 Apr 45; returned New York P/E 3 Jan 46 and moved to Ft Bragg N.C. 16 Jan 46 where active thru 1946.

Campaigns: *Sicily, Naples-Foggia, Normandy, Rhineland, Ardennes-Alsace, Central Europe*
Aug 45 Loc: Ludwiglust Germany

Typical Organization (1944/45):

325th Glider Infantry Regiment
504th Parachute Infantry Regiment*
505th Parachute Infantry Regiment**
 HHB Division Artillery
319th Glider Field Artillery Bn (75mm)
320th Glider Field Artillery Bn (75mm)
376th Prcht Field Artillery Bn (75mm)
456th Prcht Field Artillery Bn (75mm)
 80th Airborne Antiaircraft Battalion
 82nd Airborne Signal Company

307th Airborne Engineer Battalion
307th Airborne Medical Company
 82nd Counter Intelligence Corps Det
Headquarters Special Troops
Hqs Company, 82nd Airborne Division
Military Police Platoon
Reconnaissance Platoon
782nd Airborne Ordnance Maintenance Company
407th Airborne Quartermaster Company
 82nd Parachute Maintenance Company

507th Parachute Infantry Regiment *(attached 14 Jan 44–1 Mar 45)*
508th Parachute Infantry Regiment *(attached 14 Jan 44–21 Jan 45, 23 Jan 45–past 9 May 45)*
517th Parachute Infantry Regiment *(attached 1 Jan 45–11 Jan 45, 23 Jan 45–26 Jan 45, 3 Feb 45–5 Feb 45,*
                    9 Feb 45–10 Feb 45)
551st Parachute Infantry Battalion *(attached 26 Dec 44–13 Jan 45, 21 Jan 45–27 Jan 45)*
740th Tank Battalion *(attached 30 Dec 44–11 Jan 45, 27 Jan 45–7 Feb 45)*
605th Tank Destroyer Battalion *(attached 29 Apr 45–30 Apr 45, 2 May 45–7 May 45)*
628th Tank Destroyer Battalion *(attached 2 Jan 45–11 Jan 45)*
629th Tank Destroyer Battalion *(attached 1 Feb 45–19 Feb 45)*
643rd Tank Destroyer Battalion *(attached 4 Jan 45–5 Jan 45)*
580th AAA Auto-Wpns Battalion *(attached 28 Apr 45–30 Apr 45)*
634th AAA Auto-Wpns Battalion *(attached 6 Feb 45–19 Feb 45)*

 *Assigned to division 15 Aug 42 and replaced 327th Infantry Regt relieved same date.
 **Assigned to division 10 Feb 43 and replaced 326th Infantry Regt relieved 4 Feb 43.

Overseas Wartime Assignments:

NATO - 10 May 43
II Corps - 10 Jul 43
Seventh Army - 13 Aug 43
British 10 Corps (attached) - 26 Sep 43
NATO - 8 Nov 43
ETO - 20 Nov 43
VIII Corps - 19 Feb 44
VII Corps - 6 Jun 44
VIII Corps - 19 Jun 44
Ninth Army *(attached)* - 13 Jul 44
XVIII (A/B) Corps - 12 Aug 44

First Allied (A/B) Army - 17 Sep 44
British 1 (A/B) Corps (attached) - 17 Sep 44
British 30 Corps (attached) - 9 Oct 44
Canadian 2 Corps (attached) - 9 Nov 44
VIII Corps *(attached)* - 17 Dec 44
V Corps - 18 Dec 44
XVIII (A/B) Corps - 19 Dec 44
First Allied (A/B) Army - 18 Jan 45
III Corps - 14 Feb 45
First Allied (A/B) Army - 19 Feb 45
XXII Corps *(attached)* - 31 Mar 45
XVIII (A/B) Corps - 30 Apr 45

Commanders: MG Omar N. Bradley: Mar 42
       MG Matthew B. Ridgway: Jun 42
       MG James M. Gavin: Aug 44

Killed in Action: 1,619   *Wounded in Action:* 6,560   *Died of Wounds:* 332

82nd Airborne Division Combat Narrative

The division landed at Casablanca North Africa on 10 May 43 and trained. The 505th Prcht Inf and 3rd Bn 504th Prcht Inf parachuted to take high ground near Ponte Olivo airfield northeast of Gela Sicily on 9 Jul 43. Despite the wide scattering of the assault, objectives were seized and units linked up with 1st Inf Div the next day. The 504th Prcht Inf was parachuted in the Gela area 11 Jul 43 with heavy losses from both German and allied antiaircraft fire. The division was moved up to the front by motor and reinforced by the 39th Inf on 12 Jul 43. The crossings of Fiume delle Canno were secured 18 Jul 43 and the division pushed along the coastal highway, seizing the Marsala-Trapani area of the western coast by 23 Jul 43.

The 504th Prcht Inf was parachuted south of the Sele River near Salerno Italy on 13 Sep 43 as the 325th Glider Inf was brought into the beachhead amphibiously 15 Sep 43. 505th Prcht Inf was parachuted near the Sele River the following night to reinforce the air assault. The 504th Prcht Inf began its attack to recover Altavilla 16 Sep 43 and the division fought toward Naples, which it reached 1 Oct 43 and moved into the next day for security duty. The 504th Prcht Inf moved up in combat and had captured Gallo by 29 Oct 43. It then battled in the Winter Line commencing with attacks up Hill 687 on 15 Dec 43, and the 504th Prcht Inf assaulted Anzio Beach 22–23 Jan 44. It participated in heavy combat there along the Mussolini Canal and left in late March 1944 to rejoin the division, which had moved to England via Ireland 9 Dec 43.

The division air-assaulted behind Utah Beach Normandy France between Ste Mère-Eglise and Carentan on 6 Jun 44, being reinforced by the 325th Glider Inf the next day, which arrived both by air assault and through the beachhead by sea. The 504th Prcht Inf did not participate in this assault, but the division was reinforced by both the attached 507th and 508th Prcht Inf. The division remained under strong German pressure along the Merderit River and crossed with the 325th Glider Inf to secure a bridgehead at La Fière 9 Jun 44. The next day the 505th Prcht Inf captured Montebourg Station, and on 12 Jun 44 the 508th Prcht Inf crossed the Douve at Beuzeville-la-Bastille and reached Baupt the following day. The 325th Glider Inf and 505th Prcht Inf reached St Sauveur-le-Vicomte 16 Jun 44 and the division established a bridgehead at Pont l'Abbé 19 Jun 44. The division then attacked down the west coast of the Cotentin Peninsula and gained Hill 131 on 3 Jul 44 and the day after seized Hill 95 overlooking La Haye-du-Puits. It returned to England 13 Jul 44 for rehabilitation.

The division air-assaulted in the Nijmegen-Grave region of Holland on 17 Sep 44, took the Maas Bridge at Grave and the Maas-Waal Canal Bridge at Heumen, as well as Nijmegen-Groesbeek Ridge. The next day attempts to take Nijmegen Highway Bridge failed, and on 19 Sep 44 the division contacted the *British Guards Armd Div* at Grave. The 504th Prcht Inf attacked across the Waal River in assault boats 20 Sep 44 and seized the Railroad Bridge, and the division fought along Nijmegen-Groesbeek Ridge. The division was relieved 11 Nov 44, but on 17 Dec 44 was moved to the front in response to the German Ardennes Counteroffensive. It attacked 20 Dec 44 in the Vielsalm–St Vith region and the 504th Prcht Inf took Monceau and forced German units back across the Amblève River the next day. Further German assaults along the Salm hit the 505th Prcht Inf in the Trois Ponts area 22 Dec 44 and by 24 Dec 44 the division lost Manhay. On 25 Dec 44 it withdrew from the Vielsalm salient. It attacked northeast of Bra 27 Dec 44 and reached Salm by 4 Jan 45. Comté was cleared 8 Jan 45 and Herresbach fell 28 Jan 45. The division attacked the *West Wall* 2 Feb 45 where it was relieved 4 Feb 45, and then drove to the Roer River near Bergstein in an attack 7–10 Feb 45. The division crossed the Roer River on 17 Feb 45 and then moved to Reims for rehabilitation. It took over the 86th Inf Div sector on the Rhine 4 Apr 45 and performed security duty in Cologne until 25 Apr 45. The division attacked from the Elbe River 30 Apr 45 in the Bleckede area and pushed toward the Elbe River. The German 21st Army surrendered to the division on 2 May 45 as the 504th Prcht Inf drove to Forst Carrenzien. The division was engaged in mopping up when hostilities were declared ended on 7 May 45.

83rd Infantry Division

No Distinctive
Insignia Authorized

15 Aug 42 activated at Cp Atterbury Ind and moved to Tenn Maneuver Area 23 Jun 43 where participated in the Second Army No.2 Tennessee Maneuvers; arrived Cp Breckinridge Ky 9 Sep 43 and staged at Cp Shanks N.Y. 31 Mar 44 until departed New York P/E 6 Apr 44; arrived England 16 Apr 44 and landed in France 19 Jun 44; crossed into Luxembourg 25 Sep 44 and into Germany 6 Dec 44; moved to Belgium 27 Dec 44 and re-entered Germany 22 Feb 45; moved into Holland 21 Mar 45 and returned to Germany 28 Mar 45; returned New York P/E 26 Mar 46 and inactivated at Cp Kilmer N.J. 27 Mar 46.

Campaigns: *Normandy, Northern France, Rhineland, Ardennes-Alsace, Central Europe*
Aug 45 Loc: Wernigerode Germany

Typical Organization (1944/45):

329th Infantry Regiment
330th Infantry Regiment
331st Infantry Regiment
 HHB Division Artillery
322nd Field Artillery Battalion (105mm)
323rd Field Artillery Battalion (105mm)
324th Field Artillery Battalion (155mm)
908th Field Artillery Battalion (105mm)
 83rd Reconnaissance Troop, Mecz
 70th Tank Battalion *(attached 17 Jul 44–18 Jul44)*
736th Tank Battalion *(attached 6 Feb 45–9 May 45)*
746th Tank Battalion *(attached 5 Jul 44–16 Jul 44)*
774th Tank Battalion *(attached 28 Aug 44–24 Dec 44, 26 Jan 45–3 Feb 45)*
629th Tank Destroyer Battalion *(attached 9 Dec 44–23 Dec 44, 1 Jan 45–30 Jan 45)*
643rd Tank Destroyer Battalion *(attached 2 Feb 45–9 May 45)*
772nd Tank Destroyer Battalion *(attached 22 Dec 44–1 Jan 45)*
801st Tank Destroyer Battalion *(attached 10 Apr 45–12 Apr 45)*
802nd Tank Destroyer Battalion *(attached 1 Jul 44–7 Dec 44)*
807th Tank Destroyer Battalion *(attached 29 Sep 44–11 Oct 44)*
453rd AAA Auto-Wpns Battalion *(attached 1 Jul 44–past 9 May 45)*
473rd AAA Auto-Wpns Battalion *(attached 22 Aug 44–19 Sep 44)*

308th Engineer Combat Battalion
308th Medical Battalion
 83rd Counter Intelligence Corps Det
Headquarters Special Troops
Hqs Company, 83rd Infantry Division
Military Police Platoon
783rd Ordnance Light Maintenance Company
 83rd Quartermaster Company
 83rd Signal Company

Overseas Wartime Assignments:

VIII Corps - 8 Apr 44
XV Corps - 1 Aug 44
VIII Corps - 3 Aug 44
Ninth Army - 10 Sep 44
XX Corps - 21 Sep 44
VIII Corps - 11 Oct 44

XX Corps - 8 Nov 44
VIII Corps - 11 Nov 44
XIX Corps - 22 Dec 44
VII Corps - 26 Dec 44
XIX Corps - 16 Feb 45
XIII Corps - 8 May 45

Commanders: MG Frank W. Milburn: Aug 42
               MG Robert C. Macon: Jan 44

Killed in Action: 3,161   *Wounded in Action:* 11,807   *Died of Wounds:* 459

83rd Infantry Division Combat Narrative

The division landed across Omaha Beach France on 19 Jun 44, took over defensive positions, and attacked against strong opposition toward Périers 4 Jul 44. St Eny fell 9 Jul 44 and the division regrouped along the Ays River 15 Jul 44. The division renewed its attack 26 Jul 44 as part of the Operation COBRA Breakout and in heavy combat crossed the Taute River the next day. After consolidation the division followed the 6th Armd Div and reached the fortified city of St Malo 4 Aug 44. It began the Battle of St Malo the same day and forced back German defenders to the strongpoints of The Citadel and Dinard 9 Aug 44 after combined assaults. Dinard fell after severe fighting 15 Aug 44 and The Citadel surrendered after further combat on 17 Aug 44, marking the end of the battle.

The division moved south to protect the north bank of the Loire River west of Orleans 27 Aug 44, and assembled south of Rennes for patrolling and reconnaissance operations. After air, naval, and artillery preparation, divisional elements made an amphibious assault and took Ile de Cézembre, off St Malo, on 2 Sep 44. On 16 Sep 44 the division accepted the surrender of a large isolated German force while screening the Loire. It moved to the Moselle River at Remich on 25 Sep 44. The division then advanced in heavy combat to the *West Wall* across the Sauer as the 329th Inf fought the Battle for Grevenmacher 1–5 Oct 44 and then took Echternach 7 Oct 44. As part of Operation UNICORN the division took Le Stromberg Hill near Basse Knoz after extended fighting on 5 Nov 44 and defeated several counterattacks.

The division relieved the 4th Inf Div on 7 Dec 44, and attacked to clear the west bank of the Roer on 10 Dec 44 as the 330th Inf took Strass and the 331st Inf took Gey. The division contained a German attack toward Guerzenich on 16 Dec 44 and cleared both Roelsdorf and Lendersdorf the following day. It relieved the 5th Armd Div in line on 22 Dec 44 and fought the Battle for Winden 23–25 Dec 44, then moved into the Havelange area 27 Dec 44 where it relieved the 2nd Armd Div. The division was then engaged in heavy fighting to reduce the German salient at Rochefort. Attacking through the 3rd Armd Div on 9 Jan 45 the division took both Petite Langlir and Langlir against strong opposition 12 Jan 45, gaining a bridgehead across the Langlir-Ronce River. The division mopped up Honvelez 14 Jan 45, battled at Bovigny 15 Jan 45, and consolidated along the east edge of the Bois de Ronce, taking both Bovigny and Courtil on 19 Jan 45. It then moved back to Belgium and Holland for rehabilitation 22 Jan 45. From 23–27 Feb 45 the 330th Inf fought with the 29th Inf Div in the Schleiden area.

The division attacked 1 Mar 45 as part of Operation GRENADE in the advance to the Rhine. The 331st Inf reached the Erft River southwest of Neuss, which the 329th Inf captured 2 Mar 45, as the division repulsed German counter-attacks from Kapellen. The 330th Inf reached the bridge at Oberkassel the next day but that structure was blown up as the regiment approached. The division then assumed defensive positions.

The division crossed the Rhine south of Wesel on 29 Mar 45 and drove across the Muenster Plain, mopping up resistance along the Lippe River and establishing a small bridgehead at Hamm 1–2 Apr 45. The division relieved the 8th Armd Div near Neuhaus and took the town the next day. It resumed the attack 4 Apr 45. The 329th Inf crossed the Weser at Bodenwerder 6 Apr 45 and Halle fell. The division next dashed across the Leine River in the Alfeld-Greene area 8 Apr 45 and the 330th Inf pushed through the Harz Mountains 10 Apr 45. The 329th reached the Elbe River at Barby 12 Apr 45 as the 331st took Nienburg on the Saale River. The 329th and 331st Inf established a bridgehead across the Elbe at Barby the following day and held it against German counterattacks 16 and 18 Apr 45. The 320th Inf of 35th Inf Div was attached to division, crossed the Saale, and mopped up between Saale and Elbe Rivers until relieved by the 330th Inf on 21 Apr 45. The 329th Inf occupied Zerbst on 28 Apr 45 from which the 125th Cav Sqdn moved east to contact advancing Soviet Army forces. The division turned over the Elbe River Bridgehead to the 30th Inf Div on 6 May 45 and hostilities were declared over the next day.

84th Infantry Division

No Distinctive Insignia Authorized

15 Oct 42 activated at Cp Howze Tex and moved to the La Maneuver Area 17 Sep 43 where participated in the Third Army No.4 Louisiana Maneuvers; moved to Cp Claiborne La 16 Nov 43 and staged at Cp Kilmer N.J. 5 Sep 44 until departed New York P/E 20 Sep 44; arrived England 4 Oct 44 and landed in France 1 Nov 44; crossed into Holland 5 Nov 44 and entered Germany 17 Nov 44; crossed into Belgium 21 Dec 44 and returned to Holland 3 Feb 45 and Germany 7 Feb 45; returned New York P/E 20 Jan 46 and inactivated at Cp Kilmer N.J. 21 Jan 46.

Campaigns: *Rhineland, Ardennes-Alsace, Central Europe*
Aug 45 Loc: Salzwedel Germany

Typical Organization (1944/45):

333rd Infantry Regiment
334th Infantry Regiment
335th Infantry Regiment
 HHB Division Artillery
325th Field Artillery Battalion (105mm)
326th Field Artillery Battalion (105mm)
327th Field Artillery Battalion (155mm)
909th Field Artillery Battalion (105mm)
 84th Reconnaissance Troop, Mecz
771st Tank Battalion *(attached 20 Dec 44–22 Mar 45, 2 Apr 45–30 Jun 45)*
701st Tank Battalion *(attached 10 Dec 44–20 Dec 44)*
605th Tank Destroyer Battalion *(attached 2 Mar 45–7 Mar 45)*
638th Tank Destroyer Battalion *(attached 1 Dec 44–22 Jun 45)*
473rd AAA Auto-Wpns Battalion *(attached 1 Dec 44–10 Dec 44)*
557th AAA Auto-Wpns Battalion *(attached 1 Dec 44–27 Jan 45, 2 Feb 45–9 May 45)*

309th Engineer Combat Battalion
309th Medical Battalion
 84th Counter Intelligence Corps Det
Headquarters Special Troops
Hqs Company, 84th Infantry Division
Military Police Platoon
784th Ordnance Light Maintenance Company
 84th Quartermaster Company
 84th Signal Company

Overseas Wartime Assignments:

Ninth Army - 10 Sep 44
III Corps - 21 Sep 44
XIX Corps - 4 Nov 44
XIII Corps - 8 Nov 44
British 30 Corps (attached) - 11 Nov 44

XIII Corps - 23 Nov 44
XVIII (A/B) Corps *(attached)* - 20 Dec 44
VII Corps - 21 Dec 44
XVIII (A/B) Corps - 23 Jan 45
XIII Corps - 3 Feb 45

Commanders: MG John H. Hildring: Oct 42   MG Roscoe B. Woodruff: Mar 44
MG Stonewall Jackson: Feb 43   MG Alexander R. Bolling: Jun 44
MG Robert B. McClure: Oct 43

Killed in Action: 1,284   *Wounded in Action:* 5,098   *Died of Wounds:* 154

84th Infantry Division Combat Narrative

The division landed across Omaha Beach France 1–4 Nov 44 and moved to Gulpen Holland 5–12 Nov 44. It detached the 335th Inf to fight in the Wuerselen area 11–27 Nov 44. The division initiated attacks to reduce the Geilenkirchen salient north of Aachen, supported by British flail tanks and searchlights, on 18 Nov 44. Prummern fell 20 Nov 44 as the 334th Inf won the Battle of Mahogany Hill 19–22 Nov 44 by surprise attack on the latter date. The 333rd Inf assaulted Muellendorf 22 Nov 44 but lost advance elements in the attack, and the offensive was halted the next day as efforts to take Wurm and Beeck failed.

On 29 Nov 44, omitting artillery preparation, the division began the drive on the Roer River as the 335th Inf reached Lindern and repulsed counterattacks, and took Beeck the following day. The 334th Inf took Leiffarth and cleared the high ground northeast of Beeck and Lindern on 2 Dec 44. A German counterattack penetrated lines at Leiffarth on 16 Dec 44, but the front was restored and the division took both Wurm and Muellendorf on 18 Dec 44.

The division was moved to Marche Belgium in response to the German Ardennes Counteroffensive and organized a perimeter defense there 21–22 Dec 44. Fighting in mixed sleet and snow, German assaults pierced the division positions between Hargimont and Rochefort 23 Dec 44 and drove through Verdenne the next day. The division recovered that town 25 Dec 44 and repulsed German attacks toward Ménil the next day, then turned to reduce the pocket between Verdenne and Bourdon 27 Dec 44. The division started its offensive to help reduce the German Ardennes salient on 3 Jan 45 as it followed the 2nd Armd Div toward Houffalize. It took Consy 6–9 Jan 45, cleared the main crossroads southeast of Manhay, and captured Laroche 11 Jan 45. It gained its final objectives of Nadrin, Filly, Petite and Grande Mormont 14 Jan 45 and consolidated. After a brief rehabilitation, the division took over the 83rd Inf Div–3rd Armd Div sector 21 Jan 45 and attacked to take Gouvy and Beho 22 Jan 45 and Ourthe 23 Jan 45.

The division relieved the 102nd Inf Div in the Linnich-Himmerich sector 7 Feb 45 and prepared for the Roer River crossings. It crossed at Linnich on 23 Feb 45 and repulsed a German counterattack near Rurich. The 335th Inf had expanded the bridgehead to Houverath 25 Feb 45 as the 334th Inf cleared Hetzerath and Granterath. Against strong opposition, the 333rd Inf reached the Niers Canal at Oedt 1 Mar 45 and then crossed it near Suechteln the next day. The 335th Inf captured Krefeld 2–3 Mar 45, and the division reached the Rhine River 5 Mar 45. The 335th Inf fought at Baerl against the well-defended Rheinhausen Railroad Bridge, and the 334th Inf reached the Admiral Scheer Highway Bridge at Homberg, but it was destroyed. The division then took up defensive positions along the Rhine for the rest of the month.

The division began its assembly and crossed the Rhine 1 Apr 45, and then went into the attack. The 335th Inf forced the Weser River south of Neesen and gained surprise to establish a bridgehead astride the Weser Gebirge on 6 Apr 45. The 334th Inf seized a bridge over the Leine River near Guemmer 8 Apr 45, and the division advanced to capture Hannover on 10 Apr 45. The division overtook advancing armor to reach the Elbe River 14 Apr 45 and relieved the 5th Armd Div there 16 Apr 45. The division cleared the Wahrenberg-Pretzetze sector along the Elbe 21–22 Apr 45, and established defensive positions. On 2 May 45 it made contact with advancing Soviet Army forces near Below and Abbendorft. The division was on occupation duty when hostilities were declared ended on 7 May 45.

85th Infantry Division

No Distinctive Insignia Authorized

15 May 42 activated at Cp Shelby Miss as the 85th Division and redesignated there 1 Aug 42 as the 85th Infantry Division; moved to the La Maneuver Area 6 Apr 43 and participated in the Third Army No.2 Louisiana Maneuvers; moved to Cp Young Calif 23 Jun 43 where took part in the Desert Training Center No.3 California Maneuvers; transferred to Ft Dix N.J. 7 7 Oct 43 and staged at Cp Patrick Henry Va 18 Dec 43 until departed Hampton Roads P/E 24 Dec 43; arrived North Africa 2 Jan 44 and departed 24 Mar 44; arrived Italy 27 Mar 44; returned to Hampton Roads P/E 25 Aug 45 and inactivated at Cp Patrick Henry Va the same date.

Campaigns: *Rome-Arno, North Apennines, Po Valley*
Aug 45 Loc: *Fagianeria Italy*

Typical Organization (1944/45):

337th Infantry Regiment
338th Infantry Regiment
339th Infantry Regiment
 HHB Division Artillery
328th Field Artillery Battalion (105mm)
329th Field Artillery Battalion (105mm)
403rd Field Artillery Battalion (155mm)
910th Field Artillery Battalion (105mm)
 85th Reconnaissance Troop, Mecz

310th Engineer Combat Battalion
310th Medical Battalion
 85th Counter Intelligence Corps Det
Headquarters Special Troops
Hqs Company, 85th Infantry Division
Military Police Platoon
785th Ordnance Light Maintenance Company
 85th Quartermaster Company
 85th Signal Company

Overseas Wartime Assignments:

Fifth Army - March 44
II Corps - 25 Jul 44
IV Corps - 20 Aug 44
II Corps - 26 Aug 44
IV Corps - 23 Nov 44

II Corps - 8 Jan 45
Fifth Army - 18 Mar 45
IV Corps - 17 Apr 45
II Corps - 30 Apr 45

Commanders: MG Wade H. Haislip: May 42
MG John B. Coulter: Feb 43

Killed in Action: 1,561   *Wounded in Action:* 6,314   *Died of Wounds:* 175

85th Infantry Division Combat Narrative

The division landed at Casablanca North Africa 2 Jan 44 and received amphibious training at Port aux Poules 1 Feb–23 Mar 44, embarked for Italy, and arrived at Naples Italy 15–27 Mar 44. It moved into line west of Minturno on 10 Apr 44, except for a selected advance detachment which had been on the Minturno-Castelforte front since 28 Mar 44. The division held defensive positions north of the Garigliano River facing the Gustav Line for a month. It attacked 11 May 44 and the 339th Inf was engaged in the Battle of M. Scauri 11–16 May 44; the 338th Inf cleared Cave d'Argilla, Hill 131, and reached Highway 7 and Ausonia Road 15 May 44; and the 337th Inf overran Castellonorato and was halted below M.Campese 16 May 44. It continued heavy fighting the 338th Inf took Formia 17–18 May 44 and then was landed at Sperlonga without opposition, fought through a railroad tunnel, and pushed on to M.Leano 23 May 44 as the 339th Inf took Sonnino. The 337th Inf began its drive on Terracina 21 May 44, recovered part of M.S.Croce, and after sustained combat took an evacuated Terracina on 24 May 44; opening the road to the Anzio beachhead. The division then crossed the Amaseno River with the 339th Inf 25 May 44 and pursued the retreating German forces into the hills west of Priverno. It consolidated the following day, moved into Sezze 27 May 44, and closed into the Rocca Massima–Giulianello area 29 May 44 to relieve the 3rd Inf Div at the end of the month.

The division attacked into the Lariano sector 31 May 44 as the 337th and 338th Inf stormed M.Artemisio and captured the town of Lariano. The division fought the Battle for M.Ceraso 1–2 Jun 44, which was captured by the 337th Inf, as the 338th Inf reached Highway 6 at S.Cesareo and the 339th Inf took M. Fiore. Frascati was captured on 3 Jun 44 and the division sped up Via Tuscolana through Rome 5 Jun 44 and advanced to the Viterbo River before being relieved 10 Jun 44. After rehabilitation it took over the Arno River Line, relieving the *New Zealand 2nd Div* in the Montelupo area 16 Aug 44, and next the 91st Inf Div below Fucecchio on 18 Aug 44.

The division began the attack to force the Il Giogo Pass of the Gothic Line on 13 Sep 44. The 339th Inf fought the Battle for M.Veruca 13–17 Sep 44; the 338th Inf fought the Battle for M.Altuzzo 14–17 Sep 44; and on the latter date the 337th Inf gained M.Pratone. By 18 Sep 44 the division had broken through the Gothic Line and started pursuit operations the next day into the valleys, crossing the Santerno River at S.Pellegrino with the 337th Inf on 20 Sep 44. The 338th Inf seized Firenzuola 21 Sep 44 as the 339th Inf took M.Frena and M.Coloreta. The 337th Inf fought the Battle for M.la Fine 23–24 Sep 44 as mud, rain, and heavy opposition slowed the division's advance. The 338th Inf finally took M.Canda after severe fighting 28 Sep 44, the division battling up the crest of Torre Poggioli and into Sambuco the day previous. The 337th and 338th Inf fought the Battle for La Martina 1–2 Oct 44 as the 337th Inf cleared the ridge between the Idice and Sillaro Rivers and was subjected to heavy counterattacks 3–4 Oct 44. The division took Quinzano 4 Oct 44 and fought the Battle for M.Bibele 4–5 Oct 44. The 337th Inf fought the Battle for Hill 566 until 9 Oct 44 and the 338th Inf fought the Battle for Hill 578 10–13 Oct 44 and the Battle for M.delle Formiche 9–12 Oct 44. The division continued forward above Monterenzio and attacked M.Fano 19 Oct 44, renewed the attack and Hill 459 switched hands 22–23 Oct 44, and on 24 Oct 44 reached Mt Mezzano overlooking the Po Valley. The division then discontinued its offensive on 26 Oct 44.

The division held defensive lines near Pizzano 27 Oct–22 Nov 44 and then was relieved for rehabilitation 23 Nov 44. On 9–17 Jan 45 the division relieved the *British 1st Div* in the M.Grande area and then the division passed to army reserve on 18 Mar 45. It relieved the 1st Armd Div 17 Apr 45 and advanced to reach Gesso and the outskirts of Bologna on 20 Apr 45. The division pushed through the Po Valley as German resistance collapsed, and crossed the Panaro at Camposanto over an intact bridge 22 Apr 45. The division reached the Po River at Quingentole and established a bridgehead without opposition 23–24 Apr 45. On 26 Apr 45 the division crossed the Adige River in the Verona area and on 1 May 45 began clearing the Piave Valley. The surrender of German forces in Italy ended hostilities there on 2 May 45.

86th Infantry Division

No Distinctive
Insignia Authorized

15 Dec 42 activated at Cp Howze Tex and moved to the La Maneuver Area 21 Nov 43 where participated in the Third Army No.5 Louisiana Maneuvers; arrived Cp Livingston La 24 Jan 44 and Cp Cooke Calif 6 Sep 44; moved to Cp San Luis Obispo Calif 1 Oct 44 for amphibious training; returned to Cp Cooke Calif 23 Nov 44 and to Cp San Luis Obispo Calif 4 Dec 44; staged at Cp Myles Standish Mass 5 Feb 45 until departed Boston P/E 19 Feb 45; arrived in France 1 Mar 45 and entered Germany 27 Mar 45; arrived New York P/E 17 Jun 45 and arrived Cp Gruber Okla 21 Jun 45; staged at Cp Stoneman Calif 14 Aug 45 until departed San Francisco P/E 21 Aug 45; arrived Philippines 7 Sep 45 where inactivated 30 Dec 46.

Campaigns: *Central Europe*
Aug 45 Loc: Camp Stoneman California

Typical Organization (1944/45):

341st Infantry Regiment
342nd Infantry Regiment
343rd Infantry Regiment
 HHB Division Artillery
331st Field Artillery Battalion (105mm)
332nd Field Artillery Battalion (105mm)
404th Field Artillery Battalion (155mm)
911th Field Artillery Battalion (105mm)
 86th Reconnaissance Troop, Mecz
787th Tank Battalion *(attached 2 May 45–10 May 45)*
648th Tank Destroyer Battalion *(attached 15 Apr 45–18 Apr 45)*
807th Tank Destroyer Battalion *(attached 21 Apr 45–10 May 45)*
446th AAA Auto-Wpns Battalion *(attached 1 Apr 45–4 Apr 45)*
839th AAA Auto-Wpns Battalion *(attached 8 Apr 45–10 May 45)*

311th Engineer Combat Battalion
311th Medical Battalion
 86th Counter Intelligence Corps Det
Headquarters Special Troops
Hqs Company, 86th Infantry Division
Military Police Platoon
786th Ordnance Light Maintenance Company
 86th Quartermaster Company
86th Signal Company

Overseas Wartime Assignments:

Fifteenth Army - 30 Jan 45
VII Corps - 22 Mar 45
XXII Corps - 30 Mar 45
XVIII (A/B) Corps - 5 Apr 45

Third Army - 19 Apr 45
III Corps - 22 Apr 45
XV Corps - 2 May 45

Commanders: MG Alexander E. Anderson: Sep 42
 MG Harris M. Melasky: Jan 43
 MG Paul J. Mueller: Jan 46

Killed in Action: 136   *Wounded in Action:* 618   *Died of Wounds:* 25

86th Infantry Division Combat Narrative

The division arrived in France on 1 Mar 45, moved to Koln Germany, and relieved the 8th Inf Div in defensive positions near Weiden 28–29 Mar 45. The 341st Inf was detached to reinforce the 97th Inf Div in the Sieg River assault 5–9 Apr 45. The division moved across the Rhine at Eibelshausen on 5 Apr 45 and made its first attack 9 Apr 45 with the 342nd Inf, which advanced northward to Hotolpe-Altenhundem and overran Attendorn on 11 Apr 45. The division continued on to the Ruhr to participate in the reduction of the Ruhr pocket, the 341st Inf taking Hagen on 14 Apr 45. The 342nd Inf seized Hohenlimburg and the 343rd Inf cleared towns along the Lenne River up to the Ruhr by 15 Apr 45. The division was then engaged in light mopping-up activities and moved to Ansbach 21 Apr 45 where it continued the advance. It attacked 24 Apr 45 with both 341st and 342nd Inf which reached Eichstatt and the Altmuhl River, establishing a bridgehead there the following day. The 341st Inf cleared a wooded area near the Gungolding Bridge site and then crossed there 26 Apr 45 to reach the Danube River. The 342nd Inf sped to the Danube at Ingolstadt and crossed the same day, followed by the 341st Inf which crossed over the Danube 27–28 Apr 45.

The division secured the bridge over the Amper Canal on 29 Apr 45 and continued to the Isar River at Friesing. There it crossed in assault boats under heavy fire during the night of 29–30 Apr 45. The 342nd and 343rd Inf reached the Mittl Isar Canal and crossed it at Eitting on 30 Apr 45. The division then moved to the outskirts of Wasserburg 2 May 45, but was ordered east instead to Salzburg. The division was in that region when hostilities were declared ended on 7 May 45.

87th Infantry Division

No Distinctive Insignia Authorized

15 Dec 42 activated at Cp McCain Miss and moved to Tenn Maneuver Area 3 Dec 43 where participated in the Second Army No.4 Tennessee Maneuvers; arrived Ft Jackson S.C. 20 Jan 44 and staged at Cp Kilmer N.J. 10 Oct 44 until departed New York P/E 4 Nov 44; arrived England 12 Nov 44 and landed in France 5 Dec 44; crossed into Belgium 12 Jan 45 and into Luxembourg 21 Jan 45; re-entered Belgium 3 Feb 45 and entered Germany 16 Mar 45; returned New York P/E 11 Jul 45 and arrived Ft Benning Ga 14 Jul 45 where inactivated 21 Sep 45.

Campaigns: *Rhineland, Ardennes-Alsace, Central Europe*
Aug 45 Loc: Fort Benning Georgia

Typical Organization (1944/45):

345th Infantry Regiment
346th Infantry Regiment
347th Infantry Regiment
HHB Division Artillery
334th Field Artillery Battalion (105mm)
335th Field Artillery Battalion (155mm)
336th Field Artillery Battalion (105mm)
912th Field Artillery Battalion (105mm)
87th Reconnaissance Troop, Mecz

312th Engineer Combat Battalion
312th Medical Battalion
87th Counter Intelligence Corps Det
Headquarters Special Troops
Hqs Company, 87th Infantry Division
Military Police Platoon
787th Ordnance Light Maintenance Company
87th Quartermaster Company
87th Signal Company

735th Tank Battalion *(attached 1 Feb 45–9 Mar 45, 15 Mar 45–9 May 45)*
761st Tank Battalion *(attached 20 Dec 44–23 Dec 44, 1 Jan 45–15 Jan 45, 26 Jan 45–1 Feb 45)*
607th Tank Destroyer Battalion *(attached 3 Feb 45–6 Mar 45, 15 Mar 45–9 May 45)*
610th Tank Destroyer Battalion *(attached 14 Dec 44–22 Dec 44)*
691st Tank Destroyer Battalion *(attached 22 Dec 44–24 Dec 44, 8 Jan 45–26 Jan 45)*
704th Tank Destroyer Battalion *(attached 17 Dec 44–19 Dec 44)*
811th Tank Destroyer Battalion *(attached 26 Jan 45–28 Jan 45)*
549th AAA Auto-Wpns Battalion *(attached 24 Dec 44–9 May 45)*

Overseas Wartime Assignments:

Third Army - 25 Nov 44
III Corps - 4 Dec 44
XII Corps - 11 Dec 44
XV Corps - 21 Dec 44

VIII Corps - 29 Dec 44
XII Corps - 14 Jan 45
VIII Corps - 25 Jan 45

Commanders: MG Percy W. Clarkson: Dec 42
MG Eugene M. Landrum: Oct 43
MG Frank L. Culin Jr: Apr 44

Killed in Action: 1,154   *Wounded in Action:* 4,342   *Died of Wounds:* 141

160

87th Infantry Division Combat Narrative

The division landed in France 1–5 Dec 44 and took over the Metz sector from the 5th Inf Div, where Ft Jeanne d'Arc was still holding out, on 8 Dec 44. The division then moved to the Gross Rederching area of the Saar-German border 11–12 Dec 44 and relieved the 26th Inf Div. Attacking on 14 Dec 44 the division took Rimling in heavy combat and by 15 Dec 44 the 347th Inf had taken Oberailbrach and the heights overlooking the Blies. The division continued clearing operations in the outer portions of the *West Wall* until its offensive was ordered stopped on 18 Dec 44. The division was then transferred to counter the German Ardennes Counteroffensive.

The division took Moircy on 30 Dec 44 but lost it to counterattack the following day, and finally secured it on 1 Jan 45 as Jenneville was captured. On 3 Jan 45 the division had elements surrounded in the woods east of St Hubert, and was halted near Pironpré, west of Bastogne, the next day. It was forced out of Bonnerue 6 Jan 45, which was not recaptured until the 347th Inf retook it 11 Jan 45. The division fought the Battle of Tillet 6–10 Jan 45, which ended as it crossed the Ronce River east of Petite Langlir. The division contacted the British at the Ourthe River 13 Jan 45. The division then moved to Luxembourg to take over the 4th Inf Div zone along the Sauer from Echternach to Wasserbilling on 17 Jan 45, the 346th Inf taking the latter on 23 Jan 45. On 26 Jan 45 the division relieved the 17th A/B Div beyond Wattermal Belgium and the 346th Inf took Espeler and several other towns south of St Vith. The division took over that sector 28 Jan 45. The division attacked from the heights west of the Our River 29 Jan 45 and assaulted the *West Wall*. Manderfeld and Auw fell as the division crossed into Germany 1 Feb 45. Its reconnaissance troop entered Roth 3 Feb 45 as the division consolidated, then fought the Battle for the Schnee Eifel Crossroads east of Kobscheid 6–7 Feb 45. The 345th Inf captured Olzheim 8 Feb 45 and then took Neuendorf the following day. The division went on the defensive 10 Feb 45.

The 345th and 346th Inf attacked on 26 Feb 45 against the well-defended remaining *West Wall* positions. Despite armored assistance, the pillboxes and obstacles made advance difficult and Ormont was not captured until 1 Mar 45. The 346th and 347th Inf cleared to the Kyll River by 4 Mar 45 as the 345th Inf took Reuth. The division crossed the Kyll 6 Mar 45 and attacked with three regiments in line the next day and advanced rapidly to seize the Ahrhutte bridge intact over the Ahr River on 8 Mar 45. Dollendorf also fell that day, and on 9 Mar 45 the division was withdrawn for rehabilitation.

The division closed into defend the Koblenz-Lehmen sector along the Moselle River on 14 Mar 45. The 345th and 347th Inf assaulted across the river in the Winnigen-Kolberg sector 16 Mar 45 against light resistance. The 345th Inf then fought house-to-house in the Battle of Koblenz 17–19 Mar 45 which ended with the fall of Fort Constantine. The 347th Inf captured Oberspray 19 Mar 45 and the division was relieved on 23 Mar 45. The division crossed the Rhine against strong opposition on 25 Mar 45 and was counterattacked at the bridgehead in the Braubach-Boppard area. The bridgehead, however, was expanded to the Lahn River line by 27 Mar 45 where the division took over responsibility for the Diez-Limburg area as the 345th Inf took Niederselters. The division relieved the 90th Inf Div north of the Werra and commenced clearing Thuringer Wald 7 Apr 45 against scattered resistance. The division advanced to the Saale River near Rudolstadt by 12 Apr 45, and on the following day crossed at Etzelbach, Schwarza, and Saalfeld. The division assaulted across the Weisse-Elster River 16 Apr 45 and took Plauen the next day. The division then took up defensive positions four miles from the Czechoslovakian border 20 Apr–4 May 45. It took Falkenstein 6 May 45 and was in that area when hostilities were declared ended as of 7 May 45.

88th Infantry Division

No Distinctive Insignia Authorized

15 Jul 42 activated at Cp Gruber Okla as the 88th Division and redesignated there 1 Aug 42 as the 88th Infantry Division; moved to the La Maneuver Area 16 Jun 43 where participated in the Third Army No.3 Louisiana Maneuvers; arrived Ft Sam Houston Tex 29 Aug 43 and staged at Cp Patrick Henry Va 8 Nov 43 until departed Hampton Roads P/E 6 Dec 43; arrived North Africa 15 Dec 43 and arrived in Italy 6 Feb 44 where remained active thru 1946.

Campaigns: *Rome-Arno, North Apennines, Po Valley*
Aug 45 Loc: Desenzano Italy

Typical Organization (1944/45):

349th Infantry Regiment	313th Engineer Combat Battalion
350th Infantry Regiment	313th Medical Battalion
351st Infantry Regiment	88th Counter Intelligence Corps Det
HHB Division Artillery	Headquarters Special Troops
337th Field Artillery Battalion (105mm)	Hqs Company, 88th Infantry Division
338th Field Artillery Battalion (105mm)	Military Police Platoon
339th Field Artillery Battalion (155mm)	788th Ordnance Light Maintenance Company
913th Field Artillery Battalion (105mm)	88th Quartermaster Company
88th Reconnaissance Troop, Mecz	88th Signal Company

Overseas Wartime Assignments:

Fifth Army - 5 Feb 44	II Corps - 1 Jun 44
II Corps - 28 Feb 44	IV Corps - 8 Jul 44
IV Corps - 28 May 44	II Corps - 25 Jul 44

Commanders: MG John E. Sloan: Jul 42   BG James C. Fry: Jul 45
MG Paul W. Kendall: Sep 44   MG Bryant E. Moore: Nov 45

Killed in Action: 2,298   *Wounded in Action:* 9,225   *Died of Wounds:* 258

88th Infantry Division Combat Narrative

The division arrived at Casablanca North Africa on 15 Dec 43 and moved to Magenta Algeria for training on 28 Dec 43. It arrived in Naples Italy on 6 Feb 44 and staged in the Piedmont d'Alife area and relieved the 36th Inf Div on M.Castellone 28 Feb 44. A detachment went into the line before Cassino 27 Feb 44 and the division relieved the British along the Garigliano River near Minturno 5 Mar 44 which it then defended. On 11 May 44 the 350th and 351st Inf attacked toward Rome against strong opposition, the 351st Inf losing a company approaching S.Maria Infante 12 May 44. The Germans then offered only rearguard resistance and on 15 May 44 the division pushed through an undefended Spigno. The 351st Inf came under heavy fire 18 May 44 in attempts to take M.Grande, and the 349th and 350th Inf advanced from Rocca Secca across the Amaseno Valley 26 May 44. The division was relieved 29 May 44 and the 349th Inf detached to the Anzio beachhead where it linked up. On 2 Jun 44 the 351st Inf overran S.Cesareo and cut Highway 6 and after a battle on the outskirts of the city, the division pushed through Rome 4 Jun 44 along the Via Prenestina. After continuing across the Tiber River to Bassanelio the division was withdrawn for rehabilitation on 11 Jun 44.

The division went into defensive positions near Pomerance 5 Jul 44 and took over the 1st Armd Div zone 8 Jul 44, attacking with the 349th and 350th Inf which took Volterra the next day. The advance came to a temporary halt on the last heights overlooking the Arno River above Palaia, which had fallen the previous day, on 18 Jul 44. The division then cleared the region below the Arno in heavy combat 20–25 Jul 44. It then rested and sent the 350th Inf to assist in Livorno operations 21 Aug 44, and was reinforced by the attachment of the 442nd Inf to the division 20 Aug–2 Sep 44. The division crossed the Arno River 1 Sep 44 and continued advancing until relieved 6 Sep 44 for regroupment.

The division was committed back to the front 21 Sep 44 and the 349th and 350th Inf advanced rapidly along the Santerno River Valley toward Imola. The division battled on M.Acuto and repulsed counterattacks 24 Sep 44, seized M.Pratolungo and M.del Puntale 26 Sep 44, and ran into strong German opposition. The 350th Inf fought the Battle for M.Battaglia 27 Sep–13 Oct 44 until relieved by the British who continued the struggle; the 351st Inf battled up M.Cappello 30 Sep 44; and the 349th Inf captured Belvedore on 1 Oct 44 and then Sassoleone 3 Oct 44. The division fought the Battle for Hill 587 5–8 Oct 44 which it then abandoned, as the 351st Inf fought the Battle of Gesso Ridge 10–12 Oct 44 and the 350th Inf, later joined by the 349th Inf, fought the Battle of M.delle Tombe 11–16 Oct 44. The division regrouped on 15 Oct 44 and pushed toward the M.Cuccoli-M.Grande Range. M.Grande was taken by the 350th Inf, with heavy air and artillery support and interdiction to prevent counterattack, 20 Oct 44. Vedriano was taken but lost to counterattack 23–24 Oct 44, and as further efforts to deepen the M.Grande salient failed, the offensive was halted 26 Oct 44.

The division then maintained defensive positions and later relieved the 85th Inf Div on 22 Nov 44. It was relieved in line 13 Jan 45 for rehabilitation, and then relieved the 91st Inf Div and reentered the line 24 Jan 45 in the Loiano-Livergnano sector. On 6 Mar 45 the division was relieved astride Highway 6, but the division resumed attacking 15 Apr 45 for the Bologna Offensive. It fought the Battle for M.Monterumici 16–17 Apr 45. The 350th Inf took M.Mario 18 Apr 45 and the division established positions west of the Reno River the next day. It attacked again 20 Apr 45 and the 351st Inf crossed the Panaro River between Camposanto and Finale 22 Apr 45. The division reached the Po River near Carbonarai 23 Apr 45 and captured large numbers of German troops before they could cross over. The division itself crossed the Po the following day and captured Verona against scattered resistance 25–26 Apr 45. It cleared Vicenza 28 Apr 45 and crossed the Brenta River on 30 Apr 45. The division was advancing through the Dolomite Alps toward Innsbruck Austria when the German forces in Italy surrendered 2 May 45, ending hostilities in the division's area.

89th Infantry Division

No Distinctive Insignia Authorized

15 Jul 42 activated at Cp Carson Colo as the 89th Division and redesignated there as the 89th Infantry Division 10 Aug 42; reorganized and redesignated as the 89th Light Division (Truck) 1 Aug 43 and moved to the La Maneuver Area 17 Nov 43 where participated in the Third Army No.5 Maneuvers; next moved to the Hunter-Liggett Mil Res Calif 5 Feb 44 where took part in the III Corps No.1 California Maneuvers testing the light division concept; arrived Cp Butner N.C. 27 May 44 and redesignated the 89th Infantry Division there 15 Jun 44; staged at Cp Myles Standish Mass 29 Dec 44 until departed Boston P/E 10 Jan 45; arrived France 21 Jan 45 and crossed into Luxembourg 8 Mar 45 and entered Germany 10 Mar 45; arrived New York P/E 16 Dec 45 and inactivated at Cp Shanks N.Y. on 17 Dec 45.

Campaigns: *Rhineland, Central Europe*
Aug 45 Loc: Werdau Germany

Typical Organization (1943):

353rd Infantry Regiment
354th Infantry Regiment
355th Infantry Regiment
 HHB Division Artillery
340th Field Artillery Battalion (75mm)
341st Field Artillery Battalin (75mm)
914th Field Artillery Battalion (75mm)
579th Field Artillery Antitank Battery

314th Engineer Combat Battalion
314th Medical Battalion
729th Antiaircraft Artillery Machine Gun Bn
Division Headquarters
Hqs Company, 89th Light Division
Military Police Platoon
Ordnance Light Maintenance Platoon
Quartermaster Truck Company
Signal Platoon

Typical Organization (1944/45):

353rd Infantry Regiment
354th Infantry Regiment
355th Infantry Regiment
 HHB Division Artillery
340th Field Artillery Battalion (105mm)
341st Field Artillery Battalion (105mm)
563rd Field Artillery Battalion (155mm)
914th Field Artillery Battalion (105mm)
 89th Reconnaissance Troop, Mecz
707th Tank Battalion *(attached 6 Apr 45–30 Apr 45)*
748th Tank Battalion *(attached 25 Mar 45–6 Apr 45)*
602nd Tank Destroyer Battalion *(attached 12 Mar 45–29 May 45)*
811th Tank Destroyer Battalion *(attached 6 Mar 45–12 Mar 45)*
550th AAA Auto-Wpns Battalion *(attached 5 Mar 45–31 May 45)*

314th Engineer Combat Battalion
314th Medical Battalion
 89th Counter Intelligence Corps Det
Headquarters, Special Troops
Hqs Company, 89th Infantry Division
Military Police Platoon
714th Ordnance Light Maintenance Company
405th Quartermaster Company
 89th Signal Company

Overseas Wartime Assignments:

Fifteenth Army - 21 Jan 45
XII Corps - 4 Mar 45
VIII Corps - 23 Mar 45

Commanders: MG William H. Gill: Jul 42
  MG Thomas D. Finley: Feb 43

Killed in Action: 292   *Wounded in Action:* 692   *Died of Wounds:* 33

89th Infantry Division Combat Narrative

The division landed at Le Havre France on 21 Jan 45 and moved up to Sauer River near Echternach on 11 Mar 45. It attached 12 Mar 45 with the 353rd and 355th Inf toward the Cochem-Alf sector of the Moselle, and by 16 Mar 45 the 353rd and 354th Inf attacked across the river in the Bullay area and gained a small bridgehead. The 355th Inf crossed the Moselle at Alf 18 Mar 45 and advanced forward behind the 11th Armd Div. The division then cleared southward to the Nahe from Bad Kreusnach westward. It crossed the Nahe River 20 Mar 45 and cleared bypassed resistance.

The division assaulted across the Rhine River on 26 Mar 45 under intense fire in the Wellmich-Oberwesel region. The 354th Inf secured Weyer, the 353rd Inf captured Dorscheid, and the 355th Inf crossed at Boppard and moved along the eastern bank of the river to take Kestert. The bridgehead was expanded the next day toward Weisbaden and forward elements seized Strueth. The 355th Inf took Lorch after heavy fighting 28 Mar 45 as the 353rd Inf battled through Hinter Wald. The 355th Inf then cleared the Rhine bend west of Weisbaden and the division reached the line from Neuhof to Eltville 30 Mar 45 and then consolidated and mopped up.

The division concentrated in the Hersfeld area and attacked 5 Apr 45. The 353rd Inf overcame strong opposition at Eisenach 6 Apr 45 and the division cleared the Thuringer Wald, securing Friedrichroda, reputed German strongpoint and Nazi Redoubt, 8 Apr 45. By 10 Apr 45 the 354th and 355th Inf had advanced to the Gera River at Rudisleben, Arnstadt, and east of Espenfeld. The division next moved through Bad Berka to the Saale River in the Rothenstein area 12 Apr 45. The 353rd and 355th Inf cleared the Rothenstein-Beutelsdorf sector west of the Saale by the end of the following day. The division then sped east from the Saale to the Weisse-Elster and Weida Rivers between Gera and Zeulenroda and crossed 15 Apr 45. It reached the Pliesse River on 16 Apr 45 and assaulted Werdau which fell the next day, as the division established a bridgehead across the Zwick Mulde River near Zwickau. On 18 Apr 45 the 354th and 355th expanded the bridgehead to overrun Zwickau and Wilkau and other small towns. The advance was halted on order 23 Apr 45, and the division engaged in security and patrolling until hostilities were declared ended on 7 May 45.

90th Infantry Division

No Distinctive
Insignia Authorized

25 Mar 42 activated at Cp Barkeley Tex as the 90th Division and redesignated there as the 90th Infantry Division 20 May 42; redesignated the 90th Motorized Division 15 Sep 42 and moved to La Maneuver Area to participate in the Third Army No.1 Louisiana Maneuvers 28 Jan 43; returned to Cp Barkeley Tex 1 Apr 43 where redesignated as the 90th Infantry Division 1 May 43; went to Cp Young Calif 12 Sep 43 where participated in the Desert Training Center No.3 California Maneuvers; arrived Ft Dix N.J. 26 Sep 43 and staged at Cp Kilmer N.J. 17 Mar 44 until departed New York P/E 23 Mar 44; arrived in England 4 Apr 44 and landed in France 8 Jun 44; entered Germany 24 Nov 44 and returned to France 22 Dec 44; crossed into Luxembourg 7 Jan 45 and into Belgium 22 Jan 45; returned to Luxembourg 29 Jan 45 and to Germany 8 Feb 45 and entered Czechoslovakia 5 May 45; returned to New York P/E 24 Dec 45 and inactivated at Cp Shanks N.Y. 27 Dec 45.

Campaigns: *Normandy, Northern France, Rhineland, Ardennes-Alsace, Central Europe*
Aug 45 Loc: Eisenstein Germany

Typical Organization (1944/45):

357th Infantry Regiment	315th Engineer Combat Battalion
358th Infantry Regiment	315th Medical Battalion
359th Infantry Regiment	90th Counter Intelligence Corps Det
HHB Division Artillery	Headquarters Special Troops
343rd Field Artillery Battalion (105mm)	Hqs Company, 90th Infantry Division
344th Field Artillery Battalion (105mm)	Military Police Platoon
345th Field Artillery Battalion (155mm)	790th Ordnance Light Maintenance Company
915th Field Artillery Battalion (105mm)	90th Quartermaster Company
90th Reconnaissance Troop, Mecz	90th Signal Company

712th Tank Battalion *(attached 28 Jun 44–7 Jul 44, 15 Jul 44–30 Sep 44)*
746th Tank Battalion *(attached 12 Jun 44–15 Jun 44)*
607th Tank Destroyer Battalion *(attached 20 Jun 44–2 Nov 44, 20 Nov 44–27 Nov 44)*
773rd Tank Destroyer Battalion *(attached 2 Nov 44–9 May 45)*
774th Tank Destroyer Battalion *(attached 21 Dec 44–6 Jan 45)*
803rd Tank Destroyer Battalion *(attached 4 Jul 44–15 Jul 44)*
807th Tank Destroyer Battalion *(attached 20 Dec 44–24 Dec 44)*
537th AAA Auto-Wpns Battalion *(attached 16 Jun 44–7 Jul 44, 15 Jul 44–26 May 45)*

Overseas Wartime Assignments:

Third Army - 5 Mar 44
VII Corps - 27 Mar 44
VIII Corps - 19 Jun 44
Third Army - 30 Jul 44
V Corps *(attached)* - 17 Aug 44

XV Corps - 25 Aug 44
XX Corps - 26 Aug 44
III Corps - 6 Jan 45
VIII Corps - 26 Jan 45
XII Corps - 12 Mar 45

Commanders: MG Henry Terrell Jr: Mar 42
     BG Jay W. MacKelvie: Jan 44
     MG Eugene M. Landrum: Jul 44
     MG Raymond S. McClain: Aug 44

MG James A. Van Fleet: Oct 44
MG Lowell W. Rooks: Feb 45
MG Herbert L. Earnest: Mar 45

Killed in Action: 3,342   *Wounded in Action:* 14,386   *Died of Wounds:* 588

90th Infantry Division Combat Narrative

The division's 359th Inf, attached to 4th Inf Div, assaulted Utah Beach France on 6 Jun 44. The remainder of the division attacked 10 Jun 44 and the 358th Inf fought the Battle of Pont l'Abbé 10–12 Jun 44. The division halted in the Golleville-Urville area 17 Jun 44 after heavy combat and took up defensive positions. Advancing in heavy rain, the division attacked 3 Jul 44 south down the west coast of the Contentin Peninsula and fought the Battle of La Haye-du-Puits–Mont Castre Forest 6–10 Jul 44. It regrouped along the Ays River 15 Jul 44 but was forced out of St Germain-sur-Sèves on 22 Jul 44. It managed to establish a bridgehead across the Sèves River 26 Jul 44 and crossed the Taute at Périers the following day, being relieved at Mayenne 6 Aug 44. The division then entered the Battle for the Falaise Gap and took La Bourg–St Léonard after heavy fighting 17 Aug 44 and the Forêt de Gouffern the next day, closing the Falaise-Argentan Gap 19 Aug 44. On 22 Aug 44 the division was withdrawn for rehabilitation.

The division attacked again 27 Aug 44 behind 7th Armd Div and crossed the Meuse near Etain on 6 Sep 44, defeating a major German armored attack between Landres and Mairy 8 Sep 44. The division cleared Thionville west of the Moselle by 12 Sep 44 and then battled the German fortifications west of Metz 15–17 Sep 44 as the 357th Inf tried to take the Kellermann Works and the 359th Inf tried to take Ft Jeanne d'Arc. The efforts were unsuccessful, and the division resumed the attacks on the Metz forts 26 Sep 44 but the 359th Inf was halted in the 26–27 Sep 44 Battle of Gravelott–St Hubert Farm Road. The division reattacked 3 Oct 44 toward Maizières-lès-Metz on the northern approaches to Metz. It fought the Battle of the Slag Pile 3–7 Oct 44, and fought house-to-house in Maizières-lès-Metz 7–30 Oct 44, combat being centered about the well-defended Hotel de Ville.

The 358th and 359th Inf assaulted across the Moselle River at Malling and Cattenom on 9 Nov 44, the former then fighting the Battle of Ft Koenigsmacker 9–11 Nov 44. German counterattacks hit the bridgehead 10, 12, and 15 Nov 44; Kerling was lost 10 Nov 44 but regained 13 Nov 44; and the bridgehead expanded despite minefields as the 357th Inf captured Hackenberg Works 16–17 Nov 44. The division then pursued the withdrawing German forces and the 359th Inf reached the Nied River at Condé Northern 18 Nov 44. The division attacked toward the Saare River 25 Nov 44 which it reached 29 Nov 44 and cleared south of Merzig. On 6 Dec 44 the division assaulted across the Saare between Rehlingen and Wallerfangen against heavy opposition. The Battle for the Dillingen Bridgehead and *West Wall* fortifications was fought 6–18 Dec 44, when the division withdrew from the bridgehead 19 Dec 44 and regrouped back on the west bank of the Saare by 22 Dec 44.

The division attacked on 9 Jan 45 and cut the Bastogne-Wiltz Road at Doncels 11 Jan 45. It captured Bras 13 Jan 45 and fought the Battle of Oberwampach 16–18 Jan 45. The 357th Inf attacked across the Clerft River at Binsfeld 23 Jan 45. The division then crossed the Our River with the 357th Inf at Oberhausen and the 358th Inf at Stupbach on 29 Jan 45, and consolidated after taking Heckusheid with the latter and Gros Langenfeld with the 359th Inf on 1 Feb 45. The division renewed its advance on 5 Feb 45 in the Brandscheid area against heavy opposition as it entered the main *West Wall* defenses around Habscheid 7 Feb 45. The 358th Inf fought the Battle for Hill 519 on 8–9 Feb 45 and captured Watzerath 11 Feb 45, after which the division regrouped. On 18 Feb 45 it renewed its assault through the *West Wall* to the Pruem River which it reached at Waxweiler 23 Feb 45; the Battles for Lichtenborn and Binscheid being fought 20–22 Feb 45 and 20–21 Feb 45, respectively. The division was relieved 25 Feb 45.

The division renewed its offensive 4 Mar 45 and crossed the Kyll River the next day, moved to the Kelberg area 9 Mar 45, and mopped up. The division assaulted across the Moselle River in the Kattenes-Moselkern region 14 Mar 45, and attacked across the Nahe River 19 Mar 45 to capture Mainz on 22 Mar 45. It crossed the Rhine 24 Mar 45 and the 357th and 358th Inf assaulted across the Main River in the Doeringheim area 28 Mar 45. The division crossed the Werra 2 Apr 45, cleared Thuringer Wald, and closed along the Saal River 15 Apr 45. It crossed into Czechoslovakia at Prex 18 Apr 45 and was advancing on Prague when hostilities were declared ended on 7 May 45.

91st Infantry Division

No Distinctive
Insignia Authorized

15 Aug 42 activated at Cp White Oreg and moved 1 Sep 43 to the IV Corps No.1 Oregon Maneuvers; transferred to Cp Adair Oreg 2 Nov 43 and staged at Cp Patrick Henry Va 30 Mar 44 until departed Hampton Roads P/E 14 Apr 44; arrived in North Africa 21 Apr 44 and landed in Italy 19 Jun 44; returned to Hampton Roads P/E 10 Sep 45 and moved to Cp Rucker Ala 14 Sep 45 where inactivated 1 Dec 45.

Campaigns: *Rome-Arno, North Apennines, Po Valley*
Aug 45 Loc: Angoris Italy

Typical Organization (1944/45):

361st Infantry Regiment
362nd Infantry Regiment
363rd Infantry Regiment
 HHB Division Artillery
346th Field Artillery Battalion (105mm)
347th Field Artillery Battalion (105mm)
348th Field Artillery Battalion (155mm)
916th Field Artillery Battalion (105mm)
 91st Reconnaissance Troop, Mecz

316th Engineer Combat Battalion
316th Medical Battalion
 91st Counter Intelligence Corps Det
Headquarters Special Troops
Hqs Company, 91st Infantry Division
Military Police Platoon
791st Ordnance Light Maintenance Company
 91st Quartermaster Company
 91st Signal Company

Overseas Wartime Assignments:

Fifth Army - Jun 44
IV Corps - 12 Jul 44
II Corps - 31 Jul 44

Commanders: MG Charles H. Gerhardt: Aug 42
MG William G. Livesay: Jul 43

Killed in Action: 1,400   *Wounded in Action:* 6,748   *Died of Wounds:* 175

91st Infantry Division Combat Narrative

The division arrived in North Africa on 18 Apr–10 May 44 and trained at Arzew and Renan. It moved to Italy by echelon through 19 Jun 44. The 361st Inf landed at Anzio Italy 1 Jun 44 and closed at Velletri to reinforce the 36th Inf Div 9 Jun 44, and assaulted north of Rome on 12 Jun 44. The regiment reinforced the advance of 1st Armd Div 21 Jun 44 and attacked Casole d'Elsa 3–4 Jul 44, after which it reverted to division. The 363rd Inf was committed to combat on 4 Jul 44 during the attack on Hill 675, and overran M.Vase northeast of Castellini on 6 Jul 44, but lost it to German counterattack the next day. The division entered combat for the first time as a whole on 13 Jul 44 when it attacked toward the Arno despite strong opposition near Chianni, entering the evacuated town the following day. The 361st Inf captured Ponsacco and the 362nd crossed the Era River after passing through Capannoli 17 Jul 44. The 363rd Inf entered the outskirts of Livorno on 18 Jul 44 and dashed north to enter Pisa 24 Jul 44. The rest of the division reached the Arno River at Pontedera 21–22 Jul 44 and then cleared the south bank area against light resistance. The division then went into defensive positions along the Arno until 18 Aug 44 when it was relieved in line below Fucecchio and began training near Certaldo.

The division assembled east of Highway 65 9 Sep 44 and crossed the Sieve River the next day, going into the attack at M.Calvi, Monticelli, and Altuzzo on 12 Sep 44. The division was heavily engaged in this assault on the Gothic Line as the 361st and 363rd Inf fought the Battle for M.Monticelli 12–18 Sep 44. The 362nd Inf fought at M.Calvi 14–18 Sep 44 as it battled through the Futa Pass, took the Antitank Ditch below S.Lucia 16 Sep 44, and cleared S.Lucia itself by 21 Sep 44. The rest of the division reached the Saterno River the same day, and after heavy combat took M.Beni on 25 Sep 44. Supported by tanks and aircraft, the division fought the Battle for M.Oggioli 27–28 Sep 44, and attacked toward Loiano commencing 1 Oct 44. After severe fighting the town fell 5 Oct 44. The 361st Inf fought the Battle for M.Castellari 7–8 Oct 44 as the rest of the division fought the Battle for Livergnano Escarpment 9–15 Oct 44 and the Battle for M.delle Formiche 10–11 Oct 44. Livergnano itself fell 14 Oct 44, and then the division assumed defensive positions below Pianoro on 31 Oct 44. On 22 Nov 44 it was relieved in line and retired for rehabilitation, and then assumed static defensive lines until relieved again on 24 Jan 45. The division relieved the 34th Inf Div in line on 13 Feb 45 in the Idice Valley sector, and had the *Italian Legano Group* attached to it 18 Mar 45. On 20 Mar 45 the division retired to Gagliano and Villanova to prepare for a new offensive.

The division took over the 34th Inf Div zone astride Highway 65 on 5 Apr 45. On 17 Apr 45 the division attacked up Highway 65 and took its objectives of M.Adone, M.Posigliano, Pianoro, and M.Arnigo the next day. It started pursuit operations toward Bologna against slight resistance 20 Apr 45, taking M.Sabbiuno the next day, and crossing the 362nd Inf at Sermide on the Po River 24 Apr 45. The division then swung to the northeast and reached Cerea 25 Apr 45 and crossed the Adige River at Legnano the next day. It crossed the Brenta River 29 Apr 45 and on 30 Apr 45 took Treviso north of Venice. It was in that area when all German forces in Italy surrendered on 2 May 45.

92nd Infantry Division (Colored)

No Distinctive Insignia Authorized

15 Oct 42 activated at Ft McClellan Ala and moved to Ft Huachuca Ariz 5 May 43; participated in Fourth Army No.6 Louisiana Maneuvers 24 Jan–5 Apr 44 and returned to Ft Huachuca Ariz 7 Apr 44; staged at Cp Patrick Henry 17 Sep 44 until departed Hampton Roads P/E 22 Sep 44; arrived in Italy 16 Oct 44; arrived New York P/E 26 Nov 45 and inactivated at Cp Kilmer N.J. 28 Nov 45.

Campaigns: *North Apennines, Po Valley*
Aug 45 Loc: Torre Del Lago Italy

Typical Organization (1944):

365th Infantry Regiment (Cld)
370th Infantry Regiment (Cld)
371st Infantry Regiment (Cld)
HHB Division Artillery (Cld)
597th Field Artillery Battalion (105mm)(Cld)
598th Field Artillery Battalion (105mm)(Cld)
599th Field Artillery Battalion (105mm)(Cld)
600th Field Artillery Battalion (155mm)(Cld)
92nd Reconnaissance Troop (Mecz)(Cld)

317th Engineer Combat Battalion (Cld)
317th Medical Battalion (Cld)
Headquarters Special Troops (Cld)
Hqs Company, 92nd Infantry Division (Cld)
Military Police Platoon (Cld)
792nd Ordnance Light Maintenance Co (Cld)
92nd Quartermaster Company (Cld)
92nd Signal Company (Cld)

Typical Organization (1945):

370th Infantry Regiment (Cld)*
442nd Infantry Regiment *(Nisei)***
473rd Infantry Regiment**
365th Infantry Regiment (Training)(Cld)
371st Infantry Regiment (Security)(Cld)
HHB Division Artillery (Cld)
597th Field Artillery Battalion (105mm)(Cld)
598th Field Artillery Battalion (105mm)(Cld)
599th Field Artillery Battalion (105mm)(Cld)
600th Field Artillery Battalion (105mm)(Cld)

317th Engineer Combat Battalion (Cld)
317th Medical Battalion (Cld)
Headquarters Special Troops (Cld)
Hqs Company, 92nd Infantry Division (Cld)
Military Police Platoon (Cld)
792nd Ordnance Light Maintenance Co (Cld)
92nd Quartermaster Company (Cld)
92nd Signal Company (Cld)
92nd Reconnaissance Troop (Mecz)(Cld)

*Rebuilt 24 Feb–17 Mar 45 from selected personnel of 365th, 370th, and 371st Inf Regts.
**442nd Inf Regt and 473rd Inf Regt attached 30 Mar 45 and 24 Feb 45, respectively.

Overseas Wartime Assignments:

Fifth Army - 4 Nov 44
IV Corps - 25 Dec 44
Fifth Army - 3 Apr 45

Commanders: MG Edward M. Almond: Oct 42
BG John E. Wood: Aug 45

Killed in Action: **548**   *Wounded in Action:* **2,187**   *Died of Wounds:* **68**

92nd Infantry Division (Colored) Combat Narrative

The 370th Inf arrived in Naples Italy 1 Aug 44 and went into line with the 1st Armd Div on 23 Aug 44, participating in the advance against negligible German resistance across the Arno River and the occupation of Lucca. Task Force 92, comprised of the 370th Inf and CCB of the 1st Armd Div, continued the advance on 25 Sep 44 along the Serchio Valley north of Pescia. On 29 Sep 44 the task force gained control of Highway 12 along Lima Creek and reached La Lima the next day. Task Force 92 assumed responsibility for the coast sector below M.Cauala on the approach to Massa 5 Oct 44 as the remainder of the division arrived throughout October, the task force being dissolved 6 Nov 44.

The division began a protracted struggle for M.Cauala on 6 Oct 44, supporting tanks and tank destroyers being unable initially to cross swollen streams to reinforce troops driving on the mountain the next day. After reaching the slopes of M.Cauala the division was forced back by German fire 8 Oct 44, pushed to the top without opposition on 9 Oct 44 but later in the same day withdrew. After four attempts were made to gain and hold the mountain, another major push was made 12 Oct 44 which reached the crest, but again division forces were forced to retire. Efforts to take the mountain were then suspended for a few days as the division concentrated on patrol activities. M.Cauala fell undefended to a patrol on 17 Oct 44, but after further unsuccessful attempts to push northeast from the mountain, the division went on the defensive in the coast sector 23 Oct 44. The 371st Inf arrived in Livorno 18 Oct 44 and entered the line 31 Oct 44, while the 365th Inf arrived in Italy 29 Oct–8 Nov 44 and entered the front 8–9 Nov 44. The fourth regiment, the separate 366th Inf, was attached to the division on 26 Nov 44. Additionally, on 23 Dec 44 the division in the Lucca area was reinforced with two brigades of the Indian 8th Div and the 337th and 339th Inf of the 85th Inf Div.

The German counterattack against the division along the Serchio drove in its outposts on 26 Dec 44, precipitating a general withdrawal. The following day part of the 366th Inf abandoned its positions and the division made further withdrawals. Elements of the Indian 8th Division then passed through the retreating division to make patrol contact with German forces which promptly pulled back. The Indian 8th Division was placed in reserve on 10 Jan 45 and the division again given responsibility for the Serchio Valley. The 365th and 366th Inf made a limited attack to improve positions in the Serchio Valley and recovered lightly guarded Gallicano, Castelvecchio, and Albiano with ease on 4 Feb 45. The division then began indecisive fighting for the heights on either side of the Serchio, with the 366th Inf at M.Faeto and the 365th Inf at Lama di Sotto Ridge. As the division gave ground east of the river, it also crossed a heavily mined area to capture the Cinquale Canal on 8 Feb 45. However, on 11 Feb 45 it broke off all further attacks and withdrew its bridgehead across the Cinquale Canal.

The division was thoroughly reorganized commencing 1 Mar 45, the transition being completed 3 Apr 45. The 366th Inf was withdrawn and disposed into two engineer general service regiments; the 473rd Inf, attached 24 Feb 45, replaced the 370th Inf which in turn was reconstituted in a rear area from selected officers and men of the division's original three regiments; the 442nd (Nisei) attached; and the 365th and 371st Inf withdrawn, the former south of Viareggio as a replacement training center. On 5 Apr 45 the new division attacked along the Ligurian coast with the 370th and 442nd Inf leading, the former falling back immediately under counterattack but the latter taking M.Fragolita. As the 370th Inf remained pinned, the 442nd Inf went on to take M.Cerrata and then stormed and seized M.Belvedere 7 Apr 45. On 8 Apr 45 the 473rd Inf replaced the 370th Inf in line and continued the attack up Highway 1 as the latter withdrew to the rear. On 10 Apr 45 the division entered an evacuated Massa, but then was unable to make much headway against strong opposition along the coast. The division finally captured Aulla on 25 Apr 45 and reached Genoa against disorganized resistance on 27 Apr 45. It took Alessandria on 28 Apr 45, and the 473rd Inf linked up with French troops on the Franco-Italian border 30 Apr 45. It was in the vicinity of Alessandria and Pavin when German forces in Italy surrendered on 2 May 45.

93rd Infantry Division (Colored)

No Distinctive Insignia Authorized

15 May 42 activated at Ft Huachuca Ariz and moved 9 Apr 43 to the Third Army No.2 Louisiana Maneuvers; participated 8 Jul 43 in the Desert Training Center No.3 California Maneuvers; staged at Cp Stoneman Calif 15 Jan 44 until departed San Francisco P/E 24 Jan 44; arrived Guadalcanal 7 Feb 44 (Div HHC departed 19 Feb 44 and arrived 5 Mar 44); arrived Stirling Island Treasury Islands 7 Jun 44; arrived Hollandia New Guinea 30 Oct 44; arrived Morotai Island 5 Apr 45 and landed in Philippines 9 Oct 45; returned to San Francisco P/E 1 Feb 46 and inactivated at Cp Stoneman Calif 3 Feb 46.

Campaigns: Northern Solomons, Bismarck Archipelago, New Guinea
Aug 45 Loc: Morotai Island

Typical Organization (1944/45):

25th Infantry Regiment (Cld)	318th Engineer Combat Battalion (Cld)
368th Infantry Regiment (Cld)	318th Medical Battalion (Cld)
369th Infantry Regiment (Cld)	93rd Counter Intelligence Corps Det (Cld)
HHB Division Artillery (Cld)	Headquarters, Special Troops (Cld)
593rd Field Artillery Battalion (105mm)(Cld)	Hqs Company, 93rd Infantry Division (Cld)
594th Field Artillery Battalion (105mm)(Cld)	Military Police Platoon (Cld)
595th Field Artillery Battalion (105mm)(Cld)	793rd Ordnance Light Maintenance Co (Cld)
596th Field Artillery Battalion (155mm)(Cld)	93rd Quartermaster Company (Cld)
93rd Reconnaissance Troop, Mecz (Cld)	93rd Signal Company (Cld)

Overseas Wartime Assignments:

U.S. Army Forces in South Pacific - 11 Feb 44	Eighth Army - 4 Nov 44
XIV Corps - 15 Jun 44	XI Corps *(attached)* - 5 Jan 45
Provisional Island Cmd APO 706 - 8 Jul 44	Eighth Army Area Cmd *(attached)* - 20 Jan 45

Commanders: MG Charles P. Hall: May 42   MG Raymond G. Lehman: May 43
MG Fred W. Miller: Oct 42   MG Harry H. Johnson: Aug 44

Killed in Action: 12   *Wounded in Action:* 121   *Died of Wounds:* 5

93rd Infantry Division (Colored) Combat Narrative

The division moved to Guadalcanal by echelon 11 Jan–5 Mar 44, where its elements were parceled out to various islands throughout the Pacific for the duration of the war.

The 25th Inf Regt engaged in labor details at docks and warehouses on Guadalcanal 6–23 Mar 44 and arrived at Empress Augusta Bay Bougainville 28 Mar 44. There it was attached to Americal Div. It conducted limited offensive operations, crossing the Laruma River 2 Apr 44 and patrolling in the Torokina Valley 7–12 Apr 44, and against Japanese along the Kuma and East-West Trails during May. Between 26 May and 21 Jun 44 the regiment displaced to the Green Islands where it engaged in construction of fortifications, defense of installations, and trained. It moved from the Green Islands to Finschhafen New Guinea 12 Oct–10 Nov 44 where it defended the area and supplied labor details for port duty until 30 Mar 45. The regiment departed New Guinea 31 Mar 45 and arrived on Morotai Island by 12 Apr 45 where supplied stevedore crews at the port, trained, and conducted offensive operations in the Bosoboso area of eastern Morotai. These tasks were continued until the end of the war.

The 368th Inf Regt arrived at Bakina Russell Islands on 7 Feb 44 and furnished fatigue details at docks, warehouses, and supply dumps. It moved to New Georgia Island 14 Jun–3 Jul 44 and there engaged in patrols, guarded radar and radio equipment, and engaged in dock and port duties. The regiment arrived in Hollandia New Guinea 14–30 Oct 44 to furnish details for supply operations with the secondary mission of security in the area. Between 2 and 29 Apr 45 it moved to Morotai Island where it defended military installations and cleared the area between the Pilowo and Bobo Rivers. The regiment departed Morotai Island 29 Jun 45 and arrived at Zamboanga Philippines 1 Jul 45 to assume responsibility for the base. It conducted patrols and training there while a battalion was detached to take over responsibility for security of Palawan Island from the 41st Inf Div, and another battalion was sent to mop up Jolo Island. The regiment engaged in these activities until the end of the war.

The 369th Inf Regt arrived at New Georgia Island from Guadalcanal 29 Feb–12 Mar 44. There it defended the island until relieved by the 368th Inf Regt and departed 26 Jun 44. It arrived at Emirau in the St Matthias Island Group on 28 Jun 44, and was disposed tactically throughout the islands where improved fortifications and maintained defenses. The 3rd Battalion was detached to Los Negros Island Admiralty Islands and landed 29 Sep 44. The 2nd Battalion was detached to Biak Island where it arrived 1 Oct 44, followed by the rest of the regiment on 31 Oct 44. There the regiment, less 3rd Bn, supplied labor details and made some tactical patrols. On 1 Apr 45 it left Biak Island and arrived on Morotai Island 4 Apr 45. The next day elements were sent to Sansapor New Guinea and Middelburg Island, and the 3rd Battalion rejoined the regiment on Morotai about 10 Apr 45. The regiment then engaged in mopping up and establishing outposts on western Morotai until the end of the war.

The division headquarters and other assigned components engaged in cargo loading on Guadalcanal 6 Mar–4 Jun 44 and then moved to Stirling Island in the Treasury Group 5–7 Jun 44. There it assumed defensive missions and engaged in labor details until moved to Hollandia New Guinea 30 Oct 44. The division was responsible for loading and unloading of supplies and maintained outposts until departed 1 Apr 45. On 5 Apr 45 it arrived on Morotai Island and took over port operations and control of its elements on the island until the end of the war.

94th Infantry Division

No Distinctive
Insignia Authorized

15 Sep 42 activated at Ft Custer Mich and moved to Cp Phillips Kans 16 Nov 42; 3 Sep 43 participated in the Second Army No.3 Tennessee Maneuvers; transferred to Cp McCain Miss 29 Nov 43; staged at Cp Shanks N.Y. 25 Jul 44 until departed New York P/E 6 Aug 44; arrived in England 11 Aug 44 and landed in France 8 Sep 44; entered Germany 8 Jan 45; returned New York P/E 6 Feb 46 and inactivated at Cp Kilmer N.J. 7 Feb 46.

Campaigns: *Northern France, Rhineland, Ardennes-Alsace, Central Europe*
Aug 45 Loc: Dusseldorf Germany

Typical Organization (1944/45):

301st Infantry Regiment
302nd Infantry Regiment
376th Infantry Regiment
 HHB Division Artillery
301st Field Artillery Battalion (105mm)
356th Field Artillery Battalion (105mm)
390th Field Artillery Battalion (155mm)
919th Field Artillery Battalion (105mm)
 94th Reconnaissance Troop, Mecz
778th Tank Battalion *(attached 16 Feb–19 Mar 45, 23 Mar 45–24 Mar 45)*
691st Tank Destroyer Battalion *(attached 4 Mar 45 only)*
704th Tank Destroyer Battalion *(attached 23 Jan 45–4 Mar 45)*
774th Tank Destroyer Battalion *(attached 7 Jan 45–past 9 May 45)*
465th AAA Auto-Wpns Battalion *(attached 7 Jan 45–12 Jun 45)*
473rd AAA Auto-Wpns Battalion *(attached 17 Sep 44–27 Nov 44)*

319th Engineer Combat Battalion
319th Medical Battalion
 94th Counter Intelligence Corps Det
Headquarters, Special Troops
Hqs Company, 94th Infantry Division
Military Police Platoon
794th Ordnance Light Maintenance Company
 94th Quartermaster Company
 94th Signal Company

Overseas Wartime Assignments:

XIII Corps - 27 Jul 44
Ninth Army - 23 Sep 44
12th Army Group - 9 Oct 44

XX Corps - 6 Jan 45
XXII Corps - 29 Mar 45

Commanders: MG Harry J. Malony: Sep 42
BG Louis J. Fortier: May 45
MG Allison J. Barnett: Aug 45

Killed in Action: 1,009   *Wounded in Action:* 4,789   *Died of Wounds:* 147

94th Infantry Division Combat Narrative

The division landed across Utah Beach France 8 Sep 44 and relieved the 6th Armd Div at Lorient and St Nazaire, where German garrisons were besieged, 10–16 Sep 44. The division engaged in containment activities there until relieved by the 66th Inf Div on 1 Jan 45. It then moved into positions in the Saar-Moselle Triangle on 7 Jan 45 and relieved the 90th Inf Div south of Wasserbilling, facing the strongly fortified switch positions of the *West Wall.*

The division attacked 14 Jan 45 to improve its defensive positions in the area and became engaged in heavy combat. The 376th Inf fought the Battle of Tettingen and Butzdorf 14–18 Jan 45, losing the latter town which was not retaken until 26 Jan 45. The 302nd Inf cleared pillbox fortifications and held Tettingen against a strong German counterattack 21 Jan 45. The division fought the Battle of Nenning 20–23 Jan 45; the Battle of Orscholz—eastern terminus of the switch position—20 Jan 45, which was broken off after heavy losses; and the Battle of Berg 23–25 Jan 45. From 1–2 Feb 45 the division made a limited objective attack and cleared the Campholz Woods southeast of Tettingen. The 301st Inf fought house-to-house and captured Sinz 7–8 Feb 45. The 301st and 376th Inf fought the Battle for Bannholz Woods 9–10 Feb 45 but were driven back, while the 302nd Inf renewed its assault on pillboxes east of Campholz 15 Feb 45 but was repulsed. The division then regrouped.

Supported by heavy artillery and air support, the division attacked with all three regiments 19 Feb 45 to breach the *West Wall* switch-line defenses and clear the Berg-Munzingen Highway. It then followed the 10th Armed Div and cleared the Saar-Moselle Triangle below Orscholz and Saarburg by 21 Feb 45. The division assaulted across the Saar in spite of strong German opposition the next day; the 376th Inf, after delays caused by lack of assault-boats and then German fire, establishing the Ockfen Bridgehead, and the 301st and 302nd Inf crossing opposite Serrig to establish the Serrig-Taben Bridgehead. Heavy fighting continued, but by 26 Feb 45 the two bridgeheads were joined, permitting a heavy pontoon bridge to be put in at Saarburg. The division then expanded to the northeast to protect the 10th Armd Div drive on Trier and to strengthen the combined Saarburg Bridgehead. A German counterattack 5 Mar 45 against the 302nd Inf penetrated its lines, forcing the division to restore its front and clear infiltrators out of the bridgehead until 8 Mar 45.

The division crossed the Ruwer River by ford and bridge on 13 Mar 45 to attack out of the bridgehead and by 16 Mar 45 had broken through to the Hermeskeil-Nonnweiler line. It followed the 12th Armd Div and reached the Rhine 21 Mar 45, participating in the Battle for Ludwigshafen 22–24 Mar 45. On 25 Mar 45 the division was withdrawn for rehabilitation in the Baumholder area, and moved by rail and motor to Krefeld 3 Apr 45 where it relieved the 102nd Inf Div along the Rhine. There it assumed responsibility for containing the western side of the Ruhr Pocket. With the pocket's reduction by mid-April the division relieved the 101st A/B Div 18 Apr 45, and assumed military government duties; first in the Krefeld vicinity and later around Dusseldorf. It was in that status when hostilities were declared at an end on 7 May 45.

95th Infantry Division

No Distinctive Insignia Authorized

15 Jul 42 activated as 95th Division at Cp Swift Tex where redesignated 95th Infantry Division 1 Aug 42; moved to Ft Sam Houston Tex 5 Dec 42 and sent 19 Jun 43 to the Third Army No.3 Louisiana Maneuvers; transferred to Cp Polk La 24 Aug 43 and participated 18 Oct 43 in the Desert Training Center No.4 California Maneuvers; arrived Indiantown Gap Mil Res Pa 18 Feb 44 where participated in the West Virginia Mountain Training Maneuvers 1 May–1 Jul 44; staged at Cp Myles Standish Mass 21 Jul 44 until departed Boston P/E 10 Aug 44; arrived England 17 Aug 44; and landed in France 15 Sep 44; crossed into Belgium 31 Jan 45 and entered Germany 2 Mar 45; returned to Boston P/E 29 Jun 45 and arrived Cp Shelby Miss 3 Jul 45 where inactivated on 15 Oct 45.

Campaigns: *Northern France, Rhineland, Ardennes-Alsace, Central Europe*
Aug 45 Loc: Camp Shelby Mississippi

Typical Organization (1944/45):

377th Infantry Regiment
378th Infantry Regiment
379th Infantry Regiment
 HHB Division Artillery
358th Field Artillery Battalion (105mm)
359th Field Artillery Battalion (105mm)
360th Field Artillery Battalion (155mm)
920th Field Artillery Battalion (105mm)
 95th Reconnaissance Troop, Mecz
709th Tank Battalion *(attached 16 Feb 45–21 Apr 45)*
735th Tank Battalion *(attached 20 Oct 44–29 Nov 44)*
761st Tank Battalion *(attached 2 Feb 45–13 Feb 45)*
778th Tank Battalion *(attached 11 Nov 44–28 Jan 45)*
607th Tank Destroyer Battalion *(attached 1 Nov 44–2 Feb 45)*
614th Tank Destroyer Battalion *(attached 20 Nov 44–23 Nov 44)*
705th Tank Destroyer Battalion *(attached 15 Oct 44–2 Nov 44)*
773rd Tank Destroyer Battalion *(attached 25 Oct 44–7 Nov 44)*
774th Tank Destroyer Battalion *(attached 20 Oct 44–26 Oct 44)*
802nd Tank Destroyer Battalion *(attached 3 Feb 45–21 Apr 45)*
809th Tank Destroyer Battalion *(attached 7 Apr 45–13 Apr 45)*
818th Tank Destroyer Battalion *(attached 20 Oct 44–26 Oct 44)*
473rd AAA Auto-Wpns Battalion *(attached 7 Apr 45–13 Apr 45)*
547th AAA Auto-Wpns Battalion *(attached 5 Oct 44–21 May 45)*

320th Engineer Combat Battalion
320th Medical Battalion
 95th Counter Intelligence Corps Det
Headquarters, Special Troops
Hqs Company, 95th Infantry Division
Military Police Platoon
795th Ordnance Light Maintenance Company
 95th Quartermaster Company
 95th Signal Company

Overseas Wartime Assignments:

XIII Corps - 27 Jul 44
III Corps - 5 Sep 44
XX Corps - 10 Oct 44
VIII Corps - 29 Jan 45
Ninth Army - 5 Feb 45
British 8 Corps (attached) - 13 Feb 45

XIX Corps - 22 Feb 45
XIII Corps - 26 Feb 45
XIX Corps - 30 Mar 45
XXII Corps - 31 Mar 45
XIX Corps - 2 Apr 45
XVI Corps - 9 Apr 45

Commander: MG Harry L. Twaddle: Jul 42

Killed in Action: 1,205   *Wounded in Action:* 4,945   *Died of Wounds:* 167

95th Infantry Division Combat Narrative

The division arrived in France on 15 Sep 44 and was stationed near Norroy-le-Sec 1–14 Oct 44. It moved into line 19 Oct 44 in the Moselle River Bridgehead and south of Metz, and patrolled the Seille River near Cheminot. On 1 Nov 44 the division was relieved in the Arnaville Bridgehead, and on 8 Nov 44 went into the attack as the 377th Inf crossed the Moselle River and gained the Uckange Bridgehead, and also began the reduction of a German pocket west of the river near Maizières-lès-Metz. The 378th Inf established another bridgehead across the Moselle at Thionville on 11 Nov 44 and fought for Fort Yutz 11–13 Nov 44, the 377th Inf defeating a major counterattack at its bridgehead the same day. The division then attacked toward Metz as the 379th Inf fought into the Seven Dwarfs Fortifications 14 Nov 44, the 378th Inf seized Fort d'Ilange 14–15 Nov 44, and the 377th Inf stormed Bertrange 13 Nov 44. Advancing slowly through the Metz forts and bypassing strongpoints, the division reached Metz as it overran Fort St Julien and Fort Bellacroix on 18 Nov 44. The division battled through Metz until 22 Nov 44 when the city was cleared, and then was relieved despite the continued existence of isolated German garrisons in some surrounding forts on 23 Nov 44. The division attacked across the Nied River on 25 Nov 44 after intensive artillery preparation as the 377th and 378th Inf pushed into an abandoned sector of the Maginot Line. In a rapid drive, the 377th Inf crossed into Germany 28 Nov 44.

By 29 Nov 44 the division was strongly opposed on the Saar heights in front of Saarlautern and underwent ten coun-terattacks on that day alone. It gained the heights the following day, and after heavy air preparation the division attacked on 1 Dec 44 to reach and cross the Saar River. The 377th Inf fought through St Barbara 29 Nov–2 Dec 44, and the 379th Inf battled into Saarlautern the same day and crossed the bridge there 4 Dec 44, driving into the *West Wall*. In house-to-house fighting and combat through mazes of pillboxes, the Saarlautern Bridgehead Battles commenced the same day. The 379th and later 377th Inf fought the Battle of Fraulautern, and the 379th Inf fought the Battle for Saarlautern-Roden, until the division was relieved in line on 18 Dec 44 as the 5th Inf Div took over the fighting. The 378th Inf battled for Ensdorf 5–20 Dec 44 when it was withdrawn to the west bank of the Saar. With the Saarlautern Bridgehead consolidated, the division reassembled. It defeated a strong counterattack at Saarlautern 20 Jan 45 and improved positions until relieved in the bridgehead sector on 29 Jan 45. It went to army reserve 3 Feb 45 and moved to the Maastricht area of Holland. On 14 Feb 45 the division moved into the line near Meerselo and was relieved there 23 Feb 45. It assembled near Juelich Germany on 1 Mar 45.

The division attacked toward the Rhine River on 4 Mar 45; the 378th Inf driving through Uerdingen to take Rhein-hausen 5 Mar 45 while the 379th Inf eliminated the German pocket at the *Adolph Hitler* Bridge in south Uerdingen the same day. From 12 Mar–1 Apr 45 the division defended the Neuss sector along the west bank of the Rhine, and then was relieved and assembled at Beckum 3 Apr 45. The 378th and 379th Inf attacked across the Lippe River/Canal in the Hamm-Lippborn area against the Ruhr Pocket on 4 Apr 45. Fighting through diminishing resistance, the 378th Inf took Hamm 7 Apr 45 as the division formed Task Force Twaddle to finish clearing the Ruhr Pocket until 14 Apr 45. The 378th and 379th Inf took Kamen 10 Apr 45 and the 377th Inf (Task Force Faith) reduced the Ruhr-Mohne Pocket 7–12 Apr 45. The 378th Inf fought through ruined Dortmund 12–13 Apr 45, after which the division maintained positions on the north bank of the Ruhr River. The division was assigned military government duties on 15 Apr 45, detaching the 378th Inf to the Bremen Enclave Military District 1–6 May 45. The division was in this capacity when hostilities were declared ended on 7 May 45.

No Distinctive
Insignia Authorized

96th Infantry Division

15 Aug 42 activated at Cp Adair Oreg and moved to Ft Lewis Wash 10 May 43; sent to the Oregon Maneuver Area 12 Jul 43 and returned to Cp Adair Oreg 6 Aug 43; participated 5 Sep 43 in the IV Corps No.1 Oregon Maneuvers; transferred to Cp White Oreg 1 Nov 43 and arrived at Cp San Luis Obispo Calif 22 Apr 44 and Cp Beale Calif 2 Jul 44; staged at Cp Stoneman Calif 16 Jul 44 until departed San Francisco P/E 23 Jul 44; arrived Hawaii 28 Jul 44 and departed 15 Sep 44; arrived Eniwetok Anchorage 26 Sep 44 and departed for Manus Island 28 Sep 44 where it arrived 3 Oct 44; left Manus Island 14 Oct 44 and assaulted Leyte Philippine Islands 20 Oct 44; departed Leyte 25–27 Mar 45 for Okinawa Island which assaulted on 1 Apr 45; returned to Philippines 31 Jul 45 and arrived Los Angeles P/E 2 Feb 46; inactivated at Cp Anza Calif 3 Feb 46.

Campaigns: *Leyte, Ryukyus*
Aug 45 Loc: Mindoro Philippine Islands

Typical Organization (1944/45):

381st Infantry Regiment
382nd Infantry Regiment
383rd Infantry Regiment
HHB Division Artillery
361st Field Artillery Battalion (105mm)
362nd Field Artillery Battalion (105mm)
363rd Field Artillery Battalion (155mm)
921st Field Artillery Battalion (105mm)
96th Reconnaissance Troop, Mecz

321st Engineer Combat Battalion
321st Medical Battalion
96th Counter Intelligence Corps Det
Headquarters, Special Troops
Hqs Company, 96th Infantry Division
Military Police Platoon
796th Ordnance Light Maintenance Company
96th Quartermaster Company
96th Signal Company

Overseas Wartime Assignments:

Central Pacific Base Command - 19 Jul 44
Tenth Army - 10 Feb 45
XXIV Corps - 22 Feb 45

Eighth Army - 31 Jul 45
Eighth Army Area Cmd *(attached)* - 31 Jul 45

Commander: MG James L. Bradley: Aug 42

Killed in Action: 1,563   *Wounded in Action:* 7,181   *Died of Wounds:* 473

96th Infantry Division Combat Narrative

The division arrived in Hawaii 23–31 Jul 44, and trained on Oahu where it prepared for operations on Yap. The division moved to Eniwetok Island 11 Sep 44 and was informed its participation in Yap operations was cancelled 15 Sep 44, and it was diverted to Leyte Island Philippines instead. The division remained afloat at Eniwetok Anchorage until departed 28 Sep 44 for Manus Island, where it arrived 3 Oct 44 and there remained afloat until leaving for Leyte 14 Oct 44. The division landed near Dulag 20 Oct 44 and took San Jose and advanced inland across swampy terrain against pillboxes; the 381st and 383rd Inf fighting at Catmon Hill 21–29 Oct 44 and completing mop-up there 1 Nov 44, and the 382nd Inf taking Tigbao 22 Oct 44 and then fighting the Battle for Tatnauan 26–28 Oct 44. The 383rd Inf pushed across the Guinarona River despite supply difficulties, and the 382nd Inf attacked toward Bloody Ridge west of Dagami on 2 Nov 44, repulsing Japanese counterattacks 4–5 Nov 44, and battling on the ridge 5–7 Nov 44 with clearance completed 10 Nov 44. The division completed the relief of the 7th Inf Div in the Tanauan-Dagami-Dulag sector about 4 Nov 44 and assumed responsibility for its defense. It patrolled and mopped up, securing the western Dagami heights and Alto Peak by 25 Dec 44. On that day Leyte Island was declared secured, but the division continued mopping up operations and relieved the 11th A/B Div of tactical responsibility on Leyte 14 Jan 45. Two battalions were sent to Samar to relieve the 1st Cav Div of garrison duty at Catabalogan. On 10 Feb 45 the division was relieved of all combat duty in the Philippines and trained for Okinawa operations. It embarked 14 Mar 45 and made landing rehearsals near Vincay 17–19 Mar 45 and departed for Okinawa 25–27 Mar 45.

The division landed south of Bishi River on Okinawa against light resistance on 1 Apr 45 and drove down the western coast toward the Uchitomari area by 4 Apr 45. The 383rd Inf fought the Battle for Cactus Ridge 5–7 Apr 45 as Uchitomari fell; and then tackled Kakazu Ridge commencing 8 Apr 45, a surprise attack storming the ridge 9 Apr 45 but the next day it was forced off. The 381st and 383rd Inf attacked up its slopes again 10 Apr 45 and the division was subjected to major Japanese counterattacks 12–14 Apr 45, after which the 27th Inf Div took over the battle. On 17 Apr 45 the division was moved to a new zone of action on the Tanabaru-Nishibaru defenses. The 381st Inf pushed through

Kaniku 19 Apr 45 and fought the Battle for Nishibaru Ridge 19–24 Apr 45 as the 382nd Inf fought on Tombstone Ridge 19–20 Apr 45. Task Force Bradford was formed from three divisions to destroy the Kakazu Pocket, and the division secured the high ground in the Tanabaru-Nishibaru area against slackened opposition by 24 Apr 45.

The 381st and 383rd Inf attacked Maeda Escarpment assisted by flamethrowing tanks on 26 Apr 45 and met strong opposition on the reverse slopes. The division was relieved in line, still engaged in the battle for Maeda Escarpment, 29–30 Apr 45. The division was rehabilitated 1–8 May 45 and relieved the 7th Inf Div at the eastern end of the Shuri Line on 10 May 45. The 383rd Inf attacked Conical Hill 11 May, held it against a major counterattack 13 May 45, and secured it by 15 May 45. The 382nd Inf fought the Battle for Dick Hill mass 11–18 May 45 as the 381st Inf fought the Battle of Sugar Hill 18–21 May 45. The 383rd Inf fought the Battle for King Hill 19–20 May 45 and then the Battle for Love Hill 22–30 May 45. The 382nd and 383rd Inf fought the Battle for Oboe Hill and Hen Hill 21–30 May 45. By 31 May 45 the division had cleared its zone north of the Yonabaru-Shuri-Naha Road and started pursuit operations.

The division cleared opposition near Chan on 1 Jun 45 and drove southwest. The 381st Inf fought the Battle for Yaeju-Dake Escarpment 6–14 Jun 45 and took Yuza-Dake Peak on 16 Jun 45. The 383rd Inf was engaged in the Battle for Yuza 11–12 Jun 45. The division attacked into the Aragachi-Medeera area 18–22 Jun 44, when Okinawa was declared secure, and then turned to mopping up operations on the island. On 1 Jul 45 it moved to Kamizato for rehabilitation, and then left Okinawa 22 Jul 45. It arrived in Mindoro Philippines 1 Aug 45 where stationed at the end of the war.

97th Infantry Division

No Distinctive Insignia Authorized

25 Feb 43 activated at Cp Swift Tex and moved 20 Oct 43 to the Third Army No.5 Louisiana Maneuvers; transferred to Ft Leonard Wood Mo 31 Jan 44 and moved to Cp San Luis Obispo Calif 9 Jul 44; arrived Cp Cooke Calif 30 Sep 44 and staged at Cp Kilmer N.J. 13 Feb 45 until departed New York P/E 19 Feb 45; arrived France 1 Mar 45 and entered Germany 28 Mar 45; returned New York P/E 26 Jun 45 and sent to Ft Bragg N.C. 28 Jun 45; arrived Ft Lawton Wash 22 Aug 45 and departed Seattle P/E 1 Sep 45; arrived Philippines 14 Sep 45 and Japan 24 Sep 45 where inactivated 31 Mar 46.

Campaigns: *Central Europe*
Aug 45 Loc: Fort Bragg North Carolina

Typical Organization (1944/45):

303rd Infantry Regiment
386th Infantry Regiment
387th Infantry Regiment
 HHB Division Artillery
303rd Field Artillery Battalion (105mm)
365th Field Artillery Battalion (105mm)
389th Field Artillery Battalion (155mm)
922nd Field Artillery Battalion (105mm)
 97th Reconnaissance Troop, Mecz
782nd Tank Battalion *(attached 20 Apr 45–past 9 May 45)*
630th Tank Destroyer Battalion *(attached 18 Apr 45–20 Apr 45)*
820th Tank Destroyer Battalion *(attached 20 Apr 45–past 9 May 45)*
444th AAA Auto-Wpns Battalion *(attached 20 Apr 45–past 9 May 45)*
542nd AAA Auto-Wpns Battalion *(attached 2 Apr 45–4 Apr 45)*

322nd Engineer Combat Battalion
322nd Medical Battalion
 97th Counter Intelligence Corps Det
Headquarters, Special Troops
Hqs Company, 97th Infantry Division
Military Police Platoon
797th Ordnance Light Maintenance Company
 97th Quartermaster Company
 97th Signal Company

Overseas Wartime Assignments:

Fifteenth Army - 30 Jan 45
XXII Corps - 28 Mar 45
First Army - 1 Apr 45
XVIII (A/B) Corps - 10 Apr 45
Third Army - 19 Apr 45

XII Corps - 22 Apr 45
First Army - 28 Apr 45
V Corps - 30 Aug 45
Third Army - 6 May 45

Commanders: BG Louis A. Craig: Feb 43
BG Milton B. Halsey: Jan 44
MG Herman F. Kramer: Sep 45

Killed in Action: 188   *Wounded in Action:* 721   *Died of Wounds:* 26

97th Infantry Division Combat Narrative

The division arrived at Le Havre France 1 Mar 45 and crossed the German border 28 Mar 45, taking over the zone of the 95th Inf Div in the vicinity of Neuss on 1 Apr 45. From 4–6 Apr 45 it relieved the 78th Inf Div along the south bank of the Sieg River. After artillery preparation, the 386th Inf attacked across the Sieg in assault boats on 7 Apr 45 as the division drove against the Ruhr Pocket. The 303rd Inf captured Siegburg in street-to-street fighting 9–10 Apr 45, and the division pushed on Düsseldorf through densely wooded and well-defended terrain. The 303rd Inf took the I.G. Farben Chemical Works near Leverkusen, and the 386th and 387th Inf reached the Berg Neukirchen-Burscheid Railway on 15 Apr 45. The division cleared Solingen 17 Apr 45, and the following day the 303rd Inf seized Düsseldorf virtually unopposed, eliminating the Ruhr Pocket. It was relieved 20 Apr 45 and in turn relieved the 2nd Cav Group in the As-Arzberg Line 22–24 Apr 45. On 25 Apr 45 the 386th and 387th Inf attacked toward Cherb Czechoslovakia which was taken the next day. The latter regiment captured Cherb Airfield on 28 Apr 45, and the division attacked 2 May 45 to improve positions. The division attacked toward Pilsen 5 May 45, and reached Konstantinovy Lazne Czechoslovakia 7 May 45 when hostilities were declared at an end.

98th Infantry Division

No Distinctive Insignia Authorized

15 Sep 42 activated at Cp Breckinridge Ky and moved 6 Sep 43 to Second Army No.3 Tennessee Maneuvers; transferred to Cp Rucker Ala 16 Nov 43; staged at Ft Lawton Wash 5 Apr 44 until departed Seattle P/E 13 Apr 44; arrived Hawaii 19 Apr 44 and Japan 27 Sep 45 where inactivated 16 Feb 46.

Campaigns: *Pacific Theater without Inscription*
Aug 45 Loc: Fort Hase Hawaii

Typical Organization (1944/45):

389th Infantry Regiment
390th Infantry Regiment
391st Infantry Regiment
 HHB Division Artillery
367th Field Artillery Battalion (105mm)
368th Field Artillery Battalion (105mm)
369th Field Artillery Battalion (155mm)
923rd Field Artillery Battalion (105mm)
 98th Reconnaissance Troop, Mecz

323rd Engineer Combat Battalion
323rd Medical Battalion
 98th Counter Intelligence Corps Det
Headquarters, Special Troops
Hqs Company, 98th Infantry Division
Military Police Platoon
798th Ordnance Light Maintenance Company
 98th Quartermaster Company
 98th Signal Company

Overseas Wartime Assignments:

U.S. Army Forces Central Pacific - 19 Apr 44
Central Pacific Base Command - 1 Jul 44
IX Corps - 14 May 45

U.S. Army Forces Central Pacific - 22 Jun 45
U.S. Army Forces Middle Pacific - 1 Jul 45

Commanders: MG Paul L. Ransom: Sep 42
 MG George W. Griner Jr: Nov 43
 BG Josef R. Sheetz: Jun 44
 MG Ralph C. Smith: Jul 44

BG Josef R. Sheetz: Aug 44
BG Wayne C. Zimmerman: Oct 44
MG Arthur M. Harper: Oct 44

Killed in Action: None   *Wounded in Action:* None   *Died of Wounds:* None

98th Infantry Division Combat Narrative

The division arrived in Hawaii with the 389th Inf on 19 Apr 44 and was assigned to defend the Kauai District. On 28 Apr 44 the 391st Inf arrived and was tasked to defend Maui District; followed by the 390th Inf which arrived 4 May 44 and moved to Kauai, and then relieved the 38th Inf Div of the ground defense mission on Oahu 26 May 44. The division was relieved of defense missions in the Kauai and Maui Districts on 2 Nov 44 and assembled on Oahu. There the 389th Inf relieved the 390th Inf for the Oahu defense mission on 5 Dec 44, and the 391st Inf relieved the 389th Inf in turn on 18 Mar 45. The division was relieved of ground defense responsibilities on Oahu 31 May 45 and began intensive training, and on 28 Jul 45 was alerted for participation in the invasion of Japan. It was preparing for this role in Hawaii when the war ended.

99th Infantry Division

15 Nov 42 activated at Cp Van Dorn Miss and moved 16 Sep 43 to Third Army No.4 Louisiana Maneuvers; transferred to Cp Maxey Tex 19 Nov 43; staged at Cp Myles Standish Mass 13 Sep 44 until departed Boston P/E 30 Sep 44; arrived England 10 Oct 44 and landed in France 3 Nov 44; entered Germany 12 Nov 44; arrived Hampton Roads P/E 26 Sep 45 and inactivated Cp Patrick Henry Va 27 Sep 45.

No Distinctive
Insignia Authorized

Campaigns: *Rhineland, Ardennes-Alsace, Central Europe*
Aug 45 Loc: Pfeffenhausen Germany

Typical Organization (1944/45):

393rd Infantry Regiment
394th Infantry Regiment
395th Infantry Regiment
 HHB Division Artillery
370th Field Artillery Battalion (105mm)
371st Field Artillery Battalion (105mm)
372nd Field Artillery Battalion (155mm)
924th Field Artillery Battalion (105mm)
 99th Reconnaissance Troop, Mecz
750th Tank Battalion *(attached 28 Jan 45–5 Feb 45)*
786th Tank Battalion *(attached 23 Feb 45–9 May 45)*
629th Tank Destroyer Battalion *(attached 22 Feb 45–9 May 45)*
644th Tank Destroyer Battalion *(attached 28 Jan 45–8 Feb 45)*
801st Tank Destroyer Battalion *(attached 9 Nov 44–3 Feb 45)*
814th Tank Destroyer Battalion *(attached 8 Feb 45–13 Feb 45)*
817th Tank Destroyer Battalion *(attached 13 Feb 45–22 Feb 45)*
535th AAA Auto-Wpns Battalion *(attached 11 Dec 44–9 May 45)*

324th Engineer Combat Battalion
324th Medical Battalion
 99th Counter Intelligence Corps Det
Headquarters, Special Troops
Hqs Company, 99th Infantry Division
Military Police Platoon
799th Ordnance Light Maintenance Company
 99th Quartermaster Company
 99th Signal Company

Overseas Wartime Assignments:

V Corps - 4 Nov 44
2nd Inf Division *(attached)* - 18 Dec 44
V Corps - 7 Jan 45

VII Corps - 20 Feb 45
III Corps - 9 Mar 45

Commanders: MG Thompson Lawrence: Nov 42
MG Walter E. Lauer: Jul 43
BG Frederick H. Black: Aug 45

Killed in Action: 993   *Wounded in Action:* 4,177   *Died of Wounds:* 141

99th Infantry Division Combat Narrative

The division landed at Le Havre France on 3 Nov 44 and assembled at Aubel Belgium, and entered the line north of the Roer River between Schmidt and Monschau on 9 Nov 44. After a period of defensive patrolling, the division attacked toward the Roer and Urft Dams on 13 Dec 44 against heavy resistance from the *West Wall*. On 16 Dec 44 the German Ardennes Counteroffensive hit the division which initially held at Hofen but gave ground to the south. The division was partially surrounded and suffered heavy losses as it retreated to new defensive positions before Elsenborn Ridge on 19 Dec 44. The next day German forces temporarily breached the lines west of Wirtzfeld, but the division reestablished its front. From 21 Dec 44–29 Jan 45 the division was rebuilt on the front and maintained defensive positions. It attacked with the 393rd Inf into the Elsenbuchel Woods east of Elsenborn on 30 Jan 45 and gained its objectives in the Monschau Forest 1 Feb 45. It was then withdrawn into reserve except for the 395th Inf which was detached to assist the 1st Inf Div in the *West Wall* near Hellenthal 3–5 Feb 45. On 5 Feb 45 the division relieved the 1st Inf Div, but on 11 Feb 45 was itself relieved in line and moved to Waimes Belgium for rehabilitation. On 20 Feb 45 it moved to the Aubel and Clermont areas.

The division attacked again, reinforced by the 4th Cav Group, on 2 Mar 45 with the 393rd Inf as it crossed the Erft River at Glesch and took Neurath. The detached 395th Inf meanwhile assisted the 3rd Armd Div at Pfaffendorf Bridgehead 1–3 Mar 45. The division sped along the Erft on a broad front and reached the Rhine at Grimlinghausen 5 Mar 45, the 395th Inf capturing Udesheim the next day. On 8 Mar 45 the division was relieved and moved to Stadt-Meckenheim area 9 Mar 45. It crossed the Rhine at Remagen 10–11 Mar 45 and took over the southern flank of the bridgehead, withstanding counterattacks and expanding it thru the Honnigen Wald into Honnigen which fell to the 394th Inf after heavy combat by 16 Mar 45. The 395th Inf reached the Wied River 17 Mar 45 and the division made limited attacks to improve positions.

The 393rd and 395th Inf attacked across the Wied River 22 Mar 45 and advanced past Kurtscheid the next day, cutting the Koln-Frankfurt Highway near Willroth on 25 Mar 45 as the 394th Inf crossed the Wied also. Driving east behind the 9th Armd Div, the 393rd Inf cleared to the Dill River line northwest of Wetzlar and relieved the armor of crossing in the Asslar-Hermannstein region on 28 Mar 45. The following day the 394th Inf relieved the 7th Armd Div at Giessen. The division was relieved at Wetzlar 30 Mar 45 and deployed to the Gemuenden area on 1 Apr 45. On 4 Apr 45 it relieved the 9th Inf Div in the Schwarzenau area.

The division began its attack on the Ruhr Pocket with the 393rd and 394th Inf in assault on 5 Apr 45, taking Wingeshausen the next day as it cleared resistance bypassed by the 7th Armd Div. On 9 Apr 45 the division crossed the Lenne River and the 394th Inf secured Bracht and the 395th Inf cleared the Saalhausen-Langener sector. By 16 Apr 45 all resistance in the eastern portion of the Ruhr Pocket collapsed as Iserlohn garrison surrendered to the division. It then started toward its assembly area at Trossenfurt, northwest of Bamberg, and relieved the 42nd Inf Div of responsibility for Fuerth on 21 Apr 45. The division attacked again on 23 Apr 45 as the 394th and 395th Inf followed in the wake of the 14th Armd Div to advance to the Allersberg-Holpoltstein line by the end of the day. Against heavy opposition, it reached the Altmuhr River at Dietfurt and Kinding 25 Apr 45 and then pushed rapidly to the Danube from the Altmuhl Bridgeheads the following day. The 393rd Inf assaulted across the Danube River on 27 Apr 45 at Eining, followed that same day by the 395th Inf which was repulsed in the Neustadt area. After sharp combat the bridgehead was expanded and the division then advanced to the Isar River against little or no resistance. On 30 Apr–1 May 45 the division crossed the Isar with the 393rd Inf at Landshut and the 395th Inf in the Moosburg area to cover bridging operations of the 14th Armd Div. The division then continued its advance without opposition to the Inn River and Giesenhausen when hostilities were declared ended on 7 May 45.

100th Infantry Division

No Distinctive
Insignia Authorized

15 Nov 42 activated at Ft Jackson S.C. and moved 17 Nov 43 to Second Army No.4 Tennessee Maneuvers; transferred to Ft Bragg N.C. 18 Jan 44 and staged at Cp Kilmer N.J. 30 Sep 44 until departed New York P/E 6 Oct 44; arrived in France 20 Oct 44 and entered Germany 22 Mar 45; arrived Hampton Roads P/E 10 Jan 46 and inactivated same date at Cp Patrick Henry Va.

Campaigns: *Rhineland, Ardennes-Alsace, Central Europe*
Aug 45 Loc: Goppingen Germany

Typical Organization (1944/45):

397th Infantry Regiment	325th Engineer Combat Battalion
398th Infantry Regiment	325th Medical Battalion
399th Infantry Regiment	100th Counter Intelligence Corps Det
HHB Division Artillery	Headquarters, Special Troops
373rd Field Artillery Battalion (155mm)	Hqs Company, 100th Infantry Division
374th Field Artillery Battalion (105mm)	Military Police Platoon
375th Field Artillery Battalion (105mm)	800th Ordnance Light Maintenance Company
925th Field Artillery Battalion (105mm)	100th Quartermaster Company
100th Reconnaissance Troop, Mecz	100th Signal Company
781st Tank Battalion *(attached 7 Dec 44–21 Dec 44, 23 Feb 45–23 Apr 45)*	
824th Tank Destroyer Battalion *(attached 26 Nov 44–24 Apr 45)*	
898th AAA Auto-Wpns Battalion *(attached 7 Nov 44–11 May 45)*	

Overseas Wartime Assignments:

VI Corps - 1 Nov 44	VI Corps - 25 Mar 45
XV Corps - 27 Nov 44	Seventh Army - 25 Apr 45
XXI Corps - 22 Mar 45	

Commanders: MG Withers A. Burress: Nov 42
BG Andrew C. Tychsen: Sep 45

Killed in Action: 883   *Wounded in Action:* 3,539   *Died of Wounds:* 101

100th Infantry Division Combat Narrative

The division arrived at Marseille France on 20 Oct 44 and elements went into combat at St Remy in the Vosges Mountains on 1 Nov 44. From 1–9 Nov 44 the division relieved the 45th Inf Div, and attacked on 12 Nov 44 as the 397th and 399th Inf crossed the Meurthe River at Baccarat to outflank Raon-l'Etape. Defeating a German counterattack on 13 Nov 44 the division advanced into Raon-l'Etape 18 Nov 44, which fell after the 397th Inf seized the Quarry Strongpoint. The division took Moyonmoutier without opposition 21 Nov 44 and overran St Blaise 23 Nov 44, the Vosges Mtns advance being halted on 26 Nov 44. The division arrived in the Saarebourg sector and relieved the 44th Inf Div on 27 Nov 44, where elements held the Saverne Gap Bridgehead while the rest of the division rehabilitated.

The division began the drive on Bitche 3 Dec 44, clearing Meisenthal and surrounding Mouterhouse by 6 Dec 44 and fighting the Battle for Lemberg 8–9 Dec 44 and the Battle for Reyersweiler 11–13 Dec 44. The division then fought the Battle for Fort Schiesseck, near Bitche, 14–20 Dec 44. The division was then ordered into holding positions south of Bitche due to the German Ardennes Counteroffensive. The German NORDWIND Offensive of 1 Jan 45 caused the division to give ground, but by 8 Jan 45 it was improving its positions on local attacks. The division attacked again toward Bitche on 15 Mar 45 and fought past Maginot forts to take the town the next day. On 18 Mar 45 the division was relieved from the line and reached the Rhine on 24 Mar 45.

The division crossed the Rhine on 31 Mar 45 and relieved the 63rd Inf Div near Neckargemund. It attacked 1 Apr 45 southeast along the Neckar River behind the 10th Armd Div against disorganized resistance. The 398th Inf crossed the Neckar at Neckargartach and established a bridgehead in heavy combat. The division then fought the Battle for Heilbronn 4–12 Apr 45, which fell only after house-to-house fighting. The 398th Inf fought the Battle for Jagstfeld 6–11 Apr 45 while attempting to expand its Offenau Bridgehead. The division then rapidly advanced behind the 10th Armd Div and took Loewenstein on 16 Apr 45. The 397th Inf reached the Murr River at Sulzbach 19–20 Apr 45; the 398th Inf crossed the Murr at Murrhardt 19 Apr 45; and the 399th Inf battled for the heights at Beilstein in the Neckar River Valley 18–19 Apr 45. The division then drove rapidly to Stuttgart which it reached on 21 Apr 45 as bridges were taken across the Rems River. The division mopped up pockets of resistance east of Stuttgart along the Neckar and confined further activity to patrolling. It relocated to Goppingen 30 Apr 45 for military government duty, and was serving in that capacity when hostilities were declared ended on 7 May 45.

101st Airborne Division

No Distinctive Insignia Authorized

15 Aug 42 activated at Cp Claiborne La and transferred to Ft Bragg N.C. 29 Sep 42; 7 Jun 43 moved to Springfield Tenn for Second Army No.1 Tennessee Maneuvers; returned to Ft Bragg N.C. 20 Jul 43; arrived at New York P/E 31 Aug 43 and departed 5 Sep 43; arrived England 15 Sep 43 and air-assaulted Normandy France 6 Jun 44; returned to England 13 Jul 44 and air-assaulted Nijmegen-Arnhem Holland 17 Sep 44; moved to France 28 Nov 44 and crossed into Belgium 18 Dec 44 and entered Germany 4 Apr 45; inactivated in France 30 Nov 45.

Campaigns: *Normandy, Rhineland, Ardennes-Alsace, Central Europe*
Aug 45 Loc: Mourmelon Le Grande France

Typical Organization (1944):

327th Glider Infantry Regiment
401st Glider Infantry Regiment*
502nd Parachute Infantry Regiment
HHB Division Artillery
321st Glider Field Artillery Bn (75mm)
377th Prcht Field Artillery Bn (75mm)
907th Glider Field Artillery Bn (75mm)
81st Airborne Antiaircraft Battalion

326th Airborne Engineer Battalion
326th Airborne   Medical Company
101st Counter Intelligence Corps Det
Hqs Company, 101st Airborne Division
Military Police Platoon
Reconnaissance Platoon
801st Airborne Ordnance Maintenance Company
426th Airborne Quartermaster Company
101st Signal Company

*Disbanded 1 Mar 45 in France.

Typical Organization (1945):

327th Glider Infantry Regiment
502nd Parachute Infantry Regiment
506th Parachute Infantry Regiment**
 HHB Division Artillery
321st Glider Field Artillery Bn (75mm)
377th Prcht Field Artillery Bn (75mm)
463rd Prcht Field Artillery Bn (75mm)
907th Glider Field Artillery Bn (75mm)
 81st Airborne Antiaircraft Battalion
101st Signal Company

326th Airborne Engineer Battalion
326th Airborne Medical Company
101st Counter Intelligence Corps Det
Headquarters, Special Troops
Hqs Company, 101st Airborne Division
Military Police Platoon
Reconnaissance Platoon
801st Airborne Ordnance Maintenance Company
426th Airborne Quartermaster Company
101st Parachute Maintenance Company

**Assigned 1 Mar 45; previously attached 15 Sep 43–1 Mar 45.

Combat Attachments (1944/45):

501st Parachute Infantry Regiment *(attached 1 May 44–past 9 May 45)*
506th Parachute Infantry Regiment *(attached 15 Sep 43–1 Mar 45)*
509th Parachute Infantry Battalion *(attached 22 Nov 44–18 Dec 44)*
759th Tank Battalion *(attached 28 Jun 44–8 Jul 44)*
774th Tank Battalion *(attached 5 May 45–9 May 45)*
611th Tank Destroyer Battalion *(attached 6 Jan 45–7 Jan 45)*
705th Tank Destroyer Battalion *(attached 20 Dec 44–18 Dec 45)*
807th Tank Destroyer Battalion *(attached 20 Jan 45–25 Feb 45)*
813th Tank Destroyer Battalion *(attached 5 May 45–9 May 45)*
567th AAA Auto-Wpns Battalion *(attached 23 Feb 45–27 Feb 45)*

Overseas Wartime Assignments:

VIII Corps - 22 Jan 44
First Army - 13 Mar 44
VII Corps - 6 Jun 44
VIII Corps - 15 Jun 44
Ninth Army - 15 Jul 44
XVIII (A/B) Corps - 12 Aug 44
First Allied (A/B) Army - 18 Sep 44
British 1 (A/B) Corps - 21 Sep 44
British 8 Corps - 23 Sep 44
British 12 Corps - 28 Sep 44
Canadian 2 Corps (attached) - 9 Nov 44

VIII Corps *(attached)* - 17 Dec 44
III Corps - 26 Dec 44
VIII Corps - 29 Dec 44
First Allied (A/B) Army - 19 Jan 45
VI Corps - 26 Jan 45
XVIII (A/B) Corps - 28 Feb 45
XXII Corps *(attached)* - 1 Apr 45
First Allied (A/B) Army - 6 Apr 45
VI Corps - 23 Apr 45
XXI Corps - 4 May 45

Commanders: MG William C. Lee: Aug 42
MG Maxwell D. Taylor: Mar 44
BG Anthony C. McAuliffe: Dec 44
MG Maxwell D. Taylor: Dec 44

BG William M. Gillmore: Sep 45
BG Gerald St.C Mickle: Sep 45
BG Stuart Cutler: Oct 45

Killed in Action: 1,766   *Wounded in Action:* 6,388   *Died of Wounds:* 324

101st Airborne Division Combat Narrative

The division air-assaulted into the Normandy France region 6 Jun 44 and secured the beach exits in the St Martin–de Varreville–Pouppeville area. The next day the 506th Prcht Inf moved south from Cauloville but was stopped near St Côme-dur-Mont. The division began the battle for Carentan on 8 Jun 44 and the 502nd Prcht Inf engaged in heavy combat on the causeway as envelopment operations continued 10 Jun 44. As the 502nd Prcht Inf and 327th Glider Inf moved to the outskirts of Carentan on 11 Jun 44 the German defenders withdrew, allowing the 506th Prcht Inf to seize it the following day. The division repulsed counterattacks and maintained its positions until relieved by the 83rd Inf Div on 27 Jun 44. It moved to Cherbourg and relieved the 4th Inf there 30 Jun 44. The division returned to England 13 Jul 44 for rehabilitation.

The division air-assaulted in Holland on 17 Sep 44 to seize the bridges at Veghel and Zon, north of Eindhoven. The former was captured but the Germans demolished the Zon Bridge as the paratroopers approached it. A footbridge was improvised at Zon and the division then advanced toward Eindhoven which it cleared the next day. It contacted the *British Guards Armd Div* but failed to take the bridge intact over the Wilhelmina Canal southeast of Best. The division contained counterattacks toward Zon on 19 Sep 44 and maintained its positions at Eindhoven, Zon, St Oedenrode and Veghel. After heavy combat the division advanced to take Schijndel 21 Sep 44 and forced the German defenders to withdraw from Veghel 22 Sep 44. The 506th Prcht Inf reopened the Veghel-Uden Highway on 23 Sep 44 which had been cut the previous day. It then forced the German defenders to abandon the Koevering roadblock on 25 Sep 44 in an enveloping attack. The division was relieved of its positions and withdrew to France for rehabilitation on 28 Nov 44.

The division was released from reserve 17 Dec 44 in response to the German Ardennes Counteroffensive, and arrived at Bastogne 19 Dec 44. There it established defensive lines as the city was encircled the next day. The division refused the German demand for surrender, although surrounded, on 22 Dec 44. It continued to hold its perimeter against repeated attacks. The 4th Armd Div reached the division lines on 26 Dec 44. The division continued to maintain its positions and on 9 Jan 45 the 506th Prcht Inf attacked out to take Recogne. The Bois Jacques was cleared after that, and by 13 Jan 45 the 506th Prcht Inf captured Foy as the 327th Glider Inf moved toward Bourcy. Neville fell to the 506th Prcht Inf 15 Jan 45, and moved on to seize Rachamps the following day as the 502nd Prcht Inf fought toward Bourcy. Bourcy and Hardigny were both taken by the division on 17 Jan 45. By 22 Jan 45 it closed in to the Drulingen-Sarraltroff area and by 26 Jan 45 moved into the Hochfelden zone. The following day the division assumed defensive lines along the Moder River.

The division was relieved by the 36th Inf Div on 25 Feb 45 and assembled at Mourmelon France for rehabilitation. It was then moved to the Ruhr Pocket on 31 Mar 45 and took over the 97th Inf Div sector 4 Apr 45. The division next moved to the Memmingen region 27 Apr 45 and on 30 Apr 45 was given the task of policing the Kaufbeuren-Saulgrub-Wertach-Kempten zone. It moved to the Miesbach area 1 May 45 and relieved the 4th Inf Div on 4 May 45. The division reached Berchtesgaden when hostilities were declared ended on 7 May 45.

102nd Infantry Division

No Distinctive Insignia Authorized

15 Sep 42 activated at Cp Maxey Tex and moved 16 Sep 43 to Third Army No.4 Louisiana Maneuvers; transferred to Cp Swift Tex 18 Nov 43 and arrived at Ft Dix N.J. 23 Jun 44; staged at Cp Kilmer N.J. 6 Sep 44 until departed New York P/E 12 Sep 44; arrived France 23 Sep 44; crossed into Belgium 31 Oct 44; crossed into Holland same date and entered Germany 29 Nov 44; returned to New York P/E 11 Mar 46 and inactivated at Cp Kilmer N.J. 12 Mar 46.

Campaigns: *Rhineland, Central Europe*
Aug 45 Loc: Gardelegen Germany

Typical Organization (1944/45):

405th Infantry Regiment
406th Infantry Regiment
407th Infantry Regiment
 HHB Division Artillery
379th Field Artillery Battalion (105mm)
380th Field Artillery Battalion (105mm)
381st Field Artillery Battalion (155mm)
927th Field Artillery Battalion (105mm)
102nd Reconnaissance Troop, Mecz
701st Tank Battalion *(attached 4 Apr 45–2 Jul 45)*
744th Tank Battalion *(attached 20 Dec 44–23 Dec 44)*
771st Tank Battalion *(attached 4 Nov 44–20 Dec 44)*
605th Tank Destroyer Battalion *(attached 15 Feb 45–2 Mar 45)*
771st Tank Destroyer Battalion *(attached 4 Nov 44–30 Mar 45, 10 Apr 45–17 Apr 45, 27 Apr 45–3 Jul 45)*
473rd AAA Auto-Wpns Battalion *(attached 8 Dec 44–9 Dec 44)*
548th AAA Auto-Wpns Battalion *(attached 11 Nov 44–25 Jun 45)*
556th AAA Auto-Wpns Battalion *(attached 2 Nov 44–11 Nov 44)*

327th Engineer Combat Battalion
327th Medical Battalion
102nd Counter Intelligence Corps Det
Headquarters, Special Troops
Hqs Company, 102nd Infantry Division
Military Police Platoon
802nd Ordnance Light Maintenance Company
102nd Quartermaster Company
102nd Signal Company

Overseas Wartime Assignments:

Ninth Army - 28 Aug 44
III Corps - 5 Sep 4
XVI Corps - 10 Oct 44

XIX Corps - 3 Nov 44
XIII Corps - 7 Nov 44

Commanders: MG John B. Anderson: Sep 42
MG Frank A. Keating: Jan 44

Killed in Action: 932   *Wounded in Action:* 3,668   *Died of Wounds:* 145

102nd Infantry Division Combat Narrative

The division arrived at Cherbourg France on 23 Sep 44 and trained near Valognes. The division entered combat in increments; the 405th Inf attached to 2nd Armd Div 26 Oct–3 Nov 44, the 406th Inf attached to the 30th Inf Div 25 Oct–6 Nov 44, and the 407th Inf attached to the 29th Inf Div 28 Oct–3 Nov 44. The 405th Inf was detached from the division until 2 Dec 44 and fought at Beeck. The division entered the line from the Wurm River to Waurichen on 3 Nov 44 and attacked toward the Roer River on 29 Nov 44. The 406th Inf took Linnich 1 Dec 44, and the 407th cleared Welz and took Flossdorf on 2 Dec 44. The division then consolidated along the Roer River and conducted defensive patrolling 4–19 Dec 44, when it took over the Wurm River sector from Wurm to Barmen and trained for river crossings. The division conducted a minor operation with the 11th Cav Group on 26 Jan 45 to clear the Brachelen-Himmerich-Randerath triangle west of the Roer against negligible resistance.

The division crossed the Roer at Roerdorf on 23 Feb 45 and by 25 Feb 45 the 405th Inf captured Ralshoven, the 406th Inf cleared Katzem, and the 407th Inf took Lovenich. Erkelenz fell the next day and on 27 Feb 45 the 407th Inf seized Rheindahlen. The 405th and 406th Inf overran Viersen and secured a bridgehead over the Niers Canal on 1 Mar 45 as the division bypassed Munchen-Gladbach, then battled through Krefeld 2–3 Mar 45 and reached the Rhine. During the rest of March the division defended its sector along the Rhine from Homburg south to Dusseldorf.

The division crossed the Rhine River at Wesel 3–4 Apr 45 and moved rapidly forward, mopping up resistance behind the 5th Armd Div toward the Weser River. The division crossed at Hameln on 9 Apr 45 as the 407th Inf was motored to begin clearing the Oberkirchen region east of the Weser. After clearing German opposition in the Wesergebirge with the fall of Wilsede and Hessich-Oldendorf on 12 Apr 45, the division advanced toward the Elbe River against little or no opposition. The division reached the Elbe, overtaking the armor, on 14 Apr 45 and relieved the 5th Armd Div along the river 16 Apr 45. It then outposted along the river and relieved the 35th Inf Div along the river on 26 Apr 45. It maintained defensive positions along the Elbe fifty miles from Berlin until hostilities were declared ended on 7 May 45.

103rd Infantry Division

No Distinctive
Insignia Authorized

15 Nov 42 activated at Cp Claiborne La and moved 17 Sep 43 to the Third Army No.4 Louisiana Maneuvers; transferred to Cp Howze Tex 22 Nov 43; staged at Cp Shanks N.Y. 24 Sep 44 until departed New York P/E Oct 44; arrived France 20 Oct 44 and entered Germany 23 Mar 45 and Austria 2 May 45; returned to New York P/E 18 Sep 45 and inactivated at Cp Kilmer N.J. 20 Sep 45.

Campaigns: *Rhineland, Ardennes-Alsace, Central Europe*
Aug 45 Loc: Innsbruck Austria

Typical Organization (1944/45):

409th Infantry Regiment	328th Engineer Combat Battalion
410th Infantry Regiment	328th Medical Battalion
411th Infantry Regiment	103rd Counter Intelligence Corps Det
HHB Division Artillery	Headquarters, Special Troops
382nd Field Artillery Battalion (105mm)	Hqs Company, 103rd Infantry Division
383rd Field Artillery Battalion (105mm)	Military Police Platoon
384th Field Artillery Battalion (155mm)	803rd Ordnance Light Maintenance Company
928th Field Artillery Battalion (105mm)	103rd Quartermaster Company
103rd Reconnaissance Troop, Mecz	103rd Signal Company

756th Tank Battalion *(attached 22 Feb 45–31 Mar 45)*
761st Tank Battalion *(attached 10 Mar 45–28 Mar 45)*
781st Tank Battalion *(attached 17 Jan 45–5 Feb 45, 23 Apr 45–5 May 45)*
614th Tank Destroyer Battalion *(attached 30 Apr 45–5 May 45)*
824th Tank Destroyer Battalion *(attached 24 Apr 45–5 May 45)*
354th AAA Auto-Wpns Battalion *(attached 29 Mar 45–9 May 45)*

Overseas Wartime Assignments:

Seventh Army - 1 Nov 44
VI Corps - 6 Nov 44
XV Corps - 22 Dec 44
XXI Corps - 9 Jan 45

VI Corps - 16 Jan 45
Seventh Army - 29 Mar 45
VI Corps - 19 Apr 45

Commanders: MG Charles G. Haffner Jr: Nov 42
MG Anthony C. McAuliffe: Jan 45
BG John N. Robinson: Aug 45

Killed in Action: 720   *Wounded in Action:* 3,329   *Died of Wounds:* 101

103rd Infantry Division Combat Narrative

The division arrived at Marseille France on 20 Oct 44 and relieved the 3rd Inf Div at Chevry 8–9 Nov 44. It attacked toward St Dié in the Vosges Mountains 16 Nov 44 and fought through strong opposition to clear the hill mass below the town, crossed the Meurthe River 20–21 Nov 44, and took the evacuated objective of St Dié the next day with the 409th Inf. The division then outflanked Steige Pass 23–24 Nov 44, and followed in the wake of the 14th Armd Div toward Sélestat which it helped clear in house-to-house fighting 2–4 Dec 44. The division crossed the Zintzel River at Griesbach 10 Dec 44 as it fought the Battle of Mertzwiller, overcame rearguard resistance at Climbach, and crossed the Lauter River into Germany on 15 Dec 44. The division was then relocated to the Sarreguemines area to defend against the German Ardennes Counteroffensive which never reached its sector. On 14 Jan 45 the division moved to Reichshofen to take over the zone of Task Force Herren (70th Inf Div) along the Sauer River which was accomplished 17 Jan 45. A limited attack by the division at Soufflenheim was repulsed 19 Jan 45, and in view of German force concentrations it withdrew to the Moder River.

The German attacks of 22 Jan 45 forced the division from Offwiller, and the next day the division was pushed back past Rothbach. Further German attacks on Bischoltz and Mulhausen were defeated 24–25 Jan 45, and by 26 Jan 45 the division had cleared Schillersdorf and restored its lines. The division then took over the zone of the 101st A/B Div 5 Feb 45.

The division went on the offensive 15 Mar 45 and the next day took Zinswiller and Oberbronn and reached the outskirts of Reichshoffen which fell 17 Mar 45. The division fought the Battle for Nieder Schlettenbach 18–20 Mar 45 and the Battle for Reisdorf 19–21 Mar 45. The division reached Klingenmuenster and mopped up west of the Rhine River from 22 Mar 45 until it relieved the 71st Inf Div along the Rhine from Oppau to south of Speyer 28–29 Mar 45. It then engaged in occupational duty until returned to the front.

The division started its offensive from Kirchheim on 21 Apr 45 as it followed the advance of the 10th Armd Div and cleared bypassed resistance. By 23 Apr 45 it had closed the German escape routes southeast from Stuttgart, and reached the Danube northeast of Ulm on 25 Apr 45 which it crossed the next day. Continuing to follow the 10th Armd Div the 411th Inf took Landsberg, the 410th Inf reached the Lech River at Lechbruck, and the 409th Inf cleared Schongau on 28 Apr 45. The division began negotiations for the surrender of Innsbruck on 2 May 45 as the 409th Inf continued on to reach the Inn River at Telf and Zirl the following day. On 4 May 45 the division accepted the formal surrender of Innsbruck, as the 409th Inf moved to the Brenner Pass and effected junction with Fifth Army forces from Italy. All hostilities ceased in the division's sector on 5 May 45 with the surrender of German forces in southern Germany.

104th Infantry Division

No Distinctive
Insignia Authorized

15 Sep 42 activated at Cp Adair Oreg and moved 7 Aug 43 to the IV Corps No.1 Oregon Maneuvers; participated 10 Nov 43 in the Desert Training Center No.4 California Maneuvers; transferred to Cp Carson Colo 11 Mar 44; staged at Cp Kilmer N.J. 16 Aug 44 until departed New York P/E 27 Aug 44; arrived France 7 Sep 44 and crossed into Belgium 21 Oct 44 and into Holland 30 Oct 44; entered Germany 7 Nov 44; returned to New York P/E 3 Jul 45 and arrived Cp San Luis Obispo Calif 9 Jul 45 where inactivated on 20 Dec 45.

Campaigns: *Northern France, Rhineland, Central Europe*
Aug 45 Loc: Camp San Luis Obispo California

Typical Organization (1944/45):

413th Infantry Regiment
414th Infantry Regiment
415th Infantry Regiment
 HHB Division Artillery
385th Field Artillery Battalion (105mm)
386th Field Artillery Battalion (105mm)
387th Field Artillery Battalion (155mm)
929th Field Artillery Battalion (105mm)
104th Reconnaissance Troop, Mecz
750th Tank Battalion *(attached 16 Nov 44-23 Dec 44, 6 Feb 45-22 May 45)*
784th Tank Battalion *(attached 31 Dec 44-3 Feb 45)*
692nd Tank Destroyer Battalion *(attached 29 Oct 44-7 Mar 45)*
817th Tank Destroyer Battalion *(attached 1 Apr 45-9 Jun 45)*
555th AAA Auto-Wpns Battalion *(attached 26 Oct 44-24 May 45)*

329th Engineer Combat Battalion
329th Medical Battalion
104th Counter Intelligence Corps Det
Headquarters, Special Troops
Hqs Company, 104th Infantry Division
Military Police Platoon
804th Ordnance Light Maintenance Company
104th Quartermaster Company
104th Signal Company

Overseas Wartime Assignments:

Ninth Army - 28 Aug 44
III Corps - 5 Sep 44
Ninth Army - 15 Oct 44
First Army - 5 Nov 44

VII Corps - 8 Nov 44
XIX Corps - 22 Dec 44
VII Corps - 3 Feb 45

Commanders: MG Gilbert R. Cook: Jun 42
MG Terry de la Mesa Allen: Oct 43
BG Charles K. Gailey Jr: Nov 45

Killed in Action: 971   *Wounded in Action:* 3,657   *Died of Wounds:* 143

104th Infantry Division Combat Narrative

The division arrived in France on 7 Sep 44 and moved into the line with *Canadian First Army* along the Antwerp-Breda Highway near Wuestwezel Belgium on 23 Oct 44. It attacked on 25 Oct 44 with three regiments abreast and stormed Zundert with the assistance of British tanks on 27 Oct 44. The 415th Inf reached the Mark River 30 Oct 44, failed in its first crossing attempt the next day, and then assaulted across after heavy artillery preparation on 2 Nov 44 and established a bridgehead in the Standdaarbuiten area. Zevenbergen was captured and the division reached the Maas River 5 Nov 44, departing for Aachen the next day while leaving elements to fight at Moerdijk with the *Polish 1st Armd Div* 6-7 Nov 44.

The division relieved the 1st Inf Div 8-10 Nov 44 and attacked toward the Donnersberg and Eschweiler Woods against heavy opposition on 16 Nov 44. The division fought the Battle for the Donnersberg 16-18 Nov 44 and then battled through the Eschweiler-Weisweiler industrial complex north of the Inde River 19-25 Nov 44, which was secured with the fall of Weisweiler after house-to-house fighting on the latter date. The division then mopped up and reached the Inden River 28 Nov 44, taking the bridge at Inden intact, and fighting the Battle for Lammersdorf 28-30 Nov 44 and the Battle for Inden 28 Nov-2 Dec 44. The division crossed the Inden River at Lucherberg by surprise attack on 2 Dec 44 and established a bridgehead which was subjected to strong German counterattacks 3-5 Dec 44. The division renewed its offensive 10 Dec 44 to clear the west bank of the Roer, and the 414th Inf fought the Battle for Pier 10-12 Dec 44 while the 415th Inf took Merken 11 Dec 44. The division reached the Roer River 13 Dec 44, and defended the Inden-Pier-Schophoven region until 24 Dec 44 when relieved and took over the 83rd Inf Div zone. It was engaged in defensive positions near Duren and Merken until 22 Feb 45.

The division attacked across the Roer 23 Feb 45 with the 415th Inf at Huchem and Stammeln and the 413th Inf at Birkesdorf, which mopped up Dueren as it captured the marshaling yards northeast of the city the following day. The 415th Inf fought the Battle for Arnoldsweiler 24-25 Feb 45, and then the division followed behind the 3rd Armd Div clearing bypassed resistance. It relieved the armor on the Erft River at Sindorf 28 Feb 45. The 413th and 414th Inf assaulted across the Erft Canal on 1 Mar 45 and overran Ichendorf and then defended the bridgehead against German counterattack. In heavy combat the division fought the Battle for Cologne 3-7 Mar 45, after which it took over the 8th Inf Div zone 8-14 Mar 45 and maintained defensive positions along the Rhine. It relieved the 3rd Armd Div also along the Rhine 16-17 Mar 45.

The division crossed the Rhine at Honnef 21–22 Mar 45 and attacked east of the Remagen Bridgehead, the 413th Inf overrunning the airfield east of Eudenbach the following day. After mopping up and consolidating, the division began the offensive against the Ruhr Pocket 25 Mar 45 and followed the 3rd Armd Div to eliminate scattered resistance. The division repulsed strong German attacks near Medebach and captured Paderborn 1 Apr 45 and took Rimbeck the next day. The 415th Inf fought the Battle for Kuestelberg 2–3 Apr 45 and the 413th Inf cleared Forst Hardehausen 4 Apr 45. The division regrouped the next day and then moved to the Weser River. The 415th Inf crossed the Weser at Bursfelde 7 Apr 45 and the 413th Inf crossed at Gieselwerder the following day. The division moved into blocking positions around the Harz Mountains until it crossed the Salle River and fought the Battle for Halle, which finally fell after house-to-house fighting 14–19 Apr 45. The 415th Inf captured Bitterfeld 20–21 Apr 45 and the division reached the Mulde River on the latter date. The division made contact with advancing Soviet Army forces at Pretzsch on 26 Apr 45.

106th Infantry Division

No Distinctive
Insignia Authorized

15 Mar 43 activated at Ft Jackson S.C. and moved 24 Jan 44 to Second Army No.5 Tennessee Maneuvers; transferred to Cp Atterbury Ind 28 Mar 44; staged at Cp Myles Standish Mass 10 Oct 44 until departed Boston P/E 10 Nov 44; arrived England 17 Nov 44 and landed in France 6 Dec 44; crossed into Belgium 10 Dec 44 and returned to France 16 Mar 45; entered Germany 25 Apr 45; arrived New York P/E 1 Oct 45 and inactivated at Cp Shanks N.Y. 2 Oct 45.

Campaigns: *Rhineland, Ardennes-Alsace, Central Europe*
Aug 45 Loc: Bad Ems Germany

Typical Organization (1944):

422nd Infantry Regiment*	81st Engineer Combat Battalion
423rd Infantry Regiment*	331st Medical Battalion
424th Infantry Regiment	106th Counter Intelligence Corps Det
HHB Division Artillery	Headquarters, Special Troops
589th Field Artillery Battalion (105mm)	Hqs Company, 106th Infantry Division
590th Field Artillery Battalion (105mm)	Military Police Platoon
591st Field Artillery Battalion (105mm)	806th Ordnance Light Maintenance Company
592nd Field Artillery Battalion (155mm)	106th Quartermaster Company
106th Reconnaissance Troop, Mecz	106th Signal Company
820th Tank Destroyer Battalion *(attached 8 Dec 44–4 Jan 45)*	
440th AAA Auto-Wpns Battalion *(attached 17 Dec 44–25 Dec 44)*	
563rd AAA Auto-Wpns Battalion *(attached 9 Dec 44–18 Dec 44)*	
634th AAA Auto-Wpns Battalion *(attached 8 Dec 44–18 Dec 44)*	

*Destroyed in Schnee Eifel salient 19 Dec 44 near Schonberg; rebuilt in France but did not rejoin division until 16 May 45.

Typical Organization (1945):

3rd Infantry Regiment*	81st Engineer Combat Battalion
159th Infantry Regiment*	331st Medical Battalion
424th Infantry Regiment	106th Counter Intelligence Corps Det
HHB Division Artillery	Headquarters, Special Troops
589th Field Artillery Battalion (105mm)	Hqs Company, 106th Infantry Division
590th Field Artillery Battalion (105mm)	Military Police Platoon
591st Field Artillery Battalion (105mm)	806th Ordnance Light Maintenance Company
592nd Field Artillery Battalion (155mm)	106th Quartermaster Company
106th Reconnaissance Troop, Mecz	106th Signal Company

*Attached to division 16 Mar 45–past 9 May 45 to replace 422nd, 423rd Inf Regts.

Overseas Wartime Assignments:

VIII Corps - 29 Nov 44	Fifteenth Army - 10 Mar 45
XVIII (A/B) Corps - 20 Dec 44	Advanced Section, Communications Zone
V Corps - 6 Feb 45	*(attached)* - 15 Apr 45

Commanders: MG Alan W. Jones: Mar 43
BG Herbert T. Perrin: Dec 44
MG Donald A. Stroh: Feb 45

Killed in Action: 417   *Wounded in Action:* 1,278   *Died of Wounds:* 53   *Prisoners:* 6,697**

**6,500 eventually returned to military control after being captured in the German Ardennes Counteroffensive.

106th Infantry Division Combat Narrative

The division landed in France on 6 Dec 44 and replaced the 2nd Inf Div in the Schnee Eifel sector of Belgium on 11 Dec 44. The German Ardennes Counteroffensive struck the division on 16 Dec 44, the 424th Inf being at Winterspelt and the 422nd and 423rd Inf Regts being in the Schnee Eifel salient. Both 422nd and 423rd Inf surrendered on 19 Dec 44 after being encircled in their area near Schonberg the previous day. The 424th Inf was pushed back across the Our River, losing most of its equipment, and joined other divisional remnants to hold St Vith 20–21 Dec 44, being reinforced by the 112th Inf of 28th Inf Div 19–23 Dec 44. From 24 to 30 Dec 44 the 424th Inf was attached to the 7th Armd Div and participated in heavy combat around Manhay, and then was withdrawn to Anthisnes Belgium. The 424th Inf took over defense of the Wanne-Wanneranval region 9 Jan 45 and the division had a second regiment attached, the separate 517th Prcht Inf, 11–17 Jan 45. On 15 Jan 45 the division consolidated and cleared Ennal. It then assembled at Stavelot on 18 Jan 45 and the 424th Inf was again attached to the 7th Armd Div 23–28 Jan 45 where it fought at Meyerode and around St Vith. The division moved to Hunnigen 7 Feb 45 and the 424th Inf was attached to the 99th Inf Div 5–9 Feb 45. The 424th Inf then advanced along the high ground between the Berk and Simmer River until it reached Olds on 7 Mar 45. It was then sent for rehabilitation and the division given a security mission along the Rhine River until 15 Mar 45, when the division was withdrawn to St Quentin to be rebuilt.

The division was reconstituted 16 Mar 45 when the 3rd Inf and 159th Inf were attached to replace its surrendered regiments. It then moved back into Germany 25 Apr 45, but was relegated to duty processing prisoners and performing military occupation of secure areas. The 422nd and 423rd Inf were newly formed in France from replacements and attached to the 66th Inf Div for training purposes 15 Apr 45, and were still in this capacity when hostilities were declared ended on 7 May 45.

American Division

No Distinctive Insignia Authorized

24 May 42 organized on New Caledonia from units assigned to Task Force 6814 and mobile command forces stationed on islands to include 70th Coast Artillery Regt; I Island Command organized about 10–18 Nov 42 to relieve division of responsibility for such elements not scheduled to Guadalcanal; division arrived Guadalcanal by echelon 12 Nov–8 Dec 42 (Hqs arrived latter date); moved by echelon to Fiji Islands 1 Mar–10 Apr 43 (Hqs arrived 29 Mar 43); division reorganized there 1 May 43 and HHC 51st Inf Brigade redesignated HHC American Division 1 May 43 and Task Force 6814 concurrently disbanded; Special Troops activated 1 Oct 43; division moved by echelon to Bougainville 17 Dec 43–12 Jan 44 (Hqs arrived 12 Jan 44); moved by echelon to Leyte Philippine Islands 8–28 Jan 45 (Hqs arrived 26 Jan 45); division moved to Cebu Philippines 26 Mar 45; arrived Japan 8 Sep 45; arrived Seattle P/E 9 Dec 45 and inactivated at Ft Lawton Wash 12 Dec 45.

Campaigns: *Guadalcanal, Northern Solomons, Leyte, Southern Philippines*
Aug 45 Loc: Cebu Island Philippines

Typical Organization (1944/45):

132nd Infantry Regiment
164th Infantry Regiment
182nd Infantry Regiment
HHB Division Artillery
221st Field Artillery Battalion (155mm)
245th Field Artillery Battalion (105mm)
246th Field Artillery Battalion (105mm)
247th Field Artillery Battalion (105mm)
21st Reconnaissance Troop, Mecz

57th Engineer Combat Battalion
121st Medical Battalion
182nd Counter Intelligence Corps Det
Headquarters, Special Troops
Hqs Company, American Division
Military Police Platoon
721st Ordnance Light Maintenance Company
125th Quartermaster Company
26th Signal Company

Overseas Wartime Assignments:

United States War Department - 24 May 42
U.S. Army Forces South Pacific - 26 Jul 42
XIV Corps - 2 Jan 43
II Island Command *(attached)* - 29 Mar 43
XIV Corps *(attached)* - 15 Dec 43
XIV Corps - 14 Jun 44

U.S. Army Forces Northern Solomons - 15 Nov 44
Eighth Army - 22 Jan 45
X Corps *(attached)* - 1 Feb 45
Eighth Army Area Cmd *(attached)* - 24 Feb 45
Eighth Army - 11 Mar 45
XI Corps - 1 Jul 45

Commanders: MG Alexander M. Patch: May 42
BG Edmund B. Sebree: Jan 43
MG John R. Hodge: May 43

MG Robert B. McClure: Apr 44
MG William H. Arnold: Nov 44

Killed in Action: 981   *Wounded in Action:* 3,052   *Died of Wounds:* 176

Americal Division Combat Narrative

The Americal Division had its origin in Task Force 6814 which was formed 14 Jan 42 with the mission of occupying and defending New Caledonia, and departed New York on 23 Jan 42. The force landed in Australia 26 Feb 42 and was sent to New Caledonia 6 Mar 42, arriving there 12 Mar 42 and establishing Hqs at Noumea. There the force organized the defenses and built installations on New Caledonia and New Hebrides. The Americal Division was organized from Task Force 6814 units on 27 May 42, its name being a contraction of the words "America" and "New Caledonia." The 164th Inf left for Guadalcanal 9 Oct 42 and arrived there under air attack on 13 Oct 42. The regiment defended Henderson Field against a major Japanese counterattack 24 Oct 42, and then attacked 5–11 Nov 42 participating in the Battle at Koli Point and Gavaga Creek. The 182nd Inf arrived on Guadalcanal 12 Nov 42 and participated in the renewed offensive toward Kokumbona and Poha River 18–23 Nov 42. The division Hqs and 132nd Inf landed on Guadalcanal 8 Dec 42; the latter attacking Mt Austen 17 Dec 42 and engaged in very heavy combat at the Gifu Strongpoint 24 Dec 42–9 Jan 43, when relieved in line by the 25th Inf Div. On 16 Jan 43 the 182nd Inf participated in the drive along the west coast, and on 1 Feb 43 the 132nd Inf landed at Verahue and reached Tenaro Village by 9 Feb 43. The division then occupied defensive positions and moved to the Fiji Islands in echelon 1 Mar–10 Apr 43. There the division was reorganized as the HHC of 51st Inf Bde was redesignated the HHC of Americal Div and Task Force 6814 was disbanded 1 May 43.

The division moved to Bougainville 17 Dec 43–12 Jan 44, the 182nd Inf entering the front line 2 Jan 44 and the 132nd Inf entering 9 Jan 44. A Japanese counterattack 10 Mar 44 took the south knob of key Hill 260 from the 182nd Inf and it wasn't recovered until the Japanese abandoned it on 15 Mar 44. In Apr 44 the division pushed east of the Mavavia River and secured Hill Masses 165, 155, 500, and 501 and extended the outpost line past the Torokina River. The division continued patrolling in the Torokina, Numa Numa, and Laruma sectors until relieved by the *Australian 3rd Div* on 10 Dec 44. From 11 Dec 44–7 Jan 45 the division conducted amphibious training and prepared for movement to the Philippines.

The division moved to the Philippines by echelon 8–28 Jan 45 where it relieved the 77th Inf Div on Leyte Island and established a command post at Capoocan 25 Jan 45. The division took control of the tactical mission on Leyte northwest of the Jaro-Valencia-Palompon line on 5 Feb 45 and began pushing toward the west coast of the island. On 19 Feb 45 the 1st Bn 182nd Inf landed on northwest Samar as a provisional task force and cleared the San Bernardino Strait from northwest Samar through Balicuatros Islands and west to Capul and Naranjo Islands by 26 Feb 45. Meanwhile, the division opened its attack at Villaba on Leyte and completed its encirclement of the Japanese in the northwest coastal sector and mopped up until 10 Mar 45.

The 1st Bn 132nd Inf landed on Burias and Ticao Islands 3 Mar 45, meeting opposition on the former on 6 Mar 45 and eliminating the Japanese forces there by 10 Mar 45. While the 164th Inf continued to mop up in western Leyte under Eighth Army, the rest of the division prepared for operations on Cebu Island. On 10 Apr 45 the 164th Inf rejoined the division from its mission. The division left Leyte 24 Mar 45, and after a one-hour naval bombardment, the division landed at Talisay Cebu and took Cebu City the next day. The 182nd Inf fought the Battle of Go Chan Hill 28–29 Mar 45 and then battled to clear the other hills, being counterattacked heavily on Bolo Ridge 1 Apr 45. The 132nd Inf was counterattacked approaching Hill 27 on 7 Apr 45, but took both Hills 20 and 26 by 10 Apr 45. The 3rd Bn 164th Inf landed on Bohol Island 11 Apr 45 and destroyed Japanese forces there by 25 Apr 45. Meanwhile the division on Cebu fought the Battle of Babay Ridge 12–17 Apr 45, and then continued combat on the island until 20 Jun 45. The 164th Inf landed near Looc on Negros Oriental Island on 26 Apr 45 and fought the Battle for the Palimpinon Heights until 28 May 45, the Japanese forces being destroyed on the island near Balasbalas 7–12 Jun 45. The division then reassembled on Cebu Island and engaged in training for the invasion of Japan from 21 Jun 45 until the end of the war.

Composite Army-Marine Division (CAM)

No Distinctive
Insignia Authorized

The Composite Army-Marine Division was merely a convenient term for the force formed by Marine and Army units during the Jan 43 drive to the west on Guadalcanal. It consisted of the 6th Marines, 147th Inf, 182nd Inf, artillery of the American and 2nd Marine Division, and the 2nd Marine Division staff also serving as the CAM Division staff. The name first appeared in a XIV Corps Field Order on 25 Jan 43, but the division itself had no administrative identity.

Campaigns: *Guadalcanal*

Composite Army-Marine Division Combat Narrative

The CAM Division was formed in the area facing high ground immediately south of Kokumbona Guadalcanal in January 1943. It opened a full-scale attack on 22 Jan 43 with the 6th Marines on the right, the 147th Inf in the center, and the 182nd Inf on the left, with naval gunfire support. In close combat the division cleared a ravine west of Hill 94 which had initially halted the advance, and by 24 Jan 43 linked up with the 25th Inf Div on the high ground above Kokumbona. After reaching the Poha River the division was ordered into pursuit operations. It opened this final offensive on 26 Jan 43 and advanced rapidly along the narrow coastal corridor against slight opposition. The division fought the Battle of Bonegi River 30 Jan–2 Feb 43 and then continued to the Umasami River northwest of Tassafaronga Point on 5 Feb 43. Evacuation of the Japanese forces had been completed 7–8 Feb 43 and the campaign for Guadalcanal terminated 9 Feb 43. The CAM Division was then discontinued.

Philippine Division

No Distinctive
Insignia Authorized

Stationed at Ft Mckinley Philippine Islands and surrendered to Japanese forces at Bataan Philippines 9 Apr 42.

Campaigns: *Philippine Islands*

Typical Organization (1941):

31st Infantry Regiment
45th Infantry Regiment (PS)
57th Infantry Regiment (PS)
12th Field Artillery Brigade, HHB
23rd Field Artillery (PS) (one battalion)
24th Field Artillery (PS) (two battalions)
12th Quartermaster Regiment (PS)
12th Signal Company (PS)

14th Engineers (PS)
Headquarters
Headquarters and Headquarters Det
Hqs Company, Philippine Division
12th Medical Regiment (PS) (partial)
12th Military Police Company (PS)
 4th Veterinary Company (PS)
12th Ordnance Company (PS)

Overseas Wartime Assignments:

U.S. Army Forces in the Far East - 8 Dec 41
Bataan Defense Force - 24 Dec 41
U.S. Army Forces in the Far East - 6 Jan 42
II Philippine Corps - 26 Jan 42
I Philippine Corps - 7 Apr 42

Commanders: MG Jonathan M. Wainwright: Nov 40
BG Maxwell S. Lough: Dec 41

Killed in Action: Undetermined   *Wounded in Action:* Undetermined   *Died of Wounds:* Unknown

Philippine Division Combat Narrative

The division was stationed at Fort McKinley Luzon Philippines as part of U.S. Army Forces in the Far East (USAFFE) Reserve on 8 Dec 41 and instructed to prepare defensive positions at Bamban-Arayat. It moved to Clark Field 10 Dec 41 in response to a false report that Japanese paratroopers had landed there, and then was moved to the Subic Bay area. It organized defensive positions there and then the division command post was relocated to Abucay on 14 Dec 41 and on 24 Dec 41 became a subordinate command of the Bataan Defense Force. The 31st Inf moved to the vicinity of Zig-Zag to cover forces withdrawing from central and southern Luzon, and the 57th Inf was moved to cover the Calumpit Bridges over the Pampanga River on the Gueagera-Porac Line. The division then organized the main and reserve positions on Bataan Peninsula, the division headquarters being located to KP 137.5 on Pilar-Bagac Road 25 Dec 41. The 31st Inf moved to the west side of the Olongapo Road near Layac Junction 3–5 Jan 42 and held the position until 7 Jan 42, losing Company E and most guns of the 23rd FA during the engagement.

The division headquarters moved to Damalog Trail, 2 miles west of East Road on 5 Jan 42. The 57th Inf on the main battle line near Abucay had its outpost line driven in on 9 Jan 42, and on 12 Jan 42 was subjected to a main Japanese attack which breached its lines. The positions were restored by counterattack, and the next day another main attack pierced the lines and again a counterattack restored them. The division was reverted to U.S. Army Forces in the Far East Reserve on 6 Jan 42 and established its advance command post near KP 144 on the Pilar-Bagac Road 15 Jan 42. A Japanese breakthrough in the 51st Div (PA) sector was counterattacked by the 31st and 45th Inf on 16 Jan 42, the counterattacking forces suffering a series of mishaps and after five days of continual combat were defeated with heavy losses. The division withdrew to the Reserve Battle Line in the Pilar-Bagac area on 26 Jan 42 as a result.

The division was assigned to II Philippine Corps on 26 Jan 42 and placed in command of Sub-Sector D of the corps area and its infantry regiments detached. The division headquarters was located at the south end of Trail 44-A, southeast of Mt Samat. The division units countered Japanese patrol activities and limited objective attacks from 27 Jan–27 Mar 42, participating in the Battle of the Points and the reduction of the Toul Pocket. The major Japanese attack of 28 Mar 42 struck the division which was no longer able to coordinate counterattacks. The 31st and 45th Inf both counterattacked on 6 Apr 42 but were unsuccessful, sustained very heavy losses, and were forced back to the Mamala River. The remnants of the 57th Inf were unable to link up with the 45th Inf, and the 31st Inf was destroyed as a combat entity. The division was assigned to I Philippine Corps 7 Apr 42, and on 8 Apr 42 the 57th Inf was lost on the Alangan River. The rest of the division, to include the 45th Inf, surrendered on 9 Apr 42.

1st Airborne Task Force (Provisional Seventh Army Airborne Division)

No Distinctive
Insignia Authorized

15 Jul 44 organized near Rome Italy to control air-assault forces scheduled to invade southern France; air-assaulted southern France 15 Aug 44; discontinued in France 23 Nov 44.

Campaigns: *Southern France, Rhineland*

Typical Organization (1944):

HHC, 1st Airborne Task Force
British 2nd Independent Parachute Brigade
517th Parachute Infantry Regiment
1st Battalion, 551st Parachute Infantry Regt
509th Parachute Infantry Battalion
550th Airborne Infantry Battalion (Glider)
460th Parachute Field Artillery Battalion
463rd Parachute Field Artillery Battalion
602nd Field Artillery Battalion (75mm Pack)
645th Tank Destroyer Battalion
British 64th Light Artillery Battalion
1st Special Service Force*

596th Airborne Engineer Company
887th Airborne Engineer Aviation Company
512th Airborne Signal Company
676th Medical Collecting Company
334th Quartermaster Depot Supply Company
Provisional Airborne Military Police Platoon
Provisional Pathfinder Detachment
Co A, 2nd Chemical Mortar Battalion
Co A, 83rd Chemical Mortar Battalion
Antitank Company, 442nd Infantry Regt
British Allied Air Supply Base
British 1st Independent Parachute Platoon

*Attached 22 Aug 44 to replace the *British 2nd Prcht Bde* and later assigned.

Overseas Wartime Assignments:

Seventh Army - 15 Jul 44
VI Corps - 15 Aug 44

Seventh Army - 20 Aug 44
6th Army Group - 15 Oct 44

Commander: MG Robert T. Frederick

1st Airborne Task Force Combat Narrative

8 Jul 44 formed in Italy as the Seventh Army Airborne Division (Provisional) and organized 15 Jul 44 as the 1st Airborne Task Force, and commenced training near Rome Italy on 20 Jul 44. As RUGBY Force, it air-assaulted the French Mediterranean coast in the Le Muy–Le Luc area 15 Aug 44 to block German access to the invasion beaches. Le Muy was taken the following day as the force consolidated and made contact with the 36th Inf Div 17 Aug 44.

The Task Force became responsible for the Fayence–La Napoule line on 20 Aug 44 and began clearing the region around La Napoule in the coast sector the next day and advanced on Cannes. The 509th Prcht Inf Bn, followed by the 1st Bn, 551st Prcht Inf, occupied Cannes without opposition 24 Aug 44 as the 1st Special Service Force seized both Grasse and Valbonne and then linked up in the Cannes area. The Task Force crossed the Var River 29 Aug 44 and drove through Nice to Beaulieu without opposition on 30 Aug 44. It then cleared a strongpoint at La Turbia on 2 Sep 44 and pushed through Menton to the Italian border 8 Sep 44. The Task Force was then assigned defensive positions in the Alps along the Franco-Italian border.

Part III

Infantry of the U.S. Army
in World War II

Chapter 12

Infantry Brigades

Brigades:

1 Special Service Force, 1 A/B, 2 A/B, 1–6, 8, 10, 12, 14, 16, 18, 21–23, 51–76, 79–82, 85–90, 92, 5332 (Prov), Provisional Parachute Group

1st Special Service Force

9 Jul 42 activated at Ft William Harrison Montana as a joint U.S.-Canadian unit composed of a service battalion and three small regiments specially trained in airborne, amphibious, mountain, and winter commando tactics and drawn from elite volunteers; moved to Cp Bradford Vermont 15 Apr 43 and to Ft Ethan Allen Vermont on 23 May 43; arrived San Francisco P/E 4 Jul 43 and departed 10 Jul 43; arrived in the Aleutian Islands 25 Jul 43 and landed on evacuated Kiska Island 15 Aug 43 and Segula Island 17 Aug 43; arrived at Cp Stoneman Calif 1 Sep 43 and returned to Ft Ethan Allen Vermont 9 Sep 43; staged at Cp Patrick Henry Va 20 Oct 43 until departed Hampton Roads P/E 27 Oct 43; arrived at Casablanca North Africa 5 Nov 43 and landed at Naples Italy 19 Nov 43 and went into line at Santa Maria with the 36th Inf Div; attacked well-defended Monte la Difensa 3–6 Dec 43 and Monte la Remetanea 6–9 Dec 43; took Hill 720 (M.Sammucro) 25 Dec 43 and battled up M.Vischiataro 8 Jan 44; landed at Anzio Italy 2 Feb 44 where deployed along the Mussolini Canal until 10 May 44; fought at M.Arrestino 25 May 44 and at Rocca Massima 27 May 44; took Colle Ferro 2 Jun 44 and entered Rome 4 Jun 44; invaded the Iles d'Hyeres off southern France 14 Aug 44 and took Grasse 27 Aug 44; fought at Vence 1 Sep 44 and was at Mentone 7 Sep 44 when deployed to the Italian-Franco border; remained there until 30 Nov 44 and inactivated in France on 5 Dec 44.

Campaigns: *Aleutian Islands, Naples-Foggia, Anzio, Rome-Arno, Southern France, Rhineland*

1st Airborne Infantry Brigade

20 Jul 42 activated at Ft Benning Ga as the 1st Parachute Infantry Brigade which supervised the training of attached parachute units under the Airborne Command; moved to Ft Meade S.D. on 6 Apr 43 where redesignated the 1st Airborne Infantry Brigade on 6 Jul 43; participated in the Airborne Command Maneuvers at Alliance Nebr 1–15 Aug 43 and transferred to Ft Bragg N.C. 4 Dec 43; arrived at Cp Mackall N.C. 16 Dec 43 where inactivated on 27 Jan 44.

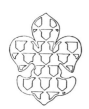

1st Infantry Brigade

Stationed at Ft Wadsworth N.Y. assigned to 1st Division where inactivated on 11 Oct 39.

2nd Airborne Infantry Brigade

20 Jun 43 activated at Cp Mackall N.C. and arrived in northern Ireland 8 Jan 44 where the two parachute infantry regiments planned for its use, the 501st and 508th, were transferred to control of the 101st and 82nd Airborne Divisions respectively; brigade HHC placed under the 82nd Airborne Division where it served until inactivation on 15 Jan 45.

Campaigns: *Normandy, Rhineland*

2nd Infantry Brigade

Stationed at Ft Ontario N.Y. assigned to 1st Division and relieved from assignment on 16 Oct 39; moved to Pierrepont N.Y. 29 Mar 40 and returned to Ft Ontario N.Y. 1 Jun 40 where inactivated the same date.

3rd Infantry Brigade

Stationed at Ft Sam Houston Tex assigned to 2nd Division where inactivated on 9 Oct 39.

4th Infantry Brigade

Stationed at Ft Francis E. Warren Wyo assigned to 2nd Division where inactivated 16 Oct 39.

5th Infantry Brigade

Stationed at Vancouver Barracks Wash assigned to 3rd Division where inactivated 16 Oct 39.

6th Infantry Brigade

Stationed at Ft Douglas Ariz assigned to 3rd Division where inactivated 12 Oct 39.

8th Infantry Brigade

Stationed at Ft McPherson Ga assigned to 4th Division and moved to Ft Benning Ga 8 Apr 40; returned to Ft McPherson Ga 28 Apr 40 and inactivated there on 22 Jun 40.

10th Infantry Brigade

Stationed at Ft Benjamin Harrison assigned to 5th Division where inactivated 10 Oct 39.

12th Infantry Brigade

Stationed at Ft Sheridan Ill assigned to 6th Division where inactivated 2 Oct 39.

14th Infantry Brigade

Stationed at Ft Snelling Minn assigned to 7th Division and moved to Cp Joseph T. Robinson Ark 4 Nov 40; returned to Ft Snelling Minn 17 Feb 40 and inactivated there on 1 Jun 40.

16th Infantry Brigade

Stationed at Ft George G. Meade Md assigned to 8th Division where inactivated 1 Jul 40.

18th Infantry Brigade

Stationed at Boston Mass assigned to 9th Division; departed United States 21 Oct 39 and arrived Ft William D. Davis Panama Canal Zone on 27 Oct 39 where inactivated 15 Jul 40.

21st Infantry Brigade

Stationed at Schofield Barracks Hawaii assigned to Hawaiian Division and disbanded 1 Oct 41.

22nd Infantry Brigade

Stationed at Schofield Barracks Hawaii assigned to Hawaiian Division and disbanded 1 Oct 41.

23rd Infantry Brigade

Stationed at Ft William McKinley Philippine Islands assigned to the Philippine Division where inactivated 19 Apr 41.

51st Infantry Brigade   Massachusetts National Guard

16 Jan 41 inducted into federal service at Quincy Mass assigned to the 26th Division and moved to Cp Edwards Mass 25 Jan 41; departed New York P/E 23 Jan 42 and relieved from assignment to the 26th Division; arrived New Caledonia 26 Feb 42 and departed 22 Nov 42; landed on Guadalcanal 26 Nov 42 where served until 24 Mar 43; arrived in Fiji Islands 29 Mar 43 where Hq & Hq Company redesignated Hq & Hq Company Americal Division on 1 May 43.

Campaigns: *Guadalcanal*

52nd Infantry Brigade   Massachusetts National Guard

16 Jan 41 inducted into federal service at Worcester Mass assigned to the 26th Division and moved to Cp Edwards Mass 25 Jan 41 where Hq disbanded on 12 Feb 42 and Hq Company redesignated 26th Reconnaissance Troop, 28th Division.

53rd Infantry Brigade   New York National Guard

15 Oct 40 inducted into federal service at Albany N.Y. assigned to the 27th Division and moved to Ft McClellan Ala 25 Oct 40; transferred to Riverside Calif 21 Dec 41 and to Ft Ord Calif 22 Jan 42; departed San Francisco P/E 10 Mar 42 and arrived Hawaii 21 Mar 42; there Hq disbanded on 1 Sep 42 and Hq Company redesignated 27th Reconnaissance Troop, 27th Division.

Campaigns: *Pacific Theater without inscription*

54th Infantry Brigade   New York National Guard

15 Oct 40 inducted into federal service at New York N.Y. assigned to the 27th Division and moved to Ft McClellan Ala 26 Oct 40; transferred to Riverside Calif 21 Dec 41 and to Ft Ord Calif 22 Jan 42; departed San Francisco P/E 30 Mar 42 and arrived Hawaii 8 Apr 42 where disbanded on 1 Sep 42.

Campaigns: *Pacific Theater without inscription*

55th Infantry Brigade   Pennsylvania National Guard

17 Feb 41 inducted into federal service at Washington Pa assigned to 28th Division and moved to Indiantown Gap Mil Res Pa 28 Feb 41; transferred to Cp Livingston La 18 Jan 42 where Hq disbanded 17 Feb 42 and Hq Company redesignated 28th Reconnaissance Troop, 28th Division.

56th Infantry Brigade   Pennsylvania National Guard

17 Feb 41 inducted into federal service at Columbia Pa assigned to 28th Division and moved to Indiantown Gap Mil Res Pa 27 Feb 41; transferred to Cp Beauregard La 18 Jan 42 where Hq disbanded 5 Feb 42 and Hq Company redesignated Hq Company, 28th Infantry Division.

57th Infantry Brigade   New Jersey National Guard

16 Sep 40 inducted into federal service at Elizabeth N.J. assigned to 44th Division and moved to Ft Dix N.J. 21 Sep 40; transferred to Cp Claiborne La 16 Jan 42 where Hq disbanded on 20 Feb 42 and Hq Company redesignated 44th Reconnaissance Troop, 44th Infantry Division.

58th Infantry Brigade   Maryland National Guard

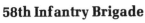

3 Feb 41 inducted into federal service at Baltimore Md assigned to 29th Division and moved to Ft George G. Meade Md 6 Feb 41 where disbanded on 28 Feb 42.

59th Infantry Brigade   Georgia National Guard

16 Sep 40 inducted into federal service at Macon Ga assigned to 30th Division and moved to Ft Jackson S.C. 20 Sep 40; there Hq disbanded 24 Feb 42 and Hq Company redesignated 30th Reconnaissance Troop, 30th Infantry Division.

60th Infantry Brigade   North Carolina National Guard

16 Sep 40 inducted into federal service at Leaksville N.C. assigned to 30th Division and moved to Ft Jackson S.C. 22 Sep 40 where disbanded on 16 Feb 42.

61st Infantry Brigade

Louisiana National Guard

25 Nov 40 inducted into federal service at Baton Rouge La assigned to 31st Division and moved to Cp Blanding Fla 14 Dec 40; there Hq disbanded on 10 Feb 42 and Hq Company redesignated 31st Reconnaissance Troop, 31st Infantry Division.

62nd Infantry Brigade

Florida and Alabama National Guard

25 Nov 40 inducted into federal service at Birmingham Ala assigned to 31st Division and moved to Cp Blanding Fla 13 Dec 40; transferred to Cp Bowie Tex on 23 Feb 42 where disbanded on 27 Feb 42.

63rd Infantry Brigade

Michigan National Guard

15 Oct 40 inducted into federal service at Detroit Mich assigned to 32nd Division and moved to Cp Beauregard La 25 Oct 40; transferred to Cp Livingston La on 19 Feb 41 where disbanded on 31 Jan 42.

64th Infantry Brigade

Wisconsin National Guard

15 Oct 40 inducted into federal service at Sparta Wis assigned to 32nd Division and moved to Cp Beauregard La 22 Oct 40; transferred to Cp Livingston La 14 Feb 41 where Hq disbanded on 16 Jan 42 and Hq Company redesignated 32nd Reconnaissance Troop, 32nd Division.

65th Infantry Brigade

Illinois National Guard

5 Mar 41 inducted into federal service at Pontiac Ill assigned to 33rd Division and moved to Cp Forrest Tenn 12 Mar 41 where Hq disbanded 12 Feb 42 and Hq Company redesignated 33rd Reconnaissance Troop, 33rd Division.

66th Infantry Brigade

Illinois National Guard

5 Mar 41 inducted into federal service at Oak Park Ill assigned to 33rd Division and moved to Cp Forrest Tenn 12 Mar 41 where disbanded on 21 Feb 42.

67th Infantry Brigade

Iowa National Guard

10 Feb 41 inducted into federal service at Des Moines Iowa assigned to 34th Division and moved to Cp Claiborne La 20 Feb 41; transferred to Ft Dix N.J. 11 Jan 42 where Hq disbanded on 16 Jan 42 and Hq Company redesignated 34th Reconnaissance Troop, 34th Infantry Division.

68th Infantry Brigade

North Dakota and Minnesota National Guard

10 Feb 41 inducted into federal service at Northfield Minn; assigned to 34th Division and moved to Cp Claiborne La 20 Feb 41; transferred to Ft Dix N.J. 11 Jan 42 where disbanded on 30 Jan 42.

69th Infantry Brigade   Nebraska and Kansas National Guard

23 Dec 40 inducted into federal service at Omaha Nebr assigned to 35th Division and moved to Cp Joseph T. Robinson Ark 7 Jan 41; transferred to Ft Ord Calif 23 Dec 41 and to Cp San Luis Obispo Calif 17 Jan 42; there Hq disbanded on 3 Feb 42 and Hq Company redesignated 35th Reconnaissance Troop, 35th Infantry Division.

70th Infantry Brigade   Missouri National Guard

23 Dec 40 inducted into federal service at Jefferson City Mo assigned to 35th Division and moved to Cp Joseph T. Robinson Ark 5 Jan 41; transferred to Ft Ord Calif 23 Dec 41 where disbanded on 3 Feb 42.

71st Infantry Brigade   Texas National Guard

25 Nov 40 inducted into federal service at San Antonio Tex assigned to 36th Division and moved to Cp Bowie Tex 18 Dec 40; there Hq disbanded on 31 Jan 42 and Hq Company redesignated 36th Reconnaissance Troop, 36th Infantry Division.

72nd Infantry Brigade   Texas National Guard

25 Nov 40 inducted into federal service at Dallas Tex assigned to 36th Division and moved to Cp Bowie Tex 5 Dec 40 where disbanded on 31 Jan 42.

73rd Infantry Brigade   Ohio National Guard

15 Oct 40 inducted into federal service at Cleveland Ohio assigned to 37th Division and moved to Cp Shelby Miss 22 Oct 40 where disbanded on 31 Jan 42.

74th Infantry brigade   Ohio National Guard

15 Oct 40 inducted into federal service at Columbus Ohio assigned to 37th Division and moved to Cp Shelby Miss 20 Oct 40; there Hq disbanded on 31 Jan 42 and Hq Company redesignated 37th Reconnaissance Troop, 37th Infantry Division.

75th Infantry Brigade   Kentucky National Guard

17 Jan 41 inducted into federal service at Bowling Green Ky assigned to 38th Division and moved to Cp Shelby Miss 26 Jan 41 where disbanded on 10 Feb 42.

76th Infantry Brigade   Indiana National Guard

17 Jan 41 inducted into federal service at Shelbyville Ind assigned to 38th Division and moved to Cp Shelby Miss on 27 Jan 41; there Hq disbanded on 10 Feb 42 and Hq Company redesignated 38th Reconnaissance Troop, 38th Infantry Division.

79th Infantry Brigade   California National Guard

3 Mar 41 inducted into federal service at Sacramento Calif assigned to 40th Division and moved to Cp San Luis Obispo Calif 10 Mar 41; transferred to Balboa Park San Diego Calif on 9 Dec 41 where disbanded on 5 Feb 42.

80th Infantry Brigade   California National Guard

3 Mar 41 inducted into federal service at Los Angeles Calif assigned to 40th Division and moved to Cp San Luis Obispo Calif 11 Mar 41; transferred to San Diego Calif 9 Dec 41 where Hq disbanded 5 Feb 42 and Hq Company redesignated 40th Reconnaissance Troop, 40th Infantry Division.

81st Infantry Brigade   Washington National Guard

16 Sep 40 inducted into federal service at Spokane Wash assigned to 41st Division and moved to Cp Murray Wash 20 Sep 40; transferred to Ft Lewis Wash 20 Mar 41 where disbanded on 14 Feb 42.

82nd Infantry Brigade

Oregon National Guard

16 Sep 40 inducted into federal service at Portland Oreg assigned to 41st Division and moved to Cp Murray Wash 23 Sep 40; transferred to Ft Lewis Wash 20 Mar 41 where Hq disbanded on 16 Feb 42 and Hq Company redesignated 41st Reconnaissance Troop, 41st Infantry Division.

85th Infantry Brigade

Connecticut National Guard

24 Feb 41 inducted into federal service at New London Conn assigned to 43rd Division and moved to Cp Blanding Fla 15 Mar 41; transferred to Cp Shelby Miss 7 Feb 42 where disbanded on 10 Feb 42.

86th Infantry Brigade

Vermont and Maine National Guard

24 Feb 41 inducted into federal service at Rutland Vermont assigned to 43rd Division and moved to Cp Blanding Fla 18 Mar 41; transferred to Cp Shelby Miss 14 Feb 42 where disbanded on 19 Feb 42.

87th Infantry Brigade

New York National Guard

16 Sep 40 inducted into federal service at Buffalo N.Y. assigned to 44th Division and moved to Ft Dix N.J. 22 Sep 40; transferred to Cp Claiborne La 16 Jan 42 where disbanded on 20 Feb 42.

88th Infantry Brigade

Virginia National Guard

3 Feb 41 inducted into federal service at Berryville Va assigned to 29th Division and moved to Ft George G. Meade Md 8 Feb 41; there Hq disbanded on 28 Feb 42 and Hq Company redesignated 29th Reconnaissance Troop, 29th Infantry Division.

89th Infantry Brigade

Colorado and Arizona National Guard

16 Sep 40 inducted into federal service at Chandler Ariz assigned to 45th Division and moved to Ft Sill Okla 24 Sep 40; transferred to Cp Barkeley Tex 28 Feb 41 and disbanded there on 23 Feb 42.

90th Infantry Brigade

Oklahoma National Guard

16 Sep 40 inducted into federal service at Durant Okla assigned to 45th Division and moved to Ft Sill Okla 24 Sep 40; transferred to Cp Barkeley Tex 28 Feb 41 where Hq disbanded on 22 Feb 42 and Hq Company redesignated 45th Reconnaissance Troop, 45th Infantry Division.

92nd Infantry Brigade

Puerto Rico National Guard

15 Oct 40 inducted into federal service at Cp Tortuguero Puerto Rico as a separate infantry brigade and moved to Caguas Puerto Rico on 26 Sep 41; returned to Cp Tortuguero Puerto Rico on 11 Oct 41 where disbanded on 24 Jul 42.

Campaigns: *American Theater without inscription*

5332nd Brigade, Provisional

26 Jul 44 activated in Burma and assigned to the Northern Combat Area Command and composed of 124th Cavalry Regt, 475th Infantry Regt, *Chinese 1st Separate Regt*, and 612th and 613th Field Artillery Battalions; also known as MARS Task Force; assembled near Mong Wi Burma and attacked the Burma Road in the Namhpakka area commencing 17 Jan 45; fought at Loi-kang Ridge and seized the Hpa-pen area heights on 2 Feb 45; moved to China by air in echelon 14 Mar–14 May 45 where inactivated in late May 45.

Campaigns: *Central Burma, India-Burma*

Provisional Parachute Group

25 Feb 41 organized at Ft Benning Ga under the Chief of Infantry to develop tactical doctrine and provide training cadre for the parachutist school and units being trained there; redesignated the Airborne Command at Ft Benning Ga on 21 Mar 42.

Chapter 13

Infantry Regiments

Regiments:

1 Filipino, 2 Filipino, 1–39, 41, 43(PS), 45(PS), 46–56, 57(PS), 58–60, 62, 63, 65–68, 71, 85–91, 101–106, 108–121, 123–138, 140–145, 147–169, 172, 174–176, 179–182, 184–190, 193, 194, 197, 198, 201, 222, 232, 242, 253–255, 259–264, 271–276, 289–291, 295–307, 309–311, 313–315, 317–331, 333–335, 337–339, 341–343, 345–347, 349–351, 353–355, 357–359, 361–372, 376–379, 381–383, 385–387, 389–391, 393–395, 397–399, 401, 405–407, 409–411, 413–415, 417, 422–424, 434, 442, 473–476, 480, 501–509, 511, 513, 515, 517, 541, 542, 551, 777, 800, 2677 OSS, 5307 Composite Provisional Unit, 6615 Ranger Force (Prov)

1st Filipino Infantry Regiment (Separate)

13 Jul 42 activated at Salinas Calif with personnel from the 1st Filipino Inf Bn and moved to Cp San Luis Obispo Calif 23 Aug 42; attached to VII Corps 1 Oct 42 and moved to Ft Ord Calif 14 Oct 42; transferred to Cp Beale Calif 8 Jan 43 and attached to II Armored Corps 21 Feb 43; sent to Hunter-Liggett Mil Res Calif 2 May 43; returned to Cp Beale Calif 24 Sep 43 where attached to Fourth Army 31 Oct 43 and to III Corps 15 Jan 44; staged at Cp Stoneman Calif 1 Apr 44 until departed San Francisco P/E 6 Apr 44; arrived in Oro Bay New Guinea 27 Apr 44 under U.S. Army Forces in the South Pacific Area; departed New Guinea 17 Jan 45 and landed on Leyte Philippine Islands 8 Feb 45; formed part of provisional task force to clear northwest coast of Samar and islands in the Bernardino Strait on 14 Feb 45; took responsibility for Biri 23 Feb 45; began to clear Mauo area of Samar 28 Feb 45; attached to Eighth Army 8 Mar 45 and the next day assumed responsibility for final mop-up of Samar island; returned to San Francisco P/E 9 Apr 46 and inactivated at Cp Stoneman Calif 10 Apr 46.

Campaigns: *New Guinea, Leyte*
Aug 45 Loc: Tacloban Philippine Islands, less 1st Bn at Ormoc Philippine Islands

1st Infantry Regiment (6th Infantry Division)

Stationed at Cp Jackson S.C. and assigned to 6th Division 16 Oct 39; transferred to Ft Benning Ga 9 Apr 40 and Sabine La-Tex Mnvr Area 8 May 40; moved to Ft Francis E. Warren Wyo 3 Jun 40 and Ft Leavenworth Kans 2 Apr 41; arrived at Ft Leonard Wood Mo 20 May 41 and participated in Tenn Maneuvers; sent to Cp Young Calif 10 Dec 42 and to Cp San Luis Obispo Calif 23 Mar 43; departed San Francisco P/E 19 Sep 43 and arrived in Hawaii 26 Sep 43; departed Hawaii 26 Jan 44 and arrived at Milne Bay New Guinea 7 Feb 44 which departed 1 Jun 44 to move to Toem area 14 Jun 44; assaulted Sansapor 30 Jul 44 and left New Guinea 26 Dec 44; assaulted Lingayen Gulf Philippine Islands on Luzon 9 Jan 45 *(10–23 Feb 45 in Sixth Army Reserve) (attached 38th Inf Div 28 Apr–1 May 45) (attached XI Corps 10–25 Jun 45)*; arrived for occupation duty in Korea 24 Oct 45 where active thru 1946.

Campaigns: *New Guinea, Luzon*
Aug 45 Loc: Bagabag Philippine Islands

2nd Filipino Infantry Regiment (Separate)

21 Nov 42 activated at Ft Ord Calif and moved to Cp Cooke Calif 11 Jan 43 where attached to II Corps 1 Feb 43; arrived Hunter-Liggett Mil Res Calif 8 Oct 43 and attached to Fourth Army 1 Nov 43; returned to Cp Cooke Calif 11 Nov 43 and attached to III Corps 15 Jan 44; there inactivated 27 Mar 44 and assets transferred to 2nd Filipino Infantry Bn.

2nd Infantry Regiment (5th Infantry Division)

Stationed at Ft Wayne Mich as part of 6th Division until assigned to 5th Division on 16 Oct 39; transferred to Ft McClellan Ala 3 Nov 39 and to Ft Benning Ga 11 Apr 40; transferred to Cp Beauregard La 11 May 40 and returned to Ft Wayne Mich 1 Jun 40; sent to Ft Custer Mich 25 Sep 40 and staged at New York P/E 10 Jan 42 where departed 26 Feb 42; arrived in Iceland for security duty 3 Mar 42; arrived in England 9 Aug 43 and landed in France 9 Jul 44 *(attached 2nd Armd Div 10–15 Sep 44)*; entered Germany 8 Feb 45; returned to New York P/E 18 Jul 45 and moved to Cp Campbell Ky on 22 Jul 45 where active thru 1946.

Campaigns: *Normandy, Northern France, Rhineland, Ardennes-Alsace, Central Europe*
Aug 45 Loc: Camp Campbell Kentucky

3rd Infantry Regiment (Separate)

Black leather strap
with buff leather strap
in middle

Stationed at Ft Jackson S.C. and assigned to 6th Division 16 Oct 39 and moved to Ft Benning Ga 12 Apr 40 and to Sabine La Mnvr area 8 May 40; arrived at Ft Snelling Minn 1 Jun 40 where relieved from 6th Division 10 May 41; 3rd Bn departed New York P/E 20 Jan 41 to defend St John's Newfoundland and moved to Ft Pepperrell Newfoundland in Nov 41; 1st Bn inactivated 1 Jun 41 and used as nucleus for the 63rd Infantry Regt at Ft Leonard Wood Mo; remainder of regt relocated to Cp Ripley Minn 13 Sep 41 and returned to Ft Snelling Minn 26 Sep 41; new 1st Bn activated in Newfoundland 14 Feb 42; regt arrived Boston P/E 22 Jun 42 and departed 2 Jul 42; arrived at Ft Pepperrell Newfoundland 6 Jul 42 where assigned to Newfoundland Base Command on 20 Jul 42; 2nd Bn inactivated in Greenland 1 Sep 42 to become basis of 73rd Inf Battalion there; regt returned to Boston P/E 17 Sep 43 and moved to Cp Butner N.C. 22 Sep 43 where attached to XII Corps and new 2nd Bn activated on 22 Oct 43; transferred to Ft Benning Ga 8 Mar 44 where assigned to Replacement & School Command to provide cadre for the infantry school; staged at Cp Myles Standish Mass 27 Feb 45 until departed Boston P/E 8 Mar 45; landed at Le Havre France 18 Mar 45 and initially provided a reserve to contain German garrison at St Nazaire; attached 106th Inf Div 16 Mar–23 Jun 45 during which time crossed into Germany 26 Apr 45 and processed prisoners; inactivated at Berlin Germany on 20 Nov 46.

Campaigns: *American Theater without inscription, Northern France*
Aug 45 Loc: Babenhausen Germany

4th Infantry Regiment (Separate)

Cloth shoulder loop

Stationed at Ft George Wright Wash as part of 3rd Division until moved to Ft Ord Calif 22 Jan 40 where relieved from division on 15 May 40; returned to Ft George Wright Wash 23 May 40 and served at Ft Lewis Wash 1–26 Aug 40 and returned to Ft George Wright Wash; departed Seattle P/E 24 Dec 40 and arrived Anchorage Alaska 3 Jan 41 where assigned to Alaskan Defense Command; arrived on Kodiak Island 23 Nov 42 and on Unalaska Island 30 Nov 42 and posted to Adak Island 8 Dec 42; assaulted Attu Island 11 May 43 and participated in the Battle for Fish Hook Ridge; returned to Seattle P/E 2 Dec 43 and moved to Ft Lewis Wash same date; arrived Ft Benning Ga 23 Jan 44 and assigned there to the Replacement & School Command; effective 1 Nov 45 transferred (less personnel and equipment) to the 25th Inf Div in Japan where active thru 1946, its personnel and equipment of 1 Nov 45 being merged into the 4th Inf Div at Cp Butner N.C.

Campaigns: *Aleutian Islands*
Aug 45 Loc: Fort Benning Georgia

5th Infantry Regiment (71st Infantry Division)

Stationed at Ft Williams Maine as part of 9th Division and dispatched to reinforce Panama Canal Zone under the 18th Inf Brigade on 7 Nov 39 where stationed at Cp Paraiso Panama Canal Zone; relieved from division 15 Jul 40 and assigned to Panama Canal Dept; departed Balboa Panama 26 Jan 43 and arrived at New Orleans P/E same date; transferred to Cp Van Dorn Miss where attached to 99th Inf Div 27 Jan 43 and to Third Army 1 Mar 43; relocated to Cp Carson Colo 25 Jul 43 where assigned to 71st Light Division 10 Jul 43; moved to Hunter-Liggett Mil Res Calif 9 Feb 44 and to Ft Benning Ga 24 May 44; staged at Cp Kilmer N.J. 13 Jan 45 until departed New York P/E 26 Jan 45; arrived in France on 6 Feb 45 *(attached to 100th Inf Div 11–14 Mar 45)* and entered Germany 23 Mar 45; entered Austria on 3 May 45 where inactivated on 15 Nov 46.

Campaigns: *Rhineland, Central Europe*
Aug 45 Loc: Westheim Germany

6th Armored Infantry Regiment (1st Armored Division)

Stationed at Cp Joseph T. Robinson Ark as the 6th Infantry and part of the 6th Division until 16 Oct 39 when assigned to 14th Inf Brigade; arrived Jefferson Barracks Mo 7 Feb 40 and moved to Ft Knox Ky 2 Mar 40; relocated to Monroe La 7 May 40 and returned to Jefferson Barracks Mo 1 Jul 40; there redesignated 15 Jul 40 as 6th Infantry (Armored) and assigned to 1st Armored Division; returned to Ft Knox Ky 7 Aug 40 and participated in the La and Carolina Maneuvers; returned to Ft Knox Ky 7 Dec 41 where redesignated the 6th Armored Infantry Regiment 1 Jan 42; staged at Ft Dix N.J. 8 Apr 42 until departed New York P/E 31 May 42; arrived in Ireland 11 Jun 42 and landed in North Africa 21 Dec 42; landed in Italy 28 Oct 43 where redesignated at Bolgheri as the 6th, 11th, and 14th Armored Infantry Battalions on 27 Jun 44.

Campaigns: *Algeria–French Morocco, Tunisia, Naples-Foggia, Anzio, Rome-Arno*

7th Infantry Regiment (3rd Infantry Division)

Stationed at Vancouver Barracks Wash as part of 3rd Division and moved to Ft Lewis Wash 7 Feb 41; transferred to Ft Ord Calif 4 May 42 and to Cp Pickett Va 17 Sep 42; departed Hampton Roads P/E 27 Oct 42 and assaulted Fedala North Africa on 8 Nov 42; assaulted Licata Sicily 10 Jul 43 and landed in Italy 18 Sep 43; assaulted Anzio Italy 22 Jan 44 and assaulted southern France 15 Aug 44; entered Germany 13 Mar 45 and entered Austria 5 May 45; arrived New York P/E 4 Sep 46 and moved to Cp Campbell Ky 8 Sep 46 where remained active thru 1946.

Campaigns: *Algeria–French Morocco, Tunisia, Sicily, Naples-Foggia, Anzio, Rome-Arno, Southern France, Rhineland, Ardennes-Alsace, Central Europe*
Aug 45 Loc: Salzburg Austria

8th Infantry Regiment (4th Infantry Division)

Stationed at Ft Moultrie S.C. as part of the 4th Division and moved to Ft Benning Ga 28 Jun 40 and participated in La and Carolina Maneuvers; transferred to Cp Gordon Ga 18 Dec 41 and to Ft Jackson S.C. 1 Dec 43; staged at Cp Kilmer N.J. 9 Jan 44 until departed New York P/E 18 Jan 44; arrived in England 29 Jan 44 and assaulted Normandy France 6 Jun 44 *(attached 9th Inf Div 10–11 Aug 44)*; crossed into Belgium 6 Sep 44 and initially entered Germany 11 Sep 44; crossed into Luxembourg 12 Dec 44 *(attached 83rd Inf Div 7–12 Dec 44)*; returned to Belgium 28 Jan 45 and to Germany 7 Feb 45; returned to New York P/E 10 Jul 45 and moved to Cp Butner N.C. 13 Jul 45 where inactivated on 25 Feb 46.

Campaigns: *Normandy, Northern France, Rhineland, Ardennes-Alsace, Central Europe*
Aug 45 Loc: Camp Butner North Carolina

9th Infantry Regiment (2nd Infantry Division)

Stationed at Ft Sam Houston Tex as part of 2nd Division and moved to Cp McCoy Wis 24 Nov 42; staged at Cp Shanks N.Y. 27 Sep 43 until departed New York P/E 8 Oct 43; arrived England 19 Oct 43 and landed in France on 12 Jun 44; crossed into Belgium 3 Oct 44 and entered Germany same date; arrived Boston P/E 19 Jul 45 and moved to Cp Swift Tex 23 Jul 45; transferred to Cp Stoneman Calif 29 Mar 46 and to Ft Lewis Wash 16 Apr 46, where active thru 1946.

Campaigns: *Normandy, Northern France, Rhineland, Ardennes-Alsace, Central Europe*
Aug 45 Loc: Camp Swift Texas

10th Infantry Regiment (5th Infantry Division)

Stationed at Ft Thomas Ky as part of the 5th Division and moved to Ft McClellan Ala 7 Nov 39; transferred to Ft Benning Ga 9 Apr 40 and to Cp Beauregard La 11 May 40; returned to Ft Thomas Ky 1 Jun 40 and relocated to Ft Custer Mich 3 Dec 40; staged at Cp Kilmer N.J. 1 Sep 41 until departed New York P/E 5 Sep 41; arrived on Iceland 16 Sep 41 for security duty until 5 Aug 43; arrived in England 9 Aug 43 and landed in France 9 Jul 44 *(attached 95th Inf Div 30 Nov–1 Dec 44)* *(attached 4th Inf Div 22–24 Dec 44)*; entered Germany 8 Feb 45; returned to New York P/E 18 Jul 45 and moved to Cp Campbell Ky 22 Jul 45 where inactivated on 20 Sep 46.

Campaigns: *Normandy, Northern France, Rhineland, Ardennes-Alsace, Central Europe*
Aug 45 Loc: Camp Campbell Kentucky

10th Infantry Regiment (27th Division)   New York National Guard

15 Oct 40 inducted into federal service at Albany N.Y. as part of the 27th Division and moved to Ft McClellan Ala 26 Oct 40, where redesignated 106th Inf Regt on 11 Dec 40.

11th Infantry Regiment (5th Infantry Division)

Stationed at Ft McClellan Ala as part of the 5th Division and moved to Ft Benning Ga 7 Apr 40; transferred to Cp Beauregard La 11 May 40 and to Ft Benjamin Harrison Ind 31 May 40; relocated to Ft Custer Mich 6 Jan 41; dispatched companies to Bermuda and Trinidad in Apr 41; staged at Cp Kilmer N.J. 3 Apr 42 until departed New York P/E 7 Apr 42; arrived on Iceland 21 Apr 42 for security duty until 5 Aug 43; arrived in England 9 Aug 43 and landed in France 9 Jul 44; entered Germany 8 Feb 45 *(attached 4th Armd Div 8–11 Mar 45)*; arrived Boston P/E 20 Jul 45 and moved to Cp Campbell Ky 23 Jul 45 where inactivated on 20 Sep 46.

Campaigns: *Normandy, Northern France, Rhineland, Ardennes-Alsace, Central Europe*
Aug 45 Loc: Camp Campbell Kentucky

12th Infantry Regiment (4th Infantry Division)

Stationed at Ft Howard Md as part of the 8th Division and moved to Arlington Cantonment Va 3 Sep 40; transferred to Ft Dix N.J. 12 Jun 41 and attached to First Army 26 Jun 41; arrived at Ft Benning Ga 24 Oct 41 and assigned to 4th Motorized Division; redesignated 12th Infantry Regiment (Motorized) on 9 Sep 42; sent to Cp Gordon Ga 21 Dec 41 and returned to Ft Dix N.J. 18 Apr 43 where redesignated the 12th Infantry Regiment 1 Aug 43; transferred to Cp Gordon Johnston Fla 25 Feb 43 and to Ft Jackson S.C. 30 Nov 43; staged at Cp Kilmer N.J. 11 Jan 44 until departed New York P/E 18 Jan 44; arrived in England 29 Jan 44 and assaulted Normandy France 6 Jun 44 *(attached 30th Inf Div 7–13 Aug 44)*; crossed into Belgium 6 Sep 44 and entered Germany 11 Sep 44 *(attached 28th Inf Div 7–10 Nov 44)*; crossed into Luxembourg 12 Dec 44 *(attached to 87th Inf Div 9–18 Jan 45)*; returned to Belgium 28 Jan 45 and reentered Germany 7 Feb 45; returned to New York P/E 12 Jul 45 and moved to Cp Butner N.C. 15 Jul 45 where inactivated on 27 Feb 46.

Campaigns: *Normandy, Northern France, Rhineland, Ardennes-Alsace, Central Europe*
Aug 45 Loc: Camp Butner North Carolina

13th Infantry Regiment (9th Division) (I)

Stationed at Ft Devens Mass as part of the 9th Division and moved to Ft William D. Davis Panama Canal Zone 27 Oct 39; there inactivated on 14 Jun 40.

13th Infantry Regiment (8th Infantry Division) (II)

14 Jul 40 activated at Ft Jackson S.C. as part of the 8th Division as the 13th Infantry Regiment; redesignated 13th Infantry Regiment (Motorized) 9 Apr 42; commenced the Tennessee Maneuvers 10 Sep 42 and moved to Cp Forrest Tenn 10 Nov 42 and then to Ft Leonard Wood Mo 29 Nov 42; transferred to Cp Young Calif 20 Mar 43 where redesignated the 13th Infantry Regiment on 1 May 43; returned to Cp Forrest Tenn 16 Aug 43 and staged at Cp Kilmer N.J. 25 Nov 43 until departed New York P/E 5 Dec 43; arrived in England 15 Dec 43 and landed in France 3 Jul 44 *(attached 4th Armd Div 27 Jul–3 Aug 44)*; entered Germany 19 Nov 44 *(attached 3rd Armd Div 26 Feb–17 Mar 45) (attached 82nd A/B Div 28–30 Apr 45)*; arrived at Hampton Roads P/E 10 Jul 45 and moved to Ft Leonard Wood Mo 13 Jul 45 where inactivated on 18 Nov 45.

Campaigns: *Normandy, Northern France, Rhineland, Central Europe*
Aug 45 Loc: Fort Leonard Wood Missouri

14th Infantry Regiment (71st Infantry Division)

Stationed at Ft William D. Davis Panama Canal Zone and arrived at San Francisco P/E 18 Jun 43; transferred to Cp Carson Colo 21 Jun 43 under Third Army and assigned to the 71st Light Division on 10 Jul 43; moved to Hunter-Liggett Mil Res Calif 10 Feb 44 and to Ft Benning Ga 24 May 44; staged at Cp Kilmer N.J. 16 Jan 45 until departed New York P/E 26 Jan 45; arrived in France 6 Feb 45 and entered Germany 22 Mar 45 and Austria 4 May 45; inactivated in Germany on 1 Sep 46.

Campaigns: *Rhineland, Northern France*
Aug 45 Loc: Gunzburg Germany

15th Infantry Regiment (3rd Infantry Division)

Stationed at Ft Lewis Wash where assigned to the 3rd Division on 12 Jan 40; sent to Ft Ord Calif 22 Jan 40 and returned to Ft Lewis Wash 19 May 40; returned to Ft Ord Calif 4 May 42 and transferred to Cp Pickett Va 16 Sep 42 where remained until departed Hampton Roads P/E on 27 Oct 42; assaulted Fedala North Africa 8 Nov 42; assaulted Licata Sicily 10 Jul 43; landed in Italy 18 Sep 43 and assaulted Anzio Italy 22 Jan 44; assaulted southern France 15 Aug 44 and entered Germany on 13 Mar 45 *(attached to 12th Armd Div 24–25 Apr 45)* and Austria on 5 May 45; arrived New York P/E 4 Sep 46 and moved to Cp Campbell Ky 8 Sep 46 where remained active thru 1946 (at zero strength).

Campaigns: *Algeria-French Morocco, Tunisia, Sicily, Naples-Foggia, Anzio, Rome-Arno, Southern France, Rhineland, Ardennes-Alsace, Central Europe*
Aug 45 Loc: Werfeu Austria

16th Infantry Regiment (1st Infantry Division)

Stationed at Ft Jay N.Y. as part of the 1st Division and moved to Ft Benning Ga 19 Nov 39 and later participated in the La Maneuvers May 40; transferred to Ft Devens Mass 24 Feb 41 and to Cp Blanding Fla 23 Feb 42; returned to Ft Benning Ga 22 May 42 and sent to Indiantown Gap Mil Res Pa 6 Jun 42; departed New York P/E 1 Aug 42 and arrived in Scotland 7 Aug 42 and in England 9 Aug 42; returned to Scotland 24 Sep 42 and assaulted Oran North Africa 8 Nov 42; assaulted Gela Sicily 10 Jul 43 and arrived in England 5 Nov 43; assaulted Normandy France 6 Jun 44 and crossed into Belgium 5 Sep 44; entered Germany 15 Sep 44 *(attached V Corps 5–15 Dec 44)*; returned to Belgium 12 Dec 44 and reentered Germany 6 Feb 45 *(attached 8th Inf Div 6–8 Feb 45) (attached VII Corps 7–8 Aug 45)*; remained active in Germany thru 1946.

Campaigns: *Algeria-French Morocco, Tunisia, Sicily, Normandy, Northern France, Rhineland, Ardennes-Alsace, Central Europe*
Aug 45 Loc: Bamberg Germany

17th Infantry Regiment (7th Infantry Division)

Stationed at Ft Crook Neb as part of the 7th Division and moved to Ft Joseph T. Robinson Ark on 9 Nov 39; returned to Ft Crook Neb 18 Feb 40; transferred to Ft Ord Calif 10 Sep 40 and sent to Santa Rosa Calif 9 Dec 41; relocated to Cp San Luis Obispo Calif 23 Apr 42 and deployed to Antelope Valley Mnvr area 22 Jun 42 where redesignated the 17th Infantry Regiment (Motorized) on 15 Jul 42; participated in the Calif Maneuvers commencing 12 Aug 42; returned to Cp San Luis Obispo Calif 20 Oct 42 where redesignated the 17th Infantry Regiment on 1 Jan 43; arrived at Ft Ord Calif 15 Jan 43 and departed San Francisco P/E 24 Apr 43; assaulted Attu Island Aleutians on 11 May 43; arrived in Hawaii 17 Sep 43, assaulted Kwajalein Atoll 31 Jan 44, and returned to Hawaii 15 Feb 44; departed Hawaii 15 Sep 44 and arrived Eniwetok Atoll 25 Sep 44 and Manus Island 3 Oct 44 enroute to Philippine Islands; *(placed in XXIV Corps Reserve 20-22 Oct 44)* assaulted Leyte Island Philippines 22 Oct 44 *(attached 11th A/B Div 22-27 Nov 44)*; departed Leyte 27 Mar 45 and assaulted Okinawa 1 Apr 45; arrived in Korea on 8 Sep 45 for occupation duty where active thru 1946.

Campaigns: *Aleutian Islands, Eastern Mandates, Leyte, Ryukyus*
Aug 45 Loc: Okinawa

18th Infantry Regiment (1st Infantry Division)

Stationed at Ft Benning Ga as part of the 1st Division and moved to La Mnvr area 10 May 40; transferred to Ft Hamilton N.Y. 5 Jun 40 and to Ft Devens Mass 27 Feb 41; sent to Cp Blanding Fla 23 Feb 42 and returned to Ft Benning Ga on 22 May 42; arrived Indiantown Gap Mil Res Pa 6 Jun 42 and departed New York P/E 2 Aug 42; arrived in England 7 Aug 42 and assaulted Oran North Africa on 8 Nov 42; served as initial reserve force off Sicily and landed at Scoglitti Sicily 13 Jul 43; arrived in England 8 Nov 43 and assaulted Normandy France 6 Jun 44; crossed into Belgium 3 Sep 44 and entered Germany 15 Sep 44, where active duty thru 1946.

Campaigns: *Algeria-French Morocco, Tunisia, Sicily, Normandy, Northern France, Rhineland, Ardennes-Alsace, Central Europe*
Aug 45 Loc: Windsheim Germany

19th Infantry Regiment (24th Infantry Division)

Stationed at Schofield Barracks Hawaii as part of the Hawaiian Division until assigned to the 24th Infantry Division on 26 Aug 41; departed Hawaii 30 Jul 43 and arrived 8 Aug 43 in Australia; arrived Goodenough Island 26 Jan 44 and assaulted Tanahmerah Bay New Guinea 22 Apr 44; departed Humboldt Bay New Guinea 7-12 Oct 44 and assaulted Leyte Island Philippines on 20 Oct 44 *(attached Sixth Army 20 Nov 44-1 Jan 45)* and assaulted Mindoro Philippines 15 Dec 44 *(attached Eighth Army 1 Jan-1 Feb 45)*; assaulted Romblon and Simara Islands 12 Mar 45 and Malabang Mindanao on 17 Apr 45; arrived in Japan for occupation duty 22 Oct 45 where active thru 1946.

Campaigns: *Central Pacific, New Guinea, Leyte, Luzon, Southern Philippines*
Aug 45 Loc: Davao Mindanao Philippine Islands

20th Infantry Regiment (6th Infantry Division)

Stationed at Ft Francis E. Warren Wyo as part of the 2nd Division and assigned to the 6th Division there on 16 Oct 39; moved to Cp Jackson S.C. 17 Nov 39 and to Ft Benning Ga 10 Apr 40; participated in La Maneuvers of May 40 and returned to Ft Francis E. Warren Wyo 28 May 40; transferred to Ft Leavenworth Kans 1 Apr 41 and to Ft Leonard Wood Mo 20 May 41 where redesignated the 20th Infantry Regiment (Motorized) on 1 Oct 42; participated in the Tenn Maneuvers and moved to Cp Young Calif 3 Dec 42; relocated to Cp San Luis Obispo Calif 25 Mar 43 where redesignated the 20th Infantry Regiment on 1 May 43; departed San Francisco P/E 20 Sep 43 and arrived in Hawaii 26 Sep 43; departed Hawaii 8 Feb 44 and landed at Milne Bay New Guinea 18 Feb 44 *(attached as ALAMO Force Reserve 10 Jul-25 Aug 44)*; assaulted Lingayen Gulf Luzon Philippine Islands 9 Jan 45 *(attached Provost Marshal General, U.S. Army Forces in the Far East 18 Apr-1 Jun 45 at Manila) (attached 37th Inf Div 7-12 Jun 45)*; arrived in Korea for occupation duty on 18 Oct 45 where remained active thru 1946.

Campaigns: *New Guinea, Luzon*
Aug 45 Loc: Bagabag Philippine Islands

21st Infantry Regiment (24th Infantry Division)

Stationed at Schofield Barracks Hawaii as part of the Hawaiian Division until assigned to the 24th Infantry Division on 26 Aug 41; departed Hawaii 30 Jul 43 and arrived in Australia 8 Sep 43; arrived Goodenough Island 15 Feb 44 and assaulted Tanahmerah Bay New Guinea 22 Apr 44; *(attached to Sixth Army 23 Sep–2 Nov 44)* assaulted Panoan Island Philippines on 20 Oct 44; *(attached Sixth Army 27 Dec 44–1 Feb 45)* made company-level assaults on Marindupue 3 Jan 45 and Nasugbu Point Luzon 29 Jan 45; assaulted Lubang 24 Feb 45 and assaulted Malabang Mindanao on 17 Apr 45 *(placed in X Corps Reserve 25–28 Apr 45)*; arrived in Japan for occupation duty on 22 Oct 45 where remained active thru 1946.

Campaigns: *Central Pacific, New Guinea, Leyte, Luzon, Southern Philippines*
Aug 45 Loc: Davao Mindanao Philippine Islands

22nd Infantry Regiment (4th Infantry Division)

Stationed at Ft McClellan Ala as part of the 4th Division and moved to Ft Benning Ga 21 Feb 41; transferred to Cp Gordon Ga 27 Dec 41 where redesignated the 22nd Infantry Regiment (Motorized) on 9 Sep 42; relocated to Ft Dix N.J. 16 Apr 43 where redesignated the 22nd Infantry Regiment on 1 Aug 43; moved to Cp Gordon Johnston Fla 28 Sep 43 and to Ft Jackson S.C. 1 Dec 43; staged at Cp Kilmer N.J. 8 Jan 44 until departed New York P/E 18 Jan 44; arrived England 29 Jan 44 and assaulted Normandy France 6 Jun 44 *(attached 2nd Armd Div 19 Jul–2 Aug 44)*; crossed into Belgium 6 Sep 44 and entered Germany 11 Sep 44 *(attached 83rd Inf Div 3–7 Dec 44)*; crossed into Luxembourg 12 Dec 44, returned to Belgium 28 Jan 45, and reentered Germany 7 Feb 45; returned to New York P/E 12 Jul 45 and moved to Cp Butner N.C. 13 Jul 45 where inactivated on 5 Mar 46.

Campaigns: *Normandy, Northern France, Rhineland, Ardennes-Alsace, Central Europe*
Aug 45 Loc: Camp Butner North Carolina

23rd Infantry Regiment (2nd Infantry Division)

Stationed at Ft Sam Houston Tex as part of the 2nd Division and moved to Cp McCoy Wis 24 Nov 42; staged at Cp Shanks, N.Y. 29 Sep 43 until departed New York P/E 8 Oct 43; arrived England 18 Oct 43 and landed in France 12 Jun 44; crossed into Belgium 3 Oct 44 and entered Germany same date *(attached 99th Inf Div 16–18 Dec 44)* *(attached 1st Inf Div 13–24 Jan 45)*; returned New York P/E 20 Jul 45 and moved to Cp Swift Tex 25 Jul 45; transferred to Cp Stoneman Calif 30 Mar 46 and to Ft Lewis Wash 16 Apr 46; active thru 1946.

Campaigns: *Normandy, Northern France, Rhineland, Ardennes-Alsace, Central Europe*
Aug 45 Loc: Camp Swift Texas

24th Infantry Regiment (Colored) (Separate)

Stationed at Ft Benning Ga and participated in the Carolina Maneuvers of Oct-Dec 41; departed San Francisco P/E 4 Apr 42 and arrived in New Hebrides 4 May 42; arrived on Guadalcanal 28 Aug 43 and assigned to XIV Corps; 1st Bn deployed to Bougainville Mar-May 44 for perimeter defense duty; departed Guadalcanal 8 Dec 44 and landed on Saipan and Tinian 19 Dec 44 for garrison duty which included mopping up remaining Japanese forces there; assigned to Pacific Ocean Area Command 15 Mar 45, to Central Pacific Base Command 15 May 45, and to Western Pacific Base Command 22 Jun 45; left Saipan and Tinian 9 Jul 45 and arrived Kerama Island Group off Okinawa 29 Jul 45; active on Okinawa thru 1946.

Campaigns: *Northern Solomons, Western Pacific*
Aug 45 Loc: Okinawa

25th Infantry Regiment (Colored) (93rd Infantry Division)

Stationed at Ft Huachuca Ariz where attached to Third Army until assigned to 93rd Infantry Division on 1 Jan 42; moved to Cp Young Calif 8 Jul 43 and departed San Francisco P/E 24 Jan 44; arrived Guadalcanal by echelon 7 Feb–5 Mar 44 and arrived on Bougainville 28 Mar 44 *(attached to American Division 28 Mar–12 Jun 44) (attached XIV Corps 12 Jun–8 Jul 44)*; arrived in Green Islands 8 Jul 44 *(attached to Provisional Island Command APO 293 8 Jul–10 Oct 44) (attached XIV Corps 10 Oct 44–12 Apr 45)*; left Green Islands in echelon and arrived Finschhafen New Guinea 10 Nov 44; moved to Morotai Island 12 Apr 45 where rejoined division; arrived in Philippines 9 Oct 45 and returned to San Francisco P/E 1 Feb 46 and inactivated at Cp Stoneman Calif 3 Feb 46.

Campaigns: *Northern Solomons, Bismarck Archipelago, New Guinea*
Aug 45 Loc: Morotai Island

26th Infantry Regiment (1st Infantry Division)

Stationed at Plattsburg Barracks N.Y. as part of the 1st Division and moved to Ft Devens Mass 27 Feb 41; transferred to Cp Blanding Fla 23 Feb 42 and to Ft Benning Ga 22 May 42; relocated to Indiantown Gap Mil Res Pa 6 Jun 42 and departed New York P/E 6 Aug 42; arrived in England 10 Aug 42 and in Scotland 22 Sep 42; assaulted North Africa 8 Nov 42 and assaulted Gela Sicily on 10 Jul 43; returned to England 5 Nov 43 and assaulted Normandy France 6 Jun 44 *(attached to 29th Inf Div 17 May–7 Jun 44) (attached to 4th Inf Div 29–30 Jul 44)*; crossed into Belgium 3 Sep 44 and entered Germany 15 Sep 44 *(attached 99th Inf Div 17–18 Dec 44)*; active in Germany thru 1946.

Campaigns: *Algeria-French Morocco, Tunisia, Sicily, Normandy, Northern France, Rhineland, Ardennes-Alsace, Central Europe*
Aug 45 Loc: Heilsbronn Germany

27th Infantry Regiment (25th Infantry Division)

Stationed at Schofield Barracks Hawaii and assigned to the Hawaiian Division until 26 Aug 41 when assigned to the 25th Infantry Division; departed Hawaii 6 Dec 42 and landed on Guadalcanal 1 Jan 43; landed on New Georgia Island 2 Aug 43 *(attached to 43rd Inf Div 10–24 Sep 43)*; cleared Arundel and Sagekarasa Islands in Sep 43; assaulted Kolombangara Island 6 Oct 43; reassembled on Guadalcanal 25 Oct 43 and arrived in New Hebrides 20 Nov 43, in New Zealand 26 Nov 43, and in New Caledonia 27 Feb 44; departed New Caledonia 17 Dec 44 and arrived Manus Island 29 Dec 44 enroute to landing on 11 Jan 45 in the Mabilao area of Lingayen Gulf Luzon Philippines; sent to Japan for occupation duty 27 Oct 45 where remained active thru 1946.

Campaigns: *Central Pacific, Guadalcanal, Northern Solomons, Luzon*
Aug 45 Loc: Bamban Philippine Islands

28th Infantry Regiment (8th Infantry Division)

Stationed at Ft Niagara N.Y. as part of the 1st Division until 22 Jun 40 when assigned to the 8th Division; moved to Cp Jackson S.C. 2 Dec 40 where redesignated as the 28th Infantry Regiment (Motorized) on 9 Apr 42 and participated in the Tenn Maneuvers of Sep-Nov 42; transferred to Ft Leonard Wood Mo 28 Nov 42 and to Cp Young Calif 20 Mar 43 where redesignated the 28th Infantry Regiment on 1 May 43; arrived Cp Forrest Tenn 17 Aug 43 and staged at Cp Kilmer N.J. 23 Nov 43 until departed New York P/E 5 Dec 43; arrived in England 16 Dec 43 and landed in France 3 Jul 44 *(attached 6th Armd Div 18–21 Aug 44)*; crossed into Luxembourg 30 Sep 44 and entered Germany 19 Nov 44; arrived at Hampton Roads P/E 6 Jul 45 and moved to Ft Leonard Wood Mo on 9 Jul 45 where inactivated 1 Nov 45.

Campaigns: *Normandy, Northern France, Rhineland, Central Europe*
Aug 45 Loc: Fort Leonard Wood Missouri

29th Infantry Regiment (Separate)

Stationed at Ft Benning Ga as part of the 4th Division until relieved 16 Oct 39; participated in La Maneuvers 6–30 May 40; 1 Jun 42 assigned Replacement & School Command with Infantry School Brigade; transferred to Ft Jackson S.C. 5 May 43 and staged at Cp Myles Standish Mass 30 Jul 43 until departed Boston P/E 7 Aug 43; arrived Iceland 13 Aug 43 and departed 5 Feb 44; arrived England 8 Feb 44 and landed in France 27 Aug 44 where guarded lines of communication; moved to Belgium 19 Dec 44 and defended Meuse River crossings; entered Germany 9 Apr 45 where inactivated on 31 Oct 46.

Campaigns: *Northern France, Rhineland, Ardennes-Alsace, Central Europe*
Aug 45 Loc: Frankfurt Germany

30th Infantry Regiment (3rd Infantry Division)

Stationed at Presidio of San Francisco Calif as part of the 3rd Division and moved to Ft Ord Calif 12 Jan 40; returned to Presidio of San Francisco 15 May 40 and relocated to Ft Lewis Wash 31 Mar 41; returned to Ft Ord Calif 2 May 42 and arrived at Cp Pickett Va 21 Sep 42; departed Hampton Roads P/E 27 Oct 42 and assaulted Fedala North Africa 8 Nov 42; assaulted Licata Sicily 10 Jul 43; landed in Italy on 18 Sep 43 and assaulted Anzio Italy 22 Jan 44; assaulted southern France 15 Aug 44 and entered Germany 13 Mar 45 and Austria 5 May 45; arrived New York P/E 4 Sep 46 and moved to Cp Campbell Ky 8 Sep 46 where continued on active duty through 1946 at zero strength (records cadre only).

Campaigns: *Algeria-French Morocco, Tunisia, Sicily, Naples-Foggia, Anzio, Rome-Arno, Southern France, Rhineland, Ardennes-Alsace, Central Europe*
Aug 45 Loc: Salzburg Austria

31st Infantry Regiment (Philippine Division)

Stationed at Manila until 3 Jan 40 when moved to Luzon defenses and then to Bataan *(attached II Philippine Corps 26 Jan–7 Apr 42)* where surrendered to Japanese forces 9 Apr 42.

Campaigns: *Philippine Islands*

32nd Infantry Regiment (7th Infantry Division)

1 Jul 40 activated at Ft Ord Calif and assigned to 7th Division and redesignated as the 32nd Infantry Regiment (Motorized) on 18 Nov 41; moved to Cp San Luis Obispo Calif 16 May 42 and participated in California Maneuvers 13–25 Jun 42 in Antelope Valley; redesignated as 32nd Infantry Regiment 1 Jan 43 and transferred to Ft Ord Calif 15 Jan 43; departed San Francisco P/E 15 Apr 43 and assaulted Attu Island Aleutians 11 May 43; left Aleutians 1 Sep 43 and arrived in Hawaii 17 Sep 43; departed Hawaii 22 Jan 44 and assaulted Kwajalein Atoll 1 Feb 44; returned to Hawaii 15 Feb 44 and left 15 Sep 44, arriving at Eniwetok 25 Sep 44 and Manus Island 3 Oct 44 en route to Philippine Islands where assaulted Leyte Island 20 Oct 44; departed Leyte 27 Mar 45 and assaulted Okinawa 1 Apr 45; arrived in Korea for occupation duty 8 Sep 45 where remained active thru 1946.

Campaigns: *Aleutian Islands, Eastern Mandates, Leyte, Ryukyus*
Aug 45 Loc: Okinawa

33rd Infantry Regiment (Separate)

Stationed at Ft Clayton Panama Canal Zone under the Panama Canal Department and moved to Trinidad 11 Dec 41 under the Trinidad Base Command; arrived New York P/E 13 Mar 44 and assigned to XXI Corps; arrived at Cp Claiborne La 15 Mar 44 where inactivated 26 Jun 44.

Campaigns: *American Theater without Inscription*

34th Infantry Regiment (8th Division) (I)

Stationed at Ft George G. Meade Md as part of the 8th Division and transferred to Ft Benning Ga on 6 Apr 40, where inactivated on 5 Jun 40.

34th Infantry Regiment (24th Infantry Division) (II)

1 Jul 40 activated at Cp Jackson S.C. as part of the 8th Division, moved to Winnsboro Mnvr Area S.C. 25 Sep 41 and returned to Cp Jackson S.C. 26 Nov 41; arrived San Francisco P/E 3 Dec 41 and departed 16 Dec 41; arrived Schofield Barracks Hawaii 21 Dec 41 where assigned to the 24th Infantry Division 12 Jun 43; departed Hawaii 9 Aug 43 and arrived Australia 25 Aug 43 and landed on Goodenough Island 15 Feb 44 *(attached as Task Force RECKLESS Reserve 27 Mar–14 May 44)*; landed in New Guinea 22 Apr 44 *(attached to HURRICANE Task Force 15 Jun–17 Jul 44 for Biak operations with 41st Inf Div)*; assaulted Leyte Island Philippines 20 Oct 44 *(attached 32nd Inf Div 17 Nov–2 Dec 44) (attached XI Corps 19 Jan–28 Feb 45)*; 3rd Bn assaulted Corregidor Island on 16 Feb 45; arrived in Japan for occupation duty 22 Oct 45 where remained active thru 1946.

Campaigns: *New Guinea, Leyte, Luzon, Southern Philippines*
Aug 45 Loc: Davao Mindanao Philippine Islands

35th Infantry Regiment (25th Infantry Division)

Stationed at Schofield Barracks Hawaii as part of the Hawaiian Division until 26 Aug 41 when assigned to the 25th Infantry Division; departed Hawaii 25 Nov 42 and landed on Guadalcanal 17 Dec 42 *(attached to Northern Landing Force Task Force 31 on 11 Aug 43)* and assaulted Vella LaVella Island 15 Aug 43; returned to Guadalcanal 20 Oct 43; moved to New Caledonia 13 Feb 44 and returned to Guadalcanal 21 Dec 44; arrived Manus Island 29 Dec 44 enroute to Philippines where landed 11 Jan 45 in Lingayen Gulf Luzon *(attached as Sixth Army Reserve 20 Nov 44–28 Jan 45)*; arrived Japan for occupation duty on 7 Oct 45 where remained active thru 1946.

Campaigns: *Central Pacific, Guadalcanal, Northern Solomons, Luzon*
Aug 45 Loc: Bambam Philippine Islands

36th Armored Infantry Regiment (3rd Armored Division)

15 Apr 41 activated at Cp Beauregard La as the 36th Infantry Regiment (Armored) assigned to the 3rd Armored Division; moved to Cp Polk La 13 Jun 41 where redesignated the 36th Armored Infantry Regiment on 1 Jan 42; transferred to Indio Calif 20 Jul 42 and to Cp Pickett Va 1 Nov 42; relocated to Indiantown Gap Mil Res Pa 13 Jan 43 and departed New York P/E 27 Aug 43; landed in England 16 Sep 43 and in France 25 Jun 44; crossed into Belgium 19 Dec 44 and entered Germany 7 Feb 45, where inactivated on 10 Nov 45.

Campaigns: *Normandy, Northern France, Rhineland, Ardennes-Alsace, Central Europe*
Aug 45 Loc: Mulheim Germany

37th Infantry Regiment (Separate)

4 Mar 41 activated, less HHC, at Ft Francis E. Warren Wyo and moved to Ft Greely Alaska on 13 Jul 41 and HHC activated at Unalaska 1 Aug 41; moved to Adak Island 26 Nov 42 and to Atka 24 Aug 43; arrived at Prince Rupert P/E Canada on 28 Jan 44 and departed 5 Feb 44; arrived Cp White Oreg 8 Feb 44 under Fourth Army and attached to III Corps 15 Feb 44; transferred to Cp Phillips Kans 26 Apr 44 under XVI Corps and assigned to XXXVI Corps on 17 Jul 44; arrived at Ft Benning Ga 14 Aug 44 under Replacement & School Command where inactivated on 5 Feb 45.

Campaigns: *Aleutian Islands*

38th Infantry Regiment (2nd Infantry Division)

Stationed at Ft Douglas Utah as part of 3rd Division until assigned to 2nd Division on 16 Oct 39; moved to Cp Bullis Tex 9 Nov 39 and to Ft Sam Houston Tex 27 Jan 40 where participated in maneuvers; transferred to Cp McCoy Wis 24 Nov 42 and staged at Cp Shanks N.Y. 30 Sep 43 until departed New York P/E 8 Oct 43; arrived England 19 Oct 43 and landed in France 12 Jun 44 *(attached VIII Corps 21–30 Aug 44)*; crossed into Belgium 3 Oct 44 and entered Germany same date *(attached 78th Inf Div 8 Mar 45 only) (attached 9th Armd Div 25 Mar–5 Apr 45)*; crossed into Czechoslovakia 5 May 45; returned to New York P/E 20 Jul 45 and moved to Cp Swift Tex 25 Jul 45; transferred to Cp Carson Colo 28 Apr 46 where remained active thru 1946.

Campaigns: *Normandy, Northern France, Rhineland, Ardennes-Alsace, Central Europe*
Aug 45 Loc: Camp Swift, Texas

39th Infantry Regiment (9th Infantry Division)

9 Aug 40 activated at Ft Bragg N.C. and assigned to 9th Division; located at Chester S.C. Mnvr area 23 Sep–1 Dec 41; returned to Ft Bragg N.C. and staged at Ft Dix N.J. 18 Sep 42 until departed New York P/E 26 Sep 42; arrived England 6 Oct 42 and assaulted North Africa 8 Nov 42; landed in Sicily 31 Jul 43 and returned to England 25 Nov 43; landed in France 10 Jun 44 *(attached to 4th Inf Div 11–15 Jun 44) (attached 1st Inf Div 4–7 Aug 44) (attached 4th Inf Div 7–9 Aug 44)*; crossed into Belgium 2 Sep 44 and entered Germany 14 Sep 44; returned to Belgium 26 Oct 44 and reentered Germany 5 Dec 44; returned to Belgium 19 Dec 44 and reentered Germany 28 Jan 45 *(attached 2nd Inf Div 8–12 Feb 45 and 17–22 Feb 45) (attached to 7th Armd Div 7–8 Mar 45) (attached to 78th Inf Div 11–16 Mar 45)*; inactivated at Bad Tolz Germany on 30 Nov 46.

Campaigns: *Algeria-French Morocco, Tunisia, Sicily, Normandy, Northern France, Rhineland, Ardennes-Alsace, Central Europe*
Aug 45 Loc: Aichach Germany

41st Armored Infantry Regiment (2nd Armored Division)

15 Jul 40 activated at Ft Benning Ga as the 41st Infantry Regiment (Armored) assigned to the 2nd Armored Division; redesignated there as the 41st Armored Infantry Regiment on 1 Jan 42; moved to Monroe S.C. 10 Jul 42 and to Ft Bragg N.C. 15 Aug 42; staged at Ft Dix N.J. 3 Nov 42 until departed New York P/E 11 Dec 42; landed in North Africa 25 Dec 42 less elements which assaulted Fedala 8 Nov 42; assaulted Sicily 10 Jul 43 and arrived in England 25 Nov 43; landed in France 9 Jun 44, crossed into Belgium 2 Sep 44 and into Holland 16 Sep 44; entered Germany 19 Sep 44; returned to Belgium 22 Dec 44 and to Holland 3 Feb 45; reentered Germany 25 Feb 45; returned to New York P/E 1 Feb 46 and moved to Cp Hood Tex 6 Feb 46 where broken up on 25 Mar 46 and reorganized as various divisional components.

Campaigns: *Algeria-French Morocco, Sicily, Normandy, Northern France, Rhineland, Ardennes-Alsace, Central Europe*
Aug 45 Loc: Burgdorf Germany

No Distinctive
Insignia Authorized

43rd Infantry Regiment (Philippine Scouts)

1 Apr 41 1st Battalion activated in Luzon Philippine Islands and was attached to the Bataan Defense Force and Philippine Division before being destroyed by Japanese forces on Bataan 6 Apr 42; Companies C and E at Zamboanga on Mindanao lost near Dalirig on 9 May 42.

Campaigns: *Philippine Islands*

45th Infantry Regiment (Philippine Scouts) (Philippine Division)

Stationed at Ft William McKinley Philippines as part of the Philippine Division and surrendered to Japanese forces on Bataan 9 Apr 42.

Campaigns: *Philippine Islands*

46th Armored Infantry Regiment (5th Armored Division)

No Distinctive
Insignia Authorized

1 Oct 41 activated at Ft Knox Ky as the 46th Infantry Regiment (Armored) assigned to 5th Armored Division and redesignated the 46th Armored Infantry Regiment on 1 Jan 42; moved to Cp Cooke Calif 16 Feb 42 and participated in the Aug-Oct 42 Calif Maneuvers; transferred to Tenn Mnvr area 23 Mar 43 and to Pine Camp N.Y. 28 Jun 43 where redesignated, less 1st and 2nd Bns, as the 46th Armored Infantry Battalion on 20 Sep 43. 1st and 2nd Bns redesignated 47th and 15th Armored Infantry Battalions, respectively.

47th Infantry Regiment (9th Infantry Division)

10 Aug 40 activated at Ft Bragg N.C. assigned to the 9th Division, participated in maneuvers at Chester S.C. 30 Sep–30 Nov 41, and returned to Ft Bragg N.C.; moved to Solomons Island Md for amphibious training 23 Jun 42; arrived at Hampton Roads P/E 15 Oct 42 and departed 27 Oct 42; assaulted Safi North Africa 8 Nov 42 and landed in Sicily 31 Jul 43; arrived England 25 Nov 43 and landed in France 9 Jun 44; crossed into Belgium 2 Sep 44 *(attached to 3rd Armd Div 8–10 Sep 44)*; entered Germany 14 Sep 44 *(attached to 3rd Armd Div 25 Oct–10 Nov 44) (attached 1st Inf Div 10 Nov–1 Dec 44) (attached to V Corps 17–25 Dec 44) (attached to 9th Armd Div 7–9 Mar 45)*; inactivated in Germany on 31 Dec 46.

Campaigns: *Algeria-French Morocco, Tunisia, Sicily, Normandy, Northern France, Rhineland, Ardennes-Alsace, Central Europe*
Aug 45 Loc: Schrobenhausen Germany

48th Armored Infantry Regiment (7th Armored Division)

No Distinctive
Insignia Authorized

2 Mar 42 activated at Cp Polk La assigned to the 7th Armored Division, participated in La maneuvers 15 Sep–9 Nov 42, and returned to Cp Polk; transferred to Cp Young Calif 17 Mar 43 and to Ft Benning Ga 11 Aug 43, where redesignated, less 1st and 2nd Bns, as the 48th Armored Infantry Battalion on 20 Sep 43. 1st and 2nd Bns redesignated 38th and 23rd Armored Infantry Battalions, respectively.

49th Armored Infantry Regiment (8th Armored Division)

No Distinctive
Insignia Authorized

1 Apr 42 activated at Ft Knox Ky assigned to the 8th Armored Division and moved to Cp Campbell Ky 8 Jan 43 and to Cp Polk La 5 Mar 43, where redesignated, less 1st and 2nd Bns, as the 49th Armored Infantry Battalion on 20 Sep 43. 1st and 2nd Battalions redesignated 58th and 7th Armored Infantry Battalions, respectively.

50th Armored Infantry Regiment (6th Armored Division)

No Distinctive
Insignia Authorized

15 Feb 42 activated at Ft Knox Ky assigned to the 6th Armored Division and moved to Cp Chaffee Ark 20 Mar 42 where participated in the Aug-Sep 42 La maneuvers; transferred to Cp Young Calif 11 Oct 42 and to Cp Cooke Calif 19 Mar 43; there redesignated, less 1st and 2nd Bns, as the 50th Armored Infantry Battalion on 20 Sep 43. 1st and 2nd Battalions redesignated 44th and 9th Armored Infantry Battalions, respectively.

51st Armored Infantry Regiment (4th Armored Division)

14 Apr 41 activated at Pine Camp N.Y. as the 51st Infantry Regiment (Armored) assigned to the 4th Armored Division, where redesignated the 51st Armored Infantry Regiment on 1 Jan 42; moved to the Tenn Mnvr area 30 Sep 42 and to Cp Young Calif 27 Nov 42; transferred to Cp Bowie Tex 13 Jun 43 where redesignated, less 1st and 2nd Bns, as the 51st Armored Infantry Battalion on 10 Sep 43. 1st and 2nd Bns redesignated 53rd and 10th Armored Infantry Battalions, respectively.

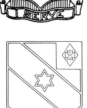

52nd Armored Infantry Regiment (9th Armored Division)

15 Jul 42 activated at Ft Riley Kans assigned to the 9th Armored Division and moved to Cp Young Calif 18 Jun 43, where redesignated, less 1st, 2nd, and 3rd Bns, as the 52nd Armored Infantry Battalion on 9 Oct 43. 3rd Bn disbanded and 1st and 2nd Bns redesignated 60th and 27th Armored Infantry Battalions, respectively.

53rd Infantry Regiment (Separate)

1 Aug 40 activated at Ft Ord Calif assigned to 7th Division until 7 Nov 41; moved to the Sacramento Fairgrounds Calif 8 Dec 41 and to the Ogden Utah State Armory 24 Jan 42; transferred to the Presidio of San Francisco Calif 18 Apr 42 and departed San Francisco P/E 18 Jun 42; arrived Ft Randall Alaska 26 Jun 42 and relocated to Adak Island 22 Aug 42; attached to Amphibious Force #9 21 Jul 43 and landed on evacuated Kiska Island 15 Aug 43; departed the Aleutian Islands 22 Sep 44 and arrived Seattle P/E 2 Oct 44 under Fourth Army; moved to Cp Swift Tex 12 Oct 44 and to Cp Shelby Miss 18 Feb 45 where assigned to Replacement & School Command; transferred to Cp Hood Tex 9 Jul 45 and assigned to the Tank Destroyer Replacement Training Center the next day; arrived at Cp Callan Calif 6 Aug 45 under XXXVI Corps where inactivated on 11 Sep 45.

Campaigns: *Aleutian Islands*
Aug 45 Loc: Camp Callan California

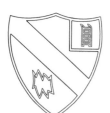

54th Armored Infantry Regiment (10th Armored Division)

15 Jul 42 activated at Ft Benning Ga assigned to the 10th Armored Division and moved to the Tenn Mnvr area 27 Jun 43; transferred to Cp Gordon Ga 4 Sep 43 where redesignated, less 1st, 2nd, and 3rd Bns, as the 54th Armored Infantry Battalion on 20 Sep 43. 3rd Bn disbanded and 1st and 2nd Bns redesignated 61st and 20th Armored Infantry Battalions, respectively.

No Distinctive
Insignia Authorized

55th Armored Infantry Regiment (11th Armored Division)

15 Aug 42 activated at Cp Polk La assigned to the 11th Armored Division and moved to the La Mnvr area 25 Jun 43; transferred to Cp Barkeley Tex 22 Aug 43 where redesignated, less 1st, 2nd, and 3rd Bns, as the 55th Armored Infantry Battalion on 20 Sep 43. 3rd Bn disbanded and 1st and 2nd Bns redesignated 63rd and 21st Armored Infantry Battalions, respectively.

No Distinctive
Insignia Authorized

56th Armored Infantry Regiment (12th Armored Division)

15 Sep 42 activated at Cp Campbell Ky assigned to the 12th Armored Division and moved to Tenn Mnvr area 6 Sep 43 where redesignated, less 1st and 2nd Bns, as the 56th Armored Infantry Battalion on 11 Nov 43. 1st and 2nd Bns redesignated 66th and 17th Armored Infantry Battalions, respectively.

57th Infantry Regiment (Philippine Scouts) (Philippine Division)

Stationed at Ft William McKinley Philippines assigned to the Philippine Division and surrendered to Japanese forces at Bataan 9 Apr 42.

Campaigns: *Philippine Islands*

No Distinctive
Insignia Authorized

58th Infantry Regiment (Separate)

24 Apr 42 activated at Ft Lewis Wash and staged at Cp Murray Wash in May 42, arriving at Ft Glenn Alaska late May 42; transferred to Dutch Harbor Alaska in Jun 42 where Headquarters disbanded 26 Jan 44 and 1st and 2nd Bns redesignated 203rd and 204th Infantry Battalions same date; 3rd Bn redesignated 205th Infantry Battalion 10 Feb 44.

Campaigns: *Aleutian Islands*

No Distinctive
Insignia Authorized

59th Armored Infantry Regiment (13th Armored Division)

15 Oct 42 activated at Cp Beale Calif assigned to the 13th Armored Division, where redesignated, less 1st and 2nd Bns, as the 59th Armored Infantry Battalion on 20 Sep 43. 1st and 2nd Bns redesignated 67th and 16th Armored Infantry Battalions, respectively.

60th Infantry Regiment (9th Infantry Division)

10 Aug 40 activated at Ft Bragg N.C. assigned to the 9th Division, moved to Chester S.C. 26 Sep 41 for maneuvers, and returned to Ft Bragg N.C.; transferred to Norfolk Va for amphibious training 18 Sep 42 and departed Hampton Roads P/E 27 Oct 42; assaulted North Africa 8 Nov 42 and landed in Sicily 31 Jul 43; arrived in England 25 Nov 43 and landed in France 11 Jun 44; crossed into Belgium 2 Sep 44 and entered Germany 15 Sep 44 *(attached 104th Inf Div 18–21 Dec 44) (attached 2nd Armd Div 22–23 Dec 44) (attached 9th Armd Div 4–5 Mar 45) (attached 7th Armd Div 8–9 Mar 45) (attached 3rd Armd Div 22–24 Apr 45)*; inactivated in Germany on 28 Dec 46.

Campaigns: *Algeria–French Morocco, Tunisia, Sicily, Normandy, Northern France, Rhineland, Ardennes-Alsace, Central Europe*

Aug 45 Loc: Giesenfeld Germany

No Distinctive
Insignia Authorized

62nd Armored Infantry Regiment (14th Armored Division)

15 Nov 42 activated at Cp Chaffee Ark assigned to the 14th Armored Division, where redesignated, less 1st and 2nd Bns, as the 62nd Armored Infantry Battalion on 20 Sep 43; 1st and 2nd Battalions redesignated 68th and 19th Armored Infantry Battalions, respectively.

63rd Infantry Regiment (6th Infantry Division)

1 Jun 41 activated at Ft Leonard Wood Mo assigned to the 6th Division and redesignated the 63rd Infantry Regiment (Motorized) in Oct 42; moved to Cp Young Calif 9 Dec 42 and to Cp San Luis Obispo Calif 28 Mar 43 where redesignated 63rd Infantry Regiment on 1 May 43; staged at Cp Stoneman Calif 16 Jul 43 until departed San Francisco P/E 21 Jul 43; arrived Hawaii 29 Jul 43 and departed 26 Jan 44; arrived at Milne Bay New Guinea on 31 Jan 44 and landed in the Toem Bay area 14 Jun 44; assaulted Sansapor New Guinea on 30 Jul 44 and assaulted Lingayen Gulf Luzon Philippines 10 Jan 45 *(attached to I Corps 10 Jan–11 Jan 45) (attached 43rd Inf Div 12–30 Jan 45)*; arrived in Korea for occupation duty 18 Oct 45 where active thru 1946.

Campaigns: *New Guinea, Luzon*
Aug 45 Loc: Bagabag Philippine Islands

65th Infantry Regiment (Puerto Rican) (Separate)

Stationed at San Juan Puerto Rico and moved to Ft Miles Puerto Rico 1 Feb 40; served between Salinas and Ft Buchanan (ex-Ft Miles) until transferred to Cp Tortuguero Puerto Rico 4 Nov 42; arrived Ft Clayton Panama Canal Zone 14 Jan 43 and New Orleans P/E 21 Jan 44; staged at Cp Patrick Henry Va 29 Jan 44 until departed Hampton Roads P/E 26 Mar 44; arrived in North Africa 5 Apr 44 and landed in France 30 Sep 44; 3rd Bn sent to Corsica where attached to 12th Air Force 13 Dec 44 and later fought in the Maritime Alps; remainder of regiment entered Germany 2 Apr 45 *(attached to 63rd Inf Div 30 Apr–12 May 45)*; returned to Puerto Rico 9 Nov 45 and stationed at Ponce Air Base (Losey Field) Puerto Rico 4 Dec 45; served briefly on Trinidad and returned to Cp O'Reilly Puerto Rico 6 Feb 46 and moved to Henry Barracks where remained active thru 1946.

Campaigns: *Rome-Arno, Rhineland, Ardennes-Alsace, Central Europe*
Aug 45 Loc: Feudenheim Germany

66th Infantry Regiment (Light Tanks) (2nd Armored Division)

15 Jan 40 activated at Ft Benning Ga assigned to the 2nd Armored Division and moved to Cp Beauregard La 11 May 40 for maneuvers; returned to Ft Benning Ga 2 Jun 40 where redesignated the 66th Armored Regiment (Light) on 15 Jul 40.

66th Infantry Regiment (71st Infantry Division)

15 Jul 43 activated at Cp Carson Colo and assigned to the 71st Light Division; moved to Hunter-Liggett Mil Res Calif 12 Feb 44 and to Ft Benning Ga 24 May 44; staged at Cp Kilmer N.J. 17 Jan 45 until departed New York P/E 26 Jan 45; arrived in France 6 Feb 45 *(attached to 100th Inf Div 12–14 Mar 45)*; entered Germany 23 Mar 45; returned to New York P/E 3 Apr 46 and inactivated at Cp Kilmer N.J. on 5 Apr 46.

Campaigns: *Rhineland, Central Europe*
Aug 45 Loc: Dillingen Germany

67th Infantry Regiment (Medium Tanks)

5 Jun 40 activated at Ft Benning Ga where redesignated 67th Armored Regiment 15 Jul 40.

68th Infantry Regiment (Light Tanks)

1 Jan 40 1st and 2nd Battalions activated at Ft Benning Ga and 1st Bn inactivated 5 Jun 40; 2nd Bn redesignated 2nd Bn, 68th Armored Regiment, there on 15 Jul 40.

71st Infantry Regiment (44th Infantry Division)   New York National Guard

16 Sep 40 inducted into federal service at New York N.Y. assigned to the 44th Division and moved to Ft Dix N.J. 23 Sep 40; participated in Carolina Maneuvers 26 Sep–6 Dec 41 and returned to Ft Dix N.J.; moved to Cp Claiborne La 16 Jan 42 and to Ft Lewis Wash 25 Feb 42; transferred to Vancouver Barracks Wash 22 Apr–1 Jun 42 and to Salem Oreg 1 Dec 42–21 Jan 43; relocated to Ft Lewis Wash 21 Jan 43 and to La Mnvr area 27 Jan 44; arrived at Cp Phillips Kans 8 Apr 44 and staged at Cp Myles Standish Mass 23 Aug 44 until departed Boston P/E 5 Sep 44; landed in France on 15 Sep 44 *(attached to 79th Inf Div 18–24 Oct 44)* and entered Germany 25 Mar 45 and Austria 30 Apr 45; arrived at New York P/E 20 Jul 45 and moved to Cp Chaffee Ark 24 Jul 45 where inactivated on 23 Nov 45.

Campaigns: *Northern France, Rhineland, Ardennes-Alsace, Central Europe*
Aug 45 Loc: Camp Chaffee Arkansas

85th Mountain Infantry Regiment (10th Mountain Division)

No Distinctive
Insignia Authorized

15 Jul 43 activated at Cp Hale Colo assigned to the 10th Light Division as the 85th Infantry Regiment and moved to Cp Swift Tex 25 Jun 44 where redesignated the 85th Mountain Infantry Regiment on 6 Nov 44; staged at Cp Patrick Henry Va 24 Dec 44 until departed Hampton Roads P/E 4 Jan 45; arrived in Italy 13 Jan 45 and arrived back in New York P/E 10 Aug 45; moved to Cp Carson Colo 14 Aug 45 where inactivated 30 Nov 45.

Campaigns: *North Apennines, Po Valley*
Aug 45 Loc: Cp Carson Colorado

86th Mountain Infantry Regiment (10th Mountain Division)

No Distinctive
Insignia Authorized

1 May 43 activated at Cp Hale Colo as the 86th Infantry Regiment and assigned to the Mountain Training Center; moved to Cp Swift Tex 25 Jun 43 where assigned to the 10th Light Division 15 Jul 43 and redesignated the 86th Mountain Infantry Regiment on 6 Nov 44; staged at Cp Patrick Henry Va 2 Dec 44 until departed Hampton Roads P/E 10 Dec 44; arrived in Italy 23 Dec 44 and returned to Hampton Roads P/E 7 Aug 45; moved to Cp Carson Colo 11 Aug 45 where inactivated on 27 Nov 45.

Campaigns: *North Apennines, Po Valley*
Aug 45 Loc: Camp Carson Colorado

87th Mountain Infantry Regiment (10th Mountain Division)

15 Nov 41 1st Battalion activated at Ft Lewis Wash as the 1st Bn, 87th Infantry Mountain Regiment assigned to the Mountain Training Center and remainder of regiment activated there 25 May 42; transferred to Hunter-Liggett Mil Res Calif 19 Nov 42 and to Cp Hale Colo 29 Dec 42; arrived at Ft Ord Calif 14 Jun 43 where assigned to Amphibious Training Force #9 on 14 Jul 43 and departed San Francisco P/E 29 Jul 43; arrived on Adak Island 4 Aug 43 and landed on evacuated Kiska Island 15 Aug 43; sent to Port Edward P/E Canada on 17 Dec 43 and moved to Cp Carson Colo 24 Dec 43; there redesignated the 87th Infantry Regiment 22 Feb 44 and assigned to 10th Light Division same date; transferred to Cp Swift Tex 28 Jun 44 where redesignated the 87th Mountain Infantry Regiment on 6 Nov 44; staged at Cp Patrick Henry Va 24 Dec 44 until departed Hampton Roads P/E 4 Jan 45; arrived in Italy 13 Jan 45 and returned to Hampton Roads P/E 11 Aug 45; moved to Cp Carson Colo 16 Aug 45 where inactivated on 21 Nov 45.

Campaigns: *Aleutian Islands, North Apennines, Po Valley*
Aug 45 Loc: Camp Carson Colorado

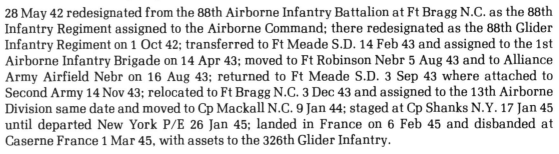

88th Glider Infantry Regiment (13th Airborne Division)

28 May 42 redesignated from the 88th Airborne Infantry Battalion at Ft Bragg N.C. as the 88th Infantry Regiment assigned to the Airborne Command; there redesignated as the 88th Glider Infantry Regiment on 1 Oct 42; transferred to Ft Meade S.D. 14 Feb 43 and assigned to the 1st Airborne Infantry Brigade on 14 Apr 43; moved to Ft Robinson Nebr 5 Aug 43 and to Alliance Army Airfield Nebr on 16 Aug 43; returned to Ft Meade S.D. 3 Sep 43 where attached to Second Army 14 Nov 43; relocated to Ft Bragg N.C. 3 Dec 43 and assigned to the 13th Airborne Division same date and moved to Cp Mackall N.C. 9 Jan 44; staged at Cp Shanks N.Y. 17 Jan 45 until departed New York P/E 26 Jan 45; landed in France on 6 Feb 45 and disbanded at Caserne France 1 Mar 45, with assets to the 326th Glider Infantry.

Campaigns: *Central Europe*

89th Infantry Regiment (Separate)

No Distinctive
Insignia Authorized

Activated by companies as follows: Co A - 15 Oct 41 Ft Dix N.J.; HHC, 3rd Bn - 2 Jan 41 Ft Snelling Minn; Co I - 1 Jun 41 Bermuda; Co K - 2 Jan 41 Ft Snelling Minn; Co L - 20 Jun 41 Bermuda; Co M - 1 Sep 41 Ft Jackson S.C.; guarded several island complexes in the Antilles Command on Jamaica and Bermuda; inactivated as follows: HHC, 3rd Bn and Cos I, K, and M - 21 Oct 43 Ft Benning Ga; Co A - 19 Nov 43 Antilles; Co L - 30 Jul 44 Cp Pickett Va.

Campaigns: *American Theater without Inscription*

90th Infantry Regiment (Separate)

No Distinctive
Insignia Authorized

15 Jul 43 activated at Cp Hale Colo assigned to the 10th Light Division until 22 Feb 44 when transferred to Cp Carson Colo under XVI Corps; assigned to XXXVI Corps on 17 Jul 44 and moved to Cp Gruber Okla 1 Dec 44; there assigned to the Replacement & School Command on 9 Feb 45 and relocated to Cp Rucker Ala 17 Feb 45 where inactivated 10 Aug 45.

91st Infantry Regiment (Separate)

No Distinctive
Insignia Authorized

10 Mar 42 3rd Battalion, less Cos I and K, activated at Cp Blanding Fla from assets of Cos K and M of the 102nd Infantry Regt; departed Cp Blanding Fla 19 Apr 42 and staged at Cp Pendleton Va until departed Hampton Roads P/E 7 Jul 42; stationed on Ascension Island until transferred to the Philippines in late 1945 where the remainder of the regiment was activated on 31 Dec 46.

Campaigns: *American Theater without inscription*

Aug 45 Loc: Ascension Island

101st Infantry Regiment (26th Infantry Division)　　　Massachusetts National Guard

16 Jan 41 inducted into federal service at Boston Mass assigned to the 26th Division and moved to Cp Edwards Mass 23 Jan 41; moved to A.P.Hill Mil Res Va 25 Jun 42 and to Ft George G. Meade Md 12 Oct 42; transferred to Ft Jackson S.C. 29 Jan 43 and to Cp Gordon Ga 20 Apr 43; relocated to Cp Campbell Ky 5 Sep 43 and to the Tenn Mnvr area 22 Jan 44; returned to Ft Jackson S.C. 30 Mar 44 and staged at Cp Shanks N.Y. 22 Aug 44 until departed New York P/E 27 Aug 44; landed in France on 7 Sep 44 and crossed into Luxembourg on 20 Dec 44; returned to France 28 Jan 45 and entered Germany 4 Feb 45; returned to France again 19 Feb 45 and reentered Germany 23 Feb 45; entered Czechoslovakia 6 May 45; arrived Boston P/E 29 Dec 45 and inactivated at Cp Myles Standish Mass same date.

Campaigns: *Northern France, Rhineland, Ardennes-Alsace, Central Europe*
Aug 45 Loc: Horni Plana Czechoslovakia

102nd Infantry Regiment (Separate)　　　Connecticut National Guard

24 Feb 41 inducted into federal service at New Haven Conn assigned to the 43rd Division and moved to Cp Blanding Fla 15 Mar 41; arrived at Charleston P/E 15 Jan 42, less most of 3rd Bn which assets transferred into 91st Inf Regt later, and departed 27 Jan 42 as part of Task Force 5614; arrived at Bora Bora Society Islands 17 Feb 42 and relieved from assignment to 43rd Infantry Division on 19 Feb 42 and assigned to GHQ; assigned to III Island Base Command 1 Oct 43 and moved to Espiritu Santo 8 Apr 44 where assigned to South Pacific Base Command; arrived in Hawaii 22 Nov 44 under Central Pacific Base Command and assigned to the Combat Training Command there; Co K served on Leyte Island Philippines and inactivated there 10 Apr 45; remainder of regiment, less 2nd Bn, inactivated in Hawaii 10 Apr 45 and 2nd Bn inactivated there on 30 Jun 46.

Campaigns: *Western Pacific* (det only), *Leyte* (Co K only)
Aug 45 Loc: Schofield Barracks Hawaii, less Co F on Christmas Island

103rd Infantry Regiment (43rd Infantry Division)　　　Maine National Guard

24 Feb 41 inducted into Federal service at Portland Maine assigned to the 43rd Division and moved to Cp Blanding Fla 13 Mar 41; transferred to Cp Shelby Miss 14 Feb 42 and to Ft Ord Calif 7 Sep 42; departed San Francisco P/E 30 Sep 42 and arrived in New Zealand 25 Oct 42; arrived Noumea New Caledonia 7 Nov 42 and departed 13 Feb 43; landed on Guadalcanal 17 Feb 43 and landed in Russell Islands 21 Feb 43; assaulted New Georgia 30 Jun 43 and 3rd Bn landed at Laiana New Guinea 14 Jul 43; regiment returned to New Zealand 17 Feb 44 and arrived Aitape New Guinea 22 Jul 44; departed New Guinea 26 Dec 44 and assaulted Lingayen Gulf Luzon Philippine Islands 9 Jan 45 *(attached 1st Cav Div 8–12 Mar 45) (attached XIV Corps 1–31 Jul 45)*; arrived in Japan for occupation duty 13 Sep 45 and returned to San Francisco P/E 9 Oct 45; inactivated at Cp Stoneman Calif on 1 Nov 45.

Campaigns: *Guadalcanal, Northern Solomons, New Guinea, Luzon*
Aug 45 Loc: Cabanatuan Philippine Islands

104th Infantry Regiment (26th Infantry Division)　　　Massachusetts National Guard

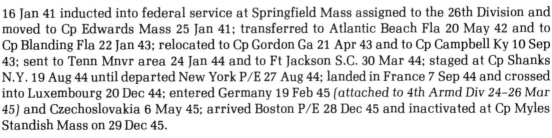

16 Jan 41 inducted into federal service at Springfield Mass assigned to the 26th Division and moved to Cp Edwards Mass 25 Jan 41; transferred to Atlantic Beach Fla 20 May 42 and to Cp Blanding Fla 22 Jan 43; relocated to Cp Gordon Ga 21 Apr 43 and to Cp Campbell Ky 10 Sep 43; sent to Tenn Mnvr area 24 Jan 44 and to Ft Jackson S.C. 30 Mar 44; staged at Cp Shanks N.Y. 19 Aug 44 until departed New York P/E 27 Aug 44; landed in France 7 Sep 44 and crossed into Luxembourg 20 Dec 44; entered Germany 19 Feb 45 *(attached to 4th Armd Div 24–26 Mar 45)* and Czechoslovakia 6 May 45; arrived Boston P/E 28 Dec 45 and inactivated at Cp Myles Standish Mass on 29 Dec 45.

Campaigns: *Northern France, Rhineland, Ardennes-Alsace, Central Europe*
Aug 45 Loc: Chaulsing Czechoslovakia

105th Infantry Regiment (27th Infantry Division)　　　　**New York National Guard**

15 Oct 40 inducted into federal service at Troy N.Y. assigned to the 27th Division and moved to Ft McClellan Ala 25 Oct 40; moved to Riverside Calif 21 Dec 41 and to Ft Ord Calif 22 Jan 42; departed San Francisco P/E 10 Mar 42 and arrived in Hawaii 17 Mar 42; 3rd Bn landed on Makin Island 20 Nov 43 and returned to Hawaii 2 Dec 43; regiment left Hawaii 31 May 44 and landed on Saipan 16–17 Jun 44 *(attached to Army Garrison Force 244 on Saipan 15–30 Jul 44)*; arrived Espiritu Santo 4 Sep 44 and departed 25 Mar 45; assaulted Tsugen Shima off Okinawa 10 Apr 45 and landed on Okinawa 12–13 Apr 45; arrived in Japan for occupation duty 12 Sep 45 where inactivated on 12 Dec 45.

Campaigns: *Central Pacific, Western Pacific, Ryukyus*
Aug 45 Loc: Okinawa

106th Infantry Regiment (27th Infantry Division)　　　　**New York National Guard**

11 Dec 40 redesignated from 10th Infantry Regiment (N.Y. NG) at Ft McClellan Ala and assigned to the 27th Division; moved to Cp Forrest Tenn 30 May 41 and returned to Ft McClellan Ala 30 Jun 41; transferred to Corona Calif 21 Dec 41 and to Ft Ord Calif 22 Jan 42; departed San Francisco P/E 10 Mar 42 and arrived Hawaii 15 Mar 42; designated reserve for projected Marshall Islands operations on 3 Oct 43 and attached to V Amphibious Corps for training 14 Dec 43; departed Hawaii 23 Jan 44 and 2nd Bn occupied Majuro Atoll 1 Feb–5 Mar 44, remainder of regiment assaulted Eniwetok 19 Feb 44 and arrived back in Hawaii 13 Apr 44; landed on Saipan 20 Jun 44 and departed 4 Sep 44; arrived Espiritu Santo 13 Sep 44 and left 20 Mar 45 *(attached 96th Inf Div 11–16 Apr 45)*; landed on Okinawa 12 Apr 45 and 2nd Bn attached Island Command APO 245 as Ie Shima garrison on 3 May 45; regiment arrived in Japan 12 Sep 45 and arrived at Seattle P/E 31 Dec 45; inactivated at Ft Lawton Wash on 31 Dec 45.

Campaigns: *Eastern Mandates, Western Pacific, Ryukyus*
Aug 45 Loc: Okinawa

108th Infantry Regiment (40th Infantry Division)　　　　**New York National Guard**

15 Oct 40 inducted into federal service at Syracuse N.Y. assigned to the 27th Division and moved to Ft McClellan Ala 26 Oct 40; moved to the Los Angeles County Fairgrounds at Pomona Calif 21 Dec 41 and to Ft Ord Calif 22 Jan 42; departed San Francisco P/E 7 Apr 42 and arrived Hawaii 17 Apr 42 where relieved from the 27th and assigned to the 40th Infantry Division on 1 Sep 42; departed Hawaii 21 Jan 44 and arrived Guadalcanal 4 Feb 44 which departed 22 Apr 44; arrived Cape Gloucester New Britain 28 Apr 44 and left 9 Dec 44 *(attached as XIV Corps Reserve 30 Nov 44–10 Jan 45)*; landed at Lingayen Gulf Luzon Philippine Islands 10 Jan 45; left Luzon 8 Mar 45 and arrived at Leyte 13 Mar 45 and assaulted Macjalar Bay Mindanao 10 May 45 *(attached Eighth Army Area Command 13 Mar–24 May 45) (attached X Corps 25 May–28 Jun 45)*; rejoined division on Panay 29 Jun 45 and departed Philippines 29 Jul 45 and served on occupation duty in Korea 1 Nov 45–15 Mar 46; returned to San Francisco P/E 5 Apr 46 and inactivated at Cp Stoneman Calif on 7 Apr 46.

Campaigns: *Bismarck Archipelago, Leyte, Luzon, Southern Philippines*
Aug 45 Loc: Cotabato Philippine Islands

109th Infantry Regiment (28th Infantry Division)　　　　**Pennsylvania National Guard**

17 Feb 41 inducted into federal service at Scranton Pa assigned to the 28th Division and moved to Indiantown Gap Mil Res Pa 1 Mar 41; transferred to Cp Livingston La 11 Jan 42 and to Cp Gordon Johnston Fla 23 Jan 43; arrived at Cp Pickett Va 6 Jun 43 and staged at Cp Myles Standish Mass 1 Oct 43 until departed Boston P/E 20 Oct 43; arrived England 29 Oct 43 and landed in France 22 Jul 44; crossed into Belgium 7 Sep 44 and into Luxembourg 8 Sep 44 *(attached to 9th Armd Div 20–22 Dec 44) (attached 10th Armd Div 22–26 Dec 44)*; returned to Belgium 27 Dec 44 and to France 2 Jan 45; reentered Belgium 1 Feb 45 and entered Germany 21 Feb 45; returned to Boston P/E 2 Aug 45 and moved to Cp Shelby Miss 7 Aug 45 where inactivated on 22 Oct 45.

Campaigns: *Normandy, Northern France, Rhineland, Ardennes-Alsace, Central Europe*
Aug 45 Loc: Camp Shelby Mississippi

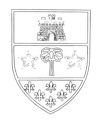

110th Infantry Regiment (28th Infantry Division)   Pennsylvania National Guard

17 Feb 41 inducted into federal service at Washington Pa assigned to the 28th Division and moved to Indiantown Gap Mil Res Pa 28 Feb 41; transferred to Cp Livingston La 19 Jan 42 and to Cp Gordon Johnston Fla 19 Jan 43; arrived at Cp Pickett Va 10 Jun 43 and staged at Cp Shanks N.Y. 27 Sep 43 until departed New York P/E 8 Oct 43; arrived England 18 Oct 43 and landed in France 22 Jul 44; crossed into Belgium 7 Sep 44 and into Holland 8 Sep 44 and entered Germany 11 Sep 44; returned to Belgium 18 Dec 44 and to France 2 Jan 45; reentered Belgium 19 Feb 45 and Germany 21 Feb 45; arrived Boston P/E 2 Aug 45 and moved to Cp Shelby Miss 6 Aug 45 where inactivated on 25 Oct 45.

Campaigns: *Normandy, Northern France, Rhineland, Ardennes-Alsace, Central Europe*
Aug 45 Loc: Camp Shelby Mississippi

111th Infantry Regiment (Separate)   Pennsylvania National Guard

17 Feb 41 inducted into federal service at Philadelphia Pa assigned to the 28th Division and moved to Indiantown Gal Mil Res Pa 27 Feb 41; transferred to Baltimore Md 20 Dec 41 and to Ft Monroe Va 18 Jan 42 where relieved from the 28th Division 17 Feb 42 and assigned to the Eastern Defense Command 30 Apr 42; further attached to the Chesapeake Bay sector 8 Feb 43 and relocated to Cp Pendleton Va 15 Oct 43; staged at Cp Stoneman Calif 3 Nov 43 and departed San Francisco P/E 9 Nov 43; arrived Hawaii 12 Nov 43 under Central Pacific Base Command; 1st Bn assaulted Kwajalein 31 Jan 44 and remained as the garrison while Co I assaulted Ujelan Atoll near Eniwetok 22 Apr 44; regiment moved to Peleliu 1 Feb 45 where attached Western Pacific Base Command 15 May 45; departed 2 Nov 45 and arrived Los Angeles P/E 21 Nov 45 and inactivated at Cp Anza Calif on 22 Nov 45.

Campaigns: *Central Pacific, Eastern Mandates, Western Pacific*
Aug 45 Loc: Peleliu Island Palau Islands

112th Infantry Regiment (28th Infantry Division)   Pennsylvania National Guard

17 Feb 41 inducted into federal service at Kane Pa assigned to the 28th Division and moved to Indiantown Gap Mil Res Pa 27 Feb 41; transferred to Cp Livingston La 11 Jan 42 and to Cp Gordon Johnston Fla 17 Jan 43; arrived at Cp Pickett Va 2 Jun 43 and staged at Cp Myles Standish Mass 28 Sep 43 until departed Boston P/E 8 Oct 43; arrived England 18 Oct 43 and landed in France 22 Jul 44; crossed into Belgium 7 Sep 44 and into Holland 8 Sep 44; entered Germany 11 Sep 44 *(attached 5th Armd Div 13-26 Sep 44) (attached 8th Inf Div 15-19 Nov 44)* and returned to Belgium 18 Dec 44 *(attached to 106th Inf Div 19-23 Dec 44) (attached to 30th Inf Div 5-11 Jan 45)*; entered Germany again 21 Feb 45 *(attached to 78th Inf Div 19-25 Apr 45)*; returned to Boston P/E 3 Aug 45 and moved to Cp Shelby Miss 6 Aug 45 where inactivated on 6 Dec 45.

Campaigns: *Normandy, Northern France, Rhineland, Ardennes-Alsace, Central Europe*
Aug 45 Loc: Camp Shelby Mississippi

113th Infantry Regiment (Separate)   New Jersey National Guard

16 Sep 40 inducted into federal service at Newark N.J. assigned to the 44th Division and moved to Ft Dix N.J. 24 Sep 40; transferred to Freehold N.J. 15 Dec 41 and to Ft Hancock N.J. 23 Dec 41 where relieved from the 44th Division on 16 Feb 42 and assigned to GHQ 20 Feb 42; reassigned to the Eastern Defense Command 30 Apr 42 and relocated to Ft Hamilton N.Y. 19 Mar 43; transferred to Cp Pickett Va 30 Mar 44 under XIII Corps and attached to Second Army there 25 Oct 44; moved to Ft Jackson S.C. 23 Dec 44 where assigned to Replacement & School Command on 9 Feb 45; arrived at Cp Rucker Ala 17 Feb 45 where inactivated on 25 Sep 45.

Aug 45 Loc: Camp Rucker Alabama

114th Infantry Regiment (44th Infantry Division)   New Jersey National Guard

16 Sep 40 inducted into federal service at Camden N.J. assigned to the 44th Division and moved to Ft Dix N.J. 23 Sep 40; transferred to Salem Oreg 16 Jan 42 and to Ft Lewis Wash 26 Feb 42; sent to La Mnvr area 3 Feb 44 and to Cp Phillips Kans 8 Apr 44; staged at Cp Myles Standish Mass 26 Aug 44 until departed Boston P/E 5 Sep 44; arrived in France 15 Sep 44 *(attached to 79th Inf Div 17–24 Oct 44)*; entered Germany 17 Mar 45 and Austria 1 Apr 45; arrived New York P/E 20 Jul 45 and moved to Cp Chaffee Ark 24 Jul 45 where inactivated on 16 Nov 45.

Campaigns: *Northern France, Rhineland, Ardennes-Alsace, Central Europe*
Aug 45 Loc: Camp Chaffee Arkansas

115th Infantry Regiment (29th Infantry Division)   Maryland National Guard

3 Feb 41 inducted into federal service at Frederick Md assigned to the 29th Division and moved to Ft George G. Meade Md 18 Feb 41; transferred to A.P. Hill Mil Res Va 22 Apr 42 and to the Carolina Mnvr area 8 Jul 42; arrived Cp Blanding Fla 19 Aug 42 and staged at Cp Kilmer N.J. 20 Sep 42 until departed New York P/E 5 Oct 42; arrived England 11 Oct 42 *(attached 1st Inf Div 2–7 Jun 44)* and assaulted Normandy France 6 Jun 44; crossed into Belgium and Holland both on 27 Sep 44 and entered Germany 30 Sep 44; returned to New York P/E 16 Jan 46 and inactivated at Cp Kilmer N.J. on 17 Jan 46.

Campaigns: *Normandy, Northern France, Rhineland, Central Europe*
Aug 45 Loc: Bremen Germany

116th Infantry Regiment (29th Infantry Division)   Virginia National Guard

3 Feb 41 inducted into federal service at Staunton Va assigned to the 29th Division and moved to Ft George G. Meade Md 20 Feb 41; transferred to A.P. Hill Mil Res Va 22 Apr 42 and to the Carolina Mnvr area 8 Jul 42; arrived Cp Blanding Fla 19 Aug 42 and staged at Cp Kilmer N.J. 20 Sep 42 until departed New York P/E 27 Sep 42; arrived England 2 Oct 42 *(attached 1st Inf Div 17 May–7 Jun 44)* and assaulted Normandy France 6 Jun 44; crossed into Belgium and Holland both on 28 Sep 44 and entered Germany 12 Oct 44 *(attached 75th Inf Div 1–7 Apr 45)*; returned to New York P/E 4 Jan 46 and inactivated at Cp Kilmer N.J. on 6 Jan 46.

Campaigns: *Normandy, Northern France, Rhineland, Central Europe*
Aug 45 Loc: Lehe Germany

117th Infantry Regiment (30th Infantry Division)   Tennessee National Guard

16 Sep 40 inducted into federal service at Jackson Tenn assigned to the 30th Division and moved to Ft Jackson S.C. 24 Sep 40; transferred to Ft Benning Ga 13 Sep 42 and served as Inf School demonstration regiment for river crossings; relocated to Cp Blanding Fla 1 Mar 43 and to Tullahoma Tenn 30 May 43; arrived at Cp Atterbury Ind 15 Nov 43 and staged at Cp Myles Standish Mass 28 Jan 44 until departed Boston P/E 11 Feb 44; arrived England 23 Feb 44 and landed in France 14 Jun 44; crossed into Belgium 4 Sep 44 and into Holland 12 Sep 44 and entered Germany 19 Sep 44; returned to Belgium 18 Dec 44 and reentered Germany 2 Feb 45; returned to Holland 6 Mar 45 and returned to Germany 18 Mar 45; arrived New York P/E 21 Aug 45 and moved to Ft Jackson S.C. 24 Aug 45 where inactivated on 24 Nov 45.

Campaigns: *Normandy, Northern France, Rhineland, Ardennes-Alsace, Central Europe*
Aug 45 Loc: Shipment #10390-F at sea

118th Infantry Regiment (Separate) **South Carolina National Guard**

16 Sep 40 inducted into federal service at Charleston S.C. assigned to the 30th Division and moved to Ft Jackson S.C. 21 Sep 40; staged at Cp Kilmer N.J. 4 Aug 42 and departed New York P/E 5 Aug 42; arrived Iceland for security duty 19 Aug 42 where relieved from assignment to the 30th Division on 24 Aug 42; departed Iceland 29 Oct 43 and arrived in England 6 Nov 43 and in Ireland 6 Jan 44; returned to England 1 May 44 and landed in France 13 Dec 44 and defended the Meuse River bridge at Givet during the German Ardennes Counteroffensive; entered Germany 26 May 45 and returned to New York P/E 14 Jan 46 and inactivated at Cp Kilmer N.J. on 15 Jan 46.

Campaigns: *Northern France, Rhineland*
Aug 45 Loc: Feudenheim Germany

No Distinctive
Insignia Authorized

119th Infantry Regiment (30th Infantry Division) **North Carolina National Guard**

7 Sep 42 activated at Ft Jackson S.C. and assigned to 30th Infantry Division; moved to Cp Blanding Fla 4 Oct 42 and Tullahoma Tenn on 30 May 43; transferred to Cp Atterbury Ind 8 Nov 43 and staged at Cp Myles Standish Mass 31 Jan 44 until departed Boston P/E 11 Feb 44; arrived England 23 Feb 44 and landed in France 10 Jun 44; crossed into Belgium 2 Sep 44 and into Holland 13 Sep 44; entered Germany 17 Sep 44 and returned to Belgium 17 Dec 44 *(attached to XVIII A/B Corps 19–20 Dec 44)*; reentered Germany 3 Feb 45 *(attached 2nd Armd Div 2–17 Apr 45)*; returned Boston P/E 19 Aug 45 and moved to Cp Jackson S.C. 21 Aug 45 where inactivated on 24 Nov 45.

Campaigns: *Normandy, Northern France, Rhineland, Ardennes-Alsace, Central Europe*
Aug 45 Loc: Shipment #10390-G at sea

120th Infantry Regiment (30th Infantry Division) **North Carolina National Guard**

16 Sep 40 inducted into federal service at Raleigh N.C. assigned to the 30th Division and moved to Ft Jackson S.C. 22 Sep 40; transferred to Cp Blanding Fla 4 Oct 42 and to Tullahoma Tenn 27 May 43; relocated to Cp Atterbury Ind 15 Nov 43 and staged at Cp Myles Standish Mass 1 Feb 44 until departed Boston P/E 11 Feb 44; arrived England 22 Feb 44 and landed in France 10 Jun 44; crossed into Belgium 2 Sep 44 and into Holland 13 Sep 44; entered Germany 17 Sep 44 and returned to Belgium 17 Dec 44; reentered Germany 3 Feb 45 and arrived New York P/E 21 Aug 45; moved to Cp Jackson S.C. 24 Aug 45 where inactivated on 24 Nov 45.

Campaigns: *Normandy, Northern France, Rhineland, Ardennes-Alsace, Central Europe*
Aug 45 Loc: Shipment #10390-H loading in England

121st Infantry Regiment (8th Infantry Division) **Georgia National Guard**

16 Sep 40 inducted into federal service at Macon Ga assigned to the 30th Division and moved to Ft Jackson S.C. 23 Sep 40; transferred to Chester S.C. 27 Sep 41 where relieved from the 30th Division and assigned to the 8th Division 22 Nov 41; returned to Cp Jackson S.C. 30 Nov 41 where redesignated the 121st Infantry Regiment (Motorized) on 9 Apr 42 and sent to Tenn Mnvr area 7 Nov 42; relocated to Ft Leonard Wood Mo 3 Dec 42 and to Cp Young Calif 20 Mar 43 where redesignated the 121st Infantry Regiment 1 Apr 43; arrived at Cp Forrest Tenn 21 Aug 43 and staged at Cp Kilmer N.J. 27 Nov 43 until departed New York P/E 5 Dec 43; arrived England 15 Dec 43 and landed in France 1 Jul 44 *(attached 83rd Inf Div 6–15 Aug 44)*; crossed into Luxembourg and Germany both on 19 Nov 44 *(attached to 82nd A/B Div 29–30 Apr 45)*; arrived Boston P/E 11 Jul 45 and moved to Ft Leonard Wood Mo 13 Jul 45 where inactivated on 20 Oct 45.

Campaigns: *Normandy, Northern France, Rhineland, Ardennes-Alsace, Central Europe*
Aug 45 Loc: Ft Leonard Wood Missouri

123rd Infantry Regiment (33rd Infantry Division)

No Distinctive
Insignia Authorized

28 Sep 42 activated at Ft Lewis Wash and assigned to the 33rd Infantry Division and moved to Cp Young Calif 13 Apr 43 and to Cp Stoneman Calif 24 Jun 43; departed San Francisco P/E 7 Jul 43 and arrived Hawaii 14 Jul 43; departed Hawaii 26 Apr 44 and arrived Finschhafen New Guinea 11 May 44; arrived Maffin Bay New Guinea 1 Sep 44 *(attached TORNADO Task Force 1-25 Sep 44)*; departed Toem New Guinea 26 Jan 45 and landed on Luzon Philippine Islands 10 Feb 45 *(attached 43rd Inf Div 13-15 Feb 45)*; arrived Japan 26 Sep 45 for occupation duty and inactivated there on 5 Feb 46.

Campaigns: *New Guinea, Luzon*
Aug 45 Loc: Baguio Philippine Islands

124th Infantry Regiment (Separate) (I)   Florida National Guard

25 Nov 40 inducted into federal service at Jacksonville Fla assigned to the 31st Division and moved to Cp Blanding Fla 18 Dec 40 where relieved from division on 15 Dec 41; arrived at Ft Benning Ga 11 Jan 42 under the Infantry School and then assigned to Replacement & School Command 1 Jun 42; transferred to Ft Jackson S.C. 12 Oct 43 under XII Corps and later IX Corps 20 Jan 44; there inactivated 2 Mar 44.

124th Infantry Regiment (31st Infantry Division) (II)   Florida National Guard

5 Apr 44 activated in Australia and assigned to the 31st Infantry Division using the assets of the disbanded 154th Infantry Regt; arrived Dobodura New Guinea on 24 Apr 44 and transferred to Aitape New Guinea 2-6 Jul 44 *(attached to PERSECUTION Task Force 2 Jul-9 Sep 44)*; rejoined division 11 Sep 44 at Maffin Bay New Guinea and assaulted Morotai Island 15 Sep 44; departed Morotai 18 Apr 45 and arrived at Parang Mindanao Philippine Islands 3 May 45; arrived San Francisco P/E 14 Dec 45 and inactivated at Cp Stoneman Calif on 16 Dec 45.

Campaigns: *New Guinea, Southern Philippines*
Aug 45 Loc: Valencia Mindanao Philippine Islands

125th Infantry Regiment (Separate)   Michigan National Guard

LET THE DRUM BEAT

15 Oct 40 inducted into federal service at Detroit Mich assigned to 32nd Division and moved to Cp Beauregard La 25 Oct 40; transferred to Cp Livingston La 19 Feb 41 where relieved from the 32nd Division on 8 Dec 41 and assigned to Fourth Army; relocated to Los Angeles Calif 29 Dec 41 and to Municipal Plunge Griffith Park Calif 7 Jan 42; sent to Gilroy Calif 21 Apr 42 and to Ft Ord Calif 14 Sep 43 and returned to Gilroy Calif 5 Oct 43; transferred to Cp Maxey Tex 4 Feb 44 where assigned to XXIII Corps 9 Apr 44 and XXXVI Corps 19 Sep 44 and Replacement & School Command 17 Nov 44; moved to Cp Gruber Okla 10 Dec 44 where assigned to XXXVI Corps 13 Dec 44 and to Replacement & School Command 16 Feb 45; arrived at Cp Rucker Ala 25 Feb 45 where inactivated on 20 Sep 45.

Aug 45 Loc: Camp Rucker Alabama

126th Infantry Regiment (32nd Infantry Division)   Michigan National Guard

15 Oct 40 inducted into federal service at Grand Rapids Mich assigned to 32nd Division and moved to Cp Beauregard La 27 Oct 40; transferred to Cp Livingston La 19 Feb 41 and to Ft Devens Mass 26 Feb 42; departed San Francisco P/E 13 Apr 42 and arrived in Australia 14 May 42; arrived at Port Moresby New Guinea 18-28 Sep 42 *(attached to 7th Australian Division 19 Nov 42-9 Jan 43)*; withdrew from New Guinea and returned to Australia 21 Jan-21 Feb 43 and arrived at Goodenough Island 23 Oct 43 *(attached to LAZARETTO Task Force 25 Oct-27 Nov 43)*; 15 Dec 43 landed at Milne Bay New Guinea and assaulted Saidor New Guinea 2 Jan 44 *(attached to MICHAELMAS Task Force 20 Dec 43-18 Feb 44)*; landed on Morotai Island 16 Sep 44 *(attached TRADEWIND Task Force 15-19 Aug 44) (attached XI Corps 20 Aug-2 Oct 44)*; rejoined division at sea 9-14 Nov 44 while in transit to the Philippine Islands and landed at Leyte 14 Nov 44; landed at Lingayen Gulf Luzon 27 Jan 45 *(attached as Sixth Army Reserve 30 Jan-15 Feb 45) (attached to 25th Inf Div 23 May-30 Jun 45)*; arrived in Japan for occupation duty 22 Oct 45 where inactivated on 28 Feb 46.

Campaigns: *Papua, New Guinea, Leyte, Luzon*
Aug 45 Loc: Anabat Philippine Islands

127th Infantry Regiment (32nd Infantry Division)   Michigan National Guard

15 Oct 40 inducted into federal service at Grandon Wis assigned to 32nd Division and moved to Cp Beauregard La 24 Oct 40; transferred to Cp Livingston La 15 Feb 41 and to Ft Devens Mass 27 Feb 42; departed San Francisco P/E 22 Apr 42 and arrived Australia 14 May 42; departed Brisbane Australia 14 Nov 42 and arrived Port Moresby New Guinea 27 Nov 42; returned to Australia by echelon 21 Jan–21 Feb 43 and arrived at Milne Bay New Guinea 23 Oct 43 *(attached as ALAMO Force Reserve 25 Oct 43–22 Apr 44)*; assaulted Aitape New Guinea on 22 Apr 44 *(attached PERSECUTION Task Force 23 Apr–4 May 44)*; departed New Guinea 9 Nov 44 and landed on Leyte Island Philippines 14 Nov 44; landed on Lingayen Gulf Luzon 27 Jan 45; arrived in Japan 19 Oct 45 for occupation duty and inactivated there 28 Feb 46.

Campaigns: *Papua, New Guinea, Leyte, Luzon*
Aug 45 Loc: Anabat Philippine Islands

128th Infantry Regiment (32nd Infantry Division)   Wisconsin National Guard

15 Oct 40 inducted into federal service at Oshkosh Wis assigned to 32nd Division and moved to Cp Beauregard La 23 Oct 40; transferred to Cp Livingston La 15 Feb 41 and to Ft Devens Mass 28 Feb 42; departed San Francisco P/E 22 Apr 42 and arrived in Australia 14 May 42; departed Australia 17 Sep 42 and arrived Port Moresby New Guinea 23 Sep 42; left New Guinea by echelon and returned to Australia 21 Jan–21 Feb 43; arrived Goodenough Island 23 Oct 43 and landed at Saidor New Guinea 19 Jan 44 *(attached MICHAELMAS Task Force 19 Jan–18 Feb 44) (attached ALAMO Force Reserve 12 May–8 Jun 44)*; departed New Guinea 9 Nov 44 and landed on Leyte Island Philippines 14 Nov 44; landed on Lingayen Gulf Luzon 27 Jan 45; arrived in Japan 19 Oct 45 where inactivated on 28 Feb 46.

Campaigns: *Papua, New Guinea, Leyte, Luzon*
Aug 45 Loc: Anabat Philippine Islands

129th Infantry Regiment (37th Infantry Division)   Illinois National Guard

5 Mar 41 inducted into federal service at Sycamore Ill assigned to 33rd Division and moved to Cp Forrest Tenn 20 Mar 41 and to La Mnvr area 10 Aug 41; returned to Cp Forrest Tenn 7 Oct 41 and departed San Francisco P/E 24 Aug 42, less 1st Bn which was detached to furnish cadre to another infantry regiment; arrived Fiji Islands 20 Sep 42 where new 1st Bn raised 1 Feb 43 *(attached to 37th Inf Div 19 Sep 42–30 Jul 43)*; departed Fiji Islands 11 Mar 43 and arrived at Espiritu Santo 13 Mar 43 under IV Island Command where relieved from 33rd and assigned to the 37th Infantry Division on 31 Jul 43; arrived Guadalcanal 4 Nov 43 and departed 11 Nov 43; arrived Bougainville 13 Nov 43 and left 13 Dec 44; landed at Lingayen Gulf Luzon on 9 Jan 45 *(attached to XIV Corps 21–24 Jan 45) (attached to 40th Inf Div 1–2 Feb 45) (attached to 33rd Inf Div 27 Mar–10 Apr 45)*; arrived at Los Angeles P/E 12 Dec 45 and inactivated at Cp Anza Calif on 13 Dec 45.

Campaigns: *Northern Solomons, Luzon*
Aug 45 Loc: San Jose Philippine Islands

130th Infantry Regiment (33rd Infantry Division)   Illinois National Guard

5 Mar 41 inducted into federal service at Decatur Ill assigned to 33rd Division and moved to Cp Forrest Tenn 21 Mar 41 and participated in the Aug-Oct 41 La Maneuvers; transferred to Ft Lewis Wash 13 Sep 42 and to Cp Young Calif 10 Apr 43; staged at Cp Stoneman Calif 15 Jun 43 until departed San Francisco P/E 21 Jun 43; arrived in Hawaii 27 Jun 43 and departed 26 Apr 44; arrived Finschhafen New Guinea 19 May 44 and departed New Guinea 11 Dec 44; arrived Morotai Island 18 Dec 44 and left 3 Feb 45; arrived at Lingayen Gulf Luzon 10 Feb 45 *(attached to 43rd Inf Div 14–15 Feb 45)*; arrived in Japan for occupation duty on 25 Sep 45 where inactivated on 5 Feb 46.

Campaigns: *New Guinea, Luzon*
Aug 45 Loc: Baguio Philippine Islands

131st Infantry Regiment (Separate)   Illinois National Guard

5 Mar 41 inducted into federal service at Chicago Ill assigned to 33rd Division and moved to Cp Forrest Tenn 22 Mar 41 and participated in the Aug-Oct 41 La Maneuvers; relieved from the 33rd Division at Cp Forrest Tenn 21 Feb 42 and assigned to VI Corps; moved to Ft Brady Mich 24 Mar 42 and guarded the Sault Sainte Marie Locks; assigned to IX Corps 20 Sep 43 and transferred to Cp Van Dorn Miss 24 Sep 43; assigned to the Replacement & School Command 5 Oct 43 and arrived at Ft Benning Ga 20 Oct 43; 3rd Bn sent to England and assets used to form 2nd Bn 156th Infantry Regt; remainder of 131st Infantry Regiment inactivated at Ft Benning Ga on 26 Feb 44.

132nd Infantry Regiment (American Division)   Illinois National Guard

5 Mar 41 inducted into federal service at Chicago Ill assigned to 33rd Division and moved to Cp Forrest Tenn 26 Mar 41 and participated in the Aug-Oct 41 La Maneuvers; relieved from the 33rd Division at Cp Forrest Tenn 14 Jan 42 and assigned to Task Force 6814; departed New York P/E 20 Jan 42 and arrived in Australia 27 Feb 42 which left 6 Mar 42; arrived in New Caledonia 12 Mar 42 where assigned to the Americal Division 24 May 42 and arrived on Guadalcanal 8 Dec 42; departed Guadalcanal 6 Apr 43 and arrived in Fiji Islands 10 Apr 43 which left 1 Jan 44; arrived Bougainville 12 Jan 44 and departed 14 Jan 45; landed on Leyte Island Philippines 26 Jan 45 and assaulted Cebu Island 26 Mar 45; arrived in Japan 8 Sep 45 where inactivated on 15 Nov 45.

Campaigns: *Guadalcanal, Northern Solomons, Leyte, Southern Philippines*
Aug 45 Loc: Baguio Philippine Islands

133rd Infantry Regiment (34th Infantry Division)   Iowa National Guard

10 Feb 41 inducted into federal service at Sioux City Iowa assigned to 34th Division and moved to Cp Claiborne La 1 Mar 41; staged at Ft Dix N.J. 5 Jan 42 until departed New York P/E 14 Jan 42; arrived Northern Ireland 26 Jan 42 and landed in North Africa on 3 Jan 43; arrived in Italy 21 Sep 43; arrived Hampton Roads P/E 3 Nov 45 and inactivated at Cp Patrick Henry Va on the same date.

Campaigns: *Tunisia, Naples-Foggia, Anzio, Rome-Arno, North Apennines, Po Valley*
Aug 45 Loc: Iseo Italy

134th Infantry Regiment (35th Infantry Division)   Nebraska National Guard

23 Dec 40 inducted into federal service at Omaha Nebr assigned to the 35th Division and moved to Cp Joseph T. Robinson Ark 7 Jan 41; transferred to Ft Ord Calif 23 Dec 41 and to Cp San Luis Obispo Calif 17 Jan 42; relocated to Presidio of San Francisco Calif 26 Mar 42, to Inglewood Los Angeles Calif 24 Apr 42, and to Ojai Calif 19 May 42; returned to Cp San Luis Obispo Calif 19 Jan 43 and moved to Cp Rucker Ala 27 Mar 43 and to the Tenn Mnvr area 17 Nov 43; arrived at Cp Butner N.C. 21 Jan 44 and staged at Cp Kilmer N.J. 2 May 44 until departed New York P/E 12 May 44; arrived England 25 May 44 and landed in France 5 Jul 44 *(attached to XIX Corps 13-15, 17-19 Sep 44) (attached to 6th Armd Div 22-27 Nov 44)*; crossed into Belgium 26 Dec 44 *(attached to 6th Armd Div 18 Jan-1 Feb 45)*; crossed into Luxembourg 22 Jan 45 and into Germany 6 Feb 45 and entered Holland 2 Mar 45; reentered Germany 3 Mar 45 *(attached to 79th Inf Div 13-14 Mar 45, 25-26 Mar 45 and 13-15 Apr 45)*; returned to New York P/E 10 Sep 45 and moved to Cp Breckinridge Ky 12 Sep 45 where inactivated on 21 Nov 45.

Campaigns: *Normandy, Northern France, Rhineland, Ardennes-Alsace, Central Europe*
Aug 45 Loc: Bopparol Germany

135th Infantry Regiment (34th Infantry Division)   Minnesota National Guard

10 Feb 41 inducted into federal service at Minneapolis Minn assigned to 34th Division and moved to Cp Claiborne La 27 Feb 41; staged at Ft Dix N.J. 10 Jan 42 until departed New York P/E 30 Apr 42; arrived in Northern Ireland 15 May 42 and landed in North Africa 3 Jan 43; arrived in Italy on 21 Sep 43; arrived Hampton Roads P/E 3 Nov 45 and inactivated at Cp Patrick Henry Va the same date.

Campaigns: *Tunisia, Naples-Foggia, Anzio, Rome-Arno, North Apennines, Po Valley*
Aug 45 Loc: Iseo Italy

136th Infantry Regiment (33rd Infantry Division)

1 Apr 42 activated at Cp Forrest Tenn assigned to 33rd Infantry Division and moved to Ft Lewis Wash 16 Sep 42; transferred to Cp Young Calif 4 Apr 43 and staged at Cp Stoneman Calif 28 Jun 43 and departed San Francisco P/E 8 Jul 43; arrived in Hawaii 15 Jul 43 and departed 30 Apr 44; arrived at Finschhafen New Guinea 11 May 44 and landed on Morotai Island 18 Dec 44 and departed 3 Feb 45; arrived at Lingayen Gulf Luzon Philippine Islands 10 Feb 45 and sent to Japan 25 Sep 45 where inactivated on 5 Feb 46.

Campaigns: *New Guinea, Luzon*
Aug 45 Loc: Baguio Philippine Islands

137th Infantry Regiment (35th Infantry Division)   **Kansas National Guard**

23 Dec 40 inducted into federal service at Wichita Kans assigned to the 35th Division and moved to Cp Joseph T. Robinson Ark 7 Jan 41; transferred to Ft Ord Calif 23 Dec 41 and to the Presidio of San Francisco Calif 14 Jan 42; sent to Long Beach Calif 23 Apr 42 and to Cp San Luis Obispo Calif 2 Feb 43; relocated to Cp Rucker Ala 31 Mar 43 and to the Tenn Mnvr area 17 Nov 43; arrived at Cp Butner N.C. 21 Jan 44 and staged at Cp Kilmer N.J. 3 May 44 until departed New York P/E 12 May 44; arrived England 25 May 44 and landed in France 8 Jul 44 *(attached to 4th Armd Div 20–24 Aug 44)*; entered Germany 18 Nov 44 and crossed into Belgium 27 Dec 44; returned to France 18 Jan 45 and reentered Germany 5 Feb 45; crossed into Holland 23 Feb 45 and returned to Germany 26 Feb 45 *(attached 30th Inf Div 14 Apr 45 only)*; arrived Boston P/E 31 Aug 45 and moved to Cp Breckinridge Ky 4 Sep 45 where inactivated on 5 Dec 45.

Campaigns: *Normandy, Northern France, Rhineland, Ardennes-Alsace, Central Europe*
Aug 45 Loc: Shipment #10201-G loading in France

138th Infantry Regiment (Separate)   **Missouri National Guard**

23 Dec 40 inducted into federal service at St Louis Mo assigned to 35th Division and moved to Cp Joseph T. Robinson Ark 5 Jan 41; transferred to Ft Ord Calif 23 Dec 41 and to Ft Lewis Wash 6 Jan 42 where relieved from the 35th Division on 3 Feb 42 and assigned to GHQ; departed Seattle P/E 14 May 42 and arrived at Ft Randall Alaska 22 May 42; 1st Bn stationed at Cold Bay, 2nd Bn at Juneau, and 3rd Bn at Naknek, Bethel, Umnak, Atka, and Galena; under Alaskan Defense Command until departed Alaska 3 Jun 44 and arrived at Prince Rupert P/E Canada 8 Jun 44; arrived Cp Shelby Miss 9 Jun 44 under IX Corps where inactivated on 20 Jul 44.

Campaigns: *Aleutian Islands*

140th Infantry Regiment (Separate)   **Missouri National Guard**

23 Dec 40 inducted into federal service at Sikeston Mo assigned to the 35th Division and moved to Cp Joseph T. Robinson Ark 4 Jan 41; transferred to Ft Ord Calif 23 Dec 41 and to San Francisco Calif 25 Dec 41; relocated to Cp San Luis Obispo Calif 25 Mar 42 and to San Diego Calif 22 Apr 42 where relieved from the 35th Division on 27 Jan 43 and assigned to the Southern California Sector of Western Defense Command; transferred to Cp Howze Tex 5 Feb 44 and assigned to XXIII Corps on 10 Apr 44 and to XXXVI Corps on 19 Sep 44; assigned to Replacement & School Command 17 Nov 44 and moved to Cp Swift Tex 10 Dec 44 and to Cp Rucker Ala 23 Feb 45; there inactivated on 20 Sep 45.

Aug 45 Loc: Camp Rucker Alabama

141st Infantry Regiment (36th Infantry Division)   Texas National Guard

25 Nov 40 inducted into federal service at San Antonio Tex assigned to the 36th Division and moved to Cp Bowie Tex 27 Dec 40; transferred to Cp Blanding Fla 20 Feb 42 and to Wadesboro N.C. 9 Jul 42; relocated to Cp Edwards Mass 17 Aug 42 and departed New York P/E 1 Apr 43; arrived in North Africa 13 Apr 43 and assaulted Salerno Italy 9 Sep 43; assaulted southern France 15 Aug 44 *(attached to 3rd Inf Div 7–8 Sep 44) (attached to 100th Inf Div 1–4 Jan 45 and 18–23 Jan 45) (attached to VI Corps 23–29 Jan 45)*; entered Germany 22 Mar 45 and Austria on 5 May 45; arrived at Hampton Roads P/E 22 Dec 45 and inactivated at Cp Patrick Henry Va the same date.

Campaigns: *Naples-Foggia, Anzio, Rome-Arno, Southern France, Rhineland, Ardennes-Alsace, Central Europe*
Aug 45 Loc: Balubeuren Germany

142nd Infantry Regiment (36th Infantry Division)   Texas National Guard

25 Nov 40 inducted into federal service at Fort Worth Tex assigned to the 36th Division and moved to Cp Bowie Tex 13 Dec 40; transferred to Cp Blanding Fla 18 Feb 42 and to the Carolina Mnvr area 9 Jul 42; relocated to Cp Edwards Mass 17 Aug 42 and to A.P. Hill Mil Res Va 7 Mar 43; staged at Ft Dix N.J. 17 Mar 43 until departed New York P/E 2 Apr 43; arrived North Africa 13 Apr 43 and assaulted Salerno Italy 9 Sep 43; assaulted southern France 15 Aug 44; entered Germany 23 Dec 44 *(attached to XXI Corps 14–18 Jan 45)* and Austria 4 May 45; arrived Hampton Roads P/E 15 Dec 45 and inactivated at Cp Patrick Henry Va on the same date.

Campaigns: *Naples-Foggia, Anzio, Rome-Arno, Southern France, Rhineland, Ardennes-Alsace, Central Europe*
Aug 45 Loc: Kirchberg Germany

143rd Infantry Regiment (36th Infantry Division)   Texas National Guard

25 Nov 40 inducted into federal service at Waco Tex assigned to the 36th Division and moved to Cp Bowie Tex 5 Jan 41; transferred to Cp Blanding Fla 20 Feb 42 and to the Carolina Mnvr area 8 Jul 42; relocated to Cp Edwards Mass 17 Aug 42 and departed New York P/E 1 Apr 43; arrived North Africa 13 Apr 43 and assaulted Salerno Italy 9 Sep 43; assaulted southern France 15 Aug 44 and entered Germany 22 Mar 45 and Austria 5 May 45; arrived Hampton Roads P/E 22 Dec 45 and inactivated at Cp Patrick Henry Va the same date.

Campaigns: *Naples-Foggia, Anzio, Rome-Arno, Southern France, Rhineland, Ardennes-Alsace, Central Europe*
Aug 45 Loc: Langenau Germany

144th Infantry Regiment (Separate)   Texas National Guard

25 Nov 40 inducted into federal service at Fort Worth Tex assigned to the 36th Division and moved to Cp Bowie Tex 7 Jan 41; transferred to Ft Lewis Wash 14 Dec 41 and to Portland Oreg 21 Dec 41 where relieved from the 36th Division on 1 Feb 42 and assigned to GHQ; relocated to San Francisco Calif 20 Apr 42 and to Santa Rosa Calif 7 May 42 under the Western Defense Command; transferred to Atlantic Beach Fla 21 Jan 43 under Eastern Defense Command and to Cp Van Dorn Miss 23 Mar 44 where assigned to XXI Corps on 18 Apr 44; moved to Cp Swift Tex 5 Jan 45 and to Cp Rucker Ala 4 Apr 45 under Replacement & School Command; there inactivated on 20 Sep 45.

Aug 45 Loc: Camp Rucker Alabama

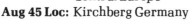

145th Infantry Regiment (37th Infantry Division)   Ohio National Guard

15 Oct 40 inducted into federal service at Cleveland Ohio assigned to the 37th Division and moved to Cp Shelby Miss 22 Oct 40; transferred to Indiantown Gap Mil Res Pa 18 Feb 42 and to Cp Stoneman Calif 11 May 42; departed San Francisco P/E 26 May 42 and arrived in New Zealand 12 Jun 42; departed 12 Jul 42 and arrived Suva Fiji Islands 15 Jul 42 which left 1 Apr 43; arrived on Guadalcanal 3 Apr 43 (3rd Bn attached 1st Marine Raider Force and assaulted New Georgia 3 Jul 43); arrived Rendova Island 11 Jul 43 *(attached to 43rd Inf Div 15-23 Jul 43)* and landed on New Georgia 20 Jul 43; returned to Guadalcanal 4-9 Sep 43 and departed 17 Nov 43; arrived Bougainville 19 Nov 43 *(attached XIV Corps 30 Nov 44-10 Jan 45)*; assaulted Lingayen Gulf Luzon Philippine Islands 9 Jan 45 *(attached to XIV Corps 20-21 Jan 45) (attached Provost Marshal General U.S. Army Forces in the Far East 2 Mar-18 Apr 45 at Manila) (attached 6th Inf Div 18-30 Apr 45) (attached 38th Inf Div 30 Apr-2 Jun 45)*; returned to San Francisco P/E 12 Dec 45 and inactivated at Cp Stoneman Calif on 13 Dec 45.

Campaigns: *Northern Solomons, Luzon*
Aug 45 Loc: San Jose Philippine Islands

147th Infantry Regiment (Separate)   Ohio National Guard

15 Oct 40 inducted into federal service at Cincinnati Ohio assigned to the 37th Division and moved to Cp Shelby Miss 24 Oct 40; transferred to Indiantown Gap Mil Res Pa 18 Feb 42 and departed Hampton Roads P/E 6 Apr 42; arrived Togatabu Fiji Islands 1 May 42 and 1st Bn landed near Aola River Guadalcanal 4 Nov 42 without opposition; 3rd Bn landed at Koli Point Guadalcanal 29 Nov 42 and regiment consolidated under XIV Corps *(attached to CAM Division 16-29 Jan 43)*; advanced along coast and moved to Pt Cruz area 19 Jan 43 and seized Hill 95 on 22 Jan 43; battled across the Bonegi River 31 Jan-2 Feb 43 against strong opposition and reached Umasani 4 Feb 43 to find Japanese evacuated; arrived New Hebrides 15 May 43 enroute to Samoa which reached 18 May 43 where relieved from the 37th Infantry Division about 31 Jul 43; arrived New Caledonia 2 Apr 44 enroute to Guadalcanal which reached 7 Apr 44; 11 Apr 44 assumed garrison duties on Emirau St Matthias Islands, returned to Guadalcanal 3 Jul 44 and to New Caledonia 8 Jul 44 where assigned to New Caledonia Island Command 1 Sep 44 and South Pacific Base Command 28 Feb 45; departed New Caledonia 5 Mar 45, assigned to Pacific Ocean Area Command 15 Mar 45, and arrived at Iwo Jima 21 Mar 45 as the garrison force and assumed security duties 26 Mar 45; became the garrison of Iwo Jima 4 Apr 45 and assigned to Pacific Base Command on 25 Jun 45; sent 1st Bn to occupy Tinian 30 Jun 45; assigned to Tenth Army 5 Oct 45 and landed on Okinawa 25 Oct 45 and departed 28 Nov 45; arrived Seattle P/E 12 Dec 45 and inactivated at Vancouver Barracks Wash on 15 Dec 45.

Campaigns: *Guadalcanal, Northern Solomons, Western Pacific, Air Offensive-Japan*
Aug 45 Loc: Iwo Jima, less 1st Bn on Tinian

148th Infantry Regiment (37th Infantry Division)   Ohio National Guard

15 Oct 40 inducted into federal service at Columbus Ohio assigned to the 37th Division and moved to Cp Shelby Miss 24 Oct 40; transferred to Indiantown Gap Mil Res Pa 18 Feb 42 and departed San Francisco P/E 10 May 42; arrived Fiji Islands 10 Jun 42 and departed 14 Apr 43; arrived on Guadalcanal 19 Apr 43 and departed 31 May 43; landed on Banika Russell Islands 7 Jun 43; 3rd Bn attached 1st Marine Raider Force and assaulted New Georgia 3 Jul 43; arrived New Georgia 17 Jul 43 *(attached to 43rd Inf Div 15-23 Jul 43)* and returned to Guadalcanal 6-10 Sep 43; landed on Bougainville 5 Nov 43 *(attached to 3rd Marine Division there)*; assaulted Lingayen Gulf Luzon Philippine Islands 9 Jan 45 *(attached 25th Inf Div 30 Apr-31 May 45)*; arrived at Los Angeles P/E 30 Oct 45 and inactivated at Cp Anza Calif on 9 Nov 45.

Campaigns: *Northern Solomons, Luzon*
Aug 45 Loc: San Jose Philippine Islands

149th Infantry Regiment (38th Infantry Division)   Kentucky National Guard

17 Jan 41 inducted into federal service at Louisville Ky assigned to the 38th Division and moved to Cp Shelby Miss 26 Jan 41; transferred to Cp Carabelle Fla 23 Nov 42 and to Cp Livingston La 21 Jan 43; departed New Orleans P/E 1 Jan 44 and arrived in Hawaii 20 Jan 44; departed Hawaii 14 Jun 44 and arrived at Oro Bay New Guinea on 1 Jul 44; left New Guinea 30 Nov 44 and landed on Leyte Philippine Islands 14 Dec 44 *(attached to XXIV Corps 6–9 Dec 44) (elements attached to 11th A/B Div 9 Dec 44–about 5 Jan 45)*; landed on Luzon 29 Jan 45 *(attached to 6th Inf Div 30 Apr–3 May 45)*; arrived at Los Angeles P/E 30 Oct 45 and inactivated at Cp Anza Calif on 9 Nov 45.

Campaigns: *New Guinea, Leyte, Luzon*
Aug 45 Loc: Manila Philippine Islands

150th Infantry Regiment (Separate)   West Virginia National Guard

17 Jan 41 inducted into federal service at Welch W.Va assigned to the 38th Division and moved to Cp Shelby Miss 27 Jan 41; departed New Orleans P/E 30 Dec 41 and arrived at Ft Clayton Panama Canal Zone 4 Jan 42 where relieved from assignment to the 38th Division on 10 Feb 42; assigned to the Panama Canal Department and performed garrison duties there until inactivated on 1 Feb 46.

Campaigns: *American Theater without Inscription*
Aug 45 Loc: Ft Clayton Panama, less 3rd Bn at Ft Davis and Co K at Ft Gulick, Canal Zone

151st Infantry Regiment (38th Infantry Division)   Indiana National Guard

17 Jan 41 inducted into federal service at Indianapolis Ind assigned to the 38th Division and moved to Cp Shelby Miss 29 Jan 41; relocated to Cp Carabelle Fla 23 Nov 42 and to Cp Livingston La 21 Jan 43; departed New Orleans P/E 1 Jan 44 and arrived in Hawaii 20 Jan 44; departed 14 Jun 44 and arrived at Oro Bay New Guinea on 1 Jul 44; left New Guinea 30 Nov 44 and landed on Leyte Philippine Islands 14 Dec 44 *(attached to 24th Inf Div 31 Jan–7 Feb 45)*; assaulted Bataan 15 Feb 45, Caballo Island 27 Mar 45, and El Fraile Island 13 Apr 45 *(attached to 6th Inf Div 29–30 Apr 45)*; arrived Los Angeles P/E 2 Nov 45 and inactivated at Cp Anza Calif on 9 Nov 45.

Campaigns: *New Guinea, Leyte, Luzon*
Aug 45 Loc: Manila Philippine Islands

152nd Infantry Regiment (38th Infantry Division)   Indiana National Guard

17 Jan 41 inducted into federal service at Indianapolis Ind assigned to 38th Division and moved to Cp Shelby Miss 30 Jan 41; relocated to Cp Carabelle Fla 23 Nov 42 and to Cp Livingston La 15 Jan 43; departed New Orleans P/E 3 Jan 44 and arrived in Hawaii 21 Jan 44; left Hawaii 1 Jul 44 and arrived in New Guinea on 16 Jul 44; landed on Leyte Philippine Islands 14 Dec 44 and landed on Luzon 29 Jan 45 *(attached to 6th Inf Div 25–30 Apr 45)*; arrived at Los Angeles P/E 30 Oct 45 and inactivated at Cp Anza Calif on 9 Nov 45.

Campaigns: *New Guinea, Leyte, Luzon*
Aug 45 Loc: Manila Philippine Islands

153rd Infantry Regiment (Separate)   Arkansas National Guard

23 Dec 40 inducted into federal service at Conway Ark, assigned to the Second Army and moved to Cp Joseph T. Robinson Ark 3 Jan 41; transferred to Cp Forrest Tenn 28 May 41 and returned to Cp Joseph T. Robinson Ark 1 Jul 41 where assigned to Fourth Army on 1 Aug 41; staged at Cp Murray Wash 20 Aug 41 until departed Seattle P/E 12 Apr 42 and arrived at Ft Glenn Alaska 25 Apr 42, less 1st and 3rd Bns which departed previously on 1 Sep 41 for duty at Seward, Nome, Yakutat, and Annette; assigned to the Alaskan Department and 2nd Bn arrived on Adak Feb 43 and Kiska 15 Aug 43; regiment departed Alaska 28 Feb 44 and arrived at Prince Rupert P/E Canada 13 Mar 44; arrived at Cp Shelby Miss 21 Mar 44 under IX Corps and inactivated there on 30 Jun 44.

Campaigns: *Aleutian Islands*

154th Infantry Regiment (31st Infantry Division)

No Distinctive Insignia Authorized

20 Sep 42 activated at Cp Shelby Miss and assigned to the 31st Infantry Division; moved to La Mnvr area 24 Jun 43 and to Cp Pickett Va 2 Sep 43; staged at Cp Patrick Henry Va 8 Jan 44 until departed Hampton Roads P/E 9 Feb 44; arrived in New Guinea on 22 Feb 44 where disbanded on 5 Apr 44 and assets used to fill the 124th Infantry Regiment.

Campaigns: *New Guinea*

155th Infantry Regiment (31st Infantry Division)   **Mississippi National Guard**

20 Nov 40 inducted into federal service at Vicksburg Miss assigned to the 31st Division and moved to Cp Blanding Fla 21 Dec 40; transferred to Cp Bowie Tex 24 Feb 42 and to Mansfield La 28 Jul 42; relocated to Cp Shelby Miss 22 Sep 42 and to the La Mnvr area 25 Jun 43; arrived at Cp Pickett Va 28 Aug 43 and staged at Cp Patrick Henry Va 4 Feb 44 until departed Hampton Roads P/E 2 Mar 44; arrived at Oro Bay New Guinea 4 Apr 44 and departed Maffin Bay New Guinea 12 Sep 44; assaulted Morotai Island 15 Sep 44 and left 18 Apr 45; landed at Parang Mindanao Philippine Islands 22 Apr 45; arrived at San Francisco P/E 11 Dec 45 and inactivated at Cp Stoneman Calif on 12 Dec 45.

Campaigns: *New Guinea, Southern Philippines*
Aug 45 Loc: Valencia Mindanao Philippine Islands

156th Infantry Regiment (Separate)   **Louisiana National Guard**

25 Nov 40 inducted into federal service at New Orleans La assigned to the 31st Division and moved to Cp Blanding Fla 22 Dec 40; transferred to Cp Bowie Tex 26 Feb 42 where relieved from the 31st Division on 14 Jul 42; staged at Ft Dix N.J. 19 Sep 42 until departed New York P/E 26 Sep 42; arrived in England 6 Oct 42 and 2nd Bn sent to Oran Algeria for military police duties due to its French linguistic ability where it later was redesignated the 202nd Infantry Battalion; regiment assigned to the U.S. Army Assault Training Center at Woolacombe England in Jul 43 and new 2nd Bn formed from the 3rd Bn, 131st Inf Regt; headquarters detachment and Co L assaulted Normandy France on 6 Jun 44 and entire regiment ashore by 24 Jun 44; returned to England 6 Jul 44 and returned to France by echelon 18 Aug–3 Sep 44; guarded flanks of allied advance and Red Ball Express highway; 2nd Bn detached to guard Supreme Headquarters Allied Expeditionary Force headquarters from 15 Oct 44; remainder of regiment moved in mid-Nov 44 to provide security duty at the U.S. Embassy, U.S. Naval Headquarters and other command facilities in Paris France; regiment, less 2nd Bn, moved to Normandy coast in mid-Dec 44 where contained German garrisons on the Channel Islands; returned to New York P/E 11 Mar 46 and inactivated at Cp Kilmer, N.J. on 13 Mar 46.

Campaigns: *Northern France, Central Europe, Normandy–Co L, Rhineland–Co F*
Aug 45 Loc: Le Mans France

157th Infantry Regiment (45th Infantry Division)   **Colorado National Guard**

16 Sep 40 inducted into federal service at Denver Colo assigned to the 45th Division and moved to Ft Sill Okla 26 Sep 40; transferred to Cp Barkeley Tex 28 Feb 41 and to Ft Devens Mass 22 Apr 42; relocated briefly to Cp Edwards Mass 8 Aug 42 and returned to Ft Devens Mass 21 Aug 42; moved to Pine Camp N.Y. 11 Nov 42 and to Cp Pickett Va 20 Jan 43; departed Hampton Roads P/E 25 May 43 and arrived in North Africa 22 Jun 43; assaulted Scoglitti Sicily 9–11 Jul 43 and assaulted Salerno Italy 9 Sep 43; assaulted southern France 15 Aug 44 (attached to 44th Inf Div 25–27 Nov 44) and entered Germany 17 Mar 45; arrived at Boston P/E 10 Sep 45 and moved to Cp Bowie Tex 17 Sep 45 where inactivated on 3 Dec 45.

Campaigns: *Sicily, Naples-Foggia, Anzio, Rome-Arno, Southern France, Rhineland, Ardennes-Alsace, Central Europe*
Aug 45 Loc: Munchen Germany

158th Infantry Regiment (Separate)　　　　　　　　　　　Arizona National Guard

16 Sep 40 inducted into federal service at Tucson Ariz assigned to the 45th Division and moved to Ft Sill Okla 23 Sep 40; relocated to Cp Barkeley Tex 28 Feb 41 and to the Panama Canal Zone 31 Dec 41 where relieved from assignment to the 45th Division on 11 Feb 42; shipped to Brisdbane Australia in Jan 43 and moved to Port Moresby New Guinea in Feb 43 and later to Milne Bay in May 43; *(attached BYPRODUCT Task Force 1 Jun–4 Aug 43)* landed on Kiriwini Trobriand Islands 23–30 Jun 43 without opposition *(attached to the DIRECTOR Task Force 25 Nov 43–20 May 44)*; landed at Arawe New Britain 27 Dec 43 and defeated Japanese forces there by 17 Jan 44; *(attached TORNADO Task Force 21 May–22 Jun 44)* landed at Toem New Guinea 21 May 44 and went into line at the Tor River 23 May 44 and fought the Battle for Lone Tree Hill there 26–29 May 44; relieved at Toem 5 Jun 44 and attacked 8 Jun 44 in the Hollandia-Aitape area to reach the Tirfoam River 9 Jun 44 where relieved in line 14 Jun 44; *(attached CYCLONE Task Force 22 Jun–25 Sep 44)* assaulted Noemfoor Island 2 Jul 44 and seized Kornasoren airfield 4 Jul 44 without opposition; *(attached Eighth Army 28 Sep 44–9 Jan 45)* landed on Luzon Philippine Islands 11 Jan 45 and drove up Route 251 and occupied Damortis 13 Jan 45; *(attached 43rd Inf Div 13 Jan–3 Mar 45)* began combat at Amlang 14 Jan 45 and fought Battle for Blue Ridge 18–21 Jan 45 and the Battle for Cataguintingan Ridge 24–26 Jan 45; moved into reserve near Tarlac on 15 Feb 45; *(attached to 11th A/B Div 3–24 Mar 45)* began offensive to open Balayan and Batangas Bays on 5 Mar 45 and after heavy combat cleared the Calumpan Peninsula by 16 Mar 45; *(attached to XIV Corps 25 Mar–15 Jun 45)* assaulted Legaspi area of Bicol Peninsula Luzon 1 Apr 45 and battled for ridge near Daraga 1–9 Apr 45, reaching the west coast of the peninsula at Bulan on 8 Apr 45; assaulted Cituinan Hill 12–27 Apr 45 and patrolled the Anayan area commencing 1 May 45 *(attached XI Corps 15 Jun 45–past 14 Aug 45)*; arrived in Japan for occupation duty and inactivated there on 17 Jan 46.

Campaigns: *New Guinea, Bismarck Archipelago, Luzon*
Aug 45 Loc: Naga Philippine Islands

159th Infantry Regiment (Separate)　　　　　　　　　　　California National Guard

3 Mar 41 inducted into federal service at Oakland Calif assigned to the 40th Division and moved to Cp San Luis Obispo Calif 14 Mar 41 where relieved from the 40th and assigned to the 7th Division on 29 Sep 41; there redesignated the 159th Infantry Regiment (Motorized) on 29 Oct 41 and transferred to Ft Ord Calif 3 Dec 41 and to the Presidio of San Francisco Calif 15 Feb 42; returned to Cp San Luis Obispo Calif 22 Apr 42 where redesignated the 159th Infantry Regiment on 1 Jan 43; staged at Fort Ord Calif 1 Feb 43 until departed San Francisco P/E 25 Jun 43 *(attached to Amphibious Training Force #9 5 May–28 Jun 43)*; landed on Attu Island 9 Jul 43 and relieved the 17th Infantry Regt as the garrison force; relieved from the 7th Infantry Division on 23 Aug 43 and assigned to the Alaskan Department; departed Attu on 9 Aug 44 and arrived Seattle P/E 20 Aug 44; transferred to Cp Swift Tex 28 Aug 44 under XXIII Corps and assigned to Fourth Army 1 Sep 44; moved to Cp Callan Calif 20 Dec 44 and returned to Cp Swift Tex 25 Jan 45; staged at Cp Kilmer N.J. 27 Feb 45 until departed New York P/E 7 Mar 45; arrived in France 18 Mar 45 where attached to the 106th Infantry Division throughout European service and entered Germany on 25 Apr 45; returned to New York P/E 4 Nov 45 and inactivated at Cp Shanks N.Y. on the same date.

Campaigns: *Aleutian Islands, Northern France*
Aug 45 Loc: Namedy Germany

160th Infantry Regiment (40th Infantry Division)   California National Guard

3 Mar 41 inducted into federal service at Los Angeles Calif assigned to the 40th Division and moved to Cp San Luis Obispo Calif 11 Mar 41; transferred to Ft Lewis Wash 29 Apr 42 and departed San Francisco P/E 26 Sep 42; arrived Hawaii 4 Oct 42 where assigned to the 27th Infantry Division 1 Sep 42 and reassigned to the 40th Infantry Division on 30 Oct 42; departed Hawaii 25 Dec 43 and arrived Guadalcanal 4 Jan 44; landed at Cape Gloucester New Britain 28 Apr 44 and departed 9 Dec 44; arrived at Huon Gulf New Guinea 18 Dec 44 and assaulted Lingayen Gulf Luzon Philippine Islands on 9 Jan 45; landed on Panay Island 26 Mar 45 and on Negros Island 30 Mar 45; returned to San Francisco P/E 5 Apr 46 and inactivated at Cp Stoneman Calif on 7 Apr 46.

Campaigns: *Bismarck Archipelago, Luzon, Southern Philippines*
Aug 45 Loc: Los Negros Philippine Islands

161st Infantry Regiment (25th Infantry Division)   Washington National Guard

16 Sep 40 inducted into federal service at Spokane Wash assigned to the 41st Division and moved to Cp Murray Wash 23 Sep 40; transferred to Ft Lewis Wash 20 Mar 41 and to the Presidio of San Francisco Calif 11 Dec 41; departed San Francisco P/E 16 Dec 41 and arrived in Hawaii 21 Dec 41 *(attached to 25th Inf Div 23 Jul–2 Aug 42)*; relieved from assignment to the 41st and assigned to the 25th Infantry Division on 3 Aug 42 and departed Hawaii 16 Dec 42; arrived Guadalcanal 4 Jan 43 *(attached to 37th Inf Div 22 Jul–6 Aug 43)* and landed on Rendova 20 Jul 43; returned to Guadalcanal 17 Oct 43 and departed 1 Nov 43; arrived New Zealand on 9 Nov 43 and departed 21 Feb 44 for New Caledonia where landed 26 Feb 44 and departed on 17 Dec 44, landed at Lingayen Gulf Luzon Philippine Islands on 11 Jan 45; arrived in Japan for occupation duty 28 Oct 45 and inactivated there on 1 Nov 45.

Campaigns: *Guadalcanal, Northern Solomons, Luzon*
Aug 45 Loc: Bambam Philippine Islands

162nd Infantry Regiment (41st Infantry Division)   Oregon National Guard

16 Sep 40 inducted into federal service at Portland Oreg assigned to the 41st Division and moved to Cp Murray Wash 23 Sep 40; transferred to Ft Lewis Wash 20 Mar 41 and to Ft Dix N.J. 24 Feb 42; departed New York P/E 1 Mar 42 and arrived Australia 9 Apr 42; departed Australia on 8 Feb 43 and arrived at Port Moresby and Oro Bay New Guinea; left New Guinea 28 Sep 43 and returned to Australia 3 Oct 43; departed 11 Mar 44 and landed at Finschhafen New Guinea 23 Mar 44 and assaulted Hollandia New Guinea 22 Apr 44; assaulted Biak Island 27 May 44 and departed 2 Feb 45; arrived on Mindoro Philippine Islands 9 Feb 45 and assaulted Zamboanga Mindanao on 10 Mar 45 *(attached to X Corps 4 May–6 Jun 45)* *(attached Central Task Force 6–8 Jun 45)* *(attached to 24th Inf Div 8 Jun–4 Jul 45)* *(attached to X Corps 5–6 Jul 45)*; inactivated in Japan on 31 Dec 45.

Campaigns: *New Guinea, Luzon, Southern Philippines*
Aug 45 Loc: Zamboanga Mindanao Philippine Islands

163rd Infantry Regiment (41st Infantry Division)   Montana National Guard

No Distinctive
Insignia Authorized

16 Sep 40 inducted into federal service at Billings Montana assigned to 41st Division and moved to Cp Murray Wash 23 Sep 40; transferred to Ft Lewis Wash 20 Mar 41 and departed San Francisco P/E 7 Apr 42; arrived Australia 7 Apr 42 and departed 21 Dec 42; arrived Port Moresby New Guinea 27 Dec 42 *(attached to Australian 7th Div 27 Dec 42–25 Jan 43)*; departed New Guinea 16 Jul 43 and returned to Australia 17 Jul 43; returned to New Guinea 23 Mar 44 *(attached PERSECUTION Task Force 23 Mar–7 May 44)* and assaulted Aitape New Guinea 22 Apr 44; *(attached TORNADO Task Force 12 May–29 May 44)* assaulted Wadke-Toem New Guinea 17 May 44 and arrived on Biak Island 31 May 44 which departed 29 Jan 45; arrived on Mindoro Philippine Islands 9 Feb 45 and assaulted Zamboanga Mindanao 10 Mar 45; assaulted Sanga Sanga 2 Apr 45 and assaulted Jolo Island 9 Apr 45; inactivated in Japan 31 Dec 45.

Campaigns: *Papua, New Guinea, Luzon, Southern Philippines*
Aug 45 Loc: Zamboanga Mindanao Philippine Islands

164th Infantry Regiment (American Division)   North Dakota National Guard

10 Feb 41 inducted into federal service at Fargo N.D. assigned to the 34th Division and moved to Cp Claiborne La 27 Feb 41 where relieved from assignment to the 34th Division on 8 Dec 41 and attached to the Fourth Army; transferred to Ft Ord Calif 17 Dec 41 and assigned to GHQ 30 Jan 42 and departed San Francisco P/E 19 Mar 42; arrived Australia 7 Apr 42 and New Caledonia 19 Apr 42 where assigned to the American Division 24 May 42; departed New Caledonia 9 Oct 42 and arrived on Guadalcanal 13 Oct 42 *(attached to 1st Marine Div 13 Oct–9 Dec 42)*; departed Guadalcanal 1 Mar 43 and arrived in Fiji Islands 5 Mar 43; departed 18 Dec 43 and arrived on Bougainville 25 Dec 43 which left 8 Jan 45; arrived on Leyte Philippine Islands 21 Jan 45 *(attached Eighth Army Area Command 7 Mar–5 Apr 45)* and antitank company participated in assault on Cebu Island 26 Mar 45; remainder of regiment landed on Cebu 10 Apr 45 and on Negros Occidental 26 Apr 45 *(attached to Eighth Army 1 Jul 45–past 14 Aug 45)*; arrived in Japan for occupation duty on 8 Sep 45 and arrived at Seattle P/E 22 Nov 45; inactivated at Ft Lawton Wash 24 Nov 45.

Campaigns: *Guadalcanal, Northern Solomons, Leyte, Southern Philippines*
Aug 45 Loc: Cebu Island Philippine Islands

165th Infantry Regiment (27th Infantry Division)   New York National Guard

15 Oct 41 inducted into federal service at New York N.Y. assigned to the 27th Division and moved to Ft McClellan Ala 26 Oct 41; transferred to Riverside Calif 21 Dec 41 and to Ft Ord Calif 22 Jan 42; departed San Francisco P/E 30 Mar 42 and arrived Hawaii on 8 Apr 42 where assigned to the 40th Infantry Division 3 Sep 42 but reassigned to the 27th Infantry Division on 30 Oct 42; departed Hawaii 10 Nov 43 and landed on Makin Atoll 20 Nov 43; departed Makin, less 3rd Bn, 24 Nov 43 and returned to Hawaii 2 Dec 43 and 3rd Bn returned 1 Jan 44; departed Hawaii 31 May 44 and landed on Saipan 17 Jun 44 *(attached to 4th Marine Div 17–18 Jun 44, 26 Jun–1 Jul 44)* *(attached to 2nd Marine Div 8–11 Jul 44)*; arrived at Espiritu Santo 4 Sep 44 and departed 25 Mar 45; landed on Okinawa 9 Apr 45 *(attached to XXIV Corps 9–15 Apr 45)*; arrived in Japan for occupation duty 12 Sep 45; arrived Seattle P/E 31 Dec 45 and inactivated at Ft Lawton Wash same date.

Campaigns: *Central Pacific, Western Pacific, Ryukyus*
Aug 45 Loc: Okinawa

166th Infantry Regiment (Separate)   Ohio National Guard

15 Oct 40 inducted into federal service at Columbus Ohio assigned to 37th Division and moved to Cp Shelby Miss 25 Oct 40 where relieved from 37th Division on 16 Jan 42; moved to New Orleans La 12 Feb 42 and 1st Bn detached to Task Force 1291 for service on Aruba and Curacao Islands in Caribbean until 1 Sep 43 when battalion returned less personnel; 18 Apr 42 assigned to Southern Defense Command at New Orleans less 2nd Bn at Texas City Tex; transferred to Ft Barrancas Fla 2 Oct 42, less 1st and 2nd Bns, and returned to Cp Shelby Miss 15 Apr 43 under Third Army where 2nd Bn rejoined regiment; relocated to Ft Sill Okla 20 Sep 43 where assigned to Replacement & School Command on 1 Feb 44 and inactivated same date, less 2nd and 3rd Bns which were inactivated 22 Feb 44 at Cp Hood Tex and 12 Feb 45 at Ft Sill Okla, respectively.

No Distinctive
Insignia Authorized

167th Infantry Regiment (31st Infantry Division)   Alabama National Guard

25 Nov 40 inducted into federal service at Gadsden Ala assigned to the 31st Division and moved to Cp Blanding Fla 20 Dec 40; transferred to Mansfield La 28 Jul 42 and to Cp Shelby Miss 22 Sep 42 and participated in La Maneuvers 25 Jun–24 Aug 43; arrived at Cp Pickett Va 30 Aug 43 and staged at Cp Patrick Henry Va 23 Feb 44 until departed Hampton Roads P/E 2 Mar 44; arrived Oro Bay New Guinea 7 Apr 44 and Toem New Guinea 14 Jul 44; departed Maffin Bay 12 Sep 44 and assaulted Morotai Island 15 Sep 44; arrived at Sansapor New Guinea 15 Nov 44, less 2nd Bn which assaulted Mapia Island same date; departed New Guinea 15 Apr 45, less 2nd Bn, and arrived Parang Mindanao Philippine Islands 22 Apr 45 where 2nd Bn rejoined regiment from Morotai 3 May 45; arrived San Francisco P/E 7 Dec 45 and inactivated at Cp Stoneman Calif on 20 Dec 45.

Campaigns: *New Guinea, Western Pacific, Southern Philippines*
Aug 45 Loc: Valencia Mindanao Philippine Islands

168th Infantry Regiment (34th Infantry Division)   Iowa National Guard

10 Feb 41 inducted into federal service at Des Moines Iowa assigned to the 34th Division and moved to Cp Claiborne La 3 Mar 41; staged at Ft Dix N.J. 8 Jan 42 until departed New York P/E 30 Apr 42; arrived Ireland 13 May 42 and Scotland 23 Aug 42; assaulted Algiers vicinity North Africa 8 Nov 42 and landed in Italy 21 Sep 43; returned to Hampton Roads P/E 3 Nov 45 and inactivated at Cp Patrick Henry Va on the same date.

Campaigns: *Algeria–French Morocco, Tunisia, Anzio, Rome-Arno, North Apennines, Po Valley*
Aug 45 Loc: Iseo Italy

169th Infantry Regiment (43rd Infantry Division)   Connecticut National Guard

24 Feb 41 inducted into federal service at Hartford Conn assigned to the 43rd Division and moved to Cp Blanding Fla 15 Mar 41; transferred to Cp Shelby Miss 17 Feb 42 and to Ft Ord Calif 7 Sep 42; departed San Francisco P/E 30 Sep 42 and arrived in New Zealand 22 Oct 42 which left 23 Nov 42; arrived Noumea New Caledonia 28 Nov 42 and departed 16 Feb 43; landed at Koli Point Guadalcanal 19 Feb 43 and in Russell Islands 22 Feb 43; Cos A and B assaulted Baraulu Island 30 Jun 43 and regiment moved to Rendova 4 Jul 43; Co L assaulted Baanga Island 12 Aug 43 and 3rd Bn assaulted Vella Cela 13 Aug 43; regiment returned to New Zealand 25 Feb 44; *(attached PERSECUTION Task Force 10 Jun–16 Aug 44)* landed at Aitape New Guinea 14 Jul 44 and departed 26 Dec 44; assaulted Lingayen Gulf Luzon Philippine Islands 9 Jan 45 *(attached to I Corps 17–26 Feb 45) (attached to XI Corps 31 Mar–3 May 45)*; arrived Japan 13 Sep 45 and returned to San Francisco P/E 29 Oct 45 and inactivated at Cp Stoneman Calif on 1 Nov 45.

Campaigns: *Guadalcanal, Northern Solomons, New Guinea, Luzon*
Aug 45 Loc: Cabanatuan Philippine Islands

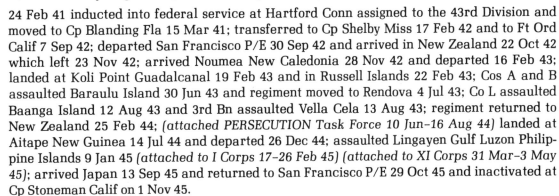

172nd Infantry Regiment (43rd Infantry Division)   Vermont National Guard

24 Feb 41 inducted into federal service at Brattleboro Vt assigned to the 43rd Division and moved to Cp Blanding Fla 5 Mar 41; transferred to Cp Shelby Miss 15 Feb 42 and to Ft Ord Calif 7 Sep 42; departed San Francisco P/E 5 Oct 42 and arrived at Espiritu Santo 26 Oct 42 *(attached to Espiritu Santo Base Command 26 Oct 42–21 Mar 43)*; arrived at Guadalcanal 23 Mar 43 *(attached XIV Corps 23 Mar–14 Apr 43) (attached to 37th Inf Div 15 Apr–29 Jun 43)*; landed on Rendova 30 Jun 43 and Co A and Antitank Co assaulted Sasavele Island same date; assaulted Arundel 27 Aug 43 and reassembled on Rendova 25 Sep 43 *(attached to IV Island Command 27 Jan–15 Feb 44)*; arrived in New Zealand by 26 Mar 44 and moved to New Guinea 4–22 Jul 44; departed 26 Dec 44 and assaulted Lingayen Gulf Luzon Philippine Islands 9 Jan 45; arrived in Japan 13 Sep 45 for occupation duty; returned to San Francisco P/E 8 Oct 45 and inactivated at Cp Stoneman Calif on 1 Nov 45.

Campaigns: *Northern Solomons, New Guinea, Luzon*
Aug 45 Loc: Cabanatuan Philippine Islands

174th Infantry Regiment (Separate)   New York National Guard

16 Sep 40 inducted into federal service at Buffalo N.Y. assigned to the 44th Division and moved to Ft Dix N.J. 24 Sep 40; transferred to Cp Claiborne La 16 Jan 42 and to Ft Lewis Wash 4 May 42; relocated to Ojai Calif 5 Jan 43 and to San Fernando Calif 27 Jan 43 where relieved of assignment to the 44th Division same date and assigned to the Western Defense Command; assigned to III Corps 22 Jan 44 and moved to Cp White Oreg 4 Feb 44; transferred to Cp Chaffee Ark 28 Mar 44 under XVI Corps and assigned XXXVI Corps 17 Jul 44; relocated to Cp Gruber Okla 9 Dec 44 and to Cp Rucker Ala 3 Apr 45 under Replacement & School Command where inactivated on 26 Sep 45.

Aug 45 Loc: Camp Rucker Alabama

175th Infantry Regiment (29th Infantry Division)   Maryland National Guard

3 Feb 41 inducted into federal service at Baltimore Md assigned to the 29th Division and moved to Ft George G. Meade Md 17 Feb 41; relocated to A.P. Hill Mil Res Va 22 Apr 42 and to Carolina Mnvr area 8 Jul 42; arrived Cp Blanding Fla 19 Aug 42 and staged at Cp Kilmer N.J. 20 Sep 42 until departed New York P/E 5 Oct 42; arrived England 11 Oct 42 and assaulted Normandy France on 6 Jun 44; crossed into both Belgium and Holland 27 Sep 44 and entered Germany 30 Sep 44 *(attached Ninth Army 17–24 Mar 45) (attached XIII Corps 20–26 Apr 45)*; returned to New York P/E 15 Jan 46 and inactivated at Cp Kilmer N.J. on 16 Jan 46.

Campaigns: *Normandy, Northern France, Rhineland, Central Europe*
Aug 45 Loc: Osterholz Germany

176th Infantry Regiment (Separate)   Virginia National Guard

3 Feb 41 inducted into federal service at Richmond Va assigned to the 29th Division and moved to Ft George G. Meade Md 17 Feb 41; detached to guard Washington D.C. 17 Dec 41 and attached to the Washington Provisional Brigade; relieved from assignment to the 29th Division 11 Mar 42 and assigned to GHQ; served as White House Honor Guard, Presidential Special Guard, guard for the Capitol and other government buildings as well as for the Combined Chiefs of Staff; performed ceremonial and escort functions and engaged in protective security for scattered vital capitol-area facilities; relocated to A.P. Hill Mil Res Va on 20 Feb 43 where assigned to the Replacement & School Command 1 Apr 43; arrived at Ft Benning Ga 11 Apr 43 as School Troops; inactivated there on 10 Jul 44.

179th Infantry Regiment (45th Infantry Division)   Oklahoma National Guard

16 Sep 40 inducted into federal service at Oklahoma City Okla assigned to 45th Division and moved to Ft Sill Okla 26 Sep 40; transferred to Cp Barkeley Tex 28 Feb 41 and to Ft Devens Mass 22 Apr 42; relocated to Pine Camp N.Y. 9 Nov 42 and to Cp Pickett Va 16 Jan 43; staged at Cp Patrick Henry Va 25 May 43 until departed Hampton Roads P/E 8 Jun 43; landed in North Africa 22 Jun 43 and assaulted Scoglitti Sicily 9 Jul 43; assaulted Salerno Italy 9 Sep 43 and Anzio Italy 22 Jan 44; assaulted southern France 15 Aug 44 *(attached 36th Inf Div 23–24 Aug 44) (attached VI Corps 3–7 Sep 44)* and entered Germany 17 Mar 45; arrived at New York P/E 14 Sep 45 and moved to Cp Bowie Tex 17 Sep 45 where inactivated on 19 Nov 45.

Campaigns: *Sicily, Naples-Foggia, Anzio, Rome-Arno, Southern France, Rhineland, Ardennes-Alsace, Central Europe*
Aug 45 Loc: Munchen Germany

180th Infantry Regiment (45th Infantry Division)   Oklahoma National Guard

16 Sep 40 inducted into federal service at Muskogee Okla assigned to the 45th Division and moved to Ft Sill Okla 26 Sep 40; transferred to Cp Barkeley Tex 28 Feb 41 and to Ft Devens Mass 25 Apr 42; relocated to Pine Camp N.Y. 10 Nov 42 and to Cp Pickett Va 24 Jan 43; staged at Cp Patrick Henry Va 25 May 43 until departed Hampton Roads P/E 8 Jun 43; landed in North Africa 22 Jun 43 and assaulted Scoglitti Sicily 9 Jul 43; assaulted Salerno Italy 10 Sep 43, landed at Anzio, and assaulted southern France 15 Aug 44; entered Germany 17 Mar 45; arrived New York P/E 14 Sep 45 and moved to Cp Bowie Tex 17 Sep 45 where inactivated on 29 Nov 45.

Campaigns: *Sicily, Naples-Foggia, Anzio, Rome-Arno, Southern France, Rhineland, Ardennes-Alsace, Central Europe*
Aug 45 Loc: Munchen Germany

181st Infantry Regiment (Separate)   Massachusetts National Guard

16 Jan 41 inducted into federal service at Worcester Mass assigned to the 26th Division and moved to Cp Edwards Mass 25 Jan 41 where relieved of assignment to the 26th Division on 27 Jan 42; transferred to Boston Mass 11 May 42 and to Framingham Mass 27 May 42 where assigned to the Eastern Defense Command 8 Feb 43 and provided coastal security for the New England sector; arrived Ft Dix N.J. 5 Dec 43 under XIII Corps where inactivated on 8 Feb 44.

182nd Infantry Regiment (Americal Division)   Massachusetts National Guard

16 Jan 41 inducted into federal service at Charlestown Mass assigned to the 26th Division and moved to Cp Edwards Mass 25 Jan 41 where relieved of assignment to the 26th Division on 14 Jan 42; assigned to Task Force 6814 and departed New York P/E 22 Jan 42; arrived in Australia 26 Feb 42 and in New Caledonia 12 Mar 42 where assigned to the Americal Division on 24 May 42; landed Guadalcanal on 12 Nov 42 *(attached to CAM Div 16–30 Jan 43)* and departed 23 Mar 43; arrived Fiji Islands 29 Mar 43 and left 20 Dec 43; arrived at Bougainville 28 Dec 43 where remained until 14 Jan 45; arrived at Leyte Philippine Islands on 28 Jan 45 and elements assaulted Biri Island 20 Feb 45; assaulted Cebu Island 26 Mar 45; arrived in Japan for occupation duty on 8 Sep 45; arrived at Seattle P/E 29 Nov 45 and inactivated at Ft Lawton Wash on 2 Dec 45.

Campaigns: *Guadalcanal, Northern Solomons, Leyte, Southern Philippines*
Aug 45 Loc: Cebu Philippine Islands

184th Infantry Regiment (7th Infantry Division)   California National Guard

3 Mar 41 inducted into federal service at Sacramento Calif assigned to 40th Division and moved to Cp San Luis Obispo Calif 11 Mar 41; transferred to San Diego Calif 9 Dec 41 and to Ft Lewis Wash 29 Apr 42; relocated to the Presidio of San Francisco Calif 14 Jun 42 where relieved from assignment to the 40th Division and assigned to Western Defense Command on 16 Jun 42; moved to Ft Ord Calif 17 Nov 42 where attached to 7th Inf Div 20 Jan 43 and to Amphibious Training Force #9 on 4 May 43; departed San Francisco P/E 10 Jul 43 and arrived at Adak Island 24 Jul 43 where assigned to the 7th Infantry Division on 27 Aug 43; departed 1 Sep 43 and arrived Hawaii 17 Sep 43 which left 20 Jan 44; assaulted Kwajalein 31 Jan 44 and returned to Hawaii 15 Feb 44; left Hawaii 15 Sep 44 and arrived Eniwetok 25 Sep 44 and Manus Island 3 Oct 44 enroute to Philippine Islands where assaulted Leyte on 20 Oct 44; departed Leyte 25 Mar 45 and landed on Okinawa 1 Apr 45; arrived in Korea for occupation duty 8 Sep 45 and inactivated there on 20 Jan 46.

Campaigns: *Aleutian Islands, Eastern Mandates, Leyte, Ryukyus*
Aug 45 Loc: Okinawa

185th Infantry Regiment (40th Infantry Division)   California National Guard

3 Mar 41 inducted into federal service at Fresno Calif assigned to 40th Division and moved to Cp San Luis Obispo Calif 15 Mar 41; transferred to Ft Lewis Wash 29 Apr 42 and staged at Cp Stoneman Calif 14 Aug 42 until departed San Francisco P/E 23 Aug 42; arrived Hawaii 3 Sep 42 and departed 13 Jan 44; arrived Guadalcanal 21 Jan 44 and Cape Gloucester New Britain on 23 Apr 44; departed 9 Dec 44 and arrived Manus Island enroute to New Guinea where landed 18 Dec 44; returned to Manus Island and departed 27–31 Dec 44 enroute to Philippine Islands where landed at Lingayen Gulf Luzon on 9 Jan 45; assaulted Negros Island 29 Mar 45 and returned to San Francisco P/E 5 Apr 46; inactivated at Cp Stoneman Calif on 7 Apr 46.

Campaigns: *Bismarck Archipelago, Luzon, Southern Philippines*
Aug 45 Loc: Negros Philippine Islands

186th Infantry Regiment (41st Infantry Division)   Oregon National Guard

16 Sep 40 inducted into federal service at Portland Oreg assigned to 41st Division and moved to Cp Murray Wash 23 Sep 40; transferred to Ft Lewis Wash 20 Mar 41 and departed San Francisco P/E 22 Apr 42; arrived in Australia 14 May 42 and moved by air to the Buna-Gona area of New Guinea about 25 Jan 43; returned to Australia in Jul 43 and returned to New Guinea 11 Mar 44 where assaulted Hollandia 27 Apr 44; assaulted Biak Island 27 May 44 and departed 2 Feb 45; assaulted Palawan Island Philippines 28 Feb 45 and rejoined division at Zamboanga Mindanao on 27 Mar 45; inactivated in Japan 31 Dec 45.

Campaigns: *Papua, New Guinea, Luzon, Southern Philippines*
Aug 45 Loc: Zamboanga Mindanao Philippine Islands

187th Glider Infantry Regiment (11th Airborne Division)

25 Feb 43 activated at Cp Mackall N.C. and assigned to the 11th Airborne Division; moved to Cp Polk La 9 Jan 44 and staged at Cp Stoneman Calif 29 Apr 44 until departed San Francisco P/E 6 May 44; arrived New Guinea 29 May 44 and departed 11 Nov 44; arrived on Leyte Philippine Islands 18 Nov 44 and assaulted Nasugbu Point Luzon on 31 Jan 45 *(attached to Provost Marshal General U.S. Army Forces in the Far East 1 Jun–27 Jul 45 at Manila)*; arrived at Okinawa 12 Aug 45 and Japan 30 Aug 45 for occupation duty where active thru 1946.

Campaigns: *New Guinea, Leyte, Luzon*
Aug 45 Loc: Lipa Batangas Philippine Islands

188th Parachute Infantry Regiment (11th Airborne Division)

25 Feb 43 activated at Cp Mackall N.C. as the 188th Glider Infantry Regiment and assigned to the 11th Airborne Division; moved to Cp Polk La 8 Jan 44 and staged at Cp Stoneman Calif 29 Apr 44 until departed San Francisco P/E 17 May 44; arrived New Guinea 11 Jun 44 and Leyte Philippine Islands on 18 Nov 44; assaulted Nasugbu Point Luzon 31 Jan 45 and redesignated as the 188th Parachute Infantry Regiment on 20 Jul 45; arrived Okinawa on 12 Aug 45 and Japan on 30 Aug 45 where active on occupation duty thru 1946.

Campaigns: *New Guinea, Leyte, Luzon*
Aug 45 Loc: Lipa Batangas Philippine Islands

189th Glider Infantry Regiment (13th Airborne Division)

13 Aug 43 activated at Ft Bragg N.C. and assigned to the 13th Airborne Division; there disbanded on 8 Dec 43.

190th Glider Infantry Regiment (13th Airborne Division)

13 Aug 43 activated at Ft Bragg N.C. and assigned to the 13th Airborne Division; there disbanded on 4 Dec 43.

193rd Glider Infantry Regiment (17th Airborne Division)

15 Apr 43 activated at Cp Mackall N.C. and assigned to the 17th Airborne Division and moved to the Tenn Mnvr area 7 Feb 44; transferred to Cp Forrest Tenn 24 Mar 44 and staged at Cp Myles Standish Mass 14 Aug 44 until departed Boston P/E 20 Aug 44; arrived England 28 Aug 44 and landed in France 31 Dec 44; moved immediately into Belgium *(attached to 101st A/B Div 3–7 Jan 45 and 14–18 Jan 45)* where disbanded on 1 Mar 45.

Campaigns: *Rhineland, Ardennes-Alsace, Central Europe*

194th Glider Infantry Regiment (17th Airborne Division)

15 Apr 43 activated at Cp Mackall N.C. and assigned to the 17th Airborne Division and moved to Tenn Mnvr area 7 Feb 44; transferred to Cp Forrest Tenn 24 Mar 44 and staged at Cp Myles Standish Mass 14 Aug 44 until departed Boston P/E 20 Aug 44; arrived England 28 Aug 44 and landed in France 24 Dec 44; crossed into Belgium 25 Dec 44 and returned to France 11 Feb 45; air-assaulted Wesel Germany 24 Mar 45 *(attached to 95th Inf Div 5–13 Apr 45)*; arrived Boston P/E 14 Sep 45 and inactivated at Cp Myles Standish Mass same date.

Campaigns: *Rhineland, Ardennes-Alsace, Central Europe*
Aug 45 Loc: Vittel France

197th Infantry Regiment (Separate)

No Distinctive Insignia Authorized

29 Jan 43 2nd Battalion activated on Adak Island Alaska with personnel and equipment from the 2nd Bn, 134th Infantry Regt and employed to garrison Aleutian Islands; departed Alaska and sent to the United States where inactivated at Cp Chaffee Ark on 26 Jun 44.

Campaigns: *Aleutian Islands*

198th Infantry Regiment (Separate)

No Distinctive Insignia Authorized

9 Feb 43 1st Battalion activated in Alaska with personnel and equipment from the 1st Bn, 71st Infantry Regt and employed to garrison Aleutian Islands; there redesignated as the 206th Infantry Battalion on 26 Jan 44.

Campaigns: *Aleutian Islands*

201st Infantry Regiment (Separate)   West Virginia National Guard

6 Jan 41 inducted into federal service at Morgantown W. Va and moved to Ft Benjamin Harrison Ind 10 Jan 41 where attached to Second Army; staged at Cp Murray Wash 5 Aug 41 until departed Seattle P/E 12 Sep 41; arrived Kodiak Alaska 16 Sep 41 and transferred to Adak Island in Nov 42 and to Amchitka in Jan 43; departed Alaska 22 Mar 44 and returned to Seattle P/E 2 Apr 44; moved to Cp Carson Colo 10 Apr 44 under XVI Corps and assigned to XXXVI Corps on 17 Jul 44; relocated to Ft Jackson S.C. 18 Sep 44 under IX Corps and assigned to XXIII Corps 25 Sep 44; arrived at Cp Rucker Ala 3 Mar 45 under Replacement & School Command and inactivated there on 26 Sep 45.

Campaigns: *Aleutian Islands*
Aug 45 Loc: Camp Rucker Alabama

222nd Infantry Regiment (42nd Infantry Division)

No Distinctive Insignia Authorized

14 Jul 43 activated at Gp Gruber Okla and assigned to the 42nd Infantry Division and staged at Cp Kilmer N.J. 12 Nov 44 until departed New York P/E 25 Nov 44; arrived in France 8 Dec 44 and entered Germany 18 Mar 45; inactivated in Austria on 30 Jun 46.

Campaigns: *Rhineland, Ardennes-Alsace, Central Europe*
Aug 45 Loc: Schwarz Germany

232nd Infantry Regiment (42nd Infantry Division)

No Distinctive Insignia Authorized

14 Jul 43 activated at Cp Gruber Okla and assigned to the 42nd Infantry Division and staged at Cp Kilmer, N.J. 16 Nov 44 until departed New York P/E 25 Nov 44; arrived in France 7 Dec 44 and entered Germany 18 Mar 45; inactivated in Austria on 30 Jun 46.

Campaigns: *Rhineland, Ardennes-Alsace, Central Europe*
Aug 45 Loc: Schwarz Germany

242nd Infantry Regiment (42nd Infantry Division)

14 Jul 43 activated at Cp Gruber Okla and assigned to the 42nd Infantry Division and staged at Cp Kilmer N.J. 12 Nov 44 until departed New York P/E 25 Nov 44; arrived in France 8 Dec 44 and entered Germany 18 Mar 45; inactivated in Austria on 30 Jun 46.

Campaigns: *Rhineland, Ardennes-Alsace, Central Europe*
Aug 45 Loc: St Johann Austria

253rd Infantry Regiment (63rd Infantry Division)

15 Jun 43 activated at Cp Blanding Fla and assigned to the 63rd Infantry Division and moved to Cp Van Dorn Miss 23 Aug 43; staged at Cp Shanks N.Y. 6 Nov 44 until departed New York P/E 25 Nov 44; landed in France 7 Dec 44 *(attached to 44th Inf Div 31 Dec 44–6 Feb 45)* and entered Germany 20 Mar 45; arrived Boston P/E 27 Sep 45 and inactivated at Cp Myles Standish Mass on 28 Sep 45.

Campaigns: *Rhineland, Ardennes-Alsace, Central Europe*
Aug 45 Loc: Tauberbischofsheim Germany

254th Infantry Regiment (63rd Infantry Division)

15 Jun 43 activated at Cp Blanding Fla and assigned to the 63rd Infantry Division and moved to Cp Van Dorn Miss 25 Aug 43; staged at Cp Shanks N.Y. 8 Nov 44 until departed New York P/E 25 Nov 44; landed in France on 9 Dec 44 *(attached to 3rd Inf Div 28 Dec 44–9 Feb 45)* *(attached to 100th Inf Div 9–17 Feb 45)*; entered Germany on 20 Mar 45 and returned to New York P/E 28 Sep 45 and inactivated at Cp Kilmer N.J. on 29 Sep 45.

Campaigns: *Rhineland, Ardennes-Alsace, Central Europe*
Aug 45 Loc: Greglingen Germany

255th Infantry Regiment (63rd Infantry Division)

15 Jun 43 activated at Cp Blanding Fla and assigned to the 63rd Infantry Division and moved to Cp Van Dorn Miss 25 Aug 43; staged at Cp Shanks N.Y. 11 Nov 44 until departed New York P/E 25 Nov 44; landed in France on 7 Dec 44 *(attached to 100th Inf Div 31 Dec 44–19 Jan 45)* *(attached to 44th Inf Div 19 Jan–6 Feb 45)*; entered Germany on 20 Mar 45 and returned to New York P/E 28 Sep 45; inactivated at Cp Kilmer N.J. on 29 Sep 45.

Campaigns: *Rhineland, Ardennes-Alsace, Central Europe*
Aug 45 Loc: Kunzelsau Germany

259th Infantry Regiment (65th Infantry Division)

16 Aug 43 activated at Cp Shelby Miss and assigned to the 65th Infantry Division; staged at Cp Shanks N.Y. 28 Dec 44 until departed New York P/E on 10 Jan 45; arrived in France on 21 Jan 45 and entered Germany 20 Mar 45; inactivated in Austria on 31 Aug 45.

Campaigns: *Rhineland, Central Europe*
Aug 45 Loc: Urfahr Austria

260th Infantry Regiment (65th Infantry Division)

16 Aug 43 activated at Cp Shelby Miss and assigned to the 65th Infantry Division; staged at Cp Shanks N.Y. 30 Dec 44 until departed New York P/E 10 Jan 45; arrived in France on 21 Jan 45 and entered Germany 20 Mar 45; inactivated in Austria on 31 Aug 45.

Campaigns: *Rhineland, Central Europe*
Aug 45 Loc: Kirchschlag Austria

261st Infantry Regiment (65th Infantry Division)

No Distinctive
Insignia Authorized

16 Aug 43 activated at Cp Shelby Miss and assigned to the 65th Infantry Division; staged at Cp Shanks N.Y. 31 Dec 44 until departed New York P/E 10 Jan 45; arrived in France on 21 Jan 45 and entered Germany 20 Mar 45 *(attached to 11th Armd Div 28–29 Mar 45) (attached to 6th Armd Div 29 Mar–4 Apr 45)*; inactivated in Austria on 31 Aug 45.

Campaigns: *Rhineland, Central Europe*
Aug 45 Loc: Enns Austria

262nd Infantry Regiment (66th Infantry Division)

No Distinctive
Insignia Authorized

15 Apr 43 activated at Cp Blanding Fla and assigned to the 66th Infantry Division; moved to Cp Joseph T. Robinson Ark 12 Aug 43 and to Cp Rucker Ala 17 Apr 44; staged at Cp Shanks N.Y. 30 Oct 44 until departed New York P/E 15 Nov 44; arrived in England 26 Nov 44 and landed in France 25 Dec 44; entered Germany on 28 May 45; returned to New York P/E 7 Nov 45 and inactivated at Cp Shanks N.Y. on 8 Nov 45.

Campaigns: *Northern France*
Aug 45 Loc: Villepail France

263rd Infantry Regiment (66th Infantry Division)

No Distinctive
Insignia Authorized

15 Apr 43 activated at Cp Blanding Fla and assigned to the 66th Infantry Division; moved to Cp Joseph T. Robinson Ark 13 Aug 43 and to Cp Rucker Ala 23 Apr 44; staged at Cp Shanks N.Y. 30 Oct 44 until departed New York P/E 15 Nov 44; arrived in England 26 Nov 44 and landed in France 29 Dec 44; entered Germany on 27 May 45; returned to New York P/E 31 Oct 45 and inactivated at Cp Shanks N.Y. on 1 Nov 45.

Campaigns: *Northern France*
Aug 45 Loc: Villepail France

264th Infantry Regiment (66th Infantry Division)

No Distinctive
Insignia Authorized

15 Apr 43 activated at Cp Blanding Fla and assigned to the 66th Infantry Division; moved to Cp Joseph T. Robinson Ark 15 Aug 43 and to Cp Rucker Ala 21 Apr 44; staged at Cp Shanks N.Y. 2 Nov 44 until departed New York P/E 15 Nov 44; arrived in England 26 Nov 44 and landed in France 25 Dec 44; entered Germany on 27 May; returned to New York P/E 6 Nov 45 and inactivated at Cp Shanks N.Y. on 8 Nov 45.

Campaigns: *Northern France*
Aug 45 Loc: Villepail France

271st Infantry Regiment (69th Infantry Division)

No Distinctive
Insignia Authorized

15 May 43 activated at Cp Shelby Miss and assigned to the 69th Infantry Division and staged at Cp Kilmer N.J. 2 Nov 44 until departed New York P/E 15 Nov 44; arrived England 26 Nov 44 and landed in France 24 Jan 45; crossed into Belgium 9 Feb 45 and into Germany 8 Mar 45 *(attached to 2nd Inf Div 18–19 Apr 45)*; returned to New York P/E 19 Sep 45 and inactivated at Cp Kilmer N.J. 22 Sep 45.

Campaigns: *Rhineland, Central Europe*
Aug 45 Loc: Mucheln Germany

272nd Infantry Regiment (69th Infantry Division)

15 May 43 activated at Cp Shelby Miss and assigned to the 69th Infantry Division; staged at Cp Kilmer N.J. 4 Nov 44 until departed New York P/E 15 Nov 44; arrived England 26 Nov 44 and landed in France 24 Jan 45; crossed into Belgium 9 Feb 45 and into Germany 8 Mar 45 *(attached to 104th Inf Div 1–6 May 45)*; returned to New York P/E 19 Sep 45 and inactivated at Cp Kilmer N.J. on 22 Sep 45.

Campaigns: *Rhineland, Central Europe*
Aug 45 Loc: Zeitz Germany

273rd Infantry Regiment (69th Infantry Division)

15 May 43 activated at Cp Shelby Miss and assigned to the 69th Infantry Division; staged at Cp Kilmer N.J. 4 Nov 44 until departed New York P/E 15 Nov 44; arrived England 26 Nov 44 and landed in France 24 Jan 45; crossed into Belgium 9 Feb 45 and into Germany 8 Mar 45 *(attached to V Corps 16–25 Mar 45)*; returned to New York P/E 16 Sep 45 and inactivated at Cp Kilmer N.J. on 18 Sep 45.

Campaigns: *Rhineland, Central Europe*
Aug 45 Loc: Trebsen Germany

274th Infantry Regiment (70th Infantry Division)

15 Jun 43 activated at Cp Adair Oreg and assigned to the 70th Infantry Division and moved to Ft Leonard Wood Mo 29 Jul 44; staged at Cp Myles Standish Mass 18 Nov 44 until departed Boston P/E 1 Dec 44; arrived in France 10 Dec 44 *(attached to 79th Inf Div 1–2 Jan 45)* *(attached to 45th Inf Div 3–17 Jan 45)* *(attached to 103rd Inf Div 17–22 Jan 45)* *(attached to 45th Inf Div 22–29 Jan 45)* *(attached to 100th Inf Div 29 Jan–8 Feb 45)*; entered Germany 27 Mar 45; arrived in New York P/E 9 Oct 45 and inactivated at Cp Kilmer N.J. on 11 Oct 45.

Campaigns: *Rhineland, Ardennes-Alsace, Central Europe*
Aug 45 Loc: Schierstein Germany

275th Infantry Regiment (70th Infantry Division)

15 Jun 43 activated at Cp Adair Oreg and assigned to the 70th Infantry Division and moved to Ft Leonard Wood Mo 29 Jul 44; staged at Cp Myles Standish Mass 19 Nov 44 until departed Boston P/E 6 Dec 44; arrived in France 15 Dec 44 and entered Germany 27 Mar 45; arrived New York P/E 9 Oct 45 and inactivated at Cp Kilmer N.J. on 11 Oct 45.
on 11 Oct 45.

Campaigns: *Rhineland, Ardennes-Alsace, Central Europe*
Aug 45 Loc: Kamberg Germany

276th Infantry Regiment (70th Infantry Division)

15 Jun 43 activated at Cp Adair Oreg and assigned to the 70th Infantry Division and moved to Ft Leonard Wood Mo 29 Jul 44; staged at Cp Myles Standish Mass 20 Nov 44 until departed Boston P/E 6 Dec 44; arrived in France 15 Dec 44 and entered Germany 27 Mar 45; arrived New York P/E Oct 45 and inactivated at Cp Kilmer N.J. on 11 Oct 45.

Campaigns: *Rhineland, Ardennes-Alsace, Central Europe*
Aug 45 Loc: Lohr Germany

289th Infantry Regiment (75th Infantry Division)

15 Apr 43 activated at Ft Leonard Wood Mo and assigned to the 75th Infantry Division; moved to La Mnvr area 24 Jan 44 and to Cp Breckinridge Ky 7 Apr 44; staged at Cp Shanks N.Y. 17 Oct 44 until departed New York P/E 22 Oct 44; arrived England 3 Nov 44 and landed in France 13 Dec 44; crossed into Holland 18 Dec 44 and into Belgium next day *(attached to 3rd Armd Div 24–29 Dec 44)* and returned to France 27 Jan 45; reentered Belgium 17 Feb 45 and Holland 18 Feb 45 *(attached British 8 Corps 4–10 Mar 45)*; entered Germany 10 Mar 45 and arrived at Hampton Roads P/E 23 Nov 45; inactivated at Cp Patrick Henry Va on the same date.

Campaigns: *Rhineland, Ardennes-Alsace, Central Europe*
Aug 45 Loc: Sissone France

No Distinctive Insignia Authorized

290th Infantry Regiment (75th Infantry Division)

15 Apr 43 activated at Ft Leonard Wood Mo and assigned to the 75th Infantry Division; moved to La Mnvr area 24 Jan 44 and to Cp Breckinridge Ky 7 Apr 44; staged at Cp Shanks N.Y. 16 Oct 44 until departed New York P/E 22 Oct 44; arrived England 2 Nov 44 and landed in France 13 Dec 44; crossed into Holland 18 Dec 44 and into Belgium next day *(attached to 3rd Armd Div 23–31 Dec 44) (attached to 83rd Inf Div 31 Dec 44–1 Jan 45) (attached to 84th Inf Div 1–10 Jan 45)*; returned to France 27 Jan 45 and reentered Belgium 17 Feb 45 and Holland 18 Feb 45 *(attached to British 6th A/B Div 20–21 Feb 45)*; entered Germany 10 Mar 45 *(attached to 30th Inf Div 26–27 Mar 45) (attached to 8th Armd Div 27–30 Mar 45)*; arrived Hampton Roads P/E 17 Nov 45 and inactivated at Cp Patrick Henry Va on 18 Nov 45.

Campaigns: *Rhineland, Ardennes-Alsace, Central Europe*
Aug 45 Loc: Le Havre France

No Distinctive Insignia Authorized

291st Infantry Regiment (75th Infantry Division)

15 Apr 43 activated at Ft Leonard Wood Mo and assigned to the 75th Infantry Division; moved to La Mnvr area 24 Jan 44 and to Cp Breckinridge Ky 7 Apr 44; staged at Cp Shanks N.Y. 18 Oct 44 until departed New York P/E 22 Oct 44; arrived England 2 Nov 44 and landed in France 13 Dec 44; crossed into Holland 18 Dec 44 and into Belgium next day *(attached to 3rd Armd Div 24–29 Dec 44)* and returned to France 27 Jan 45; reentered Belgium 17 Feb 45 and Holland 18 Feb 45 *(attached British 8 Corps 4–10 Mar 45)*; entered Germany 10 Mar 45 and arrived at Hampton Roads P/E 23 Nov 45; inactivated at Cp Patrick Henry Va on the same date.

Campaigns: *Rhineland, Ardennes-Alsace, Central Europe*
Aug 45 Loc: Suippes France

No Distinctive Insignia Authorized

295th Infantry Regiment (Puerto Rican) (Separate)   Puerto Rico National Guard

15 Oct 40 inducted into federal service at Cp Tortuguero Puerto Rico and assigned to the Caribbean Defense Command; moved to Caguas Puerto Rico 26 Sep 41 and returned to Cp Tortuguero on 11 Oct 41; transferred to Cp O'Reilly Puerto Rico 2 Feb 44 and departed San Juan Puerto Rico 20 Sep 44; arrived Panama Canal Zone 24 Sep 44 where inactivated on 20 Feb 46.

Campaigns: *American Theater without Inscription*
Aug 45 Loc: Fort William D. Davis Panama Canal Zone; less AT Co at David Panama, Cos B and D at Seymour Island Galapagos, Co C at Salinas Ecuador, Cos A and B at Fort Clayton and Co L at Fort Randolph Panama Canal Zone.

296th Infantry Regiment (Puerto Rican) (Separate)   Puerto Rico National Guard

15 Oct 40 inducted into federal service at Cp Tortuguero Puerto Rico and variously assigned to the Panama Mobile Force, Antilles Dept, etc; served at Cp Tortuguero until departed San Juan Puerto Rico 12 Jan 44; arrived at Panama Canal Zone 14 Jan 44 and returned to Puerto Rico 4 Apr 45; departed Puerto Rico 8 May 45 and arrived in Hawaii 25 Jun 45 under the Central Pacific Base Command; returned to Cp O'Reilly Puerto Rico on 6 Mar 46 and inactivated there on 12 Mar 46.

Campaigns: *American Theater without Inscription, Pacific Theater without Inscription*
Aug 45 Loc: Kahuku Army Airbase Hawaii

297th Infantry Regiment (Separate)   Alaska National Guard

15 Sep 41 1st Battalion inducted into federal service at Juneau Alaska and moved to Ft Richardson Alaska for duty; redesignated in Alaska as the 208th Infantry Battalion on 26 Jan 44.

Campaigns: *Pacific Theater without inscription*

298th Infantry Regiment (Separate)   Hawaii National Guard

15 Oct 40 inducted into federal service at Honolulu Hawaii and assigned to the 25th Infantry Division on 1 Oct 41 and stationed at Schofield Barracks Hawaii where guarded Oahu; relieved from assignment to the 25th and assigned to the 24th Infantry Division on 23 Jul 42; relieved from assignment to the 24th Infantry Division on 12 Jun 43 but remained attached until 16 Jul 43; assigned to the Hawaiian Department until arrived on Espiritu Santo 4 Dec 43 under U.S. Army Forces in the South Pacific Area; landed on Guadalcanal 22 Jan 44 and assigned to Central Pacific Base Command on 10 Nov 44 and returned to Hawaii 22 Nov 44; regiment inactivated, less 1st Bn, there on 10 Apr 45 and the 1st Bn inactivated on Hawaii 22 Jan 46.

Campaigns: *Central Pacific*
Aug 45 Loc: 1st Battalion at Schofield Barracks Hawaii, less Co B at Bellows Field

299th Infantry Regiment (Separate)   Hawaii National Guard

15 Oct 40 inducted into federal service at Honolulu Hawaii and assigned to the 24th Infantry Division on 1 Oct 41; stationed at Schofield Barracks Hawaii and transferred to Iolani Barracks Honolulu on 4 Jun 41; there inactivated on 21 Jul 42 and assets transferred to the 298th Infantry Regt.

Campaigns: *Central Pacific*

300th Infantry Regiment (Separate)

10 Dec 42 activated at Ft Benning Ga under the Replacement & School Command to serve as a crack demonstration regiment for the Infantry School; moved to Cp McCain Miss 4 Apr 44 under XXI Corps and assigned to the IX Corps 22 Aug 44; transferred to Ft Jackson S.C. on 28 Aug 44, assigned to XXIII Corps on 25 Sep 44 and to Second Army on 20 Oct 44; arrived at Cp Rucker Ala 5 Apr 45 under Replacement & School Command where inactivated on 26 Sep 45.

Aug 45 Loc: Camp Rucker Alabama

301st Infantry Regiment (94th Infantry Division)

15 Sep 42 organized at Ft Custer Mich and assigned to the 94th Infantry Division and moved to Cp Phillips Kans 16 Nov 42; transferred to the Tenn Mnvr area 6 Sep 43 and to Cp McCain Miss 28 Nov 43; staged at Cp Shanks N.Y. 26 Jul 44 until departed New York P/E 6 Aug 44; arrived in England 11 Aug 44 and landed in France 14 Sep 44; entered Germany 8 Jan 45; returned to New York P/E 1 Feb 46 and inactivated at Cp Kilmer N.J. on 4 Feb 46.

Campaigns: *Northern France, Rhineland, Ardennes-Alsace, Central Europe*
Aug 45 Loc: Mehmann Germany

302nd Infantry Regiment (94th Infantry Division)

15 Sep 42 organized at Ft Custer Mich and assigned to the 94th Infantry Division; transferred to Cp Phillips Kans 18 Nov 42 and to Cp McCain Miss 28 Nov 43; staged at Cp Shanks N.Y. 26 Jul 44 until departed New York P/E 6 Aug 44; arrived England 11 Aug 44 and landed in France 14 Sep 44; entered Germany 8 Jan 45 *(attached to 28th Inf Div 6–10 Jan 45)*; returned to New York P/E 29 Jan 46 and inactivated at Cp Kilmer N.J. on 30 Jan 46.

Campaigns: *Northern France, Rhineland, Ardennes-Alsace, Central Europe*
Aug 45 Loc: Dusseldorf Germany

303rd Infantry Regiment (97th Infantry Division)

25 Feb 43 organized at Cp Swift Tex and assigned to the 97th Infantry Division; moved to the La Mnvr area 19 Oct 43 and to Ft Leonard Wood Mo 31 Jan 44; transferred to Cp San Luis Obispo Calif 17 Jul 44 and to Cp Callan Calif 11 Oct 44; arrived at Cp Cooke Calif 1 Nov 44 and staged at Cp Kilmer N.J. 6 Feb 45 until departed New York P/E 19 Feb 45; arrived in France 1 Mar 45 and entered Germany 28 Mar 45 *(attached to 78th Inf Div 3–6 Apr 45)*; returned to New York P/E 23 Jun 45 and moved to Ft Bragg N.C. 28 Jun 45; staged at Ft Lawton Wash 23 Aug 45 until departed Seattle P/E 30 Aug 45; arrived Philippine Islands 16 Sep 45 and in Japan 24 Sep 45 where inactivated on 31 Mar 46.

Campaigns: *Central Europe*
Aug 45 Loc: Fort Bragg North Carolina

304th Infantry Regiment (76th Infantry Division)

15 Jun 42 organized at Ft George G. Meade Md and assigned to the 76th Division; moved to A.P. Hill Mil Res Va on 4 Jul 43 and to Cp McCoy Wis 4 Oct 43; staged at Cp Myles Standish Mass 14 Nov 44 until departed Boston P/E 24 Nov 44; arrived England 4 Dec 44 and landed in France 12 Jan 45; crossed into Belgium and Luxembourg both on 23 Jan 45 and entered Germany 28 Feb 45; disbanded there on 31 Aug 45.

Campaigns: *Rhineland, Ardennes-Alsace, Central Europe*
Aug 45 Loc: Altenberg Germany

305th Infantry Regiment (77th Infantry Division)

25 Mar 42 organized at Ft Jackson S.C. and assigned to the 77th Division; moved to La Mnvr area 25 Jan 43 and to Cp Young Calif 23 Apr 43; transferred to Indiantown Gap Mil Res Pa 1 Oct 43 and to the W.Va Mnvr area 18 Nov 43; arrived Cp Pickett Va 4 Dec 43 and staged at Cp Stoneman Calif 15 Mar 44 until departed San Francisco P/E 27 Mar 44; arrived Hawaii 1 Apr 44 and departed 1 Jul 44; landed on Guam 21 Jul 44 *(attached to 1st Prov Marine Brigade 21–24 Jul 44)* and departed 3 Nov 44; arrived Manus Island 15 Nov 44 en route to Philippine Islands where landed 23 Nov 44 on Leyte Island; assaulted Ormoc Leyte on 7 Dec 44 and left the Philippines on 21 Mar 45; Co B assaulted Amura Shima 27 Mar 45 and other elements assaulted both Aka Shima and Zamami Shima 26 Mar 45; assaulted Ie Shima on 16 Apr 45; posted 1st and 2nd Bns as garrisons to Ie Shima and Zamami Shima respectively and remainder of regiment landed on Okinawa 27 Apr 45; 1st and 2nd Bns rejoined division on Okinawa 7 May 45 and 24 May 45 respectively *(regiment attached to 96th Inf Div 16–23 Jun 45)*; departed Okinawa 7 Jul 45 and arrived on Cebu Philippines 17 Jul 45; arrived in Japan 5 Oct 45 where inactivated on 15 Mar 46.

Campaigns: *Western Pacific, Leyte, Ryukyus*
Aug 45 Loc: Cebu Philippine Islands

306th Infantry Regiment (77th Infantry Division)

25 Mar 42 organized at Ft Jackson S.C. and assigned to the 77th Division; moved to La Mnvr area 25 Jan 43 and to Cp Young Calif 23 Apr 43; transferred to W.Va Mnvr area 7 Oct 43 and to Indiantown Gap Mil Res Pa 28 Oct 43; arrived Cp Pickett Va 23 Nov 43 and staged at Cp Stoneman Calif 16 Mar 44 until departed San Francisco P/E 24 Mar 44; arrived Hawaii 1 Apr 44 and departed 1 Jul 44; landed on Guam 23 Jul 44 and left 3 Nov 44; arrived Manus Island 15 Nov 44 enroute to Philippine Islands where landed 23 Nov 44 on Leyte *(attached to 11th A/B Div 28 Nov–3 Dec 44)*; assaulted Ormoc Leyte on 7 Dec 44 and left Philippines 18 Mar 45; 1st Bn assaulted Geruma Shima and 2nd Bn assaulted Hokaji Shima on 26 Mar 45 while other elements assaulted Amuro Shima and Tokashiki Shima 27 Mar 45; 2nd Bn assaulted Keise Shima 31 Mar 45 and regiment next assaulted Ie Shima on 16 Apr 45; landed on Okinawa 27 Apr 45 and departed 7 Jul 45; arrived Cebu Island Philippines 17 Jul 45 and arrived Japan 5 Oct 45 where inactivated on 15 Mar 46.

Campaigns: *Western Pacific, Leyte, Ryukyus*
Aug 45 Loc: Cebu Philippine Islands

307th Infantry Regiment (77th Infantry Division)

25 Mar 42 organized at Ft Jackson S.C. and assigned to the 77th Division; moved to La Mnvr area 25 Jan 43 and to Cp Young Calif 23 Apr 43; transferred to Indiantown Gap Mil Res Pa 5 Oct 43 and to Cp Pickett Va 11 Nov 43; staged at Cp Stoneman Calif 19 Mar 44 until departed San Francisco P/E 25 Mar 44; arrived Hawaii 1 Apr 44 and departed 9 Jul 44; landed on Guam 23 Jul 44 and left 3 Nov 44; arrived Manus Island 15 Nov 44 enroute to Philippine Islands where landed 23 Nov 44 on Leyte; assaulted Ormoc Leyte on 7 Dec 44 and 2nd Bn detached for duty on Samar 30 Nov–14 Dec 44; departed Philippine Islands 18 Mar 45 and assaulted Yakabi Shima 26 Mar 45 and Co G assaulted Kuba Shima 27 Mar 45; assaulted Ie Shima 16–17 Apr 45 and landed on Okinawa 27 Apr 45; departed 27 Jun 45 and arrived Cebu Island Philippines 10 Jul 45; arrived Japan 5 Oct 45 where inactivated on 15 Mar 46.

Campaigns: *Western Pacific, Leyte, Ryukyus*
Aug 45 Loc: Cebu Philippine Islands

309th Infantry Regiment (78th Infantry Division)

15 Aug 42 organized at Cp Butner N.C. and assigned to the 78th Infantry Division; moved to Tenn Mnvr area 24 Jan 44 and to Cp Pickett Va 29 Mar 44; staged at Cp Kilmer N.J. 5 Oct 44 until departed New York P/E 14 Oct 44; arrived England 25 Oct 44 and landed in France 22 Nov 44; crossed into Belgium 27 Nov 44 and into Germany 7 Dec 44 *(attached to 9th Inf Div 8–12 Feb 45)* *(attached to 9th Armd Div 8–11 Mar 45)*; inactivated in Germany on 22 May 46.

Campaigns: *Rhineland, Ardennes-Alsace, Central Europe*
Aug 45 Loc: Melsungen Germany

310th Infantry Regiment (78th Infantry Division)

15 Aug 42 organized at Cp Butner N.C. and assigned to the 78th Infantry Division; moved to Tenn Mnvr area 24 Jan 44 and to Cp Pickett Va 30 Mar 44; staged at Cp Kilmer N.J. 3 Oct 44 until departed New York P/E 14 Oct 44; arrived England 25 Oct 44 and landed in France 22 Nov 44; crossed into Belgium 27 Nov 44 and into Germany 7 Dec 44 *(attached to 9th Armd Div 10–14 Mar 45)*; inactivated in Germany on 15 Jun 46.

Campaigns: *Rhineland, Ardennes-Alsace, Central Europe*
Aug 45 Loc: Bad Wildungen Germany

311th Infantry Regiment (78th Infantry Division)

15 Aug 42 organized at Cp Butner N.C. and assigned to the 78th Infantry Division; moved to Tenn Mnvr area 24 Jan 44 and to Cp Pickett Va 30 Mar 44; staged at Cp Kilmer N.J. 3 Oct 44 until departed New York P/E 14 Oct 44; arrived England 25 Oct 44 and landed in France 22 Nov 44; crossed into Belgium 27 Nov 44 and into Germany 7 Dec 44 *(attached to 8th Inf Div 10–23 Dec 44) (attached to 9th Armd Div 8–11 Mar 45)*; inactivated in Germany on 22 May 46.

Campaigns: *Rhineland, Ardennes-Alsace, Central Europe*
Aug 45 Loc: Hersfeld Germany

313th Infantry Regiment (79th Infantry Division)

15 Jun 42 organized at Cp Pickett Va and assigned to the 79th Division; moved to Cp Blanding Fla 28 Aug 42 and to Tenn Mnvr area 10 Mar 43; transferred to Cp Forrest Tenn 19 Jun 43 and to Cp Young Calif 15 Aug 43; arrived at Cp Phillips Kans 11 Dec 43 and staged at Cp Myles Standish Mass 31 Mar 44 until departed Boston P/E 7 Apr 44; arrived England 16 Apr 44 and landed in France 12 Jun 44 *(attached to 45th Inf Div 1–14 Jan 45)*; crossed into Belgium 17 Feb 45 and into Holland 22 Feb 45; entered Germany 3 Mar 45; arrived New York P/E 13 Dec 45 and inactivated at Cp Kilmer N.J. on 15 Dec 45.

Campaigns: *Normandy, Northern France, Rhineland, Ardennes-Alsace, Central Europe*
Aug 45 Loc: Kraslice Czechoslovakia

314th Infantry Regiment (79th Infantry Division)

15 Jun 42 organized at Cp Pickett Va and assigned to the 79th Division; moved to Cp Blanding Fla 28 Aug 42 and to Tenn Mnvr area 12 Mar 43; transferred to Cp Forrest Tenn 19 Jun 43 and to Cp Young Calif 12 Aug 43; arrived at Cp Phillips Kans 8 Dec 43 and staged at Cp Myles Standish Mass 30 Mar 44 until departed Boston P/E 7 Apr 44; arrived England 16 Apr 44 and landed in France 14 Jun 44 *(attached to 45th Inf Div 1–14 Jan 45)*; crossed into Belgium 17 Feb 45 and into Holland 22 Feb 45 *(attached XVI Corps 23 Feb–1 Mar 45)* and entered Germany 3 Mar 45; arrived New York P/E 13 Dec 45 and inactivated at Cp Kilmer N.J. on 15 Dec 45.

Campaigns: *Normandy, Northern France, Rhineland, Ardennes-Alsace, Central Europe*
Aug 45 Loc: Kynsperk Germany

315th Infantry Regiment (79th Infantry Division)

15 Jun 42 organized at Cp Pickett Va and assigned to the 79th Division; moved to Cp Blanding Fla 2 Sep 42 and to Tenn Mnvr area 8 Mar 43; arrived at Cp Forrest Tenn 19 Jun 43 and at Cp Young Calif 18 Aug 43; transferred to Cp Phillips Kans 6 Dec 43 and staged at Cp Myles Standish Mass 29 Mar 44 until departed Boston P/E 7 Apr 44; arrived England 7 Apr 44 and landed in France 14 Jun 44 *(attached to 14th Armd Div 13–21 Jan 45)*; crossed into Belgium 17 Feb 45 and into Holland 22 Feb 45 and entered Germany 3 Mar 45; arrived New York P/E 10 Dec 45 and inactivated at Cp Kilmer N.J. 11 Dec 45.

Campaigns: *Normandy, Northern France, Rhineland, Ardennes-Alsace, Central Europe*
Aug 45 Loc: Bochum Germany

317th Infantry Regiment (80th Infantry Division)

15 Jul 42 organized at Cp Forrest Tenn and assigned to the 80th Division; moved to Tenn Mnvr area 23 Jun 43 and to Cp Phillips Kans 6 Sep 43; arrived at Calif-Ariz Mnvr area 8 Dec 43 and at Ft Dix N.J. 3 Apr 44; staged at Cp Kilmer N.J. 19 Jun 44 until departed New York P/E 1 Jul 44; arrived England 7 Jul 44 and landed in France 3 Aug 44; crossed into Luxembourg 20 Dec 44 and into Germany 18 Feb 45 and into Austria 5 May 45; returned to New York P/E 10 Jan 46 and inactivated at Cp Kilmer N.J. on the same date.

Campaigns: *Northern France, Rhineland, Ardennes-Alsace, Central Europe*
Aug 45 Loc: Hoheuschwangau Germany

318th Infantry Regiment (80th Infantry Division)

16 Jul 42 organized at Cp Forrest Tenn and assigned to the 80th Division; moved to Tenn Mnvr area 22 Jun 43 and to Cp Phillips Kans 7 Sep 43; arrived at Calif-Ariz Mnvr area 5 Dec 43 and at Ft Dix N.J. 20 Mar 44; staged at Cp Kilmer N.J. 23 Jun 44 until departed New York P/E 1 Jul 44; arrived England 7 Jul 44 and landed in France 3 Aug 44; crossed into Luxembourg 20 Dec 44 *(two battalions attached to the 4th Armd Div 24–28 Dec 44) (two battalions attached to 4th Inf Div 26 Jan 45–25 Feb 45)* and entered Germany 18 Feb 45 *(attached to 76th Inf Div 1–3 Mar 45) (attached to 10th Armd Div 16–18 Mar 45)*; entered Austria on 5 May 45; returned to New York P/E 17 Jan 46 and inactivated at Cp Kilmer N.J. on 18 Jan 46.

Campaigns: *Northern France, Rhineland, Ardennes-Alsace, Central Europe*
Aug 45 Loc: Kempten Germany

319th Infantry Regiment (80th Infantry Division)

16 Jul 42 organized at Cp Forrest Tenn and assigned to the 80th Division; moved to Tenn Mnvr area 22 Jun 43 and to Cp Phillips Kans 8 Sep 43; arrived at Calif-Ariz Mnvr area 2 Dec 43 and at Ft Dix N.J. 20 Mar 44; staged at Cp Kilmer N.J. 21 Jun 44 until departed New York P/E 1 Jul 44; arrived England 7 Jul 44 and landed in France on 3 Aug 44 *(attached to XX Corps 10–15 Aug 44) (attached to VIII Corps 16–21 Aug 44) (attached to XII Corps 22–27 Aug 44) (attached to 4th Armd Div 11–15 Sep 44) (attached to 4th Inf Div 26–28 Jan 45) (attached to 4th Armd Div 29 Jan–4 Feb 45)*; entered Germany 18 Feb 45 *(attached to 76th Inf Div 8–9 Mar 45)* and Austria on 5 May 45; returned to New York P/E 17 Jan 46 and inactivated at Cp Kilmer N.J. on 18 Jan 46.

Campaigns: *Northern France, Rhineland, Ardennes-Alsace, Central Europe*
Aug 45 Loc: Mendelheim Germany

320th Infantry Regiment (35th Infantry Division)

26 Jan 43 activated at Cp San Luis Obispo Calif and assigned to the 35th Infantry Division; moved to Cp Rucker Ala 2 Apr 43 and to the Tenn Mnvr area 17 Nov 43; transferred to Cp Butner N.C. 31 Jan 44 and staged at Cp Kilmer N.J. 4 May 44 until departed New York P/E 12 May 44; arrived England 26 May 44 and landed in France 7 Jul 44 *(attached to 4th Armd Div 19–24 Sep 44)*; crossed into Luxembourg 27 Dec 44 and into Belgium 8 Jan 45 *(attached to 6th Armd Div 10–18 Jan 45)* and returned to France 19 Jan 45; entered Holland 31 Jan 45 and Germany on 4 Feb 45 *(attached to 83rd Inf Div 15–21 Mar 45) (attached to 75th Inf Div 6–13 Apr 45) (attached to XIX Corps 13–21 Apr 45)*; returned to New York P/E 10 Sep 45 and moved to Cp Breckinridge Ky 12 Sep 45, where inactivated on 21 Nov 45.

Campaigns: *Normandy, Northern France, Rhineland, Ardennes-Alsace, Central Europe*
Aug 45 Loc: Neuweid Germany

321st Infantry Regiment (81st Infantry Division)

15 Jun 42 organized at Cp Rucker Ala and assigned to the 81st Division; moved to Tenn Mnvr area 19 Apr 43 and to Cp Young Calif 15 Jul 43; transferred to Cp San Luis Obispo Calif 21 Nov 43 and to Cp Beale Calif 21 Apr 44; staged at Cp Stoneman Calif 23 Jun 44 until departed San Francisco P/E 1 Jul 44; arrived in Hawaii 8 Jul 44 and departed on 8 Aug 44; arrived Guadalcanal 24 Aug 44 and left 7 Sep 44 for Angaur Island where landed on 17 Sep 44 until 22 Sep 44; arrived Peleliu Island 23 Sep 44 *(attached to 1st Marine Div 23 Sep–20 Oct 44)*; Co I assaulted Fais Island 24 Dec 44 and other elements assaulted Garakayo 9 Oct 44; departed Peleliu Island 8 Feb 45 and arrived New Caledonia about 15 Feb 45 and departed 3 May 45; arrived Manus Island 9 May 45 enroute to the Philippine Islands where arrived on Leyte 16 May 45; arrived in Japan for occupation duty on 25 Sep 45 where inactivated on 20 Jan 46.

Campaigns: *Western Pacific, Leyte*
Aug 45 Loc: Leyte Philippine Islands

322nd Infantry Regiment (81st Infantry Division)

15 Jun 42 organized at Cp Rucker Ala and assigned to the 81st Division; moved to Tenn Mnvr area 2 Apr 43 and to Cp Young Calif 11 Jul 43; transferred to Cp San Luis Obispo Calif 21 Nov 43 and to Cp Beale Calif 27 Apr 44; staged at Cp Stoneman Calif 23 Jun 44 until departed San Francisco P/E 29 Jun 44; arrived in Hawaii 4 Jul 44 and departed on 12 Aug 44; arrived Guadalcanal 24 Aug 44 and left 7 Sep 44 for Angaur Island which assaulted 17 Sep 44; moved to Peleliu Island 19 Oct 44 and departed 6 Dec 44 for New Caledonia; departed Caledonia 3 May 45 and landed on Leyte Philippine Islands 16 May 45; arrived in Japan for occupation duty 25 Sep 45 and inactivated there on 20 Jan 46.

Campaigns: *Western Pacific, Leyte*
Aug 45 Loc: Leyte Philippine Islands

323rd Infantry Regiment (81st Infantry Division)

15 Jun 42 organized at Cp Rucker Ala and assigned to the 81st Division; moved to Tenn Mnvr area 20 Apr 43 and to Cp Young Calif 16 Jul 43; transferred to Cp San Luis Obispo Calif 19 Nov 43 and to Cp Beale Calif 27 Apr 44; staged at Cp Stoneman Calif 24 Jun 44 until departed San Francisco P/E 3 Jul 44; arrived in Hawaii 8 Jul 44 and departed on 12 Aug 44; assaulted Ulithi Atoll 21 Sep 44 and assaulted Ngulu Atoll 16 Oct 44 in the Palau Islands which departed 20 Jan 45 for New Caledonia; departed New Caledonia 3 May 45 and landed on Leyte Philippine Islands 16 May 45; arrived in Japan for occupation duty 25 Sep 45 and inactivated there on 20 Jan 46.

Campaigns: *Western Pacific, Leyte*
Aug 45 Loc: Leyte Philippine Islands

324th Infantry Regiment (44th Infantry Division)

1 Feb 43 activated at Ft Lewis Wash and assigned to the 44th Infantry Division; moved to La Mnvr area 1 Feb 44 and to Cp Phillips Kans 10 Apr 44; staged at Cp Myles Standish Mass 24 Aug 44 until departed Boston P/E 5 Sep 44; arrived in France 15 Sep 44 *(attached 79th Inf Div 19–24 Oct 44)* and entered Germany 25 Mar 45 *(attached to VI Corps 8–10 Apr 45)* *(attached to 4th Inf Div 10–19 Apr 45)* and entered Austria 30 Apr 45; arrived at New York P/E 20 Jul 45 and moved to Cp Chaffee Ark 24 Jul 45 where inactivated 1 Nov 45.

Campaigns: *Northern France, Rhineland, Ardennes-Alsace, Central Europe*
Aug 45 Loc: Camp Chaffee Arkansas

325th Glider Infantry Regiment (82nd Airborne Division)

25 Mar 42 organized at Cp Claiborne La as the 325th Infantry Regiment and assigned to the 82nd Division and attached to IV Corps 1 Aug 42; there redesignated the 325th Glider Infantry Regiment on 15 Aug 42 and assigned to the 82nd Airborne Division; moved to Ft Bragg N.C. 4 Oct 42 and staged at Cp Edwards Mass 19 Apr 43 until departed New York P/E 28 Apr 43; landed in North Africa 10 May 43 and landed on Sicily 9 Jul 43; returned to North Africa 19 Aug 43 and to Sicily 4 Sep 43; landed in Italy 13 Sep 43 and arrived Northern Ireland on 9 Dec 43 and England 14 Feb 44; assaulted Normandy France on 6 Jun 44 and returned to England 13 Jul 44; assaulted Nijmegen-Arnhem Holland 17 Sep 44 and crossed into France 14 Nov 44; entered Belgium 18 Dec 44 and Germany 30 Jan 45; returned to France 19 Feb 45 and to Germany 2 Apr 45; returned to New York P/E 3 Jan 46 and moved to Ft Bragg N.C. 16 Jan 46; active there thru 1946.

Campaigns: *Sicily, Naples-Foggia, Normandy, Rhineland, Ardennes-Alsace, Central Europe*
Aug 45 Loc: Epinal France

326th Glider Infantry Regiment (13th Airborne Division)

25 Mar 42 organized at Cp Claiborne La as the 326th Infantry Regiment and assigned to the 82nd Division; there redesignated as the 326th Glider Infantry Regiment 6 Aug 42; moved to Ft Bragg N.C. 4 Oct 42 where relieved from assignment to the 82nd Airborne Division 4 Feb 43 and assigned to the Airborne Command; transferred to Alliance Army Airbase Nebr 25 Feb 43 and returned to Ft Bragg N.C. 7 Dec 43; assigned to the 13th Airborne Division on 8 Dec 43 and relocated to Cp Mackall N.C. 14 Jan 44; staged at Cp Shanks N.Y. 16 Jan 45 until departed New York P/E 26 Jan 45; landed in France 6 Feb 45; returned to New York P/E 27 Aug 45 and moved back to Ft Bragg N.C. 30 Aug 45 where inactivated on 25 Feb 46.

Campaigns: *Central Europe*
Aug 45 Loc: Auxerre France scheduled on Shipment #10580-F

327th Glider Infantry Regiment (101st Airborne Division)

25 Mar 42 organized at Cp Claiborne La as the 327th Infantry Regiment and assigned to the 82nd Division *(attached to IV Corps 1-4 Aug 42) (attached to 101st A/B Div 5-14 Aug 42)*; redesignated as the 327th Glider Infantry Regiment 15 Aug 42 and assigned to the 101st Airborne Division; moved to Ft Bragg N.C. 29 Sep 42 and staged at Cp Shanks N.Y. 28 Aug 43 until departed New York P/E 5 Sep 43; arrived England 15 Sep 43 and assaulted Normandy France 6 Jun 44; returned to England 13 Jul 44 and assaulted Nijmegen-Arnhem Holland 17 Sep 44; returned to France 25 Nov 44 and entered Germany 27 Apr 45; inactivated in France on 30 Nov 45.

Campaigns: *Normandy, Rhineland, Ardennes-Alsace, Central Europe*
Aug 45 Loc: Berchtesgaden Germany

328th Infantry Regiment (26th Infantry Division)

12 Feb 43 activated at Ft Jackson S.C. and assigned to the 26th Infantry Division; moved to Cp Gordon Ga 21 Apr 43 and to Cp Campbell Ky 5 Sep 43; transferred to Tenn Mnvr area 24 Jan 44 and returned to Ft Jackson S.C. 31 Mar 44; staged at Cp Shanks N.Y. 18 Aug 44 until departed New York P/E 27 Aug 44; arrived England 7 Sep 44 and landed in France on same date *(attached to 80th Inf Div 2-15 Oct 44)*; crossed into Luxembourg 30 Dec 44 and into Germany 19 Feb 45 *(attached to the 4th Armd Div 26-28 Mar 45) (attached to 11th Armd Div 3-6 May 45)*; entered Czechoslovakia 6 May 45; arrived Boston P/E 28 Dec 45 and inactivated at Cp Myles Standish Mass on 29 Dec 45.

Campaigns: *Northern France, Rhineland, Ardennes-Alsace, Central Europe*
Aug 45 Loc: Vlachova Czechoslovakia

329th Infantry Regiment (83rd Infantry Division)

15 Aug 42 organized at Cp Atterbury Ind and assigned to the 83rd Infantry Division; moved to Tenn Mnvr area 22 Jun 43 and to Cp Breckinridge Ky 12 Sep 43; staged at Cp Shanks N.Y. 28 Mar 44 until departed New York P/E 6 Apr 44; arrived in England 18 Apr 44 and landed in France 19 Jun 44; crossed into Luxembourg 25 Sep 44 and entered Germany 6 Dec 44 *(attached to 4th Inf Div 7-10 Dec 44) (attached to 9th Inf Div 13 Dec 44 only)*; crossed into Belgium 27 Dec 44 *(attached to 84th Inf Div 21-22 Jan 45)* and returned to Germany 22 Feb 45; entered Holland 21 Mar 45 and reentered Germany 28 Mar 45; returned to New York P/E 5 Apr 46 and inactivated at Cp Kilmer N.J. 6 Apr 46.

Campaigns: *Normandy, Northern France, Rhineland, Ardennes-Alsace, Central Europe*
Aug 45 Loc: Deggendorf Germany

330th Infantry Regiment (83rd Infantry Division)

15 Aug 42 organized at Cp Atterbury Ind and assigned to the 83rd Infantry Division; moved to Tenn Mnvr area 23 Jun 43 and to Cp Breckinridge Ky 12 Sep 43; staged at Cp Shanks N.Y. 30 Mar 44 until departed New York P/E 6 Apr 44; arrived in England 19 Apr 44 and landed in France 19 Jun 44; crossed into Luxembourg 25 Sep 44 (*attached to the 4th Inf Div 3–7 Dec 44*) and entered Germany 6 Dec 44 (*attached to VII Corps 27 Dec 44–1 Jan 45*); entered Belgium 27 Dec 44 (*attached to 3rd Armd Div 1–7 Jan 45*); returned to Germany 22 Feb 45 (*attached to 29th Inf Div 23–27 Feb 45*); entered Holland 21 Mar 45 and reentered Germany 28 Mar 45 (*attached to XIX Corps 5–7 Apr 45 and 13–20 Apr 45*); returned to New York P/E 27 Mar 46 and inactivated at Cp Kilmer N.J. the same date.

Campaigns: *Normandy, Northern France, Rhineland, Ardennes-Alsace, Central Europe*
Aug 45 Loc: Freyung Germany

331st Infantry Regiment (83rd Infantry Division)

15 Aug 42 organized at Cp Atterbury Ind and assigned to the 83rd Infantry Division; moved to Tenn Mnvr area 23 Jun 43 and to Cp Breckinridge Ky 12 Sep 43; staged at Cp Shanks N.Y. 31 Mar 44 until departed New York P/E 6 Apr 44; arrived England 19 Apr 44 and landed in France 19 Jun 44; crossed into Luxembourg 25 Sep 44 and entered Germany 6 Dec 44; crossed into Belgium 27 Dec 44 (*attached to 3rd Armd Div 29–31 Dec 44*) (*attached to 2nd Armd Div 27 Feb–1 Mar 45*) and returned to Germany 22 Feb 45; entered Holland 21 Mar 45 and reentered Germany 28 Mar 45 (*attached to XIX Corps 10–11 Apr 45*); returned to New York P/E 29 Mar 46 and inactivated at Cp Kilmer N.J. on 30 Mar 46.

Campaigns: *Normandy, Northern France, Rhineland, Ardennes-Alsace, Central Europe*
Aug 45 Loc: Griesbach Czechoslovakia

No Distinctive
Insignia Authorized

333rd Infantry Regiment (84th Infantry Division)

15 Oct 42 organized at Cp Howze Tex and assigned to the 84th Infantry Division; moved to the La Mnvr area 17 Sep 43 and to Cp Claiborne La 16 Nov 43; staged at Cp Kilmer N.J. 6 Sep 44 until departed New York P/E 20 Sep 44; arrived England 1 Oct 44 and landed in France 1 Nov 44; entered Germany 13 Nov 44 and Belgium 21 Dec 44; crossed into Holland 3 Feb 45 and returned to Germany 7 Feb 45; returned New York P/E 20 Jan 46 and inactivated at Cp Kilmer N.J. on 27 Jan 46.

Campaigns: *Rhineland, Ardennes-Alsace, Central Europe*
Aug 45 Loc: Leutershausen Germany

334th Infantry Regiment (84th Infantry Division)

15 Oct 42 organized at Cp Howze Tex and assigned to the 84th Infantry Division; moved to La Mnvr area 13 Sep 43 and to Cp Claiborne La 17 Nov 43; staged at Cp Kilmer N.J. 7 Sep 44 until departed New York P/E 20 Sep 44; arrived England 1 Oct 44 and landed in France 1 Nov 44; crossed into Germany 13 Nov 44 and into Belgium 21 Dec 44 and Holland 3 Feb 45; returned to Germany 7 Feb 45; returned to New York P/E 20 Jan 46 and inactivated at Cp Kilmer N.J. on 21 Jan 46.

Campaigns: *Rhineland, Ardennes-Alsace, Central Europe*
Aug 45 Loc: Wiesloch Germany

335th Infantry Regiment (84th Infantry Division)

15 Oct 42 organized at Cp Howze Tex and assigned to the 84th Infantry Division; moved to La Mnvr area 14 Sep 43 and to Cp Claiborne La 17 Nov 43; staged at Cp Kilmer N.J. 9 Sep 44 until departed New York P/E 29 Sep 44; arrived England 10 Oct 44 and landed in France 4 Nov 44 (*attached to 30th Inf Div 11–12 Nov 44*); entered Germany 13 Nov 44 (*attached to 2nd Armd Div 22–24 Nov 44*) (*attached to 102nd Inf Div 24–27 Nov 44*) and entered Belgium 21 Dec 44 (*attached 3rd Armd Div 18–21 Jan 45*); entered Holland 3 Feb 45 and returned to Germany 7 Feb 45; returned New York P/E 22 Jan 46 and inactivated at Cp Kilmer N.J. 23 Jan 46.

Campaigns: *Rhineland, Ardennes-Alsace, Central Europe*
Aug 45 Loc: Schwetzingen Germany

337th Infantry Regiment (85th Infantry Division)

15 May 42 organized at Cp Shelby Miss and assigned to the 85th Infantry Division; moved to La Mnvr area 8 Apr 43 and to Cp Young Calif 13 Jun 43; arrived at Ft Dix N.J. 12 Oct 43 and staged at Cp Patrick Henry Va 20 Dec 43 until departed Hampton Roads P/E 24 Dec 43; landed in North Africa on 2 Jan 44 and arrived in Italy 27 Mar 44; returned to Hampton Roads P/E 25 Aug 45 and inactivated at Cp Patrick Henry Va that same date.

Campaigns: *Rome-Arno, North Apennines, Po Valley*
Aug 45 Loc: Fagianeria Italy

338th Infantry Regiment (85th Infantry Division)

15 May 42 organized at Cp Shelby Miss and assigned to the 85th Infantry Division; moved to La Mnvr area 7 Apr 43 and to Cp Young Calif 23 Jun 43; arrived at Ft Dix N.J. 10 Oct 43 and staged at Cp Patrick Henry Va 19 Dec 43 until departed Hampton Roads P/E 24 Dec 43; landed in North Africa on 2 Jan 44 and arrived in Italy 27 Mar 44; returned to Hampton Roads P/E 25 Aug 45 and inactivated at Cp Patrick Henry Va that same date.

Campaigns: *Rome-Arno, North Apennines, Po Valley*
Aug 45 Loc: Fagianeria Italy

339th Infantry Regiment (85th Infantry Division)

15 May 42 organized at Cp Shelby Miss and assigned to the 85th Infantry Division; moved to La Mnvr area 6 Apr 43 and to Cp Young Calif 23 Jun 43; arrived at Ft Dix N.J. 9 Oct 43 and staged at Cp Patrick Henry Va 15 Dec 43 until departed Hampton Roads P/E 24 Dec 43; landed in North Africa 2 Jan 44 and arrived in Italy 27 Mar 44; returned to Hampton Roads P/E 25 Aug 45 and inactivated at Cp Patrick Henry Va that same date.

Campaigns: *Rome-Arno, North Apennines, Po Valley*
Aug 45 Loc: Fagianeria Italy

341st Infantry Regiment (86th Infantry Division)

15 Dec 42 organized at Cp Howze Tex and assigned to the 86th Infantry Division; moved to the La Mnvr area 22 Nov 43 and to Cp Livingston La 25 Jan 44; transferred to Cp Cooke Calif 15 Sep 44 and staged at Cp Myles Standish Mass 15 Feb 45 until departed Boston P/E 19 Feb 45; landed in France 1 Mar 45 and entered Germany 27 Mar 45 *(attached to 82nd A/B Div 5 Apr 45 only) (attached to 97th Inf Div 6–9 Apr 45)*; arrived New York P/E 17 Jun 45 and moved to Cp Gruber Okla 21 Jun 45; staged at Cp Stoneman Calif 14 Aug 45 until departed San Francisco P/E 21 Aug 45; arrived in the Philippine Islands 7 Sep 45 where inactivated on 30 Dec 46.

Campaigns: *Central Europe*
Aug 45 Loc: Camp Stoneman California

342nd Infantry Regiment (86th Infantry Division)

15 Dec 42 organized at Cp Howze Tex and assigned to the 86th Infantry Division; moved to the La Mnvr area 20 Nov 43 and to Cp Livingston La 25 Jan 44; transferred to Cp Cooke Calif 14 Sep 44; staged at Cp Myles Standish Mass 13 Feb 45 until departed Boston P/E 19 Feb 45; landed in France on 1 Mar 45 and entered Germany 27 Mar 45; arrived at New York P/E 17 Jun 45 and moved to Cp Gruber Okla 21 Jun 45; staged at Cp Stoneman Calif 14 Aug 45 until departed San Francisco P/E 17 Sep 45; arrived in the Philippine Islands 20 Nov 45 where inactivated on 30 Dec 46.

Campaigns: *Central Europe*
Aug 45 Loc: Camp Stoneman California

343rd Infantry Regiment (86th Infantry Division)

15 Dec 42 organized at Cp Howze Tex and assigned to the 86th Infantry Division; moved to La Mnvr area 23 Nov 43 and to Cp Livingston La 25 Jan 44; transferred to Cp Cooke Calif 12 Sep 44 and to Cp San Luis Obispo Calif 1 Oct 44; staged at Cp Myles Standish Mass 10 Feb 45 until departed Boston P/E 19 Feb 45; landed in France 1 Mar 45 and entered Germany 27 Mar 45; arrived New York P/E 17 Jun 45 and moved to Cp Gruber Okla 21 Jun 45; staged at Cp Stoneman Calif 14 Aug 45 until departed San Francisco P/E 17 Sep 45; arrived Philippine Islands 20 Nov 45 where inactivated on 30 Dec 46.

Campaigns: *Central Europe*
Aug 45 Loc: Camp Stoneman California

345th Infantry Regiment (87th Infantry Division)

15 Dec 42 organized at Cp McCain Miss and assigned to the 87th Infantry Division; moved to Tenn Mnvr area 2 Dec 43 and to Ft Jackson S.C. 20 Jan 44; staged at Cp Kilmer N.J. 10 Oct 44 until departed New York P/E 17 Oct 44; arrived England 22 Oct 44 and landed in France 5 Dec 44; crossed into Belgium 12 Jan 45 *(attached to 17th A/B Div 15–16 Jan 45)* and into Luxembourg 21 Jan 45; returned to Belgium 3 Feb 45 and entered Germany 16 Mar 45; returned to New York P/E 11 Jul 45 and moved to Ft Benning Ga 14 Jul 45 where inactivated on 21 Sep 45.

Campaigns: *Rhineland, Ardennes-Alsace, Central Europe*
Aug 45 Loc: Fort Benning Georgia

346th Infantry Regiment (87th Infantry Division)

15 Dec 42 organized at Cp McCain Miss and assigned to the 87th Infantry Division; moved to the Tenn Mnvr area 2 Dec 43 and to Ft Jackson S.C. 21 Jan 44; staged at Cp Kilmer N.J. 12 Oct 44 until departed New York P/E 17 Oct 44; arrived England 22 Oct 44 and landed in France 5 Dec 44; crossed into Belgium 12 Jan 45 *(attached to 4th Inf Div 14–16 Jan 45)* and into Luxembourg 21 Jan 45; returned to Belgium 3 Feb 45 and entered Germany 16 Mar 45; arrived Boston P/E 19 Jul 45 and moved to Ft Benning Ga 22 Jul 45 where inactivated on 21 Sep 45.

Campaigns: *Rhineland, Ardennes-Alsace, Central Europe*
Aug 45 Loc: Fort Benning Georgia

347th Infantry Regiment (87th Infantry Division)

15 Dec 42 organized at Cp McCain Miss and assigned to the 87th Infantry Division; moved to the Tenn Mnvr area 2 Dec 43 and to Ft Jackson S.C. 20 Jan 44; staged at Cp Kilmer N.J. 14 Oct 44 until departed New York P/E 17 Oct 44; arrived England 22 Oct 44 and landed in France 5 Dec 44; crossed into Belgium 12 Jan 45 *(attached to 4th Inf Div 14–16 Jan 45)* and into Luxembourg 21 Jan 45; returned to Belgium 3 Feb 45 and entered Germany 16 Mar 45; arrived New York P/E 11 Jul 45 and moved to Ft Benning Ga 14 Jul 45 where inactivated on 21 Sep 45.

Campaigns: *Rhineland, Ardennes-Alsace, Central Europe*
Aug 45 Loc: Fort Benning Georgia

349th Infantry Regiment (88th Infantry Division)

15 Jul 42 organized at Cp Gruber Okla and assigned to the 88th Infantry Division; moved to La Mnvr area 16 Jun 43 and to Ft Sam Houston Tex 30 Aug 43; staged at Cp Patrick Henry Va 4 Dec 43 until departed Hampton Roads P/E 16 Dec 43; arrived North Africa 25 Dec 43 and landed in Italy 6 Feb 44 where active thru 1946.

Campaigns: *Rome-Arno, North Apennines, Po Valley*
Aug 45 Loc: Bolzano Italy

350th Infantry Regiment (88th Infantry Division)

15 Jul 42 organized at Cp Gruber Okla and assigned to the 88th Infantry Division; moved to La Mnvr area 15 Jun 43 and to Ft Sam Houston Tex 30 Aug 43; staged at Cp Patrick Henry Va 23 Nov 43 until departed Hampton Roads P/E 3 Dec 43; landed in North Africa 20 Dec 43 and arrived Italy 12 Feb 44 where active thru 1946.

Campaigns: *Rome-Arno, North Apennines, Po Valley*
Aug 45 Loc: Modena Italy

351st Infantry Regiment (88th Infantry Division)

15 Jul 42 organized at Cp Gruber Okla and assigned to the 88th Infantry Division; moved to La Mnvr area 16 Jun 43 and to Ft Sam Houston Tex 26 Aug 43; staged at Cp Patrick Henry Va 4 Nov 43 until departed Hampton Roads P/E 12 Nov 43; landed in North Africa 4 Dec 43 and arrived in Italy 6 Feb 44 where active thru 1946.

Campaigns: *Rome-Arno, North Apennines, Po Valley*
Aug 45 Loc: Ghedi Italy

No Distinctive
Insignia Authorized

353rd Infantry Regiment (89th Infantry Division)

15 Jul 42 organized at Cp Carson Colo and assigned to the 89th Division; redesignated as the 353rd Infantry Regiment (Light) on 1 Aug 43 and moved to the La Mnvr area 18 Nov 43; transferred to Hunter-Liggett Mil Res Calif 30 Jan 44 and Cp Butner N.C. 27 May 44 where redesignated the 353rd Infantry Regiment on 15 Jun 44; staged at Cp Myles Standish Mass 30 Dec 44 until departed Boston P/E 10 Jan 45; landed in France 21 Jan 45 and crossed into Luxembourg 8 Mar 45 and entered Germany 10 Mar 45; arrived Hampton Roads P/E 18 Dec 45 and inactivated at Cp Patrick Henry Va the same date.

Campaigns: *Rhineland, Central Europe*
Aug 45 Loc: Duclair France

354th Infantry Regiment (89th Infantry Division)

15 Jul 42 organized at Cp Carson Colo and assigned to the 89th Division; redesignated as the 354th Infantry Regiment (Light) on 1 Aug 43 and moved to the La Mnvr area 19 Nov 43; transferred to Hunter-Liggett Mil Res Calif 1 Feb 44 and to Cp Butner N.C. 27 May 44 where redesignated the 354th Infantry Regiment on 15 Jun 44; staged at Cp Myles Standish Mass 31 Dec 44 until departed Boston P/E 10 Jan 45; landed in France 21 Jan 45 and crossed into Luxembourg 8 Mar 45 and entered Germany 10 Mar 45; arrived New York P/E 24 Dec 45 and inactivated at Cp Kilmer N.J. 25 Dec 45.

Campaigns: *Rhineland, Central Europe*
Aug 45 Loc: Cany Barville France

355th Infantry Regiment (89th Infantry Division)

15 Jul 42 organized at Cp Carson Colo and assigned to the 89th Division; redesignated as the 355th Infantry Regiment (Light) on 1 Aug 43 and moved to the La Mnvr area 20 Nov 43; transferred to Hunter-Liggett Mil Res Calif 2 Feb 44 and to Cp Butner N.C. 29 May 44 where redesignated the 355th Infantry Regiment on 15 Jun 44; staged at Cp Myles Standish Mass 31 Dec 44 until departed Boston P/E 10 Jan 45; landed in France 24 Jan 45 and crossed into Luxembourg 8 Mar 45 and entered Germany 10 Mar 45 *(attached to 11th Armd Div 17–21 Mar 45) (attached to 4th Armd Div 3–6 Apr 45)*; arrived New York P/E 18 Dec 45 and inactivated at Cp Kilmer N.J. 20 Dec 45.

Campaigns: *Rhineland, Central Europe*
Aug 45 Loc: Yvetot France

357th Infantry Regiment (90th Infantry Division)

25 Mar 42 organized at Cp Barkeley Tex and assigned to the 90th Division; redesignated as the 357th Infantry Regiment (Motorized) on 15 Sep 42 and moved to La Mnvr area 28 Jan 43; returned to Cp Barkeley Tex 1 Apr 43 where redesignated the 357th Infantry Regiment on 1 May 43; transferred to Cp Young Calif 5 Sep 43 and to Ft Dix N.J. 1 Jan 44; staged at Cp Kilmer N.J. 15 Mar 44 until departed New York P/E 24 Mar 44; arrived in England 4 Apr 44 and landed in France 8 Jun 44; entered Germany 24 Nov 44 and returned to France 22 Dec 44; crossed into Luxembourg 6 Jan 45 and into Belgium 22 Jan 45; returned to Luxembourg 27 Jan 45 and reentered Germany on 29 Jan 45 *(attached to 5th Inf Div 23–24 Mar 45)* *(attached to XII Corps 8–15 Apr 45)*; entered Czechoslovakia 5 May 45; returned to New York P/E 26 Dec 45 and inactivated at Cp Kilmer N.J. on 27 Dec 45.

Campaigns: *Normandy, Northern France, Rhineland, Ardennes-Alsace, Central Europe*
Aug 45 Loc: Neustadt Germany

358th Infantry Regiment (90th Infantry Division)

25 Mar 42 organized at Cp Barkeley Tex and assigned to the 90th Division; redesignated as the 358th Infantry Regiment (Motorized) on 15 Sep 42 and moved to La Mnvr area 28 Jan 43; returned to Cp Barkeley Tex 1 Apr 43 where redesignated the 358th Infantry Regiment on 1 May 43; transferred to Cp Young Calif 7 Sep 43 and to Ft Dix N.J. 3 Jan 44; staged at Cp Kilmer N.J. 15 Mar 44 until departed New York P/E 24 Mar 44; arrived England 9 Apr 44 and landed in France 6 Jun 44; entered Germany 23 Nov 44 *(attached to 10th Armd Div 19–24 Nov 44)* and returned to France 22 Dec 44; entered Luxembourg 7 Jan 45 and Belgium 12 Jan 45; returned to Luxembourg 23 Jan 45 and to Belgium 27 Jan 45; reentered Germany 29 Jan 45 and entered Czechoslovakia 5 May 45; arrived at Boston P/E 25 Dec 45 and inactivated Cp Myles Standish Mass on 26 Dec 45.

Campaigns: *Normandy, Northern France, Rhineland, Ardennes-Alsace, Central Europe*
Aug 45 Loc: Nabburg Germany

359th Infantry Regiment (90th Infantry Division)

25 Mar 42 organized at Cp Barkeley Tex and assigned to the 90th Division; redesignated as the 359th Infantry Regiment (Motorized) on 15 Sep 42 and moved to the La Mnvr Area 28 Jan 43; returned to Cp Barkeley Tex 1 Apr 43 where redesignated the 359th Infantry Regiment on 1 May 43; transferred to Cp Young Calif 12 Sep 43 and to Ft Dix N.J. 5 Jan 44; staged at Cp Kilmer N.J. 14 Mar 44 until departed New York P/E 24 Mar 44; arrived England 5 Apr 44 *(attached to 4th Inf Div 6–10 Jun 44)* and assaulted Normandy France 6 Jun 44 *(attached to the 9th Inf Div 16–17 Jun 44)*; entered Germany 25 Nov 44 and returned to France 22 Dec 44; crossed into Luxembourg 7 Jan 45 and into Belgium 22 Jan 45; returned to Luxembourg 23 Jan 45 and to Belgium 31 Jan 45; reentered Germany same date *(attached to 4th Armd Div 16–19 Mar 45 and 29 Mar–3 Apr 45)* *(attached to 26th Inf Div 6–10 Apr 45)* and entered Czechoslovakia 7 May 45; returned to New York P/E 24 Dec 45 and inactivated at Cp Kilmer N.J. on 26 Dec 45.

Campaigns: *Normandy, Northern France, Rhineland, Ardennes-Alsace, Central Europe*
Aug 45 Loc: Amberg Germany

361st Infantry Regiment (91st Infantry Division)

15 Aug 42 organized at Cp White Oreg and assigned to the 91st Infantry Division; moved to Oreg Mnvr area 3 Sep 43 and to Cp Adair Oreg 4 Nov 43; staged at Cp Patrick Henry Va 25 Mar 44 until departed Hampton Roads P/E 13 Apr 44; arrived North Africa 21 Apr 44 and landed in Italy 27 May 44; returned to Hampton Roads P/E 26 Aug 45 and moved to Cp Rucker Ala 29 Aug 45 where inactivated on 13 Nov 45.

Campaigns: *Rome-Arno, North Apennines, Po Valley*
Aug 45 Loc: Shipment #22026-K at sea

362nd Infantry Regiment (91st Infantry Division)

15 Aug 42 organized at Cp White Oreg and assigned to the 91st Infantry Division; moved to Oreg Mnvr area 1 Sep 43 and to Cp Adair Oreg 2 Nov 43; staged at Cp Patrick Henry Va 30 Mar 44 until departed Hampton Roads P/E 13 Apr 44; arrived North Africa 21 Apr 44 and landed in Italy 19 Jun 44; returned to Hampton Roads P/E 10 Sep 45 and moved to Cp Rucker Ala 14 Sep 45 where inactivated on 17 Nov 45.

Campaigns: *Rome-Arno, North Apennines, Po Valley*
Aug 45 Loc: Lucinico Italy

363rd Infantry Regiment (91st Infantry Division)

15 Aug 42 organized at Cp White Oreg and assigned to the 91st Infantry Division; moved to Oreg Mnvr area 1 Sep 43 and to Cp Adair Oreg 3 Nov 43; staged at Cp Patrick Henry Va 30 Mar 44 until departed Hampton Roads P/E 13 Apr 44; arrived in North Africa 30 Apr 44 and landed in Italy 19 Jun 44; returned to Hampton Roads P/E 30 Aug 45 and moved to Cp Rucker Ala 14 Sep 45 where inactivated on 27 Nov 45.

Campaigns: *Rome-Arno, North Apennines, Po Valley*
Aug 45 Loc: Merna Italy

364th Infantry Regiment (Colored) (Separate)

No Distinctive
Insignia Authorized

10 Jun 42 redesignated from the 367th Infantry Regiment, less 1st Bn, at Cp Claiborne La and 1st Bn activated 13 Jun 42; attached to Third Army until moved to Phoenix Ariz 19 Jun 42 where attached to the Western Defense Command Southern Frontier Sector on 20 Sep 42; transferred to Cp Van Dorn Miss 27 May 43 where assigned to the IX Corps on 5 Aug 43; staged at Ft Lawton Wash 31 Dec 43 until departed Seattle P/E 15 Jan 44; arrived in Alaska 24 Jan 44 and sent to garrison duty on Adak Island 6 Feb 44 where relieved the 138th Infantry Regt in May 44; inactivated at Adak Island Alaska on 15 May 46 and 1st and 2nd Bns redesignated 80th and 81st Infantry Battalions respectively.

Campaigns: *Pacific Theater without Inscription*
Aug 45 Loc: Camp Earle Alaska, less 1st Battalion on Amchitka Island and 2nd Battalion on Shemya Island

365th Infantry Regiment (Colored) (92nd Infantry Division)

No Distinctive
Insignia Authorized

15 Oct 42 activated at Cp Atterbury Ind and assigned to the 92nd Infantry Division; moved to Ft Huachuca Ariz 10 May 43 and staged at Cp Patrick Henry Va 17 Sep 44 until departed Hampton Roads P/E 2 Oct 44; arrived in Italy 27 Oct 44 and returned to Hampton Roads P/E 27 Nov 45 and inactivated at Cp Patrick Henry Va the same date.

Campaigns: *North Apennines, Po Valley*
Aug 45 Loc: Torre Del Lago Italy, less 3rd Battalion at Novi Ligure Italy

366th Infantry Regiment (Colored) (Separate)

10 Feb 41 activated at Ft Devens Mass and assigned to the Eastern Defense Command on 30 Apr 42; attached to 1st Service Command 1 May 43 and to XIII Corps 1 Sep 43; moved to A.P. Hill Mil Res Va 14 Oct 43 and to Cp Atterbury Ind 23 Nov 43 under XX Corps; assigned XXII Corps 21 Jan 44 and staged at Cp Patrick Henry Va 22 Mar 44 until departed Hampton Roads P/E 28 Mar 44; arrived North Africa 6 Apr 44 and attached to 15th Air Force for airfield security duties from Sardinia to the Adriatic coast; assigned to Fifth Army 4 Nov 44 and arrived Livorno Italy 21 Nov 44 for attachment to the 92nd Infantry Division until 25 Feb 45, disbanded in Italy on 28 Mar 45 and personnel transferred into the 224th and 226th Engineer General Service Regiments.

Campaigns: *Rome-Arno, North Apennines*

367th Infantry Regiment (Colored) (Separate)

No Distinctive Insignia Authorized

25 Mar 41 activated at Cp Claiborne La and 1st Bn transferred to Charleston P/E for shipment to Liberia in Apr 42 but due to shipping shortage finally departed 8 Feb 43; due to manifest cargo-marking complications 1st Bn redesignated 367th Infantry Battalion 9 Jun 42 and remainder of regiment then redesignated as the 364th Infantry Regiment 10 Jun 42 since the number sequence 367 was now allotted to the former 1st Battalion.

368th Infantry Regiment (Colored) (93rd Infantry Division)

1 Mar 41 activated at Ft Huachuca Ariz and assigned to the 93rd Infantry Division on 1 Jan 42; moved to the La Mnvr area 9 Apr 43 and to Cp Young Calif 8 Jul 43; staged at Cp Stoneman Calif 16 Jan 44 until departed San Francisco P/E 24 Jan 44; arrived at Bakina Russell Islands 7 Feb 44 and departed 14 Jun 44; landed on New Georgia 15 Jun 44 *(attached to VI Island Command 8 Jul–14 Oct 44)* and arrived at Hollandia New Guinea 30 Oct 44; left New Guinea 5 Apr 45 and arrived on Morotai Island 11 Apr 45 with the rear detachment joining it there 29 Apr 45; departed 29 Jun 45 and arrived at Zamboanga Philippine Islands 1 Jul 45 where relieved the 41st Inf Div *(attached to X Corps 1 Jul 45–past 14 Aug 45)*; returned to San Francisco P/E 1 Feb 46 and inactivated at Cp Stoneman Calif on 3 Feb 46.

Campaigns: *New Guinea, Northern Solomons, Southern Philippines*
Aug 45 Loc: Zamboanga Mindanao Philippine Islands

369th Infantry Regiment (Colored) (93rd Infantry Division)

No Distinctive Insignia Authorized

15 May 42 activated at Ft Huachuca Ariz and assigned to the 93rd Infantry Division; moved to La Mnvr area 9 Apr 43 and to Cp Young Calif 8 Jul 43; staged at Cp Stoneman Calif 25 Jan 44 until departed San Francisco P/E 29 Jan 44; arrived Guadalcanal 11 Feb 44 and New Georgia 29 Feb 44 *(attached to VI Island Command on New Georgia)*; departed 26 Jun 44 and arrived on Emirau Island 28 Jun 44 *(attached to Provisional Island Command APO 198 at Emirau 8 Jul–10 Oct 44)*; 3rd Bn sent to Los Negros Island 29 Sep 44 and the 2nd Bn sent to Biak Island 1 Oct 44; regiment left Emirau 14–31 Oct 44 and arrived on Biak 1 Nov 44 *(attached to 41st Inf Div 10 Oct 44–28 Jan 45) (attached to 3rd Engineer Special Brigade 28 Jan–15 Jul 45)*; arrived on Morotai Island 4 Apr 45 and Co C arrived on Jolo Island Philippines 29 Jun 45; returned to San Francisco P/E 1 Feb 46 and inactivated at Cp Stoneman Calif on 3 Feb 46.

Campaigns: *Northern Solomons, New Guinea, Bismarck Archipelago*
Aug 45 Loc: Morotai Island, less 2nd Battalion on Biak Island, Co C on Jolo Island Philippines and Co G on Middleburg Island off New Guinea

370th Infantry Regiment (Colored) (92nd Infantry Division)

No Distinctive Insignia Authorized

15 Oct 42 activated at Cp Breckinridge Ky and assigned to the 92nd Infantry Division; moved to Ft Huachuca Ariz 5 May 43 and staged at Cp Patrick Henry Va 3 Jul 44 until departed Hampton Roads P/E 15 Jul 44; arrived Italy 24 Jul 44 and returned to Hampton Roads P/E 27 Nov 45 and inactivated at Cp Patrick Henry Va the same date.

Campaigns: *Rome-Arno, North Apennines, Po Valley*
Aug 45 Loc: Viareggio Italy

371st Infantry Regiment (Colored) (92nd Infantry Division)

No Distinctive Insignia Authorized

15 Oct 42 activated at Cp Joseph T. Robinson Ark and assigned to the 92nd Infantry Division; moved to Ft Huachuca Ariz 8 May 43 and staged at Cp Patrick Henry Va 12 Sep 44 until departed Hampton Roads P/E 22 Sep 44; arrived Italy 18 Oct 44 and arrived New York P/E 24 Nov 45 and inactivated at Cp Kilmer N.J. on 28 Nov 45.

Campaigns: *Rome-Arno, North Apennines, Po Valley*
Aug 45 Loc: Torre Del Lago Italy, less 3rd Battalion at Aversa and Co M at Secondigliano

372nd Infantry Regiment (Colored) (Separate)   **Ohio, New Jersey, Massachusetts, Maryland, D.C. National Guard**

10 Mar 41 inducted into federal service at the following stations: Hqs from Washington D.C. and Ohio, 1st Bn from New Jersey, 2nd Bn at Columbus Ohio, 3rd Bn at Boston Mass and Service Co from Maryland; moved to Ft Dix N.J. 17 Mar 41 and to New York N.Y. on 17 Dec 41 where assigned to the Eastern Defense Command 1 May 42; provided security and duty in greater New York City vicinity and assigned to the 2nd Service Command there 21 Jan 44; transferred to Cp Breckinridge Ky 20 Apr 44 under XXII Corps and to Ft Huachuca Ariz 11 Nov 44 under Fourth Army; staged at Ft Lawton Wash 24 Apr 45 until departed Seattle P/E 29 Apr 45; arrived Hawaii 9 May 45 where assigned to the Central Pacific Base Command on 15 May 45; inactivated there on 31 Jan 46.

Campaigns: *Pacific Theater without Inscription*
Aug 45 Loc: Schofield Barracks Hawaii, less 2nd Battalion at Hilo, Co D at Bellows Field, Co F at Kauai, Co G at Maui, Co H at Molokai, Co I at Aiea, and Co K at Fort Shafter Hawaii

376th Infantry Regiment (94th Infantry Division)

15 Sep 42 organized at Ft Custer Mich and assigned to the 94th Infantry Division; moved to Cp Phillips Kans 16 Nov 42 and to the Tenn Mnvr area 4 Sep 43; transferred to Cp McCain Miss 28 Nov 43 and staged at Cp Shanks N.Y. 29 Jul 44 until departed New York P/E 6 Aug 44; arrived England 11 Aug 44 and landed in France 14 Sep 44; entered Germany on 8 Jan 45 *(attached to 10th Armd Div 19 Feb–3 Mar 45)*; returned to New York P/E 28 Jan 46 and inactivated at Cp Kilmer N.J. on 29 Jan 46.

Campaigns: *Northern France, Rhineland, Ardennes-Alsace, Central Europe*
Aug 45 Loc: Wuppertal Germany

377th Infantry Regiment (95th Infantry Division)

15 Jul 42 organized at Cp Swift Tex and assigned to the 95th Infantry Division; moved to Ft Sam Houston Tex 3 Dec 42 and to La Mnvr area 21 Jun 43; transferred to Cp Polk La 24 Aug 43 and to Cp Young Calif 14 Oct 43; relocated to Indiantown Gap Mil Res Pa 22 Feb 44 and staged at Cp Myles Standish Mass 27 Jul 44 and departed Boston P/E 10 Aug 44; arrived England 17 Aug 44 and landed in France 15 Sep 44; crossed into Belgium 31 Jan 45 and entered Germany 2 Mar 45 *(attached to 2nd Armd Div 29 Mar–2 Apr 45)*; arrived Hampton Roads P/E 27 Jun 45 and moved to Cp Shelby Miss 2 Jul 45 where inactivated on 11 Oct 45.

Campaigns: *Northern France, Rhineland, Ardennes-Alsace, Central Europe*
Aug 45 Loc: Camp Shelby Mississippi

378th Infantry Regiment (95th Infantry Division)

15 Jul 42 organized at Cp Swift Tex and assigned to the 95th Infantry Division; moved to Ft Sam Houston Tex 1 Dec 42 and to La Mnvr area 19 Jun 43; transferred to Cp Polk La 24 Aug 43 and to Cp Young Calif 16 Oct 43; relocated to Indiantown Gap Mil Res Pa 18 Feb 44 and staged at Cp Myles Standish Mass 27 Jul 44 and departed Boston P/E 6 Aug 44; arrived England 12 Aug 44 and landed in France 15 Sep 44; crossed into Belgium 31 Jan 45 and entered Germany 2 Mar 45 *(attached to British 8 Corps 4–8 Apr 45)*; returned to Boston P/E 29 Jun 45 and moved to Cp Shelby Miss 3 Jul 45 where inactivated on 23 Oct 45.

Campaigns: *Northern France, Rhineland, Ardennes-Alsace, Central Europe*
Aug 45 Loc: Camp Shelby Mississippi

379th Infantry Regiment (95th Infantry Division)

15 Jul 42 organized at Cp Swift Tex and assigned to the 95th Division; moved to Ft Sam Houston Tex 2 Dec 42 and to La Mnvr area 24 Jun 43; transferred to Cp Polk La 27 Aug 43 and to Cp Young Calif 22 Oct 43; relocated to Indiantown Gap Mil Res Pa 18 Feb 44 and staged at Cp Myles Standish Mass 23 Jul 44 until departed Boston P/E 10 Aug 44; arrived England 17 Aug 44 and landed in France 15 Sep 44; crossed into Belgium 31 Jan 45 and entered Germany 2 Mar 45 *(attached to 2nd Armd Div 1-4 Mar 45)*; returned to Boston P/E 1 Jul 45 and moved to Cp Shelby Miss 4 Jul 45 where inactivated on 12 Oct 45.

Campaigns: *Northern France, Rhineland, Ardennes-Alsace, Central Europe*
Aug 45 Loc: Camp Shelby Mississippi

381st Infantry Regiment (96th Infantry Division)

15 Aug 42 organized at Cp Adair Oreg and assigned to the 96th Infantry Division; moved to Ft Lewis Wash 7 May 43 and to Oreg Mnvr area 15 Jul 43; transferred to Cp White Oreg 1 Nov 43 and to Cp San Luis Obispo Calif 30 Apr 44; transferred to Cp Beale Calif 12 Jun 44 and staged at Cp Stoneman Calif 18 Jul 44 until departed San Francisco P/E 23 Jul 44; arrived Hawaii 29 Jul 44 and departed 15 Sep 44 *(attached as Sixth Army Reserve 26 Sep–27 Oct 44)* and landed on Leyte Philippine Islands 22 Oct 44 *(attached to Sixth Army 12–19 Nov 44)*; departed 27 Mar 45 and assaulted Okinawa 1 Apr 45; arrived on Palawan Island 31 Jul 45; arrived at Los Angeles P/E 2 Feb 46 and inactivated at Cp Anza Calif on 3 Feb 46.

Campaigns: *Leyte, Ryukyus*
Aug 45 Loc: Mindoro Philippine Islands

382nd Infantry Regiment (96th Infantry Division)

15 Aug 42 organized at Cp Adair Oreg and assigned to the 96th Infantry Division; moved to Ft Lewis Wash 3 May 43 and to Oreg Mnvr area 13 Jul 43; transferred to Cp White Oreg 2 Nov 43 and to Cp San Luis Obispo Calif 28 Apr 44; relocated to Cp Beale Calif 27 Jun 44 and staged at Cp Stoneman Calif 17 Jul 44 until departed San Francisco P/E 23 Jul 44; arrived Hawaii 28 Jul 44 and departed 15 Sep 44; assaulted Leyte Philippine Islands on 20 Oct 44 *(attached to 11th A/B Div 12–14 Dec 44) (attached as XXIV Corps Reserve 8 Feb–2 Apr 45)*; landed on Okinawa 2 Apr 45 and arrived on Palawan Island 31 Jul 45; arrived Los Angeles P/E 2 Feb 46 and inactivated at Cp Anza Calif on 3 Feb 46.

Campaigns: *Leyte, Ryukyus*
Aug 45 Loc: Mindoro Philippine Islands

No Distinctive
Insignia Authorized

383rd Infantry Regiment (96th Infantry Division)

15 Aug 42 organized at Cp Adair Oreg and assigned to the 96th Infantry Division; moved to Ft Lewis Wash 12 May 43 and to Oreg Mnvr area 12 Jul 43; transferred to Cp White Oreg 2 Nov 43 and to Cp San Luis Obispo Calif 26 Apr 44; relocated to Cp Beale Calif 4 Jul 44 and staged at Cp Stoneman Calif 16 Jul 44 until departed San Francisco P/E 23 Jul 44; arrived Hawaii 29 Jul 44 and departed 15 Sep 44; assaulted Leyte Philippine Islands on 20 Oct 44 and assaulted Okinawa 1 Apr 45 *(attached as XXIV Corps Reserve 16–29 Apr 45) (attached to 77th Inf Div 29–30 Apr 45)*; arrived on Palawan Island 31 Jul 45; arrived at Los Angeles P/E 2 Feb 46 and inactivated at Cp Anza Calif on 3 Feb 46.

Campaigns: *Leyte, Ryukyus*
Aug 45 Loc: Mindoro Philippine Islands

No Distinctive
Insignia Authorized

385th Infantry Regiment (76th Infantry Division)

15 Jun 42 organized at Ft George G. Meade Md and assigned to the 76th Division; moved to A.P. Hill Mil Res Va 24 Jul 43 and to Cp McCoy Wis 2 Oct 43; staged at Cp Myles Standish Mass 15 Nov 44 until departed Boston P/E 24 Nov 44; arrived in England 4 Dec 44 and landed in France 12 Jan 45; crossed into Belgium 23 Jan 45 and into Luxembourg 25 Jan 45 and entered Germany 1 Mar 45; inactivated there on 31 Aug 45.

Campaigns: *Rhineland, Ardennes-Alsace, Central Europe*
Aug 45 Loc: Zwickau Germany

386th Infantry Regiment (97th Infantry Division)

25 Feb 43 organized at Cp Swift Tex and assigned to the 97th Infantry Division; moved to La Mnvr area 18 Oct 43 and to Ft Leonard Wood Mo 31 Jan 44; transferred to Cp San Luis Obispo Calif 15 Jul 44 and to Cp Callan Calif 29 Aug 44; relocated to Cp Cooke Calif 10 Oct 44 and staged at Cp Kilmer N.J. 8 Feb 45 until departed New York P/E 19 Feb 45; landed in France 1 Mar 45 and entered Germany 28 Mar 45 *(attached to 78th Inf Div 5-6 Apr 45)*; arrived at Boston P/E 25 Jun 45 and moved to Ft Bragg N.C. 27 Jun 45; staged at Ft Lawton Wash 24 Aug 45 until departed Seattle P/E 28 Aug 45; arrived in the Philippine Islands 16 Sep 45 and inactivated in Japan on 31 Mar 46.

Campaigns: *Central Europe*
Aug 45 Loc: Fort Bragg North Carolina

387th Infantry Regiment (97th Infantry Division)

25 Feb 43 organized at Cp Swift Tex and assigned to the 97th Infantry Division; moved to La Mnvr area 23 Oct 43 and to Ft Leonard Wood Mo 31 Jan 44; transferred to Cp San Luis Obispo Calif 17 Jul 44 and to Cp Callan Calif 29 Aug 44; relocated to Cp Cooke Calif 22 Oct 44 and staged at Cp Kilmer N.J. 10 Feb 45 until departed New York P/E 19 Feb 45; landed in France 1 Mar 45 and entered Germany 28 Mar 45 *(attached to 78th Inf Div 4-6 Apr 45)*; returned to New York P/E 28 Jun 45 and moved to Ft Bragg N.C. 2 Jul 45; staged at Ft Lawton Wash 25 Aug 45 until departed Seattle P/E 28 Aug 45; arrived in the Philippine Islands 16 Sep 45 and inactivated in Japan on 31 Mar 46.

Campaigns: *Central Europe*
Aug 45 Loc: Fort Bragg North Carolina

389th Infantry Regiment (98th Infantry Division)

15 Sep 42 organized at Cp Breckinridge Ky and assigned to the 98th Infantry Division; moved to Tenn Mnvr area 6 Sep 43 and to Cp Rucker Ala 15 Nov 43; staged at Ft Lawton Wash 6 Apr 44 until departed Seattle P/E 13 Apr 44; arrived in Hawaii 19 Apr 44 where served on Kauai and Oahu *(attached to Central Pacific Base Command 5 Dec 44-18 Mar 45)*; arrived in Japan for occupation duty 5 Oct 45 where inactivated on 16 Feb 46.

Campaigns: *Pacific Theater without Inscription*
Aug 45 Loc: Fort Hase Hawaii

390th Infantry Regiment (98th Infantry Division)

15 Sep 42 organized at Cp Breckinridge Ky and assigned to the 98th Infantry Division; moved to Tenn Mnvr area 6 Sep 43 and to Cp Rucker Ala 12 Nov 43; staged at Ft Lawton Wash 15 Apr 44 until departed Seattle P/E 28 Apr 44; arrived in Hawaii 4 May 44 and served at Kauai and Oahu *(attached to 38th Inf Div 26 May-1 Jun 44)* *(attached to U.S. Army Forces in Central Pacific Area 1 Jun-1 Jul 44)* *(attached to Central Pacific Base Command 1 Jul-12 Nov 44)*; arrived in Japan 5 Oct 45 where inactivated on 16 Feb 46.

Campaigns: *Pacific Theater without Inscription*
Aug 45 Loc: Fort Hase Hawaii

No Distinctive
Insignia Authorized

391st Infantry Regiment (98th Infantry Division)

15 Sep 42 organized at Cp Breckinridge Ky and assigned to the 98th Infantry Division; moved to Tenn Mnvr area 7 Sep 43 and to Cp Rucker Ala 20 Nov 43; staged at Ft Lawton Wash 17 Apr 44 until departed Seattle P/E 22 Apr 44; arrived in Hawaii 28 Apr 44 and served at Maui and Oahu *(attached to Central Pacific Base Command 2 Nov 44-31 Mar 45)*; arrived in Japan 5 Oct 45 where inactivated on 16 Feb 46.

Campaigns: *Pacific Theater without Inscription*
Aug 45 Loc: Fort Hase Hawaii

393rd Infantry Regiment (99th Infantry Division)

15 Nov 42 organized at Cp Van Dorn Miss and assigned to the 99th Infantry Division; moved to the La Mnvr area 13 Sep 43 and to Cp Maxey Tex 19 Nov 43; staged at Cp Myles Standish Mass 14 Sep 44 until departed Boston P/E 30 Sep 44; arrived England 10 Oct 44 and landed in France 1 Nov 44 and entered Germany 12 Nov 44; arrived Hampton Roads P/E 20 Sep 45 and inactivated at Cp Patrick Henry Va the same date.

Campaigns: *Rhineland, Ardennes-Alsace, Central Europe*
Aug 45 Loc: Lohr Germany

394th Infantry Regiment (99th Infantry Division)

15 Nov 42 organized at Cp Van Dorn Miss and assigned to the 99th Infantry Division; moved to the La Mnvr area 14 Sep 43 and to Cp Maxey Tex 17 Nov 43; staged at Cp Myles Standish Mass and departed Boston P/E 30 Sep 44; arrived England 11 Oct 44 and landed in France 1 Nov 44 *(attached to 9th Inf Div 10–14 Nov 44)* and entered Germany 12 Nov 44 *(attached to 9th Inf Div 11 Mar 45)*; arrived Hampton roads P/E 29 Sep 45 and inactivated at Cp Patrick Henry Va the same date.

Campaigns: *Rhineland, Ardennes-Alsace, Central Europe*
Aug 45 Loc: Kitzingen Germany

395th Infantry Regiment (99th Infantry Division)

15 Nov 42 organized at Cp Van Dorn Miss and assigned to the 99th Infantry Division; moved to the La Mnvr area 16 Sep 43 and to Cp Maxey Tex 17 Nov 43; staged at Cp Myles Standish Mass 17 Sep 44 until departed Boston P/E 30 Sep 44; arrived in England 9 Oct 44 and landed in France 1 Nov 44 *(attached to 9th Inf Div 9–13 Nov 44)* and entered Germany 12 Nov 44 *(attached to 1st Inf Div 3–5 Feb 45) (attached to 3rd Armd Div 1–3 Mar 45) (attached to III Corps 12–13 Mar 45)*; returned to Boston P/E 28 Sep 45 and inactivated at Cp Myles Standish Mass on 29 Sep 45.

Campaigns: *Rhineland, Ardennes-Alsace, Central Europe*
Aug 45 Loc: Hammelburg Germany

397th Infantry Regiment (100th Infantry Division)

15 Nov 42 organized at Ft Jackson S.C. and assigned to the 100th Infantry Division; moved to Tenn Mnvr area 16 Nov 43 and to Ft Bragg N.C. 18 Jan 44; staged at Cp Kilmer N.J. 25 Sep 44 until departed New York P/E 6 Oct 44; arrived in France 20 Oct 44 *(attached to 45th Inf Div 6–9 Nov 44 and 28 Nov–5 Dec 44)* and entered Germany 22 Mar 45; arrived at Hampton Roads P/E 10 Jan 46 and inactivated at Cp Patrick Henry Va the same date.

Campaigns: *Rhineland, Ardennes-Alsace, Central Europe*
Aug 45 Loc: Goppingen Germany

398th Infantry Regiment (100th Infantry Division)

15 Nov 42 organized at Ft Jackson S.C. and assigned to the 100th Infantry Division; moved to Tenn Mnvr area 11 Nov 43 and to Ft Bragg N.C. 18 Jan 44; staged at Cp Kilmer N.J. 26 Sep 44 until departed New York P/E 6 Oct 44; arrived in France 20 Oct 44 *(attached to 45th Inf Div 6–9 Nov 44)* and entered Germany 22 Mar 45; arrived at New York P/E 7 Jan 46 and inactivated at Cp Kilmer N.J. on 8 Jan 46.

Campaigns: *Rhineland, Ardennes-Alsace, Central Europe*
Aug 45 Loc: Backnang Germany

399th Infantry Regiment (100th Infantry Division)

15 Nov 42 organized at Ft Jackson S.C. and assigned to the 100th Infantry Division; moved to Tenn Mnvr area 10 Nov 43 and to Ft Bragg N.C. 18 Jan 44; staged at Cp Kilmer N.J. 29 Sep 44 until departed New York P/E 6 Oct 44; arrived in France 20 Oct 44 *(attached to 45th Inf Div 2-9 Nov 44)* and entered Germany 22 Mar 45; returned to New York P/E 28 Jan 46 and inactivated at Cp Kilmer N.J. on 29 Jan 46.

Campaigns: *Rhineland, Ardennes-Alsace, Central Europe*
Aug 45 Loc: Kirchheim Germany

No Distinctive
Insignia Authorized

401st Glider Infantry Regiment (101st Airborne Division)

15 Aug 42 activated at Cp Claiborne La and assigned to the 101st Airborne Division; moved to Ft Bragg N.C. 1 Oct 42 and staged at Cp Shanks N.Y. 30 Aug 43 until departed New York P/E 5 Sep 43; arrived England 18 Oct 43 and assaulted Normandy France 6 Jun 44; returned to England and regiment, less 2nd Bn, assaulted Nijmegen-Arnhem Holland on 17 Sep 44; returned to France 28 Nov 44 and disbanded there on 1 Mar 45; assets to 327th Glider Infantry.

Campaigns: *Normandy, Rhineland, Ardennes-Alsace, Central Europe*

405th Infantry Regiment (102nd Infantry Division)

15 Sep 42 organized at Cp Maxey Tex and assigned to the 102nd Infantry Division; moved to La Mnvr area 15 Sep 43 and to Cp Swift Tex 18 Nov 43; transferred to Ft Dix N.J. 2 Jul 44 and staged at Cp Kilmer N.J. 5 Sep 44 until departed New York P/E 12 Sep 44; landed in France on 23 Sep 44 *(attached to 2nd Armd Div 26 Oct-3 Nov 44)* and crossed into Belgium and Holland both on 31 Oct 44 *(attached to 84th Inf Div 19 Nov-2 Dec 44)*; entered Germany 29 Nov 44 where inactivated on 1 Jun 46.

Campaigns: *Rhineland, Central Europe*
Aug 45 Loc: Arnstadt Germany

406th Infantry Regiment (102nd Infantry Division)

15 Sep 42 organized at Cp Maxey Tex and assigned to the 102nd Infantry Division; moved to La Mnvr area 15 Sep 43 and to Cp Swift Tex 18 Nov 43; relocated to Ft Dix N.J. 2 Jul 44 and staged at Cp Kilmer N.J. 5 Sep 44 until departed New York P/E 12 Sep 44; landed in France on 23 Sep 44 *(attached to 30th Inf Div 25 Oct-6 Nov 44)* and crossed into both Holland and Belgium 31 Oct 44 *(attached to 2nd Armd Div 6-25 Nov 44)* and entered Germany 29 Nov 44; returned to New York P/E 16 Mar 46 and inactivated at Cp Kilmer N.J. same date.

Campaigns: *Rhineland, Central Europe*
Aug 45 Loc: Rudolstadt Germany

407th Infantry Regiment (102nd Infantry Division)

15 Sep 42 organized at Cp Maxey Tex and assigned to the 102nd Infantry Division; moved to La Mnvr area 15 Sep 43 and to Cp Swift Tex 18 Nov 43; relocated to Ft Dix N.J. 2 Jul 44 and staged at Cp Kilmer N.J. 3 Sep 44 until departed New York P/E 12 Sep 44; landed in France on 23 Sep 44 *(attached to 29th Inf Div 28 Oct-3 Nov 44)* and crossed into both Holland and Belgium 31 Oct 44; entered Germany 29 Nov 44 *(attached to XIII Corps 27 Feb 45 and 12-17 Apr 45) (attached to 5th Armd Div 17-18 Apr 45) (attached to XIII Corps 18-26 Apr 45)*; returned to New York P/E 13 Mar 46 and inactivated at Cp Kilmer N.J. 16 Mar 46.

Campaigns: *Rhineland, Central Europe*
Aug 45 Loc: Ohrdruf Germany

409th Infantry Regiment (103rd Infantry Division)

15 Nov 42 organized at Cp Claiborne La and assigned to the 103rd Infantry Division; moved to La Mnvr area 17 Sep 43 and to Cp Howze Tex 21 Nov 43; staged at Cp Shanks N.Y. 25 Sep 44 until departed New York P/E 6 Oct 44; landed in France 20 Oct 44 *(attached to 45th Inf Div 15–17 Jan 45)* and entered Germany 23 Mar 45 and Austria 2 May 45; returned to New York P/E 18 Sep 45 and inactivated at Cp Shanks N.Y. on 19 Sep 45.

Campaigns: *Rhineland, Ardennes-Alsace, Central Europe*
Aug 45 Loc: Innsbruck Austria

410th Infantry Regiment (103rd Infantry Division)

15 Nov 42 organized at Cp Claiborne La and assigned to the 103rd Infantry Division; moved to La Mnvr area 17 Sep 43 and to Cp Howze Tex 21 Nov 43; staged at Cp Shanks N.Y. 27 Sep 44 until departed New York P/E 6 Oct 44; landed in France 20 Oct 44 and entered Germany 23 Mar 45 and Austria 2 May 45; arrived Boston P/E 19 Sep 45 and inactivated at Cp Myles Standish Mass on 20 Sep 45.

Campaigns: *Rhineland, Ardennes-Alsace, Central Europe*
Aug 45 Loc: Motz Germany

411th Infantry Regiment (103rd Infantry Division)

15 Nov 42 organized at Cp Claiborne La and assigned to the 103rd Infantry Division; moved to La Mnvr area 17 Sep 43 and to Cp Howze Tex 21 Nov 43; staged at Cp Shanks N.Y. 27 Sep 44 until departed New York P/E 6 Oct 44; landed in France 20 Oct 44 *(attached to 79th Inf Div 19–21 Jan 45)* and entered Germany 23 Mar 45 and Austria 2 May 45; returned to New York P/E 18 Sep 45 and inactivated at Cp Kilmer N.J. on 20 Sep 45.

Campaigns: *Rhineland, Ardennes-Alsace, Central Europe*
Aug 45 Loc: Imst Austria

413th Infantry Regiment (104th Infantry Division)

15 Aug 42 organized at Cp Adair Oreg and assigned to the 104th Infantry Division; moved to Oreg Mnvr area 5 Aug 43 and to Calif-Ariz Mnvr area 7 Nov 43; arrived at Cp Carson Colo 11 Mar 44 and staged at Cp Kilmer N.J. 17 Aug 44 until departed New York P/E 27 Aug 44; landed in France 7 Sep 44 and crossed into Belgium 21 Oct 44 and into Holland 30 Oct 44; entered Germany 7 Nov 44 *(attached to 1st Inf Div 21–23 Mar 45)*; returned to New York P/E 3 Jul 45 and moved to Cp Shelby Miss 15 Jul 45; transferred to Cp San Luis Obispo Calif 15 Aug 45 where inactivated on 13 Dec 45.

Campaigns: *Northern France, Rhineland, Central Europe*
Aug 45 Loc: Entrained from Camp Shelby Mississippi to Camp San Luis Obispo California

414th Infantry Regiment (104th Infantry Division)

15 Aug 42 organized at Cp Adair Oreg and assigned to the 104th Infantry Division; moved to Oreg Mnvr area 5 Aug 43 and to Calif-Ariz Mnvr area 10 Nov 43; arrived at Cp Carson Colo 11 Mar 44 and staged at Cp Kilmer N.J. 17 Aug 44 until departed New York P/E 27 Aug 44; landed in France 7 Sep 44 and crossed into Belgium 18 Oct 44 and into Holland 30 Oct 44; entered Germany 7 Nov 44 *(attached to 3rd Armd Div 23 Mar–12 Apr 45)*; returned to New York P/E 11 Jul 45 and moved to Cp Shelby Miss 15 Jul 45; transferred to Cp San Luis Obispo Calif 15 Aug 45 where inactivated on 11 Dec 45.

Campaigns: *Northern France, Rhineland, Central Europe*
Aug 45 Loc: Entrained from Camp Shelby Mississippi to Camp San Luis Obispo California

415th Infantry Regiment (104th Infantry Division)

15 Aug 42 organized at Cp Adair Oreg and assigned to the 104th Infantry Division; moved to Oreg Mnvr area 7 Aug 43 and to Calif-Ariz Mnvr area 12 Nov 43; arrived at Cp Carson Colo 11 Mar 44 and staged at Cp Kilmer N.J. 19 Aug 44 until departed New York P/E 27 Aug 44; landed in France 7 Nov 44 and crossed into Belgium 21 Oct 44 and into Holland 30 Oct 44; entered Germany 7 Nov 44; returned to New York P/E 11 Jul 45 and moved to Cp Shelby Miss 15 Jul 45; transferred to Cp San Luis Obispo Calif 15 Aug 45 where inactivated on 17 Dec 45.

Campaigns: *Northern France, Rhineland, Central Europe*
Aug 45 Loc: Entrained from Camp Shelby Mississippi to Camp San Luis Obispo California

417th Infantry Regiment (76th Infantry Division)

15 Jun 42 organized at Ft George G. Meade Md and assigned to the 76th Division; moved to A.P. Hill Mil Res Va 5 Jul 43 and to Cp McCoy Wis 1 Oct 43; staged at Cp Myles Standish Mass 15 Nov 44 until departed Boston P/E 24 Nov 44; arrived in England 4 Dec 44 and landed in France 11 Jan 45; crossed into Belgium on 22 Jan 45 and into Luxembourg on 25 Jan 45 *(attached to 5th Inf Div 3–11 Feb 45)*; entered Germany 1 Mar 45 *(attached to 10th Armd Div 4–12 Mar 45)* where inactivated on 31 Aug 45.

Campaigns: *Rhineland, Ardennes-Alsace, Central Europe*
Aug 45 Loc: Griez Germany

No Distinctive
Insignia Authorized

422nd Infantry Regiment (106th Infantry Division)

15 Mar 43 activated at Ft Jackson S.C. and assigned to the 106th Infantry Division; moved to Tenn Mnvr area 24 Jan 44 and to Cp Atterbury Ind 30 Mar 44; staged at Cp Myles Standish Mass 14 Oct 44 until departed Boston P/E 19 Oct 44; arrived England 28 Oct 44 and landed in France 5 Dec 44; crossed into Belgium 10 Dec 44 and effectively destroyed in the Schnee Eifel salient 18 Dec 44; rebuilt in France 16 Mar 45 *(attached to 66th Inf Div 15 Apr–15 May 45)* and entered Germany 25 Apr 45; arrived New York P/E 1 Oct 45 and inactivated at Cp Kilmer N.J. on 2 Oct 45.

Campaigns: *Northern France, Rhineland, Ardennes-Alsace*
Aug 45 Loc: Mayen Germany

No Distinctive
Insignia Authorized

423rd Infantry Regiment (106th Infantry Division)

15 Mar 43 activated at Ft Jackson S.C. and assigned to the 106th Infantry Division; moved to Tenn Mnvr area 24 Jan 44 and to Cp Atterbury Ind 29 Mar 44; staged at Cp Myles Standish Mass 10 Oct 44 until sent to Exch.Jersey N.J. 16–17 Oct 44 and departed New York P/E 17 Oct 44; arrived England 22 Oct 44 and landed in France 5 Dec 44; crossed into Belgium 10 Dec 44 and effectively destroyed in Schnee Eifel salient 18 Dec 44; rebuilt in France 16 Mar 45 *(attached to 66th Inf Div 15 Apr–15 May 45)* and entered Germany 25 Apr 45; arrived New York P/E 1 Oct 45 and inactivated at Cp Shanks N.Y. on 2 Oct 45.

Campaigns: *Northern France, Rhineland, Ardennes-Alsace*
Aug 45 Loc: Mayen Germany

No Distinctive
Insignia Authorized

424th Infantry Regiment (106th Infantry Division)

15 Mar 43 activated at Ft Jackson S.C. and assigned to the 106th Infantry Division; moved to Tenn Mnvr area 24 Jan 44 and to Cp Atterbury Ind 28 Mar 44; staged at Cp Myles Standish Mass 12 Oct 44, sent to Jersey City N.J. 19 Oct 44, and departed New York P/E 21 Oct 44; arrived in England 28 Oct 44 and landed in France 5 Dec 44; crossed into Belgium 10 Dec 44 *(attached to 7th Armd Div 24–30 Dec 44 and 23–28 Jan 45)* *(attached to 99th Inf Div 5–9 Feb 45)*; returned to France 16 Mar 45 and entered Germany 25 Apr 45; returned to New York P/E 5 Oct 45 and inactivated at Cp Shanks N.Y. on 6 Oct 45.

Campaigns: *Northern France, Rhineland, Ardennes-Alsace*
Aug 45 Loc: Ingelheim Germany

434th Infantry Regiment (Separate)

20 Jun 41 Headquarters detachment and Companies A, E, and I activated at Ft Jackson S.C. and sent to the Caribbean area; inactivated at St Lucia British West Indies on 16 Oct 42 less Co E inactivated at Antigua British West Indies 19 Nov 43 and Companies A and I inactivated at Cp Claiborne La on 5 May 44.

442nd Infantry Regiment (Nisei) (Separate)

1 Feb 43 activated at Cp Shelby Miss and attached to Third Army and later to IX Corps on 5 Aug 43; staged at Cp Patrick Henry Va 24 Apr 44 until departed Hampton Roads P/E less 1st Bn 3 May 44; arrived in Italy 28 May 44 where placed under 34th Inf Div and during Jun 44 cleared the villages of Belvedore and Sasetta; attacked toward Livorno 3 Jul 44 against strong opposition above Rosignano and seized Luciana 17 Jul 44; Livorno fell 19 Jul 44 and attached to IV Corps 7 Aug 44; in ZI 1st Bn relieved from regiment 10 Aug 44 and redesignated the 171st Infantry Battalion and concurrently the 100th Infantry Battalion in Italy (Separate) assigned to the regiment; occupied frontal sector west of Florence under 88th Inf Div on 20 Aug 44 and by 2 Sep 44 had reached Sesto; antitank company assaulted southern France 15 Aug 44 and remainder of regiment arrived there 10 Oct 44 *(attached to 36th Inf Div 11 Oct– 9 Nov 44 and 9–18 Nov 44)*; 15 Oct 44 attacked toward Bruyeres and battled in the Foret Domaniale de Champ 25–30 Oct 44 to rescue the isolated 1st Bn, 141st Inf Regt; relieved the 1st Special Service Force on the Franco-Italian border 28 Nov 44; returned to Italy under Fifth Army 25 Mar 45 and attached to 92nd Inf Div 30 Mar 45; attacked toward Massa in the Ligurian coastal sector on 5 Apr 45 and took M.Cerreta and M.Belvedere in heavy combat 6–7 Apr 45; occupied Carrara without opposition on 11 Apr 45; arrived New York P/E 3 Jul 46 and moved to Ft Belvoir Va on 4 Jul 46; departed New York P/E 21 Jul 46 and arrived in Hawaii 9 Sep 46 where inactivated on 15 Aug 46.

Campaigns: *Naples-Foggia, Anzio, Rome-Arno, North Apennines, Rhineland, Po Valley*
Aug 45 Loc: Ghedi Italy

473rd Infantry Regiment (Separate)

14 Jan 45 activated at Montecatini Italy and formed from HHC 2nd Armored Group with 1st Bn from 435th AAA Automatic Weapons Bn, 2nd Bn from 532nd AAA Automatic Weapons Bn, and 3rd Bn from 900th AAA Automatic Weapons Bn; attached to the 92nd Inf Div 24 Feb 45 and committed into the attack in the Ligurian coastal sector on 8 Apr 45; crossed the Parmignola Canal 17 Apr 45 and reached Turin on 30 Apr 45 where linked up with troops at the Franco-Italian border; inactivated in Italy on 14 Sep 45.

Campaigns: *North Apennines, Po Valley*
Aug 45 Loc: Catarozzo Italy

474th Infantry Regiment (Separate)

6 Jan 45 activated in France with personnel from the 1st Special Service Force with the 99th Infantry Battalion joined as the third battalion on 25 Jan 45; trained at Barneville and attached to Third Army and moved to Aachen for consolidation 2 Apr 45; entered Germany 5 Apr 45 and arrived in Norway 7 Jun 45; arrived at New York P/E 25 Oct 45 and inactivated at Cp Shanks N.Y. on 26 Oct 45.

Campaigns: *Central Europe*
Aug 45 Loc: Drammen Norway

475th Infantry Regiment (Long Range Penetration, Special)

10 Aug 44 activated at Ledo India from personnel of the 5307th Composite Unit, Provisional, and assigned to the Northern Combat Area Command and further to the 5332nd Brigade, Provisional, also known as MARS Task Force; opened offensive 15 Oct 44 to clear northern Burma and open a supply route to China and on 15 Nov 44 began march from Cp Landis to assist the *Chinese 22nd Div* near Si-u; ordered to relieve the *Chinese 22nd Div* in the Mo-hlaing area on 6 Dec 44; counterattacked to restore positions there on 9 Dec 44 and began holding action in the Mo-hlaing/Tonk-wa Burma area the following day, less 1st Bn sent to Shwegu vicinity; repelled strong Japanese counterattacks 13–14 Dec 44 and on the latter date made contact with the *British 36th Div* at Katha; relieved at Tonk-wa on 31 Dec 44 and marched toward Mong Wi where attacked from commencing 8 Jan 45; fought the Battle for Loi-kang Ridge 3–4 Feb 45 and entered China in Apr 45; inactivated in China on 1 Jul 45.

Campaigns: *India-Burma, Central Burma*

No Distinctive Insignia Authorized

476th Armored Infantry Regiment (16th Armored Division)

15 Jul 43 activated at Cp Chaffee Ark and assigned to the 16th Armored Division; there redesignated, less 1st and 2nd Bns, as the 18th Armored Infantry Battalion on 10 Sep 43; 1st and 2nd Bns redesignated the 64th and 69th Armored Infantry Battalions, respectively.

No Distinctive Insignia Authorized

480th Armored Infantry Regiment (20th Armored Division)

15 Mar 43 activated at Cp Campbell Ky and assigned to the 20th Armored Division; there redesignated, less 1st and 2nd Bns, as the 8th Armored Infantry Battalion on 10 Sep 43; 1st and 2nd Bns redesignated the 65th and 70th Armored Infantry Battalions, respectively.

No Distinctive Insignia Authorized

501st Parachute Infantry Regiment (Separate)

24 Feb 42 1st Battalion redesignated from the 501st Parachute Battalion and remainder of regiment activated at Cp Toccoa Ga on 15 Nov 42; 1st Bn inactivated 2 Nov 42 in Australia and assets used to form the 2nd Bn, 503rd Prcht Inf there, and new 1st Bn activated at Cp Toccoa Ga on 15 Nov 42; assigned to the Airborne Command 15 Dec 42 and moved to Ft Benning Ga on 23 Mar 43 and to Cp Mackall N.C. 13 Apr 43 where assigned to the 2nd Airborne Brigade 3 Sep 43; staged at Cp Myles Standish Mass 2 Jan 44 until departed Boston P/E 18 Jan 44; arrived in England 31 Jan 44 and attached to the 101st Airborne Division in May 44 past the end of hostilities in Europe; assaulted Normandy France to capture the Douve River locks at La Barquette 6 Jun 44 and returned to England 13 Jul 44; assaulted Nijmegen-Arnhem Holland on 17 Sep 44 and captured Beghel; moved to Rheims France 28 Nov 44 for rehabilitation and sent to Bastogne Belgium 18 Dec 44 where fought until Jan 45; entered Germany 4 Apr 45 where inactivated on 20 Aug 45.

Campaigns: *Normandy, Rhineland, Ardennes-Alsace, Central Europe, Pacific Theater without Inscription*
Aug 45 Loc: Bad Gastein Germany

502nd Parachute Infantry Regiment (101st Airborne Division)

24 Feb 42 1st Battalion redesignated from the 502nd Parachute Battalion and remainder of regiment activated at Ft Benning Ga on 2 Mar 42; assigned to the 101st Airborne Division 15 Aug 42 and moved to Ft Bragg N.C. 24 Sep 42; staged at Cp Shanks N.Y. 25 Aug 43 until departed New York P/E 5 Sep 43; arrived in England 18 Sep 43 and assaulted Normandy France 6 Jun 44; returned to England 13 Jul 44 and assaulted Nijmegen-Arnhem Holland 17 Sep 44 *(attached to 82nd A/B Div 4–5 Oct 44)* and entered Germany 4 Apr 45 where inactivated on 30 Nov 45.

No Distinctive Insignia Authorized

Campaigns: *Normandy, Rhineland, Ardennes-Alsace, Central Europe*
Aug 45 Loc: Kossen Austria

503rd Parachute Infantry Regiment (Separate)

No Distinctive
Insignia Authorized

24 Feb 42 1st and 2nd Battalions redesignated at Ft Benning Ga from the 503rd and 504th Parachute Battalions respectively, and remainder of regiment activated there on 2 Mar 42; moved to Ft Bragg N.C. 21 Mar 42 under the Airborne Command where 3rd Bn activated 8 Jun 42; staged at Cp Stoneman Calif 16 Oct 42 until departed San Francisco P/E, less 2nd Bn, on 19 Oct 42; arrived in Australia where new 2nd Bn raised 2 Nov 42 from 1st Bn, 501st Prcht Inf; original 2nd Bn redesignated 2nd Bn, 509th Prcht Inf on 2 Nov 42 in England; left Australia 18 Aug 43 and arrived Port Moresby New Guinea 20 Aug 43; air-assaulted Nadzab on the Markam River near Lae unopposed on 5 Sep 43 and relieved in area 17 Sep 43; returned to Australia 27 Jan 44 and landed back in New Guinea 14 Apr 44; HHC and 1st Bn parachuted onto Kamiri airfield Noemfoor Island 3 Jul 44 and 3rd Bn airdropped next day; due to high casualties incurred in drops despite lack of Japanese opposition the 2nd Bn arrived via sea 11 Jul 44; 1st Bn fought Battle for Hill 670, 13–16 Jul 44; Hill 380 near Inasi taken 10 Aug 44 and by 17 Aug 44 remaining Japanese forces on Noemfoor defeated; departed 9 Nov 44 and landed on Leyte Philippine Islands 18 Nov 44; invaded Mindoro at San Agustin 15 Dec 44 and secured San Jose same date; seized Palauan on island 5 Jan 45 and terminated operations on Mindoro 15 Jan 45; parachuted onto Corregidor Island 16 Feb 45 and 1st Bn reinforced by landing craft the following day *(attached to XI Corps 16 Feb–8 Mar 45)*; Corregidor cleared by 2 Mar 45 and regiment served as garrison; arrived at Pulupandan Negros Island on 7 Apr 45 and went into the offensive there 9 Apr 45 *(attached to 40th Inf Div 9 Apr–1 Jul 45)*; after heavy combat 15–22 Apr 45 took Hill 3155 and opened drive toward Hill 4055 on 11 May 45; assumed responsibility for mop-up of Negros 4 Jul 45 until end of hostilities; arrived Los Angeles P/E 23 Dec 45 and inactivated at Cp Anza Calif on 25 Dec 45.

Campaigns: *New Guinea, Leyte, Luzon, Southern Philippines*
Aug 45 Loc: Iloilo Philippine Islands

504th Parachute Infantry Regiment (82nd Airborne Division)

No Distinctive
Insignia Authorized

1 May 42 activated at Ft Benning Ga and assigned to the Airborne Command; assigned to the 82nd Airborne Division on 15 Aug 42 and moved to Ft Bragg N.C. 30 Sep 42; staged at Cp Edwards Mass 18 Apr 43 until departed New York P/E 10 May 43; landed in North Africa 10 May 43 and assaulted Gela Sicily on 9 Jul 43; assaulted Salerno Italy 9 Sep 43 with 3rd Bn and completed arrival there 18 Oct 43; assaulted Anzio Italy 22 Jan 44 and departed Italy 10 Apr 44; arrived England 23 Apr 44 where remained until assaulted Nijmegen-Arnhem Holland on 17 Sep 44; relocated to France 15 Nov 44 *(attached to 75th Inf Div 1–3 Jan 45)* and crossed into Belgium 26 Jan 45 and returned to France 22 Feb 45 and entered Germany 8 Apr 45; returned to New York P/E 3 Jan 46 and moved to Ft Bragg N.C. 16 Jan 46 where remained active thru 1946.

Campaigns: *Sicily, Naples-Foggia, Anzio, Rhineland, Ardennes-Alsace, Central Europe*
Aug 45 Loc: Rambervillers France

505th Parachute Infantry Regiment (82nd Airborne Division)

No Distinctive
Insignia Authorized

6 Jul 42 activated at Ft Benning Ga and assigned to the Airborne Command; assigned to the 82nd Airborne Division on 10 Feb 43 and moved to Ft Bragg N.C. 12 Feb 43; staged at Cp Edwards Mass 21 Apr 43 until departed New York P/E 28 Apr 43; landed in North Africa 10 May 43 and assaulted Gela Sicily on 9 Jul 43; returned to North Africa 19 Aug 43 and to Sicily 4 Sep 43; landed in Italy 13 Sep 43 and departed 19 Nov 43; arrived Ireland 9 Dec 43 and England 14 Feb 44; assaulted Normandy France 6 Jun 44 and returned to England 13 Jul 44; assaulted Nijmegen-Arnhem Holland 17 Sep 44; returned to France 14 Nov 44 and crossed into Belgium 18 Dec 44 and entered Germany 30 Jan 45; returned to France 19 Feb 45 and reentered Germany 2 Apr 45; returned to New York P/E 3 Jan 46 and moved to Ft Bragg N.C. 16 Jan 46 where remained active thru 1946.

Campaigns: *Sicily, Naples-Foggia, Normandy, Rhineland, Ardennes-Alsace, Central Europe*
Aug 45 Loc: Epinal France

506th Parachute Infantry Regiment (101st Airborne Division)

20 Jul 42 activated at Cp Toombs Ga, renamed Cp Toccoa Ga 21 Aug 42, and moved to Ft Benning Ga 9 Dec 42 where attached to the Airborne Command 15 Dec 42; transferred to Cp Mackall N.C. 26 Feb 43 *(attached to the 101st Airborne Division 1 Jun 43–1 Mar 45)*; relocated to Sturgis Army Airfield Ky 6 Jun 43 and to Ft Bragg N.C. 23 Jul 43; staged at Cp Shanks N.Y. 29 Aug 43 until departed New York P/E 5 Sep 43; arrived England 15 Sep 43 and assaulted Normandy France on 6 Jun 44; returned to England 13 Jul 44 and assaulted Nijmegen-Arnhem Holland 17 Sep 44; entered Germany 4 Apr 45 *(attached to 4th Inf Div 2–3 May 45)*; was assigned 101st A/B Div 1 Mar 45; inactivated there on 30 May 45.

Campaigns: *Normandy, Rhineland, Ardennes-Alsace, Central Europe*
Aug 45 Loc: Zell-am-see Austria

507th Parachute Infantry Regiment (17th Airborne Division)

20 Jul 42 activated at Ft Benning Ga and assigned to the Airborne Command; moved to Barksdale Field La 7 Mar 43 and to Alliance Army Airfield Nebr 23 Mar 43 where assigned to the 1st Airborne Infantry Brigade on 14 Apr 43; staged at Cp Shanks N.Y. 23 Nov 43 until departed New York P/E 5 Dec 43; arrived England 16 Dec 43 *(attached to 82nd A/B Div 14 Jan–27 Aug 44)* and assaulted Normandy France on 6 Jun 44; returned to England 13 Jul 44 *(attached to 17th A/B Div 27 Aug 44–1 Mar 45)* and landed in France 24 Dec 44; crossed into Belgium 25 Dec 44 and returned to France 11 Feb 45 where assigned to the 17th Airborne Division on 1 Mar 45; assaulted Wesel Germany 24 Mar 45 *(attached to XIX Corps 31 Mar–2 Apr 45)*; arrived Boston P/E 15 Sep 45 and inactivated at Cp Myles Standish Mass on 16 Sep 45.

Campaigns: *Normandy, Rhineland, Ardennes-Alsace, Central Europe*
Aug 45 Loc: Vittel France

508th Parachute Infantry Regiment (Separate)

20 Oct 42 activated at Cp Blanding Fla and assigned to the Airborne Command; moved to Ft Benning Ga 5 Feb 43 and to Cp Mackall N.C. 25 Mar 43; staged at Cp Shanks N.Y. 20 Dec 43 until departed New York P/E 29 Dec 43; arrived northern Ireland 8 Jan 44 *(attached to the 82nd Airborne Division 14 Jan 44–20 Jan 45)* and England 13 Mar 44; assaulted Normandy France on 6 Jun 44 and returned to England 13 Jul 44; assaulted Nijmegen-Arnhem Holland 17 Sep 44 and returned to France 20 Nov 44; crossed into Belgium 26 Jan 45 *(attached to 7th Armd Div 21–23 Jan 45)* *(attached to 82nd A/B Div 24 Jan 45–past end of hostilities)*; returned to New York P/E 24 Nov 46 and inactivated at Cp Kilmer N.J. on 25 Nov 46.

Campaigns: *Normandy, Rhineland, Ardennes-Alsace, Central Europe*
Aug 45 Loc: Sissone France

509th Parachute Infantry Regiment (Separate)

2 Nov 42 the 2nd Battalion redesignated from 2nd Bn 503rd Prcht Infantry in England and assaulted Oran and Youks Les Bains North Africa 8–15 Nov 42; attached to 82nd Airborne Division for assault of Sicily on 9 Jul 43; assaulted Salerno Italy 9 Sep 43 and parachuted onto Avellino 14 Sep 43; badly decimated in ensuing battle and withdrawn from front to guard Fifth Army Headquarters in Italy; redesignated at Venafro as the 509th Parachute Infantry Battalion on 10 Dec 43.

Campaigns: *Algeria-French Morocco, Tunisia, Sicily, Naples-Foggia*

511th Parachute Infantry Regiment (11th Airborne Division)

5 Jan 43 activated at Cp Toccoa Ga and assigned to the Airborne Command; moved to Cp Mackall N.C. 21 Feb 43 where assigned to the 11th Airborne Division on 25 Feb 43; transferred to Ft Benning Ga 14 May 43 and returned to Cp Mackall N.C. 14 Jun 43; relocated to Cp Polk La 5 Jan 44 and staged at Cp Stoneman Calif 29 Apr 44 until departed San Francisco P/E 8 May 44; arrived in New Guinea 29 May 44 and arrived on Leyte Philippine Islands 18 Nov 44; assaulted Tagaytay Ridge Luzon on 3 Feb 45 and arrived in Okinawa 12 Aug 45 enroute to Japan for occupation duty; arrived in Japan 30 Aug 45 where active thru 1946.

Campaigns: *New Guinea, Leyte, Luzon*
Aug 45 Loc: Okinawa

513th Parachute Infantry Regiment (17th Airborne Division)

No Distinctive Insignia Authorized

11 Jan 43 activated at Ft Benning Ga and assigned to the 13th Airborne Division and moved to Ft Bragg N.C. 1 Nov 43 and to Cp Mackall N.C. 15 Jan 44; transferred to Tenn Mnvr area 4 Mar 44 where relieved from assignment to the 13th and assigned to the 17th Airborne Division on 10 Mar 44; relocated to Cp Forrest Tenn 24 Mar 44 and staged at Cp Myles Standish Mass 13 Aug 44 until departed Boston P/E 20 Aug 44; arrived in England 28 Aug 44 and landed in France 24 Dec 44; crossed into Belgium 25 Dec 44 and returned to France 11 Feb 45; returned to Belgium 21 Mar 45 and assaulted Wesel Germany 24 Mar 45; arrived at Boston P/E 14 Sep 45 and inactivated at Cp Myles Standish Mass the same date.

Campaigns: *Rhineland, Ardennes-Alsace, Central Europe*
Aug 45 Loc: Vittel France

515th Parachute Infantry Regiment (13th Airborne Division)

No Distinctive Insignia Authorized

31 May 43 activated at Ft Benning Ga and assigned to the Airborne Command; moved to Cp Mackall N.C. 19 Jan 44 under XIII Corps where assigned to the 13th Airborne Division on 10 Mar 44; staged at Cp Shanks N.Y. 19 Jan 45 until departed New York P/E 26 Jan 45; arrived in France 6 Feb 45 and returned to New York P/E 22 Aug 45; moved to Ft Bragg N.C. 26 Aug 45 where inactivated on 25 Feb 46.

Campaigns: *Central Europe*
Aug 45 Loc: Shipment #10580-G at sea

517th Parachute Infantry Regiment (13th Airborne Division)

No Distinctive Insignia Authorized

15 Mar 43 activated at Cp Toccoa Ga and assigned to the Airborne Command and to the 17th Airborne Division 15 Apr 43; moved to Cp Mackall N.C. 8 Aug 43 and to the Tenn Mnvr area 8 Feb 44; returned to Cp Mackall N.C. 5 Mar 44 where relieved from the 17th Airborne Division on 10 Mar 44 and attached to Second Army; staged at Cp Patrick Henry Va 7 May 44 until departed Hampton Roads P/E 17 May 44; arrived Italy 28 May 44 and committed into combat under IV Corps along Highway 1 north of Rome on 17 Jun 44; assaulted southern France 15 Aug 44 and took St Vallier on 24 Aug 44 *(attached to XVIII A/B Corps 22 Nov–16 Dec 44)* *(attached to 30th Inf Div 17–27 Dec 44)* *(attached to 7th Armd Div 28–29 Dec 44)* *(attached to 82nd A/B Div 1–11 Jan 45)*; attacked 13 Jan 45 to take Henumont *(attached 106th Inf Div 11–17 Jan 45)* *(attached to 82nd A/B. Div 23–26 Jan 45 and 3–4 Feb 45)* and moved to Bergstein area 4 Feb 45; attacked through heavily mined area toward Schmidt-Nideggen road on 6–7 Feb 45 *(attached to 78th Inf Div 4–7 Feb 45)* and assembled near Huertgen on 9 Feb 45 *(attached to 82nd A/B Div 9–10 Feb 45)* *(attached to 13th A/B Div 11 Feb–1 Mar 45)*; assigned to the 13th Airborne Division on 1 Mar 45 and arrived at New York P/E 20 Aug 45; moved to Ft Bragg N.C. 23 Aug 45 where inactivated on 25 Feb 46.

Campaigns: *Southern France, Rhineland, Ardennes-Alsace, Central Europe*
Aug 45 Loc: Shipment #10580-H at sea

541st Parachute Infantry Regiment (Separate)

No Distinctive Insignia Authorized

12 Aug 43 activated at Ft Benning Ga and assigned to the Airborne Command; moved to Cp Mackall N.C. 14 Oct 43 and assigned to XIII Corps on 1 Mar 44; returned to Ft Benning Ga 29 Jul 44 and assigned to the Replacement & School Command on 7 Jul 44 and attached to the Airborne Center on 16 Nov 44; returned to Cp Mackall N.C. 23 Nov 44 and staged at Cp Stoneman Calif 23 May 45 and departed San Francisco P/E 5 Jun 45; arrived at Manila Philippine Islands on 10 Jul 45 and assets used to form 3rd Bns for the 187th and 188th Parachute Infantry Regiments; inactivated at Lipa Luzon on 10 Aug 45.

Campaigns: *Pacific Theater without Inscription*
Aug 45 Loc: Manila Philippine Islands

542nd Parachute Infantry Regiment (Separate)

1 Sep 43 activated at Ft Benning Ga and assigned to the Airborne Command; assigned to the Replacement & School Command on 29 Feb 44 and redesignated there as the 542nd Parachute Infantry Battalion on 17 Mar 44.

551st Parachute Infantry Regiment (Separate)

26 Nov 42 1st Battalion activated at Ft Kobbe Panama Canal Zone and arrived in Italy about June 1944; assaulted southern France 15 Aug 44 under the 1st Airborne Task Force and moved into Belgium where attached to the 82nd Airborne Division 26 Dec 44–13 Jan 45 and 21–27 Jan 45; inactivated in Europe on 10 Feb 45.

Campaigns: *Rome-Arno, Southern France, Rhineland, Ardennes-Alsace, American Theater without Inscription*

777th Infantry Regiment (Separate)

Jun 44 Cannon Company activated at Cp Cooke Calif where disbanded on 24 Jul 44.

800th Infantry Regiment (Separate)

5 Jun 43 Cannon Company activated at Cp Roberts Calif where redesignated the Cannon Company of 147th Infantry Regiment on 1 Apr 44.

2677th Office of Strategic Services Regiment

15 Jul 44 organized at Algiers North Africa under Fifth Army and transferred to Caserta Italy where absorbed into OSS Operational Group Command on 27 Nov 44.

Campaigns: *Rome-Arno*

5307th Composite Unit, Provisional

10 Oct 43 organized at Deogarh India as the 5307th Composite Regiment, Provisional, and activated 1 Jan 44 under U.S. Army Forces in China-Burma-India; 2 Jan 44 redesignated as the 5307th Composite Unit, Provisional, also known as GALAHAD Force and *Merrill's Marauders*; organized into three long-range penetration battalions and entered Hukawing Valley Burma on 12 Feb 44; assigned to the Northern Combat Area Command on 8 May 44 and operated behind Japanese front lines, capturing Myitkyina Airfield along the Irrawaddy river 17 May 44; 3rd Bn defeated at Charpate 24 May 44 and 2nd Bn driven from Namkwi 26 May 44; battled at Myitkyina until captured city 3 Aug 44 where disbanded on 10 Aug 44 and assets transferred to 475th Infantry Regiment.

Campaigns: *India-Burma*

6615th Ranger Force, Provisional

Summer 1943 formed in North Africa to protect Fifth Army left flank during impending Italian operations and organized with the 1st, 3rd, and 4th Ranger Inf Battalions, 83rd Chemical Mortar Bn, and 2nd Bn, 509th Prcht Infantry; assaulted Salerno Italy on 9 Sep 43 and subordinate units variously attached and reattached during the Naples-Foggia campaign; assaulted Anzio Italy 22 Jan 44 and effectively destroyed at Cisterna di Littoria Italy on 30 Jan 44.

Campaigns: *Naples-Foggia, Anzio*

Chapter 14

Infantry Battalions

Battalions:

1 Filipino, 1 Parachute, 1 Ranger, 1 Recon, 2 Filipino, 2 Provisional, 2 Ranger, 3 Army Defense, 3 Ranger, 4 Army Defense, 4-6 Ranger, 6-10 Armored Infantry, 10 Mountain Antitank, 11 Armored Infantry, 14-21 Armored Infantry, 23 Armored Infantry, 27 Armored Infantry, 38 Armored Infantry, 44 Armored Infantry, 46-56 Armored Infantry, 58-70 Armored Infantry, 73, 75 Composite Training, 88 Airborne, 93 Infantry Antitank, 94 Infantry Antitank, 99 Infantry Antitank, 99-101, 101-105 Infantry Antitank, 122, 170, 171, 202-210, 367 Armored Infantry, 470-472, 501-504 Parachute, 509 Parachute, 526-540 Armored Infantry, 542 Parachute, 550 Airborne, 555 Parachute, 2671 OSS Special Recon, 5217 Special Recon

⭐ EXAMPLE — HOW TO USE THIS TABLE

Unit Designation and Type	Date Formed and Location (Source of Unit)/Inactivation and Location	August 1945 Location

Overseas Wartime Locations followed by - **Campaign Key Numbers** and PE return to United States, if applicable or space allows
(notes and remarks in parenthesis)

2nd Ranger Infantry Battalion 1 Apr 43 Cp Forrest Tenn as 2nd Ranger Bn/23 Oct 45 Cp Patrick Henry Va   Dol Lukavice Czechoslovakia
NYPE: 23 Nov 43   England: 29 Nov 43   France-ETO: 6 Jun 44 - **25,26,30,32,34**   HRPE: 22 Oct 45 *(redes Ranger Inf Bn 1 Aug 43)*

In this example, the 2nd Ranger Infantry Battalion was originally formed at Camp Forrest, Tennessee, as the 2nd Ranger Battalion on 1 April 1943. The unit was redesignated as the 2nd Ranger Infantry Battalion on 1 August 1943. It *departed* New York Port of Embarkation on 23 November 1943 and *arrived* in England on 29 November 1943. It landed in France–European Theater of Operations on 6 June 1944 and participated in the Ardennes-Alsace, Central European, Normandy, Northern France, and Rhineland campaigns. This information was derived by indexing the bold-faced campaign key numbers with Appendix I. In August 1945 it was at Dol Lukavice, Czechoslovakia. The battalion arrived at Hampton Roads Port of Embarkation on 22 October 1945 and was inactivated at Camp Patrick Henry, Virginia, on 23 October 1945.

BATTALION DESIGNATION AND TYPE	FORMED (SOURCE OF UNIT)/INACTIVATION *Active through 1946	AUGUST 1945 LOCATION

1st Filipino Infantry Battalion 1 Apr 42 Cp San Luis Obispo Calif / 11 Jul 42 Cp San Luis Obispo Calif   *(attached VII Corps)*

1st Parachute Battalion 16 Sep 40 Ft Benning Ga / 1 Oct 40 Ft Benning Ga redes 501st Prcht Bn

1st Ranger Infantry Battalion 19 Jun 42 Carrickfergus N.Ireland as 1st Ranger Bn / 15 Aug 44 U.S.A. *(destroyed at*
N.Ireland: 19 Jun 42   N.Africa: 8 Nov 42   Sicily: 9 Jul 43   Italy: 9 Sep 43 - **23,24,29,35,36,38**   Z.I:15 Apr 44   *Anzio 31 Jan 44)*
(redes Ranger Inf Bn 1 Aug 43)

1st Reconnaissance Battalion, Special 20 Nov 44 Hollandia New Guinea (5217th Rcn Bn)/15 Aug 45 Manila Philippines   Manila Philippines
New Guinea: 20 Nov 44   Philippines: 19 Jul 45 - **15** *(note: teams inserted into Philippines throughout service) (Filipino personnel)*

2nd Filipino Infantry Battalion 27 Mar 44 Cp Cooke Calif (1st Bn, 2nd Filipino Inf) / 21 Dec 45 Philippines   Manila Philippines
SFPE: 14 Jun 44   New Guinea: 5 Jul 44   Philippines: Unknown - **15**

2nd Provisional Infantry Battalion 8 Dec 44 Ft Read Trinidad / *   Cp Robinson Ark
Trinidad: 8 Dec 44   NOPE: 13 Dec 44 *(R&S Cmd 13 Dec 44)*

2nd Ranger Infantry Battalion 1 Apr 43 Cp Forrest Tenn as 2nd Ranger Bn / 23 Oct 45 Cp Patrick Henry Va   Dol Lukavice Czechoslovakia
NYPE: 23 Nov 43   England: 29 Nov 43   France-ETO: 6 Jun 44 - **25,26,30,32,34**   HRPE: 22 Oct 45 *(redes Ranger Inf Bn 1 Aug 43)*

3rd Army Defense Battalion 11 Oct 43 Oahu Hawaii / 25 Sep 44 Hawaii
Hawaii: 11 Oct 43   Kwajalein: 1 Feb 44   Eniwetok: 19 Feb 44 - **10** *(attached to 7th Inf Div for assault on Kwajalein)*

3rd Ranger Infantry Battalion 21 May 43 Nemours Morocco as 3rd Ranger Bn / 15 Aug 44 U.S.A. *(destroyed at*
N.Africa: 21 May 43   Sicily: 1 Aug 43   Italy: 9 Sep 43 - **24,29,35,36**   Z.I: 15 Apr 44 *(Provisional until 21 Jul 43)*   *Anzio 31 Jan 44)*
(redes Ranger Inf Bn 1 Aug 43)

4th Army Defense Battalion 11 Oct 43 Oahu Hawaii / 5 Feb 45 Kwajalein
Hawaii: 11 Oct 43   Kwajalein: 1 Feb 44 - **10** *(attached to 7th Inf Div for assault on Kwajalein)*

4th Ranger Infantry Battalion 29 May 43 N.Africa as 4th Ranger Bn / 24 Oct 44 Cp Butner N.C. *(decimated at*
N.Africa: 29 May 43   Sicily: 9 Jul 43   Italy: 9 Sep 43 - **24,29,35,36** *(Provisional until 21 Jul 43)*   *Anzio 31 Jan 44)*
(redes Ranger Inf Bn 1 Aug 43)

5th Ranger Infantry Battalion 1 Sep 43 Cp Forrest Tenn / 22 Oct 45 Cp Myles Standish Mass   Markt Grafing Germany
NYPE: 8 Jan 44   England: 17 Jan 44   France-ETO: 6 Jun 44 - **25,26,30,32,34**   BPE: 21 Oct 45

6th Armored Infantry Battalion 20 Jul 44 Bolgheri Italy (6th Armd Inf) / 1 May 46 Germany redes 12th Constab Sqdn   Salzburg Austria
Italy: 20 Jul 44 - **29,31,33,35,38** *(assigned 1st Armd Div)*

6th Ranger Infantry Battalion 24 Sep 44 Hollandia New Guinea (98th FA Bn) / 30 Dec 45 Japan   Clark Field, Philippines
New Guinea: 24 Sep 44   Philippines: 17 Oct 44 - **13,14,15**

7th Armored Infantry Battalion 15 Sep 43 Cp Polk La (2nd Bn, 49th Armd Inf) / 13 Nov 45 Cp Myles Standish Mass   Pilsen Czechoslovakia
NYPE: 7 Nov 44   England: 18 Nov 44   France-ETO: 2 Feb 45 - **25,26,34**   BPE: 12 Nov 45 *(assigned 8th Armd Div)*

8th Armored Infantry Battalion 10 Sep 43 Cp Campbell Ky (480th Armd Inf) / 2 Apr 46 Cp Hood Tex   Cp Cooke Calif
BPE: 6 Feb 45   France-ETO: 17 Feb 45 - **26**   NYPE: 6 Aug 45 *(assigned 20th Armd Div)*

9th Armored Infantry Battalion 15 Sep 43 Cp Cooke Calif (2nd Bn, 50th Armd Inf) / 18 Sep 45 Cp Shanks N.Y.   Jena Germany
NYPE: 11 Feb 44   England: 22 Feb 44   France-ETO: 19 Jul 44 - **25,26,30,32,34**   NYPE: 17 Sep 45 *(assigned 6th Armd Div)*

BATTALION DESIGNATION AND TYPE	FORMED (SOURCE OF UNIT) / INACTIVATION	AUGUST 1945 LOCATION

10th Armored Infantry Battalion   10 Sep 43 Cp Bowie Tex (2nd Bn, 51st Armd Inf) / 1 May 46 Germany redes 10th   Kelheim Germany
BPE: 29 Dec 43   England: 9 Jan 44   France-ETO: 13 Jul 44 - **25,26,30,32,34** *(assigned 4th Armd Div)*   Constab Sqdn

10th Mountain Inf Antitank Battalion   6 Nov 44 Cp Swift Tex (727th AAA Mg Bn) / 17 Nov 45 Cp Carson Colo   Shipment #22050-0 unloading
HRPE: 6 Jan 45   Italy: 18 Jan 45 - **31,33**   HRPE: 10 Aug 45 *(assigned 10th Mtn Div)*

11th Armored Infantry Battalion   20 Jul 44 Bolgheri Italy (2nd Bn, 6th Armd Inf) / 1 May 46 Germany redes 11th   Salzburg Austria
Italy: 20 Jul 44 - **29,31,33,35,38** *(assigned 1st Armd Div)*   Constab Sqdn

14th Armored Infantry Battalion   20 Jul 44 Bolgheri Italy (3rd Bn, 6th Armd Inf) / 1 May 46 Germany redes 14th   Salzburg Austria
Italy: 20 Jul 44 - **29,31,33,35,38** *(assigned 1st Armd Div)*   Constab Sqdn

15th Armored Infantry Battalion   20 Sep 43 Pine Camp N.Y. (2nd Bn, 46th Armd Inf) / 8 Oct 45 Cp Myles Standish   Bad Sachsa Germany
NYPE: 11 Feb 44   England: 23 Feb 44   France-ETO: 25 Jul 44 - **25,26,30,32,34**   BPE: 7 Oct 45 *(assigned 5th Armd Div)*   Mass

16th Armored Infantry Battalion   20 Sep 43 Cp Beale Calif (2nd Bn, 59th Armd Inf) / 9 Nov 45 Cp Cooke Calif   Cp Cooke Calif
·NYPE: 18 Jan 45   England: 29 Jan 45   France-ETO: 29 Jan 45 - **26,34**   HRPE: 23 Jul 45 *(assigned 13th Armd Div)*

17th Armored Infantry Battalion   15 Sep 43 Tenn Mnvr Area (2nd Bn, 56th Armd Inf) / 3 Dec 45 Cp Kilmer N.J.   Tannhausen Germany
NYPE: 20 Sep 44   England: 2 Oct 44   France-ETO: 9 Nov 44 - **25,26,34**   NYPE: 1 Dec 45 *(assigned 12th Armd Div)*

18th Armored Infantry Battalion   10 Sep 43 Cp Chaffee Ark (476th Armd Inf) / 16 Oct 45 Cp Myles Standish Mass   Flashenhutte Germany
NYPE: 5 Feb 45   France-ETO: 17 Feb 45 - **26**   BPE: 15 Oct 45 *(assigned 16th Armd Div)*

19th Armored Infantry Battalion   15 Sep 43 Cp Chaffee Ark (2nd Bn, 62nd Armd Inf) / 16 Sep 45 Cp Patrick Henry Va   Taufkirchen Germany
NYPE: 14 Oct 44   France-ETO: 28 Oct 44 - **25,26,34**   HRPE: 16 Sep 45 *(assigned 14th Armd Div)*

20th Armored Infantry Battalion   15 Sep 43 Cp Gordon Ga (2nd Bn, 54th Armd Inf) / 13 Oct 45 Cp Patrick Henry Va   Murnau Germany
NYPE: 12 Sep 44   France-ETO: 23 Sep 44 - **25,26,34**   HRPE: 13 Oct 45 *(assigned 10th Armd Div)*

21st Armored Infantry Battalion   20 Sep 43 Cp Barkeley Tex (2nd Bn, 55th Armd Inf) / 31 Aug 45 Austria   Spital Austria
NYPE: 29 Sep 44   England: 9 Oct 44   France-ETO: 23 Dec 44 - **25,26,34** *(assigned 11th Armd Div)*

23rd Armored Infantry Battalion   20 Sep 43 Ft Benning Ga (2nd Bn, 48th Armd Inf) / 11 Oct 45 Cp Kilmer N.J.   Eilenberg Germany
NYPE: 7 Jun 44   England: 13 Jun 44   France-ETO: 11 Aug 44 - **25,26,32,34**   NYPE: 10 Oct 45 *(assigned 7th Armd Div)*

27th Armored Infantry Battalion   9 Oct 43 Cp Young Calif (2nd Bn, 52nd Armd Inf) / 13 Oct 45 Cp Patrick Henry Va   Wunsiedel Germany
NYPE: 20 Aug 44   England: 26 Aug 44   France-ETO: 29 Sep 44 - **25,26,34**   HRPE: 12 Oct 45 *(assigned 9th Armd Div)*

38th Armored Infantry Battalion   20 Sep 43 Ft Benning Ga (1st Bn, 48th Armd Inf) / 11 Oct 45 Cp Shanks N.Y.   Dessau Germany
NYPE: 7 Jun 44   England: 13 Jun 44   France-ETO: 11 Aug 44 - **25,26,32,34**   NYPE: 10 Oct 45 *(assigned 7th Armd Div)*

44th Armored Infantry Battalion   20 Sep 43 Cp Cooke Calif (1st Bn, 50th Armd Inf) / 19 Sep 45 Cp Shanks N.Y.   Sommerda Germany
NYPE: 11 Feb 44   England: 22 Feb 44   France-ETO: 19 Jul 44 - **25,26,30,32,34**   NYPE: 18 Sep 45 *(assigned 6th Armd Div)*

46th Armored Infantry Battalion   20 Sep 43 Pine Camp N.Y. (46th Armd Inf) / 13 Oct 45 Cp Myles Standish Mass   Erfurt Germany
NYPE: 11 Feb 44   England: 25 Feb 44   France-ETO: 23 Jul 44 - **25,26,30,32,34**   BPE: 12 Oct 45 *(assigned 5th Armd Div)*

47th Armored Infantry Battalion   20 Sep 43 Pine Camp N.Y. (1st Bn, 47th Armd Inf) / 8 Oct 45 Cp Myles Standish Mass   Werther Klein Germany
NYPE: 11 Feb 44   England: 25 Feb 44   France-ETO: 23 Jul 44 - **25,26,30,32,34**   BPE: 7 Oct 45 *(assigned 5th Armd Div)*

48th Armored Infantry Battalion   20 Sep 43 Ft Benning Ga (48th Armd Inf) / 8 Oct 45 Cp Myles Standish Mass   Roitzsch   Czechoslovakia
NYPE: 7 Jun 44   England: 13 Jun 44   France-ETO: 11 Aug 44 - **25,26,32,34**   BPE: 7 Oct 45 *(assigned 7th Armd Div)*

49th Armored Infantry Battalion   20 Sep 43 Cp Polk La (49th Armd Inf) / 11 Nov 45 Cp Kilmer N.J.   Rokycany Czechoslovakia
NYPE: 7 Nov 44   England: 18 Nov 44   France-ETO: 2 Feb 45 - **25,26,34**   NYPE: 10 Nov 45 *(assigned 8th Armd Div)*

50th Armored Infantry Battalion   20 Sep 43 Cp Cooke Calif (50th Armd Inf) / 18 Sep 45 Cp Shanks N.Y.   Eisenberg Germany
NYPE: 11 Feb 44   England: 22 Feb 44   France-ETO: 19 Jul 44 - **25,26,30,32,34**   NYPE: 17 Sep 45 *(assigned to 6th Armd Div)*

51st Armored Infantry Battalion   10 Sep 43 Cp Bowie Tex (51st Armd Inf) / 1 May 46 Germany redes 51st Constab   Parsberg Germany
BPE: 29 Dec 43   England: 9 Jan 44   France-ETO: 13 Jul 44 - **25,26,30,32,34** *(assigned 4th Armd Div)*   Sqdn

52nd Armored Infantry Battalion   9 Oct 43 Cp Polk La (52nd Armd Inf) / 13 Oct 45 Cp Patrick Henry Va   Schonwald Germany
NYPE: 20 Aug 44   England: 26 Aug 44   France-ETO: 29 Sep 44 - **25,26,34**   HRPE: 12 Oct 45 *(assigned 9th Armd Div)*

53rd Armored Infantry Battalion   10 Sep 43 Cp Bowie Tex (1st Bn, 51st Armd Inf) / 1 May 46 Germany redes 53rd   Essenbach Germany
BPE: 29 Dec 43   England: 8 Jan 44   France-ETO: 13 Jul 44 - **25,26,30,32,34** *(assigned 4th Armd Div)*   Constab Sqdn

54th Armored Infantry Battalion   20 Sep 43 Cp Gordon Ga (54th Armd Inf) / 13 Oct 45 Cp Patrick Henry Va   Oberau Germany
NYPE: 12 Sep 44   France-ETO: 23 Sep 44 - **25,26,34**   HRPE: 13 Oct 45 *(assigned 10th Armd Div)*

55th Armored Infantry Battalion   20 Sep 43 Cp Barkeley Tex (55th Armd Inf) / 31 Aug 45 Austria   Ried Germany
NYPE: 29 Sep 44   England 9 Oct 44   France-ETO: 23 Dec 44 - **25,26,34** *(assigned 11th Armd Div)*

BATTALION DESIGNATION AND TYPE	FORMED (SOURCE OF UNIT)/INACTIVATION	AUGUST 1945 LOCATION

56th Armored Infantry Battalion 11 Nov 43 Tenn Mnvr Area (56th Armd Inf) / 5 Dec 45 Cp Kilmer N.J. Hopfingen Germany
NYPE: 20 Sep 44   England: 2 Oct 44   France-ETO: 9 Nov 44 - **25,26,34**   NYPE: 4 Dec 45 (assigned 12th Armd Div)

58th Armored Infantry Battalion 20 Sep 43 Cp Polk La (1st Bn, 49th Armd Inf)/11 Nov 45 Cp Kilmer N.J. Klatovy Czechoslovakia
NYPE: 7 Nov 44   England: 18 Nov 44   France-ETO: 2 Feb 45 - **25,26,34**   NYPE: 10 Nov 45 (assigned 8th Armd Div)

59th Armored Infantry Battalion 20 Sep 43 Cp Beale Calif (59th Armd Inf) / 9 Nov 45 Cp Cooke Calif Cp Cooke Calif
NYPE: 18 Jan 45   England: 29 Jan 45   France-ETO: 29 Jan 45 - **26,34**   HRPE: 23 Jul 45 (assigned 13th Armd Div)

60th Armored Infantry Battalion 3 Oct 43 Cp Young Calif (1st Bn, 52nd Armd Inf) / 13 Oct 45 Cp Patrick Henry Va Coburg Germany
NYPE: 20 Aug 44   England: 26 Aug 44   France-ETO: 29 Sep 44 - **25,26,34**   HRPE: 12 Oct 45 (assigned 9th Armed Div)

61st Armored Infantry Battalion 20 Sep 43 Cp Gordon Ga (1st Bn, 54th Armd Inf)/23 Oct 45 Cp Patrick Henry Va Mittenwald Germany
NYPE: 12 Sep 44   France-ETO: 23 Sep 44 - **25,26,34**   HRPE: 23 Oct 45 (assigned 10th Armd Div)

62nd Armored Infantry Battalion 20 Sep 43 Cp Chaffee Ark (62nd Armd Inf) / 20 Sep 45 Cp Myles Standish Mass Burghausen Germany
NYPE: 14 Oct 44   France-ETO: 28 Oct 44 - **25,26,34**   BPE: 18 Sep 45 (assigned 14th Armd Div)

63rd Armored Infantry Battalion 20 Sep 43 Cp Barkeley Tex (1st Bn, 55th Armd Inf)/31 Aug 45 Austria Bad Hall Germany
NYPE: 29 Sep 44   England: 9 Oct 44   France-ETO: 23 Dec 44 - **25,26,34** (assigned 11th Armd Div)

64th Armored Infantry Battalion 10 Sep 43 Ft Knox Ky (1st Bn, 476th Armd Inf) / 13 Oct 45 Cp Myles Standish Mass Ceminy Germany
NYPE: 5 Feb 45   France-ETO: 17 Feb 45 - **26**   BPE: 12 Oct 45 (assigned 16th Armd Div)

65th Armored Infantry Battalion 10 Sep 43 Cp Campbell Ky (1st Bn, 480th Armd Inf) / 2 Apr 46 Cp Hood Tex Cp Cooke Calif
BPE: 6 Feb 45   France-ETO: 17 Feb 45 - **26**   NYPE: 6 Aug 45 (assigned 20th Armd Div)

66th Armored Infantry Battalion 11 Nov 43 Tenn Mnvr Area (1st Bn, 56th Armd Inf) / 5 Dec 45 Cp Kilmer N.J. Ellwangen Germany
NYPE: 20 Sep 44   England: 2 Oct 44   France-ETO: 9 Nov 44 - **25,26,34**   NYPE: 4 Dec 45 (assigned 12th Armd Div)

67th Armored Infantry Battalion 20 Sep 43 Cp Beale Calif (1st Bn, 59th Armd Inf)/12 Nov 45 Cp Cooke Calif Cp Cooke Calif
NYPE: 18 Jan 45   England: 29 Jan 45   France-ETO: 29 Jan 45 - **26,34**   NYPE: 23 Jul 45 (assigned 13th Armd Div)

68th Armored Infantry Battalion 20 Sep 43 Cp Chaffee Ark (1st Bn, 62nd Armd Inf) / 19 Sep 45 Cp Myles Standish Mass Ampfling Germany
NYPE: 14 Oct 44   France-ETO: 28 Oct 44 - **25,26,34**   BPE: 17 Sep 45 (assigned 14th Armd Div)

69th Armored Infantry Battalion 10 Sep 43 Cp Chaffee Ark (2nd Bn, 476th Armd Inf) /14 Oct 45 Cp Shanks N.Y. Prachomety Czechoslovakia
NYPE: 5 Feb 45   France-ETO: 17 Feb 45 - **26**   NYPE: 13 Oct 45 (assigned 16th Armd Div)

70th Armored Infantry Battalion 10 Sep 43 Cp Campbell Ky (2nd Bn, 480th Armd Inf) / 20 Mar 46 Cp Hood Tex Cp Cooke Calif
BPE: 6 Feb 45   France-ETO: 19 Feb 45 - **26**   NYPE: 6 Aug 45 (assigned 20th Armd Div)

73rd Infantry Battalion 1 Sep 42 Greenland (2nd Bn, 3rd Inf) /23 Jun 44 Cp Butner N.C.
Greenland: 1 Sep 42   BPE: 7 Mar 44 (four line companies of Bn activated at Ft Snelling Minn 1 Sep 42 and arrived in Greenland on 11 Nov 42)
(Greenland Base Cmd)

75th Composite Infantry Training Battalion 15 Jun 42 Cp Edwards Mass /12 Dec 43 Cp Pickett Va   (Amphibious Training Cmd)

88th Airborne Infantry Battalion 10 Oct 41 Ft Benning Ga /15 Jun 42 Ft Bragg N.C. redes 88th Inf Regt
(Airborne Command)

93rd Infantry Antitank Battalion 1 Jun 40 Ft Benning Ga as 93rd Antitank Bn/15 Dec 41 redes 893rd Tank Destroyer Bn
(93rd Antitank Bn redes 93rd Inf Bn [Antitank] 6 Jul 40 which was redes 93rd Infantry Antitank Bn 21 Jul 41) (II Army Corps)

94th Infantry Antitank Battalion 1 Jun 40 Ft Benning Ga 94th Antitank Bn/15 Dec 41 redes 894th Tank Destroyer Bn
(94th Antitank Bn redes 94th Bn [Antitank] 6 Jul 40 which was redes 94th Infantry Antitank Bn 24 Jul 41) (IV Army Corps)

99th Infantry Antitank Battalion 24 Jul 40 Ft Lewis Wash /15 Dec 41 redes 899th Tank Destroyer Bn
(99th Antitank Bn redes 99th Inf Antitank Bn 24 Jul 41) (IX Army Corps)

99th Infantry Battalion (Separate) 15 Aug 43 Cp Ripley Minn / 2 Nov 45 Cp Myles Standish Mass Drammen Norway
NYPE: 5 Sep 43   England: 15 Sep 43   France-ETO: 21 Jun 44 - **25,30,32,34**   BPE: 1 Nov 45 (personnel of Norwegian ancestry)
(assigned 474th Inf 25 Jan 45)

100th Infantry Battalion (Nisei) 15 Jun 42 Oakland Calif /15 Aug 46 Hawaii Ghedi Italy
NYPE: 21 Aug 43   N.Africa: 2 Sep 43   Italy: 25 Nov 43   France: 15 Aug 44   Italy: 25 Mar 45 - **29,31,33,34,35,37**   Hawaii: 9 Aug 46
(assigned 442nd Inf 10 Aug 44)
The task of guarding the Hawaiian Islands had been shared by the 298th and 299th Infantry Regiments, Hawaiian National Guard units that had been called into federal service in 1940. By late 1941 many of their enlisted men and some of their officers were of Japanese ancestry. When sufficient replacements from the mainland finally arrived in May 1942, the Hawaiian Department withdrew these "Nisei" troops from the 298th and 299th Infantry Regiments, organized them into a provisional battalion, and on 5 Jun 1942 shipped them to the mainland. This group of 29 officers and 1,277 enlisted men officially became the 100th Infantry Battalion at Oakland, California, on 15 Jun 1942.

101st Infantry Battalion (Separate) 15 Dec 42 Cp Atterbury Ind / 27 May 43 Cp Atterbury Ind (personnel of Austrian ancestry)

BATTALION DESIGNATION AND TYPE	FORMED (SOURCE OF UNIT) / INACTIVATION	AUGUST 1945 LOCATION

101st Infantry Antitank Battalion NY NG
(redes Inf AT Bn 24 Jul 41)
6 Jan 41 Albany N.Y. as Antitank Bn / 15 Dec 41 Ft Benning Ga redes 801st TD Bn

102nd Infantry Antitank Battalion NY NG
(redes Inf AT Bn 24 Jul 41)
13 Jan 41 Hempstead N.Y. as Antitank Bn / 15 Dec 41 Cp Shelby Miss redes 802nd TD Bn

103rd Infantry Antitank Battalion Wash NG
(redes Inf AT Bn 24 Jul 41)
10 Feb 41 Tacoma Wash as Antitank Bn / 15 Dec 41 Ft Lewis Wash redes 803rd TD Bn

104th Infantry Antitank Battalion N.M. NG
(redes Inf AT Bn 24 Jul 41)
6 Jan 41 Santa Fe N.M. as Antitank Bn / 15 Dec 41 Cp San Luis Obispo Calif redes 804th TD Bn

105th Infantry Antitank Battalion Pa. NG
(redes Inf AT Bn 24 Jul 41)
3 Feb 41 Harrisburg Pa as Antitank Bn / 15 Dec 41 Ft George G. Meade redes 805th TD Bn

122nd Infantry Battalion (Separate)
5 Jan 43 Cp Carson Colo / 23 Aug 46 Cairo Egypt — Cairo Egypt
Charleston PE: 24 Dec 43   Egypt: 21 Jan 44 *(122nd Inf Bn redes* **Third Contingent, Unit "B," Operational Group,** *Office of Strategic Services* [OSS] *1 Oct 43 at Cp Carson Colo) (personnel of Greek ancestry)*

170th Infantry Battalion (Separate)
2 Jan 43 Ft Sill Okla / 14 Feb 44 Cp Bowie Tex   *(R&S Cmd Arty Sch 2 Jan 43)*

171st Infantry Battalion (Separate)
(attached Second Army)
5 Sep 44 Cp Shelby Miss (1st Bn, 442nd Inf) / 19 Feb 45 Cp Shelby Miss

202nd Infantry Battalion (Separate)
(North African Service Cmd)
1 Sep 43 N.Africa (2nd Bn, 156th Inf) / 25 Feb 44 N.Africa

203rd Infantry Battalion (Separate)
Alaska: 26 Jan 44   SPE: 16 Dec 44 *(R&S Cmd 18 Feb 45)*
26 Jan 44 Alaska (1st Bn, 58th Inf) / 2 Mar 45 Cp Shelby Miss

204th Infantry Battalion (Separate)
Alaska: 26 Jan 44   SPE: 4 Jan 45 *(R&S Cmd 15 Feb 45)*
26 Jan 44 Ft Glenn Alaska (2nd Bn, 58th Inf) / 8 Mar 45 Cp Shelby Miss

205th Infantry Battalion (Separate)
Alaska: 10 Feb 44   Attu I: 7 Aug 44 SPE: 10 Jan 45 *(R&S Cmd 15 Feb 45)*
10 Feb 44 Ft Mears Alaska (3rd Bn, 58th Inf) / 8 Mar 45 Cp Shelby Miss

206th Infantry Battalion (Separate)
Alaska: 26 Jan 44   SPE: 14 Feb 45 *(R&S Cmd 14 Apr 45)*
26 Jan 44 Alaska (1st Bn, 198th Inf) / 9 May 45 Cp Shelby Miss

207th Infantry Battalion (Separate)
Dutch West Indies: 1 Sep 43   Trinidad: 22 Feb 44
1 Sep 43 Curacao Dutch West Indies (elmts 166th Inf) / 28 Feb 46 Trinidad — Ft Read Trinidad

208th Infantry Battalion (Separate)
Alaska: 26 Jan 44   SPE: 24 Feb 45 *(R&S Cmd 14 Apr 45)*
26 Jan 44 Alaska (1st Bn, 297th Inf) / 16 May 45 Cp Shelby Miss

209th Infantry Battalion (Separate)
Dutch West Indies: 1 Jun 44   Puerto Rico: 26 Jul 44
1 Jun 44 Aruba Dutch West Indies / 28 Feb 46 Puerto Rico — Losey Field Puerto Rico

210th Infantry Battalion (Separate)
Dutch West Indies: 1 Jun 44   Puerto Rico: 26 Jul 44
1 Jun 44 Curacao Dutch West Indies / 28 Feb 46 Puerto Rico — Losey Field Puerto Rico

367th Armored Infantry Battalion (Cld)
NYPE: 7 Feb 43   Morocco: 19 Feb 43   Marshall Liberia: 10 Mar 43   Morocco-Algeria: 21 Jan 44 - **35**
9 Jun 42 Cp Davis N.C. (1st Bn, 367th Inf) / 10 Jan 45 Corsica

470th Infantry Battalion (Separate)
Newfoundland: 10 Aug 43   BPE: 7 Sep 45
10 Aug 43 Ft Pepperrell Newfoundland (3rd Bn, 3rd Inf) / 8 Sep 45 Cp Myles Standish Mass — Newfoundland

471st Infantry Battalion (Separate)
10 Aug 43 Ft McAndrew Newfoundland (1st Bn, 3rd Inf) / 1 Jun 45 Newfoundland

472nd Infantry Battalion (Separate)
3 Sep 43 Ft Brady Mich (1st Bn, 131st Inf) / 10 May 44 Cp Rucker Ala

501st Parachute Battalion
1 Oct 40 Ft Benning Ga (1st Prcht Bn) / 15 Feb 42 Ft Benning Ga redes 1st Bn 501st Prcht Inf

502nd Parachute Battalion
(attached Chief of Infantry)
1 Jul 41 Ft Benning Ga / 24 Feb 42 Ft Benning Ga redes 1st Bn 502nd Prcht Inf

503rd Parachute Infantry Battalion
(attached Chief of Infantry)
22 Aug 41 Ft Benning Ga / 24 Feb 42 Ft Benning Ga redes 1st Bn 503rd Prcht Inf

504th Parachute Infantry Battalion
(attached Chief of Infantry)
5 Oct 41 Ft Benning Ga / 24 Feb 42 Ft Benning Ga consolidated with 2nd Bn 503rd Prcht Inf

509th Parachute Infantry Battalion
Italy: 10 Dec 43   France-ETO: 15 Aug 44 - **24,25,29,34,35,37** *(assigned 101st A/B Div 18 Nov 44–18 Dec 44)*
10 Dec 43 Venafro Italy (2nd Bn, 509th Prcht Inf) / 1 Mar 45 France

BATTALION DESIGNATION AND TYPE	FORMED (SOURCE OF UNIT)/INACTIVATION	*Active through 1946	AUGUST 1945 LOCATION

526th Armored Infantry Battalion
20 Mar 43 Ft Knox Ky / 25 Nov 45 Germany — Wiesbaden Germany
NYPE: 19 Mar 44   England: 12 Apr 44   France-ETO: 24 Aug 44 - **25,26,32,34**

527th Armored Infantry Battalion
20 Mar 43 Ft Knox Ky /12 Jun 44 Ft Knox Ky — *(R&S Cmd 19 Feb 44)*

528th Armored Infantry Battalion
20 Mar 43 Ft Knox Ky / 31 Aug 43 Ft Knox Ky — *(Armored Force)*

529th Armored Infantry Battalion
28 Mar 43 Cp Cooke Calif / 31 Aug 43 Cp Cooke Calif — *(II Corps 31 Mar 43)*

530th Armored Infantry Battalion
28 Mar 43 Cp Cooke Calif / 31 Aug 43 Cp Cooke Calif — *(II Corps 31 Mar 43)*

531st Armored Infantry Battalion
28 Mar 43 Cp Cooke Calif / 31 Aug 43 Cp Cooke Calif — *(II Corps 28 Mar 43)*

532nd Armored Infantry Battalion
10 May 43 Cp Chaffee Ark / 31 Aug 43 Cp Chaffee Ark — *(Armored Force)*

533rd Armored Infantry Battalion
25 May 43 Cp Chaffee Ark / 31 Aug 43 Cp Chaffee Ark — *(Armored Force)*

534th Armored Infantry Battalion
(Armored Force)
31 Mar 43 Cp Chaffee Ark / 27 Oct 43 Cp Chaffee Ark redes 534th Amphib Tractor Bn

535th Armored Infantry Battalion
31 Mar 43 Cp Polk La /10 Jan 44 Cp Cooke Calif — *(Third Army 1 May 43)*

536th Armored Infantry Battalion
(Third Army 1 May 43)
31 Mar 43 Cp Polk La / 29 Jan 44 Ft Ord Calif redes 536th Amphib Tractor Bn

537th Armored Infantry Battalion
25 May 43 Cp Campbell Ky / 31 Aug 43 Cp Campbell Ky — *(Second Army 11 Jul 43)*

538th Armored Infantry Battalion
27 May 43 Ft Benning Ga / 31 Aug 43 Ft Benning Ga — *(Armored Force)*

539th Infantry Battalion
31 Mar 43 Ft Riley Kans / 31 Aug 43 Ft Riley Kans — *(Armored Force)*

540th Armored Infantry Battalion
31 Mar 43 Cp Beale Calif / 31 Aug 43 Cp Beale Calif — *(II Corps)*

542nd Parachute Infantry Battalion
(Airborne Center)
17 Mar 44 Ft Benning Ga (542nd Prcht Inf) /1 Jul 45 Cp Mackall N.C.

550th Airborne Infantry Battalion
1 Jul 41 Howard Field Panama Canal Zone /1 Mar 45 Cheniers France, assets to 3rd Bn,
Panama: 1 Jul 41   SFPE: 30 Aug 43   HRPE: 23 Apr 44   Italy: 24 May 44   Sicily: 1 Jun 44   194th Glider Infantry
France-ETO: 15 Aug 44 - **25,34,35,37**

555th Parachute Infantry Battalion (Cld)
25 Nov 44 Cp Mackall N.C. / * — Pendleton Field Oreg

2671st Special Reconnaissance Battalion
1 Aug 44 Caserta Italy (Fifth Army Operational Group)/1 Oct 45 Austria — Salzburg Austria
Italy: 1 Aug 44 (**OSS** *Operational Group in N.Africa since 4 May 43)* - **29,31,33,35**   *(Office of Strategic Services)*

5217th Reconnaissance Battalion, Special   8 Oct 43 Cp Tabragalba Australia/20 Nov 44 New Guinea redes 1st Rcn Bn, Special
Australia: 8 Oct 43   New Guinea: 21 Nov 43 *(Teams inserted into Philippines since inception) (Filipino personnel)*

*Active through 1946

Chapter 15

Chemical Mortar Battalions

Battalions:

1–3, 71, 72, 80–100, 443, 483, 534, 537, 560, 781, 782

⭐ EXAMPLE — HOW TO USE THIS TABLE

Unit Designation and Type	Date Formed and Location (Source of Unit) / Inactivation and Location	August 1945 Location

Overseas Wartime Locations followed by - **Campaign Key Numbers** and PE return to United States, if applicable or space allows
(notes and remarks in parenthesis)

100th Chemical Mortar Battalion   30 Aug 44 La Fagianeria Italy as Chem Bn (Mtz) (637th AAA Bn) /13 Oct 45 Cp Myles   Filigare Italy
Italy: 30 Aug 44 - **31,33,35**   BPE: 12 Oct 45 *(redes Chem Mor Bn 15 Nov 44)*   Standish Mass

In this example, the 100th Chemical Mortar Battalion was formed as the 100th Chemical Battalion (Motorized) from the 637th Antiaircraft Artillery Battalion at La Fagianeria, Italy, on 30 August 1944. The previous service of that unit can be tracked in Chapter 38. It served in the North Apennines, Po Valley, and Rome-Arno campaigns. This information was derived by indexing the boldfaced campaign key numbers with Appendix I. It was redesignated as the 100th Chemical Mortar Battalion on 15 November 1944 and was located in Filigare, Italy, during August 1945. It arrived at Boston Port of Embarkation on 12 October 1945 and was inactivated at Camp Myles Standish, Massachusetts, on 13 October 1945.

BATTALION DESIGNATION AND TYPE	FORMED (SOURCE OF UNIT) / INACTIVATION *Active through 1946	AUGUST 1945 LOCATION

1st Chemical Mortar Battalion, Co A   P   Hawaii / 12 Mar 42 Hawaii redes 91st Chem Co

2nd Chemical Mortar Battalion   P   Edgewood Arsenal Md as Chem Bn (Mtz) / 26 Jul 46 Germany   Niehendorf Germany
HRPE: 4 Jun 43   N.Africa: 22 Jun 43   Sicily: 10 Jul 43   Italy: 9 Sep 43   France-ETO: 15 Aug 44 - **25,26,29,34,35,36,37**
(redes Chem Mor Bn 31 Dec 44)

3rd Chemical Mortar Battalion   1 Jan 42 Ft Benning as Chem Bn (Mtz) / 2 Jan 46 Cp Patrick Henry Va   Gmunden Austria
BPE: 20 Apr 43   N.Africa: 28 Apr 43   Sicily: 10 Jul 43   Italy: 28 Oct 43   France-ETO: 15 Aug 44 - **25,26,29,34,35,36,37**
(redes Chem Mor Bn 11 Mar 45)

71st Chemical Mortar Battalion   7 Dec 44 Cp Shelby Miss (479th AAA Bn) / 18 Jan 46 Vancouver Bks Wash   **USS** *Zeilin* **(AP.9)** at sea
SPE: 22 Jul 45 Okinawa: 22 Aug 45 - **19**   SPE: 17 Jan 46

72nd Chemical Mortar Battalion   7 Dec 44 Cp Shelby Miss (560th AAA Bn) / 18 Apr 46 Hawaii   Oahu Hawaii
SPE: 20 Jun 45   Hawaii: 26 Jun 45

80th Chemical Mortar Battalion   30 Jun 44 Cp Swift Tex as Chem Bn (Mtz)/1 Feb 46 Cp Stoneman Calif   Philippine Islands
SFPE: 26 Jan 45   Philippines: 26 Feb 45 - **13,20**   SFPE: 30 Jan 46 *(redes Chem Mor Bn 4 Mar 45)*

81st Chemical Mortar Battalion   25 Apr 42 Ft D.A. Russell Tex as Chem Bn (Mtz) / 7 Nov 45 Ft Leonard Wood Mo   Branau Germany
NYPE: 21 Oct 43   England: 2 Nov 43   France-ETO: 6 Jun 44 - **25,26,30,32,34**   NYPE: 2 Sep 45 *(redes Chem Mor Bn 22 Feb 45)*

82nd Chemical Mortar Battalion   25 Apr 42 Ft Bliss Tex as Chem Bn (Mtz) /*   Philippine Islands
SFPE: 27 Jun 43   New Caledonia: 19 Jul 43   Guadalcanal: 3 Nov 43   Bougainville: 15 Jan 44   Philippines: 11 Jan 45 - **3,14,16**
(redes Chem Mor Bn 16 Mar 45)

83rd Chemical Mortar Battalion   10 Jun 42 Cp Gordon Ga as Chem Bn (Mtz) / 26 Nov 45 Cp Myles Standish Mass   Hall Germany
BPE: 29 Apr 43   N.Africa: 11 May 43   Sicily: 10 Jul 43   Italy: 9 Sep 43   France-ETO: 15 Aug 44 - **24,25,26,29,34,35,36,37**
(redes Chem Mor Bn 31 Dec 44)

84th Chemical Mortar Battalion   5 Jun 42 Cp Rucker Ala as Chem Bn (Mtz) / 25 Sep 45 Italy   Lucca Italy
BPE: 29 Apr 43   N.Africa: 11 May 43   Italy: 9 Sep 43 - **24,29,31,33,35** *(redes Chem Mor Bn 8 Nov 44)*

85th Chemical Mortar Battalion   5 Jun 43 Ft. D.A. Russell Tex as Chem Bn (Mtz) / 31 May 46 Philippines   Philippine Islands
SFPE: 20 Jul 44   New Guinea: 24 Aug 44   Los Negros I: 4 Oct 44   Philippines: 20 Oct 44 - **3,13,14,15** *(redes Chem Mor Bn 17 Dec 44)*

86th Chemical Mortar Battalion   17 May 43 Cp Swift Tex as Chem Bn (Mtz)/*   Cp Campbell Ky
NYPE: 19 Apr 44   England: 26 Apr 44   France-ETO: 30 Jun 44 - **25,26,30,32,34**   NYPE: 10 Jul 45 *(redes Chem Mor Bn 15 Feb 45)*

87th Chemical Mortar Battalion   22 May 43 Cp Rucker Ala as Chem Bn (Mtz) / 6 Nov 45 Ft Benning Ga   Ft Benning Ga
NYPE: 31 Mar 44   England: 7 Apr 44   France-ETO: 6 Jun 44 - **25,26,30,32,34**   NYPE: 2 Aug 45 *(redes Chem Mor Bn 26 Apr 45)*

88th Chemical Mortar Battalion   29 May 43 Cp Rucker Ala as Chem Bn (Mtz) / 29 Dec 45 Cp Anza Calif   Ie Shnima
SFPE: 30 Apr 44   Hawaii: 6 May 44   Saipan (Co C only): 17 Jun 44   Philippines: 20 Oct 44   Okinawa: 1 Apr 45   Ie Shima 16 Apr 45 -
13,19,21 *(redes Chem Mor Bn 15 Feb 45)*

89th Chemical Mortar Battalion   15 Nov 43 Cp Roberts Calif as Chem Bn (Mtz) / 29 Oct 45 Ft Jackson S.C.   Ft Jackson, S.C.
BPE: 19 Nov 44   England: 2 Dec 44   France-ETO: Feb 45 - **26,34**   NYPE: 5 Jul 45 *(redes Chem Mor Bn 17 Dec 44)*

90th Chemical Mortar Battalion   10 Feb 44 Ft Bragg N.C. as Chem Bn (Mtz) / 20 Feb 46 Ft Jackson S.C.   Ft Jackson S.C.
NYPE: 22 Oct 44   England: 2 Nov 44   France-ETO: 3 Feb 45 - **26,34**   NYPE: 6 Jul 45 *(redes Chem Mor Bn 3 Dec 44)*

BATTALION DESIGNATION AND TYPE	FORMED (SOURCE OF UNIT)/INACTIVATION *Active through 1946	AUGUST 1945 LOCATION
91st Chemical Mortar Battalion BPE: 11 Oct 44 England: 19 Oct 44 France-ETO: 21 Oct 44 - 25,26,34 NYPE: 10 Jul 45 (redes Chem Mor Bn 22 Feb 45)	15 Feb 44 Cp Joseph T Robinson as Chem Bn (Mtz) / *	Cp Swift Tex
92nd Chemical Mortar Battalion England: 9 Feb 44 France-ETO: 27 Jun 44 - 25,26,30,32,34 NYPE: 3 Aug 45 (redes Chem Mor Bn 15 Dec 44)	9 Feb 44 Brockley Combe England as Chem Bn (Mtz) / 27 Oct 45 Cp San Luis Obispo Calif	Shipment #10106-U unloading
93rd Chemical Mortar Battalion NYPE: 20 Jan 45 France-ETO: 29 Jan 45 - 26 NYPE: 4 Jul 45 (redes Chem Mor Bn 18 Nov 44)	24 Mar 44 Cp Rucker Ala as Chem Bn (Mtz) / 20 Oct 45 Ft Bragg N.C.	Ft Bragg N.C.
94th Chemical Mortar Battalion NYPE: 21 Jan 45 England: 30 Jan 45 France-ETO: 4 Mar 45 - 26,34 NYPE: 13 Jul 45 (redes Chem Mor Bn 11 Jan 45)	24 Mar 44 Ft Jackson S.C. as Chem Bn (Mtz) / 5 Nov 45 Cp Shelby Miss	Cp Shelby Miss
95th Chemical Mortar Battalion NYPE: 18 Jan 45 France-ETO: 29 Jan 45 - 26 NYPE: 6 Jul 45 (redes Chem Mor Bn 14 Nov 44)	1 Apr 44 Cp Polk La as Chem Bn (Mtz)/19 Dec 45 Cp Shelby Miss	Cp Shelby Miss
96th Chemical Mortar Battalion NYPE: 11 Feb 45 England: 18 Feb 45 France-ETO: 10 Mar 45 - 26 NYPE: 13 Feb 46 (redes Chem Mor Bn 11 Jan 45)	1 Apr 44 Cp Livingston La as Chem Bn (Mtz) / 14 Feb 46 Cp Kilmer N.J.	
97th Chemical Mortar Battalion NYPE: 3 Feb 45 England: 13 Feb 45 France-ETO: 26 Feb 45 - 26 NYPE: 6 Jul 45 (redes Chem Mor Bn 16 Feb 45)	5 May 44 Ft Leonard Wood as Chem Bn (Mtz) / 23 Nov 45 Cp Polk La	Cp Polk La
98th Chemical Mortar Battalion New Guinea: 24 Jun 44 Philippines: 9 Jan 45 - 14,15 LAPE: 24 Dec 45 (redes Chem Mor Bn 20 Mar 45)	24 Jun 44 Buna New Guinea (641st TD Bn) as Chem Bn (Mtz) / 26 Dec 45 Cp Anza Calif	Philippine Islands
99th Chemical Mortar Battalion Italy: 28 Aug 44 France-ETO: 24 Nov 44 - 25,26,34,35 NYPE: 6 Jul 45 (redes Chem Mor Bn 31 Dec 44)	28 Aug 44 Casserta Italy as Chem Bn (Mtz) (442nd AAA Bn) / 18 Oct 45 Cp Chaffee	Cp Chaffee Ark
100th Chemical Mortar Battalion Italy: 30 Aug 44 - 31,33,35 BPE: 12 Oct 45 (redes Chem Mor Bn 15 Nov 44)	30 Aug 44 La Fagianeria Italy as Chem Bn (Mtz) (637th AAA Bn)/13 Oct 45 Cp Myles Standish Mass	Filigare Italy
443rd Chemical Mortar Battalion	1 Jul 45 Cp Hood Tex (443rd FA Bn) / 22 Sep 45 Cp Hood Tex	Cp Hood Tex
483rd Chemical Mortar Battalion	1 Jul 45 Cp Hood Tex (483rd FA Bn) / 22 Sep 45 Cp Hood Tex	Cp Hood Tex
534th Chemical Mortar Battalion	5 Jul 45 Cp Gruber Okla (534th FA Bn) / 8 Sep 45 Cp Gruber Okla	Cp Gruber Okla
537th Chemical Mortar Battalion	5 Jul 45 Cp Gruber Okla (537th FA Bn) / 8 Sep 45 Cp Gruber Okla	Cp Gruber Okla
560th Chemical Mortar Battalion	9 Jul 45 Ft Bragg N.C. (560th FA Bn) / 22 Sep 45 Ft Bragg N.C.	Ft Bragg N.C.
781st Chemical Mortar Battalion	5 Jul 45 Cp Bowie Tex (781st FA Bn) / 8 Sep 45 Cp Bowie Tex	Cp Bowie Tex
782nd Chemical Mortar Battalion	5 Jul 45 Cp Bowie Tex (782nd FA Bn) / 8 Sep 45 Cp Bowie Tex	Cp Bowie Tex

*Active through 1946

Chapter 16

Miscellaneous Infantry Organizations

Army Garrison Forces:

Anguar Island/APO 264, Apanama, Baker/APO 457, Canton/APO 914, Christmas Island/
APO 915, Eighth Army Area Cmd/APO 248, Engebi Island, Fanning Island/APO 967, Hawaii
District/APO 960, Guam/APO 246, Ie Shima/APO 245, Iwo Jima/APO 86, Kikai Jima/APO 458,
Kwajalein/APO 241, Makin/Seventh, Maui/APO 961, Kauai/APO 962, Miyako Jima/APO 457,
Okinawa/APO 331, Palmyra/APO 458, Saipan/APO 244, Tarawa/APO 240, Tinian/APO 247

Other Infantry Organizations:

Alamo Scouts, Alaska Scouts, Jingpaw or *Kachin Rangers*

GARRISON FORCE	FORMED (SOURCE OF GARRISON)/INACTIVATION
Army Garrison Force APO 264 Anguar Island (Palau Is) Service as Garrison: 30 Sep 44–12 Jul 45	22 Aug 44 Oahu Hawaii/12 Jul 45 Anguar Island
Army Garrison Force Apamama or Abemama (Gilbert Is) Service as Garrison: 16 Mar 44–18 Oct 44	22 Feb 44 Oahu Hawaii/22 Dec 44 Hawaii
Army Task Force APO 457 Baker Island Service as Garrison: 1 Sep 43–26 Mar 44	11 Aug 43 Oahu Hawaii/10 Apr 44 Hawaii
Army Garrison Force APO 914 Canton Island Service as Garrison: 30 Jun 44–past 14 Aug 45	30 Jun 44 (Canton Def Force which had landed 13 Feb 42)/unknown
Army Garrison Force APO 915 Christmas Island Service as Garrison: 30 Jun 44–past 14 Aug 45	30 Jun 44 (Task Force which had landed 11 Feb 42)/unknown
Army Garrison Force APO 248 (Eighth Army Area Command) Service as Garrison: 20 Oct 44–past 14 Aug 45 Campaigns: Leyte	17 Jun 44 Ft Kamehameha Hawaii/unknown
Army Garrison Force Engebi Island (Marshall Is) Service as Garrison: 19 Feb 44–20 Sep 44	19 Feb 44 (3rd Army Def Bn) Kwajalein/25 Sep 44 Hawaii
Army Garrison Force APO 967 Fanning Island Service as Garrison: 10 Nov 42–7 Jul 45	10 Nov 42 (Co L 21st Inf) Fanning I/12 Jul 45 Hawaii
Army Garrison Force APO 960 Hawaii District Service as Garrison: 30 Jun 44–past 14 Aug 45	30 Jun 44 (Garrison Force of 5 May 41)/unknown
Army Garrison Force APO 246 Guam (Marianas Is) Service as Garrison: 2 Aug 44–past 14 Aug 45 Campaigns: Western Pacific	26 May 44 Oahu Hawaii/unknown
Army Garrison Force APO 245 Ie Shima (Ryukyus Is) Service as Garrison: 16 Apr 45–past 14 Aug 45 Campaigns: Ryukyus	24 Jan 45 Oahu Hawaii/5 Oct 45 Okinawa
Army Garrison Force APO 86 Iwo Jima Service as Garrison: 19 Feb 45–past 14 Aug 45 Campaigns: Air Offensive Japan	2 Dec 44 Ft Kamehameha Hawaii/2 Sep 45 Iwo Jima
Army Garrison Force APO 458 Kikai Jima (Ryukyus Is) Service as Garrison: never served outside Hawaii	14 Mar 45 Schofield Bks Hawaii/26 Jul 45 Hawaii
Army Garrison Force APO 241 Kwajalein (Marshall Is) Service as Garrison: 1 Feb 44–8 Aug 45	11 Oct 43 (3rd & 4th Army Def Bus) Hawaii/8 Aug 45 Kwajalein
7th Garrison Force Makin Atoll (Gilbert Is) Service as Garrison: 21 Nov 43–3 Feb 45	7 Oct 43 Oahu Hawaii/3 Feb 45 Makin Atoll
Army Garrison Force APO 961 Maui District (Hawaii Is) Service as Garrison: 30 Jun 44–past 14 Aug 45 Campaigns: Central Pacific	30 Jun 44 Maui, Molokai, Lanai, Kahoolawe/unknown
Army Garrison Force APO 962 Kauai District (Hawaiian Is) Service as Garrison: 30 Jun 44–past 14 Aug 45	30 Jun 44 Kauai, Nilhau/unknown
Army Garrison Force APO 457 Miyako Jima (Ryukyus) Service as Garrison: never served outside Hawaii	11 Mar 45 Schofield Bks Hawaii/15 Jul 45 Hawaii
Army Garrison Force APO 331 Okinawa (Ryukyus) Service as Garrison: 1 Apr 45–past 14 Aug 45 Campaigns: Ryukyus	13 Dec 44 Schofield Bks Hawaii/5 Oct 45 Okinawa
Army Task Force APO 458 Palmyra (Line Is south of Oahu) Service as Garrison: 7 Oct 43–unknown	30 Sep 43 Oahu Hawaii/16 May 44 Hawaii
Army Garrison Force APO 244 Saipan (Marianas Is) Service as Garrison: 16 Jun 44–past Aug 45 Campaigns: Western Pacific	11 Apr 44 Oahu Hawaii/unknown
Army Garrison Force APO 240 Tarawa (Gilbert Is) Service as Garrison: 15 Mar 44–unknown	22 Feb 44 Oahu Hawaii/22 Dec 44 Hawaii
Army Garrison Force APO 247 Tinian (Marianas Is) Service as Garrison: 17 Oct 44–past 14 Aug 45 Campaigns: Western Pacific	26 May 44 Oahu Hawaii/27 Mar 46 West Pac Base Cmd

Alamo Scouts

27 Dec 43 first of ten teams of Alamo Scouts initiated training at the *Alamo Scout Training Center* at Fergusson Island near Goodenough Island New Guinea; assigned to Sixth Army and performed over sixty combat and intelligence-gathering raids in both New Guinea and the Philippine Islands.

Campaigns: *Leyte*

Alaskan Scouts

1 Oct 41 activated as the Alaskan Defense Command Scout Detachment (Provisional) at Ft Richardson Alaska and composed of Eskimo, Indian, Aleut, and prospector volunteers; assaulted both Attu and Kiska and redesignated the 1st Combat Intelligence Platoon *(Alaskan Scouts)* on 6 Nov 44.

Campaigns: *Aleutian Islands*

Jingpaw or Kachin Rangers

May 42 OSS Detachment 101 arrived in India and stationed at New Delhi; recruited force from the Kachin hill tribe of north-central Burma residing in area where the Ledo Road was constructed and assaulted Ramree Island Burma on 27 Jan 45; assaulted Lawksawk Burma 9–13 Apr 45 and 11 May 45; assaulted Mongkung Burma 11 Apr 45 and assaulted Heshi Burma 23 Apr 45; assaulted both Indaw and Rangoon Burma on 2 May 45; OSS Detachment 101 discontinued on 12 Jul 45.

Campaigns: *India-Burma, Central Burma*

Part IV

Armored Forces of the U.S. Army in World War II

Chapter 17

Armored Brigades

1st Armored Brigade

15 Jul 40 activated at Ft Knox Ky and assigned 1st Armored Division; moved to Cp Polk La 1 Sep 41 and to the Ft Jackson S.C. area 30 Oct 41; there disbanded 1 Jan 42.

2nd Armored Brigade

15 Jul 40 activated at Ft Benning Ga and assigned 2nd Armored Div; moved to Panama City Fla 13 Dec 40 and returned Ft Benning Ga 17 Dec 40; arrived Grand Cane La 12 Aug 41 and returned Ft Benning Ga 29 Sep 41; transferred to the Ft Jackson S.C. area 2 Nov 41 and arrived back at Ft Benning Ga 1 Dec 41 where disbanded Jan 42.

3rd Armored Brigade

15 Apr 41 activated at Cp Beauregard La and assigned 3rd Armored Division; moved to Cp Polk La 11 Jun 41 where disbanded 1 Jan 42.

4th Armored Brigade

15 Apr 41 activated at Pine Camp N.Y. and assigned 4th Armored Division; disbanded there 1 Jan 42.

5th Armored Brigade

1 Oct 41 activated at Ft Knox Ky and assigned 5th Armored Division where disbanded 1 Jan 42.

Provisional Tank Brigade

Stationed at Ft Benning Ga and participated in the 1940 Louisiana Maneuvers; formed the nucleus of the 2nd Armored Division and discontinued 15 Jul 40.

Chapter 18

Armored Groups

Groups:

1–20, 1 Prov, 1 Prov *(Chinese-American)*, Provisional Armored (Task Force Butler), Provisional (Amphib), Provisional

1st Armored Group (I)

20 Mar 43 activated at Ft Knox Ky under the Armored Force where redesignated 17th Armored Group on 20 Nov 43.

1st Armored Group (II)

11 Feb 41 activated as the 1st Tank Group at Ft Knox Ky and moved to Ft Benning Ga 4 Jul 41; arrived Fulton La 13 Aug 41 and Hoffman N.C. 7 Oct 41; transferred to Ft George C. Meade Md 4 Dec 41 where inactivated 1 Mar 42 but reactivated on the same date there; sent to Indiantown Gap Mil Res Pa on 1 Aug 42 and departed New York P/E 31 Aug 42; arrived in England 5 Sep 42 and landed in North Africa 17 Jan 43; landed in Italy 27 Oct 43 where redesignated 1st Armored Group at Annuziata Italy 19 Mar 44; operated as a combat armored group in Italy; landed in southern France on 23 Sep 44 and functioned as the VI Corps armored section; inactivated at Marseille France on 20 Sep 45.

Campaigns: *Naples-Foggia, Rome-Arno, Rhineland, Ardennes-Alsace, Central Europe*
Aug 45 Loc: Hohenschambach Germany

2nd Armored Group (I)

28 Mar 43 activated at Cp Cooke Calif under the Armored Force and assigned to II Armored Corps 31 Mar 43; moved to Ft Ord Calif 20 Oct 43 attached to Fourth Army and redesignated there as the 18th Armored Group on 30 Nov 43.

2nd Armored Group (II)

1 Mar 42 activated at Cp Bowie Tex as the 2nd Tank Group and moved to Indio Calif 19 Apr 42 where assigned Desert Training Center 1 Mar 42; staged at Ft Dix N.J. 22 Feb 43 until departed New York P/E 5 Mar 43; landed in North Africa 18 Mar 43 and arrived in Italy 26 Nov 43 where redesignated 2nd Armored Group at Roccaravindola on 19 Mar 44; operated as a combat armored group in Italy and attached to Task Force 45 (45th AAA Brigade) as a line unit on 26 Jul 44; disbanded at Montecatini Italy 19 Dec 44 and concurrently reconstituted there as HHC 473rd Infantry Regiment.

Campaigns: *Naples-Foggia, Rome-Arno, North Apennines*

3rd Armored Group (I)

31 Mar 43 activated at Cp Chaffee Ark under the Armored Force and redesignated there as the 12th Tank Group 14 Sep 43.

3rd Armored Group (II)

1 Mar 42 activated at Ft Lewis Wash as the 3rd Tank Group and moved to Cp Young Calif 23 Nov 42 and assigned Desert Training Center; transferred to Cp Pickett Va 13 Jun 43 and assigned XIII Corps; arrived Ft Dix N.J. 2 Sep 43 and staged at Cp Shanks N.Y. 14 Oct 43 until departed New York P/E 21 Oct 43; arrived in England 2 Nov 43 where redesignated 3rd Armored Group at East Allington, Cornwall, on 4 Jan 44; assaulted Normandy France 6 Jun 44 and functioned as the V Corps armored section; inactivated in Germany on 30 Sep 45.

Campaigns: *Normandy, Northern France, Rhineland, Ardennes-Alsace, Central Europe*
Aug 45 Loc: Ellrich Germany

4th Armored Group

23 Apr 42 activated in Hawaii as the 4th Tank Group (Light) where redesignated 4th Armored Group 25 Nov 43; trained, prepared, and rehabilitated tank and amphibious units for Pacific operations; departed Hawaii 22 Jun 45 and arrived Leyte Philippines 11 Jul 45; returned to San Francisco P/E 11 Jan 46 and inactivated at Cp Stoneman Calif 12 Jan 46.

Campaigns: *Pacific Theater without inscription*
Aug 45 Loc: Leyte Philippine Islands

5th Armored Group (Colored)

20 May 42 activated at Cp Claiborne La as the 5th Tank Group (Colored) and moved to Cp Hood Tex 15 Sep 43 where assigned to the Tank Destroyer Center; there redesignated as 5th Armored Group (Colored) 22 Nov 43; moved to Ft Huachuca Ariz 29 Apr 44 and assigned XXIII Corps 1 May 44; returned to Cp Hood Tex 2 Jul 44 where inactivated 1 Dec 44.

6th Armored Group

23 Apr 42 activated at Cp Bowie Tex as the 6th Tank Group and moved to Cp Young Calif 6 May 43 where assigned Desert Training Center; staged at Cp Shanks N.Y. 14 Dec 43 until departed New York P/E 8 Jan 44; arrived in England 17 Jan 44 where redesignated 6th Armored Group at Littlehampton on 1 Feb 44; assaulted France 6 Jun 44 and operated as a line armored group until 16 Jul 44 when it began functioning as VII Corps armored section; entered Belgium 6 Sep 44 and Germany 13 Sep 44; arrived Boston P/E 21 Oct 45 and inactivated at Cp Myles Standish Mass 22 Oct 45.

Campaigns: *Normandy, Northern France, Rhineland, Ardennes-Alsace, Central Europe*
Aug 45 Loc: Obeturn Germany

7th Armored Group

2 Jul 42 activated at Cp Hood Tex as the 7th Tank Group and moved to La Maneuver Area 26 Sep 43; located to Cp Swift Tex 15 Dec 43 and redesignated 7th Armored Group same date and assigned XVIII Corps; staged at Cp Shanks N.Y. 1 Feb 44 until departed New York P/E 1 Mar 44; arrived in England 7 Mar 44 and landed in France 3 Jul 44; functioned as XIX Corps armored section; crossed into Belgium 3 Sep 44 and into Holland 20 Sep 44; restructured as the Ninth Army Rest Area Headquarters 10 Mar 45 and entered Germany 12 Apr 45; arrived Boston P/E 25 Nov 45 and inactivated Cp Myles Standish Mass 26 Nov 45.

Campaigns: *Normandy, Northern France, Rhineland, Central Europe*
Aug 45 Loc: Innstadt Germany

8th Armored Group

10 Aug 42 activated at Cp Rucker Ala as the 8th Tank Group and moved to Ft Knox Ky 4 May 43; arrived Cp Shelby Miss 4 Nov 43 where redesignated 8th Armored Group 2 Dec 43; staged at Cp Shanks N.Y. 3 Feb 44 and departed New York P/E 11 Feb 44; arrived England 23 Feb 44 and landed in France 31 Jul 44 where functioned as XX Corps armored section; crossed into Luxembourg 28 Dec 44 and entered Germany 27 Mar 45; arrived Boston P/E 25 Nov 45 and inactivated at Cp Myles Standish Mass 26 Nov 45.

Campaigns: *Northern France, Ardennes-Alsace, Central Europe*
Aug 45 Loc: Kelheim Germany

9th Armored Group

10 Sep 42 activated at Cp Campbell Ky as the 9th Tank Group and moved 19 Aug 43 to the Desert Training Center Ariz where redesignated 9th Armored Group on 8 Dec 43; staged at Cp Shanks N.Y. 23 Mar 44 until departed New York P/E 31 Mar 44; arrived in England 6 Apr 44 and landed in France 12 Nov 44; crossed into Belgium 10 Dec 44 and committed into combat 18 Dec 44; served as XVIII Corps armored section commencing 23 Dec 44 and entered Germany 15 Feb 45; began functioning as III Corps armored section on 19 Feb 45 and inactivated in Germany 24 Oct 45.

Campaigns: *Rhineland, Ardennes-Alsace, Central Europe*
Aug 45 Loc: Kothen Germany

10th Armored Group

1 Mar 43 activated at Ft Lewis Wash as the 10th Tank Group and moved to Oreg Maneuver Area 5 Sep 43 under IV Corps; stationed at Yakima Wash 24 Oct 43 and went to the Calif-Ariz Maneuver Area 28 Nov 43 where redesignated 10th Armored Group 9 Dec 43; transferred to Ft Knox Ky 1 May 44 and staged at Cp Kilmer N.J. 20 Jul 44 until departed New York P/E 26 Jul 44; arrived in England 5 Aug 44 and landed in France on 29 Aug 44; committed into combat 18 Jan 45 as CCR, 8th Armored Division; entered Holland 8 Feb 45 and entered Germany 1 Mar 45 where inactivated on 1 May 46.

Campaigns: *Northern France, Rhineland, Ardennes-Alsace, Central Europe*
Aug 45 Loc: Duderstadt Germany

11th Armored Group

28 Jul 43 activated at Cp Campbell Ky as the 11th Tank Group and moved to the Tenn Maneuver Area 16 Nov 43 where redesignated 11th Armored Group 5 Dec 43; returned to Cp Campbell Ky by the end of the year and departed Boston P/E 28 Feb 44; arrived in England 8 Mar 44 and landed in France 18 Jul 44; committed into combat 31 Jul 44 and entered Germany 19 Mar 45 where inactivated on 1 May 46.

Campaigns: *Normandy, Northern France, Rhineland, Ardennes-Alsace, Central Europe*
Aug 45 Loc: Apolda Germany

12th Armored Group

14 Sep 43 redesignated from the 3rd Armored Group as the 12th Tank Group at Cp Chaffee Ark and moved to Cp Howze Tex 10 Nov 43 with X Corps; redesignated there as the 12th Armored Group on 13 Dec 43 and assigned XVIII Corps 10 Jan 44 and then XXIII Corps 1 Feb 44; staged at Cp Myles Standish Mass 26 Sep 44 until departed Boston P/E 4 Oct 44; arrived in England 12 Oct 44 and landed in France 15 Oct 44; functioned as CCR, 9th Armored Division; crossed into Luxembourg 2 Dec 44 and into Belgium 19 Dec 44; returned to France 31 Dec 44 and to Belgium 20 Jan 45; entered Germany 31 Mar 45; arrived at New York P/E 1 Jul 45 and moved to Cp Gruber Okla 11 Jul 45 where inactivated on 20 Oct 45.

Campaigns: *Rhineland, Ardennes-Alsace, Central Europe*
Aug 45 Loc: Camp Gruber Oklahoma

13th Armored Group

1 Nov 43 activated at Ft Lewis Wash under IV Corps and moved to Ft Ord Calif 21 Feb 44 with III Corps; staged at Cp Stoneman Calif 5 Oct 44 until departed San Francisco P/E 21 Oct 44; arrived in New Guinea 12 Nov 44 and landed in Philippine Islands 11 Jan 45; returned San Francisco P/E 10 Jan 46 and inactivated at Cp Stoneman Calif 12 Jan 46.

Campaigns: *Luzon*
Aug 45 Loc: Clark Field Philippines

14th Armored Group

28 Oct 43 activated at Ft Jackson S.C. under XII Corps and moved to Tenn Maneuver Area 25 Feb 44 with IX Corps; arrived at Ft Campbell Ky 24 Mar 44 and assigned XXII Corps; moved to Ft Knox Ky 19 Sep 44 with Replacement & School Command and inactivated there 10 Mar 45.

15th Armored Group

28 Oct 43 activated at Cp Rucker Ala under III Corps and moved to Tenn Maneuver Area 22 Jan 44 under IX Corps; arrived Ft Jackson S.C. 29 Feb 44 and assigned to XXIII Corps 25 Sep 44; arrived Cp Shelby Miss 11 Oct 44 and moved to Ft Jackson S.C. 20 Nov 44 where inactivated 23 Feb 46.

Aug 45 Loc: Fort Jackson South Carolina

16th Armored Group

8 Nov 43 activated at Cp Pickett Va under XIII Corps and moved to Cp Chaffee Ark 28 Feb 44 under XVI Corps; arrived Cp Phillips Kans 14 Apr 44 and assigned XXXVI Corps 17 Jul 44; transferred to Cp Carson Colo 2 Aug 44 where inactivated 11 Sep 44.

17th Armored Group

20 Nov 43 redesignated from 1st Armored Group at Ft Knox Ky and staged at Cp Kilmer N.J. 2 Apr 44 until departed New York P/E 20 Apr 44; arrived England 26 Apr 44 and landed in France 5 Aug 44 and committed into combat 13 Aug 44; functioned as XII Corps armored section; crossed into Luxembourg 21 Dec 44 and entered Germany 3 Mar 45; inactivated in Belgium 30 Apr 46.

Campaigns: *Northern France, Rhineland, Ardennes-Alsace, Central Europe*
Aug 45 Loc: Regensburg Germany

18th Armored Group

30 Nov 43 redesignated from 2nd Armored Group at Ft Ord Calif and assigned III Corps 15 Jan 44 and XXXVI Corps 4 Jul 45; inactivated there 27 Nov 45.

Aug 45 Loc: Fort Ord California

19th Armored Group

24 Aug 44 activated at Kaiaka Bay Camp Hawaii from officers of the 715th Amphibious Tractor Battalion; assumed training responsibilities, LVT maintenance, and water driving course instruction; inactivated 10 Apr 45 in Hawaii and assets transferred to the Combat Training Command.

Campaigns: *Pacific Theater without inscription*

20th Armored Group

26 Aug 44 activated at Schofield Barracks Hawaii from assets of the Provisional Armored Group there; departed Hawaii 15 Sep 44 and landed at Leyte Philippines 21 Oct 44 attached to XXIV Corps; assaulted Okinawa 1 Apr 45 and inactivated in Korea 8 Jun 46.

Campaigns: *Leyte, Ryukyus*
Aug 45 Loc: Okinawa

Provisional Armored Group

7 Jun 44 established at Schofield Barracks Hawaii where assigned to XXIV Corps; discontinued 26 Aug 44 and assets transferred to 20th Armored Group.

Campaigns: *Pacific Theater without inscription*

Provisional Armored Group (Amphibious)

15 Feb 45 organized under the 77th Infantry Division and composed of 708th Amphibious Tank and 715th and 773rd Amphibious Tractor Battalions; group participated in the Kerama Retto, Kiese Shima, and Ie Shima phases of the Okinawa campaign from 26 Mar–26 Apr 45.

Campaigns: *Ryukyus*

Provisional Armored Group (Task Force Butler)

18 Aug 44 organized near Le Muy southern France under the command of Brig. Gen. F. B. Butler, deputy commander VI Corps; discontinued in France 30 Aug 44.

Campaigns: *Southern France*

1st Provisional Tank Group

21 Nov 41 activated at Ft Stotsenburg Philippine Islands with the arrival of 192nd and 194th Tank Battalions and 17th Ordnance Company; surrendered on Bataan to Japanese forces 9 Apr 42.

Campaigns: *Philippine Islands*

1st Provisional Tank Group (Chinese-American)

1 Oct 43 activated at Ramgarh India and arrived Ledo 1 Jan 44; entered Burma 20 Jan 44 and supported *Chinese 22nd Div* and Galahad Force commencing 3 Mar 44 in combat; in China Mar 45.

Campaigns: *India-Burma, Central Burma*
Aug 45 Loc: Sookeratung India

Chapter 19

Armored Regiments

Regiments:

1–5, 7–9, 11, 13, 14, 16, 20, 31–37, 40–48, 66–69, 80, 81, Armored Force Demonstration

1st Armored Regiment

15 Jul 40 redesignated from 1st Cavalry Regiment at Ft Knox Ky as 1st Armored Regiment (Light) and assigned 1st Armored Division; moved to Cp Polk La 1 Sep 41 and to the Ft Jackson S.C. area 30 Oct 41; returned to Ft Knox Ky 7 Dec 41 where redesignated 1st Armored Regiment 1 Jan 42; staged at Ft Dix N.J. 10 Apr 42 until departed New York P/E 13 May 42; arrived Northern Ireland 11 Jun 42 and elements assaulted Oran North Africa 8–10 Nov 42, the regiment completely ashore by 21 Dec 42; landed in Italy 8 Nov 43 where regiment, less 2nd Bn, redesignated 1st Tank Battalion 20 Jul 44 and 2nd Bn disbanded.

Campaigns: *Algeria–French Morocco, Naples–Foggia, Anzio, Rome–Arno*

2nd Armored Regiment (Light)

15 Apr 41 activated at Cp Beauregard La and assigned 3rd Armored Division; there redesignated 32nd Armored Regiment (Light) 8 May 41.

2nd Armored Regiment

15 Jul 42 activated at Ft Riley Kans with personnel and equipment from 2nd Cavalry Regiment and assigned 9th Armored Division; moved to Cp Young Calif 14 Jun 43 where regiment (less 1st and 3rd Bns, Band, Maint Co, Serv Co, and Rcn Co) redesignated 2nd Tank Battalion 9 Oct 43; 1st and 3rd Bns and Rcn Co redesignated 776th and 19th Tank Bns and Troop D 89th Cav Rcn Sqdn respectively and remainder disbanded.

3rd Armored Regiment (Light)

15 Apr 41 activated at Cp Beauregard La and assigned 3rd Armored Division; there redesignated 33rd Armored Regiment (Light) 8 May 41.

3rd Armored Regiment

15 Jul 42 activated at Ft Benning Ga with personnel and equipment from 3rd Cavalry Regiment and assigned 10th Armored Division; moved to Murfreesboro Tenn 23 Jun 43 and to Cp Gordon Ga 5 Sep 43; there regiment (less 1st and 3rd Bns, Band, Maint Co, Serv Co, and Rcn Co) redesignated 3rd Tank Battalion 20 Sep 43; 1st and 3rd Bns and Rcn Co redesignated 777th and 21st Tank Bns and Troop D 90th Cav Rcn Sqdn respectively and remainder disbanded.

4th Armored Regiment (Medium)

15 Apr 41 activated at Cp Beauregard La and assigned 3rd Armored Division; there redesignated 40th Armored Regiment (Medium) 8 May 41.

5th Armored Regiment (Light)

15 Apr 41 activated at Pine Camp N.Y. and assigned 4th Armored Division; there redesignated 35th Armored Regiment (Light) 8 May 41.

5th Armored Regiment

15 Jul 43 activated at Cp Chaffee Ark and assigned 16th Armored Division; there regiment (less 1st and 3rd Bns, Band, Maint Co, Serv Co, and Rcn Co) redesignated 5th Tank Battalion 10 Sep 43; 1st and 3rd Bns and Rcn Co redesignated 717th and 26th Tank Bns and Troop D 23rd Cav Rcn Sqdn respectively and remainder disbanded.

7th Armored Regiment (Light)

15 Apr 41 activated at Pine Camp N.Y. and assigned 4th Armored Division; there redesignated 37th Armored Regiment (Light) 8 May 41.

8th Armored Regiment (Medium)

15 Apr 41 activated at Pine Camp N.Y. and assigned 4th Armored Division; there redesignated 80th Armored Regiment (Medium) 8 May 41.

9th Armored Regiment

15 Mar 43 activated at Cp Campbell Ky and assigned 20th Armored Division; there regiment (less 1st and 3rd Bns, Band, Maint Co, Serv Co, and Rcn Co) redesignated 9th Tank Battalion 10 Sep 43; 1st and 3rd Bns and Rcn Co redesignated 718th and 27th Tank Battalions and Troop D 33rd Cav Rcn Sqdn respectively and remainder disbanded.

11th Armored Regiment

15 Jul 42 activated at Ft Benning Ga with personnel and equipment from 11th Cavalry Regiment and assigned 10th Armored Division; moved to Murfreesboro Tenn 22 Jun 43 and to Cp Gordon Ga 5 Sep 43; there regiment (less 3rd Bn, Band, Maint Co, Serv Co, and Rcn Co) redesignated 11th Tank Battalion 20 Sep 43; 3rd Bn and Rcn Co redesignated 712th Tank Bn and Troop E 90th Cav Rcn Sqdn respectively and remainder disbanded.

13th Armored Regiment

15 Jul 40 redesignated from 13th Cavalry Regiment at Ft Knox Ky as 13th Armored Regiment (Light) and assigned 1st Armored Division; moved to Cp Polk La 1 Sep 41 and to Ft Jackson S.C. area 30 Oct 41; returned to Ft Knox Ky 7 Dec 41 where redesignated 13th Armored Regiment 1 Jan 42; staged at Ft Dix N.J. 10 Apr 42 until departed New York P/E 13 May 42; arrived in Northern Ireland 11 Jun 42 and elements assaulted North Africa 8 Nov 42, the entire regiment ashore by 21 Dec 42; landed in Italy 28 Oct 43; redesignated (less HHC 1st Bn, HHC 2nd Bn, Cos A, B, and C, 3rd Bn, Maint Co, and Rcn Co) at Bolgheri as 13th Tank Battalion 20 Jul 44; 3rd Bn and Maint Co redesignated 4th Tank Bn and Rcn Co redesignated Troop D 81st Cav Rcn Sqdn and remainder disbanded.

Campaigns: *Algeria–French Morocco, Tunisia, Naples-Foggia, Anzio, Rome-Arno*

14th Armored Regiment

15 Jul 42 activated at Ft Riley Kans with personnel and equipment from 14th Cavalry Regiment and assigned 9th Armored Division; moved to Desert Training Center Calif 13 Jun 43; there redesignated (less 3rd Bn, Band, Maint Co, Serv Co, and Rcn Co) as 14th Tank Battalion 9 Oct 43; 3rd Bn and Rcn Co redesignated 711th Tank Bn and Troop E 89th Cav Rcn Sqdn respectively and remainder disbanded.

16th Armored Regiment

15 Jul 43 activated at Cp Chaffee Ark and assigned 16th Armored Division; there redesignated (less 3rd Bn, Band, Main Co, Serv Co, and Rcn Co) as 16th Tank Battalion 10 Sep 43; 3rd Bn and Rcn Co redesignated 787th Tank Bn and Troop E 23rd Cav Rcn Sqdn respectively and remainder disbanded.

20th Armored Regiment

15 Mar 43 activated at Cp Campbell Ky and assigned 20th Armored Division; there redesignated (less 3rd Bn, Band, Maint Co, Serv Co, and Rcn Co) as 20th Tank Battalion 10 Sep 43; 3rd Bn and Rcn Co redesignated 788th Tank Bn and Troop E 33rd Cav Rcn Sqdn respectively and remainder disbanded.

31st Armored Regiment (Light)

1 Oct 41 activated at Ft Knox Ky and assigned 5th Armored Division; inactivated there 1 Jan 42.

31st Armored Regiment

2 Mar 42 activated at Cp Polk La and assigned 7th Armored Division and moved to Desert Training Center 13 Mar 43; arrived Ft Benning Ga 5 Aug 43 where redesignated (less 1st and 3rd Bns, Band, Maint Co, Serv Co, and Rcn Co) as 31st Tank Battalion 20 Sep 43; 1st and 3rd Bns and Rcn Co redesignated 774th and 17th Tank Bns and Troop D 87th Cav Rcn Sqdn respectively and remainder disbanded.

32nd Armored Regiment

8 May 41 redesignated from 2nd Armored Regiment at Cp Beauregard La as 32nd Armored Regiment (Light) and assigned to 3rd Armored Division; moved to Cp Polk La 11 Jun 41 and to Indio Calif 26 Jul 42; redesignated 32nd Armored Regiment 1 Jan 42; arrived at Cp Pickett Va 9 Nov 42 and Indiantown Gap Mil Res Pa 17 Jan 43; departed New York P/E 5 Sep 43 and arrived in England 16 Sep 43; landed in France 23 Jun 44 and crossed into Belgium 2 Sep 44 and entered Germany 8 Feb 45; inactivated there 10 Nov 45.

Campaigns: *Normandy, Northern France, Rhineland, Ardennes-Alsace, Central Europe*
Aug 45 Loc: Gross Umstadt Germany

33rd Armored Regiment

8 May 41 redesignated from 3rd Armored Regiment at Cp Beauregard La as 33rd Armored Regiment (Light) assigned to 3rd Armored Division; moved to Cp Polk La 11 Jun 41 and redesignated 33rd Armored Regiment 1 Jan 42; sent to Indio Calif 18 Jul 42 and Cp Pickett Va 7 Nov 42; arrived Indiantown Gap Mil Res Pa 20 Jan 42 and departed New York P/E 5 Sep 43; arrived in England 18 Sep 43 and landed in France 23 Jun 44; crossed into Belgium 2 Sep 44 and into Germany 12 Sep 44; returned to Belgium 19 Dec 44 and entered Germany again 7 Feb 45 where inactivated 10 Nov 45.

Campaigns: *Normandy, Northern France, Rhineland, Ardennes-Alsace, Central Europe*
Aug 45 Loc: Russelsheim Germany

34th Armored Regiment

1 Oct 41 activated at Ft Knox Ky as 34th Armored Regiment (Light) and assigned 5th Armored Division; moved to Cp Cooke Calif 16 Feb 42 and to Tenn Maneuver Area 24 Mar 43; arrived at Pine Camp N.Y. 24 Jun 43 where redesignated (less 1st and 3rd Bns, Maint Co, Serv Co, and Rcn Co) as 34th Tank Battalion 20 Sep 43; 1st and 3rd Bns and Rcn Co redesignated 772nd Tank and 10th Tank Bns and Troop D 85th Cav Rcn Sqdn respectively and remainder disbanded.

35th Armored Regiment

8 May 41 redesignated from 5th Armored Regiment at Pine Camp N.Y. as 35th Armored Regiment (Light) assigned to 4th Armored Division; moved to Cp Forrest Tenn 2 Oct 42 and Cp Young Calif 17 Nov 42; arrived Cp Bowie Tex 12 Jun 43 where redesignated (less 1st and 3rd Bns, Maint Co, Serv Co and Rcn Co) as 35th Tank Battalion 10 Sep 43; 1st and 3rd Bns and Rcn Co redesignated 771st and 8th Tank Battalions and Troop D 25th Cav Rcn Sqdn and remainder disbanded.

36th Armored Regiment

1 Apr 42 activated at Ft Knox Ky and assigned 8th Armored Division; moved to Cp Campbell Ky 9 Jan 43 and Cp Polk La 5 Mar 43 where redesignated (less 1st and 3rd Bns, Band, Maint Co, Serv Co and Rcn Co) as 36th Tank Battalion 20 Sep 43; 1st and 3rd Bns and Rcn Co redesignated 775th and 18th Tank Battalions and Troop D 88th Cav Rcn Sqdn respectively and remainder disbanded.

37th Armored Regiment

8 May 41 redesignated from 7th Armored Regiment as 37th Armored Regiment (Light) and assigned to 4th Armored Division at Pine Camp N.Y.; moved to Cp Forrest Tenn 2 Oct 42 and Cp Young Calif 17 Nov 42 and Cp Bowie Tex 12 Jun 43; there redesignated (less 3rd Bn, Maint Co, Serv Co and Rcn Co) as 37th Tank Battalion 10 Sep 43; 3rd Bn and Rcn Co redesignated 706th Tank Bn and Troop E 25th Cav Rcn Sqdn respectively and remainder disbanded.

40th Armored Regiment (Medium)

8 May 41 redesignated from 4th Armored Regiment at Cp Beauregard La assigned to 3rd Armored Division; inactivated there 1 Jan 42.

40th Armored Regiment

2 Mar 42 activated at Cp Polk La and assigned to 7th Armored Division; moved to Desert Training Center Cp Young Calif 21 Mar 43 and arrived Ft Benning Ga 13 Aug 43; there redesignated (less 3rd Bn, Maint Co, Serv Co and Rcn Co) as 40th Tank Battalion 20 Sep 43; 3rd Bn and Rcn Co redesignated 709th Tank Bn and Troop E 87th Cav Rcn Sqdn respectively and remainder disbanded.

41st Armored Regiment

15 Aug 42 activated at Cp Polk La and assigned 11th Armored Division; moved to Cp Barkeley Tex 3 Sep 43 where redesignated (less 1st and 3rd Bns, Band, Maint Co, Serv Co and Rcn Co) as 41st Tank Battalion 20 Sep 43; 1st and 3rd Bns and Rcn Co redesignated 778th and 22nd Tank Bns and Troop D 41st Cav Rcn Sqdn respectively and remainder disbanded.

42nd Armored Regiment

15 Aug 42 activated at Cp Polk La and assigned 11th Armored Division; moved to Cp Barkeley Tex 4 Sep 43 where redesignated (less 3rd Bn, Band, Maint Co, Serv Co and Rcn Co) as 42nd Tank Battalion 20 Sep 43; 3rd Bn and Rcn Co redesignated 713th Tank Bn and Troop E 41st Cav Rcn Sqdn respectively and remainder disbanded.

43rd Armored Regiment

15 Sep 42 activated at Cp Campbell Ky and assigned 12th Armored Division; moved to Tenn Maneuver Area 6 Sep 43 where redesignated (less 1st and 3rd Bns, Band, Maint Co, Serv Co and Rcn Co) as 43rd Tank Battalion 11 Nov 43; 1st and 3rd Bns and Rcn Co redesignated 779th and 23rd Tank Bns and Troop D 92nd Cav Rcn Sqdn respectively; remainder disbanded.

44th Armored Regiment

15 Sep 42 activated at Cp Campbell Ky and assigned 12th Armored Division; moved to Tenn Maneuver Area 6 Sep 43 where redesignated (less 3rd Bn, Maint Co, Serv Co and Rcn Co) as 44th Tank Battalion 11 Nov 43; 3rd Bn and Rcn Co Co redesignated 714th Tank Bn and Troop E 92nd Cav Rcn Sqdn respectively and remainder disbanded.

45th Armored Regiment

15 Oct 42 activated at Cp Beale Calif and assigned 13th Armored Division; there redesignated (less 1st and 3rd Bns, Band, Maint Co, Serv Co and Rcn Co) as 45th Tank Battalion 20 Sep 43; 1st and 3rd Bns and Rcn Co redesignated 780th and 24th Tank Bns and Troop D 93rd Cav Rcn Sqdn respectively and remainder disbanded.

46th Armored Regiment

15 Oct 42 activated at Cp Beale Calif and assigned 13th Armored Division; there redesignated (less 3rd Bn, Band, Maint Co, Serv Co and Rcn Co) as 46th Tank Battalion 20 Sep 43; 3rd Bn and Rcn Co redesignated 715th Tank Bn and Troop E 93rd Cav Rcn Sqdn respectively and remainder disbanded.

47th Armored Regiment

15 Nov 42 activated at Cp Chaffee Ark and assigned 14th Armored Division; there redesignated (less 1st and 3rd Bns, Band, Maint Co, Serv Co and Rcn Co) as 47th Tank Battalion 20 Sep 43; 1st and 3rd Bns and Rcn Co redesignated 786th and 25th Tank Bns and Troop D 94th Cav Rcn Sqdn respectively and remainder disbanded.

48th Armored Regiment

15 Nov 42 activated at Cp Chaffee Ark and assigned 14th Armored Division; there redesignated (less 3rd Bn, Maint Co, Band, Serv Co and Rcn Co) as 48th Tank Battalion 20 Sep 43; 3rd Bn and Rcn Co redesignated 716th Tank Bn and Troop E 94th Cav Rcn Sqdn respectively and remainder disbanded.

66th Armored Regiment

15 Jul 40 redesignated from 66th Infantry Regiment (Light Tanks) as 66th Armored Regiment (Light) at Ft Benning Ga and assigned 2nd Armored Division; moved to Monroe N.C. 10 Jul 42 and to Ft Bragg N.C. 15 Aug 42; redesignated 66th Armored Regiment 1 Jan 42; staged at Ft Dix N.J. 7 Nov 42 (less 1st Bn which assaulted North Africa 8 Nov 42) until departed New York P/E 11 Dec 42 and landed North Africa 25 Dec 42; assaulted Licata Sicily 10 Jul 43 and sent to England 25 Nov 43; landed in France 9 Jun 44 and crossed into Belgium 2 Sep 44 and into Holland 16 Sep 44; first entered Germany 19 Sep 44 and returned to Belgium 22 Dec 44 and to Holland 3 Feb 45; reentered Germany 24 Feb 45; returned New York P/E 29 Jan 46 and moved to Cp Hood Tex 4 Feb 46; inactivated there 25 Mar 46.

Campaigns: *Algeria–French Morocco, Sicily, Normandy, Northern France, Rhineland, Ardennes-Alsace, Central Europe*

Aug 45 Loc: Lebenstadt Germany

67th Armored Regiment

15 Jul 40 redesignated from 67th Infantry Regiment (Medium Tanks) at Ft Benning Ga as 67th Armored Regiment (Medium) and assigned 2nd Armored Division; redesignated 67th Armored Regiment 1 Jan 42 and moved to Carolina Maneuver Area 10 Jul 42 and to Ft Bragg N.C. 15 Aug 42; staged at Ft Dix N.J. 5 Nov 42 and departed New York P/E 11 Dec 42 and arrived in North Africa 25 Dec 42 where elements had assaulted Fedala and Safi 8 Nov 42; assaulted Licata and Scoglitti Sicily 9 Jul 43 and moved to England 25 Nov 43; landed in France 11 Jun 44 and crossed into Belgium 6 Sep 44 and into Holland 16 Sep 44; first entered Germany 4 Oct 44 and returned to Belgium 22 Dec 44 and to Holland 14 Feb 45; reentered Germany 23 Feb 45; returned to New York P/E 29 Jan 46 and moved to Cp Hood Tex 4 Feb 46 where inactivated 25 Mar 46.

Campaigns: *Algeria–French Morocco, Tunisia, Sicily, Normandy, Northern France, Rhineland, Ardennes-Alsace, Central Europe*

Aug 45 Loc: Heerte Germany

68th Armored Regiment (Light)

1 Aug 40 activated (less 2nd Bn redesignated from 2nd Bn, 68th Infantry Regiment (Light Tanks and already active) at Ft Benning Ga as 68th Armored Regiment (Light) and assigned 2nd Armored Division; inactivated there 8 Jan 42.

68th Armored Regiment

15 Feb 42 activated at Ft Knox Ky and assigned 6th Armored Division; moved to Cp Chaffee Ark 20 Mar 42 and to Cp Young Calif 12 Oct 42; arrived at Cp Cooke Calif 20 Mar 43 where redesignated (less 1st and 3rd Bns, Band, Maint Co, Serv Co and Rcn Co) as 68th Tank Battalion 20 Sep 43; 1st and 3rd Bns and Rcn Co redesignated 773rd and 15th Tank Bns and Troop D 86th Cav Rcn Sqdn respectively and remainder disbanded.

69th Armored Regiment (Medium)

31 Jul 40 activated at Ft Knox Ky and assigned 1st Armored Division; transferred to Cp Polk La 1 Sep 41 and to the Ft Jackson S.C. Maneuver Area 30 Oct 41; returned to Ft Knox Ky where inactivated 10 Jan 42.

69th Armored Regiment

15 Feb 42 activated at Ft Knox Ky and assigned to 6th Armored Division; moved to Cp Chaffee Ark 20 Mar 42 and to the Desert Training Center Calif 15 Oct 42; arrived Cp Cooke Calif 20 Mar 43 where redesignated (less 3rd Bn, Maint Co, Serv Co and Rcn Co) as 69th Tank Battalion 20 Sep 43; 3rd Bn and Rcn Co redesignated 708th Tank Bn and Troop E 86th Cav Rcn Sqdn respectively and remainder disbanded.

80th Armored Regiment (Medium)

8 May 41 redesignated from 8th Armored Regiment at Pine Camp N.Y. and assigned 4th Armored Division; inactivated there 5 Jan 42.

80th Armored Regiment

1 Apr 42 activated at Ft Knox Ky and assigned 8th Armored Division and moved to Cp Campbell Ky 7 Jan 43; arrived Cp Polk La 5 Mar 43 where redesignated (less 3rd Bn, Band, Maint Co, Serv Co and Rcn Co) as 80th Tank Battalion 20 Sep 43; 3rd Bn and Rcn Co redesignated 710th Tank Bn and Troop E 88th Cav Rcn Sqdn respectively and remainder disbanded.

81st Armored Regiment

1 Oct 41 activated at Ft Knox Ky as 81st Armored Regiment (Medium) and assigned 5th Armored Division; redesignated as 81st Armored Regiment 1 Jan 42; moved to Cp Cooke Calif 16 Feb 42 and to Calif Maneuver Area 14 Aug 42; returned Cp Cooke Calif 19 Nov 42 and moved to Tenn Maneuver Area 24 Mar 43; arrived Pine Camp N.Y. 24 Jun 43 where redesignated (less 3rd Bn, Band, Maint Co, Serv Co and Rcn Co) as 81st Tank Battalion 20 Sep 43; 3rd Bn and Rcn Co redesignated 707th Tank Bn and Troop E 85th Cav Rcn Sqdn respectively and remainder disbanded.

Armored Force School Demonstration Regiment

1 Feb 42 activated at Ft Knox Ky under a special T/O and consisted of HHC, Maint Co and Serv Co, tank battalion of 2 medium and 1 light tank companies, and another battalion with 1 rifle co, 1 engr co, 1 rcn co, and 1 artillery battery; inactivated there 24 Jan 45.

Chapter 20

Amphibian Tank and Tractor Battalions

Battalions:

40, 69, 80, 534–536, 539, 540, 658, 672, 708, 715, 718, 720, 726–728, 737–739, 742, 747, 764, 773, 776, 780, 788, 795, 826, Provisional

⭐ EXAMPLE — HOW TO USE THIS TABLE

Unit Designation and Type   Date Formed and Location (Source of Unit)/Inactivation and Location   August 1945 Location

Overseas Wartime Locations followed by - **Campaign Key Numbers** and PE return to United States, if applicable or space allows
(notes and remarks in parenthesis)

672nd Amphibian Tractor Bn   15 Apr 44 Ft Ord Calif (672nd TD Bn)/24 Dec 45 Cp Stoneman Calif   Manila Philippines less Co A
SFPE: 23 Sep 44 Bougainville: 9 Sep 44 Lingayen Gulf Philippines: 9 Jan 45 Balikpapan Borneo: 1 Jul 45 - **14,15,16** SFPE: 24 Dec 45 at Morotai Island

In this example, the 672nd Amphibian Tractor Battalion was redesignated from the 672nd Tank Destroyer Battalion on 15 April 1944 at Fort Ord, California. Earlier service of this unit can be tracked by looking up the service of the 672nd Tank Destroyer Battalion in Chapter 28. The 672nd Amphibian Tractor Battalion *departed* San Francisco Port of Embarkation on 23 September 1944 and *arrived* on Bougainville 9 September 1944. It landed at Lingayen Gulf, Philippines, on 9 January 1945 and at Balikpapan, Borneo, on 1 July 1945. The battalion participated in the Luzon, New Guinea, and Northern Solomons campaigns. This information was derived by indexing the boldfaced campaign key numbers with Appendix I. It was located in Manila, Philippines, in August 1945, less Company A which was on Morotai Island. The 672nd Amphibian Tractor Battalion returned to San Francisco Port of Embarkation on 24 December 1945 and was inactivated the same day at Camp Stoneman, California.

BATTALION DESIGNATION AND TYPE	FORMED (SOURCE OF UNIT)/INACTIVATION	AUGUST 1945 LOCATION
40th Amphibian Tractor Bn Germany: 25 Jul 45 NYPE: 21 Feb 46	25 Jul 45 Hardheim Germany (40th Tank Bn) / 22 Feb 46 Cp Kilmer N.J.	Terneuzen Holland
69th Amphibian Tractor Bn Germany: 11 Jul 45 NYPE: 6 Mar 46	11 Jul 45 Germany (69th Tank Bn) / 8 Mar 46 Cp Kilmer N.J.	Ettersburg Germany
80th Amphibian Tractor Bn Czechoslovakia: 11 Jul 45 NYPE: 20 Feb 46	11 Jul 45 Czechoslovakia (80th Tank Bn) / 22 Feb 46 Cp Kilmer N.J.	Hattorf Germany
534th Amphibian Tractor Bn SFPE: 8 Feb 44 Hawaii: 15 Feb 44 Saipan: 15 Jun 44 Tinian: 24 Jul 44 Hawaii: 29 Aug 44 Okinawa: 21 Jul 45 Philippines: 22 Aug 45 - **21** SFPE: 7 Jan 46	27 Oct 43 Ft Ord Calif (534th Armd Inf Bn) / 8 Jan 46 Cp Anza Calif	Ulithi enroute to Philippines
535th Amphibian Tractor Bn	30 Jun 45 Ft Ord Calif / 10 Nov 45 Ft Ord Calif	Ft Ord Calif
536th Amphibian Tractor Bn SPE: 8 Jun 44 Hawaii: 17 Jun 44 Leyte Philippines: 20 Oct 44 Ormoc I Philippines: 7 Dec 44 Okinawa: 1 Apr 45 - **13,19**	29 Jan 44 Ft Ord Calif (536th Armd Inf Bn) / 15 Apr 46 Okinawa	Okinawa
539th Amphibian Tractor Bn SPE: 17 Oct 44 Hawaii: 24 Oct 44 New Caledonia: 14 Feb 45 Philippines: 27 Jun 45 - **13** SFPE: 4 Jan 46	14 Apr 44 Ft Ord Calif (cadre fm 706th TD Bn) / 7 Jan 46 Cp Stoneman Calif	Leyte Philippines
540th Amphibian Tractor Bn SPE: 27 Oct 44 Hawaii: 4 Nov 44 New Caledonia: 28 Feb 45 Philippines: 22 Jun 45 - **13** SFPE: 4 Jan 46	14 Apr 44 Ft Ord Calif (cadre fm 706th TD Bn) / 7 Jan 46 Cp Stoneman Calif	Leyte Philippines
658th Amphibian Tractor Bn SFPE: 23 Sep 44 New Guinea: 17 Oct 44 New Britain I: 28 Oct 44 Lingayen Gulf Philippines: 9 Jan 45 Palawan I: 28 Feb 45 Zamboanga Mindanao: 10 Mar 45 Cebu I: 26 Mar 45 Sanga Sanga I: 2 Apr 45 Jolo I: 9 Apr 45 Malabang Mindanao: 17 Apr 45 Macajalar Bay Philippines: 10 May 45 - **3,13,14,20** SFPE: 13 Jan 46	15 Apr 44 Ft Ord Calif (658th TD Bn)/15 Jan 46 Cp Stoneman Calif	Bacolod Philippines
672nd Amphibian Tractor Bn SFPE: 23 Sep 44 Bougainville: 9 Sep 44 Lingayen Gulf Philippines: 9 Jan 45 Balikpapan Borneo: 1 Jul 45 - **14, 15,16** SFPE: 24 Dec 45	15 Apr 44 Ft Ord Calif (672nd TD Bn) / 24 Dec 45 Cp Stoneman Calif	Manila Philippines less Co A at Morotai Island
708th Amphibian Tank Bn SFPE: 24 Dec 43 Hawaii: 31 Dec 43 Kwajalein: 1 Feb 44 Majuro I: 17 Feb 44 Hawaii: 14 Mar 44 Philippines: 25 Feb 45 Ryukyus (Aka Shima, Zamami Shima, Geruma Shima, Hokai Shima): 26 Mar 45 Ryukyus (Amura Shima, Kuba Shima, Tokashika Shima): 27 Mar 45 Keise Shima: 31 Mar 45 Ie Shima I:16 Apr 45 Okinawa: 25 Apr 45 Philippines: 17 Jul 45 - **10,19,21** *(reorganized as Amphib Trac Bn during Marshalls campaign)*	27 Oct 43 Ft Ord Calif (708th Tank Bn) / 25 Jan 46 Philippines	Cebu I. less Co C at Okinawa
715th Amphibian Tractor Bn SFPE: 6 Jan 44 Hawaii: 15 Jan 44 Saipan: 15 Jun 44 Hawaii: 18 Aug 44 Philippines: 27 Feb 45 Ryukyus (Yakabi Shima, Aka Shima, Zamami Shima): 26 Mar 45 Ryukyus (Amura Shima, Kuba Shima): 27 Mar 45 Ie Shima I: 16 Apr 45 - **19,21** SFPE: 11 Jan 46	27 Oct 43 Ft Ord Calif (715th Tank Bn) / 13 Jan 46 Cp Stoneman Calif	Okinawa
718th Amphibian Tractor Bn SPE: 29 Jul 44 Hawaii: 9 Aug 44 Leyte Philippines: 20 Oct 44 Ormoc I Philippines: 7 Dec 44 Okinawa: 1 Apr 45 - **13,19**	15 Apr 44 Ft Ord Calif (718th Tank Bn) / 15 Apr 46 Okinawa	Okinawa
720th Amphibian Tractor Bn SPE: 30 Oct 44 Hawaii: 5 Nov 44 SPE: 21 Dec 45	14 Apr 44 Ft Ord Calif / 23 Dec 45 Vancouver Barracks Wash	Okinawa
726th Amphibian Tractor Bn SPE: 8 Jun 44 Hawaii: 15 Jun 44 Angaur I: 17 Sep 44 Garakayo: 9 Oct 44 Ngeregone: 15 Nov 44 Saipan: 30 Apr 45 Okinawa: 30 May 45 - **21** SPE: 1 Mar 46	26 Jan 44 Ft Ord Calif / 2 Mar 46 Ft Lawton Wash	Okinawa

BATTALION DESIGNATION AND TYPE	FORMED (SOURCE OF UNIT)/INACTIVATION	AUGUST 1946 LOCATION

727th Amphibian Tractor Bn   26 Jan 44 Ft Ord Calif / 15 Mar 46 Okinawa   Dagupan Philippines
SFPE: 16 Jun 44   New Guinea: 5 Jul 44   Leyte Philippines: 20 Oct 44   Lingayen Gulf Philippines: 9 Jan 45   Labuan I: 10 Jan 45
Tarakan I: 1 May 45   Balikpapan Borneo: 1 Jul 45 - **13,14,15**   Okinawa: 20 Oct 45

728th Amphibian Tractor Bn   15 Jan 44 Ft Ord Calif (775th TD Bn) / 15 Dec 45 Philippines   Mindoro Philippines
SPE: 7 Aug 44   Hawaii: 14 Aug 44   Leyte Philippines: 20 Oct 44   Okinawa: 1 Apr 45 - **13,19**

737th Amphibian Tractor Bn   11 Jul 45 Vilshofen Germany (737th Tank Bn) / 15 Nov 45 Ft Ord Calif   Shipment #10447-A at sea aboard **SS** *Tim Dwight*
Germany: 11 Jul 45   BPE: 16 Aug 45

738th Amphibian Tractor Bn   16 Jul 45 Jesberg Germany (738th Tank Bn) / 20 Nov 45 Ft Ord Calif   Shipment #10447-B at sea aboard **SS** *Lyman Abbott*
Germany: 16 Jul 45   BPE: 19 Aug 45

739th Amphibian Tractor Bn   11 Jul 45 Detmold Germany (739th Tank Bn) / 21 Nov 45 Ft Ord Calif   Shipment #10447-C at sea
Germany: 11 Jul 45   NYPE: 18 Aug 45

742nd Amphibian Tank Bn   15 Aug 44 Ft Ord Calif (742nd Tank Bn) / 20 Feb 46 Ft Ord Calif   Arriving Cp Cooke Calif

747th Amphibian Tank Bn   10 Jul 45 Jaderberg Germany (747th Tank Bn) / 6 Mar 46 Cp Kilmer N.J.   Jaderberg Germany
Germany: 10 Jul 45   NYPE: 5 Mar 46

764th Amphibian Tractor Bn   3 Aug 44 Ft Ord Calif (764th Tank Bn) / 20 Feb 46 Ft Ord Calif   Cp Cooke Calif

773rd Amphibian Tractor Bn   20 Oct 43 Ft Ord Calif as Amphibian Tank Bn (773rd Tank Bn) / 15 Apr 46 Japan   Leyte Philippines
SFPE: 8 Feb 44   Hawaii: 15 Feb 44   Saipan: 15 Jun 44   Tinian: 24 Jul 44   Hawaii: 17 Aug 44   Geruma, Hokaji Shima: 26 Mar 45
Tokashiki Shima: 27 Mar 45   Keise Shima: 31 Mar 45   Ie Shima I: 16 Apr 45 - **19,21** *(redes Amphib Tractor 10 Jan 44)*

776th Amphibian Tank Bn   28 Jan 44 Ft Ord Calif (776th Tank Bn) / 21 Jan 46 Cp Anza Calif   Okinawa
SPE: 8 Jun 44   Hawaii: 15 Jun 44   Angaur I: 17 Sep 44   Leyte Philippines: 20 Oct 44   Negeregong I: 15 Nov 44
Okinawa: 1 Apr 45 - **13,19,21**   LAPE: 20 Jan 46

780th Amphibian Tank Bn   8 Apr 44 Ft Ord Calif (780th Tank Bn) / 1 Jan 46 Cp Stoneman Calif   Okinawa
SPE: 9 Jul 44   Hawaii: 15 Jul 44   Leyte Philippines: 20 Oct 44   Okinawa: 1 Apr 45 - **13,19**   SFPE: 30 Dec 45

788th Amphibian Tractor Bn   15 Apr 44 Ft Ord Calif (788th Tank Bn) / 15 Dec 45 Philippines   Mindoro Philippines
SPE: 29 Jul 44   Hawaii: 9 Aug 44   Leyte Philippines: 20 Oct 44   Okinawa: 1 Apr 45 - **13,19**

795th Amphibian Tank Bn   30 Jun 45 Ft Ord Calif / 3 Nov 45 Ft Ord Calif   Ft Ord Calif

826th Amphibian Tractor Bn   18 Apr 44 Ft Ord Calif (826th TD Bn) / 24 Dec 45 Cp Stoneman Calif   Luzon Philippines
SFPE: 16 Aug 44   New Guinea: 4 Sep 44   Leyte Philippines: 20 Oct 44   Lingayen Gulf Philippines: 9 Jan 45 - **3,13,14,15,20**
SFPE: 23 Dec 45

Provisional Amphibian Tractor Bn   1 Jan 44 Waianae Amphib Training Center Hawaii (708th Amphib Tank Bn) / 14 Feb 44
Hawaii: 1 Jan 44   Kwajalein: 31 Jan 44 - **10** *(formed from assets of 708th Amphib Tank Bn and AT companies*   discontinued
of the 17th, 32nd, and 184th Infantry Regiments for Kwajalein invasion)

Chapter 21

Tank Battalions

Battalions:

1–6 Prov (*Chinese-American*), 1–5, 8–11, 13–28, 31, 34–37, 40–48, 68–70, 80, 81, 192–194, 662, 701, 702, 706–718, 735–764, 766, 767, 771–782, 784–788, 812, Prov

✪ EXAMPLE — HOW TO USE THIS TABLE

Unit Designation and Type	Date Formed and Location (Source of Unit)/Inactivation and Location	August 1945 Location

Overseas Wartime Locations followed by - **Campaign Key Numbers** and PE return to United States, if applicable or space allows
(notes and remarks in parenthesis)

771st Tank Battalion	10 Sep 43 Cp Bowie Tex (1st Bn, 35th Armd Regt)/1 May 46 Germany redes 71st	Lauenstein Germany
BPE: 17 Aug 44 England: 25 Aug 44 France-ETO: 15 Oct 44 - **25,26,34** *(N–10 Sep 43* **PP; X)**	Constab Sqdn	

In this example, the 771st Tank Battalion was redesignated from the 1st Battalion, 35th Armored Regiment on 10 September 1943 at Camp Bowie, Texas. Earlier service of this unit can be tracked by looking up the service of the 35th Armored Regiment in Chapter 19. The 771st Tank Battalion *departed* Boston Port of Embarkation on 17 August 1944 and *arrived* in England on 25 August 1944. It landed in France–European Theater of Operations on 15 October 1944 and participated in the Ardennes-Alsace, Central European, and Rhineland campaigns of World War II. This information was derived by indexing the boldfaced campaign key numbers with Appendix I. It was located in Lauenstein, Germany, in August 1945, and was redesignated as the 71st Constabulary Squadron on 1 May 1946 in Germany. The 771st Tank Battalion was organized as a medium tank battalion under Table of Organization 17–25 dated 15 September 1943, effective 10 September 1943 pending publication of final Table of Organization. This information was derived by using the Index of lettered note codes given below. The battalion was never reorganized under a different Table of Organization during its actual wartime service **(X)**. In other words, it always served as a medium tank battalion.

E = T/O 17-55 dtd 15 Jan 44 Airborne Tank Bn		**K** = T/O 17-15 dtd 11 Nov 44 Light Tank Bn
F = T/O 17-26S dtd 15 Sep 43 Tank Bn (Medium) Special*		**L** = T/O 17-15 dtd 1 Mar 42 Tank Bn (Light)
G = T/O 17-85S dtd 21 Jun 43 Tank Bn, Medium (Special)*		**M** = T/O 17-85 dtd 23 Jun 42 Tank Bn (Medium)
H = T/O 27-45S dtd 4 Dec 43 Medium Tank Bn, Special*		**N** = T/O 17-25 dtd 15 Sep 43 Medium Tank Bn
I = T/O 17-75 dtd 23 Jun 42 Tank Bn (Light)		**O** = T/O 17-25 dtd 18 Nov 44 Medium Tank Bn
J = T/O 17-15 dtd 12 Nov 43 Light Tank Bn		**PP** = Pending publication of final T/O

X = Never reorganized under different T/O, or reorganized past end of hostilities in theater of operations applicable to that unit.

*****F, G, H** are mine-clearing tank battalion organizations.

In some cases, to conserve space, T/O letter keys are not given if coincides with formation of battalion and the type is obvious as organized under the applicable T/O.

BATTALION DESIGNATION AND UNIT	FORMED (SOURCE OF UNIT)/INACTIVATION *Active through 1946	AUGUST 1945 LOCATION
1st Tank Battalion Italy: 20 Jul 44 - **31,33,35** *(N–20 Jul 44;* **X)** *(1st Armd Div)*	20 Jul 44 Bolgheri Italy (1st Armd Regt)/1 May 46 Germany redes 1st Constab Sqdn	Salzburg Austria
1st Tank Battalion, Provisional India: 1 Oct 43 Burma: 20 Jan 44 - **5,12** *(Chinese-American)*	1 Oct 43 Ramgarh India / Phased into Kuomintang Army by end of war	Sookeratung India
2nd Tank Battalion NYPE: 20 Aug 44 England: 26 Aug 44 France-ETO: 9 Oct 44 - **25,26,34** HRPE: 7 Oct 45 *(N–9 Oct 43;* **O**–*19 Apr 45) (9th Armd Div)*	9 Oct 43 Cp Young Calif (2nd Armd Regt) / 7 Oct 45 Cp Patrick Henry Va	Kulmbach Germany
2nd Tank Battalion, Provisional India: 1 Oct 43 Burma: 20 Jan 44 - **5,12** *(Chinese-American)*	1 Oct 43 Ramgarh India / Phased into Kuomintang Army by end of war	Sookeratung India
3rd Tank Battalion NYPE: 13 Sep 44 France-ETO: 23 Sep 44 - **25,26,34** HRPE: 13 Oct 45 *(N–20 Sep 43;* **O**–*5 May 45) (10th Armd Div)*	20 Sep 43 Cp Gordon Ga (3rd Armd Regt) / 13 Oct 45 Cp Patrick Henry Va	Oberammergau Germany
3rd Tank Battalion, Provisional India: 1 Oct 43 Burma: 20 Jan 44 - **5,12** *(Chinese-American)*	1 Oct 43 Ramgarh India / Phased into Kuomintang Army by end of war	Sookeratung India
4th Tank Battalion Italy: 20 Jul 44 - **31,33,35** *(N–20 Jul 44,* **X)** *(1st Armd Div)*	20 Jul 44 Bolgheri Italy (3rd Bn, 13th Armd Regt) / 1 May 46 Germany redes 72nd Constab Sqdn	Salzburg Austria
4th Tank Battalion, Provisional India: 1 Oct 43 Burma: 20 Jan 44 - **5,12** *(Chinese-American)*	1 Oct 43 Ramgarh India / Phased into Kuomintang Army by end of war	Sookeratung India
5th Tank Battalion NYPE: 5 Feb 45 France-ETO: 16 Feb 45 - **26** *(N–10 Sep 43* **PP;** **O**–*16 May 45) (16th Armd Div)*	10 Sep 43 Cp Chaffee Ark (5th Armd Regt) / 16 Oct 45 Cp Shanks N.Y.	Tepl Czechoslovakia
5th Tank Battalion, Provisional India: 1 Oct 43 Burma: 20 Jan 44 - **5,12** *(Chinese-American)*	1 Oct 43 Ramgarh India / Phased into Kuomintang Army by end of war	Sookeratung India

BATTALION DESIGNATION AND TYPE	FORMED (SOURCE OF UNIT)/INACTIVATION	AUGUST 1945 LOCATION

6th Tank Battalion, Provisional   1 Oct 43 Ramgarh India / Phased into Kuomintang Army by end of war   Sookeratung India
India: 1 Oct 43   Burma: 20 Jan 44 - **5,12** *(Chinese-American)*

8th Tank Battalion   10 Sep 43 Cp Bowie Tex (3rd Bn, 35th Armd Regt)/1 May 46 Germany redes 8th   Vilsiburg Germany
BPE: 29 Dec 43   England: 8 Jan 44   France-ETO: 13 Jul 44 - **25,26,30,32,34** *(N–10 Sep 43 PP; X) (4th Armd Div)*   Constab Sqdn

9th Tank Battalion   10 Sep 43 Cp Campbell Ky (9th Armd Regt) / 2 Apr 46 Cp Hood Tex   Cp Cooke Calif
BPE: 6 Feb 45   France-ETO: 17 Feb 45 - **26**   NYPE: 6 Aug 45 *(N–10 Sep 43; O–20 May 45) (20th Armd Div)*

10th Tank Battalion   20 Sep 43 Pine Camp N.Y. (3rd Bn, 34th Armd Regt) / 9 Oct 45 Cp Myles Standish   Benneckenstein Germany
NYPE: 11 Feb 44   England: 23 Feb 44   France-ETO: 25 Jul 44 - **25,26,30,32,34**   BPE: 8 Oct 45 *(N–20 Sep 43; O–1 May 45)*   Mass
(5th Armd Div)

11th Tank Battalion   20 Sep 43 Cp Gordon Ga (11th Armd Regt) / 13 Oct 45 Cp Patrick Henry Va   Schongau Germany
NYPE: 13 Sep 44   France-ETO: 23 Sep 44 - **25,26,34**   HRPE: 13 Oct 45 *(N–20 Sep 43; O–5 May 45) (10th Armd Div)*

13th Tank Battalion   20 Jul 44 Italy (13th Armd Regt) / 1 May 46 Germany redes 13th Constab Sqdn   Salzburg Austria
Italy: 20 Jul 44 - **31,33,35** *(N–20 Jul 44; X) (1st Armd Div)*

14th Tank Battalion   9 Oct 43 Desert Training Center Calif (14th Armd Regt) /13 Oct 45 Cp Patrick Henry   Lichtenfels Germany
NYPE: 20 Aug 44   England: 26 Aug 44   France-ETO: 9 Oct 44 - **25,26,34**   HRPE: 12 Oct 45 *(N–9 Oct 43; O–19 Apr 45)*   Va
(9th Armd Div)

15th Tank Battalion   20 Sep 43 Cp Cooke Calif (3rd Bn, 68th Armd Regt) / 25 Feb 46 Cp Kilmer N.J.   Jena, Germany
NYPE: 11 Feb 44   England: 24 Feb 44   France-ETO: 22 Jul 44 - **25,26,30,32,34**   NYPE: 20 Feb 46 *(N–20 Sep 43; O–20 May 45)*
(6th Armd Div until 19 Jul 45)

16th Tank Battalion   10 Sep 43 Cp Chaffee Ark (16th Armd Regt) / 14 Oct 45 Cp Shanks N.Y.   Krukanice Czechoslovakia
NYPE: 5 Feb 45   France-ETO: 17 Feb 45 - **26**   NYPE: 13 Oct 45 *(N–10 Sep 43 PP; O–16 May 45) (16th Armd Div)*

17th Tank Battalion   20 Sep 43 Ft Benning Ga (3rd Bn, 31st Armd Regt) / 11 Oct 45 Cp Kilmer N.J.   Krostitz Germany
NYPE: 7 Jun 44   England: 13 Jun 44   France-ETO: 11 Aug 44 - **25,26,32,34**   NYPE: 10 Oct 45 *(N–20 Sep 43; X) (7th Armd Div)*

18th Tank Battalion   20 Sep 43 Cp Polk La (3rd Bn, 36th Armd Regt) / 11 Nov 45 Cp Shanks N.Y.   Clausthal-Zellerfeld Germany
NYPE: 7 Nov 44   England: 18 Nov 44   France-ETO: 7 Jan 45 - **25,26,34**   NYPE: 10 Nov 45 *(N–20 Sep 43; O–1 May 45) (8th Armd Div)*

19th Tank Battalion   9 Oct 43 Cp Polk La (3rd Bn, 2nd Armd Regt) / 9 Oct 45 Cp Patrick Henry Va   Hof Germany
NYPE: 20 Aug 44   England: 26 Aug 44   France-ETO: 9 Oct 44 - **25,26,34**   HRPE: 8 Oct 45 *(N–9 Oct 43; O–19 Apr 43) (9th Armd Div)*

20th Tank Battalion   19 Sep 43 Cp Campbell Ky (20th Armd Regt) / 2 Apr 46 Cp Hood Tex   Cp Cooke Calif
BPE: 6 Feb 45   France-ETO: 17 Feb 45 - **26**   NYPE: 6 Aug 45 *(N–19 Sep 43; O–20 May 45) (20th Armd Div)*

21st Tank Battalion   20 Sep 43 Cp Gordon Ga (3rd Bn, 3rd Armd Regt) /19 Oct 45 Cp Myles Standish Mass   Garmisch-Partenkirchen
NYPE: 13 Sep 44   England: 23 Sep 44   France-ETO: 23 Sep 44 - **25,26,34**   BPE: 18 Oct 45 *(N–20 Sep 43; O–5 May 45) (10th Armd Div)*   Germany

22nd Tank Battalion   20 Sep 43 Cp Barkeley Tex (3rd Bn, 41st Armd Regt) / 31 Aug 45 Germany   Haslach Germany
NYPE: 29 Sep 44   France: 2 Oct 44   England: 5 Oct 44   France-ETO: 17 Dec 44 - **25,26,34** *(N–20 Sep 43; X) (11th Armd Div)*

23rd Tank Battalion   11 Nov 43 Tennessee Maneuver Area (3rd Bn, 43rd Armd Regt) / 3 Dec 45 Cp Kilmer   Augsburg Germany
NYPE: 20 Sep 44   England: 2 Oct 44   France-ETO: 16 Nov 44 - **25,26,34**   NYPE: 1 Dec 45 *(N–11 Nov 43; X) (12th Armd Div)*   N.J.

24th Tank Battalion   20 Sep 43 Cp Beale Calif (3rd Bn, 45th Armd Regt) / 14 Nov 45 Cp Cooke Calif   Cp Cooke Calif
NYPE: 18 Jan 45   France-ETO: 29 Jan 45 - **26,34**   HRPE: 23 Jul 45 *(N–20 Sep 43; O–16 May 45) (13th Armd Div)*

25th Tank Battalion   15 Sep 43 Cp Chaffee Ark (3rd Bn, 47th Armd Regt) /16 Sep 45 Cp Patrick Henry Va   Toging Germany
NYPE: 14 Oct 44   France-ETO: 28 Oct 44 - **25,26,34**   HRPE: 16 Sep 45 *(N–20 Sep 43; X) (14th Armd Div)*

26th Tank Battalion   10 Sep 43 Cp Chaffee Ark (3rd Bn, 5th Armd Regt) /16 Oct 45 Cp Myles Standish   Dal Jamne Germany
NYPE: 5 Feb 45   France-ETO: 17 Jan 45 - **26**   BPE: 15 Oct 45 *(N–10 Sep 43 PP; O–16 May 45) (16th Armd Div)*   Mass

27th Tank Battalion   10 Sep 43 Cp Campbell Ky (3rd Bn, 9th Armd Regt) / 2 Apr 46 Cp Hood Tex   Cp Cooke Calif
BPE: 6 Feb 45   France-ETO: 19 Feb 45 - **26**   NYPE: 6 Aug 45 *(N–20 Sep 43; O–20 May 45) (20th Armd Div)*

28th Tank Battalion   6 Dec 43 Ft Knox Ky as Airborne Tank Bn / 13 Jan 46 Cp Stoneman Calif   Shipment #2209-C **USS** *Elmore*
LAPE: 5 Aug 45   Philippines: 30 Aug 45   SFPE: 11 Jan 46 *(activated under proposed undated T/O; E—19 Feb 44; redes fm A/B under*   **(APA.42)**
N–20 Oct 44; O–10 Feb 45)

31st Tank Battalion   20 Sep 43 Ft Benning Ga (31st Armd Regt)/11 Oct 45 Cp Shanks N.Y.   Bitterfeld Germany
NYPE: 7 Jun 44   England: 13 Jun 44   France-ETO: 11 Aug 44 - **25,26,32,34**   NYPE: 9 Oct 45 *(N–20 Sep 43; X) (7th Armd Div)*

34th Tank Battalion   20 Sep 43 Pine Camp N.Y. (34th Armd Regt) / 8 Oct 45 Cp Myles Standish Mass   Sommerds Germany
NYPE: 11 Feb 44   England: 23 Feb 44   France-ETO: 25 Jul 44 - **25,26,30,32,34**   BPE: 7 Oct 45 *(N–20 Sep 43; O–1 May 45) (5th Armd Div)*

35th Tank Battalion   10 Sep 43 Cp Bowie Tex (35th Armd Regt) /1 May 46 Germany redes 35th Constab   Strakonice Czechoslovakia
BPE: 29 Dec 43   England: 9 Jan 44   France-ETO: 13 Jul 44 - **25,26,30,32,34** *(N–10 Sep 43 PP; X) (4th Armd Div)*   Sqdn

BATTALION DESIGNATION AND TYPE　　　　**FORMED (SOURCE OF UNIT)/INACTIVATION**　　　　**AUGUST 1945 LOCATION**

36th Tank Battalion　　　　20 Sep 43 Cp Polk La (36th Armd Regt)/11 Nov 45 Cp Kilmer N.J.　　　　Northeim Germany
NYPE: 7 Nov 44　　England: 18 Nov 44　　France-ETO: 3 Jan 45 - **25,26,34**　　NYPE: 10 Nov 45 *(N–20 Sep 43; O–1 May 45) (8th Armd Div)*

37th Tank Battalion　　　　10 Sep 43 Cp Bowie Tex (37th Armd Regt)/1 May 46 Germany redes 37th Constab　　　　Neumarkt Germany
BPE: 29 Dec 43　　England: 8 Jan 44　　France-ETO: 11 Jul 44 - **25,26,30,32,34** *(N–10 Sep 43 PP;X) (4th Armd Div)*　　　　Sqdn

40th Tank Battalion　　　　20 Sep 43 Ft Benning Ga (40th Armd Regt)/25 Jul 45 Germany redes 40th Amphibian
NYPE: 7 Jun 44　　England: 13 Jun 44　　France-ETO: 11 Aug 44 - **25,26,32,34** *(N–20 Sep 43) (7th Armd Div until 25 Jul 43)*　　　　Tractor Bn

41st Tank Battalion　　　　20 Sep 43 Cp Barkeley Tex (41st Armd Regt)/31 Aug 45 Austria　　　　Linz Austria
NYPE: 29 Sep 44　　England: 11 Oct 44　　France-ETO: 11 Dec 44 - **25,26,34** *(N–20 Sep 43) (11th Armd Div)*

42nd Tank Battalion　　　　20 Sep 43 Cp Barkeley Tex (42nd Armd Regt) / 31 Aug 45 Germany　　　　Leonfelden Germany
NYPE: 29 Sep 44　　England: 11 Oct 44　　France-ETO: 18 Dec 44 - **25,26,34** *(N–20 Sep 43; X) (11th Armd Div)*

43rd Tank Battalion　　　　11 Nov 43 Tennessee Maneuver Area (43rd Armd Regt) / 3 Dec 45 Cp Kilmer N.J.　　　　Ellwangen Germany
NYPE: 20 Sep 44　　France-ETO: 2 Oct 44 - **25,26,34**　　NYPE: 1 Dec 45 *(N–11 Nov 43; X) (12th Armd Div)*

44th Tank Battalion　　　　11 Nov 43 Tennessee Maneuver Area (44th Armd Regt) / 10 May 46 Japan　　　　Manila Philippines
Portland Sub-P/E: 23 Mar 44　　Australia: 21 Apr 44　　New Guinea: 11 May 44　　Admiralty I: 25 Sep 44
Philippines: 20 Oct 44 - **3,13,14,15** *(N–11 Nov 43; O–9 Feb 45) (12th Armd Div until 11 Feb 44)*

45th Tank Battalion　　　　20 Sep 43 Cp Beale Calif (45th Armd Regt) / 13 Nov 45 Cp Cooke Calif　　　　Cp Cooke Calif
NYPE: 18 Jan 45　　France-ETO: 30 Jan 45 - **26,34**　　BPE: 27 Jul 45 *(N–20 Sep 43; O–16 May 45) (13th Armd Div)*

46th Tank Battalion　　　　20 Sep 43 Cp Beale Calif (46th Armd Regt) / 13 Nov 45 Cp Cooke Calif　　　　Cp Cooke Calif
NYPE: 18 Jan 45　　England: 29 Jan 45　　France-ETO: 29 Jan 45 - **26,34**　　NYPE: 23 Jul 45 *(N–20 Sep 43; O–16 May 45) (13th Armd Div)*

47th Tank Battalion　　　　20 Sep 43 Cp Chaffee Ark (47th Armd Regt) / 16 Sep 45 Cp Patrick Henry Va　　　　Muhldorfer Hart Germany
NYPE: 14 Oct 44　　France-ETO: 28 Oct 44 - **25,26,34**　　HRPE: 16 Sep 45 *(N–20 Sep 43; X) (14th Armd Div)*

48th Tank Battalion　　　　20 Sep 43 Cp Chaffee Ark (48th Armd Regt) / 16 Sep 45 Cp Patrick Henry Va　　　　Klettham Germany
NYPE: 14 Oct 44　　France-ETO: 28 Oct 44 - **25,26,34**　　HRPE: 16 Sep 45 *(N–20 Sep 43; X) (14th Armd Div)*

68th Tank Battalion　　　　20 Sep 43 Cp Cooke Calif (68th Armd Regt) / 29 Dec 45 Cp Patrick Henry Va　　　　Buttstadt Germany
NYPE: 11 Feb 44　　England: 24 Feb 44　　France-ETO: 22 Jul 44 - **25,26,30,32,34**　　HRPE: 29 Dec 45 *(N–20 Sep 43; O–20 May 45)*
(6th Armd Div until 19 Jul 45)

69th Tank Battalion　　　　20 Sep 43 Cp Cooke Calif (69th Armd Regt) /11 Jul 45 Germany redes 69th Amphibian
NYPE: 11 Feb 44　　England: 26 Feb 44　　France-ETO: 21 Jul 44 - **25,26,30,32,34** *(N–20 Sep 43; O–20 May 45)*　　　　Tractor Bn
(6th Armd Div until 11 Jul 45)

70th Tank Battalion　　　　15 Jul 40 Ft George G. Meade Md (pers of 1st Bn, 67th Armd Regt) /1 Jun 46 Germany　　　　Bamberg Germany
NYPE: 13 Jan 43　　N.Africa: 26 Jan 43 (Co A: 8 Nov 42)　　Sicily: 11 Jul 43　　England: 28 Nov 43　　France-ETO: 6 Jun 44 -
23,25,26,30,32,34,36,38 *(activated as Tank Bn [Medium]; redes Tank Bn [Light Tank] 7 Oct 41; Tank Bn [Light] under L–9 May 42;*
Tank Bn under N–1 Dec 43; X)

80th Tank Battalion　　　　20 Sep 43 Cp Polk La (80th Armd Regt) 11 Jul 45 Czechoslovakia redes 80th Amphibian
NYPE: 7 Nov 44　　England: 18 Nov 44　　France-ETO: 6 Jan 45 - **25,26,34** *(N–20 Sep 43; O–1 May 45)*　　　　Tractor Bn
(8th Armd Div until 11 Jul 45)

81st Tank Battalion　　　　20 Sep 43 Pine Camp N.Y. (81st Armd Regt) / 8 Oct 45 Cp Myles Standish Mass　　　　Bleicherode Germany
NYPE: 11 Feb 44　　England: 23 Feb 44　　France-ETO: 25 Jul 44 - **25,26,30,32,34**　　BPE: 7 Oct 45 *(N–20 Sep 43; O–1 May 45) (5th Armd Div)*

191st Tank Battalion　　　　20 Feb 41 Ft George G Meade Md *(see remarks)* / 7 Dec 45 Cp Patrick Henry Va　　　　Hohenkamer Germany
NYPE: 28 Feb 43　　N.Africa: 9 Mar 43　　Italy: 9 Sep 43　　France-ETO: 15 Aug 44 - **24,25,26,29,34,35,37**　　HRPE: 6 Dec 45
(org as Tank Bn [Light] w/Cos A,B,C,D fm 27th [NY NG], 26th [Mass NG], 29th [Va NG], 43rd [Conn NG] Tank Cos respectively;
Tank Bn [Medium] M–8 Aug 42; N–22 Dec 43; O–20 Apr 45)

192nd Tank Battalion (Light)　　　　20 Dec 40 Ft Knox Ky *(see remarks)* / 9 Apr 42 Bataan Philippines
SFPE: 27 Oct 41　　Philippines: Nov 41 - **18** *(org as Tank Bn [Light] w/Cos A,B,C,D fm 32nd [Wis NG], 33rd [Ill NG], 37th [Ohio NG],*
38th [Ky NG] Tank Cos respectively)

193rd Tank Battalion　　　　20 Jan 41 Ft Benning Ga *(see remarks)* / 21 Jan 46 Cp Stoneman Calif　　　　Okinawa
SFPE: 23 Dec 41　　Hawaii: 7 Jan 42　　Makin I: 20 Nov 43　　Hawaii: 3 Dec 43　　Espiritu Santo: 16 Jan 45　　Okinawa: 8 Apr 45 - **6,21**
SFPE: 18 Jan 46 *(I–1 Jan 43; N–17 Dec 43; O–17 Jun 45) (org as Tank Bn [Light] w/Cos A,B,C,D, fm 30th [Ga NG], 31st [Ala NG],*
36th [Tex NG], 45th [Colo NG] Tank Cos respectively)

194th Tank Battalion (Light)　　　　12 Mar 41 Ft Lewis Wash *(see remarks)* / 9 Apr 42 Bataan Philippines, less Co B
SFPE: 5 Sep 41　　Philippines: 26 Sep 41 - **18** *(org as Tank Bn [Light] w/Cos A,B,C, fm 34th [Minn NG], 35th [Mo NG],*
40th [Calif NG] Tank Cos respectively) (Co B did not accompany the battalion in its movement to the Philippines, and was subsequently
redesignated as the 602nd Medium Tank Company)

662nd Tank Battalion　　　　17 Dec 44 Ft Knox Ky (662nd TD Bn) / 24 Feb 45 Ft Knox Ky　　　　*(N–17 Dec 44; X)*

BATTALION DESIGNATION AND TYPE   **FORMED (SOURCE OF UNIT)/INACTIVATION**   *Active through 1946   **AUGUST 1945 LOCATION**

701st Tank Battalion   1 Mar 43 Cp Campbell Ky as Tank Bn (Medium) / 25 Dec 45 Cp Kilmer N.J.   Gotha Germany
NYPE: 22 Apr 44   England: 30 Apr 44   France-ETO: 24 Aug 44 - **26,32,34**   NYPE: 24 Dec 45 (**F**–6 *Nov 43; Medium Tank Bn, Special*
H–*8 Feb 44; Tank Bn* **N**–*31 Oct 44;* **O**–*15 Apr 45*)

702nd Tank Battalion   1 Mar 43 Cp Campbell Ky as Tank Bn (Medium) / 19 Sep 45 Cp Patrick Henry Va   Gmunden Austria
NYPE: 22 Apr 44   England: 30 Apr 44   France-ETO: 6 Aug 44 - **25,26,32,34**   HRPE: 19 Sep 45 (**N**–*20 Oct 43,* **X**)
(6th Armd Div past 11 Jul 45)

706th Tank Battalion   10 Sep 43 Cp Bowie Tex (3rd Bn, 37th Armd Regt) / 30 Sep 46 Philippines   Okinawa
SPE: 22 Mar 44   Hawaii: 29 Mar 44   Guam: 22 Jul 44   Philippines: 23 Nov 44   Ie Shima I: 16 Apr 45   Okinawa: 25 Apr 45 - **13,19,21**
*(***N**–*10 Sep 43* **PP**, **O**–*11 Aug 45)*

707th Tank Battalion   20 Sep 43 Pine Camp N.Y. (3rd Bn, 81st Armd Regt) /8 Oct 45 Cp Myles Standish   Eisfeld Germany
BPE: 11 Feb 44   England: 23 Feb 44   France-ETO: 1 Sep 44 - **25,26,32,34**   BPE: 7 Oct 45 (**N**–*20 Sep 43;* **O**–*12 Jul 45)*   Mass
(12 Jul 45 assigned 7th Armd Div)

708th Tank Battalion   20 Sep 43 Cp Cooke Calif (3rd Bn, 69th Armd Regt)/27 Oct 43 Ft Ord Calif redes
708th Amphibian Tank Bn

709th Tank Battalion   20 Sep 43 Ft Benning Ga (3rd Bn, 40th Armd Regt) / 10 Apr 46 Cp Kilmer N.J.   Eger Germany
BPE: 28 Feb 44   England: 8 Mar 44   France-ETO: 11 Jul 44 - **25,26,30,32,34**   NYPE: 9 Apr 46 (**N**–*20 Sep 43;* **O**–*15 Apr 45)*

710th Tank Battalion   20 Sep 43 Cp Polk La (3rd Bn, 80th Armd Regt) / 17 Jan 46 Cp Anza Calif   Leyte Philippines
SPE: 15 Jun 44   Hawaii: 22 Jun 44   Palau I: 17 Sep 44   New Caledonia: 23 Dec 44   Philippines: 17 May 45 - **13,21**
*(***N**–*20 Sep 43;* **O**–*5 Mar 45)*   LAPE: 16 Jan 46

711th Tank Battalion   9 Oct 43 Desert Training Center Calif (3rd Bn, 14th Armd Regt)/21 Jan 46 Ft Lawton   Okinawa
SPE: 22 Mar 44   Hawaii: 29 Mar 44   Philippines: 4 Feb 45   Okinawa: 1 Apr 45 - **19**   SPE: 18 Jan 46 (**N**–*9 Oct 43;* **X**)   Wash

712th Tank Battalion   20 Sep 43 Cp Gordon Ga (3rd Bn, 11th Armd Regt)/27 Oct 45 Cp Kilmer N.J.   Amberg Germany
BPE: 28 Feb 44   England: 8 Mar 44   France-ETO: 29 Jun 44 - **25,26,30,32,34**   NYPE: 25 Oct 45 (**N**–*20 Sep 43;* **X**)

713th Tank Bn (Armored Flamethrower)   20 Sep 43 Cp Barkeley Tex (3rd Bn, 42nd Armd Regt)/14 Feb 46 Korea   Okinawa
SPE: 14 Aug 44   Hawaii: 21 Aug 44   Philippines: 16 Mar 45   Okinawa: 7 Apr 45 - **19**
*(***N**–*20 Sep 43; Provisional Armored Flamethrower - 11th Jan 45)*

714th Tank Battalion   11 Nov 43 Tennessee Maneuver Area (3rd Bn, 44th Armd Regt) / 4 Dec 45 Cp Kilmer   Wertingen Germany
NYPE: 20 Sep 44   France-ETO: 2 Oct 44 - **25,26,34**   NYPE: 3 Dec 45 (**N**–*11 Nov 43;* **X**) *(assigned 12th Armd Div 7 Mar 44)*   N.J.

715th Tank Battalion   20 Sep 43 Cp Beale Calif (3rd Bn, 46th Armd Regt) / 27 Oct 43 Ft Ord Calif redes
715th Amphibian Tractor Bn

716th Tank Battalion   20 Sep 43 Cp Chaffee Ark (3rd Bn, 48th Armd Regt) /19 Dec 45 Cp Stoneman Calif   Davao Mindanao less Co B at
SFPE: 2 Jun 44   New Guinea: 2 Jul 44   Philippines: 9 Jan 45 - **13,14,15,20**   SFPE: 17 Dec 45 (**N**–*20 Sep 43;* **O**–*9 Feb 45)*   Macajalar Bay and Co C at Iloilo

717th Tank Battalion   3 Sep 43 Cp Chaffee Ark (1st Bn, 5th Armd Regt) / *   Cp Swift Tex
NYPE: 26 Dec 44   England: 7 Jan 45   France-ETO: 7 Feb 45 - **26,34**   NYPE: 5 Jul 45 (**N**–*c.10 Sep 43* **PP**; **O**–*15 Apr 45)*

718th Tank Battalion   10 Sep 43 Cp Campbell Ky (1st Bn, 9th Armd Regt)/15 Apr 44 Ft Ord Calif redes
718th Amphibian Tractor Bn

735th Tank Battalion   10 Jan 43 Ft Lewis Wash as Tank Bn, Medium (cadre fm 743rd Tank Bn) / 25 Oct 45   Muhltroff Germany
BPE: 11 Feb 44   England: 23 Feb 44   France-ETO: 11 Jul 44 - **25,26,30,32,34**   BPE: 24 Oct 45   Cp Myles Standish Mass
*(***N**–*1 Nov 43;* **O**–*30 Apr 45)*

736th Tank Battalion   1 Feb 43 Cp Rucker Ala as Tank Bn, Medium/11 Nov 45 Cp Kilmer N.J.   Baddeckensted Germany
NYPE: 31 Mar 44   England: 6 Apr 44   France-ETO: 24 Aug 44 - **25,26,30,32,34**   NYPE: 10 Nov 45 *(redes Tank Bn, Medium [Special]*
G–*2 Jul 43; Medium Tank Bn, Special* **H**–*8 Feb 44; Tank Bn under* **N**–*31 Oct 44;* **O**–*15 Apr 45) (assigned 8th Armd Div 12 Jul 45)*

737th Tank Battalion   1 Feb 43 Ft Lewis Wash as Tank Bn, Medium (pers fm 743rd Tank Bn) /11 Jul 45
Germany redes 737th Amphibian Tractor Bn
BPE: 11 Feb 44   England: 23 Feb 44   France-ETO: 13 Jul 44 - **25,26,30,32,34** (**N**–*1 Nov 43;* **X**)

738th Medium Tank Bn, Special   1 Mar 43 Ft Benning Ga as Tank Bn, Medium/16 Jul 45 Germany redes 738th Amphibian
NYPE: 22 Apr 44   England: 30 Apr 44   France-ETO: 10 Nov 44 - **25,26,34** *(Tank Bn, Medium [Special]* **G**–*19 Nov 43;*   Tractor Bn
Medium Tank Bn, Special **H**–*4 Dec 43)*

739th Medium Tank Bn, Special   1 Mar 43 Ft Lewis Wash as Tank Bn, Medium /11 Jul 45 Germany redes 739th Amphibian
NYPE: 26 Jul 44   England: 6 Aug 44   France-ETO: 4 Nov 44 - **25,26,34** *(Tank Bn, Medium [Special]* **G**–*5 Dec 43;*   Tractor Bn
Medium Tank Bn, Special **H**–*8 Feb 44)*

740th Tank Battalion   1 Mar 43 Ft Knox Ky as Tank Bn, Medium / 23 Jul 46 Germany   Witzenhausen Germany
NYPE: 26 Jul 44   England: 6 Aug 44   France-ETO: 30 Oct 44 - **25,26,34** *(Tank Bn, Medium [Special]* **G**–*10 Sep 43;*
Medium Tank Bn, Special **H**–*8 Feb 44; Tank Bn* **N**–*31 Oct 44)*

BATTALION DESIGNATION AND TYPE	FORMED (SOURCE OF UNIT)/INACTIVATION *Active through 1946	AUGUST 1945 LOCATION

741st Tank Battalion
15 Mar 42 Ft George G Meade Md as Tank Bn, Medium / 27 Oct 45 Cp Kilmer N.J.   Rosutka Germany
NYPE: 20 Oct 43   England: 2 Nov 43   France-ETO: 6 Jun 44 - **25,26,30,32,34**   NYPE: 25 Oct 45
(M–1 Sep 42; Tank Bn N–1 Dec 43; O–30 Apr 45)

742nd Light Tank Battalion
1 May 42 Ft Lewis Wash as Tank Bn, Light / 15 Aug 44 Ft Ord Calif redes 742nd
(J–20 Dec 43; X)   Amphibian Tank Bn

743rd Tank Battalion
16 May 42 Ft Lewis Wash as Tank Bn, Light / 27 Nov 45 Cp Myles Standish Mass   Meltheuer Germany
NYPE: 17 Nov 43   England: 25 Nov 43   France-ETO: 6 Jun 44 - **25,26,30,32,34**   BPE: 26 Nov 45 *(redes Tank Bn, Medium M–Oct 42;*
Tank Bn N–2 Dec 43; O–15 Apr 45) (partially configured as flamethrower in Nov 44)

744th Light Tank Battalion
27 Apr 42 Cp Bowie Tex as Tank Bn, Light / 2 Nov 45 Cp Patrick Henry Va   Olpe Germany
BPE: 28 Dec 43   England: 9 Jan 44   France-ETO: 30 Jun 44 - **25,26,30,32,34**   HRPE: 2 Nov 45 *(Light Tank Bn J–8 Mar 44; K–24 Mar 45)*

745th Tank Battalion
15 Aug 42 Cp Bowie Tex as Tank Bn, Medium / 27 Oct 45 Cp Kilmer N.J.   Chet Czechoslovakia
NYPE: 19 Aug 43   England: 25 Aug 43   France-ETO: 6 Jun 44 - **25,26,30,32,34**   NYPE: 25 Oct 45
(M–1 Sep 42; Tank Bn N–2 Dec 43; O–30 Apr 45)

746th Tank Battalion
20 Aug 42 Cp Rucker Ala as Tank Bn, Medium / 26 Oct 45 Cp Shanks N.Y.   Gaimersheim Germany
NYPE: 29 Jan 44   England: 9 Feb 44   France-ETO: 6 Jun 44 - **25,26,30,32,34**   NYPE: 25 Oct 45 *(Tank Bn N–22 Oct 43; O–30 Apr 45)*

747th Tank Battalion
10 Nov 42 Cp Bowie Tex as Tank Bn, Medium /14 Jul 45 Germany redes 747th Amphibian
NYPE: 11 Feb 44   England: 23 Feb 44   France-ETO: 7 Jun 44 - **26,30,32,34** *(Tank Bn N–22 Nov 43; O–15 Apr 45)*   Tank Bn
(partially configured as Flamethrower, Nov 44)

748th Tank Battalion
20 Aug 42 Cp Rucker Ala as Tank Bn, Medium /19 Sep 45 Cp Patrick Henry Va   Hart Germany
NYPE: 31 Mar 44   England: 6 Apr 44   France-ETO: 18 Jul 44 - **25,26,32,34**   HRPE: 19 Sep 45 *(redes Tank Bn, Medium [Special] under*
G–20 Apr 43 PP; Medium Tank Bn, Special under H–8 Feb 44; Tank Bn under N–31 Oct 44; O–16 May 45) (assigned 6th Armd Div 19 Jul 45)

749th Tank Battalion
2 Dec 42 Cp Bowie Tex as Tank Bn, Medium /19 Sep 45 Cp Shanks N.Y.   Langenbourg Germany
NYPE: 11 Feb 44   England: 23 Feb 44   France-ETO: 6 Jun 44 - **25,26,30,32,34**   NYPE: 18 Sep 45 *(Tank Bn N–22 Nov 43; O–30 Apr 45)*
(assigned 6th Armd Div 12 Jul 45)

750th Tank Battalion
1 Jan 43 Ft Knox Ky as Tank Bn, Medium /16 Dec 45 Cp Kilmer N.J.   Bernburg Germany
BPE: 15 Sep 44   England: 22 Sep 44   France-ETO: 3 Oct 44 - **25,26,34**   NYPE: 14 Dec 45 *(Tank Bn N–18 Oct 43; O–30 Apr 45)*

751st Tank Battalion
1 Jun 41 Ft Benning Ga as Tank Bn, Medium /1 Oct 45 Italy   Prato Centenaro Italy
NYPE: 5 Aug 42   England: 17 Aug 42   N.Africa: 15 Jan 43   Italy: 9 Sep 43 - **24,29,31,33,35,38** *(Tank Bn under N–5 Dec 43 Riardo Italy; X)*

752nd Tank Battalion
1 Jun 41 Ft Lewis Wash as Tank Bn, Medium / *   Bolzano Italy
NYPE: 5 Aug 42   England: 18 Aug 42   N.Africa: 17 Jan 43   Italy: 12 Jan 44 - **29,31,33,35,38** *(M–1 Oct 42; Tank Bn under N–18 Jan 44;*
O–20 Jun 45) (known as 2642nd Armored Replacement Battalion 21 Mar 43–18 Jan 44 - per 3rd Ind Hqs Fifth Army which GO# 31
inactivating Tank Bn was rescinded)

753rd Tank Battalion
1 Jun 41 Ft Benning Ga as Tank Bn, Medium /15 Jan 46 Cp Patrick Henry Va   Kaufbeuren Germany
HRPE: 24 Apr 43   N.Africa: 26 May 43   Sicily: 10 Jul 43   Italy: 9 Sep 43   France-ETO: 15 Aug 44 - **25,26,29,34,35,36,37**
(M–9 Sep 42; Tank Bn N–29 Mar 44; O–20 Apr 45)

754th Tank Battalion
1 Jun 41 Pine Camp N.Y. as Tank Bn, Medium/31 Dec 46 Korea   Manila Philippines less Co D at
NYPE: 23 Jan 42   New Caledonia: 12 Mar 42   Guadalcanal: 14 Aug 43 (Co C arrived Guad 4 May 43)   Bougainville: 1 Jan 44   Bagabag Philippines
Philippines: 9 Jan 45 - **14,16** *(redes Tank Bn [Light] 15 Jan 42; I–7 Nov 42; Tank Bn under N–15 Nov 43; O–9 Feb 45)*
(attached Americal Div 24 May 42–3 Apr 43)

755th Tank Battalion
1 Jun 41 Cp Bowie Tex as Tank Bn, Medium / 8 Sep 45 Italy   La Marchesa Italy
NYPE: 6 Aug 42   England: 17 Aug 42   N.Africa: 17 Jan 43   Italy: 3 Nov 43 - **29,31,33,35** *(Tank Bn under N–10 Jan 44; O–24 Apr 45)*

756th Tank Battalion
1 Jun 41 Ft Lewis Wash as Tank Bn, Light / 8 Feb 46 Cp Kilmer N.J.   Salzburg Austria
NYPE: 13 Jan 43   N.Africa: 25 Jan 43 (Cos A,C in N.Africa– 8 Nov 42)   Italy:17 Sep 43   France-ETO: 15 Aug 44 - **23,25,26,29,34,35,37**
NYPE: 7 Feb 46 *(I–21 Aug 42; redes Tank Bn St Agata Italy under N–15 Dec 43; O–20 Apr 45)*

757th Tank Battalion
1 Jun 41 Ft Ord Calif as Tank Bn, Light / 8 Oct 45 Italy   Manzano Italy
NYPE: 5 Mar 43   N.Africa: 18 Mar 43   Italy: 28 Oct 43 - **29,31,33,35** *(L–19 Mar 42; Tank Bn under N–12 Jan 44; O–18 Apr 45)*

758th Light Tank Bn (Cld)
1 Jun 41 Ft Knox Ky as Tank Bn, Light / 25 Sep 45 Italy   Bassina Italy
HRPE: 22 Oct 44   Italy: 17 Nov 44 - **31,33** *(I–24 Aug 42; K–3 May 45)*

759th Light Tank Battalion
1 Jun 41 Ft Knox Ky as Tank Bn, Light / 28 Dec 45 Cp Myles Standish Mass   Ermsleben Germany
BPE: 20 Aug 42   Iceland: 31 Aug 42   England: 9 Aug 43   France-ETO: 16 Jun 44 - **25,26,30,32,34**   BPE: 27 Dec 45 *(J–7 Mar 44; K–9 Apr 45)*

760th Tank Battalion
1 Jun 41 Cp Bowie Tex as Tank Bn, Light / 14 Sep 45 Italy   Modena Italy
NYPE: 13 Jan 43   N.Africa: 26 Jan 43   Italy: 30 Oct 43 - **29,31,33,35** *(redes Medium Tank Bn 27 Nov 41; M–25 Aug 42;*
Tank Bn under N–22 Nov 43; O–18 Apr 45)

761st Tank Battalion (Cld)
1 Apr 42 Cp Claiborne La as Tank Bn, Light / 1 Jun 46 Germany   Bissingen Germany
NYPE: 27 Aug 44   England: 7 Sep 44   France-ETO: 16 Oct 44 - **25,26,32,34** *(I–10 Aug 42; Tank Bn under N–29 Oct 43; X)*

BATTALION DESIGNATION AND TYPE	FORMED (SOURCE OF UNIT)/INACTIVATION	AUGUST 1945 LOCATION

762nd Tank Battalion — 23 Apr 42 Schofield Bks Hawaii as Tank Bn, Light / 10 Apr 45 Hawaii
Hawaii: 23 Apr 42   Saipan: 16 Jun 44 (less Cos A and C)   Hawaii: 25 Aug 44 - **21** *(Tank Bn under* **N**–*19 Nov 43;* **X***)*

763rd Tank Battalion — 23 Apr 42 Hawaii as Tank Bn, Light / 2 Dec 45 Philippines — Leyte Philippines
Hawaii: 23 Apr 42   Philippines: 20 Oct 44   Okinawa: 1 Apr 45 - **13,19** *(Tank Bn under* **N**–*19 Nov 43,* **X***)*

764th Light Tank Battalion — 24 Oct 42 Ft Benning Ga as Tank Bn, Light / 3 Aug 44 Ft Ord Calif redes 764th
(J–7 Feb 44; **X***)* — Amphibian Tractor Bn

766th Tank Battalion — 8 Feb 43 Hawaii as Tank Bn, Light (Prov Tank Bn) / 4 Apr 45 Hawaii
Hawaii: 8 Feb 43   Kwajalein I: (Co B only - never landed) 1 Feb 44   Eniwetok I: (Co C only) 18 Feb 44   Saipan: (Co D only): 17 Jun 44 -
10,21 *(Tank Bn under* **N**–*19 Nov 43;* **X***)*

767th Tank Battalion — 8 Feb 43 Schofield Barracks Hawaii as Tank Bn, Light (Prov Tank Bn)/31 Mar 46 — Schofield Barracks Hawaii
Hawaii: 8 Feb 43   Marshall I: Feb 44   Philippines: 20 Oct 44 - **10,13** *(I–8 Feb 43; Tank Bn under* **N**–*19 Nov 43;* **O**–*11 May 45)*   Japan

771st Tank Battalion — 10 Sep 43 Cp Bowie Tex (1st Bn, 35th Armd Regt) / 1 May 46 Germany redes 71st — Lauenstein Germany
BPE: 17 Aug 44   England: 25 Aug 44   France-ETO: 15 Oct 44 - **25,26,34** *(N*–*10 Sep 43* **PP***;* **X***)*   Constab Sqdn

772nd Tank Battalion — 20 Sep 43 Pine Camp N.Y. (1st Bn, 34th Armd Regt) / 14 Nov 45 Cp Shelby Miss — Cp Shelby Miss
BPE: 26 Jan 45   France-ETO: 6 Feb 45 - **26,34**   HRPE: 5 Jul 45 *(N*–*20 Sep 43;* **O**–*20 Apr 45)*

773rd Tank Battalion — 20 Sep 43 Cp Cooke Calif (1st Bn, 68th Armd Regt) / 20 Oct 43 Ft Ord Calif redes
773rd Amphibian Tank Bn

774th Tank Battalion — 20 Sep 43 Ft Benning Ga (1st Bn, 31st Army Regt) / 26 Jul 46 Germany — Elbensee Germany
NYPE: 2 Jul 44   England: 12 Jul 44   France-ETO: 25 Aug 44 - **25,26,30,32,34** *(N*–*20 Sep 43;* **O**–*22 Jul 45)*

775th Tank Battalion — 20 Sep 43 Cp Polk La (1st Bn, 36th Armd Regt) / 5 Jan 46 Cp Stoneman Calif — Dagupan Philippines less Co C
SFPE: 28 May 44   New Guinea: 20 Jun 44   Philippines: 11 Jan 45 - **14,15**   SFPE: 3 Jan 46 *(N*–*20 Sep 43;* **O**–*9 Feb 45)*   at San Jose Philippines

776th Tank Battalion — 9 Oct 43 Desert Training Center Calif (1st Bn, 2nd Armd Regt) / 28 Jan 44 Ft Ord Calif
redes 776th Amphibian Tank Bn

777th Tank Battalion — 20 Sep 43 Cp Gordon Ga (1st Bn, 3rd Armd Regt) / 24 Oct 45 Cp San Luis Obispo Calif — Cp San Luis Obispo Calif
NYPE: 17 Dec 44   England: 29 Dec 44   France-ETO: 6 Feb 45 - **26,34**   BPE: 6 Jul 45 *(N*–*20 Sep 43;* **O**–*30 Apr 45)*

778th Tank Battalion — 20 Sep 43 Cp Barkeley Tex (1st Bn, 41st Armd Regt) / 20 Oct 46 Germany — Salnau Czechoslovakia
BPE: 5 Sep 44   England: 15 Sep 44   France-ETO: 15 Sep 44 - **25,26,32,34** *(N*–*15 Sep 43 eff 27 Jul 44;* **O**–*16 May 45)*

779th Tank Battalion — 11 Nov 43 Tennessee Maneuver Area (1st Bn, 43rd Armd Regt)/16 Jan 46 Cp Stone- — Shipment #9605-A
SFPE: 21 Jul 45   Philippines: 8 Sep 45   SFPE: 14 Jan 46 *(N*–*11 Nov 43;* **O**–*22 Feb 45)*   man Calif

780th Tank Battalion — 20 Sep 43 Cp Beale Calif (1st Bn, 45th Armd Regt) / 8 Apr 44 Ft Ord Calif redes
780th Amphibian Tank Bn

781st Tank Battalion — 2 Jan 43 Ft Knox Ky as Tank Bn, Light / 19 Feb 46 Cp Campbell Ky — Cp Campbell Ky
NYPE: 14 Oct 44   France-ETO: 28 Oct 44 - **25,26,34** *(redes Tank Bn under* **N**–*18 Oct 43;* **O**–*20 Apr 45)*

782nd Tank Battalion — 1 Feb 43 Cp Campbell Ky as Tank Bn, Light / 25 Feb 46 Fr Bragg N.C. — Ft Bragg N.C.
NYPE: 3 Jan 45   France-ETO: 16 Jan 45 - **26**   NYPE: 1 Jan 46 *(redes Tank Bn under* **N**–*19 Oct 43;* **X***)*

784th Tank Battalion (Cld) — 1 Apr 43 Cp Claiborne La as Tank Bn, Light / 29 Apr 46 Cp Kilmer N.J. — Kelbreg Germany
NYPE: 30 Oct 44   England: 10 Nov 44   France-ETO: 25 Dec 44 - **26,34**   NYPE: 28 Apr 46 *(Tank Bn under* **N**–*29 Oct 43;* **X***)*

785th Tank Battalion — 1 Mar 43 Ft Knox Ky as Tank Bn, Light / 19 Jan 46 Cp Stoneman Calif — Shipment #9451-P
SFPE: 28 Jul 45   Philippines: 3 Sep 45   SFPE: 17 Jan 46 *(Tank Bn under* **N**–*22 Oct 43;* **X***)*

786th Tank Battalion — 20 Sep 43 Cp Chaffee Ark (1st Bn, 47th Armd Regt) / 8 Nov 45 Cp Gruber Okla — Cp Gruber Okla
NYPE: 1 Dec 44   England: 8 Dec 44   France-ETO: 23 Jan 45 - **26,34**   BPE: 6 Jul 45 *(N*–*20 Sep 43;* **X***)*

787th Tank Battalion — 10 Sep 43 Cp Chaffee Ark (3rd Bn, 16th Armd Regt) / 21 Feb 46 Ft Jackson S.C. — Ft Jackson S.C.
NYPE: 2 Mar 45   France-ETO: 12 Mar 45 - **26**   HRPE: 11 Jul 45 *(N*–*10 Sep 43* **PP***;* **X***)*

788th Tank Battalion — 10 Sep 43 Cp Campbell Ky (3rd Bn, 20th Armd Regt) / 15 Apr 44 Ft Ord Calif redes
788th Amphibian Tractor Bn

812th Tank Battalion — 28 Nov 44 Ft Jackson S.C. (812th TD Bn) / 2 Nov 45 Ft Jackson S.C. *(N*–*28 Nov 44;* **X***)* — Ft Jackson S.C.

Provisional Tank Battalion — 7 Sep 42 Oahu Hawaii (AT Co, 25th Inf Div) / 8 Feb 43 discontinued in Hawaii
(assets to 766th and 767th Tank Bns)

*Active through 1946

Part V

Cavalry of the U.S. Army in World War II

Chapter 22

Cavalry Brigades

Brigades:

1–5, 7, 56, 316 Provisional, Washington Provisional

1st Cavalry Brigade

Stationed at Ft Clark Tex and assigned to 1st Cavalry Division; moved to Toyahuale Tex 13 Oct 39 and to Ft Bliss Tex 6 Nov 39; returned to Ft Clark Tex 4 Feb 40 where stationed except at Jasper Tex 26 Apr–30 May 40 and Cravens La 12–25 Aug 40; transferred to Ft Bliss Tex 6 Feb 41 where stationed except for maneuvers at Sabine Area La 8 Aug–4 Oct 41 and Mansfield La 27 Jul–21 Sep 42; staged at Cp Stoneman Calif 21 Jun 43 until departed San Francisco P/E 3 Jul 43; arrived in Australia 24 Jul 43 and moved to New Guinea 22 Feb 44; formed BREWER Task Force until 18 May 44 during which time assaulted Los Negros Island 28 Feb 44; assaulted Leyte Philippines 20 Oct 44 and moved to Luzon Philippines 27 Jan 45; arrived in Japan 2 Sep 45 where active thru 1946.

Campaigns: *New Guinea, Bismarck Archipelago, Leyte, Luzon*
Aug 45 Loc: Lucena Batangas Philippine Islands

2nd Cavalry Brigade

Stationed at Ft Bliss Tex and assigned to 1st Cavalry Division with the following relocations due to maneuvers: Toyahuale Tex 11–28 Oct 39; Louisiana Maneuver Area 25 Apr–28 May 40, 12–22 Aug 40, 10 Aug–4 Oct 41; 27 Jul–21 Sep 42; staged at Cp Stoneman Calif 18 Jun 43 until departed San Francisco P/E 26 Jun 43; arrived in Australia 11 Jul 43; advance elements arrived New Guinea 19 Dec 43 and brigade ashore by 22 Feb 44 in Oro Bay area; landed on Los Negros Island 9 Mar 44; assaulted Leyte Philippines 20 Oct 44 and moved to Luzon 27 Jan 45; arrived in Japan 2 Sep 45 where active thru 1946.

Campaigns: *New Guinea, Bismarck Archipelago, Leyte, Luzon*
Aug 45 Loc: Lucena Batangas Philippine Islands

3rd Cavalry Brigade

15 Oct 40 activated at Ft Riley Kans and assigned to 2nd Cavalry Division; participated in Arkansas Maneuvers 26 Aug–1 Oct 41 and returned to Ft Riley Kans 4 Oct 41; moved to Phoenix Ariz 16 Dec 41 and returned to Ft Riley Kans 27 Jun 42 where redesignated as the 9th Armored Division Train 15 Jul 42.

4th Cavalry Brigade (Colored)

21 Feb 41 activated at Ft Riley Kans and assigned to Army Ground Forces; participated in Arkansas Maneuvers 26 Aug–1 Oct 41 and returned to Ft Riley Kans 4 Oct 41; moved to Cp Lockett Calif 28 Jun 42 and assigned Western Defense Command and later Third Army on 23 Nov 42; assigned to 2nd Cavalry Division 25 Feb 43 and left Cp Lockett Calif 30 Jan 44; staged at Cp Patrick Henry Va 4 Feb 44 until departed Hampton Roads P/E 28 Feb 44; arrived North Africa 12 Mar 44 and inactivated there 23 Mar 44.

5th Cavalry Brigade (Colored)

25 Feb 43 activated at Ft Clark Tex and assigned to 2nd Cavalry Division; staged at Cp Patrick Henry Va 23 Jan 44 until departed Hampton Roads P/E 30 Jan 44; arrived North Africa 9 Feb 44 where inactivated 12 Jun 44. Its assets became the basis of the 6400th Ordnance Ammunition Battalion (Provisional) (Colored).

7th Cavalry Brigade (Mechanized)

Active at Black Lake N.Y. and returned to Ft Knox Ky on 13 Sep 39; composed of the 1st and 13th Cavalry Regiments, 68th Field Artillery Battalion, 7th Reconnaissance and Support Squadron, 7th Signal Troop, 4th Medical Troop, 47th Mechanized Engineer Troop, and a quartermaster maintenance company; moved to Monroe La and participated in the Louisiana Maneuvers 7–27 May 40 which were instrumental in developing the armored division concept; returned to Ft Knox Ky 31 May 40 where HHT redesignated HHC 1st Armored Division on 15 Jul 40.

56th Cavalry Brigade   Texas National Guard

18 Nov 40 inducted into federal service at San Antonio Tex and moved to Ft Bliss Tex 27 Nov 40 where assigned to Third Army and attached to 1st Cavalry Division; moved to Ft McIntosh Tex 6 Feb 41 and returned to Ft Bliss Tex 28 May 41; participated in Louisiana Maneuvers 15 Aug–2 Oct 41 and transferred to Ft McIntosh Tex 4 Oct 41 under Third Army; moved to Ft D.A. Russell Tex 2 Nov 43 and returned to Ft McIntosh Tex 23 Dec 43 and assigned to Fourth Army 21 Jan 44; HHT redesignated there as the 56th Cavalry Reconnaissance Troop (Mecz) on 12 May 44.

316th Cavalry Brigade, Provisional

9 Mar 45 formed in Germany when the 3rd and 16th Cavalry Groups combined to assist the north flank of XII Corps on the Moselle River; attacked toward Waldrach and Nieder-Fall on 14 Mar 45; primary mission of brigade was to clear the Trier-Hermeskeil Road after which it was discontinued.

Campaigns: *Central Europe*

Washington Provisional Brigade

Stationed at Ft Myer Va where it had been organized in Sep 36 with the 3rd Cavalry Regiment as its main component; other assets included the 1st Bn, 16th Field Artillery (75mm Gun, Horse-Drawn) - past 16 Dec 40 replaced by Btry C, 55th Field Artillery (75mm Gun, Horse-Drawn), and the 703rd Military Policy Battalion; discontinued on 5 May 42.

Chapter 23

Cavalry Groups

Groups:

2–4, 6, 11, 14–16, 29, 101, 102, 104, 106, 107, 113, 115

2nd Cavalry Group (Mechanized)

22 Dec 43 redesignated from 2nd Cavalry Regiment (Mecz) at Ft Jackson S.C. with 2nd and 42nd Cav Rcn Sqdns attached; staged at Ft Hamilton N.Y. 2 Apr 44 until departed New York P/E 10 Apr 44; arrived England 16 Apr 44 and landed in France 19 Jul 44; protected lines of communication from Cherbourg to Carentan and was committed to combat 2 Aug 44; drove to Loire River and joined XII Corps at Le Mans 10 Aug 44 and protected its right flank; encountered the German 11th *Panzer* Div at Luneville 18 Sep 44; attached to 26th Inf Div 12 Oct 44–22 Nov 44 and entered Germany 5 Dec 44; returned to France 7 Dec 44; crossed into Luxembourg 23 Dec 44 and guarded XII Corps' right flank along Moselle River until 1 Mar 45 when entered Germany at Wasserbilling on the *West Wall*; reached the Rhine 16 Mar 45 and crossed 25 Mar 45; entered Czechoslovakia 5 May 45; redesignated as the 2nd Constabulary Regiment in Germany 1 May 46.

Campaigns: *Normandy, Northern France, Rhineland, Ardennes-Alsace, Central Europe*
Aug 45 Loc: Brenner Pass Austria

3rd Cavalry Group (Mechanized)

3 Nov 43 redesignated from 3rd Cavalry Regiment (Mecz) at Cp Gordon Ga with 3rd and 43rd Cav Rcn Sqdns attached; moved to Tenn Maneuver Area 15 Nov 43 and returned to Cp Gordon Ga 15 Jan 44; staged at Cp Myles Standish Mass 12 Jun 44 until departed Boston P/E 22 Jun 44; arrived in England 30 Jun 44 and landed in France 9 Aug 44; committed to combat 10 Aug 44 with XX Corps in Le Mans area; its 3rd Sqdn was used as infantry to assault Fort Driant at Metz; group reunited mid-Oct 44 and held XX Corps' north flank; crossed into Germany 29 Nov 44 and returned to France 7 Dec 44; held defensive positions along the *West Wall* and entered Germany 28 Feb 45 operating in front of or on flanks of XX Corps; crossed the Rhine 29 Mar 45 and entered Austria 5 May 45; returned to New York P/E 21 Dec 45 and was inactivated at Cp Kilmer N.J. 22 Dec 45.

Campaigns: *Northern France, Rhineland, Ardennes-Alsace, Central Europe*
Aug 45 Loc: Radstadt Austria

4th Cavalry Group (Mechanized)

21 Dec 43 redesignated from 4th Cavalry Regiment (Mecz) in England with 4th and 24th Cav Rcn Sqdns attached; assaulted Normandy France 6 Jun 44 under VII Corps and group HHT arrived 15 Jun 44 and participated in battle for Cherbourg; attached to 2nd Armored Div during battle for St Lo; protected south flank of VII Corps and crossed into Belgium 3 Sep 44 and into Germany 14 Sep 44; moved to Huertgen Forest and maintained contact between 2nd Armored Div and 8th Inf during German Ardennes Counteroffensive; moved back into Belgium 22 Dec 44 and fought at Aachen; entered Germany 4 Feb 45 and crossed the Roer; crossed the Rhine at Bonn and helped seal the Ruhr Pocket; redesignated as the 4th Constabulary Regiment in Germany 1 May 46.

Campaigns: *Normandy, Northern France, Rhineland, Ardennes-Alsace, Central Europe*
Aug 45 Loc: Rammelburg Germany

6th Cavalry Group (Mechanized)

1 Jan 44 redesignated from 6th Cavalry Regiment (Mecz) at Tanderagee Ireland with 6th and 28th Cav Rcn Sqdns attached; landed in France 9 Jul 44 where used as information service for Third Army until 1 Dec 44 when committed to combat near St Avold France; entered Luxembourg 31 Dec 44 to locate German forces in the Bastogne vicinity and then reduced German units between 26th and 35th Inf Divs in the Lintage-Saar area where it remained until 13 Jan 45; crossed into Germany 25 Feb 45 with VIII Corps and attacked through Bauler, Waxweiler and Lasel; mopped up along Berlin autobahn and protected VIII Corps' southern flank; redesignated as the 6th Constabulary Regiment in Germany 1 May 46.

Campaigns: *Normandy, Northern France, Rhineland, Ardennes-Alsace, Central Europe*
Aug 45 Loc: Sonneberg Germany

11th Cavalry Group (Mechanized)

5 May 43 activated at Cp Young Calif with the 36th and 44th Cav Rcn Sqdns attached; moved to Ft Bragg N.C. 31 Jan 44 and to Atlantic Beach Fla 15 Mar 44; arrived Cp Gordon Ga 1 Jun 44 and departed New York P/E 29 Sep 44; arrived England 10 Oct 44 and landed in France 26 Nov 44 and moved into Holland 8 Dec 44; went into the line in Germany 12 Dec 44 and protected the Roer River sector; recrossed into Holland 3 Feb 45 and reentered Germany 27 Feb 45 on the left flank of 84th Inf Div; held defensive line along Rhine near Dusseldorf 12 Mar 44 under XIII Corps and crossed the Rhine at Wesel 1 Apr 45; screened XIII Corps' northern flank and saw action during the battle of Munster and the seizure of the Ricklingen Bridge over the Leine River; redesignated the 11th Constabulary Regiment in Germany 1 May 46.

Campaigns: *Rhineland, Central Europe*
Aug 45 Loc: Gross Iselde Germany

14th Cavalry Group (Mechanized)

12 Jul 43 activated at Ft Lewis Wash with the 18th and 32nd Cav Rcn Sqdns attached; moved to Cp White Oreg 1 Nov 43 and to Cp Maxey Tex 20 Apr 44; staged at Cp Shanks N.Y. 18 Aug 44 until departed New York P/E 28 Aug 44; arrived England 3 Sep 44 and landed in France 27 Sep 44; crossed into Luxembourg 19 Oct 44 and committed to combat along the *West Wall* 20 Oct 44; crossed into Belgium 13 Dec 44 and suffered heavy losses near Manderfield during the German Ardennes Counteroffensive; attached the Roer River line 28 Jan 45 and crossed into Germany 6 Feb 45 where helped eliminate the Ruhr Pocket; redesignated as the 14th Constabulary Regiment in Germany 1 May 46.

Campaigns: *Rhineland, Ardennes-Alsace, Central Europe*
Aug 45 Loc: Erlangen Germany

15th Cavalry Group (Mechanized)

15 Mar 44 redesignated from the 15th Cavalry Regiment (Mecz) in Trowbridge England with the 15th and 17th Cav Rcn Sqdns attached; landed in France 5 Jul 44 and committed to combat 2 Aug 44 near Avranches for the assault on Brest; remained at St Nazaire and Lorient until relieved by 66th Inf Div and performed screening missions for Ninth Army until 13 Feb 45; attached to XIV Corps and crossed into Holland 16 Feb 45 and entered Germany 3 Mar 45; redesignated as the 15th Constabulary Regiment in Germany 1 May 46.

Campaigns: *Northern France, Rhineland, Central Europe*
Aug 45 Loc: Montabaur Germany

16th Cavalry Group (Mechanized)

22 Nov 43 redesignated from the 16th Cavalry Regiment (Mecz) at Ft Devens Mass with the 16th and 19th Cav Rcn Sqdns; moved to Framingham Mass 28 Nov 43 and to Cp Pickett Va 26 May 44; remained there except for training at A.P. Hill Mil Res Va 13–31 Jul 44 and 9 Aug–20 Sep 44; staged at Cp Shanks N.Y. 14 Nov 44 until departed New York P/E 21 Nov 44; arrived in England 27 Nov 44 and landed in France 27 Feb 45; assigned to Third Army and went into line alongside 3rd Cav Group 8 Mar 45 and entered Germany 9 Mar 45; actively engaged in the Saar-Moselle triangle near Trier and protected XX Corps' left flank during drive into Germany; crossed the Rhine near Mainz 29 Mar 45 and went to Fifteenth Army 7 Apr 45; redesignated as the 16th Constabulary Regiment in Germany 28 Aug 46.

Campaigns: *Rhineland, Central Europe*
Aug 45 Loc: Rosarth Germany

29th Cavalry Group (Mechanized)

1 May 44 activated at Ft Riley Kans using assets of the 29th Cav Regt and assigned to Replacement & School Command with 127th, 128th, and 129th Cav Rcn Sqdns attached; inactivated there 6 Feb 45.

101st Cavalry Group (Mechanized)

21 Dec 43 redesignated from the 101st Cavalry Regiment (Mecz) at Cp Ashby Va with the 101st and 116th Cav Rcn Sqdns attached; moved to Ft Story Va 11 Jan 44 and to Cp Campbell Ky 3 Jul 44; staged at Cp Kilmer N.J. 25 Oct 44 until departed New York P/E 30 Oct 44; arrived England 12 Nov 44 and landed in France 31 Jan 45; assigned to XV Corps and entered Germany 9 Feb 45 where attacked along the Saar River line 14 Mar 45; moved to protect lines of communications in XXI Corps zone and screened the advance of 4th Inf Div past 1 Apr 45 and later the 12th Armored Div; arrived Boston P/E 24 Oct 45 and inactivated at Cp Myles Standish Mass 25 Oct 45.

Campaigns: *Rhineland, Central Europe*
Aug 45 Loc: Erbach Germany

310

102nd Cavalry Group (Mechanized)

2 Jan 44 redesignated from the 102nd Cavalry Regiment (Mecz) in Exeter England with the 38th and 102nd Cav Rcn Sqdns attached; landed in France 8 Jun 44 to protect V Corps' flanks; crossed into Belgium 7 Sep 44 and into Germany 14 Sep 44; moved into Luxembourg 16 Sep 44 and back to Belgium 27 Sep 44 and reentered Germany 10 Nov 44; held defensive positions along the *West Wall* and held its area against the German Ardennes Counteroffensive; returned to France 14 Mar 45 and returned to Germany 31 Mar 45 and screened V Corps' advance; fought at Colmar and reached Czechoslovakia 8 May 45; arrived Boston P/E 21 Oct 45 and was inactivated at Cp Myles Standish Mass 22 Oct 45.

Campaigns: *Normandy, Northern France, Rhineland, Ardennes-Alsace, Central Europe*
Aug 45 Loc: Dobrany Czechoslovakia

104th Cavalry Group (Mechanized)

1 Jan 44 redesignated from the 104th Cavalry Regiment (Mecz) at Salem Oreg with 104th and 119th Cav Rcn Sqdns attached; moved to Ft Lewis Wash 27 Jan 44; arrived Cp Gruber Okla under XVI Corps 30 Jun 40 where inactivated 15 Aug 44.

106th Cavalry Group (Mechanized)

14 Mar 44 redesignated from 106th Cavalry Regiment (Mecz) in England with the 106th and 121st Cav Rcn Sqdns attached; landed in France 2 Jul 44 and mopped up German forces in Normandy area under VIII Corps; helped seal the Falaise Pocket and fought as infantry in the Foret de Parroy alongside the 44th and 79th Inf Divs; helped to capture Strassbourg in Nov 44 and entered Germany 23 Dec 44; returned to France 12 Feb 45 and reentered Germany 20 Mar 45 and captured Salzburg Austria; arrived Boston P/E 21 Oct 45 and inactivated at Cp Myles Standish Mass 22 Oct 45.

Campaigns: *Normandy, Northern France, Rhineland, Ardennes-Alsace, Central Europe*
Aug 45 Loc: St Wolfgang Austria

107th Cavalry Group (Mechanized)

1 Jan 44 redesignated from the 107th Cavalry Regiment (Mecz) at Santa Rosa Calif with 45th and 115th Cav Rcn Sqdns attached; moved to Cp Polk La 8 Jul 44 under XXI Corps and inactivated there 6 Mar 45.

113th Cavalry Group (Mechanized)

1 Feb 44 redesignated from the 113th Cavalry Regiment (Mecz) in Hampshire England with the 113th and 125th Cav Rcn Sqdns attached; landed in France 2 Jul 44 and committed to combat at St Jean de Haye 4 Jul 44 and attacked St Lô with the 35th Inf Div 28 Jul 44; joined the 2nd Armored Div at Percy and protected the XIX Corps to Mortain and helped seal the Falaise Gap; entered Belgium 5 Sep 44 and Holland 13 Sep 44; entered Germany 26 Nov 44 and moved to the northern edge of Huertgen Forest during the German Ardennes Counteroffensive; assaulted the Roer River in Feb 45 and screened between XIX and XIII Corps during the Rhine crossings; assisted in sealing the Harz Mountains Pocket in Apr 45; returned to New York P/E 25 Oct 45 and inactivated at Cp Shanks N.Y. 26 Oct 45.

Campaigns: *Normandy, Northern France, Rhineland, Central Europe*
Aug 45 Loc: Niederflorsheim Germany

115th Cavalry Group (Mechanized)

1 Jan 44 redesignated from the 115th Cavalry Regiment (Mecz) at Ft Lewis Wash with the 104th and 107th Cav Rcn Sqdns attached; moved to Santa Anita Calif 27 Jan 44 and Wilmington Calif 5 Feb 44; arrived Cp Hood Tex 15 Jun 44 and staged at Cp Shanks N.Y. 25 Dec 44 until departed New York P/E 3 Jan 45; landed in France 15 Jan 45 and relieved the 15th Cav Group at St Nazaire; entered combat 10 Feb 45 and entered Germany 22 Apr 45 protecting right flank of VI Corps from Stuttgart until Innsbruck; entered Austria 3 May 45; arrived Boston P/E 21 Oct 45 and inactivated at Cp Myles Standish Mass 22 Oct 45.

Campaigns: *Rhineland, Central Europe*
Aug 45 Loc: Nesselwang Germany

Chapter 24

Cavalry Regiments

Regiments:

1–16, 26–29, 101, 102, 104, 106, 107, 112, 113, 115, 124

1st Cavalry Regiment (Mechanized)

Stationed at Ft Knox Ky and moved to Monroe La 8 May 40 to participate in the Louisiana Maneuvers as part of the experimental armored division; returned to Ft Knox Ky 31 May 40 where redesignated the 1st Armored Regiment 15 Jul 40.

2nd Cavalry Regiment (Horse)

Stationed at Ft Riley Kans as part of the 2nd Cavalry Division where remained except for training at Onamia Minn 7–18 Aug 40, Arkansas 26 Aug–1 Oct 41, and Phoenix Ariz 16 Dec 41–24 Jun 42; inactivated at Ft Riley Kans 15 Jul 42 with personnel and equipment being transferred to the 2nd Armored Regiment.

2nd Cavalry Regiment (Mechanized)

15 Jan 43 activated at Ft Jackson S.C. under XII Corps and later Second Army 1 Mar 43; reassigned to XII Corps 5 Aug 43 and moved to Lebanon Tenn 3 Sep 43; returned to Ft Jackson S.C. 21 Nov 43 where redesignated HHT 2nd Cavalry Group and 2nd and 43rd Cavalry Reconnaissance Squadrons on 22 Dec 43.

3rd Cavalry Regiment (Horse-Mechanized)

Stationed at Ft Myer Va as an elite guard unit for the Washington D.C. area under the Washington Provisional Brigade; sent to training at Norwood N.Y. 8–26 Aug 40 and returned to Ft Myer Va 28 Aug 40; moved to Ft Oglethorpe Ga 21 Feb 42 and to Ft Benning Ga 8 Jul 42; there inactivated 15 Jul 42 with personnel and equipment being transferred to the 3rd Armored Regiment.

3rd Cavalry Regiment (Mechanized)

15 Mar 43 activated at Cp Gordon Ga under III Corps where redesignated HHT 3rd Cavalry Group and 3rd and 43rd Cavalry Reconnaissance Squadrons on 3 Nov 43.

4th Cavalry Regiment (Mechanized)

Active at Ft Meade S.D. as the 4th Cavalry Regiment (Horse-Mechanized) under Second Army; sent to Cp Joseph T Robinson Ark 26 Nov 39 and to Sabine Maneuver Area La on 25 Apr 40; returned to Ft Meade S.D. 2 Jun 40 and went to Lincoln Minn for training 19 Jul 40 and moved back to Ft Meade S.D. 20 Aug 40; transferred to Ft Riley Kans 18 Aug 41 and to Ft Meade S.D. 9 Oct 41 where redesignated 4th Cavalry Regiment (Mechanized) 16 Apr 42; assigned to XI Corps 19 Aug 42; relocated to Tenn Maneuver Area 10 Sep 42 and returned to Ft Meade S.D. 12 Nov 42; sent to Cp Young Calif 24 Jan 43 and assigned to the Desert Training Center there; relocated to Cp Maxey Tex 3 Aug 43 under X Corps; staged at Cp Shanks N.Y. 22 Nov 43 until departed New York P/E 5 Dec 43; arrived in England 15 Dec 43 where redesignated HHT 4th Cavalry Group and the 4th and 24th Cavalry Reconnaissance Squadrons on 21 Dec 43.

Campaigns: *European Theater without inscription*

5th Cavalry Regiment (Infantry)

The 5th Cavalry Regiment (Horse) was stationed at Ft Clark Tex as part of the 1st Cavalry Division and trained briefly at Toyahvale Tex 13–30 Oct 39; moved to Ft Bliss Tex 6 Nov 39 relocated to Ft Clark Tex 4 Feb 40 from where it went to the Louisiana Maneuver Area 27 Apr–29 May 40 and 12–23 Aug 40; moved again to Ft Bliss Tex 6 Feb 41 and from there went to the Louisiana Maneuver Area 8 Aug–4 Oct 41 and 27 Jul–21 Sep 42; dismounted and reorganized as infantry 28 Feb 43; staged at Cp Stoneman Calif 20 Jun 43 until departed San Francisco P/E 2 Jul 43; arrived Australia 24 Jul 43 and reorganized partly under cavalry and partly under infantry T/Os 4 Dec 43; landed at Oro Bay New Guinea 22 Feb 44 and landed on the east coast of Los Negros Island 29 Feb 44; there captured Momote Airdrome 2 Mar 44 and completed conquest of island by 24 Mar 44; assaulted Leyte Island Philippines 20 Oct 44 under X Corps until 27 Oct 44; landed on Luzon Philippines 27 Jan 45 and attached to 37th Inf Div 16 Feb 45–2 Mar 45; reorganized wholly under infantry T/O (but retained cavalry designation) on 20 Jul 45; arrived Japan 2 Sep 45 where active thru 1946.

Campaigns: *New Guinea, Bismarck Archipelago, Leyte, Luzon*
Aug 45 Loc: Lucena Philippine Islands

6th Cavalry Regiment (Mechanized)

Assigned to the 3rd Cavalry Dvision as the 6th Cavalry Regiment (Horse-Mechanized) and stationed at Ft Oglethorpe Ga until 1 Dec 39 when relieved from division; relocated to Ft Benning Ga 11 Apr–5 May 40 and to Alexandria La 8–27 May 40; went back to Ft Oglethorpe Ga 30 May 40 and returned to Alexandria La 13–21 Aug 40 and to Ragley La 26 Jul–1 Oct 41 and to Chester S.C. 6 Nov–1 Dec 41; transferred from Ft Oglethorpe Ga to Cp Blanding Fla 18 Feb 42 where redesignated 6th Cavalry Regiment (Mechanized) on 21 Jul 42; moved to Ft Jackson S.C. 2 Nov 42 and to Ft Oglethorpe Ga 16 Apr 43; participated in maneuvers at Lebanon Tenn 18 Apr–20 Jun 43 and returned to Ft Jackson S.C.; staged at Cp Shanks N.Y. 8 Oct 43 until departed New York P/E 12 Oct 43; arrived England 18 Oct 43 where redesignated HHT 6th Cavalry Group and the 6th and 28th Cavalry Reconnaissance Squadrons on 1 Jan 44.

Campaigns: *European Theater without inscription*

7th Cavalry Regiment (Infantry)

The 7th Cavalry Regiment (Horse) was stationed at Ft Bliss Tex as part of the 1st Cavalry Division except for training at the Louisiana Maneuver Area on the following dates — 26 Apr–28 May 40, 12–22 Aug 40, and 8 Aug–4 Oct 41; it was dismounted on 28 Feb 43 and staged at Cp Stoneman Calif 18 Jun 43 until departed San Francisco P/E 26 Jun 43; arrived in Australia 11 Jul 43 where reorganized partly under infantry and partly under cavalry T/Os 4 Dec 43; moved to Oro Bay New Guinea 22 Feb 44 and landed on Los Negros Island to reinforce the beachhead 4 Mar 44, securing Lombrum Plantation; cleared Hauwei Island 12–13 Mar 44; arrived Lugos Mission on Manus Island 15 Mar 44; assaulted Leyte Philippines 20 Oct 44, reaching the Visayan Sea in late December and reassembled with division near Tunga 7 Jan 45; landed on Luzon 27 Jan 45; reorganized wholly under infantry T/O (but retained cavalry designation) on 20 Jul 45; moved to Japan 2 Sep 45 where active thru 1946.

Campaigns: *Bismarck Archipelago, New Guinea, Leyte, Luzon*
Aug 45 Loc: Lucena Batangas Philippine Islands

8th Cavalry Regiment (Infantry)

The 8th Cavalry Regiment (Horse) was active at Ft Bliss Tex as part of the 1st Cavalry Division where it remained except for maneuvers in Louisiana at Sabine 26 Apr–28 May 40, Cravens 13–24 Aug 40, and Leesville 10 Aug 41–21 Sep 42; it was dismounted 28 Feb 43 and staged at Cp Stoneman Calif 18 Jun 43 until departed San Francisco P/E 26 Jun 43; arrived Australia 11 Jul 43 and reorganized partly under cavalry and partly under infantry T/O 4 Dec 43; moved to Oro Bay New Guinea 22 Feb 44 and landed on Manus Island 15 Mar 44 where it overran the Lugos Mission and seized Lorengau Airdrome against fierce resistance; after mopping up the island by 5 May 44 it next landed at La Paz Samar Island Philippines 24 Oct 44 where it patrolled until 8 Jan 45; rejoined the division on Leyte and landed on Luzon Philippines 27 Jan 45; attached to XI Corps 5–29 Jun 45; reorganized wholly as infantry (but retained its cavalry designation) 20 Jul 45; moved to Japan 2 Sep 45 where active thru 1946.

Campaigns: *New Guinea, Bismarck Archipelago, Leyte, Luzon*
Aug 45 Loc: Lucena Batangas Philippine Islands

9th Cavalry Regiment (Horse) (Colored)

Stationed at Ft Riley Kans as part of the 3rd Cavalry Division until 10 Oct 40 when transferred to the 2nd Cavalry Division; trained in the Arkansas Maneuver Area 26 Aug–1 Oct 41 and returned to Ft Riley Kans; transferred to Ft Clark Tex 4 Jul 42; staged at Cp Patrick Henry Va 23 Jan 44 until departed Hampton Roads P/E 31 Jan 44; arrived North Africa 9 Feb 44 where inactivated 7 Mar 44 at Assi-Ben-Okba Algeria and assets transferred to provisional port companies.

Campaigns: *European Theater without inscription*

10th Cavalry Regiment (Horse) (Colored)

Stationed at Ft Leavenworth Kans as part of the 3rd Cavalry Division until 10 Oct 40 when transferred to the 2nd Cavalry Division; moved to Ft Riley Kans 14 Mar 41 and trained in the Arkansas Maneuver Area 26 Aug–1 Oct 41 and returned to Ft Riley Kans; moved to Cp Lockett Calif 30 Jun 42; staged at Cp Patrick Henry Va 15 Feb 44 until departed Hampton Roads P/E 3 Mar 44; arrived North Africa 12 Mar 44 where inactivated on 20 Mar 44 at Assi-Ben-Okba Algeria and assets transferred to 6486th Engineer Battalion.

Campaigns: *European Theater without inscription*

11th Cavalry Regiment (Horse)

Stationed at the Presidio of Monterey Calif as part of the 2nd Cavalry Division and moved to Ft Ord Calif 16–27 Jan 40 and Cp Clayton Calif 15 Apr–15 May 40 for temporary training; participated in maneuvers at Ft Lewis Wash 4–29 Aug 40 and returned to Presidio of Monterey Calif 31 Aug 40 where relieved from 2nd Cav Div in Oct 40; transferred to Seeley Calif 7 Nov 41 and next moved to Live Oaks Calif 24 Jul 41; returned to Cp Seeley Calif 17 Sep 41 and to Cp Lockett Calif 10 Dec 41; assigned to the Armored Force 12 Jun 42 and relocated to Ft Benning Ga 10 Jul 42; inactivated there 15 Jul 42 with personnel and equipment being transferred to the 11th Armored Regiment.

12th Cavalry Regiment (Infantry)

Stationed at Ft Brown Tex as the 12th Cavalry Regiment (Horse) and part of the 1st Cavalry Division; transferred to Ft Clark Tex 16 Sep 39 and to Ft Bliss Tex 6 Nov 39; returned to Ft Brown Tex 3 Feb 40 and went to the Louisiana Maneuvers from there at Sabine 27 Apr–29 May 40 and at Cravens 13–26 Aug 40; went to Ft Bliss Tex 7 Feb 41 and participated in Louisiana Maneuvers from there 6 Aug–4 Oct 41 and 27 Jul–21 Sep 42; dismounted on 28 Feb 43; staged at Cp Stoneman Calif 20 Jun 43 until departed San Francisco Calif 3 Jul 43; arrived in Australia 24 Jul 43 where it was reorganized partly under infantry and partly under cavalry T/O 4 Dec 43; moved to Oro Bay New Guinea 26 Jan 44 and reinforced the beachhead on Los Negros Island 6 Mar 44, taking Salami and Prlaka; on 1 Apr 44 began operations against the small islands off Mokerang in the Admiralties; assaulted Leyte Philippines 20 Oct 40 and took San Jose; landed on Luzon Philippines 27 Jan 45; attached to the 37th Inf Div 16 Feb–1 Mar 45; reorganized wholly as infantry (but retained its cavalry designation) on 20 Jul 45; moved to Japan 2 Sep 45 where active thru 1946.

Campaigns: *New Guinea, Bismarck Archipelago, Leyte, Luzon*
Aug 45 Loc: Lucena Batangas Philippine Islands

13th Cavalry Regiment (Mechanized)

Stationed at Ft Knox Ky assigned to the 7th Cavalry Brigade; participated in the Louisiana Maneuvers at Monroe 7–27 May 40; returned to Ft Knox Ky 31 May 40 where redesignated as the 13th Armored Regiment 15 Jul 40.

14th Cavalry Regiment (Horse)

Stationed at Ft Des Moines Iowa as part of the 2nd Cavalry Division; served briefly at Cp Joseph T Robinson Ark 23 Nov 39–9 Feb 40 and then returned to Ft Des Moines Iowa; transferred to Ft Riley Kans 28 May 40 from where participated in maneuvers at Crossett Ark 27 Aug–1 Oct 41 and Tucson Ariz 15 Dec 41–26 Jun 42; returned to Ft Riley Kans where inactivated 15 Jul 42 and personnel and equipment transferred to the 14th Armored Regiment.

15th Cavalry Regiment (Mechanized)

No Distinctive
Insignia Authorized

22 Mar 42 activated at Ft Riley Kans and attached to Second Army; moved to Cp Maxey Tex 23 Jan 43 under X Corps and participated in maneuvers in Louisiana 18 Jun–28 Aug 43; relocated to the Desert Training Center Calif 20 Aug 43; staged at Cp Shanks N.Y. 14 Feb 44 until departed New York P/E 1 Mar 44; arrived England 7 Mar 44 where redesignated as HHT 15th Cavalry Group and the 15th and 17th Cavalry Reconnaissance Squadrons on 15 Mar 44.

Campaigns: *European Theater without inscription*

16th Cavalry Regiment (Mechanized)

No Distinctive
Insignia Authorized

15 Jun 42 activated at Cp Forrest Tenn under III Corps where trained except for exercises at Ft Oglethorpe Ga 8 Jul 42–14 Feb 43 and Lebanon Tenn 27 Jun–27 Aug 43; relocated to Ft Devens Mass 24 Oct 43 and placed under the Eastern Defense Command where redesignated as HHT 16th Cavalry Group and the 16th and 19th Cavalry Reconnaissance Squadrons on 22 Nov 43.

26th Cavalry Regiment (Horse) (Philippine Scouts)

Active in the Philippines and moved to positions along the Bamban River near Ft Stotsenburg Luzon 8 Dec 41; attached to the 11th Inf Div (PS) in northern Luzon 21 Dec 41 and screened the right flank of the North Luzon Force, defending the withdrawal of the 71st Inf Div (PS) with delaying actions; fought continuously from Damortis to the Tayug River as the last United States Army cavalry unit to conduct mounted combat; forced to destroy its horses and then fought dismounted and in Jan 42 attacked to restore the front between I and II Corps and there was enveloped by Japanese forces; surrendered remnants 9 Apr 42 on Bataan.

Campaigns: *Philippine Islands*

27th Cavalry Regiment (Horse) (Colored)

No Distinctive
Insignia Authorized

25 Feb 43 activated at Ft Clark Tex as part of the 2nd Cavalry Division; staged at Cp Patrick Henry Va 23 Jan 44 until departed Hampton Roads P/E 28 Feb 44; arrived North Africa 9 Mar 44 where inactivated 27 Mar 44 at Assi-Ben-Okba Algeria and assets transferred to form the 6404th Port Battalion.

Campaigns: *European Theater without inscription*

28th Cavalry Regiment (Horse) (Colored)

No Distinctive
Insignia Authorized

25 Feb 43 activated at Cp Lockett Calif as part of the 2nd Cavalry Division's 4th Brigade; attached to II Armored Corps there 9 Oct 43 and to Fourth Army 25 Oct 43; attached to III Corps 14 Jan 44; staged at Cp Patrick Henry Va 15 Feb 44 until departed Hampton Roads P/E 3 Mar 44; arrived in North Africa 12 Mar 44 where inactivated 31 Mar 44 at Assi-Ben-Okba Algeria and assets transferred to form the 6487th Engineer Battalion.

Campaigns: *European Theater without inscription*

29th Cavalry Regiment (Composite School)

No Distinctive
Insignia Authorized

23 Jan 43 activated at Ft Riley Kans under the Replacement & School Command and inactivated there 1 May 44.

101st Cavalry Regiment (Horse-Mechanized)   New York National Guard

27 Jan 41 inducted into federal service at Brooklyn N.Y. and attached First Army; moved to Ft Devens Mass 4 Feb 41 and participated in maneuvers at the Ft Jackson–Ft Bragg Area 2 Oct–3 Dec 41; returned to Ft Devens Mass 7 Dec 41 and assigned to VI Corps 1 May 42; went to Pine Camp N.Y. for exercises 4 Sep–24 Oct 42; assigned to Eastern Defense Command 1 Jan 43; transferred from Ft Devens Mass to Ft George G Meade Md 12 Mar 43 and to Cp Ashby Va 15 Oct 43 where redesignated as HHT 101st Cavalry Group and the 101st and 116th Cavalry Reconnaissance Squadrons 21 Dec 43.

102nd Cavalry Regiment (Horse-Mechanized)   New Jersey National Guard

6 Jan 41 inducted into federal service at Newark N.J. and moved to Ft Jackson S.C. 16 Jan 41; assigned to I Army Corps and participated in maneuvers in the Ft Jackson–Ft Bragg Area 23 Sep–2 Dec 41; returned to Ft Jackson S.C. and attached to III Corps 6 Aug 42; transferred to Ft Dix N.J. 16 Sep 42 where staged until departed New York P/E 26 Sep 42; arrived England 6 Oct 42 where remained until redesignated as HHT 102nd Cavalry Group and the 102nd and 117th Cavalry Reconnaissance Squadrons there on 2 Jan 44. The 2nd Battalion had been transferred from England 26 Dec 42 and arrived North Africa on 31 Dec 42. There it was redesignated later as the 117th Cavalry Reconnaissance Squadron at Douera Algeria.

Campaigns: *European Theater without inscription*

104th Cavalry Regiment (Horse-Mechanized)   Pennsylvania National Guard

17 Feb 41 inducted into federal service at Harrisburg Pa and moved to Indiantown Gap Mil Res Pa 1 Mar 41 under II Corps; from there participated in maneuvers at A.P. Hill Mil Res Va 5–20 Aug 41, Ft Jackson–Ft Bragg Area 29 Sep–6 Dec 41; attached to First Army 5 Feb 42 and moved to Philadelphia Pa 4 Apr 42; relocated to Pittsburgh Pa 6 Jul 42 under VI Corps; returned to Indiantown Gap Mil Res Pa 9 Nov 42 and assigned to XII Corps 24 Nov 42 after moving to Ft Jackson S.C. 18 Nov 42; relocated to Salem Oreg 11 Jan 43 under the Western Defense Command; there redesignated as HHT 104th Cavalry Group and the 104th and 119th Cavalry Reconnaissance Squadrons on 1 Jan 44.

106th Cavalry Regiment (Horse-Mechanized)   Illinois National Guard

25 Nov 40 inducted into federal service at Urbana Ill and moved to Cp Livingston La 3 Jan 41 under V Corps; from there participated in maneuvers at Hineston La 21–24 Jun 41, Kinisatchie La 27 Jun–13 Aug 41, Dry Creek La 13 Aug–29 Sep 41, and the Louisiana Maneuver Area 15 Sep–10 Nov 42; assigned Third Army 12 Jan 42 and IV Corps 1 May 42; assigned to XV Corps 1 Mar 43 and transferred to Burkeville Tex 25 Jun 43 after which it went to Cp Hood Tex 25 Aug 43 under the Tank Destroyer Center; staged at Cp Shanks N.Y. 20 Feb 44 until departed New York P/E 27 Mar 44; arrived in England 9 Mar 44 where redesignated as HHT 106th Cavalry Group and the 106th and 121st Cavalry Reconnaissance Squadrons on 14 Mar 44.

Campaigns: *European Theater without inscription*

107th Cavalry Regiment (Horse-Mechanized)   Ohio National Guard

5 Mar 41 inducted into federal service at Cleveland Ohio and moved to Cp Forrest Tenn 16 Mar 41 under VII Corps; from there participated in maneuvers at the Sabine Maneuver Area Ark 16 Aug–5 Oct 41 and Ft Jackson–Ft Bragg Area 7 Nov–1 Dec 41; relocated to Ft Ord Calif 24 Dec 41 and then to the Desert Training Center at Cp Young Calif 3 Aug 42 and assigned to the center there; attached to II Armored Corps and moved to Ft Ord Calif 11 Dec 42 and next to Santa Rosa Calif 14 Jan 43 under the Northern California Sector of the Western Defense Command; there redesignated as HHT 107th Cavalry Group and the 22nd and 107th Cavalry Reconnaissance Squadrons on 1 Jan 44.

112th Cavalry Regiment (Special)   Texas National Guard

18 Nov 40 inducted into federal service at Dallas Tex and moved to Ft Bliss Tex as (Horse) 28 Nov 40; moved to Ft Clark Tex 6 Feb 41 and returned to Ft Bliss Tex 27 May 41; went to the Louisiana Maneuver Area 12 Aug 41 and then back to Ft Clark Tex 4 Oct 41; staged at Cp Stoneman Calif 11 Jul 42 until departed San Francisco P/E 20 Jul 42; arrived New Caledonia 11 Aug 42 and operated as a mounted regiment attached to the First Island Command; arrived Australia 17 May 43 where dismounted; moved to New Guinea 21 Jun 43 and landed on Woodlark Island 1 Jul 43; arrived Goodenough Island 1 Dec 43 and staged for the invasion of New Britain; landed at Arawe 15 Dec 43 and took Cape Mercus and small offshore islands to disrupt Japanese supply routes; went to Finschhafen New Guinea 9 Jun 44 and reinforced 32nd Inf Div to assist in defeating Japanese forces at Wewak; reorganized as 112th Cavalry Regiment (Special) 1 Oct 44; arrived in the Philippines 14 Nov 44 and attached to 1st Cavalry Division to clear Ormoc Valley sector; landed on Luzon Philippines 27 Jan 45 and kept supply lines open to Manila, operating into the Santa Inez Valley; arrived Japan 3 Sep 45 and inactivated there 27 Jan 46.

Campaigns: *New Guinea, Bismarck Archipelago, Luzon*
Aug 45 Loc: Manila Philippines

113th Cavalry Regiment (Horse-Mechanized)
Iowa National Guard

13 Jan 41 inducted into federal service at Des Moines Iowa and moved to Cp Bowie Tex 25 Jan 41 under VIII Corps; participated in maneuvers at Pelican La 25 Jul–19 Sep 42 and returned to Cp Bowie Tex; transferred to Cp Hood Tex 15 Dec 42 and trained at Cp Livingston La 26 Aug–13 Sep 43 and the Louisiana Maneuver Area 13 Sep–15 Nov 43; transferred to Cp Polk La 15 Nov 43 under III Armored Corps until attached to XXI Corps 25 Dec 43; staged at Cp Myles Standish Mass 9 Jan 44 until departed Boston P/E 18 Jan 44; arrived England 28 Jan 44 where redesignated HHT 113th Cavalry Group and the 113th and 125th Cavalry Reconnaissance Squadrons on 1 Feb 44.

Campaigns: *European Theater without inscription*

115th Cavalry Regiment (Horse-Mechanized)
Wyoming National Guard

24 Feb 41 inducted into federal service at Cheyenne Wyoming and moved to Ft Lewis Wash 10 Mar 41 under Fourth Army; from there participated in Maneuvers at Hunter-Liggett Mil Res Calif 28 May–16 Jun 41 and Corvallis Wash 9 Dec 41–28 Jan 42; moved to Salem Oreg 28 Jan 42 and returned to Ft Lewis Wash 1 May 42; there redesignated as HHT 115th Cavalry Group and the 115th and 126th Cavalry Reconnaissance Squadrons on 1 Jan 44.

124th Cavalry Regiment (Special)
Texas National Guard

18 Nov 40 inducted into federal service at Houston Tex as the 124th Cavalry Regiment (Horse) and moved to Ft Bliss Tex 28 Nov 40 under the 56th Cavalry Brigade; sent to Ft Brown Tex 5 Feb 41 and returned to Ft Bliss Tex 29 May 41; participated in the Louisiana Maneuvers 12 Aug–2 Oct 41 and then went to Ft Brown Tex 4 Oct 41; served at Ft D.A. Russell Tex 4 Nov–22 Dec 43 and returned to Ft Brown Tex; transferred to Ft Riley Kans 12 May 44 under Fourth Army; staged at Cp Anza Calif 10 Jul 44 until departed Los Angeles P/E 25 Jul 44; arrived India 26 Aug 44 where redesignated and reorganized as the 124th Cavalry Regiment (Special) 20–25 Sep 44; flown to Myitkyina Burma and entered combat as part of the MARS Task Force in Oct 44; established roadblocks on the Burma Road during drive to reopen the route below Nankam Burma; regiment moved over 300 miles in enemy territory relying on airdrop alone to establish a roadblock at Nampakka Burma; contacted the Japanese 15 Jan 45 and moved south along the Burma Road to arrive at Lashio Burma by 23 Mar 45; flown to China 26 Apr–14 May 45 where inactivated on 1 Jul 45 at Kunming China.

Campaigns: *Central Burma, India-Burma*

Chapter 25

Cavalry Squadrons and Reconnaissance Battalions

Reconnaissance Battalions:

1–8, 81–94, 96, 100

Reconnaissance Squadrons:

U.S. Military Academy, 2–4, 6, 15–19, 22–25, 27, 28, 30, 32–36, 38, 41–45, 81, 85–94, 101, 102, 104, 106, 107, 113, 115–117, 119, 121, 125–129

⭐ EXAMPLE — HOW TO USE THIS TABLE

Unit Designation and Type	Date Formed and Location (Source of Unit)/Inactivation and Location	August 1945 Location

Overseas Wartime Locations followed by - **Campaign Key Numbers** and PE return to United States, if applicable or space allows
(notes and remarks in parenthesis)

81st Cavalry Rcn Squadron (Mechanized)	12 May 41 Ft Knox Ky (1st Arm Rcn Bn)/1 May 46 Germany redes 81st Constab	Salzburg Austria
NYPE: 13 May 42 N.Ireland: 13 Jun 42 N.Africa: 21 Dec 42 Italy: 28 Oct 43 - **24,29,31,33,35,38**		Sqdn
(initially desig 81st Armd Rcn Bn and redes 81st Cav Rcn Sqdn [Mecz] 20 Jul 44 in Italy) (assigned 1st Armd Div)		

In this example, the 81st Cavalry Reconnaissance Squadron (Mechanized) was formed from the 1st Armored Reconnaissance Battalion on 12 May 1941 at Fort Knox, Kentucky. By reading the notes under this unit, we can see it was initially designated the 81st Armored Reconnaissance Battalion and wasn't redesignated as the 81st Cavalry Reconnaissance Squadron (Mechanized) until 20 July 1944 when it was in Italy. The unit was assigned to the 1st Armored Division. It *departed* New York Port of Embarkation on 13 May 1942 and arrived in Northern Ireland 13 June 1942, landed in North Africa on 21 December 1942, and in Italy on 28 October 1943. It participated in the Anzio, Naples-Foggia, North Apennines, Po Valley, Rome-Arno, and Tunisian campaigns. This information was derived by indexing the boldfaced campaign key numbers with Appendix I. In August 1945 the 81st Cavalry Reconnaissance Squadron was located in Salzburg, Austria, and was redesignated as the 81st Constabulary Squadron in Germany on 1 May 1946.

SQUADRON/BATTALION DESIGNATION AND TYPE	FORMED (SOURCE OF UNIT) / INACTIVATION *Active through 1946	AUGUST 1945 LOCATION
U.S. Military Academy Cavalry Sqdn (Cld)	15 Nov 40 West Point N.Y. / *	West Point N.Y.
1st Reconnaissance Battalion *(assigned Third Army)*	3 Jan 41 Ft Bliss Tex / 8 May 41 Ft Bliss Tex redes 91st Cav Rcn Sqdn	
1st Reconnaissance Battalion (Armored) *(assigned 1st Armd Div)*	15 Jul 40 Ft Knox Ky / 12 May 41 Ft Knox Ky redes 81st Rcn Bn	
2nd Reconnaissance Battalion (Armored) *(assigned 2nd Armd Div)*	15 Jul 40 Ft Benning Ga / 8 May 41 Ft Benning Ga redes 82nd Rcn Bn	
2nd Cavalry Rcn Squadron (Mechanized) NYPE: 2 Apr 44 England: 5 May 44 France: 20 Jul 44 Lux: 23 Dec 44 Germany: 3 Mar 45 - **25,26,30,32,34** *(attached 2nd Cav Gp)*	22 Dec 43 Ft Jackson S.C. (1st Sqdn, 2nd Cav) / *	Neukirchen Germany
3rd Reconnaissance Battalion (Armored) *(assigned 3rd Armd Div)*	15 Apr 41 Cp Beauregard La / 8 May 41 Cp Beauregard La redes 83rd Rcn Bn	
3rd Reconnaissance Squadron *(1st Cav Div until 2 Mar 43)*	15 Nov 42 Ft Bliss Tex / 25 Oct 43 Cp Maxey Tex redes 38th Cav Rcn Sqdn	
3rd Cavalry Rcn Squadron (Mechanized) NYPE: 2 Jul 44 England: 14 Jul 44 France: 9 Aug 44 Germany: 18 Nov 44 Austria: 4 May 45 - **25,26,32,34** NYPE: 10 Jul 45 *(attached 3rd Cav Gp)*	3 Nov 43 Cp Gordon Ga (1st Sqdn, 3rd Cav) / *	Ft Bragg N.C.
4th Reconnaissance Battalion (Armored) *(assigned 4th Armd Div)*	15 Apr 41 Pine Camp N.Y. / 1 Jan 42 Pine Camp N.Y. redes 84th Rcn Bn	
4th Reconnaissance Squadron *(4th Inf Div until 30 Jul 43)*	10 Jun 42 Cp Gordon Ga / 5 Jan 44 Ft Jackson S.C. redes 34th Cav Rcn Sqdn	
4th Cavalry Rcn Squadron (Mechanized) England: 21 Dec 43 France: 6 Jun 44 Belgium: 3 Sep 44 Germany: 4 Feb 45 - **25,26,30,32,34** *(attached 4th Cav Gp)*	21 Dec 43 Singleton England (1st Sqdn, 4th Cav) / 1 May 46 Austria redes 4th Constab Sqdn	Helbra Germany
5th Reconnaissance Squadron (Cld) *(assigned 2nd Cav Div)*	25 Feb 43 Ft Clark Tex / 1 Jan 44 Ft Clark Tex redes 35th Cav Rcn Sqdn (Cld)	
6th Reconnaissance Squadron *(6th Mtz Div until 17 Jun 43)*	25 Jun 42 Ft Leonard Wood Mo / 2 Jan 44 Cp White Oreg redes 30th Cav Rcn Sqdn	
6th Cavalry Rcn Squadron (Mechanized) N.Ireland: 1 Jan 44 England: 13 May 44 France: 10 Jul 44 Lux: 25 Dec 44 Belgium: 28 Dec 44 Germany: 23 Feb 45 - **25,26,30,32,34** *(attached 6th Cav Gp)*	1 Jan 44 Gilford N.Ireland (1st Sqdn, 6th Cav) / *	Hildaburghausen Germany
7th Reconnaissance Squadron SFPE: 26 Jun 43 Australia: 11 Jul 43 *(1st Cav Div 2 Mar 43)*	16 Jun 42 Cp San Luis Obispo Calif / 4 Dec 43 Australia	
8th Reconnaissance Squadron *(8th Mtz Div until 7 May 43)*	10 Jun 42 Ft Jackson S.C. / 23 Dec 43 Cp Young Calif redes 44th Cav Rcn Sqdn	

SQUADRON/BATTALION DESIGNATION AND TYPE	FORMED (SOURCE OF UNIT)/INACTIVATION *Active through 1946	AUGUST 1945 LOCATION

15th Cavalry Rcn Squadron (Mechanized)   12 Mar 44 Trowbridge England (1st Sqdn, 15th Cav) / *
England: 12 Mar 44   France: 5 Jul 44   Holland: 16 Feb 45   Germany: 9 Mar 45 - **26,30,32,34** (attached 15th Cav Gp)

Verl Germany

16th Cavalry Rcn Squadron (Mechanized)   22 Dec 43 Framingham Mass (Rcn Sqdn, 16th Cav) / 10 Feb 46 Cp Hood Tex
NYPE: 21 Nov 44   England: 27 Nov 44   France: 28 Feb 45 - **26,34**   NYPE: 25 Aug 45 (attached 16th Cav Gp)

Rosrath Germany sch to SWPA Shipment #R4645-D

17th Cavalry Rcn Squadron (Mechanized)   12 Mar 44 Trowbridge England (2nd Sqdn, 15th Cav) / *
England: 12 Mar 44   France: 15 Jul 44   Holland: 16 Oct 44   Germany: 23 Nov 44 - **26,30,32,34** (attached 15th Cav Gp)

Wiedenburck Germany

18th Cavalry Rcn Squadron (Mechanized)   8 Jul 43 Ft Lewis Wash as 18th Rcn Sqdn / *
NYPE: 28 Aug 44   England: 3 Sep 44   France: 27 Sep 44   Belgium: 19 Oct 44   Germany: 6 Feb 45 - **25,26,34**   BPE: 10 Jul 45
(18th Rcn Sqdn redesignated as 18th Cavalry Rcn Sqdn [Mecz] 11 Nov 43 at Cp White Oreg) (attached 14th Cav Gp)

Cp Gruber Okla

19th Cavalry Rcn Squadron (Mechanized)   22 Dec 43 Saco Maine (2nd Sqdn, 16th Cav) / 10 Nov 45 Cp Campbell Ky
NYPE: 21 Nov 44   England: 27 Nov 44   France-ETO: 27 Feb 45 - **26,34**   BPE: 25 Aug 45 (attached to 16th Cav Gp-

Birkenfeld Germany sch to SWPA, Shipment #R4645-C

22nd Cavalry Rcn Squadron (Mechanized)   1 Jan 44 San Rafael Calif (1st Sqdn, 107th Cav) / 15 Aug 44 Cp Gruber Okla

23rd Cavalry Rcn Squadron (Mechanized)   10 Sep 43 Cp Chaffee Ark (96th Arm Rcn Bn) / 15 Oct 45 Cp Shanks N.Y.
NYPE: 5 Feb 45   France: 17 Feb 45   Germany: 19 Apr 45   Czech: 8 May 45 - **26**   NYPE: 14 Oct 45 (assigned 16th Armd Div)

Kuttenplan Czechoslovakia

24th Cavalry Rcn Squadron (Mechanized)   21 Dec 43 Singleton England (2nd Sqdn, 4th Cav) / *
England: 21 Dec 43   France: 16 Jun 44   Belgium: 5 Sep 44   Germany: 1 Feb 45 - **25,26,30,32,34** (attached 4th Cav Gp)

Ballenstadt Germany

25th Cavalry Rcn Squadron (Mechanized)   10 Sep 43 Cp Bowie Tex (84th Rcn Bn) / 1 May 46 Germany
BPE: 29 Dec 43   England: 9 Jan 44   France: 13 Jul 44   Belgium: 21 Dec 44   Lux: 11 Jan 45   Germany: 22 Feb 45 - **25,26,30,32,34**
(assigned 4th Armd Div)

Frontenhausen Germany

27th Cavalry Rcn Squadron (Mechanized)   14 Mar 43 Panama Canal Zone / 1 Dec 43 Cp Maxey Tex redes 32nd Cav Rcn Sqdn
Panama Canal Zone: 14 Mar 43   SFPE: 10 Sep 43

28th Cavalry Rcn Squadron (Mechanized)   1 Jan 44 Gilford N.Ireland (2nd Sqdn, 6th Cav) / *
N.Ireland: 1 Jan 44   England: 13 May 44   France: 10 Jul 44   Lux: 24 Dec 44   Belgium: 24 Dec 44   Germany: 24 Feb 45 - **25,26,30,32,34**
(attached 6th Cav Gp)

Sonneberg Germany

30th Cavalry Rcn Squadron (Mechanized)   2 Jan 44 Cp White Oreg (6th Rcn Sqdn) / 6 Feb 45 Ft Riley Kans   (R&S Cmd 17 Aug 44)

32nd Cavalry Rcn Squadron (Mechanized)   1 Dec 43 Cp Maxey Tex (27th Cav Rcn Sqdn) / 8 Sep 45 Cp Bowie Tex
NYPE: 28 Aug 44   England: 3 Sep 44   France-ETO: 4 Oct 44 - **25,26,34**   NYPE: 10 Jul 45 (attached 14th Cav Gp)

Camp Bowie Tex

33rd Cavalry Rcn Squadron (Mechanized)   19 Sep 43 Cp Campbell Ky (100th Arm Rcn Bn) / 2 Apr 46 Cp Hood Tex
BPE: 6 Feb 45   France: 17 Feb 45   Germany: 4 Apr 45 - **26**   NYPE: 2 Aug 45 (assigned 20th Armd Div)

Camp Cooke Calif

34th Cavalry Rcn Squadron (Mechanized)   5 Jan 44 Ft Jackson S.C. (4th Rcn Sqdn) / 3 Mar 45 Ft Riley Kans

35th Cavalry Rcn Squadron (Cld) (Mecz)   1 Jan 44 Ft Clark Tex (5th Rcn Sqdn Cld) / 25 Mar 44 North Africa
HRPE: 28 Feb 44   N.Africa: 12 Mar 44 (assigned 2nd Cav Div)

36th Cavalry Rcn Squadron (Mechanized)   22 Dec 43 Cp Young Calif (90th Rcn Sqdn) / 26 Oct 45 Cp Patrick Henry Va
NYPE: 29 Sep 44   England: 12 Oct 44   France-ETO: 26 Nov 44 - **26,34**   HRPE: 25 Oct 45

Sievershausen Germany

38th Cavalry Rcn Squadron (Mechanized)   25 Oct 43 Cp Maxey Tex (3rd Rcn Sqdn) / 28 Nov 45 Cp Kilmer N.J.
NYPE: 15 Nov 43   England: 20 Nov 43   France: 12 Jun 44   Belgium: 4 Sep 44   Germany: 30 Mar 45 - **25,26,30,32,34**
NYPE: 27 Nov 45 (attached 102nd Cav Gp)

Prestice Czechoslovakia

41st Cavalry Rcn Squadron (Mechanized)   10 Sep 43 Cp Barkeley Tex (91st Arm Rcn Sqdn) / 31 Aug 45 Germany
NYPE: 29 Sep 44   England: 9 Oct 44   France-ETO: 16 Dec 44 - **25,26,34** (assigned 11th Armd Div)

Urfahr Austria

42nd Cavalry Rcn Squadron (Mechanized)   22 Dec 43 Ft Jackson S.C. (2nd Sqdn, 2nd Cav) / 22 Dec 45 Germany redes 42nd
NYPE: 22 Apr 44   England: 5 May 44   France: 20 Jul 44   Lux: 23 Dec 44   Germany: 5 Mar 45 - **25,26,30,32,34**   Constab Sqdn
(attached 2nd Cav Gp)

Lam Germany

43rd Cavalry Rcn Squadron (Mechanized)   3 Nov 43 Cp Gordon Ga (2nd Sqdn, 3rd Cav) / *
BPE: 22 Jun 44   England: 29 Jun 44   France: 7 Aug 44   Germany: 28 Nov 44 - **25,26,32,34**   HRPE: 5 Jul 45 (attached 3rd Cav Gp)

Cp Bowie Tex

44th Cavalry Rcn Squadron (Mechanized)   23 Dec 43 Cp Young Calif (8th Rcn Sqdn) / 29 Sep 45 Ft Bragg N.C.
NYPE: 29 Sep 44   England: 10 Oct 44   France-ETO: 26 Nov 44 - **26,34**   NYPE: 2 Aug 45 (attached 11th Cav Gp)

Ft Bragg N.C.

45th Cavalry Rcn Squadron (Mechanized)   20 Apr 44 Cp Hood Tex / 26 Feb 45 Ft Knox Ky   (R&S Cmd 17 Feb 45)

81st Cavalry Rcn Squadron (Mechanized)   12 May 41 Ft Knox Ky (1st Arm Rcn Bn) / 1 May 46 Germany redes 81st Constab
NYPE: 13 May 42   N.Ireland: 13 Jun 42   N.Africa: 21 Dec 42   Italy: 28 Oct 43 - **24,29,31,33,35,38**   Sqdn
(initially desig 81st Armd Rcn Bn and redes 81st Cav Rcn Sqdn [Mecz] 20 Jul 44 in Italy) (assigned 1st Armd Div)

Salzburg Austria

SQUADRON/BATTALION DESIGNATION AND TYPE	FORMED (SOURCE OF UNIT)/INACTIVATION *Active through 1946	AUGUST 1945 LOCATION

82nd Armored Reconnaissance Battalion   8 May 41 Ft Benning Ga (2nd Arm Rcn Bn) / 25 Mar 46 Cp Hood Tex — Drutte Germany
NYPE: 11 Dec 42   N.Africa: 8 Nov 42   Sicily: 10 Jul 43   England: 25 Nov 43   France-ETO: 7 Jun 44 - **23,25,26,30,32,34,36**
NYPE: 29 Jan 46 *(assigned 2nd Armd Div)*

83rd Armored Reconnaissance Battalion   8 May 41 Cp Beauregard La (3rd Arm Rcn Bn) /10 Nov 45 Germany — Darmstadt Germany
NYPE: 5 Sep 43   England: 18 Sep 43   France-ETO: 23 Jun 44 - **25,26,30,32,34** *(assigned 3rd Armd Div)*

84th Armored Reconnaissance Battalion   1 Jan 42 Pine Camp N.Y. (4th Arm Rcn Bn) /10 Sep 43 Cp Bowie Tex redes 25th Cav Rcn Sqdn
(assigned 4th Armd Div)

85th Cavalry Rcn Squadron (Mechanized)   1 Oct 41 Ft Knox Ky as 85th Arm Rcn Bn /11 Oct 45 Cp Kilmer N.J. — Langensalza Germany
NYPE: 11 Feb 44   England: 23 Feb 44   France-ETO: 25 Jul 44 - **25,26,30,32,34**   NYPE: 10 Oct 45
(85th Arm Rcn Bn redes 85th Cav Rcn Sqdn [Mecz] 20 Sep 43 at Pine Camp N.Y.) (assigned 5th Armd Div)

86th Cavalry Rcn Squadron (Mechanized)   15 Feb 42 Ft Knox Ky as 86th Arm Rcn Bn /19 Sep 45 Cp Myles Standish Mass — Kahla Germany
NYPE: 11 Feb 44   England: 23 Feb 44   France-ETO: 19 Jul 44 - **25,26,30,32,34**   BPE: 18 Sep 45
(86th Arm Rcn Bn redes 86th Cav Rcn Sqdn [Mecz] 10 Sep 43 at Cp Cooke Calif) (assigned 6th Armd Div)

87th Cavalry Rcn Squadron (Mechanized)   2 Mar 42 Cp Polk La as 87th Arm Rcn Bn / 9 Oct 45 Cp Shanks N.Y. — Osternienburg Germany
NYPE: 7 Jun 44   England: 13 Jun 44   France-ETO: 11 Aug 44 - **25,26,32,34**   NYPE: 8 Oct 45
(87th Arm Rcn Bn redes 87th Cav Rcn Sqdn [Mecz] 10 Sep 43 at Ft Benning Ga) (assigned 7th Armd Div)

88th Cavalry Rcn Squadron (Mechanized)   1 Apr 42 Ft Knox Ky as 88th Arm Rcn Bn /13 Nov 45 Cp Patrick Henry Va — Hardegsen Germany
NYPE: 7 Nov 44   England: 18 Nov 44   France-ETO: 5 Jan 45 - **25,26,34**   HRPE: 12 Nov 45
(88th Arm Rcn Bn redes 88th Cav Rcn Sqdn [Mecz] 10 Sep 43 at Cp Polk La) (assigned 8th Armd Div)

89th Cavalry Rcn Squadron (Mechanized)   15 Jul 42 Ft Riley Kans (92nd Cav Rcn Sqdn) /13 Oct 45 Cp Patrick Henry Va — Bayreuth Germany
NYPE: 20 Aug 44   England: 26 Aug 44   France-ETO: 28 Sep 44 - **25,26,34**   HRPE: 12 Oct 45
(initially desig 89th Armd Rcn Bn and redes 89th Cav Rcn Sqd [Mecz] 19 Oct 43 at Desert Training Center Cp Young Calif)
(assigned 9th Armd Div)

90th Cavalry Rcn Squadron (Mechanized)   15 Jul 42 Ft Benning Ga as 90th Arm Rcn Bn /13 Oct 45 Cp Patrick Henry Va — Rottenbuch Germany
NYPE: 12 Sep 44   France-ETO: 23 Sep 44 - **25,26,34**   HRPE: 13 Oct 45
(90th Arm Rcn Bn redes 90th Cav Rcn Sqdn [Mecz] 10 Sep 43 at Cp Gordon Ga) (assigned 10th Armd Div)

90th Reconnaissance Squadron   15 Sep 42 Cp Barkeley Tex/22 Dec 43 Cp Young Calif redes 41st Cav Rcn Sqdn
(90th Mtz Div 15 Sep 43)

91st Armored Reconnaissance Battalion   15 Aug 42 Cp Polk La /10 Sep 43 Cp Barkeley Tex redes 41st Cav Rcn Sqdn
(assigned 11th Armd Div)

91st Cavalry Rcn Squadron (Mechanized)   8 May 41 Ft Bliss Tex (1st Rcn Sqdn) / 2 Nov 45 Cp Myles Standish Mass — Barbarolo Italy
NYPE: 11 Dec 42   N.Africa: 25 Dec 42   Sicily: 19 Jul 43   Italy: 20 Oct 43 - **29,31,33,35,36,38**   BPE: 1 Nov 45 *(attached Fifth Army)*

92nd Cavalry Rcn Squadron (I) (Mechanized) 19 Mar 42 Ft Riley Kans /15 Jul 42 Ft Riley Kans redes 89th Arm Rcn Bn
(assigned 2nd Cavalry Div)

92nd Cavalry Rcn Squadron (II) (Mechanized) 15 Feb 42 Cp Campbell Ky as 92nd Arm Rcn Bn / 3 Dec 45 Cp Kilmer N.J. — Dischingen Germany
NYPE: 20 Sep 44   England: 1 Oct 44   France-ETO: 9 Nov 44 - **25,26,34**   NYPE: 1 Dec 45
(92nd Arm Rcn Bn redes 92nd Cav Rcn Sqdn [Mecz] 10 Sep 43 in the Tennessee Maneuver Area) (assigned 12th Armd Div)

93rd Cavalry Rcn Squadron (Mechanized)   15 Oct 42 Cp Beale Calif as 93rd Arm Rcn Bn /12 Nov 45 Cp Cooke Calif — Cp Cooke Calif
NYPE: 26 Jan 45   France-ETO: 6 Feb 45 - **26,34**   BPE: 27 Jul 45
(93rd Arm Rcn Bn redes 93rd Cav Rcn Sqdn [Mecz] 10 Sep 43 at Cp Beale Calif) (assigned 13th Armd Div)

94th Cavalry Rcn Squadron (Mechanized)   15 Nov 42 Cp Chaffee Ark as 94th Arm Rcn Bn /16 Sep 45 Cp Patrick Henry Va — Gars Germany
NYPE: 14 Oct 44   France-ETO: 28 Oct 44 - **25.26.34**   HRPE: 16 Sep 45
(94th Arm Rcn Bn redes 94th Cav Rcn Sqdn [Mecz] 20 Sep 43 at Cp Chaffee Ark) (assigned 14th Armd Div)

96th Armored Reconnaissance Battalion   15 Jul 43 Cp Chaffee Ark /10 Sep 43 Cp Chaffee Ark redes 23rd Cav Rcn Sqdn
(assigned 16th Armd Div)

100th Armored Reconnaissance Battalion   15 Mar 43 Cp Campbell Ky /19 Sep 43 Cp Campbell Ky redes 33rd Cav Rcn Sqdn
(assigned 20th Armd Div)

101st Cavalry Rcn Squadron (Mechanized)   23 Dec 43 Cp Somerset Md (1st Sqdn 101st Cav) / 7 Sep 45 Cp Campbell Ky — Cp Campbell Ky
NYPE: 30 Oct 44   England: 12 Nov 44   France-ETO: 2 Feb 45 - **26**   NYPE: 11 Jul 45 *(attached 101st Cav Gp)*

102nd Cavalry Rcn Squadron (Mechanized)   2 Jan 44 Exeter England (1st Sqdn, 102nd Cav) / 22 Oct 45 Cp Shanks N.Y. — Pilsen Czechoslovakia
England: 2 Jan 44   France: 7 Jun 44   Belgium: 4 Sep 44   Germany: 13 Sep 44   Czech: 7 May 45 - **25,26,30,32,34**   NYPE: 22 Oct 45
(attached 102nd Cav Gp)

104th Cavalry Rcn Squadron (Mechanized)   1 Jan 44 Salem Oreg (1st Sqdn, 104th Cav) /15 Nov 45 Cp Hood Tex — Bensberg Germany sch to SWPA Shipment #R4645-A
NYPE: 5 Feb 45   England: 16 Feb 45   France-ETO: 4 Mar 45 - **26,32**   NYPE: 3 Sep 45 *(attached to 115th Cav Gp)*

SQUADRON/BATTALION DESIGNATION AND TYPE	FORMED (SOURCE OF UNIT)/INACTIVATION	AUGUST 1945 LOCATION

106th Cavalry Rcn Squadron (Mechanized)   15 Mar 44 England (1st Sqdn, 106th Cav) / 24 Oct 45 Cp Shanks N.Y.
England: 15 Mar 44   France: 30 Jun 44   Germany: 24 Dec 44   Austria: 5 May 45 - **25,26,30,32,34**   NYPE: 23 Oct 45
(attached 106th Cav Gp)

Mittenwald Germany

107th Cavalry Rcn Squadron (Mechanized)   1 Jan 44 Santa Rosa Calif (2nd Sqdn, 107th Cav) /16 Nov 45 Cp Bowie Tex
NYPE: 3 Jan 45   France: 15 Jan 45   Germany: 23 Apr 45 - **26,32,34**   HRPE: 21 Aug 45 *(attached 115th Cav Gp)*

Nesselwang Germany sch to
SWPA, Shipment #R4645-B

113th Cavalry Rcn Squadron (Mechanized)   1 Feb 44 Middle Wallop England (1st Sqdn, 113th Cav) / 21 Oct 45 Cp Myles Standish
England: 1 Feb 44   France: 1 Jul 44   Belgium: 5 Sep 44   Holland: 13 Sep 44   Germany: 22 Sep 44 - **26,30,32,34**   Mass
BPE: 20 Oct 45 *(attached 113th Cav Gp)*

Budlingen Germany

115th Cavalry Rcn Squadron (Mechanized)   1 Jan 44 Ft Lewis Wash (1st Sqdn, 115th Cav) / 6 Mar 45 Cp Polk La
(Fourth Army 4 Jul 44)

116th Cavalry Rcn Squadron (Mechanized)   21 Dec 43 Cp Somerset Md (2nd Sqdn, 101st Cav) / 10 Nov 45 Cp Campbell Ky
NYPE: 30 Oct 44   England: 12 Nov 44   France: 31 Jan 45   Germany: 9 Feb 45 - **26,34**   NYPE: 26 Aug 45 *(attached 101st Cav Gp)*

Lindenfels Germany

117th Cavalry Rcn Squadron (Mechanized)   30 Nov 43 Douera Algeria (2nd Sqdn, 102nd Cav) / 25 Nov 45 Germany
N.Africa: 30 Nov 43   Italy: 16 May 44   France-ETO: 15 Aug 44 - **25,26,34,35,37** *(attached Seventh Army)*

Ober Erlenbach Germany

119th Cavalry Rcn Squadron (Mechanized)   1 Jan 44 Salem Oreg (2nd Sqdn, 104th Cav)/15 Aug 44 Cp Gruber Okla

121st Cavalry Rcn Squadron (Mechanized)   15 Mar 44 England (2nd Sqdn, 106th Cav)/23 Oct 45 Cp Shanks N.Y.
England: 15 Mar 44   France: 17 Jul 44   Germany: 24 Dec 44   Austria: 4 May 45 - **25,26,30,32,34**   NYPE: 22 Oct 45
(attached 106th Cav Gp)

St Gilgen Austria

125th Cavalry Rcn Squadron (Mechanized)   1 Feb 44 Hampshire England (2nd Sqdn, 113th Cav) / 23 Oct 45 Cp Shanks N.Y.
England: 1 Feb 44   France: 28 Jun 44   Belgium: 2 Sep 44   Holland: 8 Sep 44   Germany: 28 Jan 45 - **26,30,32,34**   NYPE: 22 Oct 45
(attached 113th Cav Gp)

Friedberg Germany

126th Cavalry Rcn Squadron (Mechanized)   1 Jan 44 Ft Lewis Wash (2nd Sqdn, 115th Cav) /15 Aug 44 Ft Jackson S.C.

127th Cavalry Rcn Squadron (Mechanized)   1 May 44 Ft Riley Kans / 22 Sep 44 Ft Riley Kans   *(R&S Cmd 1 May 44)*

128th Cavalry Rcn Squadron (Mechanized)   1 May 44 Ft Riley Kans / 22 Sep 44 Ft Riley Kans   *(R&S Cmd 1 May 44)*

129th Cavalry Rcn Squadron (Mechanized)   1 May 44 Ft Riley Kans / 6 Feb 45 Ft Riley Kans   *(R&S Cmd 1 May 44)*

*Active through 1946.

Part VI

Tank Destroyers of the U.S. Army in World War II

Chapter 26

Tank Destroyer Brigades

Brigades:

1, 2

1st Tank Destroyer Brigade

18 Nov 42 activated at Cp Hood Tex and transferred to Cp Claiborne La on 26 Feb 43; participated in the Louisiana Maneuvers 15 Sep–15 Nov 43; arrived Cp Shanks N.Y. 28 Dec 43 where staged until departed New York P/E 2 Jan 44; arrived England on 10 Jan 44 and landed in France 11 Jul 44; on 1 Aug 44 was used to establish "Task Force A" as a headquarters to command armored forces in exploitation of the Brittany Peninsula after the Allied breakthrough at Avranches; operated in this area as a separate combat command of VIII Corps and "Task Force A" dissolved after mission completion on 22 Sep 44; began functioning as the Third Army tank destroyer section commencing 30 Sep 44 in which capacity it remained; served on occupation duty in Germany until 31 Oct 45 and inactivated thereafter.

Campaigns: *Normandy, Northern France, Rhineland, Ardennes-Alsace, Central Europe*

2nd Tank Destroyer Brigade

24 Nov 42 activated at Cp Hood Tex under the Tank Destroyer Center; moved to Cp Forrest Tenn 11 Apr 43 under Second Army and to Tenn Maneuver Area 19 Apr 43; returned to Cp Forrest Tenn 26 Aug 43 and transferred to Cp Breckinridge Ky 5 Oct 43 and to Tenn Maneuver Area again 8 Nov 43; arrived back at Cp Breckinridge Ky 20 Nov 43 and assigned XX Corps; disbanded there on 8 Mar 44.

Chapter 27

Tank Destroyer Groups

Groups:

1–24

1st Tank Destroyer Group

30 Mar 42 activated at Cp Bowie Tex and moved to Cp Sutton N.C. 8 May 42 and to Ft Bragg N.C. 28 May 42; arrived Indiantown Gap Mil Res Pa 3 Aug 42 and departed New York P/E 19 Aug 42; arrived England 31 Aug 42 and landed in North Africa 16 Jan 43; sent into Italy 28 Oct 43 but withdrawn 18 Nov 43; returned England 9 Dec 43 and landed in France 13 Jun 44; functioned as VII Corps Traffic Control Section; crossed into Belgium 8 Sep 44 and entered Germany 17 Sep 44; returned to Belgium 23 Dec 44 and reentered Germany 6 Feb 45 where inactivated 5 Nov 45.

Campaigns: *Tunisia, Naples-Foggia, Normandy, Northern France, Rhineland, Ardennes-Alsace, Central Europe*
Aug 45 Loc: Marburg Germany

2nd Destroyer Group

15 Mar 42 activated at Ft Sam Houston Tex and moved to Cp Hood Tex 1 Jul 42; transferred to Cp Claiborne La 9 Apr 43 and staged at Cp Kilmer N.J. 15 Dec 43 until departed New York P/E 29 Dec 43; arrived in England 8 Jan 44 and landed in France 26 Jun 44; functioned as XIX Corps antitank section; crossed into Belgium 3 Sep 44 and into Holland 20 Sep 44; returned to Belgium 28 Sep 44 and to Holland 3 Nov 44; entered Germany 22 Dec 44 where inactivated 5 Nov 45.

Campaigns: *Normandy, Northern France, Rhineland, Central Europe*
Aug 45 Loc: Korschenborich Germany

3rd Tank Destroyer Group

30 Mar 42 activated at Cp Bowie Tex and transferred to Cp Pickett Va 18 Jun 43; arrived Ft Dix N.J. 2 Sep 43 and staged at Cp Shanks N.Y. 14 Oct 43 until departed New York P/E 21 Oct 43; arrived England 2 Nov 43 and landed in France 8 Jun 44; functioned as the V Corps antitank section; entered Belgium 9 Sep 44 and Luxembourg 16 Sep 44; returned to Belgium 4 Oct 44 and entered Germany 26 Feb 45; arrived in Czechoslovakia 8 May 45; returned to New York P/E 21 Feb 46 and inactivated at Cp Kilmer N.J. 22 Feb 46.

Campaigns: *Normandy, Northern France, Rhineland, Ardennes-Alsace, Central Europe*
Aug 45 Loc: Volkmarsen Germany

4th Tank Destroyer Group

1 Sep 42 activated at Cp Hood Tex and moved to Ft Lewis Wash 15 Feb 43 under IX Corps; transferred to IV Corps 15 Mar 43 and III Corps 15 Jan 44; staged at Cp Kilmer N.J. 10 Apr 44 until departed New York P/E 21 Apr 44; arrived England 26 Apr 44 and landed in France 19 Jul 44; functioned as the XX Corps antitank section; entered Germany 6 Dec 44 and arrived Boston P/E 27 Jul 45; arrived Ft Jackson S.C. 2 Sep 45 where inactivated 26 Oct 45.

Campaigns: *Normandy, Northern France, Rhineland, Ardennes-Alsace, Central Europe*
Aug 45 Loc:

5th Tank Destroyer Group

1 Sep 42 activated at Cp Hood Tex and moved to Desert Training Center Cp Young Calif 23 Apr 43; transferred to Cp Gruber Okla 19 Nov 43 and assigned X Corps; staged at Cp Kilmer N.J. 27 Dec 43 until departed New York P/E 2 Jan 44; arrived England 10 Jan 44 and landed in France 12 Jul 44; functioned as the XV Corps antitank section; entered Germany 18 Mar 45 and Austria 5 May 45; returned New York P/E 2 Dec 45 and inactivated Cp Shanks N.Y. 4 Dec 45.

Campaigns: *Normandy, Northern France, Rhineland, Ardennes-Alsace, Central Europe*
Aug 45 Loc: Sarrebourg France

6th Tank Destroyer Group

1 Sep 42 activated at Cp Hood Tex and moved to Desert Training Center Cp Young Calif 8 Jan 43; transferred to Cp Maxey Tex 31 Jul 43 and attached Third Army; staged at Cp Kilmer N.J. 16 Jan 44 until departed New York P/E 29 Jan 44; arrived England 5 Feb 44 and landed in France 25 Jul 44; functioned as XIII Corps antitank section; crossed into Belgium 24 Oct 44 and inactivated in Germany 1 May 46 when redesignated 5th Constabulatory Regiment.

Campaigns: *Normandy, Northern France, Rhineland, Central Europe*
Aug 45 Loc: Dulken Germany

7th Tank Destroyer Group

1 Sep 42 activated at Cp Hood Tex and moved to Cp Bowie Tex 18 Nov 42; returned to Cp Hood Tex 20 Jan 43 and transferred to Cp Shelby Miss 6 Mar 43 and XV Corps; staged at Cp Kilmer N.J. 2 Feb 44 until departed New York P/E 9 Feb 44; arrived in England 18 Feb 44 and landed in France 18 Jul 44; functioned as the VIII Corps antitank section; crossed into Luxembourg 23 Oct 44 and into Belgium 19 Dec 44; returned to Luxembourg 31 Jan 45 and entered Germany 6 Mar 45 where active until 25 Mar 46.

Campaigns: *Normandy, Northern France, Rhineland, Ardennes-Alsace, Central Europe*
Aug 45 Loc: Diez Germany

8th Tank Destroyer Group

13 Oct 42 activated at Cp Hood Tex and moved to Cp Bowie Tex 15 Jan 43; returned to Cp Hood Tex 12 Mar 43 and transferred to Cp Rucker Ala 1 Jun 43 where assigned III Corps 28 Aug 43; arrived Ft Dix N.J. in Apr 44 and staged at Cp Myles Standish Mass 22 Aug 44 until departed Boston P/E 5 Sep 44; arrived England 15 Sep 44 and landed in France 21 Oct 44; functioned as the III Corps antitank section; crossed into Luxembourg 19 Dec 44 and into Belgium 20 Dec 44; returned to Luxembourg 24 Dec 44 and recrossed into Belgium 23 Feb 45; entered Germany 24 Feb 45; arrived New York P/E 7 Jul 45 and arrived Cp Bowie Tex 12 Jul 45 where inactivated 20 Oct 45.

Campaigns: *Northern France, Rhineland, Ardennes-Alsace, Central Europe*
Aug 45 Loc: Camp Bowie Texas

9th Tank Destroyer Group

13 Oct 42 activated at Cp Hood Tex and moved to Cp Bowie Tex 4 Dec 42; returned to Cp Hood Tex 5 Mar 43 and moved to Tenn Maneuver Area 18 Jun 43; transferred to Cp Atterbury Ind 29 Aug 43 under IV Armored Corps and assigned XX Corps 9 Oct 43 and XXII Corps 25 Jan 44; staged at Cp Kilmer N.J. 31 Mar 44 until departed New York P/E 3 May 44; arrived in England 16 May 44 and landed France 31 Jul 44; functioned as XII Corps Advanced Information Center; crossed into Luxembourg 21 Dec 44 and entered Germany 9 Mar 45; arrived Hampton Roads P/E 9 Aug 45 and moved to Cp Hood Tex 13 Aug 45 where inactivated 1 Nov 45.

Campaigns: *Northern France, Rhineland, Ardennes-Alsace, Central Europe*
Aug 45 Loc: Shipment #10106-M unloading Cp Patrick Henry Virginia

10th Tank Destroyer Group

13 Feb 43 activated at Cp Bowie Tex and moved to Cp Hood Tex 1 Apr 43; attached to Third Army and transferred to Many La (La Mnvr Area) 27 Jun 43 where assigned to X Corps 5 Aug 45; arrived at Cp Gruber Okla 26 Aug 43 and assigned to Desert Training Center and moved to Cp Young Calif 14 Nov 43; relocated to Cp Cooke Calif 26 Feb 44 and assigned to III Corps; arrived at Cp Howze Tex 3 May 44 and assigned to XXIII Corps; there disbanded 25 May 44.

11th Tank Destroyer Group

20 Feb 43 activated at Cp Bowie Tex and moved to Cp Hood Tex 23 Mar 43; attached to Third Army and transferred to La Maneuver Area 17 Jul 43; moved to Cp Swift Tex 25 Aug 43 and assigned VIII Corps; returned to La Maneuver Area 16 Sep 43 and assigned XVIII Corps 8 Nov 43; returned to Cp Swift Tex 19 Nov 43 where assigned XXIII Corps 1 Feb 44; arrived Cp Howze Tex 5 May 44 and disbanded there 25 May 44.

12th Tank Destroyer Group

27 Feb 43 activated at Cp Bowie Tex and moved to Cp Hood Tex 14 Apr 43; sent to Desert Training Center Cp Young Calif 27 Jul 43 and moved to Cp Claiborne La 31 Jan 44 under XXI Corps; transferred to Cp Livingston La 26 May 44; staged at Cp Shanks N.Y. 17 Sep 44 until departed New York P/E 24 Sep 44; arrived in England 30 Sep 44 and landed in France 2 Oct 44; functioned as XVI Corps antitank section; crossed into Belgium 15 Dec 44 and into Holland 31 Dec 44; entered Germany 3 Mar 45; arrived Hampton Roads P/E 27 Jun 45 and moved to Cp Hood Tex 3 Jul 45 where inactivated 1 Nov 45.

Campaigns: *Rhineland, Central Europe*
Aug 45 Loc: Camp Hood Texas

13th Tank Destroyer Group

6 Mar 43 activated at Cp Bowie Tex and moved to Cp Hood Tex 12 May 43; sent to Tenn Maneuver Area 25 Aug 43 under XII Corps and arrived Cp Gordon Ga 9 Nov 43 where assigned IX Corps 20 Jan 44; moved to Ft Jackson S.C. 27 Mar 44 and assigned XXIII Corps 25 Sep 44; staged at Ft Lawton Wash 19 Dec 44 until departed Seattle P/E 28 Dec 44; arrived Hawaii 5 Jan 45 and departed in Jul 45; arrived 9 Jul 45 at Leyte Philippine Islands; moved to Mindoro 5 Aug 45; inactivated in the Philippines 12 Nov 45.

Campaigns: *Pacific Theater without inscription*
Aug 45 Loc: Mindoro Philippine Islands

14th Tank Destroyer Group

13 Mar 43 activated at Cp Bowie Tex and moved to Cp Hood Tex 15 May 43; transferred to Cp Phillips Kans 21 Aug 43 under XI Corps and to Tenn Maneuver Area 10 Nov 43 under Second Army; arrived Cp Campbell Ky 15 Jan 44 and assigned XX Corps and later XXII Corps 25 Jan 44; inactivated there 20 May 44.

15th Tank Destroyer Group

20 Mar 43 activated at Cp Bowie Tex and moved to Cp Hood Tex 20 May 43; transferred to Cp Cooke Calif 17 Sep 43 under II Armored Corps and went to the Calif-Ariz Maneuver Area 23 Jan 44; relocated to Cp Gruber Okla 18 Mar 44 and assigned XVI Corps and later XXXVI Corps 17 Jul 44; inactivated there 25 Aug 44.

16th Tank Destroyer Group

3 Apr 43 activated at Cp Bowie Tex and moved to Cp Hood Tex 9 May 43; transferred to Ft Jackson S.C. 18 Oct 43 and assigned XII Corps; sent to Tenn Maneuver Area 21 Jan 44 and to Cp Breckinridge Ky 24 Mar 44 with XXII Corps; staged at Cp Kilmer N.J. 15 Oct 44 until departed New York P/E 1 Nov 44; arrived England 9 Nov 44 and landed in France 17 Feb 45; functioned as the XXI Corps antitank section; entered Germany 23 Mar 45 and arrived Boston P/E 4 Sep 45; moved to Cp Swift Tex Sep 45 where inactivated 10 Nov 45.

Campaigns: *Rhineland, Central Europe*
Aug 45 Loc: France

17th Tank Destroyer Group

10 Apr 43 activated at Cp Bowie Tex and moved to Cp Hood Tex 16 May 43; returned to Cp Bowie Tex 18 Oct 43 with VIII Corps; moved to La Maneuver Area 15 Nov 43 under XVIII Corps and relocated to Cp Bowie Tex 28 Jan 44 where assigned XXIII Corps 1 Feb 44; arrived Cp Swift Tex 25 Apr 44 where disbanded 30 Aug 44.

18th Tank Destroyer Group

17 Apr 43 activated at Cp Bowie Tex and moved to Cp Hood Tex 7 May 43; transferred to Cp Joseph T. Robinson Ark 12 Nov 43 under IX Corps and went to Cp Claiborne La 24 Dec 43 where assigned XXI Corps 7 Jan 44; went to La Maneuver Area 3 Feb 44 and to Cp Howze Tex 6 Apr 44 where assigned XXIII Corps; arrived at Cp Polk La 23 Jul 44 and assigned XXI Corps 19 Sep 44; moved to Ft Knox Ky 6 Feb 45 where inactivated 20 Feb 45.

19th Tank Destroyer Group

1 May 43 activated at Cp Hood Tex and moved to Cp Gruber Okla 20 Jan 44 with XVI Corps; sent to La Maneuver Area 26 Feb 44 under Fourth Army and arrived Cp Rucker Ala 13 Apr 44 with IX Corps where disbanded 20 May 44.

20th Tank Destroyer Group

8 May 43 activated at Cp Hood Tex and moved to Cp Maxey Tex 12 Feb 44 under XXIII Corps; arrived at Cp Bowie Tex 26 Apr 44 and staged at Cp Myles Standish Mass 27 Sep 44 until departed Boston P/E 4 Oct 44; arrived in England 12 Oct 44 and landed in France 15 Oct 44; functioned as Ninth Army Rear Detachment; crossed into Holland 24 Dec 44 and entered Germany 10 Mar 45; returned to Boston P/E 4 Sep 45 and moved immediately to Cp Gruber Okla where inactivated 23 Nov 45.

Campaigns: *Rhineland, Central Europe*
Aug 45 Loc: France

21st Tank Destroyer Group

15 May 43 activated at Cp Hood Tex and moved to Cp Shelby Miss 16 Feb 44 under IX Corps where inactivated 22 Nov 45.

Aug 45 Loc: Camp Shelby Mississippi

22nd Tank Destroyer Group

5 Jun 43 activated Cp Hood Tex and assigned Replacement & School Command 17 Feb 44; inactivated at Ft Knox Ky 20 Feb 45.

23rd Tank Destroyer Group

12 Jun 43 activated at Cp Hood Tex and assigned XXIII Corps 18 Feb 44; staged at Cp Myles Standish Mass 26 Sep 44 until departed Boston P/E 11 Oct 44; arrived in England 18 Oct 44 and landed in France 21 Oct 44; crossed into Belgium 26 Nov 44 and entered Germany 10 Mar 45; arrived New York P/E 1 Jul 45 and moved to Ft Bragg N.C. 4 Jul 45 where inactivated 26 Oct 45.

Campaigns: *Rhineland, Ardennes-Alsace, Central Europe*
Aug 45 Loc: Fort Bragg North Carolina

24th Tank Destroyer Group

19 Jun 43 activated at Cp Hood Tex and assigned XXIII Corps 18 Feb 44 and Fourth Army 19 Sep 44; inactivated there 23 Dec 44.

Chapter 28

Tank Destroyer Battalions

Battalions:

601–603, 605–612, 614, 626–638, 640, 641, 643–672, 679, 691, 692, 701–706, 771–776, 795, 801–829, 846, 893, 894, 899

⭐ EXAMPLE — HOW TO USE THIS TABLE

Unit Designation and Type   Date Formed and Location (Source of Unit)/Inactivation and Location   August 1945 Location
Overseas Wartime Locations followed by - **Campaign Key Numbers** and PE return to United States, if applicable or space allows
(notes and remarks in parenthesis)

803rd Tank Destroyer Bn (S-P) (M10-M36)   15 Dec 41 Ft Lewis Wash as Heavy S-P (103rd Inf AT Bn)/1 Dec 45 Cp Kilmer N.J.   Luxembourg, Luxembourg
NYPE: 24 Jun 43   England: 6 Jul 43   France-ETO: 13 Jun 44 - **25,26,30,32,34**   NYPE: 29 Nov 45 *(A–1 Nov 43, B–15 Sep 44)*

In this example, the 803rd Tank Destroyer Battalion (Self-Propelled) was redesignated from the 103rd Infantry Anti-tank Battalion on 15 December 1941 at Fort Lewis, Washington. Earlier service can be tracked by looking up the 103rd Infantry Antitank Battalion in Chapter 14. The 803rd Tank Destroyer Battalion, initially formed as a heavy self-propelled type, *departed* New York Port of Embarkation on 24 Jun 1943, *arrived* in England on 6 July 1943, and landed in France–European Theater of Operations 13 June 1944. It participated in the Ardennes-Alsace, Central European, Normandy, Northern France, and Rhineland campaigns. This information was derived by indexing the boldfaced campaign key numbers with Appendix I. It was located in Luxembourg in August 1945, returned to New York Port of Embarkation 29 November 1945, and inactivated at Camp Kilmer, New Jersey, on 1 December 1945. Equipment type varied during the war and this is indicated by parenthesized remarks. On the first line, just after the unit title is the type **(S-P)**. This is the *final* wartime type of the battalion. Next is **(M10-M36)**, which in this table represents tank destroyer vehicles used during *combat* operations, and represents sequential outfittings. In this case the battalion went into combat equipped with **M10** tank destroyers and was later refitted with **M36** tank destroyers. On the second line are the Table of Organization notes on the battalion. In this case, reference is made to the index of lettered note codes given below which relate that the 803rd Tank Destroyer Battalion was reorganized from Heavy Self-Propelled to Self-Propelled under the 27 January 1943 Table of Organization 18-25 on 1 November 1943, and was reorganized under the 15 March 1944 Table of Organization 18-25 on 15 September 1944.

A = T/O 18-25 Tank Destroyer Battalion dated 27 January 1943 (Self-Propelled)
B = T/O 18-25 Tank Destroyer Battalion dated 15 March 1944 (Self-Propelled)
C = T/O 18-35 Tank Destroyer Battalion dated 7 May 1943 (Towed 3-inch Gun)
D = T/O 18-35 Tank Destroyer Battalion dated 1 September 1944 (Towed 3-inch Gun)
X = not reorganized under a different T/O for the remainder of the war or unit service
c. = circa, such as c.8 May 43 would mean about 8 May 43, usually Earliest Practical Date afterwards

A or **C** (initial S-P or Towed T/Os) are not recorded if in fact the given unit was activated under that particular T/O, in which case the effective date of the T/O would coincide with the unit's formation date. This would only be applicable to 1943, as all Tank Destroyer units (Towed or Self-Propelled) were under T/O 18-25 dated 8 Jun 42 prior to the introduction of **A** and **C** series.

Unless otherwise stated, units that served entirely stateside during the war were not usually reorganized under later **B** or **D** T/Os.

Example: *(A–24 May 43,* **Towed AT Gun** *C–11 Dec 43,* **S-P** *B–5 Apr 45)*
In this case the battalion was reorganized as Self-Propelled under the 27 Jan 43 18-25 T/O on 24 May 43, was reorganized as a towed 3-inch gun battalion under the 18-35 T/O dated 7 May 1943 on 11 Dec 43, and was finally re-equipped as a Self-Propelled battalion under T/O 18-25 dated 15 Mar 44 effective 5 Apr 1945.

Equipment type varied during the war, so that **(M10-M36)** represents sequential outfittings. **(M3)** refers to the M3 75mm gun motor carriage mounted on the halftrack. Note that **S-P** simply means tracked tank destroyers.

BATTALION DESIGNATION AND TYPE   **FORMED (SOURCE OF UNIT) / INACTIVATION**   **AUGUST 1945 LOCATION**

601st Tank Destroyer Bn (S-P) (M3-M10-M36)   16 Dec 41 Ft Devens Mass as Lt Towed / 18 Oct 45 Cp Shanks N.Y.   Toul France
NYPE: 2 Aug 42   Scotland: 7 Aug 42   N.Africa: 8 Nov 42   Sicily: 30 Jul 43   Italy: 9 Sep 43
France-ETO: 15 Aug 44 - **23,24,25,26,29,34,35,36,37,38**   NYPE: 17 Oct 45 *(S-P in 1942, A–19 Nov 43, B–15 Jun 44)*

602nd Tank Destroyer Bn (S-P) (M18)   15 Dec 41 Ft Sam Houston Tex as Lt Towed/ 23 Nov 45 Cp Myles Standish Mass   Wittlich Germany
NYPE: 18 Jul 44   England: 29 Jul 44   France-ETO: Aug 44 - **25,26,32,34**   BPE: 22 Nov 45 *(S-P in 1942, A–21 May 43, B–8 Nov 44)*

603rd Tank Destroyer Bn (S-P) (M18)   15 Dec 41 Ft Lewis Wash as Lt Towed/15 Dec 45 Cp Kilmer N.J.   Chateau-Salins France
NYPE: 11 Apr 44   England: 16 Apr 44   France-ETO: 22 Jul 44 - **24,26,30,32,34**   NYPE: 14 Dec 45 *(S-P in 1942, A–30 Jun 43, B–8 Nov 44)*

605th Tank Destroyer Bn (S-P) *(see note)*   16 Dec 41 Ft Custer Mich as Lt Towed / 4 Nov 45 Cp Myles Standish Mass   Viersen Germany
NYPE: 10 Dec 44   England: 16 Dec 44   France-ETO: 26 Jan 45 - **26,34**   BPE: 3 Nov 45
(S-P in 1942, **Towed AT Gun** *C–3 Mar 44, D–22 Dec 44,* **S-P** *B–past March 45)*

BATTALION DESIGNATION AND TYPE	FORMED (SOURCE OF UNIT)/INACTIVATION	AUGUST 1945 LOCATION

606th Tank Destroyer Bn (S-P)   16 Dec 41 Ft Leonard Wood Mo as Lt Towed / 28 Feb 45 Cp Hood Tex
(S-P in 1942, A–9 Mar 44, X) (R&S Cmd 23 Nov 44)

607th Tank Destroyer Bn (S-P) (M36)   9 Dec 41 Ft Ord Calif as Lt Towed / 27 Oct 45 Cp Kilmer N.J.   Lissendorf Germany
BPE: 13 Apr 44   England: 21 Apr 44   France-ETO: 16 Jun 44 - **25,26,30,32,34**   NYPE: 25 Oct 45
(S-P in 1942, A–25 May 43, Towed AT Gun C–15 Dec 43, S-P B–21 Nov 44)

608th Tank Destroyer Bn (S-P)   15 Dec 41 Ft Jackson S.C. as Lt Towed / 20 Dec 43 Cp Atterbury Ind
(S-P in 1942, A–20 Jun 43, X) (Personnel to other TD Bns)

609th Tank Destroyer Bn (S-P) (M18)   15 Dec 41 Ft Bragg N.C. as Lt Towed/13 Nov 45 Cp Breckinridge Ky   Trier Germany
NYPE: 11 Aug 44   England: 22 Aug 44   France-ETO: 20 Sep 44 - **25,26,32,34**   NYPE: 7 Sep 45 *(S-P in 1942, A–25 Jun 43, B–28 Apr 44)*

610th Tank Destroyer Bn (S-P) (M36)   10 Apr 42 Cp Barkeley Tex / 7 Dec 45 Cp Myles Standish Mass   Prum Germany
NYPE: 3 Jun 44   England: 12 Jun 44   France-ETO: 1 Aug 44 - **25,26,32,34**   BPE: 6 Dec 45
(A–c.8 May 43, Towed AT Gun C–5 Dec 43, S-P B–11 Oct 44 in ETO)

611th Tank Destroyer Bn (Towed AT Gun)   1 May 42 Cp Polk La / 20 Feb 45 Ft Knox Ky   *(C–8 Jul 43, X)*

612th Tank Destroyer Bn (S-P) (M18)   25 Jun 42 Cp Swift Tex / 27 Oct 45 Cp Kilmer N.J.   Bonn Germany
NYPE: 7 Apr 44   England: 15 Apr 44   France-ETO: 14 Jun 44 - **25,26,30,32,34**   NYPE: 25 Oct 45
(A–c.8 May 43, Towed AT Gun C–21 Dec 43, S-P B–28 Dec 44)

614th Tank Destroyer Bn (Cld) (Towed AT Gun)   25 Jul 42 Cp Carson Colo / 31 Jan 46 Cp Kilmer N.J.   Bouxwiller France
NYPE: 27 Aug 44   England: 7 Sep 44   France-ETO: 7 Sep 44 - **25,26,32,34**   NYPE: 30 Jan 46 *(C–2 Jul 43, X)*

626th Tank Destroyer Bn (S-P)   15 Dec 41 Cp Edwards Mass as Lt Towed / 20 Dec 43 Cp Gordon Ga
(S-P–31 May 42, A–15 May 43, X)

627th Tank Destroyer Bn (S-P)   15 Dec 41 Ft McClellan Ala as Lt Towed / 10 Apr 45 Hawaii
SFPE: 23 Jun 42   Hawaii: 5 Jul 42 *(past 7 Jan 45 functioned as prov Quartermaster Bn)* *(S-P in 1942, A–1 Jul 43, B–25 Feb 44)*
(turned in all equipment on 15 Jan 45)

628th Tank Destroyer Bn (S-P) (M10-M36)   15 Dec 41 Indiantown Gap Pa as Lt Towed / 14 Nov 45 Cp Myles Standish Mass   Neersen Germany
NYPE: 29 Jan 44   England: 5 Feb 44   France-ETO: 31 Jul 44 - **25,26,32,34**   BPE: 13 Nov 45 *(S-P in 1942, A–8 May 43, B–15 Sep 44)*

629th Tank Destroyer Bn (S-P) (M10)   15 Dec 41 Ft George G Meade Md as Lt Towed / 3 Dec 45 Cp Kilmer N.J.   Neurath Germany
NYPE: 1 Jan 44   England: 8 Jan 44   France-ETO: 2 Jul 44 - **25,26,30,32,34**   NYPE: 2 Dec 45 *(S-P in 1942, A–19 May 43, B–15 Sep 44)*

630th Tank Destroyer Bn (S-P) (M36)   15 Dec 41 Ft Jackson S.C. as Lt Towed / 31 Mar 46 Cp Kilmer N.J.   Iversheim Germany
NYPE: 3 Jun 44   England: 12 Jun 44   France-ETO: 23 Jul 44 - **25,26,32,34**   NYPE: 28 Mar 46 *(S-P in 1942)*

631st Tank Destroyer Bn (S-P) (M10)   15 Dec 41 Cp Blanding Fla as Lt Towed / 16 Dec 45 Cp Kilmer N.J.   Langgreis Germany
NYPE: 26 Jul 44   England: 5 Aug 44   France-ETO: 31 Aug 44 - **25,26,32,34**   NYPE: 15 Dec 45 *(S-P in 1942)*

632nd Tank Destroyer Bn (S-P) (M10)   15 Dec 41 Cp Livingston La as Lt Towed / 1 Jan 46 Cp Stoneman Calif   Philippine Islands
SFPE: 12 May 42   Australia: 12 May 42   New Guinea: 28 Oct 43   Philippines: 20 Oct 44 - **13,14,15**   SFPE: 30 Dec 45
(S-P in 1942, A–5 Apr 44, B–10 May 44)

633rd Tank Destroyer Bn (S-P) (M18)   16 Dec 41 Cp Forrest Tenn as Lt Towed / 30 Oct 45 Ft Bragg N.C.   Ft Bragg N.C.
NYPE: 31 Mar 45   France-ETO: 12 Apr 45 - **26**   NYPE: 10 Jul 45 *(S-P in 1942, A–13 May 43, X)*

634th Tank Destroyer Bn (S-P) (M10)   16 Dec 41 Cp Claiborne La as Lt Towed / 29 Nov 45 Cp Kilmer N.J.   Versailles France
NYPE: 29 Dec 43   England: 8 Jan 44   France-ETO: Jun 44 - **25,26,30,32,34**   NYPE: 29 Nov 45 *(S-P in 1942, A–8 May 43, B–15 Sep 44)*

635th Tank Destroyer Bn (S-P) (M10)   15 Dec 41 Cp Joseph T Robinson Ark as Lt Towed / 27 Dec 45 Cp Myles Standish   Leipzig Germany
NYPE: 9 Feb 44   England: 18 Feb 44   France-ETO: 4 Jul 44 - **25,26,30,32,34**   BPE: 26 Oct 45   Mass
(S-P A–Jun 43, B–15 Feb 45)

636th Tank Destroyer Bn (S-P) (M10)   15 Dec 41 Cp Bowie Tex as Lt Towed / 7 Dec 45 Cp Myles Standish Mass   Brumath France
NYPE: 2 Apr 43   N.Africa: 13 Apr 43   Italy: 12 Sep 43   France-ETO: 15 Aug 44 - **24,25,26,29,34,35,37**   BPE: 3 Dec 45
(S-P in 1942, A–4 Jan 44, X)

637th Tank Destroyer Bn (S-P) (M18)   19 Dec 41 Cp Shelby Miss as Lt Towed / 25 Jan 46 Japan   Philippine Islands
SFPE: 26 May 42   Fiji I: 28 Jun 42   Espiritu Santo: 8 Jul 44   Bougainville: 19 Oct 44   Philippines: 9 Jan 45 - **14**
(S-P in 1942, A–14 Jan 44, B–10 May 44)

638th Tank Destroyer Bn (S-P) (M18)   15 Dec 41 Cp Shelby Miss as Lt Towed / 7 Nov 45 Ft Benning Ga   Ft Benning Ga
NYPE: 30 Aug 44   France-ETO: 9 Sep 44 - **25,26,32,34**   BPE: Jul 45

640th Tank Destroyer Bn (S-P) (M10)   19 Dec 41 Cp San Luis Obispo Calif at Lt Towed / 13 Jan 46 Cp Anza Calif   Philippine Islands
SFPE: 4 Sep 42   Hawaii: 12 Sep 42;   Guadalcanal: 5 Feb 44   New Britian: 3 May 44   Philippines: 9 Jan 45 - **3,14,20**
(S-P in 1942, A–1 Jul 43, B–28 Oct 44)

641st Tank Destroyer Bn   18 Dec 41 Ft Lewis Wash as Lt Towed / 24 Jun 44 New Guinea redes 98th Chem
NYPE: 4 Mar 42   Australia: 9 Apr 42   New Guinea: 21 Jan 43 - **3,15,17**   Mortar Bn

BATTALION DESIGNATION AND TYPE	FORMED (SOURCE OF UNIT) / INACTIVATION	AUGUST 1945 LOCATION
643rd Tank Destroyer Bn (S-P) (M18)	15 Dec 41 Cp Blanding Fla as Lt Towed / 6 Nov 45 Cp San Luis Obispo Calif	Cp San Luis Obispo Calif

BPE: 5 Sep 44   France-ETO: 15 Sep 44 - **25,26,34**   HRPE: 5 Jul 45 *(S-P in 1942,* **A**–*19 May 43,* **Towed AT Gun C**–*21 Dec 43,* **S-P B**–*13 Dec 44)*

644th Tank Destroyer Bn (S-P) (M10)	15 Dec 41 Ft Dix N.J. as Lt Towed / 5 Dec 45 Cp Patrick Henry Va	Bergerhausen Germany

NYPE: 2 Jan 44   N.Ireland: 11 Jan 44   England: 13 May 44   France-ETO: 12 Jul 44 - **25,26,30,32,34**   HRPE: 5 Dec 45
(S-P in 1942, **A**–*13 May 43,* **B**–*15 Nov 44)*

645th Tank Destroyer Bn (S-P) (M10-M36)	15 Dec 41 Cp Barkeley Tex as Lt S-P / 30 Oct 45 Cp Myles Standish Mass	Hambach France

NYPE: 28 Apr 43   N.Africa: 26 May 43   Italy: 9 Sep 43   France-ETO: 15 Aug 44 - **24,25,26,29,34,35,37**   BPE: 29 Oct 45
*(***A**–*15 Jan 44,* **B**–*19 Jul 44)*

646th Tank Destroyer Bn (S-P) (Cld)   15 May 42 Ft Huachuca Ariz / 1 May 44 Indiantown Gap Mil Res Pa
*(***A**–*past 8 May 43,* **X***)*

647th Tank Destroyer Bn (S-P)   6 Mar 43 Cp Bowie Tex / 12 May 44 Cp Van Dorn Miss   *(personnel to 144th Inf)*

648th Tank Destroyer Bn (Towed AT Gun)	6 Mar 43 Cp Bowie Tex / 16 Dec 45 Cp Kilmer N.J.	Schwabach Germany

NYPE: 10 Dec 44   England: 19 Dec 44   France-ETO: 26 Jan 45 - **26,34**   NYPE: 13 Dec 45
(S-P in 1942, **Towed AT Gun C**–*3 Mar 44,* **S-P B**–*24 May 45)*

649th Tank Destroyer Bn (Cld) (Towed AT Gun)   31 Mar 43 Cp Bowie Tex / 24 Apr 44 Hampton Roads P/E
(personnel to Army Service Forces)

650th Tank Destroyer Bn (S-P)   13 Mar 43 Cp Bowie Tex / 25 Mar 44 Cp Bowie redes 425th Armd FA Bn

651st Tank Destroyer Bn (S-P)   13 Mar 43 Cp Bowie Tex / 29 May 44 Cp Howze Tex   *(personnel to 140th Inf)*

652nd Tank Destroyer Bn (S-P)	20 Mar 43 Cp Bowie Tex / 16 Sep 45 Cp Shelby Miss	Cp Shelby Miss

*(***A**–*c.8 May 43,* **B**–*26 Jun 44)*

653rd Tank Destroyer Bn (S-P)   20 Mar 43 Cp Bowie Tex / 10 May 44 Cp Van Dorn Miss   *(personnel to 144th Inf)*

654th Tank Destroyer Bn (Light) (S-P) (M10-M36)	15 Dec 41 Ft Benning Ga / 13 Nov 45 Cp Patrick Henry Va	Venlo Holland

NYPE: 7 Oct 43   England: 19 Oct 43   N.Ireland: 20 Oct 43   England: 29 Apr 44   France-ETO: 11 Jul 44 - **25,26,30,32,34**   HRPE: 13 Nov 45

655th Tank Destroyer Bn (S-P)   3 Apr 43 Cp Bowie Tex / 10 Apr 44 Cp Hood Tex
(personnel to 493rd and 869th Ordnance Heavy Automotive Maint Cos)

656th Tank Destroyer Bn (S-P) (M18-M36)	3 Apr 43 Cp Bowie Tex / 1 Nov 46 Cp Campbell Ky	Cp Campbell Ky

NYPE: 16 Dec 44   England: 28 Dec 44   France-ETO: 6 Feb 45 - **26,34**   HRPE: 2 Jul 45
*(***S-P** *in 1942,* **A**–*c.8 May 43,* **B**–*1 Dec 44)*

657th Tank Destroyer Bn (S-P)   10 Apr 43 Cp Bowie Tex / 10 Apr 44 Cp Hood Tex
(Personnel to 493rd and 869th Ordnance Heavy Automotive Maint Cos)

658th Tank Destroyer Bn (S-P)   10 Apr 43 Cp Bowie Tex / 15 Apr 44 Ft Ord Calif redes 658th Amphibious Tractor Bn

659th Tank Destroyer Bn (Cld) (Towed AT Gun)   15 May 43 Cp Hood Tex / 1 Dec 44 Cp Livingston La   *(R&S Cmd 23 Nov 44*

660th Tank Destroyer Bn (S-P) (School Troops)   17 Apr 43 Cp Bowie Tex / 25 May 44 Cp Carson Colo
(battalion served as Tank Destroyer Center School Troops 7 May 43 until 18 Feb 44 when assigned R&S Cmd) (personnel to 201st Inf)

661st Tank Destroyer Bn (S-P) (M18)	17 Apr 43 Cp Bowie Tex / 10 Feb 46 Cp Hood Tex	Cp Shelby Miss

NYPE: 10 Jan 45   France-ETO: 23 Jan 45 - **26,34**   BPE: 6 Jul 45 *(***B**–*5 Jun 44)*

662nd Tank Destroyer Bn (Towed AT Gun)   1 May 43 Cp Hood Tex / 17 Dec 44 Ft Knox Ky redes 662nd Tank Bn

662nd Tank Destroyer Bn (Towed AT Gun)   1 May 43 Cp Hood Tex / 17 Dec 44 Ft Knox Ky redes 662nd Tank Bn
(R&S Cmd 17 Feb 44)

663rd Tank Destroyer Bn (S-P)   1 May 43 Cp Hood Tex / 25 Mar 44 Cp Bowie redes 426th Armd FA Bn

664th Tank Destroyer Bn (S-P)   8 May 43 Cp Hood Tex / 12 May 44 Cp Maxey Tex   *(personnel to 125th Inf)*

665th Tank Destroyer Bn (S-P)   8 May 43 Cp Hood Tex / 17 May 44 Cp Maxey Tex   *(personnel to 125th Inf)*

666th Tank Destroyer Bn (S-P)   15 May 43 Cp Hood Tex / 25 Mar 44 Cp Bowie Tex redes 427th Armd FA Bn

667th Tank Destroyer Bn (S-P)   5 Jun 43 Cp Hood Tex / 3 Jun 44 Cp Maxey Tex   *(personnel to 125th Inf)*

668th Tank Destroyer Bn (S-P)   5 Jun 43 Cp Hood Tex / 25 Mar 44 Cp Bowie Tex redes 428th Armd FA Bn

669th Tank Destroyer Bn (Cld) (Towed AT Gun)   19 Jun 43 Cp Hood Tex / 15 Nov 44 Ft Huachuca Ariz

670th Tank Destroyer Bn (S-P)   12 Jun 43 Cp Hood Tex / 10 Apr 45 Hawaii
SPE: 28 Dec 44   Hawaii: 5 Jan 45 *(***B**–*28 Apr 44)*

BATTALION DESIGNATION AND TYPE	FORMED (SOURCE OF UNIT) / INACTIVATION	AUGUST 1945 LOCATION

671st Tank Destroyer Bn (S-P) (M18) 12 Jun 43 Cp Hood Tex /17 Jan 46 Cp Anza Calif — Philippine Islands
SPE: 28 Dec 44   Hawaii: 5 Jan 45   Philippines: Jul 45   LAPE: 16 Jan 46 *(B–16 May 44)*

672nd Tank Destroyer Bn (S-P) 19 Jun 43 Cp Hood Tex /15 Apr 44 Ft Ord Calif redes 672nd Amphibious Tractor Bn

679th Tank Destroyer Bn (Cld) (Towed AT Gun) 26 Jun 43 Cp Hood Tex / 27 Oct 45 Cp Kilmer N.J. — Bolzanetto Italy
NYPE: 10 Jan 45   France-ETO: 21 Jan 45   Italy: 1 Mar 45 - **31,33**   NYPE: 26 Oct 45 *(C–15 Jul 43, X)*

691st Tank Destroyer Bn (S-P) (M36) 15 Dec 41 Ft Bliss Tex as Lt S-P/13 Apr 46 Cp Kilmer N.J. — Offenbach Germany
BPE: 26 Jul 44   England: 1 Aug 44   France-ETO: 27 Aug 44 - **25,26,30,32,34**   NYPE: 12 Apr 46
(Towed AT Gun C–22 Dec 43, D–26 Jan 45, S-P B–20 Mar 45)

692nd Tank Destroyer Bn (S-P) (M10) 10 Apr 42 Cp Gordon Ga as Lt S-P/8 Feb 46 Cp Swift Tex — Brauweiler Germany
NYPE: 12 Sep 44   England: 23 Sep 44   France-ETO: 25 Sep 44 - **25,26,34**   BPE: 26 Aug 45
(A–c.8 May 43, Towed AT Gun C–1 Mar 44, S-P B–7 Feb 45)

701st Tank Destroyer Bn (S-P) (M3-M10) 15 Dec 41 Ft Knox Ky as Heavy S-P/29 Oct 45 Ft Leonard Wood Mo — Shipment #22006-T at sea
NYPE: 31 May 42   Ireland: 11 Jun 42   Scotland: 27 Oct 42   England: 28 Oct 42   N.Africa: 10 Dec 42
Italy: 29 Oct 43 - **23,29,31,33,35,38**   BPE: 22 Aug 45 *(A–9 Sep 43, B–27 Jul 44)*

702nd Tank Destroyer Bn (S-P) (M10-M36) 15 Dec 41 Ft Benning Ga as Heavy S-P/3 Oct 45 Cp Myles Standish Mass — Glehn Germany
BPE: 15 Feb 44   England: 22 Feb 44   France-ETO: 11 Jun 44 - **25,26,30,32,34**   BPE: 2 Oct 45 *(A–29 Apr 43, B–15 Sep 44)*

703rd Tank Destroyer Bn (S-P) (M10-M36) 15 Dec 41 Cp Polk La as Heavy S-P / 3 Jan 46 Cp Kilmer N.J. — Cologne Germany
NYPE: 4 Sep 43   England: 15 Sep 43   France-ETO: 1 Jul 44 - **25,26,30,32,34**   NYPE: 2 Jan 46

704th Tank Destroyer Bn (S-P) (M18) 15 Dec 41 Pine Camp N.Y. as Heavy S-P / 24 Oct 45 Cp Shanks N.Y. — Ulmen Germany
BPE: 27 Feb 44   England: 12 Mar 44   France-ETO: 13 Jul 44 - **25,26,30,32,34**   NYPE: 24 Oct 45 *(A–25 May 43, B–8 Nov 44)*

705th Tank Destroyer Bn (S-P) (M18) 15 Dec 41 Ft Knox Ky as Heavy S-P / 16 Nov 45 Cp Patrick Henry Va — Trois Vierges Luxembourg
NYPE: 18 Apr 44   England: 28 Apr 44   France-ETO: 17 Jul 44 - **25,26,30,32,34**   HRPE: 16 Nov 45 *(A–19 May 43, B–8 Nov 44)*

706th Tank Destroyer Bn (S-P) 30 Mar 42 Cp Chaffee Ark as Heavy S-P /14 Apr 44 Ft Ord Calif
(personnel to 539th, 540th, and 720th Amphibious Tractor Battalions) (A–19 May 43, X)

771st Tank Destroyer Bn (S-P) (M10-M36) 15 Dec 41 Ft Ethan Allen Vt as Heavy S-P/1 Dec 45 Cp Kilmer N.J. — Viersen Germany
NYPE: 21 Oct 43   England: 2 Nov 43   France-ETO: 28 Sep 44 (Co A in France since 4 Sep 44) - **26,32,34**   NYPE: 29 Nov 45
(A–15 May 43, B–1 Dec 44)

772nd Tank Destroyer Bn (Towed AT Gun) 16 Dec 41 Ft Leonard Wood as Heavy S-P / 24 Sep 45 Cp Shelby Miss — Cp San Luis Obispo Calif
NYPE: 29 Sep 44   England: 10 Oct 44   France-ETO: 20 Dec 44 - **25,26,34**   NYPE: 28 Jul 45
(A–18 May 43, Towed AT Gun C–11 Mar 44, D–1 Mar 45)

773rd Tank Destroyer Bn (S-P) (M10-M36) 15 Dec 41 Cp Shelby Miss as Heavy S-P / 23 Oct 45 Cp Patrick Henry Va — Berresheim Germany
NYPE: 29 Jan 44   England: 9 Feb 44   France-ETO: 8 Aug 44 - **25,26,32,34**   HRPE: 22 Oct 45 *(A–27 Jun 43, B–8 Nov 44)*

774th Tank Destroyer Bn (S-P) (M36) 15 Dec 41 Cp Blanding Fla as Heavy S-P / 29 Oct 45 Cp Kilmer N.J. — Thionville France
NYPE: 3 Jun 44   England: 12 Jun 44   France-ETO: 8 Aug 44 - **25,26,30,32,34** *(Towed AT Gun C–15 Dec 43, S-P B–26 Jan 45)*

775th Tank Destroyer Bn (S-P) 16 Dec 41 Forrest Tenn as Heavy S-P /15 Apr 44 Ft Ord Calif redes 728th
Amphibious Tractor Bn

776th Tank Destroyer Bn (S-P) (M10-M36) 20 Dec 41 Ft Lewis Wash as Heavy S-P/25 Nov 45 Cp Kilmer N.J. — Insviller Germany
NYPE: 13 Jan 43   N.Africa: 26 Jan 43   Italy: 19 Sep 43   France-ETO: 4 Oct 44 - **25,26,29,34,35,38**   NYPE: 23 Nov 45 *(A–19 Dec 43, X)*

795th Tank Destroyer Bn (Cld) (S-P) 16 Dec 41 Ft Custer Mich as Heavy S-P / 24 Apr 44 Hampton Roads P/E
(A–c.8 May 43, X)

801st Tank Destroyer Bn (S-P) (M18) 15 Dec 41 Ft Benning Ga as Heavy S-P (101st Inf AT Bn)/29 Nov 45 Cp Myles — Steinheim Germany
BPE: 28 Feb 44   England: 8 Mar 44   France-ETO: 13 Jun 44 - **25,26,30,32,34**   BPE: 28 Nov 45   Standish Mass
(A–24 May 43, Towed AT Gun C–11 Dec 43, S-P B–5 Apr 45)

802nd Tank Destroyer Bn (S-P) 15 Dec 41 Cp Shelby Miss as Heavy S-P (102nd Inf AT Bn)/1 Dec 45 Cp Kilmer N.J. — Wadersloh Germany
NYPE: 7 Apr 44   England: 15 Apr 44   France-ETO: 1 Jul 44 - **25,26,30,32,34**   NYPE: 29 Nov 45
(A–17 May 43, Towed AT Gun C–22 Dec 43, S-P B–1 Mar 45)

803rd Tank Destroyer Bn (S-P) (M10-M36) 15 Dec 41 Ft Lewis Wash as Heavy S-P (103rd Inf AT Bn)/1 Dec 45 Cp Kilmer N.J. — Luxembourg, Luxembourg
NYPE: 24 Jun 43   England: 6 Jul 43   France-ETO: 13 Jun 44 - **25,26,30,32,34**   NYPE: 29 Nov 45 *(A–1 Nov 43, B–15 Sep 44)*

804th Tank Destroyer Bn (S-P) (M10) 15 Dec 41 Cp San Luis Obispo Calif as Heavy S-P (104th Inf AT Bn)/10 Dec 45 — Cp Hood Tex
NYPE: 5 Aug 42   England: 17 Aug 42   N.Africa: 31 Mar 43   Italy: 8 Feb 44 - **31,33,35**   HRPE: 31 Jul 45   Cp Hood Tex
(A–9 Sep 43, B–15 Jun 44)

805th Tank Destroyer Bn (Towed AT Gun) 15 Dec 41 Ft George G Meade Md as Heavy S-P (105th Inf AT Bn)/2 Nov 45 Cp — Cp Hood Tex
NYPE: 5 Aug 42   England: 18 Aug 42   N.Africa: 17 Jan 43   Italy: 28 Oct 44 - **24,29,31,33,35,38**   HRPE: 31 Jul 45   Hood Tex
(C–30 Sep 44) (also had M3)

BATTALION DESIGNATION AND TYPE	FORMED (SOURCE OF UNIT)/INACTIVATION	AUGUST 1945 LOCATION

806th Tank Destroyer Bn (S-P) (M10) 15 Mar 42 Cp Gordon Ga as Heavy S-P/12 Jan 46 Cp Anza Calif — SS *Poelau Laut* at sea
SFPE: 12 Aug 45   Eniwetok Atoll: 1 Sep 45   Philippines: 8 Oct 45   LAPE: 11 Jan 46 (**A**–*31 May 43*, **B**–*15 Nov 44*)

807th Tank Destroyer Bn (Towed AT Gun) 1 Mar 42 Cp Cooke Calif as Heavy S-P/22 Sep 45 Cp Hood Tex — Cp Cooke Calif
NYPE: 11 Aug 44   England: 22 Aug 44   France-ETO: 18 Sep 44 - **25,26,34**   HRPE: 16 Jul 45 (**C**–*22 Dec 43*, **D**–*10 Mar 45*)

808th Tank Destroyer Bn (S-P) (M36) 27 Mar 42 Cp Joseph T Robinson Ark as Heavy S-P / 26 Sep 45 Cp Rucker Ala — Cp Howze Tex
NYPE: 11 Aug 44   England: 22 Aug 44   France-ETO: 19 Sep 44 - **26,34**   NYPE: 2 Aug 45 (**Towed AT Gun C**–*5 Jul 43*, **S-P B**–*27 Jan 45*)

809th Tank Destroyer Bn (S-P) (M18-M36) 14 Mar 42 Cp Forrest Tenn / 8 Sep 45 Cp Bowie Tex — Cp Bowie Tex
NYPE: 30 Nov 44   England: 8 Dec 44   France-ETO: Jan 45 - **26,34**   BPE: 10 Jul 45 (**A**–*c.8 May 43*, **B**–*15 Nov 44*)

810th Tank Destroyer Bn (S-P) 18 Mar 42 Cp Forrest Tenn / 20 Dec 43 Cp Forrest Tenn
(personnel to other TD units)

811th Tank Destroyer Bn (S-P) (M18) 10 Apr 42 Cp Gordon Ga as Heavy S-P / 20 Feb 46 Cp Butner N.C. — Beurig Germany
BPE: 5 Sep 44   France-ETO: 15 Sep 44 - **25,26,34**   NYPE: 27 Aug 45 (**A**–*7 Jun 43*, **B**–*28 Apr 44*)

812th Tank Destroyer Bn (Towed AT Gun) 10 Apr 42 Cp Gordon Ga as Heavy S-P / 28 Nov 44 Ft Jackson S.C. redes 812th Tank Bn
(C-1 Mar 44)

813th Tank Destroyer Bn (S-P) (M3-M10-M36) 15 Dec 41 Ft Bragg N.C. as Heavy S-P / 25 Nov 45 Cp Myles Standish Mass — Bocholtz Holland
NYPE: 5 Aug 42   England: 17 Aug 42   N.Africa: 14 Dec 42   Sicily: 15 Jul 43   England: Dec 43   France-ETO: 27 Jun 44 - **25,26,30,32,34,35,38**   BPE: 24 Nov 45 *(in Sicily as POW escort unit only, with no equipment)* (**A**–*c.8 May 43*, **B**–*25 Oct 44*)

814th Tank Destroyer Bn (S-P) (M10-M36) 1 May 42 Cp Polk La as Heavy S-P/20 Sep 45 Germany — Esch Germany
BPE: 15 Feb 44   England: 22 Feb 44   France-ETO: 8 Aug 44 - **25,26,32,34** (**A**–*c.8 May 43*, **B**–*1 Dec 44*)

815th Tank Destroyer Bn (Towed AT Gun) 11 May 42 Cp Cooke Calif as Heavy S-P/27 Sep 44 New Guinea
SFPE: 10 Mar 44   New Guinea: 30 Mar 44

816th Tank Destroyer Bn (Towed AT Gun) 11 May 42 Cp Cooke Calif as Heavy S-P/20 Feb 45 Ft Knox Ky
(C-15 Mar 44, D-31 Oct 44)

817th Tank Destroyer Bn (S-P) (M18) 1 Jun 42 Cp Chaffee Ark as Heavy S-P / 4 Apr 46 Cp Kilmer N.J. — Warburg Germany
BPE: 24 Jul 44   Scotland: 31 Jul 44   England: 2 Aug 44   France-ETO: 25 Aug 44 - **26,32,34**   NYPE: 3 Apr 46
(Towed AT Gun C–*5 Jul 43*, **S-P B**–*27 Mar 45*)

818th Tank Destroyer Bn (S-P) (M10-M36) 15 Dec 41 Ft Sill Okla as Heavy S-P / 30 Oct 45 Cp Shanks N.Y. — Burik Germany
NYPE: 20 Oct 43   N.Ireland: 1 Nov 43   England: 13 May 44   France-ETO: 15 Jul 44 - **25,26,30,32,34**   NYPE: 29 Oct 45

819th Tank Destroyer Bn (S-P) (M10) 1 Jun 42 Cp Chaffee Ark as Heavy S-P / 2 Nov 45 Palau Islands — Palau Islands
SFPE: 15 Mar 44   Hawaii: 21 Mar 44   Palau I: 1 Feb 45 - **21** (**Towed AT Gun C**–*1 Jul 43*, **S-P B**–*11 Nov 44*)

820th Tank Destroyer (S-P) (M18) 25 Jun 42 Cp Swift Tex as Heavy S-P / 8 Sep 45 Cp Swift Tex — Cp Swift Tex
BPE: 7 Oct 44   England: 15 Oct 44   France-ETO: 15 Oct 44 - **25,26,34**   HRPE: 10 Jul 45 (**Towed AT Gun C**–*12 Jul 43*, **S-P B**–*10 Mar 45*)

821st Tank Destroyer Bn (S-P) (M10) 25 Jul 42 Cp Carson Colo as Heavy S-P / 17 Feb 46 Cp Kilmer N.J. — Rheydt Germany
BPE: 6 Apr 44   England: 17 Apr 44   France-ETO: 26 Jun 44 - **26,30,32,34**   NYPE: 16 Feb 46 (**Towed AT Gun C**–*9 Jul 43*, **S-P B**–*18 Dec 44*)

822nd Tank Destroyer Bn (S-P) (M18) 25 Jul 42 Cp Carson Colo as Heavy S-P / 8 Sep 45 Cp Gruber Okla — Cp Gruber Okla
NYPE: 23 Nov 44   England: 4 Dec 44   France-ETO: 23 Jan 45 - **26,34**   BPE: 6 Jul 45 (**Towed AT Gun C**–*14 Jul 43*, **S-P B**–*20 Apr 45*)

823rd Tank Destroyer Bn (S-P) (M10) 25 Jul 42 Cp Carson Colo as Heavy S-P / 24 Oct 45 Cp Shanks N.Y. — Echt Holland
BPE: 6 Apr 44   England: 17 Apr 44   France-ETO: 26 Jun 44 - **25,26,30,32,34**   NYPE: 23 Oct 45
(Towed AT Gun C–*14 Jul 43*, **S-P B**–*18 Dec 44*)

824th Tank Destroyer Bn (S-P) (M18) 10 Aug 42 Cp Gruber Okla as Heavy S-P/11 Sep 45 Ft Jackson S.C. — Ft Jackson S.C.
NYPE: 14 Oct 44   France-ETO: 28 Oct 44 - **25,26,34**   NYPE: 12 Jul 45 *(Towed AT Gun C*–*18 Jul 43*, **S-P B**–*11 Mar 45*)

825th Tank Destroyer Bn (S-P) (M10) 10 Aug 42 Cp Gruber Okla as Heavy S-P/9 Mar 46 Cp Kilmer N.J. — Verdun France
NYPE: 30 May 44   England: 5 Jun 44   France-ETO: Jul 44 - **25,26,32,34** *(Towed AT Gun C*–*12 Jul 43*, **S-P B**–*past 18 Jan 45*)

826th Tank Destroyer Bn (S-P) 21 Dec 41 Cp Roberts Calif as Heavy S-P/18 Apr 44 Ft Ord Calif redes 826th Amphibious Tractor Bn

827th Tank Destroyer Bn (Cld) (S-P) (M18) 24 Apr 42 Cp Forrest Tenn as Heavy S-P / 2 Dec 45 Cp Patrick Henry Va — Sarrebourg France
NYPE: 3 Nov 44   France-ETO: 13 Nov 44 - **25,26,34** (**A**–*21 Jul 43*, **Towed AT Gun C**–*12 Jun 43*, **S-P B**–*27 Jul 44*)

828th Tank Destroyer Bn (Cld) (S-P) 30 May 42 Ft Knox Ky as Heavy S-P / 7 Dec 43 Ft Huachuca Ariz
(personnel to 150th, 373rd, 390th, 393rd, and 394th Quartermaster Truck Cos) (**A**–*31 May 43*, **X**)

829th Tank Destroyer Bn (Cld) (Towed AT Gun) 25 Jul 42 Cp Gruber Okla as Heavy S-P / 27 Mar 44 Cp Hood Tex
(personnel to Eighth Service Command) (**C**–*10 Jul 43*)

BATTALION DESIGNATION AND TYPE	FORMED (SOURCE OF UNIT)/INACTIVATION	AUGUST 1945 LOCATION

846th Tank Destroyer Bn (Cld) (Towed AT Gun) 15 Dec 41 Cp Livingston La as Heavy S-P/13 Dec 43 Cp Swift Tex
(personnel to VIII Corps of Third Army) (C–c.2 Jul 43)

893rd Tank Destroyer Bn (S-P) (M10) 15 Dec 41 Ft George G Meade Md as Heavy S-P (93rd AT Bn) /13 Feb 46 NYPE   Altendorf Germany
NYPE: 9 Jan 44   England: 17 Jan 44   France-ETO: 1 Jul 44 - **25,26,30,32,34**   NYPE: 7 Feb 46 *(A–24 Jun 43, B–15 Sep 44)*

894th Tank Destroyer Bn (S-P) (M3-M10) 15 Dec 41 Ft Benning Ga as Heavy S-P (94th AT Bn) / 8 Sep 45 Italy   Piancenza Italy
NYPE: 6 Aug 42   England: 17 Aug 42   N.Africa: 17 Jan 43   Italy: Sep 43 - **29,31,33,35,38** *(A–9 Sep 43, B–11 Dec 44)*

899th Tank Destroyer Bn (S-P) (M10-M36) 15 Dec 41 Ft Lewis Wash as Heavy S-P (99th AT Bn) / 27 Dec 45 Cp Kilmer N.J.   Venwegen Germany
NYPE: 13 Jan 43   N.Africa: 26 Jan 43   England: 10 Dec 43   France-ETO: 6 Jun 44 - **25,26,30,32,34,35,38**   NYPE: 27 Dec 45
(A–9 Sep 43, B–15 Sep 44)

Organizational Notes: Equipment type varied during the war so that **(M10-M36)** represents sequential outfittings. **(M3)** refers to the M3 75mm gun motor carriage mounted on the halftrack. Below are the exact T/O tables which reflect unit authorizations. Note that **S-P** simply means tracked tank destroyers.

A = T/O 18-25 Tank Destroyer Battalion dated 27 January 1943 (Self-Propelled)
B = T/O 18-25 Tank Destroyer Battalion dated 15 March 1944 (Self-Propelled)
C = T/O 18-35 Tank Destroyer Battalion dated 7 May 1943 (Towed 3-inch Gun)
D = T/O 18-35 Tank Destroyer Battalion dated 1 September 1944 (Towed 3-inch Gun)
X = not reorganized under a different T/O for the remainder of the war or unit service
c. = circa, such as c.8 May 43 would mean about 8 May 43, usually Earliest Practical Date afterwards

A or **C** (initial S-P or Towed T/Os) are not recorded if in fact the given unit was activated under that particular T/O, in which case the effective date of the T/O would coincide with the unit's formation date. This would only be applicable to 1943, as all Tank Destroyer units (towed or Self-Propelled) were under T/O 18-25 dated 8 Jun 42 prior to the introduction of **A** and **C** series.

Unless otherwise stated, units which served entirely stateside during the war were not usually reorganized under later **B** or **D** T/Os.

Example: A–*24 May 43,* **Towed AT Gun C**–*11 Dec 43,* **S-P B**–*5 Apr 45*

In this case the battalion was reorganized as Self-Propelled under the 27 Jan 43 18-25 T/O on 24 May 43, was reorganized as a towed 3-inch gun battalion under the 18-35 T/O dtd 7 May 1943 on 11 Dec 43, and was finally re-equipped as a Self-Propelled battalion under T/O 18-25 dtd 15 Mar 44 effective 5 Apr 1945.

Part VII

Field Artillery of the U.S. Army in World War II

Chapter 29

Corps Artillery

Corps Artillery:

I–XVI, XIX–XXIV, XXXII, XXXVI

I Corps Artillery

18 Jan 44 redesignated from HHB 147th Field Artillery Regiment at Rockhampton Australia and moved to Goodenough Island 7 Mar 44; arrived in Biak-Hollandia area New Guinea 22 Apr 44; landed at Lingayen Gulf Philippines 9 Jan 45; sent to Japan 25 Sep 45 where inactivated 31 May 46.

Campaigns: *New Guinea, Luzon*
Aug 45 Loc: Luzon Philippine Islands

II Corps Artillery

12 Mar 44 redesignated from HHB 71st Field Artillery Brigade in Italy where inactivated 15 Oct 45.

Campaigns: *Rome-Arno, North Apennines, Po Valley*
Aug 45 Loc: Vincenza Italy

III Corps Artillery

10 Aug 43 redesignated from HHB 14th Field Artillery Brigade at the Tennessee Maneuver Area and moved to Cp Forrest Tenn 26 Aug 43; arrived at Cp Gordon Ga 16 Sep 43 and Ft Ord Calif 16 Jan 44; went to Presidio of Monterey Calif 8 May 44 and staged at Cp Shanks N.Y. 2 Sep 44 until departed New York P/E 12 Sep 44; arrived in England 23 Sep 44 and landed in France 12 Oct 44; crossed into Luxembourg 19 Dec 44 and into Belgium 20 Dec 44; returned to Luxembourg 20 Jan 45 and entered Germany 12 Feb 45; arrived Boston P/E 6 Jul 45 and moved to Cp Polk La 11 Jul 45 where inactivated 10 Oct 46.

Campaigns: *Rhineland, Ardennes-Alsace, Central Europe*
Aug 45 Loc: Camp Polk Louisiana

IV Corps Artillery

18 Aug 43 redesignated from HHB 75th Field Artillery Brigade at Ft Lewis Wash and moved to Oregon Maneuver Area 30 Aug 43 and to Calif-Ariz Maneuver Area 9 Nov 43; staged at Cp Patrick Henry Va 20 Feb 44 until departed Hampton Roads P/E 7 Mar 44; arrived in North Africa 16 Mar 44 and arrived in Italy 27 Mar 44; arrived New York P/E 11 Oct 45 where inactivated 13 Oct 45.

Campaigns: *Rome-Arno, North Apennines, Po Valley*
Aug 45 Loc: Moglia Italy

V Corps Artillery

14 Feb 44 redesignated from HHB 76th Field Artillery Brigade in England and landed in France 6 Jun 44; crossed into Belgium 9 Sep 44 and into Luxembourg 15 Sep 44; returned to Belgium 4 Oct 44 and entered Germany 27 Oct 44; arrived New York P/E 11 Jul 45 and moved to Ft Jackson S.C. 13 Jul 45 where inactivated 15 Jun 46.

Campaigns: *Normandy, Northern France, Rhineland, Ardennes-Alsace, Central Europe*

Aug 45 Loc: Fort Jackson South Carolina

VI Corps Artillery

10 Dec 43 redesignated from HHB 18th Field Artillery Brigade in Italy and moved to southern France 16 Aug 44; entered Germany 25 Mar 45 where inactivated 10 Feb 46.

Campaigns: *Naples-Foggia, Rome-Arno, Southern France, Rhineland, Ardennes-Alsace, Central Europe*
Aug 45 Loc: Sternberg Germany

VII Corps Artillery

13 Mar 44 redesignated from HHB 17th Field Artillery Brigade in England and landed in France 12 Jun 44; crossed into Belgium 5 Sep 44 and into Germany 15 Sep 44; returned to Belgium 1 Oct 44 and reentered Germany 1 Nov 44; went back to Belgium 23 Dec 44 and entered Germany again 4 Feb 45; arrived Hampton Roads P/E 9 Jul 45 and moved to Cp San Luis Obispo Calif 15 Jul 45; arrived Ft Ord Calif 20 Sep 45 where inactivated 15 Nov 45.

Campaigns: *Normandy, Northern France, Rhineland, Ardennes-Alsace, Central Europe*
Aug 45 Loc: Camp San Luis Obispo California

VIII Corps Artillery

9 Aug 43 redesignated from HHB 72nd Field Artillery Brigade at Cp Bowie Tex and moved to Ft Slocum N.Y. 30 Nov 43; left New York P/E 13 Dec 43 and arrived in England 19 Dec 43; landed in France 2 Jul 44 and crossed into Belgium 3 Oct 44; returned to France 18 Dec 44 and moved back into Belgium 20 Dec 44; entered Germany 23 Jan 45; arrived Boston P/E 31 Jul 45 and moved to Cp Bowie Tex 5 Aug 45; arrived Cp Gruber Okla 27 Sep 45 where inactivated 23 Oct 45.

Campaigns: *Normandy, Northern France, Rhineland, Ardennes-Alsace, Central Europoe*
Aug 45 Loc: Camp Bowie Texas

IX Corps Artillery

30 Aug 43 redesignated from HHB 74th Field Artillery Brigade at Cp Shelby Miss and moved to La Maneuver Area 19 Nov 43; arrived Cp Gordon Ga 30 Jan 44 and Ft McPherson Ga 19 Apr 44; staged at Ft Lawton Wash 22 Aug 44 until departed Seattle P/E 27 Aug 44; arrived Hawaii 2 Sep 44 and left 29 Jun 45; arrived Leyte Philippines 15 Jul 45 and went to Japan 5 Oct 45 where inactivated 31 Dec 45.

Campaigns: *Pacific Theater without inscription*
Aug 45 Loc: Leyte Philippine Islands

X Corps Artillery

1 Sep 43 redesignated from HHB 73rd Field Artillery Brigade at Cp Gruber Okla and moved to Calif-Ariz Maneuver Area 19 Jan 44; arrived Cp Beale Calif 25 Apr 44 and staged at Cp Stoneman Calif 1 Jul 44 until departed San Francisco P/E 11 Jul 44; arrived New Guinea 30 Jul 44 and assaulted Leyte Philippines 20 Oct 44; arrived Japan 7 Oct 45 where inactivated 28 Feb 46.

Campaigns: *New Guinea, Leyte, Southern Philippines*
Aug 45 Loc: Macajalar Bay Mindanao Philippines

XI Corps Artillery

14 Aug 43 redesignated from HHB 19th Field Artillery Brigade at Cp Phillips Kans and moved to Ft Riley Kans 5 Oct 43; arrived at Lebanon Tenn 10 Nov 43 and at Cp Tyson Tenn 14 Jan 44; staged at Cp Stoneman Calif 5 Mar 44 until departed San Francisco P/E 10 Mar 44; arrived Finschhafen New Guinea 22 Apr 44 and landed Cape Cretin-Aitape New Guinea 28 Jun 44; landed on Morotai Island and 15 Sep 44 and on Leyte Philippines 14 Nov 44; arrived on Luzon 29 Jan 45 and sent to Japan 15 Sep 45 where inactivated 15 Mar 46.

Campaigns: *New Guinea, Leyte, Luzon*
Aug 45 Loc: Manila Philippine Islands

XII Corps Artillery

11 Aug 43 redesignated from HHB 22nd Field Artillery Brigade at Ft Bragg N.C. and moved to Ft Jackson S.C. 11 Oct 43; arrived at Tenn Maneuver Area 25 Jan 44 and Cp Forrest Tenn 10 Mar 44; moved to Ft Slocum N.Y. 1 Apr 44 and departed New York P/E 10 Apr 44; arrived in England 16 Apr 44 and landed in France 27 Jul 44; crossed into Luxembourg 21 Dec 44 and entered Germany 8 Mar 45 where inactivated 15 Dec 45.

Campaigns: *Northern France, Rhineland, Ardennes-Alsace, Central Europe*
Aug 45 Loc: Regensburg Germany

XIII Corps Artillery

18 Aug 43 redesignated from HHB 15th Field Artillery Brigade at Cp Pickett Va and moved to Ft Bragg N.C. 18 Jan 44; arrived A.P. Hill Mil Res Va 25 May 44 and Ft Dix N.J. 6 Jun 44; staged at Cp Shanks N.Y. 8 Jul 44 and departed New York P/E 15 Jul 44; arrived in England 21 Jul 44 and landed in France 5 Oct 44; crossed into Belgium 19 Oct 44 and into Holland 9 Nov 44; entered Germany 2 Mar 45; arrived Hampton Roads P/E 9 Jul 45 and moved to Cp Cooke Calif 15 Jul 45 where inactivated 25 Sep 45.

Campaigns: *Rhineland, Central Europe*
Aug 45 Loc: Camp Cooke California

XIV Corps Artillery

Activated Nov 43 on Guadalcanal and moved to Bougainville 10 Dec 43; landed at Lingayen Gulf Philippines 9 Jan 45; arrived in Japan Nov 45 and inactivated 13 Dec 45 at Ft Lawton Wash.

Campaigns: *Northern Solomons, Luzon*
Aug 45 Loc: Canlubang Philippine Islands

XV Corps Artillery

17 Aug 43 redesignated from 16th Field Artillery Brigade at the California-Arizona Maneuver Area and moved to Ft Slocum N.Y. 1 Dec 43; departed New York P/E 14 Dec 43 and arrived England 20 Dec 43; landed in France 11 Jul 44 and entered Germany 21 Mar 45 and Austria 5 May 45; inactivated in Germany 31 Mar 46.

Campaigns: *Northern France, Rhineland, Ardennes-Alsace, Central Europe*
Aug 45 Loc: Salzburg Austria

XVI Corps Artillery

10 Dec 43 redesignated from HHB 172nd Field Artillery Group at Ft Riley Kans and staged at Cp Shanks N.Y. 8 Sep 44 until departed New York P/E 20 Sep 44; arrived in England via Scotland 25 Sep 44 and landed in France 28 Sep 44; crossed into Belgium 30 Nov 44 and into Holland 22 Dec 44; entered Germany 7 Mar 45; returned New York P/E 6 Dec 45 and inactivated at Cp Kilmer N.J. 7 Dec 45.

Campaigns: *Rhineland, Central Europe*
Aug 45 Loc: Bad Meinberg Germany

XIX Corps Artillery

10 Oct 43 redesignated from HHB 141st Field Artillery Brigade at Cp Gordon Ga and moved to La Maneuver Area 30 Oct 43 and to Cp Polk La 15 Nov 43; staged at Ft Hamilton N.Y. 10 Jan 44 until departed New York P/E 18 Jan 44; arrived in England 28 Jan 44 and landed in France 24 Jun 44; crossed into Belgium 3 Sep 44 and into Holland 15 Sep 44; entered Germany 20 Nov 44 and inactivated in France 5 Sep 45.

Campaigns: *Normandy, Northern France, Rhineland, Central Europe*
Aug 45 Loc: Friedberg Germany

XX Corps Artillery

21 Oct 43 activated at Indiantown Gap Mil Res Pa and moved to Ft Leonard Wood Mo 11 Nov 43; staged at Ft Slocum N.Y. 2 Feb 44 until departed New York P/E 11 Feb 44; arrived England 20 Feb 44 and landed in France 27 Jul 44; entered Germany 27 Mar 45 where inactivated 1 Mar 46.

Campaigns: *Normandy, Northern France, Rhineland, Ardennes-Alsace, Central Europe*
Aug 45 Loc: St Martin France

XXI Corps Artillery

29 Dec 43 redesignated from HHB 112th Field Artillery Brigade at Cp Polk La and moved to Ft Slocum N.Y. 26 Oct 44; departed New York P/E 3 Nov 44 and arrived in England 9 Nov 44; landed France 25 Dec 44 and entered Germany 18 Mar 45; inactivated in Austria 10 Oct 45.

Campaigns: *Rhineland, Ardennes-Alsace, Central Europe*
Aug 45 Loc: Pluderhausen Germany

XXII Corps Artillery

15 Jan 44 activated at Ft Leonard Wood Mo and moved to Cp Campbell Ky 14 Apr 44; arrived Ft Bragg N.C. 4 Aug 44 and staged at Cp Shanks N.Y. 21 Nov 44 until departed New York P/E 30 Nov 44; arrived in England 8 Dec 44 and landed in France 21 Jan 45; crossed into Belgium 20 Mar 45 and entered Germany 27 Mar 45 where inactivated 20 Jan 46.

Campaigns: *Rhineland, Central Europe*
Aug 45 Loc: Pilsen Czechoslovakia

XXIII Corps Artillery

15 Jan 44 activated at Cp Bowie Tex and moved to Ft McPherson Ga 23 Sep 44; staged at Cp Kilmer N.J. 2 Dec 44 until departed New York P/E 10 Dec 44; arrived England via Scotland 18 Dec 44 and landed France 29 Mar 45; entered Germany 9 Apr 45 where inactivated 10 Feb 46.

Campaigns: *European Theater without inscription*
Aug 45 Loc: Oberstein Germany

XXIV Corps Artillery

31 May 44 redesignated from HHB 225th Field Artillery Group on Hawaii and departed 15 Sep 44; assaulted Leyte Philippines 20 Oct 44 and landed on Okinawa 1 Apr 45; arrived Korea 8 Sep 45 where inactivated 12 Feb 46.

Campaigns: *Leyte, Ryukyus*
Aug 45 Loc: Okinawa

XXXII Corps Artillery

17 Oct 44 redesignated from HHB 427th Field Artillery Group at Ft Bragg N.C. (Corps never organized and HHB only component on active duty); attached to Second Army there and inactivated at Ft Bragg N.C. 15 Oct 45.

Aug 45 Loc: Fort Bragg N.C.

XXXVI Corps Artillery

10 Jul 44 activated at Ft Riley Kans and moved to Cp Gruber Okla 14 Jan 45; arrived Cp Callan Calif 28 Jun 45 where inactivated 25 Sep 45.

Aug 45 Loc: Camp Callan California

Chapter 30

Field Artillery Brigades

Brigades:

Fort Bragg Prov, 1–4, 6, 11, 13–19, 22, 26, 31–34, 46, 51–63, 65, 66, 68–76, 141

Fort Bragg Provisional Field Artillery Brigade

1 Aug 41 organized Ft Bragg N.C. and attached to First Army; participated in the Carolina Maneuvers Sep-Dec 41; discontinued at Ft Bragg N.C. 8 Jul 42.

1st Field Artillery Brigade

Stationed at Ft Hoyle Md as part of 1st Division where disbanded 16 Oct 39.

2nd Field Artillery Brigade

Stationed at Ft Sam Houston Tex as part of 2nd Division where disbanded 7 Oct 39.

3rd Field Artillery Brigade

Stationed at Ft Lewis Wash as part of 3rd Division where disbanded 16 Oct 39.

4th Field Artillery Brigade

Stationed at Ft Sill Okla as part of 4th Division where disbanded 14 Nov 39.

6th Field Artillery Brigade

Stationed at Ft Sheridan Ill as part of 6th Division where disbanded 2 Oct 39.

11th Field Artillery Brigade

Stationed at Schofield Barracks Hawaii as part of Hawaiian Division where redesignated HHB, 24th Infantry Division Artillery 26 Aug 41.

13th Field Artillery Brigade

Stationed at Ft Bragg N.C. and attached to I Army Corps; participated in Louisiana Maneuvers May and Aug 40 and Carolina Maneuvers Sep-Nov 41; transferred to Cp Blanding Fla 29 Mar 42 under II Army Corps; participated in Carolina Maneuvers Jul 42; departed New York P/E 6 Aug 42 and arrived England 17 Aug 42; landed in North Africa 5 Dec 42; arrived Sicily 13 Aug 43 and landed in Italy 21 Sep 43; landed in southern France 25 Aug 44; crossed into Germany 24 Mar 45; returned to New York P/E 26 Feb 46 and moved immediately to Cp Kilmer N.J. where inactivated 27 Feb 46.

Campaigns: *Naples-Foggia, Rome-Arno, Southern France, Rhineland, Central Europe*
Aug 45 Loc: Donauworth Germany

14th Field Artillery Brigade

23 Oct 42 activated at Cp Haan Calif and attached to Fourth Army; arrived at Cp Forrest Tenn 27 May 42 and assigned III Army Corps; relocated to Cp Gordon Ga 12 May 43; returned to Cp Forrest Tenn 22 Jun 43 and redesignated HHB, III Corps Artillery in the Tennessee Maneuver Area 10 Aug 43.

15th Field Artillery Brigade

15 Jun 42 activated at Ft Bragg N.C. and assigned to I Army Corps; transferred to Ft Sill Okla 28 Oct 42 under XII Army Corps; returned Ft Bragg N.C. 25 Jun 43 and arrived Cp Pickett Va 10 Aug 43 where redesignated HHB, XIII Corps Artillery 18 Aug 43.

16th Field Artillery Brigade

15 Jul 42 activated at Cp Gruber Okla under the X Army Corps; participated in both Louisiana Maneuvers of Nov-Dec 42 and Jul-Aug 43; arrived at the California-Arizona Maneuver Area on 10 Aug 43 where redesignated HHB, XV Corps Artillery 17 Aug 43.

17th Field Artillery Brigade

19 Jan 43 activated at Ft Sill Okla and staged at Cp Myles Standish Mass 20 Feb 44 until departed Boston P/E 28 Feb 44; arrived in England 8 Mar 44 where redesignated as HHB, VII Corps Artillery on 13 Mar 44.

Campaigns: *European Theater without inscription*

18th Field Artillery Brigade

1 Jun 40 activated at Ft Sill Okla and assigned to VIII Army Corps; participated in the Louisiana Maneuvers of Aug-Oct 41 and transferred to Cp Bowie Tex 5 Feb 42; staged at Cp Myles Standish Mass 13 Aug 43 until departed New York P/E 21 Aug 43; arrived in North Africa 2 Sep 43 and immediately dispatched to Italy where it was redesignated as HHB, VI Corps Artillery on 10 Dec 43.

Campaigns: *Naples-Foggia*

19th Field Artillery Brigade

5 Aug 43 activated at Ft Leonard Wood Mo and assigned to the IV Armored Corps; arrived at Cp Phillips Kans on 13 Aug 43 where redesignated HHB, XI Corps Artillery 14 Aug 43.

22nd Field Artillery Brigade

15 Jul 42 activated at Ft Bragg N.C. and assigned to the Second Army; remained at Ft Bragg N.C. where it was redesignated as HHB, XII Corps Artillery on 11 Aug 43.

26th Field Artillery Brigade

1 Jun 41 activated at Cp Roberts Calif and departed San Francisco P/E 21 Nov 41; arrived in Australia on 22 Dec 41 and dispatched to reinforce allied forces on Java Island where it served 11 Jan 42-27 Feb 42; returned to Australia on 4 Mar 42 where it was inactivated 5 Jul 42.

Campaigns: *East Indies*

31st Field Artillery Brigade

7 Dec 43 activated at Ft Sill Okla where it was inactivated on 12 Feb 45.

32nd Field Artillery Brigade

16 Feb 44 redesignated from HHB, 403rd Field Artillery Group at Cp Shelby Miss and assigned to the IX Corps; staged at Cp Kilmer N.J. 29 Mar 44 until departed New York P/E 10 Apr 44; arrived in England 16 Apr 44; assigned to First Army 10 Jun 44 and landed in France 27 Jun 44; crossed into Belgium 20 Sep 44 and into Holland 23 Sep 44; entered Germany 26 Oct 44 but returned to Belgium 27 Dec 44; reentered Germany 6 Feb 45 where inactivated on 24 May 46.

Campaigns: *Normandy, Northern France, Rhineland, Ardennes-Alsace, Central Europe*
Aug 45 Loc: Frankenberg Germany

33rd Field Artillery Brigade

16 Mar 44 redesignated from HHB, 166th Field Artillery Group at Gp Gordon Ga; staged at Cp Kilmer N.J. 25 Jun-2 Jul 44; departed New York P/E 2 Jul 44 and arrived England 12 Jul 44; assigned First Army 10 Jun 44 and landed in France 27 Aug 44; crossed into Luxembourg 25 Feb 45; entered Germany 27 Feb 45; arrived Hampton Roads P/E and inactivated at Cp Patrick Henry Va 10 Dec 45.

Campaigns: *Normandy, Northern France, Rhineland, Ardennes-Alsace, Central Europe*
Aug 45 Loc: Miesbach Germany

348

34th Field Artillery Brigade

15 Mar 44 redesignated from HHB, 181st Field Artillery Group at Cp Beale Calif; assigned III Corps; staged at Cp Shanks N.Y. 25 Jun–2 Jul 44; departed New York P/E 2 Jul 44 and arrived England 12 Jul 44; landed in France 18 Aug 44; crossed into Belgium 20 Oct 44 and Holland 17 Nov 44; entered Germany 25 Nov 44; returned Hampton Roads P/E and inactivated at Cp Patrick Henry Va 16 Nov 45.

Campaigns: *Northern France, Rhineland, Central Europe*
Aug 45 Loc: Backnang Germany

46th Field Artillery Brigade (Colored)

10 Feb 41 activated at Cp Livingston La and assigned Third Army; attached IV Corps 28 Jan 43 and VIII Corps 16 Jul 43; there redesignated as HHB, 46th Field Artillery Group 16 Sep 43.

51st Field Artillery Brigade   Massachusetts National Guard

16 Jan 41 inducted into federal service at Boston Mass as part of 26th Division; arrived Cp Edwards Mass 24 Jan 41 where redesignated HHB, 26th Division Artillery 12 Feb 42.

52nd Field Artillery Brigade   New York National Guard

15 Oct 40 inducted into federal service at Jamaica N.Y. as part of 27th Division; moved to Ft McClellan Ala 25 Oct 40; relocated to Riverside Calif 21 Dec 41 and Ft Ord Calif 22 Jan 42; departed San Francisco P/E 10 Mar 42 and arrived in Hawaii 17 Mar 42 where redesignated HHB, 27th Division Artillery 1 Sep 42.

Campaigns: *Pacific Theater without inscription*

53rd Field Artillery Brigade   Pennsylvania National Guard

17 Feb 41 inducted into federal service at Pittsburgh Pa as part of 28th Division; transferred to Indiantown Gap Mil Res Pa 26 Feb 41; arrived Cp Beauregard La 18 Jan 42 where redesignated HHB, 28th Division Artillery 7 Feb 42.

54th Field Artillery Brigade   Virginia National Guard

3 Feb 41 inducted into federal service at Richmond Va as part of 29th Division; arrived Ft George G. Meade Md 6 Feb 41 where redesignated as HHB, 29th Division Artillery 28 Feb 42.

55th Field Artillery Brigade   Georgia National Guard

16 Sep 40 inducted into federal service at Savannah Ga as part of 30th Division; arrived Ft Jackson S.C. 19 Sep 40 where redesignated HHB, 30th Division Artillery 5 Feb 42.

56th Field Artillery Brigade
Florida National Guard

25 Nov 40 inducted into federal service at Avon Park Fla as part of 31st Division; moved to Cp Blanding Fla 14 Dec 40; arrived Cp Bowie Tex 25 Feb 42 where redesignated HHB, 31st Division Artillery 27 Feb 42.

57th Field Artillery Brigade
Wisconsin National Guard

15 Oct 40 inducted into federal service at Whitefish Bay Wis as part of 32nd Division; moved to Cp Beauregard La 21 Oct 40; arrived Cp Livingston La 14 Feb 41 where redesignated HHB, 32nd Division Artillery 16 Jan 42.

58th Field Artillery Brigade
Illinois National Guard

5 Mar 41 inducted into federal service at Chicago Ill as part of 33rd Division; arrived Cp Forrest Tenn 12 Mar 41 where redesignated HHB, 33rd Division Artillery 12 Feb 42.

59th Field Artillery Brigade
Minnesota National Guard

10 Feb 41 inducted into federal service at Minneapolis Minn as part of 34th Division; arrived Cp Claiborne La 20 Feb 41; transferred to Ft Dix N.J. 9 Jan 42 where redesignated HHB, 34th Division Artillery 30 Jan 42.

60th Field Artillery Brigade
Kansas National Guard

23 Dec 40 inducted into federal service at Topeka Kans as part of 35th Division; moved to Cp Joseph T. Robinson Ark 5 Jan 41 and transferred to Ft Ord Calif 23 Dec 41; arrived Cp San Luis Obispo Calif 18 Jan 42 where redesignated HHB, 35th Division Artillery 3 Feb 42.

61st Field Artillery Brigade (I)
Texas National Guard

25 Nov 40 inducted into federal service at San Antonio Tex as part of 36th Division; arrived Cp Bowie Tex 7 Jan 41 where redesignated HHB, 36th Division Artillery 31 Jan 42.

61st Field Artillery Brigade (II)

18 Jul 44 redesignated from HHB, 222nd Field Artillery Group at Ft Jackson S.C. and assigned IX Corps; transferred to Ft McPherson Ga 19 Jul 44 and relocated to Cp Hood Tex 6 Oct 44; staged at Cp Shanks N.Y. 25 Dec 44–10 Jan 45; departed New York P/E 10 Jan 45 and arrived in France 21 Jan 45; entered Germany 6 Apr 45 where inactivated 25 Mar 46.

Campaigns: *European Theater without inscription*
Aug 45 Loc: Krefeld Germany

62nd Field Artillery Brigade   Ohio National Guard

15 Oct 40 inducted into federal service at Dayton Ohio as part of 37th Division; arrived at Cp Shelby Miss 22 Oct 40 where redesignated HHB, 37th Division Artillery 16 Jan 42.

63rd Field Artillery Brigade   Kentucky National Guard

17 Jan 41 inducted into federal service at Louisville Ky as part of 38th Division; arrived Cp Shelby Miss 28 Jan 41 where redesignated HHB, 38th Division Artillery 10 Feb 42.

65th Field Artillery Brigade   Utah National Guard

3 Mar 41 inducted into federal service at Salt Lake City Utah as part of 40th Division; arrived Cp San Luis Obispo Calif 18 Mar 41 where redesignated HHB, 40th Division Artillery 5 Feb 42.

66th Field Artillery Brigade   Washington National Guard

16 Sep 40 inducted into federal service at Seattle Wash as part of 41st Division; arrived Cp Murray Wash 29 Sep 40 and transferred to Ft Lewis Wash 20 Mar 41 where redesignated HHB, 41st Division Artillery 14 Feb 42.

68th Field Artillery Brigade   Rhode Island National Guard

24 Feb 41 inducted into federal service at Providence R.I. as part of 43rd Division; arrived Cp Blanding Fla 19 Mar 41 and moved to Cp Shelby Miss 16 Feb 42 where redesignated HHB, 43rd Division Artillery 19 Feb 42.

69th Field Artillery Brigade   New Jersey National Guard

16 Sep 40 inducted into federal service at Camden N.J. as part of 44th Division; arrived Ft Dix N.J. 24 Sep 40 and moved to Cp Claiborne La 16 Jan 42 where redesignated HHB, 44th Division Artillery 20 Feb 42.

70th Field Artillery Brigade   Oklahoma National Guard

16 Sep 40 inducted into federal service at Oklahoma City Okla as part of 45th Division; arrived Ft Sill Okla 24 Sep 40; arrived Cp Barkeley Tex 3 Mar 41 where redesignated HHB, 45th Division Artillery 11 Feb 42.

71st Field Artillery Brigade

New York National Guard

3 Feb 41 inducted into federal service at New York N.Y. and assigned First Army; moved to Ft Ethan Allen Vt 18 Feb 41 and assigned VI Army Corps; assigned XIII Corps 30 Dec 42; arrived Cp Forrest Tenn 15 Jun 43; staged at Ft Dix N.J. 17 Jul–9 Aug 43; departed New York P/E 21 Aug 43 and arrived North Africa 2 Sep 43 and moved into Italy in October 43 where redesignated HHB, II Corps Artillery near Cassino 12 Mar 44.

Campaigns: *Naples-Foggia, Rome-Arno*

72nd Field Artillery Brigade

Michigan National Guard

7 Apr 41 inducted into federal service at Lansing Mich; moved to Ft Knox Ky 17 Apr 41 under V Army Corps; arrived Ft Leonard Wood Mo 2 Jun 41 and assigned XI Corps 2 Sep 42; arrived Cp Bowie Tex 4 Aug 43 where redesignated as HHB, VIII Corps Artillery 9 Aug 43.

73rd Field Artillery Brigade

Pennsylvania National Guard

13 Jan 41 inducted into federal service at Philadelphia Pa; arrived Cp Shelby Miss 18 Jan 41 and assigned V Army Corps; participated in Louisiana Maneuvers of Aug-Oct 41; arrived Cp Sutton N.C. 23 Mar 42 and sent to Cp Blanding Fla 13 Oct 42; participated in Tennessee Maneuvers Apr-Jun 43; arrived Cp Gruber Okla 20 Aug 43 where redesignated as HHB, X Corps Artillery 1 Sep 43.

74th Field Artillery Brigade

Georgia National Guard

24 Feb 41 inducted into federal service at Cp Blanding Fla and assigned IV Army Corps; transferred to Cp Shelby Miss 27 Mar 42 where redesignated as HHB, IX Corps Artillery 30 Aug 43.

75th Field Artillery Brigade

Tennessee National Guard

24 Feb 41 inducted into federal service at Cp Forrest Tenn and assigned VII Army Corps; transferred to Cp Roberts Calif 26 Dec 41 and assigned IV Corps 23 Jul 43; arrived Ft Lewis Wash 6 Aug 43 where redesignated HHB, IV Corps Artillery 18 Aug 43.

76th Field Artillery Brigade

California National Guard

1 Apr 41 inducted into federal service at Ft Francis E. Warren Wyo and assigned IX Army Corps; transferred to Ft Lewis Wash 14 Dec 41; sent to Cp Young Calif 16 Apr 43 and assigned IV Corps 15 Mar 43; arrived Ft Leonard Wood Mo 23 Aug 43; staged at Cp Shanks N.Y. 1–21 Oct 43; departed New York P/E 21 Oct 43 and arrived England 3 Nov 43 where redesignated HHB, V Corps Artillery 14 Feb 44.

Campaigns: *European Theater without inscription*

141st Field Artillery Brigade

31 Aug 43 redesignated from HHB, 141st Field Artillery Group at Gp Gordon Ga where redesignated HHB, XIX Corps Artillery 10 Oct 43.

Chapter 31

Field Artillery Groups

Groups:

5, 6, 17, 18, 30, 35, 36, 40, 46, 77, 79, 112, 119, 137, 141, 142, 144, 153, 166, 168, 172–174, 177–179, 181–183, 186–188, 190, 191, 193–196, 202–205, 207–214, 218–220, 222–225, 228, 250, 252, 258, 333, 349–351, 353, 401–411, 413–432, 442, 472, 578, 1 Provisional, 2 Provisional, 1 Provisional Gun

1st Field Artillery Group (Provisional)

Organized at Ft Stotsenburg Phillipines as part of North Luzon Force in late 41 with Btry A 23rd Field Artillery Regt and Btrys B and C, 86th Field Artillery Regt; surrendered to Japanese forces 9 Apr 42.

Campaigns: *Philippine Islands*

1st Provisional Gun Group

23 Mar 44 activated at Schofield Barracks Hawaii from assets of the 55th Coast Artillery Regiment; departed Hawaii for Saipan on 27 May 44; while enroute to the Marianas Islands aboard the **USS** *Sumter* **(APA.52)** it was transformed into the nucleus of the 420th Field Artillery Group 31 May 44.

2nd Field Artillery Group (Provisional)

Organized on Luzon as part of the South Luzon Force in late 41 in the Philippines with HHB and Btry A, 86th Field Artillery Regt; surrendered to Japanese forces 9 Apr 42.

Campaigns: *Philippine Islands*

5th Field Artillery Group (Motorized)

5 Sep 42 activated at Cp Young Calif as the 5th Armored Artillery Group; staged at Cp Kilmer N.J. 19 Dec 42 until departed New York P/E 14 Jan 43; arrived North Africa 25 Jan 43 and landed Sicily 11 Jul 43 where redesignated 5th Field Artillery Group 14 Aug 43; arrived England 9 Dec 43; landed France 20 Jul 44 and entered Germany 22 Nov 44; returned to France 29 Nov 44 and to Germany 3 Dec 44; reentered France 7 Dec 44 and Germany 3 Feb 45; arrived Boston P/E 21 Oct 45 and inactivated at Cp Myles Standish Mass 22 Oct 45.

Campaigns: *Tunisia, Sicily, Normandy, Northern France, Rhineland, Ardennes-Alsace, Central Europe*
Aug 45 Loc: Mattinghofen Austria

6th Field Artillery Group (Motorized)

5 Sep 42 activated at Cp Chaffee Ark as the 6th Armored Artillery Group; staged at Cp Shanks N.Y. 14 Aug 43 until departed New York P/E 21 Aug 43; landed North Africa 2 Sep 43 and Italy 23 Oct 43 where redesignated 6th Field Artillery Group 10 Dec 43; landed southern France 15 Aug 44 and entered Germany 23 Mar 45; arrived Boston P/E 21 Oct 45 and inactivated at Cp Myles Standish Mass 22 Oct 45.

Campaigns: *Naples-Foggia, Rome-Arno, Southern France, Rhineland, Ardennes-Alsace, Central Europe*
Aug 45 Loc: Murnau Germany

17th Field Artillery Group (Motorized)

1 Mar 44 redesignated from HHB 17th Field Artillery Regt in Traverecce Italy; landed in France 2 Sep 44 and entered Germany 6 Dec 44; returned to France 22 Mar 45 and reentered Germany 28 Mar 45; arrived New York P/E 26 Feb 46 and inactivated at Cp Kilmer N.J. 27 Feb 46.

Campaigns: *Rome-Arno, Southern France, Rhineland, Ardennes-Alsace, Central Europe*
Aug 45 Loc: Harburg Germany

18th Field Artillery Group (Motorized)

8 Feb 43 redesignated from HHC 18th Field Artillery Regt at Ft Sill Okla; moved to Cp Young Calif 9 Oct 43; staged at Cp Shanks N.Y. 19 Mar 44 until departed New York P/E 31 Mar 44; arrived England 8 Apr 44 and landed in France 20 Jun 44; crossed into Belgium 3 Sep 44 and into Germany 2 Oct 44; recrossed into Belgium 23 Dec 44 and reentered Germany 2 May 45; returned New York P/E 31 Dec 45 and inactivated at Cp Kilmer N.J. 3 Jan 46.

Campaigns: *Normandy, Northern France, Rhineland, Ardennes-Alsace, Central Europe*
Aug 45 Loc: Suhl Germany

30th Field Artillery Group (Motorized)

18 May 44 redesignated from HHB 30th Field Artillery Regt at Cp Pickett Va; moved to Cp Butner N.C. 17 Jul 44; staged at Cp Kilmer N.J. 9 Nov 44 until departed New York P/E 21 Nov 44; arrived England 27 Nov 44 and landed France 5 Feb 45; entered Germany 28 Mar 45 where inactivated 31 Jul 46.

Campaigns: *Rhineland, Central Europe*
Aug 45 Loc: Neuberg Germany

35th Field Artillery Group (Motorized)

1 Mar 43 redesignated from HHB 35th Field Artillery Regt at Cp Shelby Miss; moved to La Maneuver Area 31 Jul 43; staged at Cp Shanks N.Y. 15 Aug 43 until departed New York P/E 21 Aug 43; landed in North Africa 2 Sep 43 and arrived in Italy 11 Nov 43; arrived in France 5 Sep 44 and entered Germany 24 Mar 45 where inactivated 25 Mar 46.

Campaigns: *Naples-Foggia, Rome-Arno, Anzio, Southern France, Rhineland, Ardennes-Alsace, Central Europe*
Aug 45 Loc: Tutzing Germany

36th Field Artillery Group (Motorized)

5 Mar 44 redesignated from HHB 36th Field Artillery Regt at Pantano Italy and assaulted southern France 15 Aug 44; entered Germany 28 Mar 45 and Austria on 5 May 45; arrived New York P/E 3 Apr 46 and inactivated at Cp Kilmer N.J. 4 Apr 46.

Campaigns: *Rome-Arno, Southern France, Rhineland, Central Europe*
Aug 45 Loc: Heilbronn Germany

40th Field Artillery Group (Motorized)

1 Mar 43 redesignated from HHB 40th Field Artillery Regt at Cp Forrest Tenn; moved to Cp Polk La 1 Dec 43; staged at Cp Kilmer N.J. 28 Mar 44 until departed New York P/E 10 Apr 44; arrived England 16 Apr 44 and landed in France 18 Jul 44; entered Germany 5 Dec 44 and returned to France 28 Jan 45; arrived back in Germany 19 Feb 45 where inactivated on 15 Mar 46.

Campaigns: *Normandy, Northern France, Rhineland, Ardennes-Alsace, Central Europe*
Aug 45 Loc: Trier Germany

46th Field Artillery Group (Motorized) (Colored) (I)

16 Sep 43 redesignated from HHB 46th Field Artillery Brigade at Cp Livingston La and inactivated there on 31 Jan 44.

46th Field Artillery Group (Motorized) (Colored) (II)

31 Dec 44 activated at Marseille France from assets of the 8th Antiaircraft Artillery Group and entered Germany 18 Feb 45; returned to France 19 Feb 45 and sent back to Germany 29 Mar 45; arrived New York P/E 14 Nov 45 and inactivated at Cp Kilmer N.J. on 16 Nov 45.

Campaigns: *Rhineland, Central Europe*
Aug 45 Loc: Unter Haching Germany

77th Field Artillery Group (Motorized)

24 Feb 44 redesignated from HHB 77th Field Artillery Regt at Capriati Italy and served in Italy until inactivated there on 25 Sep 45.

Campaigns: *Rome-Arno, North Apennines, Po Valley*
Aug 45 Loc: Bassano Italy

79th Field Artillery Group (Motorized)

23 Feb 43 redesignated from HHB 79th Field Artillery Regt at Ft Bragg N.C.; staged at Cp Kilmer N.J. 30 Mar 44 until departed New York P/E 10 Apr 44; arrived England 16 Apr 44 and landed in France 4 Jul 44; crossed into Holland 23 Sep 44 and Germany 30 Oct 44; entered Belgium 29 Dec 44 and reentered Germany 6 Feb 45 where inactivated 30 Jun 46.

Campaigns: *Normandy, Northern France, Rhineland, Ardennes-Alsace, Central Europe*
Aug 45 Loc: Frankenburg Germany

112th Field Artillery Group (Motorized)

1 May 43 redesignated from HHB 112th Field Artillery Regt as Ft Jackson S.C. and moved to Cp Polk La 24 Dec 43; redesignated there as HHB, XXI Corps Artillery 29 Dec 43.

119th Field Artillery Group (Motorized)

8 Feb 43 redesignated from HHB, 119th Field Artillery Regt at Ft Leonard Wood Mo; moved to Cp Young Calif 23 Aug 43; staged at Cp Myles Standish Mass 5 Feb 44 until departed Boston P/E 27 Feb 44; arrived England 8 Mar 44 and landed in France 26 Jun 44; crossed into Belgium 8 Sep 44 and into Holland 13 Sep 44; entered Germany 14 Oct 44; arrived Hampton Roads P/E 16 Nov 45 and inactivated at Cp Patrick Henry Va 16 Nov 45.

Campaigns: *Normandy, Northern France, Rhineland, Ardennes-Alsace, Central Europe*
Aug 45 Loc: Ortenberg Germany

137th Field Artillery Group (Motorized)

8 Feb 43 redesignated from HHB, 137th Field Artillery Regt at Cp Gruber Okla 8 Feb 43; moved to La Maneuver Area 20 Apr 43 and returned to Cp Gruber Okla 11 Jun 43; arrived at Cp Cooke Calif 25 Sep 43 where inactivated 9 Oct 43.

141st Field Artillery Group (Motorized)

7 Mar 43 redesignated from HHB 141st Field Artillery Regt at Cp Blanding Fla; moved to Tenn Maneuver Area 19 Apr 43 and to Cp Gordon Ga 21 Jun 43; there redesignated 141st Field Artillery Brigade 31 Aug 43.

142nd Field Artillery Group (Motorized)

8 Feb 43 redesignated from HHB 142nd Field Artillery Regt at Cp Bowie Tex; moved to La Maneuver Area 8 Jun 43 and staged at Cp Shanks N.Y. 27 Sep 43 until departed New York P/E 21 Oct 43; arrived England 3 Nov 43 and landed in France 14 Jun 44; crossed into Belgium 3 Sep 44 and Germany 18 Sep 44; recrossed into Belgium 23 Dec 44 and into Germany 4 Feb 45; arrived Boston P/E 29 Oct 45 and inactivated at Cp Myles Standish Mass 30 Oct 45.

Campaigns: *Normandy, Northern France, Rhineland, Ardennes-Alsace, Central Europe*
Aug 45 Loc: Sondershausen Germany

144th Field Artillery Group (Motorized)

8 Feb 43 redesignated from HHB 144th Field Artillery Regt at Ft Lewis Wash; moved to Cp Young Calif 20 Apr 43 and Ft Leonard Wood Mo 19 Aug 43; staged at Cp Myles Standish Mass 22 Nov 43 until departed Boston P/E 28 Dec 43; arrived England 8 Jan 44 and landed in France 16 Jul 44; entered Germany 23 Mar 45 and Austria 7 May 45 where inactivated 23 Apr 46.

Campaigns: *Normandy, Northern France, Rhineland, Ardennes-Alsace, Central Europe*
Aug 45 Loc: Thalham Germany

153rd Field Artillery Group (Motorized)

14 Aug 44 redesignated from HHB 153rd Coast Artillery Group (155mm Gun) at Ft Bragg N.C.; staged at Cp Shanks N.Y. 2 Mar 45 until departed New York P/E 7 Mar 45; arrived in France 18 Mar 45 and entered Germany 10 Apr 45; arrived Boston P/E 31 Jul 45 and arrived Ft Jackson S.C. 2 Aug 45 where inactivated 22 Feb 46.

Campaigns: *Central Europe*
Aug 45 Loc: Fort Jackson South Carolina

166th Field Artillery Group (Motorized)

7 Mar 43 redesignated from HHB 166th Field Artillery Regt at Cp Blanding Fla; moved to Cp Gordon Ga 18 Mar 43 where redesignated 33rd Field Artillery Brigade 16 Mar 44.

168th Field Artillery Group (Motorized)

1 Mar 43 redesignated from HHB 168th Field Artillery Regt at Cp San Luis Obispo Calif; moved to Cp Roberts Calif 7 Apr 43; staged at Cp Stoneman Calif 27 Oct 43 until departed San Francisco P/E 1 Nov 43; arrived Australia 18 Nov 43 and landed in New Guinea 8 Mar 44; arrived Philippines 21 Jan 45 and inactivated in Japan 15 Dec 45.

Campaigns: *New Guinea, Luzon*
Aug 45 Loc: Rosales Philippines

172nd Field Artillery Group (Motorized)

1 Mar 43 redesignated from HHB 172nd Field Artillery Regt at Cp Shelby Miss; moved to La Maneuver Area 25 Jun 43 and Desert Training Center Calif 12 Sep 43; arrived at Ft Riley Kans 10 Dec 43 where redesignated HHB XVI Corps Artillery same date.

173rd Field Artillery Group (Motorized)

8 Feb 43 redesignated from HHB 173rd Field Artillery Regt at Cp Gruber Okla; moved to Cp Maxey Tex 1 Mar 43 and returned Cp Gruber Okla 24 Aug 43; staged at Cp Shanks N.Y. 14 Mar 44 until departed New York P/E 29 Mar 44; arrived England 8 Apr 44 and landed in France 22 Jul 44; entered Germany 17 Mar 45 and Austria 8 May 45; returned New York P/E 26 Nov 45 and inactivated at Cp Kilmer N.J. 27 Nov 45.

Campaigns: *Normandy, Northern France, Rhineland, Ardennes-Alsace, Central Europe*
Aug 45 Loc: Salzburg Austria

174th Field Artillery Group (Motorized)

25 Feb 43 redesignated from HHB 174th Field Artillery Regt at Cp Bowie Tex; staged at Cp Shanks N.Y. 13 Mar 44 until departed New York P/E 28 Mar 44; arrived England 8 Apr 44 and landed in France 29 Jun 44; crossed into Belgium 3 Oct 44 and back into France 22 Dec 44; recrossed into Belgium 1 Feb 45 and entered Germany 5 Feb 45; arrived Boston P/E 24 Oct 45 and inactivated at Cp Myles Standish Mass 25 Oct 45.

Campaigns: *Normandy, Northern France, Rhineland, Ardennes-Alsace, Central Europe*
Aug 45 Loc: Schmalkalden Germany

177th Field Artillery Group (Motorized)

8 Feb 43 redesignated from HHB 177th Field Artillery Regt at Ft Leonard Wood Mo and moved to Cp McCoy Wis 12 Mar 43; transferred to Ft Riley Kans 7 Oct 43, Gallatin Tenn 22 Dec 43, Cp Forrest Tenn 14 Jan 44, and Cp Tyson Tenn 22 Feb 44; arrived Cp Myles Standish Mass 22 Apr 44 and Boston 4 May 44 but transferred to Ft Dix N.J. same date; arrived New York P/E 26 Jun 44 and departed 2 Jul 44; arrived England 14 Jul 44 and landed in France 16 Aug 44; crossed into Luxembourg 21 Dec 44, entered Germany 21 Feb 45 and entered Czechoslovakia 6 May 45; arrived Boston P/E 24 Oct 45 and inactivated at Cp Myles Standish Mass 25 Oct 45.

Campaigns: *Northern France, Rhineland, Ardennes-Alsace, Central Europe*
Aug 45 Loc: Bogen Germany

178th Field Artillery Group (Motorized)

24 Feb 44 redesignated from HHB 178th Field Artillery Regt in Venafro Italy where remained until inactivated 15 Oct 45.

Campaigns: *Rome-Arno, North Apennines, Po Valley*
Aug 45 Loc: Bassano Italy

179th Field Artillery Group (Motorized)

1 Mar 43 redesignated from HHB 179th Field Artillery Regt at Cp Shelby Miss; moved to Cp Joseph T. Robinson Ark 1 Jul 43 and returned Cp Shelby Miss 3 Dec 43; arrived Cp Polk La 25 Feb 44; staged at Cp Kilmer N.J. 28 Mar 44 until departed New York P/E 10 Apr 44; arrived England 16 Apr 44 and landed in France 27 Jun 44; crossed into Belgium 18 Sep 44 and into Germany 21 Sep 44; recrossed into Belgium 25 Dec 44; reentered Germany 7 Feb 45; arrived Hampton Roads P/E 23 Oct 45 and inactivated at Cp Patrick Henry Va same date.

Campaigns: *Normandy, Northern France, Rhineland, Ardennes-Alsace, Central Europe*
Aug 45 Loc: Frankenberg Germany

181st Field Artillery Group (Motorized)

1 Mar 43 redesignated from HHB 181st Field Artillery Regt at Desert Training Center Calif and moved to Cp Roberts Calif 17 Oct 43; arrived Cp Beale Calif 13 Mar 44 where redesignated 34th Field Artillery Brigade 15 Mar 44.

182nd Field Artillery Group (Motorized)

1 Mar 43 redesignated from HHB 182nd Field Artillery Regt at Ft Leonard Wood Mo and moved to Desert Training Center Calif 23 Aug 43; arrived Ft Bragg N.C. 28 Nov 43; staged at Cp Shanks N.Y. 17 Mar 44 until departed New York P/E 31 Mar 44; arrived England 8 Apr 44 and landed in France 12 Aug 44; crossed into Luxembourg 22 Dec 44 and entered Germany 23 Feb 45; returned to New York P/E 27 Nov 45 and inactivated at Cp Kilmer N.J. 28 Nov 45.

Campaigns: *Northern France, Rhineland, Ardennes-Alsace, Central Europe*
Aug 45 Loc: Straubing Germany

183rd Field Artillery Group (Motorized)

8 Feb 43 redesignated from HHB 183rd Field Artillery Regt at Ft Lewis Wash; moved to Cp Young Calif 16 Apr 43 and Ft Ord Calif 6 Aug 43; staged at Cp Kilmer N.J. 20 Jul 44 until departed New York P/E 26 Jul 44; arrived England 5 Aug 44 and landed in France 21 Aug 44; crossed into Luxembourg 21 Dec 44 and into Belgium 6 Jan 45; entered Germany 25 Feb 45; arrived Boston P/E 20 Oct 45 and inactivated at Cp Myles Standish Mass 21 Oct 45.

Campaigns: *Northern France, Rhineland, Ardennes-Alsace, Central Europe*
Aug 45 Loc: Regensburg Germany

186th Field Artillery Group (Motorized)

18 Feb 45 redesignated from HHB 186th Field Artillery Regt at Ft Ethan Allen Vermont; moved to A.P. Hill Mil Res Va 20 Mar 43 and Cp Forrest Tenn 16 Jun 43; arrived Elkins W.Va 1 Sep 43 and Indiantown Gap Mil Res Pa 12 Oct 43 where inactivated 21 Oct 43.

187th Field Artillery Group (Motorized)

8 Feb 43 redesignated from HHB 187th Field Artillery Regt at Ft Ethan Allen Vermont; moved to A.P. Hill Mil Res Va 20 Mar 43 and Cp Forrest Tenn 15 Jun 43; arrived Ft Dix N.J. 4 Sep 43 and staged at Cp Kilmer N.J. 8 Oct 43 until departed New York P/E 21 Oct 43; arrived England 3 Nov 43 and landed in France 11 Jun 44; crossed into Luxembourg and Belgium both 10 Sep 44 and first entered Germany 16 Sep 44; crossed back into Luxembourg 19 Sep 44 and into Belgium 22 Sep 44; reentered Luxembourg 28 Sep 44 and Belgium 4 Oct 44; entered Germany again 27 Oct 44; returned to Belgium 27 Jan 45 and Germany 4 Feb 45; entered Czechoslovakia 4 May 45; returned to New York P/E 16 Dec 45 and inactivated at Cp Kilmer N.J. 17 Dec 45.

Campaigns: *Normandy, Northern France, Rhineland, Ardennes-Alsace, Central Europe*
Aug 45 Loc: Strakonice Czechoslovakia

188th Field Artillery Group (Motorized)

17 Feb 43 redesignated from HHB 188th Field Artillery Regt at Yakima Wash and moved to Cp Young Calif 21 Apr 43; arrived Gp Gruber Okla 20 Aug 43 and staged at Cp Shanks N.Y. 22 Nov 43 until departed New York P/E 5 Dec 43; arrived England 17 Dec 43 and landed in France 12 Jun 44; crossed into Belgium 4 Sep 44 and into Germany 15 Sep 44; returned to Belgium 21 Dec 44 and Germany 3 Feb 45; arrived Boston P/E 29 Oct 45 and inactivated at Cy Myles Standish Mass 30 Oct 45.

Campaigns: *Normandy, Northern France, Rhineland, Ardennes-Alsace, Central Europe*
Aug 45 Loc: Lutzen Germany

190th Field Artillery Group (Motorized)

1 Nov 43 redesignated from HHB 190th Field Artillery Regt in England; landed in France 8 Jun 44 and crossed into Belgium 10 Sep 44 and entered Germany 27 Oct 44; returned to Belgium 21 Dec 44 and Germany 3 Feb 45; entered Czechoslovakia 5 May 45; arrived Hampton Roads P/E 31 Dec 45 and inactivated at Cp Patrick Henry Va same date.

Campaigns: *Normandy, Northern France, Rhineland, Ardennes-Alsace, Central Europe*
Aug 45 Loc: Horazdovice Czechoslovakia

191st Field Artillery Group (Motorized)

8 Feb 43 redesignated from HHB 191st Field Artillery Regt at Cp Roberts Calif; staged at Cp Stoneman Calif 2 Nov 43 until departed San Francisco P/E 24 Nov 43; arrived New Guinea 9 Dec 43 and landed in the Philippines 13 Jan 45; returned to San Francisco P/E 10 Jan 46 and inactivated at Cp Stoneman Calif 12 Jan 46.

Campaigns: *New Guinea, Luzon*
Aug 45 Loc: Manila Philippines

193rd Field Artillery Group (Motorized)

23 Feb 43 redesignated from HHB 193rd Field Artillery Regt at Ft Bragg N.C.; transferred to Ft Sill Okla 20 Apr 43 and Cp Gruber Okla 14 Jan 44; staged at Cp Kilmer N.J. 28 Mar 44 until departed New York P/E 10 Apr 44; arrived England 18 Apr 44 and landed in France 23 Jul 44; first entered Germany 3 Dec 44; crossed into Belgium 20 Dec 44 and into Luxembourg 22 Dec 44; returned to Belgium 30 Dec 44 and Luxembourg 27 Jan 45; entered Germany again 26 Feb 45; arrived Boston P/E 20 Oct 45 where inactivated at Cp Myles Standish Mass 21 Oct 45.

Campaigns: *Normandy, Northern France, Rhineland, Ardennes-Alsace, Central Europe*
Aug 45 Loc: Freising Germany

194th Field Artillery Group (Motorized)

8 Feb 43 redesignated from HHB 194th Field Artillery Regt at Ft Bragg N.C.; staged at Ft Dix N.J. 12 Aug 43 until departed New York P/E 21 Aug 43; arrived North Africa 2 Sep 43 and landed in Italy 5 Nov 43; arrived in France 1 Oct 44; entered Germany 17 Mar 45 and Austria 5 May 45; returned New York P/E 20 Dec 45 and inactivated at Cp Kilmer N.J. 21 Dec 45.

Campaigns: *Naples-Foggia, Rome-Arno, North Apennines, Rhineland, Ardennes-Alsace, Central Europe*
Aug 45 Loc: Salzburg Austria

195th Field Artillery Group (Motorized)

1 Mar 43 redesignated from HHB 195th Field Artillery Regt at Ft Ord Calif; moved to Cp Young Calif 30 Apr 43 and Ft Leonard Wood Mo 20 Aug 43; staged at Cp Shanks N.Y. 14 Mar 44 until departed New York P/E 29 Mar 44; arrived in England 8 Apr 44 and landed in France 23 Jul 44; first entered Germany 5 Dec 44; returned to France 21 Dec 44 and Germany 22 Feb 45; arrived Boston P/E 24 Oct 45 and inactivated at Cp Myles Standish Mass 25 Oct 45.

Campaigns: *Normandy, Northern France, Rhineland, Ardennes-Alsace, Central Europe*
Aug 45 Loc: Leuggreis Germany

196th Field Artillery Group (Motorized)

1 Mar 43 redesignated from HHB 196th Field Artillery Regt at Ft Sill Okla; moved to Cp Gordon Ga 19 Jun 43; staged at Cp Kilmer N.J. 3 Feb 44 until departed New York P/E 11 Feb 44; arrived in England 23 Feb 44 and landed in France 18 Jul 44; crossed into Belgium 15 Oct 44 and into Holland 31 Oct 44; entered Germany 21 Nov 44; arrived Hampton Roads P/E 26 Oct 45 and inactivated at Cp Patrick Henry Va same date.

Campaigns: *Normandy, Northern France, Rhineland, Central Europe*
Aug 45 Loc: Gersfeld Germany

202nd Field Artillery Group (Motorized)

1 Mar 43 redesignated from HHB 202nd Field Artillery Regt at Hornbeck La and moved to Boyce La 10 Jul 43; arrived Cp Howze Tex 25 Aug 43; staged at Cp Shanks N.Y. 3 Feb 44 until departed New York P/E 11 Feb 44; arrived in England 23 Feb 44 and landed in France 18 Jul 44; entered Belgium 1 Oct 44 and Germany 31 Oct 44; returned to New York P/E 27 Nov 45 and inactivated at Cp Kilmer N.J. 28 Nov 45.

Campaigns: *Normandy, Northern France, Rhineland, Central Europe*
Aug 45 Loc: Fallersleben Germany

203rd Field Artillery Group (Motorized)

1 Mar 43 redesignated from HHB 203rd Field Artillery Regt at Ft Bragg N.C. and arrived Ft Jackson S.C. 9 Jun 43; moved to Tenn Maneuver Area 24 Feb 44 and to Cp Forrest Tenn 28 Mar 44; staged at Cp Kilmer N.J. 18 Jul 44 until departed New York P/E 26 Jul 44; arrived in England 5 Aug 44 and landed in France 4 Sep 44; first entered Germany 17 Dec 44; crossed into Luxembourg 20 Dec 44 and Belgium 21 Dec 44; returned to Luxembourg 23 Dec 44 and Germany 24 Feb 45; returned to New York P/E 25 Nov 45 and inactivated at Cp Kilmer N.J. 27 Nov 45.

Campaigns: *Northern France, Rhineland, Ardennes-Alsace, Central Europe*
Aug 45 Loc: Eissenach Germany

204th Field Artillery Group (Motorized)

1 Mar 43 redesignated from HHB 204th Field Artillery Regt at Cp Forrest Tenn; moved to Cp Gordon Ga 13 May 43 and Cp Rucker Ala 18 Jun 43; arrived Tenn Maneuver Area 29 Feb 44 and Ft Riley Kans 28 Mar 44; staged at Cp Kilmer N.J. 17 Jul 44 until departed New York P/E 26 Jul 44; arrived in England 5 Aug 44 and landed in France 26 Aug 44; entered Germany 8 Dec 44; arrived in Boston P/E 21 Oct 45 and inactivated at Cp Myles Standish Mass on 22 Oct 45.

Campaigns: *Northern France, Rhineland, Ardennes-Alsace, Central Europe*
Aug 45 Loc: Seewalchen Austria

205th Field Artillery Group (Motorized)

23 Mar 44 activated at Cp Gordon Ga and moved to Ft Jackson S.C. 20 Oct 44; staged at Cp Shanks N.Y. 27 Dec 44 until departed New York P/E 10 Jan 45; arrived in France 21 Jan 45 and entered Germany 21 Feb 45; arrived at Boston P/E 13 Nov 45 and inactivated at Cp Myles Standish Mass 14 Nov 45.

Campaigns: *Rhineland, Central Europe*
Aug 45 Loc: Suhlendorf Germany

207th Field Artillery Group (Motorized)

23 Mar 44 activated at Ft Leonard Wood Mo and staged at Ft Lawton Wash 22 Dec 44 until departed Seattle P/E 1 Jan 45; arrived in Hawaii 6 Jan 45 and landed in the Philippines 27 Jul 45; arrived at San Francisco P/E 11 Jan 46 and inactivated at Cp Stoneman Calif 12 Jan 46.

Campaigns: *Pacific Theater without inscription*
Aug 45 Loc: Leyte Philippines

208th Field Artillery Group (Motorized)

1 Mar 43 redesignated from HHB 208th Field Artillery Regt at Cp Forrest Tenn; moved to Cp Polk La 29 Nov 43 and staged at Cp Shanks N.Y. 13 Mar 44 until departed New York P/E 23 Mar 44; arrived in England 3 Apr 44 and landed in France 14 Jul 44; entered Germany 17 Mar 45 and Austria 5 May 45; returned to New York P/E 26 Nov 45 and inactivated at Cp Shanks N.Y. 27 Nov 45.

Campaigns: *Normandy, Northern France, Rhineland, Ardennes-Alsace, Central Europe*
Aug 45 Loc: Salzburg Austria

209th Field Artillery Group (Motorized)

23 Mar 44 activated at Cp Rucker Ala and moved to Ft Bragg N.C. 16 Dec 44; staged at Cp Shanks N.Y. 2 Mar 45 until departed New York P/E 7 Mar 45; arrived in France 18 Mar 45 and entered Germany 14 Apr 45; returned to New York P/E 2 Aug 45 and arrived Cp Bowie Tex 6 Aug 45 where inactivated 20 Oct 45.

Campaigns: *Central Europe*
Aug 45 Loc: Camp Bowie Texas

210th Field Artillery Group (Motorized)

24 Jan 44 activated at Cp Maxey Tex and moved to Ft Sill Okla 2 Sep 44; staged at Cp Myles Standish Mass 15 Dec 44 until departed Boston P/E 22 Dec 44; arrived in England 29 Dec 44 and landed in France 10 Mar 45; entered Germany 18 Mar 45; arrived New York P/E 25 Jan 46 and inactivated at Cp Kilmer N.J. 26 Jan 46.

Campaigns: *Rhineland, Central Europe*
Aug 45 Loc: Marburg Germany

211th Field Artillery Group (Motorized)

15 Feb 44 activated at Ft Bragg N.C. and staged at Cp Shanks N.Y. 12 Aug 44 until departed New York P/E 17 Aug 44; arrived in England 25 Aug 44 and landed in France 24 Sep 44; crossed into Belgium 21 Oct 44 and into Holland 25 Oct 44; entered Germany same date and inactivated there 5 Jul 46.

Campaigns: *Rhineland, Ardennes-Alsace, Central Europe*
Aug 45 Loc: Nuernburg Germany

212th Field Artillery Group (Motorized)

20 Apr 44 activated at Ft Riley Kans; staged at Cp Kilmer N.J. 19 Jan 45 until departed New York P/E 5 Feb 45; arrived in France 17 Feb 45 and crossed into Belgium 29 Mar 45; entered Germany 30 Mar 45 where inactivated 30 Apr 46.

Campaigns: *Central Europe*
Aug 45 Loc: Aachen Germany

213th Field Artillery Group (Motorized)

17 Apr 44 activated at Cp Joseph T. Robinson Ark and moved to Ft Sill Okla 23 Nov 44 where inactivated 1 Mar 45.

214th Field Artillery Group (Motorized)

17 Mar 44 activated at Cp Van Dorn Miss; moved to Cp Polk La 30 Oct 44 and Ft Sill Okla 18 Nov 44; staged at Cp Shanks N.Y. 26 Mar 45 until departed New York P/E 8 Apr 45; arrived in France 19 Apr 45 and entered Germany 30 Apr 45; returned to New York P/E 16 Jul 45 and arrived in Cp Shelby Miss 20 Jul 45 where inactivated 12 Nov 45.

Campaigns: *European Theater without inscription*
Aug 45 Loc: Camp Shelby Mississippi

218th Field Artillery Group (Motorized)

20 Apr 44 activated at Cp Chaffee Ark and moved to Cp Bowie Tex 28 Dec 44; departed San Francisco P/E 29 May 45 and arrived in the Philippine Islands 22 Jun 45 where inactivated 11 Feb 46.

Campaigns: *Luzon*
Aug 45 Loc: San Jose Philippine Islands

219th Field Artillery Group (Motorized)

9 Mar 44 activated at Cp Shelby Miss; staged at Cp Shanks N.Y. 8 Dec 44 until departed New York P/E 16 Dec 44; arrived in England 21 Dec 44 and landed in France 18 Mar 45 and entered Germany where inactivated 8 May 46.

Campaigns: *Rhineland, Central Europe*
Aug 45 Loc: Fulda Germany

220th Field Artillery Group (Motorized)

6 Mar 44 activated at Cp Hood Tex; staged at Cp Shanks N.Y. 30 Nov 44 until departed New York P/E 9 Dec 44; arrived in England 20 Dec 44 and landed in France 2 Mar 45; entered Germany 15 Mar 45; returned to New York P/E 23 Oct 45 and inactivated at Cp Shanks N.Y. 24 Oct 45.

Campaigns: *Rhineland, Central Europe*
Aug 45 Loc: Grunwald Germany

222nd Field Artillery Group (Motorized)

12 Jan 44 activated at Cp Gordon Ga and moved to Ft Jackson S.C. 17 Apr 44 where redesignated 61st Field Artillery Brigade 18 Jul 44.

223rd Field Artillery Group (Motorized)

21 Feb 44 activated at Cp Bowie Tex; staged at Ft Lawton Wash 15 Oct 44 until departed Seattle P/E 23 Oct 44; arrived in Hawaii 28 Oct 44 where inactivated 25 Apr 46.

Campaigns: *Pacific Theater without inscription*
Aug 45 Loc: Schofield Barracks Hawaii

224th Field Artillery Group (Motorized)

21 Feb 44 activated at Cp Hood Tex; staged at Cp Shanks N.Y. 17 Dec 44 until departed New York P/E 26 Dec 44; arrived in England 7 Jan 45 and landed in France 10 Mar 45; crossed into Belgium 17 Mar 45 and entered Germany same date; returned to New York P/E 21 Feb 46 and inactivated at Cp Kilmer N.J. 22 Feb 46.

Campaigns: *Rhineland, Central Europe*
Aug 45 Loc: Sangerhausen Germany

225th Field Artillery Group (Motorized)

3 Feb 44 redesignated from HHB 225th Field Artillery Regt in Hawaii where redesignated HHB, XXIV Corps Artillery 31 May 44.

Campaigns: *Pacific Theater without inscription*

228th Field Artillery Group (Motorized)

8 Feb 43 redesignated from HHB 228th Field Artillery Regt at Ft Bragg N.C.; moved to Tenn Maneuver Area 10 Sep 43 and Calif-Ariz Maneuver Area 22 Nov 43; staged at Cp Myles Standish Mass 5 Feb 44 until departed Boston P/E 11 Feb 44; arrived in England 23 Feb 44 and landed in France 24 Jun 44; entered Holland 19 Sep 44 and Germany 20 Nov 44; returned to Boston P/E 13 Nov 45 and inactivated at Cp Myles Standish Mass 14 Nov 45.

Campaigns: *Normandy, Northern France, Rhineland, Central Europe*
Aug 45 Loc: Lich Germany

250th Field Artillery Group (Motorized)

18 May 44 redesignated from HHB 250th Coast Artillery Regt (155mm Gun) at Cp Gruber Okla; staged at Cp Shanks N.Y. 19 Jan 45 until departed New York P/E 11 Feb 45; arrived in England 18 Feb 45 and landed in France 11 Mar 45; entered Germany 31 Mar 45; returned to New York P/E 12 Nov 45 and inactivated at Cp Kilmer N.J. 14 Nov 45.

Campaigns: *Central Europe*
Aug 45 Loc: Frankenforde Germany

252nd Field Artillery Group (Motorized)

20 May 44 redesignated from HHB 252nd Coast Artillery Regt (155mm Gun) at Ft Jackson S.C.; staged at Cp Shanks N.Y. 27 Dec 44 until departed New York P/E 10 Jan 45; arrived in France 23 Jan 45 and entered Germany 20 Feb 45; returned to New York P/E 27 Nov 45 and inactivated at Cp Kilmer N.J. 29 Nov 45.

Campaigns: *Rhineland, Central Europe*
Aug 45 Loc: Mattighofen Germany

258th Field Artillery Group (Motorized)

8 Feb 45 redesignated from HHB 258th Field Artillery Regt at Pine Camp N.Y.; moved to A.P. Hill Mil Res Va 12 Mar 43 and Indiantown Gap Mil Res Pa 11 Oct 43; arrived Ft Dix N.J. 14 Dec 43 and staged at Cp Shanks N.Y. 13 Jan 44 until departed New York P/E 22 Jan 44; arrived in England 28 Jan 44 and landed in France 8 Jul 44; crossed into Holland 16 Sep 44 and into Germany 19 Nov 44; arrived Boston P/E 24 Sep 45 and inactivated at Cp Myles Standish Mass 25 Sep 45.

Campaigns: *Normandy, Northern France, Rhineland, Central Europe*
Aug 45 Loc: Alsfeld Germany

333rd Field Artillery Group (Motorized) (Colored)

10 Mar 43 redesignated from HHB 333rd Field Artillery Regt at Cp Gruber Okla; staged at Cp Shanks N.Y. 4 Feb 44 until departed New York P/E 11 Feb 44; arrived in England 23 Feb 44 and landed in France 29 Jun 44; crossed into Belgium 1 Oct 44 and returned to France 28 Dec 44; reentered Belgium 12 Jan 45 and entered Germany 1 Feb 45; arrived at Hampton roads P/E 29 Dec 45 and inactivated at Cp Patrick Henry Va 30 Dec 45.

Campaigns: *Normandy, Northern France, Rhineland, Ardennes-Alsace, Central Europe*
Aug 45 Loc: Freising Germany

349th Field Artillery Group (Motorized) (Colored)

12 Feb 43 redesignated from HHB 349th Field Artillery Regt at Ft Sill Okla; arrived at Cp Hood Tex 20 Jul 44; staged at Cp Myles Standish Mass 5 Oct 44 until departed Boston P/E 11 Oct 44; arrived in France 21 Oct 44; crossed into Belgium 27 Dec 44 and into Holland same date; entered Germany 1 Feb 45 where inactivated 24 May 46.

Campaigns: *Rhineland, Central Europe*
Aug 45 Loc: Murrhardt Germany

350th Field Artillery Group (Motorized) (Colored)

1 Apr 43 redesignated from HHB 350th Field Artillery Regt at Cp Livingston La where inactivated 1 Mar 44.

351st Field Artillery Group (Motorized) (Colored)

1 Apr 43 redesignated from HHB 351st Field Artillery Regt at Cp Livingston La; moved to Ft Sill Okla 24 Mar 44 and Cp Gruber Okla 19 Jul 44; staged at Cp Myles Standish Mass 1 Dec 44 until departed Boston P/E 12 Dec 44; arrived in England 20 Dec 44 and landed in France 18 Feb 45; entered Belgium 1 Mar 45 and Germany 4 Mar 45 where inactivated 15 Jun 46.

Campaigns: *Rhineland, Central Europe*
Aug 45 Loc: Hilpolstein Germany

353rd Field Artillery Group (Motorized) (Colored)

1 Apr 43 redesignated from HHB 353rd Field Artillery at Cp Livingston La where inactivated on 1 Mar 44.

401st Field Artillery Group (Motorized)

1 Feb 43 activated at Cp Swift Tex; moved to Cp Bowie Tex 14 Aug 43 and Ft Sill Okla 18 Sep 43; arrived at Cp Polk La 3 Jun 44 and staged at Cp Shanks N.Y. 4 Sep 44 until departed New York P/E 24 Sep 44; arrived in Scotland 30 Sep 44 and England 1 Oct 44; landed in France 2 Oct 44; entered Belgium 14 Dec 44 and Germany 23 Dec 44; returned to Belgium 31 Dec 44 and to Germany 7 Feb 45; returned to New York P/E 16 Feb 46 and inactivated at Cp Kilmer N.J. 17 Feb 46.

Campaigns: *Northern France, Rhineland, Ardennes-Alsace, Central Europe*
Aug 45 Loc: Roth Germany

402nd Field Artillery Group (Motorized)

15 Mar 43 activated at Cp Butner N.C. and moved to Ft Bragg N.C. 18 Dec 43; staged at Cp Kilmer N.J. 26 Jun 44 until departed New York P/E 2 Jul 44; arrived in England 12 Jul 44 and landed in France 16 Aug 44; crossed into Belgium 3 Oct 44 and returned to France 21 Dec 44; recrossed into Belgium 22 Dec 44 and entered Luxembourg 27 Dec 44; returned to Belgium 29 Dec 44 and to Luxembourg 26 Jan 45; reentered Belgium 30 Jan 45 and entered Germany 7 Feb 45; returned to New York P/E 25 Oct 45 and inactivated at Cp Kilmer N.J. 26 Oct 45.

Campaigns: *Northern France, Rhineland, Ardennes-Alsace, Central Europe*
Aug 45 Loc: Meiningen Germany

403rd Field Artillery Group (Motorized)

1 Mar 43 activated at Cp Shelby Miss where redesignated the 32nd Field Artillery Brigade on 16 Feb 44.

404th Field Artillery Group (Motorized)

1 Apr 43 activated at Cp Bowie Tex and moved to Cp Hood Tex 17 Mar 44; staged at Cp Shanks N.Y. 25 Jun 44 until departed New York P/E 2 Jul 44; arrived in England 12 Jul 44 and landed in France 13 Sep 44; crossed into Luxembourg 21 Dec 44 and entered Germany 7 Feb 45; returned to New York P/E on 22 Oct 45 and inactivated at Cp Shanks N.Y. on 23 Oct 45.

Campaigns: *Northern France, Rhineland, Ardennes-Alsace, Central Europe*
Aug 45 Loc: Bodendorf Germany

405th Field Artillery Group (Motorized)

15 Apr 43 activated at Cp Phillips Kans and moved to Ft Riley Kans 4 Dec 43; transferred to Gallatin Tenn 19 Dec 43 and to Cp Campbell Ky 1 Feb 44; staged at Cp Patrick Henry Va 20 Jun 44 until departed Hampton Roads P/E 1 Jul 44; arrived in Italy 15 Jul 44 and landed in France on 29 Sep 44; entered Germany 19 Mar 45; arrived in Boston P/E 29 Oct 45 and inactivated at Cp Myles Standish Mass on 30 Oct 45.

Campaigns: *Rome-Arno, Rhineland, Ardennes-Alsace, Central Europe*
Aug 45 Loc: Assebrouck Belgium

406th Field Artillery Group (Motorized)

1 Apr 43 activated at Cp Maxey Tex; staged at Cp Shanks N.Y. 1 Feb 44 until departed New York P/E 11 Feb 44; arrived in England 23 Feb 44 and landed in France 13 Jun 44; crossed into Belgium 8 Sep 44; entered Germany 13 Sep 44 and Czechoslovakia 5 May 45; returned to New York P/E 25 Oct 45 and inactivated at Cp Shanks N.Y. 26 Oct 45.

Campaigns: *Normandy, Northern France, Rhineland, Ardennes-Alsace, Central Europe*
Aug 45 Loc: Osek Czechoslovakia

407th Field Artillery Group (Motorized)

5 Aug 43 activated at Cp Marshall N.C.; moved to Ft Benning Ga 20 Mar 44 and Cp Rucker Ala 1 Jun 44; staged at Cp Kilmer N.J. 17 Sep 44 until departed New York P/E 24 Sep 44; arrived in England 30 Sep 44 and landed in France 3 Oct 44; entered Belgium 10 Dec 44 and Germany 23 Dec 44; inactivated in Austria 30 Apr 46.

Campaigns: *Rhineland, Central Europe*
Aug 45 Loc: Scharding Austria

408th Field Artillery Group (Motorized)

6 Nov 43 activated at Ft Ord Calif and moved to Cp Cooke Calif 2 Dec 43; moved to Ft Sill Okla 24 Feb 44 and Cp Polk La 3 Sep 44; staged at Cp Kilmer N.J. 24 Oct 44 until departed New York P/E 1 Nov 44; arrived England 9 Nov 44 and landed in France 31 Dec 44; entered Belgium 6 Jan 45 and Germany 6 Feb 45; returned to New York P/E 28 Jan 46 and inactivated at Cp Kilmer N.J. 29 Jan 46.

Campaigns: *Rhineland, Ardennes-Alsace, Central Europe*
Aug 45 Loc: Hersbruck Germany

409th Field Artillery Group (Motorized)

6 Nov 43 activated at Cp Roberts Calif and moved to Ft Bragg N.C. 8 May 44; staged at Cp Stoneman Calif 17 May 45 until departed San Francisco P/E 29 May 45; arrived in the Philippine Islands 22 Jun 45; returned to San Francisco P/E 10 Jan 46 and inactivated at Cp Stoneman Calif 12 Jan 46.

Campaigns: *Pacific Theater without inscription*
Aug 45 Loc: San Jose Philippine Islands

410th Field Artillery Group (Motorized)

21 Dec 43 activated at Ft Dix N.J. and moved to Cp Butner N.C. 5 Jan 44; staged at Cp Kilmer N.J. 21 Jul 44 until departed New York P/E 11 Aug 44; arrived in England 22 Aug 44 and landed in France 6 Sep 44; entered Luxembourg 21 Dec 44 and Germany 26 Feb 45; returned to New York P/E 25 Oct 45 and inactivated at Cp Kilmer N.J. 26 Oct 45.

Campaigns: *Northern France, Rhineland, Ardennes-Alsace, Central Europe*
Aug 45 Loc: Cham Germany

411th Field Artillery Group (Motorized)

21 Dec 43 activated at Ft Lewis Wash and moved to Ft Bragg N.C. 12 May 44; staged at Cp Kilmer N.J. 24 Oct 44 until departed New York P/E 30 Oct 44; arrived in England 12 Nov 44 and landed in France 23 Feb 45; entered Germany 6 Mar 45; returned to New York P/E 25 Oct 45 and inactivated at Cp Shanks N.Y. 26 Oct 45.

Campaigns: *Rhineland, Central Europe*
Aug 45 Loc: Ellingen Germany

413th Field Artillery Group (Motorized)

7 Jan 44 activated at Cp Gruber Okla; moved to Cp Carson Colo 28 Feb 44 and returned to Cp Gruber Okla 23 Sep 44; staged at Cp Kilmer N.J. 10 Nov 44 until departed New York P/E 21 Nov 44; arrived in England 27 Nov 44 and landed in France 11 Feb 45; entered Germany 17 Mar 45; returned to New York P/E 6 Mar 46 and inactivated at Cp Kilmer N.J. 8 Mar 46.

Campaigns: *Rhineland, Central Europe*
Aug 45 Loc: Hall Germany

414th Field Artillery Group (Motorized)

1 Jan 44 activated at Cp Beale Calif; moved to Cp Bowie Tex 7 Mar 44 and Cp Hood Tex 15 Jan 45; staged at Cp Stoneman Calif 10 Jun 45 until departed San Francisco P/E 15 Jun 45; arrived in the Philippine Islands 10 Jul 45; returned to San Francisco P/E 26 Dec 45 and inactivated at Cp Stoneman Calif 28 Dec 45.

Campaigns: *Pacific Theater without inscription*
Aug 45 Loc: Manila Philippines

415th Field Artillery Group (Motorized)

31 Mar 44 activated at Cp Forrest Tenn and moved to Ft Jackson S.C. 27 Sep 44 where it remained active through 1946.

416th Field Artillery Group (Motorized)

31 Mar 44 activated at Cp Chaffee Ark and staged at Cp Myles Standish Mass 19 Nov 44 until departed Boston P/E 2 Dec 44; arrived in England 12 Dec 44 and entered Luxembourg 6 Mar 45; entered Germany 10 Mar 45; arrived in New York P/E 27 Oct 45 and inactivated at Cp Kilmer N.J. 28 Oct 45.

Campaigns: *Rhineland, Central Europe*
Aug 45 Loc: Auerbach Germany

417th Field Artillery Group (Motorized)

28 Apr 44 activated at Cp Breckinridge Ky; moved to Ft Sill Okla 23 Sep 44 and Cp Hood Tex 2 Dec 44; staged at Cp Kilmer N.J. 18 Jan 45 until departed New York P/E 5 Feb 45; arrived in England 16 Feb 45 and landed in France 6 Mar 45; entered Germany 1 Apr 45; arrived at Boston P/E 19 Aug 45 and transferred to Cp Gruber Okla 23 Aug 45 where inactivated 14 Feb 46.

Campaigns: *Central Europe*
Aug 45 Loc: Shipment #10160-B at sea returning to USA.

418th Field Artillery Group (Motorized)

25 Apr 44 activated at Cp Barkeley Tex and moved to Cp Bowie Tex 28 Sep 44; staged at Ft Lawton Wash 22 Dec 44 until departed Seattle P/E 1 Jan 45; arrived in Hawaii 6 Jan 45 and departed 6 Jul 45; arrived in the Philippines 27 Jul 45; returned to San Francisco P/E 11 Jan 46 where inactivated at Cp Stoneman Calif on 12 Jan 46.

Campaigns: *Pacific Theater without inscription*
Aug 45 Loc: Leyte Philippine Islands

419th Field Artillery Group (Motorized)

31 May 44 activated aboard the **USS** *George F. Elliot* **(AP.105)** enroute from Hawaii to Saipan from assets of the 225th Field Artillery Group; remained aboard ship while at Eniwetok 7–12 Jun 44 and landed on Saipan 16 Jun 44; landed on Tinian Island 27 Jul 44; departed Tinian 29 Nov 44 and landed in the Philippine Islands 6 Dec 44; landed on Okinawa 4 Apr 45 where inactivated on 15 Feb 46.

Campaigns: *Western Pacific, Leyte, Ryukyus*
Aug 45 Loc: Okinawa

420th Field Artillery Group (Motorized)

31 May 44 activated aboard the **USS** *Sumter* **(APA.52)** enroute from Hawaii to Saipan from assets of the 1st Provisional Gun Group; remained aboard ship while at Eniwetok 7–12 Jun 44; landed on Saipan 15 Jun 44 and departed 29 Nov 44; landed in the Philippine Islands 6 Dec 44 and landed on Okinawa 5 Apr 45 where inactivated on 8 Nov 45.

Campaigns: *Western Pacific, Leyte, Ryukyus*
Aug 45 Loc: Okinawa

421st Field Artillery Group (Motorized)

2 Aug 44 activated at Nemi Italy from assets of the Rome Area Command as well as 13th Field Artillery Brigade and 17th Field Artillery Group and 36th Infantry Division Artillery; departed Italy 20 Sep 44 and landed in France 24 Sep 44; entered Germany 25 Mar 45 and arrived at New York P/E 17 Oct 45; inactivated at Cp Kilmer N.J. on 19 Oct 45.

Campaigns: *Rhineland, Central Europe*
Aug 45 Loc: Herrachine Germany

422nd Field Artillery Group (Motorized)

8 Feb 43 redesignated from HHB 422nd Field Artillery Regt at Louisiana Maneuver Area and moved to Cp Bowie Tex 21 Feb 43; transferred to Ft Sill Okla 5 Mar 43 and to Cp Howze Tex 9 Mar 44; staged at Cp Kilmer N.J. 20 Jul 44 until departed New York P/E 26 Jul 44; arrived in England 5 Aug 44 and landed in France 28 Aug 44; crossed into Belgium 7 Sep 44 and into Luxembourg 6 Nov 44; returned to Belgium 28 Dec 44 and entered Germany 6 Feb 45, arrived back at New York P/E 18 Nov 45 and inactivated at Cp Kilmer N.J. on 20 Nov 45.

Campaigns: *Northern France, Rhineland, Ardennes-Alsace, Central Europe*
Aug 45 Loc: Bad Soden Germany

423rd Field Artillery Group (Motorized)

23 Jul 44 activated at Cecina Italy from assets of both IV Corps Artillery and 88th Infantry Division Artillery; assigned Fifth Army and remained in Italy until inactivated 8 Oct 45.

Campaigns: *Rome-Arno, North Apennines, Po Valley*
Aug 45 Loc: Loiano Italy

424th Field Artillery Group (Motorized)

28 Jul 44 activated at Cecina Italy from II Corps Artillery and 34th Infantry Division Artillery assets; assigned Fifth Army and remained in Italy until inactivated 3 Aug 45.

Campaigns: *Rome-Arno, North Apennines, Po Valley*
Aug 45 Loc: Novaro Italy

425th Field Artillery Group (Motorized)

31 Jul 44 activated Cp Joseph T. Robinson Ark and moved to Cp Bowie Tex 31 Dec 44; staged at Ft Hamilton N.Y. 4 Apr 45 until departed New York P/E 8 Apr 45; arrived in France 19 Apr 45 and entered Germany 30 Apr 45; returned to New York P/E 16 Jul 45 and arrived at Cp Hood Tex 21 Jul 45; sent to Cp Polk La 15 Mar 46 and returned to Cp Hood Tex 19 Dec 46 where active thru 1946.

Campaigns: *Central Europe*
Aug 45 Loc: Camp Hood Texas

426th Field Artillery Group (Motorized)

31 Jul 44 activated at Ft Jackson S.C. and staged at Cp Shanks N.Y. 19 Jan 45 until departed New York P/E 3 Feb 45; arrived in England 11 Feb 45 and landed in France 6 Mar 45; entered Germany 28 Mar 45; returned to New York P/E 11 Nov 45 and inactivated at Cp Kilmer N.J. 12 Nov 45.

Campaigns: *Rhineland, Central Europe*
Aug 45 Loc: Trier Germany

427th Field Artillery Group (Motorized)

25 Aug 44 activated at Ft Bragg N.C. where redesignated as HHB XXXII Corps Artillery 17 Oct 44.

428th Field Artillery Group (Motorized)

25 Aug 44 activated at Ft Leonard Wood Mo and moved to Cp Chaffee Ark 17 Nov 44; staged at Cp Patrick Henry Va 4 Mar 45 until departed Hampton Roads P/E 17 Mar 45; arrived in Italy 23 Mar 45 where inactivated 30 Sep 45.

Campaigns: *North Appenines, Po Valley*
Aug 45 Loc: Naples Italy

429th Field Artillery Group (Motorized)

31 Oct 44 activated at Cp Gruber Okla and moved to Cp Hood Tex 20 Nov 45 where inactivated 10 Feb 46.

Aug 45 Loc: Camp Gruber Oklahoma

430th Field Artillery Group (Motorized)

25 Sep 44 activated at Cp Hood Tex and moved to Cp Anza Calif 13 Jul 45 and departed Los Angeles P/E 22 Jul 45; arrived in Philippines 17 Aug 45; returned to San Francisco P/E 26 Dec 45 and inactivated at Cp Stoneman Calif 28 Dec 45.

Campaigns: *Pacific Theater without inscription*
Aug 45 Loc: Shipment #2209-D loading at Los Angeles

431st Field Artillery Group (Motorized)

16 Oct 44 activated at Cp Gruber Okla where inactivated 20 Oct 45.

Aug 45 Loc: Camp Gruber Oklahoma

432nd Field Artillery Group (Motorized)

26 Feb 45 activated at Cp Bowie Tex and moved to Cp Hood Tex 21 May 45; returned to Cp Bowie Tex 4 Jun 45 where inactivated 2 Nov 45.

Aug 45 Loc: Camp Bowie Texas

442nd Field Artillery Group (Motorized)

25 Sep 44 activated at Ft Bragg N.C. where inactivated 31 Oct 46.

Aug 45 Loc: Fort Bragg North Carolina

472nd Field Artillery Group (Motorized)

6 Mar 43 redesignated from HHB 472nd Field Artillery Regt at Cp Gordon Ga and moved to Ft Sill Okla 17 Jun 43; arrived at Cp Chaffee Ark 8 Apr 44 and staged at Cp Shanks N.Y. 19 Aug 44 until departed New York P/E 28 Aug 44; arrived in England 3 Sep 44 and landed in France 26 Sep 44; crossed into Belgium 20 Oct 44 and into Holland 30 Oct 44; entered Germany 22 Nov 44; arrived at Hampton Roads P/E 16 Nov 45 and inactivated at Cp Patrick Henry Va same date.

Campaigns: *Rhineland, Central Europe*
Aug 45 Loc: Schluchtern Germany

578th Field Artillery Group (Motorized)

23 Feb 43 redesignated from 578th Field Artillery Regt at Ft Bragg N.C. where inactivated 23 Feb 44.

Chapter 32

Field Artillery Regiments

Regiments:

1–21, 23–26, 28–31, 34–36, 40, 47, 65–68, 72, 76, 77, 79, 80–83, 87, 88, 99, 101–128, 130–139, 141–148, 150–152, 156–158, 160, 161, 162, 165, 166, 168, 172–174, 176, 177–196, 200, 202–204, 208, 218, 222, 225, 228, 258, 333, 349–351, 353, 422, 472, 578

1st Field Artillery Regiment (75mm Gun) (Truck-D)

Stationed at Ft Sill Okla and assigned to 6th Division; redesignated there as 1st Field Artillery Battalion 1 Oct 40.

2nd Field Artillery Regiment (75mm Gun) (Truck-D)

1st Battalion active in Canal Zone and redesignated there at Ft Clayton as 2nd Field Artillery Battalion 13 Jan 41.

3rd Field Artillery Regiment (75mm Gun) (Horse-D)

2nd Battalion active at Ft Sheridan Ill and inactivated there 1 Jun 40. 1st Battalion activated 1 Oct 39 at Ft Riley Kans and assigned to 2nd Cavalry Division where redesignated 3rd Field Artillery Battalion 1 Jan 41.

4th Field Artillery Regiment (75mm How) (Pack)

1st Battalion active at Ft Bragg N.C. and remainder of regiment (less 2nd Bn) activated there 1 Jun 40 where redesignated as 4th Field Artillery Battalion 16 Dec 40.

5th Field Artillery Regiment (155mm How) (Truck-D)

Stationed at Madison Barracks N.Y. as part of 18th FA Bde and redesignated there as 5th Field Artillery Battalion 1 Oct 40.

6th Field Artillery Regiment (75mm Gun) (Horse-D)

Stationed at Ft Hoyle Md as part of GHQ Reserve until assigned to 8th Division 22 Jun 40; inactivated 1 Aug 40, less 1st Bn which was redesignated as 6th Field Artillery Battalion 4 Jan 41.

7th Field Artillery Regiment (75mm Gun) (Truck-D)

Stationed primarily at Ft Ethan Allen Vt and assigned to 1st Division where redesignated as 7th Field Artillery Battalion 1 Oct 40.

8th Field Artillery Regiment (75mm Gun) (Truck-D)

Stationed in Hawaii as part of 11th FA Bde, Hawaiian Division, where redesignated 8th Field Artillery Battalion 1 Oct 41.

9th Field Artillery Regiment (75mm Gun) (Truck-D)

2nd Battalion active at Ft Lewis Wash and assigned to 3rd FA where redesignated as 9th Field Artillery Battalion 1 Oct 40.

10th Field Artillery Regiment (75mm Gun) (Truck-D)

Stationed at Ft Lewis Wash and assigned to 3rd Division where redesignated 10th Field Artillery Battalion 1 Oct 40.

11th Field Artillery Regiment (155mm How) (Truck-D)

Stationed at Schofield Barracks Hawaii as part of 11th FA Bde, Hawaiian Division, where redesignated 11th Field Artillery Battalion 26 Aug 41.

12th Field Artillery Regiment (155mm How) (Truck-D)

Stationed at Ft Sam Houston Tex as part of 2nd FA Bde where redesignated as 12th Field Artillery Battalion 1 Oct 40.

13th Field Artillery Regiment (75mm Gun) (Truck-D)

Stationed at Schofield Barracks Hawaii as part of 11th FA Bde, Hawaiian Division, where redesignated as 13th Field Artillery Battalion 1 Oct 41.

14th Field Artillery Regiment (105mm How) (Armored)

15 Jul 40 activated at Ft Benning Ga where assigned to 2nd Armored Division and redesignnated there as 14th Armored Field Artillery Battalion 1 Jan 42.

15th Field Artillery Regiment (75mm Gun) (Truck-D)

Stationed at Ft Sam Houston Tex as part of 2nd FA Bde where redesignated as 15th Field Artillery Battalion 1 Oct 40.

16th Field Artillery Regiment (75mm Gun) (Horse-D)

3 Jan 41 activated at Ft Myer Va and redesignated there as 16th Field Artillery Battalion 13 Jan 41.

17th Field Artillery Regiment (155mm How) (Truck-D)

Stationed at Ft Bragg N.C. with 13th FA Bde, I Army Corps; transferred 29 Mar 42 to Cp Blanding Fla and 2nd Bn activated; departed New York P/E 5 Aug 42; arrived in England 17 Aug 42 and left 26 Nov 42; landed in North Africa 6 Dec 42; landed in Sicily 16 Jul 43; moved to Italy 17 Oct 43 where redesignated HHB, 17th Field Artillery Group 1 Mar 44. 1st Bn redesignated 17th Field Artillery Battalion same date; 2nd Bn redesignated 630th Field Artillery Battalion 14 Feb 44.

Campaigns: *Naples-Foggia, Rome-Arno, Sicily*

18th Field Artillery Regiment (Composite School Troops)

Stationed at Ft Sill Okla where served as the artillery demonstration and training regiment and was assigned to Replacement & School Command. Initially, its 1st Bn was 75mm Gun (Horse-D) while the 2nd Bn was 155mm How (Truck-D). Later its 1st Bn became a composite weapons battalion, and its 2nd Bn converted to 105mm howitzers. The 3rd Bn was activated 1 Jun 40 as a 155mm howitzer battalion. The 4th Bn was activated 1 Mar 41 and outfitted with 105mm howitzers. Battery K was detached and served at Ft Bragg N.C. On 8 Feb 43 regiment was designated HHB, 18th Field Artillery Group, and 1st–4th Bns redesignated 685th, 687th, 689th, and 693rd Field Artillery Battalions, respectively.

19th Field Artillery Regiment (75mm Gun) (Truck-D)

5 Oct 39 activated at Ft Knox Ky and assigned to 5th FA Bde where it was redesignated 19th Field Artillery Battalion 1 Oct 40.

20th Field Artillery Regiment

1 Jun 40 activated at Ft Benning Ga where redesignated 20th Field Artillery Battalion 1 Oct 40.

21st Field Artillery Regiment (155mm How) (Truck-D)

6 Oct 39 activated at Ft Knox Ky and assigned to 5th FA Bde where it was redesignated 21st Field Artillery Battalion 1 Oct 40.

No Distinctive
Insignia Authorized

23rd Field Artillery Regiment (2.95-inch Gun) (Pack) (Philippine Scouts)

Battery A active with remainder of 1st Battalion activated 14 Mar 41 as part of the Philippine Division at Ft Stotsenberg Philippines; surrendered to Japanese forces on Bataan 9 Apr 42.

Campaigns: *Philippine Islands*

24th Field Artillery Regiment (75mm Gun) (Truck-D) (Philippine Scouts)

Stationed at Ft Stotsenberg Philippines as part of the Philippine Division and surrendered to Japanese forces on Bataan 9 Apr 42.

Campaigns: *Philippine Islands*

25th Field Artillery Regiment (75mm Gun) (Truck-D)

2nd Battalion active at Henry Barracks Puerto Rico where redesignated as 25th Field Artillery Battalion 30 Dec 40.

26th Field Artillery Regiment (75mm Gun) (Truck-D)

1 Aug 40 activated at Ft Bragg N.C. and assigned to 9th Division where redesignated as 26th Field Artillery Battalion 1 Oct 40.

28th Field Artillery Regiment (155mm How) (Truck-D)

1 Jun 40 activated at Cp Jackson S.C. and assigned to 8th Division where it was redesignated 28th Field Artillery Battalion 1 Oct 40.

No Distinctive
Insignia Authorized

29th Field Artillery Regiment (75mm Gun) (Truck-D)

1 Aug 40 activated at Ft Benning Ga and assigned to 4th Division where it was redesignated 29th Field Artillery Battalion 1 Oct 40.

No Distinctive
Insignia Authorized

30th Field Artillery Regiment (155mm How) (Truck-D)

4 Jun 41 activated at Cp Roberts Calif and assigned to 26th FA Bde and III Corps; moved to San Jose Calif 11 Dec 41, Los Gatos Calif 12 Dec 41, Orange Calif 5 Jan 42; departed San Francisco P/E 26 May 42 and arrived at Ft Greely Alaska 31 May 42; departed Alaska 13 Apr 44 and returned to San Francisco P/E 20 Apr 44; transferred to Ft Lawton Wash 20 Apr 44; relocated to Cp Pickett Va where redesignated HHB, 30th Field Artillery Brigade 18 May 44 and 1st and 2nd Bns redesignated 521st and 550th Field Artillery Battalions, respectively.

Campaigns: *Aleutian Islands*

No Distinctive
Insignia Authorized

31st Field Artillery Regiment (155mm How) (Truck-D)

1 Jul 40 activated at Cp Ord Calif and assigned to 7th Division where redesignated as 31st Field Artillery Battalion 1 Oct 40.

No Distinctive
Insignia Authorized

34th Field Artillery Regiment

1 Aug 40 activated at Ft Bragg N.C. where redesignated 34th Field Artillery Battalion 1 Oct 40.

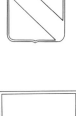

35th Field Artillery Regiment (155mm Gun) (Motorized)

10 Feb 41 activated at Cp Blanding Fla and assigned to 74th FA Bde and IV Army Corps; transferred to Cp Shelby Miss 27 Mar 42 where redesignated HHB, 35th Field Artillery Group 1 Mar 43. 1st and 2nd Bns redesignated 976th and 977th Field Artillery Battalions, respectively.

36th Field Artillery Regiment (155mm Gun) (Motorized)

10 Oct 39 activated at Ft Bragg N.C. and attached to I Army Corps; departed New York P/E 10 Aug 42 and arrived in Scotland 17 Aug 42; departed England 25 Nov 42 and landed in North Africa 8 Dec 42; landed completely at Sicily 8 Aug 43; landed in Italy 21 Sep 43; assaulted Anzio Italy 22 Jan 44; redesignated in Pantano Italy as HHB, 36th Field Artillery Group 5 Mar 44. 1st and 2nd Bns redesignated 36th and 633rd Field Artillery Battalions, respectively.

Campaigns: *Tunisia, Sicily, Naples-Foggia, Rome-Arno, Anzio*

40th Field Artillery Regiment (155mm How) (Truck-D)

4 Jun 41 activated at Cp Roberts Calif and assigned 26th FA Bde and III Army Corps; later assigned 14th FA Bde; arrived at Cp Forrest Tenn 13 Jul 42 where redesignated HHB, 40th Field Artillery Group 1 Mar 43. 1st and 2nd Bns redesignated 974th and 975th Field Artillery Battalions, respectively.

No Distinctive
Insignia Authorized

47th Field Artillery Regiment (105mm How) (Truck-D)

1 Jun 41 activated at Ft Bragg N.C. and assigned First Army; 2nd Bn detached to Cp Gordon Ga 29 Dec 41; regiment redesignated as 47th Field Artillery Battalion, less 2nd Bn which was redesignated 44th Field Artillery Battalion 26 Jan 42.

No Distinctive
Insignia Authorized

65th Field Artillery Regiment (105mm How) (Armored)

1 Oct 41 activated at Ft Knox Ky where redesignated 65th Armored Field Artillery Battalion 1 Jan 42.

66th Field Artillery Regiment (105mm How) (Armored)

15 Apr 41 activated at Pine Camp N.Y. and assigned 4th Armored Division where redesignated 66th Armored Field Artillery Battalion 1 Jan 42.

67th Field Artillery Regiment (105mm How) (Armored)

15 Apr 41 activated at Cp Beauregard La and assigned 3rd Armored Division; moved to Cp Polk La 11 Jun 41 where redesignated 67th Armored Field Artillery Battalion 1 Jan 42.

68th Field Artillery Regiment (105mm How) (Armored)

1 Mar 40 activated at Ft Knox Ky and assigned 1st Armored Division 15 Jul 40 where redesignated 68th Armored Field Artillery Battalion 1 Jan 42.

72nd Field Artillery Regiment (105mm How) (Truck-D)

1 Jun 41 activated at Ft Bragg N.C. and assigned First Army; arrived at Ft Sill Okla 13 Feb 42; departed New York P/E 4 Mar 42 and landed on New Caledonia 9 Apr 42; assigned to Americal Division 24 May 42; inactivated there 15 Aug 42.

Campaigns: *Pacific Theater without inscription*

76th Field Artillery Regiment

Stationed at Ft Francis E. Warren Wyo as part of 3rd Division; assigned GHQ Reserve 16 Oct 39; moved to Presidio of Monterey Calif 17 May 40; arrived at Ft Lewis Wash 5 Aug 40; transferred to Ft Ord Calif 1 Sep 40 where redesignated 76th Field Artillery Battalion 22 Jan 41.

77th Field Artillery Regiment (155mm How) (Truck-D)

Stationed at Ft D. A. Russell Tex under 4th Division; assigned to 18th FA Bde and VIII Army Corps and moved to Cp Bowie Tex on 27 Jan 42; departed New York P/E 7 Feb 43 and landed in North Africa on 19 Feb 43; assaulted Licata Sicily 9–11 Jul 43 and landed in Italy 29 Oct 43 where redesignated HHB, 77th Field Artillery Group on 24 Feb 44. 1st and 2nd Battalions redesignated 634 and 631st Field Artillery Battalions, respectively.

Campaigns: *Sicily, Naples-Foggia, Rome-Arno, Anzio*

79th Field Artillery Regiment (240mm How) (Motorized)

1 Jun 41 activated at Ft Bragg N.C. and assigned to the 12th FA Bde, First Army, and later to 22nd FA Bde, Second Army; redesignated there as HHB, 79th Field Artillery Group on 23 Feb 43. 1st and 2nd Battalions redesignated 697th and 698th Field Artillery Battalions, respectively.

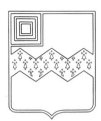

80th Field Artillery Regiment (155mm How) (Truck-D)

12 Oct 39 activated at Ft Lewis Wash and assigned to the 6th Division on 16 Oct 39; arrived at Ft Des Moines Iowa 31 May 40 where redesignated 80th Field Artillery Battalion on 1 Oct 40.

No Distinctive
Insignia Authorized

81st Field Artillery Regiment

1 Jul 40 activated at Ft Lewis Wash where redesignated 81st Field Artillery Battalion on 16 Dec 40.

82nd Field Artillery Regiment (75mm Gun) (Horse-D)

Stationed at Ft Bliss Tex as part of the 1st Cavalry Division where redesignated the 82nd Field Artillery Battalion on 3 Jan 41.

83rd Field Artillery Regiment (75mm Gun) (Horse-D)

1 Jun 40 activated at Ft Benning Ga and arrived Ft Jackson S.C. 19 Oct 40 where it was redesignated the 83rd Field Artillery Battalion on 16 Dec 40.

No Distinctive
Insignia Authorized

86th Field Artillery Regiment (155mm Gun) (Philippine Scouts)

See 86th Field Artillery Battalion.

Campaigns: *Philippine Islands*

No Distinctive
Insignia Authorized

87th Field Artillery Regiment

15 Jul 40 1st Battalion activated at Ft William E. Davis Panama Canal Zone where it was redesignated the 87th Field Artillery Battalion on 16 Dec 40.

No Distinctive
Insignia Authorized

88th Field Artillery Regiment (75mm Gun) (Philippine Scouts)

19 Apr 41 partially activated at Ft Stotsenberg Philippines and surrendered to Japanese forces on Bataan 9 Apr 42.

Campaigns: *Philippine Islands*

99th Field Artillery Regiment (75mm How) (Pack)

31 Jul 40 activated at Ft Hoyle Md where it was redesignated 99th Field Artillery Battalion 16 Dec 40, less 2nd Bn which was redesignated 98th Field Artillery Battalion at Ft Lewis Wash 13 Jan 41.

101st Field Artillery Regiment (75mm Gun) (Truck-D)   Massachusetts National Guard

16 Jan 41 inducted into federal service at Boston Mass as part of 51st FA Bde, 26th Division; arrived at Cp Edwards Mass 24 Jan 41 where Hq inactivated 12 Feb 42. 1st and 2nd Bns redesignated 101st and 212th Field Artillery Battalions, respectively, 3 Feb 42.

102nd Field Artillery Regiment (75mm Gun) (Truck-D)   Massachusetts National Guard

16 Jan 41 inducted into federal service at Salem Mass as part of 51st FA Bde, 26th Division; arrived at Cp Edwards Mass 25 Jan 41 where Hq disbanded 12 Feb 42. 1st and 2nd Bns redesignated 211th and 102nd Field Artillery Battalions, respectively, 3 Feb 42.

103rd Field Artillery Regiment (75mm Gun) (Truck-D)   Rhode Island National Guard

24 Feb 41 inducted into federal service at Providence R.I. as part of 68th FA Bde, 43rd Division; arrived at Cp Blanding Fla 17 Mar 41 where Hq disbanded 20 Feb 42. 1st and 2nd Bns redesignated 103rd and 169th Field Artillery Battalions, respectively, 10 Feb 42.

104th Field Artillery Regiment (75mm Gun) (Truck-D)   New York National Guard

15 Oct 40 inducted into federal service at Jamaica N.Y. as part of 52nd FA Bde, 27th Division; transferred to Ft McClellan Ala 25 Oct 40; relocated to Ft Ord Calif 22 Jan 42; departed San Francisco P/E 10 Mar 42 and arrived in Hawaii 16 Apr 42 where Hq disbanded 30 Aug 42. 1st and 2nd Bns redesignated 249th and 104th Field Artillery Battalions, respectively, 1 Sep 42.

Campaigns: *Pacific Theater without inscription*

105th Field Artillery Regiment (75mm Gun) (Truck-D)   New York National Guard

15 Oct 40 inducted into federal service at New York N.Y. as part of 52nd FA Bde, 27th Division; transferred to Ft McClellan Ala 25 Oct 40; relocated to Ft Ord Calif 22 Jan 42; departed San Francisco P/E 30 Mar 42 and arrived in Hawaii 4 Apr 42 where HHB disbanded at Ft Shafter 1 Sep 42. 1st and 2nd Bns redesignated 226th and 105th Field Artillery Battalions, respectively, 1 Sep 42.

Campaigns: *Pacific Theater without inscription*

106th Field Artillery Regiment (155mm How) (Truck-D)   New York National Guard

15 Oct 40 inducted into federal service at Buffalo N.Y. as part of 52nd FA Bde, 27th Division; transferred to Ft McClellan Ala 25 Oct 40; relocated to Ft Ord Calif 22 Jan 42; departed San Francisco P/E 29 Mar 42 and arrived in Hawaii 9 Apr 42 where HHB redesignated HHB, 225th Field Artillery Regiment 1 Sep 42 and 1st and 2nd Bns redesignated 106th Field Artillery Battalion and 1st Battalion, 225th Field Artillery Regiment, respectively.

Campaigns: *Pacific Theater without inscription*

107th Field Artillery Regiment (75mm Gun) (Truck-D)   Pennsylvania National Guard

17 Feb 41 inducted into federal service at Pittsburgh Pa as part of 53rd FA Bde, 28th Division; moved to Indiantown Gap Mil Res Pa 26 Feb 41; arrived at Cp Beauregard La 22 Jan 42 where HHB disbanded 7 Feb 42. 1st and 2nd Bns redesignated 107th and 229th Field Artillery Battalions, respectively.

108th Field Artillery Regiment (155mm How) (Truck-D)   Pennsylvania National Guard

17 Feb 41 inducted into federal service at Philadelphia Pa as part of 53rd FA Bde, 28th Division; moved to Indiantown Gap Mil Res Pa 26 Feb 41; arrived at Cp Beauregard La 22 Jan 42 where HHB redesignated HHB, 193rd FA Regiment 7 Feb 42. 1st and 2nd Bns redesignated 1st Battalion, 193rd FA Regiment and 108th Field Artillery Battalion, respectively.

109th Field Artillery Regiment (75mm Gun) (Truck-D)   Pennsylvania National Guard

17 Feb 41 inducted into federal service at Wilkes-Barre Pa as part of 53rd FA Bde, 28th Division; moved to Indiantown Gap Mil Res Pa 26 Feb 41; arrived at Cp Livingston La 19 Jan 42 where Hq was disbanded 7 Feb 42. 1st Bn redesignated 2nd Battalion, 193rd FA Regiment and 2nd Bn (at Cp Beauregard La) redesignated 109th Field Artillery Battalion same date.

110th Field Artillery Regiment (75mm Gun) (Truck-D)   Maryland National Guard

3 Feb 41 inducted into federal service at Pikesville Md as part of 54th FA Bde, 29th Division; arrived at Ft George G. Meade Md 20 Feb 41 where Hq disbanded 28 Feb 42. 1st and 2nd Bns redesignated 110th and 224th Field Artillery Battalions, respectively.

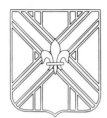

111th Field Artillery Regiment (75mm Gun) (Truck-D)   Virginia National Guard

3 Feb 41 inducted into federal service at Hampton Va as part of 54th FA Bde, 29th Division; arrived at Ft George G. Meade Md 20 Feb 41 where Hq disbanded 28 Feb 42. 1st and 2nd Bns redesignated 111th and 227th Field Artillery Battalions, respectively.

112th Field Artillery Regiment (75mm Gun) (Truck-D)   New Jersey National Guard

27 Jan 41 inducted into federal service at Trenton N.J.; moved to Ft Bragg N.C. 8 Feb 41; arrived at Ft Sill Okla 16 Mar 42 and assigned to Field Artillery School 1 May 42; transferred to Ft Jackson S.C. 22 Apr 43 where HHB redesignated HHB, 112th Field Artillery Group 1 May 43. 1st and 2nd Bns redesignated 695th and 696th Field Artillery Battalions, respectively.

113th Field Artillery Regiment (155mm How) (Truck-D)   North Carolina National Guard

16 Sep 40 inducted into federal service at Dunn N.C.; arrived at Ft Jackson S.C. 1 Oct 40 where part of 55th FA Bde, 30th Division; redesignated there as HHB, 196th FA Regiment and 1st and 2nd Bns redesignated 113th Field Artillery Battalion and 2nd Battalion, 196th FA Regiment, all on 7 Feb 42.

114th Field Artillery Regiment (155mm How) (Truck-D)   Mississippi National Guard

25 Nov 40 inducted into federal service at Greenville Miss as part of 56th FA Bde, 31st Division; arrived at Cp Blanding Fla 21 Dec 40 where HHB redesignated HHB, 137th FA Regiment 10 Feb 42. 1st and 2nd Bns redesignated 114th Field Artillery Battalion and 1st Battalion, 137th FA Regiment, respectively.

No Distinctive
Insignia Authorized

115th Field Artillery Regiment (75mm Gun) (Truck-D)   Tennessee National Guard

16 Sep 40 inducted into federal service at Memphis Tenn as part of 55th FA Bde, 30th Division; arrived at Ft Jackson S.C. 26 Sep 40 where HHB disbanded 7 Feb 42 and 1st and 2nd Bns redesignated 115th Field Artillery Battalion and 1st Battalion, 196th FA Regiment, respectively.

116th Field Artillery Regiment (75mm Gun) (Truck-D)   Florida National Guard

25 Nov 40 inducted into federal service at St. Petersburg Fla as part of 56th FA Bde, 31st Division; arrived at Cp Blanding Fla 19 Dec 40 where 1st and 2nd Bns redesignated 10 Feb 42 as 116th and 149th Field Artillery Battalions, respectively. Regimental HHB moved to Cp Bowie Tex 24 Feb 42 where disbanded 27 Feb 42.

117th Field Artillery Regiment (75mm Gun) (Truck-D)　　Alabama National Guard

25 Nov 40 inducted into federal service at Florala Ala as part of 56th FA Bde, 31st Division; arrived at Cp Blanding Fla 17 Dec 40 where 1st and 2nd Bns redesignated 117th Field Artillery Battalion and 2nd Battalion, 137th FA Regiment respectively. Regimental Hq moved to Cp Bowie Tex 23 Feb 42 where disbanded 27 Feb 42.

118th Field Artillery Regiment (75mm Gun) (Truck-D)　　Georgia National Guard

16 Sep 40 inducted into federal service at Savannah Ga as part of 55th FA Bde, 30th Division; arrived at Ft Jackson S.C. 27 Sep 40 where Hq inactivated 7 Feb 42. 1st and 2nd Bns redesignated 118th and 230th Field Artillery Battalions, respectively.

119th Field Artillery Regiment (155mm Gun) (Motorized)　　Michigan National Guard

7 Apr 41 inducted into federal service at Lansing Mich; arrived at Ft Knox Ky 17 Apr 41; transferred to Ft Leonard Wood Mo 2 Jun 41 and assigned 72nd FA Bde, XI Corps; redesignated there HHB, 119th Field Artillery Group 8 Feb 43. 1st and 2nd Bns redesignated 978th and 979th Field Artillery Battalions, respectively.

120th Field Artillery Regiment (75mm Gun) (Truck-D)　　Wisconsin National Guard

15 Oct 40 inducted into federal service at Superior Wis as part of 57th FA Bde, 32nd Division; transferred to Cp Beauregard La 25 Oct 40; arrived at Cp Livingston La 14 Feb 41 where regiment, less 2nd Bn, redesignated 120th Field Artillery Battalion 31 Jan 42. 2nd Bn redesignated 129th Field Artillery Battalion.

121st Field Artillery Regiment (155mm How) (Truck-D)　　Wisconsin National Guard

15 Oct 40 inducted into federal service at Abbotsford Wis as part of 57th FA Bde, 32nd Division; transferred to Cp Beauregard La 25 Oct 40; arrived at Cp Livingston La 13 Feb 41; 1st Bn relocated to Ft Devens Mass 4 Jan 42; redesignated HHB, 173rd FA Regiment at Cp Livingston La 16 Jan 42. 1st and 2nd Bns redesignated 121st Field Artillery Battalion and 2nd Battalion, 173rd FA Regiment, respectively.

122nd Field Artillery Regiment (75mm Gun) (Truck-D)　　Illinois National Guard

5 Mar 41 inducted into federal service at Chicago Ill as part of 58th FA Bde, 33rd Division; arrived at Cp Forrest Tenn 15 Mar 41 where HHB disbanded 21 Feb 42. 1st and 2nd Bns redesignated 122nd and 210th Field Artillery Battalions, respectively.

123rd Field Artillery Regiment (155mm How) (Truck-D)   Illinois National Guard

5 Mar 41 inducted into federal service at Monmouth Ill as part of 58th FA Bde, 33rd Division; arrived at Cp Forrest Tenn 18 Mar 41; relocated to Cp Robinson Ark 16 Aug 41 where HHB redesignated HHB, 208th FA Regiment 12 Feb 42. 1st and 2nd Bns redesignated 123rd Field Artillery Battalion and 2nd Battalion, 200th FA Regiment, respectively. The 2nd Battalion had been detached and had departed New York P/E 23 Jan 42 and was redesignated en route to New Caledonia.

124th Field Artillery Regiment (75mm Gun) (Truck-D)   Illinois National Guard

5 Mar 41 inducted into federal service at Chicago Ill as part of 58th FA Bde, 33rd Division; arrived at Cp Forrest Tenn 17 Mar 41 where Hq disbanded 12 Feb 42. 1st Bn redesignated 1st Battalion, 208th FA Regiment at Arkadelphia Ark and 2nd Bn redesignated 124th Field Artillery Battalion same date.

125th Field Artillery Regiment (75mm Gun) (Truck-D)   Minnesota National Guard

10 Feb 41 inducted into federal service at Duluth Minn as part of 59th FA Bde, 34th Division; transferred to Cp Claiborne La 5 Mar 41; arrived at Ft Dix N.J. 10 Jan 42 where Hq disbanded 30 Jan 42. 1st and 2nd Bns redesignated 125th Field Artillery Battalion and 2nd Battalion, 194th FA Regiment, respectively.

No Distinctive
Insignia Authorized

126th Field Artillery Regiment (75mm Gun) (Truck-D)   Wisconsin National Guard

15 Oct 40 inducted into federal service at Green Bay Wis as part of 57th FA Bde, 32nd Division; transferred to Cp Beauregard La 22 Oct 40; arrived at Cp Livingston La 14 Feb 41 where redesignated, less 2nd Bn, as 126th Field Artillery Battalion 31 Jan 42. 2nd Bn redesignated 1st Battalion, 173rd FA Regiment 16 Jan 42.

127th Field Artillery Regiment (155mm How) (Truck-D)   Kansas National Guard

23 Dec 40 inducted into federal service at Topeka Kans as part of 60th FA Bde, 35th Division; moved to Cp Joseph T. Robinson Ark 4 Jan 41; transferred to Ft Ord Calif 23 Dec 41; arrived at Cp San Luis Obispo Calif 17 Jan 42 where Hq disbanded 22 Mar 42. 1st and 2nd Bns redesignated 1st Battalion, 195th FA Regiment and 127th Field Artillery Battalion on 3 Feb 42.

128th Field Artillery Regiment (75mm Gun) (Truck-D)   Missouri National Guard

25 Nov 40 inducted into federal service at Columbia Mo; moved to Ft Jackson S.C. 10 Dec 40 and assigned to First Army; relocated to Cp Blanding Fla 3 Dec 41; arrived at Cp Chaffee Ark 15 Sep 42 where inactivated, less 1st Battalion, on 26 Sep 42. 1st Bn redesignated 128th Armored Field Artillery Battalion.

130th Field Artillery Regiment (75mm Gun) (Truck-D)   Kansas National Guard

23 Dec 40 inducted into federal service at Topeka Kans as part of 60th FA Bde, 35th Division; moved to Cp Joseph T. Robinson Ark 5 Jan 41; relocated to Ft Ord Calif 19 Dec 41; arrived at Cp San Luis Obispo Calif 17 Jan 42 where HHB disbanded 3 Feb 42. 1st and 2nd Bns redesignated 130th and 154th Field Artillery Battalions, respectively.

131st Field Artillery Regiment (75mm Gun) (Truck-D)   Texas National Guard

25 Nov 40 inducted into federal service at Plainview Tex as part of 61st FA Bde, 36th Division; arrived at Cp Bowie Tex 11 Jan 41; 2nd Bn detached and sent to San Francisco P/E which departed 21 Nov 41 and arrived in Australia, deployed to Malang Java where surrendered 8 Mar 42 to Japanese forces; regimental Hq disbanded at Cp Bowie Tex 31 Jan 42. 1st Bn redesignated 131st Field Artillery Battalion there.

Campaigns: *East Indies* (2nd Battalion only)

132nd Field Artillery Regiment (75mm Gun) (Truck-D)   Texas National Guard

25 Nov 40 inducted into federal service at Corsicana Tex as part of 61st FA Bde, 36th Division; arrived at Cp Bowie Tex 10 Jan 41 where HHB disbanded 31 Jan 42. 1st and 2nd Bns redesignated 132nd and 155th Field Artillery Battalions.

133rd Field Artillery Regiment (155mm How) (Truck-D)   Texas National Guard

25 Nov 40 inducted into federal service at San Antonio Tex as part of 61st FA Bde, 36th Division; arrived at Cp Bowie Tex 11 Jan 41 where Hq disbanded 31 Jan 42. 1st and 2nd Bns redesignated 133rd Field Artillery Battalion and 2nd Battalion, 202nd FA Regiment, respectively.

134th Field Artillery Regiment (75mm Gun) (Truck-D)   Ohio National Guard

15 Oct 40 inducted into federal service at Columbus Ohio as part of 62nd FA Bde, 37th Division; arrived at Cp Shelby Miss 24 Oct 40 where redesignated, less 2nd Battalion, as 134th Field Artillery Battalion 16 Jan 42. 2nd Bn redesignated 140th Field Artillery Battalion.

135th Field Artillery Regiment (75mm Gun) (Truck-D)   Ohio National Guard

15 Oct 40 inducted into federal service at Cleveland Ohio as part of 62nd FA Bde, 37th Division; arrived at Cp Shelby Miss 25 Oct 40 where redesignated, less 2nd Battalion, as 135th Field Artillery Battalion 16 Jan 42. 2nd Bn redesignated 1st Battalion, 174th FA Regiment.

136th Field Artillery Regiment (155mm How) (Truck-D)   Ohio National Guard

15 Oct 40 inducted into federal service at Columbus Ohio as part of 62nd FA Bde, 37th Division; arrived at Cp Shelby Miss 26 Oct 40 where HHB redesignated HHB, 174th FA Regiment 16 Jan 41. 1st and 2nd Bns redesignated 136th Field Artillery Battalion and 2nd Battalion, 174th FA Regiment, respectively.

No Distinctive
Insignia Authorized

137th Field Artillery Regiment (155mm How) (Truck-D)

10 Feb 42 redesignated from HHB, 114th Field Artillery at Cp Blanding Fla. 1st Bn formerly 2nd Bn, 114th FA and 2nd Bn formerly 2nd Bn, 117th FA; arrived at Cp Bowie Tex 25 Feb 42 and assigned to 16th FA Bde, X Corps; arrived at Cp Gruber Okla 25 Aug 42 where HHB redesignated HHB, 137th Field Artillery Group 8 Feb 43. 1st and 2nd Bns redesignated 932nd and 933rd Field Artillery Battalions, respectively.

138th Field Artillery Regiment (75mm Gun) (Truck-D)   Kentucky National Guard

17 Jan 41 inducted into federal service at Louisville as part of 63rd FA Bde, 38th Division; arrived at Cp Shelby Miss 29 Jan 41 where HHB inactivated 10 Feb 42. 1st Bn redesignated 138th Field Artillery Battalion. 2nd Bn detached and departed San Francisco P/E 3 Dec 41; arrived in Hawaii 21 Dec 41 where redesignated 198th Field Artillery Battalion 10 Feb 42.

Campaigns: *Pacific Theater without inscription*

139th Field Artillery Regiment (75mm Gun) (Truck-D)   Indiana National Guard

17 Jan 41 inducted into federal service at Indianapolis Ind as part of 63rd FA Bde, 38th Division; arrived at Cp Shelby Miss 1 Feb 41 where Hq disbanded 10 Feb 42. 1st and 2nd Bns redesignated 139th and 163rd Field Artillery Battalions, respectively.

141st Field Artillery Regiment (155mm How) (Truck-D)   Louisiana National Guard

13 Jan 41 inducted into federal service at New Orleans La; arrived at Cp Shelby Miss 20 Jan 41 where assigned to V Army Corps; transferred to Cp Sutton N.C. 23 Mar 42 and assigned to 73rd FA Bde and VII Corps; arrived at Cp Blanding Fla 15 Oct 42 where HHB redesignated HHB, 141st Field Artillery Group 7 Mar 43. 1st and 2nd Bns redesignated 934th and 935th Field Artillery Battalions, respectively.

142nd Field Artillery Regiment (155mm How) (Truck-D)   Arkansas National Guard

6 Jan 41 inducted into federal service at Texarkana Ark; transferred to Ft Sill Okla 17 Jan 41 and assigned to 18th FA Bde and VIII Corps; arrived at Cp Bowie Tex 5 Feb 42 where HHB redesignated HHB, 142nd Field Artillery Group 8 Feb 43. 1st and 2nd Bns designated 936th and 937th Field Artillery Battalions, respectively. 3rd Bn had been disbanded 25 Jan 41 at Ft Sill Okla.

143rd Field Artillery Regiment (75mm Gun) (Truck-D)   California National Guard

3 Mar 41 inducted into federal service at Stockton Calif as part of 65th FA Bde, 40th Division; arrived at Cp San Luis Obispo Calif 16 Mar 41 where HHB redesignated HHB, 204th FA Regiment 5 Feb 42. 1st and 2nd Bns redesignated 143rd and 164th Field Artillery Battalions, respectively.

144th Field Artillery Regiment (155mm Gun) (Motorized)   California National Guard

3 Feb 41; inducted into federal service at Santa Barbara Calif; transferred to Ft Lewis Wash 18 Feb 41 and assigned to 76th FA Bde and IX Army Corps; there redesignated HHB, 144th Field Artillery Group 8 Feb 43. 1st and 2nd Bns redesignated 980th and 981st Field Artillery Battalions, respectively.

145th Field Artillery Regiment (75mm Gun) (Truck-D)   Utah National Guard

3 Mar 41 inducted into federal service at Salt Lake City Utah as part of 65th FA Bde, 40th Division; transferred to Cp San Luis Obispo Calif 18 Mar 41; regiment, less 1st Bn, departed San Francisco P/E 12 Dec 41 and arrived in Hawaii 17 Dec 41 where HHB disbanded 6 Jun 42. 1st Bn redesignated 213th Field Artillery Battalion in El Cajon Calif 24 Mar 42 while 2nd Bn redesignated 145th Field Artillery Battalion in Hawaii 6 Jun 42.

Campaigns: *Pacific Theater without inscription*

146th Field Artillery Regiment (75mm Gun) (Truck-D)   Washington National Guard

16 Sep 40 inducted into federal service at Seattle Wash as part of 66th FA Bde, 41st Division; transferred to Cp Murray Wash 23 Sep 40; arrived at Ft Lewis Wash 20 Mar 41 where Hq disbanded 14 Feb 42. 1st and 2nd Bns redesignated 146th and 167th Field Artillery Battalions, respectively.

147th Field Artillery Regiment (75mm Gun) (Truck-D)   South Dakota National Guard

25 Nov 40 inducted into federal service at Sioux Falls S.D.; transferred to Ft Ord Calif 8 Dec 40 and assigned to Fourth Army; re-equipped with 105mm How; departed San Francisco P/E 22 Nov 41 and arrived in Australia 23 Dec 41; landed 6 Aug 43 in New Guinea; HHB returned to Australia and redesignated HHB, I Corps Artillery 18 Jan 44. 1st and 2nd Bns redesignated 260th and 147th Field Artillery Battalions on 31 Dec 43, respectively.

Campaigns: *New Guinea*

148th Field Artillery Regiment (75mm Gun) (Truck-D)   Idaho National Guard

16 Sep 40 inducted into federal service at Coeur d'Alene Idaho as part of 65th FA Bde, 41st Division; transferred to Cp Murray Wash 24 Sep 40; arrived at Ft Lewis Wash 20 Mar 41; departed San Francisco P/E, less 2nd Bn, 21 Nov 41 and arrived in Australia 6 Jan 42; departed Darwin Australia 16–18 Feb 42 but convoy returned to Australia where HHB disbanded 17 Jun 42. 1st Bn redesignated 148th Field Artillery Battalion. 2nd Bn, which moved from Ft Lewis Wash to Port Angeles Wash 28 Dec 41 redesignated there as 205th Field Artillery Battalion 14 Feb 42.

Campaigns: *Pacific Theater without inscription*

150th Field Artillery Regiment (155mm How) (Truck-D)   Indiana National Guard

17 Jan 41 inducted into federal service at Indianapolis Ind as part of 63rd FA Bde, 38th Division; arrived at Cp Shelby Miss 29 Jan 41 where Hq disbanded 10 Feb 42. 1st and 2nd Bns redesignated 150th Field Artillery Battalion and 2nd Battalion, 208th FA Regiment, respectively. 3rd Bn disbanded 18 Feb 41.

151st Field Artillery Regiment (75mm Gun) (Truck-D)   Minnesota National Guard

10 Feb 41 inducted into federal service at Minneapolis Minn as part of 59th FA Bde, 34th Division; transferred to Cp Claiborne La 6 Mar 41; arrived at Ft Dix N.J. 10 Jan 42 where Hq disbanded 30 Jan 42. 1st Bn departed New York P/E 14 Jan 42 and arrived in Northern Ireland 25 Jan 42 where redesignated 151st Field Artillery Battalion 30 Jan 42. 2nd Bn redesignated at Ft Dix as 175th Field Artillery Battalion 30 Jan 42.

152nd Field Artillery Regiment (75mm Gun) (Truck-D)   Maine National Guard

24 Feb 41 inducted into federal service at Bangor Maine as part of 68th FA Bde, 43rd Division; transferred to Cp Blanding Fla 14 Mar 41 where 1st and 2nd Bns redesignated 1st Battalion, 203rd FA Regiment and 152nd Field Artillery Battalion respectively on 10 Feb 42; HHB arrived at Cp Shelby Miss 14 Feb 42 where redesignated HHB, 203rd Field Artillery Regiment 19 Feb 42.

156th Field Artillery Regiment (75mm Gun) (Truck-D)   New York National Guard

16 Sep 40 inducted into federal service at Newburgh N.Y. as part of 69th FA Bde, 44th Division; transferred to Ft Dix N.J. 25 Sep 40; arrived at Cp Claiborne La 16 Jan 42 where HHB disbanded 16 Feb 42. 1st and 2nd Bns redesignated 156th and 170th Field Artillery Battalions, respectively.

157th Field Artillery Regiment (155mm How) (Truck-D)   New Jersey National Guard

16 Sep 40 inducted into federal service at Camden N.J. as part of 69th FA Bde, 44th Division; transferred to Ft Dix N.J. 18 Sep 40; arrived at Cp Claiborne La 16 Jan 42 where Hq disbanded 20 Feb 42. 1st Bn redesignated 1st Battalion, 228th FA Regiment there 20 May 42. 2nd Bn had been disbanded Ft Dix N.J. 7 Jan 41. 3rd Bn had been redesignated 2nd Bn 6 Jan 41 and was redesignated 157th Field Artillery Battalion at Cp Claiborne La 20 Feb 42.

158th Field Artillery Regiment (75mm How) (Truck-D)   Oklahoma National Guard

16 Sep 40 inducted into federal service at Anadarko Okla as part of 70th FA Bde, 45th Division; arrived at Ft Sill Okla 24 Sep 40 where HHB disbanded 22 Feb 42. 1st Bn redesignated there as 158th Field Artillery Battalion 11 Feb 42. 2nd Bn had transferred to Cp Barkeley Tex 7 Mar 41 and departed New Orleans P/E 29 Dec 41, arriving in Canal Zone 6 Jan 42 where redesignated 207th Field Artillery Battalion 11 Feb 42.

160th Field Artillery Regiment (75mm Gun) (Truck-D)   Oklahoma National Guard

16 Sep 40 inducted into federal service at Tulsa Okla as part of 70th FA Bde, 45th Division; transferred to Ft Sill Okla 24 Sep 40; arrived at Cp Barkeley Tex 28 Jan 41 where HHB disbanded 22 Feb 42. 1st and 2nd Bns redesignated 160th and 171st Field Artillery Battalions, respectively.

161st Field Artillery Regiment (75mm Gun) (Truck-D)   Kansas National Guard

23 Dec 40 inducted into federal service at Topeka Kans as part of 60th FA Bde, 35th Division; transferred to Cp Joseph T. Robinson Ark 4 Jan 41; relocated to Ft Ord Calif 24 Dec 41; arrived at Cp San Luis Obispo Calif 17 Jan 42 where HHB redesignated HHB, 195th FA Regiment 3 Feb 42. 1st and 2nd Battalions redesignated 161st Field Artillery Battalion and 2nd Battalion, 195th FA Regiment, respectively.

No Distinctive
Insignia Authorized

162nd Field Artillery Regiment (75mm Gun) (Truck-D)   Puerto Rico National Guard

15 Oct 40 1st Bn only inducted into federal service at Henry Barracks, Puerto Rico where redesignated 162nd Field Artillery Battalion 31 May 42.

Campaigns: *American Theater without inscription*

No Distinctive
Insignia Authorized

165th Field Artillery Regiment (75mm Gun) (Truck-D)   New Jersey National Guard

16 Sep 40 inducted into federal service at East Orange N.J. as part of 69th FA Bde, 44th Division; transferred to Ft Dix N.J. 24 Sep 40; arrived at Cp Claiborne La 16 Jan 42 where Hq disbanded 20 Feb 42. 1st Bn, which had moved from Ft Dix N.J. 3 Jan 42 and arrived at Ft Hancock N.J. 3 Jan 42, redesignated there as 199th Field Artillery Battalion 20 Feb 42. 2nd Bn redesignated 165th Field Artillery Battalion at Cp Claiborne La same date.

166th Field Artillery Regiment (155mm How) (Truck-D)   Pennsylvania National Guard

13 Jan 41 inducted into federal service at Philadelphia Pa; relocated to Cp Shelby Miss 23 Jan 41 and assigned to V Army Corps; transferred to Cp Sutton N.C. 23 Mar 42 and assigned to 73rd FA Bde and VII Corps; arrived at Cp Blanding Fla 15 Oct 42 where HHB redesignated HHB, 166th Field Artillery Group 7 Mar 43. 1st Bn redesignated 938th Field Artillery Battalion, and 2nd Bn, which moved to Ft Sill Okla 15 Dec 42 from Cp Blanding Fla, redesignated 939th Field Artillery Battalion.

168th Field Artillery Regiment (155mm Gun) (Motorized)   Colorado National Guard

24 Feb 41 inducted into federal service at Denver Colo; arrived Cp Forrest Tenn 11 Mar 41 and assigned to VII Army Corps; assigned to 75th FA Bde; transferred to Cp Roberts Calif 28 Dec 41 and assigned to II Armored Corps; arrived at Cp San Luis Obispo Calif 2 Feb 42 where HHB redesignated HHB 168th Field Artillery Group 1 Mar 43. 1st and 2nd Bns redesignated 8 Feb 43 as 168th and 983rd Field Artillery Battalions, respectively.

172nd Field Artillery Regiment (155mm How) (Truck-D) New Hampshire National Guard

24 Feb 41 inducted into federal service at Manchester N.H.; transferred to Cp Blanding Fla 14 Feb 41 and assigned to IV Army Corps; arrived at Cp Shelby Miss 27 Mar 42 where HHB redesignated HHB, 172nd Field Artillery Group 1 Mar 43. 1st and 2nd Bns redesignated 172nd and 941st Field Artillery Battalions, respectively.

No Distinctive
Insignia Authorized

173rd Field Artillery Regiment (155mm Gun) (Motorized)

16 Jan 42 redesignated from HHB 121st Field Artillery at Cp Livingston La; 1st Bn formerly 2nd Bn, 126th FA and 2nd Bn formerly 2nd Bn, 121st FA; arrived at Cp Gruber Okla 12 Aug 42 and assigned to 16th FA Bde and X Corps where HHB redesignated HHB 173rd Field Artillery Group 8 Feb 43. 1st and 2nd Bns redesignated 173rd and 985th Field Artillery Battalions, respectively.

No Distinctive
Insignia Authorized

174th Field Artillery Regiment (155mm Gun) (Motorized)

16 Jan 42 redesignated from HHB 136th Field Artillery at Cp Shelby Miss; 1st Bn formerly 2nd Bn, 135th FA and 2nd Bn formerly 2nd Bn, 136 FA; arrived at Cp Bowie Tex and assigned to 18th FA Bde and VIII Corps where HHB redesignated as HHB 174th Field Artillery Group 25 Feb 43. 1st and 2nd Bns redesignated 174th and 987th Field Artillery Battalions, respectively.

176th Field Artillery Regiment (155mm How) (Truck-D)   Pennsylvania National Guard

3 Feb 41 inducted into federal service at Pittsburgh Pa as part of 54th FA Bde, 29th Division; arrived at Ft George G. Meade Md 20 Feb 41 where HHB redesignated HHB, 228th FA Regiment 28 Feb 42. 1st and 2nd Bns redesignated 176th Field Artillery Battalion and 2nd Battalion, 228th FA Regiment, respectively.

No Distinctive
Insignia Authorized

177th Field Artillery Regiment (155mm How) (Truck-D)   Michigan National Guard

7 Apr 41 inducted into federal service at Detroit Mich; transferred to Ft Knox Ky 19 Apr 41 and assigned to Second Army; arrived at Ft Leonard Wood Mo 2 Jun 41 and assigned to 72nd FA Bde and XI Corps where redesignated as HHB 177th Field Artillery Group 8 Feb 43. 1st and 2nd Bns redesignated 177th and 943rd Field Artillery Battalions, respectively.

178th Field Artillery Regiment (155mm How) (Truck-D)   South Carolina National Guard

27 Jan 41 inducted into federal service at Abbeville S.C.; arrived at Ft Bragg N.C. and assigned to I Army Corps; departed New York P/E 6 Aug 42 and arrived in Scotland 17 Aug 42; landed in North Africa 6 Dec 42; invaded Sicily 16 Jul 43; and landed in Italy 30 Sep 43 where HHB redesignated HHB 178th Field Artillery Group 24 Feb 44. 1st and 2nd Bns redesignated 178th and 248th Field Artillery Battalions, respectively.

Campaigns: *Tunisia, Sicily, Naples-Foggia, Rome-Arno*

179th Field Artillery Regiment (155mm How) (Truck-D)   Georgia National Guard

24 Feb 41 inducted into federal service at Atlanta Ga; sent to Cp Blanding Fla 3 Mar 41 and assigned to IV Army Corps; arrived at Cp Shelby Miss 27 Mar 43 where HHB redesignated HHB, 179th Field Artillery Group 1 Mar 43. 1st and 2nd Battalions redesignated 179th and 945th Field Artillery Battalions, respectively.

180th Field Artillery Regiment (155mm How) (Truck-D)   Massachusetts National Guard

16 Jan 41 inducted into federal service at Boston Mass as part of 51st FA Bde, 26th Division; arrived at Cp Edwards Mass 28 Jan 41 and departed New York P/E, less 2nd Bn, 23 Jan 42 and HHB was redesignated while at sea en route to New Caledonia HHB, 200th FA Regiment 3 Feb 42. In like manner 1st Bn was redesignated 1st Battalion, 200th FA Regiment. 2nd Bn redesignated 180th Field Artillery Battalion same date at Cp Edwards Mass.

Campaigns: *Pacific Theater without inscription*

181st Field Artillery Regiment (155mm How) (Truck-D)   Tennessee National Guard

24 Feb 41 inducted into federal service at Chattanooga Tenn; transferred to Cp Forrest Tenn 4 Mar 41 and assigned to VII Army Corps; arrived at Cp Roberts Calif 27 Dec 41 and assigned to 75th FA Bde and II Armored Corps; assigned to Desert Training Center there 14 Aug 42 where HHB redesignated HHB, 181st Field Artillery Group 1 Mar 43. 1st and 2nd Bns redesignated 181st and 947th Field Artillery Battalions, respectively, on 8 Feb 43.

182nd Field Artillery Regiment (155mm How) (Truck-D)   Michigan National Guard

7 Apr 41 inducted into federal service at Detroit Mich; transferred to Ft Knox Ky 18 Apr 41 and assigned to Second Army; arrived at Ft Leonard Wood Mo 2 Jun 41 and assigned to 72nd FA Bde and XI Corps; redesignated there as HHB, 182nd Field Artillery Group 1 Mar 43. 1st and 2nd Bns redesignated 182nd and 949th Field Artillery Battalions 8 Feb 43, respectively.

183rd Field Artillery Regiment (155mm How) (Truck-D)   Idaho National Guard

1 Apr 41 inducted into federal service at Boise Idaho; transferred to Ft Francis E. Warren Wyo and assigned to IX Army Corps 15 Apr 41; arrived at Ft Lewis Wash 14 Dec 41 and assigned to 76th FA Bde where HHB redesignated HHB, 183rd Field Artillery Group 8 Feb 43. 1st and 2nd Bns redesignated 183rd and 951st Field Artillery Battalions, respectively.

184th Field Artillery Regiment (155mm How) (Truck-D) (Colored)   Illinois N. G.

6 Jan 41 inducted into federal service at Chicago Ill; arrived at Ft Custer Mich 15 Jan 41 and assigned to Second Army where HHB disbanded 16 Jan 43. 1st and 2nd Bns redesignated 930th and 931st Field Artillery Battalions, respectively.

185th Field Artillery Regiment (155mm How) (Truck-D)   **Iowa National Guard**

10 Feb 41 inducted into federal service at Boone Iowa as part of 54th FA Bde, 34th Division; transferred to Cp Claiborne La 4 Mar 41; arrived at Ft Dix N.J. 10 Jan 42 where HHB redesignated HHB, 194th FA Regiment 30 Jan 42. 1st and 2nd Bns redesignated 1st Battalion, 194th FA Regiment and 185th Field Artillery Battalion, respectively.

186th Field Artillery Regiment (155mm How) (Truck-D)   **New York National Guard**

27 Jan 41 inducted into federal service at Brooklyn N.Y.; arrived at Madison Barracks N.Y. 7 Feb 41 and assigned to 71st FA Bde and VI Army Corps; arrived at Ft Ethan Allen Vt 7 Jun 41 where HHB was redesignated HHB, 186th Field Artillery Group 18 Feb 43. 1st and 2nd Bns redesignated 186th and 953rd Field Artillery Battalions, respectively.

187th Field Artillery Regiment (155mm How) (Truck-D)   **New York National Guard**

3 Feb 41 inducted into federal service at Brooklyn N.Y.; arrived at Ft Ethan Allen Vt 19 Feb 41 and assigned to 71st FA Bde and VI Army Corps; redesignated HHB there as HHB, 187th Field Artillery Group 8 Feb 43. 1st and 2nd Bns redesignated 187th and 955th Field Artillery Battalions, respectively.

No Distinctive
Insignia Authorized

188th Field Artillery Regiment (155mm How) (Truck-D)   **North Dakota National Guard**

1 Apr 41 inducted into federal service at Bismarck, N.D.; relocated to Ft Francis E. Warren Wyo 16 Apr 41 and assigned to 76th FA Bde and IX Army Corps; arrived at Ft Lewis Wash 15 Dec 41; sent to Yakima Wash 2 Nov 42 where HHB redesignated HHB, 188th Field Artillery Group 17 Feb 43. 1st and 2nd Bns redesignated 188th and 957th Field Artillery Battalions, respectively, on 8 Feb 43.

189th Field Artillery Regiment (155mm How) (Truck-D)   **Oklahoma National Guard**

16 Sep 40 inducted into federal service at Enid Okla as part of 70th FA Bde, 45th Division; transferred to Ft Sill Okla 24 Sep 40; arrived at Cp Barkeley Tex 7 Mar 41; returned, less 1st Bn, to Ft Sill Okla 25 Jan 42 where HHB redesignated HHB, 202nd FA Regiment 11 Feb 42. 1st Bn redesignated 189th Field Artillery Battalion same date at Cp Barkeley Tex. 2nd Bn redesignated 1st Bn, 202nd FA Regiment at Ft Sill Okla 11 Feb 42.

190th Field Artillery Regiment (155mm Gun) (Motorized)   **Pennsylvania National Guard**

13 Jan 41 inducted into federal service at Tyrone Pa; arrived at Cp Shelby Miss 3 Feb 41 and assigned to V Army Corps; departed New York P/E 31 Aug 42 and arrived at Northern Ireland 8 Sep 42; transferred to England 3 Jan 43 where HHB redesignated HHB, 190th Field Artillery Group 1 Nov 43. 1st and 2nd Bns redesignated 190th and 200th Field Artillery Battalions there, respectively.

Campaigns: *European Theater without inscription*

191st Field Artillery Regiment (155mm How) (Truck-D)   Tennessee National Guard

No Distinctive
Insignia Authorized

24 Feb 41 inducted into federal service at Nashville Tenn; transferred to Cp Forrest Tenn and assigned to VII Army Corps; arrived at Cp Roberts Calif 27 Jan 42 and assigned to 75th FA Bde and II Armored Corps; HHB redesignated there as HHB, 191st Field Artillery Group 8 Feb 43. 1st and 2nd Bns redesignated 191st and 959th Field Artillery Battalions, respectively.

192nd Field Artillery Regiment (155mm How) (Truck-D)   Connecticut National Guard

24 Feb 41 inducted into federal service at New London Conn as part of 68th FA Bde, 43rd Division; arrived at Cp Blanding Fla 18 Mar 41 where 1st and 2nd Bns redesignated 2nd Battalion, 203rd FA Regiment and 192nd Field Artillery Battalion, respectively, 10 Feb 42; regimental HHB sent to Cp Shelby Miss 16 Feb 42 where disbanded 20 Feb 42.

193rd Field Artillery Regiment (105mm How) (Truck-D)

No Distinctive
Insignia Authorized

7 Feb 42 redesignated from HHB, 108th Field Artillery at Cp Beauregard La; 1st Bn formerly 1st Bn, 108th FA and 2nd Bn formerly 1st Bn, 109th FA; moved to Cp Livingston La 27 Feb 42 under 22nd FA Bde and Second Army; arrived at Ft Bragg N.C. 15 Aug 42 where HHB redesignated HHB, 193rd Field Artillery Group 23 Feb 43. 1st and 2nd Bns redesignated 193rd and 688th Field Artillery Battalions, respectively.

194th Field Artillery Regiment (8-inch How) (Motorized)

No Distinctive
Insignia Authorized

30 Jan 42 redesignated from HHB, 185th Field Artillery at Ft Dix N.J.; 1st Bn formerly 1st Bn, 185th FA and 2nd Bn formerly 2nd Bn, 125th FA; assigned to 15th FA Bde and XII Army Corps; arrived at Ft Bragg N.C. 12 Mar 43 where HHB redesignated HHB, 194th Field Artillery Group 8 Feb 43. 1st and 2nd Bns redesignated 194th and 995th Field Artillery Battalions, respectively.

195th Field Artillery Regiment (8-inch How) (Motorized)

No Distinctive
Insignia Authorized

3 Feb 42 redesignated from HHB, 161st Field Artillery at Cp San Luis Obispo Calif; 1st Bn formerly 1st Bn, 127th FA and 2nd Bn formerly 2nd Bn, 161st FA; arrived at Ft Ord Calif 28 Apr 42 and assigned to II Armored Corps where HHB redesignated HHB, 195th Field Artillery Group 1 Mar 43. 1st and 2nd Bns redesignated 195th and 997th Field Artillery Battalions, respectively.

196th Field Artillery Regiment (105mm How) (Truck-D)

No Distinctive
Insignia Authorized

7 Feb 42 redesignated from HHB, 113th Field Artillery at Ft Jackson S.C.; 1st Bn formerly 2nd Bn, 115th FA and 2nd Bn formerly 2nd Bn, 113th FA; arrived at Ft Sill Okla 26 Aug 42 where assigned to Replacement and School Command there; HHB redesignated HHB, 196th Field Artillery Group 1 Mar 43. 1st and 2nd Bns redesignated 196th and 690th Field Artillery Battalions, respectively.

200th Field Artillery Regiment (155mm How) (Truck-D)

No Distinctive
Insignia Authorized

3 Feb 42 redesignated from HHB, 180th Field Artillery at sea en route to New Caledonia; 1st Bn formerly 1st Bn, 180th FA and 2nd Bn formerly 2nd Bn, 123rd FA; arrived New Caledonia 26 Feb 42 and assigned to Americal Division 24 May 42; HHB disbanded there 15 Aug 42 and 1st and 2nd Bns redesignated 221st and 223rd Field Artillery Battalions, respectively.

Campaigns: *Pacific Theater without inscription*

202nd Field Artillery Regiment (155mm How) (Truck-D)

No Distinctive
Insignia Authorized

11 Feb 42 redesignated from HHB, 189th Field Artillery at Ft Sill Okla; 1st Bn from 2nd Bn, 189th FA and 2nd Bn formerly 2nd Bn, 133rd FA; moved to Cp Barkeley Tex 22 Feb 42 and assigned to 16th FA Bde and X Corps; transferred to Cp Gruber Okla 6 Aug 42; arrived at Hornbeck La 26 Feb 43 and HHB redesignated there as HHB, 202nd Field Artillery Group 1 Mar 43. 1st and 2nd Bns redesignated 202nd and 961st Field Artillery Battalions, respectively.

203rd Field Artillery Regiment (155mm How) (Truck-D)

No Distinctive
Insignia Authorized

19 Feb 42 redesignated from HHB, 152nd Field Artillery at Cp Shelby Miss; 1st Bn formerly 1st Bn, 152nd FA and 2nd Bn formerly 1st Bn, 192nd FA; arrived at Ft Bragg N.C. and assigned to 15th FA Bde and XII Corps; HHB redesignated there as HHB, 203rd Field Artillery Group 1 Mar 43. 1st and 2nd Bns redesignated 203rd and 963rd Field Artillery Battalions, respectively.

204th Field Artillery Regiment (155mm How) (Truck-D)

No Distinctive
Insignia Authorized

5 Feb 42 redesignated from HHB, 143rd Field Artillery at Cp San Luis Obispo Calif; 1st Bn formerly 2nd Bn, 222nd FA and 2nd Bn formerly 1st Bn, 218th FA; transferred to Ft Lewis Wash 2 Apr 42; arrived at Cp Forrest Tenn 21 Dec 42 where HHB redesignated HHB, 204th Field Artillery Group; 1st and 2nd Bns redesignated 204th and 965th Field Artillery Battalions, respectively; all on 1 Mar 43.

208th Field Artillery Regiment (155mm Gun) (Motorized)

No Distinctive
Insignia Authorized

12 Feb 42 redesignated from HHB, 123rd Field Artillery at Cp Joseph T. Robinson Ark; 1st Bn formerly 1st Bn, 214th FA and 2nd Bn formerly 2nd Bn, 150th FA; arrived at Cp Forrest Tenn 7 Oct 42 and assigned to 14th FA Bde and III Corps where HHB redesignated HHB, 208th Field Artillery Group 1 Mar 43. 1st and 2nd Bns redesignated 208th and 989th Field Artillery Battalions, respectively.

218th Field Artillery Regiment (115mm How) (Truck-D)   **Oregon National Guard**

16 Sep 40 inducted into federal service at Portland Oreg as part of 66th FA Bde, 41st Division; transferred to Cp Murray Wash 19 Sep 40; arrived at Ft Lewis Wash 20 Mar 41 where Hq disbanded 14 Feb 42. 1st and 2nd Bns redesignated 2nd Battalion, 204th FA Regiment and 218th Field Artillery Battalions, respectively. (3rd Battalion had been redesignated as 2nd Bn 31 Jan 41 after original regimental 2nd Bn HHB disbanded that date.)

222nd Field Artillery Regiment (155mm How) (Truck-D)   **Utah National Guard**

3 Mar 41 inducted into federal service at Salt Lake City Utah as part of 65th FA Bde, 40th Division; arrived at Cp San Luis Obispo Calif 18 Mar 41 where Hq disbanded 4 Feb 42. 1st and 2nd Bns redesignated 222nd Field Artillery Battalion and 1st Battalion, 204th FA Regiment, respectively, 5 Feb 42.

No Distinctive
Insignia Authorized

225th Field Artillery Regiment (155mm How) (Truck-D)

1 Sep 42 redesignated from HHB, 106th Field Artillery in Hawaii where HHB redesignated HHB, 225th Field Artillery Group 3 Feb 44; 1st Bn (formerly 2nd Bn, 106th FA) redesignated 225th Field Artillery Battalion.

Campaigns: *Pacific Theater without inscription*

No Distinctive
Insignia Authorized

228th Field Artillery Regiment (155mm How) (Truck-D)

28 Feb 42 redesignated from HHB, 176th Field Artillery at Ft George G. Meade Md; 1st Bn formerly 1st Bn, 157th FA and 2nd Bn formerly 2nd Bn, 176th FA; arrived at Ft Bragg N.C. 28 Jul 42 and assigned to 15th FA Bde and XII Corps; HHB redesignated there as HHB, 228th Field Artillery Group 8 Feb 43. 1st and 2nd Bns redesignated 228th and 967th Field Artillery Battalions, respectively.

258th Field Artillery Regiment (155mm Gun) (Motorized)   **New York National Guard**

3 Feb 41 inducted into federal service at New York N.Y.; transferred to Ft Ethan Allen Vt and assigned to 71st FA Bde and VI Army Corps; moved to Madison Barracks N.Y. 2 Jun 41; arrived at Pine Camp N.Y. 18 May 42 where HHB redesignated HHB, 258th Field Artillery Group 8 Feb 43. 1st and 2nd Bns redesignated 258th and 991st Field Artillery Battalions, respectively.

No Distinctive
Insignia Authorized

333rd Field Artillery Regiment (155mm How) (Truck-D) (Colored)

5 Aug 42 activated at Cp Gruber Okla and assigned to Third Army; HHB redesignated there as HHB, 333rd Field Artillery Group 10 Mar 43. 1st and 2nd Bns redesignated 333rd and 969th Field Artillery Battalions, respectively.

349th Field Artillery Regiment (155mm Gun) (Motorized) (Colored)

1 Aug 40 activated at Ft Sill Okla and assigned to VIII Army Corps; later assigned to Replacement and School Command there and re-equipped as 75mm Gun (Truck-D); HHB redesignated there as HHB, 349th Field Artillery Group 12 Feb 43. 1st and 2nd Bns redesignated 349th and 686th Field Artillery Battalions, respectively.

350th Field Artillery Regiment (155mm How) (Truck-D) (Colored)

10 Feb 41 activated at Cp Livingston La and assigned to 46th FA Bde and Third Army; HHB redesignated there as HHB, 350th Field Artillery Group 1 Apr 43. 1st and 2nd Bns redesignated 350th and 971st Field Artillery Battalions, respectively.

351st Field Artillery Regiment (155mm How) (Truck-D) (Colored)

10 Feb 41 activated at Cp Livingston La and assigned to 46th FA Bde and Third Army; HHB redesignated there as HHB, 351st Field Artillery Group 1 Apr 43. 1st and 2nd Bns redesignated 351st and 973rd Field Artillery Battalions, respectively.

353rd Field Artillery Regiment (155mm Gun) (Motorized) (Colored)

10 Feb 41 activated at Cp Livington La and assigned to 46th FA Bde and Third Army; HHB redesignated as HHB, 353rd Field Artillery Group 1 Apr 43. 1st and 2nd Bns redesignated 353rd and 993rd Field Artillery Battalions, respectively.

422nd Field Artillery Regiment (105mm How) (Truck-D)

15 Jul 42 activated at Cp Bowie Tex and assigned to Third Army; deployed to Louisiana Maneuver Area 31 Jan 43 and there HHB redesignated as HHB, 422nd Field Artillery Group 8 Feb 43. 1st and 2nd Bns redesignated 691st and 692nd Field Artillery Battalions, respectively.

472nd Field Artillery Regiment (105mm How) (Truck-D)

1 Aug 42 activated at Cp Gordon Ga and assigned to Second Army; HHB redesignated there as HHB, 472nd Field Artillery Group 6 Mar 43. 1st and 2nd Bns redesignated 472nd and 694th Field Artillery Battalions, respectively.

578th Field Artillery Regiment (8-inch How) (Motorized) (Colored)

15 Jun 42 activated at Ft Bragg N.C. and assigned to 22nd FA Bde, Second Army; HHB redesignated there as HHB, 578th Field Artillery Group 23 Feb 43. 1st and 2nd Bns redesignated 578th and 999th Field Artillery Battalions, respectively.

Chapter 33

Field Artillery and Rocket Battalions

Observation Battalions:

1–3, 7, 8, 12–17, 285–294

Rocket Battalions having no Field Artillery branch designator:

1, 2

Battalions:

1–22, 25–34, 36–39, 41–71, 73–84, 86, 87, 89–95, 97–99, 101–111, 113–118, 120–136, 138–141, 143, 145–165, 167–183, 185–200, 202–205, 207–213, 215–232, 240–278, 280–284, 301–329, 331–351, 353, 355, 356, 358–365, 367–377, 379–387, 389–405, 412–414, 419–429, 433–436, 440, 443, 450, 456–458, 460, 462–467, 472, 477, 483, 484, 489–501, 512, 514–519, 521, 522, 526, 527–553, 557–561, 563, 564, 566, 569, 570, 573, 575, 576, 578, 580, 583, 589–605, 607–613, 616–618, 623, 624, 626–628, 630, 631, 633–635, 655–677, 680, 681, 685–698, 718, 720, 721, 724, 725, 730–734, 736, 738–784, 786–791, 793, 795, 797, 798, 801–805, 808, 809, 861–863, 867–872, 879–884, 897–899, 901–916, 919–925, 927–943, 945, 947, 949, 951, 953, 955, 957, 959, 961, 963, 965, 967, 969, 971, 973–981, 983, 985, 987, 989, 991, 993, 995, 997, 999, 1114, 1125, First Provisional Gun

⭐ EXAMPLE — HOW TO USE THIS TABLE

Unit Designation and Type   Date Formed and Location (Source of Unit)/Inactivation and Location   August 1945 Location

Overseas Wartime Locations followed by - **Campaign Key Numbers** and PE return to United States, if applicable or space allows
(notes and remarks)

104th Field Artillery Bn (105mm How Trk-D)   1 Sep 42 Ft Shafter Hawaii (2nd Bn, 104th FA)/31 Dec 45 Ft Lawton Wash   Okinawa
Hawaii: 1 Sep 42   Saipan: 17 Jun 44   Espiritu Santo: 4 Sep 44   Okinawa: 9 Apr 45 - **10,19,21**   SPE: 31 Dec 45 *(27th Inf Div)*

In this example, the 104th Field Artillery Battalion was equipped with truck-drawn 105mm howitzers and organized at Fort Shafter, Hawaii, from the 2nd Battalion of the 104th Field Artillery on 1 September 1942. The reader may research the battalion's previous existence under the 104th Field Artillery Regiment in this book. The battalion went to Saipan 17 June 1944, to Espiritu Santo on 4 September 1944, and to Okinawa on 9 April 1945, where it was still stationed in August 1945. It is credited with the Eastern Mandates, Ryukyus, and Western Pacific campaigns. This information was derived by indexing the boldfaced campaign key numbers with Appendix I. Note these key number codes are in numerical sequence rather than chronological order, but since the appendix displays all campaign dates, they can be easily arranged by time sequence if desired. The battalion returned to the Seattle Port of Embarkation on 31 December 1945 and was inactivated that same day at Fort Lawton, Washington. Finally, it served under the 27th Infantry Division.

BATTALION DESIGNATION AND TYPE	FORMED (SOURCE OF UNIT)/INACTIVATION *Active through 1946	AUGUST 1945 LOCATION

1st Field Artillery Bn (105mm How Trac-D)   1 Oct 40 Ft Sill Okla (1st FA) / *   Bagabag Philippines
SFPE: 2 Oct 43   Hawaii: 11 Oct 43   New Guinea: 31 Jan 44   Philippines: 29 Dec 44 - **14,15** *(6th Inf Div)*

1st Field Artillery Observation Bn   P   Ft Bragg N.C. / 31 Dec 45 New York P/E   Donauworth Germany
NYPE: 5 Aug 42   England: 17 Aug 42   N.Africa: 6 Dec 42   Sicily: 10 Jul 43   Italy: 10 Sep 43
France-ETO: 16 Aug 44 - **26,29,34,35,36,37,38,39**   NYPE: 30 Dec 45 *(nondiv)*

1st Rocket Battalion (4.5 inch Trk-D)   4 Jan 45 Ft Sill Okla (121st AAA Gun Bn)/13 Apr 45 Ft Sill Okla redes 421st
Rocket FA Bn *(nondiv)*

2nd Field Artillery Bn (155mm How Trac-D)   13 Jan 41 Ft Clayton Canal Zone (2nd FA) / 29 Mar 46 Cp Kilmer N.J.   Sterbfritz Germany
Panama: 13 Jan 41   SFPE: 10 Sep 43   BPE: 29 Jun 44   England: 9 Jul 44   France-ETO: 16 Aug 44 - **26,32,34**   NYPE: 28 Aug 46
(Truck-D until 1944) (nondiv)

2nd Field Artillery Observation Bn   1 Jun 40 Ft Sill Okla / 25 Dec 45 Cp Patrick Henry Va   Starnberg Germany
NYPE: 21 Aug 43   N.Africa: 2 Sep 43   Italy: 19 Nov 43   France-ETO: 22 Aug 44 - **24,25,26,29,34,35,37**   HRPE: 25 Dec 45 *(nondiv)*

2nd Rocket Battalion (4.5-inch Trk-D)   4 Jan 45 Ft Sill Okla (769th AAA Gun Bn)/12 Apr 45 Ft Sill Okla redes 422nd
Rocket FA Bn *(nondiv)*

3rd Armored Field Artillery Bn   1 Jul 41 Ft Riley Kans (3rd FA) / 20 Oct 46 Germany   Munchberg Germany
NYPE: 20 Aug 44   England: 26 Aug 44   France-ETO: 29 Sep 44 - **25,26,34** *(formerly 75mm How [H-D] with 2nd Cav Div until 14 Jul 42
when assigned 9th Armd Div)*

3rd Field Artillery Observation Bn   1 Jun 41 Ft Bragg N.C./1 Dec 45 New York P/E   Salzburg Austria
NYPE: 2 Jan 44   England: 10 Jan 44   France-ETO: 17 Jul 44 - **25,26,30,32,34**   NYPE: 29 Nov 45 *(assigned FA School in U.S.) (nondiv)*

4th Field Artillery Bn (155mm How Trac-D)   16 Dec 40 Ft Bragg N.C. (4th FA) / 10 Dec 46 Leyte Philippines   Leyte Philippines
SFPE: 4 Apr 42   New Hebrides: 4 May 42   Guadalcanal: 4 Mar 44   New Guinea: 10 Oct 44   Philippines: 9 Aug 45
(75mm How Pk in 1941) (nondiv)

5th Field Artillery Bn (155mm How Trac-D)   1 Oct 40 Madison Bks N.Y. (5th FA) / *   Triesdorf Germany
NYPE: 1 Aug 42   England: 7 Aug 42   N.Africa: 8 Nov 42   Sicily: 10 Jul 43   England: 8 Nov 43
France-ETO: 6 Jun 44 - **23,25,26,30,32,34,36,38** *(1st Inf Div)*

6th Field Artillery Bn (105mm How Trac-D)   4 Jan 41 Ft Bragg N.C. (6th FA) / 18 Dec 45 Cp Anza Calif   San Jose Philippines
SFPE: 16 Jul 42   Fiji I: 8 Aug 42   New Hebrides: 13 Mar 43   Guadalcanal: 3 Nov 43   Bougainville: 13 Nov 43
Philippines: 9 Jan 45 - **14,16** *(37th Inf Div)*

7th Field Artillery Bn (105mm How Trk-D)   1 Oct 40 Ft Ethan Allen Vt (7th FA) / *   Gunzenhausen Germany
NYPE: 1 Aug 42   England: 7 Aug 42   N.Africa: 8 Nov 42   Sicily: 10 Jul 43   England: 8 Nov 43
France-ETO: 6 Jun 44 - **23,25,26,30,32,34,36,38** *(1st Inf Div)*

7th Field Artillery Observation Bn   1 Jun 41 Ft Bragg N.C. / 10 Feb 46 Cp Hood Tex   Shipment #10077-F at sea
NYPE: 24 Apr 44   England: 6 May 44   France-ETO: 19 Jul 44 - **25,26,30,32,34**   NYPE: 26 Aug 45 *(nondiv)*

8th Field Artillery Bn (105mm How Trac-D)   1 Oct 41 Ft Shafter Hawaii (8th FA) / *   Bamban Philippines
Hawaii: 1 Oct 41   Guadalcanal: 23 Dec 42   New Zealand: 9 Nov 43   New Caledonia: 9 Feb 44   Philippines: 11 Jan 45 - **6,11,14**
(25th Inf Div)

BATTALION DESIGNATION AND TYPE   **FORMED (SOURCE OF UNIT)/INACTIVATION** *Active through 1946   **AUGUST 1945 LOCATION**

8th Field Artillery Observation Bn   1 Jun 41 Ft Sill Okla / 28 Dec 45 Cp Myles Standish Mass   Butzbach Germany
NYPE: 10 Feb 44   England: 22 Feb 44   France-ETO: 26 Jun 44 - **26,30,32,34**   BPE: 27 Dec 45 *(nondiv)*

9th Field Artillery Bn (155mm How Trk-D)   1 Oct 40 Ft Lewis Wash (9th FA) / *   Hellbrunn Germany
HRPE: 27 Oct 42   N.Africa: 8 Nov 42   Sicily: 10 Jul 43   Italy: 18 Sep 43   France-ETO: 15 Aug 44 - **23,24,25,26,29,34,35,36,37,38**
NYPE: 4 Sep 46 *(3rd Inf Div)*

10th Field Artillery Bn (105mm How Trk-D)   1 Oct 40 Ft Lewis Wash (10th FA) / *   St Leonhard Austria
HRPE: 27 Oct 42   N.Africa: 8 Nov 42   Sicily: 10 Jul 43   Italy: 18 Sep 43   France-ETO: 15 Aug 44 - **23,24,25,26,29,34,35,36,37,38**
NYPE: 4 Sep 46 *(3rd Inf Div)*

11th Field Artillery Bn (155mm How Trac-D)   1 Oct 41 Schofield Bks Hawaii (11th FA) / *   Davao Mindanao Philippines
Hawaii: 1 Oct 41   Australia: 8 Aug 43   Goodenough I: 15 Feb 44   New Guinea: 22 Apr 44   Philippines: 20 Oct 44 - **6,13,14,15,20**
(24th Inf Div)

12th Field Artillery Bn (155mm How Trac-D)   1 Oct 40 Ft Sam Houston Tex (12th FA) / *   Cp Swift Tex
NYPE: 8 Oct 43   England: 18 Oct 43   France-ETO: 7 Jun 44 - **25,26,30,32,34**   NYPE: 20 Jul 45 *(2nd Inf Div)*

12th Field Artillery Observation Bn   17 Mar 42 Ft Sill Okla / 29 Dec 45 Cp Patrick Henry Va   Wathlingen Germany sch to
NYPE: 11 Feb 44   England: 23 Feb 44   France-ETO: 30 Jun 44 - **26,30,32,34**   HRPE: 29 Dec 45 *(nondiv)*   SWPA under Shipment #R5065-SS

13th Field Artillery Bn (105mm How Trac-D)   1 Oct 41 Schofield Bks Hawaii (13th FA) / *   Davao Mindanao Philippines
Hawaii: 1 Oct 41   Australia: 8 Aug 43   Goodenough I: 12 Feb 44   New Guinea: 22 Apr 44   Philippines: 20 Oct 44 - **6,13,14,15,20**
(24th Inf Div)

13th Field Artillery Observation Bn   1 Apr 42 Ft Bragg N.C. / 8 Mar 46 Cp Kilmer N.J.   Sangerhausen Germany
NYPE: 2 Dec 43   England: 13 Dec 43   France-ETO: 7 Jun 44 - **25,26,30,32,34**   NYPE: 7 Mar 46 *(nondiv)*

14th Armored Field Artillery Bn   1 Jan 42 Ft Benning Ga (14th FA) / *   Salzgitter Germany
NYPE: 11 Dec 42   N.Africa: 25 Dec 42   Sicily: 10 Jul 43   England: 25 Nov 43   France-ETO: 10 Jun 44 - **23,25,26,30,32,34,36**
NYPE: 5 Feb 46 *(2nd Armd Div)*

14th Field Artillery Observation Bn   1 Jun 42 Ft Sill Okla / 24 May 46 Germany   Backnang Germany
NYPE: 2 Jul 44   England: 12 Jul 44   France-ETO: 18 Aug 44 - **25,26,30,32,34** *(nondiv)*

15th Field Artillery Bn (105mm How Trk-D)   1 Oct 40 Ft Sam Houston Tex (15th FA) / *   Cp Swift Tex
NYPE: 6 Oct 43   England: 18 Oct 43   France-ETO: 7 Jun 44 - **25,26,30,32,34**   BPE: 19 Jul 45 *(2nd Inf Div)*

15th Field Artillery Observation Bn   1 May 42 Ft Bragg N.C. / 15 Mar 46 Italy   Filigara Italy
NYPE: 21 Aug 43   N.Africa: 2 Sep 43   Italy: 23 Oct 43 - **24,29,31,33,35** *(nondiv)*

16th Armored Field Artillery Bn   3 Jan 41 Ft Myer Va / 26 Jul 46 Germany   Kronach Germany
NYPE: 20 Aug 44   England: 26 Aug 44   France-ETO: 29 Sep 44 - **25,26,34**
(initially 75mm Gun H-D FA Bn until assigned to 9th Armd Div 3 Jun 42)

16th Field Artillery Observation Bn   15 Jun 42 Ft Bragg N.C. / 24 Oct 45 Cp Kilmer N.J.   Frankenhain Germany
NYPE: 22 Jun 44   England: 29 Jun 44   France-ETO: 19 Aug 44 - **25,26,30,32,34**   NYPE: 23 Oct 45 *(nondiv)*

17th Field Artillery Bn (155mm How Trac-D)   1 Mar 44 Pozzilli Italy (1st Bn, 17th FA) / 16 Apr 46 Cp Kilmer N.J.   Feldofing Germany
Italy: 1 Mar 44   France-ETO: 9 Sep 44 - **25,26,34,35,37**   NYPE: 15 Apr 46 *(nondiv)*

17th Field Artillery Observation Bn   15 Jun 42 Ft Lewis Wash / 2 Jan 46 Cp Kilmer N.J.   Susice Czechoslovakia
NYPE: 21 Oct 43   England: 2 Nov 43   France-ETO: 8 Jun 44 - **25,26,30,32,34**   NYPE: 1 Jan 46 *(nondiv)*

18th Field Artillery Bn (105mm Trk-D)   9 Aug 43 Cp Gordon Ga (685th FA Bn) / 3 Mar 46 Cp Kilmer N.J.   Beichlingen Germany
NYPE: 11 Feb 44   England: 23 Feb 44   France-ETO: 6 Jul 44 - **25,26,30,32,34**   NYPE: 2 Mar 46 *(nondiv)*

19th Field Artillery Bn (105mm Trk-D)   1 Oct 40 Ft Knox Ky (19th FA)/20 Sep 46 Cp Campbell Ky   Cp Campbell Ky
NYPE: 31 Mar 42   Iceland: 10 May 42   England: 9 Aug 43   France-ETO: 11 Jul 44 - **25,26,30,32,34**   BPE: 16 Jul 43 *(5th Inf Div)*

20th Field Artillery Bn (155mm How Trac-D)   1 Oct 40 Ft Benning Ga (20th FA) / 13 Feb 46 Cp Butner N.C.   Cp Butner N.C.
NYPE: 18 Jan 44   England: 29 Jan 44   France-ETO: 6 Jun 44 - **25,26,30,32,34**   NYPE: 10 Jul 45 *(4th Inf Div)*

21st Field Artillery Bn (155mm How Trac-D)   1 Oct 40 Ft Knox Ky (21st FA) / 20 Sep 46 Cp Campbell Ky   Cp Campbell Ky
NYPE: 1 May 42   Iceland: 11 May 42   England: 9 Aug 43   France-ETO: 11 Jul 44 - **25,26,30,32,34**   BPE: 10 Jul 45 *(5th Inf Div)*

22nd Armored Field Artillery Bn   15 Apr 41 Pine Camp N.Y. / 1 May 46 Germany redes 22nd Constab Sqdn   Beilingries Germany
BPE: 29 Dec 43   England: 9 Jan 44   France-ETO: 13 Jul 44 - **25,26,30,32,34** *(105mm How until redes Armd FA Bn 1 Jan 42) (4th Armd Div)*

25th Field Artillery Bn (105mm How Trk-D)   30 Dec 40 Henry Bks Puerto Rico (2nd Bn, 25th FA) / 21 Mar 46 Cp Kilmer N.J.   Homberg Germany
Puerto Rico: 30 Dec 40   NOPE: 20 May 43   NYPE: 24 Sep 44   England: 30 Sep 44   France-ETO: 2 Oct 44 - **25,26,34**
NYPE: 20 Mar 46 *(nondiv)*

26th Field Artillery Bn (105mm How Trk-D)   1 Oct 40 Ft Bragg N.C. (26th FA) / 20 Nov 46 Germany   Jetzendorf Germany
NYPE: 26 Sep 42   N.Africa: 8 Nov 42   Sicily: 15 Jul 43   England: 27 Nov 43   France-ETO: 9 Jun 44 - **23,25,26,30,32,34,36,38** *(9th Inf Div)*

BATTALION DESIGNATION AND TYPE	FORMED (SOURCE OF UNIT)/INACTIVATION *Active through 1946	AUGUST 1945 LOCATION

27th Armored Field Artillery Bn   15 Jul 40 Ft Knox Ky / 1 May 46 Italy   Salzburg Austria
NYPE: 11 May 42   N.Ireland: 20 May 42   N.Africa: 21 Dec 42   Italy: 9 Sep 43 - **23,24,29,31,33,35,38**
(105mm How; redes Armd FA Bn 1 Jan 42) (1st Armd Div)

28th Field Artillery Bn (155mm How Trac-D)   1 Oct 40 Ft Jackson S.C. (28th FA) / 25 Oct 45 Ft Leonard Wood Mo   Ft Leonard Wood Mo
NYPE: 5 Dec 43   England: 16 Dec 43   France-ETO: 3 Jul 44 - **26,30,32,34**   HRPE: 6 Jul 45 *(8th Inf Div)*

29th Field Artillery Bn (105mm How Trk-D)   1 Oct 40 Ft Benning Ga (29th FA) / 14 Feb 46 Cp Butner N.C.   Cp Butner N.C.
NYPE: 18 Jan 44   England: 29 Jan 44   France-ETO: 6 Jun 44 - **25,26,30,32,34**   NYPE: 10 Jul 45 *(4th Inf Div)*

30th Field Artillery Bn (155mm How Trac-D)   1 May 45 Germany (521st FA Bn) / *   Ft Bragg N.C.
Germany: 1 May 45 - **26**   NYPE: 2 Aug 45 *(nondiv)*

31st Field Artillery Bn (155mm How Trac-D)   1 Oct 40 Ft Ord Calif (31st FA) / *   Okinawa
SFPE: 12 Jul 43   Alaska: 19 Jul 43   Hawaii: 15 Sep 43   Philippines: 20 Oct 44   Okinawa: 1 Apr 45 - **2,10,13,19** *(7th Inf Div)*

32nd Field Artillery Bn (105mm How Trk-D)   1 Oct 40 Ft Ethan Allen Vt / *   Feuchtwangen Germany
NYPE: 1 Aug 42   Scotland: 7 Aug 42   N.Africa: 8 Nov 42   Sicily: 10 Jul 43   England: 8 Nov 43
France-ETO: 6 Jun 44 - **23,25,26,30,32,34,36,38** *(1st Inf Div)*

33rd Field Artillery Bn (105mm How Trk-D)   1 Oct 40 Ft Ethan Allen Vt / *   Heidenheim Germany
NYPE: 1 Aug 42   Scotland: 7 Aug 42   N.Africa: 8 Nov 42   Sicily: 10 Jul 43   England: 8 Nov 43
France-ETO: 6 Jun 44 - **23,25,26,30,32,34,36,38** *(1st Inf Div)*

34th Field Artillery Bn (155mm How Trac-D)   1 Oct 40 Ft Bragg N.C. (34th FA) / 20 Nov 46 Germany   Pfaffenhofen Germany
NYPE: 12 Dec 42   N.Africa: 25 Dec 42   Sicily: 15 Jul 43   England: 25 Nov 43   France-ETO: 9 Jun 44 - **25,26,30,32,34,36,38**
(9th Inf Div)

36th Field Artillery Bn (155mm How Trac-D)   5 Mar 44 Nettuno Italy (1st Bn, 36th FA) / 8 Jan 46 Cp Kilmer N.J.   Holzhausen Germany
Italy: 5 Mar 44   France-ETO: 15 Aug 44 - **24,25,26,29,34,35,37**   NYPE: 7 Jan 46 *(nondiv)*

37th Field Artillery Bn (105mm How Trk-D)   1 Oct 40 Ft Sam Houston Tex / *   Cp Swift Tex
NYPE: 6 Oct 43   England: 8 Oct 43   France-ETO: 7 Jun 44 - **25,26,30,32,34**   NYPE: 20 Jul 45 *(2nd Inf Div)*

38th Field Artillery Bn (105mm How Trk-D)   1 Oct 40 Ft Ethan Allen Vt / *   Cp Swift Tex
NYPE: 7 Oct 43   England: 8 Oct 43   France-ETO: 7 Jun 44 - **25,26,30,32,34**   NYPE: 20 Jul 45 *(2nd Inf Div)*

39th Field Artillery Bn (105mm How Trk-D)   1 Oct 40 Ft Lewis Wash / *   Hallines France
HRPE: 27 Oct 42   N.Africa: 8 Nov 42   Sicily: 10 Jul 43   Italy: 18 Sep 43   France-ETO: 15 Aug 44 - **23,24,25,26,29,34,35,36,37,38**
NYPE: 4 Sep 46 *(3rd Inf Div)*

41st Field Artillery Bn (105mm How Trk-D)   1 Oct 40 Ft Lewis Wash / *   Salzburg Austria
HRPE: 27 Oct 42   N.Africa: 8 Nov 42   Sicily: 10 Jul 43   Italy: 18 Sep 43   France-ETO: 15 Aug 44 - **23,24,25,26,29,34,35,36,37,38**
NYPE: 4 Sep 46 *(3rd Inf Div)*

42nd Field Artillery Bn (105mm How Trk-D)   1 Oct 40 Ft Benning Ga / 14 Feb 46 Cp Butner N.C.   Cp Butner N.C.
NYPE: 18 Jan 44   England: 29 Jan 44   France-ETO: 6 Jun 44 - **25,26,30,32,34**   NYPE: 10 Jul 45 *(4th Inf Div)*

43rd Field Artillery Bn (105mm How Trk-D)   1 Jun 41 Ft Jackson S.C. / 20 Oct 45 Ft Leonard Wood Mo   Ft Leonard Wood Mo
NYPE: 5 Dec 43   England: 16 Dec 43   France-ETO: 3 Jul 44 - **26,30,32,34**   HRPE: 9 Jul 45 *(8th Inf Div)*

44th Field Artillery Bn (105mm How Trk-D)   29 Dec 41 Cp Gordon Ga (2nd Bn, 47th FA) / 18 Feb 46 Cp Butner N.C.   Cp Butner N.C.
NYPE: 18 Jan 44   England: 29 Jan 44   France-ETO: 6 Jun 44 - **25,26,30,32,34**   NYPE: 10 Jul 45 *(4th Inf Div)*

45th Field Artillery Bn (105mm How Trk-D)   1 Jun 41 Ft Jackson S.C. / 20 Oct 45 Ft Leonard Wood Mo   Ft Leonard Wood Mo
NYPE: 5 Dec 43   England: 15 Dec 43   France-ETO: 3 Jul 44 - **26,30,32,34**   HRPE: 9 Jul 45 *(8th Inf Div)*

46th Field Artillery Bn (105mm How Trk-D)   14 Oct 40 Ft Knox Ky / 20 Sep 46 Cp Campbell Ky   Cp Campbell Ky
NYPE: 29 Apr 42   Iceland: 11 May 42   England: 9 Aug 43   France-ETO: 11 Jul 44 - **25,26,30,32,34**   BPE: 16 Jul 45 *(5th Inf Div)*

47th Armored Field Artillery Bn   26 Jan 42 Ft Bragg N.C. (47th FA) / 9 Oct 45 Cp Myles Standish Mass   Diedorf Germany
NYPE: 11 Feb 44   England: 23 Feb 44   France-ETO: 25 Jul 44 - **25,26,30,32,34**   BPE: 8 Oct 45 *(105mm How Trk-D until 9 Sep 42)*
(9th Armd Div since 9 Sep 42)

48th Field Artillery Bn (105mm How Trk-D)   1 Jun 41 Ft Ord Calif / *   Okinawa
SFPE: 24 Apr 43   Attu: 11 May 43   Adak I: 15 Jul 43   Hawaii: 15 Sep 43   Philippines: 20 Oct 44   Okinawa: 1 Apr 45 - **2,10,13,19**
(7th Inf Div)

49th Field Artillery Bn (105mm How Trk-D)   1 Jun 41 Ft Ord Calif / *   Okinawa
SFPE: 24 Apr 43   Attu: 11 May 43   Hawaii: 15 Sep 43   Philippines: 20 Oct 44   Okinawa: 1 Apr 45 - **2,10,13,19** *(7th Inf Div)*

50th Field Artillery Bn (105mm How Trk-D)   1 Oct 40 Ft Knox Ky / 20 Sep 46 Adak Alaska   Cp Campbell Ky
NYPE: 18 Feb 42   Iceland: 3 Mar 42   England: 9 Sep 43   France-ETO: 10 Jul 44 - **25,26,30,32,34**   BPE: 16 Jul 45   SFPE: 14 Sep 46
(5th Inf Div)

BATTALION DESIGNATION AND TYPE	FORMED (SOURCE OF UNIT)/INACTIVATION *Active through 1946	AUGUST 1945 LOCATION

51st Field Artillery Bn (105mm How Trac-D)   1 Oct 40 Ft Sill Okla / *
SFPE: 20 Sep 43   Hawaii: 11 Oct 43   New Guinea: 31 Jan 44   Philippines: 9 Jan 45 - **14,15** *(6th Inf Div)*

Bagabag Philippines

52nd Field Artillery Bn (105mm How Trac-D)   1 Oct 41 Schofield Bks Hawaii / *
Hawaii: 1 Oct 41   Australia: 8 Aug 43   Goodenough I: 15 Feb 44   New Guinea: 22 Apr 44   Philippines: 20 Oct 44 - **6,13,14,15,21**
(24th Inf Div)

Davao Mindanao Philippines

53rd Field Artillery Bn (105mm How Trac-D)   1 Oct 40 Ft Sill Okla / *
SFPE: 21 Jul 43   Hawaii: 29 Jul 43   New Guinea: 31 Jan 44   Philippines: 9 Jan 45 - **14,15** *(6th Inf Div)*

Bagabag Philippines

54th Armored Field Artillery Bn   15 Apr 41 Cp Beauregard La / 10 Nov 45 Germany
NYPE: 5 Sep 43   England: 16 Sep 43   France-ETO: 23 Jun 44 - **25,26,30,32,34** *(105mm How Trk-D until 1 Jan 42) (3rd Armd Div)*

Oberau Germany

55th Field Artillery Bn (155mm How Trac-D)   18 Jun 43 Ft Bragg N.C. / 15 Apr 46 Philippines
SFPE: 27 Sep 44   New Guinea: 20 Oct 44   Philippines: 11 Jan 45 - **14,15** *(105mm How Trk-D until 1944) (nondiv)*

Luzon Philippines

56th Field Artillery Bn (105mm How Trk-D)   1 Jun 41 Ft Jackson S.C. / 20 Oct 45 Ft Leonard Wood Mo
NYPE: 5 Dec 43   England: 15 Dec 43   France-ETO: 3 Jul 44 - **26,30,32,34**   HRPE: 9 Jul 45   *(8th Inf Div)*

Ft Leonard Wood Mo

57th Field Artillery Bn (105mm How Trk-D)   1 Jun 41 Ft Ord Calif / *
SFPE: 6 Jul 43   Attu: 9 Jul 43   Hawaii: 15 Sep 43   Philippines: 20 Oct 44   Okinawa: 1 Apr 45 - **2,10,13,19**   *(7th Inf Div)*

Okinawa

58th Armored Field Artillery Bn   1 Oct 41 Ft Knox Ky / 26 Jul 46 Austria
NYPE: 2 Nov 42   N.Africa: 11 Nov 42   Sicily: 14 Jul 43   England: 9 Dec 43   France-ETO: 6 Jun 44 - **25,26,30,32,34,36,38**
(relieved from 5th Armd Div 1 Sep 42) (nondiv)

Endorf Germany

59th Armored Field Artillery Bn   15 Feb 42 Ft Knox Ky / 4 Dec 45 Cp Myles Standish Mass
NYPE: 21 Aug 43   N.Africa: 2 Sep 43   Italy: 23 Oct 43   France-ETO: 15 Aug 44 - **25,26,29,34,37**   BPE: 3 Dec 45
(relieved from 6th Armd Div 7 Dec 42) (nondiv)

Aufkirchen Germany

60th Field Artillery Bn (105mm Trk-D)   1 Oct 40 Ft Bragg N.C. / 20 Nov 46 Germany
NYPE: 27 Oct 42   N.Africa: 8 Nov 42   Sicily: 15 Jul 43   England: 26 Nov 43   France-ETO: 9 Jun 44 - **23,25,26,30,32,34,36,38** *(9th Inf Div)*

Strasshof Austria

61st Field Artillery Bn (105mm Trac-D)   3 Jan 41 Ft Bliss Tex / *
SFPE: 3 Jul 43   Australia: 24 Jul 43   New Guinea: 21 Dec 43   Admiralty I: 16 Mar 44   Philippines: 20 Oct 44 - **3,13,14,15**
(initially 75mm How H-D) (1st Cav Div)

Lucena Philippines

62nd Armored Field Artillery Bn   10 Feb 41 Ft Bliss Tex / 29 Nov 45 Cp Kilmer N.J.
NYPE: 2 Nov 42   N.Africa: 11 Nov 42   Sicily: 10 Jul 43   England: 9 Dec 43   France-ETO: 6 Jun 44 - **25,26,30,32,34,36,38**
(105mm How Trk-D until 28 Aug 42) (nondiv)

Zatavi Czechoslovakia

63rd Field Artillery Bn (105mm How Trac-D)   1 Oct 41 Schofield Bks Hawaii / *
Hawaii: 1 Oct 41   Australia: 8 Aug 43   Goodenough I: 15 Feb 44   New Guinea: 22 Apr 44   Philippines: 20 Oct 44 - **6,13,14,15,20**
(24th Inf Div)

Davao Mindanao Philippines

64th Field Artillery Bn (105mm How Trac-D)   1 Oct 41 Oahu Hawaii / *
Hawaii: 1 Oct 41   Guadalcanal: 23 Dec 42   Russell I: Jul 43   Vella Lavella: 17 Aug 43   New Zealand: 9 Nov 43
New Caledonia: 24 Feb 44   Philippines: 11 Jan 45 - **6,11,14,16** *(25th Inf Div)*

Bambam Philippines

65th Armored Field Artillery Bn   1 Jan 42 Ft Knox Ky (65th FA) / 25 Nov 45 Cp Myles Standish Mass
NYPE: 14 Jan 43   N.Africa: 26 Jan 43   Sicily: 15 Jul 43   England: 9 Dec 43   France-ETO: 6 Jun 44 - **26,30,32,34,36,38**
(relieved from 5th Armd Div 1 Sep 42) (nondiv)

Schluchtern Germany

66th Armored Field Artillery Bn   1 Jan 42 Pine Camp N.Y. (66th FA) / 1 May 46 Germany redes 66th Constab Sqdn
BPE: 29 Dec 43   England: 9 Jan 44   France-ETO: 13 Jul 44 - **25,26,30,32,34** *(4th Armd Div)*

Rottenburg Germany

67th Armored Field Artillery Bn   1 Jan 42 Cp Polk La (67th FA) / 10 Nov 45 Germany
NYPE: 5 Sep 43   England: 15 Sep 43   France-ETO: 24 Jun 44 - **25,26,30,32,34** *(3rd Armd Div)*

Buchschlag Germany

68th Armored Field Artillery Bn   1 Jan 42 Ft Knox Ky (68th FA) / 1 Jan 46 Germany redes 68th Constab Sqdn
NYPE: 15 May 42   N.Ireland: 20 May 42   N.Africa: 21 Dec 42   Italy: 28 Oct 43 - **24,29,31,33,35,38** *(1st Armd Div)*

Salzburg Austria

69th Armored Field Artillery Bn   15 Feb 42 Ft Knox Ky / 2 Mar 46 Cp Kilmer N.J.
NYPE: 21 Aug 43   N.Africa: 4 Sep 43   Italy: 23 Oct 43   France-ETO: 15 Aug 44 - **24,25,26,29,34,35,37**
(relieved from 6th Armd Div 7 Dec 42) (nondiv)

Diessen Germany

70th Field Artillery Bn (105mm How Trk-D)   9 Jan 41 Ft Jackson S.C. / 9 Dec 45 Cp Patrick Henry Va
BPE: 7 Aug 43   Iceland: 13 Aug 43   England: 30 Jul 44   France-ETO: 10 Sep 44 - **26,32,34**   HRPE: 9 Dec 45
(75mm Gun H-D with GHQ in 1941) (nondiv)

Selters Germany

71st Armored Field Artillery Bn   9 Jan 41 Ft Jackson S.C. / 7 Oct 45 Cp Kilmer N.J.
NYPE: 11 Feb 44   England: 23 Feb 44   France-ETO: 1 Aug 44 - **25,26,30,32,34**   NYPE: 6 Oct 45
(75mm Gun H-D with GHQ until assigned 1 Sep 42 to 5th Armd Div)

Ershausen Germany

BATTALION DESIGNATION AND TYPE	FORMED (SOURCE OF UNIT)/INACTIVATION *Active through 1946	AUGUST 1945 LOCATION

73rd Armored Field Artillery Bn   19 Mar 42 Ft Riley Kans / 9 Oct 45 Cp Patrick Henry Va   Naila Germany
NYPE: 20 Aug 44   England: 26 Aug 44   France-ETO: 29 Sep 44 - **25,26,34**   HRPE: 9 Oct 45
(105mm How Trk-D until 15 Jul 42 when assigned 9th Armd Div)

74th Field Artillery Bn (105mm Trk-D)   22 Jan 41 Ft Ord Calif / 31 Oct 46 Ft Jackson S.C.   Ft Jackson S.C.
NYPE: 26 Dec 44   England: 7 Jan 45   France-ETO: 7 Jan 45 - **26,34**   NYPE: 5 Jul 45 *(initially 75mm Gun H-D thru 1941) (nondiv)*

75th Field Artillery Bn (155mm How Trac-D)   22 Jan 41 Ft Ord Calif / 10 Feb 46 Cp Hood Tex   Cp Carson Colo
SPE: 22 Jun 42   Alaska: 8 Jul 42   SPE: 1 May 44   HRPE: 28 Mar 45   Italy: 7 Apr 45 - **2,33**   HRPE: 9 Aug 45
(75mm Gun H-D thru 1941) (relieved from 7th Inf Div 6 Apr 41)

76th Field Artillery Bn (105mm How Trk-D)   22 Jan 41 Ft Ord Calif (76th FA) / 27 Nov 45 Cp Kilmer N.J.   Stachy Czechoslovakia
NYPE: 2 Jul 44   England: 13 Jul 44   France-ETO: 12 Aug 44 - **26,34**   NYPE: 26 Nov 45
(75mm Gun H-D relieved from 7th Inf Div Jun 41) (nondiv)

77th Field Artillery Bn (Cld) (75mm How H-D)   25 Feb 43 Ft Clark Tex / 26 Feb 44 North Africa
HRPE: 1 Feb 44   N.Africa: 20 Feb 44   *(2nd Cav Div)*

77th Field Artillery Bn (155mm Gun Trac-D)   15 May 45 Konigsdorf Germany (634th FA Bn) / 4 Jan 46 Cp Kilmer N.J.   Unter Windach Germany
Germany: 15 May 45   NYPE: 3 Jan 46   *(nondiv)*

78th Armored Field Artillery Bn   15 Jul 40 Ft Benning Ga / *   Ringelheim Germany
NYPE: 12 Dec 42   N.Africa: 25 Dec 42   Sicily: 10 Jul 43   England: 25 Nov 43   France-ETO: 7 Jun 44 - **23,25,26,30,32,34,36**
NYPE: 30 Jan 46 *(2nd Armd Div)*

79th Field Artillery Bn (Cld) (75mm How H-D)   25 Feb 43 Ft Clark Tex / 10 Mar 44 North Africa
HRPE: 12 Feb 44   N.Africa: 3 Mar 44   *(2nd Cav Div)*

80th Field Artillery Bn (155mm How Trac-D)   1 Oct 40 Ft Des Moines Iowa (80th FA) / *   Bagabag Philippines
SFPE: 20 Sep 43   Hawaii: 26 Sep 43   New Guinea: 31 Jan 44   Philippines: 9 Jan 45 - **14,15**   *(6th Inf Div)*

81st Field Artillery Bn (155mm How Trac-D)   16 Dec 40 Ft Lewis Wash (81st FA)/7 Feb 46 Cp Kilmer N.J.   Steinbach Hall Germany sch to
SPE: 10 Feb 41   Alaska: 15 Feb 41   SPE: 10 Dec 43   NYPE: 28 Aug 44   England: 3 Sep 44   France-ETO: 2 Oct 44 - **25,26,34**   SWPA under Shipment #R6604-HHH
NYPE: 6 Feb 46   *(nondiv)*

82nd Field Artillery Bn (105mm How Trac-D)   3 Jan 41 Ft Bliss Tex (82nd FA) / *   Lucena Philippines
SFPE: 4 Jun 43   Australia: 23 Jun 43   New Guinea: 22 Feb 44   Admiralty I: 16 Mar 44   Philippines: 20 Oct 44 - **3,13,14,15**
(75mm How H-D thru 1941) (1st Cav Div)

83rd Armored Field Artillery Bn   9 Jan 41 Ft Sill Okla (83rd FA) / 7 Oct 45 Cp Patrick Henry Va   Seiberg Germany
NYPE: 11 Feb 44   England: 23 Feb 44   France-ETO: 25 Jul 44 - **25,26,30,32,34**   HRPE: 7 Oct 45
(105mm How Trk-D until 21 Oct 42) (relieved from 8th Div Jun 41) (nondiv)

84th Field Artillery Bn (105mm How Trk-D)   1 Oct 40 Ft Bragg N.C. / 20 Nov 46 Germany   Schweikenkirchen Germany
NYPE: 13 Jan 43   N.Africa: 26 Jan 43   Sicily: 31 Jul 43   England: 25 Nov 43   France-ETO: 9 Jun 44 - **23,25,26,30,32,34,36,38** *(9th Inf Div)*

86th Field Artillery Bn (155mm How) (P.S.)   19 Apr 41 Ft Stotsenburg Philippines / 6 May 42 Philippines
Philippines: 19 Apr 41 - **18** *(assigned to 1st FA Group, Provisional during Philippine Islands campaign) (surrendered 9 Apr 42) (nondiv)*

87th Armored Field Artillery Bn   3 Jan 41 Ft William E Davis Panama / 31 Dec 45 Cp Kilmer N.J.   Sangerhausen Germany
Canal Zone: 3 Jan 41   NYPE: 7 Apr 43   NYPE: 2 Jan 44   England: 8 Jan 44   France-ETO: 9 Jun 44 - **25,26,30,32,34**   NYPE: 30 Dec 45
(battalion was 105mm How Trk-D at Ft Knox Ky until re-equipped in later 1943, having left its mechanized equipment behind in Panama Canal Zone where initially redesignated Armored Field Artillery Bn 1 Jun 42 from 105mm How Trk-D; however, it retained the title of 87th Armored Field Artillery Bn) (nondiv)

89th Field Artillery Bn (105mm How Trac-D)   1 Oct 41 Ft Shafter Hawaii / 15 Dec 46 Japan   Bambam Philippines
Hawaii: 1 Oct 41   Guadalcanal: 23 Dec 42   New Zealand: 9 Nov 43   New Caledonia: 8 Feb 44   Philippines: 11 Jan 45 - **6,11,14**
(25th Inf Div)

90th Field Artillery Bn (155mm How Trac-D)   1 Oct 41 Schofield Bks Hawaii / *   Bambam Philippines
Hawaii: 1 Oct 41   Guadalcanal: 23 Dec 42   New Zealand: 9 Nov 43   New Caledonia: 8 Feb 44   Philippines: 11 Jan 45 - **6,11,14**
(25th Inf Div)

91st Armored Field Artillery Bn   1 Jan 42 Ft Knox Ky /1 May 46 Germany redes 91st Constab Sqdn   Salzburg Austria
NYPE: 30 May 42   N.Ireland: 11 Jun 42   England: 30 Oct 42   N.Africa: 21 Dec 42   Italy: 1 Nov 43 - **24,29,31,33,35,38** *(1st Armd Div)*

92nd Armored Field Artillery Bn   8 Jan 42 Ft Benning Ga / *   Salzgitter Germany
NYPE: 12 Dec 42   N.Africa: 25 Dec 42   Sicily: 10 Jul 43   England: 25 Nov 43   France-ETO: 7 Jun 44 - **25,26,30,32,34,36**
NYPE: 1 Feb 46 *(2nd Armd Div)*

93rd Armored Field Artillery Bn   15 Feb 42 Ft Knox Ky / 29 Nov 45 Cp Kilmer N.J.   Heilbronn Germany
NYPE: 21 Aug 43   N.Africa: 2 Sep 43   Italy: 23 Oct 43   France-ETO: 15 Aug 44 - **25,26,29,34,35,37**   NYPE: 28 Nov 45
(relieved from 6th Armd Div 7 Dec 42) (nondiv)

94th Armored Field Artillery Bn   9 Jan 42 Pine Camp N.Y. /1 May 46 redes 94th Constab Sqdn Germany   Biedenberg Germany
BPE: 29 Dec 43   England: 9 Jan 44   France-ETO: 13 Jul 44 - **25,26,30,32,34** *(4th Armd Div)*

BATTALION DESIGNATION AND TYPE	FORMED (SOURCE OF UNIT)/INACTIVATION *Active through 1946	AUGUST 1945 LOCATION

95th Armored Field Artillery Bn   1 Jan 42 Ft Knox Ky / 9 Oct 45 Cp Myles Standish Mass   Uder Germany
NYPE: 11 Feb 44   England: 23 Feb 44   France-ETO: 25 Jul 44 - **25,26,30,32,34**   BPE: 8 Oct 45 *(5th Armd Div)*

97th Field Artillery Bn (105mm How Trac-D)   4 Jan 41 Ft Bragg N.C. / 31 Jan 46 Cp Stoneman Calif   Dulag Philippines
SFPE: 15 Mar 42   New Caledonia: 5 Apr 42   Guadalcanal: 16 Jan 43   New Caledonia: 13 Dec 43   Philippines: 21 May 45 - **11,13**
(75mm How Pk thru 1941) (nondiv)

98th Field Artillery Bn (75mm How Pack)   13 Jan 41 Ft Lewis Wash / 24 Sep 44 New Guinea redes 6th Ranger Inf Bn
HRPE: 27 Dec 42   Australia: 30 Jan 43   New Guinea: 26 Aug 44 - **15** *(nondiv)*

99th Field Artillery Bn (105mm How Trac-D)   16 Dec 40 Edgewood Arsenal Md (99th FA) / *   Lucena Philippines
SFPE: 23 May 43   Australia: 23 Jun 43   Los Negros: 28 Feb 44   Admiralty I: 16 Mar 44   Philippines: 20 Oct 44 - **3,13,14,15**
(75mm How Pk thru 1941) (1st Cav Div)

101st Field Artillery Bn (105mm How Trk-D)   3 Feb 42 Cp Edwards Mass (1st Bn, 101st FA) / 25 Dec 45 Cp Patrick Henry Va   Cernice Czechoslovakia
NYPE: 27 Aug 44   France-ETO: 7 Sep 44 - **25,26,32,34**   HRPE: 25 Dec 45 *(26th In Div)*

102nd Field Artillery Bn (105mm How Trk-D)   3 Feb 42 Cp Edwards Mass (2nd Bn, 102nd FA) / 25 Dec 45 Cp Patrick Henry Va   Rozmital Czechoslovakia
NYPE: 27 Aug 44   France-ETO: 7 Sep 44 - **25,26,32,34**   HRPE: 25 Dec 45 *(26th Inf Div)*

103rd Field Artillery Bn (105mm How Trac-D)   10 Feb 42 Cp Blanding Fla (1st Bn, 103rd FA) / 22 Oct 45 Cp Stoneman Calif   Cabanatuan Philippines
SFPE: 5 Oct 42   New Hebrides: 26 Oct 42   New Georgia: 30 Jun 43   Guadalcanal: 28 Jun 44   New Zealand: 17 Feb 44
New Guinea: 22 Jul 44   Philippines: 9 Jan 45 - **14,15,16**   SFPE: 19 Oct 45 *(43rd Inf Div)*

104th Field Artillery Bn (105mm How Trk-D)   1 Sep 42 Ft Shafter Hawaii (2nd Bn, 104th FA) / 31 Dec 45 Ft Lawton Wash   Okinawa
Hawaii: 1 Sep 42   Saipan: 17 Jun 44   Espiritu Santo: 4 Sep 44   Okinawa: 9 Apr 45 - **10,19,21**   SPE: 31 Dec 45 *(27th Inf Div)*

105th Field Artillery Bn (105mm How Trk-D)   1 Sep 42 Ft Shafter Hawaii (1st Bn, 105th FA) / 31 Dec 45 Ft Lawton Wash   Okinawa
Hawaii: 1 Sep 42   Saipan: 17 Jun 44   Espiritu Santo: 4 Sep 44   Okinawa: 9 Apr 45 - **10,19,21**   SPE: 31 Dec 45 *(27th Inf Div)*

106th Field Artillery Bn (155mm How Trac-D)   1 Sep 42 Ft Shafter Hawaii (1st Bn, 106th FA) / 31 Dec 45 Ft Lawton Wash   Okinawa
Hawaii: 1 Sep 42   Saipan: 17 Jun 44   Espiritu Santo: 4 Sep 44   Okinawa: 9 Apr 45 - **10,19,21**   SPE: 31 Dec 45 *(27th Inf Div)*

107th Field Artillery Bn (105mm How Trk-D)   7 Feb 42 Cp Beauregard La (1st Bn, 107th FA) / 27 Oct 45 Cp Shelby Miss   Cp Shelby Miss
BPE: 11 Oct 43   England: 18 Oct 43   France-ETO: 22 Jul 44 - **25,26,30,32,34**   BPE: 2 Aug 45 *(28th Inf Div)*

108th Field Artillery Bn (155mm How Trac-D)   7 Feb 42 Cp Beauregard La (2nd Bn, 108th FA) / 25 Oct 45 Cp Shelby Miss   Cp Shelby Miss
BPE: 11 Oct 43   England: 18 Oct 43   France-ETO: 22 Jul 44 - **25,26,30,32,34**   BPE: 2 Aug 45 *(28th Inf Div)*

109th Field Artillery Bn (105mm How Trk-D)   7 Feb 42 Cp Beauregard La (2nd Bn, 109th FA; / 30 Oct 45 Cp Shelby Miss   Cp Shelby Miss
BPE: 30 Sep 43   England: 1 Nov 43   France-ETO: 22 Jul 44 - **25,26,30,32,34**   BPE: 2 Aug 45 *(28th Inf Div)*

110th Field Artillery Bn (105mm How Trk-D)   28 Feb 42 Ft George G Meade Md (1st Bn, 110th FA) / 6 Jan 45 Cp Kilmer N.J.   Rodenkirchen Germany
NYPE: 5 Oct 42   England: 11 Oct 42   France-ETO: 6 Jun 44 - **26,30,32,34**   NYPE: 4 Jan 46 *(29th Inf Div)*

111th Field Artillery Bn (105mm How Trk-D)   28 Feb 42 Ft George G Meade Md (1st Bn, 111th FA) / 6 Jan 45 Cp Kilmer N.J.   Tossens Germany
NYPE: 27 Sep 42   England: 2 Oct 42   France-ETO: 6 Jun 44 - **26,30,32,34**   NYPE: 4 Jan 46 *(29th Inf Div)*

113th Field Artillery Bn (155mm How Trac-D)   7 Feb 42 Ft Jackson S.C. (1st Bn, 113th FA) / 20 Nov 45 Ft Jackson S.C.   Shipment #10390-N at sea
BPE: 11 Feb 44   England: 23 Feb 44   France-ETO: 10 Jun 44 - **25,26,30,32,34**   NYPE: 21 Aug 45 *(30th Inf Div)*

114th Field Artillery Bn (155mm How Trac-D)   10 Feb 42 Cp Blanding Fla (1st Bn, 114th FA) / 21 Dec 45 Cp Stoneman Calif   Valencia Mindanao Philippines
HRPE: 9 Feb 44   New Guinea: 17 Mar 44   Morotai: 17 Sep 44   Philippines: 22 Apr 45 - **15,20**   SFPE: 19 Dec 45 *(31st Inf Div)*

115th Field Artillery Bn (105mm How Trk-D)   7 Feb 42 Ft Jackson S.C. (1st Bn, 115th FA) / 20 Apr 46 Germany   Weiler Germany
BPE: 21 Aug 42   Iceland: 31 Aug 42   England: 6 Nov 43   France-ETO: 23 Sep 44 - **25,26,32,34**
(relieved from 30th Inf Dvi 24 Aug 42) (nondiv)

116th Field Artillery Bn (105mm How Trac-D)   10 Feb 42 Cp Blanding Fla (1st Bn, 116th FA) / 20 Dec 45 Cp Stoneman Calif   Valencia Mindanao Philippines
HRPE: 2 Mar 44   New Guinea: 7 Apr 44   Morotai: 15 Sep 44   Philippines: 22 Apr 45 - **15,20**   SFPE: 20 Dec 45 *(31st Inf Div)*

117th Field Artillary Bn (105mm How Trac-D)   10 Feb 42 Cp Blanding Fla (1st Bn, 117th FA) / 8 Dec 45 Cp Stoneman Calif   Valencia Mindanao Philippines
HRPE: 2 Mar 44   New Guinea: 7 Apr 44   Morotai: 16 Sep 44   Philippines: 22 Apr 45 - **15,20**   SFPE: 7 Dec 45 *(31st Inf Div)*

118th Field Artillery Bn (105mm How Trk-D)   7 Feb 42 Ft Jackson S.C. (1st Bn, 118th FA) /13 Nov 45 Ft Jackson S.C.   Shipment #10390-K in England
HRPE: 11 Feb 44   England: 23 Feb 44   France-ETO: 10 Jun 44 - **25,26,30,32,34**   NYPE: 21 Aug 45 *(30th Inf Div)*

120th Field Artillery Bn (105mm How Trac-D)   31 Jan 42 Cp Livingston La (1st Bn, 120th FA) / 28 Feb 46 Japan   Anabat Philippines
SFPE: 22 Apr 42   Australia: 14 May 42   Goodenough I: 28 Oct 43   New Guinea: 2 Jan 44   Philippines: 14 Nov 44 - **13,14,15** *(32nd Inf Div)*

121st Field Artillery Bn (155mm How Trac-D)   16 Jan 42 Ft Devens Mass (1st Bn, 121st FA) / 28 Feb 46 Japan   Anabat Philippines
SFPE: 22 Apr 42   Australia: 14 May 42   Goodenough I: 28 Oct 43   New Guinea: 8 Jan 44   Biak I: 27 May 44
Philippines: 14 Nov 44 - **13,14,15** *(32nd Inf Div)*

BATTALION DESIGNATION AND TYPE	FORMED (SOURCE OF UNIT)/INACTIVATION	AUGUST 1945 LOCATION

122nd Field Artillery Bn (105mm How Trac-D) 12 Feb 42 Cp Forrest Tenn (1st Bn, 122nd FA) / 5 Feb 46 Japan — Baguio Philippines
SFPE: 8 Jul 43   Hawaii: 15 Jul 43   New Guinea: 11 May 44   Morotai: 18 Dec 44   Philippines: 10 Feb 45 - **14,15** (33rd Inf Div)

123rd Field Artillery Bn (155mm How Trac-D) 12 Feb 42 Cp Forrest Tenn (1st Bn, 123rd FA)/5 Feb 46 Japan — Baguio Philippines
SFPE: 8 Jul 43   Hawaii: 15 Jul 43   New Guinea: 19 May 44   Morotai: 18 Dec 44   Philippines: 10 Feb 45 - **14,15** (33rd Inf Div)

124th Field Artillery Bn (105mm How Trac-D) 12 Feb 42 Cp Forrest Tenn (2nd Bn, 124th FA) / 5 Feb 46 Japan — Baguio Philippines
SFPE: 21 Jun 43   Hawaii: 27 Jun 43   New Guinea: 19 May 44   Morotai: 18 Dec 44   Philippines: 10 Feb 45 - **14,15** (33rd Inf Div)

125th Field Artillery Bn (105mm How Trk-D) 30 Jan 42 Ft Dix N.J. (1st Bn, 125th FA) / 3 Nov 45 Cp Patrick Henry Va — Iseo Italy
NYPE: 30 Apr 42   N.Ireland: 13 May 42   Scotland: 13 Dec 42   N.Africa: 3 Jan 43   Italy: 21 Sep 43 - **24,29,31,33,35,38**   HRPE: 3 Nov 45
(34th Inf Div)

126th Field Artillery Bn (105mm How Trac-D) 31 Jan 42 Cp Livingston La (1st Bn, 126th FA) / 28 Feb 46 Japan — Anabat Philippines
SFPE: 22 Apr 42   Australia: 14 May 42   Goodenough I: 28 Oct 43   New Guinea: 8 Jan 44   Philippines: 14 Nov 44 - **13,14,15** (32nd Inf Div)

127th Field Artillery Bn (155mm How Trac-D) 3 Feb 42 Cp San Luis Obispo Calif (2nd Bn, 127th FA) / 20 Nov 45 Cp Breckinridge — Sobernheim Germany
NYPE: 12 May 44   England: 26 May 44   France-ETO: 6 Jul 44 - **25,26,30,32,34**   NYPE: 10 Sep 45 (35th Inf Div)   Ky

128th Armored Field Artillery Bn 26 Sep 42 Cp Chaffee Ark (1st Bn, 128th FA) / 27 Nov 45 Cp Kilmer N.J. — Weimar Germany
NYPE: 11 Feb 44   England: 23 Feb 44   France-ETO: 22 Jul 44 - **25,26,30,32,34**   NYPE: 26 Nov 45 (assigned 6th Armd Div 11 Oct 42)
(6th Armd Div)

129th Field Artillery Bn (105mm How Trac-D) 16 Jan 42 Cp Livingston La (2nd Bn, 120th FA) / 28 Feb 46 Japan — Anabat Philippines
SFPE: 22 Apr 42   Australia: 14 May 42   Goodenough I: 28 Oct 43   New Guinea: 8 Jan 44   Philippines: 14 Nov 44 - **13,14,15** (32nd Inf Div)

130th Field Artillery Bn (105mm How Trk-D) 3 Feb 42 Cp San Luis Obispo Calif (1st Bn, 130th FA) /11 Dec 45 Cp M Standish — Wach Germany
NYPE: 2 Dec 44   England: 12 Dec 44   France-ETO: 13 Feb 45   BPE: 10 Dec 45 (relieved from 35th Inf Div 27 Jan 43) (nondiv)   Mass

131st Field Artillery Bn (105mm How Trk-D) 31 Jan 42 Cp Bowie Tex (1st Bn, 131st FA) / 26 Dec 45 Cp Patrick Henry Va — Bolzheim Germany
NYPE: 2 Apr 43   N.Africa: 13 Apr 43   Italy: 9 Sep 43   France-ETO: 15 Aug 44   HRPE: 26 Dec 45 - **24,25,26,29,34,35,37** (36th Inf Div)

132nd Field Artillery Bn (105mm How Trk-D) 31 Jan 42 Cp Bowie Tex (1st Bn, 132nd FA) /18 Dec 45 Cp Patrick Henry Va — Erolzheim Germany
NYPE: 2 Apr 43   N.Africa: 13 Apr 43   Italy: 9 Sep 43   France-ETO: 15 Aug 44   HRPE: 18 Dec 45 - **24,25,26,29,34,35,37** (36th Inf Div)

133rd Field Artillery Bn (155mm How Trk-D) (I) 31 Jan 42 Cp Bowie Tex (1st Bn, 133rd FA) / 5 Nov 42 Cp Edwards Mass redes
(36th Inf Div)   155th FA Bn

133rd Field Artillery Bn (105mm How Trk-D) (II) 5 Nov 42 Cp Edwards Mass (155th FA Bn) /18 Dec 45 Cp Patrick Henry Va — Schwendi Germany
NYPE: 2 Apr 43   N.Africa: 13 Apr 43   Italy: 9 Sep 43   France-ETO: 15 Aug 44 - **24,25,26,29,34,35,37**   HRPE: 18 Dec 45
(When the 36th Div was triangularized, it was authorized the 131st, 132nd, 133rd and 155th FA Bns. Since the 133rd FA had been the
division's 155mm How regiment, in order to conform gun caliber (155mm) to unit title (155th FA Bn) the 133rd FA's 1st Bn (155mm) was
redes the 155th FA Bn, and this 133rd FA Bn was formed from the 105mm-equipped 155th FA Bn which had been redes from the 2nd Bn of
the 132nd FA which was the actual source of the new 133rd FA Bn) (36th Inf Div)

134th Field Artillery Bn (105mm How Trk-D) 16 Jan 42 Cp Shelby Miss (134th FA) /13 Oct 45 Ft Bragg N.C. — Ft Bragg N.C.
NYPE: 7 Apr 42   Australia: 9 May 42   Woodlark I: 1 Jul 43   New Guinea: 26 Jan 44   Australia: 30 Jan 44 - **15**   SFPE: 21 Jan 44
(relieved from 37th Inf Div 2 Jun 43) (nondiv)

135th Field Artillery Bn (105mm How Trac-D) 16 Jan 42 Cp Shelby Miss (1st Bn, 135th FA) /13 Dec 45 Cp Anza Calif — San Jose Philippines
SFPE: 26 May 42   New Zealand: 12 Jun 42   Fiji I: 28 Jun 42   Guadalcanal: 5 Apr 43   New Guinea: 22 Jul 43   New Georgia: 22 Jul 43
Bougainville: 8 Nov 43   Philippines: 9 Jan 45 - **14,16**   LAPE: 12 Dec 45 (37th Inf Div)

136th Field Artillery Bn (105mm How Trac-D) 16 Jan 42 Cp Shelby Miss (1st Bn, 136th FA) /13 Dec 45 Cp Anza Calif — San Jose Philippines
SFPE: 26 May 42   New Zealand: 12 Jun 42   Fiji I: 28 Jun 42   Guadalcanal: 5 Apr 43   New Guinea: 22 Jul 43   New Georgia: 22 Jul 43
Bougainville: 8 Nov 43   Philippines: 9 Jan 45 - **14,16**   LAPE: 12 Dec 45 (37th Inf Div)

138th Field Artillery Bn (105mm How Trac-D) 10 Feb 42 Cp Shelby Miss (1st Bn, 138th FA) /1 Nov 45 Cp Anza Calif — Manila Philippines
NOPE: 1 Jan 44   Hawaii: 20 Jan 44   New Guinea: 2 Aug 44   Philippines: 14 Dec 44 - **13,14,15**   LAPE: 31 Oct 45 (38th Inf Div)

139th Field Artillery Bn (105mm How Trac-D) 10 Feb 42 Cp Shelby Miss (1st Bn, 139th FA) /1 Nov 45 Cp Anza Calif — Manila Philippines
NOPE: 1 Jan 44   Hawaii: 20 Jan 44   New Guinea: 2 Aug 44   Philippines: 14 Dec 44 - **13,14,15**   LAPE: 31 Oct 45 (38th Inf Div)

140th Field Artillery Bn (105mm How Trac-D) 16 Jan 42 Cp Shelby Miss (2nd Bn, 134th FA) /18 Dec 45 Cp Stoneman Calif — San Jose Philippines
SFPE: 26 May 42   New Zealand: 12 Jun 42   Fiji I: 28 Jun 42   Guadalcanal: 5 Apr 43   New Georgia: 18 Apr 43   Bougainville: 2 Nov 43
Philippines: 9 Jan 45 - **14,16**   SFPE: 11 Dec 45 (37th Inf Div)

141st Field Artillery Bn (155mm How Trac-D) 30 Jul 43 Cp Gordon Ga (1st Bn, 141st FA) /16 Dec 45 Cp Kilmer N.J. — Deining Germany
NYPE: 21 Aug 43   N.Africa: 2 Sep 43   Italy: Nov 43   France-ETO: 15 Aug 44 - **24,26,29,34,35,37**   NYPE: 14 Dec 45 (nondiv)

143rd Field Artillery Bn (105mm How Trac-D) 5 Feb 42 Ventura Calif (1st Bn, 143rd FA) / 7 Apr 46 Cp Stoneman Calif — Negros Philippines
SFPE: 26 Aug 42   Hawaii: 5 Sep 42   Guadalcanal: 4 Jan 44   New Britain: 23 Apr 44   Philippines: 9 Jan 45 - **3,14,20**   SFPE: 5 Apr 46
(entire service with 40th Inf Div except when assigned to 27th Inf 1 Sep 42–30 Oct 42 in Hawaii) (40th Inf Div)

BATTALION DESIGNATION AND TYPE	FORMED (SOURCE OF UNIT) / INACTIVATION	AUGUST 1945 LOCATION

145th Field Artillery Bn (155mm How Trac-D) 6 Jun 42 Hawaii (2nd Bn, 145th FA) / 26 Jan 46 Korea   Okinawa
Hawaii: 6 Jun 42 Kwajalein: 31 Jan 44 Hawaii: 24 Feb 44 Saipan: 17 Jun 44 Tinian: 24 Jul 44 Philippines: 6 Dec 44
Okinawa: 1 Apr 45 - **10,13,19,21** (nondiv)

146th Field Artillery Bn (105mm How Trac-D)   14 Feb 42 Ft Lewis Wash (1st Bn, 146th FA) / 31 Dec 45 Japan   Zamboanga Philippines
SFPE: 22 Apr 42 Australia: 14 May 42 New Guinea: 25 Jan 43 Biak I: 27 May 44 Philippines: 9 Feb 45 - **14,15,20** (41st Inf Div)

147th Field Artillery Bn (105mm How Trac-D)   31 Dec 43 Kiriwina I (2nd Bn, 147th FA) /17 Jan 46 Japan   Manila Philippines
Kiriwina, Trobriand I: 31 Dec 43 New Guinea: 6 Apr 44 Noemfoor I: 2 Jul 44 Philippines: 11 Jan 45 - **3,14,15** (nondiv)

148th Field Artillery Bn (105mm How Trac-D)   17 Jun 42 Australia (1st Bn, 148th FA) /17 Jan 46 Japan   Manila Philippines
Australia: 17 Jun 42 New Britain: 15 Dec 43 New Guinea: 19 Jun 43 Philippines: 29 Nov 44 - **3,13,14,15** (nondiv)

149th Field Artillery Bn (105mm How Trac-D)   10 Feb 42 Cp Blanding Fla (2nd Bn, 116th FA) / 21 Dec 45 Cp Stoneman Calif   Valencia Mindanao Philippines
HRPE: 9 Feb 44 New Guinea: 15 Mar 44 Morotai: 15 Sep 44 Mapia I: 15 Nov 44 Philippines: 30 Apr 45 - **15,20,21** SFPE: 21 Dec 45
(31st Inf Div)

150th Field Artillery Bn (155mm How Trac-D)   10 Feb 42 Cp Shelby Miss (1st Bn, 150th FA) /1 Nov 45 Cp Anza Calif   Manila Philippines
NOPE: 1 Jan 44 Hawaii: 21 Jan 44 New Guinea: 24 Jul 44 Philippines: 14 Dec 44 - **13,14,15** LAPE: 31 Oct 45 (38th Inf Div)

151st Field Artillery Bn (105mm How Trk-D)   30 Jan 42 N.Ireland (1st Bn, 151st FA) / 3 Nov 45 Cp Patrick Henry Va   Iseo Italy
N.Ireland: 30 Jan 42 N.Africa: 10 Aug 43 Italy: 9 Sep 43 - **24,29,31,33,35,38** HRPE: 3 Nov 45 (34th Inf Div)

152nd Field Artillery Bn (105mm How Trac-D)   10 Feb 42 Cp Blanding Fla (2nd Bn, 152nd FA) /14 Oct 45 Cp Stoneman Calif   Cabanatuan Philippines
SFPE: 1 Oct 42 New Zealand: 22 Oct 42 New Caledonia: 17 Nov 42 Guadalcanal: 15 Feb 43 Russell I: 21 Feb 43
New Zealand: 17 Feb 44 Wickham I: 30 Jun 43 New Guinea: 22 Jul 44 Philippines: 9 Jan 45 - **11,14,15,16** SFPE: 10 Oct 45 (43rd Inf Div)

153rd Field Artillery Bn (8-inch Gun Trac-D)   15 Nov 42 Ft Bliss Tex / 3 Dec 45 Cp Shanks N.Y.   Walheim Germany
NYPE: 3 May 44 England: 15 May 44 France-ETO: 26 Jun 44 - **25,26,30,32,34** NYPE: 2 Dec 45
(105mm How Trk-D in Z.I.; relieved from 1st Cav Div 15 Mar 43) (nondiv)

154th Field Artillery Bn (155mm How Trac-D)   3 Feb 42 Cp San Luis Obispo Calif (2nd Bn, 130th FA) /1 Jan 46 Cp Stoneman Calif   Shipment #2892-J
SPE: 27 Jul 42 Alaska: 11 Aug 42 SPE: 1 May 44 SFPE: 12 Jul 45 Philippines: Aug 45 - **2** SFPE: 30 Dec 45
(relieved from 35th Inf Div 12 Jan 43) (nondiv)

155th Field Artillery Bn (105mm How Trk-D) (I)   31 Jan 42 Cp Bowie Tex (2nd Bn, 132nd FA) /5 Nov 42 Cp Edwards Mass redes
(36th Inf Div)   133rd FA Bn

155th Field Artillery Bn (155mm How Trac-D) (II)   5 Nov 42 Cp Edwards Mass (133rd FA Bn) /18 Dec 45 Cp Patrick Henry Va   Orsenhausen Germany
NYPE: 2 Apr 43 N.Africa: 13 Apr 43 Italy: 9 Sep 43 France-ETO: 15 Aug 44 - **24,25,26,29,34,35,37** HRPE: 18 Dec 45
(see note - 133rd FA Bn) (36th Inf Div)

156th Field Artillery Bn (105mm How Trk-D)   20 Feb 42 Cp Claiborne La (1st Bn, 156th FA) / 5 Nov 45 Cp Chaffee Ark   Cp Chaffee Ark
BPE: 5 Sep 44 France-ETO: 15 Sep 44 - **25,26,32,34** NYPE: 20 Jul 45 (44th Inf Div)

157th Field Artillery Bn (155mm How Trac-D)   20 Feb 42 Cp Claiborne La (2nd Bn, 157th FA) /12 Nov 45 Cp Chaffee Ark   Cp Chaffee Ark
BPE: 5 Sep 44 France-ETO: 15 Sep 44 - **25,26,32,34** NYPE: 20 Jul 45 (44th Inf Div)

158th Field Artillery Bn (105mm How Trk-D)   11 Feb 42 Ft Sill Okla (1st Bn, 158th FA) / 24 Nov 45 Cp Bowie Tex   Munchen Germany
HRPE: 3 Jun 43 N.Africa: 22 Jun 43 Sicily: 9 Jul 43 Italy: 9 Sep 43 France-ETO: 15 Aug 44 - **24,25,26,29,34,35,36,37**
NYPE: 12 Sep 45 (45th Inf Div)

159th Field Artillery Bn (Cld) (105mm How Trac-D) 25 Feb 43 Ft Clark Tex /15 Feb 44 Cp Crowder Mo   (2nd Cav Div)

160th Field Artillery Bn (105mm How Trk-D)   11 Feb 42 Cp Barkeley Tex (1st Bn, 160th FA) / 24 Nov 45 Cp Bowie Tex   Munchen Germany
HRPE: 4 Jun 43 N.Africa: 22 Jun 43 Sicily: 9 Jul 43 Italy: 9 Sep 43 France-ETO: 15 Aug 44 - **24,25,26,29,34,35,36,37**
NYPE: 12 Sep 45 (45th Inf Div)

161st Field Artillery Bn (105mm How Trek-D)   3 Feb 42 Cp San Luis Obispo Calif (1st Bn, 161st FA) / 20 Nov 45 Cp Breckinridge   Baumholder Germany
NYPE: 12 May 44 England: 25 May 44 France-ETO: 6 Jul 44 - **25,26,30,32,34** NYPE: 10 Sep 45 (35th Inf Div)   Ky

162nd Field Artillery Bn (105mm How Trk-D)   31 May 42 Puerto Rico (1st Bn, 162nd FA) / 6 May 46 Puerto Rico   Waldkatzenbach Germany
Puerto Rico: 31 May 42 Canal Zone: Unknown NOPE: 30 Jul 44 NYPE: 8 Apr 45 France-ETO: 19 Apr 45 - **26** Puerto Rico: 9 Nov 45
(nondiv)

163rd Field Artillery Bn (105mm How Trac-D)   10 Feb 42 Cp Shelby Miss (2nd Bn, 139th FA) /1 Nov 45 Cp Anza Calif   Manila Philippines
NOPE: 1 Jan 44 Hawaii: 20 Jan 44 New Guinea: 20 Jul 44 Philippines: 14 Dec 44 - **13,14,15** LAPE: 31 Oct 45 (38th Inf Div)

164th Field Artillery Bn (105mm How Trac-D)   5 Feb 42 El Cajon Calif (2nd Bn, 143rd FA) /7 Apr 46 Ft Mason Calif   Negros Philippines
SFPE: 4 Sep 42 Hawaii: 12 Sep 42 Guadalcanal: 5 Feb 44 New Britain: 23 Apr 44 Philippines: 9 Jan 45 - **3,13,14** SFPE: 5 Apr 46
(entire service with 40th Inf Div except 1 Sep 42-1 Apr 43 in Hawaii when temporarily relieved of assignment to division) (40th Inf Div)

165th Field Artillery Bn (155mm How Trac-D)   20 Feb 42 Cp Claiborne La (2nd Bn, 165th FA) /15 Apr 46 Philippines   Shipment #4122-B unloading
SPE: 19 Jul 42 Alaska: 1 Aug 42 SPE: 24 May 44 SFPE: 26 Jun 45 Philippines: 26 Jul 45 - **2** (105mm How Trk-D until late 44)
(relieved from 44th Inf Div 27 Jan 43) (nondiv)

BATTALION DESIGNATION AND TYPE	FORMED (SOURCE OF UNIT)/INACTIVATION	AUGUST 1945 LOCATION

167th Field Artillery Bn (105mm How Trac-D)   14 Feb 42 Ft Lewis Wash (2nd Bn, 146th FA) / 31 Dec 45 Japan   Zamboanga Philippines
SFPE: 19 Mar 42   Australia: 6 Apr 42   New Guinea: 25 Jan 43   Biak I: 27 May 44   Philippines: 9 Feb 45 - **14,15,20** *(41st Inf Div)*

168th Field Artillery Bn (155mm Gun Trac-D)   8 Feb 43 Cp San Luis Obispo Calif (1st Bn, 168th FA) /17 Jan 46 Cp Stoneman   Rosales, Philippines
SFPE: 1 Nov 43   Australia: 18 Nov 43   New Guinea: 22 Apr 44   Philippines: 11 Jan 45 - **14,15**   SFPE: 15 Jan 46 *(nondiv)*   Calif

169th Field Artillery Bn (105mm How Trac-D)   10 Feb 42 Cp Blanding Fla (2nd Bn, 103rd FA) / 22 Oct 45 Cp Stoneman Calif   Cabanatuan Philippines
SFPE: 1 Oct 42   New Zealand: 27 Oct 42   New Caledonia: 28 Nov 42   Guadalcanal: 23 Feb 43   Russell I: 12 Mar 43
New Georgia: 22 Jun 43   New Guinea: 22 Jul 44   Philippines: 9 Jan 45 - **11,14,15,16**   SFPE: 19 Oct 45 *(43rd Inf Div)*

170th Field Artillery Bn (105mm How Trk-D)   20 Feb 42 Cp Claiborne La (2nd Bn, 156th FA) /12 Nov 45 Cp Hood Tex   Cp Hood Tex
NYPE: 16 Dec 44   England: 21 Dec 44   France-ETO: 4 Mar 45 - **26,34**   HRPE: 19 Jul 45 *(relieved from 44th Inf Div 27 Jan 43) (nondiv)*

171st Field Artillery Bn (105mm How Trk-D)   11 Feb 42 Cp Barkeley Tex (2nd Bn, 160th FA) / 24 Nov 45 Cp Bowie Tex   Munchen Germany
HRPE: 4 Jun 43   N.Africa: 22 Jun 43   Sicily: 9 Jul 43   Italy: 11 Sep 43   France-ETO: 15 Aug 44 - **24,25,26,29,34,35,36,37**
NYPE: 12 Sep 45 *(45th Inf Div)*

172nd Field Artillery Bn (4.5-inch Gun Trac-D)   10 Mar 43 Cp Shelby Miss (1st Bn, 172nd FA) /19 Nov 45 Cp Patrick Henry Va   Eschwege Germany
BPE: 24 Mar 44   England: 4 Apr 44   France-ETO: 14 Jun 44 - **25,26,30,32,34**   HRPE: 19 Nov 45 *(155mm How Trk-D until late 1943)*
(nondiv)

173rd Field Artillery Bn (155mm Gun Trk-D)   8 Feb 43 Cp Gruber Okla (1st Bn, 173rd FA) /11 Sep 45 Italy   Quinzano Italy
NYPE: 21 Aug 43   N.Africa: 2 Sep 43   Italy: 26 Nov 43 - **29,31,33,35** *(nondiv)*

174th Field Artillery Bn (155mm Gun S-P)   25 Feb 43 Cp Bowie Tex (1st Bn, 174th FA) / 23 Dec 45 Cp Kilmer N.J.   Linz Austria
NYPE: 27 Feb 44   England: 9 Mar 44   France-ETO: 1 Jul 44 - **25,26,30,32,34**   NYPE: 22 Dec 45 *(nondiv)*

175th Field Artillery Bn (105mm How Trk-D)   30 Jan 42 Ft Dix N.J. (2nd Bn, 151st FA) / 3 Nov 45 Cp Patrick Henry Va   Iseo Italy
NYPE: 30 Apr 42   England: 13 May 42   N.Africa: 3 Jan 43   Italy: 21 Sep 43 - **23,24,29,31,33,35,38**   HRPE: 3 Nov 45 *(34th Inf Div)*

176th Field Artillery Bn (4.5-inch Gun Trac-D)   28 Feb 42 Ft George G Meade Md (1st Bn, 176th FA) / 5 Dec 45 Cp Kilmer N.J.   Moosburg Germany
BPE: 2 Jul 44   England: 9 Jul 44   France-ETO: 17 Aug 44 - **25,26,32,34**   NYPE: 4 Dec 45 *(105mm How Trk-D until 1944) (nondiv)*

177th Field Artillery Bn (155mm How Trac-D)   8 Feb 43 Ft Leonard Wood Mo (1st Bn, 177th FA) / 30 Nov 45 Cp Shanks N.Y.   Rinsingen Germany
NYPE: 10 Apr 44   England: 17 Apr 44   France-ETO: 17 Jul 44 - **25,26,30,32,34** *(Truck-D in Z.I.)*   NYPE: 28 Nov 45 *(nondiv)*

178th Field Artillery Bn (155mm How Trac-D)   24 Feb 44 Venafro Italy (1st Bn, 178th FA) /1 Nov 45 Italy   Grantorto Italy
Italy: 24 Feb 44 - **31,33** *(nondiv)*

179th Field Artillery Bn (155mm How Trac-D)   1 Mar 43 Cp Shelby Miss (1st Bn, 179th FA) / 9 Dec 45 Cp Patrick Henry Va   Bogen Germany
BPE: 3 Jul 44   England: 12 Jul 44   France-ETO: 13 Aug 44 - **25,26,30,32,34**   HRPE: 9 Dec 45 *(Truck-D until 1944) (nondiv)*

180th Field Artillery Bn (155mm How Trac-D)   3 Feb 42 Cp Edwards Mass (2nd Bn, 180th FA) /1 Jan 46 Cp Patrick Henry Va   Krumau Germany
NYPE: 27 Aug 44   France-ETO: 7 Sep 44 - **25,26,32,34**   HRPE: 1 Jan 46 *(26th Inf Div)*

181st Field Artillery Bn (155mm How Trac-D)   8 Feb 43 Cp Roberts Calif (1st Bn, 181st FA) / 21 Dec 45 Cp Stoneman Calif   Davao Mindanao Philippines
SFPE: 27 Oct 43   Australia: 13 Nov 43   Goodenough I: 24 Dec 43   New Guinea: 19 Apr 44   Philippines: 9 Jan 45 - **14,15,20**
SFPE: 21 Dec 45 *(Truck-D prior to being sent overseas) (nondiv)*

182nd Field Artillery Bn (155mm How Trac-D)   8 Feb 43 Ft Leonard Wood Mo (1st Bn, 182nd FA) / 3 Dec 45 Cp M Standish Mass   Salzburg Austria
NYPE: 10 Apr 44   England: 16 Apr 44   France-ETO: 25 Jul 44 - **25,26,30,32,34**   HRPE: 2 Dec 45 *(Truck-D until sent overseas) (nondiv)*

183rd Field Artillery Bn (155mm How Trac-D)   8 Feb 43 Ft Lewis Wash (1st Bn, 183rd FA) / 30 Oct 45 Cp Myles Standish Mass   Rassla Germany
BPE: 5 Dec 43   England: 17 Dec 43   France-ETO: 15 Jun 44 - **25,26,30,32,34**   HRPE: 29 Oct 45 *(Truck-D until sent overseas) (nondiv)*

185th Field Artillery Bn (155mm How Trac-D)   30 Jan 42 Ft Dix N.J. (2nd Bn, 185th FA) / 3 Nov 45 Cp Patrick Henry Va   Iseo Italy
NYPE: 30 Apr 42   N.Ireland: 13 May 42   N.Africa: 3 Jan 43   Italy: 21 Sep 43 - **23,24,29,31,33,35,38**   HRPE: 3 Nov 45 *(34th Inf Div)*

186th Field Artillery Bn (155mm How Trac-D)   8 Feb 43 Ft Ethan Allen Vt (1st Bn, 186th FA) /14 Dec 45 Cp Patrick Henry Va   Strakonice Czechoslovakia
NYPE: 21 Oct 43   England: 3 Nov 43   France-ETO: 8 Jun 44 - **25,26,30,32**   HRPE: 14 Dec 45 *(nondiv)*

187th Field Artillery Bn (155mm How Trac-D)   8 Feb 43 Ft Ethan Allen Vt (1st Bn, 187th FA) / 5 Jan 46 Cp Patrick Henry Va   Babylon Czechoslovakia
NYPE: 21 Oct 43   England: 3 Nov 43   France-ETO: 7 Jun 44 - **25,26,30,32,34**   HRPE: 5 Jan 46 *(nondiv)*

188th Field Artillery Bn (155mm How Trac-D)   8 Feb 43 Yakima Wash (1st Bn, 188th FA) / 27 Oct 45 Cp Myles Standish Mass   Bachra Germany
NYPE: 5 Dec 43   England: 15 Dec 43   France-ETO: 11 Jun 44 - **25,26,30,32,34**   BPE: 26 Oct 45 *(Truck-D in Z.I.) (nondiv)*

189th Field Artillery Bn (155mm How Trac-D)   11 Feb 42 Cp Barkeley Tex (1st Bn, 189th FA) / 24 Nov 45 Cp Bowie Tex   Munchen Germany
HRPE: 3 Jun 43   N.Africa: 22 Jun 43   Sicily: 9 Jul 43   Italy: 9 Sep 43   France-ETO: 15 Aug 44 - **24,25,26,29,34,35,36,37**
NYPE: 12 Sep 45 *(45th Inf Div)*

190th Field Artillery Bn (155mm Gun Trac-D)   1 Nov 43 England (1st Bn, 190th FA) /10 Dec 45 Cp Patrick Henry Va   Janovice Czechoslovakia
England: 1 Nov 43   France-ETO: 7 Jun 44 - **25,26,30,32,34**   HRPE: 10 Dec 45 *(nondiv)*

191st Field Artillery Bn (155mm How Trac-D)   8 Feb 43 Cp Roberts Calif (1st Bn, 191st FA) / 3 Dec 45 Cp Shanks N.Y.   Eisenach Germany
BPE: 2 Jul 44   England: 9 Jul 44   France-ETO: 13 Aug 44 - **25,26,32,34**   NYPE: 2 Dec 45 *(Truck-D until sent overseas) (nondiv)*

BATTALION DESIGNATION AND TYPE	FORMED (SOURCE OF UNIT)/INACTIVATION	AUGUST 1945 LOCATION

192nd Field Artillery Bn (155mm How Trac-D)   10 Feb 42 Cp Blanding Fla (2nd Bn, 192nd FA)/22 Oct 45 Cp Stoneman Calif   Cabanatuan Philippines
SFPE: 1 Oct 42   New Zealand: 22 Oct 42   New Caledonia: 30 Dec 42   New Georgia: 30 Jun 43   Guadalcanal: 28 Jan 44
New Guinea: 22 Jul 44   Philippines: 9 Jan 45 - **11,14,15,16**   SFPE: 19 Oct 45   *(43rd Inf Div)*

193rd Field Artillery Bn (105mm How Trk-D)   23 Feb 43 Ft Bragg N.C. (1st Bn, 193rd FA) / 24 Nov 45 Cp Myles Standish Mass   Wasungen Germany
BPE: 12 Aug 44   England: 22 Aug 44   France-ETO: 10 Dec 44 - **25,26,34**   BPE: 23 Nov 45   *(nondiv)*

194th Field Artillery Bn (8-inch How Trk-D)   8 Feb 43 Ft Bragg N.C. (1st Bn, 194th FA) /13 Dec 45 Cp Patrick Henry Va   Utting Germany
NYPE: 21 Aug 43   N.Africa: 2 Sep 43   Italy: 11 Nov 43   France-ETO: 20 Nov 44 - **24,25,26,29,31,33,35**   HRPE: 13 Dec 45 *(nondiv)*

195th Field Artillery Bn (8-inch How Trac-D)   1 Mar 43 Ft Ord Calif (1st Bn, 195th FA) / 28 Nov 45 Cp Myles Standish Mass   Grossenehrich Germany
NYPE: 11 Feb 44   England: 23 Feb 44   France-ETO: 16 Jun 44 - **25,26,30,32,34**   BPE: 27 Nov 45   *(nondiv)*

196th Field Artillery Bn (105mm How Trk-D)   8 Feb 43 Ft Sill Okla (1st Bn, 196th FA) / 26 Nov 45 Cp Patrick Henry Va   Mies Czechoslovakia
NYPE: 11 Feb 44   England: 23 Feb 44   France-ETO: 8 Jul 44 - **25,26,30,32,34**   HRPE: 26 Nov 45   *(nondiv)*

197th Field Artillery Bn (105mm How Trk-D)   7 Sep 42 Ft Jackson S.C. /13 Nov 45 Ft Jackson S.C.   Shipment #10390-L in England
BPE: 11 Feb 44   England: 25 Feb 44   France-ETO: 10 Jun 44 - **25,26,30,32,34**   NYPE: 21 Aug 45   *(30th Inf Div)*

198th Field Artillery Bn (155mm How Trac-D)   10 Feb 42 Hawaii (2nd Bn, 138th FA) / 21 Jan 46 Cp Anza Calif   Okinawa
Hawaii: 10 Feb 42   Philippines: 20 Oct 44   Okinawa: 3 Apr 45 - **13,19**   LAPE: 20 Jan 46 *(relieved from 38th Inf Div 1 Mar 42) (nondiv)*

199th Field Artillery Bn (4.5-inch Gun Trac-D)   20 Feb 42 Ft Hancock N.J. (1st Bn, 199th FA) / 23 Oct 45 Cp Shanks N.Y.   Hermneskiel Germany
NYPE: 11 Aug 44   England: 22 Aug 44   France-ETO: 11 Sep 44 - **32**   NYPE: 22 Oct 45 *(105mm How Trk-D until 1944) (nondiv)*

200th Field Artillery Bn (155mm Gun Trac-D)   1 Nov 43 England (2nd Bn, 190th FA) /16 Dec 45 Cp Kilmer N.J.   Sedlitz Germany
England: 1 Nov 43   France-ETO: 7 Jun 44 - **25,26,30,32,34**   NYPE: 14 Dec 45   *(nondiv)*

202nd Field Artillery Bn (155mm How Trac-D)   1 Mar 43 La Mnvr Area (1st Bn, 202nd FA) / 2 Dec 45 Cp Shanks N.Y.   Obertrum Germany
BPE: 18 Jan 44   England: 29 Jan 44   France-ETO: 3 Jul 44 - **25,26,30,32,34**   NYPE: 1 Dec 45 *(Truck-D until sent overseas) (nondiv)*

203rd Field Artillery Bn (155mm How Trac-D)   8 Feb 43 Ft Bragg N.C. (1st Bn, 203rd FA) / 26 Oct 45 Cp Patrick Henry Va   Friedberg Germany
NYPE: 21 Feb 44   England: 29 Feb 44   France-ETO: 21 Jun 44 - **26,30,32,34**   HRPE: 26 Oct 45 *(Truck-D until sent overseas) (nondiv)*

204th Field Artillery Bn (155mm How Trk-D)   1 Mar 43 Cp Forrest Tenn (1st Bn, 204th FA) / 29 Nov 45 Cp Kilmer N.J.   Steinhofen Germany
NYPE: 28 Mar 44   England: 8 Apr 44   France-ETO: 19 Jul 44 - **25,26,30,32,34**   NYPE: 28 Nov 45   *(nondiv)*

205th Field Artillery Bn (105mm How Trac-D)   14 Feb 42 Port Angeles Wash (2nd Bn, 148th FA) / 31 Dec 45 Japan   Zamboanga Philippines
SFPE: 22 Apr 42   Australia: 14 May 42   New Guinea: 25 Jan 43   Biak I: 27 May 44   Philippines: 9 Feb 45 - **14,15,20**   *(41st Inf Div)*

207th Field Artillery Bn (8-inch How Trac-D)   11 Feb 42 Panama (2nd Bn, 158th FA) /16 Nov 45 Cp Kilmer N.J.   Tann Germany
Panama: 11 Feb 42   SFPE: 25 Jun 43   NYPE: 26 Jul 44   England: 5 Aug 44   France-ETO: 9 Sep 44 - **26,32,34**   NYPE: 14 Nov 45
(105mm How Trk-D until 1944) (nondiv)

208th Field Artillery Bn (155mm Gun Trac-D)   1 Mar 43 Cp Forrest Tenn (1st Bn, 208th FA) / 9 Apr 46 Cp Kilmer N.J.   Henndorf Austria
NYPE: 6 Apr 44   England: 16 Apr 44   France-ETO: 16 Jul 44 - **25,26,30,32,34**   NYPE: 8 Apr 46   *(nondiv)*

209th Field Artillery Bn (155mm How Trac-D)   1 Apr 42 Ft Lewis Wash / 2 Nov 46 Cp Polk La   Entrained to Cp Bowie Tex
SPE: 14 May 42   Alaska: 21 May 42   SPE: 17 May 44   NYPE: 27 Feb 45   France-ETO: 11 Mar 45 - **2,26**   NYPE: 16 Jul 45 *(nondiv)*

210th Field Artillery Bn (105mm How Trac-D)   12 Feb 42 Cp Forrest Tenn (2nd Bn, 122nd FA) / 5 Feb 46 Japan   Baguio Philippines
SFPE: 6 Jul 43   Hawaii: 11 Jul 43   New Guinea: 12 May 44   Morotai: 18 Dec 44   Philippines: 10 Feb 45 - **14,15** *(33rd Inf Div)*

211th Field Artillery Bn (4.5-inch Gun Trac-D)   3 Feb 42 Cp Edwards Mass (1st Bn, 102nd FA) / 9 Mar 46 Cp Kilmer N.J.   Herford Germany
NYPE: 11 Aug 44   England: 22 Aug 44   France-ETO: 15 Sep 44 - **26,32,34**   NYPE: 7 Mar 46 *(105mm How Trk-D until 1944) (nondiv)*

212th Armored Field Artillery Bn   3 Feb 42 Cp Edwards Mass (2nd Bn, 101st FA) / 21 Sep 45 Cp Patrick Henry Va   Holzdorf Germany
NYPE: 11 Feb 44   England: 23 Feb 44   France-ETO: 19 Jul 44 - **25,26,30,32,34**   HRPE: 20 Sep 45
(105mm How Trk-D until assigned 6th Armd Div 1 Sep 42) (6th Armd Div)

213th Field Artillery Bn (105mm How Trac-D)   24 Mar 42 El Cajon Calif (1st Bn, 145th FA) / 7 Apr 46 Ft Mason Calif   Negros Philippines
SFPE: 23 Aug 42   Hawaii: 1 Sep 42   Guadalcanal: 21 Jan 44   New Britain: 23 Apr 44   Philippines: 9 Jan 45 - **3,14,20**   SFPE: 5 Apr 46
(40th Inf Div)

215th Field Artillery Bn (155mm How Trac-D)   21 Jan 43 Ft Bragg N.C. less Btry A formed 15 Jun 42 / 28 Oct 45 Cp Patrick Henry   Branau Germany
NYPE: 20 Sep 44   England: 1 Oct 44   France-ETO: 10 Dec 44 - **25,26,34**   HRPE: 27 Oct 45
(Glider FA Bn, 75mm How Pk, 17 Oct 42–23 Jan 44) (nondiv)

216th Field Artillery Bn (105mm How Trk-D)   6 Jan 43 Cp San Luis Obispo Calif / 20 Nov 45 Cp Breckinridge Ky   Oberkirchen Germany
NYPE: 12 May 44   England: 26 May 44   France-ETO: 6 Jul 44 - **25,26,30,32,34**   NYPE: 10 Sep 45   *(35th Inf Div)*

217th Field Artillery Bn (105mm How Trk-D)   1 Feb 43 Ft Lewis Wash /19 Nov 45 Cp Chaffee Ark   Cp Chaffee Ark
BPE: 5 Sep 44   France-ETO: 15 Sep 44 - **25,26,32,34**   NYPE: 20 Jul 45   *(44th Inf Div)*

BATTALION DESIGNATION AND TYPE	FORMED (SOURCE OF UNIT) / INACTIVATION	AUGUST 1945 LOCATION

218th Field Artillery Bn (155mm How Trac-D)   14 Feb 42 Ft Lewis Wash (2nd Bn, 218th FA) / 31 Dec 45 Japan   Zamboanga Philippines
SFPE: 22 Apr 42   Australia: 14 May 42   New Guinea: 30 Jun 43   Biak I: 27 May 44   Philippines: 9 Feb 45 - **14,15,20** *(41st Inf Div)*

219th Field Artillery Bn (105mm How Trk-D)   12 Jan 43 El Cajon Calif / 20 Nov 45 Cp Breckinridge Ky   Birkenfeld Germany
NYPE: 12 May 44   England: 25 May 44   France-ETO: 6 Jul 44 - **25,26,30,32,34**   NYPE: 10 Sep 45   *(35th Inf Div)*

220th Field Artillery Bn (105mm How Trk-D)   1 Feb 43 Ft Lewis Wash / 7 Nov 45 Cp Chaffee Ark   Cp Chaffee Ark
BPE: 5 Sep 44   France-ETO: 15 Sep 44 - **25,26,32,34**   NYPE: 20 Jul 45   *(44th Inf Div)*

221st Field Artillery Bn (155mm How Trac-D)   17 Jul 42 New Caledonia (1st Bn, 200th FA) / 26 Nov 45 Seattle P/E   Cebu Philippines
New Caledonia: 17 Jul 42   Guadalcanal: 5 Jan 43   Fiji I: 10 Apr 43   Bougainville: 12 Jan 44   Philippines: 26 Jan 45 - **11,13,16,20**
(Americal Div)

222nd Field Artillery Bn (155mm How Trac-D)   5 Feb 42 Cp San Luis Obispo Calif (1st Bn, 222nd FA) / 7 Apr 46 Ft Mason Calif   Negros Philippines
SFPE: 23 Aug 42   Hawaii: 4 Sep 42   Guadalcanal: 31 Dec 43   New Britain: 23 Apr 44   Philippines: 9 Jan 45 - **3,14,20**
SFPE: 5 Apr 46   *(40th Inf Div)*

223rd Field Artillery Bn (155mm Gun Trac-D)   15 Aug 42 New Caledonia (2nd Bn, 200th FA) / 24 Dec 45 Cp Anza Calif   Tacloban Philippines
New Caledonia: 15 Aug 42   Philippines: 18 Jul 45   LAPE: 24 Dec 45 *(Bn relieved from Americal Div 26 Feb 43) (nondiv)*

224th Field Artillery Bn (105mm How Trk-D)   28 Feb 42 Ft George G Meade Md (2nd Bn, 110th FA) / 16 Jan 46 Cp Kilmer N.J.   Blexen Germany
NYPE: 5 Oct 42   England: 11 Oct 42   France-ETO: 6 Jun 44 - **26,30,32,34**   NYPE: 15 Jan 46   *(29th Inf Div)*

225th Field Artillery Bn (155mm How Trac-D)   3 Feb 44 Hawaii (1st Bn, 225th FA) / 21 Jan 46 Ft Lawton Wash   Okinawa
Hawaii: 3 Feb 44   Saipan: 17 Jun 44   Tinian I: 27 Jul 44   Philippines: 6 Dec 44   Okinawa: 2 Apr 45 - **13,19,21**   SPE: 18 Jan 46 *(nondiv)*

226th Field Artillery Bn (155mm Gun Trac-D)   1 Sep 42 Hawaii (2nd Bn, 105th FA) / 21 Jan 46 Cp Anza Calif   Okinawa
Hawaii: 1 Sep 42   Philippines: 20 Oct 44   Okinawa: 14 Jun 45 - **13,19**   LAPE: 20 Jan 46 *(nondiv)*

227th Field Artillery Bn (155mm How Trac-D)   28 Feb 42 Ft George G Meade Md (2nd Bn, 111th FA) / 16 Jan 46 Cp Kilmer N.J.   Broke Germany
NYPE: 27 Sep 42   England: 2 Oct 42   France-ETO: 6 Jun 44 - **26,30,32,34**   NYPE: 15 Jan 46   *(29th Inf Div)*

228th Field Artillery Bn (155mm How Trac-D)   8 Feb 43 Ft Bragg N.C. (1st Bn, 228th FA) / 27 Oct 45 Cp Myles Standish Mass   Lollar Germany
NYPE: 14 Feb 44   England: 23 Feb 44   France-ETO: 28 Jun 44 - **26,30,32,34**   BPE: 26 Oct 45 *(Truck-D until sent overseas) (nondiv)*

229th Field Artillery Bn (105mm How Trk-D)   7 Feb 42 Cp Beauregard La (2nd Bn, 107th FA) / 22 Oct 45 Cp Shelby Miss   Cp Shelby Miss
BPE: 11 Oct 43   England: 18 Oct 43   France-ETO: 22 Jul 44 - **25,26,30,32,34**   BPE: 2 Aug 45   *(28th Inf Div)*

230th Field Artillery Bn (105mm How Trk-D)   7 Feb 42 Ft Jackson S.C. (2nd Bn, 118th FA) / 13 Nov 45 Ft Jackson S.C.   Shipment #10390-M at sea
BPE: 11 Feb 44   England: 25 Feb 44   France-ETO: 10 Jun 44 - **25,26,30,32,34**   NYPE: 21 Aug 45   *(30th Inf Div)*

231st Armored Field Artillery Bn   15 Sep 42 Cp Chaffee Ark / 21 Sep 45 Cp Myles Standish Mass   Blankenhain Germany
NYPE: 11 Feb 44   England: 23 Feb 44   France-ETO: 19 Jul 44 - **25,26,30,32,34**   BPE: 20 Sep 43   *(6th Armed Div)*

232nd Field Artillery Bn (105mm How Trk-D)   14 Jul 43 Cp Gruber Okla / 30 Jun 46 Salzburg Austria   Kufstein Austria
NYPE: 6 Jan 45   France-ETO: 18 Jan 45 - **25,26,34**   *(42nd Inf Div)*

240th Field Artillery Bn (155mm Gun Trac-D)   20 Aug 42 Cp White Oreg / 3 Oct 45 Cp Shanks N.Y.   Feucht Germany
NYPE: 22 Jun 44   England: 28 Jun 44   France-ETO: 10 Aug 44 - **25,26,32,34**   NYPE: 2 Oct 45 *(Truck-D until sent overseas) (nondiv)*

241st Field Artillery Bn (105mm How Trk-D)   20 Aug 42 Cp White Oreg / 10 Dec 45 Cp Patrick Henry Va   Markt Schwaben Germany
NYPE: 2 Jul 44   England: 12 Jul 44   France-ETO: 20 Aug 44 - **25,26,32,34**   HRPE: 10 Dec 45 *(nondiv)*

242nd Field Artillery Bn (105mm How Trk-D)   20 Aug 42 Cp White Oreg / 30 Nov 45 Cp Shanks N.Y.   Landsberg Germany
NYPE: 2 Jul 44   England: 12 Jul 44   France-ETO: 24 Aug 44 - **25,26,32,34**   NYPE: 28 Nov 45 *(nondiv)*

243rd Field Artillery Bn (8-inch Gun Trac-D)   8 Aug 42 Cp Shelby Miss / 22 Feb 46 Cp Kilmer N.J.   Bad Aibling Germany
NYPE: 22 Jun 44   England: 28 Jun 44   France-ETO: 7 Aug 44 - **25,26,32,34**   NYPE: 21 Feb 46 *(105mm How Trk-D until sent overseas) (nondiv)*

244th Field Artillery Bn (Captured Weapons)   8 Aug 42 Cp Shelby Miss / 19 Feb 46 Cp Kilmer N.J.   Cham Germany
NYPE: 2 Jul 44   England: 13 Jul 44   France-ETO: 31 Jul 44 - **25,26,30,32,34**   NYPE: 18 Feb 46 *(initially 105mm How Trk-D until 1944 when reorg as 155mm Gun Trac-D but in ETO outfitted with German 150mm, 100mm, 88mm and French 155mm Schneider cannons) (nondiv)*

245th Field Artillery Bn (105mm How Trac-D)   15 Aug 42 New Caledonia / 26 Nov 45 Ft Lewis Wash   Cebu Philippines
New Caledonia: 15 Aug 42   Guadalcanal: 12 Nov 42   Fiji I: 29 Mar 43   Bougainville: 12 Jan 44   Philippines: 26 Jan 45 - **11,13,16,20**
SPE: 25 Nov 45 *(Americal Division)*

246th Field Artillery Bn (105mm How Trac-D)   15 Aug 42 New Caledonia / 24 Nov 45 Ft Lewis Wash   Cebu Philippines
New Caledonia: 15 Aug 42   Guadalcanal: 12 Nov 42   Fiji I: 29 Mar 43   Bougainville: 12 Jan 44   Philippines: 26 Jan 45 - **11,13,16,20**
SPE: 23 Nov 45 *(Americal Division)*

247th Field Artillery Bn (105mm How Trac-D)   15 Aug 42 New Caledonia / 10 Dec 45 Ft Lewis Wash   Cebu Philippines
New Caledonia: 15 Aug 42   Guadalcanal: 12 Nov 42   Fiji I: 29 Mar 43   Bougainville: 12 Jan 44   Philippines: 26 Jan 45 - **11,13,16,20**
SPE: 9 Dec 45 *(Americal Division)*

BATTALION DESIGNATION AND TYPE	FORMED (SOURCE OF UNIT) / INACTIVATION *Active through 1946	AUGUST 1945 LOCATION

248th Field Artillery Bn (155mm How Trac-D)   24 Feb 44 St. Elia Italy (2nd Bn, 178th FA) / 25 Nov 45 Italy   Montorio Italy
Italy: 24 Feb 44 - **29,31,33,35** *(nondiv)*

249th Field Artillery Bn (105mm How Trac-D)   1 Sep 42 Hawaii (1st Bn, 104th FA) / 31 Dec 45 Ft Lawton Wash   Okinawa
Hawaii: 1 Sep 42   Saipan: 17 Jun 44   Espiritu Santo: 4 Sep 44   Okinawa: 9 Apr 45 - **19,21**   SPE: 31 Dec 45 *(nondiv)*

250th Field Artillery Bn (105mm How Trk-D)   25 Sep 42 Cp Maxey Tex / 8 Mar 46 Cp Kilmer N.J.   Obermoos Germany
NYPE: 11 Feb 44   England: 23 Feb 44   France-ETO: 24 Jul 44 - **25,26,30,32,34**   NYPE: 7 Mar 46 *(nondiv)*

251st Field Artillery Bn (105mm How Trac-D)   25 Sep 42 Cp Maxey Tex / 24 Dec 45 Cp Stoneman Calif   San Jose Philippines
SFPE: 29 Mar 44   Australia: 20 Apr 44   New Guinea: Unknown   Philippines: 21 Jan 45 - **14,15**   SFPE: 24 Dec 45 *(Truck-D in Z.I.)* *(nondiv)*

252nd Field Artillery Bn (105mm How Trk-D)   26 Oct 42 Cp McCoy Wis / 10 Dec 45 Cp Patrick Henry Va   Steinau Germany
NYPE: 11 Aug 44   England: 22 Aug 44   France-ETO: 18 Oct 44 - **26,34**   HRPE: 10 Dec 45 *(nondiv)*

253rd Armored Field Artillery Bn   26 Oct 42 Cp McCoy Wis / 21 Sep 45 Cp Myles Standish Mass   Kreuzburg Germany
NYPE: 2 Jul 44   England: 12 Jul 44   France-ETO: 19 Aug 44 - **25,26,30,32**   BPE: 20 Sep 45 *(105mm How Trk-D until 14 Jan 44)* *(nondiv)*

254th Field Artillery Bn (155mm How Trac-D)   21 Jan 43 Cp Gordon Ga / 11 Nov 45 Cp Kilmer N.J.   Steinbach Unter Germany
BPE: 17 Aug 44   England: 25 Aug 44   France-ETO: 1 Oct 44 - **25,26,34**   NYPE: 10 Nov 45 *(105mm How Trk-D until 1944)* *(nondiv)*

255th Field Artillery Bn (105mm How Trk-D)   21 Jan 43 Cp Gordon Ga / 3 Dec 45 Cp Myles Standish Mass   Wiechtach Germany
NYPE: 2 Jul 44   England: 12 Jul 44   France-ETO: 13 Aug 44 - **25,26,32,34**   BPE: 2 Dec 45 *(nondiv)*

256th Field Artillery Bn (8-inch Gun Trac-D)   21 Jan 43 Cp Gordon Ga / 13 Mar 46 Cp Kilmer N.J.   Ludwigsburg Germany
NYPE: 22 Jun 44   England: 28 Jun 44   France-ETO: 7 Aug 44 - **26,32,34**   NYPE: 12 Mar 46 *(105mm How Trk-D until 1944)* *(nondiv)*

257th Field Artillery Bn (155mm How Trac-D)   21 Jan 43 Cp Gordon Ga / 6 Oct 45 France   Hohenaltheim Germany
NYPE: 29 Sep 44   England: 9 Oct 44   France-ETO: 24 Dec 44 - **25,26,32,34** *(105mm How Trk-D until 1944)* *(nondiv)*

258th Field Artillery Bn (155mm Gun S-P)   8 Feb 43 Pine Camp N.Y. (1st Bn, 258th FA) / 19 Dec 45 Cp Myles Standish Mass   Lehrbach Germany
NYPE: 22 Jan 44   England: 28 Jan 44   France-ETO: 2 Jul 44 - **26,30,32,34**   BPE: 18 Dec 45 *(nondiv)*

259th Field Artillery Bn (4.5-inch Gun Trac-D)   25 Jan 43 Cp Swift Tex / 10 Mar 46 Cp Kilmer N.J.   Witzenhausen Germany
NYPE: 11 Aug 44   England: 22 Aug 44   France-ETO: 16 Sep 44 - **25,26,32,34**   NYPE: 9 Mar 46 *(105mm How Trk-D until 1944)* *(nondiv)*

260th Field Artillery Bn (105mm How Trac-D)   31 Dec 43 Milne Bay New Guinea (1st Bn, 147th FA) / 10 Jun 45 Finschhafen New Guinea
New Guinea: 31 Dec 43 - **3,15** *(nondiv)*

261st Field Artillery Bn (155mm Gun Trac-D)   1 Feb 43 Cp Swift Tex / 13 Feb 46 Cp Bowie Tex   Shipment #10447-E unloading
BPE: 4 Oct 44   England: 12 Oct 44   France-ETO: 8 Dec 44 - **26,34**   HRPE: 13 Aug 45 *(105mm How Trk-D until 1944)* *(nondiv)*

262nd Armored Field Artillery Bn   1 Feb 43 Cp Swift Tex / 15 Sep 45 Cp Shelby Miss   Cp Shelby Miss
(105mm How Trk-D until 1944 when reorg as Trac-D and on 27 Nov 44 redes Armd FA Bn; served at Ft Sill FA School 18 Sep 43–8 Jun 44) *(nondiv)*

263rd Field Artillery Bn (105mm How Trk-D)   12 Feb 43 Ft Jackson S.C. / 25 Dec 45 Cp Patrick Henry Va   Hohenfurth Germany
NYPE: 27 Aug 44   England: 7 Sep 44   France-ETO: 8 Sep 44 - **25,26,32,34**   HRPE: 25 Dec 45 *(26th Inf Div)*

264th Field Artillery Bn (8-inch How Trac-D)   1 Feb 43 Cp Swift Tex / 8 Jan 46 Cp Kilmer N.J.   Abenberg Germany
NYPE: 26 Jul 44   England: 6 Aug 44   France-ETO: 9 Sep 44 - **25,26,32,34**   NYPE: 7 Jan 46 *(105mm How Trk-D until 1944)* *(nondiv)*

265th Field Artillery Bn (240mm How Trac-D)   1 Mar 43 Cp Shelby Miss / 31 Dec 45 Cp Kilmer N.J.   Hilleraleben Germany
NYPE: 18 Jul 44   England: 28 Jul 44   France-ETO: 31 Aug 44 - **26,32,34**   NYPE: 30 Dec 45 *(105mm How Trk-D until 1944)* *(nondiv)*

266th Field Artillery Bn (240mm How Trac-D)   1 Mar 43 Cp Shelby Miss / 21 Dec 45 Cp Myles Standish Mass   Frankenburg Germany
NYPE: 21 Apr 44   England: 26 Apr 44   France-ETO: 4 Jul 44 - **25,26,30,32,34**   BPE: 20 Dec 45 *(105mm How Trk-D until 1944)* *(nondiv)*

267th Field Artillery Bn (240mm How Trac-D)   1 Mar 43 Cp Shelby Miss / 12 Feb 46 Cp Kilmer N.J.   Auerbach Germany sch to
NYPE: 23 Jul 44   England: 28 Jul 44   France-ETO: 2 Sep 44 - **25,26,32,34**   NYPE: 11 Feb 46 *(105mm How Trk-D until 1944)* *(nondiv)*   SWPA under Shipment #R4085-HH

268th Field Artillery Bn (8-inch Gun Trac-D)   1 Mar 43 Cp Shelby Miss / 19 Dec 45 Cp Myles Standish Mass   Allendorf Germany
NYPE: 15 Jul 44   England: 21 Jul 44   France-ETO: 27 Aug 44 - **25,26,32,34**   BPE: 18 Dec 45 *(105mm How Trk-D until 1944)* *(nondiv)*

269th Field Artillery Bn (240mm How Trac-D)   15 Mar 43 Cp Butner N.C. / 29 Nov 45 Cp Kilmer N.J.   Morbach Germany
NYPE: 20 Apr 44   England: 27 Apr 44   France-ETO: 24 Jul 44 - **25,26,30,32,34**   NYPE: 27 Nov 45 *(105mm How Trk-D until 1944)* *(nondiv)*

270th Field Artillery Bn (240mm How Trac-D)   15 Mar 43 Cp Butner N.C. / 25 Oct 45 Cp Myles Standish Mass   Bad Aibling Germany
NYPE: 6 Apr 44   England: 13 Apr 44   France-ETO: 24 Jul 44 - **25,26,30,32,34**   BPE: 24 Oct 45 *(105mm How Trk-D until 1944)* *(nondiv)*

271st Field Artillery Bn (105mm How Trac-D)   11 Oct 43 Australia / *   Lucena Philippines
Australia: 11 Oct 43   New Guinea: 22 Feb 44   Admiralty I: 16 Mar 44   Philippines: 20 Oct 44 - **3,13,14,15** *(1st Cav Div)*

BATTALION DESIGNATION AND TYPE	FORMED (SOURCE OF UNIT)/INACTIVATION *Active through 1946	AUGUST 1945 LOCATION

272nd Field Artillery Bn (240mm How Trac-D) 15 Mar 43 Cp Butner N.C./27 Nov 45 Cp Kilmer N.J.
NYPE: 21 Apr 44 England: 26 Apr 44 France-ETO: 7 Aug 44 - **25,26,32,34** NYPE: 26 Nov 45 *(105mm How Trk-D until 1944) (nondiv)*
Ludwigsburg Germany

273rd Field Artillery Bn (155mm Gun Trac-D) 1 Mar 43 Cp Beale Calif / 27 Dec 45 Cp Kilmer N.J.
BPE: 2 Jul 44 England: 9 Jul 44 France-ETO: 28 Aug 44 - **25,26,30,32,34** NYPE: 26 Dec 45 *(105mm How Trk-D until sent overseas) (nondiv)*
Arbing Germany

274th Armored Field Artillery Bn 15 Apr 43 Cp Phillips Kans / *
NYPE: 2 Jul 44 England: 12 Jul 44 France-ETO: 19 Aug 44 - **25,26,32,34** HRPE: 10 Jul 45 *(105mm How Trk-D until 1 Feb 44) (nondiv)*
Cp Bowie Tex

275th Armored Field Artillery Bn 15 Apr 43 Cp Phillips Kans / 8 Sep 45 Cp Bowie Tex
NYPE: 2 Jul 44 England: 14 Jul 44 France-ETO: 6 Sep 44 - **25,26,32,34** BPE: 3 Jul 45 *(105mm How Trk-D until 1 Feb 44) (nondiv)*
Cp Bowie Tex

276th Armored Field Artillery Bn 15 Apr 43 Cp Phillips Kans /18 Oct 45 Ft Bragg N.C.
NYPE: 2 Jul 44 England: 12 Jul 44 France-ETO: 24 Aug 44 - **25,26,32,34** NYPE: 10 Jul 45 *(105mm How Trk-D until 1 Feb 44) (nondiv)*
Ft Bragg N.C.

277th Field Artillery Bn (240mm How Trac-D) 6 May 43 Cp McCoy Wis /1 Jul 46 France
NYPE: 15 Jul 44 England: 21 Jul 44 France-ETO: 30 Aug 44 - **25,26,32,34** *(105mm How Trk-D until 1944) (nondiv)*
Roth Germany

278th Field Artillery Bn (240mm How Trac-D) 6 May 43 Cp McCoy Wis/19 Jan 46 Cp Kilmer N.J.
NYPE: 15 Jul 44 England: 21 Jul 44 France-ETO: 30 Aug 44 - **25,26,32,34** NYPE: 18 Jan 46 *(105mm How Trk-D until 1944) (nondiv)*
Neuhof Germany

280th Field Artillery Bn (105mm How Trk-D) 10 May 43 Cp Cooke Calif / 9 Mar 46 Cp Kilmer N.J.
BPE: 7 Sep 44 England: 14 Sep 44 France-ETO: 18 Sep 44 - **25,26,32,34** NYPE: 8 Mar 46 *(nondiv)*
Wesenuffer Germany

281st Field Artillery Bn (105mm How Trk-D) 10 May 43 Cp Cooke Calif / 4 Dec 45 Cp Kilmer N.J.
NYPE: 30 Oct 44 England: 11 Nov 44 France-ETO: Unknown - **26,34** NYPE: 2 Dec 45 *(nondiv)*
Schwabach Germany

282nd Field Artillery Bn (105mm How Trk-D) 25 Jun 43 Cp Rucker Ala / 6 Oct 45 France
NYPE: 22 Jun 44 England: 29 Jun 44 France-ETO: 10 Aug 44 - **25,26,32,34** *(nondiv)*
Suhl Germany

283rd Field Artillery Bn (105mm How Trk-D) 25 Jun 43 Cp Rucker Ala /14 Sep 45 Cp Patrick Henry Va
NYPE: 22 Jun 44 England: 29 Jun 44 France-ETO: 9 Aug 44 - **26,32,34** HRPE: 14 Sep 45 *(nondiv)*
Furstenfeldbruck Germany

284th Field Artillery Bn (105mm How Trk-D) 25 Jun 43 Cp Rucker Ala /14 Dec 45 Cp Myles Standish Mass
NYPE: 2 Jul 44 England: 9 Jul 44 France-ETO: 17 Aug 44 - **25,26,32,34** BPE: 13 Dec 45 *(nondiv)*
Munich Germany

285th Field Artillery Observation Bn 11 Jan 43 Cp Gruber Okla / 23 Oct 45 Cp Patrick Henry Va
NYPE: 19 Aug 44 England: 31 Aug 44 France-ETO: Unknown - **25,26,34** HRPE: 23 Oct 45
(assigned FA School Ft Sill 18 Aug 43–11 Aug 44) (nondiv)
Meiningen Germany

286th Field Artillery Observation Bn 15 Apr 43 Ft Bragg N.C. / 30 Oct 45 Cp Myles Standish Mass
NYPE: 28 Aug 44 England: 3 Sep 44 France-ETO: 23 Sep 44 - **25,26,34** BPE: 29 Oct 45 *(nondiv)*
Regensburg Germany

287th Field Artillery Observation Bn 20 May 43 Cp Bowie Tex / 21 Jan 46 Cp Anza Calif
SPE: 10 Jun 44 Hawaii: 16 Jun 44 Philippines: 20 Oct 44 Okinawa: Unknown - **13,19** LAPE: 20 Jan 46 *(nondiv)*
Okinawa

288th Field Artillery Observation Bn 1 Aug 43 Ft Leonard Wood Mo / 31 Jul 46 Germany
NYPE: 29 Sep 44 England: 10 Oct 44 France-ETO: 9 Dec 44 - **25,26,34** *(nondiv)*
Neunhof Germany

289th Field Artillery Observation Bn 20 Nov 43 Cp Roberts Calif /15 Feb 46 Philippines
SFPE: 8 Sep 44 New Guinea: 2 Oct 44 Philippines: 13 Jan 45 - **14,15** *(nondiv)*
Dagupan Philippines

290th Field Artillery Observation Bn 20 Oct 43 Ft Leonard Wood Mo/26 Oct 45 Cp Kilmer N.J.
NYPE: 12 Sep 44 England: 23 Sep 44 France-ETO: 25 Sep 44 - **34** NYPE: 25 Oct 45 *(nondiv)*
Airfield Germany

291st Field Artillery Observation Bn 12 Jan 44 Cp Gordon Ga /1 Dec 45 Cp Kilmer N.J.
BPE: 11 Oct 44 England: 18 Oct 44 France-ETO: 22 Oct 44 - **25,26,34** NYPE: 29 Nov 45 *(nondiv)*
Dirlos Germany

292nd Field Artillery Observation Bn 21 Feb 44 Cp Bowie Tex /15 Jul 46 Ft Bragg N.C.
NYPE: 23 Nov 44 England: 4 Dec 44 France-ETO: 4 Feb 45 - **26,34** NYPE: 2 Aug 45 *(nondiv)*
Ft Bragg N.C.

293rd Field Artillery Observation Bn 15 Mar 44 Cp Hood Tex/6 Nov 45 Ft Jackson S.C.
NYPE: 5 Feb 45 France-ETO: 17 Feb 45 - **32** BPE: 23 Jun 45 *(nondiv)*
Ft Jackson S.C.

294th Field Artillery Observation Bn 15 Apr 44 Ft Jackson S.C./26 Oct 45 Cp Bowie Tex
NYPE: 3 Jan 45 France-ETO: 15 Jan 45 - **26** NYPE: 4 Jul 45 *(nondiv)*
Cp Bowie Tex

301st Field Artillery Bn (105mm How Trk-D) 15 Sep 42 Ft Custer Mich / 3 Feb 46 Cp Kilmer N.J.
NYPE: 6 Aug 44 England: 11 Aug 44 France-ETO: 14 Sep 44 - **25,26,32,34** NYPE: 2 Feb 46 *(94th Inf Div)*
Lewerkussen Germany

302nd Field Artillery Bn (105mm How Trk-D) 15 Jun 42 Ft George G Meade Md / 31 Aug 45 Germany
BPE: 10 Dec 44 England: 20 Dec 44 France-ETO: 12 Jan 45 - **25,26,34** *(76th Inf Div)*
Triptiz Germany

303rd Field Artillery Bn (105mm How Trk-D) 25 Feb 43 Cp Swift Tex/31 Mar 46 Japan
NYPE: 19 Feb 45 France-ETO: 1 Mar 45 NYPE: 23 Jun 45 SPE: 1 Sep 45 Philippines: 19 Sep 45 - **26** *(97th Inf Div)*
Ft Bragg N.C.

BATTALION DESIGNATION AND TYPE	FORMED (SOURCE OF UNIT)/INACTIVATION *Active through 1946	AUGUST 1945 LOCATION

304th Field Artillery Bn (105mm How Trk-D)   25 Mar 42 Ft Jackson Miss /15 Mar 46 Japan
SFPE: 24 Mar 44   Hawaii: 31 Mar 44   Guam: 21 Jul 44   Philippines: 23 Nov 44   Ie Shima: 16 Apr 45   Okinawa: 20 Apr 45 - **13,19,21**
(77th Inf Div)

Cebu Philippines

305th Field Artillery Bn (105mm How Trk-D)   25 Mar 42 Ft Jackson Miss /15 Mar 46 Japan
SFPE: 27 Mar 44   Hawaii: 1 Apr 44   Guam: 21 Jul 44   Philippines: 23 Nov 44   Ie Shima: 16 Apr 45   Okinawa: 20 Apr 45 - **13,19,21**
(77th Inf Div)

Cebu Philippines

306th Field Artillery Bn (155mm How Trac-D)   25 Mar 42 Ft Jackson Miss /15 Mar 46 Japan
SFPE: 24 Mar 44   Hawaii: 31 Mar 44   Guam: 21 Jul 44   Philippines: 23 Nov 44   Ie Shima: 16 Apr 45   Okinawa: 20 Apr 45 - **13,19,21**
(77th Inf Div)

Cebu Philippines

307th Field Artillery Bn (105mm How Trk-D)   15 Aug 42 Cp Butner N.C. / 24 May 46 Germany
NYPE: 14 Oct 44   England: 25 Oct 44   France-ETO: 22 Nov 44 - **25,26,34** *(78th Inf Div)*

Hofgeismar Germany

308th Field Artillery Bn (105mm How Trk-D)   15 Aug 42 Cp Butner N.C. / 25 Apr 46 Cp Kilmer N.J.
NYPE: 14 Oct 44   England: 25 Oct 44   France-ETO: 22 Nov 44 - **25,26,34**   NYPE: 24 Apr 46 *(78th Inf Div)*

Helsa Germany

309th Field Artillery Bn (155mm How Trac-D)   15 Aug 42 Cp Butner N.C. /19 Apr 46 Cp Kilmer N.J.
NYPE: 14 Oct 44   England: 25 Oct 44   France-ETO: 22 Nov 44 - **25,26,34**   NYPE: 18 Apr 46 *(78th Inf Div)*

Kassel Germany

310th Field Artillery Bn (105mm How Trk-D)   15 Jun 42 Cp Pickett Va / 20 Dec 45 Cp Kilmer N.J.
BPE: 7 Apr 44   England: 16 Apr 44   France-ETO: 14 Jun 44 - **25,26,30,32,34**   NYPE: 19 Dec 45 *(79th Inf Div)*

Eger Czechoslovakia

311th Field Artillery Bn (105mm How Trk-D)   15 Jun 42 Cp Pickett Va / 21 Dec 45 Cp Kilmer N.J.
BPE: 7 Apr 44   England: 16 Apr 44   France-ETO: 14 Jun 44 - **25,26,30,32,34**   NYPE: 20 Dec 45 *(79th Inf Div)*

Milikov Czechoslovakia

312th Field Artillery Bn (155mm How Trac-D)   15 Jun 42 Cp Pickett Va /17 Dec 45 Cp Patrick Henry Va
BPE: 7 Apr 44   England: 16 Apr 44   France-ETO: 14 Jun 44 - **25,26,30,32,34**   HRPE: 17 Dec 45 *(79th Inf Div)*

Eger Czechoslovakia

313th Field Artillery Bn (105mm How Trk-D)   15 Jul 42 Cp Forrest Tenn /10 Jan 46 Cp Kilmer N.J.
NYPE: 22 Jun 44   England: 7 Jul 44   France-ETO: 3 Aug 44 - **25,26,32,34**   NYPE: 8 Jan 46 *(80th Inf Div)*

Ottobeuren Germany

314th Field Artillery Bn (105mm How Trk-D)   15 Jul 42 Cp Forrest Tenn/5 Jan 46 Cp Kilmer N.J.
NYPE: 1 Jul 44   England: 7 Jul 44   France-ETO: 3 Aug 44 - **25,26,32,34**   NYPE: 3 Jan 46 *(80th Inf Div)*

Ober Gunzberg Germany

315th Field Artillery Bn (155mm How Trac-D)   15 Jul 42 Cp Forrest Tenn / 5 Jan 46 Cp Kilmer N.J.
NYPE: 22 Jun 44   England: 7 Jul 44   France-ETO: 3 Aug 44 - **25,26,32,34**   NYPE: 3 Jan 46 *(80th Inf Div)*

Memzingersberg Germany

316th Field Artillery Bn (105mm How Trk-D)   15 Jun 42 Cp Rucker Ala /20 Jan 46 Japan
SFPE: 5 Jul 44   Hawaii: 11 Jul 44   Guadalcanal: 24 Aug 44   Palau I: 15 Sep 44   New Caledonia: 14 Jan 45
Philippines: 16 May 45 - **13,21** *(81st Inf Div)*

Leyte Philippines

317th Field Artillery Bn (105mm How Trk-D)   15 Jun 42 Cp Rucker Ala/20 Jan 46 Japan
SFPE: 5 Jul 44   Hawaii: 11 Jul 44   Guadalcanal: 24 Aug 44   Palau I: 15 Sep 44   New Caledonia: 14 Jan 45
Philippines: 16 May 45 - **13,21** *(81st Inf Div)*

Leyte Philippines

318th Field Artillery Bn (155mm How Trac-D)   15 Jun 42 Cp Rucker Ala / 20 Jan 46 Japan
SFPE: 5 Jul 44   Hawaii: 11 Jul 44   Guadalcanal: 24 Aug 44   Palau I: 15 Sep 44   New Caledonia: 14 Jan 45
Philippines: 16 May 45 - **13,21** *(81st Inf Div)*

Leyte Philippines

319th Glider Field Artillery Bn (75mm Pk How)   25 Mar 42 Cp Claiborne La /*
NYPE: 28 Apr 43   N.Africa: 10 May 43   Sicily: 4 Sep 43   Italy: 10 Sep 43   Ireland: 9 Dec 43   England: 14 Feb 44   France: 6 Jun 44
England: 13 Jul 44   Holland: 17 Sep 44 - **25,26,29,30,34,36**   NYPE: 3 Jan 46 *(105mm How Trk-D until 6 Aug 42) (82nd A/B Div)*

Epinal France

320th Glider Field Artillery Bn (75mm Pk How)   25 Mar 42 Cp Claiborne La /*
NYPE: 28 Apr 43   N.Africa: 10 May 43   Sicily: 4 Sep 43   Italy: 13 Sep 43   Ireland: 9 Dec 43   England: 14 Feb 44   France: 6 Jun 44
England: 13 Jul 44   Holland: 17 Sep 44 - **25,26,29,30,34,36**   NYPE: 3 Jan 46 *(105mm How Trk-D until 6 Aug 42) (82nd A/B Div)*

Crouton France

321st Glider Field Artillery Bn (75mm Pk How)   25 Mar 42 Cp Claiborne La /3 Nov 45 Germany
NYPE: 5 Sep 43   England: 15 Sep 43   France: 6 Jun 44   England: 13 Jul 44   Holland: 17 Sep 44 - **25,26,30,34**
(155mm How Trk-D until 6 Aug 42, relieved from 82nd A/B Div 15 Aug 42 and assigned to 101st A/B Div) (101st A/B Div)

Grossmain France

322nd Field Artillery Bn (105mm How Trk-D)   15 Aug 42 Cp Atterbury Ind / 22 Mar 46 Cp Kilmer N.J.
NYPE: 6 Apr 44   England: 18 Apr 44   France-ETO: 19 Jun 44 - **25,26,30,32,34**   NYPE: 21 Mar 46 *(83rd Inf Div)*

Obernzell Germany

323rd Field Artillery Bn (105mm How Trk-D)   15 Aug 42 Cp Atterbury Ind / 25 Mar 46 Cp Kilmer N.J.
NYPE: 6 Apr 44   England: 16 Apr 44   France-ETO: 19 Jun 44 - **25,26,30,32,34**   NYPE: 24 Mar 46 *(83rd Inf Div)*

Passau Germany

324th Field Artillery Bn (155mm How Trac-D)   15 Aug 42 Cp Atterbury Ind/22 Mar 46 Cp Kilmer N.J.
NYPE: 6 Apr 44   England: 16 Apr 44   France-ETO: 19 Jun 44 - **25,26,30,32,34**   NYPE: 21 Mar 46 *(83rd Inf Div)*

Tittling Germany

325th Field Artillery Bn (105mm How Trk-D)   15 Oct 42 Cp Howze Tex /24 Jan 46 Cp Kilmer N.J.
NYPE: 20 Sep 44   England: 1 Oct 44   France-ETO: 4 Nov 44 - **25,26,34**   NYPE: 23 Jan 46 *(84th Inf Div)*

Neckarelz Germany

BATTALION DESIGNATION AND TYPE	FORMED (SOURCE OF UNIT)/INACTIVATION *Active through 1946	AUGUST 1945 LOCATION

326th Field Artillery Bn (105mm How Trk-D)   15 Oct 42 Cp Howze Tex / 21 Jan 46 Cp Kilmer N.J.
NYPE: 20 Sep 44   England: 1 Oct 44   France-ETO: 4 Nov 44 - **25,26,34**   NYPE: 20 Jan 46 *(84th Inf Div)*
Rappenau Germany

327th Field Artillery Bn (155mm How Trac-D)   15 Oct 42 Cp Howze Tex / 29 Jan 46 Cp Kilmer N.J.
NYPE: 29 Sep 44   England: 10 Oct 44   France-ETO: 4 Nov 44 - **25,26,34**   NYPE: 28 Jan 46 *(84th Inf Div)*
Helmstadt Germany

328th Field Artillery Bn (105mm How Trk-D)   15 May 42 Cp Shelby Miss / 25 Aug 45 Cp Patrick Henry Va
HRPE: 24 Dec 43   N.Africa: 1 Jan 44   Italy: 27 Mar 44 - **31,33,35**   HRPE: 25 Aug 45 *(85th Inf Div)*
Fagianeria Italy

329th Field Artillery Bn (105mm How Trk-D)   15 May 42 Cp Shelby Miss / 25 Aug 45 Cp Patrick Henry Va
HRPE: 28 Dec 43   N.Africa: 7 Jan 44   Italy: 27 Mar 44 - **31,33,35**   HRPE: 25 Aug 45 *(85th Inf Div)*
Fagianeria Italy

331st Field Artillery Bn (105mm How Trk-D)   15 Dec 42 Cp Howze Tex / 30 Dec 46 Philippines
BPE: 19 Feb 45   France-ETO: 1 Mar 45 - **26**   NYPE: 17 Jun 45   SFPE: 15 Aug 45   Philippines: 12 Sep 45 *(86th Inf Div)*
San Francisco P/E

332nd Field Artillery Bn (105mm How Trk-D)   15 Dec 42 Cp Howze Tex / 30 Dec 46 Philippines
BPE: 19 Feb 45   France-ETO: 1 Mar 45 - **26**   NYPE: 17 Jun 45   SFPE: 18 Aug 43   Philippines: 12 Sep 45 *(86th Inf Div)*
Entrained to Cp Stoneman Calif

333rd Field Arty Bn (Cld) (155mm How Trac-D)   9 Mar 43 Cp Gruber Okla (1st Bn, 333rd FA) /10 Jun 45 Germany
NYPE: 11 Feb 44   England: 18 Feb 44   France-ETO: 29 Jun 44 - **25,26,30,32,34** *(155mm How Trk-D until sent overseas) (nondiv)*

334th Field Artillery Bn (105mm How Trk-D)   15 Dec 42 Cp McCain Miss / 21 Sep 45 Ft Benning Ga
NYPE: 4 Nov 44   England: 12 Nov 44   France-ETO: 5 Dec 44 - **25,26,34**   HRPE: 16 Jul 45 *(87th Inf Div)*
Ft Benning Ga

335th Field Artillery Bn (155mm How Trac-D)   15 Dec 42 Cp McCain Miss / 21 Sep 45 Ft Benning Ga
NYPE: 4 Nov 44   England: 12 Nov 44   France-ETO: 5 Dec 44 - **25,26,34**   HRPE: 13 Jul 45 *(87th Inf Div)*
Ft Benning Ga

336th Field Artillery Bn (105mm How Trk-D)   15 Dec 42 Cp McCain Miss / 21 Sep 45 Ft Benning Ga
NYPE: 4 Nov 44   England: 12 Nov 44   France-ETO: 5 Dec 44 - **25,26,34**   HRPE: 16 Jul 45 *(87th Inf Div)*
Ft Benning Ga

337th Field Artillery Bn (105mm How Trk-D)   15 Jul 42 Cp Gruber Okla / *
HRPE: 24 Nov 43   N.Africa: 15 Dec 43   Italy: 6 Feb 44 - **31,33,35** *(88th Inf Div)*
Aversa Italy

338th Field Artillery Bn (105mm How Trk-D)   15 Jul 42 Cp Gruber Okla / *
HRPE: 2 Dec 43   N.Africa: 22 Dec 43   Italy: 6 Feb 44 - **31,33,35** *(88th Inf Div)*
Fagianeria Italy

339th Field Artillery Bn (155mm How Trac-D)   15 Jul 42 Cp Gruber Okla / *
HRPE: 2 Dec 43   N.Africa: 22 Dec 43   Italy: 6 Feb 44 - **31,33,35** *(88th Inf Div)*
Ghedi Italy

340th Field Artillery Bn (105mm How Trk-D)   15 Jul 42 Cp Carson Colo /19 Dec 45 Cp Kilmer N.J.
BPE: 10 Jan 45   France-ETO: 21 Jan 45 - **26,34**   NYPE: 17 Dec 45 *(89th Inf Div)*
Duclair France

341st Field Artillery Bn (105mm How Trk-D)   15 Jul 42 Cp Carson Colo /19 Dec 45 Cp Kilmer N.J.
BPE: 10 Jan 45   France-ETO: 21 Jan 45 - **26,34**   NYPE: 17 Dec 45 *(89th Inf Div)*
Werdau Germany

342nd Armored Field Artillery Bn   15 Jul 42 Cp Carson Colo /19 Feb 46 Ft Bragg N.C.
HRPE: 14 Oct 44   Italy: 28 Oct 44   France-ETO: 7 Dec 44 - **25,26,34**   BPE: 29 Jul 45
(155mm How Trk-D until 10 Sep 43, relieved from 89th Inf Div 1 Aug 43) (nondiv)
Ft Bragg N.C.

343rd Field Artillery Bn (105mm How Trk-D)   25 Mar 42 Cp Barkeley Tex / 22 Dec 45 Cp Patrick Henry Va
NYPE: 23 Mar 44   England: 4 Apr 44   France-ETO: 6 Jun 44 - **25,26,30,32,34**   HRPE: 22 Dec 45 *(90th Inf Div)*
Weiden Germany

344th Field Artillery Bn (105mm How Trk-D)   25 Mar 42 Cp Barkeley Tex / 22 Dec 45 Cp Patrick Henry Va
NYPE: 24 Mar 44   England: 9 Apr 44   France-ETO: 7 Jun 44 - **25,26,30,32,34**   HRPE: 22 Dec 45 *(90th Inf Div)*
Maxmilianshutte Germany

345th Field Artillery Bn (155mm How Trac-D)   25 Mar 42 Cp Barkeley Tex / 22 Dec 45 Cp Patrick Henry Va
NYPE: 23 Mar 44   England: 5 Apr 44   France-ETO: 7 Jun 44 - **25,26,30,32,34**   HRPE: 22 Dec 45 *(90th Inf Div)*
Neunberg Germany

346th Field Artillery Bn (105mm How Trk-D)   15 Aug 42 Cp White Oreg /15 Sep 45 Cp Rucker Ala
HRPE: 3 Apr 44   N.Africa: 21 Apr 44   Italy: 27 May 44 - **31,33,35**   BPE: 10 Sep 45 *(91st Inf Div)*
Percotta Italy

347th Field Artillery Bn (105mm How Trk-D)   15 Aug 42 Cp White Oreg / 27 Nov 45 Cp Rucker Ala
HRPE: 13 Apr 44   N.Africa: 30 Apr 44   Italy: 27 May 44 - **31,33,35**   BPE: 10 Sep 45 *(91st Inf Div)*
Goriza Italy

348th Field Artillery Bn (155mm How Trac-D)   15 Aug 42 Cp White Oreg / 27 Nov 45 Cp Rucker Ala
HRPE: 13 Apr 44   N.Africa: 30 Apr 44   Italy: 27 May 44 - **31,33,35**   BPE: 10 Sep 45 *(91st Inf Div)*
Cormons Italy

349th Field Arty Bn (Cld) (155mm How Trac-D)   12 Feb 43 Ft Sill Okla (1st Bn, 349th FA) / *
NYPE: 30 Oct 44   England: 10 Nov 44   France-ETO: 10 Feb 45 - **26,34** *(105mm How Trk-D until 1944) (nondiv)*
Greding Germany

350th Field Arty Bn (Cld) (155mm How Trac-D)   1 Apr 43 Cp Livingston La (1st Bn, 350th FA)/7 Aug 46 Cp Kilmer N.J.
NYPE: 16 Dec 44   England: 21 Dec 44   France-ETO: 22 Feb 45 - **26,34**   NYPE: 4 Aug 46 *(Truck-D until sent overseas) (nondiv)*
Munkheim Germany

351st Field Arty (Cld) (155mm How Trac-D)   1 Apr 43 Cp Livingston La (1st Bn, 351st FA) /10 Aug 46 Cp Kilmer N.J.
NYPE: 16 Dec 44   England: 21 Dec 44   France-ETO: 25 Feb 45 - **26,34**   NYPE: 9 Aug 46 *(Truck-D until sent overseas) (nondiv)*
Hilpolstein Germany

BATTALION DESIGNATION AND TYPE	FORMED (SOURCE OF UNIT)/INACTIVATION *Active through 1946	AUGUST 1945 LOCATION

353rd Field Arty Bn (Cld) (155mm Gun Trac-D)   1 Apr 43 Cp Livingston La (1st Bn, 353rd FA)/19 Mar 44 Cp Van Dorn Miss redes
1697th Engr Comb Bn (Cld)

355th Field Artillery Bn (105mm How Trk-D)   15 Jun 42 Ft George G Meade Md / 31 Aug 45 Germany   Weida Germany
BPE: 10 Dec 44   England: 20 Dec 44   France-ETO: 12 Jan 45 - **25,26,34** (76th Inf Div)

356th Field Artillery Bn (105mm How Trk-D)   15 Sep 42 Ft Custer Mich / 8 Feb 46 Cp Kilmer N.J.   Huckeswagen Germany
NYPE: 6 Aug 44   England: 11 Aug 44   France-ETO: 14 Sep 44 - **25,26,32,34**   NYPE: 7 Feb 46 (94th Inf Div)

358th Field Artillery Bn (105mm How Trk-D)   15 Jul 42 Cp Swift Tex /15 Oct 45 Cp Shelby Miss   Cp Shelby Miss
BPE: 6 Aug 44   England: 12 Aug 44   France-ETO: 15 Sep 44 - **25,26,32,34**   BPE: 29 Jun 45 (95th Inf Div)

359th Field Artillery Bn (105mm How Trk-D)   15 Jul 42 Cp Swift Tex /15 Oct 45 Cp Shelby Miss   Cp Shelby Miss
BPE: 6 Aug 44   England: 12 Aug 44   France-ETO: 15 Sep 44 - **25,26,32,34**   BPE: 29 Jun 45 (95th Inf Div)

360th Field Artillery Bn (155mm How Trac-D)   15 Jul 42 Cp Swift Tex /15 Oct 45 Cp Shelby Miss   Cp Shelby Miss
BPE: 6 Aug 44   England: 12 Aug 44   France-ETO: 15 Sep 44 - **25,26,32,34**   BPE: 29 Jun 45 (95th Inf Div)

361st Field Artillery Bn (105mm How Trk-D)   15 Aug 42 Cp Adair Oreg / 3 Feb 46 Cp Anza Calif   Mindoro Philippines
SFPE: 26 Jul 44   Hawaii: 31 Jul 44   Philippines: 20 Oct 44   Okinawa: 1 May 45 - **13,19**   LAPE: 2 Feb 46 (96th Inf Div)

362nd Field Artillery Bn (105mm How Trk-D)   15 Aug 42 Cp Adair Oreg / 3 Feb 46 Cp Anza Calif   Mindoro Philippines
SFPE: 28 Jul 44   Hawaii: 2 Aug 44   Philippines: 20 Oct 44   Okinawa: 1 May 45 - **13,19**   LAPE: 2 Feb 46 (96th Inf Div)

363rd Field Artillery Bn (155mm How Trac-D)   15 Aug 42 Cp Adair Oreg / 3 Feb 46 Cp Anza Calif   Mindoro Philippines
SFPE: 28 Jul 44   Hawaii: 2 Aug 44   Philippines: 20 Oct 44   Okinawa: 1 May 45 - **13,19**   LAPE: 2 Feb 46 (96th Inf Div)

364th Field Artillery Bn (155mm How Trac-D)   15 Jun 42 Ft George G Meade Md / 31 Aug 45 Germany   Gera Germany
BPE: 10 Dec 44   England: 20 Dec 44   France-ETO: 12 Jan 45 - **25,26,34** (76th Inf Div)

365th Field Artillery Bn (105mm How Trk-D)   25 Feb 43 Cp Swift Tex / 31 Mar 46 Japan   Ft Bragg N.C.
NYPE: 19 Feb 45   France-ETO: 1 Mar 45   NYPE: 23 Jun 45   SPE: 1 Sep 45   Philippines: 19 Sep 45 - **26** (97th Inf Div)

367th Field Artillery Bn (105mm How Trk-D)   15 Sep 42 Cp Breckinridge Ky /16 Feb 46 Japan   Ft Hase Hawaii
SPE: 13 Apr 44   Hawaii: 19 Apr 44   Japan: 27 Sep 45 (98th Inf Div)

368th Field Artillery Bn (105mm How Trk-D)   15 Sep 42 Cp Breckinridge Ky /16 Feb 46 Japan   Ft Hase Hawaii
SPE: 17 Apr 44   Hawaii: 22 Apr 44   Japan: 27 Feb 45 (98th Inf Div)

369th Field Artillery Bn (155mm How Trac-D)   15 Sep 42 Cp Breckinridge Ky /16 Feb 46 Japan   Ft Hase Hawaii
SPE: 29 Apr 44   Hawaii: 4 May 44   Japan: 27 Feb 45 (98th Inf Div)

370th Field Artillery Bn (105mm How Trk-D)   15 Nov 42 Cp Van Dorn Miss / 27 Sep 45 Cp Patrick Henry Va   Hassfurt Germany
BPE: 30 Sep 44   England: 9 Oct 44   France-ETO: 1 Nov 44 - **25,26,34**   HRPE: 27 Sep 45 (99th Inf Div)

371st Field Artillery Bn (105mm How Trk-D)   15 Nov 42 Cp Van Dorn Miss / 27 Sep 45 Cp Patrick Henry Va   Schweinfurt Germany
BPE: 30 Sep 44   England: 10 Oct 44   France-ETO: 1 Nov 44 - **25,26,34**   HRPE: 27 Sep 45 (99th Inf Div)

372nd Field Artillery Bn (155mm How Trac-D)   15 Nov 42 Cp Van Dorn Miss / 29 Sep 45 Cp Patrick Henry Va   Ebern Germany
BPE: 30 Sep 44   England: 9 Oct 44   France-ETO: 1 Nov 44 - **25,26,34**   HRPE: 27 Sep 45 (99th Inf Div)

373rd Field Artillery Bn (155mm How Trac-D)   15 Nov 42 Ft Jackson S.C. /10 Jan 46 Cp Patrick Henry Va   Gmund Germany
NYPE: 6 Oct 44   France-ETO: 20 Oct 44 - **25,26,34**   HRPE: 10 Jan 46 (100th Inf Div)

374th Field Artillery Bn (105mm How Trk-D)   15 Nov 42 Ft Jackson S.C. /12 Jan 46 Cp Kilmer N.J.   Welzheim Germany
NYPE: 6 Oct 44   France-ETO: 20 Oct 44 - **25,26,34**   NYPE: 11 Jan 46 (100th Inf Div)

375th Field Artillery Bn (105mm How Trk-D)   15 Nov 42 Ft Jackson S.C. /11 Jan 46 Cp Patrick Henry Va   Le Havre France
NYPE: 6 Oct 44   France-ETO: 20 Oct 44 - **25,26,34**   HRPE: 11 Jan 46 (100th Inf Div)

376th Prcht Field Artillery Bn (75mm Pk How)   16 Aug 42 Cp Claiborne La / *   Epinal France
NYPE: 28 Apr 43   N.Africa: 10 May 43   Sicily: 9 Jul 43   Italy: 13 Sep 43   N.Ireland: 9 Dec 43   France: 6 Jun 44
England: 13 Jul 44   Holland: 17 Sep 44 - **24,25,26,29,30,34,35,36**   NYPE: 3 Jan 46 (82nd A/B Div)

377th Prcht Field Artillery Bn (75mm Pk How)   16 Aug 42 Cp Claiborne La /31 Nov 45 Germany   Unken Austria
NYPE: 5 Sep 43   England: 18 Oct 43   France: 6 Jun 44   England: 13 Jul 44   Holland: 17 Sep 44 - **25,26,30,34** (101st A/B Div)

379th Field Artillery Bn (105mm How Trk-D)   15 Sep 42 Cp Maxey Tex / 21 Mar 46 Cp Kilmer N.J.   Tabarz Germany
NYPE: 12 Sep 44   France-ETO: 23 Sep 44 - **26,34**   NYPE: 20 Mar 46 (102nd Inf Div)

380th Field Artillery Bn (105mm How Trk-D)   15 Sep 42 Cp Maxey Tex /14 Mar 46 Cp Kilmer N.J.   Grafentonna Germany
NYPE: 12 Sep 44   France-ETO: 23 Sep 44 - **26,34**   NYPE: 13 Mar 46 (102nd Inf Div)

381st Field Artillery Bn (155mm How Trac-D)   15 Sep 42 Cp Maxey Tex /14 Mar 46 Cp Kilmer N.J.   Sundhausen Germany
NYPE: 12 Sep 44   France-ETO: 23 Sep 44 - **26,34**   NYPE: 13 Mar 46 (102nd Inf Div)

BATTALION DESIGNATION AND TYPE	FORMED (SOURCES OF UNIT)/INACTIVATION *Active through 1946	AUGUST 1945 LOCATION
382nd Field Artillery Bn (105mm How Trk-D) NYPE: 6 Oct 44 France-ETO: 20 Oct 44 - **25,26,34**	15 Nov 42 Cp Claiborne La / 22 Sep 45 Cp Patrick Henry Va HRPE: 22 Sep 45 *(103rd Inf Div)*	Sellrain Austria
383rd Field Artillery Bn (105mm How Trk-D) NYPE: 6 Oct 44 France-ETO: 20 Oct 44 - **25,26,34**	15 Nov 42 Cp Claiborne La / 22 Sep 45 Cp Shanks N.Y. NYPE: 21 Sep 45 *(103rd Inf Div)*	Axams Austria
384th Field Artillery Bn (155mm How Trac-D) NYPE: 6 Oct 44 France-ETO: 20 Oct 44 - **25,26,34**	15 Nov 42 Cp Claiborne La / 22 Sep 45 Cp Patrick Henry Va NYPE: 22 Sep 45 *(103rd Inf Div)*	Igls Austria
385th Field Artillery Bn (105mm How Trk-D) NYPE: 27 Aug 44 France-ETO: 7 Sep 44 - **26,32,34**	15 Sep 42 Cp Adair Oreg /10 Dec 45 Cp San Luis Obispo Calif NYPE: 3 Jul 45 *(104th Inf Div)*	Cp San Luis Obispo Calif
386th Field Artillery Bn (105mm How Trk-D) NYPE: 27 Aug 44 France-ETO: 7 Sep 44 - **26,32,34**	15 Sep 42 Cp Adair Oreg / 6 Nov 45 Cp San Luis Obispo Calif NYPE: 3 Jul 45 *(104th Inf Div)*	Cp San Luis Obispo Calif
387th Field Artillery Bn (155mm How Trac-D) NYPE: 27 Aug 44 France-ETO: 7 Sep 44 - **26,32,34**	15 Sep 42 Cp Adair Oreg /10 Dec 45 Cp San Luis Obispo Calif NYPE: 3 Jul 45 *(104th Inf Div)*	Cp San Luis Obispo Calif
389th Field Artillery Bn (155mm How Trac-D) NYPE: 19 Feb 45 France-ETO: 1 Mar 45 - **26** NYPE: 23 Jun 45 SPE: 17 Sep 45	25 Feb 43 Cp Swift Tex / 31 Mar 46 Japan *(97th Inf Div)*	Ft Bragg N.C.
390th Field Artillery Bn (155mm How Trac-D) NYPE: 6 Aug 44 England: 11 Aug 44 France-ETO: 14 Sep 44 - **25,26,32,34** NYPE: 4 Feb 46	15 Sep 42 Ft Custer Mich / 5 Feb 46 Cp Kilmer N.J. *(94th Inf Div)*	Langenfeld Germany
391st Armored Field Artillery Bn NYPE: 5 Sep 43 England: 15 Sep 43 France-ETO: 25 Jun 44 - **25,26,30,32,34**	1 Aug 42 Cp Polk La /10 Nov 45 Germany *(3rd Armd Div)*	Neu Isenberg Germany
392nd Field Artillery Bn (105mm How Trk-D) NYPE: 6 Jan 45 France-ETO: 18 Jan 45	14 Jul 43 Cp Gruber Okla / 30 Jun 46 Austria *(42nd Inf Div)*	Thiersee Germany
393rd Field Artillery Bn (105mm How Trac-D)	20 Apr 44 Ft Riley Kans /7 Mar 45 Cp Hood Tex *(Truck-D until late 1944)*	(nondiv)
394th Field Artillery Bn (105mm How Trk-D) NYPE: 8 Apr 45 France-ETO: 19 Apr 45 BPE: 10 Jul 45 *(nondiv)*	20 Apr 44 Ft Riley Kans / *	Ft Jackson S.C.
395th Armored Field Artillery Bn NYPE: 5 Feb 45 France-ETO: 19 Feb 45 - **26** NYPE: 12 Oct 45	15 Jul 43 Cp Chaffee Ark /13 Oct 45 Cp Shanks N.Y. *(16th Armd Div)*	Schonewalde Germany
396th Armored Field Artillery Bn NYPE: 5 Feb 45 France-ETO: 19 Feb 45 - **26** NYPE: 12 Oct 45	15 Jul 43 Cp Chaffee Ark /13 Oct 45 Cp Shanks N.Y. *(16th Armd Div)*	Mies Czechoslovakia
397th Armored Field Artillery Bn NYPE: 5 Feb 45 France-ETO: 19 Feb 45 - **26** NYPE: 12 Oct 45	15 Jul 43 Cp Chaffee Ark /13 Oct 45 Cp Shanks N.Y. *(16th Armd Div)*	Plana Czechoslovakia
398th Armored Field Artillery Bn NYPE: 7 Nov 44 England: 18 Nov 44 France-ETO: 10 Jan 45 - **25,26,34** NYPE: 11 Nov 45	1 Apr 42 Ft Knox Ky /12 Nov 45 Cp Kilmer N.J. *(8th Armd Div)*	Litice Czechoslovakia
399th Armored Field Artillery Bn NYPE: 7 Nov 44 England: 18 Nov 44 France-ETO: 10 Jan 45 - **25,26,34** NYPE: 11 Nov 45	1 Apr 42 Ft Knox Ky /12 Nov 45 Cp Kilmer N.Y. *(8th Armd Div)*	Horsice Czechoslovakia
400th Armored Field Artillery Bn NYPE: 22 Apr 44 England: 30 Apr 44 France-ETO: 17 Jul 44 - **25,26,30,32,34** HRPE: 9 Oct 45	5 Apr 43 Ft Knox Ky / 9 Oct 45 Cp Patrick Henry Va *(nondiv)*	Happurg Germany
401st Field Artillery Bn (105mm How Trk-D) BPE: 8 Mar 45 France-ETO: 18 Mar 45 - **26,32** NYPE: 22 Mar 46 *(nondiv)*	20 Apr 44 Ft Riley Kans / 23 Mar 46 Cp Kilmer N.J.	Heilbronn Germany
402nd Field Artillery Bn (105mm How Trk-D) NYPE: 6 Jan 45 France-ETO: 18 Jan 45 - **26,34** *(42nd Inf Div)*	14 Jul 43 Cp Gruber Okla / 30 Jun 46 Austria	Kufstein Germany
403rd Field Artillery Bn (155mm How Trk-D) HRPE: 31 Dec 43 N.Africa: 9 Jan 44 Italy: 27 Mar 44 - **31,33,35** HRPE: 25 Aug 45	15 May 42 Cp Shelby Miss/25 Aug 45 Cp Patrick Henry Va *(85th Inf Div)*	Fagianeria Italy
404th Field Artillery Bn (155mm How Trac-D) BPE: 19 Feb 45 France-ETO: 1 Mar 45 NYPE: 17 Jun 45 SFPE: 21 Aug 45 Philippines: 7 Sep 45 - **26**	15 Dec 42 Cp Howze Tex / 30 Dec 46 Philippines *(86th Inf Div)*	Entrained to San Francisco
405th Armored Field Artillery Bn NYPE: 7 Nov 44 England: 18 Nov 44 France-ETO: 10 Jan 45 - **25,26,34** NYPE: 12 Nov 45	1 Apr 42 Ft Knox Ky /12 Nov 45 Cp Kilmer N.J. *(8th Armd Div)*	Letnany Czechoslovakia
412th Armored Field Artillery Bn BPE: 6 Feb 45 France-ETO: 17 Feb 45 - **26** NYPE: 2 Aug 45	15 Mar 43 Cp Campbell Ky / 2 Apr 46 Cp Hood Tex *(20th Armd Div)*	Cp Cooke Calif
413th Armored Field Artillery Bn BPE: 6 Feb 45 France-ETO: 17 Feb 45 - **26** NYPE: 2 Aug 45	15 Mar 43 Cp Campbell Ky / 2 Apr 46 Cp Hood Tex *(20th Armd Div)*	Cp Cooke Calif
414th Armored Field Artillery Bn BPE: 6 Feb 45 France-ETO: 17 Feb 45 - **26** NYPE: 2 Aug 45	15 Mar 43 Cp Campbell Ky / 2 Apr 46 Cp Hood Tex *(20th Armd Div)*	Cp Cooke Calif

BATTALION DESIGNATION AND TYPE	FORMED (SOURCE OF UNIT)/INACTIVATION *Active through 1946	AUGUST 1945 LOCATION

419th Armored Field Artillery Bn
15 Jul 42 Ft Benning Ga /18 Oct 45 Cp Patrick Henry Va
NYPE: 13 Sep 44   France-ETO: 23 Sep 44 - **25,26,34**   HRPE: 18 Oct 45 *(10th Armd Div)*
Flecken Austria

420th Armored Field Artillery Bn
15 Jul 42 Ft Benning Ga /18 Oct 45 Cp Patrick Henry Va
NYPE: 13 Sep 44   France-ETO: 23 Sep 44 - **25,26,34**   HRPE: 18 Oct 45 *(10th Armd Div)*
Benediktbeuren Germany

421st Rocket Field Arty Bn (4.5-in. Rocket Trk-D)   12 Apr 45 Ft Sill Okla (1st Rocket Bn) /15 Jan 46 Ft Lawton Wash
SPE: 6 Jun 45   Hawaii: 12 Jun 45   Okinawa: 24 Jul 45 - **19**   SPE: 14 Jan 46 *(nondiv)*
Okinawa

422nd Rocket Field Arty Bn (4.5-in Rocket Trk-D)   12 Apr 45 Ft Sill Okla (2nd Rocket Bn) /1 Jan 46 Ft Stoneman Calif
SFPE: 1 Jun 45   Philippines: 11 Jul 45   SFPE: 30 Dec 45 *(nondiv)*
Manila Philippines

423rd Armored Field Artillery Bn
15 Jul 42 Ft Benning Ga /18 Oct 45 Cp Patrick Henry Va
NYPE: 13 Sep 44   France-ETO: 23 Sep 44 - **25,26,34**   HRPE: 18 Oct 45 *(10th Armd Div)*
Huttenberg Austria

424th Field Artillery Bn (105mm How Trk-D)   20 Apr 44 Ft Riley Kans / 5 Feb 45 Ft Benning Ga
(R&S Cmd 13 Nov 44) (nondiv)

425th Armored Field Artillery Bn   25 Mar 44 Cp Bowie Tex (650th TD Bn) /17 Feb 45 Ft Knox Ky   *(nondiv)*

426th Armored Field Artillery Bn   25 Mar 44 Cp Bowie Tex (663rd TD Bn) /8 Jan 46 Cp Anza Calif
SPE: 1 Feb 45   Hawaii: 9 Feb 45   Philippines: 16 Jul 45   LAPE: 7 Jan 46 *(nondiv)*
Leyte Philippines

427th Armored Field Artillery Bn   25 Mar 44 Cp Bowie Tex (666th TD Bn) / 28 Dec 45 Cp Stoneman Calif
SPE: 8 Feb 45   Hawaii: 15 Feb 45   Philippines: 20 Jul 45   SFPE: 27 Dec 45 *(nondiv)*
Leyte Philippines

428th Armored Field Artillery Bn   25 Mar 44 Cp Bowie Tex (668th TD Bn) / 8 Jan 46 Cp Anza Calif
SPE: 8 Feb 45   Hawaii: 15 Feb 45   Philippines: 16 Jul 45   LAPE: 7 Jan 46
Leyte Philippines

429th Field Artillery Bn (155mm How Trac-D)   16 Oct 44 Cp Gruber Okla /1 Jan 46 Cp Stoneman Calif
SFPE: 20 Jun 45   Philippines: 16 Jul 45   SFPE: 30 Dec 45 *(initially 4.5-inch Gun Trac-D until 1945) (nondiv)*
Shipment #4122-H unloading

433rd Field Artillery Bn (155mm Gun Trac-D)   25 Sep 44 Ft Jackson S.C. /17 Jan 46 Cp Stoneman Calif
LAPE: 3 Aug 45   Philippines: 23 Aug 45   SFPE: 15 Jan 46 *(initially 4.5-inch Gun Trac-D until 1945) (nondiv)*
Shipment #2209-B at sea

434th Armored Field Artillery Bn   2 Mar 42 Cp Polk La /11 Oct 45 Cp Kilmer N.J.
NYPE: 7 Jun 44   England: 13 Jun 44   France-ETO: 11 Aug 44 - **25,26,32,34**   NYPE: 10 Oct 45 *(7th Armd Div)*
Halle Germany

435th Field Artillery Bn (8-inch How Trac-D)   21 Aug 44 Cp Gruber Okla/20 Apr 46 Hawaii
Portland Sub-PE: 28 Jun 45   Hawaii: 6 Jul 45 *(nondiv)*
Schofield Barracks Hawaii

436th Field Artillery Bn (8-inch How Trac-D)   21 Aug 44 Cp Gruber Okla / 5 Oct 45 Cp Hood Tex   *(nondiv)*
Cp Gruber Okla

440th Armored Field Artillery Bn   2 Mar 42 Cp Polk La /11 Oct 45 Cp Kilmer N.J.
NYPE: 7 Jun 44   England: 13 Jun 44   France-ETO: 11 Aug 44 - **25,26,32,34**   NYPE: 10 Oct 45 *(7th Armd Div)*
Halle Germany

443rd Field Artillery Bn (8-inch How Trac-D)   25 Sep 44 Cp Hood Tex /1 Jul 45 Cp Hood Tex redes 443rd Chem Mortar Bn
(nondiv)

450th Field Artillery Bn (8-inch How Trac-D)   25 Sep 44 Cp Hood Tex / 30 Jun 45 Cp Hood Tex   *(nondiv)*

456th Prcht Field Artillery Bn (75mm Pk How)   24 Sep 42 Ft Bragg N.C. / *
NYPE: 28 Apr 43   N.Africa: 10 May 43   Sicily: 9 Jul 43   N.Africa: 19 Aug 43   Sicily: 4 Sep 43   Italy: 13 Sep 43
N.Ireland: 9 Dec 43   England: 14 Feb 44   France: 6 Jun 44   England: 13 Jul 44   Holland: 17 Sep 44 - **25,26,29,30,34,35**
(assigned 82nd A/B Div 10 Feb 43) (82nd A/B Div)
Epinal France

457th Prcht Field Artillery Bn (75mm Pk How)   5 Jan 43 Ft Bragg N.C. / *
SFPE: 6 May 44   New Guinea: 28 May 44   Philippines: 18 Nov 44   Okinawa: 12 Aug 45 - **13,14,15**
(assigned 11th A/B Div 23 Feb 43) (11th A/B Div)
Okinawa *(arriving via air)*

458th Prcht Field Artillery Bn (75mm Pk How)   20 Feb 43 Ft Bragg N.C. / 25 Feb 46 Ft Bragg N.C.
NYPE: 26 Jan 45   France-ETO: 14 Feb 45 - **26**   NYPE: 20 Aug 45 *(13th A/B Div)*
Shipment #10580-P at sea

460th Prcht Field Artillery Bn (75mm Pk How)   15 Apr 43 Cp Mackall N.C. / 25 Feb 46 Ft Bragg N.C.
HRPE: 17 May 44   'Italy: 31 May 44   France-ETO: 15 Aug 44 - **25,26,34**   NYPE: 20 Aug 45 *(assigned 17th A/B Div until 10 Mar 44; attached 1st A/B Task Force for invasion of southern France; assigned 13th A/B Div 22 Feb 45) (13th A/B Div)*
Shipment #10580-R at sea

462nd Prcht Field Artillery Bn (75mm Pk How)   16 Jun 43 Cp Mackall N.C. / 21 Dec 45 Cp Anza Calif
SFPE: 12 Mar 44   Australia: 29 Mar 44   New Guinea: 14 Apr 44   Noemfoor I: 3 Jul 44   Philippines: 18 Nov 44 - **13,14,15**
LAPE: 18 Dec 45 *(nondiv)*
Iloilo Philippines

463rd Prcht Field Artillery Bn (75mm Pk How)   20 Feb 44 Nettuno Italy / 30 Nov 45 Germany
Italy: 20 Feb 44   France-ETO: 15 Aug 44 - **24,25,26,34,35,37**
(attached to 101st A/B Div 9 Dec 44 and assigned 1 Mar 45) (101st A/B Div)
Bayers France

BATTALION DESIGNATION AND TYPE	FORMED (SOURCE OF UNIT)/INACTIVATION *Active through 1946	AUGUST 1945 LOCATION

464th Prcht Field Artillery Bn (75mm Pk How) 1 Aug 44 Cp Mackall N.C./25 Oct 45 Cp Mackall N.C.
NYPE: 10 Feb 45   France-ETO: 24 Feb 45 - **26,34**   NYPE: 13 Aug 45 *(not assigned 17th A/B Div until 4 Jun 45) (nondiv)*
Shipment #10563-A at NYPE

465th Field Artillery Bn (8-inch How Trac-D) 1 Mar 43 Ft Bragg N.C./10 Dec 46 Philippines
HRPE: 23 Jul 44   New Guinea: 24 Aug 44   Philippines: 28 Oct 44 - **13,14,15** *(75mm Pk How Trk-D until 15 Jan 44) (nondiv)*
Luzon Philippines

466th Prcht Field Artillery Bn (75mm Pk How) 1 Aug 43 Cp Mackall N.C./16 Sep 45 Cp Myles Standish Mass
BPE: 20 Aug 44   England: 28 Aug 44   France-ETO: 24 Dec 44 - **25,26,34**   BPE: 15 Sep 45 *(assigned to 17th A/B Div 10 Mar 44)*
(17th A/B Div)
Vittel France

467th Prcht Field Arty Bn (75mm Pk How((I) 15 Mar 44 Cp Mackall N.C. / 30 Jul 44 Cp Mackall N.C.   *(nondiv)*

467th Prcht Field Arty Bn (75mm Pk How) (II) 20 Dec 44 Cp Mackall N.C. /1 Jul 45 Cp Mackall N.C.   *(A/B Center)*

472nd Glider Field Artillery Bn (75mm Pk How) 6 Mar 43 Cp Gordon Ga (1st Bn, 472nd FA) / *
SFPE: 26 Aug 44   New Guinea: 9 Sep 44   Philippines: 14 Nov 45   Okinawa: 12 Aug 45 - **14,15** *(assigned to 11th A/B Div 20 Jul 45)*
(105mm How Trk-D until 1944 when reorg as 105mm How Trac-D) redes as Glider FA Bn 75mm Pk How 20 Jul 45 in Philippines) (11th A/B Div)
Okinawa *(arriving via air)*

477th Field Artillery Observation Bn 15 Jun 44 Ft Sill Okla /15 May 46 Hawaii
SPE: 3 Apr 45   Hawaii: 11 Apr 45 *(nondiv)*
Schofield Barracks Hawaii

483rd Field Artillery Bn (8-inch How Trac-D) 25 Sep 44 Cp Hood Tex /1 Jul 45 Cp Hood Tex redes 483rd Chem Mortar Bn *(nondiv)*

484th Field Artillery Bn (8-inch How Trac-D) 25 Sep 44 Cp Hood Tex / 30 Jun 45 Cp Hood Tex   *(nondiv)*

489th Armored Field Artillery Bn 1 Mar 42 Cp Polk La / 9 Oct 45 Cp Shanks N.Y.
NYPE: 7 Jun 44   England: 13 Jun 44   France-ETO: 11 Aug 44 - **25,26,32,34**   NYPE: 8 Oct 45 *(7th Armd Div)*
Buschdorf Germany

490th Armored Field Artillery Bn 15 Aug 42 Cp Polk La / 31 Aug 45 Austria
NYPE: 29 Sep 44   England: 11 Oct 44   France-ETO: 16 Dec 44 - **25,26,34** *(11th Armd Div)*
Altausee Austria

491st Armored Field Artillery Bn 15 Aug 42 Cp Polk La / 31 Aug 45 Austria
NYPE: 29 Sep 44   England: 10 Oct 44   France-ETO: 16 Dec 44 - **25,26,34** *(11th Armd Div)*
Steyermuhl Austria

492nd Armored Field Artillery Bn 15 Aug 42 Cp Polk La / 31 Aug 45 Austria
NYPE: 29 Sep 44   England: 11 Oct 44   France-ETO: 16 Dec 44 - **25,26,34** *(11th Armd Div)*
Bad Ischl Austria

493rd Armored Field Artillery Bn 15 Sep 42 Cp Campbell Ky / 3 Dec 45 Cp Kilmer N.J.
NYPE: 20 Sep 44   England: 1 Oct 44   France-ETO: 9 Nov 44 - **25,26,34**   NYPE: 1 Dec 45 *(12th Armd Div)*
Mergelstetten Germany

494th Armored Field Artillery Bn 15 Sep 42 Cp Campbell Ky /1 Dec 45 Cp Kilmer N.J.
NYPE: 20 Sep 44   England: 1 Oct 44   France-ETO: 9 Nov 44 - **25,26,34**   NYPE: 30 Nov 45 *(12th Armd Div)*
Steinheim Germany

495th Armored Field Artillery Bn 15 Sep 42 Cp Campbell Ky / 4 Dec 45 Cp Kilmer N.J.
NYPE: 20 Sep 44   England: 1 Oct 44   France-ETO: 9 Nov 44 - **25,26,34**   NYPE: 3 Dec 45 *(12th Armd Div)*
Giengen Germany

496th Armored Field Artillery Bn 15 Oct 42 Cp Beale Calif / 3 Nov 45 Cp Cooke Calif
NYPE: 18 Jan 45   France-ETO: 29 Jan 45 - **26,34**   HRPE: 23 Jul 45 *(13th Armd Div)*
Cp Cooke Calif

497th Armored Field Artillery Bn 15 Oct 42 Cp Beale Calif / 3 Nov 45 Cp Cooke Calif
NYPE: 18 Jan 45   France-ETO: 29 Jan 45 - **26,34**   HRPE: 23 Jul 45 *(13th Armd Div)*
Cp Cooke Calif

498th Armored Field Artillery Bn 15 Oct 42 Cp Beale Calif /10 Nov 45 Cp Cooke Calif
NYPE: 18 Jan 45   France-ETO: 29 Jan 45 - **26,34**   HRPE: 23 Jul 45 *(13th Armd Div)*
Cp Cooke Calif

499th Armored Field Artillery Bn 15 Nov 42 Cp Chaffee Ark /16 Sep 45 Cp Patrick Henry Va
NYPE: 14 Oct 44   France-ETO: 28 Oct 44 - **25,26,34**   HRPE: 16 Sep 45 *(14th Armd Div)*
Erding Germany

500th Armored Field Artillery Bn 15 Nov 42 Cp Chaffee Ark / 23 Sep 45 Cp Myles Standish Mass
NYPE: 14 Oct 44   France-ETO: 28 Oct 44 - **25,26,34**   BPE: 22 Sep 45 *(14th Armd Div)*
Wasserburg Germany

501st Armored Field Artillery Bn 15 Nov 42 Cp Chaffee Ark/23 Sep 45 Cp Myles Standish Mass
NYPE: 14 Oct 44   France-ETO: 28 Oct 44 - **25,26,34**   BPE: 22 Sep 45 *(14th Armd Div)*
Altotting Germany

512th Field Artillery Bn (105mm How Trk-D) 25 Jun 43 Cp Rucker Ala / 24 Dec 45 Cp Kilmer N.J.
NYPE: 2 Jul 44   Scotland: 14 Jul 44   France-ETO: 23 Aug 44   NYPE: 22 Dec 45 - **25,26,32,34** *(nondiv)*
Plauen Germany

514th Field Artillery Bn (155mm Gun Trac-D) 6 Nov 43 Ft Lewis Wash /18 Feb 46 Ft Jackson S.C.
NYPE: 27 Sep 44   England: 3 Oct 44   France-ETO: 9 Oct 44 - **25,26,32,34**   NYPE: 20 Aug 45 *(nondiv)*
Shipment #10447-D at sea

515th Field Artillery Bn (155mm Gun Trac-D) 6 Nov 43 Ft Lewis Wash /12 Feb 46 Cp Kilmer N.J.
NYPE: 30 Oct 44   England: 12 Nov 44   France-ETO: 31 Jan 45 - **26,34**   NYPE: 11 Feb 46 *(nondiv)*
Ohringen Germany

516th Field Artillery Bn (155mm Gun Trac-D) 25 Nov 43 Cp Shelby Miss / 9 Apr 46 Cp Kilmer N.J.
NYPE: 27 Sep 44   England: 3 Oct 44   France-ETO: 10 Dec 44 - **26,34**   NYPE: 8 Apr 46 *(Truck-D until sent overseas) (nondiv)*
Halle Germany

BATTALION DESIGNATION AND TYPE	FORMED (SOURCE OF UNIT)/INACTIVATION *Active through 1946	AUGUST 1945 LOCATION

517th Field Artillery Bn (155mm Gun Trac-D)   5 Jan 44 Ft Bragg N.C. / 25 Jan 46 Japan   Leyte Philippines
SFPE: 18 Oct 44   Bougainville: 10 Nov 44   Philippines: 14 Jan 45 - **14** *(nondiv)*

518th Field Artillery Bn (155mm How Trk-D)   17 Apr 44 Cp Joseph T Robinson Ark /12 Feb 45 Ft Sill Okla
(R&S Cmd 6 Dec 44) (nondiv)

519th Rocket Field Arty Bn (4.5-in. Rocket Trk-D)   17 Apr 44 Cp Joseph T. Robinson Ark /11 Sep 45 Ft Sill Okla   Ft Sill Okla
(105mm How Trk-D until reorg as Rocket FA 20 Jun 45 at Ft Sill Okla) (R&S Cmd 13 Nov 44) (nondiv)

521st Field Artillery Bn (155mm How Trac-D)   18 May 44 Cp Pickett Va (1st Bn, 30th FA) /1 May 45 Germany redes 30th FA Bn
NYPE: 27 Feb 45   France-ETO: 11 Mar 45 *(nondiv)*

522nd Field Arty Bn (Nisei) (105mm How Trk-D)   1 Feb 43 Cp Shelby Miss/31 Dec 45 Cp Kilmer N.J.   Mertingen Germany
HRPE: 3 May 44   Italy: 28 May 44   France-ETO: 29 Sep 44 - **26,31,34,35**   NYPE: 29 Dec 45 *(personnel of Japanese ancestry)*

526th Rocket Field Arty Bn (4.5-in. Rocket Trk-D)   17 Apr 44 Cp Joseph T Robinson Ark / 20 Nov 45 Ft Sill Okla   Ft Sill Okla
(105mm How Trk-D until reorg as Rocket FA 15 Apr 45 at Ft Sill Okla) (R&S Cmd 13 Nov 44) (nondiv)

527th Field Artillery Bn (8-inch How Trac-D)   18 May 44 Cp Gruber Okla (3rd Bn, 250th CA)/24 Sep 45 Italy   Pacengo Italy
HRPE: 18 Feb 45   Italy: 1 Mar 45 - **31,33** *(155mm Gun Trac-D until late 1944) (nondiv)*

528th Field Artillery Bn (155mm Gun Trac-D)   21 Feb 44 Cp Hood Tex /1 Nov 46 Cp Hood Tex   Shipment #10077-C at sea
NYPE: 30 Oct 44   England: 13 Nov 44   France-ETO: 8 Feb 45 - **26,34**   NYPE: 18 Aug 45 *(nondiv)*

529th Field Artillery Bn (8-inch How Trac-D)   22 Mar 44 Cp Hood Tex /11 Feb 46 Cp Kilmer N.J.   Rheyt Germany sch to SWPA
NYPE: 27 Feb 45   France-ETO: 11 Mar 45 - **26**   NYPE: 11 Feb 46 *(155mm Gun Trac-D until late 1944) (nondiv)*   under Shipment #R6604-A

530th Field Artillery Bn (155mm Gun Trac-D)   20 May 44 Ft Jackson S.C. (3rd Bn, 252nd CA) / 30 Sep 45 Italy   Isola Italy
NYPE: 1 Mar 45   Italy: 15 Mar 45 - **31,33,35** *(nondiv)*

531st Field Artillery Bn (155mm Gun Trac-D)   31 May 44 Schofield Barracks Hawaii (First Prov Gun Bn) /1 Jan 46 Cp Stoneman   Okinawa
Hawaii: 31 May 44   Saipan: 17 Jun 44   Tinian: 27 Jul 44   Philippines: 6 Dec 44   Okinawa: 2 Apr 45 - **13,19,21**   Calif
SFPE: 21 Dec 45 *(nondiv)*

532nd Field Artillery Bn (155mm Gun Trac-D)   31 May 44 Schofield Barracks Hawaii (32nd CA Bn)/22 Dec 45 Ft Lawton Wash   Okinawa
Hawaii: 31 May 44   Saipan: 22 Jun 44   Philippines: 6 Dec 44   Kamiyama Shima: 31 Mar 45   Okinawa: 14 May 45 - **13,19,21**
SPE: 21 Dec 45 *(nondiv)*

533rd Rocket Field Arty Bn (4.5-in. Rocket Trk-D)   25 Sep 44 Cp Hood Tex/*   Cp Hood Tex
(8-inch How Trac-D until reorg as Rocket FA 10 Jun 45 at Cp Polk La) (nondiv)

534th Field Artillery Bn (8-inch How Trac-D)   16 Oct 44 Cp Gruber Okla / 5 Jul 45 Cp Gruber Okla redes 534th Chem Mortar Bn
(nondiv)

535th Field Artillery Bn (8-inch How Trk-D)   18 May 44 Cp Gruber Okla (1st Bn, 250th CA) / 29 Nov 45 Cp Shanks N.Y.   Mulchen Gladbeck Germany
NYPE: 19 Feb 45   France-ETO: 3 Jan 45 - **26**   NYPE: 27 Nov 45 *(155mm Gun Trk-D until late 1944) (nondiv)*

536th Field Artillery Bn (8-inch How Trk-D)   18 May 44 Cp Gruber Okla (2nd Bn, 250th CA) / 25 Nov 45 Italy   Rosa Italy
HRPE: 18 Feb 45   Italy: 1 Mar 45 - **31,33** *(155mm Gun Trk-D until late 1944) (nondiv)*

537th Field Artillery Bn (8-inch How Trac-D)   16 Oct 44 Cp Gruber Okla / 5 Jul 45 Chicago Ill redes 537th Chem Mortar Bn *(nondiv)*

538th Field Artillery Bn (240mm How Trac-D)   30 Aug 44 Ft Bragg N.C. (286th CA Bn) /14 Dec 45 Cp Myles Standish Mass   Rhaunen Germany
NYPE: 23 Mar 45   France-ETO: 3 Apr 45 - **26**   BPE: 13 Dec 45 *(nondiv)*

539th Field Artillery Bn (240mm How Trac-D)   30 Aug 44 Ft Bragg N.C. (287th CA Bn) / 28 Dec 45 Cp Myles Standish Mass   Zeweiv Germany
NYPE: 22 Mar 45   France-ETO: 3 Apr 45   BPE: 27 Dec 45 *(nondiv)*

540th Field Artillery Bn (155mm Gun Trac-D)   20 May 44 Ft Jackson S.C. (2nd Bn, 252nd CA) /13 Dec 45 Cp Gruber Okla   Cp Gruber Okla
NYPE: 19 Feb 45   France-ETO: 3 Mar 45 - **32**   NYPE: 23 Jun 45 *(nondiv)*

541st Field Artillery Bn (155mm Gun Trac-D)   20 May 44 Ft Jackson S.C. (1st Bn, 252nd CA) /13 Dec 46 Cp Kilmer N.J.   Ft Jackson S.C.
NYPE: 5 Feb 45   France-ETO: 17 Feb 45 - **26**   NYPE: 16 Jul 45 *(nondiv)*

542nd Field Artillery Bn (155mm How Trac-D)   14 Jul 43 Cp Gruber Okla / 30 Jun 46 Austria   Kufstein Austria
NYPE: 6 Jan 45   France-ETO: 18 Jan 45 - **26,34** *(42nd Inf Div)*

543rd Field Artillery Bn (240mm How Trac-D)   12 Jan 44 Ft Bragg N.C. / 28 Dec 45 Cp Stoneman Calif   Leyte Philippines
SPE: 28 Dec 44   Hawaii: 4 Jan 45   Philippines: 17 Jul 45   SFPE: 27 Dec 45 *(nondiv)*

544th Field Artillery Bn (240mm How Trac-D)   12 Jan 44 Ft Bragg N.C./26 Jan 46 Cp Anza Calif   Dagupan Philippines
SFPE: 20 Oct 44   New Guinea: 13 Nov 44   Philippines: 19 Feb 45 - **14,15**   LAPE: 25 Jan 46 *(nondiv)*

545th Field Artillery Bn (240mm How Trac-D)   21 Apr 44 Ft Jackson S.C. / 8 Jan 46 Cp Anza Calif   Leyte Philippines
SPE: 28 Dec 44   Hawaii: 4 Jan 45   Philippines: 13 Jul 45   LAPE: 7 Jan 46 *(nondiv)*

BATTALION DESIGNATION AND TYPE	FORMED (SOURCE OF UNIT)/INACTIVATION *Active through 1946	AUGUST 1945 LOCATION

546th Field Artillery Bn (155mm Gun Trk-D)   18 Apr 44 Cp Shelby Miss / 5 Jan 46 Cp Patrick Henry Va   Baumholder Germany
NYPE: 3 Jan 45   France-ETO: 16 Jan 45 - **26**   HRPE: 5 Jan 46 *(nondiv)*

547th Field Artillery Bn (155mm Gun Trk-D)   13 Apr 44 Cp Hood Tex / 20 Mar 46 Cp Kilmer N.J.   Kornwestheim Germany
NYPE: 8 Dec 44   England: 21 Dec 44   France-ETO: 17 Feb 45 - **26,34**   NYPE: 19 Mar 46 *(nondiv)*

548th Field Artillery Bn (155mm Gun Trk-D)   13 Apr 44 Cp Hood Tex/25 Dec 45 Cp Kilmer N.J.   Bamberg Germany
NYPE: 1 Nov 44   England: 9 Nov 44   France-ETO: 4 Feb 45 - **26,34**   NYPE: 21 Dec 45 *(nopndiv)*

549th Field Artillery Bn (155mm Gun Trk-D)   13 Apr 44 Cp Hood Tex / 5 Jan 46 Cp Patrick Henry Va   Eichstatt Germany
NYPE: 9 Dec 44   England: 20 Dec 44   France-ETO: 20 Feb 45 - **26,34**   HRPE: 5 Jan 46 *(nondiv)*

550th Field Artillery Bn (155mm How Trac-D)   18 May 44 Cp Pickett Va (2nd Bn, 30th FA) / 8 Feb 46 Cp Swift Tex   Cp Swift Tex
NYPE: 27 Feb 45   France-ETO: 11 Mar 45   NYPE: 6 Aug 45 *(nondiv)*

551st Field Artillery Bn (240mm How Trac-D)   21 Jan 43 Ft Bragg N.C./27 Nov 45 Cp Kilmer N.J.   Battenberg Germany
NYPE: 21 Mar 44   England: 27 Mar 44   France-ETO: 26 Jun 44 - **25,26,30,32,34**   NYPE: 26 Nov 45 *(nondiv)*

552nd Field Artillery Bn (240mm How Trac-D)   15 Aug 43 Ft Bragg N.C. / 26 Nov 45 Cp Myles Standish Mass   Bottendorf Germany
NYPE: 6 Apr 44   England: 13 Apr 44   France-ETO: 29 Jun 44 - **25,26,30,32,34**   BPE: 25 Nov 45 *(nondiv)*

553rd Field Artillery Bn (240mm How Trac-D)   21 Aug 44 Ft Bragg N.C. /11 Feb 46 Cp Kilmer N.J.   Yvetot France sch to SWPA
NYPE: 23 Mar 45   France-ETO: 3 Apr 45   NYPE: 10 Feb 46 *(nondiv)*   under Shipment #R4085-GG

557th Field Artillery Bn (155mm Gun S-P)   15 May 43 Cp Gruber Okla /14 Feb 46 Cp Cooke Calif   Cp Cooke Calif
NYPE: 2 Jul 44   England: 12 Jul 44   France-ETO: 12 Aug 44 - **25,26,32,34**   BPE: 20 Jul 45 *(nondiv)*

558th Field Artillery Bn (155mm Gun S-P)   10 May 43 Cp Roberts Calif /10 Feb 46 Cp Hood Tex   Conflans France sch to SWPA
NYPE: 2 Jul 44   England: 12 Jul 44   France-ETO: 12 Aug 44 - **25,26,32,34**   NYPE: 24 Aug 45 *(nondiv)*   under Shipment #R4645-E

559th Field Artillery Bn (155mm Gun Trk-D)   1 Jul 43 Cp Joseph T Robinson Ark / 24 Oct 45 Cp Myles Standish Mass   Ober Massfeld Germany
NYPE: 10 Apr 44   England: 16 Apr 44   France-ETO: 1 Jul 44 - **25,26,30,32,34**   BPE: 23 Oct 45 *(nondiv)*

560th Field Artillery Bn (240mm How Trac-D)   25 Sep 44 Ft Bragg N.C. / 9 Jul 45 Ft Bragg redes 560th Chem Mortan Bn   *(nondiv)*

561st Field Artillery Bn (155mm Gun Trk-D)   9 Jul 43 Cp Joseph T Robinson Ark / 6 Oct 45 France   Kipfenberg Germany
NYPE: 7 Apr 44   England: 15 Apr 44   France-ETO: 30 Jun 44 - **25,26,30,32,34** *(nondiv)*

563rd Field Artillery Bn (155mm How Trac-D)   15 Jun 44 Cp Butner N.C. /19 Dec 45 Cp Kilmer N.J.   St Pierre de Manneville France
BPE: 10 Jan 45   France-ETO: 21 Jan 45 - **34**   NYPE: 17 Dec 45 *(89th Inf Div)*

564th Field Artillery Bn (155mm How Trac-D)   26 May 44 Ft Benning Ga / 9 Mar 46 Cp Kilmer N.J.   Neuburg Germany
NYPE: 26 Jan 45   France-ETO: 6 Feb 45 - **26,34**   NYPE: 8 Mar 46 *(71st Inf Div)*

566th Field Artillery Bn (105mm How Trk-D)   17 Apr 44 Cp Joseph T Robinson Ark /12 Feb 45 Ft Sill Okla   *(nondiv)*

569th Field Artillery Bn (105mm How Trk-D)   17 Apr 44 Cp Van Dorn Miss / 20 Feb 46 Ft Bragg N.C.   Ft Bragg N.C.
NYPE: 8 Apr 45   France-ETO: 19 Apr 45   HRPE: 3 Jul 45 *(nondiv)*

570th Field Artillery Bn (8-inch Gun Trac-D)   21 Apr 44 Ft Jackson S.C. /10 Dec 45 Philippines   Shipment #4122-C unloading
SFPE: 7 Jul 45   Philippines: 3 Aug 45 *(nondiv)*

573rd Field Artillery Bn (8-inch Gun Trac-D)   21 Apr 44 Ft Jackson S.C. /10 Dec 45 Philippines   Shipment #4122-D unloading
SFPE: 7 Jul 45   Philippines: 3 Aug 45 *(nondiv)*

575th Field Artillery Bn (8-inch Gun Trac-D)   20 Jul 44 Terricciola Italy /19 Dec 45 Cp Myles Standish Mass   Mannheim Germany
Italy: 20 Jul 44   France-ETO: 16 Aug 44 - **25,26,34,37**   BPE: 18 Dec 45 *(Btry A and B not formed until 18 Nov 44) (nondiv)*

576th Field Artillery Bn (8-inch How S-P)   16 Oct 44 Ft Bragg N.C. / *   Ft Bragg, N.C.
(nondiv) (organized under proposed T/O and still experimental in Aug 45)

578th Field Arty Bn (Cld) (8-inch How Trac-D)   23 Feb 43 Ft Bragg N.C. (1st Bn, 578th FA) /2 Nov 45 Germany   Eschenstruth Germany
NYPE: 6 Apr 44   England: 13 Apr 44   France-ETO: 17 Jul 44 - **25,26,30,32,34** *(nondiv)*

580th Field Artillery Bn (105mm How Trk-D)   17 Apr 44 Cp Van Dorn Miss / 8 Sep 45 Cp Gruber Okla   Cp Gruber Okla
NYPE: 8 Apr 45   France-ETO: 19 Apr 45   BPE: 26 Jun 45 *(nondiv)*

583rd Field Artillery Bn (105mm How Trk-D)   17 Apr 44 Cp Van Dorn Miss/8 Sep 45 Cp Gruber Okla   Cp Gruber Okla
NYPE: 8 Apr 45   France-ETO: 19 Apr 45   BPE: 26 Jun 45 *(nondiv)*

589th Field Artillery Bn (105mm How Trk-D)   15 Mar 43 Ft Jackson S.C. / 3 Oct 45 Cp Patrick Henry Va   Nachtsheim Germany
BPE: 10 Nov 44   England: 17 Nov 44   France-ETO: 6 Dec 44 - **25,32,34**   HRPE: 3 Oct 45 *(106th Inf Div)*

590th Field Artillery Bn (105mm How Trk-D)   15 Mar 43 Ft Jackson S.C. / 3 Oct 45 Cp Patrick Henry Va   Nachtsheim Germany
BPE: 10 Nov 44   England: 17 Nov 44   France-ETO: 6 Dec 44 - **25,32,34**   HRPE: 3 Oct 45 *(106th Inf Div)*

BATTALION DESIGNATION AND TYPE	FORMED (SOURCE OF UNIT)/INACTIVATION	AUGUST 1945 LOCATION

591st Field Artillery Bn (105mm How Trk-D)   15 Mar 43 Ft Jackson S.C. / 3 Oct 45 Cp Patrick Henry Va — *Gross Garrach Austria*
BPE: 10 Nov 44   England: 17 Nov 44   France-ETO: 6 Dec 44 - **25,32,34**   HRPE: 3 Oct 45 *(106th Inf Div)*

592nd Field Artillery Bn (155mm How Trac-D)   15 Mar 43 Ft Jackson S.C. / 3 Oct 45 Cp Patrick Henry Va — *Heilbronn Germany*
BPE: 10 Nov 44   England: 17 Nov 44   France-ETO: 6 Dec 44 - **25,32,34**   HRPE: 3 Oct 45 *(106th Inf Div)*

593rd Field Arty Bn (Cld) (105mm How Trac-D)   15 May 42 Ft Huachuca Ariz / 3 Feb 46 Cp Stoneman Calif — *Morotai Island*
SFPE: 31 Jan 44   Guadalcanal: 17 Feb 44   Bougainville: 29 Mar 44   Green I: 17 Jul 44   New Guinea: 11 Jan 45
Morotai: 7 Apr 45 - **3,15,16** *(93rd Inf Div)*

594th Field Arty Bn (Cld) (105mm How Trac-D)   15 May 42 Ft Huachuca Ariz / 3 Feb 46 Cp Stoneman Calif — *Zamboanga Philippines*
SFPE: 31 Jan 44   Guadalcanal: 17 Feb 44   Russell I: 28 Feb 44   New Georgia: 14 Jun 44   New Guinea: 18 Nov 44
Morotai: 11 Apr 45 - **3,15,16** *(93rd Inf Div)*

595th Field Arty Bn (Cld) (105mm How Trac-D)   15 May 42 Ft Huachuca Ariz / 3 Feb 46 Cp Stoneman Calif — *Morotai Island*
SFPE: 31 Jan 44   Guadalcanal: 17 Feb 44   New Georgia: 12 Mar 44   Emirau I: 7 Jul 44   Biak I: 19 Nov 44
Morotai: 7 Apr 45 - **3,15,16** *(93rd Inf Div)*

596th Field Arty Bn (Cld) (155mm How Trac-D)   15 May 42 Ft Huachuca Ariz / 3 Feb 46 Cp Stoneman Calif — *Morotai Island*
SFPE: 31 Jan 44   Guadalcanal: 17 Feb 44   Treasury I: 21 Jun 44   New Guinea: 16 Nov 44   Morotai: 7 Apr 45 - **3,15,16** *(93rd Inf Div)*

597th Field Arty Bn (Cld) (105mm How Trk-D)   15 Oct 42 Cp Atterbury Ind / 24 Nov 45 Cp Myles Standish Mass — *Torre Del Lago Italy*
HRPE: 20 Sep 44   Italy: 4 Oct 44 - **31,33**   BPE: 23 Nov 45 *(92nd Inf Div)*

598th Field Arty Bn (Cld) (105mm How Trk-D)   15 Oct 42 Cp Breckinridge Ky / 24 Nov 45 Cp Myles Standish Mass — *Torre Del Lago Italy*
HRPE: 15 Jul 44   Italy: 24 Nov 44 - **31,33,35**   BPE: 23 Nov 45 *(92nd Inf Div)*

599th Field Arty Bn (Cld) (105mm How Trk-D)   15 Oct 42 Cp Joseph T Robinson Ark / 24 Nov 45 Cp Myles Standish Mass — *Torre Del Lago Italy*
HRPE: 20 Sep 44   Italy: 4 Oct 44 - **31,33**   BPE: 23 Nov 45 *(92nd Inf Div)*

600th Field Arty Bn (Cld) (155mm How Trac-D)   15 Oct 42 Ft McClellan Ala / 24 Nov 45 Cp Myles Standish Mass — *Torre Del Lago Italy*
HRPE: 12 Sep 44   Italy: 7 Oct 44 - **31,33**   BPE: 23 Nov 45 *(92nd Inf Div)*

601st Field Artillery Bn (75mm Pk How)   16 Apr 42 Ft Bragg N.C. / 25 Oct 45 Cp Shanks N.Y. — *Oberau Germany*
SFPE: 29 Jul 43   Alaska: 4 Aug 43   SPE: 2 Dec 43   HRPE: 2 Feb 44   Italy: 29 Feb 44   France-ETO: 15 Oct 44 - **2,26,29,34,35**
NYPE: 23 Oct 45 *(nondiv)*

602nd Field Artillery Bn (75mm Pk How)   20 Jul 42 Cp Carson Colo / 22 Dec 45 Cp Kilmer N.J. — *Landsberg Germany*
SFPE: 29 Jul 43   Alaska: 4 Aug 43   SPE: 2 Dec 43   HRPE: 1 Feb 44   N.Africa: 29 Feb 44   Italy: 1 Mar 44
France-ETO: 15 Aug 44 - **2,26,29,34,35,37**   NYPE: 21 Dec 45 *(nondiv)*

603rd Field Artillery Bn (75mm Pk How)

     Only Btry A (75mm Pk How) of the 603rd FA Bn was active; raised 10 Feb 42 at Charleston Sub-P/E and inactivated 10 Oct 43 on Guadalcanal.

604th Field Artillery Bn (75mm Pk How)   11 Jan 43 Cp Carson Colo / 10 Nov 45 Cp Carson Colo — *Shipment #22050-J at HRPE*
HRPE: 6 Jan 45   Italy: 18 Jan 45 - **31,33**   HRPE: 9 Aug 45 *(assigned to 10th Mtn Div 15 Jul 43) (10th Mtn Div)*

605th Field Artillery Bn (75mm Pk How)   11 Jan 43 Cp Carson Colo / 8 Nov 45 Cp Carson Colo — *Shipment #22050-K at HRPE*
HRPE: 6 Jan 45   Italy: 18 Jan 45 - **31,33**   HRPE: 9 Aug 45 *(assigned to 10th Mtn Div 15 Jul 43) (10th Mtn Div)*

607th Field Artillery Bn (105mm How Trk-D)   10 May 43 Cp Carson Colo / 10 Mar 46 Cp Kilmer N.J. — *Rain Germany*
NYPE: 26 Jan 45   France-ETO: 6 Feb 45 - **26,34**   NYPE: 9 Mar 46 *(75mm Pk How until 19 May 44) (15 Jul 43 asgnd 71st Light Div)*
(71st Inf Div)

608th Field Artillery Bn (105mm How Trk-D)   10 May 43 Cp Carson Colo / 11 Mar 46 Cp Kilmer N.J. — *Hemerlen Germany*
NYPE: 26 Jan 45   France-ETO: 6 Feb 45 - **26,34**   NYPE: 10 Mar 46 *(75mm Pk How until 19 May 44) (15 Jul 43 assigned 71st Light Div)*
(71st Inf Div)

609th Field Artillery Bn (105mm How Trk-D)   14 May 43 Cp Carson Colo / 9 Mar 46 Cp Kilmer N.J. — *Donauworth Germany*
NYPE: 26 Jan 45   France-ETO: 6 Feb 45 - **26,34**   NYPE: 8 Mar 46 *(75mm Pk How until 19 May 44) (15 Jul 43 assigned 71st Light Div)*
(71st Inf Div)

610th Field Artillery Bn (75mm Pk How)   17 Dec 43 Cp Gruber Okla / 31 Jul 44 Cp Carson Colo   *(nondiv)*

611th Field Artillery Bn (75mm Pk How)   17 Dec 43 Cp Gruber Okla / 6 Feb 45 Ft Riley Kans   *(nondiv)*

612th Field Artillery Bn (75mm Pk How)   17 Dec 43 Cp Gruber Okla / 25 Aug 45 Kunming China — *Kunming China*
LAPE: 25 Jul 44   India: 26 Aug 44   China: 29 Apr 45 - **5,12** *(nondiv)*

613th Field Artillery Bn (75mm Pk How)   17 Dec 43 Cp Gruber Okla / 25 Aug 45 Kunming China — *Kunming China*
LAPE: 22 Oct 44   India: 23 Nov 44   China: 9 May 45 - **5,12** *(nondiv)*

616th Field Artillery Bn (75mm Pk How)   15 Jul 43 Cp Hale Colo / 27 Nov 45 Cp Carson Colo — *Shipment #22050-L at HRPE*
HRPE: 5 Jan 45   Italy: 23 Jan 45 - **31,33**   HRPE: 13 Aug 45 *(10th Mtn Div)*

BATTALION DESIGN AND TYPE	FORMED (SOURCE OF UNIT) / INACTIVATION	AUGUST 1945 LOCATION

617th Field Artillery Observation Bn 31 Jul 44 Ft Bragg N.C. /10 Dec 45 Cp Hood Tex — Cp Hood Tex
HRPE: 28 Mar 45   Italy: 7 Apr 45 - **33,35**   HRPE: 20 Jul 45 *(nondiv)*

618th Field Artillery Observation Bn 31 Jul 44 Ft Riley Kans / 6 Dec 45 Cp Gruber Okla   *(nondiv)* — Cp Gruber Okla

623rd Field Artillery Observation Bn 15 Jan 45 Ft Sill Okla / 7 Dec 45 Ft Sill Okla   *(R&S Cmd 15 Jan 45)* — *Ft Sill Okla*

624th Field Artillery Observation Bn 25 Aug 44 Ft Leonard Wood Mo / 28 Dec 45 Cp Stoneman Calif — Manila Philippines
SFPE: 17 Jun 45   Philippines: 9 Jul 45   SFPE: 26 Dec 45 *(nondiv)*

626th Field Artillery Bn (105mm How Trk-D) 17 Apr 44 Cp Van Dorn Miss /19 Feb 45 Ft Sill Okla   *(R&S Cmd 18 Nov 44)*

627th Field Artillery Bn (105mm How Trk-D) 20 Apr 44 Cp Chaffee Ark / 5 Sep 46 Germany — Heilbronn Germany
NYPE: 7 Mar 45   France-ETO: 18 Mar 45 - **26,32** *(nondiv)*

628th Rocket Field Arty Bn (4.5-in. Rocket Trk-D) 20 Apr 44 Cp Chaffee Ark /11 Sep 45 Ft Sill Okla — Ft Sill Okla
(105mm How Trk-D until reorg as Rocket FA 1 Aug 45 at Ft Sill Okla) (R&S Cmd 13 Feb 45)

630th Field Artillery Bn (8-inch How Trac-D) 14 Feb 44 Viticuso Italy (2nd Bn, 17th FA) / 22 Feb 46 Cp Kilmer N.J. — Hall Germany
Italy: 14 Feb 44   France-ETO: 9 Sep 44 - **26,34,35,37**   NYPE: 21 Feb 46 *(nondiv)*

631st Field Artillery Bn (155mm How Trac-D) 24 Feb 44 Cassino Italy (2nd Bn, 77th FA) / 8 Sep 45 Italy — Molinetto Italy
Italy: 24 Feb 44 - **31,33,35** *(nondiv)*

633rd Field Artillery Bn (155mm Gun Trac-D) 5 Mar 44 Mignano Italy (2nd Bn, 36th FA) / 8 Sep 45 Italy — Modena Italy
Italy: 5 Mar 44 - **31,33,35** *(nondiv)*

634th Field Artillery Bn (155mm Gun Trac-D) 24 Feb 44 Anzio Italy (1st Bn, 77th FA) /15 May 45 Germany redes 77th FA Bn
Italy: 24 Feb 44   France-ETO: 16 Aug 44 - **25,26,34,35,37** *(nondiv)*

635th Field Artillery Bn (155mm Gun Trk-D) 13 Apr 44 Cp Hood Tex / 6 Jan 46 Cp Patrick Henry Va — Neuberg Germany
NYPE: 9 Dec 44   England: 20 Dec 44   France-ETO: 17 Feb 45 - **26,32,34**   HRPE: 6 Jan 46 *(nondiv)*

655th Field Artillery Bn (8-inch How Trac-D) 13 Apr 44 Cp Hood Tex /18 Jan 46 Cp Anza Calif — Davao Philippines
SFPE: 17 Dec 44   Philippines: 2 Jan 45 - **13,20**   LAPE: 17 Jan 46 *(nondiv)*

656th Field Artillery Bn (8-inch How Trac-D) 20 Apr 44 Cp Rucker Ala /1 Dec 45 Cp Kilmer N.J. — Berg Reichenstein Germany
NYPE: 30 Nov 40   England: 8 Dec 44   France-ETO: 3 Mar 45 - **26,34**   NYPE: 29 Nov 45 *(nondiv)*

657th Field Artillery Bn (8-inch How Trk-D) 20 Apr 44 Cp Rucker Ala / 29 Nov 45 Cp Kilmer N.J. — Cologne Germany
NYPE: 5 Feb 45   England: 16 Feb 45   France-ETO: 27 Feb 45 - **32**   NYPE: 28 Nov 45 *(nondiv)*

658th Field Artillery Bn (8-inch How Trac-D) 10 Apr 44 Cp Forrest Tenn / 2 Jan 46 Cp Kilmer N.J. — Aachen Germany
NYPE: 11 Feb 45   France-ETO: 23 Feb 45   NYPE: 1 Jan 46 *(nondiv)*

659th Field Artillery Bn (8-inch How Trac-D) 10 Apr 44 Cp Forrest Tenn / 6 Apr 46 Cp Kilmer N.J. — Juchen Germany
NYPE: 11 Feb 45   France-ETO: 23 Feb 45 - **26**   NYPE: 6 Apr 46 *(nondiv)*

660th Field Artillery Bn (8-inch How Trac-D) 7 Apr 44 Ft Leonard Wood Mo / 20 Apr 46 Germany — Schlotheim Germany
NYPE: 21 Nov 44   England: 27 Nov 44   France-ETO: 9 Mar 45 - **26,34** *(nondiv)*

661st Field Artillery Bn (8-inch How Trac-D) 7 Apr 44 Ft Leonard Wood Mo /10 Feb 46 Cp Hood Tex — Shipment #10077-D at NYPE
NYPE: 31 Jan 45   England: 8 Feb 45   France-ETO: 25 Feb 45   NYPE: 11 Aug 45 *(nondiv)*

662nd Field Artillery Bn (8-inch How Trac-D) 7 Apr 44 Ft Leonard Wood Mo /1 Dec 45 Cp Myles Standish Mass — Bad Aibling Germany
BPE: 18 Dec 44   England: 27 Dec 44   France-ETO: 16 Mar 45 - **26,34**   BPE: 30 Nov 45 *(nondiv)*

663rd Field Artillery Bn (8-inch How Trk-D) 13 Apr 44 Cp Chaffee Ark / 29 Dec 45 Cp Kilmer N.J. — Suhl Germany
NYPE: 1 Dec 44   England: 12 Dec 44   France-ETO: Feb 45 - **26,34**   NYPE: 28 Dec 45 *(nondiv)*

664th Field Artillery Bn (155mm How Trac-D) 21 Feb 44 Cp Maxey Tex /1 Mar 46 Ft Sill Okla   *(R&S Cmd 23 Aug 44)* — *Ft Sill Okla*

665th Field Artillery Bn (155mm How Trac-D) 21 Feb 44 Cp Maxey Tex /11 Feb 46 Cp San Luis Obispo Calif — Cp San Luis Obispo Calif
NYPE: 27 Feb 45   France-ETO: 11 Mar 45   NYPE: 10 Jul 45 *(nondiv)*

666th Field Artillery Bn (155mm How Trac-D) 21 Feb 44 Cp Bowie Tex / 20 Nov 45 Cp Myles Standish Mass — Scharding Austria
BPE: 10 Nov 44   Scotland: 17 Nov 44   France-ETO: 24 Dec 44 - **25,26,34**   BPE: 19 Nov 45 *(nondiv)*

667th Field Artillery Bn (155mm How Trac-D) 21 Feb 44 Cp Bowie Tex / 29 Jan 46 Cp Kilmer N.J. — Furth Germany
BPE: 10 Nov 44   Scotland: 17 Nov 44   France-ETO: 31 Dec 44 - **25,26,34**   NYPE: 28 Jan 46 *(nondiv)*

668th Field Artillery Bn (155mm How Trac-D) 21 Feb 44 Cp Bowie Tex / 20 Apr 46 Hawaii — Schofield Barracks Hawaii
SPE: 23 Oct 44   Hawaii: 28 Oct 44 *(nondiv)*

669th Field Artillery Bn (155mm How Trac-D) 21 Feb 44 Cp Bowie Tex / 28 Feb 46 Hawaii — Schofield Barracks Hawaii
SPE: 23 Oct 44   Hawaii: 28 Oct 44 *(nondiv)*

BATTALION DESIGNATION AND TYPE	FORMED (SOURCE OF UNIT)/INACTIVATION *Active through 1946	AUGUST 1945 LOCATION

670th Field Artillery Bn (155mm How Trac-D)   23 Mar 44 Cp Gordon Ga/17 Nov 45 Cp Myles Standish Mass
BPE: 26 Jan 45   France-ETO: 6 Feb 45 - **26**   BPE: 16 Nov 45 *(nondiv)*
Furth Germany

671st Field Artillery Bn (155mm How Trac-D)   23 Mar 44 Cp Gordon Ga / 28 Oct 45 Cp Patrick Henry Va
BPE: 19 Feb 45   France-ETO: 1 Mar 45 - **34**   HRPE: 27 Oct 45 *(nondiv)*
Kyllburg Germany

672nd Field Artillery Bn (155mm How Trac-D)   23 Mar 44 Cp Gordon Ga /13 Oct 45 Cp Kilmer N.J.
BPE: 26 Jan 45   France-ETO: 6 Feb 45 - **26**   NYPE: 12 Oct 45 *(nondiv)*
Bielstein Germany

673rd Field Artillery Bn (155mm How Trac-D)   23 Mar 44 Cp Gordon Ga / 4 Dec 45 Cp Patrick Henry Va
NYPE: 11 Feb 45   France-ETO: 23 Feb 45   HRPE: 4 Dec 45 *(nondiv)*
Oberstein Germany

674th Prcht Field Artillery Bn (75mm Pk How)   25 Feb 43 Cp Mackall N.C./*
SFPE: 6 May 44   New Guinea: 28 May 44   Philippines: 18 Nov 44   Okinawa: 12 Aug 45 - **13,14,15** *(Glider FA until 20 Jul 45)*
(11th A/B Div)
Okinawa *(arriving via air)*

675th Glider Field Artillery Bn (75mm Pk How)   25 Feb 43 Cp Mackall N.C. / *
SFPE: 3 May 44   New Guinea: 28 May 44   Philippines: 18 Nov 44   Okinawa: 12 Aug 45 - **13,14,15** *(11th A/B Div)*
Okinawa *(arriving via air)*

676th Glider Field Artillery Bn (75mm Pk How)   13 Aug 43 Ft Bragg N.C./25 Feb 46 Ft Bragg N.C.
NYPE: 26 Jan 45   France-ETO: 6 Feb 45 - **26**   NYPE: 20 Aug 45 *(13th A/B Div)*
Shipment #10580-M at sea

677th Glider Field Artillery Bn (75mm Pk How)   13 Aug 43 Ft Bragg N.C. / 25 Feb 46 Ft Bragg N.C.
NYPE: 26 Jan 45   France-ETO: 6 Feb 45 - **26**   NYPE: 20 Aug 45 *(13th A/B Div)*
Shipment #10580-N at sea

680th Glider Field Artillery Bn (75mm Pk How)   15 Apr 43 Cp Mackall N.C. /14 Sep 45 Cp Myles Standish Mass
BPE: 20 Aug 44   England: 28 Aug 44   France-ETO: 24 Dec 44 - **25,26,34**   BPE: 14 Sep 45 *(17th A/B Div)*
Vittel France

681st Glider Field Artillery Bn (75mm Pk How)   15 Apr 43 Cp Mackall N.C. /14 Sep 45 Cp Myles Standish Mass
BPE: 20 Aug 44   England: 28 Aug 44   France-ETO: 24 Dec 44 - **25,26,34**   BPE: 14 Sep 45 *(17th A/B Div)*
Vittel France

685th Field Artillery Bn (105mm How Trk-D)   8 Feb 43 Ft Sill Okla (1st Bn, 18th FA) / 9 Aug 43 Cp Gordon Ga redes 18th FA Bn
(nondiv)

686th Field Arty Bn (Cld) (155mm How Trac-D)   12 Feb 43 Ft Sill Okla (2nd Bn, 349th FA) / *
NYPE: 30 Oct 44   England: 10 Nov 44   France-ETO: 1 Feb 45 - **26,34** *(75mm Gun Trk-D until late 1943 when reorg as 105mm How Trk-D; reorg as 155mm How in 1944) (nondiv)*
Unter Baar Germany

687th Field Artillery Bn (105mm How Trk-D)   8 Feb 43 Ft Sill Okla (2nd Bn, 18th FA) /1 May 46 Cp Kilmer N.J.
BPE: 11 Feb 44   England: 23 Feb 44   France-ETO: 17 Jul 44 - **25,26,30,32,34**   NYPE: 30 Apr 46 *(nondiv)*
Schmalkalden Germany

688th Field Artillery Bn (105mm How Trk-D)   23 Feb 43 Ft Bragg N.C. (2nd Bn, 193rd FA) / 2 Dec 45 Cp Myles Standish Mass
NYPE: 11 Aug 44   England: 22 Aug 44   France-ETO: 13 Sep 44 - **32**   BPE: 1 Dec 45 *(nondiv)*
Trier Germany

689th Field Artillery Bn (155mm How Trac-D)   8 Feb 43 Ft Sill Okla (3rd Bn, 18th FA) / 23 Dec 45 Cp Patrick Henry Va
BPE: 2 Jul 44   England: 9 Jul 44   France-ETO: 22 Aug 44 - **25,26,32,34**   HRPE: 23 Dec 45 *(Truck-D until sent overseas) (nondiv)*
Osterhofen Germany

690th Field Artillery Bn (105mm How Trk-D)   8 Feb 43 Ft Sill Okla (2nd Bn, 196th FA) / 29 Oct 45 Cp Kilmer N.J.
NYPE: 11 Feb 44   England: 23 Feb 44   France-ETO: 8 Jul 44 - **25,26,30,32,34**   NYPE: 28 Oct 45 *(nondiv)*
Leipzig Germany

691st Field Artillery Bn (105mm How Trk-D)   8 Feb 43 La Mnvr Area (1st Bn, 422nd FA) / 8 Mar 46 Cp Kilmer N.J.
BPE: 12 Aug 44   England: 22 Aug 44   France-ETO: 18 Sep 44 - **26,34**   NYPE: 6 Mar 46 *(nondiv)*
Marburg Germany

692nd Field Artillery Bn (105mm How Trk-D)   8 Feb 43 La Mnvr Area (2nd Bn, 422nd FA) / 20 Mar 46 Cp Kilmer N.J.
NYPE: 11 Aug 44   England: 22 Aug 44   France-ETO: 15 Sep 44 - **26,32,34**   NYPE: 19 Mar 46 *(nondiv)*
Neustadt Germany

693rd Field Artillery Bn (105mm How Trk-D)   8 Feb 43 Ft Sill Okla (4th Bn, 18th FA) / 29 Mar 46 Cp Kilmer N.J.
BPE: 11 Feb 44   England: 23 Feb 44   France-ETO: 14 Jul 44 - **25,26,30,32,34**   NYPE: 28 Mar 46 *(nondiv)*
Salzburg Austria

694th Field Artillery Bn (105mm How Trac-D)   6 Mar 43 Cp Gordon Ga (2nd Bn, 472nd FA) /16 Jan 46 Cp Stoneman Calif
SFPE: 26 Aug 44   New Guinea: 15 Sep 44   Philippines: 10 Jan 45 - **14,15**   SFPE: 14 Jan 46 *(Truck-D until sent overseas) (nondiv)*
San Fernando Philippines

695th Armored Field Artillery Bn   1 May 43 Ft Jackson S.C. (1st Bn, 112th FA) / 2 Nov 45 Cp Myles Standish Mass
NYPE: 11 Feb 44   England: 23 Feb 44   France-ETO: Jul 44 - **25,26,30,34**   BPE: 1 Nov 45 *(105mm How Trk-D until 26 Aug 43) (nondiv)*
Hersfeld Germany

696th Armored Field Artillery Bn   1 May 43 Ft Jackson S.C. (2nd Bn, 112th FA) / 27 Oct 45 Cp Patrick Henry Va
NYPE: 11 Feb 44   England: 23 Feb 44   France-ETO: 28 Jul 44 - **25,26,30,32,34**   HRPE: 27 Oct 45 *(105mm How Trk-D until 26 Aug 43)*
(nondiv)
Hungen Germany

697th Field Artillery Bn (240mm How Trac-D)   23 Feb 43 Ft Bragg N.C. (1st Bn, 79th FA)/12 Feb 46 Cp Kilmer N.J.
HRPE: 24 Dec 43   N.Africa: 12 Jan 44   Italy: 22 Jan 44   France-ETO: 25 Oct 44 - **25,26,29,31,34,35**   NYPE: 11 Feb 46 *(nondiv)*
Ertnelming France sch to SWPA under Shipment #R4085-JJ

698th Field Artillery Bn (240mm How Trac-D)   23 Feb 43 Ft Bragg N.C. (2nd Bn, 79th FA)/14 Feb 46 Cp Kilmer N.J.
HRPE: 23 Dec 43   N.Africa: 12 Jan 44   Italy: 25 Jan 44   France-ETO: 25 Oct 44 - **24,25,26,31,34,35**   NYPE: 13 Feb 46 *(nondiv)*
Saverne France sch to SWPA under Shipment #R4085-KK

BATTALION DESIGNATION AND TYPE	FORMED (SOURCE OF UNIT) / INACTIVATION	AUGUST 1945 LOCATION
718th Field Artillery Bn (155mm How Trac-D) NYPE: 5 Jan 45 France-ETO: 14 Jan 45 - **26,34** BPE: 27 Sep 45 *(63rd Inf Div)*	15 Jun 43 Cp Blanding Fla / 28 Sep 45 Cp Myles Standish Mass	Altenmunster Germany
720th Field Artillery Bn (155mm How Trac-D) NYPE: 10 Jan 45 France-ETO: 21 Jan 45 - **26,34** *(65th Inf Div)*	16 Aug 43 Cp Shelby Miss / 31 Aug 45 Austria	Gallsbach Austria
721st Field Artillery Bn (155mm How Trac-D) NYPE: 1 Dec 44 England: 12 Dec 44 France-ETO: 29 Dec 44 - **32** NYPE: 11 Nov 45 *(66th Inf Div)*	15 Apr 43 Cp Blanding Fla / 13 Nov 45 Cp Shanks N.Y.	Villepail France
724th Field Artillery Bn (155mm How Trac-D) NYPE: 1 Dec 44 England: 12 Dec 44 France-ETO: 24 Jan 45 - **26,34** NYPE: 16 Sep 45 *(69th Inf Div)*	15 May 43 Cp Shelby Miss / 16 Sep 45 Cp Kilmer N.J.	Lutzen Germany
725th Field Artillery Bn (155mm How Trac-D) BPE: 8 Jan 45 France-ETO: 18 Jan 45 - **26,34** NYPE: 9 Oct 45 *(70th Inf Div)*	15 Jun 43 Cp Adair Oreg / 11 Oct 45 Cp Kilmer N.J.	Bad Orb Germany
730th Field Artillery Bn (155mm How Trac-D) NYPE: 14 Nov 44 England: 22 Nov 44 France-ETO: 13 Dec 44 - **25,26,34** HRPE: 14 Nov 45 *(75th Inf Div)*	15 Apr 43 Ft Leonard Wood Mo / 14 Nov 45 Cp Patrick Henry Va	Le Havre France
731st Field Artillery Bn (155mm Gun Trac-D) NYPE: 31 Mar 44 England: 6 Apr 44 France-ETO: 16 Jul 44 - **25,26,30,32,34** HRPE: 26 Oct 45 *(nondiv)*	18 Jan 43 Cp Maxey Tex / 26 Oct 45 Cp Patrick Henry Va	Regensburg Germany
732nd Field Arty Bn (Cld) (155mm Gun Trk-D) *(nondiv)*	21 Jan 43 Ft Bragg N.C. / 15 Mar 44 Cp Pickett Va redes 1695th Engr Comb Bn	
733rd Field Artillery Bn (155mm Gun Trac-D) NYPE: 10 Apr 44 England: 16 Apr 44 France-ETO: 2 Jul 44 - **25,26,30,32,34** NYPE: 8 Oct 45 *(nondiv)*	2 Feb 43 Cp Maxey Tex / 10 Oct 45 Cp Kilmer N.J.	Kolbermoor France
734th Field Artillery Bn (155mm Gun Trac-D) NYPE: 10 Jul 44 England: 22 Jul 44 France-ETO: 18 Aug 44 - **25,26,32,34** NYPE: 13 Dec 45 *(nondiv)*	2 Feb 43 Cp Maxey Tex / 16 Dec 45 Cp Kilmer N.J.	Eisenach Germany
736th Field Artillery Bn (8-inch How Trac-D) NYPE: 22 Jun 44 England: 28 Jun 44 France-ETO: 7 Aug 44 - **25,26,32,34** NYPE: 10 Oct 45 *(nondiv)*	25 Jun 43 Ft Ord Calif / 11 Oct 45 Cp Shanks N.Y.	Wallenberg Germany
738th Field Artillery Bn (8-inch How Trac-D) NYPE: 16 Jun 44 England: 28 Jun 44 France-ETO: 10 Aug 44 - **25,26,30,32,34** NYPE: 16 Dec 45 *(Truck-D until 1944) (nondiv)*	25 Jun 43 Ft Ord Calif / 17 Dec 45 Cp Kilmer N.J.	Strauberg Germany
739th Field Artillery Bn (8-inch How Trac-D) NYPE: 15 Jul 44 England: 21 Jul 44 France-ETO: 28 Aug 44 - **25,26,30,32,34** *(Truck-D until 1944) (nondiv)*	25 Jun 43 Ft Jackson S.C. / 20 Apr 46 Germany	Nidda Germany
740th Field Artillery Bn (8-inch How Trac-D) NYPE: 22 Jun 44 England: 28 Jun 44 France-ETO: 10 Aug 44 - **25,26,32,34** BPE: 10 Oct 45 *(nondiv)*	25 Jun 43 Ft Jackson S.C. / 11 Oct 45 Cp Myles Standish Mass	Regenstauf Germany
741st Field Artillery Bn (8-inch How Trac-D) NYPE: 2 Jul 44 England: 12 Jul 44 France-ETO: 13 Sep 44 - **25,26,30,32,34** NYPE: 1 Dec 45 *(Truck-D until 1944) (nondiv)*	25 Jun 43 Ft Jackson S.C. / 2 Dec 45 Cp Shanks N.Y.	Neuberg Germany
742nd Field Artillery Bn (8-inch How Trk-D) NYPE: 1 Dec 44 England: 12 Dec 44 France-ETO: 15 Feb 45 - **26,34** HRPE: 26 Oct 45 *(nondiv)*	13 Apr 44 Cp Chaffee Ark / 26 Oct 45 Cp Patrick Henry Va	Henfenfeld Germany
743rd Field Artillery Bn (8-inch How Trk-D) NYPE: 30 Nov 44 England: 8 Dec 44 France-ETO: 3 Mar 45 - **26,34** *(nondiv)*	13 Apr 44 Cp Chaffee Ark / 6 Oct 45 France	Bad Salzschlirt Germany
744th Field Artillery Bn (8-inch How Trk-D) NYPE: 1 Dec 44 England: 12 Dec 44 France-ETO: 23 Feb 45 - **26,34** NYPE: 25 Oct 45 *(nondiv)*	13 Apr 44 Cp Chaffee Ark / 26 Oct 45 Cp Kilmer N.J.	Feldkirchen Germany
745th Field Artillery Bn (8-inch How Trk-D) NYPE: 16 Dec 44 England: 21 Dec 44 France-ETO: 14 Mar 45 - **26,34** BPE: 3 Dec 45 *(nondiv)*	18 Apr 44 Cp Shelby Miss / 4 Dec 45 Cp Myles Standish Mass	Braunau Germany
746th Field Artillery Bn (8-inch How Trk-D) NYPE: 17 Dec 44 England: 27 Dec 44 France-ETO: 16 Mar 45 - **26** NYPE: 25 Oct 45 *(nondiv)*	18 Apr 44 Cp Shelby Miss / 26 Oct 45 Cp Kilmer N.J.	Turnich Germany
747th Field Artillery Bn (8-inch How Trk-D) NYPE: 17 Dec 44 England: 27 Dec 44 France-ETO: 16 Mar 45 - **26,34** BPE: 11 Dec 45 *(nondiv)*	18 Apr 44 Cp Shelby Miss / 12 Dec 45 Cp Myles Standish Mass	Korwestheim Germany
748th Field Artillery Bn (8-inch How Trk-D) NYPE: 17 Dec 44 England: 27 Dec 44 France-ETO: 16 Mar 45 - **26,34** NYPE: 21 Dec 45 *(nondiv)*	18 Apr 44 Cp Shelby Miss / 22 Dec 45 Cp Kilmer N.J.	Weisenburg Germany
749th Field Artillery Bn (8-inch How Trac-D) SPE: 28 Dec 44 Hawaii: 5 Jan 45 Okinawa: 1 Apr 45 - **19** *(nondiv)*	21 Feb 44 Cp Hood Tex / 31 Mar 46 Korea	Okinawa
750th Field Artillery Bn (8-inch How Trac-D) SPE: 28 Dec 44 Hawaii: 4 Jan 45 Okinawa: 1 Apr 45 - **19** SPE: 21 Dec 45 *(nondiv)*	21 Feb 44 Cp Hood Tex / 23 Dec 45 Vancouver Barracks Wash	Okinawa
751st Field Artillery Bn (155mm How Trac-D) BPE: 24 Jul 44 England: 30 Jul 44 France-ETO: 30 Aug 44 - **25,26,32,34** *(Truck-D until 1944) (nondiv)*	18 Jan 43 Cp Bowie Tex / 30 Jun 46 Germany	Neuhof Germany

BATTALION	FORMED (SOURCE OF UNIT) / INACTIVATION	AUGUST 1945 LOCATION
752nd Field Artillery Bn (155mm How Trac-D) 18 Jan 43 Cp Bowie Tex / 3 Oct 45 Cp Shanks N.Y. BPE: 2 Jul 44 England: 9 Jul 44 France-ETO: 19 Aug 44 - **25,26,32,34** NYPE: 2 Oct 45 *(Truck-D until 1944) (nondiv)*		Hammerdorf Germany
753rd Field Artillery Bn (155mm How Trac-D) 1 Apr 43 Cp Beale Calif /17 Dec 45 Cp Kilmer N.J. NYPE: 26 Jul 44 England: 5 Aug 44 France-ETO: 7 Sep 44 - **26,32,34** NYPE: 16 Dec 45 *(Truck-D until 1944) (nondiv)*		Gersfeld Germany
754th Field Artillery Bn (155mm How Trac-D) 15 Aug 43 Ft Leonard Wood Mo / 3 Dec 45 Cp Myles Standish Mass NYPE: 11 Aug 44 England: 22 Aug 44 France-ETO: 14 Sep 44 - **26,34** BPE: 3 Dec 45 *(Truck-D until 1944) (nondiv)*		Andorf Germany
755th Field Artillery Bn (155mm How Trac-D) 15 Aug 43 Ft Leonard Wood Mo / 21 Dec 45 Cp Kilmer N.J. NYPE: 11 Aug 44 England: 22 Aug 44 France-ETO: 18 Sep 44 - **25,26,34** NYPE: 19 Dec 45 *(Truck-D until 1944) (nondiv)*		Pappenheim Germany
756th Field Artillery Bn (155mm How Trac-D) 15 Aug 43 Ft Ord Calif / 26 Jan 46 Cp Anza Calif NOPE: 22 Aug 44 New Guinea: 2 Oct 44 Philippines: 10 Jan 45 - **3,14** LAPE: 25 Jan 46 *(Truck-D until sent overseas) (nondiv)*		Manila Philippines
757th Field Artillery Bn (155mm How Trac-D) 15 Aug 43 Ft Ord Calif /16 Jan 46 Cp Stoneman Calif NOPE: 22 Aug 44 New Guinea: 2 Oct 44 Philippines: 13 Jan 45 - **14** SFPE: 14 Jan 46 *(Truck-D until sent overseas) (nondiv)*		Manila Philippines
758th Field Artillery Bn (155mm How Trac-D) 25 Nov 43 Cp Maxey Tex / 7 Feb 46 Cp Kilmer N.J. NYPE: 24 Sep 44 England: 30 Sep 44 France-ETO: 6 Oct 44 - **25,26,34** NYPE: 5 Feb 46 *(Truck-D until early 1944) (nondiv)*		Fulda Germany
759th Field Artillery Bn (155mm How Trac-D) 23 Mar 44 Cp Rucker Ala / 22 Feb 46 Cp Kilmer N.J. NYPE: 5 Feb 45 France-ETO: 17 Feb 45 - **26** NYPE: 21 Feb 46 *(nondiv)*		Monschau Germany
760th Field Artillery Bn (155mm How Trac-D) 15 Aug 43 Ft Ord Calif / 25 Jan 46 Japan SFPE: 4 Sep 44 New Guinea: 23 Sep 44 Philippines: 22 Jan 45 - **14,15** *(Truck-D until sent overseas) (nondiv)*		Manila Philippines
761st Field Artillery Bn (155mm How Trac-D) 23 Mar 44 Cp Rucker Ala / 24 Feb 46 Cp Kilmer N.J. NYPE: 3 Feb 45 England: 11 Feb 45 France-ETO: 25 Feb 45 - **26** NYPE: 23 Feb 46 *(nondiv)*		Stolberg Germany
762nd Field Artillery Bn (155mm How Trac-D) 21 Apr 44 Ft Jackson S.C. / 3 Oct 45 Cp Shanks N.Y. NYPE: 10 Jan 45 France-ETO: 21 Jan 45 - **25,26,34** NYPE: 2 Oct 45 *(nondiv)*		Artelshofen Germany
763rd Field Artillery Bn (155mm How Trac-D) 21 Apr 44 Ft Jackson S.C. /16 Nov 45 Cp Kilmer N.J. NYPE: 10 Jan 45 France-ETO: 23 Jan 45 NYPE: 14 Nov 45 *(nondiv)*		Trier Germany
764th Field Artillery Bn (155mm How Trac-D) 5 May 44 Cp Breckinridge Ky /10 Feb 46 Cp Hood Tex NYPE: 27 Feb 45 France-ETO: 11 Mar 45 NYPE: 2 Aug 45 *(nondiv)*		Cp Hood Tex
765th Field Artillery Bn (155mm How Trac-D) 5 May 44 Cp Breckinridge Ky / 8 Sep 45 Italy HRPE: 1 Mar 45 Italy: 14 Mar 45 - **31,33,35** *(nondiv)*		Pontecchio Italy
766th Field Artillery Bn (155mm How Trac-D) 5 May 44 Cp Breckinridge Ky /12 Feb 46 Ft Jackson S.C. HRPE: 1 Mar 45 Italy: 14 Mar 45 - **31,33,35** HRPE: 18 Jul 45 *(nondiv)*		Ft Jackson S.C.
767th Field Artillery Bn (155mm How Trac-D) 5 May 44 Cp Breckinridge Ky /10 Feb 46 Cp Hood Tex NYPE: 27 Feb 45 France-ETO: 11 Mar 45 Charleston Sub-P/E: 6 Aug 45 *(nondiv)*		Shipment #10106-K unloading
768th Field Artillery Bn (155mm How Trac-D) 9 May 44 Cp Barkeley Tex / 21 Nov 45 Cp Myles Standish Mass NYPE: 23 Nov 44 England: 4 Dec 44 France-ETO: 1 Feb 45 - **26,34** BPE: 20 Nov 45 *(nondiv)*		Bad Soden Germany
769th Field Artillery Bn (155mm How Trac-D) 9 May 44 Cp Barkeley Tex /1 Jan 46 Cp Stoneman Calif SFPE: 1 Jun 45 Philippines: 11 Jul 45 SFPE: 30 Dec 45 *(nondiv)*		Manila Philippines
770th Field Artillery Bn (4.5-inch Gun Trac-D) 1 Apr 43 Cp Bowie Tex / 2 Mar 46 Cp Kilmer N.J. NYPE: 2 Jul 44 England: 12 Jul 44 France-ETO: 25 Aug 44 - **25,26,30,32,34** NYPE: 1 Mar 46 *(nondiv)*		Munich Germany
771st Field Artillery Bn (4.5-inch Gun Trac-D) 1 Apr 43 Cp Bowie Tex / 31 Dec 45 Cp Kilmer N.J. NYPE: 2 Jul 44 England: 12 Jul 44 France-ETO: 21 Aug 44 - **25,26,32,34** NYPE: 30 Dec 45 *(nondiv)*		Roding Germany
772nd Field Artillery Bn (4.5-inch Gun Trac-D) 1 Apr 43 Cp Bowie Tex/26 Oct 45 Cp Kilmer N.J. NYPE: 18 Jul 44 England: 28 Jul 44 France-ETO: 26 Aug 44 - **25,26,30,32,34** NYPE: 25 Oct 45 *(nondiv)*		Oberndorf Germany
773rd Field Artillery Bn (4.5-inch Gun Trac-D) 1 Apr 43 Cp Bowie Tex / 26 Dec 45 Cp Myles Standish Mass NYPE: 18 Jul 44 England: 28 Jul 44 France-ETO: 25 Aug 44 - **25,26,30,32,34** BPE: 25 Dec 45 *(nondiv)*		Eschwege Germany
774th Field Artillery Bn (4.5-inch Gun Trac-D) 1 May 43 Cp Beale Calif / 4 Mar 46 Cp Kilmer N.J. NYPE: 23 Jul 44 England: 28 Jul 44 France-ETO: 30 Aug 44 - **26,32,34** NYPE: 3 Mar 46 *(nondiv)*		Herzogenrath Germany
775th Field Artillery Bn (4.5-inch Gun Trac-D) 1 May 43 Cp Beale Calif / 8 Mar 46 Cp Kilmer N.J. BPE: 2 Jul 44 England: 9 Jul 44 France-ETO: 21 Aug 44 - **25,26,32,34** NYPE: 6 Mar 46 *(nondiv)*		Grunwald Germany
776th Field Artillery Bn (155mm How Trac-D) 25 Nov 43 Cp Maxey Tex / 23 Jan 46 Cp Kilmer N.J. NYPE: 27 Sep 44 England: 3 Oct 44 France-ETO: 9 Oct 44 - **25,26,34** NYPE: 22 Jan 46 *(Truck-D until sent overseas) (nondiv)*		Schleusingen Germany

BATTALION DESIGNATION AND TYPE	FORMED (SOURCE OF UNIT)/DESIGNATION	AUGUST 1945 LOCATION
777th Field Arty Bn (Cld) (4.5-inch Gun Trac-D) BPE: 11 Aug 44 England: 23 Aug 44 France-ETO: 18 Sep 44 - **26,34** *(nondiv)*	15 Apr 43 Cp Beale Calif /18 Sep 45 France	Altheim Germany
778th Field Artillery Bn (240mm How Trac-D) SFPE: 26 Jul 45 Philippines: 24 Jul 45 *(nondiv)*	14 Aug 44 Ft Bragg N.C. (290th CA Bn) /10 Dec 45 Philippines	Manila Philippines
779th Field Artillery Bn (240mm How Trac-D) SFPE: 26 Jun 45 Philippines: 24 Jul 45 *(nondiv)*	14 Aug 44 Ft Bragg N.C. (291st CA Bn) /10 Dec 45 Philippines	Manila Philippines
780th Field Artillery Bn (8-inch Gun Trac-D) SFPE: 11 Jul 45 Philippines: 3 Aug 45 *(nondiv)*	14 Aug 44 Ft Bragg N.C. (292nd CA Bn) /10 Dec 45 Philippines	Shipment #4122-B unloading
781st Field Artillery Bn (8-inch How Trk-D) *(nondiv)*	17 Aug 44 Cp Joseph T Robinson Ark (1st Bn, 30th CA) /5 Jul 45 Cp Bowie Tex redes 781st Chem Mortar Bn	
782nd Field Artillery Bn (8-inch How Trk-D) *(nondiv)*	17 Aug 44 Cp Joseph T Robinson Ark (289th CA Bn) /5 Jul 45 Cp Bowie Tex redes 782nd Chem Mortar Bn	
783rd Armored Field Artillery Bn *(8-inch How Trk-D until 9 Feb 45) (nondiv)*	17 Aug 44 Cp Joseph T Robinson Ark (46th CA Bn) / 22 Sep 45 Cp Hood Tex	Cp Hood Tex
784th Armored Field Artillery Bn *(8-inch How Trk-D until 9 Feb 45) (nondiv)*	17 Aug 44 Cp Joseph T Robinson Ark (34th CA Bn) / 8 Oct 45 Ft Bragg N.C.	Ft Bragg N.C.
786th Field Artillery Bn (8-inch How Trac-D) SFPE: 15 Jun 45 Philippines: 9 Jul 45 SFPE: 9 Jan 46 *(nondiv)*	23 Mar 44 Ft Leonard Wood Mo /11 Jan 46 Cp Stoneman Calif	Tacloban Philippines
787th Field Artillery Bn (8-inch How Trac-D) NYPE: 1 Dec 44 England: 12 Dec 44 France-ETO: Feb 45 - **26,34** NYPE: 20 Feb 46	6 Nov 43 Ft Lewis Wash/ 22 Feb 46 Cp Kilmer N.J.	Thungersheim Germany
788th Field Artillery Bn (8-inch How Trac-D) NYPE: 30 Nov 44 England: 8 Dec 44 France-ETO: 13 Feb 45 - **26,34** NYPE: 28 Mar 46 *(nondiv)*	6 Nov 43 Ft Lewis Wash / 29 Mar 46 Cp Kilmer N.J.	Horn Germany
789th Field Artillery Bn (8-inch How Trac-D) SFPE: 15 Jun 45 Philippines: 10 Jul 45 SFPE: 9 Jan 46 *(nondiv)*	23 Mar 44 Ft Leonard Wood Mo /11 Jan 46 Cp Stoneman Calif	Manila Philippines
790th Field Artillery Bn (8-inch How Trac-D) BPE: 18 Jan 45 England: 29 Jan 45 France-ETO: 29 Jan 45 - **26** NYPE: 13 Feb 46 *(nondiv)*	10 Apr 44 Cp Forrest Tenn /14 Feb 46 Cp Kilmer N.J.	Mechernich Germany
791st Field Artillery Bn (8-inch How Trac-D) BPE: 18 Jan 45 England: 20 Jan 45 France-ETO: 30 Jan 45 - **26** NYPE: 19 Aug 45 *(nondiv)*	10 Apr 44 Cp Forrest Tenn/21 Aug 45 Cp Kilmer N.J.	Shipment #10077-E at sea
793rd Field Artillery Bn (8-inch How Trac-D) NYPE: 6 Apr 44 England: 16 Apr 44 France-ETO: 26 Jun 44 - **25,26,30,32,34** BPE: 16 Dec 45 *(nondiv)*	4 Mar 43 Ft Bragg N.C. /17 Dec 45 Cp Myles Standish Mass	Wieseck Germany
795th Field Artillery Bn (Cld) (8-in. How Trk-D) *(nondiv)*	6 May 43 Ft Bragg N.c. /13 Mar 44 Ft Jackson S.C. redes 1700th Engr Comb Bn	
797th Field Artillery Bn (8-inch How Trac-D) SFPE: 20 Jun 45 Philippines: 16 Jul 45 *(nondiv)*	20 Apr 44 Cp Chaffee Ark /10 Dec 45 Philippines	Manila Philippines
798th Field Artillery Bn (105mm How Trk-D) *(FA Board 5 May 44) (nondiv)*	15 Apr 44 Ft Bragg N.C. / 20 Mar 45 Ft Bragg N.C.	

801st Field Artillery Bn (155mm How Trk-D)

   Only Btry A of the 801st FA Bn was active; (105mm How Trk-D, later 155mm How Trk-D) raised 18 May 42 at Ft Bragg N.C. and inactivated Ft Benning Ga 17 Jun 43.

802nd Field Artillery Bn (105mm How Trk-D) NYPE: 2 Jul 44 England: 12 Jul 44 France-ETO: 12 Aug 44 - **25,26,32,34** NYPE: 25 Mar 46 *(nondiv)*	6 Mar 42 Ft Benning Ga / 26 Mar 46 Cp Kilmer N.J.	Wallhausen Germany
803rd Field Artillery Bn (155mm How Trac-D) SFPE: 5 Jun 45 Philippines: 12 Jul 45 SFPE: 27 Dec 45 *(nondiv)*	9 May 44 Cp Barkeley Tex / 28 Dec 45 Cp Stoneman	Leyte Philippines
804th Field Artillery Bn (155mm How Trac-D) SFPE: 5 Jun 45 Philippines: 12 Jul 45 SFPE: 27 Dec 45 *(nondiv)*	9 May 44 Cp Barkeley Tex / 28 Dec 45 Cp Stoneman Calif	Leyte Philippines
805th Field Artillery Bn (155mm How Trac-D) BPE: 26 Jan 45 France-ETO: 6 Feb 45 - **26** BPE: 2 Oct 45 *(nondiv)*	9 May 44 Cp Barkeley Tex / 3 Oct 45 Cp Myles Standish Mass	Wermelskirchen Germany
808th Field Artillery Bn (155mm How Trac-D) NYPE: 24 Sep 44 England: 30 Sep 44 France-ETO: 3 Oct 44 - **26,34** HRPE: 23 Oct 45 *(nondiv)*	1 May 44 Cp Pickett Va (511th AAA Gun Bn) / 23 Oct 45 Cp Patrick Henry Va	Nurnberg Germany
809th Field Artillery Bn (155mm How Trac-D) NYPE: 29 Sep 44 England: 10 Oct 44 France-ETO: 16 Dec 44 - **25,26,34** BPE: 1 Dec 45 *(nondiv)*	1 May 44 Cp Pickett Va (512th AAA Gun Bn) / 2 Dec 45 Cp Myles Standish Mass	Altdorf Germany

BATTALION DESIGNATION AND TYPE	FORMED (SOURCE OF UNIT) / INACTIVATION	AUGUST 1945 LOCATION

861st Field Artillery Bn (105mm How Trk-D)   15 Jun 43 Cp Blanding Fla / 29 Sep 45 Cp Patrick Henry Va
NYPE: 5 Jan 45   France-ETO: 14 Jan 45 - **26,34**   HRPE: 29 Sep 45 *(63rd Inf Dif)*
Langenburg Germany

862nd Field Artillery Bn (105mm How Trk-D)   15 Jun 43 Cp Blanding Fla / 27 Sep 45 Cp Myles Standish Mass
NYPE: 5 Jan 45   France-ETO: 14 Jan 45 - **26,34**   BPE: 26 Sep 45 *(63rd Inf Div)*
Kirchberg Germany

863rd Field Artillery Bn (105mm How Trk-D)   15 Jun 43 Cp Blanding Fla / 29 Sep 45 Cp Patrick Henry Va
NYPE: 5 Jan 45   France-ETO: 14 Jan 45 - **26,34**   HRPE: 29 Sep 45 *(63rd Inf Div)*
Kirchberg Germany

867th Field Artillery Bn (105mm How Trk-D)   16 Aug 43 Cp Shelby Miss / 31 Aug 45 Austria
NYPE: 10 Jan 45   France-ETO: 21 Jan 45 - **26,34** *(65th Inf Div)*
Eferding Austria

868th Field Artillery Bn (105mm How Trk-D)   16 Aug 43 Cp Shelby Miss / 31 Aug 45 Austria
NYPE: 10 Jan 45   France-ETO: 21 Jan 45 - **26,34** *(65th Inf Div)*
Lambach Austria

869th Field Artillery Bn (105mm How Trk-D)   16 Aug 43 Cp Shelby Miss / 31 Aug 45 Austria
NYPE: 10 Jan 45   France-ETO: 21 Jan 45 - **26,34** *(65th Inf Div)*
Wels Austria

870th Field Artillery Bn (105mm How Trk-D)   15 Apr 43 Cp Blanding Fla / 6 Nov 45 Cp Kilmer N.J.
NYPE: 1 Dec 44   England: 12 Dec 44   France-ETO: 25 Dec 44 - **32**   NYPE: 5 Nov 45 *(66th Inf Div)*
Villepail France

871st Field Artillery Bn (105mm How Trk-D)   15 Apr 43 Cp Blanding Fla / 6 Nov 45 Cp Kilmer N.J.
NYPE: 1 Dec 44   England: 12 Dec 44   France-ETO: 25 Dec 44 - **32**   NYPE: 5 Nov 45 *(66th Inf Div)*
Villepail France

872nd Field Artillery Bn (105mm How Trk-D)   15 Apr 43 Cp Blanding Fla / 6 Nov 45 Cp Kilmer N.J.
NYPE: 1 Dec 44   England: 12 Dec 44   France-ETO: 25 Dec 44 - **32**   NYPE: 5 Nov 45 *(66th Inf Div)*
Villepail France

879th Field Artillery Bn (105mm How Trk-D)   15 May 43 Cp Shelby Miss / 16 Sep 45 Cp Kilmer N.J.
NYPE: 1 Dec 44   England: 12 Dec 44   France-ETO: 24 Jan 45 - **26,34**   NYPE: 14 Sep 45 *(69th Inf Div)*
Louvement France

880th Field Artillery Bn (105mm How Trk-D)   15 May 43 Cp Shelby Miss / 16 Sep 45 Cp Kilmer N.J.
NYPE: 1 Dec 44   England: 12 Dec 44   France-ETO: 24 Jan 45 - **26,34**   NYPE: 14 Sep 45 *(69th Inf Div)*
Merseburg Germany

881st Field Artillery Bn (105mm How Trk-D)   15 May 43 Cp Shelby Miss / 16 Sep 45 Cp Kilmer N.J.
NYPE: 1 Dec 44   England: 13 Dec 44   France-ETO: 24 Jan 45 - **26,34**   NYPE: 14 Sep 45 *(69th Inf Div)*
Leuna Germany

882nd Field Artillery Bn (105mm How Trk-D)   15 Jun 43 Cp Adair Oreg / 11 Oct 45 Cp Kilmer N.J.
BPE: 8 Jan 45   France-ETO: 18 Jan 45 - **26,34**   NYPE: 9 Oct 45 *(70th Inf Div)*
Unlingen Germany

883rd Field Artillery Bn (105mm How Trk-D)   15 Jun 43 Cp Adair Oreg / 11 Oct 45 Cp Kilmer N.J.
BPE: 8 Jan 45   France-ETO: 18 Jan 45 - **26,34**   NYPE: 9 Oct 45 *(70th Inf Div)*
Niederrieden Germany

884th Field Artillery Bn (105mm How Trk-D)   15 Jun 43 Cp Adair Oreg / 11 Oct 45 Cp Kilmer N.J.
BPE: 8 Jan 45   France-ETO: 18 Jan 45 - **26,34**   NYPE: 9 Oct 45 *(70th Inf Div)*
Kronberg Germany

897th Field Artillery Bn (105mm How Trk-D)   15 Apr 43 Ft Leonard Wood Mo / 26 Nov 45 Cp Kilmer N.J.
NYPE: 14 Nov 44   England: 22 Nov 44   France-ETO: 13 Dec 44 - **25,26,34**   NYPE: 25 Nov 45 *(75th Inf Div)*
Le Havre France

898th Field Artillery Bn (105mm How Trk-D)   15 Apr 43 Ft Leonard Wood Mo / 26 Nov 45 Cp Kilmer N.J.
NYPE: 14 Nov 44   England: 22 Nov 44   France-ETO: 13 Dec 44 - **25,26,34**   NYPE: 25 Nov 45 *(75th Inf Div)*
Le Havre France

899th Field Artillery Bn (105mm How Trk-D)   15 Apr 43 Ft Leonard Wood Mo / 26 Nov 45 Cp Kilmer N.J.
NYPE: 14 Nov 44   England: 22 Nov 44   France-ETO: 13 Dec 44 - **25,26,34**   NYPE: 25 Nov 45 *(75th Inf Div)*
Le Havre France

901st Field Artillery Bn (105mm How Trk-D)   15 Jun 42 Ft George G Meade Md / 31 Aug 45 Germany
BPE: 10 Dec 44   England: 20 Dec 44   France-ETO: 12 Jan 45 - **25,26,34** *(76th Inf Div)*
Munchenbernsdorf Germany

902nd Field Artillery Bn (105mm How Trk-D)   25 Mar 42 Ft Jackson S.C. / 15 Mar 46 Japan
SFPE: 24 Mar 44   Hawaii: 31 Mar 44   Guadalcanal: 21 Jul 44   Philippines: 23 Nov 44   Okinawa: 20 Apr 45 - **13,19,21** *(77th Inf Div)*
Leyte Philippines

903rd Field Artillery Bn (105mm How Trk-D)   15 Aug 42 Cp Butner N.C. / 22 Apr 46 Cp Kilmer N.J.
NYPE: 14 Oct 44   England: 25 Oct 44   France-ETO: 22 Nov 44 - **25,26,34**   NYPE: 20 Apr 46 *(78th Inf Div)*
Brasselsberg Germany

904th Field Artillery Bn (105mm How Trk-D)   15 Jun 42 Cp Pickett Va / 12 Dec 45 Cp Kilmer N.J.
BPE: 7 Apr 44   England: 17 Apr 44   France-ETO: 14 Jun 44 - **25,26,30,32,34**   NYPE: 10 Dec 45 *(79th Inf Div)*
Eger Germany

905th Field Artillery Bn (105mm How Trk-D)   15 Jul 42 Cp Forrest Tenn / 6 Jan 46 Cp Kilmer N.J.
NYPE: 1 Jul 44   England: 7 Jul 44   France-ETO: 3 Aug 44 - **25,26,32,34**   NYPE: 5 Jan 46 *(80th Inf Div)*
Eisenburg Germany

906th Field Artillery Bn (105mm How Trk-D)   15 Jun 42 Cp Rucker Ala / 20 Jan 46 Japan
SFPE: 9 Jul 44   Hawaii: 17 Jul 44   Guadalcanal: 24 Aug 44   Palau I: 15 Sep 44   New Caledonia: 14 Jan 45
Philippines: 16 May 45 - **13,21** *(81st Inf Div)*
Leyte Philippines

907th Glider Field Artillery Bn (75mm Pk How)   25 Mar 42 Cp Claiborne La / 30 Nov 45 Germany
NYPE: 5 Sep 43   England: 18 Sep 43   France: 6 Jun 44   England: 13 Jul 44   Holland: 17 Sep 44 - **25,26,30,34**
(assigned 15 Aug 42 to div) (101st A/B Div)
Hohenberg Germany

BATTALION DESIGNATION AND TYPE	FORMED (SOURCE OF UNIT)/INACTIVATION *Active through 1946	AUGUST 1945 LOCATION

908th Field Artillery Bn (105mm How Trk-D)   15 Aug 42 Cp Atterbury Ind / 24 Mar 46 Cp Kilmer N.J.   Hausenberg Germany
NYPE: 6 Apr 44   England: 19 Apr 44   France-ETO: 19 Jun 44 - **25,26,30,32,34**   NYPE: 23 Mar 46 *(83rd Inf Div)*

909th Field Artillery Bn (105mm How Trk-D)   15 Oct 42 Cp Howze Tex / 23 Jan 46 Cp Kilmer N.J.   Sinaheim Germany
NYPE: 29 Sep 44   England: 10 Oct 44   France-ETO: 13 Nov 44 - **25,26,34**   NYPE: 22 Jan 46 *(84th Inf Div)*

910th Field Artillery Bn (105mm How Trk-D)   15 May 42 Cp Shelby Miss / 25 Aug 45 Cp Patrick Henry Va   Fagianeria Italy
HRPE: 28 Dec 43   N.Africa: 7 Jan 44   Italy: 27 Mar 44 - **31,33,35**   HRPE: 25 Aug 45 *(85th Inf Div)*

911th Field Artillery Bn (105mm How Trk-D)   15 Dec 42 Cp Howze Tex / 30 Dec 46 Philippines   Entrained to Cp Stoneman Calif
BPE: 19 Feb 45   France-ETO: 1 Mar 45 - **26**   NYPE: 17 Jun 45   SFPE: 18 Aug 45   Philippines: 12 Sep 45 *(86th Inf Div)*

912th Field Artillery Bn (105mm How Trk-D)   15 Dec 42 Cp McCain Miss / 21 Sep 45 Ft Benning Ga   Ft Benning Ga
NYPE: 4 Nov 44   England: 12 Nov 44   France-ETO: 5 Dec 44 - **25,26,34**   HRPE: 16 Jul 45 *(87th Inf Div)*

913th Field Artillery Bn (105mm How Trk-D)   15 Jul 42 Cp Gruber Okla / *   Livorno Italy
HRPE: 12 Nov 43   N.Africa: 3 Dec 43   Italy: 4 Feb 44 - **31,33,35** *(88th Inf Div)*

914th Field Artillery Bn (105mm How Trk-D)   15 Jul 42 Cp Carson Colo /19 Dec 45 Cp Kilmer N.J.   Doudeville France
BPE: 10 Jan 45   France-ETO: 24 Jan 45 - **26,34**   NYPE: 17 Dec 45 *(89th Inf Div)*

915th Field Artillery Bn (105mm How Trk-D)   25 Mar 42 Cp Barkeley Tex / 27 Dec 45 Cp Shanks N.Y.   Fronberg Germany
NYPE: 23 Mar 44   England: 5 Apr 44   France-ETO: 8 Jun 44 - **25,26,30,32,34**   NYPE: 24 Dec 45 *(90th Inf Div)*

916th Field Artillery Bn (105mm How Trk-D)   15 Aug 42 Cp White Oreg / 27 Nov 45 Cp Rucker Ala   Goriza Italy
HRPE: 3 Apr 44   N.Africa: 21 Apr 44   Italy: 27 May 44 - **31,33,35**   HRPE: 10 Sep 45 *(91st Inf Div)*

919th Field Artillery Bn (105mm How Trk-D)   15 Sep 42 Ft Custer Mich / 9 Feb 46 Cp Kilmer N.J.   Wermelskirchen Germany
NYPE: 6 Aug 44   England: 11 Aug 44   France-ETO: 14 Sep 44 - **25,26,32,34**   NYPE: 8 Feb 46 *(94th Inf Div)*

920th Field Artillery Bn (105mm How Trk-D)   15 Jul 42 Cp Swift Tex /15 Oct 45 Cp Shelby Miss   Cp Shelby Miss
BPE: 10 Aug 44   England: 17 Aug 44   France-ETO: 15 Sep 44 - **25,26,32,34**   BPE: 29 Jun 45 *(95th Inf Div)*

921st Field Artillery Bn (105mm How Trk-D)   15 Aug 42 Cp Adair Oreg / 3 Feb 46 Cp Anza Calif   Mindoro Philippines
SFPE: 22 Jul 44   Hawaii: 28 Jul 44   Philippines: 20 Oct 44   Okinawa: 1 Apr 45 - **13,19**   LAPE: 2 Feb 46 *(96th Inf Div)*

922nd Field Artillery Bn (105mm How Trk-D)   25 Feb 43 Cp Swift Tex / 31 Mar 46 Japan   Ft Bragg N.C.
NYPE: 19 Feb 45   France-ETO: 1 Mar 45 - **26**   NYPE: 23 Jun 45   SPE: 31 Aug 45   Philippines: 17 Sep 45 *(97th Inf Div)*

923rd Field Artillery Bn (105mm How Trk-D)   15 Sep 42 Cp Breckinridge Ky /16 Feb 46 Japan   Ft Hase Hawaii
SPE: 22 Apr 44   Hawaii: 27 Apr 44 *(98th Inf Div)*

924th Field Artillery Bn (105mm How Trk-D)   15 Nov 42 Cp Van Dorn Miss / 27 Sep 45 Cp Patrick Henry Va   Gerolzhofen Germany
BPE: 30 Sep 44   England: 10 Oct 44   France-ETO: 1 Nov 44 - **25,26,34**   HRPE: 27 Sep 45 *(99th Inf Dif)*

925th Field Artillery Bn (105mm How Trk-D)   15 Nov 42 Ft Jackson S.C. /11 Jan 46 Cp Patrick Henry Va   Le Havre France
NYPE: 6 Oct 44   France-ETO: 20 Oct 44 - **25,26,34**   HRPE: 11 Jan 46 *(100th Inf Div)*

927th Field Artillery Bn (105mm How Trk-D)   15 Sep 42 Cp Maxey Tex /14 Mar 46 Cp Kilmer N.J.   Waltershausen Germany
NYPE: 12 Sep 44   France-ETO: 23 Sep 44 - **26,34**   NYPE: 13 Mar 46 *(102nd Inf Div)*

928th Field Artillery Bn (105mm How Trk-D)   15 Nov 42 Cp Claiborne La / 22 Sep 45 Cp Patrick Henry Va   Kematau Austria
NYPE: 6 Oct 44   France-ETO: 20 Oct 44 - **25,26,34**   HRPE: 22 Sep 45 *(103rd Inf Div)*

929th Field Artillery Bn (105mm How Trk-D)   15 Sep 42 Cp Adair Oreg / 6 Nov 45 Cp San Luis Obispo Calif   Cp San Luis Obispo Calif
NYPE: 27 Aug 44   England: 7 Sep 44   France-ETO: 7 Sep 44 - **26,32,34**   NYPE: 3 Jul 45 *(104th Inf Div)*

930th Field Arty Bn (Cld) (155mm How Trk-D)   6 Jan 43 Ft Custer Mich (1st Bn, 184th FA) /1 May 44 Cp Butner N.C. redes
(nondiv)   1699th Engr Comb Bn

931st Field Arty Bn (Cld) (155mm How Trk-D)   6 Jan 43 Ft Custer Mich (2nd Bn, 184th FA) /20 Mar 44 Cp Gordon Ga redes
(nondiv)   1698th Engr Comb Bn

932nd Field Artillery Bn (8-inch How Trac-D)   8 Feb 43 Cp Blanding Fla (1st Bn, 137th FA) /10 Dec 45 Cp Patrick Henry Va   Strasswalchen Austria
NYPE: 21 Aug 43   N.Africa: 2 Sep 43   Italy: 11 Nov 43   France-ETO: 20 Nov 44 - **25,26,29,34,35**   HRPE: 10 Dec 45
(155mm How Trk-D until sent overseas) (nondiv)

933rd Field Artillery Bn (155mm How Trac-D)   10 Feb 43 Cp Gruber Okla (2nd Bn, 137th FA) / 29 Oct 45 Cp Kilmer N.J.   Neckargartach Germany
NYPE: 21 Aug 43   N.Africa: 2 Sep 43   Italy: 11 Nov 43   France-ETO: 13 Sep 44 - **26,29,34,35,37**   NYPE: 28 Oct 45
(Truck-D until sent overseas) (nondiv)

934th Field Artillery Bn (155mm How Trk-D)   7 Mar 43 Cp Blanding Fla (1st Bn, 141st FA) / 30 Jul 43 Cp Gordon Ga redes 141st
(nondiv)   FA Bn

BATTALION DESIGNATION AND TYPE	FORMED (SOURCE OF UNIT)/INACTIVATION	AUGUST 1945 LOCATION

935th Field Artillery Bn (4.5-inch Gun Trac-D)   7 Mar 43 Cp Blanding Fla (2nd Bn, 141st FA) / 26 Oct 45 Cp Patrick Henry Va   Augsburg Germany
NYPE: 21 Aug 43   N.Africa: 2 Sep 43   Italy: 11 Oct 43   France-ETO: 6 Oct 44 - **25,26,29,31,34,35**   HRPE: 26 Oct 45
(155mm How Trk-D until sent overseas) (nondiv)

936th Field Artillery Bn (155mm How Trac-D)   8 Feb 43 Cp Bowie Tex (1st Bn, 142nd FA) /16 Oct 45 Italy   San Benedetto Italy
NYPE: 21 Aug 43   N.Africa: 2 Sep 43   Italy: 11 Nov 43 - **29,31,33,35**   *(Truck-D until sent overseas) (nondiv)*

937th Field Artillery Bn (155mm How Trac-D)   8 Feb 43 Cp Bowie Tex (2nd Bn, 142nd FA) / 25 Oct 45 Cp Myles Standish Mass   Kochendorf Germany
NYPE: 21 Aug 43   N.Africa: 2 Sep 43   Italy: 11 Nov 43   France-ETO: 15 Aug 44 - **26,29,34,35,37**   BPE: 24 Oct 45
(Truck-D until sent overseas) (nondiv)

938th Field Artillery Bn (155mm How Trac-D)   7 Mar 43 Cp Blanding Fla (1st Bn, 166th FA) / 26 Oct 45 Cp Patrick Henry Va   Ammerland France
NYPE: 21 Aug 43   N.Africa: 2 Sep 43   Italy: 26 Nov 43   France-ETO: 15 Aug 44 - **24,25,26,29,34,35,37**   HRPE: 26 Oct 45
(Truck-D until sent overseas) (nondiv)

939th Field Artillery Bn (4.5-inch Gun Trac-D)   7 Mar 43 Cp Blanding Fla (2nd Bn, 166th FA) / 23 Oct 45 Cp Patrick Henry Va   Holzhausen Germany
NYPE: 21 Aug 43   N.Africa: 3 Sep 43   Italy: 20 Oct 43   France-ETO: 15 Oct 44 - **25,26,29,31,34,35**   HRPE: 23 Oct 45
(155mm How Trk-D until sent overseas) (nondiv)

940th Field Artillery Bn (155mm How Trac-D)   1 May 44 Cp Pickett Va (402nd AAA Gun Bn) / 6 Oct 45 France   Ober Kassel Germany
NYPE: 10 Jan 45   France-ETO: 21 Jan 45 - **26** *(nondiv)*

941st Field Artillery Bn (4.5-inch Gun Trac-D)   1 Mar 43 Cp Shelby Miss (2nd Bn, 172nd FA) / 23 Nov 45 Cp Myles Standish   Mitzenhausen Germany
BPE: 24 Mar 44   England: 4 Apr 44   France-ETO: 14 Jun 44 - **25,26,30,32,34**   BPE: 22 Nov 45   Mass
(155mm How Trk-D until late 1943) (nondiv)

942nd Field Artillery Bn (155mm How Trac-D)   1 May 44 Cp Pickett Va (604th AAA Gun Bn) / 4 Nov 45 Cp Kilmer N.J.   Wittlik Germany
NYPE: 10 Jan 45   France-ETO: 23 Jan 45 - **26,34**   NYPE: 2 Nov 45 *(nondiv)*

943rd Field Artillery Bn (155mm How Trac-D)   11 Nov 42 Ft Leonard Wood Mo (2nd Bn, 177th FA) / 28 Nov 45 Cp Shanks N.Y.   Rosenheim Germany
NYPE: 22 Jun 44   England: 28 Jun 44   France-ETO: 7 Aug 44 - **25,26,32,34**   NYPE: 27 Nov 45 *(Truck-D until 1944) (nondiv)*

945th Field Artillery Bn (155mm How Trac-D)   1 Mar 43 Cp Shelby Miss (2nd Bn, 179th FA) / 26 Nov 45 Cp Myles Standish Mass   Straubing Germany
BPE: 3 Jul 44   England: 12 Jul 44   France-ETO: Aug 44 - **25,26,32,34**   BPE: 25 Nov 45 *(Truck-D until 1944) (nondiv)*

947th Field Artillery Bn (155mm How Trac-D)   8 Feb 43 Cp Roberts Calif (2nd Bn, 181st FA) /1 Jan 46 Cp Stoneman Calif   Alabang Philippines
SFPE: 10 Jan 44   Goodenough I: 2 Feb 44   New Guinea: 23 Apr 44   Biak I: 28 May 44   Philippines: 23 Oct 44 - **13,14,15**
(Truck-D until late 1943) (nondiv)

949th Field Artillery Bn (155mm How Trac-D)   8 Feb 43 Ft Leonard Wood Mo (2nd Bn, 182nd FA) /1 Dec 45 Cp Kilmer N.J.   Bad Liebensted Germany
NYPE: 22 Jun 44   England: 28 Jun 44   France-ETO: 5 Aug 44 - **25,26,32,34**   NYPE: 30 Nov 45 *(Truck-D until sent overseas) (nondiv)*

951st Field Artillery Bn (155mm How Trac-D)   8 Feb 43 Ft Lewis Wash (2nd Bn, 183rd FA) /13 Oct 45 Cp Myles Standish Mass   Bad Bibra Germany
NYPE: 5 Dec 43   England: 17 Dec 43   France-ETO: 11 Jun 44 - **25,26,30,32,34**   BPE: 12 Oct 45 *(Truck-D until sent overseas) (nondiv)*

953rd Field Artillery Bn (155mm How Trac-D)   8 Feb 43 Ft Ethan Allen Vt (2nd Bn, 186th FA) / 22 Dec 45 Cp Myles Standish   Volyne Belgium
NYPE: 21 Oct 43   England: 3 Nov 43   France-ETO: 13 Jun 44 - **25,26,30,32,34**   BPE: 21 Dec 45 *(nondiv)*   Mass

955th Field Artillery Bn (155mm How Trac-D)   8 Feb 43 Ft Ethan Allen Vt (2nd Bn, 187th FA) / 22 Dec 45 Cp Kilmer N.J.   Bohumilitz Czechoslovakia
NYPE: 21 Oct 43   England: 3 Nov 43   France-ETO: 16 Jun 44 - **25,26,30,32,34**   NYPE: 21 Dec 45 *(nondiv)*

957th Field Artillery Bn (155mm How Trac-D)   8 Feb 43 Yakima Wash (2nd Bn, 188th FA) / 30 Oct 45 Cp Myles Standish Mass   Gorsleben Germany
NYPE: 5 Dec 43   England: 17 Dec 43   France-ETO: 13 Jun 44 - **25,26,30,32,34**   BPE: 29 Oct 45 *(Truck-D until sent overseas) (nondiv)*

959th Field Artillery Bn (4.5-inch Gun Trac-D)   8 Feb 43 Cp Roberts Calif (2nd Bn, 191st FA) / 5 Mar 46 Cp Kilmer N.J.   Alsfeld Germany
NYPE: 18 Apr 44   England: 26 Apr 44   France-ETO: 24 Jun 44 - **26,30,32,34**   NYPE: 4 Mar 46 *(155mm How Trk-D until late 1943) (nondiv)*

961st Field Artillery Bn (155mm How Trac-D)   1 Mar 43 La Mnvr Area (2nd Bn, 202nd FA) / 27 Nov 45 Cp Kilmer N.J.   Salzburg Austria
BPE: 18 Jan 44   England: 29 Jan 44   France-ETO: Jun 44 - **25,26,30,32,34**   NYPE: 26 Nov 45 *(Truck-D until sent overseas) (nondiv)*

963rd Field Artillery Bn (155mm How Trac-D)   8 Feb 43 Ft Bragg N.C. (2nd Bn, 203rd FA) / 27 Nov 45 Cp Kilmer N.J.   Schotten Germany
NYPE: 21 Feb 44   England: 29 Feb 44   France-ETO: 26 Jun 44 - **25,26,30,32,34**   NYPE: 27 Nov 45 *(Truck-D until 1944) (nondiv)*

965th Field Artillery Bn (155mm How Trac-D)   1 Mar 43 Cp Forrest Tenn (2nd Bn, 204th FA) / 3 Nov 45 Cp Shanks N.Y.   Kappel Germany
NYPE: 31 Mar 44   England: 8 Apr 44   France-ETO: Jul 44 - **25,26,30,32,34**   NYPE: 2 Nov 45 *(Truck-D until sent overseas) (nondiv)*

967th Field Artillery Bn (155mm How Trac-D)   8 Feb 43 Ft Bragg N.C. (2nd Bn, 228th FA) / 2 Dec 45 Cp Patrick Henry Va   Giessen Germany
NYPE: 21 Feb 44   England: 28 Feb 44   France-ETO: 26 Jun 44 - **26,30,32,34**   HRPE: 2 Dec 45 *(Truck-D until sent overseas) (nondiv)*

969th Field Arty Bn (Cld) (155mm How Trac-D)   9 Mar 43 Cp Gruber Okla (2nd Bn, 333rd FA) /15 Apr 46 Cp Kilmer N.J.   Neuhutten Germany
NYPE: 1 Mar 44   England: 7 Mar 44   France-ETO: 9 Jul 44 - **25,26,30,32,34**   NYPE: 14 Apr 46 *(Truck-D until sent overseas) (nondiv)*

971st Field Arty Bn (Cld) (155mm How Trk-D)   1 Apr 43 Cp Livingston La (2nd Bn, 350th FA) /1 Mar 44 Cp Livingston La
(nondiv)

BATTALION DESIGNATION AND TYPE	FORMED (SOURCE OF UNIT)/INACTIVATION	AUGUST 1945 LOCATION
973rd Field Arty Bn (Cld) (155mm How Trk-D) *(nondiv)*	1 Apr 43 Cp Livingston La (2nd Bn, 351st FA) /1 Apr 44 Cp Livingston La	
974th Field Artillery Bn (155mm How Trac-D) NYPE: 11 Feb 44 England: 23 Feb 44 France-ETO: 14 Jul 44 - **25,26,30,32,34** HRPE: 10 Jan 46 *(Truck-D until sent overseas) (nondiv)*	1 Mar 43 Cp Forrest Tenn (1st Bn, 40th FA) /10 Jan 46 Cp Patrick Henry Va	Sunching Germany
975th Field Artillery Bn (155mm How Trac-D) NYPE: 11 Feb 44 England: 23 Feb 44 France-ETO: 17 Jul 44 - **25,26,30,32,34** NYPE: 12 Feb 46 *(Truck-D until sent overseas) (nondiv)*	1 Mar 43 Cp Forrest Tenn (2nd Bn, 40th FA) /13 Jan 46 Cp Kilmer N.J.	Salzburg Austria
976th Field Artillery Bn (155mm Gun Trac-D) NYPE: 19 Aug 43 N.Africa: 2 Sep 43 Italy: 10 Oct 43 France-ETO: 15 Aug 44 - **24,25,26,29,34,35,37** NYPE: 5 Mar 46 *(nondiv)*	1 Mar 43 Cp Shelby Miss (1st Bn, 35th FA) / 6 Mar 46 Cp Kilmer N.J.	Wessling Germany
977th Field Artillery Bn (155mm Gun Trac-D) NYPE: 21 Aug 43 N.Africa: 2 Sep 43 Italy: 10 Oct 43 France-ETO: 15 Aug 44 - **24,25,26,29,34,35,37** HRPE: 8 Jan 46 *(nondiv)*	1 Mar 43 Cp Shelby Miss (2nd Bn, 35th FA) / 8 Jan 46 Cp Patrick Henry Va	Burgheim Germany
978th Field Artillery Bn (155mm Gun Trac-D) NYPE: 1 Mar 44 England: 7 Mar 44 France-ETO: 26 Jun 44 - **26,30,32,34** BPE: 29 Oct 45 *(nondiv)*	8 Feb 43 Ft Leonard Wood Mo (1st Bn, 119th FA) / 30 Oct 45 Cp Myles Standish Mass	Budlingen Germany
979th Field Artillery Bn (155mm Gun Trac-D) NYPE: 27 Feb 44 England: 6 Mar 44 France-ETO: 27 Jun 44 - **26,30,32,34** NYPE: 28 Oct 45 *(nondiv)*	8 Feb 43 Ft Leonard Wood Mo (2nd Bn, 119th FA) / 29 Oct 45 Cp Kilmer N.J.	Grunberg Germany
980th Field Artillery Bn (155mm Gun Trk-D) BPE: 28 Dec 43 England: 8 Jan 44 France-ETO: 6 Jun 44 - **25,26,30,32,34** BPE: 12 Nov 45 *(nondiv)*	8 Feb 43 Ft Lewis Wash (1st Bn, 144th FA) /13 Nov 45 Cp Myles Standish Mass	Sondershausen Germany
981st Field Artillery Bn (155mm Gun Trk-D) BPE: 28 Dec 43 England: 8 Jan 44 France-ETO: 13 Jun 44 - **25,26,30,32,34** NYPE: 27 Nov 45 *(nondiv)*	8 Feb 43 Yakima Wash (2nd Bn, 144th FA) / 28 Nov 45 Cp Kilmer N.J.	Bad Frankenhausen Germany
983rd Field Artillery Bn (155mm Gun Trac-D) Portland Sub-P/E: 31 Mar 44 New Guinea: 13 May 44 Philippines: 23 Oct 44 - **13,14,15,20** SFPE: 17 Dec 45 *(nondiv)*	8 Feb 43 Cp Roberts Calif (2nd Bn, 186th FA) /19 Dec 45 Cp Stoneman Calif	Davao Mindanao Philippines
985th Field Artillery Bn (155mm Gun Trac-D) NYPE: 21 Aug 43 N.Africa: 2 Sep 43 Italy: 30 Oct 43 - **29,31,33,35** *(nondiv)*	8 Feb 43 Cp Gruber Okla (2nd Bn, 173rd FA) / 8 Oct 45 Italy	Bassano Italy
987th Field Artillery Bn (155mm Gun S-P) NYPE: 13 Mar 44 England: 21 Mar 44 France-ETO: 7 Jun 44 - **25,26,30,32,34** NYPE: 19 Aug 45 *(nondiv)*	25 Feb 43 Cp Bowie Tex (2nd Bn, 174th FA) / 27 Oct 45 Cp Cooke Calif	Shipment #10160-C at sea
989th Field Artillery Bn (155mm Gun Trac-D) NYPE: 23 Mar 44 England: 3 Apr 44 France-ETO: 14 Jul 44 - **25,26,30,32,34** NYPE: 16 Feb 46 *(nondiv)*	1 Mar 44 Cp Forrest Tenn (2nd Bn, 208th FA) /17 Feb 46 Cp Kilmer N.J.	Salzburg Austria
991st Field Artillery Bn (155mm Gun S-P) NYPE: 22 Jan 44 England: 28 Jan 44 France-ETO: 11 Jul 44 - **25,26,30,32,34** BPE: 15 Nov 45 *(nondiv)*	8 Feb 43 Pine Camp N.Y. (2nd Bn, 258th FA) /16 Nov 45 Cp Myles Standish Mass	Allstedt Germany
993rd Field Arty Bn (Cld) (155mm Gun Trac-D) *(nondiv)*	1 Apr 43 Cp Livingston La (2nd Bn, 353rd FA) /19 Mar 44 Cp Swift Tex redes 1696th Engr Comb Bn	
995th Field Artillery Bn (8-inch How Trk-D) NYPE: 21 Aug 43 N.Africa: 2 Sep 43 Italy: 13 Nov 43 France-ETO: 9 Sep 44 - **25,26,29,34,35,37** NYPE: 25 Dec 45 *(nondiv)*	8 Feb 43 Ft Bragg N.C. (2nd Bn, 194th FA) / 26 Dec 45 Cp Kilmer N.J.	Starnberg Germany
997th Field Artillery Bn (8-inch How Trac-D) BPE: 15 Feb 44 England: 22 Feb 44 France-ETO: 27 Jun 44 - **25,26-30,32,34** HRPE: 20 Dec 45 *(nondiv)*	1 Mar 43 Ft Ord Calif (2nd Bn, 195th FA) / 20 Dec 45 Cp Patrick Henry Va	Schmalkalden Germany
999th Field Arty Bn (Cld) (8-inch How Trac-D) NYPE: 3 Jun 44 England: 12 Jun 44 France-ETO: 17 Jul 44 - **25,26,30,32,34** NYPE: 16 Dec 45 *(nondiv)*	23 Feb 43 Ft Bragg N.C. (2nd Bn, 578th FA) /17 Dec 45 Cp Kilmer N.J.	Ostlingen Germany
1114th Field Artillery Bn (105mm How Trk-D) Panama: 14 Jul 44 Puerto Rico: 4 Apr 45 Hawaii: 25 May 45 Puerto Rico: 6 Mar 46 *(nondiv)*	14 Jul 44 Ft Clayton Panama Canal Zone /12 Mar 46 Puerto Rico	Kahuku Army Airbase Hawaii
1125th Armored Field Artillery Bn Italy: 25 Sep 44 - **31,33,35** *(nondiv)*	25 Sep 44 Naples Italy (454th AAA Bn) /11 Sep 45 Italy	Palazzo Italy
First Prov Gun Bn (155mm Gun)	22 Mar 44 Hawaii (2nd Bn, 55th CA Regt) / 31 May 44 Hawaii redes 531st FA Bn	

*Active through 1946

Part VIII

Coast Artillery and Antiaircraft Artillery of the U.S. Army in World War II

Chapter 34

Antiaircraft Artillery and Coast Artillery Brigades

Brigades:

Hawaiian, Atlantic, Pacific, 31–59, 61–68, 70, 71, 74–76, 101, 102, 2626 Provisional, Provisional

Atlantic Coast Artillery Brigade

1 Sep 41 formed at Ft Randolph Panama Canal Zone where redesignated 75th AAA Brigade 20 Jan 44.

Campaigns: *American Theater without inscription*

Hawaiian Separate Coast Artillery Brigade

Stationed at Ft DeRussy Hawaii where redesignated Hawaiian Coast Artillery Command 1 Aug 41 which was disbanded 16 Mar 42.

Campaigns: *Central Pacific*

Pacific Coast Artillery Brigade

1 Sep 41 formed at Ft Amador Panama Canal Zone and moved to Ft Clayton Canal Zone 31 Jan 42; redesignated 76th AAA Brigade there 5 Feb 44.

Campaigns: *American Theater without inscription*

31st Antiaircraft Artillery Brigade

20 Nov 42 activated at Cp Haan Calif as the 31st Coast Artillery Brigade (AA); staged at Ft Dix N.J. 19 Mar 43 until departed New York P/E 28 Apr 43; arrived in North Africa 11 May 43 and moved to Sardinia 17 Nov 43; there redesignated as AAA Brigade 6 Jan 44 and moved to Corsica 10 Apr 44; arrived in southern France 22 Aug 44 where assigned Ninth Air Force 12 Nov 44; crossed into Belgium 8 Apr 45 and inactivated at Langenselbold Germany 30 Jun 46.

Campaigns: *Rome-Arno, Southern France, Rhineland*
Aug 45 Loc: Namur Belgium

32nd Antiaircraft Artillery Brigade

20 Nov 42 activated at Ft Bliss Tex as the 32nd Coast Artillery Brigade (AA) and redesignated there as AAA Brigade 28 May 43; staged at Cp Stoneman Calif 20 Aug 43 until departed San Francisco P/E 7 Sep 43; arrived in Australia 1 Oct 43 and landed in New Guinea 14 Oct 43; arrived on Goodenough Island 3 Nov 43 and returned to New Guinea 24 Feb 44; assaulted Leyte Philippines 20 Oct 44 and active in Philippines thru 1946.

Campaigns: *New Guinea, Leyte*
Aug 45 Loc: Leyte Philippines

33rd Antiaircraft Artillery Brigade

10 Feb 41 activated at Cp Hulen Tex as the 33rd Coast Artillery Brigade (AA) and moved to San Diego Calif 14 Dec 41 where redesignated AAA Brigade 1 Sep 43; arrived Cp Haan Calif 8 Mar 44 where disbanded 12 Apr 44.

34th Antiaircraft Artillery Brigade

10 Feb 41 activated at Ft Bragg N.C. as the 34th Coast Artillery Brigade (AA) and moved to Norfolk Va 11 Dec 41; staged at Cp Kilmer N.J. 28 Jul 42 until departed New York P/E 5 Aug 42; arrived in England via Scotland 18 Aug 42 and left 25 Nov 42; landed in North Africa 5 Dec 42 and moved to Sicily 29 Jul 43; there redesignated AAA Brigade 10 Jan 44 and landed in Italy 6 Mar 44; landed in southern France 17 Aug 44 and entered Germany 26 Mar 45; arrived at Boston P/E 1 Dec 45 and inactivated at Cp Myles Standish Mass 2 Dec 45.

Campaigns: *Tunisia, Sicily, Rome-Arno, Southern France, Rhineland, Central Europe*
Aug 45 Loc: Neckarsteinach Germany

35th Antiaircraft Artillery Brigade

20 Nov 42 activated at Cp Stewart Ga as the 35th Coast Artillery Brigade (AA) and staged at Cp Myles Standish Mass 21 Apr 43 until departed Boston P/E 28 Apr 43; landed in North Africa 11 May 43 and Italy 10 Sep 43 where redesignated AAA Brigade 14 Jun 44 at Rome; assaulted southern France 15 Aug 44 and entered Germany 26 Mar 45; arrived at New York P/E 25 Oct 45 and inactivated at Cp Kilmer N.J. 26 Oct 45.

Campaigns: *Naples-Foggia, Anzio, Rome-Arno, Southern France, Rhineland, Ardennes-Alsace, Central Europe*
Aug 45 Loc: Fussen Germany

36th Antiaircraft Artillery Brigade

10 Feb 41 activated at Cp Edwards Mass as the 36th Coast Artillery Brigade (AA) and moved to Boston Mass 17 Dec 41; transferred to Cp Kilmer N.J. 21 Sep 42 and to Washington D.C. 13 Oct 42 where redesignated AAA Brigade 1 Sep 43; arrived at Cp Davis N.C. 3 Mar 44 where disbanded 25 Mar 44.

37th Antiaircraft Artillery Brigade

10 Feb 41 activated at Cp Haan Calif under Fourth Army as the 37th Coast Artillery Brigade (AA); moved to Los Angeles Calif 5 Dec 41 where redesignated AAA Brigade 1 Sep 43; assigned to Los Angeles Air Defense Region 1 Jul 44 and moved to Ft Bliss Tex 11 Aug 45 where inactivated 5 Sep 45.

Aug 45 Loc: Fort Bliss Texas

38th Antiaircraft Artillery Brigade

10 Feb 41 activated at Cp Stewart Ga as the 38th Coast Artillery Brigade (AA) and moved to Carolina Maneuver Area 26 Sep 41; transferred back to Cp Stewart 1 Dec 41 and moved to Ft Totten N.Y. 12 Dec 41; there redesignated AAA Brigade 1 Sep 43 and went to Ft Hamilton N.Y. 2 Apr 44; departed New York P/E 7 Apr 44 and arrived in England 15 Apr 44; landed in France 18 Jul 44 and crossed into Luxembourg 8 Feb 45; entered Germany 27 Mar 45 where inactivated 30 Jun 46.

Campaigns: *Normandy, Northern France, Rhineland, Ardennes-Alsace*
Aug 45 Loc: Regensburg Germany

39th Antiaircraft Artillery Brigade

25 Feb 41 activated at Ft Bliss Tex as the 39th Coast Artillery Brigade (AA) and moved to Ft Lawton Wash 14 Dec 41 where redesignated AAA Brigade 1 Sep 43; assigned to Fourth Air Force 15 Apr 44 and transferred to Ft Bliss Tex 10 Jul 44; assigned to Replacement & School Command and moved to Cp Maxey Tex 24 Oct 44 where inactivated 26 Oct 44.

40th Antiaircraft Artillery Brigade

23 Jan 41 activated at Ft Sheridan Ill as the 40th Coast Artillery Brigade (AA) and moved to Philadelphia-Wilmington area 14 Dec 41; arrived at New York P/E 27 Jan 42 and departed 18 Feb 42; arrived in Australia 28 May 42 and landed in New Guinea 14 Feb 43 where redesignated AAA Brigade 15 Jun 44 under Sixth Army; arrived in the Philippines 14 Dec 44; sent to Japan 9 Feb 46 and arrived in Hawaii 25 May 46 where inactivated 15 Dec 46.

Campaigns: *New Guinea, East Indies, Leyte, Luzon*
Aug 45 Loc: Fort McKinley Philippine Islands

41st Coast Artillery Brigade (Antiaircraft)

14 Jan 42 activated at Cp Davis N.C. and arrived at San Francisco P/E 25 Jan 42 and departed 18 Feb 42; landed in Australia 9 Mar 42 where inactivated 15 Nov 43 at Townsville, having served in Australia as a personnel source for Hqs, U.S. Army Forces in Australia.

Campaigns: *Pacific Theater without inscription*

42nd Antiaircraft Artillery Brigade

1 Apr 42 activated at Cp Haan Calif as the 42nd Coast Artillery Brigade (AA) and staged at Cp Murray Wash 10 Oct 42 until departed Seattle P/E 17 Oct 42; arrived in Alaska 25 Oct 42 where remained until 11 Apr 44; returned to Seattle P/E 17 May 44 and arrived Cp Haan Calif 28 Apr 44 where redesignated as AAA Brigade 25 May 44; assigned to Replacement & School Command same date and moved to Cp Howze Tex 22 Oct 44 where inactivated 1 Nov 44.

Campaigns: *Aleutian Islands*

43rd Antiaircraft Artillery Brigade

1 May 42 activated at Cp Davis N.C. as the 43rd Coast Artillery Brigade (AA) and moved to Ft Fisher N.C. 9 Jun 42; arrived at Philadelphia Pa 8 Aug 42 where redesignated AAA Brigade 1 Sep 43; moved to Cp Stewart Ga 24 Mar 44 and to Mitchell Field Long Island N.Y. 22 Jul 44 under First Air Force; assigned to Replacement & School Command and moved to Cp Gordon Ga 20 Dec 44 where inactivated 27 Dec 44.

429

44th Antiaircraft Artillery Brigade

1 Jun 42 activated at Cp Hulen Tex as 44th Coast Artillery Brigade (AA) and staged at Cp Myles Standish 21 Apr 43 until departed New York P/E 28 Apr 43; arrived in North Africa 12 May 43 where redesignated AAA Brigade 26 Dec 43; arrived at Sardinia 6 Jul 44 and Corsica 3 Aug 44; landed in France 13 Nov 44 and entered Germany 27 Mar 45; arrived at Hampton Roads P/E 23 Oct 45 and inactivated at Cp Patrick Henry Va 23 Oct 45.

Campaigns: *Rome-Arno, Rhineland, Central Europe*
Aug 45 Loc: Schellenberg Germany

45th Antiaircraft Artillery Brigade

1 Jun 42 activated at Cp Stewart Ga as the 45th Coast Artillery Brigade (AA); staged at Cp Shanks N.Y. 4 Apr 43 until departed New York P/E 22 Apr 43; arrived in North Africa 30 Apr 43 and landed in Italy 22 Sep 43; there functioned as the Fifth Army Antiaircraft Command initially and was redesignated AAA Brigade at Santa Maria on 8 Apr 44; functioned as a line command unit from 5 Nov 44 until inactivation known as Task Force 45 and assigned sector of the frontline in Italy serving as infantry; inactivated at Lamestra Italy on 13 Feb 45.

Campaigns: *Naples-Foggia, Rome-Arno, North Apennines*

46th Antiaircraft Artillery Brigade

1 Feb 42 activated at Ft Bliss Tex as the 46th Coast Artillery Brigade (AA) and moved to Boston Mass 24 Jul 42 where redesignated AAA Brigade 1 Sep 43; arrived at Cp Edwards Mass 27 Mar 44 where disbanded 1 Apr 44.

47th Antiaircraft Artillery Brigade

26 Jan 42 activated at Cp Davis N.C. as the 47th Coast Artillery Brigade (AA) and moved to Indiantown Gap Pa 22 Apr 42; departed New York P/E 30 Apr 42 and arrived in Iceland 10 May 42 where redesignated AAA Brigade on 5 Sep 43; departed Iceland 30 Oct 43 and arrived in England 4 Nov 43; landed in France 30 Jun 44 and returned to New York P/E 13 Dec 45 and inactivated at Cp Kilmer N.J. on 16 Dec 45.

Campaigns: *Normandy, Northern France*
Aug 45 Loc: Paris France

48th Antiaircraft Artillery Brigade

26 Jan 42 activated at Cp Stewart Ga as the 48th Coast Artillery Brigade (AAA) and moved to Norfolk Va 23 Jul 42 where redesignated AAA Brigade 1 Sep 43; went to Lebanon Tenn 24 Jan 44 and to Campbell Army Airfield Tenn 28 Mar 44; arrived at Ft Bliss Tex 23 May 44 and staged at Seattle P/E 6 Nov 44 until departed 12 Nov 44; landed in Hawaii on 17 Nov 44 where inactivated 31 Dec 45.

Campaigns: *Pacific Theater without inscription*
Aug 45 Loc: Hickam Field Hawaii

49th Antiaircraft Artillery Brigade

1 Dec 42 activated at Cp Davis N.C. as the 49th Coast Artillery Brigade (AA) and redesignated there as AAA Brigade 28 May 43; moved to Ft McPherson Ga 9 Jun 43 and participated in Tenn Maneuvers 21 Jun 43 after which went to Cp Forrest Tenn 1 Aug 43; returned to Ft McPherson Ga 16 Aug 43; staged at Cp Kilmer N.J. 26 Nov 43 until departed New York P/E 5 Dec 43; arrived in England 16 Dec 43 and landed in France; entered Belgium 18 Dec 44 and Germany 11 Mar 45 where inactivated 15 Mar 46.

Campaigns: *Normandy, Northern France, Rhineland, Ardennes-Alsace, Central Europe*
Aug 45 Loc: Weilburg Germany

50th Antiaircraft Artillery Brigade

10 Feb 43 activated at Cp Davis N.C. as the 50th Coast Artillery Brigade (AA) where redesignated AAA Brigade 28 May 43; moved to Tenn Maneuver Area 15 Nov 43 and Cp Campbell Ky 6 Jan 44; staged at Cp Kilmer N.J. 4 Feb 44 until departed New York P/E 1 Mar 44; arrived in England 7 Mar 44 and landed in France 14 Jul 44; crossed into Belgium 8 Nov 44 and entered Germany 8 May 45; returned to New York P/E 27 Nov 45 and inactivated at Cp Shanks N.Y. 28 Nov 45.

Campaigns: *Normandy, Northern France, Rhineland, Central Europe*
Aug 45 Loc: Bayreuth Germany

51st Antiaircraft Artillery Brigade

10 Feb 43 activated at Ft Bliss Tex as the 51st Coast Artillery Brigade (AA) where redesignated AAA Brigade 28 May 43; moved to Hamilton Field Calif 25 Jul 43 and to Cp Haan Calif 21 Dec 43; staged at Cp Shanks N.Y. 1 Feb 44 until departed New York P/E 11 Feb 44; arrived in England 23 Feb 44 and landed in France 18 Jul 44; entered Germany 7 Apr 45 and returned to New York P/E 14 Dec 45 and inactivated at Cp Kilmer N.J. 15 Dec 45.

Campaigns: *Normandy, Northern France, Rhineland, Central Europe*
Aug 45 Loc: Bad Homburg Germany

52nd Antiaircraft Artillery Brigade

20 Mar 43 activated at Cp Edwards Mass as the 52nd Coast Artillery Brigade (AA) and redesignated there as AAA Brigade 5 Jun 43; moved to Tenn Maneuver Area 29 Sep 43 and to Cp Campbell Ky 30 Oct 43; staged at Cp Kilmer N.J. 14 Dec 43 until departed New York P/E 29 Dec 43; arrived in England 7 Jan 44 and landed in France 5 Jul 44; entered Belgium 9 Oct 44 and Germany 12 Apr 45; returned to New York P/E 27 Nov 45 and inactivated at Cp Shanks N.Y. 28 Nov 45.

Campaigns: *Normandy, Northern France, Rhineland, Central Europe*
Aug 45 Loc: Bad Godesburg Germany

53rd Antiaircraft Artillery Brigade

11 Jul 41 activated in Hawaii as the 53rd Coast Artillery Brigade (AA) where redesignated AAA Brigade 12 Dec 43; provided staff cadre for formation of the Hawaiian Antiaircraft Artillery Command 16 Mar 42; assigned to Tenth Army 31 Jan 45 and left Hawaii 15 Mar 45; landed on Okinawa 17 Apr 45 where inactivated 30 Jan 46.

Campaigns: *Central Pacific, Ryukyus*
Aug 45 Loc: Okinawa

54th Antiaircraft Artillery Brigade

1 Dec 42 activated at Cp Haan Calif as 54th Coast Artillery Brigade (AA) where redesignated AAA Brigade 28 May 43; moved to Cp Polk La 12 Jun 43 and staged at Cp Shanks N.Y. 24 Nov 43 until departed New York P/E 3 Dec 43; arrived in England 9 Dec 43 and landed in France 29 Jul 44; entered Germany 15 Apr 45; arrived at Boston P/E 21 Oct 45 and inactivated at Cp Myles Standish Mass 22 Oct 45.

Campaigns: *Northern France, Rhineland, Central Europe*
Aug 45 Loc: St Inglevert Belgium

55th Antiaircraft Artillery Brigade

10 Mar 43 activated at Cp Stewart Ga as the 55th Coast Artillery Brigade (AA) and redesignated there as AAA Brigade 5 Jun 43; moved to Mitchell Field Long Island N.Y. 21 Jul 43 and to Cp Davis N.C. 16 Nov 43; staged at Cp Shanks N.Y. 22 Dec 43 until departed New York P/E 2 Jan 44; arrived in England 8 Jan 44 and landed in France 24 Jun 44; crossed into Belgium 21 Oct 44 and into Holland same date; entered Germany 10 Mar 45; arrived at Hampton Roads P/E 23 Oct 45 and inactivated at Cp Patrick Henry Va same date.

Campaigns: *Normandy, Northern France, Rhineland, Central Europe*
Aug 45 Loc: Bad Lippsebringe Germany

56th Antiaircraft Artillery Brigade

10 Apr 43 activated at Cp Stewart Ga as the 56th Coast Artillery Brigade (AA) and redesignated there as AAA Brigade 28 May 43; moved to Mitchell Field Long Island N.Y. 22 Oct 43 and to Tenn Maneuver Area 29 Jan 44; arrived at Cp Forrest Tenn 25 Mar 44 and Cp Davis N.C. 20 Apr 44; staged at Cp Kilmer N.J. 3 Aug 44 until departed New York P/E 11 Aug 44; arrived in England 22 Aug 44 and landed in France 5 Sep 44; crossed into Belgium 28 Oct 44 and returned to France 5 Apr 45; entered Germany 21 Apr 45; returned to New York P/E 2 Dec 45 and inactivated Cp Shanks N.Y. 3 Dec 45.

Campaigns: *Northern France, Rhineland, Central Europe*
Aug 45 Loc: Heidelberg Germany

57th Antiaircraft Artillery Brigade

10 Apr 43 activated at Cp Haan Calif as the 57th Coast Artillery Brigade (AA) and redesignated there as AAA Brigade 28 May 43; moved to Calif-Ariz Maneuver Area 9 Nov 43 and to Hamilton Field Calif 11 Mar 44; arrived at Cp Cooke Calif 12 Jun 44 and Ft Bliss Tex 17 Aug 44; relocated to Cp Maxey Tex 2 Nov 44 where inactivated 9 Nov 44.

58th Antiaircraft Artillery Brigade

10 May 43 activated at Ft Bliss Tex as the 58th Coast Artillery Brigade (AA) where redesignated as AAA Brigade 28 May 43; moved to Cp Swift Tex 14 Jul 44 where inactivated 29 Jul 44.

59th Antiaircraft Artillery Brigade

10 May 43 activated at Cp Haan Calif as the 59th Coast Artillery Brigade (AA) where redesignated as AAA Brigade 28 May 43; moved to Hamilton Field Calif 2 Dec 43 and returned to Cp Haan Calif 19 Apr 44; transferred to Cp Beauregard La 11 Aug 44 and Ft Bliss Tex 15 Nov 44; staged at Ft Lawton Wash 6 Jan 45 until departed Seattle P/E 13 Jan 45; arrived in Hawaii 20 Jan 45 and departed 29 Jan 45; landed on Saipan 12 Feb 45 where inactivated 15 Jan 46.

Campaigns: *Western Pacific*
Aug 45 Loc: Saipan

61st Antiaircraft Artillery Brigade

10 Jul 43 activated at Cp Davis N.C. where disbanded 25 Mar 44.

62nd Antiaircraft Artillery Brigade

1 Aug 43 activated at Cp Stewart Ga and moved to Cp Gordon Ga 20 Oct 44 under Replacement & School Command where inactivated 31 Oct 44.

63rd Antiaircraft Artillery Brigade

1 Aug 43 activated at Ft Bliss Tex and sent to La Maneuver Area 6 Mar 44; moved to Mitchell Field Long Island N.Y. 1 May 44 and to Cp Stewart Ga 10 Oct 44; arrived at Ft Jackson S.C. 5 Jan 45 where inactivated 2 Feb 45.

64th Antiaircraft Artillery Brigade

10 Sep 43 activated at Cp Edwards Mass where inactivated 11 Dec 43.

65th Antiaircraft Artillery Brigade

10 Sep 43 activated at Cp Haan Calif and moved to Muroc Calif 23 May 44; returned to Cp Haan Calif 15 Sep 44 and moved to Cp Howze Tex 3 Dec 44 where inactivated 13 Dec 44.

66th Antiaircraft Artillery Brigade

1 Oct 43 activated at Cp Stewart Ga where disbanded 25 Mar 44.

67th Antiaircraft Artillery Brigade

1 Oct 43 activated at Ft Bliss Tex and inactivated there 22 Jul 44.

68th Antiaircraft Artillery Brigade

10 Aug 43 activated on New Caledonia and moved to Guadalcanal 7 Oct 43; left 11 Jun 44 and landed on Bougainville 15 Jun 44; departed Bougainville 12 Nov 44 and arrived in the Philippines 9 Jan 45 where inactivated 28 Feb 46.

Campaigns: *Northern Solomons, Luzon*
Aug 45 Loc: San Fernando Philippine Islands

70th Antiaircraft Artillery Brigade

12 Dec 43 activated on Hawaii and assigned to Central Pacific Base Command; inactivated there 31 Dec 45.

Campaigns: *Pacific Theater without inscription*
Aug 45 Loc: Hickam Field Hawaii

71st Antiaircraft Artillery Brigade

10 Dec 43 activated at Paterno Italy from assets of 2626th AAA Brigade (Provisional); later assigned to Mediterranean Theater of Operations 1 Nov 44; inactivated in Italy 8 Sep 45.

Campaigns: *Naples-Foggia, Rome-Arno, Po Valley, Naples-Foggia*
Aug 45 Loc: Ghedi Italy

74th Antiaircraft Artillery Brigade

15 Jun 43 activated at Cp Edwards Mass as the 74th Coast Artillery Brigade (AA) and redesignated there as AAA Brigade 1 May 43; moved to Mitchell Field Long Island N.Y. 11 Jan 44 and returned to Cp Edwards Mass 16 May 44; staged at Cp Kilmer N.J. 5 Aug 44 until departed New York P/E 11 Aug 44; arrived in England 22 Aug 44 and landed in France 5 Sep 44; crossed into Belgium 7 Oct 44 and returned to France 2 Nov 44; entered Holland 12 Mar 45; returned to New York P/E 26 Jun 45 and inactivated at Ft Bliss Tex 5 Sep 45.

Campaigns: *Northern France, Rhineland, Central Europe*
Aug 45 Loc: Fort Bliss Texas

75th Antiaircraft Artillery Brigade

20 Jan 44 redesignated from the Atlantic Coast Artillery Brigade at Ft Randolph Panama Canal Zone where disbanded 15 Apr 46.

Campaigns: *American Theater without inscription*
Aug 45 Loc: Ft Davis Panama Canal Zone

76th Antiaircraft Artillery Brigade

5 Feb 44 redesignated from the Pacific Coast Artillery Brigade at Ft Clayton Panama Canal Zone where disbanded 15 Apr 46.

Campaigns: *American Theater without inscription*
Aug 45 Loc: Ft Clayton Panama Canal Zone

101st Antiaircraft Artillery Brigade   Minnesota National Guard

6 Jan 41 inducted into federal service at White Bear Lake Minn as the 101st Coast Artillery Brigade (AA) and moved to Cp Haan Calif 19 Jan 41; transferred to San Francisco Calif 1 Dec 43 where redesignated AAA Brigade 1 Sep 43; returned to Cp Haan Calif 20 Apr 44 where disbanded 29 Apr 44.

102nd Antiaircraft Artillery Brigade   New York National Guard

10 Feb 41 inducted into federal service at New York N.Y. as the 102nd Coast Artillery Brigade (AA) and moved to Cp Stewart Ga 20 Feb 41; transferred to Philadelphia Pa 15 Jan 42 and to A.P. Hill Mil Res Va 19 Nov 42; moved to Ft George G. Meade Md 28 Jan 43 and returned to Cp Stewart Ga 6 Aug 43 where redesignated AAA Brigade 1 Sep 43; sent to La Maneuver Area 30 Sep 43 and to Mitchell Field Long Island N.Y. 22 Mar 44; arrived at Cp Pickett Va 2 May 44 and staged at Cp Kilmer N.J. 5 Sep 44 but returned to Cp Pickett Va; staged at Cp Stoneman Calif 25 Oct 44 and departed San Francisco P/E 17 Nov 44; landed in New Guinea 5 Dec 44 and in the Philippines 26 Feb 45; returned to San Francisco P/E 30 Dec 45 where inactivated at Cp Stoneman Calif 1 Jan 46.

Campaigns: *Luzon*
Aug 45 Loc: Clark Field Philippine Islands

2626th Antiaircraft Artillery Brigade, Provisional

1 Mar 43 organized at Casablanca North Africa as the 2626th Coast Artillery Brigade (AA) (Provisional) and assigned to II Corps; arrived in Sicily 15 Aug 43 and redesignated AAA Brigade, Provisional at Agrigento on 18 Oct 43; moved into Italy in late October 43 where discontinued on 10 Dec 43 and assets used to form the 71st Antiaircraft Artillery Brigade at Paterno.

Campaigns: *Sicily*

Provisional Coast Artillery Brigade (Antiaircraft)

7 Apr 42 organized from Groupment A in Philippine Islands and consisted of both 200th and 515th Coast Artillery (AA), fought as infantry south of Cabcaben Airfield Luzon 8 Apr 42 and surrendered to Japanese forces on Bataan 9 Apr 42.

Campaigns: *Philippine Islands*

Chapter 35

Antiaircraft Artillery, Barrage Balloon, and Coast Artillery Groups

Groups:

San Francisco, 1 Barrage Balloon, 2 Barrage Balloon, 1–51, 53–58, 61–80, 82, 83, 85–98, 103, 105–124, 134–145, 152, 153, 155, 197, 198, 202–205, 207–214, 216, 217, 251, 260, 369, 501, 502, 505, 507, 601–605, 701

San Francisco Antiaircraft Artillery Group, Provisional

27 Mar 45 activated at San Francisco Calif and discontinued there on 28 Jun 45.

1st Barrage Balloon Group (Special)

1 Feb 42 activated at Cp Tyson Tenn as 1st Barrage Balloon Group; redesignated Special at Bremerton Wash 7 May 43; inactivated at Ft Custer Mich 9 Sep 43.

1st Antiaircraft Artillery Group

17 Aug 42 activated at Ft Bliss Tex as 1st Coast Artillery Group (AA) and departed United States 1 Mar 43; arrived in North Africa 9 Mar 43 and landed in Sicily on 9 Aug 43; transferred to Sardinia 4 Dec 43; redesignated there as AAA Group 31 Dec 43 at Sassari, and moved to Corsica 25 Jul 44; landed in France 2 Nov 44 where inactivated at Marseille 13 Feb 45.

Campaigns: *Tunisia, Sicily, Rome-Arno, Rhineland*

1st Coast Artillery Group (Harbor Defense)

1 Nov 44 redesignated from 1st Coast Artillery Regiment in Panama Canal Zone where redesignated Harbor Defense of Cristobal 2 Jan 45, which was active through 1946.

Campaigns: *American Theater without inscription*

2nd Antiaircraft Artillery Group

17 Aug 42 activated at Ft Bliss Tex as 2nd Coast Artillery Group (AA) and there redesignated as AAA Group 5 Jun 43; departed United States 5 Sep 43 and arrived in England 18 Sep 43; landed at Utah Beach France on 12 Jul 44 and crossed into Belgium 24 Sep 44 and into Holland 29 Oct 44; entered Germany 3 Mar 45; returned to New York P/E in Oct 45 and inactivated at Cp Kilmer N.J. 25 Oct 45.

Campaigns: *Normandy, Northern France, Rhineland, Central Europe*
Aug 45 Loc: Olde Germany

2nd Barrage Balloon Group

1 May 43 activated at Los Angeles Calif and inactivated at Ft Custer Mich 9 Sep 43.

3rd Antiaircraft Artillery Group

17 Aug 42 activated at Cp Davis N.C. as 3rd Coast Artillery Group (AA) and redesignated AAA Group at Norfolk Va 1 Jun 43; inactivated at Cp Pickett Va on 18 Aug 44.

4th Antiaircraft Artillery Group (Searchlight Operations)

17 Aug 42 activated at Cp Stewart Ga as the 4th Coast Artillery Group (AA) and departed United States 7 Feb 43; arrived in North Africa 21 Feb 43 and landed in Sicily during August 43; arrived in Italy 26 Oct 43 where redesignated AAA Group at Foggia 1 May 44; inactivated in Italy 9 Dec 44 at Barberino and assets used to fill the 1168th Engineer Combat Group.

Campaigns: *Tunisia, Sicily, Naples-Foggia, Rome-Arno*

4th Coast Artillery Group (Harbor Defense)

1 Nov 44 redesignated from 4th Coast Artillery Regiment in Panama Canal Zone where redesignated the Harbor Defense of Balboa 2 Jan 45, which was active thru 1946.

Campaigns: *American Theater without inscription*

5th Antiaircraft Artillery Group

17 Aug 42 activated at Cp Hulen Tex as 5th Coast Artillery Group (AA) and departed United States 20 Apr 43; arrived in North Africa 11 May 43 and left Oran Algeria 21 Sep 43 and landed south of Naples Italy 21 Sep 43; redesignated AAA Group 18 Feb 44 while attached to 35th AAA Brigade under French Expeditionary Corps; arrived in Anzio Italy 25 Apr 44 and departed Naples Italy 12 Aug 44; assaulted southern France 15 Aug 44 and assigned to Seventh Army 18 Aug 44; entered Germany 31 Mar 45; returned to Boston P/E and inactivated at Cp Myles Standish Mass 15 Oct 45.

Campaigns: *Tunisia, Sicily, Naples-Foggia, Anzio, Rome-Arno, Southern France, Rhineland, Ardennes-Alsace, Central Europe*
Aug 45 Loc: Feudenheim Germany

6th Antiaircraft Artillery Group

21 Aug 42 activated at Cp Haan Calif as 6th Coast Artillery Group (AA) and redesignated AAA Group 26 May 43; departed United States 18 Aug 43 and arrived in Australia 11 Sep 43; landed in New Guinea 1 Nov 43 and moved to New Britain 11 May 44; returned to New Guinea 7 Dec 44; moved to Tacloban Leyte Philippines 1 Mar 45 but did not unload; landed in Manila Bay Luzon 11 Mar 45; inactivated in Manila Philippines 10 Dec 45.

Campaigns: *Bismarck Archipelago, New Guinea, Luzon*
Aug 45 Loc: Manila, Philippines

7th Antiaircraft Artillery Group

1 Sep 42 activated at Cp Haan Calif as 7th Coast Artillery Group (AA) and redesignated AAA Group 26 May 43; departed United States 21 Oct 43 and arrived in England 3 Nov 43; landed in France 27 Jul 44 and attached to 38th AAA Brigade and defended Nancy until 25 Jan 45; crossed into Luxembourg 19 Mar 45 and entered Germany 29 Mar 45; returned to New York P/E 16 Feb 46 and inactivated at Cp Kilmer N.J. 17 Feb 46.

Campaigns: *Northern France, Rhineland, Ardennes-Alsace, Central Europe*
Aug 45 Loc: Augsburg Germany

8th Antiaircraft Artillery Group

1 Sep 42 activated at Cp Stewart Ga as 8th Coast Artillery Group (AA) and departed United States 28 Apr 43; landed in North Africa 11 May 43 and assaulted Salerno Italy 9 Sep 43; redesignated AAA Group at San Pietro Italy 18 Feb 44; arrived in France 24 Nov 44 where inactivated 13 Feb 45 at Marseille.

Campaigns: *Naples-Foggia, Rome-Arno, North Apennines, Rhineland*

9th Antiaircraft Artillery Group

1 Sep 42 activated at Cp Hulen Tex as 9th Coast Artillery Group (AA); departed United States 28 Apr 43 and arrived in North Africa 11 May 43; landed in Italy 17 Nov 43 and defended Bagnoli and attached to British 22nd AA Brigade; assigned to Fifth Army 25 Feb 44 and redesignated AAA Group 12 Feb 44 in Naples; landed at Anzio Italy 28 Feb 44; landed at Marseille France 2 Nov 44 and inactivated in France 13 Feb 45.

Campaigns: *Naples-Foggia, Anzio, Rome-Arno, Rhineland*

10th Antiaircraft Artillery Group

5 Oct 42 activated at the Fighter School Orlando Fla as the 10th Coast Artillery Group (AA) and redesignated AAA Group 2 Jun 43; departed United States 6 Oct 43 and arrived in Australia 29 Oct 43 and moved to New Guinea 5 Nov 43 where attached to Fifth Air Force to act as advisory staff antiaircraft section; moved to Biak Island 3–6 Nov 44 and to Leyte Philippines 15 Nov 44; arrived on San Jose Mindoro Island 2 Feb 45; inactivated on Luzon Philippines 20 Jan 46.

Campaigns: *Bismarck Archipelago, New Guinea, Leyte, Luzon, Ryukyus*
Aug 45 Loc: Clark Field Philippines

11th Antiaircraft Artillery Group

20 Jan 43 activated at Cp Davis N.C. as the 11th Coast Artillery Group (AA) and redesignated AAA Group 26 May 43; departed United States 29 Dec 43 and arrived in England 9 Jan 44; assaulted Utah Beach Normandy France 6 Jun 44 and attached to 49th AAA Brigade; entered Belgium 6 Sep 44 and entered Germany 12 Mar 45; moved to Remagen Bridge on Rhine 26 Mar 45 where remained until 11 Apr 45; inactivated in Germany 6 Oct 45.

Campaigns: *Normandy, Northern France, Rhineland, Ardennes-Alsace, Central Europe*
Aug 45 Loc: Apolds Germany

12th Antiaircraft Artillery Group

20 Jan 43 activated at Cp Davis N.C. as the 12th Coast Artillery Group (AA) and redesignated AAA Group 26 May 43; departed United States 29 Dec 43 and arrived in England 10 Jan 44; landed over Omaha Beach 11–15 Jun 44 in France and supported XIX Corps in ETO; crossed into Holland 20 Sep 44 and entered Germany 22 Dec 44; inactivated there 6 Oct 45.

Campaigns: *Normandy, Northern France, Rhineland, Central Europe*
Aug 45 Loc: Lauterbach Germany

13th Antiaircraft Artillery Group

20 Jan 43 activated at Cp Stewart Ga as the 13th Coast Artillery Group (AA) and redesignated AAA Group 26 May 43; departed United States 29 Sep 43 and arrived on Espiritu Santo 16 Oct 43; arrived on Guadalcanal 5 Nov 43 and Russell Island 9 Nov 43 where in charge of antiaircraft defenses there until moved to Green Island 25 May 44; landed at Samar Philippines 27 Feb 45 and inactivated at Leyte Philippines 20 Jan 46.

Campaigns: *Northern Solomons, Bismarck Archipelago, Southern Philippines*
Aug 45 Loc: Samar Island Philippines

14th Antiaircraft Artillery Group

20 Jan 43 activated at Cp Stewart Ga as the 14th Coast Artillery Group (AA) and redesignated AAA Group 26 May 43; departed United States 1 Oct 43 and arrived in New Caledonia 18 Oct 43; went to New Hebrides 1 Nov 43 and landed on Guadalcanal 3 Nov 43; landed on Florida Island 5 Nov 43 and Emirau Island 25 Mar 44; arrived in New Guinea 22 Dec 44 and landed in Philippines 22 Jan 45 where inactivated 16 Dec 45.

Campaigns: *Northern Solomons, Bismarck Archipelago, Luzon*
Aug 45 Loc: San Fernando Philippine Islands

15th Antiaircraft Artillery Group

20 Jan 43 activated at Cp Haan Calif as the 15th Coast Artillery Group (AA) and redesignated AAA Group 26 May 43; departed United States 15 Nov 43 and arrived in Australia 8 Dec 43 and New Guinea at Dobodura 14 Dec 43; attached to Task Force Brewer and landed on Los Negros Island 9–26 Mar 44; supported 1st Cav Div on Koruniat and Ndorilo Islands 1 Apr 44; arrived at Morotai Island 15 Oct 44 and landed in Philippines 20 Jun 45 where inactivated on Leyte 10 Dec 45.

Campaigns: *New Guinea, Bismarck Archipelago, Leyte*
Aug 45 Loc: Leyte Philippine Islands

15th Coast Artillery Group (Harbor Defense)

13 Aug 44 redesignated from 15th Coast Artillery Regiment on Hawaii where inactivated 10 Apr 45. It helped operate the quartermaster depot in Hawaii.

Campaigns: *Pacific Theater without inscription*

16th Antiaircraft Artillery Group

20 Jan 43 activated at Cp Edwards Mass as the 16th Coast Artillery Group (AA) and redesignated AAA Group 26 May 43; departed New York P/E 2 Jan 44 and arrived in England 8 Jan 44; assaulted Omaha Beach France 6 Jun 44 and crossed into Belgium 7 Sep 44; crossed into Luxembourg 22 Oct 44 and defended Luxembourg city until returned to Belgium 4 Feb 45; entered Germany 14 Feb 45 and returned to New York P/E and inactivated at Cp Kilmer N.J. 11 Oct 45.

Campaigns: *Normandy, Northern France, Rhineland, Ardennes-Alsace, Central Europe*
Aug 45 Loc: Forchheim Germany

16th Coast Artillery Group (Harbor Defense)

13 Aug 44 redesignated from 16th Coast Artillery Regiment on Hawaii where inactivated 10 Apr 45. It helped operate the Hawaiian quartermaster depot.

Campaigns: *Pacific Theater without inscription*

17th Antiaircraft Artillery Group

20 Jan 43 activated at Cp Edwards Mass as 17th Coast Artillery Group (AA) and redesignated AAA Group 26 May 43; departed United States 18 Jan 44 and arrived in England 31 Jan 44 via Scotland; arrived at Omaha Beach France 25 Jun 44 and defended Hqs SHAEF 24 Aug–23 Sep 44; crossed into Belgium 8 Nov 44 and furnished outer belt protection for Antwerp against German robot bombs; entered Germany 20 Apr 45 and attached to IX Air Force Service Command to disarm German AA guns; inactivated 20 Nov 45 at Bad Neustadt Germany.

Campaigns: *Normandy, Northern France, Rhineland, Central Europe*
Aug 45 Loc: Ober Ursel Germany

17th Coast Artillery Training Group

10 Mar 41 activated at Cp Davis N.C. where inactivated 15 May 42.

18th Coast Artillery Training Group

10 Mar 41 activated at Cp Davis N.C. where inactivated 15 May 42.

18th Antiaircraft Artillery Group

20 Jan 43 activated at Cp Edwards Mass as the 18th Coast Artillery Group (AA) and redesignated 26 May 43; departed New York P/E 23 Dec 43 and arrived in England 29 Dec 43; landed in France 7 Jun 44 and crossed into Belgium 29 Sep 44; protected river crossings over Meuse at Liege and entered Holland 6 Feb 45 and Germany 3 Mar 45; returned to New York P/E and inactivated Cp Kilmer N.J. 11 Dec 45.

Campaigns: *Normandy, Northern France, Rhineland, Ardennes-Alsace, Central Europe*
Aug 45 Loc: Lippstadt Germany

19th Antiaircraft Artillery Group

10 Feb 43 activated at Cp Davis N.C. as the 19th Coast Artillery Group (AA) and redesignated 26 May 43; departed New York P/E 23 Dec 43 and arrived in England 31 Dec 43; arrived at Utah Beach France 17 Jul 44 and engaged in Brittany and Crozon Peninsula; crossed into Belgium 20 Oct 44 and supported Ninth Army; entered Holland 7 Nov 44 and Germany 1 Mar 45; inactivated in Belgium 29 Jun 46.

Campaigns: *Normandy, Northern France, Rhineland, Ardennes-Alsace, Central Europe*
Aug 45 Loc: Goslar Germany

20th Antiaircraft Artillery Group

10 Feb 43 activated at Cp Stewart Ga as 20th Coast Artillery Group (AA) and redesignated 26 May 43; inactivated at Ft Bliss Tex 25 Feb 45.

21st Antiaircraft Artillery Group

10 Feb 43 activated at Ft Bliss Tex as the 21st Coast Artillery Group (AA) and redesignated AAA Group 26 May 43; departed United States 11 Feb 44 and arrived in England 23 Feb 44; landed in France 14 Jul 44 and crossed into Luxembourg 28 Mar 45; entered Germany 7 Apr 45; arrived at New York P/E and inactivated Cp Kilmer N.J. 2 Oct 45.

Campaigns: *Normandy, Northern France, Rhineland, Central Europe*
Aug 45 Loc; Wiesbaden Germany

22nd Antiaircraft Artillery Group

20 Feb 43 activated at Ft Bliss Tex as the 22nd Coast Artillery Group (AA) and redesignated AAA Group 26 May 43; departed New York P/E 1 Mar 44 and arrived in England 7 Mar 44; arrived at Utah Beach France 13 Jul 44 and provided antiaircraft protection there and later Paris; crossed into Belgium 29 Oct 44 and defended Antwerp; moved to Paris 13 Feb 45 where group used for instructor teams throughout ETO in aircraft recognition; inactivated in Germany 30 Oct 45.

Campaigns: *Normandy, Northern France, Rhineland, Ardennes-Alsace*
Aug 45 Loc: Neustadt Germany

23rd Antiaircraft Artillery Group

20 Feb 43 activated at Cp Hulen Tex as the 23rd Coast Artillery Group (AA) and redesignated AAA Group 26 May 43; moved to Cp Livingston La 25 Dec 43 and staged at Cp Shanks N.Y. 2 Feb 44 until departed New York P/E 11 Feb 44; arrived in England 18 Feb 44 and landed in France 13 Jul 44; entered Germany on 17 Mar 45 and Austria 5 May 45; inactivated in Belgium 30 Apr 46.

Campaigns: *Normandy, Northern France, Rhineland, Ardennes-Alsace, Central Europe*
Aug 45 Loc: Salzburg Austria

24th Antiaircraft Artillery Group

20 Feb 43 activated at Cp Hulen Tex as the 24th Coast Artillery Group (AA) and redesignated AAA Group 26 May 43; departed Boston P/E 28 Feb 44 and arrived in England 8 Mar 44; landed in Utah Beach France 11 Jul 44 and crossed into Belgium 10 Feb 45 and entered Germany 12 Mar 45; arrived at Hampton Roads P/E and inactivated at Cp Patrick Henry Va 23 Oct 45.

Campaigns: *Normandy, Northern France, Rhineland, Ardennes-Alsace, Central Europe*
Aug 45 Loc: Mulhausen Germany

25th Antiaircraft Artillery Group

20 Feb 43 activated at Cp Haan Calif as the 25th Coast Artillery Group (AA) and redesignated AAA Group 26 May 43; departed United States 16 Jun 44 and arrived at Finschhafen New Guinea 5 Jul 44 where attached to X Corps; assaulted Leyte Philippines 20 Oct 44 where protected corps installations; inactivated in Philippines 10 Dec 45.

Campaigns: *New Guinea, Bismarck Archipelago, Leyte*
Aug 45 Loc: Tacloban Philippine Islands

26th Antiaircraft Artillery Group

10 Mar 43 activated at Cp Stewart Ga as the 26th Coast Artillery Group (AA) and redesignated AAA Group 26 May 43; departed United States 1 Mar 44 and arrived in England 7 Mar 44; landed in France 5 Jul 44 and crossed into Luxembourg 6 Oct 44 and into Holland 22 Oct 44; entered Germany 2 Mar 45; arrived at New York P/E and inactivated at Cp Kilmer N.J. 26 Oct 45.

Campaigns: *Normandy, Northern France, Rhineland, Central Europe*
Aug 45 Loc: Bad Lippsprings Germany

27th Antiaircraft Artillery Group

20 Mar 43 activated at Cp Stewart Ga as the 27th Coast Artillery Group (AA) and redesignated AAA Group 26 May 43; departed United States 24 Mar 44 and arrived in England 5 Apr 44 via Scotland; landed in France 20 Jul 44 and crossed into Luxembourg 22 Dec 44 and entered Germany 24 Feb 45; arrived at New York P/E and inactivated at Cp Kilmer N.J. 4 Jan 46.

Campaigns: *Normandy, Northern France, Rhineland, Ardennes-Alsace, Central Europe*
Aug 45 Loc: Ruhmannsfelden Germany

28th Antiaircraft Artillery Group

20 Mar 43 activated at Ft Bliss Tex and moved to Ontario Army Airfield Calif 19 Sep 43; transferred to Cp Cooke Calif 21 Jan 44, to Cp Haan Calif 14 Aug 44, and staged at Ft Lawton Wash 6 Nov 44 until departed Seattle P/E 12 Nov 44; arrived in Hawaii 17 Nov 44 where inactivated 31 Dec 45. Group was first organized as 28th Coast Artillery Group and redesignated AAA Group 26 May 43.

Campaigns: *Pacific Theater without inscription*
Aug 45 Loc: Fort Shafter, Hawaii

29th Antiaircraft Artillery Group

20 Mar 43 activated at Cp Stewart Ga as the 29th Coast Artillery Group (AA) and redesignated AAA Group 26 May 43; departed United States 7 Apr 44 and arrived in England 16 Apr 44; landed in France 4 Jul 44 and entered Belgium 9 Dec 44 and Germany only after the war; arrived at New York P/E and inactivated at Cp Kilmer N.J. 3 Dec 45.

Campaigns: *Normandy, Northern France, Rhineland, Ardennes-Alsace*
Aug 45 Loc: Liega Germany

440

30th Antiaircraft Artillery Group

30 Apr 43 activated at Cp Davis N.C. and departed New York P/E 23 Jul 44; arrived in Scotland 28 Jul 44 and moved immediately to England, operated flying bomb defenses in England 6 Aug–9 Sep 44; landed in France at Omaha Beach 28 Sep 44 and protected shipping at both Utah and Omaha beaches against flying bombs until moved to Belgium 23 Oct 44 where defended Antwerp against pilotless aircraft; entered Germany 24 Apr 45 where inactivated 14 Dec 45.

Campaigns: *Rhineland*
Aug 45 Loc: Schifferstadt Germany

31st Antiaircraft Artillery Group

30 Apr 43 activated at Cp Stewart Ga and departed United States 11 Aug 44; arrived in England 22 Aug 44 and landed at Utah Beach France 21 Sep 44 where assigned to IX Air Defense Command 10 Oct 44; moved into Belgium 16 Oct 44 and entered Germany 12 Apr 45 where defended various Rhine River crossings including Remagen; inactivated in Germany 20 Sep 46.

Campaigns: *Rhineland*
Aug 45 Loc: Bad Godesburg Germany

32nd Antiaircraft Artillery Group

30 Apr 43 activated at Cp Stewart Ga and departed New York P/E 6 Oct 44; arrived in England 18 Oct 44 and landed at Rouen France 27 Nov 44; crossed into Luxembourg 19 Dec 44 and into Belgium 20 Dec 44 where defended Bastogne against German air activity 28–31 Dec 44; entered Germany 8 Mar 45 where inactivated 30 Mar 46.

Campaigns: *Rhineland, Ardennes-Alsace, Central Europe*
Aug 45 Loc: Aachen Germany

33rd Antiaircraft Artillery Group

20 Apr 43 activated at Ft Bliss Tex and departed United States 22 Mar 44; arrived in New Guinea 20 Apr 44 and landed on Biak Island 1 Apr 45; moved to Philippines 17 Jul 45 where inactivated 10 Dec 45.

Campaigns: *New Guinea*
Aug 45 Loc: San Fernando, Philippine Islands

34th Antiaircraft Artillery Group

20 Apr 43 activated at Cp Hulen Tex and departed New York P/E 24 Jul 44; arrived in England 31 Jul 44 and landed in France 28 Aug 44; crossed into Holland 27 Dec 44 and into Belgium 28 Jan 45; returned to France 28 Jan 45 to protect lines of communication at Sarre Union-Bining; entered Germany 21 Mar 45 where inactivated 1 Jun 46.

Campaigns: *Northern France, Rhineland, Central Europe*
Aug 45 Loc: Heidenheim Germany

35th Antiaircraft Artillery Group

20 Apr 43 activated at Cp Haan Calif and departed San Francisco P/E 22 Apr 44; arrived at Finschhafen New Guinea 15 May 44 where functioned as a training agency for battalions and conducted antiaircraft schools and technical experiments for the 14th AA Command; arrived in Philippines 11 Mar 45 where furnished protection for Lingayen area; arrived in Japan 4 Nov 45 where inactivated 28 Feb 46.

Campaigns: *New Guinea, Luzon*
Aug 45 Loc: Binmaley Philippine Islands

36th Antiaircraft Artillery Group

30 Apr 43 activated at Cp Haan Calif and departed United States 6 Dec 44; arrived at Oahu Hawaii 11 Dec 44 and moved to Aiea 20 Dec 44; relocated to Hickam Field Oahu Hawaii 25 Jan 45 and was inactivated in Hawaii 15 May 46.

Campaigns: *Pacific Theater without inscription*
Aug 45 Loc: Hickam Field Hawaii

37th Antiaircraft Artillery Group

20 Apr 43 activated at Cp Haan Calif and moved to Santa Maria Army Air Base Calif 10 Nov 43; transferred to Cp Irwin Calif 10 Feb 44 and to Cp Haan Calif 19 Feb 44 where inactivated 22 Jul 44.

38th Antiaircraft Artillery Group

30 Apr 43 activated at Cp Edwards Mass and departed United States 20 Aug 44; arrived in England 28 Aug 44 and landed in France 21 Sep 44; crossed into Belgium 20 Oct 44 and into Holland 2 Mar 45; entered Germany 9 Mar 45 where inactivated 1 Jun 46.

Campaigns: *Rhineland, Ardennes-Alsace, Central Europe*
Aug 45 Loc: Wewelsburg Germany

39th Antiaircraft Artillery Group

10 May 43 activated at Cp Haan Calif and inactivated there 11 Dec 44.

40th Antiaircraft Artillery Group

10 May 43 activated at Cp Haan Calif where inactivated 29 Jul 44.

41st Antiaircraft Artillery Group

24 May 43 activated at Cp Haan Calif and inactivated at Cp Livingston La 24 Dec 44.

42nd Antiaircraft Artillery Group

24 May 43 activated at Cp Haan Calif and inactivated at Cp Howze Tex 13 Dec 44.

43rd Antiaircraft Artillery Group

20 May 43 activated at Cp Davis N.C. and departed United States 15 Nov 44; arrived in Hawaii 24 Nov 44 and landed on Okinawa 10 Jul 45 where inactivated 30 Jan 46.

Campaigns: *Ryukyus*
Aug 45 Loc: Okinawa

44th Antiaircraft Artillery Group

20 May 43 activated at Cp Stewart Ga and moved to Richmond Army Air Base Va 7 Dec 43; departed Seattle P/E 15 Nov 44 and arrived at Honolulu Hawaii 23 Nov 44 and later served at Cp Malakole Hawaii; landed on Ie Shima Island 7 Jun 45 and Zamami Shima Island 11 Jun 45; arrived on Okinawa 13 Aug 45 where served until inactivated there 30 Jun 46.

Campaigns: *Ryukyus*
Aug 45 Loc: Okinawa

45th Antiaircraft Artillery Group

10 Jun 43 activated at Ft Sheridan Ill and moved to Ft Bliss Tex 4 Sep 43 and to Tenn Maneuver Area 31 Jan 44; transferred to Ft Jackson S.C. 13 Apr 44 and departed New York P/E 11 Aug 44; arrived in England 22 Aug 44 and landed in Normandy France 21 Sep 44; crossed into Belgium 30 Oct 44 and assigned to provide anti-rocket protection to Antwerp approaches, moving to Camp de Brasachaet in direct path of V-1 air routes 1 Jan 45; moved to Wesel on the Rhine 16 Apr 45 to protect bridges; inactivated in Germany 24 Mar 46.

Campaigns: *Rhineland, Central Europe*
Aug 45 Loc: Wesel Germany

46th Antiaircraft Artillery Group

15 Jun 43 activated at Cp Edwards Mass where inactivated 30 Jun 44.

47th Antiaircraft Artillery Group

15 Jun 43 activated at Cp Edwards Mass where inactivated 30 Jun 44.

48th Antiaircraft Artillery Group

10 Jun 43 activated at Cp Edwards Mass and inactivated at Cp Pickett Va 20 Jul 44.

49th Antiaircraft Artillery Group

1 Jun 43 activated at Verona N.J. and inactivated at Cp Edwards Mass 25 Mar 44.

442

50th Antiaircraft Artillery Group

25 Aug 43 activated at Ft Bliss Tex and moved to Orlando Fla 2 Feb 44 and to Cp Gordon Ga 6 Nov 44; inactivated there 15 Nov 44.

51st Antiaircraft Artillery Group

25 Aug 43 activated at Ft Bliss Tex and inactivated at Cp Maxey Tex 4 Nov 44.

53rd Antiaircraft Artillery Group

15 Aug 43 activated at Ft Bliss Tex and inactivated at Cp Maxey Tex 2 Nov 44.

54th Antiaircraft Artillery Group

15 Aug 43 activated at Ft Bliss Tex and inactivated at Cp Maxey Tex 20 Nov 44.

55th Antiaircraft Artillery Group

10 Jul 43 activated at Ft Bliss Tex and inactivated at Cp Maxey Tex 5 Dec 44.

56th Antiaircraft Artillery Group

10 Jul 43 activated at Cp Davis N.C. and inactivated at Cp Gordon Ga 31 Oct 44.

57th Antiaircraft Artillery Group

10 Jul 43 activated at Cp Edwards Mass and inactivated at Cp Maxey Tex 15 Nov 44.

58th Antiaircraft Artillery Group

10 Jul 43 activated at Cp Hulen Tex and moved to Cp Maxey 22 Oct 44 where inactivated 29 Oct 44.

61st Antiaircraft Artillery Group

15 Oct 43 activated at Cp Haan Calif and inactivated there 22 Jul 44.

62nd Antiaircraft Artillery Group

15 Oct 43 activated at Cp Haan Calif and inactivated there 5 Aug 44.

63rd Antiaircraft Artillery Group

10 Sep 43 redesignated from the 63rd Coast Artillery Regiment in Seattle Wash and moved to Ft Bliss Tex 22 Jul 45 where inactivated 5 Sep 45.

64th Antiaircraft Artillery Group

25 Sep 43 activated at Cp Stewart Ga and inactivated at Cp Maxey Tex 15 Nov 44.

65th Antiaircraft Artillery Group

10 May 43 redesignated from 65th Coast Artillery Regiment at Ft Ord Calif and departed San Francisco P/E 24 Jul 43; arrived in Adak Alaska 30 Jul 43 where inactivated 29 Feb 44.

Campaigns: *Aleutian Islands*

66th Antiaircraft Artillery Group

25 Sep 43 activated at Cp Stewart Ga and inactivated at Cp Gordon Ga 22 Nov 44.

67th Antiaircraft Artillery Group

25 Sep 43 activated at Cp Stewart Ga and moved to Cp Campbell Ky 12 Jul 44 where inactivated 14 Jul 44.

68th Antiaircraft Artillery Group

4 Jun 44 redesignated from 68th Coast Artillery Regiment at Anzio Italy and landed at St Raphael France 19 Sep 44; 9 Dec 44 tasked to supervise all Seventh Army Lines of Communications troops and engaged in security of army installations at over 108 locations and remained in that capacity; entered Germany 30 Mar 45; returned to New York P/E 21 Dec 45 and inactivated at Cp Kilmer N.J. 22 Dec 45.

Campaigns: *Rome-Arno, Southern France, Rhineland, Ardennes-Alsace, Central Europe*
Aug 45 Loc: Fussen Germany

69th Antiaircraft Artillery Group

10 Sep 43 redesignated from 69th Coast Artillery Regiment at San Diego Calif and moved to Ft Bliss Tex 6 Mar 44; arrived at Cp Polk La 12 Jun 44 and departed Seattle P/E 13 Jan 45; arrived in Honolulu Hawaii 20 Jan 45 and sent to Saipan where arrived 12 Feb 45 and relieved the 24th Inf Regt in mopping up Japanese forces there 28 Jun–1 Aug 45; inactivated on Saipan 5 Jun 46.

Campaigns: *Western Pacific*
Aug 45 Loc: Saipan

70th Antiaircraft Artillery Group

10 Nov 43 redesignated from 70th Coast Artillery Regiment at Segi Point New Georgia Island and moved to Guadalcanal 20 Feb 44 where constructed a large Antiaircraft Artillery Training Center; landed in New Guinea 24 Nov 44 and in the Philippines 9 Jul 45 where active thru 1946.

Campaigns: *Northern Solomons, Luzon*
Aug 45 Loc: Philippine Islands

71st Antiaircraft Artillery Group

1 Sep 43 redesignated from 71st Coast Artillery Regiment in Washington D.C. and moved to La Maneuver Area 2 Feb 44 and Cp Livingston La 3 May 44; departed New York P/E 24 Aug 44 and landed in England 1 Sep 44; transferred to France 3 Oct 44 and crossed into Belgium 29 Mar 45 and Germany 4 May 45; inactivated in Germany 24 May 46.

Campaigns: *Northern France, Central Europe*
Aug 45 Loc: Mehlem Germany

72nd Antiaircraft Artillery Group

15 Sep 43 activated at Ft Randolph Panama Canal Zone where disbanded 1 Feb 46.

73rd Antiaircraft Artillery Group

15 Sep 43 activated in Panama Canal Zone where disbanded 1 Feb 46.

74th Antiaircraft Artillery Group

1 Apr 44 redesignated from 74th Coast Artillery Regiment at Cagliari Sardinia; moved to Corsica 5 Oct 44; landed in France 11 Nov 44 and inactivated at Marseille 13 Feb 45.

Campaigns: *Rome-Arno*

75th Antiaircraft Artillery Group

20 Feb 44 redesignated from 75th Coast Artillery Regiment at Ft Bliss Tex and moved to Cp Howze Tex 2 Dec 44 where inactivated 12 Dec 44.

76th Antiaircraft Artillery Group (Colored)

1 Nov 43 redesignated from 76th Coast Artillery Regiment at Espiritu Santo, New Hebrides and moved to Russell Islands 10 Jun 44; arrived in New Guinea 2 Jan 45 and Philippines 17 Aug 45; arrived at San Francisco P/E 25 Jan 46 where inactivated at Cp Stoneman Calif 27 Jan 46.

Campaigns: *Pacific Theater without inscription*

444

77th Antiaircraft Artillery Group (Colored)

1 Nov 43 redesignated from 77th Coast Artillery Regiment at Havannah Harbor New Hebrides and moved to Guadalcanal 3 Dec 43; arrived at Munda Point New Georgia 13 Dec 43 and Los Negros Admiralty Islands 8 Feb 45; returned to Los Angeles P/E 30 Dec 45 and inactivated at Cp Anza Calif 31 Dec 45.

Campaigns: *Northern Solomons*
Aug 45 Loc: Admiralty Islands

78th Antiaircraft Artillery Group

7 Feb 44 redesignated from 78th Coast Artillery Regiment on Attu Island; inactivated 3 Feb 44 at Cp Earle Alaska.

79th Antiaircraft Artillery Group

1 Sep 43 redesignated from 79th Coast Artillery Regiment at Manchester Conn and moved to Bradley Field Conn 24 Jul 44; arrived at Ft Bragg N.C. under XXII Corps 11 Aug 44 and inactivated there 24 Aug 44.

80th Antiaircraft Artillery Group

24 Mar 44 redesignated from 62nd Coast Artillery Regiment at Palermo Sicily; moved to Taranto Italy 14 Jul 44 where staged and landed in southern France 16 Aug 44; protected French Army areas and Marseilles during ETO service; inactivated in Germany 14 Dec 45.

Campaigns: *Rome-Arno, Southern France, Rhineland*
Aug 45 Loc: Neustadt Germany

82nd Antiaircraft Artillery Group

15 Sep 43 activated in Panama Canal Zone where inactivated 1 Feb 46.
Campaigns: *American Theater without inscription*

Aug 45 Loc: Fort Gulick Canal Zone

83rd Antiaircraft Artillery Group

15 Sep 43 activated in Panama Canal Zone where inactivated 1 Feb 46.
Campaigns: *American Theater without inscription*
Aug 45 Loc: Fort Clayton Canal Zone

85th Antiaircraft Artillery Group

1 Sep 43 redesignated from 85th Coast Artillery Regiment at Norfolk Va and moved to Cp Butner N.C. 8 Feb 44 under XIII Corps; arrived at Suffolk Co Long Island N.Y. 15 Apr 44 and transferred to Cp Stewart Ga 29 Jun 44; assigned to Replacement & School Command 26 Nov 44 and moved to Cp Livingston La 13 Dec 44 where inactivated 27 Dec 44.

86th Antiaircraft Artillery Group

26 May 44 activated at Ft Kamehameha Hawaii and departed 7 Jun 44; landed on Saipan 27 Jun 44 and inactivated there 15 Jan 46.

Campaigns: *Western Pacific*
Aug 45 Loc: Saipan

87th Antiaircraft Artillery Group

22 Jun 44 activated in Ledo India and disbanded in Burma 9 Jul 45.

Campaigns: *Central Burma*

88th Antiaircraft Artillery Group

15 Sep 43 activated in Panama Canal Zone where inactivated 1 Feb 46.
Campaigns: *American Theater without inscription*
Aug 45 Loc: Fort Gulick Canal Zone

89th Antiaircraft Artillery Group

1 Sep 43 redesignated from 89th Coast Artillery Regiment in Washington D.C. and moved to Ft Bragg N.C. 11 Aug 43 under XVIII Corps; inactivated there 24 Aug 44.

90th Antiaircraft Artillery Group (Colored)

25 May 44 redesignated from the 90th Coast Artillery Regiment in Oran North Africa and inactivated there 5 Dec 44.

Campaigns: *European Theater without inscription*

91st Antiaircraft Artillery Group

23 May 44 redesignated from 67th Coast Artillery Regiment Apollinare Italy and departed Naples Italy 2 Sep 44 and landed at St Tropez France 4 Sep 44; entered Germany 30 Mar 45 where inactivated 1 Jun 46.

Campaigns: *Rome-Arno, Southern France, Rhineland, Ardennes-Alsace, Central Europe*
Aug 45 Loc: Hopferau Germany

92nd Antiaircraft Artillery Group

10 Aug 43 activated in Honiton England from assets of HHB 61st Coast Artillery Regt and landed in France 4 Jul 44; crossed into Germany 8 Apr 45 where inactivated 30 Oct 45.

Campaigns: *Normandy, Northern France, Rhineland, Central Europe*
Aug 45 Loc: Nichelstadt Germany

93rd Antiaircraft Artillery Group

15 Oct 43 activated at Cp Hulen Tex and inactivated at Cp Maxey Tex 21 Nov 44.

94th Antiaircraft Artillery Group

15 May 43 redesignated from 94th Coast Artillery Regiment in Cairns Australia and landed on Goodenough Island 16 Aug 43; assaulted Tanahmerah Bay New Guinea 22 Apr 44 and arrived in Philippines 22 Nov 44 where assaulted Mindoro Island 15 Dec 44; active in Philippines past 1946.

Campaigns: *New Guinea, East Indies, Luzon, Leyte*
Aug 45 Loc: Mindoro Philippines

95th Antiaircraft Artillery Group

15 Oct 43 activated at Cp Stewart Ga and inactivated at Cp Howze Tex 17 Nov 44.

96th Antiaircraft Artillery Group

25 Sep 43 activated at Cp Stewart Ga and inactivated at Cp Gordon Ga 22 Nov 44.

97th Antiaircraft Artillery Group

12 Dec 43 redesignated from 97th Coast Artillery Regiment at Hickam Field Hawaii and departed there 15 Sep 44; assaulted Leyte Philippines 20 Oct 44 and supported 7th Inf Div in vicinity of Dulag airstrip; left Philippines 28 Mar 45 and landed on Okinawa 3 Apr 45 where inactivated 20 Feb 46.

Campaigns: *Leyte, Ryukyus*
Aug 45 Loc: Okinawa

98th Antiaircraft Artillery Group

12 Dec 43 redesignated from 98th Coast Artillery Regiment in Hawaii and served as the searchlight group in the Hawaiian Antiaircraft Artillery Command; small units from the group participated in action in Kwajalein and Eniwetok; remained active at Ft Shafter Hawaii thru 1946.

Campaigns: *Central Pacific*
Aug 45 Loc: Fort Shafter Hawaii

103rd Antiaircraft Artillery Group

5 Jul 43 activated in Orlando Fla and departed United States 6 Oct 44; arrived in England 18 Oct 44 and landed in France 2 Dec 44 and crossed into Belgium 12 Dec 44; entered Germany 8 Mar 45 where inactivated 15 Mar 46.

Campaigns: *Rhineland, Ardennes-Alsace, Central Europe*
Aug 45 Loc: Dillenburg Germany

105th Antiaircraft Artillery Group

20 Jan 43 redesignated from 504th Coast Artillery Regiment at Cp Hulen Tex as the 105th Coast Artillery Group (AA) and moved to Ft Dix N.J. 19 Mar 43; there redesignated as AAA Group 14 Apr 43 and staged at Ft Dix N.J. until departed New York P/E 28 Apr 43; arrived in North Africa 11 May 43 and landed on Sicily 10 Jul 43 in the assault; moved back to North Africa 15 Nov 43 and entered Italy 19 Jun 44; landed in southern France 15 Aug 44 and crossed into Holland 20 Mar 45; entered Germany 23 Apr 45; returned to New York P/E 27 Nov 45 and inactivated at Cp Shanks N.Y. 28 Nov 45.

Campaigns: *Sicily, Rome-Arno, Southern France, Rhineland, Central Europe*
Aug 45 Loc: Munster Germany

106th Antiaircraft Artillery Grou-

20 Jul 43 redesignated from 508th Coast Artillery Regiment at Barrafranca Sicily and moved to Corsica 6 Dec 43; redesignated from 106th Coast Artillery Group to AAA Group at Calvi 26 Jul 44 and landed in France 2 Dec 44 where inactivated 13 Feb 45 at Marseille.

Campaigns: *Sicily, Rome-Arno*

107th Antiaircraft Artillery Group

20 Jan 43 redesignated from 512th Coast Artillery Regiment at Ft Bliss Tex as the 107th Coast Artillery Group (AA) and moved to Cp Pickett Va 26 Mar 43; there redesignated as AAA Group 14 Apr 43 and staged at Cp Patrick Henry Va 26 May 43 until departed Hampton Roads P/E 3 Jun 43; arrived in Africa 22 Jun 43 and assaulted Sicily 9 Jul 43; landed in Italy 5 Nov 43 where inactivated 30 Sep 45.

Campaigns: *Sicily, Naples-Foggia, Rome-Arno, North Apennines*
Aug 45 Loc: Poggio Adorno Italy

108th Antiaircraft Artillery Group

26 May 43 redesignated from the 514th Coast Artillery Regiment at Cp Davis N.C. and moved to Cp Stewart Ga 14 Oct 43; staged at Cp Shanks N.Y. 22 Dec 43 until departed New York P/E 28 Dec 43; arrived in England 7 Jan 44 and landed in France 28 Jun 44; entered Germany 2 May 45 where inactivated 14 Dec 45.

Campaigns: *Normandy, Northern France, Rhineland, Central Europe*
Aug 45 Loc: Kaufhueren Germany

109th Antiaircraft Artillery Group

20 Jan 43 redesignated from the 86th Coast Artillery Regiment at Cp Haan Calif as the 109th Coast Artillery Group (AA) and redesignated there as AAA Group 26 May 43; moved to Cp Polk La 12 Jun 43 and staged at Cp Kilmer N.J. 16 Nov 43 until departed New York P/E 3 Dec 43; arrived in England 9 Dec 43 and assaulted Normandy France 6 Jun 44; crossed into Belgium 5 Sep 44 and first entered Germany 16 Sep 44; returned to Belgium 22 Dec 44 and reentered Germany 5 Feb 45; went back to Belgium 23 Apr 45; arrived at Hampton Roads P/E 2 Nov 45 and inactivated at Cp Patrick Henry Va same date.

Campaigns: *Normandy, Northern France, Rhineland, Ardennes-Alsace, Central Europe*
Aug 45 Loc: Verviers France

110th Antiaircraft Artillery Group

15 Jan 43 redesignated from 506th Coast Artillery Regiment at Cp Edwards Mass as the 110th Coast Artillery Group (AA) and moved to Ft Brady Mich 5 Apr 43; there redesignated AAA Group 26 May 43 and moved to Cp Edwards Mass 27 Sep 43; went to Tenn Maneuver Area 14 Jan 44 and to Farmingdale Army Air Base Long Island N.Y. 25 Apr 44; arrived at Cp Butner N.C. 12 Sep 44 where inactivated 11 Jan 45.

111th Antiaircraft Artillery Group

20 Jan 43 redesignated from 509th Coast Artillery Regiment at Ft Bliss Tex as the 111th Coast Artillery Group (AA) and redesignated there as AAA Group 26 May 43; moved to McMinnville Tenn 6 Jun 43 and to Cp Butner N.C. 20 Aug 43; staged at Cp Kilmer N.J. 15 Dec 43 until departed New York P/E 29 Dec 43; arrived in England 10 Jan 44 and landed in France 14 Mar 45; entered Germany 8 Apr 45; returned to New York P/E 21 Feb 46 and inactivated at Cp Kilmer N.J. 22 Feb 46.

Campaigns: *European Theater without inscription*
Aug 45 Loc: Trier Germany

112th Antiaircraft Artillery Group

20 Jan 43 redesignated from 510th Coast Artillery Regiment at Ft Sheridan Ill as 112th Coast Artillery Group (AA) and redesignated as AAA Group there 26 May 43; moved to Cp Atterbury Ind 8 Jun 43 and to Tenn Maneuver Area 21 Jun 43; arrived at Cp Campbell Ky 28 Aug 43 and staged at Cp Shanks N.Y. 8 Nov 43 until departed New York P/E 17 Nov 43; arrived in England 24 Nov 43 and landed in France 20 Jul 44; entered Germany 18 Mar 45 and Austria 5 May 45; arrived at Hampton Roads P/E 18 Oct 45 and inactivated at Cp Patrick Henry Va same date.

Campaigns: *Normandy, Northern France, Rhineland, Ardennes-Alsace, Central Europe*
Aug 45 Loc: Pfarrkirchen Germany

113th Antiaircraft Artillery Group

20 Jan 43 redesignated from 511th Coast Artillery Regiment at Cp Haan Calif as 113th Coast Artillery Group (AA) and redesignated there as AAA Group 26 May 43; moved to Cp Adair Oreg 6 Jul 43 and staged at Cp Myles Standish Mass 6 Jan 44 until departed Boston P/E 18 Jan 44; landed in France 30 Jun 44 and crossed into Belgium 29 Sep 44 and into Luxembourg 1 Oct 44; returned to Belgium 18 Dec 44 and entered Germany 6 Mar 45; returned to Boston P/E 15 Nov 45 and inactivated at Cp Myles Standish Mass 17 Nov 45.

Campaigns: *Normandy, Northern France, Rhineland, Ardennes-Alsace, Central Europe*
Aug 45 Loc: Eisenach Germany

114th Antiaircraft Artillery Group

20 Jan 43 redesignated from 513th Coast Artillery Regiment at Ft Bliss Tex as 114th Coast Artillery Group (AA) and moved to Cp Young Calif 11 Feb 43; there redesignated as AAA Group 15 Jun 43 and moved to Richmond Va 28 Aug 43; stationed at Cp Stewart Ga 17 Dec 43 and staged at Cp Myles Standish Mass 18 Feb 44 until departed Boston P/E 27 Feb 44; landed in England 8 Mar 44 and in France 12 Jul 44 where defended Utah Beach until 6 Oct 44 when transferred to protect Le Havre; moved to Plailly France 21 Jan 45 and established firing range; entered Germany 28 Mar 45 where inactivated 29 Dec 45.

Campaigns: *Normandy, Northern France, Rhineland*
Aug 45 Loc: Neustadt, Germany

115th Antiaircraft Artillery Group

20 Jan 43 redesignated from 606th Coast Artillery Regiment at Cp Edwards Mass as 115th Coast Artillery Group (AA) and moved to Cp Gordon Johnston Fla 29 Apr 43; arrived at Tenn Maneuver Area 27 May 43 where redesignated AAA Group 13 Jun 43 and moved to Cp Pickett Va 28 Jun 43; staged at Cp Myles Standish Mass 11 Oct 43 until departed Boston P/E 6 Nov 43; arrived in England 16 Nov 43 and landed in France 13 Jun 44; crossed into Belgium 9 Sep 44 and into Luxembourg 16 Sep 44; returned to Belgium 4 Oct 44 and entered Germany 6 Mar 45; entered Czechoslovakia 8 May 45; arrived in New York P/E 25 Oct 45 and inactivated at Cp Kilmer N.J. 26 Oct 45.

Campaigns: *Normandy, Northern France, Rhineland, Ardennes-Alsace, Central Europe*
Aug 45 Loc: Pilsen Czechoslovakia

116th Antiaircraft Artillery Group

20 Jan 43 redesignated from 607th Coast Artillery Regiment at Cp Hulen Tex as the 116th Coast Artillery Group (AA) and moved to Cp Cooke Calif 2 Mar 43; there redesignated as AAA Group 9 Jun 43 and staged at Cp Stoneman Calif 28 Sep 43 until departed San Francisco P/E 27 Oct 43; arrived in Australia 13 Nov 43 and landed on Kiriwina Island 16 Dec 43; landed in New Guinea 6 Apr 44 and assaulted Hollandia New Guinea 22 Apr 44; assaulted Noemfoor Island 2 Jul 44 and landed in Philippines 6 Apr 45 and assaulted Malabang 17 Apr 45; inactivated in Philippines 20 Jan 46.

Campaigns: *New Guinea, Luzon, Southern Philippines*
Aug 45 Loc: Cotabato Philippine Islands

117th Antiaircraft Artillery Group

20 Jan 43 redesignated from 608th Coast Artillery Regiment at Ft Bliss Tex as 117th Coast Artillery Group (AA) and redesignated there as AAA Group 20 May 43; staged at Cp Stoneman Calif 21 Jul 43 until departed San Francisco P/E 16 Aug 43; arrived in Guadalcanal 5 Sep 43 and New Guinea 17 Dec 44; arrived in Philippines 29 Aug 45 where inactivated 10 Feb 46.

Campaigns: *Pacific Theater without inscription*
Aug 45 Loc: Finschhafen New Guinea

448

118th Antiaircraft Artillery Group

20 Jan 43 redesignated from 609th Coast Artillery Regiment at Cp Edwards Mass as 118th Coast Artillery Group (AA) and redesignated there as AAA Group 26 May 43; moved to Tenn Maneuver Area 11 Oct 43 and to Cp Forrest Tenn 5 Nov 43; staged at Cp Kilmer N.J. 28 Dec 43 until departed New York P/E 4 Jan 44; arrived in England 14 Jan 44 and landed in France 24 Jul 44 on Omaha Beach; defended airfields of IX Tactical Air Command and crossed into Belgium 5 Oct 44 and into Germany 4 Apr 45; inactivated in France 20 Nov 45.

Campaigns: *Normandy, Northern France, Rhineland, Central Europe*
Aug 45 Loc: Chamonix Belgium

119th Antiaircraft Artillery Group

20 Jan 43 redesignated from 610th Coast Artillery Regiment at Cp Davis N.C. as the 119th Coast Artillery Group (AA) and redesignated there as AAA Group 26 May 43, staged at Cp Stoneman Calif 12 Sep 43 until departed San Francisco P/E 18 Sep 43; arrived in Fiji Islands 2 Oct 43 and transferred to New Guinea 30 Nov 44; arrived in Philippines 13 Mar 45 where inactivated 10 Dec 45.

Campaigns: *Luzon*
Aug 45 Loc: San Fernando Philippine Islands

120th Antiaircraft Artillery Group

20 Jan 43 redesignated from 611th Coast Artillery Regiment at Ft Bliss Tex as the 120th Coast Artillery Group (AA) and redesignated there as AAA Group 26 May 43; moved to Cp Polk La 5 Jun 43 and staged at Cp Stoneman Calif 29 Jan 43 until departed San Francisco P/E 27 Oct 43; arrived at Sydney Australia 13 Nov 43 and landed at Finschhafen New Guinea 20 Mar 44 and departed 9 Dec 44; arrived at Tarragona Leyte Philippines 8 Jan 45 and landed in Luzon Philippines 29 Jan 45 where inactivated 30 Jan 46.

Campaigns: *New Guinea, Leyte, Luzon*
Aug 45 Loc: Clark Field Philippine Islands

121st Coast Artillery Group (Antiaircraft) (Colored)

20 Jan 43 redesignated from 612th Coast Artillery Regiment at Cp Stewart Ga where inactivated 2 Apr 43.

122nd Coast Artillery Group (Antiaircraft) (Colored)

20 Jan 43 redesignated from 613th Coast Artillery Regiment at Cp Stewart Ga where inactivated 2 Apr 43.

123rd Antiaircraft Artillery Group

28 Nov 44 activated at Cp Malakole Hawaii from assets of the 70th AAA Brigade; moved to Pearl Harbor area 9 Dec 44; inactivated in Hawaii on 31 Dec 45.

Campaigns: *Pacific Theater without inscription*
Aug 45 Loc: Hickam Field Hawaii

124th Antiaircraft Artillery Group

15 Oct 43 activated at Cp Davis N.C. and inactivated at Cp Gordon Ga 31 Oct 44.

134th Antiaircraft Artillery Group

28 Oct 43 activated on Iceland using assets of the 47th AAA Brigade; arrived at New York P/E 14 Jun 45 and moved to Cp Kilmer N.J. where inactivated 16 Jun 45.

Campaigns: *European Theater without inscription*

135th Antiaircraft Artillery Group

6 Nov 43 redesignated from 66th Coast Artillery Regiment at Ft Brooke Puerto Rico and arrived at New York P/E 4 Dec 43; arrived at Cp Stewart Ga 9 Dec 43 and Cp Gordon Ga 20 Oct 44 where inactivated 31 Oct 44.

136th Antiaircraft Artillery Group

12 Dec 43 redesignated from 64th Coast Artillery Regiment at Ft Shafter Hawaii and departed 27 Mar 45; arrived on Okinawa 26 Apr 45 and moved to Ie Shima Island 12 May 45; active on Okinawa past 1946.

Campaigns: *Ryukyus*
Aug 45 Loc: Ie Shima Island

137th Antiaircraft Artillery Group

12 Dec 43 redesignated from 93rd Coast Artillery Regiment on Hawaii and departed Oahu 7 Apr 45; arrived at Eniwetok 15 Apr 45 and Ulithi Atoll 28 Apr 45; landed on Okinawa 3 May 45 and protected harbor of Naha; inactivated in Korea 25 Feb 46.

Campaigns: *Ryukyus*
Aug 45 Loc: Okinawa

138th Antiaircraft Artillery Group

12 Dec 43 redesignated from 95th Coast Artillery Regiment on Hawaii and departed 24 Jan 45; landed on Iwo Jima 19 Feb 45 and active in Japan past 1946.

Campaigns: *Air Offensive Japan*
Aug 45 Loc: Iwo Jima

139th Antiaircraft Artillery Group

12 Dec 43 redesignated from 96th Coast Artillery Regiment on Hawaii and departed 23 Jan 44; landed on Kwajalein Atoll Marshall Islands 6 Feb 44 where remained until 20 Feb 45; returned to Hawaii 20 Feb 45 where inactivated 10 Dec 46.

Campaigns: *Eastern Mandates*
Aug 45 Loc: Camp Malakole Hawaii

140th Antiaircraft Artillery Group

1 Dec 43 redesignated from 614th Coast Artillery Regiment at Cp Stewart Ga and moved to Cp Gordon Ga 1 Nov 44 where inactivated 8 Nov 44.

141st Coast Artillery Group (155mm Gun)

20 May 44 activated on New Caledonia and landed at Hollandia New Guinea 8 Jan 45; arrived at San Marcelino Luzon Philippines 30 Aug 45 and disbanded there 6 Dec 45.

Campaigns: *New Guinea, Luzon*
Aug 45 Loc: Luzon Philippine Islands

142nd Coast Artillery Group (155mm Gun)

20 May 44 activated on Guadalcanal and moved to Milne Bay New Guinea on 25 Jul 44; landed in the Philippines 1 Mar 45 and disbanded there 31 May 46.

Campaigns: *New Guinea, Luzon*
Aug 45 Loc: Manila Philippines

143rd Coast Artillery Group (155mm Gun)

31 May 44 activated at Kawailoa Hawaii from HHB 57th Coast Artillery Regt; inactivated on Sand Island Hawaii 31 Dec 45.

Campaigns: *Pacific Theater without inscription*
Aug 45 Loc: Schofield Barracks Hawaii

144th Coast Artillery Group (155mm Gun)

31 May 44 activated at Ft Ruger Hawaii and sent to New Caledonia where arrived 22 Feb 45; arrived on Okinawa 23 Jun 45 where inactivated 10 Oct 45.

Campaigns: *Ryukyus*
Aug 45 Loc: Okinawa

145th Coast Artillery Group (155mm Gun)

1 Jun 44 redesignated from 51st Coast Artillery Regiment at Port-of-Spain Trinidad where disbanded 28 Feb 46.

Campaigns: *American Theater without inscription*
Aug 45 Loc: Port-of-Spain Trinidad British West Indies

152nd Coast Artillery Group (155mm Gun) (Colored)

5 Jun 44 redesignated from 54th Coast Artillery Regiment at Ft Ord Calif and moved to Cp Livingston La 16 Jul 44 under XXI Corps where disbanded 3 Aug 44.

153rd Coast Artillery Group (155mm Gun)

12 Jun 44 redesignated from 53rd Coast Artillery Regiment at Cp Pendleton Va and moved to Ft Bragg N.C. 4 Aug 44 with XXII Corps; there redesignated as 153rd Field Artillery Group 14 Aug 44.

155th Antiaircraft Artillery Group

12 May 43 activated in Panama Canal Zone and inactivated in Puerto Rico 1 Jun 44.

Campaigns: *American Theater without inscription*

197th Antiaircraft Artillery Group

15 May 43 redesignated from 197th Coast Artillery Regiment at Townsville Australia and moved to New Guinea 13 Jul 43 and departed 28 Dec 44; assaulted Lingayen Gulf Philippines 9 Jan 45; returned to San Francisco P/E 26 Dec 45 and inactivated at Cp Stoneman Calif 28 Dec 45.

Campaigns: *New Guinea, Luzon*
Aug 45 Loc: Luzon Philippines

198th Antiaircraft Artillery Group

1 Mar 44 redesignated from 198th Coast Artillery Regiment in the Treasury Islands and moved to Bougainville 30 Sep 44; departed 19 Feb 45 and landed in Philippines 5 Mar 45; arrived at San Francisco P/E 24 Dec 45 and inactivated at Cp Anza Calif same date.

Campaigns: *Northern Solomons, Leyte*
Aug 45 Loc: Dulag Philippine Islands

202nd Antiaircraft Artillery Group

10 Sep 43 redesignated from 202nd Coast Artillery Regiment at Bremerton Wash and moved to Cp Haan Calif 3 Jun 44; transferred to Esler Field La 3 Sep 44 and to Cp Howze Tex 8 Nov 44 where inactivated 17 Nov 44.

203rd Antiaircraft Artillery Group

26 Jan 44 redesignated from 203rd Coast Artillery Regiment at Amchitka Aleutians Alaska; arrived at Seattle P/E 21 Aug 44 and arrived at Cp Bowie Tex 30 Aug 44 where inactivated 11 Oct 44.

204th Antiaircraft Artillery Group

10 Sep 43 redesignated from 204th Coast Artillery Regiment at San Diego Calif and moved to Ft Bliss Tex 4 Aug 45 where inactivated 5 Sep 45.

Aug 45 Loc: Fort Bliss Texas

205th Antiaircraft Artillery Group

10 Sep 43 redesignated from 205th Coast Artillery Regiment at Santa Monica Calif and moved to Cp Bowie Tex 20 Aug 44 under XXIII Corps where inactivated 24 Aug 44.

207th Antiaircraft Artillery Group

21 Apr 43 redesignated from the 207th Coast Artillery Regiment at Cp Edwards Mass and moved to Farmingdale Army Airfield N.Y. 14 Aug 43; transferred to Cp Davis N.C. 10 Oct 43 and staged at Cp Shanks N.Y. 5 Feb 44 until departed New York P/E 11 Feb 44; arrived in England 23 Feb 44 and landed on Omaha Beach France 9 Jun 44; crossed into Luxembourg 4 Feb 45 and entered Germany 30 Mar 45; arrived at Boston P/E 21 Dec 45 and inactivated at Cp Myles Standish Mass 22 Dec 45.

Campaigns: *Normandy, Northern France, Rhineland, Ardennes-Alsace, Central Europe*
Aug 45 Loc: Abansberg Germany

208th Antiaircraft Artillery Group

15 May 43 redesignated from 208th Coast Artillery Regiment in Townsville Australia and moved to New Guinea 13 Jul 43; designated Hqs of HURRICANE Task Force AA units and assaulted Biak Island 27 May 44; left Biak Island 1 Dec 45 and arrived in the Philippines 9 Dec 45; arrived at San Francisco P/E 17 Jan 46 and inactivated at Cp Stoneman Calif 16 Jan 46.

Campaigns: *New Guinea, East Indies*
Aug 45 Loc: Biak Island

209th Antiaircraft Artillery Group

14 Mar 44 redesignated from 209th Coast Artillery Regiment at Arpaia Italy and inactivated 15 Oct 45 in Italy.

Campaigns: *Rome-Arno, Po Valley, North Apennines*
Aug 45 Loc: Loiano Italy

210th Antiaircraft Artillery Group

14 Feb 44 redesignated from 210th Coast Artillery Regiment on Adak Island Aleutians Alaska and departed 9 Aug 44; arrived at Seattle P/E 20 Aug 44 and moved to Cp Haan Calif 28 Aug 44 and to Cp Howze Tex 22 Oct 44 where inactivated 1 Nov 44.

Campaigns: *Pacific Theater without inscription*

211th Antiaircraft Artillery Group

10 Sep 43 redesignated from 211th Coast Artillery Regiment at Vallejo Calif and moved to San Francisco Calif 20 Apr 44 under XXIII Corps; arrived at Cp Bowie Tex 22 Aug 44 where inactivated 24 Aug 44.

212th Antiaircraft Artillery Group

10 Sep 43 redesignated from 212th Coast Artillery Regiment at Paine Field Seattle Wash and staged at Ft Lawton Wash 15 Jul 44 until departed Seattle P/E 23 Jul 44; arrived at Adak Island Aleutians 3 Aug 44 and moved to Shemya Island November 44; inactivated there 3 Feb 45.

Campaigns: *Pacific Theater without inscritpion*

213th Antiaircraft Artillery Group

1 Apr 44 redesignated from 213th Coast Artillery Regiment at Bains de Puzzichello Corsica and landed in France 22 Aug 44; entered Germany 10 Apr 45 where inactivated 20 Nov 45.

Campaigns: *Rome-Arno, Southern France, Rhineland, Central Europe*
Aug 45 Loc: Heidelberg Germany

214th Antiaircraft Artillery Group

11 Nov 43 redesignated from 214th Coast Artillery Regiment on Guadalcanal which departed 26 Dec 43; arrived at Takapuna New Zealand 31 Dec 43 and landed at Finschhafen New Guinea 22 Jun 44; landed at Toem New Guinea 14 Aug 44 and left 11 Sep 44; landed on Morotai Island 15 Sep 44 where practiced amphibious landings; arrived in Philippines 8 Dec 45 and arrived at San Francisco P/E 17 Jan 46; inactivated at Cp Stoneman Calif 19 Jan 46.

Campaigns: *Guadalcanal, New Guinea*
Aug 45 Loc: Morotai

216th Antiaircraft Artillery Group

10 Sep 43 redesignated from 216th Coast Artillery Regiment in San Francisco Calif and moved to Cp Haan Calif 15 Apr 44; transferred to Cp Howze Tex 18 Nov 44 where inactivated 23 Nov 44.

217th Antiaircraft Artillery Group

10 Sep 43 redesignated from 217th Coast Artillery Regiment at Oakland-Berkeley Calif and moved to Cp Bowie Tex 20 Aug 44 where inactivated 24 Aug 44.

251st Antiaircraft Artillery Group

1 Mar 44 redesignated from 251st Coast Artillery Regiment on Bougainville under XIV Corps; left 11 Dec 44 and after brief stopovers at Lae New Guinea and Manus Admiralty Islands arrived at Lingayen Gulf Philippines 9 Jan 45; moved to Manila 8 Mar 45 where charged with protection of Manila area; arrived at San Francisco P/E 26 Dec 45 and inactivated at Cp Stoneman Calif 29 Dec 45.

Campaigns: *Luzon*
Aug 45 Loc: Manila Philippine Islands

260th Antiaircraft Artillery Group

10 Sep 43 redesignated from 260th Coast Artillery Regiment at McChord Field Wash and moved to Ft Bliss Tex 3 Jun 44; arrived at Cp Maxey Tex 24 Oct 44 where inactivated 9 Nov 44.

369th Antiaircraft Artillery Group (Colored)

12 Dec 43 redesignated from 369th Coast Artillery Regiment in Hawaii where inactivated 28 Nov 44.

Campaigns: *Pacific Theater without inscription*

501st Antiaircraft Artillery Group

10 Sep 43 redesignated from 501st Coast Artillery Regiment at San Francisco Calif and moved to Cp Haan Calif 11 Apr 44 where inactivated 22 Jul 44.

502nd Antiaircraft Artillery Group

1 Sep 43 redesignated from 502nd Coast Artillery Regiment at Paterson N.J. and moved to New York N.Y. 10 Feb 44; arrived at Ft Bragg N.C. 10 Aug 44 where inactivated 24 Aug 44.

505th Antiaircraft Artillery Group

14 Mar 44 redesignated from 505th Coast Artillery Regiment at Santa Maria Italy and moved to Naples Italy 1 Sep 44 where commenced infantry training; arrived in France at Toulon 28 Oct 44 and served as Delta Base Section advisor for AAA units 17 Nov 44 until disbanded at Marseille France 13 Feb 45.

Campaigns: *Naples-Foggia, Rome-Arno*

507th Antiaircraft Artillery Group

10 Sep 43 redesignated from 507th Coast Artillery Regiment at North Long Beach Calif and moved to Cp Haan Calif; arrived at Cp Howze Tex 10 Nov 44 where inactivated 17 Nov 44.

601st Antiaircraft Artillery Group

1 Sep 43 redesignated from 601st Coast Artillery Regiment at Philadelphia Pa and moved to Cp Davis N.C. 2 Mar 44 where inactivated 31 Aug 44.

602nd Antiaircraft Artillery Group

1 Sep 43 redesignated from 602nd Coast Artillery Regiment at New York N.Y. and moved to Cp Davis N.C. 18 Mar 44; transferred to Farmingdale Army Air Base N.Y. 6 Sep 44; arrived at Cp Gordon Ga 14 Dec 44 where inactivated 22 Dec 44.

603rd Antiaircraft Artillery Group

10 Sep 43 redesignated from 603rd Coast Artillery Regiment at Culver City Calif and moved to Los Angeles Calif 24 Jul 44 and to Muroc Calif 22 Jan 45; returned to Los Angeles 21 Apr 45 and arrived at Ft Bliss Tex 5 Aug 45 where inactivated 5 Sep 45.

Aug 45 Loc: Fort Bliss Texas

604th Antiaircraft Artillery Group

1 Sep 43 redesignated from 604th Coast Artillery Regiment at New York–Bayonne N.J. vicinity; moved to Cp Davis N.C. 18 Mar 44 and to Cp Polk La 11 Aug 44; staged at Cp Stoneman Calif 15 Jan 45 until departed San Francisco Calif 20 Jan 45; arrived in New Guinea 4 Feb 45 where disbanded 18 Mar 45.

Campaigns: *Pacific Theater without inscription*

605th Antiaircraft Artillery Group

1 Sep 43 redesignated from 605th Coast Artillery Regiment at Boston Mass and moved to Cp Edwards Mass 1 Mar 44 where disbanded 25 Mar 44.

615th Antiaircraft Artillery Group

15 Sep 43 activated in Panama Canal Zone and inactivated there 1 Feb 46.

Campaigns: *American Theater without inscription*

Aug 45 Loc: Fort Clayton Canal Zone

701st Antiaircraft Artillery Group

1 Sep 43 redesignated from 701st Coast Artillery Regiment at Newport R.I. and moved to Ft Dix N.J. under XVIII Corps 9 Jul 44; inactivated there 18 Aug 44.

Chapter 36

Coast Artillery Regiments

Regiments:

1–11, 13–16, 18–23, 30, 31, 35, 36, 39–41, 46–79, 82–100, 196–198, 200–217, 240–246, 248–253, 260, 261, 263, 265, 369, 428, 501–515, 601–615, 625, 701, Provisional

1st Coast Artillery Regiment (Harbor Defense) (Type C)

Stationed at Ft Sherman Panama Canal Zone and 3rd Bn activated 15 Mar 40; 1st and 2nd Bns activated 17 Apr 42; regimental assets used to form 1st CA Battalion and other components in area and HHB designated there as HHB 1st Coast Artillery Group 1 Nov 44.

Campaigns: *American Theater without inscription*

2nd Coast Artillery Regiment (Harbor Defense) (Type B)

Stationed at Ft Monroe Va under Harbor Defenses of Chesapeake Bay and upgraded to Type A in 1941; regiment, less 2nd Bn, redesignated there as 2nd CA Battalion 1 Oct 44 and 2nd Bn redesignated 175th CA Battalion.

3rd Coast Artillery Regiment (Harbor Defense) (Type B)

Stationed at Ft MacArthur Calif under Harbor Defenses of Los Angeles and upgraded to Type A in 1941; regiment, less 1st and 3rd Bns, redesignated there as 521st CA Battalion 18 Oct 44; 1st and 3rd Bns redesignated 520th and 522nd CA Battalions respectively.

4th Coast Artillery Regiment (Harbor Defense) (Type C)

Stationed at Ft Armador Panama Canal Zone and HHB redesignated there as HHB 4th Coast Artillery Group 1 Nov 44; other regimental assets used to form 4th CA Battalion and other components in area.

Campaigns: *American Theater without inscription*

5th Coast Artillery Regiment (Harbor Defense) (Type A)

Stationed at Ft Hamilton N.Y. under Harbor Defenses of southern New York and regimental assets raised slowly until three battalions active by Jun 41; moved to Ft Tilden N.Y. 20 May 43 where regimental assets absorbed into New York Harbor Defenses and HHB assigned to IX Corps 24 Feb 44; HHB transferred to Cp Rucker Ala 13 Mar 44 where inactivated 19 Apr 44.

6th Coast Artillery Regiment (Harbor Defense) (Type C)

Stationed at Ft Winfield Scott Calif under Harbor Defenses of San Francisco; moved to Ft Baker Calif 29 Nov 43 where HHB disbanded 18 Oct 44 and 1st–4th Bns redesignated 6th, 172nd, 173rd, and 174th CA Battalions, respectively.

7th Coast Artillery Regiment (Harbor Defense) (Type B)

Stationed at Ft Hancock N.J. under Harbor Defenses of Sandy Hook; moved to Ft Tilden N.Y. 23 Sep 42 and returned to Ft Hancock 20 May 43; there regimental assets absorbed into New York Harbor Defenses and HHB assigned to XXII Corps 23 Feb 44; HHB transferred to Ft Leonard Wood Mo 15 Mar 44 where inactivated 7 Apr 44.

8th Coast Artillery Regiment (Harbor Defense) (Type B)

Stationed at Ft Preble Maine under Harbor Defenses of Portland; 1st and 2nd Bns not completely formed until Feb 41 and Battery G (Searchlight) activated Jun 41; regimental assets absorbed into Portland Harbor Defenses and HHB assigned to IX Corps 25 Feb 44; HHB transferred to Cp Shelby Miss 27 Mar 44 where inactivated 18 Apr 44.

9th Coast Artillery Regiment (Harbor Defense) (Type A)

Stationed at Ft Banks Mass under Harbor Defenses of Boston; 1st and 2nd Bns activated 10 Feb 41 and 3rd Bn activated 1 Jun 41; regimental assets absorbed into Boston Harbor Defenses and HHB assigned to XXIII Corps 23 Feb 44; HHB transferred to Cp Hood Tex 17 Mar 44 where inactivated 12 Apr 44.

10th Coast Artillery Regiment (Harbor Defense) (Type B)

1 Jan 40 activated at Ft Adams R.I. under Harbor Defenses of Narragansett Bay; 1st and 2nd Bns activated 10 Apr 41; regimental assets absorbed into Narragansett Bay Harbor Defenses and HHB assigned to XXII Corps 25 Feb 44; HHB transferred to Cp Forrest Tenn 14 Mar 44 where inactivated 10 Apr 44.

11th Coast Artillery Regiment (Harbor Defense) (Type B)

Stationed at Ft H.G. Wright N.Y. under Harbor Defenses of Long Island Sound; moved to Winthrop N.Y. 3 Aug 40 and returned to Ft H.G. Wright 31 Aug 40; there regimental assets absorbed into Long Island Sound Harbor Defenses and HHB assigned to XXII Corps 23 Feb 44; HHB transferred to Ft Leonard Wood MO 14 Mar 44 where inactivated 7 Apr 44.

13th Coast Artillery Regiment (Harbor Defense) (Type A)

Stationed at Ft Barrancas Fla under Harbor Defenses of Key West; 2nd Bn activated 1 Aug 40 at Ft Moultrie S.C. and joined regiment at Ft Barrancas 24 Apr 42 from duty with Harbor Defenses of Charleston; 3rd Bn inactivated 17 Jan 42; relocated to Ft Pickens Fla where HHB redesignated Harbor Defense of Pensacola 31 Aug 44; 1st and 2nd Bns redesignated 181st and 13th CA Battalions, respectively. The 3rd Bn had departed Charleston P/E 27 Jan 42 and became the 276th CA Bn at Bora Bora 17 Dec 42.

14th Coast Artillery Regiment (Harbor Defense) (Type A)

Stationed at Ft Worden Wash under Harbor Defenses of Puget Sound where HHB disbanded 18 Oct 44; 1st–3rd Bns redesignated 14th, 169th, and 170th CA Battalions, respectively.

15th Coast Artillery Regiment (Harbor Defense) (Type A)

Stationed at Ft Kamehameha Hawaii and responsible for coastal defense of Pearl Harbor on Oahu Island; assigned to Central Pacific Base Command 31 Jan 44 and HHB redesignated HHB 15th Coast Artillery Group there 13 Aug 44; other regimental assets used to form several CA units in area.

Campaigns: *Central Pacific*

16th Coast Artillery Regiment (Harbor Defense) (Type A)

Stationed in Hawaii where responsible for the coastal defense of Honolulu on Oahu Island; there HHB redesignated as HHB 16th Coast Artillery Group 13 Aug 44 and other regimental assets used to form several CA units in area.

Campaigns: *Central Pacific*

18th Coast Artillery Regiment (Harbor Defense) (Type B)

1 Feb 40 activated at Ft Stevens Oreg under Harbor Defenses of Columbia and 2nd Bn activated under Harbor Defenses of San Francisco; regiment relocated to Ft Funston Calif 7 Dec 41 and moved to Ft Winfield Scott Calif 2 Dec 43; there regimental assets absorbed into San Francisco Harbor Defenses and HHB assigned to XXII Corps 14 Apr 44; HHB transferred to Cp Breckinridge Ky 1 May 44 where inactivated 5 May 44.

Campaigns: *Pacific Theater without inscription*

19th Coast Artillery Regiment (Harbor Defense) (Type A)

1 Feb 40 activated at Ft Rosecrans Calif under Harbor Defenses of San Diego and HHB disbanded there 18 Oct 44 along with 3rd Bn; 1st and 2nd Bns redesignated 19th and 523rd CA Battalions, respectively.

20th Coast Artillery Regiment (Harbor Defense) (Type A)

1 Feb 40 activated at Ft Crockett Tex under Harbor Defenses of Galveston; 1st Bn activated 1 Apr 42 and moved to Ft Travis Tex 10 Oct 42; HHB redesignated there as Harbor Defense of Galveston 31 Aug 44 and 1st Bn redesignated 20th CA Battalion.

40th Coast Artillery Regiment

27 Dec 42 Batteries A, B, C, D, and E activated in Alaska where inactivated 29 Dec 44.

Campaigns: *Aleutian Islands*

41st Coast Artillery Regiment (Harbor Defense)

21 Apr 42 activated in Hawaii as Railway Coast Artillery Regiment and redesignated as Harbor Defense 22 May 43; regiment, less Batteries A, D, and G, disbanded in Hawaii 25 May 44 and those batteries renumbered as separate units.

Campaigns: *Pacific Theater without inscription*

46th Coast Artillery Regiment (155mm Gun) (Truck-Drawn)

10 Feb 43 activated Cp Pendleton Va and attached to First Army; transferred to Cp Shelby Miss 19 Mar 44 where inactivated, less 1st Bn, 19 Apr 44; 1st Bn redesignated 46th CA Battalion.

47th Coast Artillery Regiment (155mm Gun) (Truck-Drawn)

15 Apr 43 activated at Cp Pendleton Va and moved to Cp Pickett Va 7 Feb 44; there HHB disbanded 10 Feb 44 and 1st–3rd Bns redesignated 32nd, 33rd, and 38th CA Battalions, respectively, in Hawaii.

48th Coast Artillery Regiment

1 May 42 Battery G (Searchlight) activated at San Francisco and served in the Pacific Theater before being inactivated at Ft Ray Ark 30 Jan 44.

Campaigns: *Western Pacific*

49th Coast Artillery Regiment

1 May 42 Battery G (Searchlight) activated at Los Angeles and served in the Pacific Theater before being inactivated at Cp Barkeley Tex 8 May 44.

Campaigns: *Northern Solomons*

50th Coast Artillery Regiment (155mm Gun) (Mobile)

1 Feb 42 activated at Cp Pendleton Va and moved to Ft Crockett Tex 9 Apr 42; relocated to Cp Pendleton again 4 May 42 and transferred to Ft Taylor Fla 19 Dec 42; arrived at Montauk Point Long Island N.Y. 20 May 43; sent to Ft McKinley Maine 6 Oct 43 where assigned to XIII Corps 13 Jan 44; arrived at Ft Devens Mass 21 Jan 44 where 1st Bn disbanded 28 Jan 44 and HHB disbanded 31 Jan 44; 1st and 2nd Bns redesignated 42nd and 43rd CA Battalions, respectively.

51st Coast Artillery Regiment (155mm Gun) (Mobile) (Puerto Rican)

16 Mar 42 activated at San Juan Puerto Rico and moved to Port-of-Spain Trinidad 8 Dec 43; there HHB redesignated as HHB 145th Coast Artillery Group 1 Jun 44 and 1st and 2nd Bns redesignated 51st and 52nd CA Battalions, respectively.

Campaigns: *American Theater without inscription*

52nd Coast Artillery Regiment (Railway 8-inch Gun)

Stationed at Ft Hancock N.J. under Harbor Defenses of Sandy Hook and HHB disbanded there 1 May 43; Btry F posted to Bermuda 20 Apr 41 and another battery sited in Newfoundland on 1 May 41; 1st–3rd Bns redesignated 286th, 287th, and 288th CA Battalions and Batteries E and X were used to form the 285th CA Battalion.

Campaigns: *American Theater without inscription*

21st Coast Artillery Regiment (Harbor Defense) (Type B)

1 Feb 40 activated at Ft Dupont Del under the Harbor Defenses of Delaware and moved to Ft Miles Del 10 Jun 42; there HHB redesignated as Harbor Defense of Delaware 1 Oct 44 and 1st Bn redesignated 21st CA Battalion.

22nd Coast Artillery Regiment (Harbor Defense) (Type B)

1 Feb 40 activated at Ft Constitution N.H. under Harbor Defenses of Portsmouth and moved to Ft Langdon N.H. 23 Nov 40; there HHB disbanded 7 Oct 44 and Batteries A, B, C, and G redesignated as the Harbor Defense of Portsmouth.

23rd Coast Artillery Regiment (Harbor Defense) (Type D)

27 Dec 40 redesignated from 23rd CA Battalion at Ft Rodman Mass; there redesignated as the 23rd CA Battalion (Separate) 21 Aug 43; redesignated as a regiment again at Ft Rodman 13 Sep 43 and new 2nd Bn formed from 3rd Bn, 242nd CA Regiment; there HHB redesignated 23rd CA Battalion (Separate) 6 Mar 44; 1st and 2nd Bns inactivated 12 Apr 44 and 10 Apr 44, respectively. (The 1st Battalion had departed Ft Rodman Mass on 13 Mar 44 and arrived at Ft Hood Tex on 16 Mar 44, being inactivated there 12 Apr 44 as indicated above.)

30th Coast Artillery Regiment

18 Feb 42 1st Battalion activated at Ft Lewis Wash; served in Aleutian Islands and returned to Cp Joseph T. Robinson Ark where redesignated 781st Field Artillery Battalion 24 Jul 44.

Campaigns: *Aleutian Islands*

31st Coast Artillery Regiment (Harbor Defense)

15 Jan 43 activated at Cp Pendleton Va and moved to Key West Fla 16 Apr 43; there redesignated as Harbor Defense of Key West 1 Oct 44.

35th Coast Artillery Regiment (Harbor Defense)

12 May 43 HHB and Batteries A, B, and C activated at Ft Brooke Puerto Rico and redesignated there as 35th CA Battalion 1 Nov 44.

Campaigns: *American Theater without inscription*

36th Coast Artillery Regiment (Harbor Defense)

1 Jun 43 activated in Puerto Rico and arrived at Ft Kobbe Panama Canal Zone 14 Oct 44 where HHB redesignated 36th CA Battalion 1 Nov 44.

Campaigns: *American Theater without inscription*

39th Coast Artillery Regiment

1 Jun 43 Battery B partially activated in Dutch West Indies and disbanded there 22 May 44.

Campaigns: *American Theater without inscription*

53rd Coast Artillery Regiment (155mm Gun) (Mobile)

20 Jul 42 activated Cp Pendleton Va and attached to Provisional Coast Artillery Brigade in the Chesapeake Bay Sector 17 Jul 42; attached to Southern Sector and moved to Cp Atlantic Beach Fla 19 Oct 42; assigned to XIII Corps and returned to Cp Pendleton Va 26 Mar 44 where assigned to XVIII Corps 24 May 44; HHB redesignated HHB 153rd Coast Artillery Group there 12 Jun 44 and 1st–3rd Bns redesignated 290th, 291st, and 292nd CA Battalions, respectively.

54th Coast Artillery Regiment (155mm Gun) (Mobile) (Colored)

10 Feb 41 activated at Cp Wallace Tex and attached to First Army; moved to Cp Davis N.C. 22 May 41 and then to Ft Fisher N.C. 21 Oct 41; returned to Cp Davis N.C. 24 Nov 41; transferred to Ft Cronkhite Calif 28 Feb 42 and Ft Ord Calif 5 Apr 42 where assigned to Western Defense Command 22 Apr 42; 2nd Bn departed San Francisco P/E 6 Oct 42 and arrived on Espiritu Santo 26 Oct 42 and next on Bougainville 7 Feb 44; regiment (less 2nd Bn) arrived at Capitola CCC Camp Calif 30 Jan 43 and returned to Ft Ord Calif 20 Mar 44 where assigned to III Corps 10 Apr 44; there HHB redesignated as HHB 152nd Coast Artillery Group 5 Jun 44, and 1st–3rd Bns were redesignated 606th, 49th, and 607th CA Battalions, respectively.

Campaigns: *Pacific Theater without inscription*

55th Coast Artillery Regiment (155mm Gun) (Mobile)

22 May 43 activated in Hawaii where headquarters inactivated 31 May 44; 2nd Bn invaded Saipan in Jun 44 and was later inactivated there.

Campaigns: *Western Pacific*

56th Coast Artillery Regiment (155mm Gun) (Mobile)

2 Jun 41 activated at Ft Cronkhite Calif under Harbor Defenses of San Francisco and moved to Ft Barry Calif 25 Feb 42; dispatched contingent of four reduced batteries from San Francisco P/E 19 Feb 42 which arrived in Chile late Mar 42; another element arrived at Talara Peru on 8 Mar 42 which was redesignated the 723rd and 727th CA Batteries (AA) there on 14 Aug 42; Task Force VELLUM departed New Orleans P/E 26 Feb 42 and reached Puerto de la Cruz Venezuela on 13 Mar 42; remainder of regiment returned to Ft Cronkhite Calif 3 May 42; assigned to Southern California Sector and transferred to Seaside Park Ventura Calif 8 Apr 43; moved to Campbell Ranch at Goleta Calif 23 Sep 43 and returned to Ft Cronkhite Calif 16 Jan 44 where assigned to III Corps 25 Jan 44; arrived at Cp Cooke Calif where HHB disbanded 11 Feb 44 and 1st–3rd Bns redesignated 44, 45th, and 48th CA Battalions, respectively.

Campaigns: *American Theater without inscription*

57th Coast Artillery Regiment (155mm Gun) (Mobile)

3 Jan 41 activated at Ft Monroe Va under Harbor Defenses of Chesapeake Bay and moved to Cp Pendleton Va 20 Feb 41, less battery which departed New York P/E 20 Jan 41 for duty at St John's Newfoundland; Battery B landed on Bermuda 20 Apr 41; remainder of regiment sent to Hawaii with Batteries A and D leading; regimental Hqs staged at San Francisco P/E 23 Dec 41 and departed 27 Dec 41, arriving in Hawaii 7 Jan 42; there inactivated 31 May 44.

Campaigns: *Central Pacific*

58th Coast Artillery Regiment (155mm Gun) (Mobile)

18 Oct 42 2nd Battalion activated at Puerto de la Cruz and Las Peidras Venezuela from Task Force VELLUM of 56th Coast Artillery and disbanded on 26 Jun 44; other elements formed Nov 42 from contingents of the 56th Coast Artillery stationed at Tocopilla, Barquitos Island, San Antonio, and Antofagasta in northern Chile which were withdrawn in April 43.

Campaigns: *American Theater without inscription*

59th Coast Artillery Regiment (Harbor Defense)

Stationed in Philippine Islands where headquartered at Ft Mills (Corregidor) under the Philippine Coast Artillery Command and responsible for Fts Hughes (Caballo), Drum (El Fraile) and Frank (Carabao) in Manila Bay and Ft Wint (Grande Island) in Subic Bay; surrendered to Japanese forces there 6 May 42.

Campaigns: *Philippine Islands*

60th Coast Artillery Regiment (Antiaircraft) (Semimobile)

Stationed at Ft Mills Corregidor Philippine Islands under the Philippine Coast Artillery Command and surrendered to Japanese forces there 6 May 42.

Campaigns: *Philippine Islands*

61st Coast Artillery Regiment (Antiaircraft) (Semimobile)

Stationed at Ft Sheridan Ill, attached to Second Army and departed New York P/E 26 Feb 42; arrived in Iceland 3 Mar 42 where remained until 2 Aug 43; arrived in England 8 Aug 43 and HHB inactivated at Honiton 10 Aug 43; 1st–3rd Bns redesignated 184th AAA Gun, 634th AAA Auto-Wpns, and 635th AAA Auto-Wpns Battalions, respectively.

Campaigns: *European Theater without inscription*

62nd Coast Artillery Regiment (Antiaircraft) (Mobile)

Stationed at Ft Totten N.Y. and posted batteries to Newfoundland in 1941; staged at Cp Kilmer N.J. 27 Jul 42 until departed New York P/E 31 Aug 42; arrived in England 6 Sep 42 and assaulted North Africa 11 Nov 42; landed in Sicily 18 Jul 43 where HHB redesignated HHB, 80th AAA Group 24 Mar 44; 1st–3rd Bns redesignated 62nd AAA Gun, 893rd AAA Auto-Wpns, and 331st AAA Searchlight Battalions, respectively.

Campaigns: *Algeria–French Morocco, Tunisia, Sicily*

63rd Coast Artillery Regiment (Antiaircraft) (Semimobile)

Stationed at Ft MacArthur Calif and attached to Fourth Army; moved to Ft Bliss Tex 6 Dec 40 and attached to Third Army 31 Dec 40; arrived at Seattle Wash 15 Dec 41 where HHB redesignated as HHB 63rd AAA Group 10 Sep 43; 1st–3rd Bns redesignated 63rd AAA Gun, 213th AAA Auto-Wpns, and 243rd AAA Searchlight Battalions, respectively.

64th Coast Artillery Regiment (Antiaircraft) (Semimobile)

Stationed in Hawaii where HHB redesignated HHB 136th AAA Group 12 Dec 43; 1st–3rd Bns redesignated 64th AAA Gun, 750th AAA Gun, and 864th AAA Auto-Wpns Battalions, respectively.

Campaigns: *Central Pacific*

462

65th Coast Artillery Regiment (Antiaircraft) (Semimobile)

Stationed at Ft Winfield Scott Calif and attached to Fourth Army; moved to Cp Haan Calif 16 Jan 41 and Los Angeles Calif 5 Dec 41; arrived at Ft Ord Calif 30 Apr 43 where HHB redesignated HHB 65th AAA Group 10 May 43; 1st–3rd Bns redesignated 65th AAA Gun, 255th AAA Auto-Wpns, and 245th AAA Searchlight Battalions, respectively.

66th Coast Artillery Regiment (Antiaircraft) (Semimobile)

16 Mar 42 activated in San Juan Puerto Rico with 2nd and 3rd Bns being activated 25 Aug 42 there; HHB redesignated HHB 135th AAA Group there 6 Nov 43; 1st–3rd Bns redesignated 66th AAA Gun, 910th AAA Auto-Wpns, and 293rd AAA Searchlight Battalions, respectively.

Campaigns: *American Theater without inscription*

67th Coast Artillery Regiment (Antiaircraft) (Mobile)

10 Feb 41 activated at Ft Bragg N.C. and attached to First Army (1st Bn active since 1 Jul 40 there); moved to Paterson N.J. 12 Dec 41 and Ft Hancock N.J. 2 Nov 42; arrived at A.P. Hill Military Reservation Va 20 Nov 42 and Ft Dix N.J. 28 Dec 42 where staged until departed New York P/E 13 Jan 43; landed in North Africa 28 Jan 43 and in Italy 15 Oct 43; there HHB redesignated HHB 91st AAA Group 23 May 44; 1st and 2nd Bns redesignated 67th AAA Gun and 894th AAA Auto-Wpns Battalions, respectively, and 3rd Bn disbanded.

Campaigns: *Tunisia, Naples-Foggia, Rome-Arno*

68th Coast Artillery Regiment (Antiaircraft) (Mobile)

4 Nov 39 activated at Ft Williams Maine and attached to First Army; moved to Cp Edwards Mass 16 Sep 40 and to Boston Mass 9 Dec 41; staged at Cp Kilmer N.J. 27 Jul 42 until departed New York P/E 12 Sep 42 but returned to Ft Dix N.J. same date; returned to New York P/E 26 Oct 42 and departed 2 Nov 42; landed in North Africa 11 Nov 42 with 1st Bn assaulting Fedhala 8 Nov 42; landed in Sicily 9 Aug 43 and in Italy 31 Oct 43; there assaulted Anzio 22 Jan 44 and HHB was redesignated HHB 68th AAA Group 4 Jun 44; 1st and 2nd Bns redesignated 68th AAA Gun and 895th AAA Auto-Wpns Battalions, respectively, and 3rd Bn disbanded.

Campaigns: *Tunisia, Sicily, Naples-Foggia, Anzio*

69th Coast Artillery Regiment (Antiaircraft) (Semimobile)

Stationed at Ft Crockett Tex; 2nd Bn dispatched to San Juan Puerto Rico on 25 Sep 39; moved to Cp Hulen Tex 12 Jan 41; arrived at San Diego Calif 14 Dec 41 where 1st Bn activated same date; remained there and HHB redesignated HHB 69th AAA Group 10 Sep 43; 1st–3rd Bns redesignated 69th AAA Gun, 529th AAA Auto-Wpns, and 249th AAA Searchlight Battalions, respectively.

Campaigns: *American Theater without inscription*

70th Coast Artillery Regiment (Antiaircraft) (Semimobile)

4 Nov 39 activated Ft Monroe Va and moved to Ft Moultrie S.C. 28 Jun 40; arrived at Cp Stewart Ga 16 Dec 40 and sent to Baltimore Md 11 Dec 41; staged at Ft Dix N.J. 17 Jan 42 until departed New York P/E 23 Jan 42; arrived in Australia 27 Feb 42 and in New Caledonia 12 Mar 42 where attached to Americal Division 24 May 43; landed on Guadalcanal 2 Jun 43 and attached to XIV Corps; 1st Bn assaulted Wickham Island 30 Jun 43; regiment arrived at Segi Point New Georgia 15 Oct 43 less 2nd Bn which remained on Guadalcanal; HHB redesignated in New Georgia Island as HHB 70th AAA Group 10 Nov 43 and 1st and 2nd Bns were redesignated 70th AAA Gun and 925th AAA Auto-Wpns Battalions, respectively.

Campaigns: *Northern Solomons*

71st Coast Artillery Regiment (Antiaircraft) (Semimobile)

3 Jan 41 activated at Ft Story Va and attached to First Army (less 1st Bn active there since 1 Jul 40); moved to Norfolk Va 8 Dec 41 and to Washington D.C. 7 Jan 42; there HHB redesignated HHB 71st AAA Group 1 Sep 43 and 1st–3rd Bns redesignated 71st AAA Gun, 384th AAA Auto-Wpns and 241st AAA Searchlight Battalions, respectively.

72nd Coast Artillery Regiment (Antiaircraft) (Semimobile)

1 Nov 39 activated at Ft Randolph Panama Canal Zone and Batteries A–C, G–I, K–Q, R, V, and W raised only; inactivated there 15 Sep 43 and assets used to form other units in the area.

Campaigns: *American Theater without inscription*

73rd Coast Artillery Regiment (Antiaircraft) (Semimobile)

1 Nov 39 activated at Ft Amador Panama Canal Zone and moved to Ft Clayton Panama Canal Zone 27 Jan 42 where inactivated, less 2nd Bn HHB and Batteries F and H, 15 Sep 43; cited components disbanded there 10 Dec 43.

Campaigns: *American Theater without inscription*

74th Coast Artillery Regiment (Antiaircraft) (Semimobile)

3 Jan 41 activated at Ft Monroe Va and attached to First Army; moved to Cp Pendleton Va 18 Jul 41 and to Norfolk Va 14 Dec 41 enroute to Portsmouth Va where arrived same date until transferred to A.P. Hill Mil Res Va 19 Nov 42; arrived at Ft George G. Meade Md 29 Jan 43 and staged at Cp Myles Standish Mass 20 Apr 43 until departed New York P/E 28 Apr 43; landed in North Africa 11 May 43 and Sardinia 27 Oct 43; there HHB redesignated as HHB 74th AAA Group 1 Apr 44; 1st and 2nd Bns redesignated 74th AAA Gun and 896th AAA Auto-Wpns Battalions, respectively, and 3rd Bn disbanded 1 May 44.

Campaigns: *Rome-Arno*

75th Coast Artillery Regiment (Antiaircraft) (Semimobile)

1 Jul 40 activated at Ft Lewis Wash and departed Seattle P/E 26 Nov 40; arrived at Ft Richardson Alaska 30 Nov 40 where remained until 16 Jan 44; returned to Seattle P/E 3 Feb 44 and arrived at Ft Bliss Tex 7 Feb 44 and assigned to Replacement & School Command there 26 Nov 44; transferred to Cp Howze Tex 2 Dec 44 where HHB redesignated HHB 75th AAA Group 20 Feb 44; 1st–3rd Bns redesignated 75th AAA Gun, 595th AAA Auto-Wpns and 333rd AAA Searchlight Battalions, respectively.

Campaigns: *Pacific Theater without inscription*

76th Coast Artillery Regiment (Antiaircraft) (Semimobile) (Colored)

10 Feb 41 activated at Ft Bragg N.C. (less 1st Bn active since 1 Aug 40) and moved to Philadelphia Pa 11 Dec 41; transferred to Burbank Calif and Fourth Army 26 May 42; staged at Cp Stoneman Calif 30 Jul 42 until departed San Francisco P/E 10 Aug 42; arrived at Espiritu Santo New Hebrides 2 Sep 42 where HHB redesignated HHB 76th AAA Group 1 Nov 43; 1st and 2nd Bns redesignated 76th AAA Gun and 933rd AAA Auto-Wpns Battalions, respectively, and 3rd Bn disbanded.

Campaigns: *Pacific Theater without inscription*

77th Coast Artillery Regiment (Antiaircraft) (Semimobile) (Colored)

10 Feb 41 activated at Ft Bragg N.C. and moved to Windy Hill S.C. 14 Jul 41; returned to Ft Bragg N.C. 27 Oct 41 and moved to Hartford Conn 11 Dec 41; staged at Ft Dix N.J. 25 Mar 42 until departed New York P/E 9 Apr 42; arrived at Tongatabu Island, South Tonga Islands 9 May 42 and arrived in New Hebrides 18 Apr 43; there HHB redesignated HHB 77th AAA Group 1 Nov 43 and 1st–3rd Bns redesignated 77th AAA Gun, 938th AAA Auto-Wpns, and 374th AAA Searchlight Battalions, respectively.

Campaigns: *Pacific Theater without inscription*

78th Coast Artillery Regiment (Antiaircraft) (Semimobile)

10 Feb 41 activated at Cp Haan Calif (less 1st Bn active since 1 Aug 40) and moved to Ft Mac-Arthur Calif 5 Dec 41; transferred to Long Beach Calif 29 Dec 41 and to Ft Ord Calif 31 Jan 43; departed San Francisco P/E 15 Apr 43 and attached to 7th Infantry Division; assaulted Attu Island Aleutians 11 May 43 where remained until HHB redesignated HHB 78th AAA Group 7 Feb 44; 1st–3rd Bns redesignated 78th AAA Gun, 591st AAA Auto-Wpns, and 248th AAA Searchlight Battalions, respectively.

Campaigns: *Aleutian Islands*

79th Coast Artillery Regiment (Antiaircraft) (Semimobile)

1 Jun 41 activated at Ft Bliss Tex and attached to Third Army; moved to Manchester Conn 5 Apr 42 where HHB redesignated HHB 79th AAA Group 1 Sep 43; 1st–3rd Bns redesignated 79th AAA Gun, 539th AAA Auto-Wpns, and 239th AAA Searchlight Battalions, respectively.

82nd Coast Artillery Regiment (Antiaircraft) (Semimobile)

7 Dec 40 activated at Ft Randolph Panama Canal Zone where inactivated 15 Sep 43; 1st–3rd Bns redesignated there as an AAA Gun, 590th AAA Auto-Wpns, and 298th AAA Searchlight Battalions, respectively.

Campaigns: *American Theater without inscription*

83rd Coast Artillery Regiment (Antiaircraft) (Semimobile)

7 Dec 40 activated at Ft Amador Panama Canal Zone and moved to Ft Kobbe Canal Zone 7 Oct 41 where inactivated 15 Sep 43; 3rd Bn redesignated 275th AAA Searchlight Battalion.

Campaigns: *American Theater without inscription*

84th Coast Artillery Regiment (Antiaircraft)

4 Sep 42 Batteries A and B activated at Ft Read Trinidad and disbanded 29 Feb 44.

Campaigns: *American Theater without inscription*

85th Coast Artillery Regiment (Antiaircraft) (Semimobile)

26 Jan 42 activated at Cp Davis N.C. and assigned to V Corps; moved to Norfolk Va 28 May 42 and assigned to Eastern Defense Command; there HHB redesignated as HHB 85th AAA Group 1 Sep 43; 1st–3rd Bns redesignated 85th AAA Gun, 388th AAA Auto-Wpns, and 328th AAA Searchlight Battalions, respectively.

86th Coast Artillery Regiment (Antiaircraft) (Semimobile)

1 Jun 42 activated at Cp Haan Calif where HHB redesignated HHB 109th Coast Artillery Group 20 Jan 43; 1st–3rd Bns redesignated 161st, 195th, and 222nd Coast Artillery Battalions, respectively.

87th Coast Artillery Regiment (Antiaircraft) (Semimobile)

20 Aug 42 activated in the Panama Canal Zone where remained until 21 Sep 43; arrived at New Orleans P/E 4 Oct 43 and moved to Ft Bliss Tex 6 Oct 43 where inactivated 10 Dec 43.

Campaigns: *American Theater without inscription*

88th Coast Artillery Regiment (Antiaircraft) (Semimobile)

20 Aug 42 activated in the Panama Canal Zone where inactivated 15 Sep 43.

Campaigns: *American Theater without inscription*

89th Coast Artillery Regiment (Antiaircraft) (Semimobile)

10 Aug 42 activated in Washington D.C. and HHB redesignated there as HHB 89th AAA Group 1 Sep 43; 1st–3rd Bns redesignated 89th AAA Gun, 392nd AAA Auto-Wpns, and 332nd AAA Searchlight Battalions, respectively.

90th Coast Artillery Regiment (Antiaircraft) (Semimobile) (Colored)

1 May 42 activated at Cp Stewart Ga and staged at Ft Dix N.J. 17 Mar 43 until departed New York P/E 2 Apr 43; landed in North Africa 12 Apr 43 where HHB redesignated HHB 90th AAA Group 25 May 44; 1st–3rd Bns redesignated 90th AAA Gun, 897th AAA Auto-Wpns, and 334th AAA Searchlight Battalions, respectively.

Campaigns: *European Theater without inscription*

91st Coast Artillery Regiment (Harbor Defense) (Philippine Scouts)

Stationed at Ft Mills Corregidor and Ft Drum El Fraile Island Philippines and surrendered to Japanese forces there 6 May 42.

Campaigns: *Philippine Islands*

92nd Coast Artillery Regiment (Harbor Defense) (Philippine Scouts)

Stationed at Ft Mills Corregidor and Ft Hughes Caballo Island Philippines and surrendered to Japanese forces there 6 May 42.

Campaigns: *Philippine Islands*

93rd Coast Artillery Regiment (Antiaircraft) (Semimobile)

25 Apr 41 activated at Cp Davis N.C. and moved to Barstow Calif 10 Jan 42; departed San Francisco P/E 21 May 42 and arrived in Hawaii 29 May 42 where HHB redesignated as HHB 137th AAA Group 12 Dec 43; 1st–3rd Bns redesignated 751st AAA Gun, 865th AAA Auto-Wpns, and 294th AAA Searchlight Battalions, respectively.

Campaigns: *Pacific Theater without inscription*

94th Coast Artillery Regiment (Antiaircraft) (Semimobile)

17 Apr 41 activated at Cp Davis N.C. and moved to Newport News Va on 10 Dec 41; departed New York P/E 18 Feb 42 and arrived in Australia 28 Mar 42; Batteries D, G, and K sent to New Guinea and rejoined regiment in Australia; there HHB redesignated 94th AAA Group HHB 15 May 43; 1st–3rd Bns redesignated 743rd CA, 209th CA, and 236th AAA Searchlight Battalions, respectively.

Campaigns: *Papau*

95th Coast Artillery Regiment (Antiaircraft) (Semimobile)

17 Apr 41 activated at Cp Davis N.C. and moved to Ft McDowell Calif 21 Dec 41; departed San Francisco P/E 26 Dec 41 and arrived in Hawaii 7 Jan 42 where HHB redesignated HHB 138th AAA Group 12 Dec 43; 1st–3rd Bns redesignated 93rd AAA Gun, 752nd AAA Gun, and 866th AAA Auto-Wpns Battalions, respectively.

Campaigns: *Pacific Theater without inscription*

96th Coast Artillery Regiment (Antiaircraft) (Semimobile)

15 Mar 41 activated at Cp Davis N.C. and departed San Francisco P/E 27 Feb 42; arrived in Hawaii 10 Mar 42 where HHB redesignated HHB 139th AAA Group 12 Dec 43; 1st–3rd Bns redesignated 96th AAA Gun, 753rd AAA Gun, and 867th AAA Auto-Wpns Battalions, respectively.

Campaigns: *Pacific Theater without inscription*

97th Coast Artillery Regiment (Antiaircraft) (Semimobile)

9 Oct 41 activated at Ft Kamehameha Hawaii where redesignated HHB as HHB 97th AAA Group 12 Dec 43; 1st–3rd Bns redesignated 97th AAA Gun, 754th AAA Gun, and 868th AAA Auto-Wpns Battalions, respectively.

Campaigns: *Central Pacific*

98th Coast Artillery Regiment (Antiaircraft) (Semimobile)

10 Jul 41 activated at Schofield Barracks Hawaii where HHB redesignated as HHB 98th AAA Group 12 Dec 43; 1st–3rd Bns redesignated 98th AAA Gun, 755th AAA Gun, and 869th AAA Auto-Wpns Battalions, respectively.

Campaigns: *Central Pacific*

99th Coast Artillery Regiment (Antiaircraft) (Semimobile) (Colored)

15 Apr 41 activated at Cp Davis N.C. and arrived at New Orleans P/E 22 Apr 42 where departed 26 Apr 42; arrived at Ft Read Trinidad 10 May 42 where remained until 30 Nov 43; arrived at New York P/E 4 Dec 43 and transferred to Cp Stewart Ga 9 Dec 43 where disbanded 29 Feb 44; 1st–3rd Bns redesignated 99th AAA Gun, 871st AAA Auto-Wpns, and 338th AAA Searchlight Battalions, respectively.

Campaigns: *American Theater without inscription*

100th Coast Artillery Regiment (Antiaircraft) (Semimobile) (Colored)

17 Apr 41 activated at Cp Davis N.C. and moved to Ft Custer Mich 13 Mar 42; transferred to Ft Brady Mich 8 Apr 42 and arrived at Cp Stewart Ga where disbanded 28 Apr 43; 1st and 2nd Bns redesignated 100th AAA Gun and 538th AAA Auto-Wpns Battalions, respectively, and 3rd Bn disbanded.

196th Coast Artillery Regiment (Antiaircraft)

20 Dec 42 2nd Battalion activated at Ft Amador Panama Canal Zone where inactivated 15 Sep 43.

Campaigns: *American Theater without inscription*

197th Coast Artillery Regiment (Antiaircraft) (Semimobile)   N.H. National Guard

16 Sep 40 inducted into federal service at Concord N.H. and moved to Cp Hulen Tex 30 Sep 40; transferred to Elizabeth N.J. 12 Dec 41 and staged at Ft Dix N.J. 12 Jan 42 until departed San Francisco 18 Feb 42; arrived in Australia 22 Mar 42 where HHB redesignated HHB 197th AAA Group 15 May 43; 1st–3rd Bns redesignated 744th CA, 210th CA, and 237th AAA Searchlight Battalions, respectively.

Campaigns: *Pacific Theater without inscription*

198th Coast Artillery Regiment (Antiaircraft) (Semimobile)   Delaware National Guard

16 Sep 40 inducted into federal service at Wilmington Del and moved to Cp Upton N.Y. 22 Sep 40; arrived at Cp Edwards Mass 26 Mar 41 and transferred to Ft Ontario N.Y. 5 Sep 41; sent to East Hartford Conn 9 Dec 41 and departed Charleston P/E 27 Jan 42; arrived at Bora Bora 17 Feb 42 and Efate New Hebrides 27 Feb 43; landed on Guadalcanal 17 Oct 43 and Treasury Islands 6 Nov 43 where HHB redesignated HHB 198th AAA Group 1 Mar 44; 1st–3rd Bns redesignated 736th AAA Gun, 945th AAA Auto-Wpns, and 373rd AAA Searchlight Battalions, respectively.

Campaigns: *Northern Solomons*

200th Coast Artillery Regiment (Antiaircraft) (Mobile)   New Mexico National Guard

6 Jan 41 inducted into federal service at Deming N.M. and moved to Ft Bliss Tex 15 Jan 41; departed San Francisco P/E 3 Sep 41 and arrived in Philippine Islands 20 Nov 41 and stationed at Ft Stotsenburg–Clark Field as part of Philippine Coast Artillery Command; surrendered to Japanese forces on Bataan 9 Apr 42.

Campaigns: *Philippine Islands*

201st Coast Artillery Regiment (Antiaircraft)   Puerto Rico National Guard

Jun 40 1st Battalion inducted into federal service at Ponce Puerto Rico where redesignated 123rd CA Battalion 2 Apr 41.

202nd Coast Artillery Regiment (Antiaircraft) (Semimobile)   Illinois National Guard

16 Sep 40 inducted into federal service at Chicago Ill and moved to Ft Bliss Tex 27 Sep 40; transferred to Bremerton Wash 16 Dec 41 where HHB redesignated HHB 202nd AAA Group 10 Sep 43; 1st–3rd Bns redesignated 768th AAA Gun, 396th AAA Auto-Wpns, and 242nd AAA Searchlight Battalions, respectively.

203rd Coast Artillery Regiment (Antiaircraft) (Semimobile)   Missouri National Guard

16 Sep 40 inducted into federal service at Webb City Mo and moved to Cp Hulen Tex 26 Sep 40; transferred to Los Angeles Calif 15 Dec 41 and to Ft Lewis Wash 15 Jun 42; departed Seattle P/E 18 Jun 42 and arrived at Ft Randall Alaska 26 Jun 42; transferred to Amchitka Aleutian Islands 17 Apr 43 where remained until 12 Aug 44; HHB redesignated there as HHB 203rd AAA Group 26 Jan 44; 1st–3rd Bns redesignated 86th AAA Gun, 592nd AAA Auto-Wpns, and 299th AAA Searchlight Battalions, respectively.

Campaigns: *Aleutian Islands*

204th Coast Artillery Regiment (Antiaircraft) (Semimobile)   Louisiana National Guard

6 Jan 41 inducted into federal service at Shreveport La and moved to Cp Hulen Tex 11 Jan 41; arrived at San Diego Calif 15 Dec 41 where HHB redesignated HHB 204th AAA Group 10 Sep 43; 1st–3rd Bns redesignated 769th AAA Gun, 527th AAA Auto-Wpns, and 244th Searchlight Battalions, respectively.

205th Coast Artillery Regiment (Antiaircraft) (Semimobile)   Washington National Guard

3 Feb 41 inducted into federal service at Olympia Wash and moved to Ft Lewis Wash 14 Feb 41; arrived at Santa Monica Calif 11 Dec 41 where HHB redesignated HHB 205th AAA Group 10 Sep 43; 1st–3rd Bns redesignated 770th AAA Gun, 530th AAA Auto-Wpns, and 240th AAA Searchlight Battalions, respectively.

206th Coast Artillery Regiment (Antiaircraft) (Semimobile)   Arkansas National Guard

6 Jan 41 inducted into federal service at Marianna Ark and moved to Ft Bliss Tex 18 Jan 41; staged at Cp Murray Wash 5 Aug 41 until departed Seattle P/E 27 Feb 42; arrived in Alaska 8 Mar 42 where remained until 20 Feb 44; returned to Seattle P/E 27 Feb 44 and arrived at Ft Bliss Tex where disbanded 25 Mar 44; 1st Bn disbanded at Cp Chaffee Ark 9 May 44 and 2nd and 3rd Bns redesignated 597th AAA Auto-Wpns and 339th AAA Searchlight Battalions, respectively.

Campaigns: *Aleutian Islands*

207th Coast Artillery Regiment (Antiaircraft) (Semimobile)   New York National Guard

10 Feb 41 inducted into federal service at New York N.Y. and moved to Cp Stewart Ga 20 Feb 41; transferred to Cp Pendleton Va 22 Mar 42 and to Newport R.I. 4 Apr 42; arrived at Cp Edwards Mass 8 Apr 43 where HHB redesignated as HHB 207th AAA Group 10 Sep 43; 1st–3rd Bns redesignated 771st AAA Gun, 7th AAA Auto-Wpns, and 247th AAA Searchlight Battalions, respectively.

208th Coast Artillery Regiment (Antiaircraft) (Semimobile)   Connecticut National Guard

6 Jan 41 inducted into federal service at West Hartford Conn and moved to Cp Edwards Mass 14 Jan 41; stationed at Boston 9 Dec 41 until returned to Cp Edwards Mass 13 Jan 42; departed San Francisco P/E 18 Feb 42 and arrived in Australia 9 Mar 42 and moved to Townsend; 3rd Bn activated there 13 Aug 42 and moved with 1st Bn to Port Moresby New Guinea 19 Oct 42; Batteries C and E moved to New Guinea as a provisional AA unit 15 Nov 42; HHB redesignated in Australia as HHB 208th AAA Group 15 May 43; 1st–3rd Bns redesignated 745th CA, 211th CA, and 238th AAA Searchlight Battalions, respectively.

Campaigns: *Papau*

209th Coast Artillery Regiment (Antiaircraft) (Semimobile)   New York National Guard

10 Feb 41 inducted into federal service at Rochester N.Y. and moved to Cp Stewart Ga 21 Feb 41; staged at Ft Dix N.J. 23 Apr 42 until departed New York P/E 11 May 42; arrived in Northern Ireland 18 May 42 and England 12 Dec 42; landed in North Africa 3 Jan 43 and Italy 28 Oct 43 where attached to Fifth Army; HHB designated there as HHB 209th AAA Group 14 Mar 44; 1st–3rd Bns redesignated 72nd AAA Gun, 898th AAA Auto-Wpns, and 335th AAA Searchlight Battalions, respectively.

Campaigns: *Tunisia, Naples-Foggia, Rome-Arno*

210th Coast Artillery Regiment (Antiaircraft) (Semimobile)   Michigan National Guard

24 Feb 41 inducted into federal service at Detroit Mich and moved to Ft Sheridan Ill 5 Mar 41; located at Lake Village Ark 29 Aug 41 until returned to Ft Sheridan Ill 6 Oct 41; transferred to Everett Wash 15 Dec 41 and departed Seattle P/E 29 Jun 42; arrived in Alaska 5 Jul 42 and landed on Adak Island 19 Sep 42; there HHB redesignated as HHB 210th AAA Group 19 Feb 44; 1st–3rd Bns redesignated 94th AAA Gun, 593rd AAA Auto-Wpns, and 300th AAA Searchlight Battalions, respectively.

Campaigns: *Aleutian Islands*

211th Coast Artillery Regiment (Antiaircraft) (Semimobile)   Mass. National Guard

16 Sep 40 inducted into federal service at Boston Mass and moved to Cp Edwards Mass 21 Sep 40; relocated to Cp Hulen Tex 25 Oct 40 and transferred to Vallejo Calif 14 Dec 41; there HHB redesignated as HHB 211th AAA Group 10 Sep 43; 1st–3rd Bns redesignated 772nd AAA Gun, 747th AAA Auto-Wpns, and 324th AAA Searchlight Battalions, respectively.

212th Coast Artillery Regiment (Antiaircraft) (Semimobile)   New York National Guard

10 Feb 41 inducted into federal service at New York N.Y. and moved to Cp Stewart Ga 20 Feb 41; transferred to Washington D.C. 13 Dec 41 and to Norfolk Va 8 Jan 42; arrived at Paine Field Seattle Wash 26 May 42 where HHB redesignated HHB 212th AAA Group 10 Sep 43; 1st–3rd Bns redesignated 773rd AAA Gun, 212th AAA Auto-Wpns, and 336th AAA Searchlight Battalions, respectively.

213th Coast Artillery Regiment (Antiaircraft) (Semimobile)   Pa. National Guard

15 Sep 40 inducted into federal service at Allentown Pa and moved to Cp Pendleton Va 24 Sep 40; transferred to Cp Stewart Ga 22 Feb 41 and to Ft Hamilton N.Y. 12 Dec 41; arrived at Brooklyn N.Y. 22 Dec 41 and Ft Wadsworth N.Y. 1 Jan 42; located to Bayonne N.Y. 7 Jun 42 and staged at Cp Kilmer N.J. 21 Jul 42 until moved to Ft Dix N.J. 12 Sep 42 and departed New York P/E 1 Nov 42; landed at Casablanca North Africa 18 Nov 42 and moved to Algeria 27 Mar 43; arrived at Tunisia 27 Jun 43 and landed in Italy 9 Sep 43; arrived in Corsica 16 Mar 44 where HHB redesignated as HHB 213th AAA Group 1 Apr 44; 1st–3rd Bns redesignated 73rd AAA Gun, 899th AAA Auto-Wpns, and 337th AAA Searchlight Battalions, respectively.

Campais: *Algeria–French Morocco, Tunisia, Naples-Foggia, Rome-Arno*

214th Coast Artillery Regiment (Antiaircraft) (Semimobile)   Georgia National Guard

25 Nov 40 inducted into federal service at Washington Ga and moved to Cp Stewart Ga 3 Dec 40; transferred to Ft Jackson S.C. 25 Sep 41 and returned to Cp Stewart Ga 1 Dec 41; arrived at San Francisco Calif 11 May 42 and staged at Cp Stoneman Calif 21 Sep 42 until departed San Francisco P/E 24 Sep 42; arrived in New Zealand 6 Oct 42 and New Caledonia 27 Nov 42; landed on Guadalcanal 30 Jan 43 with responsibility of Henderson Field defense; there HHB redesignated as HHB 214th AAA Group 11 Nov 43; 1st–3rd Bns redesignated 528th AAA Gun, 950th AAA Auto-Wpns, and 250th AAA Searchlight Battalions, respectively.

Campaigns: *Guadalcanal*

215th Coast Artillery Regiment (Antiaircraft) (Semimobile)   Minnesota National Guard

6 Jan 41 inducted into federal service at Mankato Minn and moved to Cp Haan Calif 19 Jan 41; staged at Cp Murray Wash 7 Aug 41 until departed Seattle P/E 29 Aug 41; arrived at Ft Greely Kodiak Alaska 3 Sep 41 where remained until 26 Feb 44; returned to Seattle P/E 29 Feb 44 and arrived at Ft Bliss Tex 22 Mar 44 where disbanded 25 Mar 44; 1st–3rd Bns redesignated 598th AAA Gun, 599th AAA Auto-Wpns, and 347th AAA Searchlight Battalions, respectively.

Campaigns: *Pacific Theater without inscription*

216th Coast Artillery Regiment (Antiaircraft) (Semimobile)   Minnesota National Guard

6 Jan 41 inducted into federal service at St Paul Minn and moved to Cp Haan Calif 19 Jan 41; moved to Longview Wash 17 Aug 41 and returned to Cp Haan Calif 6 Sep 41; arrived at San Francisco Calif 2 Dec 41 where HHB redesignated HHB 216th AAA Group 10 Sep 43; 1st–3rd Bns redesignated 774th AAA Gun, 256th AAA Auto-Wpns, and 246th AAA Searchlight Battalions, respectively.

217th Coast Artillery Regiment (Antiaircraft) (Semimobile)   Minnesota National Guard

10 Feb 41 inducted into federal service at St Cloud Minn and moved to Cp Haan Calif 24 Feb 41; transferred to Oakland-Berkeley Calif 4 Dec 41 where HHB redesignated as HHB 217th AAA Group 10 Sep 43; 1st–3rd Bns redesignated 775th AAA Gun, 257th AAA Auto-Wpns, and 344th AAA Searchlight Battalions, respectively.

240th Coast Artillery Regiment (Harbor Defense) (Type A)   Maine National Guard

16 Sep 40 inducted into federal service at Portland Maine and moved to Ft McKinley Maine 23 Sep 40 under the Harbor Defenses of Portland; transferred to Ft Williams Maine 2 Jan 42 and to Ft Levett Maine 5 Oct 44; there regiment (less HHB 3rd Bn and Btry I which had been inactivated 18 Apr 44) redesignated as 185th CA and 186th CA Battalions.

241st Coast Artillery Regiment (Harbor Defense) (Type C)   Mass. National Guard

16 Sep 40 inducted into federal service at Boston Mass and moved to Ft Andrews Mass 23 Sep 40 under the Harbor Defenses of Boston; transferred to Ft Dawes Mass 12 Dec 41 and Ft Heath Mass in Nov 43; arrived at Ft Banks Mass in Mar 44 where regimental HHB, 3rd Bn HHB and Btry L inactivated 7 Oct 44; remainder of regiment redesignated 187th CA and 241st CA Battalions, less 4th Bn which had been designated 3rd Bn, 8th CA Regt.

242nd Coast Artillery Regiment (Harbor Defense) (Type A) Connecticut National Guard

16 Sep 40 inducted into federal service at Bridgeport Conn and moved to Ft H.G. Wright N.Y. 23 Sep 40 and to Ft Terry N.Y. 7 Nov 40 under the Harbor Defenses of Long Island Sound; 3rd Bn redesignated 2nd Bn, 23rd CA Regt 13 Sep 43; remainder of regiment redesignated there as 190th CA and 242nd CA Battalions 7 Oct 44, less 2nd Bn HHB which was inactivated.

243rd Coast Artillery Regiment (Harbor Defense) (Type A)   R.I. National Guard

16 Sep 40 inducted into federal service at Providence R.I. and moved to Ft Adams R.I. 22 Sep 40 under the Harbor Defenses of Narragansett Bay; relocated to Ft Getty R.I. 14 Mar 41 where regiment redesignated 189th CA and 243rd CA Battalions 7 Oct 44, less HHB of 2nd and 3rd Bns and Btry D which were inactivated.

244th Coast Artillery Regiment (155mm Gun) (Mobile)   New York National Guard

16 Sep 40 inducted into federal service at New York N.Y. and moved to Cp Pendleton Va 23 Sep 40; served in Ft Jackson–Ft Bragg area from 29 Sep 41 until returned to Cp Pendleton 3 Dec 41; HHB and 1st Bn inactivated 17 May 44 and 2nd Bn redesignated 289th CA Battalion 5 Jun 44; 3rd Bn redesignated 259th CA Battalion 20 Jan 43 on New Caledonia.

Campaigns: *Pacific Theater without inscription*

245th Coast Artillery Regiment (Harbor Defense) (Type C)   New York National Guard

16 Sep 40 inducted into federal service at Brooklyn N.Y. and moved to Ft Hancock N.Y. 24 Sep 40 under the Harbor Defenses of Sandy Hook; transferred to Bendix N.J. 31 Oct 41 and returned to Ft Hancock N.J. 6 Nov 41; transferred to Ft Wadsworth N.Y. 20 May 43 and returned again to Ft Hancock N.J. 1 Mar 44; HHB of 1st–4th Bns and Btrys L and M inactivated there 7 Oct 44 and remainder of regiment redesignated as 192nd CA and 245th CA Battalions.

246th Coast Artillery Regiment (Harbor Defense) (Type A) Virginia National Guard

16 Sep 40 inducted into federal service at Lynchburg Va and moved to Ft Monroe Va 23 Sep 40 and Ft Story Va 19 Dec 40 under the Harbor Defenses of Chesapeake Bay; regiment, less Btrys A and B which were redesignated 246th and 247th CA Batteries, inactivated there 20 Apr 44.

248th Coast Artillery Regiment (Harbor Defense) (Type B) Washington National Guard

16 Sep 40 inducted into federal service at Tacoma Wash and moved to Ft Worden Wash 23 Sep 40 under the Harbor Defenses of Puget Sound; arrived Cp Barkeley Tex 30 Apr 44 where inactivated 8 May 44.

249th Coast Artillery Regiment (Harbor Defense) (Type B) Oregon National Guard

16 Sep 40 inducted into federal service at Salem Oreg and moved to Cp Clatsop Oreg 23 Sep 40 under the Harbor Defenses of the Columbia; arrived at Ft Stevens Oreg 6 Feb 41 where HHB inactivated 18 Oct 44; remainder of regiment redesignated 171st CA and 249th CA Battalions.

Campaigns: *Pacific Theater without inscription*

250th Coast Artillery Regiment (155mm Gun) (Mobile) California National Guard

16 Sep 40 inducted into federal service at San Francisco Calif and moved to Cp McQuaide Calif 23 Sep 40; arrived in Alaska 19 Sep 41 where it remained until 16 Mar 44; arrived at Seattle P/E 21 Mar 44 and Ft Lewis Wash 22 Mar 44 under III Corps; transferred to Cp Gruber Okla 7 Feb 44 and assigned to XVI Corps; HHB redesignated there as HHB 250th Field Artillery Group 18 May 44 and 1st–3rd Bns redesignated 535th, 536th, and 537th Field Artillery Battalions, respectively.

Campaigns: *Pacific Theater without inscription*

251st Coast Artillery Regiment (Antiaircraft) (Semimobile) California National Guard

16 Sep 40 inducted into federal service at San Diego Calif and moved to Ventura Calif 22 Sep 40 and to Cp Anza 17 Nov 40 where departed Los Angeles P/E same date, becoming the first National Guard unit to leave the continental United States for overseas duty in World War II; arrived at Ft Shafter Hawaii 23 Nov 40 and moved to Cp Malakole Hawaii 27 Jan 41; left Hawaii 22 May 42 and arrived at Viti Levo Fiji Islands 1 Jun 42; landed on Guadalcanal 23 Nov 43 and arrived at Torokina Bougainville Island 4 Dec 43 and assigned to XIV Corps; HHB redesignated there as HHB 251st AAA Group 1 Mar 44; 1st and 2nd Bns redesignated 746th AAA Gun and 951st AAA Auto-Wpns Battalions and 3rd Bn disbanded.

Campaigns: *Central Pacific, Northern Solomons*

252nd Coast Artillery Regiment (155mm Gun) (Mobile)   North Carolina National Guard

16 Sep 40 inducted into federal service at Wilmington N.C. and moved to Ft Moultrie S.C. 23 Sep 40 and Ft Screven Ga 2 Jan 41; departed New Orleans P/E 26 Apr 42 and arrived at Trinidad 10 Apr 42 where stationed on Chacachacare Island at the northern entrance to the Gulf of Paria until 4 Apr 44; arrived at New York P/E 9 Apr 44 and moved to Ft Jackson S.C. 13 Apr 44 where assigned to IX Corps and HHB redesignated HHB 252nd Field Artillery Group 20 May 44; 1st–3rd Bns redesignated 541st, 540th, and 530th Field Artillery Battalions, respectively.

Campaigns: *American Theater without inscription*

253rd Coast Artillery Regiment (155mm Gun) (Semimobile)   Puerto Rico National Guard

15 Oct 40 inducted into federal service at San Juan Puerto Rico (1st Battalion only); partially inacticated at Cp O'Reilly Puerto Rico 1 Jun 44 but retained both Btrys A and B still active in the Netherlands West Indies at the end of the war.

Campaigns: *American Theater without inscription*
Aug 45 Loc: Btry A at Curacao and Btry B at Aruba

260th Coast Artillery Regiment (Antiaircraft) (Semimobile)   D.C. National Guard

6 Jan 41 inducted into federal service at Washington D.C. and moved to Ft Bliss Tex 29 Jan 41; transferred to Puyallup Wash 14 Dec 41 and to McChord Field Wash 28 Feb 42 where HHB redesignated as HHB 260th AAA Group 10 Sep 43; 1st–3rd Bns redesignated 260th AAA Gun, 380th AAA Auto-Wpns, and 340th AAA Searchlight Battalions, respectively.

261st Coast Artillery Regiment (Harbor Defense) (Type B)   New Jersey National Guard

25 Nov 40 2nd Battalion inducted into federal service at Jersey City N.J. but was still forming when redesignated as a CA battalion 15 Jan 41 which was in turn officially activated 27 Jan 41; regiment not considered as inducted during World War II as a result.

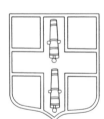

263rd Coast Artillery Regiment (Harbor Defense) (Type B)   S.C. National Guard

13 Jan 41 inducted into federal service at Greenwood S.C. and moved to Ft Moultrie S.C. 21 Jan 41 under the Harbor Defenses of Charleston; HHB redesignated there as the Harbor Defense of Charleston 7 Oct 44 and regimental assets absorbed into that command.

265th Coast Artillery Regiment (Harbor Defense) (Type B)   Florida National Guard

6 Jan 41 inducted into federal service at Jacksonville Fla and moved to Ft Crockett Tex 15 Jan 41 under the Harbor Defenses of Galveston; moved to Ft Taylor Fla 18 Apr 42 and to Ft Jackson S.C. 29 Dec 42; arrived at Ft Hancock N.J. 16 Jan 43 and staged at Ft Lawton Wash 16 Jan 44 until departed Seattle P/E 24 Jan 44; arrived in Alaska 28 Jan 44 where disbanded 31 Jul 44; regimental assets used in the 277th, 278th, and 279th CA Battalions.

369th Coast Artillery Regiment (Antiaircraft) (Colored)   New York National Guard

13 Jan 41 inducted into federal service at New York N.Y. and moved to Ft Ontario N.Y. 15 Jan 41; transferred to Cp Edwards Mass 5 Sep 41 and to Los Angeles Calif 5 May 42; staged at Cp Stoneman Calif 1 Jun 42 until departed San Francisco P/E 16 Jun 42; arrived in Hawaii 21 Jun 42 where HHB redesignated HHB 369th AAA Group 12 Dec 43; 1st and 2nd Bns redesignated as 369th AAA Gun and 870th AAA Auto-Wpns Battalions, respectively.

Campaigns: *Pacific Theater without inscription*

428th Coast Artillery Regiment (Antiaircraft) (Composite)

13 May 43 redesignated from the 428th CA Battalion (Separate) on Canton Island where it was disbanded 26 May 44.

Campaigns: *Pacific Theater without inscription*

501st Coast Artillery Regiment (Antiaircraft) (Semimobile)

1 Apr 42 activated at Cp Haan Calif and attached to Fourth Army; moved to San Francisco Calif 10 Oct 42 where HHB redesignated as HHB 501st AAA Group 10 Sep 43; 1st–3rd Bns redesignated 218th AAA Gun, 641st AAA Auto-Wpns, and 365th AAA Searchlight Battalions, respectively.

502nd Coast Artillery Regiment (Antiaircraft) (Semimobile)

1 May 42 activated at Ft Sheridan Ill and attached to Second Army; moved to Patterson N.J. 10 Oct 42 where HHB redesignated as HHB 502nd AAA Group 1 Sep 43; 1st–3rd Bns redesignated 219th AAA Gun, 642nd AAA Auto-Wpns, and 366th AAA Searchlight Battalions, respectively.

503rd Coast Artillery Regiment (Antiaircraft) (Semimobile)

7 Apr 42 activated at Ft Lewis Wash and departed Seattle P/E 22 Jun 42; arrived at Ft Glenn Alaska 29 Jun 42 where HHB inactivated 30 Dec 43; 1st and 2nd Bns redesignated 95th AAA Gun and 594th AAA Auto-Wpns Battalions, respectively, and 3rd Bn inactivated.

Campaigns: *Aleutian Islands*

504th Coast Artillery Regiment (Antiaircraft) (Semimobile)

1 Jul 42 activated at Cp Hulen Tex where HHB redesignated HHB 105th Coast Artillery Group 20 Jan 43; 1st–3rd Bns redesignated 214th CA, 630th CA, and 356th CA Battalions, respectively.

505th Coast Artillery Regiment (Antiaircraft) (Mobile)

1 Jun 42 activated at Cp Edwards Mass and moved to Indiantown Gap Mil Res Pa 29 Nov 42; departed New York P/E 8 Dec 42 and arrived in England 13 Dec 42; arrived in North Africa 4 Mar 43 and assaulted Salerno Italy 9 Sep 43; HHB redesignated as HHB 505th AAA Group 14 Mar 44 at Santa Maria Italy; 1st and 2nd Bns redesignated 87th AAA Gun and 900th AAA Auto-Wpns Battalions, respectively, and 3rd Bn disbanded.

Campaigns: *Naples-Foggia*

506th Coast Artillery Regiment (Antiaircraft) (Semimobile)

1 Jun 42 activated at Cp Edwards Mass where HHB redesignated HHB 110th Coast Artillery Group 15 Jan 43; 1st–3rd Bns redesignated 162nd CA, 196th CA, and 223rd CA Battalions, respectively.

507th Coast Artillery Regiment (Antiaircraft) (Semimobile)

1 Aug 42 activated at Cp Haan Calif and moved to North Long Beach Calif 20 Jan 43; HHB redesignated as HHB 507th AAA Group there 10 Sep 43; 1st–3rd Bns redesignated 220th AAA Gun, 643rd AAA Auto-Wpns, and 367th AAA Searchlight Battalions, respectively.

508th Coast Artillery Regiment (Antiaircraft) (Mobile)

1 Sep 42 activated at Cp Stewart Ga and moved to Ft Dix N.J. 21 Feb 43; departed New York P/E 5 Mar 43 and landed in North Africa 18 Mar 43; landed in Sicily 10 Jul 43 where HHB redesignated HHB 106th Coast Artillery Group 20 Jul 43; 1st–3rd Bns redesignated 215th CA, 637th CA, and 360th CA Battalions, respectively.

Campaigns: *Sicily*

509th Coast Artillery Regiment (Antiaircraft) (Semimobile)

10 Nov 42 activated at Ft Bliss Tex where HHB redesignated as HHB 111th Coast Artillery Group 20 Jan 43; 1st–3rd Bns redesignated 163rd CA, 197th CA, and 224th CA Battalions, respectively.

510th Coast Artillery Regiment (Antiaircraft) (Semimobile)

15 Nov 42 activated at Ft Sheridan Ill where HHB redesignated as HHB 112th Coast Artillery Group 20 Jan 43; 1st–3rd Bns redesignated 164th CA, 198th CA, and 225th CA Battalions, respectively.

511th Coast Artillery Regiment (Antiaircraft) (Semimobile)

15 Nov 42 activated at Cp Haan Calif where HHB redesignated as HHB 113th Coast Artillery Group 20 Jan 43; 1st–3rd Bns redesignated 165th CA, 199th CA, and 226th CA Battalions, respectively.

512th Coast Artillery Regiment (Antiaircraft) (Semimobile)

1 Aug 42 activated at Ft Bliss Tex where HHB redesignated as HHB 107th Coast Artillery Group 20 Jan 43; 1st–3rd Bns redesignated 216th CA, 638th CA, and 362nd CA Battalions, respectively.

513th Coast Artillery Regiment (Antiaircraft) (Semimobile)

1 Sep 42 activated at Ft Bliss Tex where HHB redesignated as HHB 114th Coast Artillery Group 20 Jan 43; 1st–3rd Bns redesignated 166th CA, 200th CA, and 227th CA Battalions, respectively.

514th Coast Artillery Regiment (Antiaircraft) (School Troops)

1 Mar 42 activated at Cp Davis N.C. where HHB redesignated as HHB 108th Coast Artillery Group 26 May 43; 1st–3rd Bns redesignated 217th CA, 639th CA, and 363rd CA Battalions, respectively.

515th Coast Artillery Regiment (Antiaircraft) (Semimobile)

19 Dec 41 activated at Ft Stotsenburg/Clark Field Philippines as a provisional antiaircraft artillery regiment by the expansion and redesignation of one battalion of the 200th Coast Artillery Regt; surrendered to Japanese forces on Bataan 9 Apr 42.

Campaigns: *Philippine Islands*

601st Coast Artillery Regiment (Antiaircraft) (Semimobile)

1 Feb 42 activated at Ft Bliss Tex and moved to Philadelphia Pa 24 May 42 where HHB redesignated as HHB 601st AAA Group 1 Sep 43; 1st–3rd Bns redesignated 601st AAA Gun, 541st AAA Auto-Wpns, and 251st AAA Searchlight Battalions, respectively.

602nd Coast Artillery Regiment (Antiaircraft) (Semimobile)

1 Mar 42 activated at Ft Bliss Tex and moved to New York N.Y. 23 Jul 42 where HHB redesignated as HHB 602nd AAA Group 1 Sep 43; 1st–3rd Bns redesignated 602nd AAA Gun, 542nd AAA Auto-Wpns, and 252nd AAA Searchlight Battalions, respectively.

603rd Coast Artillery Regiment (Antiaircraft) (Semimobile)

1 Mar 42 activated at Cp Stewart Ga and moved to Los Angeles Calif 27 Jun 42; transferred to Burbank Calif 26 Jul 42 and Culver City Calif 23 Apr 43 where HHB redesignated HHB 603rd AAA Group 10 Sep 43; 1st–3rd Bns redesignated 603rd AAA Gun, 543rd AAA Auto-Wpns, and 253rd AAA Searchlight Battalions, respectively.

604th Coast Artillery Regiment (Antiaircraft) (Semimobile)

1 Mar 42 activated at Ft Bliss Tex and moved to New York N.Y. 23 Jul 42 where HHB redesignated HHB 604th AAA Group 1 Sep 43; 1st–3rd Bns redesignated 604th AAA Gun, 544th AAA Auto-Wpns, and 254th AAA Searchlight Battalions, respectively.

605th Coast Artillery Regiment (Antiaircraft) (Semimobile)

1 Mar 42 activated at Cp Stewart Ga and moved to Boston Mass 23 Jul 42 where HHB redesignated HHB 605th AAA Group 1 Sep 43; 1st–3rd Bns redesignated 605th AAA Gun, 545th AAA Auto-Wpns, and 348th AAA Searchlight Battalions, respectively.

606th Coast Artillery Regiment (Antiaircraft) (Semimobile)

1 Aug 42 activated at Cp Edwards Mass and HHB redesignated there as HHB 115th Coast Artillery Group 20 Jan 43; 1st–3rd Bns redesignated 167th CA, 201st CA, and 228th CA Battalions, respectively.

607th Coast Artillery Regiment (Antiaircraft) (Semimobile)

1 Jun 42 activated at Cp Hulen Tex where HHB redesignated HHB 116th Coast Artillery Group 20 Jan 43; 1st–3rd Bns redesignated 168th CA, 202nd CA, and 229th CA Battalions, respectively.

608th Coast Artillery Regiment (Antiaircraft) (Semimobile)

15 Nov 42 activated at Ft Bliss Tex where HHB redesignated as HHB 117th Coast Artillery Group 20 Jan 43; 1st–3rd Bns redesignated 737th CA, 203rd CA, and 230th CA Battalions, respectively.

609th Coast Artillery Regiment (Antiaircraft) (Semimobile)

10 Dec 42 activated at Cp Edwards Mass where HHB redesignated as HHB 118th Coast Artillery Group 20 Jan 43; 1st–3rd Bns redesignated 738th CA, 204th CA, and 231st CA Battalions, respectively.

610th Coast Artillery Regiment (Antiaircraft) (Semimobile)

10 Dec 42 activated at Cp Davis N.C. where HHB redesignated as HHB 119th Coast Artillery Group 20 Jan 43; 1st–3rd Bns redesignated 739th CA, 205th CA, and 232nd CA Battalions, respectively.

611th Coast Artillery Regiment (Antiaircraft) (Semimobile)

10 Dec 42 activated at Ft Bliss Tex where HHB redesignated as HHB 120th Coast Artillery Group 20 Jan 43; 1st–3rd Bns redesignated 740th CA, 206th CA, and 233rd CA Battalions, respectively.

612th Coast Artillery Regiment (Antiaircraft) (Semimobile) (Colored)

1 Sep 42 activated at Cp Stewart Ga where HHB redesignated as HHB 121st Coast Artillery Group 20 Jan 43; 1st–3rd Bns redesignated 741st CA, 207th CA, and 234th CA Battalions, respectively.

613th Coast Artillery Regiment (Antiaircraft) (Semimobile) (Colored)

10 Dec 42 activated at Cp Stewart Ga where HHB redesignated as HHB 122nd Coast Artillery Group 20 Jan 43; 1st–3rd Bns redesignated 742nd CA, 208th CA, and 235th CA Battalions, respectively.

614th Coast Artillery Regiment (Antiaircraft) (Semimobile)

17 Apr 42 activated at Ft Randolph Panama Canal Zone; arrived at New York P/E 3 Oct 43 and arrived at Cp Davis N.C. 6 Oct 43 where assigned to Replacement & School Command 29 Oct 44; moved to Cp Stewart Ga 26 Nov 43 where HHB redesignated as HHB 140th AAA Group 1 Dec 43; 2nd and 3rd Bns redesignated 589th AAA Auto-Wpns and 297th AAA Searchlight Battalions and 1st Bn disbanded.

Campaigns: *American Theater without inscription*

615th Coast Artillery Regiment (Antiaircraft) (Semimobile)

17 Apr 42 activated at Ft Clayton Panama Canal Zone where inactivated 15 Sep 43.

Campaigns: *American Theater without inscription*

625th Coast Artillery Regiment (Harbor Defense)

3 Jan 41 1st Battalion activated at Ft Rosecrans Calif where redesignated as 1st Battalion, 19th Coast Artillery Regt 18 Oct 44.

701st Coast Artillery Regiment (Antiaircraft)

20 May 42 organized provisionally at Ft Totten N.Y. as the 701st Provisional Antiaircraft Artillery Regiment; activated 1 Oct 42 as the 701st Coast Artillery Regt and moved to Cp Myles Standish Mass 15 Mar 43; arrived at Newport R.I. 10 Apr 43 where HHB redesignated as HHB 701st AAA Group 1 Sep 43; 1st–3rd Bns redesignated 701st AAA Gun, 540th AAA Auto-Wpns, and 368th AAA Searchlight Battalions, respectively.

Provisional Coast Artillery Regiment (Antiaircraft)

13 Jan 43 raised in Puerto Rico and active there through 1946.

Campaigns: *American Theater without inscription*

Chapter 37

Harbor Defenses

Harbor Defenses:

Argentia and St John's, Balboa, Bermuda, Boston, Charleston, Chesapeake Bay, Columbia River, Cristobal, Delaware, Dutch Harbor, Eastern New York, Galveston, Honolulu, Key West, Kodiak, Long Island Sound, Los Angeles, Manila and Subic Bays, Narragansett Bay, New Bedford, New York, Pensacola, Portland, Portsmouth, Puget Sound, San Diego, San Francisco, San Juan, Seward, Sitka, Southern New York, Trinidad, Wilmington

Harbor Defenses of Argentia and St. John's

Jan 41 established at Argentia and St John's Newfoundland to guard entrances to Placentia Bay and St John's harbor, initially with elements of the 52nd, 57th, and 62nd Coast Artillery.

Campaigns: *American Theater without inscription*

Harbor Defenses of Balboa

Located on the Pacific side of the Panama Canal and initially guarded by the 4th Coast Artillery; redesignated as Harbor Defenses from the 4th Coast Artillery Group 2 Jan 45.

Campaigns: *American Theater without inscription*

Harbor Defenses of Bermuda

Apr 41 established at Ft Victoria (St George's Island), Cooper's Island, Hamilton Island, and Somerset Island in Bermuda, initially with elements of the 52nd and 57th Coast Artillery.

Campaigns: *American Theater without inscription*

Harbor Defenses of Boston

Located at Boston Mass with HHB at Ft Banks and initially guarded by the 9th Coast Artillery, reinforced in Sep 40 by the 241st Coast Artillery; composed of Ft Andrews (Boston harbor), Ft Banks (Winthrop Mass), Ft Dawes (Winthrop Mass), Ft Duvall (Hull Mass), Ft Heath (Winthrop Mass), Ft Revere (Hull Mass), Ft Ruckman (Nahant Mass), Ft Standish Outpost (Boston harbor), Ft Strong (Boston harbor), Ft Warren (Boston harbor), Ft Winthrop (Boston harbor), Marblehead Mil Res (Marblehead Mass), Sagamore Hill Gun Emplacement (Sagamore Mass), and numerous scattered tactical positions and searchlight and observation points.

Harbor Defenses of Charleston

Located at Charleston S.C. with HHB at Ft Moultrie and initially guarded by elements of the 13th Coast Artillery, reinforced in Jan 41 by the 263rd Coast Artillery; composed of Ft Moultrie (Moultrieville S.C.), Ft Sumter (Charleston S.C.); Dewees Island, Morris Island, Stoney Point combat team camp (Charleston S.C.), and various troop housing facilities.

Harbor Defenses of Chesapeake Bay

Located at the entrance to Chesapeake Bay Va with HHB at Ft Monroe Va and initially guarded by the 2nd and 57th Coast Artillery, reinforced in Sep 40 by the 246th Coast Artillery; composed of Ft John Custis (Cape Charles Va), Ft Story (Virginia Beach Va), Ft Wool (Ft Monroe Va), Cp Accomac (Accomac Va), Big Bethel subpost (Hampton Va), Fisherman's Island Mil Res, Hampton Tactical Position (Hampton Va), Middle Grounds Mil Res (Norfolk Va), and other scattered outposts at Mockhorn and Smith Islands (Townsend Va).

Harbor Defenses of Columbia River

Located at the entrance to the Columbia River between Wash and Oreg with HHB at Ft Stevens Oreg and initially guarded by the 18th Coast Artillery, reinforced in Sep 40 by the 249th Coast Artillery; composed of Ft Canby (Ilwaco Wash), Ft Columbia (Chinook Wash), Ft Stevens (Warrenton Oreg), Cp Clatsop (Clatsop Wash), and Columbia Beach Mil Res (Chinook Wash); the only seacoast fortification of the Zone of Interior to be engaged in combat during World War II was Battery David Russell (10-inch Gun) of Ft Stevens, which was fired on by a surfaced Japanese submarine on 21 Jun 42.

Campaigns: *Pacific Theater without inscription*

Harbor Defenses of Cristobal

Located on the Atlantic side of the Panama Canal and initially guarded by the 1st Coast Artillery; redesignated as Harbor Defenses from the 1st Coast Artillery Group on 2 Jan 45.

Campaigns: *American Theater without inscription*

Harbor Defenses of Delaware

Located at the entrance to Delaware Bay N.J. with HHB at Ft Miles Del and initially guarded by the 21st Coast Artillery, reinforced in Nov 40 by the 261st Coast Artillery; composed of Cape May Battery Site (Cape May N.J.), Ft Delaware (Pea Patch Island Del), Ft Dupont (Delaware City Del), Ft Miles (Lewes Del), Ft Mott (Salem N.J.), Ft Saulsbury (Milford Del) and various minor facilities.

Harbor Defenses of Dutch Harbor

22 Mar 43 formed with headquarters at Ft Schwatka (Unalaska Alaska) and subposts at Ft Leonard (Eider Point Alaska) and Ft Brumback (Summer Bay Alaska).

Campaigns: *Pacific Theater without inscription*

Harbor Defenses of Eastern New York

Located at Ft Totten (Queens New York City N.Y.) and initially guarded by the 62nd Coast Artillery; during World War II converted into an antiaircraft artillery training camp.

Harbor Defenses of Galveston

Located at Galveston Tex with HHB at Ft Crockett Tex and initially guarded by the 20th Coast Artillery, reinforced in Jan 41 by the 265th Coast Artillery; composed of Ft Crockett, Ft San Jacinto, and Ft Travis (all in Galveston Tex) as well as Aransas Pass Outpost (Aransas Pass Tex), Baytown Tactical Position (Baytown Tex), and Freeport Tactical Position (Freeport Tex).

Harbor Defenses of Honolulu

Located on Oahu Island Hawaii with HHB at Ft Shafter and initially guarded by the 15th and 16th Coast Artillery, reinforced in Nov 40 by the 251st Coast Artillery; composed of Ft Kamehameha (Pearl Harbor), Ft Weaver (Pearl Harbor), Mokapu Point (Kaneohe Bay), North Shore Oahu, Wiliwilinui Ridge, and other tactical battery sites.

Campaigns: *Central Pacific*

Harbor Defenses of Key West

Located at Key West Fla with HHB at Ft Taylor Fla and initially guarded by elements of the 13th Coast Artillery; composed of Ft Taylor (Key West Fla), Key West Barracks, and both East and West Martello Battery Sites (Key West Fla).

Harbor Defenses of Kodiak

22 Mar 43 formed with headquarters at Ft Greeley Alaska and subposts at Ft Abercrombie (Miller Point Alaska), Ft J.H. Smith (Chiniak Alaska), and Ft Tidball (Long Island Alaska).

Campaigns: *Pacific Theater without inscription*

Harbor Defenses of Long Island Sound

Located at Long Island Sound N.Y. with HHB at Ft H.G. Wright N.Y. and initially guarded by the 11th Coast Artillery, reinforced in Sep 40 by the 242nd Coast Artillery; composed of Ft Michie (Great Gull Island N.Y.), Ft Terry (Plum Island N.Y.), Ft H.G. Wright (Fishers Island N.Y.), and other installations including Cp Hero (Montauk Point N.Y.).

Harbor Defenses of Los Angeles

Located at Los Angeles Calif with HHB at Ft MacArthur Calif and initially guarded by the 3rd Coast Artillery; composed of Ft MacArthur (San Pedro Calif), Bolsa Chica Seacoast Battery (Los Angeles Calif), Oxnard Seacoast Battery (Oxnard Calif), Manhattan Beach Subpost (Manhattan Beach Calif), Point Vicente Seacoast Defenses (Los Angeles Calif), and White Point Seacoast Battery (Los Angeles Calif).

Harbor Defenses of Manila and Subic Bays

Located on Luzon Philippine Islands with HHB at Ft Mills P.I. and initially guarded by the 59th and 60th Coast Artillery as well as the 91st and 92nd Coast Artillery (Philippine Scouts); composed of Ft Drum (El Fraile Island), Ft Frank (Carabao Island), Ft Hughes (Caballo Island), Ft Mills (Corregidor Island), and Ft Wint (Grande Island in Subic Bay); evacuated Ft Wint on 24 Dec 41 and other garrisons surrendered to Japanese forces on 6 May 42.

Campaigns: *Philippine Islands*

Harbor Defenses of Narragansett Bay

Located at the entrance of Rhode Island Sound with HHB at Ft Adams R.I. and initially guarded by the 10th Coast Artillery, reinforced in Sep 40 by the 243rd Coast Artillery; composed of Ft Adams (Newport R.I.), Ft Burnside (Jamestown R.I.), Ft Church (Little Compton R.I.), Ft Getty (Jamestown R.I.), Ft Greene (Narragansett R.I.), Ft Greble (Jamestown R.I.), Ft Kearney (Saunderstown R.I.), Ft Varnum (Narragansett R.I.), Ft Wetherill (Jamestown R.I.), Brenton Point Tactical Position (Newport R.I.), Cp Burlingame (Charlestown R.I.), and miscellaneous tactical positions.

Harbor Defenses of New Bedford

Located at New Bedford Mass and Buzzards Bay with HHB at Ft Rodman Mass and guarded by the 23rd Coast Artillery; composed of Ft Rodman (New Bedford Mass), Barney's Joy Outpost (South Dartmouth Mass), Butler's Point Gun Position (New Bedford Mass), and various minor installations.

Harbor Defenses of New York (Sandy Hook)

Located at New York City and vicinity and initially known as the Harbor Defenses of Sandy Hook with HHB at Ft Hancock N.J. guarded by the 7th and 52nd Coast Artillery, reinforced in Sep 40 by the 245th Coast Artillery; composed of Ft Hancock (Sandy Hook N.J.), Ft Jay (Governors Island N.Y.), Ft Schuyler (New York N.Y.), Ft Tilden (Brooklyn N.Y.), Ft Wadsworth (Richmond N.Y.), and other coastal defense sites.

Harbor Defenses of Pensacola

Located at Pensacola Fla with HHB at Ft Barrancas Fla and initially guarded by elements of the 13th Coast Artillery; composed of Ft Barrancas, Mt McRee, and Ft Pickens (all at Pensacola Fla).

Harbor Defenses of Portland

Located at Portland Maine guarding Casco Bay with HHB at Ft Williams Maine and initially guarded by the 8th Coast Artillery, reinforced in Sep 40 by the 240th Coast Artillery; composed of Ft Levett (Cushing Island Maine), Ft Lyons (Cow Island Maine), Ft McKinley (Great Diamond Island Maine), Ft Preble (South Portland Maine), Ft Williams (Cape Elizabeth Maine), and battery sites on Jewell's Island, Long Island, and Peaks Island.

Harbor Defenses of Portsmouth

Located at Portsmouth N.H. with HHB at Cp Langdon N.H. and initially guarded by the 22nd Coast Artillery; composed of Ft Constitution (New Castle N.H.), Ft Foster (Kittery Maine), Ft Dearborn (Rye N.H.), Ft Stark (New Castle N.H.), Cp Langdon (New Castle N.H.), Gerrish Island Battery (Gerrish Island Maine), Pulpit Rock Defense Installations (Portsmouth N.H.), Salisbury Beach Outpost (Salisbury Beach Mass), and other facilities.

Harbor Defenses of Puget Sound

Located at Puget Sound Wash with HHB at Ft Worden Wash and initially guarded by the 14th Coast Artillery, reinforced in Sep 40 by the 248th Coast Artillery; composed of Ft Casey (Whidby Island Wash), Ft Hayden (Neah Bay Wash), Ft Ebey (Coupeville Wash), Ft Townsend (Port Townsend Wash), Ft Whitman (La Conner Wash), Ft Worden (Port Townsend Wash), Ft Flagler (Marrowstone Island Wash), Agate Pass Position (Port Townsend Wash), Cape George Battery Site (Port Townsend Wash), Cp Greenbank (Greenbank Wash), Middle Point (Port Townsend Wash), Partridge Point (Island Country Wash), Port Angeles Battery Site (Port Angeles Wash), Striped Peak Battery Site (Striped Peak Wash), Tibbals Bluff (Port Townsend Wash), and Willapa Bay Mil Res (Northcove Wash).

Harbor Defenses of San Diego

Located at San Diego Calif with HHB at Ft Rosecrans Calif and initially guarded by the 19th Coast Artillery; composed of Ft Rosecrans (San Diego Calif), Battery Cortez (Coronado Calif), Coronado Beach Battery (Imperial Beach Calif), and other sites.

Harbor Defenses of San Francisco

Located in the vicinity of San Francisco Calif with HHB at Ft Winfield Scott Calif and initially guarded by the 6th Coast Artillery, elements of the 18th Coast Artillery, and the 56th Coast Artillery; composed of Ft Baker, Ft Barry, Ft Cronkhite, Ft Funston, Ft Miley, Ft Winfield Scott, and the Milagara Ridge Seacoast Defense Area (all in the San Francisco Calif vicinity) as well as scattered tactical positions at Half Moon Bay, Jenner, Montara, Pigeon Point (San Mateo Calif), Point Arena, Point Marin, and Point Sur.

Harbor Defenses of San Juan

Located at San Juan Puerto Rico with HHB at Ft Brooke and initially guarded by elements of the 69th Coast Artillery; composed of San Juan harbor defenses, Roosevelt Roads and Ft Bundy overlooking Vieques Sound, and other tactical positions throughout island.

Campaigns: *American Theater without inscription*

Harbor Defenses of Seward

22 Mar 43 formed with headquarters at Ft Bulkley (Rugged Island Alaska) and a subpost at Ft McGilvray (Caines Head Alaska).

Campaigns: *Pacific Theater without inscription*

Harbor Defenses of Sitka

22 Mar 43 formed with headquarters at Ft Rosseau (Makhati Island Alaska) and subposts at Ft Piere (Biroka Alaska) and Ft Babcock (Shoals Point Alaska).

Campaigns: *Pacific Theater without inscription*

Harbor Defenses of Southern New York

Located on Long Island N.Y. and Staten Island N.Y. with HHB at Ft Hamilton N.Y. and initially guarded by the 5th Coast Artillery; composed of Ft Hamilton N.Y. and Ft Wadsworth N.Y. and other positions, all of which were merged into the Harbor Defenses of New York.

Harbor Defenses of Trinidad

Apr 41 garrisoned with elements of the 252nd Coast Artillery and located at Ft Read and Chacachacare Island at the northern entrance to the Gulf of Paria.

Campaigns: *American Theater without inscription*

Harbor Defenses of Wilmington

Located at Wilmington N.C. and composed of Kure Beach Battery (Kure Beach N.C.), Carolina Beach Tactical Position (Wilmington N.C.), and other tactical positions at Morehead City N.C. and Southport N.C.

Chapter 38

Antiaircraft Artillery, Barrage Balloon, and Coast Artillery Battalions

Battalions:

Provisional (HD), Provisional (PS), 1 Provisional, 2 Provisional, 1–4, 6, 7, 9, 12–21, 23–29, 31–38, 42–46, 48, 49, 51–58, 62–81, 85–87, 89, 90, 93–149, 152, 155, 161–181, 184–190, 192, 195–257, 259–262, 264, 266–268, 275–279, 281–283, 285–313, 315–321, 324–348, 350–363, 365–374, 376–403, 405–407, 409–411, 413–415, 417, 419–424, 427–514, 516–523, 526–595, 597–599, 601–607, 630, 633–635, 637–639, 641–643, 701, 727, 729, 731, 734, 736–755, 761–800, 811, 815–824, 832–846, 860–871, 891–903, 906, 910, 913, 925, 932, 933, 938, 945, 947, 948, 950, 951, 967, 977

⊛ EXAMPLE — HOW TO USE THIS TABLE

Unit Designation and Type	Date Formed and Location (Source of Unit) / Inactivation and Location	August 1945 Location

Overseas Wartime Locations followed by - **Campaign Key Numbers** and PE return to United States, if applicable or space allows
(notes and remarks in parenthesis)

161st AAA Gun Bn (Semimobile)	20 Jan 43 Cp Haan Calif as Sep CA Bn AA-Gun (1st Bn, 86th CA) / 26 Feb 46 Japan	San Fernando Philippines
SFPE: 23 Aug 43 Australia: 7 Sep 43 New Guinea: 14 Jan 44 Philippines: 9 Jan 45 - **14,15** *(redes from CA 15 Jun 43)*		

In this example, the 161st Antiaircraft Artillery Gun Battalion (Semimobile) was redesignated from the 1st Battalion, 86th Coast Artillery, at Camp Haan, California, on 20 January, 1943, as the 161st Separate Coast Artillery Battalion, Antiaircraft Gun. The earlier service of the unit can be tracked by looking up the service of the 86th Coast Artillery Regiment in Chapter 36. The 161st Separate Coast Artillery Battalion was redesignated as the 161st Antiaircraft Artillery Gun Battalion on 15 June 1943 (per note on second line). It *departed* San Francisco Port of Embarkation on 23 August 1943 and *arrived* in Australia on 7 September 1943. It landed in New Guinea on 14 January 1944 and in the Philippines on 9 January 1945. The battalion participated in the Luzon and New Guinea campaigns. This information was derived by indexing the boldfaced campaign key numbers with Appendix I. During August 1945 the 161st Antiaircraft Artillery Gun Battalion was located at San Fernando, Philippines, and it was inactivated in Japan on 26 February 1946.

BATTALION DESIGNATION AND TYPE	FORMED (SOURCE OF UNIT) / INACTIVATION *Active through 1946	AUGUST 1945 LOCATION
Provisional CA Bn (Harbor Defense)	12 Jan 43 Alaska / *	Alaska
Provisional CA Bn (155mm Gun) (P.S.)	14 Mar 41 Philippines / 6 May 42 Philippines	
Philippines: 14 Mar 41 - **18** *(surrendered to Japanese forces)*		
1st Provisional CA Bn (Harbor Defense)	20 May 44 Panama Canal Zone / 30 Jun 44 Cp Gruber Okla	
Panama: 20 May 44 NOPE: 14 Jun 44		
1st CA Bn (Harbor Defense)	1 Nov 44 Ft Sherman Canal Zone (1st CA) / 1 Feb 46 Panama Canal Zone	Ft Sherman Canal Zone
Panama: 1 Nov 44		
2nd Provisional CA Bn (Harbor Defense)	20 May 44 Panama Canal Zone / 21 Jun 44 Cp Van Dorn Miss	
Panama: 20 May 44 NOPE: 14 Jun 44		
2nd CA Bn (Harbor Defense)	1 Oct 44 Ft Monroe Va (2nd CA) / 1 Apr 45 Little Creek Mine Base Va	
(SE Sector 1 Oct 44)		
3rd CA Bn (Harbor Defense)	1 Dec 44 Ft MacArthur Calif (520th CA Bn) / 15 Sep 45 Ft MacArthur Calif	Ft MacArthur Calif, less Btry A at Bolsa Chica Calif
3rd Airborne AA Bn, HHD	10 Feb 43 Cp Stewart Ga / 31 Aug 45 San Marcellino Luzon Philippine Islands	Finschhafen New Guinea
SFPE: 26 Jul 43 Australia: 14 Jul 43 New Guinea: 11 Nov 43 Philippines: 27 Aug 45 - **15**		
4th CA Bn (Harbor Defense)	1 Nov 44 Ft Amador Canal Zone (1st Bn, 4th CA) / 1 Feb 46 Panama Canal Zone	Ft Amador Canal Zone, less Btry C at Seymour I Galapagos
6th CA Bn (Harbor Defense)	18 Oct 44 Ft Winfield Scott Calif (1st Bn, 6th CA) / 15 Sep 45 Ft Scott Calif	Ft Winfield Scott Calif, less Btry A at Ft Baker Calif
7th AAA Automatic Weapons Bn (Semimobile)	21 Apr 43 Cp Edwards Mass (2nd Bn, 207th CA) / 12 Jan 46 Cp Stoneman Calif	Ie Shima Island, Ryukyus
SPE: 12 Apr 44 Hawaii: 19 Apr 44 Guam: 22 Jul 44 Philippines: 23 Nov 44 Ie Shima: 16 Apr 45 Okinawa: 21 Apr 45 - **13,19,21**		
SFPE: 10 Jan 46		
9th Airborne AA Bn, HHD	10 Feb 43 Ft Bliss Tex / 31 Aug 45 San Marcellino Luzon Phillipine Islands	Subic Bay Luzon Philippines
SFPE: 26 Jul 43 Australia: 15 Aug 43 New Guinea: 11 Nov 43 Philippines: 16 Aug 45 - **15**		
12th Airborne AA Bn, HHD	10 Feb 43 Ft Bliss Tex / 20 Jun 44 Nadzab New Guinea	
SFPE: 28 Aug 43 Australia: 29 Aug 43 New Guinea: 11 Nov 43 - **15**		
13th Airborne AA Bn, HHD	3 Sep 43 Ft Bliss Tex / 6 May 44 Cp Chaffee Ark *(AA Cmd until 30 Apr 44)*	
13th CA Bn (Harbor Defense)	31 Aug 44 Ft Pickens Fla (2nd Bn, 13th CA) / 1 Apr 45 Ft Pickens Fla	
(HD of Pensacola 1 Jan 45)		
14th Airborne AA Bn, HHD	3 Sep 43 Cp Stewart Ga / 9 May 44 Cp Chaffee Ark *(AA Cmd until 5 May 44)*	
14th CA Bn (Harbor Defense)	18 Oct 44 Ft Casey Wash (1st Bn, 14th CA) / 15 Sep 45 Ft Casey Wash	Ft Casey Wash, less Btry B at Ft Ebey Wash
15th Airborne AA Bn, HHD	3 Sep 43 Cp Stewart Ga / 9 May 44 Cp Chaffee Ark *(AA Cmd until 5 May 44)*	

BATTALION DESIGNATION AND TYPE	FORMED (SOURCE OF UNIT) / INACTIVATION	AUGUST 1945 LOCATION
16th Airborne AA Bn Burma: 22 Jun 44 - **5,12**	22 Jun 44 Burma / 9 Jul 45 Burma	
17th Airborne AA Bn India: 22 Jun 44 Burma: 12 Jan 45 India: 13 May 45 - **5**	22 Jun 44 Moran Airfield India / 10 Jul 45 Dinjan India	
18th Airborne AA Bn India: 22 Jun 44 Burma: 16 Jan 45 India: 29 Jun 45 - **5**	22 Jun 44 India / 9 Jul 45 India	
19th CA Bn (Harbor Defense)	18 Oct 44 Ft Rosecrans Calif (1st Bn, 19th CA) / 15 Sep 45 Ft Rosecrans Calif	Ft Rosecrans Calif
20th CA Bn (Harbor Defense) *(HD of Galveston 31 Aug 44)*	31 Aug 44 Ft Travis Tex (1st Bn, 20th CA) / 31 Mar 45 Ft Travis Tex	
21st CA Bn (Harbor Defense)	1 Oct 44 Ft Miles Del (1st Bn, 21st CA) / 1 Apr 45 Ft Miles Del *(EDC 1 Oct 44)*	
23rd Separate CA Bn (Harbor Defense) (I)	1 Feb 40 Ft Rodman Mass / 27 Dec 40 Ft Rodman Mass redes 23rd CA Regt	
23rd Separate CA Bn (Harbor Defense) (II)	21 Aug 41 Ft Rodman Mass (23rd CA) / 13 Sep 43 Ft Rodman Mass redes 1st Bn 23rd CA	
23rd Separate CA Bn (Harbor Defense) (III)	6 Mar 44 Ft Rodman (23rd CA) / 7 Oct 44 Ft Rodman redes Btry C (Searchlight) HD of New Bedford	
24th CA Bn (Composite Harbor Defense) NYPE: 3 Feb 42 Newfoundland: 25 Mar 42 NYPE: 2 Jan 44 *(initially Separate CA Bn Harbor Defense until 10 Apr 43 when reorg as CA Bn Composite Harbor Defense) (Newfoundland Base Cmd)*	17 Jan 42 H.G. Wright LI N.Y. / 15 Jan 44 Cp Shelby Miss	
25th Separate CA Bn (Harbor Defense) NYPE: 29 Apr 44 Iceland: 10 May 42	22 Jan 42 HD of Sandy Hook N.J. / 28 Oct 43 Iceland redes 748th AAA Gun Bn	
26th Separate CA Bn (Harbor Defense) BPE: 21 Aug 42 Iceland: 31 Aug 42	28 Jan 42 Ft McKinley Maine / 28 Oct 43 Iceland redes 749th AAA Gun Bn	
27th CA Bn (6-inch Gun) (Composite) *(originally formed from Btry F, 52nd CA Regt [8-inch Ry] and Btry B, G, and H, 53rd CA Regt; changed armament to 6-inch Gun on 1 Aug 43)* *(Bermuda Base Cmd)*	20 Feb 42 Castle Harbor Bermuda / 1 Jun 44 Royal Bermuda Yacht Club Bermuda	

28th CA Bn

Following components of 28th CA Bn (Harbor Defense) raised; Btry A and 1st Plat, Btry C activated 6 Feb 42 at Cp Pendleton Va and inactivated 15 Apr 44 at Cp Hood Tex; Btry B and 2nd Plat, Btry C activated 17 Mar 42 at Cp Pendleton Va and arrived Ascension I. 14 Aug 42; inactivated there on 5 Oct 44.

29th CA Bn

Btry A and 1st Plat, Btry C of 29th CA Bn (155mm Gun) activated 6 Feb 42 at Cp Pendleton Va and inactivated 1 Jun 44 in Puerto Rico.

31st CA Bn (155mm Gun) New Caledonia: 20 Jan 43 New Hebrides: 4 Aug 43 New Guinea: 25 Jul 44 Philippines: 1 Mar 45 - **14,15** *(Separate CA Bn Harbor Defense until 1 Jun 44)*	20 Jun 43 New Caledonia (812th & 825th CA Btry) / 20 Aug 45 Philippines	Manila Philippines
32nd CA Bn (155mm Gun)	18 Feb 44 Hawaii (1st Bn, 47th CA) / 31 May 44 Hawaii	
33rd CA Bn (155mm Gun) Hawaii: 18 Feb 44 Saipan: 26 Aug 44 - **21**	18 Feb 44 Waimea Hawaii (2nd Bn, 47th CA) / 13 Dec 45 Saipan	Saipan Island
34th Separate CA Bn (Composite) *(EDC until 15 Mar 44)*	10 Jun 43 Cp Pendleton Va / 17 Aug 44 Cp Joseph T Robinson redes 784th FA Bn	
35th Bn (Harbor Defense)	1 Nov 44 Puerto Rico (35th CA) / 28 Feb 46 Puerto Rico	Ft Brooke Puerto Rico
36th CA Bn (Harbor Defense)	1 Nov 44 Ft Kobbe Canal Zone (36th CA) / 1 Feb 46 Panama Canal Zone	Ft Kobbe Canal Zone
37th CA Bn (Harbor Defense)	1 Nov 44 Ft Sherman Canal Zone / 1 Feb 46 Panama Canal Zone	Ft Sherman Canal Zone
38th CA Bn (155mm Gun) Hawaii: 15 Mar 44 Philippines: 15 Nov 44 New Caledonia: 23 Jan 45 Okinawa: 24 Jun 45 - **13,19**	15 Mar 44 Hawaii (3rd Bn, 47th CA) / 9 Oct 45 Okinawa	Okinawa
42nd CA Bn (155mm Gun) SPE: 16 Feb 44 Attu I: 5 Mar 44 SPE: 26 Nov 45	2 Feb 44 Montauk N.Y. (1st Bn, 50th CA Regt) / 28 Nov 45 Ft Lawton Wash	Cp Earle Alaska
43rd CA Bn (155mm Gun) Admiralty Islands: 5 Apr 44 Pityilu I: 16 Apr 44 - **3,15** LAPE: 30 Dec 45	5 Apr 44 Admiralty Islands (2nd Bn, 50th CA) / 31 Dec 45 Cp Anza Calif	Pityilu I, Admiralty Islands
44th CA Bn (155mm Gun) SFPE: 16 Feb 44 Hawaii: 22 Feb 44 Saipan: 26 Jul 44 Iwo Jima: 11 Apr 45 - **1,21**	22 Jan 44 Ft Cronkhite Calif (1st Bn, 56th CA) / 11 Dec 45 Iwo Jima	Iwo Jima

BATTALION DESIGNATION AND TYPE	FORMED (SOURCE OF UNIT) / INACTIVATION *Active through 1946	AUGUST 1945 LOCATION

45th CA Bn (155mm Gun)
22 Jan 44 Ft Cronkhite Calif (2nd Bn, 56th CA) / 2 Dec 45 Philippines — Cebu Philippines
SFPE: 16 Feb 44   Hawaii: 21 Feb 44   Angaur I: 12 Nov 44   Philippines: 24 May 45 - **13,21**

46th CA Bn (155mm Gun)
5 Jun 44 Cp Pendleton Va (1st Bn, 46th CA) / 17 Aug 44 Cp Joseph T Robinson Ark redes 783rd FA Bn

48th CA Bn (155mm Gun)
21 Jan 44 Ft Cronkhite Calif (3rd Bn, 56th CA) / 2 Nov 45 Peleliu Island — Peleliu Palau Islands
SFPE: 28 Feb 44   Hawaii: 5 Mar 44   Peleliu I: 11 Nov 44 - **21**

49th CA Bn (Cld) (155mm Gun)
1 Apr 44 Bougainville (2nd Bn, 54th CA) / 20 Jan 46 Philippines — Finschhafen New Guinea
Bougainville: 1 Apr 44   New Guinea: 18 Mar 45   Philippines: 27 Aug 45 - **16**

51st CA Bn (155mm Gun)
1 Jun 44 Port of Spain Trinidad (1st Bn, 51st CA) / 28 Feb 46 Trinidad — Port of Spain Trinidad

52nd CA Bn (155mm Gun)
1 Jun 44 Port of Spain Trinidad (2nd Bn, 51st CA) / 28 Feb 46 Trinidad — Port of Spain Trinidad

53rd CA Bn (Harbor Defense)
13 Aug 44 Ft Shafter Hawaii (53rd CA Btry) / 10 Apr 45 Hawaii

54th CA Bn (Harbor Defense)
13 Aug 44 Ft Kamehameha Hawaii (2nd Bn, 15th CA) / 10 Apr 46 Hawaii — Ft Kamehameha, less Btry B on Sand Island

55th CA Bn (Harbor Defense)
13 Aug 44 Hawaii / 13 Feb 45 Hawaii

56th CA Bn (Harbor Defense)
13 Aug 44 Hawaii / 10 Apr 45 Hawaii

57th CA Bn (Harbor Defense)
13 Aug 44 Hawaii / 29 Nov 46 Hawaii — Ft Hase Hawaii

58th CA Bn (Harbor Defense)
13 Aug 44 Hawaii / 10 Dec 46 Hawaii — Ft Kamehameha Hawaii

62nd AAA Gun Bn (Mobile)
24 Mar 44 Sicily (1st Bn, 62nd CA) / 13 Mar 46 Cp Kilmer N.J. — Altenstadt Germany
Sicily: 24 Mar 44   Italy: 7 Jul 44   France-ETO: 16 Aug 44 - **25,26,34,35,37**   NYPE: 12 Mar 46

63rd AAA Gun Bn (Semimobile)
10 Sep 43 Seattle Wash (1st Bn, 63rd CA) / * — Shipment #0894-A at Ulithi Atoll
SPE: 23 Jul 45   Okinawa: 21 Aug 45

64th AAA Gun Bn (Semimobile)
12 Dec 43 Ft Shafter Hawaii (1st Bn, 64th CA) / 20 May 46 Guam — Guam
Hawaii: 12 Dec 43   Guam: 10 Sep 44 - **21**

65th AAA Gun Bn (Semimobile)
10 May 43 Ft Ord Calif (1st Bn, 65th CA) / 26 Jan 45 Cp Hood Tex
SFPE: 12 Jul 43   Alaska: 22 Jul 43   SPE: 16 Dec 44 -**2** *(Amphib Tng Force #9 10 May 43)*

66th AAA Gun Bn (Semimobile)
6 Nov 43 Puerto Rico (1st Bn, 66th CA) / 27 Dec 44 Cp Gordon Ga
Puerto Rico: 6 Nov 43   NYPE: 4 Dec 44 *(R&S Cmd 17 Dec 44)*

67th AAA Gun Bn (Mobile)
23 May 44 Torino Italy (1st Bn, 67th CA) / 25 Nov 45 Cp Shanks N.Y. — Westheim Germany
Italy: 23 May 44   France-ETO: 13 Sep 44 - **25,26,34,35,37**   NYPE: 24 Nov 45

68th AAA Gun Bn (Mobile)
4 Jun 44 Anzio Italy (1st Bn, 68th CA) / 5 Apr 46 Cp Kilmer N.J. — Heidelberg Germany
Italy: 4 Jun 44   France-ETO: 15 Aug 44 - **26,34,35,37**   NYPE: 4 Apr 46

69th AAA Gun Bn (Semimobile)
10 Sep 43 San Diego Calif (1st Bn, 69th CA) / 9 Nov 44 Cp Howze Tex
(R&S Cmd 26 Oct 44)

70th AAA Gun Bn (Semimobile)
10 Nov 45 Segi Point New Georgia (1st Bn, 70th CA) / * — Dagunan Philippines
New Georgia I: 10 Nov 43   Bougainville: 23 Jun 44   New Guinea: 18 Dec 44   Manus I: 21 Dec 44   Philippines: 9 Jan 45 - **14,16**

71st AAA Gun Bn (Semimobile)
1 Sep 43 Washington D.C. (1st Bn, 71st CA) / 10 Jan 45 redes 526th AAA Gun Bn at Orlando Fla

72nd AAA Gun Bn (Mobile)
14 Mar 44 Anzio Italy (1st Bn, 209th CA) / 26 Nov 45 Cp Kilmer N.J. — Munich Germany
Italy: 14 Mar 44   France-ETO: 15 Aug 44 - **24,25,26,34,35,37**   NYPE: 25 Nov 45

73rd AAA Gun Bn (Semimobile)
23 Mar 44 Castel Volturno Italy (1st Bn, 213th CA) / 25 Jan 45 Marseille France, assets to 360th, 361st and 363rd MP Cos
Italy: 23 Mar 44   Corsica: 26 May 44   France-ETO: 8 Nov 44 - **34,35**

74th AAA Gun Bn (Mobile)
1 Apr 44 Cagliari Sardinia (1st Bn, 74th CA) / 31 Dec 44 Marseille France, assets to 370th Engr Combat Bn
Sardinia: 1 Apr 44   Corsica: 30 Jul 44   France-ETO: 16 Nov 44 - **35**

75th AAA Gun Bn (Mobile)
20th Feb 44 Ft Bliss Tex (1st Bn, 75th CA) / 25 Feb 45 Ft Bliss Tex
(AA Cmd 20 Feb 44)

76th AAA Gun Bn (Cld) (Semimobile)
1 Nov 43 New Hebrides (1st Bn, 76th CA) / 31 Dec 45 Cp Anza Calif — Admiralty Islands
New Hebrides: 1 Nov 43   New Georgia: 4 Feb 44   Vella LaVella: 10 Feb 44   New Georgia: 8 Jun 44   Los Negros I: 8 Jan 45 - **16**
LAPE: 30 Dec 45

BATTALION DESIGNATION AND TYPE	FORMED (SOURCE OF UNIT)/INACTIVATION *Active through 1946	AUGUST 1945 LOCATION

77th AAA Gun Bn (Cld) (Semimobile)   1 Nov 43 New Hebrides (1st Bn, 77th CA) / 31 Dec 45 Cp Anza Calif   Admiralty Islands
New Hebrides: 1 Nov 43   New Georgia: 8 Dec 43   Admiralty I: 8 Feb 45   LAPE: 30 Dec 45 - **16**

78th AAA Gun Bn (Semimobile)   7 Feb 44 Attu Island (1st Bn, 78th CA) / 31 Oct 45 Ft Bliss Tex   Ft Bliss Tex
Aleutians: 7 Feb 44   SPE: 8 Jan 45 *(R&S Cmd 7 Oct 45)*

79th AAA Gun Bn (Mobile)   1 Sep 43 Manchester Conn (1st Bn, 79th CA) / 31 Oct 44 Cp Gordon Ga
(R&S Cmd 20 Oct 44)

80th Airborne AA Bn   5 Sep 42 Cp Claiborne La / *   Marchais France
NYPE: 28 Apr 43   N.Africa: 10 May 43   Sicily: 9 Jul 43   Italy: 10 Sep 43   N.Ireland: 9 Dec 43   England: 15 Feb 44
France-ETO: 6 Jun 44   England: 13 Jul 44   Holland-ETO: 17 Sep 44 - **25,26,29,30,34,36**   NYPE: 3 Jan 46 *(82nd A/B Div)*

81st Airborne AA Bn   3 Sep 42 Cp Claiborne La / 30 Nov 45 Germany   Inzell Germany
NYPE: 2 Sep 43   England: 15 Sep 43   France: 6 Jun 44   England: 13 Jul 44   Holland-ETO: 17 Sep 44 - **25,26,30,34** *(101st A/B Div)*

85th AAA Gun Bn (Semimobile)   1 Sep 43 Newport News Va (1st Bn, 85th CA) / 4 Nov 44 Cp Maxey Tex
(EDC until 4 Aug 44)

86th AAA Gun Bn (Semimobile)   12 Feb 44 Alaska (1st Bn, 203rd CA) / 4 Nov 44 Cp Maxey Tex
Alaska: 12 Feb 44   SPE: 21 Aug 44 *(R&S Cmd 25 Oct 44)*

87th AAA Gun Bn (Mobile)   23 Mar 44 Santa Maria Italy (1st Bn, 505th CA) / 26 Jan 45 Miramas France,
Italy: 23 Mar 44   Corsica: 26 Mar 44   France-ETO: 5 Nov 44 - **29,35**   assets to 106th AAA Group

89th AAA Gun Bn (Mobile)   1 Sep 43 Military District Washington D.C. (1st Bn, 89th CA) / 31 Oct 44 Cp Gordon Ga
(R&S Cmd 20 Oct 44)

90th AAA Gun Bn (Cld) (Semimobile)   25 May 44 Oran North Africa (1st Bn, 90th CA) / 4 Dec 44 Pozzouli Italy
North Africa: 25 May 44   Italy: Unknown

93rd AAA Gun Bn (Semimobile)   12 Dec 43 Aiea Hawaii (1st Bn, 95th CA) / 30 Jan 46 Okinawa   Ie Shima Island Ryukyus
Hawaii: 12 Dec 43   Ie Shima: 20 Apr 45   Okinawa: 19 Nov 45 - **13,19**

94th AAA Gun Bn (Semimobile)   11 Apr 44 Adak Island (1st Bn, 210th CA) / 1 Nov 44 Cp Howze Tex
Adak I Aleutians: 11 Apr 44   SPE: 20 Aug 44 *(R&S Cmd 23 Oct 44)*

95th AAA Gun Bn (Semimobile)   8 Feb 44 Alaska (1st Bn, 503rd CA) / 24 Dec 44 Cp Maxey Tex
Alaska: 8 Feb 44   SPE: 4 Jun 44 *(R&S Cmd 20 Dec 44)*

96th AAA Gun Bn (Semimobile)   12 Dec 43 Ft Weaver Hawaii (1st Bn, 96th CA) / 7 Nov 45 Hawaii   Ft Hase Hawaii
Hawaii: 12 Dec 43   Kwajalein I: 4 Feb 44   Enrylabegan I: 7 Feb 44   Enubuj I: 15 Feb 44   Hawaii: 6 Oct 44 - **10**

97th AAA Gun Bn (Semimobile)   12 Dec 43 Schofield Bks Hawaii (1st Bn, 97th CA) / *   Ft Kamehameha Hawaii

98th AAA Gun Bn (Semimobile)   12 Dec 43 Hawaii (1st Bn, 98th CA) / 21 Jan 46 Cp Anza Calif   Okinawa
Hawaii: 12 Dec 43   Kwajalein I: 1 Feb 44   Hawaii: 5 Aug 44   Okinawa: 3 Jun 45 - **10,19**   LAPE: 20 Jan 46

99th AAA Gun Bn (Cld) (Semimobile)   29 Feb 44 Cp Stewart Ga (1st Bn, 99th CA) / 28 Aug 44 Cp Breckinridge Ky
(AA Cmd until 29 Feb 44)

100th AAA Gun Bn (Cld) (Semimobile)   20 Apr 43 Cp Stewart Ga (1st Bn, 100th CA) / 4 Dec 44 New Guinea
SFPE: 1 Nov 43   Australia: 18 Nov 43   New Guinea: 18 Feb 44 - **15**

101st AAA Auto-Wpns Bn (Air Transp.)   10 Feb 41 Hinesville Tex as Sep CA Bn AA-AW / 28 Dec 45 Cp Stoneman Calif   Manila Philippines
NYPE: 18 Feb 42   Australia: 29 Mar 42   New Guinea: 3 May 42   Philippines: 14 Mar 45 - **9,14,15**   SFPE: 25 Dec 45
(redes from CA 15 Sep 44)

101st CA Seacoast Training Bn   14 Jul 42 Ft Eustis Va / 1 Dec 43 Cp McQuade Calif
(CA Replacement Training Center)

102nd AAA Auto-Wpns Bn (Air Transp.)   6 Jan 41 Buffalo N.Y. as Sep CA Bn AA-AW / 24 Dec 45 Cp Stoneman Calif   Mindoro Philippines, less
SFPE: 18 Feb 42   Australia: 9 Mar 42   New Guinea: 7 Jul 43   Philippines: 18 Nov 44 - **9,13,14,15**   SFPE: 24 Dec 45   Btry A at Laoag Philippines
(redes from CA 15 Jun 44)

102nd CA Seacoast Training Bn   14 Jul 42 Cp Callan Calif / 1 Dec 43 Cp McQuade Calif
(CA Replacement Training Center)

103rd AAA Automatic Weapons Bn (Mobile)   24 Feb 41 Frankfort Ky as Sep CA Bn AA-AW / 1 Dec 45 Cp Kilmer N.J.   St Kynsperk Germany
NYPE: 30 Apr 44   N.Ireland: 15 May 42   N.Africa: 8 Dec 42   Sicily: 9 Jul 43   England: 9 Dec 43
France-ETO: 10 Jun 44 - **25,26,30,32,34,36** *(redes from CA 15 Nov 43)*

104th AAA Automatic Weapons Bn (Mobile)   10 Feb 41 Birmingham Ala as Sep CA Bn AA-AW / 31 Jan 46 Japan   San Marcelino Philippines
NYPE: 18 Feb 42   Australia: 28 Mar 42   New Guinea: 13 Aug 43   Goodenough I: 19 Oct 43   New Guinea: 22 Apr 44
Philippines: 22 Jun 45 - **9,14,15** *(redes from CA 15 Jun 44)*

BATTALION DESIGNATION AND TYPE	FORMED (SOURCE OF UNIT) / INACTIVATION *Active through 1946	AUGUST 1945 LOCATION

105th AAA Automatic Weapons Bn (S-P)   6 Jan 41 New Orleans La as Sep CA Bn AA-AW / 15 Sep 45 Italy   Barberino Italy
NYPE: 5 Aug 42   England: 17 Aug 42   Scotland: 24 Sep 42   N.Africa: 8 Nov 42   Sicily: 11 Jul 43   Italy: 15 Sep 43 - **23,29,31,33,35,36,38**
(redes from CA 1 Jul 44)

106th AAA Automatic Weapons Bn (S-P)   6 Jan 41 Covington Ky as Sep CA Bn AA-AW / 3 Dec 45 Cp Shanks N.Y.   Munich Germany
NYPE: 30 Apr 42   N.Ireland: 15 May 42   N.Africa: 8 Nov 42   Sicily: 10 Jul 43   Italy: 17 Sep 43
France-ETO: 15 Aug 44 - **23,24,25,26,29,34,35,36,37,38** *(redes from CA 14 Jul 44)*

107th AAA Automatic Weapons Bn (Mobile)   10 Feb 41 Dillion S.C. as Sep CA Bn AA-AW / 5 Dec 44 Pouzzila Italy
NYPE: 6 Aug 42   England: 17 Aug 42   N.Africa: 6 Dec 42   Sicily: 10 Jul 43   Italy: 19 Jun 44   France-ETO: 15 Aug 44 - **35,36,37,38**
(redes from CA 13 Nov 43)

108th AAA Gun Bn (Mobile)   10 Jan 43 Cp Edwards Mass as Sep CA Bn AA-Gun / 16 Nov 45 Cp Patrick Henry Va   Meckesheim Germany
NYPE: 21 Aug 43   N.Africa: 2 Sep 43   Italy: 19 Dec 43   France-ETO: 15 Aug 44 - **24,25,26,29,34,35,37**   HRPE: 16 Nov 45
(redes from CA 28 Jun 43)

109th AAA Gun Bn (Mobile)   10 Jan 43 Cp Edwards Mass as Sep CA Bn AA-Gun / 19 Oct 45 Cp Patrick Henry Va   Breidenbach Germany
NYPE: 16 Jul 43   England: 26 Jul 43   France-ETO: 11 Jun 44 - **25,26,30,32,34**   HRPE: 19 Oct 45 *(redes from CA 1 Oct 43)*

110th AAA Gun Bn (Mobile)   20 Jan 43 Cp Edwards Mass as Sep CA Bn AA-Gun / 6 Oct 45 Germany   Weilburg Germany
NYPE: 23 Dec 43   England: 29 Dec 43   France-ETO: 7 Jun 44 - **25,26,30,32,34** *(redes from CA 28 Jun 43)*

111th AAA Gun Bn (Semimobile)   10 Feb 43 Ft Bliss Tex as Sep CA Bn AA-Gun / 1 Dec 44 Cp Livingston La
(redes from CA 28 Jun 43)

112th AAA Gun Bn (Semimobile)   10 Feb 43 Ft Bliss Tex as Sep CA Bn AA-Gun / 20 Mar 46 Cp Kilmer N.J.   Saaralbe France
NYPE: 21 Aug 43   N.Africa: 2 Sep 43   France-ETO: 30 Aug 44 - **34,37**   NYPE: 19 Mar 46 *(redes from CA 28 Jun 43)*

113th AAA Gun Bn (Semimobile)   10 Feb 43 Ft Bliss Tex as Sep CA Bn AA-Gun / 2 Jan 46 Cp Kilmer N.J.   Les Aigalades Belgium
NYPE: 21 Aug 43   N.Africa: 2 Sep 43   England: 10 Aug 44   France-ETO: 22 Oct 44 - **25,26,34**   NYPE: 1 Jan 46 *(redes from CA 28 Jun 43)*

114th AAA Gun Bn (Semimobile)   10 Feb 43 Ft Bliss Tex as Sep CA Bn AA-Gun / 9 Jul 46 France   Romilly France
NYPE: 21 Aug 43   N.Africa: 2 Sep 43   England: 15 Sep 44   France-ETO: 15 Nov 44 - **34** *(redes from CA 28 Jun 43)*

115th AAA Gun Bn (Mobile)   20 Mar 43 Cp Davis N.C. as Sep CA Bn AA-Gun / *   Abensberg Germany
NYPE: 5 Dec 43   England: 16 Dec 43   France-ETO: 13 Jun 44 - **25,26,28,30,32,34** *(redes from CA 28 Jun 43)*

116th AAA Gun Bn (Mobile)   20 Mar 43 Cp Davis N.C. as Sep CA Bn AA-Gun / 6 Oct 45 Germany   Wetzlar Germany
NYPE: 13 Oct 43   England: 18 Oct 43   France-ETO: 7 Jun 44 - **25,26,30,32,34**   *(redes from CA 28 Jun 43)*

117th AAA Gun Bn (Mobile)   20 Mar 43 Cp Davis N.C. as Sep CA Bn AA-Gun / 27 Dec 44 Ft Jackson S.C.
(redes from CA 28 Jun 43)

118th AAA Gun Bn (Mobile)   2 Apr 43 Cp Haan Calif as Sep CA Bn AA-Gun / 15 Nov 45 Cp Kilmer N.J.   Namur Belgium
NYPE: 23 Dec 43   England: 29 Dec 43   France-ETO: 9 Jun 44 - **30,32,34**   NYPE: 13 Nov 45 *(redes from CA 28 Jun 43)*

119th AAA Gun Bn (Mobile)   2 Apr 43 Cp Haan Calif as Sep CA Bn AA-Gun / 17 Dec 45 Cp Kilmer N.J.   Biberg Germany
NYPE: 31 Mar 44   England: 8 Apr 44   France-ETO: 8 Jul 44 - **25,26,30,32,34**   NYPE: 16 Dec 45 *(redes from CA 28 Jun 43)*

120th AAA Gun Bn (Mobile)   2 Apr 43 Cp Haan Calif as Sep CA Bn AA-Gun / 4 Dec 45 Cp Patrick Henry Va   Lindhart Germany
NYPE: 23 Dec 43   England: 29 Dec 43   France-ETO: 16 Jun 44 - **25,26,28,30,32,34**   HRPE: 4 Dec 45 *(redes from CA 28 Jun 43)*

121st AAA Gun Bn (Mobile)   23 Jun 41 Reno Nev as Sep CA Bn AA-Gun / 4 Jan 45 Ft Sill Okla redes 1st Rocket Bn
(redes from CA 10 Sep 43)

122nd AAA Gun Bn (Semimobile)   27 Jan 41 Jersey City N.J. as Sep CA Bn AA-Gun / 3 Feb 45 Shemya Alaska
SPE: 23 Jul 44   Amchitka Alaska: 3 Aug 44   Shemya Alaska: 5 Nov 44 *(redes from CA 10 Sep 43)*

123rd AAA Gun Bn, Composite (Semimobile)   2 Apr 41 Puerto Rico (1st Bn, 201st CA) as Sep CA Bn AA-Gun / 31 Oct 44 Puerto Rico
Puerto Rico: 2 Apr 41   Trinidad: 23 Nov 43   Puerto Rico: 7 Jun 44
(redes from CA as 123rd AAA Gun Bn 15 Oct 43 in Puerto Rico; reorg as AAA Gun Bn, Composite 1 Jun 44 in British West Indies)

124th AAA Gun Bn (Mobile)   24 May 43 Cp Haan Calif as Sep CA Bn AA-Gun / 18 Oct 45 Cp Patrick Henry Va   Ober Kollbach Germany
BPE: 1 Jul 44   England: 8 Jul 44   France-ETO: 25 Sep 44 - **25,26,28,34**   HRPE: 18 Oct 45 *(redes from CA 28 Jun 43)*

125th AAA Gun Bn (Mobile)   24 May 43 Cp Haan Calif as Sep CA Bn AA-Gun / 27 Mar 46 Cp Kilmer N.J.   Stenay France
BPE: 1 Jul 44   England: 8 Jul 44   France-ETO: 23 Sep 44 - **25,28,34**   NYPE: 26 Mar 46 *(redes from CA 28 Jun 43)*

126th AAA Gun Bn (Mobile)   10 May 43 Cp Haan Calif as Sep CA Bn AA-Gun / 3 Jan 46 Cp Patrick Henry Va   Meiningen Germany
BPE: 1 Jul 44   England: 8 Jul 44   France-ETO: 28 Sep 44 - **25,26,28,34**   HRPE: 3 Jan 46 *(redes from CA 28 Jun 43)*

127th AAA Gun Bn (Mobile)   10 May 43 Cp Haan Calif as Sep CA Bn AA-Gun / 21 Mar 46 Cp Kilmer N.J.   Wetzlar Germany
NYPE: 2 Jul 44   England: 15 Jul 44   France-ETO: 27 Sep 44 - **25,26,28,34**   NYPE: 20 Mar 46 *(redes from CA 28 Jun 43)*

128th AAA Gun Bn (Mobile)   20 May 43 Ft Bliss Tex as Sep CA Bn AA-Gun / 30 Dec 45 Cp Kilmer N.J.   Arnshofen Germany
NYPE: 10 Apr 44   England: 16 Apr 44   France-ETO: 26 Jul 44 - **25,26,30,32,34**   NYPE: 29 Dec 45 *(redes from CA 28 Jun 43)*

BATTALION DESIGNATION AND TYPE	FORMED (SOURCE OF UNIT)/INACTIVATION *Active through 1946	AUGUST 1945 LOCATION
129th AAA Gun Bn (Mobile) NYPE: 29 Dec 43 England: 7 Jan 44 France-ETO: 27 Jun 44 - **25,26,28,30,32,34** NYPE: 6 Dec 45 *(redes from CA 28 Jun 43)*	20 May 43 Ft Bliss Tex as Sep CA Bn AA-Gun / 7 Dec 45 Cp Kilmer N.J.	Aiglsbach Germany
130th CA Bn (AA) (Gun) (Semimobile)	1 Apr 42 Ft Winfield Scott Calif / 5 May 44 Cp Breckinridge Ky	
131st AAA Gun Bn (Mobile) NYPE: 24 Jul 44 England: 31 Jul 44 France-ETO: 23 Aug 44 - **26,32,34** NYPE: 30 Dec 45 *(redes from CA 28 Jun 43)*	20 May 43 Ft Bliss Tex as Sep CA Bn AA-Gun / 31 Dec 45 Cp Kilmer N.J.	Ottending Germany
132nd AAA Gun Bn (Mobile) NYPE: 23 Jul 44 England: 28 Jul 44 France-ETO: 23 Aug 44 - **26,32,34** NYPE: 19 Feb 46 *(redes from CA 28 Jun 43)*	15 Jun 43 Cp Edwards Mass as Sep CA Bn AA-Gun / 20 Feb 46 Cp Kilmer N.J.	Holzhausen Germany
133rd AAA Gun Bn (Mobile) NYPE: 24 Jul 44 England: 31 Jul 44 France-ETO: 23 Aug 44 - **26,32,34** *(redes from CA 28 Jun 43)*	15 Jun 43 Cp Edwards Mass at Sep CA Bn AA-Gun / 31 Jul 46 Austria	Egefing France
134th AAA Gun Bn (Mobile) BPE: 3 Jul 44 England: 12 Jul 44 France-ETO: 26 Sep 44 - **25,26,28,34** NYPE: 19 Feb 46	10 Jun 43 Ft Sheridan Ill / 20 Feb 46 Cp Kilmer N.J.	Wetzlar Germany
135th AAA Gun Bn (Mobile) NYPE: 28 Aug 44 England: 3 Sep 44 France-ETO: 29 Sep 44 - **26,34** NYPE: 20 Feb 46	15 Jun 43 Cp Edwards Mass / 22 Feb 46 Cp Kilmer N.J.	Ergoldsbach Germany
136th AAA Gun Bn (Mobile) NYPE: 26 Jul 44 England: 6 Aug 44 France-ETO: 27 Aug 44 - **25,26,32,34** BPE: 11 Dec 45	15 Jun 43 Cp Edwards Mass / 12 Dec 45 Cp Myles Standish Mass	Augsburg Germany
137th AAA Gun Bn (Semimobile) SFPE: 31 Dec 44 Philippines: 14 Jan 45	10 Jun 43 Cp Edwards Mass / 18 Mar 45 Tacloban Philippines, assets to 608th MP Bn	
138th AAA Gun Bn (Mobile)	20 Jul 43 Cp Davis N.C. / 1 Dec 44 Cp Livingston La *(R&S Cmd 27 Nov 44)*	
139th AAA Gun Bn (Semimobile) SFPE: 27 Jan 45 New Guinea: 12 Feb 45 Philippines: 27 Feb 45 - **13**	20 Jul 43 Cp Davis N.C. / 18 Mar 45 Philippines	
140th AAA Gun Bn (Semimobile)	10 Jul 43 Cp Edwards Mass / 25 Jan 45 Cp Haan Calif *(AA Cmd until 11 Jun 44)*	
141st AAA Gun Bn (Mobile) BPE: 7 Sep 44 England: 14 Sep 44 France-ETO: 19 Sep 44 - **25,26,34** NYPE: 4 Apr 46	10 Jul 43 Cp Edwards Mass / 5 Apr 46 Cp Kilmer N.J.	Erwitte Germany
142nd AAA Gun Bn (Mobile) BPE: 7 Sep 44 England: 14 Sep 44 France-ETO: 18 Sep 44 - **25,26,34** NYPE: 31 Mar 46	10 Jul 43 Cp Edwards Mass / 1 Apr 46 Cp Kilmer N.J.	Herborn Germany
143rd AAA Gun Bn (Mobile) NYPE: 26 Jul 44 England: 6 Aug 44 France-ETO: 31 Aug 44 - **25,26,32,34** NYPE: 21 Dec 45	10 Jul 43 Cp Haan Calif / 22 Dec 45 Cp Kilmer N.J.	Esslingen Germany
144th AAA Gun Bn (Semimobile)	20 Jul 43 Cp Haan Calif / 30 May 44 Cp Howze Tex *(AA Cmd until 4 May 44)*	
145th AAA Gun Bn (Mobile)	1 Oct 43 Cp Stewart Ga / 9 May 44 Cp Van Dorn Miss *(AA Cmd until 4 May 44)*	
146th AAA Gun Bn (Mobile)	1 Oct 43 Ft Bliss Tex / 9 May 44 Cp Chaffee Ark *(AA Cmd until 5 May 44)*	
147th AAA Gun Bn (Mobile)	1 Oct 43 Ft Bliss Tex / 8 Nov 44 Cp Maxey Tex *(R&S Cmd 24 Oct 44)*	
148th AAA Gun Bn (Mobile)	1 Oct 43 Ft Bliss Tex / 2 Nov 44 Cp Maxey Tex *(R&S Cmd 25 Oct 44)*	
149th AAA Gun Bn (Mobile)	1 Oct 43 Ft Bliss Tex / 2 Nov 44 Cp Maxey Tex *(R&S Cmd 25 Oct 44)*	
152nd Airborne AA Bn SFPE: 6 May 44 New Guinea: 1 Jun 44 Philippines: 19 Nov 44 Okinawa: 21 Aug 45 - **13,14,15** *(11th A/B Div)*	25 Feb 43 Cp Mackall N.C. / *	Okinawa *(arriving via air)*
153rd Airborne AA Bn NYPE: 26 Jan 45 France-ETO: 6 Feb 45 - **26** NYPE: 20 Aug 45 *(13th A/B Div)*	13 Aug 43 Ft Bragg N.C. / 25 Feb 46 Ft Bragg N.C.	Shipment #10580-L at sea
155th Airborne AA Bn BPE: 17 Aug 44 England: 25 Aug 44 France-ETO: 24 Dec 44 - **25,26,34** BPE: 14 Sep 45 *(17th A/B Div)*	15 Apr 43 Cp Mackall N.C. / 14 Sep 45 Cp Myles Standish Mass	Hamborn Germany
161st AAA Gun Bn (Semimobile) SFPE: 23 Aug 43 Australia: 7 Sep 43 New Guinea: 14 Jan 44 Philippines: 9 Jan 45 - **14,15** *(redes from CA 15 Jun 43)*	20 Jan 43 Cp Haan Calif as Sep CA Bn AA-Gun (1st Bn, 86th CA) / 26 Feb 46 Japan	San Fernando Philippines
162nd AAA Gun Bn (Semimobile) *(redes from CA 1 Sep 43)*	15 Jan 43 Cp Edwards Mass as Sep CA Bn AA-Gun (1st Bn, 506th CA) / 30 Jun 44 Cp Edwards Mass	
163rd AAA Gun Bn (Semimobile) SFPE: 23 Aug 43 Australia: 7 Sep 43 New Guinea: 11 Nov 43 Woodlark I: 27 Nov 43 Goodenough I: 15 Mar 44 Philippines: 19 Mar 45 - **14,15** *(redes from CA 8 Jun 43)*	20 Jan 43 Ft Bliss Tex as Sep CA Bn AA-Gun (1st Bn, 509th CA) / 1 Feb 46 Cp Stoneman Calif	San Fernando Philippines
164th AAA Gun Bn (Semimobile) SFPE: 8 Oct 43 Guadalcanal: 11 Nov 43 Russell I: 29 Nov 43 New Guinea: 2 Jan 45 S.Narcisco: 14 Aug 45 S.Narcisco *(redes from CA 7 Jun 43)*	20 Jan 43 Ft Sheridan Ill as Sep CA Bn AA-Gun (1st Bn, 510th CA) / 15 Apr 46	Finschhafen New Guinea

BATTALION DESIGNATION AND TYPE	FORMED (SOURCE OF UNIT)/INACTIVATION	AUGUST 1945 LOCATION
165th AAA Gun Bn (Semimobile) SFPE: 18 Feb 44 New Guinea: 20 Mar 44 Biak I: 27 May 44 - **15** (redes from CA 7 Jun 43)	20 Jan 43 Cp Haan Calif as Sep CA Bn AA-Gun (1st Bn, 511th CA)/11 Feb 46 Biak Island	Biak Island
166th AAA Gun Bn (Semimobile) SFPE: 24 Sep 43 Australia: 9 Oct 43 New Guinea: 5 Feb 44 Philippines: 20 Nov 44 - **13,14,15,20** (redes from CA 19 Jun 43)	20 Jan 43 Ft Bliss Tex as Sep CA Bn AA-Gun (1st Bn, 513th CA)/11 Feb 46 Philippines	Zamboanga Philippines
167th AAA Gun Bn (Semimobile) NYPE: 28 Apr 43 N.Africa: 11 May 43 Sicily: 7 Aug 43 Sardinia: 26 Oct 43 Corsica: 16 Oct 44 France-ETO: 11 Nov 44 - **29,34,35,36** (redes from CA 1 Dec 43)	20 Jan 43 Cp Edwards Mass as Sep CA Bn AA-Gun (1st Bn, 606th CA)/4 Dec 45 Cp Patrick Henry Va	Septemes-les-Vallons France
168th AAA Gun Bn (Semimobile) SFPE: 25 Sep 43 Australia: 9 Oct 43 New Guinea: 26 Feb 44 Admiralty I: 16 Mar 44 Philippines: 20 Oct 44 - **3,13,15** (redes from CA 15 Jun 43)	20 Jan 43 Cp Hulen Tex as Sep CA Bn AA-Gun (1st Bn, 607th CA)/25 Feb 46 Philippines	Tacloban Philippines
169th CA Bn (Harbor Defense)	18 Oct 44 Cp Hayden Wash (2nd Bn, 14th CA)/15 Sep 45 Joyce Wash	Cp Hayden Wash
170th CA Bn (Harbor Defense)	18 Oct 44 Ft Worden Wash (3rd Bn, 14th CA)/15 Sep 45 Ft Worden Wash	Ft Worden Wash
171st CA Bn (Harbor Defense)	18 Oct 44 Ft Canby Wash (2nd Bn, 249th CA)/15 Sep 45 Ft Canby Wash	Ft Canby Wash
172nd CA Bn (Harbor Defense)	18 Oct 44 Ft Cronkhite Calif (2nd Bn, 6th CA)/15 Sep 45 Ft Cronkhite Calif	Ft Barry Calif, less Btry C at Ft Miley Calif
173rd CA Bn (Harbor Defense)	18 Oct 44 Ft Miley Calif (3rd Bn, 6th CA)/15 Sep 45 Ft Miley Calif	Ft Baker Calif, less Btry A at Ft Funston Calif & Btry B at Ft Cronkhite Calif
174th CA Bn (Harbor Defense)	18 Oct 44 Ft Miley Calif (4th Bn, 6th CA)/15 Sep 45 Ft Miley Calif	Ft Miley Calif, less Btry A at Ft Winfield Scott Calif & Btry B at Ft Baker Calif
175th CA Bn (Harbor Defense) (HD of Chesapeake Bay)	1 Oct 44 Ft Story Va (2nd Bn, 2nd CA)/1 Apr 45 Ft Story Va	
176th CA Bn (155mm Gun) Makin Atoll: 31 May 44 Hawaii: 20 Aug 44 Iwo Jima: 20 Apr 45 - **1**	31 May 44 Makin Atoll Gilbert Islands (elmts 57th CA)/13 Dec 45 Iwo Jima	Iwo Jima
177th CA Bn (155mm Gun) Hawaii: 31 May 44 Guam: 23 Nov 44 - **10,21** (Btry A & B in Marshalls campaigns)	31 May 44 Ft Ruger Hawaii (3rd Bn, 57th CA)/15 Jan 46 Guam	Guam
178th CA Bn (155mm Gun) Hawaii: 31 May 44 Guam: 4 Nov 44 - **10,21** (when formed Btry A and B were on Kwajalein [Btry A, 55th CA and Btry B, 57th CA] arrived in Hawaii 17 Aug 44)	31 May 44 Ft Ruger Hawaii (elmts 55th, 57th CA)/7 Feb 46 Guam	Guam
179th CA Bn (155mm Gun) Hawaii: 31 May 44 Philippines: 16 Nov 44 New Caledonia: 23 Jan 45 Okinawa: 31 Jul 45 - **13,19** (when formed Btry E on Tarawa, Btry F on Apamama; arrived in Hawaii 9 Jul 44 as Btry A and B of 179th CA Bn)	31 May 44 Kahuku Hawaii (Btry E,F, 55th CA)/10 Oct 45 Okinawa	Okinawa
180th CA Bn (155mm Gun) Hawaii: 31 May 44 Tinian: 19 Oct 44 - **21**	31 May 44 Honolulu Hawaii (Harbor Defenses of Honolulu)/13 Dec 45 Tinian	Tinian
181st CA Bn (Harbor Defense) (SDC until 1 Jan 45)	31 Aug 44 Burrwood La (1st Bn, 13th CA)/31 Mar 45 Burrwood La	
184th AAA Gun Bn (Mobile) England: 10 Aug 43 France-ETO: 16 Jun 44 - **26,28,30,32,34** BPE: 3 Dec 45	10 Aug 43 Honiton England (1st Bn, 61st CA)/4 Dec 45 Cp Myles Standish Mass	Langensalza Germany
185th CA Bn (Harbor Defense) (HD of Portland)	7 Oct 44 Peake Island Maine (1st Bn, 240th CA)/1 Apr 45 Peake Island Maine	
186th CA Bn (Harbor Defense) (HD of Portland)	7 Oct 44 Jewel Island Maine (2nd Bn, 240th CA)/1 Apr 45 Jewel Island Maine	
187th CA Bn (Harbor Defense) (HD of Boston)	7 Oct 44 Ft Ruckman Mass (2nd Bn, 241st CA)/1 Apr 45 Ft Ruckman Mass	
188th CA Bn (Harbor Defense) (HD of Narragansett Bay)	7 Oct 44 Ft Adams R.I. (1st Bn, 243rd CA)/1 Apr 45 Ft Adams R.I.	
189th CA Bn (Harbor Defense) (HD of Narragansett Bay)	7 Oct 44 Ft Adams R.I. (243rd CA)/1 Apr 45 Ft Adams R.I.	
190th CA Bn (Harbor Defense)	7 Oct 44 Ft Terry N.Y. (242nd CA)/1 Apr 45 Ft Terry N.Y. (HD of Long Island)	
192nd CA Bn (Harbor Defense) (HD of New York)	7 Oct 44 Ft Tilden N.Y. (2nd Bn, 245th CA)/1 Apr 45 Ft Tilden N.Y.	

BATTALION DESIGNATION AND TYPE	FORMED (SOURCE OF UNIT) / INACTIVATION *Active through 1946	AUGUST 1945 LOCATION

195th AAA Automatic Weapons Bn (S-P)
20 Jan 43 Cp Haan Calif as Sep CA Bn AA-AW (2nd Bn, 66th CA) /5 Dec 45 Cp
NYPE: 4 Jan 44   England: 8 Jan 44   France-ETO: 11 Jun 44 - **25,26,30,32,34**   HRPE: 5 Dec 45   Patrick Henry Va
(redes from CA 1 Mar 43)

Salzgitter Germany

196th AAA Auto-Wpns Bn (Semimobile)
15 Jan 43 Cp Edwards Mass as Sep CA Bn AA-AW (2nd Bn, 506th CA) /12 Dec 44
(redes from CA 9 May 43)
Cp Livingston La

197th AAA Automatic Weapons Bn (S-P)
20 Jan 43 Ft Bliss Tex as Sep CA Bn AA-AW (2nd Bn, 509th CA) /12 Apr 46 Cp
NYPE: 4 Jan 44   England: 8 Jan 44   France-ETO: 6 Jun 44 - **25,26,30,32,34**   NYPE: 11 Apr 46   Kilmer N.J.
(redes from CA 13 Feb 43)

Andenhausen Germany

198th AAA Auto-Wpns Bn (Semimobile)
20 Jan 43 Ft Sheridan Ill as Sep CA Bn AA-AW (2nd Bn, 510th CA) / 31 Aug 46
SFPE: 8 May 44   New Guinea: 30 Jul 44   Philippines: 9 Jan 45 - **13,16** *(redes from CA 30 Apr 43)*   Philippines

San Fernando Philippines

199th AAA Auto-Wpns Bn (Semimobile)
20 Jan 43 Cp Haan Calif as Sep CA Bn AA-AW (2nd Bn, 511th CA) / 4 Jan 46 Cp
SFPE: 16 Aug 43   Guadalcanal: 21 Sep 43   Bougainville: 15 Jan 44   Philippines: 11 Mar 45 - **13,16**   Anza Calif
(redes from CA 30 Apr 43)

Dulag Philippines
less Btry A,D at Samar

200th Separate CA Bn (AA) (Auto-Wpns)
20 Jan 43 Ft Bliss Tex (2nd Bn, 513th CA) /19 Mar 43 Cp Pickett Va redes 400th
Sep CA Bn (AA) (AW)

201st AAA Auto-Wpns Bn (Semimobile)
5 Jan 43 Cp Edwards Mass as Sep CA Bn AA-AW (2nd Bn, 606th CA /1 Oct 44
HRPE: 10 May 43   N.Africa: 23 May 43   Italy: 11 Nov 43   Corsica: 5 Apr 44   Italy: 25 Sep 44 - **29**   Bagnoli Italy
(redes from CA 12 Dec 43)

202nd AAA Auto-Wpns Bn (Semimobile)
20 Jan 43 Cp Hulen Tex as Sep CA Bn AA-AW (2nd Bn, 607th CA) /15 Dec 45
SFPE: 23 Nov 43   New Guinea: 9 Dec 43   Philippines: 12 Nov 44 - **13,14,15,20** *(redes from CA 8 May 43)*   Philippines

Zamboanga Philippines

203rd AAA Automatic Weapons Bn (S-P)
20 Jan 43 Ft Bliss Tex as Sep CA Bn AA-AW (2nd Bn, 608th CA) /15 Sep 46
NYPE: 9 Feb 44   England: 18 Feb 44   France-ETO: 26 Jun 44 - **25,26,30,32,34** *(redes from CA 13 Feb 43)*   Germany

Wetten Germany

204th AAA Auto-Wpns Bn (Semimobile)
20 Jan 43 Cp Edwards Mass as Sep CA Bn AA-AW (2nd Bn, 609th CA) /28 Nov 45
BPE: 27 Feb 44   England: 8 Mar 44   France-ETO: 19 Jun 44 - **25,26,30,32,34**   NYPE: 27 Nov 45   Cp Shanks N.Y.
(redes from CA 30 Apr 43)

Eschwege Germany

205th AAA Auto-Wpns Bn (Semimobile)
20 Jan 43 Cp Davis N.C. as Sep CA Bn AA-AW (2nd Bn, 610th CA) / 5 Apr 46
SFPE: 18 Sep 43   Fiji I: 2 Oct 43   New Georgia: 26 Nov 44   New Guinea: 30 Nov 44   Philippines: 13 Mar 45 - **14**   Philippines
(redes from CA 30 Apr 43)

Mindoro Philippines

206th AAA Auto-Wpns Bn (Semimobile)
20 Jan 43 Ft Bliss Tex as Sep CA Bn AA-AW (2nd Bn, 611th CA) /15 Jan 46 Iwo
SFPE: 16 Dec 43   Hawaii: 21 Dec 43   Saipan: 25 Jul 44   Iwo Jima: 14 Aug 45 - **1,21** *(redes from CA 30 Apr 43)*   Jima

Saipan, less Btrys C and D
on Iwo Jima

207th AAA Auto-Wpns Bn (Semimobile)
20 Jan 43 Cp Stewart Ga as Sep CA Bn AA-AW (2nd Bn, 612th CA) / 20 Jan 46
SFPE: 6 Sep 43   Australia: 28 Sep 43   New Guinea: 3 Dec 43 - **15**   LAPE: 25 Jan 46 *(redes from CA 30 Apr 43)*   Cp Anza Calif

Hollandia New Guinea

208th AAA Auto-Wpns Bn (Semimobile)
20 Jan 43 Cp Stewart Ga as Sep CA Bn AA-AW (2nd Bn, 613th CA) /4 Dec 44
SFPE: 28 Aug 43   Australia: 23 Sep 43   New Guinea: 1 Feb 44 - **15** *(redes from CA 30 Apr 43)*   New Guinea

209th AAA Automatic Weapons Bn (S-P)
15 May 43 Townsville Australia as Sep CA Bn AA-AW (2nd Bn, 94th CA) / *
Australia: 15 May 43   New Guinea: 19 May 43   Philippines: 8 Jan 45 - **14** *(redes from CA 5 Oct 44)*

San Fernando Philippines

210th AAA Auto-Wpns Bn (Semimobile)
15 May 43 Townsville Australia as Sep CA Bn AA-AW (2nd Bn, 197th CA) /
29 Dec 45 Cp Stoneman Calif
Australia: 15 May 43   New Guinea: 29 May 43   Philippines: 22 Oct 44   SFPE: 26 Dec 45 - **13,14,15** *(redes from CA 15 Jun 44)*

Clark Field Philippines

211th AAA Automatic Weapons Bn (Mobile)
15 May 43 Townsville Australia as Sep CA Bn AA-AW (2nd Bn, 208th CA) /
24 Dec 43 Cp Anza Calif
Australia: 15 May 43 New Guinea: 7 Jul 43   Admiralty I: 20 Feb 44   Philippines: 20 Oct 44 - **3,13,15**   LAPE: 24 Dec 45
(redes from CA 15 Jun 44)

Tacloban Philippines

212th AAA Auto-Wpns Bn (Semimobile)
10 Sep 43 Seattle Wash (2nd Bn, 212th CA) /11 Nov 44 Cp Howze Tex
(R&S Cmd 27 Oct 44)

213th AAA Auto-Wpns Bn (Semimobile)
10 Sep 43 Seattle Wash (2nd Bn, 63rd CA) / *

Orlando AAF Center Fla less
Btry B at Winter Garden Fla

214th AAA Gun Bn (Mobile)
20 Jan 43 Cp Hulen Tex as Sep CA Bn AA-Gun (1st Bn, 504th CA) /12 Feb 46
BPE: 28 Apr 43   N.Africa: 11 May 43   Sicily: 19 Jul 43   Corsica: 11 Jan 44   Cp Kilmer N.J.
France-ETO: 4 Sep 44 - **25,26,29,34,35,36,37**   NYPE: 11 Feb 46 *(redes from CA 13 Nov 43)*

Bad Aibling Germany

215th AAA Gun Bn (Semimobile)
20 Jan 43 Cp Stewart Ga as Sep CA Bn AA-Gun (1st Bn, 508th CA) /31 Dec 44
Gignac France, assets to 369th Engr Bn
NYPE: 5 Mar 43   N.Africa: 18 Mar 43   Sicily: Aug 43   Sardinia: 2 Dec 43   France-ETO: 15 Nov 44 - **35,36** *(redes from CA 15 Nov 43)*

BATTALION DESIGNATION AND TYPE	FORMED (SOURCE OF UNIT) / INACTIVATION	AUGUST 1945 LOCATION

216th AAA Gun Bn (Mobile)
20 Jan 43 Ft Bliss Tex as Sep CA Bn AA-Gun (1st Bn, 512th CA) /15 Nov 45 Cp
NYPE: 28 Apr 43   N.Africa: 11 May 43   Sicily: 9 Aug 43   Italy: Sep 43   France-ETO: 15 Aug 44 - **25,26,29,34,35,36,37**   Kilmer N.J.
NYPE: 13 Nov 45 *(redes from CA 13 Nov 43)*
New Ulm Germany

217th AAA Gun Bn (Mobile)
20 Jan 43 Cp Davis N.C. as Sep CA Bn AA-Gun (1st Bn, 514th CA) / 2 Jan 46
BPE: 7 Apr 44   England: 17 Apr 44   France-ETO: 25 Jun 44 - **25,26,30,32,34**   HRPE: 2 Jan 46   Cp Patrick Henry Va
(redes from CA 28 Jun 43)
Stubenag Germany

218th AAA Gun Bn (Mobile)
10 Sep 43 Benicia Arsenal Ordnance Depot Calif (1st Bn, 501st CA) / 2 Nov 44
(R&S Cmd 23 Oct 44)
Cp Maxey Tex

219th AAA Gun Bn (Mobile)
1 Sep 43 Paterson N.J. (1st Bn, 502nd CA) / 31 Oct 44 Cp Gordon Ga
(R&S Cmd 20 Oct 44)

220th AAA Gun Bn (Mobile)
10 Sep 43 North Long Beach Calif (1st Bn, 507th CA) /1 Dec 44 Cp Livingston La
(R&S Cmd 20 Nov 44)

221st CA Bn (155mm Gun)
1 Sep 44 Finschhafen New Guinea (5219th CA Btry Prov) / 2 Dec 45 New Guinea
New Guinea: 1 Sep 44 - **15**
Finschhafen New Guinea

222nd AAA Searchlight Bn
20 Jan 43 Cp Haan as CA S/L Bn (3rd Bn, 86th CA) /15 Apr 46 Philippines
SFPE: 17 Mar 44   New Guinea: 22 Apr 44   Philippines: 9 Jan 45 - **13,14,15** *(redes from CA 3 Mar 43)*
Luzon Philippines less Btry A on Biak Island & Btry B at Cotabato Mindanao Philippines

223rd AAA Searchlight Bn
15 Jan 43 Cp Edwards Mass as CA S/L Bn (3rd Bn, 506th CA) / 8 Nov 44
(redes from CA 3 Mar 43)
Cp Gordon Ga

224th AAA Searchlight Bn
20 Jan 43 Ft Bliss Tex as CA S/L Bn (3rd Bn, 509th CA) /15 Feb 46 Philippines
SFPE: 11 Jan 44   New Guinea: 29 Jan 44   Philippines: 14 Jul 45 - **15** *(redes from CA 3 Mar 43)*
Manila Philippines less det at Finschhafen New Guinea

225th AAA Searchlight Bn
20 Jan 43 Ft Sheridan Ill as CA S/L Bn (3rd Bn, 510th CA) / 31 Dec 45 Germany
NYPE: 23 Dec 43   England: 18 Jan 44   France-ETO: 18 Jun 44 - **26,30,32,34** *(redes from CA 3 Mar 43)*
Konigstein Germany

226th AAA Searchlight Bn
20 Jan 43 Cp Haan Calif as CA S/L Bn (3rd Bn, 511th CA) / 20 Dec 45 Germany
BPE: 1 Jul 44   England: 8 Jul 44   France-ETO: 25 Aug 44 - **25,26,32,34** *(redes from CA 3 Mar 43)*
Hasselt Belgium

227th AAA Searchlight Bn
20 Jan 43 Ft Bliss Tex as CA S/L Bn (3rd Bn, 513th CA) / 9 Feb 46 Cp Kilmer N.J.
SFPE: 6 Nov 43   Australia: 21 Nov 43   New Guinea: 5 Apr 44   Philippines: 23 Mar 45 - **13,14,15**   NYPE: 7 Feb 46
(redes from CA 3 Mar 43)
San Fernando Philippines less Btry B at Tacloban Philippines

228th AAA Searchlight Bn
20 Jan 43 Cp Edwards Mass at CA S/L Bn (3rd Bn, 606th CA) /10 Jul 43 Orlando
(redes from CA 20 Mar 43)
Fla

229th AAA Searchlight Bn
20 Jan 43 Cp Hulen Tex as CA S/L Bn (3rd Bn, 607th CA) /19 Feb 46 Cp Stone-
SFPE: 6 Dec 43   Australia: 24 Dec 43   New Guinea: 4 Jan 44   Morotai I: 15 Sep 44   Philippines: 9 Dec 45 - **15**   man Calif
(redes from CA 3 Mar 43)
Morotai Island less Btry B at Manila Philippines

230th AAA Searchlight Bn
20 Jan 43 Ft Bliss Tex as CA S/L Bn (3rd Bn, 608th CA) / 30 Jan 46 Okinawa
SFPE: 8 Jan 44   Hawaii: 16 Jan 44   Philippines: 21 Oct 44   Okinawa: 3 May 45 - **10,13,19,21** *(redes from CA 3 Mar 43)*
Okinawa less Btry B on Saipan and Plat of Btry C at Honolulu

231st AAA Searchlight Bn
20 Jan 43 Cp Edwards Mass as CA S/L Bn (3rd Bn, 609th CA) / 2 Jan 46 Cp Kil-
BPE: 12 Aug 44   England: 22 Aug 44   France-ETO: 25 Sep 44 - **26,32**   NYPE: 31 Dec 45 *(redes from CA 20 Mar 43)*   mer N.J.
Herstal Belgium

232nd AAA Searchlight Bn
20 Jan 43 Cp Davis N.C. as CA S/L Bn (3rd Bn, 610th CA) / 31 Oct 44 Cp Gordon Ga
(Btry B arrived New Guinea: 6 Feb 45 - 15) (redes from CA 3 Mar 43)

233rd AAA Searchlight Bn
20 Jan 43 Ft Bliss Tex as CA S/L Bn (3rd Bn, 611th CA) /1 Nov 46 Cp Hood Tex
SFPE: 1 Sep 43   Fiji I: 14 Sep 43   New Guinea: 2 Dec 44   Philippines: 20 Jul 45   SFPE: 22 Dec 45 *(redes from CA 3 Mar 43)*
Manila Philippines less Btry A at Bacolod Philippines

234th AAA Gun Bn (Cld) (Semimobile)
20 Jan 43 Cp Stewart Ga as CA S/L Bn (3rd Bn, 612th CA) /15 Jun 46 Saipan
LAPE: 19 Dec 44   India: 23 Jan 45   Saipan: 9 Jun 45 - **21** *(campaign dates 13–16 Jul 45)*
(redes from CA Searchlight Bn to AAA Gun Bn 1 Aug 43)
Saipan

235th AAA Gun Bn (Cld) (Semimobile)
20 Jan 43 Cp Stewart Ga as CA S/L Bn (3rd Bn, 613th CA) /12 Dec 44 Cp Living-
(redes from CA Searchlight Bn to AAA Gun Bn 1 Aug 43)
ston La

236th AAA Searchlight Bn
15 May 43 Townsville Australia (3rd Bn, 94th CA)/20 Apr 45 Finschhafen New
Guinea, assets to 530th MP Bn
Australia: 15 May 43   New Guinea: 1 Nov 43   Goodenough I: 27 Nov 43   New Guinea: 12 Dec 43   New Britain: 15 Dec 43
New Guinea: 26 Aug 44 - **3,13,14,15,20**

237th AAA Searchlight Bn
15 May 43 Townsville Australia (3rd Bn, 197th CA) / 29 Dec 45 Cp Anza Calif
Australia: 15 May 43   New Guinea: 27 Sep 43   Philippines: 6 Dec 44 - **3,13,14,15,20**   LAPE: 28 Dec 45
Tacloban Philippines less Btry B at Mindoro Philippines

238th AAA Searchlight Bn
15 May 43 Townsville Australia (3rd Bn, 208th CA) / 21 Apr 45 Philippines
Australia: 15 May 43   New Guinea: 25 Aug 43   Philippines: 20 Apr 45 - **3,14,15**

BATTALION DESIGNATION AND TYPE	FORMED (SOURCE OF UNIT)/INACTIVATION	AUGUST 1945 LOCATION
239th AAA Searchlight Bn	1 Sep 43 Bradley Field Hartford Conn (3rd Bn, 79th CA) / 9 Aug 44 Cp Gruber Okla	
240th AAA Searchlight Bn	10 Sep 43 Santa Monica Calif (3rd Bn, 205th CA)/5 Sep 45 Ft Bliss Tex	Ft Bliss Tex
241st AAA Searchlight Bn	1 Sep 43 Washington D.C. (3rd Bn, 71st CA) / 5 Aug 44 Cp Shelby Miss	
241st CA Bn (Harbor Defense) *(HD of Boston)*	7 Oct 44 Ft Warren Mass (1st Bn, 241st CA) / 1 Apr 45 Ft Warren Mass	
242nd CA Bn (Harbor Defense) *(HD of Long Island)*	7 Oct 44 Ft Michie N.Y. (1st Bn, 242nd CA) /1 Apr 45 Ft Michie N.Y.	
242nd AAA Searchlight Bn	10 Sep 43 Bremerton Wash (3rd Bn, 202nd CA) / 23 Jun 44 Cp Van Dorn Miss	
243rd AAA Searchlight Bn	10 Sep 43 Seattle Wash (3rd Bn, 63rd CA) / 5 Sep 45 Ft Bliss Tex	Ft Bliss Tex
244th AAA Searchlight Bn	10 Sep 43 San Diego Calif (3rd Bn, 204th CA) /17 Jun 46 Orlando Fla	Orlando Fla less Btry C at Winter Garden Fla
245th CA Bn (Harbor Defense) *(HD of New York)*	7 Oct 44 Ft Hancock N.J. (245th, CA) /1 Apr 45 Ft Hancock N.J.	
245th AAA Searchlight Bn	10 May 43 Inglewood Calif (3rd Bn, 65th CA) /12 Jun 44 Cp Haan Calif	
246th AAA Searchlight Bn	10 Sep 43 San Francisco Calif (3rd Bn, 216th CA) /30 Oct 44 Cp Haan Calif	
247th AAA Searchlight Bn *(R&S Cmd 23 Oct 44)*	21 Apr 43 Cp Edwards Mass (3rd Bn, 207th CA) / 31 Oct 44 Cp Gordon Ga	
248th AAA Searchlight Bn	10 Sep 43 Los Angeles Calif (3rd Bn, 78th CA) / 4 Nov 44 Cp Howze Tex	
249th CA Bn (Harbor Defense)	18 Oct 44 Ft Stevens Oreg (1st Bn, 249th CA) /15 Sep 45 Ft Stevens Oreg	Ft Stevens Oreg less det of Btry B at Ft Columbia Oreg
249th AAA Searchlight Bn	10 Sep 43 San Diego Calif (3rd Bn, 69th CA) /14 Jul 44 Cp Van Dorn Miss	
250th AAA Searchlight Bn Guadalcanal: 10 Nov 43 New Zealand: 10 Jan 44	10 Nov 43 Guadalcanal (3rd Bn, 214th CA) / 26 Dec 45 Cp Anza Calif New Guinea: 23 Jun 44 Philippines: 24 Aug 45 - **11,15,16,19** LAPE: 24 Dec 45	Finschhafen New Guinea less Btry A on Ie Shima Island
251st AAA Searchlight Bn	1 Sep 43 Philadelphia Pa (3rd Bn, 601st CA) / 20 Sep 44 Cp Davis N.C.	
252nd AAA Searchlight Bn *(R&S Cmd 26 Jan 45)*	1 Sep 43 New York N.Y. (3rd Bn, 602nd CA) /13 Feb 45 Cp Livingston La	
253rd AAA Searchlight Bn	10 Sep 43 Lawndale Calif (3rd Bn, 603rd CA) / 28 Aug 44 Cp Van Dorn Miss	
254th AAA Searchlight Bn	1 Sep 43 Bayonne N.J. (3rd Bn, 604th CA) /20 Sep 44 Cp Stewart Ga	
255th AAA Auto-Wpns Bn (Semimobile) SFPE: 26 Jul 43 Kiska I: 15 Aug 43 Adak I: 4 Apr 44	10 May 43 Ft Ord Calif (2nd Bn, 65th CA) / 3 Feb 45 Attu Island Alaska Attu I: 22 Nov 44 - **2**	
256th AAA Auto-Wpns Bn (Semimobile)	10 Sep 43 San Francisco Calif (2nd Bn, 216th CA) /10 Feb 44 San Francisco Calif	
257th AAA Automatic Weapons Bn (Mobile) *(R&S Cmd 22 Nov 44)*	10 Sep 43 Oakland-Berkeley Calif (2nd Bn, 217th CA) /1 Dec 44 Cp Livingston La	
259th CA Bn (155mm Gun) New Caledonia: 20 Jan 43 Guadalcanal: 22 Apr 43	20 Jan 43 New Caledonia (3rd Bn, 244th CA)/20 Aug 45 Philippines Fiji I: 11 May 44 New Guinea: 24 Jul 44 Philippines: 1 Mar 45 - **11,14,15**	Manila Philippines
260th AAA Gun Bn (Semimobile)	10 Sep 43 Pt Orchard Wash (1st Bn, 260th CA) /13 May 44 Cp Phillips Kans	
261st CA Bn (Harbor Defense) *(HD of Delaware until 15 Mar 44)*	27 Jan 41 Georgetown Del/20 Apr 44 Ft Jackson S.C.	
262nd Separate CA Bn (Harbor Defense)	20 Apr 42 Ft Rosecrans Calif / 30 Jan 43 Ft Rosecrans Calif *(HD of San Diego)*	
264th Separate CA Bn (Harbor Defense) SPE: 24 Nov 42 Alaska: 11 Dec 42 - **2**	20 Apr 42 Ft Worden Wash / 6 Nov 44 Alaska	
266th Separate CA Bn (Harbor Defense) SPE: 19 Nov 42 Alaska: 24 Nov 42 British Columbia: 6 Sep 44 SPE: 9 Sep 44	20 Apr 42 Ft Baker Calif / 9 Oct 44 Cp Shelby Miss	
267th Separate CA Bn (Harbor Defense) SPE: 6 Dec 42 Alaska: 14 Dec 42 SPE: 29 Aug 44	20 Apr 42 Ft Worden Wash / 30 Oct 44 Cp Bowie Tex	

BATTALION DESIGNATION AND TYPE	FORMED (SOURCE OF UNIT) / INACTIVATION	AUGUST 1945 LOCATION
268th CA Bn (155mm Gun)	25 Jun 42 Ft Moultrie S.C. / 20 Aug 45 Philippines	San Fernando Philippines

268th CA Bn (155mm Gun)
SFPE: 21 Jul 42   Fiji I:8 Aug 42   Tulagi I: 12 Aug 43   Bugana I: 12 Aug 43   Guadalcanal: 1 Oct 43   New Guinea: 27 Jul 44
Philippines: 1 Mar 45 - **14,15**

275th AAA Searchlight Bn
22 Nov 43 Ft Bliss Tex (3rd Bn, 83rd CA) /18 Aug 44 Cp Carson Colo

276th CA Bn (155mm Gun)
17 Dec 42 Bora Bora as Sep CA Bn Harbor Defense (3rd Bn, 13th CA) / 2 Dec 45   Oro Bay New Guinea
Philippines
Society I: 17 Dec 42   New Hebrides: 28 Feb 43   New Georgia I: 26 Dec 43   New Guinea: 30 Dec 44
Philippines: 8 Aug 45 - **16** *(redes from CA Bn Harbor Defense to CA Bn 155mm Gun 1 Jun 44 on New Georgia Island)*

277th CA Bn (155mm Gun)
31 Jul 44 Alaska (1st Bn, 265th CA) / 4 Dec 45 Ft Lawton Wash   Amchitka Island Aleutians
Alaska: 31 Jul 44   SPE: 30 Nov 45

278th CA Bn (155mm Gun)
31 Jul 44 Adak I (2nd Bn, 265th CA) / 30 Nov 45 Ft Lewis Wash   Adak Island Aleutians
Adak I: 31 Jul 44   SPE: 29 Nov 45

279th CA Bn (155mm Gun)
31 Jul 44 Alaska (3rd Bn, 265th CA) / 28 Nov 45 Ft Lawton Wash   Shemya Island Aleutians
Alaska: 31 Jul 44   SPE: 24 Nov 45

281st CA Bn (155mm Gun)
25 Feb 43 Ft Rosecrans Calif /1 Feb 45 New Caledonia
SFPE: 8 Jun 43   Bora Bora I: 20 Jun 43   New Caledonia: 4 May 44

282nd CA Bn (155mm Gun)
1 Apr 43 Cp Pendleton Va /20 May 46 Okinawa   Okinawa
SFPE: 14 Jun 43   New Caledonia: 6 Jul 43   Okinawa: 11 Jul 45

283rd CA Bn (155mm Gun)
27 Mar 43 San Francisco Calif / 20 Aug 45 Philippines   San Fernando Philippines
SFPE: 23 Jun 43   Fiji I: 18 Jul 43   Guadalcanal: 6 Feb 44   Green I: 15 Feb 44   New Guinea: 25 Jul 44   Philippines: 1 Mar 45 - **14,15**

285th CA Bn
Following components of 285th CA Bn (Railway Gun) raised—Btry A (formerly Btry E 52nd CA) activated 5 Apr 43 and inactivated 5 May 44 at Cp Breckinridge Ky and Btry B (formerly Btry X 52nd CA) activated 5 Apr 43 and inactivated 8 May 44 at Cp Barkeley Tex.

286th CA Bn (Railway Gun)
(HD of Chesapeake Bay)
1 May 43 Ft Custis Va (1st Bn, 52nd CA) / 30 Aug 44 Ft Bragg N.C. redes 538th FA Bn

287th CA Bn (Railway Gun)
(HD of Delaware)
1 May 43 Ft Miles Del (2nd Bn, 52nd CA) / 30 Aug 44 Ft Bragg N.C. redes 539th FA Bn

288th CA Bn (Railway Gun)
(in existence only one day)
1 May 43 Ft Hancock N.J. (3rd Bn, 52nd CA) /1 May 43 Ft Hancock N.J.

289th CA Bn (155mm Gun)
5 Jun 44 Cp Pendleton Va (2nd Bn, 244th CA) /17 Aug 44 Cp Joseph T Robinson Ark redes 782nd FA Bn

290th CA Bn (155mm Gun)
12 Jun 44 Cp Pendleton Va (1st Bn, 53rd CA) /14 Aug 44 Ft Bragg N.C. redes 778th FA Bn

291st CA Bn (155mm Gun)
12 Jun 44 Cp Pendleton Va (2nd Bn, 53rd CA) /14 Aug 44 Ft Bragg N.C. redes 799th FA Bn

292nd CA Bn (155mm Gun)
12 Jun 44 Cp Pendleton Va (3rd Bn, 53rd CA) /14 Aug 44 Ft Bragg N.C. redes 780th FA Bn

293rd AAA Searchlight Bn
6 Nov 43 Puerto Rico (3rd Bn, 66th CA) /12 Jun 44 Cp Stewart Ga
Puerto Rico: 6 Nov 43   NYPE: 5 Dec 43

294th AAA Searchlight Bn
12 Dec 43 Schofield Bks Hawaii (3rd Bn, 93rd CA) / 31 Aug 46 Philippines   Ft Kamehameha Hawaii less
Hawaii: 12 Dec 43 *(Btry A in Gilberts, part Btry B on Palmyra when Bn formed)* Btry C - **13,19,21**   Btry B at Ft Hase Hawaii & Btry C on Okinawa

295th AAA Searchlight Bn
12 Dec 43 Hawaii (2nd Bn, 93rd CA) / 30 Nov 45 Hawaii   Cp Malakole Hawaii less Btry A
Hawaii: 12 Dec 43   Philippines: 24 Dec 44   Iwo Jima *(Btry C only)*: 19 Feb 45   Okinawa: 1 Apr 45 - **1,13,19**   on Okinawa and Btry C on Iwo Jima

296th AAA Searchlight Bn
12 Dec 43 Ft Hase Hawaii (elmts 96th CA) / 29 Nov 45 Hawaii   Schofield Barracks Hawaii less
Hawaii: 12 Dec 43   Apamama: 11 Mar 44   Saipan *(Btry B only)*: 27 Jun 44   Hawaii *(less Btry B)*: 19 Jul 44 - **10,21**   Btry A at Cp Malakole Hawaii and Btry B on Saipan

297th AAA Searchlight Bn
(R&S Cmd 7 Nov 44)
1 Dec 43 Cp Stewart Ga (3rd Bn, 614th CA) /15 Nov 44 Cp Gordon Ga

298th AAA Searchlight Bn
(R&S Cmd 6 Nov 44)
1 Dec 43 Cp Stewart Ga (3rd Bn, 82nd CA) /15 Nov 44 Cp Gordon Ga

299th AAA Searchlight Bn
11 Apr 44 Aleutian Islands (3rd Bn, 203rd CA) / 9 Sep 44 Alaska
Alaska: 11 Apr 44

BATTALION DESIGNATION AND TYPE	FORMED (SOURCE OF UNIT) / INACTIVATION	AUGUST 1945 LOCATION
300th AAA Searchlight Bn Alaska: 14 Feb 44 SPE: 1 May 44	14 Feb 44 Adak Island Aleutians (3rd Bn, 210th CA) / 30 Oct 44 Ft Bliss Tex	
301st Separate CA Barrage Balloon Bn Norfolk Va: 20 Dec 41 Panama Canal Zone: 30 Dec 41	1 May 41 Cp Davis N.C./10 Apr 44 Cp Cooke Calif redes 47th Signal Lt Con- SFPE: 16 Dec 43 struction Bn	
302nd AA Balloon Bn, Very Low Altitude (redes from CA Barrage Balloon Bn to AA Balloon Bn, Very Low Altitude, 15 Jul 45 at Cy Tyson Tenn) (Barrage Balloon Training Center until 3 Feb 42)	1 Nov 41 Cp Davis N.C. as CA Barrage Balloon Bn /1 Aug 44 Cp Breckinridge Ky	
303rd CA Barrage Balloon Bn (Bremerton Wash 31 Dec 41–2 Sep 43)	1 Nov 41 Cp Davis N.C. / 9 Sep 43 Ft Custer Mich	
304th CA Barrage Balloon Bn (Seattle Wash 15 Jan 42–2 Sep 43)	1 Nov 41 Cp Davis N.C. / 9 Sep 43 Ft Custer Mich	
305th CA Barrage Balloon Bn SFPE: 8 Jul 42 Hawaii: 16 Jul 42	1 Nov 41 Cp Davis N.C. / 5 Nov 43 Hickam Field Hawaii, assets to 861st AAA A-W Bn	
306th CA Barrage Balloon Bn	8 Feb 42 Cp Tyson Tenn / 9 Sep 43 Ft Custer Mich (Mare I Calif 27 May 42–Aug 43)	
307th CA Barrage Balloon Bn (San Diego Calif 28 May 42–28 Aug 43)	1 Feb 42 Cp Tyson Tenn / 9 Sep 43 Ft Custer Mich	
308th CA Barrage Balloon Bn (Keyport Wash 30 May 42–29 Aug 43)	1 Mar 42 Cp Tyson Tenn / 9 Sep 43 Ft Custer Mich	
309th CA Barrage Balloon Bn (Mare I Calif 28 Jun 42–28 Aug 43)	1 Apr 42 Cp Tyson Tenn / 9 Sep 43 Ft Custer Mich	
310th CA Barrage Balloon Bn (Los Angeles Calif 23 Jan 43–27 Aug 43)	5 Jun 42 Cp Tyson Tenn / 9 Sep 43 Ft Custer Mich	
311th CA Barrage Balloon Bn (Los Angeles Calif 24 Jan 43–27 Aug 43)	5 Jun 42 Cp Tyson Tenn / 9 Sep 43 Ft Custer Mich	
312th CA Barrage Balloon Bn	5 Jun 42 Cp Tyson Tenn / 5 Nov 42 Cp Tyson Tenn (Cp Tyson Tenn; AA Cmd)	
313th AA Barrage Balloon Bn, Low Altitude Panama: 15 Jun 42 HRPE: 27 Dec 43	15 Jun 42 Panama Canal Zone as Sep CA Barrage Balloon Bn/10 Apr 44 Cp Forrest (redes from Sep CA Barrage Balloon Bn 27 Jan 44 at Ft Devens Mass) Tenn redes 48th Signal Bn	
315th CA Barrage Balloon Bn (Mitchell Field N.Y. 26 Feb 43–11 May 43)	20 Jul 42 Cp Tyson Tenn / 9 Sep 43 Ft Custer Mich	
316th AA Balloon Bn, Very Low Altitude (redes from CA Barrage Balloon Bn 15 Jul 43)	5 Dec 42 Cp Tyson Tenn as CA Barrage Balloon Bn / 7 Apr 44 Cp Forrest Tenn redes 49th Signal Bn	
317th AAA Balloon Bn (redes from CA 15 Jul 43)	5 Dec 42 Cp Tyson Tenn as CA Barrage Balloon Bn /1 Aug 44 Cp Breckinridge Ky	
318th AA Balloon Bn, Very Low Altitude (Cld) (redes from CA 1 Aug 43)	10 Dec 42 Cp Tyson Tenn as CA Barrage Balloon Bn /17 Apr 44 Cp McCain Miss	
319th AAA Balloon Bn (Cld) (redes from CA 1 Aug 43)	10 Dec 42 Cp Tyson Tenn as CA Barrage Balloon Bn / 29 Feb 44 Cp Tyson Tenn	
320th AA Balloon Bn, Very Low Altitude (Cld) NYPE: 17 Nov 43 England: 24 Nov 43 France-ETO: 6 Jun 44 NYPE: 26 Nov 44 SPE: 29 Apr 45 Hawaii: 6 May 45 - **30,32** (redes from CA 15 Jul 43)	10 Dec 42 Cp Tyson Tenn as CA Barrage Balloon Bn /14 Dec 45 Hawaii	Aiea Oahu Hawaii
321st AAA Balloon Bn (Cld) (redes from CA 15 Jul 43)	10 Dec 42 Cp Tyson Tenn as CA Barrage Balloon Bn / 29 Feb 44 Cy Tyson Tenn	
324th AAA Searchlight Bn	10 Sep 43 Vallejo Calif (3rd Bn, 211th CA) / 30 Aug 44 Vallejo Calif	
325th AAA Searchlight Bn SFPE: 14 Mar 44 Hawaii: 20 Mar 44 Okinawa: 4 Jun 45 - **19**	30 Apr 43 Cp Haan Calif / 30 Dec 46 Okinawa	Okinawa
326th AAA Searchlight Bn	10 Jun 43 Ft Bliss Tex / 25 Feb 45 Ft Bliss Tex (Orlando Fla 3 Mar 44–13 May 44)	
327th AAA Searchlight Bn (Orlando Fla 12 May 44–20 Jul 44)	10 Jun 43 Cp Edwards Mass / 30 Nov 44 Cp Livingston La	

BATTALION DESIGNATION AND TYPE	FORMED (SOURCE OF UNIT)/INACTIVATION	AUGUST 1945 LOCATION
328th AAA Searchlight Bn *(Norfolk Va 1 Sep 43–21 Jul 44)*	1 Sep 43 Norfolk Va (3rd Bn, 85th CA) / 8 Aug 44 Cp Rucker Ala	
329th AAA Searchlight Bn *(Orlando Fla 3 Jun 44–6 Nov 44)*	10 Jul 43 Cp Davis N.C. /15 Nov 44 Cp Gordon Ga	
330th AAA Searchlight Bn *(Orlando Fla 5 May 44–1 Dec 44)*	10 Jul 43 Cp Haan Calif /11 Dec 44 Cp Hood Tex	
331st AAA Searchlight Bn Sicily: 24 Mar 44 Italy: 9 Jun 44 - **35**	24 Mar 44 Palermo Sicily (3rd Bn, 62nd CA) /4 Dec 44 Pozzouli Italy, assets to Peninsular Base Sector	
332nd AAA Searchlight Bn *(Military District of Washington to 27 Feb 44)*	1 Sep 43 Washington D.C. (3rd Bn, 89th CA) /12 Jun 44 Cp Davis N.C.	
333rd AAA Searchlight Bn	20 Feb 44 Ft Bliss Tex (3rd Bn, 75th CA) /18 Aug 44 Cp Carson Colo	
334th AAA Searchlight Bn (Cld) N.Africa: 9 Mar 44 Corsica: 27 May 44 - **35**	9 Mar 44 Oran North Africa (3rd Bn, 90th CA) /9 Dec 44 Corsica	
335th AAA Searchlight Bn Italy: 1 May 44 - **35**	1 May 44 Bari Italy (3rd Bn, 209th CA) / 9 Dec 44 Naples Italy	
336th AAA Searchlight Bn *(Seattle Wash until 10 Jun 44)*	10 Sep 43 Seattle Wash (3rd Bn, 212th CA) / 26 Jun 44 Cp Gruber Okla	
337th AAA Searchlight Bn Italy: 1 Apr 44 - **35**	1 Apr 44 Arco Felice Italy (3rd Bn, 213th CA) / 24 Sep 44 Civitavecchia Italy	
338th AAA Searchlight Bn (Cld) *(AA Cmd until 11 Jul 44)*	29 Feb 44 Cp Stewart Ga (3rd Bn, 99th CA) / 31 Jul 44 Cp Rucker Ala	
339th AAA Searchlight Bn	1 Apr 44 Ft Bliss Tex (3rd Bn, 206th CA) /12 Jun 44 Ft Bliss Tex	
340th AAA Searchlight Bn	10 Sep 43 Annapolis Md (3rd Bn, 260th CA) /17 Apr 44 Cp Maxey Tex redes 76th Signal Bn	
341st AAA Searchlight Bn	5 Sep 43 Puerto Rico /1 Jun 44 Puerto Rico	
342nd AAA Searchlight Bn	15 Sep 43 Panama Canal Zone /1 Feb 46 Panama Canal Zone	Ft Davis Panama Canal Zone
343rd AAA Searchlight Bn	15 Sep 43 Panama Canal Zone /1 Feb 46 Panama Canal Zone	Ft Sherman Canal Zone
344th AAA Searchlight Bn *(Berkeley Calif until 10 Apr 44)*	10 Sep 43 Berkeley Calif (3rd Bn, 217th CA) /12 Jun 44 Cp Haan Calif	
345th AAA Searchlight Bn	15 Sep 43 Panama Canal Zone / 1 Feb 46 Panama Canal Zone	Ft Clayton Canal Zone
346th AAA Searchlight Bn	15 Sep 43 Panama Canal Zone /1 Feb 46 Panama Canal Zone	Ft Clayton Canal Zone
347th AAA Searchlight Bn At sea returning from Alaska: 1 Apr 44 Port Edward British Columbia Canada: 13 Apr 44	1 Apr 44 at sea to Port Edward Canada (3rd Bn, 215th CA) /18 Aug 44 Cp Carson Colo	
348th AAA Searchlight Bn *(HD of Boston)*	1 Sep 43 Boston Mass (3rd Bn, 605th CA) /12 Jun 44 Cp Stewart Ga	
350th AAA Searchlight Bn SFPE: 27 Oct 43 Australia: 13 Nov 43 New Guinea: 19 Feb 44 Philippines: 7 Apr 45 - **14,15** *(redes from CA 10 Apr 43 at Trigger School Orlando Fla)*	1 May 42 Cp Stewart Ga as CA S/L Bn /21 Feb 46 Philippines	Manila Philippines
351st AAA Searchlight Bn NYPE: 13 Jan 43 N.Africa: 27 Jan 43 Italy: 10 Oct 43 - **29,31,33,35,38** *(redes from CA 24 May 44)*	12 Jan 42 Cp Haan Calif as CA S/L Bn /28 Oct 44 Italy	
352nd AAA Searchlight Bn *(redes from CA 8 May 43)*	1 Mar 42 Cp Haan Calif as CA S/L Bn / 3 Jan 45 Ft Jackson S.C.	
353rd AAA Searchlight Bn NYPE: 7 Feb 43 N.Africa: 21 Feb 43 France-ETO: 17 Sep 44 - **34,35** *(redes from CA 17 Feb 44)*	1 May 42 Cp Stewart Ga as CA S/L Bn / 2 Jan 46 Cp Kilmer N.J.	Bad Mergentheim Germany
354th AAA Searchlight Bn NYPE: 7 Feb 43 N.Africa: 21 Feb 43 Italy: 3 Mar 44 - **35,38** *(redes from CA 1 May 44)*	3 Jan 42 Los Angeles Calif as CA S/L Bn / 9 Dec 44 Italy	
355th AAA Searchlight Bn NYPE: 14 Jan 43 N.Africa: 27 Jan 43 Italy: 23 Feb 44 - **35,38** *(redes from CA 1 May 44)*	1 May 42 Los Angeles Calif as CA S/L Bn / 20 Dec 44 Castelfiorentino Italy	

BATTALION DESIGNATION AND TYPE	FORMED (SOURCE OF UNIT) / INACTIVATION	AUGUST 1945 LOCATION

356th AAA Searchlight Bn
20 Jan 43 Cp Hulen Tex as CA S/L Bn / 28 Dec 45 Cp Stoneman Calif
SFPE: 11 Dec 43   Guadalcanal: 30 Dec 43   Philippines: 4 Apr 45   SFPE: 27 Dec 45 - **13**

Dulag Philippines less Btry C at Samar Philippines

357th AAA Searchlight Bn
20 Jan 43 Cp Stewart Ga as CA S/L Bn / 27 Dec 45 Cp Patrick Henry Va
NYPE: 6 Oct 44   England: 18 Oct 44   France-ETO: 27 Dec 44 - **26**   HRPE: 27 Dec 45 *(redes from CA 27 Apr 43)*

Broehuysen Germany

358th AAA Searchlight Bn
(redes from CA 24 Apr 43)
20 Jan 43 Cp Stewart Ga as CA S/L Bn / 30 Jan 45 Ft Jackson S.C.

359th AAA Searchlight Bn
(redes from CA 24 Apr 43)
10 Jan 43 Cp Edwards Mass as CA S/L Bn / 8 Nov 44 Cp Gordon Ga

360th AAA Searchlight Bn
20 Jan 43 Cp Stewart Ga as CA S/L Bn (3rd Bn, 508th CA) /15 Dec 45 Il Turiaccio
NYPE: 5 Mar 43   N.Africa: 18 Mar 43   Italy: 25 Feb 44 - **31,33,35** *(redes from CA 1 May 44)*   Italy

Modena Italy less Btry C at Motta Di Ghedi Italy

361st AAA Searchlight Bn (Cld)
1st Plat, Btry A of 361st AAA Searchlight Bn activated 1 Jan 43 at Ft Jackson S.C. and inactivated 15 Oct 43 in Alaska.

362nd AAA Searchlight Bn
20 Jan 43 Ft Bliss Tex as CA S/L Bn (3rd Bn, 512th CA) / 21 Apr 45 Philippines
SFPE: 27 Jul 43   Guadalcanal: 6 Sep 43   New Guinea: 11 Jan 45   Philippines: 20 Apr 45 - **14,16** *(redes from CA 3 Mar 43)*

363rd AAA Searchlight Bn
(redes from CA 3 Mar 43)
20 Jan 43 Cp Davis N.C. as CA S/L Bn (3rd Bn, 514th CA) / 31 Oct 44 Cp Gordon Ga

365th AAA Searchlight Bn
10 Sep 43 San Francisco Calif (3rd Bn, 501st CA) /18 Aug 44 Cp Carson Colo

366th AAA Searchlight Bn
1 Sep 43 Paterson N.J. (3rd Bn, 502nd CA) / 28 Jul 44 Cp Chaffee Ark

367th AAA Searchlight Bn
10 Sep 43 North Long Beach Calif (3rd Bn, 507th CA) /12 Jun 44 Cp Haan Calif

368th AAA Searchlight Bn
1 Sep 43 Newport R.I. (3rd Bn, 701st CA) /15 Aug 44 Ft Jackson S.C.

369th AAA Gun Bn (Cld) (Semimobile)
12 Dec 43 Hawaii (1st Bn, 369th CA) /21 Jan 46 Cp Anza Calif
Hawaii: 12 Dec 43   Okinawa: 12 Aug 45   LAPE: 20 Jan 46

Okinawa

370th AAA Searchlight Bn
1 Jun 43 Puerto Rico as CA S/L Bn /1 Jun 44 Puerto Rico   *(redes from CA 15 Oct 43)*

371st AAA Searchlight Bn
24 May 43 Portsmouth Va /12 Jun 44 Cp Davis N.C.

372nd AAA Searchlight Bn
24 May 43 Buffalo N.Y. /12 Jun 44 Cp Davis N.C.

373rd AAA Searchlight Bn
1 Mar 44 Treasury Islands (3rd Bn, 196th CA) / 29 Dec 45 Cp Stoneman Calif
Treasury I: 1 Mar 44   Bougainville: 10 Aug 44   Philippines: 9 Jan 45 - **14,16**   SFPE: 26 Dec 45

Manila Philippines less Btry B at Clark Field Philippines

374th AAA Searchlight Bn (Cld)
1 Nov 43 Espiritu Santo (3rd Bn, 77th CA) /25 Jun 45 Hollandia New Guinea
Espiritu Santo: 1 Nov 43   New Georgia I: 3 Feb 44   Admiralty I: 8 Jan 45   New Guinea: 6 Mar 45 - **3,16**

376th AAA Automatic Weapons Bn (Mobile)
15 Jul 42 Cp Stewart Ga as Sep CA Bn AA-AW/ 2 Dec 45 Cp Kilmer N.J.
NYPE: 5 Sep 43   England: 15 Sep 43   France-ETO: 15 Jun 44 - **25,26,30,32,34**   NYPE: 1 Dec 45 *(redes from CA 27 Feb 43)*

Zolling Germany

377th AAA Automatic Weapons Bn (Mobile)
15 Jul 42 Cp Stewart Ga as Sep CA Bn AA-AW/ 29 Jan 46 Cp Kilmer N.J.
NYPE: 5 Sep 43   England: 15 Sep 43   France-ETO: 14 Jun 44 - **25,26,30,32,34**   NYPE: 29 Jan 46 *(redes from CA 26 Jun 43)*

Schnaittach Germany

378th AAA Automatic Weapons Bn (Mobile)
15 Jul 42 Cp Stewart Ga as Sep CA Bn AA-AW/12 Feb 45 Ft Bragg N.C.
BPE: 10 Feb 43   Iceland: 25 Feb 43   NYPE: 27 Dec 44 *(redes from CA 5 Sep 43)*

379th AAA Automatic Weapons Bn (Mobile)
15 Jul 42 Cp Stewart Ga as Sep CA Bn AA-AW/ 5 Jun 46 Germany
NYPE: 1 Dec 44   England: 12 Dec 44   France-ETO: 19 Feb 45 - **26,34** *(redes from CA 10 May 43)*

Klotze Germany

380th AAA Auto-Wpns Bn (Semimobile)
(R&S Cmd 23 Nov 44)
10 Sep 43 McChord Field Wash (2nd Bn, 260th CA) /6 Dec 44 Cp Livingston La

381st AAA Auto-Wpns Bn (Semimobile)
20 Jan 43 Ft Sheridan Ill as Sep CA Bn AA-AW/15 Mar 45 Philippines
SFPE: 20 Jan 45   Philippines: 17 Feb 45 - **13** *(redes from CA 30 Apr 43)*

382nd AAA Auto-Wpns Bn (Semimobile)
10 Jan 43 Cp Hulen Tex as Sep CA Bn AA-AW/ 30 Jun 46 Japan
Portland Sub-P/E: 23 Mar 44   New Guinea: 21 Apr 44   Philippines: 13 Mar 45 - **14,15** *(redes from CA 30 Apr 43)*

San Fernando Philippines

383rd AAA Auto-Wpns Bn (Semimobile)
10 Jan 43 Ft Bliss Tex as Sep CA Bn AA-AW/18 Dec 45 Cp Stoneman Calif
SFPE: 23 Nov 43   Australia: 19 Dec 43   New Guinea: 22 Apr 44   Morotai I: 15 Sep 44   Philippines: 3 May 45 - **13,15**
SFPE: 16 Dec 45 *(redes from CA 30 Apr 43)*

Cotabato Philippines

384th AAA Auto-Wpns Bn (Semimobile)
(Washington D.C. until 26 Jul 44)
1 Sep 43 Washington D.C. (2nd Bn, 71st CA) /18 Aug 44 Cp Pickett Va

BATTALION DESIGNATION AND TYPE	FORMED (SOURCE OF UNIT) / INACTIVATION	AUGUST 1945 LOCATION

385th AAA Auto-Wpns Bn (Semimobile)   10 Jan 43 Cp Edwards Mass as Sep CA Bn AA-AW/ 30 Oct 45 Germany   Detmold Germany
NYPE: 29 Jan 44   England: 5 Feb 44   France-ETO: 12 Jul 44 - **25,26,30,32,34** *(redes from CA 30 Apr 43)*

386th AAA Auto-Wpns Bn (Semimobile)   10 Jan 43 Cp Edwards Mass as Sep CA Bn AA-AW/30 Oct 45 Germany   Rudesheim Germany
NYPE: 11 Feb 44   England: 18 Feb 44   France-ETO: 11 Jul 44 - **26,28,30,32,34** *(redes from CA 30 Apr 43)*

387th AAA Automatic Weapons Bn (S-P)   20 Jan 43 Cp Edwards Mass as Sep CA Bn AA-AW/ 30 Jun 46 Germany   Dingelstadt Germany
NYPE: 10 Apr 44   England: 16 Apr 44   France-ETO: 29 Jun 44 - **25,26,30,32,34** *(redes from CA 10 Apr 43)*

388th AAA Automatic Weapons Bn (S-P)   1 Sep 43 Norfolk Va (2nd Bn, 85th CA) /15 Feb 46 Ie Shima Island   Ie Shima
SPE: 29 Mar 45   Hawaii: 6 Apr 45   Ie Shima I: 10 May 45 - **19**

389th AAA Auto-Wpns Bn (Semimobile)   20 Jan 43 Cp Haan Calif as Sep CA Bn AA-AW/ 30 Jan 46 Philippines   Morotai Island
Portland Sub-P/E: 31 Mar 44   New Guinea: 1 May 44   Morotai I: 16 Sep 44   Philippines: 21 Jul 45 - **15** *(redes from CA 30 Apr 43)*

390th AAA Automatic Weapons Bn (S-P)   20 Jan 43 Cp Haan Calif as Sep CA Bn AA-AW/15 Sep 46 Germany   Dingelstadt Germany
BPE: 22 Jun 44   England: 29 Jun 44   France-ETO: 27 Jul 44 - **25,26,32,34** *(redes from CA 10 Apr 43)*

391st AAA Auto-Wpns Bn (Semimobile)   10 Jan 43 Cp Davis N.C. as Sep CA Bn AA-AW/ 27 Dec 45 Cp Kilmer N.J.   Mondorff-Bains France
BPE: 27 Feb 44   England: 8 Mar 44   France-ETO: 14 Jul 44 - **30,32,34**, Btry B entitled to 28   NYPE: 27 Dec 45 *(redes from CA 30 Apr 43)*

392nd AAA Auto-Wpns Bn (Semimobile)   1 Sep 43 Washington D.C. (2nd Bn, 89th CA) /15 May 46 Hawaii   Hickam Field Hawaii
SPE: 12 Nov 44   Hawaii: 17 Nov 44

393rd AAA Auto-Wpns Bn (Semimobile)   20 Jan 43 Cp Davis N.C. as Sep CA Bn AA-AW/1 Sep 44 Ft Dix N.J.
(redes from CA 30 Apr 43)

394th AAA Auto-Wpns Bn (Cld) (Semimobile)   20 Jan 43 Cp Davis N.C. as Sep CA Bn AA-AW/18 Mar 45 New Guinea
SFPE: 20 Jan 45   New Guinea: 4 Feb 45 *(redes from CA 30 Apr 43)*

395th AAA Auto-Wpns Bn (Cld) (Semimobile)   10 Jan 43 Cp Davis N.C. as Sep CA Bn AA-AW/15 Mar 45 Finschhafen New Guinea
SFPE: 16 Jun 44   New Guinea: 5 Jul 44 - **15** *(redes from CA 30 Apr 43)*

396th AAA Auto-Wpns Bn (Semimobile)   10 Sep 43 Bremerton Wash (2nd Bn, 202nd CA) / 9 Jan 45 Cp Livingston La
(R&S Cmd 25 Nov 44)

397th AAA Auto-Wpns Bn (Semimobile)   20 Feb 43 Ft Sheridan Ill as Sep CA Bn AA-AW/ 4 Dec 45 Cp Kilmer N.J.   Waldiesborn Germany
BPE: 27 Feb 44   England: 8 Mar 44   France-ETO: 6 Jun 44 - **25,28,30,32,34**   NYPE: 3 Dec 45
(Designated as Special AA Proving Machine-gun Battalion during assault on Normandy France) (redes from CA 30 Apr 43)

398th AAA Automatic Weapons Bn (S-P)   20 Feb 43 Cp Edwards Mass as Sep CA Bn AA-AW/ 30 Apr 46 Cp Kilmer N.J.   Siebensee Germany
BPE: 22 Jun 44   England: 29 Jun 44   France-ETO: 26 Jul 44 - **25,26,32,34**   NYPE: 29 Apr 46 *(redes from CA 1 May 43)*

399th AA Balloon Bn, Low Altitude   15 Oct 42 Ft Brady Mich as CA Barrage Balloon Bn / 30 Sep 43 Ft Sheridan Ill
(redes from CA 1 Sep 43)

400th AAA Auto-Wpns Bn (Semimobile)   19 Mar 43 Cp Pickett Va (200th CA Bn) /15 Nov 45 Cp Patrick Henry Va   La Coudray France
HRPE: 8 Jun 43   N.Africa: 22 Jun 43   Italy: 21 Sep 43   Corsica: 26 Mar 44   France-ETO: 11 Nov 44 - **29,34,35,36**
(initially Sep CA Bn AA-AW and redes 12 Dec 43 in Italy)

401st AAA Gun Bn (Mobile)   1 Apr 42 Cp Haan Calif as Sep CA Bn AA-Gun/15 Oct 45 Italy   Modena Italy
HRPE: 24 Apr 43   N.Africa: 26 May 43   Sicily: 11 Jul 43   Italy: 9 Nov 43 - **29,31,33,35,36** *(redes from CA 12 Dec 43)*

402nd AAA Gun Bn (Semimobile)   1 May 42 Ft Bliss Tex as Sep CA Bn AA-Gun /1 May 44 Cp Pickett Va redes
(redes from CA 1 Sep 43)   940th FA Bn

403rd AAA Gun Bn (Mobile)   1 Jun 42 Cp Hulen Tex as Sep CA Bn AA-Gun /15 Sep 45 Italy   Loiana Italy
NYPE: 28 Apr 43   N.Africa: 11 May 43   Sicily: 15 Aug 43   Italy: 23 Oct 43 - **29,31,33,35,36** *(redes from CA 12 Dec 43)*

405th AAA Gun Bn (Semimobile)   1 Jul 42 Ft Sheridan Ill as Sep CA Bn AA-Gun / 30 Apr 46 France   Quevillon Belgium
NYPE: 21 Oct 43   England: 3 Nov 43   France-ETO: 18 Jul 44 - **28,30,32,34** *(redes from CA 15 Jun 43)*

406th AAA Gun Bn (Semimobile)   1 Jul 42 Ft Sheridan Ill as Sep CA Bn AA-Gun / 31 Dec 44 France
NYPE: 28 Apr 43   N.Africa: 11 May 43   Sicily: 10 Aug 43   N.Africa: 15 Nov 43   Corsica: 13 Dec 43
France-ETO: 14 Nov 44 - **29,35,36** *(redes from CA 31 Dec 43)*

407th AAA Gun Bn (Semimobile)   10 Jan 43 Cp Haan Calif as Sep CA Bn AA-Gun / 30 Apr 46 France   Le Mans France
BPE: 27 Feb 44   England: 8 Mar 44   France-ETO: 23 Jun 44 - **30,32,34** *(redes from CA 7 Jun 43)*

409th AAA Gun Bn (Semimobile)   1 Aug 42 Ft Bliss Tex as Sep CA Bn AA-Gun / 25 Jan 45 Marseille France
HRPE: 10 May 43   N.Africa: 23 May 43   Italy: 19 Sep 43   Corsica: 8 Apr 44   France-ETO: 1 Nov 44 - **29,35** *(redes from CA 12 Dec 43)*

410th AAA Gun Bn (Semimobile)   15 Jun 42 Ft Bliss Tex as Sep CA Bn AA-Gun / 31 Dec 44 Miramas France, assets to
NYPE: 28 Apr 43   N.Africa: 11 May 43   Sicily: 15 Aug 43   Italy: 20 Oct 43   561st Quartermaster Group
Corsica: 21 Mar 44   France-ETO: 14 Nov 44 - **29,35,36** *(redes from CA 12 Dec 43)*

BATTALION DESIGNATION AND TYPE	FORMED (SOURCE OF UNIT)/INACTIVATION	AUGUST 1945 LOCATION

411th AAA Gun Bn (Mobile)   1 Sep 42 Cp Davis N.C. as Sep CA Bn AA-Gun / 23 Oct 45 Cp Patrick Henry Va   Ganacker Germany
NYPE: 1 Jan 44   England: 27 Jan 44   France-ETO: 9 Jun 44 - **25,26,30,32,34**   HRPE: 23 Oct 45 *(redes from CA 28 Jun 43)*

413th AAA Gun Bn (Mobile)   1 Jun 42 Cp Haan Calif as Sep CA Bn AA-Gun / 27 Oct 45 Cp Patrick Henry Va   Dillenburg Germany
NYPE: 15 Nov 43   England: 20 Nov 43   France-ETO: 7 Jun 44 - **25,26,30,32,34**   HRPE: 27 Oct 45 *(redes from CA 28 Jun 43)*

414th AAA Gun Bn (Semimobile)   9 Jun 42 Cp Stewart Ga as Sep CA Bn AA-Gun /15 Dec 45 Cp Kilmer N.J.   St Avoid Belgium
BPE: 26 Sep 42   Iceland: 22 Oct 42   England: 10 Mar 44   France-ETO: 8 Jul 44 - **25,28,30,32,34**   NYPE: 13 Dec 45
(redes from CA 22 Jun 43)

415th AAA Automatic Weapons Bn
Btry A and Btry B of 415th AAA Automatic Weapons Bn activated 22 Jul 42; Btry A at Sault Ste Marie Mich and inactivated 1 Apr 44 on New Caledonia and Btry B at Ft Ord Calif and inactivated 1 Apr 44 on New Caledonia.

417th AAA Searchlight Bn
1st Plat, Btry A and 1st Plat, Btry B of 417th AAA Searchlight Bn activated 22 Jul 42; the former at Ft Ord Calif and the latter at Sault Ste Marie Mich; both inactivated 1 Apr 44 on New Caledonia.

419th CA Bn (AA) (Composite)   3 Sep 42 Adak Island Aleutians / 31 Jul 44 Cp Swift Tex
Alaska: 3 Sep 42   SPE: Apr 44 - **2**

420th CA Bn (AA) (Composite)   17 Apr 42 Ft Raymond Alaska (205th CA elmts) /29 Jul 44 Cp Howze Tex
Alaska: 17 Apr 42   SPE: 24 Apr 44

421st AAA Bn (Composite) (Semimobile)   1 Aug 41 St Johns Newfoundland as Sep CA Bn AA (Btry B, 62nd CA) /15 Jan 44
Newfoundland: 1 Aug 41   NYPE: 2 Jan 44   Cp McCoy Wis
(redes CA Bn AA Composite 20 Sep 41 and redes AAA Composite 11 Nov 43, all in Newfoundland)

422nd AAA Bn (Composite) (Semimobile)   21 Jan 42 Cp Edwards Mass as CA Bn AA Composite /15 Jan 44 Cp McCoy Wis
NYPE: 6 Apr 42   Newfoundland: 14 Apr 42   NYPE: 2 Jan 44 *(redes from CA 11 Nov 43)*

423rd AAA Bn (Composite) (Semimobile)   10 Sep 41 Ft Bliss Tex as Sep CA Bn AA /30 Jun 45 Ft Bliss Tex
Charleston Sub-P/E: 3 Feb 42   Bermuda: 6 Feb 42   BPE: 14 May 45
(redes CA Bn AA Composite 20 Sep 41 and redes AAA Composite 1 Jun 44)

424th AAA Auto-Wpns Bn (Semimobile)   2 Jan 43 Cp Edwards Mass as Sep CA Bn AA /20 Sep 44 Cp Davis N.C.
BPE: 1 Aug 43   Greenland: 21 Aug 43   BPE: 26 Jul 44 *(redes from CA Bn AA Composite 28 Sep 43 in Greenland)*

427th CA Bn (AA) (Composite)   2 May 42 Cp Davis N.C. /10 Aug 42 Washington D.C.

427th AAA Bn (Composite) (Semimobile)   1 Sep 43 Ft Brady Mich /10 May 44 Cp Pickett Va

428th Separate CA Bn (AA) (Composite)   10 Aug 42 Hawaii /13 May 43 Canton Island redes 428th CA Regiment
Hawaii: 10 Aug 42   Canton I: 26 Aug 42

429th AAA Bn (Composite) (Semimobile)   13 May 43 Christmas I as Sep CA Bn AA / 26 May 44 Hawaii
Christmas I: 13 May 43   Hawaii: 28 Sep 43 *(redes from CA 26 Dec 43)*

430th AAA Automatic Weapons Bn (Mobile)   1 Mar 42 Cp Davis N.C. as Sep CA Bn AA-AW/11 Dec 45 Cp Patrick Henry Va   Lauterbach Germany
BPE: 20 Oct 43   England: 2 Nov 43   France-ETO: 13 Jun 44 - **26,30,32,34**   HRPE: 10 Dec 45 *(battalion initially semimobile)*
(redes from CA 15 May 43)

431st AAA Automatic Weapons Bn (Mobile)   1 Mar 42 Cp Stewart Ga as Sep CA Bn AA-AW/17 Oct 45 Cp Myles Standish   Kufstein Germany
NYPE: 5 Aug 42   England: 17 Aug 42   N.Africa: 8 Nov 42   Sicily: 10 Aug 43   Sardinia: 4 Dec 43   Mass
France-ETO: 8 Nov 44 - **23,25,26,34,36,38**   BPE: 16 Oct 45 *(redes from CA 13 Nov 43) (battalion initially semimobile)*

432nd AAA Automatic Weapons Bn (S-P)   1 Mar 42 Cp Hulen Tex as Sep CA Bn AA-AW/ 20 Sep 45 Italy   La Ca Italy
NYPE: 5 Aug 42   England: 20 Aug 42   N.Africa: 23 Nov 42   Italy: 10 Oct 43 - **29,31,33,35,38** *(battalion initially semimobile)*
(redes from CA 5 Dec 43)

433rd AAA Automatic Weapons Bn (Mobile)   1 Mar 42 Cp Stewart Ga as Sep CA Bn AA-AW/ 6 Oct 45 Germany   Eckelsheim Germany
NYPE: 7 Feb 43   N.Africa: 19 Feb 43   Sicily: 11 Jul 43   Italy: 29 Nov 43   France-ETO: 15 Sep 44 - **24,25,26,29,34,35,36,37**
(initially semimobile) (redes from CA 13 Nov 43)

434th AAA Automatic Weapons Bn (S-P)   1 Mar 42 Cp Hulen Tex as Sep CA Bn AA-AW/14 Jan 45 Montecatini Italy, assets
NYPE: 4 Aug 42   Scotland: 17 Aug 42   England: 19 Aug 42   N.Africa: 19 Jan 43   to 1st Bn, 473rd Inf Regt
Italy: 10 Oct 43 - **24,31,35,38** *(battalion initially semimobile) (redes from CA 5 Dec 43)*

435th AAA Auto-Wpns Bn (Semimobile)   1 Mar 42 Cp Hulen Tex as Sep CA Bn AA-AW/14 Jan 45 Montecatini Italy, assets
BPE: 28 Apr 43   N.Africa: 11 May 43   Italy: 22 Sep 43 - **24,29,31,35** *(redes from CA 12 Dec 43)*   to Hqs, 473rd Inf Regt

436th AAA Automatic Weapons Bn (Mobile)   20 Apr 42 Cp Hulen Tex as Sep CA Bn AA-AW/ 9 Oct 45 Cp Shanks N.Y.   Augsburg Germany
HRPE: 27 Oct 42   N.Africa: 8 Nov 42   Sicily: 9 Jul 43   France-ETO: 18 Sep 44 - **23,25,26,34,35,36,37,38**   NYPE: 8 Oct 45
(initially semimobile) (redes from CA 13 Nov 43)

BATTALION DESIGNATION AND TYPE	FORMED (SOURCE OF UNIT) / INACTIVATION	AUGUST 1945 LOCATION

437th AAA Automatic Weapons Bn (Mobile)   20 Apr 42 Cp Hulen Tex as Sep CA Bn AA-AW/ 26 Oct 44 Marseille France
NYPE: 2 Nov 42   N.Africa: 11 Nov 42   Italy: 30 Nov 43   France-ETO: 30 Aug 44 - **29,35,37** (battalion initially semimobile)
(redes from CA 12 Dec 43)

438th AAA Automatic Weapons Bn (Mobile)   6 Jun 42 Cp Edwards Mass as Sep CA Bn AA-AW/ 21 Mar 46 Cp Kilmer N.J.   Leipzig Germany
NYPE: 17 Nov 43   England: 24 Nov 43   France-ETO: 17 Jun 44 - **25,26,30,32,34**   NYPE: 20 Mar 46 (battalion initially semimobile)
(redes from CA 5 Jun 43)

439th AAA Automatic Weapons Bn (Mobile)   6 Jun 42 Cp Hulen Tex as Sep CA Bn AA-AW/ 30 Oct 45 Germany   Heckargemund Germany
NYPE: 28 Apr 43   N.Africa: 11 May 43   Italy: 13 Nov 43   France-ETO: 18 Sep 44 - **25,26,29,34,35,37** (battalion initially semimobile)
(redes from CA 12 Dec 43)

440th Automatic Weapons Bn (Mobile)   1 Jul 42 Cp Haan Calif as Sep CA Bn AA-AW/ 22 Nov 45 Cp Shanks N.Y.   Siegen Germany
NYPE: 29 Dec 43   England: 9 Jan 44   France-ETO: 7 Jul 44 - **25,26,30,32,34** (redes from CA 3 Jun 43)

441st AAA Automatic Weapons Bn (S-P)   1 Jun 42 Cp Stewart Ga as Sep CA Bn AA-AW/ 18 Oct 45 Cp Patrick Henry Va   Salzburg Austria
HRPE: 8 Jun 43   N.Africa: 22 Jun 43   Sicily: 9 Jul 43   Italy: 10 Sep 43   France-ETO: 15 Aug 44 - **24,25,26,29,34,35,36,37**
HRPE: 18 Oct 45 (redes from CA 5 Dec 43)

442nd AAA Auto-Wpns Bn (Semimobile)   1 Jun 42 Ft Bliss Tex as Sep CA Bn AA-AW/ 22 Jul 44 Oran North Africa
HRPE: 10 May 43   N.Africa: 2 Jun 43 (redes from CA 28 Nov 43)

443rd AAA Automatic Weapons Bn (S-P)   20 Apr 42 Ft Sheridan Ill as Sep CA Bn AA-AW/ 17 Feb 46 Cp Kilmer N.J.   Kempten Germany
NYPE: 26 Oct 42   N.Africa: 10 Nov 42   Sicily: 9 Jul 43   Italy: 20 Oct 43   France-ETO: 15 Aug 44 - **23,25,29,34,35,36,37,38**
NYPE: 16 Feb 46 (redes from CA 14 Apr 44)

444th AAA Automatic Weapons Bn (Mobile)   1 Jul 42 Cp Haan Calif as Sep CA Bn AA-AW/ 17 Nov 45 Cp Myles Standish Mass   Ganacker Germany
NYPE: 20 Feb 45   France-ETO: 27 Feb 45 - **26,34**   BPE: 16 Nov 45 (redes from CA 24 May 43)

445th AAA Automatic Weapons Bn (Mobile)   1 Jul 42 Cp Davis N.C. as Sep CA Bn AA-AW/ 29 Jun 46 Holland   Hagenow Germany
NYPE: 21 Feb 44   England: 28 Feb 44   France-ETO: 9 Jul 44 - **26,28,30,32,34** (battalion initially semimobile) (redes from CA 15 May 43)

446th AAA Automatic Weapons Bn (Mobile)   1 Jul 42 Cp Davis N.C. as Sep CA Bn AA-AW/ 23 Oct 45 Cp Patrick Henry Va   Wassenberg Germany
NYPE: 29 Sep 44   France-ETO: 10 Oct 44 - **25,26,34**   HRPE: 23 Oct 45 (battalion initially semimobile) (redes from CA 15 May 43)

447th AAA Automatic Weapons Bn (Mobile)   1 Jul 42 Ft Bliss Tex as Sep CA Bn AA-AW/ 25 Oct 45 Cp Myles Standish Mass   Pirmasens Germany
NYPE: 11 Feb 44   England: 23 Feb 44   France-ETO: 6 Jun 44 - **25,26,30,32,34**   BPE: 24 Oct 45 (battalion initially semimobile)
(redes from CA 3 Jun 43)

448th AAA Automatic Weapons Bn (Mobile)   1 Jul 42 Ft Bliss Tex as Sep CA Bn AA-AW/ 12 Dec 45 Cp Myles Standish Mass   Bad Kreuznach Germany
NYPE: 29 Dec 43   Scotland: 11 Jan 44   England: 27 Mar 44   France-ETO: 19 Jun 44 - **25,26,28,30,32,34** (initially semimobile)
(redes from CA 3 Jun 43)

449th AAA Automatic Weapons Bn (Mobile)   1 Jul 42 Cp Edwards Mass as Sep CA Bn AA-AW/ 26 Nov 45 Cp Kilmer N.J.   Dingolfing Germany
NYPE: 5 Dec 43   England: 16 Dec 43   France-ETO: 14 Jul 44 - **25,26,30,32,34** (battalion initially semimobile)   NYPE: 25 Nov 45
(redes from CA 25 May 43)

450th AAA Auto-Wpns Bn (Cld) (Mobile)   11 May 42 Cp Davis N.C. as Sep CA Bn AA-AW/ 26 Jan 45 Marseille France
NYPE: 6 Jan 43   England: 11 Jan 43   N.Africa: 23 Mar 43   Italy: 28 Oct 43   France-ETO: 21 Oct 44 - **29,31,33,35** (initially semimobile)
(redes from CA 12 Dec 43)

451st AAA Automatic Weapons Bn (Mobile)   1 Aug 42 Cp Stewart Ga as Sep CA Bn AA-AW/ 6 Nov 45 Cp Patrick Henry Va   Hopfeu Belgium
NYPE: 5 Mar 43   N.Africa: 18 Mar 43   Italy: 16 Sep 43   France-ETO: 15 Aug 44 - **24,25,26,29,34,35,37**   HRPE: 6 Nov 45
(initially semimobile) (redes from CA 12 Dec 43)

452nd AAA Auto-Wpns (Cld) (Mobile)   1 Aug 42 Cp Stewart Ga as Sep CA Bn AA-AW/ 17 Nov 45 Cp Myles Standish   Landau Germany
NYPE: 21 Oct 43   England: 2 Nov 43   France-ETO: 9 Jul 44 - **25,26,28,30,32,34**   BPE: 15 Nov 45   Mass
(initially semimobile) (redes from CA 15 May 43)

453rd AAA Automatic Weapons Bn (Mobile)   1 Aug 42 Ft Bliss Tex as Sep CA Bn AA-AW/ 26 Jan 46 Cp Kilmer N.J.   Blankenburg Germany
NYPE: 11 Feb 44   England: 23 Feb 44   France-ETO: 18 Jun 44 - **25,26,30,32,34**   NYPE: 25 Jan 46 (initially semimobile)
(redes from CA 5 Jun 43)

454th AAA Automatic Weapons Bn (Mobile)   1 Sep 42 Cp Stewart Ga as Sep CA Bn AA-AW/ 25 Sep 44 Italy
HRPE: 10 May 43   N.Africa: 2 Jun 43   Italy: Unknown - **35** (redes from CA 29 Jul 44)

455th AAA Automatic Weapons Bn (Mobile)   1 Sep 42 Cp Stewart Ga as Sep CA Bn AA-AW/ 17 Oct 45 Cp Myles Standish   Ainsen Germany
NYPE: 5 Sep 43   Halifax: 15 Sep 43   England: 18 Sep 43   France-ETO: 8 Jul 44 - **25,26,30,32,34**   BPE: 16 Oct 45   Mass
(redes from CA 31 May 43)

456th AAA Automatic Weapons Bn (Mobile)   1 Sep 42 Ft Sheridan Ill as Sep CA Bn AA-AW/ 23 Oct 45 Cp Patrick Henry Va   Mainburg Germany
NYPE: 21 Oct 43   England: 3 Nov 43   France-ETO: 1 Jul 44 - **25,26,30,32,34**   HRPE: 23 Oct 45 (redes from CA 1 Jun 43)

457th AAA Automatic Weapons Bn (Mobile)   1 Sep 42 Cp Hulen Tex as Sep CA Bn AA-AW/ 21 Nov 45 Cp Myles Standish Mass   Forchheim Germany
NYPE: 5 Dec 43   England: 15 Dec 43   France-ETO: 28 Jun 44 - **25,26,28,30,32,34**   BPE: 20 Nov 45 (redes from CA 15 May 43)

BATTALION DESIGNATION AND TYPE	FORMED (SOURCE OF UNIT)/INACTIVATION	AUGUST 1945 LOCATION

458th AAA Auto-Wpns Bn (Cld) (Semimobile)   1 Sep 42 Cp Stewart Ga as Sep CA Bn AA-AW/ 24 Apr 44 Cp Lee/Patrick Henry Va
(redes from CA 30 Apr 43)

459th AAA Automatic Weapons Bn (Mobile)   1 Sep 42 Cp Hulen Tex as Sep CA Bn AA-AW/ 25 Oct 45 Cp Myles Standish Mass   Eisenbach Germany
NYPE: 21 Oct 43   England: 3 Nov 43   France-ETO: 10 Jun 44 - **26,30,32,34**   BPE: 24 Oct 45 *(redes from CA 15 May 43)*

460th AAA Automatic Weapons Bn (Mobile)   1 Sep 42 Cp Hulen Tex as Sep CA Bn AA-AW/ 30 Apr 46 France   Miesbach Germany
NYPE: 21 Feb 44   England: 28 Feb 44   France-ETO: 12 Jun 44 - **25,26,30,32,34** *(redes from CA 15 May 43)*

461st AAA Automatic Weapons Bn (Molbile)   1 Sep 42 Cp Haan Calif as Sep CA Bn AA-AW/ 24 Nov 45 Cp Kilmer N.J.   Naunhof Germany
NYPE: 7 Jul 43   England: 15 Jul 43   France-ETO: 13 Jun 44 - **25,26,30,32,34**   NYPE: 23 Nov 45 *(redes from CA 14 Aug 44)*

462nd AAA Automatic Weapons Bn (Mobile)   1 Sep 42 Cp Haan Calif as Sep CA Bn AA-AW/6 Oct 45 Cp Shanks N.Y.   Pilsen Czechoslovakia
BPE: 6 Nov 43   England: 16 Nov 43   France-ETO: 11 Jun 44 - **25,26,30,32,34**   NYPE: 5 Oct 45 *(redes from CA 15 May 43)*

463rd AAA Automatic Weapons Bn (Mobile)   1 Sep 42 Cp Haan Calif as Sep CA Bn AA-AW/17 Mar 46 Cp Kilmer N.J.   Lippstadt Germany
NYPE: 22 Feb 44   England: 4 Mar 44   France-ETO: 28 Jun 44 - **25,26,30,32,34**   NYPE: 16 Mar 46 *(redes from CA 15 May 43)*

464th AAA Auto-Wpns Bn (Semimobile)   15 Oct 42 Cp Davis N.C. as Sep CA Bn AA-AW/10 Jul 45 Calcutta India
NYPE: 9 May 43   Brazil: 24 May 43   Madagascar I: 13 Jun 43   Ceylon: 18 Jun 43   India: 23 Jun 43   Burma: 12 Jan 45
India: 18 Apr 45 - **5,7,12** *(redes from CA 28 Apr 44)*

465th AAA Automatic Weapons Bn (Mobile)   15 Oct 42 Cp Davis N.C. as Sep CA Bn AA-AW/1 May 46 Germany redes Constab   Ronsdorf Germany
BPE: 22 Jun 44   England: 29 Jun 44   France-ETO: 30 Jul 44 - **25,26,32,34** *(initially semimobile)*   School Sqdn
(redes from CA 1 Feb 43)

466th AAA Auto-Wpns (Cld) (Semimobile)   15 Oct 42 Cp Stewart Ga as Sep CA Bn AA-AW/30 Nov 45 Finschhafen New   Cape Gloucester New Britain
SFPE: 29 Sep 43   Espiritu Santo: 16 Oct 43   New Britian: 20 May 44   New Guinea: 7 Dec 44 - **3,15**   Guinea
(redes from CA 30 Apr 43)

467th AAA Automatic Weapons Bn (S-P)   15 Oct 42 Cp Stewart Ga as Sep CA Bn AA-AW/16 Apr 46 Cp Kilmer N.J.   Neufohrn Germany
NYPE: 19 Jan 44   England: 30 Jan 44   France-ETO: 6 Jun 44 - **25,26,30,32,34**   NYPE: 15 Apr 46 *(initially semimobile)*
(redes from CA 13 Feb 43)

468th AAA Automatic Weapons Bn (S-P)   15 Oct 42 Cp Haan Calif as Sep CA Bn AA-AW/10 Jun 46 Germany   Prien Germany
NYPE: 2 Jul 44   England: 12 Jul 44   France-ETO: 28 Aug 44 - **25,26,30,32,34** *(initially semimobile) (redes from CA 13 Feb 43)*

469th AAA Auto-Wpns Bn (Semimobile)   15 Oct 42 Cp Davis N.C. as Sep CA Bn AA-AW/ 22 Jan 46 Cp Stoneman Calif   Dagupan Philippines
SFPE: 28 Aug 43   Australia: 29 Sep 43   New Guinea: 3 Nov 43   New Britian: 7 Jan 44   New Guinea: 8 Apr 44
Philippines: 20 Oct 44 - **3,13,14,15**   SFPE: 20 Jan 46 *(redes from CA 30 Apr 43)*

470th AAA Auto-Wpns Bn (Semimobile)   15 Oct 42 Cp Davis N.C. as Sep CA Bn AA-AW/ 24 Jan 46 Ft Lewis Wash   Negros Philippines less Btrys
SFPE: 28 Aug 43   Australia: 29 Sep 43   New Guinea: 31 Oct 43   Woodlark I: 30 Nov 43   New Guinea: 25 Mar 44   C and D at San Fernando
Philippines: 9 Jan 45 - **3,14,15,20**   SPE: 23 Jan 46 *(redes from CA 30 Apr 43)*

471st AAA Auto-Wpns Bn (Semimobile)   15 Oct 42 Cp Stewart Ga as Sep CA Bn AA-AW/ 24 Jan 46 Ft Lewis Wash   Clark Field Philippines
SFPE: 5 Jul 45   Guadalcanal: 23 Aug 43   Florida I: 24 Aug 43   Emirau I: 24 Mar 44   Philippines: 21 Jan 45 - **3,14,16**   SPE: 23 Jan 46
(redes from CA 30 Apr 43)

472nd AAA Auto-Wpns Bn (Semimobile)   15 Oct 42 Cp Stewart Ga as Sep CA Bn AA-AW/1 Jan 46 Cp Stoneman Calif   Clark Field Philippines
SFPE: 27 Aug 43   Australia: 14 Sep 43   New Guinea: 30 Dec 43   Philippines: 25 Mar 45 - **14,15**   SFPE: 30 Dec 45
(redes from CA 30 Apr 43)

473rd AAA Automatic Weapons Bn (S-P)   10 Feb 43 Cp Hulen Tex as Sep CA Bn AA-AW/1 May 46 Cp Kilmer N.J.   Elsdorf Germany
NYPE: 7 Apr 44   England: 15 Apr 44   France-ETO: 10 Jul 44 - **26,28,30,32,34**   NYPE: 30 Apr 46 *(redes from CA 10 Apr 43)*

474th AAA Automatic Weapons Bn (S-P)   15 Nov 42 Cp Edwards Mass as Sep CA Bn AA-AW/1 May 46 Germany redes   Mansfeld Germany
NYPE: 29 Jan 44   England: 5 Feb 44   France-ETO: 6 Jun 44 - **25,26,30,32,34**   64th Constab Sqdn
(initially semimobile) (redes from CA 1 Feb 43)

475th AAA Auto-Wpns Bn (Air Transp.)   15 Nov 42 Cp Edwards Mass as Sep CA Bn AA-AW/11 Jan 46 Cp Stoneman Calif   Manila Philippines
SFPE: 1 Oct 43   Guadalcanal: 21 Oct 43   New Guinea: 21 Dec 44   Philippines: 14 Jul 45   SFPE: 9 Jan 46 *(initially semimobile)*
(redes from CA 30 Apr 43)

476th AAA Auto-Wpns Bn (Semimobile)   15 Nov 42 Ft Sheridan Ill as Sep CA Bn AA-AW/15 Dec 45 Philippines   Palawan Philippines less Btrys
SFPE: 27 Oct 43   Australia: 13 Nov 43   New Guinea: 14 Apr 44   Biak I: 27 May 44   Philippines: 9 Feb 45 - **14,15,20**   C and D at Mindoro
(redes from CA 30 Apr 43)

477th AAA Auto-Wpns Bn (Cld) (Semimobile)   10 Nov 42 Cp Stewart Ga as Sep CA Bn AA-AW/ 20 Jan 46 Philippines   Oro Bay New Guinea
SFPE: 23 Aug 43   Australia: 7 Sep 43   New Guinea: 11 Jan 44   Philippines: 11 Oct 45 - **15** *(redes from CA 30 Apr 43)*

478th AAA Auto-Wpns Bn (Semimobile)   20 Nov 42 Cp Davis N.C. as Sep CA Bn AA-AW/ 4 Jan 46 Cp Stoneman Calif   Cebu Philippines less Btrys
SFPE: 27 Sep 43   Australia: 15 Oct 43   New Guinea: 5 Feb 44   Philippines: 22 Feb 45 - **13,15,20**   SFPE: 2 Jan 46   C and D at Samar
(redes from CA 30 Apr 43)

BATTALION DESIGNATION AND TYPE	FORMED (SOURCE OF UNIT)/INACTIVATION	AUGUST 1945 LOCATION
479th AAA Auto-Wpns Bn (Semimobile) *(redes from CA 30 Apr 43)*	20 Nov 42 Cp Davis N.C. as Sep CA Bn AA-AW/ 7 Dec 44 Cp Shelby Miss redes 71st Chem Mortar Bn	
480th AAA Auto-Wpns Bn (Semimobile) NYPE: 11 Feb 44 England: 18 Feb 44	15 Nov 42 Ft Bliss Tex as Sep CA Bn AA-AW/ 28 Nov 45 Cp Kilmer N.J. France-ETO: 12 Jul 44 - **28,30,32,34** NYPE: 27 Nov 45 *(redes from CA 30 Apr 43)*	Niederndorf Germany
481st AAA Auto-Wpns Bn (Semimobile) NYPE: 11 Feb 44 England: 23 Feb 44	20 Nov 42 Cp Davis N.C. as Sep CA Bn AA-AW/10 Dec 45 Cp Patrick Henry Va France-ETO: 12 Jul 44 - **26,28,30,32,34** HRPE: 10 Dec 45 *(redes from CA 30 Apr 43)*	Heilbronn Germany
482nd AAA Auto-Wpns Bn (S-P) NYPE: 11 Aug 44 England: 22 Aug 44	20 Feb 43 Cp Hulen Tex as Sep CA Bn AA-AW/ 30 Apr 46 Cp Kilmer N.J. France-ETO: 23 Sep 44 - **25,26,34** NYPE: 29 Apr 46 *(redes from CA 1 May 43)*	Eining Germany
483rd AAA Auto-Wpns Bn (Semimobile) SPE: 17 Jun 44 Hawaii: 24 Jun 44 Angaur I: 18 Sep 44	10 Feb 43 Ft Bliss Tex as Sep CA Bn AA-AW/15 Jan 46 Iwo Jima Ulithi Atoll: 24 Oct 44 Iwo Jima: 25 Feb 45 - **1,21** *(redes from CA 30 Apr 43)*	Iwo Jima
484th AAA Auto-Wpns Bn (Cld) (Semimobile) SFPE: 31 Jul 43 India: 5 Sep 43 Burma: 22 Nov 44 - **5,12**	10 Dec 42 Cp Stewart Ga as Sep CA Bn AA-AW/ 6 Jan 46 Cp Kilmer N.J. NYPE: 5 Jan 46 *(redes from CA 30 Apr 43)*	Myitkyina Burma
485th AAA Auto-Wpns Bn (Semimobile) SFPE: 16 Feb 44 Hawaii: 21 Feb 44	10 Dec 42 Cp Hulen Tex as Sep CA Bn AA-AW/ 20 Feb 46 Okinawa Philippines: 20 Oct 44 Okinawa: 1 Apr 45 - **13,19** *(redes from CA 30 Apr 43)*	Okinawa
486th AAA Automatic Weapons Bn (S-P) NYPE: 3 Dec 43 England: 9 Dec 43	10 Dec 42 Cp Davis N.C. as Sep CA Bn AA-AW/1 Jun 46 Germany France-ETO: 23 Jun 44 - **25,26,30,32,34** *(reorg as S-P in early 1943) (redes from CA 13 Feb 43)*	Grofenhausen Germany
487th AAA Auto-Wpns Bn (Semimobile) Portland Sub-P/E: 31 Mar 44 New Guinea: 12 May 44	10 Dec 42 Cp Haan Calif as Sep CA Bn AA-AW/15 Feb 46 Philippines Noemfoor I: 2 Jul 44 Philippines: 17 Apr 45 - **14,15,20** *(redes from CA 30 Apr 43)*	Macajalar Bay Philippines less Btry D at Davao Mindanao
488th AAA Auto-Wpns Bn (Semimobile) *(redes from CA 30 Apr 43)*	10 Feb 43 Ft Bliss Tex as Sep CA Bn AA-AW/ 5 Aug 44 Cp Maxey Tex	
489th AAA Automatic Weapons Bn (S-P) NYPE: 27 Feb 44 England: 9 Mar 44	10 Feb 43 Ft Bliss Tex as Sep CA Bn AA-AW/ 30 Jun 46 Germany France-ETO: 13 Jul 44 - **25,26,30,32,34** *(initially semimobile) (redes from CA 1 May 43)*	Hebramsdorf Germany
490th AAA Automatic Weapons Bn (S-P) *(redes from CA 10 Apr 43)*	10 Feb 43 Cp Stewart Ga as Sep CA Bn AA-AW/1 Dec 44 Cp Livingston La	
491st AAA Auto-Wpns Bn (Semimobile) NYPE: 10 Apr 44 England: 16 Apr 44	10 Feb 43 Cp Stewart Ga as Sep CA Bn AA-AW/ 3 Dec 45 Cp Kilmer N.J. France-ETO: 14 Jul 44 - **26,28,30,32** NYPE: 1 Dec 45 *(redes from CA 30 Apr 43)*	Hochheim Germany
492nd AAA Auto-Wpns Bn (Cld) (Semimobile) HRPE: 28 Mar 44 N.Africa: 6 Apr 44 *(redes from CA 30 Apr 43)*	10 Feb 43 Cp Stewart Ga as Sep CA Bn AA-AW/15 May 44 North Africa	
493rd AAA Auto-Wpns Bn (Cld) (Semimobile) HRPE: 28 Mar 44 N.Africa: 6 Apr 44 *(redes from CA 30 Apr 43)*	10 Feb 43 Cp Stewart Ga as Sep CA Bn AA-AW/15 May 44 North Africa	
494th AAA Gun Bn (Semimobile) Iceland: 10 Jul 42 England: 4 Nov 43	10 Jul 42 Iceland as Sep CA Bn AA-Gun (elmts 61st CA) /15 Nov 45 Cp Kilmer N.J. France-ETO: 16 Jul 44 - **28,30,32,34** NYPE: 13 Nov 45 *(redes from CA 5 Sep 43)*	Champagne France
495th AAA Gun Bn (Semimobile) Iceland: 10 Jul 42 England: 6 Nov 43	10 Jul 42 Iceland as Sep CA Bn AA-Gun (elmts 61st CA) / 30 Oct 45 Germany France-ETO: 23 Jun 44 - **26,28,30,32,34** *(redes from CA 5 Sep 43)*	Zachenberg Germany
496th AAA Gun Bn (Semimobile) Portland Sub-P/E: 16 Mar 44 New Guinea: 4 Apr 44	10 Jan 43 Cp Stewart Ga as Sep CA Bn AA-Gun /13 Jan 46 Cp Anza Calif Philippines: 3 May 45 - **15,20** LAPE: 12 Jan 46 *(redes from CA 7 Jun 43)*	Cotabato Philippines less Btry C at Davao Mindanao
497th AAA Gun Bn (Semimobile) SPE: 2 Nov 43 New Caledonia: 23 Nov 43 Guadalcanal: 15 Dec 43 *(redes from CA 7 Jun 43)*	20 Jan 43 Cp Stewart Ga as Sep CA Bn AA-Gun /15 Jan 46 Cp Stoneman Calif New Guinea: 18 Dec 44 Philippines: 14 Jul 45 SFPE: 13 Jan 46	Manila Philippines

498th CA Bn

Detachment from HHB 498th CA Bn (AA) (Gun((Semimobile), 1st Plat, Btry A and 1st Plat, Btry A all activated 1 Apr 42 on Aruba Netherlands West Indies and all inactivated there 25 Nov 43.

499th CA Bn

Detachment from HHB 499th CA Bn (AA) (Gun) (Semimobile), 1st Plat, Btry A and 2nd Plat, Btry B all activated 10 Apr 42 at Curaco Netherlands West Indies and inactivated there 25 Nov 43.

500th AAA Gun Bn (Semimobile) BPE: 1 Aug 43 Greenland: 25 Aug 43 BPE: 30 Jul 44 *(redes from CA 8 Jun 43)*	20 Jan 43 Cp Stewart Ga as Sep CA Bn AA-Gun / 20 Sep 44 Cp Davis N.C.	
501st AAA Gun Bn (Semimobile) SFPE: 16 Dec 43 Hawaii: 21 Dec 43 Saipan: 27 Jun 44 - **21** *(redes from CA 7 Jun 43)*	20 Feb 43 Cp Edwards Mass as Sep CA Bn AA-Gun / 25 Feb 46 Saipan	Saipan
502nd AAA Gun Bn (Semimobile) SFPE: 16 Dec 43 Hawaii: 21 Dec 43 Philippines: 20 Oct 44 Okinawa: 1 Apr 45 - **13,19** SPE: 13 Jan 46 *(redes from CA 7 Jun 43)*	20 Feb 43 Cp Edwards Mass as Sep CA Bn AA-Gun /15 Jan 46 Ft Lawton Wash	Okinawa

BATTALION DESIGNATION AND TYPE	FORMED (SOURCE OF UNIT) / INACTIVATION *Active through 1946	AUGUST 1945 LOCATION

503rd AAA Gun Bn (Semimobile)   10 Feb 43 Cp Stewart Ga as Sep CA Bn AA-Gun / 21 Jan 46 Cp Anza Calif   Okinawa
SFPE: 8 Jan 44   Hawaii: 16 Jan 44   Okinawa: 24 Jun 45 - **19**   LAPE: 20 Jan 46 *(redes from CA 7 Jun 43)*

504th AAA Gun Bn (Semimobile)   20 Mar 43 Cp Davis N.C. as Sep CA Bn AA-Gun / 15 Mar 46 Okinawa   Okinawa
SFPE: 12 Apr 44   Hawaii: 19 Apr 44   Philippines: 20 Oct 44   Okinawa: 1 Apr 45 - **13,19** *(redes from CA 7 Jun 43)*

505th AAA Gun Bn (Semimobile)   10 Apr 43 Cp Stewart Ga as Sep CA Bn AA-Gun / 3 Jan 46 Cp Stoneman Calif   Okinawa
SPE: 12 Aug 44   Hawaii: 21 Aug 44   Okinawa: 3 May 45 - **19**   SFPE: 1 Jan 46 *(redes from CA 7 Jun 43)*

506th AAA Gun Bn (Semimobile)   20 May 43 Cp Stewart Ga as Sep CA Bn AA-Gun / 15 Jan 46 Iwo Jima   Iwo Jima
SPE: 17 Jun 44   Hawaii: 25 Jun 44   Iwo Jima: 25 Feb 45 - **1** *(redes from CA 7 Jun 43)*

507th AAA Gun Bn (Semimobile)   20 May 43 Cp Stewart Ga as Sep CA Bn AA-Gun / 5 Apr 46 Philippines   Manila Philippines less Btry A
SFPE: 12 Jul 44   New Guinea: 31 Jul 44   Philippines: 14 Mar 45 - **14,15** *(redes from CA 7 Jun 43)*

508th AAA Gun Bn (Semimobile)   20 May 43 Cp Stewart Ga as Sep CA Bn AA-Gun / 15 Jan 46 Cp Stoneman Calif   Clark Field Philippines
SFPE: 14 Jun 44   New Guinea: 12 Jul 44   Philippines: 9 Jan 45 - **13,14,15**   SFPE: 13 Jan 46 *(redes from CA 7 Jun 43)*

509th AAA Gun Bn (Semimobile)   10 Jun 43 Cp Edwards Mass / 25 Jan 45 Cp Swift Tex

510th AAA Gun Bn (Semimobile)   15 Jun 43 Cp Edwards Mass / 18 Jan 46 Cp Anza Calif   Samar Philippines
SFPE: 27 Jun 44   New Guinea: 20 Jul 44   Philippines: 1 Dec 45 - **13,15**   LAPE: 17 Jan 46

511th AAA Gun Bn (Semimobile)   10 Jun 43 Cp Edwards Mass / 1 May 44 Cp Pickett Va redes 808th FA Bn

512th AAA Gun Bn (Semimobile)   15 Jun 43 Cp Edwards Mass / 1 May 44 Cp Pickett Va redes 809th FA Bn

513th AAA Gun Bn (Semimobile)   10 Jun 43 Cp Edwards Mass / 5 Apr 46 Philippines   Manila Philippines
SFPE: 17 Dec 44   Philippines: 2 Jan 45 - **13,14**

514th AAA Gun Bn (Semimobile)   10 Jul 43 Cp Edwards Mass / 21 Jan 46 Cp Anza Calif   Ulithi Atoll
Portland Sub-P/E: 22 Jan 45   Hawaii: 29 Jan 45   Eniwetok I: 30 Jul 45   Ulithi I: 5 Aug 45   Okinawa: 22 Aug 45   LAPE: 20 Jan 46

516th AAA Gun Bn (Semimobile)   1 Oct 43 Cp Haan Calif / 30 Nov 45 Hawaii   Hickam Field Hawaii
Portland Sub-P/E: 22 Jan 45   Hawaii: 29 Jan 45

517th AAA Gun Bn (Semimobile)   1 Oct 43 Cp Davis N.C. / 27 Dec 44 Ft Jackson S.C.

518th AAA Gun Bn (Semimobile)   12 Nov 43 New Caledonia / 15 Feb 46 Philippines   Manila Philippines
New Caledonia: 12 Nov 43   Philippines: 12 Jan 45 - **14**

519th AAA Gun Bn (Semimobile)   1 Jun 43 West Englewood N.J. / 6 May 46 France   Nacqueville France
NYPE: 27 Feb 44   England: 9 Mar 44   France-ETO: 9 Jul 44 - **30,32,34**

520th CA Bn (Harbor Defense)   18 Oct 44 Ft MacArthur Calif (1st Bn, 3rd CA) / 1 Dec 44 Ft MacArthur Calif
                                                                            redes 3rd CA Bn

521st CA Bn (Harbor Defense)   18 Oct 44 Ft MacArthur Calif (2nd Bn, 3rd CA) / 15 Sep 45 Ft MacArthur Calif   Ft MacArthur Calif

522nd CA Bn (Harbor Defense)   18 Oct 44 Huntington Beach Calif (3rd Bn, 3rd CA) / 15 Sep 45 Ft MacArthur Calif   Ft MacArthur Calif

523rd CA Bn (Harbor Defense)   18 Oct 44 Ft Rosecrans Calif (2nd Bn, 19th CA) / 15 Sep 45 Ft Rosecrans Calif   Ft Emory Calif less Btry B at Ft Rosecrans Calif

526th AAA Gun Bn (Semimobile)   10 Jan 45 Orlando Fla (71st AAA Gun Bn) / *   Winter Garden Fla less Btry A at Eglin Field, Btry B at Apopka, Btrys C,D at Orlando Fla
(AAA Composite Bn until redes AAA Gun Bn 1 Sep 45)

527th AAA Auto-Wpns Bn (Semimobile)   10 Sep 43 San Diego Calif (2nd Bn, 204th CA) / 1 Dec 44 Cp Livingston La
(R&S Cmd 22 Nov 44)

528th AAA Gun Bn (Semimobile)   10 Nov 43 New Caledonia (1st Bn, 214th CA) / 28 Dec 45 Cp Stoneman Calif   Morotai Island
New Caledonia: 10 Nov 43   Guadalcanal: 30 Jan 43   New Zealand: 10 Jan 44   New Guinea: 22 Jun 44   Morotai I: 1 Oct 44 - **15**

529th AAA Auto-Wpns Bn (Semimobile)   10 Sep 43 San Diego Calif (2nd Bn, 69th CA) / 5 Sep 45 Ft Bliss Tex   Ft Bliss Tex

530th AAA Automatic Weapons Bn (Mobile)   10 Sep 43 Santa Monica Calif (2nd Bn, 205th CA) / 3 Nov 45 Cp Shanks N.Y.   Kosslorn Germany
NYPE: 16 Dec 44   Scotland: 21 Dec 44   England: 23 Dec 44   France-ETO: 8 Mar 45 - **26,34**   NYPE: 2 Nov 45

531st AAA Automatic Weapons Bn (Mobile)   15 Jul 42 Ft Bliss Tex as Sep CA Bn AA-AW / 2 Jan 46 Cp Kilmer N.J.   Lehesten Germany
BPE: 11 Feb 44   England: 23 Feb 44   France-ETO: 15 Jun 44 - **25,26,30,32,34**   NYPE: 1 Jan 46 *(redes from CA 15 May 43)*

532nd AAA Automatic Weapons Bn (Mobile)   15 Jul 42 Ft Bliss Tex as Sep CA Bn AA-AW / 14 Jan 45 Montecatini Italy, assets to 2nd Bn, 473rd Inf Regt
NYPE: 27 Feb 43   N.Africa: 9 Mar 43   Italy: 11 Nov 43 - **29,31,35,38** *(redes from CA 12 Dec 43)*

BATTALION DESIGNATION AND TYPE	FORMED (SOURCE OF UNIT) / INACTIVATION	AUGUST 1945 LOCATION

533rd AAA Automatic Weapons Bn (Mobile)   15 Jul 42 Ft Bliss Tex as Sep CA Bn AA-AW/ 26 Oct 45 Cp Kilmer N.J.   Nesselwang Germany
NYPE: 25 Feb 43   N.Africa: 9 Mar 43   Sardinia: 17 Nov 43   France-ETO: 8 Nov 44 - **25,26,34**   NYPE: 25 Oct 45
(redes from CA 15 Dec 43)

534th AAA Automatic Weapons Bn (Mobile)   15 Jul 42 Ft Bliss Tex as Sep CA Bn AA-AW/19 Oct 45 Cp Patrick Henry Va   Fussen Germany
NYPE: 28 Apr 43   N.Africa: 11 May 43   Italy: 9 Sep 43   France-ETO: 15 Aug 44 - **24,25,26,29,35,37**   HRPE: 19 Oct 45

535th AAA Automatic Weapons Bn (Mobile)   15 Jul 42 Cp Haan Calif as Sep CA Bn AA-AW/ 24 Jun 46 Germany   Lauf Germany
NYPE: 11 Feb 44   England: 23 Feb 44   France-ETO: 6 Jun 44 - **25,26,30,32,34** *(redes from CA 15 May 43)*

536th AAA Automatic Weapons Bn (Mobile)   15 Jul 42 Cp Stewart Ga as Sep CA Bn AA-AW/16 Nov 44 Tirrenia Italy, assets to
NYPE: 27 Apr 43   N.Africa: 11 May 43   Gozo I: 28 Jun 43   Malta I: 7 Aug 43   Sicily: 15 Oct 43   287th Quartermaster Bn
Italy: 10 Jan 44 - **24,29,35** *(redes from CA 13 Nov 43)*

537th AAA Automatic Weapons Bn (Mobile)   15 Jul 42 Cp Hulen Tex as Sep CA Bn AA-AW/29 Jun 46 Germany   Aldorf Germany
NYPE: 1 Mar 44   England: 7 Mar 44   France-ETO: 17 Jun 44 - **25,26,30,32,34** *(redes from CA 15 May 43)*

538th AAA Auto-Wpns Bn (Cld) (Semimobile)   20 Apr 43 Cp Stewart Ga (2nd Bn, 100th CA) /24 Apr 44 Cp Patrick Henry /Ft Lee Va

539th AAA Auto-Wpns Bn (Semimobile)   1 Sep 43 Manchester Con (2nd Bn, 79th CA) /10 Aug 44 Cp Rucker Ala

540th AAA Auto-Wpns Bn (Semimobile)   1 Sep 43 Newport R.I. (2nd Bn, 701st CA) / 8 Nov 44 Cp Gordon Ga
(New London Conn 19 Nov 43–26 Jul 44)

541st AAA Auto-Wpns Bn (Semimobile)   1 Sep 43 Philadelphia Pa (2nd Bn, 601st CA) / 4 Jul 44 Cp Shelby Miss

542nd AAA Automatic Weapons Bn (Mobile)   1 Sep 43 New York N.Y. (2nd Bn, 602nd CA) /11 Dec 45 Germany   Euttin Germany
NYPE: 10 Dec 44   England: 16 Dec 44   France-ETO: 1 Mar 45 - **26,34**

543rd AAA Auto-Wpns Bn (Semimobile)   10 Sep 43 Inglewood Calif (2nd Bn, 603rd CA) / 5 Sep 45 Ft Bliss Tex

544th AAA Auto-Wpns Bn (Semimobile)   1 Sep 43 New York N.Y. (2nd Bn, 604th CA) /11 Aug 44 Cp Chaffee Ark

545th AAA Automatic Weapons Bn (Mobile)   1 Sep 43 Boston Mass (2nd Bn, 605th CA) / 8 Nov 44 Cp Gordon Ga

546th AAA Automatic Weapons Bn (Mobile)   10 Jan 43 Cp Haan Calif as Sep CA Bn AA-AW/ 20 Mar 46 Cp Kilmer N.J.   Wiesenberg Germany
NYPE: 20 Apr 44   England: 2 May 44   France-ETO: 14 Jul 44 - **25,26,30,32,34**   NYPE: 20 Mar 46 *(redes from CA 15 May 43)*

547th AAA Automatic Weapons Bn (Mobile)   10 Jan 43 Cp Haan Calif as Sep CA Bn AA-AW/ 29 Jun 46 Germany   Hullern Germany
NYPE: 24 Aug 44   England: 1 Sep 44   France-ETO: 29 Sep 44 - **25,26,34** *(redes from CA 15 May 43)*

548th AAA Automatic Weapons Bn (Mobile)   10 Jan 43 Cp Haan Calif as Sep CA Bn AA-AW/18 Dec 45 Cp Myles Standish   Gotha Germany
NYPE: 24 Sep 44   England: 20 Sep 44   France-ETO: 21 Oct 44 - **26,34**   BPE: 17 Dec 45 *(redes from CA 27 May 43)*   Mass

549th AAA Automatic Weapons Bn (Mobile)   20 Jan 43 Cp Edwards Mass as Sep CA Bn AA-AW/ 9 Mar 45 Cp Kilmer N.J.   Saalfeld Germany
NYPE: 29 Sep 44   England: 9 Oct 44   France-ETO: 1 Dec 44 - **25,26,34**   NYPE: 7 Mar 46 *(redes from CA 15 May 43)*

550th AAA Automatic Weapons Bn (Mobile)   10 Jan 43 Cp Edwards Mass as Sep CA Bn AA-AW/2 Nov 45 Cp Myles Standish   Sundhausen Germany
BPE: 21 Oct 43   England: 2 Nov 43   France-ETO: 18 Jun 44 - **25,26,30,32,34**   BPE: 1 Nov 45 *(redes from CA 15 May 43)*   Mass

551st AAA Automatic Weapons Bn (Mobile)   20 Jan 43 Cp Edwards Mass as Sep CA Bn AA-AW/26 Oct 45 Cp Shanks N.Y.   Regensburg Germany
BPE: 22 Jun 44   England: 29 Jun 44   France-ETO: 26 Jul 44 - **25,26,30,32,34**   NYPE: 25 Oct 45 *(redes from CA 15 May 43)*

552nd AAA Automatic Weapons Bn (Mobile)   20 Feb 43 Cp Hulen Tex as Sep CA Bn AA-AW/14 Nov 45 Cp Kilmer N.J.   Usseln Germany
NYPE: 6 Feb 44   England: 17 Sep 44   France-ETO: 15 Jun 44 - **25,26,30,32,34**   NYPE: 12 Nov 45 *(redes from CA 15 May 43)*

553rd AAA Automatic Weapons Bn (Mobile)   20 Feb 43 Cp Hulen Tex as Sep CA Bn AA-AW/ 30 Oct 45 Cp Myles Standish Mass   Elsen Germany
NYPE: 11 Aug 44   England: 22 Aug 44   France-ETO: 21 Sep 44 - **25,26,34**   BPE: 29 Oct 45 *(redes from CA 15 May 43)*

554th AAA Automatic Weapons Bn (Mobile)   20 Feb 43 Cp Hulen Tex as Sep CA Bn AA-AW/ 25 Oct 45 Cp Myles Standish Mass   Lobbend Germany
NYPE: 1 Mar 44   England: 9 Mar 44   France-ETO: 27 Jun 44 - **26,30,32,34**   BPE: 24 Oct 45 *(redes from CA 15 May 43)*

555th AAA Automatic Weapons Bn (Mobile)   20 Feb 43 Cp Hulen Tex as Sep CA Bn AA-AW/ 9 Dec 45 Cp Kilmer N.J.   Herborn Germany
NYPE: 28 Aug 44   England: 3 Sep 44   France-ETO: 2 Oct 44 - **26,34**   NYPE: 8 Dec 45 *(redes from CA 15 May 43)*

556th AAA Automatic Weapons Bn (Mobile)   20 Mar 43 Cp Davis N.C. as Sep CA Bn AA-AW/ 29 Jun 46 Belgium   Holzminden Germany
BPE: 7 Sep 44   England: 14 Sep 44   France-ETO: 18 Sep 44 - **26,34** *(redes from CA 15 May 43)*

557th AAA Automatic Weapons Bn (Mobile)   20 Mar 43 Cp Davis N.C. as Sep CA Bn AA-AW/13 Dec 45 Cp Patrick Henry Va   Selzen Germany
NYPE: 23 Jul 44   England: 28 Jul 44   France-ETO: 16 Aug 44 - **25,26,32,34**   HRPE: 13 Dec 45 *(redes from CA 15 May 43)*

558th AAA Automatic Weapons Bn (Mobile)   20 Mar 43 Cp Davis N.C. as Sep CA Bn AA-AW/14 Nov 45 Cp Shanks N.Y.   Munchen Gladbach Germany
NYPE: 30 Oct 44   England: 12 Nov 44   France-ETO: 4 Feb 45 - **26**   NYPE: 13 Nov 45 *(redes from CA 15 May 43)*

559th AAA Automatic Weapons Bn (Mobile)   20 Mar 43 Cp Davis N.C. as Sep CA Bn AA-AW/ 9 Mar 46 Cp Kilmer N.J.   Einbeck Germany
NYPE: 24 Jul 44   England: 31 Jul 44   France-ETO: 16 Aug 44 - **26,32,34**   NYPE: 8 Mar 46 *(redes from CA 15 May 43)*

BATTALION DESIGNATION AND TYPE	FORMED (SOURCE OF UNIT) / INACTIVATION *Active through 1946	AUGUST 1945 LOCATION

560th AAA Automatic Weapons Bn (Mobile) 10 Apr 43 Cp Stewart Ga as Sep CA Bn AA-AW/ 7 Dec 44 Cp Shelby Miss redes
(redes from CA 15 May 43) 72nd Chem Mortar Bn

561st AAA Automatic Weapons Bn (Mobile) 10 Apr 43 Cp Stewart Ga as Sep CA Bn AA-AW/ 8 Nov 44 Cp Gordon Ga
(redes from CA 15 May 43)

562nd AAA Automatic Weapons Bn (Mobile) 20 Apr 43 Cp Stewart Ga as Sep CA Bn AA-AW/ 30 Oct 45 Cp Myles Standish   Buren Germany
BPE: 7 Oct 44   England: 15 Oct 44   France-ETO: 18 Oct 44 - **26,34**   BPE: 29 Oct 45 *(redes from CA 15 May 43)*   Mass

563rd AAA Automatic Weapons Bn (Mobile) 20 Apr 43 Cp Stewart Ga as Sep CA Bn AA-AW/ 2 Mar 46 Cp Kilmer N.J.   Weilburg Germany
BPE: 11 Oct 44   France-ETO: 18 Oct 44 - **25,26,34**   NYPE: 1 Mar 46 *(redes from CA 15 May 43)*

564th AAA Automatic Weapons Bn (Mobile) 20 Apr 43 Cp Stewart Ga as Sep CA Bn AA-AW/ 14 Nov 45 Cp Myles Standish   Merlieux France
NYPE: 22 Oct 44   England: 2 Nov 44   France-ETO: 29 Dec 44 - **34**   BPE: 13 Nov 45 *(redes from CA 15 May 43)*   Mass

565th AAA Automatic Weapons Bn (Mobile) 10 Apr 43 Cp Stewart Ga as Sep CA Bn AA-AW/ 6 Oct 45 Germany   Forchheim Germany
NYPE: 6 Oct 44   England: 18 Oct 44   France-ETO: 15 Dec 44 - **25,26,34** *(redes from CA 15 May 43)*

566th AAA Automatic Weapons Bn (Mobile) 20 Apr 43 Cp Stewart Ga as Sep CA Bn AA-AW/ 12 Dec 45 Cp Shanks N.Y.   Holzminden Germany
NYPE: 30 Oct 44   England: 12 Nov 44   France-ETO: 26 Dec 44 - **26,34**   NYPE: 11 Dec 45 *(redes from CA 15 May 43)*

567th AAA Automatic Weapns Bn (Mobile) 10 May 43 Cp Haan Calif as Sep CA Bn AA-AW/ 16 Mar 46 Cp Kilmer N.J.   Egloffstein Germany
NYPE: 14 Oct 44   England: 25 Oct 44   France-ETO: 18 Dec 44 - **25,26,32,34**   NYPE: 16 Mar 46 *(redes from CA 15 May 43)*

568th AAA Automatic Weapons Bn (Mobile) 10 May 43 Cp Haan Calif as Sep CA Bn AA-AW/ 24 Nov 45 Cp Kilmer N.J.   Maastricht Holland
NYPE: 7 Nov 44   England: 18 Nov 44   France-ETO: 19 Nov 44 - **34**   NYPE: 22 Nov 45 *(redes from CA 15 May 43)*

569th AAA Automatic Weapons Bn (Mobile) 10 May 43 Cp Haan Calif as Sep CA Bn AA-AW/ 17 Feb 46 Cp Kilmer N.J.   Rappenau Germany
NYPE: 7 Nov 44   England: 18 Nov 44   France-ETO: 28 Jan 45 - **26,34**   NYPE: 16 Feb 46 *(redes from CA 15 May 43)*

570th AAA Automatic Weapons Bn (S-P) 10 Jun 43 Cp Edwards Mass / 30 Jun 44 Cp Edwards Mass   *(AA Cmd)*

571st AAA Automatic Weapons Bn (S-P) 10 Jun 43 Cp Edwards Mass / 10 Sep 46 Germany   Marseilles France
BPE: 10 Nov 44   England: 17 Nov 44   France-ETO: 22 Dec 44 - **25,26,34**

572nd AAA Automatic Weapons Bn (S-P) 10 Jun 43 Cp Edwards Mass / 24 Nov 45 Cp Patrick Henry Va   Feudenheim Germany
NYPE: 29 Sep 44   England: 10 Oct 44   France-ETO: 26 Nov 44 - **25,26,34**   HRPE: 24 Nov 45

573rd AAA Automatic Weapons Bn (S-P) 10 Jun 43 Cp Edwards Mass / 22 Mar 46 Cp Kilmer N.J.   Braunschweig Germany
NYPE: 16 Dec 44   England: 21 Dec 44   France-ETO: 5 Mar 45 - **26,34**   NYPE: 21 Mar 46

574th AAA Automatic Weapons Bn (S-P) 15 Jun 43 Cp Edwards Mass / 9 Dec 45 France   Rogglfing Germany
NYPE: 16 Dec 44   England: 21 Dec 44   France-ETO: 10 Mar 45 - **25,26,34**

575th AAA Automatic Weapons Bn (S-P) 10 Jul 43 Ft Bliss Tex / 20 Dec 45 Cp Patrick Henry Va   Pattendorf Germany
NYPE: 30 Oct 44   England: 11 Nov 44   France-ETO: 18 Dec 44 - **25,26,34**   HRPE: 20 Dec 45

576th AAA Automatic Weapons Bn (S-P) 10 Jul 43 Cp Davis N.C. / 27 Dec 44 Cp Livingston La   *(R&S Cmd 14 Dec 44)*

577th AAA Automatic Weapons Bn (S-P) 10 Jul 43 Cp Edwards Mass / 1 Dec 44 Cp Livingston La *(R&S Cmd 23 Nov 44)*

578th AAA Automatic Weapons Bn (S-P) 10 Jul 43 Ft Sheridan Ill / 1 Dec 44 Cp Livingston La

579th AAA Automatic Weapons Bn (S-P) 10 Jul 43 Cp Hulen Tex / 15 Apr 46 Japan   Clark Field Philippines
SFPE: 25 Mar 45   Philippines: 30 Apr 45 - **14**

580th AAA Automatic Weapons Bn (Mobile) 1 Oct 43 Cp Stewart Ga / 1 Dec 45 Cp Kilmer N.J.   Test Germany
NYPE: 16 Dec 44   England: 22 Dec 44   France-ETO: 25 Mar 45 - **26,34**   NYPE: 30 Nov 45

581st AAA Automatic Weapons Bn (Mobile) 1 Oct 43 Cp Stewart Ga / 23 Mar 46 Cp Kilmer N.J.   Wiedenhausen Germany
NYPE: 26 Dec 44   England: 7 Jan 45   France-ETO: 9 Mar 45 - **26,34**   NYPE: 21 Mar 46

582nd AAA Automatic Weapons Bn (S-P) 1 Oct 43 Ft Bliss Tex / 1 Oct 45 Ft Bliss Tex   Ft Bliss Tex

583rd AAA Automatic Weapons Bn (S-P) 1 Oct 43 Ft Bliss Tex / 9 May 44 Cp Chaffee Ark

584th AAA Automatic Weapons Bn (Mobile) 1 Oct 43 Cp Davis N.C./ 15 Dec 44 Cp Maxey Tex   *(R&S Cmd 11 Dec 44)*

585th AAA Automatic Weapons Bn (S-P) 1 Oct 43 Cp Hulen Tex / 6 May 44 Cp Chaffee Ark

586th AAA Auto-Wpns Bn (Semimobile) 1 Oct 43 Cp Hulen Tex /*   Okinawa
SPE: 5 Mar 45   Hawaii: 11 Mar 45   Okinawa: 12 Aug 45

587th AAA Automatic Weapons Bn (Mobile) 1 Oct 43 Cp Hulen Tex / 29 Oct 44 Cp Maxey Tex   *(AA Cmd)*

BATTALION DESIGNATION AND TYPE	FORMED (SOURCE OF UNIT)/INACTIVATION	AUGUST 1945 LOCATION

588th AAA Automatic Weapons Bn (Mobile) 1 Oct 43 Cp Hulen Tex / 2 Feb 45 Ft Jackson S.C.

589th AAA Automatic Weapons Bn (Mobile) 1 Dec 43 Cp Stewart Ga (2nd Bn, 614th CA) / 31 Oct 44 Cp Gordon Ga
(R&S Cmd 23 Oct 43)

590th AAA Automatic Weapons Bn (S-P) 1 Dec 43 Cp Stewart Ga (2nd Bn, 82nd CA) /10 May 44 Cp Pickett Va

591st AAA Auto-Wpns Bn (Semimobile) 7 Feb 44 Attu Island (2nd Bn, 78th CA) / 26 Jan 45 Cp Hood Tex
Aleutians: 7 Feb 44   Prince Rupert British Columbia Canada PE: 8 Dec 44   Ft Lawton Wash: 17 Dec 44

592nd AAA Auto-Wpns Bn (Semimobile) 12 Feb 44 Amchitka Island (2nd Bn, 203rd CA) /10 Nov 44 Cp Maxey Tex
Aleutians: 12 Feb 44   SPE: 16 Sep 44 *(R&S Cmd 3 Nov 44)*

593rd AAA Auto-Wpns Bn (Semimobile) 14 Feb 44 Adak Island (2nd Bn, 210th CA) /1 Nov 44 Cp Howze Tex
Aleutians: 14 Feb 44   SPE: 13 Jul 44 *(R&S Cmd 23 Oct 44)*

594th AAA Auto-Wpns Bn (Semimobile) 8 Feb 44 Ft Glenn Alaska (2nd Bn, 503rd CA) / 25 Sep 44 Cp Bowie Tex
Alaska: 8 Feb 44   SPE: 6 Aug 44

595th AAA Automatic Weapons Bn (Mobile) 20 Feb 43 Alaska (2nd Bn, 75th CA) /1 Dec 44 Cp Livingston La
Alaska: 20 Feb 43   SPE: 30 Jan 44 *(R&S Cmd 23 Nov 44)*

597th AAA Automatic Weapons Bn (Mobile) 1 Apr 44 Ft Bliss Tex (2nd Bn, 206th CA) /12 Dec 45 Cp Kilmer N.J.   Bad Lippspringe Germany
NYPE: 10 Dec 44   England: 16 Dec 44   France-ETO: 2 Mar 45 - **26,34**   NYPE: 11 Dec 45

598th AAA Gun Bn (Semimobile) 1 Jul 44 Ft Bliss Tex (1st Bn, 215th CA) / 29 Oct 44 Cp Maxey Tex
(R&S Cmd 23 Oct 44)

599th AAA Automatic Weapons Bn (Mobile) 1 Apr 44 Ft Bliss Tex (2nd Bn, 215th CA) /7 Dec 45 Cp Patrick Henry Va   Eining Germany
NYPE: 10 Dec 44   England: 16 Dec 44   France-ETO: 3 Mar 45 - **26,34**   HRPE: 7 Dec 45

601st AAA Gun Bn (Semimobile) 1 Sep 43 Philadelphia Pa (1st Bn, 601st CA) / 31 Dec 45 Germany   Labbeville France
NYPE: 13 Mar 44   England: 21 Mar 44   France-ETO: 6 Jul 44 - **28,30,32,34**

602nd AAA Gun Bn (Semimobile) 1 Sep 43 New York N.Y. (1st Bn, 602nd CA) / 26 Jan 46 Cp Kilmer N.J.   Epinal France
NYPE: 15 Mar 44   England: 21 Mar 44   France-ETO: 3 Jul 44 - **25,26,32,34**   NYPE: 25 Jan 46

603rd AAA Gun Bn (Semimobile) 10 Sep 43 Burbank Calif (1st Bn, 603rd CA) /13 May 44 Cp Phillips Kans

604th AAA Gun Bn (Semimobile) 1 Sep 43 New York N.Y. (1st Bn, 604th CA) /1 May 44 Cp Pickett Va redes 942nd
FA Bn

605th AAA Gun Bn (Semimobile) 1 Sep 43 Boston Mass (1st Bn, 605th CA) / 29 Jun 46 France   Foucarville France
NYPE: 21 Mar 44   England: 27 Mar 44   France-ETO: 9 Jul 44 - **30,32,34**

606th CA Bn (Cld) (155mm Gun) 5 Jun 44 Ft Ord Calif (1st Bn, 54th CA) / 3 Aug 44 Cp Livingston La

607th CA Bn (Cld) (155mm Gun) 5 Jun 44 Ft Ord Calif (3rd Bn, 54th CA) / 31 Jul 44 Cp Rucker Ala

630th AAA Automatic Weapons Bn (Mobile) 20 Jan 43 Cp Hulen Tex as Sep CA Bn AA-AW (2nd Bn, 504th CA)/26 Sep 45 Italy   Firenze Italy
BPE: 28 Apr 43   N.Africa: 12 May 43   Italy: 9 Sep 43 - **29,31,33,35** *(redes from CA 12 Dec 43)*

633rd AAA Automatic Weapons Bn (Mobile) 14 Aug 43 Honiton England (1st Bn, 244th CA)/6 Oct 45 Cp Shanks N.Y.   Grofenberg Germany
England: 14 Aug 43   France-ETO: 16 Jun 44 - **25,26,28,30,32,34**   NYPE: 5 Oct 45

634th AAA Automatic Weapons Bn (Mobile) 10 Aug 43 Honiton England (2nd Bn, 61st CA) / 6 Oct 45 Cp Kilmer N.J.   Forchheim Germany
England: 10 Aug 43   France-ETO: 13 Jun 44 - **25,26,28,30,32,34**   NYPE: 4 Oct 45

635th AAA Automatic Weapons Bn (Mobile) 10 Aug 43 Honiton England (3rd Bn, 61st CA) / 26 Mar 46 Cp Kilmer N.J.   Merkershausen Germany
England: 10 Aug 43   France-ETO: 9 Jul 44 - **25,26,28,30,32,34**   NYPE: 26 Mar 46

637th AAA Automatic Weapons Bn (Mobile) 20 Jan 43 Cp Stewart Ga as Sep CA Bn AA-AW (2nd Bn, 508th CA) / 22 Jul 44 Oran
NYPE: 5 Mar 43   N.Africa: 18 Mar 43 *(redes from CA 19 Nov 43)*   North Africa

638th AAA Automatic Weapons Bn (Mobile) 20 Jan 43 Ft Bliss Tex as Sep CA Bn AA-AW (2nd Bn, 512th CA) /1 Oct 44 Naples
HRPE: 9 May 43   N.Africa: 23 May 43   Corsica: 10 Jan 44   Italy: 26 Sep 44 - **29,35** *(redes from CA 31 Jan 44)*   Italy

639th AAA Automatic Weapons Bn (Mobile) 20 Jan 43 Cp Davis N.C. as Sep CA Bn AA-AW (2nd Bn, 514th CA) / 2 Jan 46 Cp   Braunfels Germany
NYPE: 29 Sep 44   France-ETO: 10 Oct 44 - **25,26,34** *(redes from CA 15 May 43)*   Kilmer N.J.

641st AAA Auto-Wpns Bn (Semimobile) 10 Sep 43 Alaska (2nd Bn, 501st CA) / 3 Feb 45 Alaska

642nd AAA Automatic Weapons Bn (Mobile) 1 Sep 43 Paterson N.J. (2nd Bn, 502nd CA) / 8 Nov 44 Cp Gordon Ga
(Ft Totten N.Y. 24 Feb–26 Jul 44)

BATTALION DESIGNATION AND TYPE	FORMED (SOURCE OF UNIT)/INACTIVATION *Active through 1946	AUGUST 1945 LOCATION
643rd AAA Automatic Weapons Bn (Mobile)	10 Sep 43 North Long Beach Calif (2nd Bn, 507th CA) / 25 Feb 45 Ft Bliss Tex	
701st AAA Gun Bn (Semimobile) *(R&S Cmd 25 Oct 44)*	1 Sep 43 Newport R.I. (1st Bn, 701st CA) / 9 Nov 44 Cp Maxey Tex	
727th AAA Machine-gun Bn *(10th Light Div)*	15 Jul 43 Cp Haan Calif / 6 Nov 44 Cp Swift Tex redes 10th Mtn Inf Bn	
729th AAA Machine-gun Bn	24 Jul 43 Cp Haan Calif /15 Jun 44 Cp Butner N.C. *(89th Light Div)*	
731st AAA Machine-Gun Bn	15 Jul 43 Cp Haan Calif / 26 May 44 Ft Benning Ga *(71st Light Div)*	
734th AAA Gun Bn (Semimobile) SFPE: 11 Nov 44 New Guinea: 1 Dec 44 Philippines: 31 Mar 45 - **14**	20 Jul 43 Cp Edwards Mass / 25 Feb 46 Philippines	Clark Field Philippines
736th AAA Gun Bn (Semimobile) Treasury I: 1 Mar 44 New Guinea: 9 Feb 45 Philippines: 15 Jul 45 - **16** SFPE: 31 Dec 45	1 Mar 44 Treasury Islands (1st Bn, 198th CA) / 2 Jan 46 Cp Stoneman Calif	Dagupan Philippines
737th AAA Gun Bn (Semimobile) SFPE: 16 Aug 43 New Caledonia: 4 Sep 43 Guadalcanal: 21 Sep 43 Tulagi I: 23 Sep 43 Emirau I: 25 Mar 44 Philippines: 13 May 45 - **3,14** SFPE: 20 Jan 46 *(redes from CA 1 Nov 43 on Tulagi Island)*	20 Jan 43 Ft Bliss Tex (1st Bn, 608th CA) as Sep CA Bn AA-Gun / 22 Jan 46 Cp Stoneman Calif	Manila Philippines
738th AAA Gun Bn (Semimobile) SFPE: 6 Jan 44 Hawaii: 15 Jan 44 Saipan: 1 Sep 44 - **21** *(redes from CA 7 Jun 43)*	20 Jan 43 Cp Edwards Mass as Sep CA Bn AA-Gun (1st Bn, 609th CA) / 25 Feb 46 Saipan	Saipan
739th AAA Gun Bn (Semimobile) SFPE: 18 Sep 43 Fiji I: 2 Oct 43 New Guinea: 1 Dec 44 Philippines: 12 Mar 45 - **14,20** *(redes from CA 7 Jun 43)*	20 Jan 43 Cp Davis N.C. as Sep CA Bn AA-Gun (1st Bn, 610th CA) /11 Feb 46 Philippines	Iloilo Philippines
740th AAA Gun Bn (Semimobile) NYPE: 11 Feb 44 England: 23 Feb 44 France-ETO: 16 Jul 44 - **28,30,32** *(redes from CA 7 Jun 43)*	20 Jan 43 Ft Bliss Tex as Sep CA Bn AA-Gun (1st Bn, 611th CA) / 9 Jul 46 France	Bolbec France
741st AAA Gun Bn (Cld) (Semimobile) SFPE: 7 Sep 43 Australia: 1 Oct 43 New Guinea: 14 Oct 43 - **3,15** *(redes from CA 8 Jun 43)*	20 Jan 43 Cp Stewart Ga as Sep CA Bn AA-Gun (1st Bn, 612th CA) /30 Jan 46 New Guinea	Hollandia New Guinea
742nd AAA Gun Bn (Cld) (Semimobile) SFPE: 29 Sep 43 Espiritu Santo: 16 Oct 43 New Britain: 20 May 44 New Guinea: 21 Nov 44 Philippines: 11 Aug 45 - **3** *(redes from CA 7 Jun 43)*	20 Jan 43 Cp Stewart Ga as Sep CA Bn AA-Gun (1st Bn, 613th CA) /11 Feb 46 Philippines	Luzon Philippines
743rd AAA Gun Bn (Mobile) Australia: 3 Apr 43 Kiriwina I: 30 Jun 43 Goodenough I: 26 Dec 43 New Guinea: 2 Jan 44 Philippines: 14 Jul 45 - **9,15** *(redes from CA 15 Jun 44)*	3 Apr 43 Australia as Sep CA Bn AA-Gun (1st Bn, 94th CA) / *	Manila Philippines
744th AAA Gun Bn (Mobile) Australia: 15 May 43 New Guinea: 12 Sep 43 Morotai I: 15 Sep 44 - **15** SFPE: 26 Dec 45 *(redes from CA 15 Jun 44)*	15 May 43 Australia as Sep CA Bn AA-Gun (1st Bn, 197th CA) / 29 Dec 45 Cp Stoneman Calif	Morotai Island
745th AAA Gun Bn (Mobile) New Guinea: 15 May 43 Noemfoor I: 2 Jul 44 Biak I: 14 Mar 45 Philippines: 23 Jun 45 - **14,15** SFPE: 5 Jan 46 *(redes from CA 15 Jun 44)*	15 May 43 New Guinea as Sep CA Bn AA-Gun (1st Bn, 208th CA) / 7 Jan 46 Cp Stoneman Calif	Clark Field Philippines
746th AAA Gun Bn (Semimobile) Bougainville: 1 Mar 44 Philippines: 9 Jan 45 - **13,16,20** SFPE: 13 Jan 46	1 Mar 44 Bougainville (1st Bn, 251st CA) /15 Jan 46 Cp Stoneman Calif	Cebu Philippines
747th AAA Auto-Wpns Bn (Semimobile)	10 Sep 43 Vallejo Calif (2nd Bn, 211th CA) / 5 Dec 45 Ft Bliss Tex	Ft Bliss Tex
748th AAA Gun Bn (Semimobile) Iceland: 28 Oct 43 NYPE: 14 Jun 45	28 Oct 43 Iceland (25th Sep CA Bn) / 22 Jun 45 Cp Kilmer N.J.	
749th AAA Gun Bn (Semimobile) Iceland: 28 Oct 43 England: 1 Jul 44 France-ETO: 25 Aug 44 - **26,28,32,34**	28 Oct 43 Iceland (26th Sep CA Bn)/25 Nov 45 Germany	Krofdorf Germany
750th AAA Gun Bn (Semimobile)	12 Dec 43 Hawaii (2nd Bn, 64th CA) / 5 Dec 46 Hawaii	Ft Shafter Hawaii
751st AAA Gun Bn (Semimobile) Hawaii: 12 Dec 43 Saipan: 15 Aug 44 - **21**	12 Dec 43 Ft Kamehameha Hawaii (1st Bn, 93rd CA) / 25 Feb 46 Saipan	Saipan, less Btrys C and D at Ft Shafter Hawaii
752nd AAA Gun Bn (Semimobile) Hawaii: 12 Dec 43 Saipan: 6 Feb 45 Iwo Jima: 11 Apr 45 - **1,21**	12 Dec 43 Hawaii (2nd Bn, 95th CA) / *	Iwo Jima
753rd AAA Gun Bn (Semimobile) Hawaii: 12 Dec 43 Kwajalein I: 4 Feb 44 Hawaii: 28 Jul 45 - **10**	12 Dec 43 Hawaii (2nd Bn, 96th CA) / *	Kwajalein Island less Btrys C and D at Hickam Field Hawaii
754th AAA Gun Bn (Semimobile)	12 Dec 43 Hawaii (2nd Bn, 97th CA) / 23 Jan 46 Hawaii	Hickam Field Hawaii
755th AAA Gun Bn (Semimobile)	12 Dec 43 Hawaii (2nd Bn, 98th CA) /18 Feb 46 Hawaii	Ft Shafter Hawaii

BATTALION DESIGNATION AND TYPE	FORMED (SOURCE OF UNIT)/INACTIVATION *Active through 1946	AUGUST 1945 LOCATION
761st AAA Gun Bn (Semimobile)	15 Sep 43 Ft Sherman Canal Zone /1 Feb 46 Ft Sherman Canal Zone	Ft Sherman Canal Zone
762nd AAA Gun Bn (Semimobile) Panama: 15 Sep 43 NOPE: 9 Sep 44	15 Sep 43 Ft Davis Canal Zone / 5 Sep 45 Ft Bliss Tex	Ft Bliss Tex
763rd AAA Gun Bn (Semimobile)	15 Sep 43 Ft Sherman Panama Canal Zone /1 Feb 46 Panama Canal Zone	Ft Davis Canal Zone
764th AAA Gun Bn (Semimobile)	15 Sep 43 Panama Canal Zone / *	Ft Gulick Canal Zone
765th AAA Gun Bn (Semimobile)	15 Sep 43 Panama Canal Zone /1 Feb 46 Panama Canal Zone	Ft Clayton Canal Zone
766th AAA Gun Bn (Semimobile)	15 Sep 43 Panama Canal Zone /15 Apr 46 Panama Canal Zone	Ft Clayton Canal Zone
767th AAA Gun Bn (Semimobile)	15 Sep 43 Panama Canal Zone /1 Feb 46 Panama Canal Zone	Ft Kobbe Canal Zone
768th AAA Gun Bn (Semimobile) SPE: 22 Jul 44 Adak I: 2 Aug 44 Cp Earle Alaska: 19 Nov 44	10 Sep 43 Bremerton Wash (1st Bn, 202nd CA) / 3 Feb 45 Cp Earle Alaska, assets to Post Headquarters	
769th AAA Gun Bn (Semimobile) (R&S Cmd 19 Dec 44)	10 Sep 43 San Diego Calif (1st Bn, 204th CA) / 4 Jan 45 Ft Sill Okla redes 2nd Rocket Bn	
770th AAA Gun Bn (Semimobile)	10 Sep 43 Santa Monica Calif (1st Bn, 205th CA) /10 Feb 44 Santa Monica Calif	
771st AAA Gun Bn (Semimobile) SFPE: 21 Jan 44 Hawaii: 31 Jan 44 Guam: 11 Nov 44 - 21	21 Apr 43 Cp Edwards Mass (1st Bn, 207th CA) /15 Jan 46 Guam	Guam
772nd AAA Gun Bn (Semimobile)	10 Sep 43 Vallejo Calif (1st Bn, 211th CA) / 30 Apr 44 Cp Howze Tex	
773rd AAA Gun Bn (Semimobile)	10 Sep 43 Seattle Wash (1st Bn, 212th CA) /13 May 44 Cp Phillips Kans	
774th AAA Gun Bn (Semimobile)	10 Sep 43 San Francisco Calif (1st Bn, 216th CA) / 8 Jun 44 Cp Howze Tex	
775th AAA Gun Bn (Semimobile)	10 Sep 43 Oakland Calif (1st Bn, 217th CA) / 6 May 44 Cp Phillips Kans	
776th AAA Auto-Wpns Bn (Semimobile) BPE: 28 Feb 44 England: 8 Mar 44 France-ETO: 24 Jul 44 - **26,28,30,32,34** BPE: 25 Nov 45 (redes from CA 30 Apr 43)	20 Mar 43 Cp Davis N.C. as Sep CA Bn AA-AW/ 26 Nov 45 Cp Myles Standish Mass	Ober Ramstadt Germany
777th AAA Automatic Weapons Bn (S-P) NYPE: 18 Apr 44 England: 26 Apr 44 France-ETO: 20 Jul 44 - **25,26,28,30,32,34** (redes from CA 1 May 43)	20 Mar 43 Ft Sheridan Ill as Sep CA Bn AA-AW/ 30 Jun 46 Germany	Wolfersdorf Germany
778th AAA Automatic Weapons Bn (S-P) NYPE: 14 Oct 44 England: 25 Oct 44 France-ETO: 19 Dec 44 - **25,26,32,34** NYPE: 30 Apr 46 (redes from CA 10 May 43)	10 Mar 43 Cp Haan Calif as Sep CA Bn AA-AW/1 May 46 Cp Kilmer N.J.	Neustadt Germany
779th AAA Auto-Wpns Bn (Semimobile) SPE: 10 Aug 44 Hawaii: 17 Aug 44 Okinawa: 13 Apr 45 - **19** (redes from CA 30 Apr 43)	10 Mar 43 Cp Haan Calif as Sep CA Bn AA-AW/ 31 Mar 46 Korea	Okinawa
780th AAA Auto-Wpns Bn (Semimobile) (redes from CA 30 Apr 43)	10 Mar 43 Cp Haan Calif as Sep CA Bn AA-AW/ 31 Jul 44 Cp Van Dorn Miss	
781st AAA Auto-Wpns Bn (Semimobile) (redes from CA 30 Apr 43)	20 Mar 43 Cp Haan Calif as Sep CA Bn AA-AW/ 5 Aug 44 Cp Maxey Tex	
782nd AAA Auto-Wpns Bn (Semimobile) (redes from CA 30 Apr 43)	20 Mar 43 Cp Haan Calif as Sep CA Bn AA-AW/12 Jun 44 Cp Haan Calif	
783rd AAA Auto-Wpns Bn (Semimobile) (redes from CA 30 Apr 43)	20 Mar 43 Cp Haan Calif as Sep CA Bn AA-AW/25 Jul 44 Cp Haan Calif	
784th AAA Auto-Wpns Bn (Semimobile) BPE: 7 Apr 44 England: 10 Apr 44 France-ETO: 14 Jul 44 - **26,30,32,34** (redes from CA 30 Apr 43)	10 Apr 43 Ft Bliss Tex as Sep CA Bn AA-AW/31 Dec 45 Germany	Handorf Germany
785th AAA Auto-Wpns Bn (Semimobile) SFPE: 22 Apr 44 New Guinea: 13 May 44 Morotai I: 19 Sep 44 Philippines: 12 Jan 46 - **15** (redes from CA 30 Apr 43)	10 Apr 43 Ft Bliss Tex as Sep CA Bn AA-AW/10 Apr 46 Philippines	Morotai Island
786th AAA Auto-Wpns Bn (Semimobile) (redes from CA 30 Apr 43)	20 Apr 43 Ft Bliss Tex as Sep CA Bn AA-AW/ 27 Jul 44 Cp Swift Tex	
787th AAA Auto-Wpns Bn (Semimobile) NYPE: 11 Aug 44 England: 22 Aug 44 France-ETO: 22 Sep 44 - **25,34** (redes from CA 30 Apr 43)	20 Apr 43 Cp Hulen Tex as Sep CA Bn AA-AW/ 27 Jun 46 Germany	Buchschwabach Germany
788th AAA Auto-Wpns Bn (Semimobile) NYPE: 11 Aug 44 England: 22 Aug 44 France-ETO: 23 Sep 44 - **25,26,32,34** (redes from CA 30 Apr 43)	20 Apr 43 Cp Hulen Tex as Sep CA Bn AA-AW/ 29 Jun 46 France	Mehlem Germany
789th AAA Auto-Wpns Bn (Semimobile) NYPE: 13 May 44 England: 25 May 44 France-ETO: 19 Sep 44 - **25,26,32,34** (redes from CA 30 Apr 43)	30 Apr 43 Cp Stewart Ga as Sep CA Bn AA-AW/18 Dec 45 Germany	Ossenberg Germany

BATTALION DESIGNATION AND TYPE	FORMED (SOURCE OF UNIT) / INACTIVATION	AUGUST 1945 LOCATION
790th AAA Auto-wpns Bn (Cld) (Semimobile) *(redes from CA 30 Apr 43)*	20 Apr 43 Cp Stewart Ga as Sep CA Bn AA-AW/24 Apr 44 Cp Patrick Henry/ Ft Lee Va	
791st AAA Auto-Wpns Bn (Semimobile) BPE: 3 Jul 44 England: 12 Jul 44 France-ETO: 18 Aug 44 - **32** NYPE: 2 Sep 43 *(redes from CA 30 Apr 43)*	20 Apr 43 Cp Stewart Ga as Sep CA Bn AA-AW/8 May 46 Cp Kilmer N.J.	Shipment #10998-B at sea
792nd AAA Auto-Wpns Bn (Semimobile) BPE: 27 Feb 44 England: 11 Mar 44 France-ETO: 15 Jul 44 - **25,26,30,32,34** NYPE: 27 Nov 45 *(redes from CA 30 Apr 43)*	20 Apr 43 Cp Stewart Ga as Sep CA Bn AA-AW/28 Nov 45 Cp Kilmer N.J.	Laugensalza Germany
793rd AAA Auto-Wpns Bn (Semimobile) SPE: 15 Nov 44 Hawaii: 23 Nov 44 *(redes from CA 30 Apr 43*	20 Apr 43 Cp Stewart Ga as Sep CA Bns AA-AW/31 Dec 45 Hawaii	Ft Hase Hawaii
794th AAA Auto-Wpns Bn (Semimobile) NYPE: 5 Oct 44 England: 13 Oct 44 France-ETO: 16 Oct 44 - **26** NYPE: 18 Jan 46 *(redes from CA 30 Apr 43)*	20 Apr 43 Cp Stewart Ga as Sep CA Bn AA-AW/20 Jan 46 Cp Kilmer N.J.	Speyer Germany
795th AAA Auto-Wpns Bn (Semimobile) BPE: 7 Apr 44 England: 16 Apr 44 France-ETO: 18 Jul 44 - **26,30,32,34** *(redes from CA 30 Apr 43)*	20 Apr 43 Cp Stewart Ga as Sep CA Bn AA-AW/31 Dec 45 Germany	Ochsenfurt Germany
796th AAA Automatic Weapons Bn (S-P) NYPE: 11 Aug 44 England: 22 Aug 44 France-ETO: 23 Sep 44 - **25,26,34** *(redes from CA 30 Apr 43)*	20 Apr 43 Cp Stewart Ga as Sep CA Bn AA-AW/17 Apr 46 Cp Kilmer N.J.	Weilheim Germany
797th AAA Automatic Weapons Bn (Mobile) *(redes from CA 30 Apr 43)*	16 Apr 43 Cp Haan Calif as Sep CA Bn AA-AW/1 Nov 44 Cp Howze Tex	
798th AAA Automatic Weapons Bn (Mobile) BPE: 10 Nov 44 England: 17 Nov 44 France-ETO: 6 Feb 45 - **26,34** NYPE: 23 Oct 45 *(redes from CA on same date it was formed)*	30 Apr 43 Cp Haan Calif as Sep CA Bn AA-AW/ 24 Oct 45 Cp Shanks N.Y.	Salzburg Austria
799th AAA Auto-Wpns Bn (Semimobile) *(redes from CA 30 Apr 43)*	16 Apr 43 Cp Haan Calif as Sep CA Bn AA-AW/19 Jul 44 Cp Gruber Okla	
800th AAA Auto-Wpns Bn (Semimobile) *(redes from CA 30 Apr 43)*	16 Apr 43 Cp Haan Calif as Sep CA Bn AA-AW/12 Jun 44 Cp Haan Calif	
811th AAA Auto-Wpns Bn (Semimobile)	17 Jul 44 Hawaii / 29 Nov 45 Hawaii	Schofield Barracks Hawaii
815th AAA Automatic Weapons Bn (Mobile) NYPE: 4 Dec 44 England: 12 Dec 44 France-ETO: 6 Mar 45 - **26,34** NYPE: 1 Mar 46 *(redes from CA 30 Apr 43)*	16 Apr 43 Cp Haan Calif as Sep CA Bn AA-AW/ 2 Mar 46 Cp Kilmer N.J.	Straubing Germany
816th AAA Auto-Wpns Bn (Semimobile) *(redes from CA on same date it was formed)*	30 Apr 43 Cp Stewart Ga as Sep CA Bn AA-AW/ 28 Jul 44 Cp Swift Tex	
817th AAA Auto-Wpns Bn (Semimobile) *(redes from CA 30 Apr 43)*	2 Apr 43 Cp Haan Calif as Sep CA Bn AA-AW/ 4 Nov 44 Cp Maxey Tex	
818th AAA Auto-Wpns Bn (Semimobile) *(redes from CA on same date it was formed)*	30 Apr 43 Cp Haan Calif as Sep CA Bn AA-AW/ 25 Jul 44 Cp Swift Tex	
819th AAA Auto-Wpns Bn (Cld) (Semimobile) *(redes from CA 30 Apr 43)*	20 Apr 43 Cp Stewart Ga as Sep CA Bn AA-AW/1 May 44 Indiantown Gap Mil Res Pa	
820th AAA Auto-Wpns Bn (Semimobile)	20 May 43 Ft Bliss Tex / 29 Jul 44 Cp Swift Tex	
821st AAA Automatic Weapons Bn (Mobile)	20 May 43 Ft Bliss Tex / 4 Nov 44 Cp Howze Tex *(R&S Cmd 24 Oct 44)*	
822nd AAA Auto-Wpns Bn (Semimobile)	10 May 43 Cp Haan Calif / 5 Oct 44 Cp Maxey Tex	
823rd AAA Auto-Wpns Bn (Semimobile)	10 May 43 Cp Haan Calif / 5 Aug 44 Cp Maxey Tex	
824th AAA Auto-Wpns Bn (Semimobile)	24 May 43 Cp Haan Calif /14 Nov 44 Cp Howze Tex *(R&S Cmd 28 Oct 44)*	
832nd AAA Auto-Wpns Bn (Semimobile)	24 May 43 Cp Haan Calif /15 Aug 44 Cp Maxey Tex	
833rd AAA Auto-Wpns Bn (Semimobile)	24 May 43 Cp Haan Calif / 8 Nov 44 Cp Howze Tex *(R&S Cmd 27 Oct 44)*	
834th AAA Automatic Weapons Bn (S-P) Portland Sub-P/E: 22 Jan 45 Hawaii: 30 Jan 45 Okinawa: 26 Apr 45 - **19**	24 May 43 Cp Haan Calif / 30 Jun 46 Korea	Okinawa
835th AAA Auto-Wpns Bn (Semimobile)	24 May 43 Cp Haan Calif / 8 Nov 44 Cp Howze Tex *(R&S Cmd 25 Oct 44)*	
836th AAA Auto-Wpns Bn (Semimobile)	20 May 43 Cp Edwards Mass /12 Dec 44 Cp Livingston La *(R&S Cmd 5 Dec 44)*	
837th AAA Auto-Wpns Bn (Semimobile)	20 May 43 Ft Sheridan Ill /1 Dec 44 Cp Livingston La *(R&S Cmd 27 Nov 44)*	
838th AAA Automatic Weapons Bn (Mobile) NYPE: 1 Dec 44 England: 12 Dec 44 France-ETO: 8 Feb 45 - **26,34** NYPE: 3 Apr 46	20 May 43 Cp Hulen Tex / 4 Apr 46 Cp Kilmer N.J.	Augsburg Germany

BATTALION DESIGNATION AND TYPE	FORMED (SOURCE OF UNIT)/INACTIVATION *Active through 1946	AUGUST 1945 LOCATION
839th AAA Automatic Weapons Bn (Mobile) BPE: 2 Dec 44 England: 12 Dec 44 France-ETO: 4 Mar 45 - **26,34** *(battalion initially semimobile)*	20 May 43 Ft Bliss Tex / 6 Oct 45 France	Schuefluigen Germany
840th AAA Auto-Wpns Bn (Semimobile) SPE: 15 Nov 44 Hawaii: 23 Nov 44	20 May 43 Cp Stewart Ga / 8 Apr 46 Hawaii	Cp Malakole Hawaii
841st AAA Auto-Wpns Bn (Semimobile)	20 May 43 Cp Stewart Ga /11 Nov 44 Cp Howze Tex *(R&S Cmd 10 Nov 44)*	
842nd AAA Auto-Wpns Bn (Semimobile) SPE: 15 Nov 44 Hawaii: 23 Nov 44	20 May 43 Cp Stewart Ga / 25 Jan 46 Hawaii	Cp Malakole Hawaii
843rd AAA Auto-Wpns Bn (Air Transp.) LAPE: 29 Jun 44 India: 7 Aug 44 Burma: 11 Oct 44	20 May 43 Cp Stewart Ga / 7 Nov 45 Cp Kilmer N.J. China: 16 Dec 44 India: 28 Sep 45 - **7,8,12** NYPE: 5 Nov 45	Myitkyina Burma less Btry B at Mogaung Burma
844th AAA Auto-Wpns Bn (Air Transp.)	20 May 43 Cp Stewart Ga / 5 Aug 44 Cp Stewart Ga *(AA Cmd)*	
845th AAA Auto-Wpns Bn (Air Transp.) *(redes from CA 30 Apr 43)*	20 Apr 43 Cp Stewart Ga as Sep CA Bn AA-AW/10 May 44 Cp Pickett Va	
846th AAA Auto-Wpns Bn (Cld) (Semimobile)	20 May 43 Cp Stewart Ga / 24 Apr 44 Cp Patrick Henry Va	
860th AAA Automatic Weapons Bn (S-P)	5 Sep 43 Puerto Rico /1 Jun 44 Puerto Rico	
861st AAA Auto-Wpns Bn (Semimobile) Hawaii: 5 Nov 43 Philippines: 8 Dec 44 Okinawa: 1 Apr 45 - **13,19**	5 Nov 43 Ft Kamehameha Hawaii (305th CA Bn) / 30 Jan 46 Okinawa	Okinawa
862nd AAA Auto-Wpns Bn (Semimobile) SFPE: 11 Jul 43 Adak I: 25 Jul 43 Kiska I: 16 Aug 43 Ft Greely Kodiak Alaska: 29 Dec 43 - **2** SPE: 8 May 44 *(Amphibian Training Force #9)*	10 May 43 Ft Ord Calif / 7 Aug 44 Cp Van Dorn Miss	
863rd AAA Auto-Wpns Bn (Semimobile) NYPE: 21 Mar 44 England: 29 Mar 44 France-ETO: 12 Jul 44 - **25,26,30,32,34** BPE: 25 Nov 45	1 Jun 43 Ft Totten N.Y. / 26 Nov 45 Cp Myles Standish Mass	Lenz Germany
864th AAA Auto-Wpns Bn (Semimobile)	12 Dec 43 Hawaii (3rd Bn, 64th CA) / *	Saipan
865th AAA Auto-Wpns Bn (Semimobile)	12 Dec 43 Hawaii (3rd Bn, 93rd CA) / *	Saipan
866th AAA Auto-Wpns Bn (Semimobile) Hawaii: 12 Dec 43 Philippines: 20 Oct 44 Okinawa: 26 Apr 45 - **13,19**	12 Dec 43 Hawaii (3rd Bn, 95th CA) / 30 Sep 46 Philippines	Okinawa
867th AAA Auto-Wpns Bn (Semimobile) Hawaii: 12 Dec 43 Kwajalein: 6 Feb 44 Engebi-Eniwetok: 19 Feb 44 Hawaii: 27 Sep 44 - **10,21**	12 Dec 43 Schofield Bks Hawaii (3rd Bn, 96th CA) / *	Cp Malakole Hawaii
868th AAA Auto-Wpns Bn (Semimobile) Hawaii: 12 Dec 43 Guam: 10 Sep 44 - **21**	12 Dec 43 Hawaii (3rd Bn, 97th CA) /15 Jan 46 Guam	Guam
869th AAA Auto-Wpns Bn (Semimobile)	12 Dec 43 Hawaii (3rd Bn, 98th CA) / 29 Nov 45 Hawaii (Btry B,C,D served on Baker I)	Hickam Field Hawaii
870th AAA Auto-Wpns Bn (Cld) (Semimobile) Hawaii: 12 Dec 43 Okinawa: 10 May 45 - **19** SPE: 13 Jan 46	12 Dec 43 Barbers Point Hawaii (2nd Bn, 369th CA) /15 Jan 46 Ft Lawton Wash	Okinawa
871st AAA Auto-Wpns Bn (Cld) (Semimobile) SFPE: 20 Jan 45 New Guinea: 4 Feb 45	29 Feb 44 Cp Stewart Ga (2nd Bn, 99th CA) /18 Mar 45 Hollandia New Guinea	
891st AAA Gun Bn (Semimobile) Panama: 15 Sep 43 NOPE: 9 Sep 44	15 Sep 43 Ft Kobbe Panama Canal Zone (1st Bn, 615th CA) / 5 Sep 45 Ft Bliss Tex	
892nd AAA Gun Bn (Semimobile)	5 Sep 43 Puerto Rico /1 Jun 44 Puerto Rico	
893rd AAA Automatic Weapons Bn (Mobile) Sicily: 24 Mar 44 Italy: 12 Jul 44 France-ETO: 16 Aug 44 - **26,34,35,37**	24 Mar 44 Sicily (2nd Bn, 62nd CA) /14 Dec 45 Germany	Maunheim Germany
894th AAA Automatic Weapons Bn (Mobile) Italy: 23 May 44 France-ETO: 1 Sep 44 - **25,26,34,35,37**	23 May 44 Mass Piscicelli Italy (2nd Bn, 67th CA) /14 Dec 45 Germany	Huttenfeld Germany
895th AAA Automatic Weapons Bn (Mobile) Italy: 4 Jun 44 France-ETO: 16 Aug 44 - **25,26,34,37** NYPE: 5 Jan 46	4 Jun 44 Santa Maria Italy (2nd Bn, 68th CA) / 6 Jan 46 Cp Kilmer N.J.	Pfronteirberg Germany
896th AAA Auto-Wpns Bn (Semimobile) Sardinia: 1 Apr 44 Corsica: 1 Sep 44 France-ETO: 13 Oct 44 - **34,35**	1 Apr 44 Cagliari Sardinia (2nd Bn, 74th CA) / 9 Jul 46 France	Cabries France
897th AAA Auto-Wpns Bn (Semimobile) North Africa: 25 May 44 France-ETO: 9 Sep 44 - **37**	25 May 44 Oran North Africa (2nd Bn, 90th CA)/15 Sep 44 St Tropez France, assets to Quartermaster truck units	

BATTALION DESIGNATION AND TYPE	FORMED (SOURCE OF UNIT) / INACTIVATION *Active through 1946	AUGUST 1945 LOCATION
898th AAA Automatic Weapons Bn (Mobile) Italy: 18 Mar 44 Corsica: 24 Aug 44 France-ETO: 25 Oct 44 - **25,26,34,35** BPE: 2 Nov 45	18 Mar 44 Montesarcchio Italy (2nd Bn, 209th CA) / 3 Nov 45 Cp Myles Standish Mass	Fendenheim Germany
899th AAA Auto-Wpns Bn (Semimobile) Italy: 14 Mar 44 France-ETO: 14 Nov 44 - **34,35**	14 Mar 44 Castel Volturno Italy (2nd Bn, 213th CA) /13 Feb 45 St Martin Vesubie France	
900th AAA Automatic Weapons Bn (Mobile) Italy: 14 Mar 44 - **29,31,35**	14 Mar 44 Santa Maria Italy (2nd Bn, 505th CA) /14 Jan 45 Montecatini Italy, assets to 3rd Bn, 473rd Inf Regt	
901st AAA Auto-Wpns Bn (Semimobile)	15 Sep 43 Panama Canal Zone /1 Feb 46 Panama Canal Zone	Ft Davis Canal Zone less det from HHB at Seymour I
902nd AAA Auto-Wpns Bn (Semimobile)	15 Sep 43 Panama Canal Zone /15 Apr 46 Panama Canal Zone	Ft Gulick Canal Zone less Btrys A, B, & D at Ft William D Davis Canal Zone & Btry C on Seymour I Galapagos
903rd AAA Auto-Wpns Bn (Semimobile)	15 Sep 43 Panama Canal Zone / *	Ft Clayton Canal Zone
906th AAA Auto-Wpns Bn (Semimobile)	15 Sep 43 Panama Canal Zone /1 Feb 46 Panama Canal Zone	Ft Clayton Canal Zone
910th AAA Automatic Weapons Bn (Mobile) Puerto Rico: 6 Nov 43 NYPE: 4 Dec 43 NYPE: 1 Dec 44 England: 12 Dec 44 France-ETO: 14 Feb 45 - **26,34** NYPE: 9 Feb 46	6 Nov 43 Puerto Rico (2nd Bn, 66th CA) /10 Feb 46 Cp Kilmer N.J.	Schreisheim Germany
913th AAA Auto-Wpns Bn (Semimobile)	6 Nov 43 Puerto Rico /1 Jun 44 Puerto Rico	
925th AAA Auto-Wpns Bn (Semimobile) Guadalcanal: 10 Nov 43 New Georgia: 22 Nov 43 Green I: 25 May 44 Bougainville: 11 Oct 44 Philippines: 11 Mar 45 - **3,13,16**	10 Nov 43 Guadalcanal (2nd Bn, 70th CA) / 31 Aug 46 Philippines	Tacloban Philippines
932nd AAA Auto-Wpns Bn (Semimobile) Galapagos I: 15 Sep 43 NOPE: 13 Jun 44	15 Sep 43 Seymour Island (2nd Bn, 19th CA) /15 Aug 44 Cp Butner N.C.	
933rd AAA Auto-Wpns Bn (Cld) (Semimobile) New Hebrides: 1 Nov 43 Russell I: 12 Dec 43 Admiralty I: 12 Dec 44 - **16** LAPE: 30 Dec 45	1 Nov 43 New Hebrides (2nd Bn, 76th CA) / 31 Dec 45 Cp Anza Calif	Admiralty Islands
938th AAA Auto-Wpns Bn (Cld) (Semimobile) New Hebrides: 1 Nov 43 New Georgia I: 5 Dec 43 New Guinea: 6 Feb 45	1 Nov 43 New Hebrides (2nd Bn, 77th CA) /15 Feb 45 New Guinea	
945th AAA Auto-Wpns Bn (Semimobile) Treasury I: 1 Mar 44 New Guinea: 9 Feb 45 Philippines: 15 Jul 45 - **16**	1 Mar 44 Treasury Islands (2nd Bn, 198th CA) /15 Feb 46 Japan	Tacloban Philippines
947th AAA Gun Bn (Semimobile) Hawaii: 26 May 44 Iwo Jima: 14 Mar 45 - **1**	26 May 44 Aiea Hawaii (429th AAA Bn) /15 Jan 46 Iwo Jima	Iwo Jima
948th AAA Gun Bn (Semimobile) Hawaii: 17 Jul 44 Ie Shima I: 4 Jun 45 - **19** LAPE: 20 Jan 46	17 Jul 44 Schofield Bks Hawaii / 21 Jan 46 Cp Anza Calif	Ie Shima Island
950th AAA Auto-Wpns Bn (Semimobile) Guadalcanal: 11 Nov 43 New Zealand: 11 Jan 44 New Guinea: 23 Jun 44 Philippines: 9 Jan 45 - **13,14,15** SFPE: 27 Dec 45	11 Nov 43 Guadalcanal (2nd Bn, 214th CA) /28 Dec 45 Cp Stoneman Calif	Clark Field Philippines
951st AAA Auto-Wpns Bn (Semimobile) Bougainville: 1 Mar 44 Philippines: 9 Jan 45 - **14,16** SFPE: 26 Dec 45	1 Mar 44 Bougainville (2nd Bn, 251st CA) / 29 Dec 45 Cp Stoneman Calif	Manila Philippines
967th AAA Gun Bn (Semimobile) Guadalcanal: 1 Nov 43 Green I: 15 Feb 44 Bougainville: 3 Oct 44 Philippines: 10 Mar 45 - **3,13,16** SFPE: 24 Dec 45	1 Nov 43 Guadalcanal (elmts 70th and 214th CA) / 28 Dec 45 Cp Stoneman Calif	Tacloban Philippines
977th AAA Auto-Wpns Bn (Semimobile) Iceland: 22 Jun 43 NYPE: 14 Jun 45	22 Jun 43 Iceland (698th, 699th CA Btry) / 22 Jun 45 Cp Kilmer N.J.	

*Active through 1946

Part IX

Engineers of the U.S. Army in World War II

Chapter 39

Engineer Brigades

Brigades:

1–6, 1–3 Provisional, 5201 Provisional, 5202 Provisional, 5220–5222 Provisional, Provisional Engineer Special Brigade Group

1st Engineer Aviation Brigade (Provisional)

5 Apr 45 raised in France from IX Engineer Command assets and inactivated in Germany on 2 Dec 45.

Campaigns: *Central Europe*
Aug 45 Loc: Buc France

1st Engineer Special Brigade

15 Jun 42 activated at Cp Edwards Mass as the 1st Engineer Amphibian Brigade with the 531st Engineer Shore Regiment and 591st Engineer Boat Regiment assigned; arrived at New York P/E 4 Aug 42 and departed 5 Aug 42; arrived in England 17 Aug 42 and then Scotland; departed Glasgow 24 Nov 42 and landed in North Africa 6 Dec 42 where redesignated 1st Engineer Special Brigade on 14 May 43; assaulted Sicily 9 Jul 43 and Italy on 9 Sep 43; returned to England on 9 Dec 43 and assaulted Utah Beach France 6 Jun 44; operated as the Utah Beach Command until 23 Oct 44 when assigned to serve as Utah District of Normandy Base Sector staff; departed France on 18 Dec 44 and arrived at New York P/E on 30 Dec 44; moved to Ft Dix N.J. and airlifted to Ft Lewis Wash on 1 Feb 45; arrived in Hawaii 14 Feb 45 from Hamilton Field Calif aerial P/E; assaulted Okinawa 1 Apr 45 and inactivated in Korea on 18 Feb 46.

Campaigns: *Sicily, Naples-Foggia, Rome-Arno, Normandy, Northern France, Ryukyus*
Aug 45 Loc: Okinawa

2nd Engineer Aviation Brigade (Provisional)

5 Apr 45 raised in France from IX Engineer Command assets and inactivated in Germany on 2 Dec 45.

Campaigns: *Central Europe*
Aug 45 Loc: Buc France

2nd Engineer Special Brigade

20 Jun 42 activated at Cp Edwards Mass as the 2nd Engineer Amphibian Brigade with the 532nd Engineer Shore, 542nd Engineer Amphibian, and 592nd Engineer Boat Regiments assigned; arrived at Cp Carrabelle Fla on 18 Oct 42 and moved to Ft Ord Calif 11 Nov 42; departed San Francisco P/E 25 Mar 43 and arrived in Australia on 17 Apr 43 where redesignated 2nd Engineer Special Brigade on 4 Jul 43; landed at Oro Bay New Guinea 25 Oct 43 and assaulted Leyte Island Philippines 20 Oct 44; arrived at Seattle P/E 16 Dec 45 and active at Ft Ord Calif through 1946.

Campaigns: *New Guinea, Leyte*
Aug 45 Loc: Leyte Philippine Islands, less detachment at Manila

3rd Engineer Aviation Brigade (Provisional)

5 Apr 45 redesignated from Headquarters IX Engineer Command in France and assigned to the Air Force Engineer Command, Provisional.

Campaigns: *Central Europe*
Aug 45 Loc: St Germain France

3rd Engineer Special Brigade

6 Aug 42 activated at Cp Edwards Mass as the 3rd Engineer Amphibian Brigade with the 533rd Engineer Shore, 543rd Engineer Amphibian, and 593rd Engineer Boat Regiments assigned; moved to Cp Carrabelle Fla 14 Nov 42 and to Ft Ord Calif 25 Apr 43 where redesignated the 3rd Engineer Special Brigade on 10 May 43; staged at Cp Stoneman Calif 12–22 Dec 43 when departed San Francisco P/E; arrived on Goodenough Island 12 Jan 44 and landed on New Guinea 24 Feb 44; landed on Biak Island 30 Sep 44 and in the Philippine Islands 24 Jul 45; arrived at Portland Oreg 20 Dec 45 where inactivated 22 Dec 45.

Campaigns: *New Guinea*
Aug 45 Loc: Luzon Philippine Islands

4th Engineer Special Brigade

1 Feb 43 activated at Ft Devens Mass as the 4th Engineer Amphibian Brigade with the 534th Engineer Shore, 544th Engineer Amphibian, and the 594th Engineer Boat Regiments assigned; moved to Cp Edwards Mass on 30 Mar 43 where redesignated as the 4th Engineer Special Brigade on 10 May 43; relocated to Cp Gordon Johnston Fla in Sep 43 and staged at Cp Stoneman Calif 21 Apr 44 until departed San Francisco P/E 28 Apr 44; arrived at Oro Bay New Guinea 18 May 44 and assaulted Morotai Island on 15 Sep 44; assaulted Lingayen Gulf Luzon Philippines 9 Jan 45; inactivated in Japan on 15 Apr 46.

Campaigns: *New Guinea, Luzon*
Aug 45 Loc: Manila Philippine Islands

5th Engineer Special Brigade

12 Nov 43 redesignated from HHC of the 1119th Engineer Combat Group at Swansea England and assaulted Omaha Beach France on 6 Jun 44; operated Omaha Beach until it was closed out 19 Nov 44; 4 Jan 45 transferred to supervise construction activities in the Seine section at Paris; sent to Le Havre 1 Apr 45; returned to the United States on 11 Jul 45 and inactivated at Cp Gordon Johnston Fla on 20 Oct 45.

Campaigns: *Normandy, Northern France, Ardennes-Alsace, Central Europe*
Aug 45 Loc: Camp Gordon Johnston Florida

6th Engineer Special Brigade

15 May 44 redesignated from HHC of the 1116th Engineer Combat Group in England and assaulted Omaha Beach France on 6 Jun 44; helped to operate Omaha Beach until 24 Dec 44 when moved 1 Jan 45 to Verdun to supervise construction; 25 Jun 45 moved to La Maison Rouge France and departed Le Havre France 14 Jul 45; arrived at Hampton Roads P/E 23 Jul 45 and moved immediately to Cp Gordon Johnston Fla where inactivated on 20 Oct 45.

Campaigns: *Normandy, Northern France, Rhineland, Central Europe*
Aug 45 Loc: Camp Gordon Johnston Florida

5201st Engineer Construction Brigade (Provisional)

13 Jun 44 activated at Hollandia New Guinea from selected personnel of the 880th Airborne Engineer Aviation Bn, 339th Engineer Construction Bn, and 931st Engineer Aviation Regiment; assaulted Leyte Island Philippines 22 Oct 44 where inactivated on 5 Dec 45.

Campaigns: *New Guinea, Leyte, Luzon*
Aug 45 Loc: Manila Philippine Islands

5202nd Engineer Construction Brigade (Provisional)

16 Jun 44 activated on Biak Island and assigned to the Sixth Army; landed on Luzon Philippine Islands on 9 Jan 45 where inactivated on 5 Dec 45.

Campaigns: *New Guinea, Leyte, Luzon*
Aug 45 Loc: Manila Philippine Islands

5220th Engineer Construction Brigade (Provisional)

23 Jul 45 activated at Engineer Section, Headquarters Sixth Army at San Fernando Luzon Philippine Islands to supervise engineer groups for the projected invasion of Japan; active organization of the brigade began 20 Aug 45; discontinued in Japan on 15 Nov 45.

Campaigns: *Pacific Theater without inscription*
Aug 45 Loc: San Fernando Philippine Islands

5221st Engineer Construction Brigade (Provisional)

11 Jul 45 activated at Manila Philippine Islands to supervise engineer groups for the projected invasion of Japan; active organization of the brigade began 1 Aug 45; discontinued in Japan.

Campaigns: *Pacific Theater without inscription*
Aug 45 Loc: Manila Philippine Islands

5222nd Engineer Construction Brigade (Provisional)

11 Jul 45 activated at Manila Philippine Islands to supervise engineer groups for the projected invasion of Japan and still organizing at the conclusion of the war; discontinued in Japan.

Campaigns: *Pacific Theater without inscription*
Aug 45 Loc: Manila Philippine Islands

Provisional Engineer Special Brigade Group

17 Feb 44 established at Pennlargaer England to control the 5th and 6th Engineer Special Brigades to be utilized in the Omaha Beach assault on Normandy France; dissolved on Omaha Beach France 26 Jun 44 and assets used to form the Headquarters, Omaha Beach Command there.

Campaigns: *Normandy*

Chapter 40

Engineer Groups

Groups:

Provisional, 19, 36, 39, 40, 427, 540, 555, 591, 595, 931, 932, 934, 1051–1061, 1067, 1101–1169, 1171–1181, 1185–1187, 1189–1200, 1338, 1347, 1348, 1350, 1378, 1497, 1521, 1523, 1524, 3188, 5207–5210 Provisional, 5212 Provisional, 5213 Provisional, 5251 Provisional, 5252 Provisional, 5255 Provisional

Engineer Combat Group (Provisional)

30 Dec 43 organized at Schofield Barracks Hawaii with personnel furnished by 34th Engineer Combat Regiment and 47th Engineer General Service Regiment; discontinued 2 May 44.

Campaigns: *Pacific Theater without inscription*

19th Engineer Combat Group

1 Mar 45 redesignated from HHC, 19th Engineer Combat Regiment in Frassineta Italy and assigned to Fifth Army; arrived at New York P/E 29 Aug 45 and arrived at Cp Shelby Miss 3 Sep 45; transferred to Cp Campbell Ky 20 Nov 45 and assigned to Second Army where stationed through 1946.

Campaigns: *North Apennines, Po Valley*
Aug 45 Loc: Livorno Italy loading Shipment #22001-F to return to USA

36th Engineer Combat Group

15 Feb 45 redesignated from HHC, 36th Engineer Combat Regiment in Sourrebourg France and assigned to Seventh Army; entered Germany 26 Mar 45 and inactivated in Austria 30 Nov 46.

Campaigns: *Central Europe*
Aug 45 Loc: Oberau Germany

39th Engineer Combat Group

17 May 45 redesignated from HHC, 39th Engineer Combat Regiment in Pisa Italy; arrived at New York P/E 29 Aug 45 and moved to Cp Swift Tex where inactivated 31 Jan 46.

Aug 45 Loc: Livorno Italy loading Shipment #22001-G to return to USA

40th Engineer Combat Group

15 Feb 45 redesignated from HHC, 40th Engineer Combat Regiment in Romanswiller France and entered Germany 23 Mar 45; arrived at New York P/E 15 Sep 45 and inactivated at Cp Kilmer N.J. 17 Sep 45.

Campaigns: *Rhineland, Central Europe*
Aug 45 Loc: Augsburg Germany

427th Engineer Construction Group

25 Apr 45 activated at Schofield Barracks Hawaii and assigned to Tenth Army 1 Jun 45; departed Hawaii 15 Jun 45 and arrived in Okinawa 15 Jul 45; inactivated in Korea 7 Jan 46.

Campaigns: *Pacific Theater without inscription*
Aug 45 Loc: Okinawa

540th Engineer Combat Group

15 Feb 45 redesignated from HHC, 540th Engineer Regiment in Lutzelbourg France and assigned to Seventh Army; entered Germany 23 Mar 45 where inactivated 25 Oct 45.

Campaigns: *Rhineland, Central Europe*
Aug 45 Loc: Landsberg Germany

555th Engineer Composite Service Group

27 Mar 45 activated in France where disbanded 12 Nov 45.

Campaigns: *European Theater without inscription*
Aug 45 Loc: France

591st Engineer Combat Group

18 Apr 45 redesignated from HHC, 1185th Engineer Combat Group in Pirmasens Germany and inactivated in France 18 Nov 45.

Campaigns: *Central Europe*
Aug 45 Loc: Salon-de-Provence France

595th Engineer Base Depot Group

6 Sep 44 activated in Hawaii where served until inactivated 13 Dec 46.

Campaigns: *Pacific Theater without inscription*
Aug 45 Loc: Ft Shafter Hawaii

931st Engineer Construction Group (Aviation)

10 Oct 44 redesignated from HHC, 931st Engineer Aviation Regiment on Morotai Island; departed Morotai 31 Dec 44 and arrived in Philippines 13 Jan 45; inactivated in Japan 15 May 46.

Campaigns: *New Guinea, Luzon*
Aug 45 Loc: Bagabag Philippines

932nd Engineer Construction Group (Aviation)

8 Oct 44 activated on Morotai Island and assigned to Southwest Pacific Area; sent to Philippines and served at Malabang; inactivated in Japan 30 Jun 46.

Campaigns: *New Guinea, Southern Philippines*
Aug 45 Loc: Cotabato Mindanao Philippines

934th Engineer Construction Group (Aviation)

1 Nov 44 activated at Finschhafen New Guinea and assigned to Southwest Pacific Area; sent to Philippines and served in Luzon; inactivated in Japan 30 Jun 46.

Campaigns: *Luzon*
Aug 45 Loc: Manila Philippines

1051st Engineer Port Construction and Repair Group

25 Nov 42 activated at Ft Screven Ga and assigned to Fourth Service Command; staged at Cp Patrick Henry Va 7–18 Jun 43; departed Hampton Roads P/E 18 Jun 43; arrived at Casablanca North Africa 29 Jun 43; landed in Sicily 4 Aug 43; moved to Italy 4 Oct 43; arrived in southern France 25 Aug 44; redesignated HHC, Engineer Port Construction and Repair (Group status deleted) 4 Feb 45. Unit crossed into Germany 29 Mar 45 and returned to France 13 May 45 where inactivated 19 Oct 46.

Campaigns: *Naples-Foggia, Sicily, Rome-Arno, Southern France, Rhineland, Central Europe*

1052nd Engineer Port Construction and Repair Group

20 Dec 42 activated at Ft Screven Ga and assigned to Fourth Service Command; staged at Cp Stoneman Calif 24 Jun–3 Jul 43; departed San Francisco P/E 3 Jul 43 and arrived at Brisbane Australia 24 Jul 43; transferred to Milne Bay New Guinea 21 Aug 43; landed at Batangas Philippines 22 Oct 44 where redesignated HHC, Engineer Port Construction and Repair (Group status deleted) 6 Jan 45. Unit inactivated in Japan 31 Jan 46.

Campaigns: *New Guinea, Leyte, Luzon*

1053rd Engineer Port Construction and Repair Group

1 Apr 43 activated at Ft Screven Ga and assigned to Fourth Service Command; staged at Cp Myles Standish Mass 19–28 Dec 43; departed Boston P/E 28 Dec 43; arrived in England 7 Jan 44 and landed in France 16 Aug 44; redesignated HHC Engineer Port Construction and Repair (Group status deleted) at Liege Belgium 2 Jan 45. Unit later left France 16 Jun 45; arrived at Manila Philippines 20 Jul 45 and was inactivated there 15 Jan 46.

Campaigns: *Northern France, Ardennes-Alsace, Central Europe, Pacific Theater without inscription*

1054th Engineer Port Construction and Repair Group

1 Apr 43 activated at Ft Screven Ga and assigned to Fourth Service Command; staged at Cp Stoneman Calif 27 Oct–15 Nov 43; departed San Francisco P/E 15 Nov 43 and arrived in Australia 5 Dec 43; deployed to Finschhafen New Guinea 24 Dec 43; landed on Leyte, Philippine Islands 5 Nov 44 where redesignated HHC, Engineer Port Construction and Repair (Group status deleted) 6 Jan 45; transferred to Luzon 11 May 45; inactivated on 20 Dec 45.

Campaigns: *New Guinea, Leyte, Luzon*

1055th Engineer Port Construction and Repair Group

1 Apr 43 activated at Ft Screven Ga and assigned to Fourth Service Command; staged at Cp Shanks N.Y. 7–23 Dec 43; departed New York P/E 23 Dec 43 and arrived in England 29 Dec 43; landed in France 14 Jun 44 where redesignated HHC, Engineer Port Construction and Repair (Group status deleted) 2 Jan 45. Unit returned to Boston P/E 10 Jul 45 and inactivated at Ft Belvoir Va 3 Jun 46.

Campaigns: *Normandy*

1056th Engineer Port Construction and Repair Group

1 Apr 43 activated at Ft Screven Ga and assigned to Fourth Service Command; staged at Cp Shanks N.Y. 7 Dec–2 Jan 44; departed New York P/E 2 Jan 44 and arrived in England 8 Jan 44; landed in France 25 Jun 44 to Cherbourg; arrived in Belgium 2 Nov 44 and redesignated there as HHC, Engineer Port Construction and Repair (Group status deleted) 2 Jan 45; crossed into Germany 13 Mar 45; arrived at Boston P/E 1 Sep 45 and inactivated at Cp Gordon Johnston Fla 20 Oct 45.

Campaigns: *Normandy, Northern France, Rhineland, Ardennes-Alsace, Central Europe*

1057th Engineer Port Construction and Repair Group

14 Aug 43 activated at Ft Screven Ga and assigned to Fourth Service Command; arrived at Cp Gordon Johnston Fla 23 Dec 43; staged at Cp Shanks N.Y. 14–21 Mar 44; departed New York P/E 21 Mar 44 and arrived in England 27 Mar 44; landed in France 7 Aug 44; redesignated as HHC, Engineer Port Construction and Repair (Group status deleted) there 2 Jan 45; crossed into Luxembourg 13 Mar 45; entered Germany 26 Mar 45; arrived at New York P/E 15 Apr 46 and inactivated there 16 Apr 46.

Campaigns: *Northern France, Rhineland, Ardennes-Alsace, Central Europe*

1058th Engineer Port Construction and Repair Group

14 Aug 43 activated at Ft Screven Ga and assigned to Fourth Service Command; arrived at Cp Gordon Johnston Fla 23 Dec 43; staged at Cp Shanks N.Y. 16–27 Feb 44; departed New York P/E 27 Feb 44 and arrived in England 9 Mar 44; landed in France 25 Aug 44; crossed into Belgium 12 Jan 45; redesignated HHC, Engineer Port Construction and Repair (Group status deleted) 2 Jan 45. Unit arrived in Germany 13 Mar 45; left France 21 Jun 45 and arrived at Manila Philippines 30 Jul 45 where inactivated 12 Dec 45.

Campaigns: *Northern France, Rhineland, Ardennes-Alsace, Central Europe, Pacific Theater without inscription*

1059 Engineer Port Construction and Repair Group

14 Aug 43 activated at Ft Screven Ga and assigned to Fourth Service Command; arrived at Cp Gordon Johnston Fla 23 Dec 43; staged at Cp Stoneman Calif 1–9 Apr 44; departed San Francisco P/E 9 Apr 44 and arrived at Milne Bay New Guinea 30 Apr 44; landed on Morotai Island 16 Sep 44 where redesignated as HHC, Engineer Port Construction and Repair (Group status deleted) 6 Jan 45. Unit landed in Philippines at Mindoro 16 Jan 45 and inactivated at Nagoya Japan 31 Jan 46.

Campaigns: *New Guinea, Luzon*

1060th Engineer Port Construction and Repair Group

22 Nov 43 activated at Cp Gordon Johnston Fla; moved to Jackson Barracks La 4 Aug 44; departed New Orleans P/E 22 Aug 44 and arrived at Hollandia New Guinea 2 Oct 44; redesignated HHC, Engineer Port Construction and Repair (Group status deleted) 6 Jan 45; invaded Lingayen Gulf Philippines 9 Jan 45 where inactivated 10 Feb 46.

Campaigns: *New Guinea, Luzon*

1061st Engineer Port Construction and Repair Group

15 Dec 43 activated at Cp Gordon Johnston Fla; staged at Cp Shanks N.Y. 19 Jul 44 until departed New York P/E 26 Jul 44; arrived in England 5 Aug 44 and landed in France 9 Aug 44 where redesignated HHC, Engineer Port Construction and Repair (Group status deleted) 2 Jan 45; departed France 16 Jun 45 and arrived at Manila Philippine Islands 20 Jul 45 where inactivated on 15 Apr 46.

Campaigns: *Northern France, Pacific Theater without inscription*
Aug 45 Loc: Manila Philippine Islands

1067th Engineer Construction Group

11 Sep 44 activated at Cp Claiborne La and staged at Cp Myles Standish Mass 26 Jan 45 until departed Boston P/E 6 Feb 45; arrived in France 19 Feb 45 and crossed into Belgium 6 Mar 45; entered Germany 20 Mar 45 and departed France 9 Jul 45; arrived at Manila Philippines 17 Aug 45 and transferred to Okinawa; inactivated in Japan on 9 Nov 45.

Campaigns: *Rhineland, Central Europe, Pacific Theater without inscription*
Aug 45 Loc: Shipment #R0598-C at sea en route to Philippines

1101st Engineer Combat Group

22 Feb 43 activated at Cp Shelby Miss and departed New York P/E 23 Dec 43; arrived in Northern Ireland via Scotland 31 Dec 43 and sent to England on 13 May 44; landed in Normandy France on 14 Jul 44; crossed into Germany 18 Mar 45 where inactivated on 30 Mar 46.

Campaigns: *Normandy, Northern France, Rhineland, Ardennes-Alsace, Central Europe*
Aug 45 Loc: Auger Germany

1102nd Engineer Combat Group

25 Feb 43 activated at Cp McCain Miss and departed the United States 31 Dec 43; arrived in England 8 Jan 44; landed in Normandy France on 6 Jul 44 and crossed into Belgium 29 Sep 44; entered Luxembourg 3 Oct 44 and Germany 7 Feb 45; inactivated in Germany on 30 Mar 46.

Campaigns: *Normandy, Northern France, Rhineland, Ardennes-Alsace, Central Europe*
Aug 45 Loc: Elsterberg Germany

1103rd Engineer Combat Group

25 Feb 43 activated at Ft Devens Mass and departed the United States on 29 Dec 43; arrived in England 10 Jan 44; landed in France on 23 Jun 44 and crossed into Luxembourg 25 Dec 44; entered Holland 1 Mar 45 and Germany 9 Mar 45; inactivated in Germany on 8 May 46.

Campaigns: *Normandy, Northern France, Rhineland, Ardennes-Alsace, Central Europe*
Aug 45 Loc: Reckinghausen Germany

1104th Engineer Combat Group

25 Mar 43 redesignated from HHC, 133rd Engineer Combat Regiment at Ft Lewis Wash and participated in Oregon Mnvrs of Aug–Oct 43; staged at Cp Shanks N.Y. 14 Dec 43 until departed New York P/E 8 Jan 44; arrived in England 17 Jan 44 and landed in France on 11 Jun 44; crossed into Belgium on 5 Sep 44 and into Holland 17 Sep 44; entered Germany 29 Nov 44; arrived at New York P/E 16 Apr 46 and inactivated there on 17 Apr 46.

Campaigns: *Normandy, Northern France, Rhineland, Ardennes-Alsace, Central Europe*
Aug 45 Loc: Gedern Germany

1105th Engineer Combat Group

15 Mar 43 redesignated from HHC 27th Engineer Combat Regiment at Cp Breckinridge Ky and departed United States 3 Dec 43; arrived in England 9 Dec 43 and landed in France on 25 Jun 44; crossed into Belgium 14 Sep 44 and entered Germany on 10 Feb 45; inactivated there on 15 Feb 46.

Campaigns: *Normandy, Northern France, Rhineland, Ardennes-Alsace, Central Europe*
Aug 45 Loc: Arnstadt Germany

1106th Engineer Combat Group

18 Mar 43 redesignated from HHC, 37th Engineer Combat Regiment at Cp Beale Calif; staged at Bay Ridge Long Island N.Y. 16 Nov 43 until departed New York P/E 26 Nov 43; arrived in England 4 Dec 43 and assaulted Normandy France 6 Jun 44; crossed into Belgium 6 Sep 44 and into Germany 29 Sep 44; group was committed as line infantry at Aachen commencing 8 Oct 44; returned to Belgium 22 Dec 44 and to Germany 4 Feb 45 where inactivated on 30 Mar 46.

Campaigns: *Normandy, Northern France, Rhineland, Ardennes-Alsace, Central Europe*
Aug 45 Loc: Gerbstadt Germany

1107th Engineer Combat Group

30 Apr 43 activated at Cp Gordon Ga and departed the United States 22 Jan 44; arrived in England on 28 Jan 44 and landed in France 18 Jul 44; crossed into Belgium 10 Oct 44 and entered Germany 4 Mar 45; arrived at Boston P/E 26 Oct 45 and inactivated at Cp Myles Standish Mass on 27 Oct 45.

Campaigns: *Normandy, Northern France, Rhineland, Ardennes-Alsace, Central Europe*
Aug 45 Loc: Neida Germany

1108th Engineer Combat Group

15 Mar 43 redesignated from HHC, 48th Engineer Combat Regiment at Cp Gruber Okla; departed the United States on 21 Aug 43 and arrived in North Africa 3 Sep 43; landed in Italy on 10 Oct 43 and transferred to the Philippine Islands 31 Aug 45; inactivated in Korea on 24 Feb 46.

Campaigns: *Naples-Foggia, Rome-Arno, North Apennines, Po Valley, Pacific Theater without inscription*
Aug 45 Loc: Shipment # R2666-A en route from Italy to Philippine Islands

1109th Engineer Combat Group

1 Apr 43 redesignated from HHC, 44th Engineer Combat Regiment at Cp McCoy Wis and participated in Tennessee Mnvrs Apr–Jun 43; staged at Ft Hamilton N.Y. 16 Nov 43 until departed New York P/E 3 Dec 43; arrived in England 9 Dec 43 and landed in France on 18 Jun 44; entered Germany 23 Mar 45; arrived at New York P/E 1 Mar 46 and inactivated at Cp Kilmer N.J. on 2 Mar 46.

Campaigns: *Normandy, Northern France, Rhineland, Ardennes-Alsace, Central Europe*
Aug 45 Loc: Salzburg Austria

1110th Engineer Combat Group

1 Apr 43 redesignated from HHC, 49th Engineer Combat Regiment at Cp Carson Colo and participated in Louisiana Mnvrs June–August 43; staged at Cp Kilmer N.J. 15 Dec 43 until departed New York P/E 22 Dec 43; arrived in England 5 Jan 44 and landed in France 11 Jun 44; crossed into Belgium 12 Sep 44 and into Germany on 12 Dec 44; returned to Belgium 22 Dec 44 and to Germany 13 Mar 45; arrived at Boston P/E 24 Oct 45 and inactivated at Cp Myles Standish Mass on 25 Oct 45.

Campaigns: *Normandy, Northern France, Ardennes-Alsace, Central Europe*
Aug 45 Loc: Eisenach Germany

1111th Engineer Combat Group

1 Apr 43 redesignated from HHC, 51st Engineer Combat Regiment at Plattsburg Barracks N.Y. and moved to Elkins West Va on 7 Sep 43; staged at Ft Dix N.J. 5 Oct 43 until departed New York P/E 3 Dec 43; arrived in England 9 Dec 43 and landed in France 29 Jun 44; crossed into Belgium on 16 Sep 44 and into Germany on 6 Feb 45; arrived at New York P/E 17 Oct 45 and inactivated at Cp Shanks N.Y. on 18 Oct 45.

Campaigns: *Normandy, Northern France, Rhineland, Ardennes-Alsace, Central Europe*
Aug 45 Loc: Castell Germany

1112th Engineer Construction Group

1 Apr 43 redesignated from HHC, 52nd Engineer Combat Regiment at Cp Butner N.C. as the 1112th Engineer Combat Group and participated in the Tennessee Mnvrs June–September 43; moved to Cp Forrest Tenn 18 Sep 43 and staged at Cp Stoneman Calif 27 Dec 43 until departed San Francisco P/E 6 Jan 44; arrived on Goodenough Island 3 Feb 44 and landed at Finschhafen New Guinea 2 May 44; landed on Biak Island 30 May 44 where redesignated as the 1112th Engineer Construction Group on 11 Jul 44; arrived at Sansapor-Mar area of New Guinea 16 Jul 44; landed on Leyte Philippine Islands on 24 Oct 44; inactivated in Japan on 20 Feb 46.

Campaigns: *New Guinea, Leyte, Luzon*
Aug 45 Loc: Clark Field Philippine Islands

1113th Engineer Construction Group

1 Apr 43 redesignated from HHC, 79th Engineer Combat Regiment at Cp Phillips Kans as Engineer Combat Group; participated in Tennessee Maneuvers Jul–Oct 43; arrived at Cp Forrest Tenn 1 Oct 43; staged at Cp Stoneman Calif 25 Dec 43 until departed San Francisco P/E 17 Jan 44; arrived on Goodenough Island 8 Feb 44; landed at Finschhafen New Guinea 2 Mar 44 and relocated to Hollandia New Guinea 22 Apr 44 where redesignated Engineer Construction Group 23 Jun 44; invaded Leyte Philippines 20 Oct 44 and landed on Okinawa 15 Jun 45; active in Japan on occupation duty through 1946.

Campaigns: *New Guinea, Leyte, Ryukyus*
Aug 45 Loc: Okinawa

1114th Engineer Combat Group

22 Mar 43 redesignated from HHC, 31st Engineer Combat Regiment at Ft Belvoir Va and assigned to the Engineer School where inactivated 18 Oct 45.

1115th Engineer Combat Group

15 Mar 43 redesignated from HHC, 82nd Engineer Combat Regiment at Cp Swift Tex; served at Cp Polk La 23 Aug–2 Nov 43 before returned to Cp Swift; staged at Cp Kilmer N.J. 15 Dec 43 until departed New York P/E 8 Jan 44; arrived in England 17 Jan 44 and landed in France 16 Jun 44; crossed into Belgium 3 Sep 44 and Holland 19 Sep 44 and entered Germany 19 Oct 44; arrived at New York P/E 27 Nov 45 where inactivated 28 Nov 45.

Campaigns: *Normandy, Northern France, Rhineland, Central Europe*
Aug 45 Loc: Wieseck Germany

1116th Engineer Combat Group

1 Apr 43 redesignated from HHC, 146th Engineer Combat Regiment at Cp Swift Tex; relocated to Amphibious Training Base Ft Pierce Fla 16 Aug 43; arrived at Cp Pickett Va 10 Oct 43; staged at Cp Kilmer N.J. 16 Dec 43 until departed New York 8 Jan 44; arrived in England 17 Jan 44 where redesignated HHC, 6th Engineer Special Brigade 15 May 44.

1117th Engineer Combat Group

1 Apr 43 redesignated from HHC, 147th Engineer Combat Regiment at Cp Swift Tex; participated in Louisiana Mnvrs Jun–Aug 43; staged at Cp Kilmer N.J. 27 Dec 43 until departed New York P/E 2 Jan 44; arrived in England 10 Jan 44; landed in France 14 Jul 44 and entered Germany 11 Mar 45; arrived at Boston P/E 19 Nov 45 where inactivated 20 Nov 45.

Campaigns: *Normandy, Northern France, Rhineland, Ardennes-Alsace, Central Europe*
Aug 45 Aug: Neustadt Germany

1118th Engineer Combat Group

1 Apr 43 redesignated from HHC, 132nd Engineer Combat Regiment at Framingham Mass; arrived at Ft Hancock N.J. 14 Apr 43; relocated to Cp Pickett Va 10 Sep 43; transferred to Ft Pierce Fla 15 Oct 43 and returned to Cp Pickett 20 Nov 43; staged at Seattle Wash 21 Mar 44 and departed 11 Apr 44; arrived in Hawaii 17 Apr 44; landed in Philippines after departing Hawaii 16 Sep 44; assaulted Ormoc Bay Leyte 7 Dec 44; landed on Ie Shima Island 18 Apr 45 where it remained until after the war and was inactivated in Japan 31 Jan 46.

Campaigns: *Leyte, Ryukyus*
Aug 45 Loc: Ie Shima Island

1119th Engineer Combat Group

7 Apr 43 redesignated from HHC, 336th Engineer General Service Regiment at Cp Rucker Ala; departed United States 21 Dec 43 and arrived in England 1 Nov 43 where redesignated HHC, 5th Engineer Special Brigade 12 Nov 43 at Swansea.

Campaigns: *European Theater without inscription*

1120th Engineer Combat Group

15 Apr 43 redesignated from HHC, 348th Engineer General Service Regiment at Cp Young Calif Desert Training Center; staged at New York P/E 16 Nov 43 until departed 3 Dec 43; arrived in England 9 Dec 43; landed in France 9 Jun 44; crossed into Belgium 6 Sep 44; first crossed into Germany 4 Oct 44; reentered Belgium 23 Dec 44 and recrossed into Germany 5 Feb 45 where inactivated 20 Jan 47.

Campaigns: *Normandy, Northern France, Rhineland, Ardennes-Alsace, Central Europe*
Aug 45 Loc: Eisleben Germany

1121st Engineer Combat Group

19 Aug 43 redesignated from HHC, 112th Engineer Combat Regiment at Devises England; assaulted Normandy France 6 Jun 44; crossed into Belgium 8 Sep 44 and entered Germany 14 Sep 44; arrived in Czechoslovakia 8 May 45; arrived at New York P/E 2 Feb 46 and inactivated at Cp Kilmer N.J. 4 Feb 46.

Campaigns: *Normandy, Northern France, Rhineland, Ardennes-Alsace, Central Europe*
Aug 45 Loc: Nurschan Czechoslovakia

1122nd Engineer Combat Group

25 Sep 43 redesignated from HHC, 35th Engineer Combat Regiment at Cp White Oreg and moved to Cp San Luis Obispo Calif 14 Apr 44; staged at Ft Lawton Wash 26 Jul 44 until Seattle P/E 1 Aug 44 departure; arrived in Hawaii 7 Aug 44; assaulted Leyte Philippines 20 Oct 44; assaulted Okinawa 1 Apr 45; inactivated in Korea on 24 Feb 46.

Campaigns: *Leyte, Ryukyus*
Aug 45 Loc: Okinawa

1123rd Engineer Combat Group

15 Jan 44 activated at Cp McCain Miss; departed United States 30 Oct 44 and arrived in England 10 Nov 44; landed in France 29 Dec 44 and crossed into Belgium 3 Jan 45; crossed into Luxembourg 15 Feb 45; entered Germany 8 Mar 45; arrived at Hampton Roads P/E and inactivated at Cp Patrick Henry Va 23 Oct 45.

Campaigns: *Rhineland, Ardennes-Alsace, Central Europe*
Aug 45 Loc: Neustadt Germany

1124th Engineer Combat Group

15 Jan 44 activated at Cp Maxey Tex; departed United States 1 Nov 44; arrived in England 9 Nov 44 and landed in France 31 Jan 45; crossed into Luxembourg 11 Feb 45; crossed into Belgium 26 Feb 45 and Holland 27 Feb 45; entered Germany 31 Mar 45 where stationed through 1946.

Campaigns: *Rhineland, Central Europe*
Aug 45 Loc: Augsburg Germany

1125th Engineer Combat Group

25 Mar 44 activated at Cp Bowie Tex; staged at Cp Shanks N.Y. 17–26 Dec 44; departed New York P/E 26 Dec 44 and arrived in England 7 Jan 45; landed in France 17 Mar 45; entered Germany 25 Mar 45; departed France 9 Jul 45 and arrived at Manila Philippines 17 Aug 45 where inactivated 10 Apr 46.

Campaigns: *Central Europe, Pacific Theater without inscription*
Aug 45 Loc: Shipment #R6604-H en route to Philippines at sea

1126th Engineer Combat Group

20 Apr 44 activated at Cp Breckinridge Ky; departed United States 9 Dec 44 and arrived in England 20 Dec 44; arrived in France 12 Mar 45 and crossed into Luxembourg on 18 Mar 45; entered Germany 20 Mar 45 where inactivated on 27 Jun 46.

Campaigns: *Rhineland, Central Europe*
Aug 45 Loc: Schallerbach Germany

1127th Engineer Combat Group

3 Apr 44 activated at Cp Swift Tex; departed United States 26 Dec 44 and arrived in England 7 Jan 45; landed in Germany 17 Apr 45; arrived in Philippine Islands 18 Aug 45 where inactivated 25 Jan 46.

Campaigns: *European Theater without inscription, Pacific Theater without inscription*
Aug 45 Loc: Shipment #R6604-G en route to Philippines at sea

1128th Engineer Combat Group

27 Dec 43 redesignated from HHC, 5th Engineer Combat Regiment at Chisledon England shortly after arrival from Iceland; landed in France 27 Jun 44 and crossed into Belgium 14 Sep 44; entered Germany 10 Mar 45 where inactivated on 30 Dec 46.

Campaigns: *Normandy, Northern France, Rhineland, Ardennes-Alsace, Central Europe*
Aug 45 Loc: Reinshartshausen Germany

1129th Engineer Combat Group

15 May 44 redesignated from HHC, 131st Engineer Combat Regiment on Bougainville Island and landed on Luzon Philippine Islands 19 Jan 45; inactivated in Japan 28 Feb 46.

Campaigns: *Luzon*
Aug 45 Loc: Manila Philippine Islands

1130th Engineer Combat Group

30 Mar 44 activated at Cp Gruber Okla and departed Boston P/E 24 Nov 44; arrived in England 4 Dec 44 and landed in France on 24 Mar 45; entered Germany 29 Mar 45 and returned to the United States 13 Sep 45 where inactivated at Cp Gruber Okla 23 Nov 45.

Campaigns: *Central Europe*
Aug 45 Loc: Hagenou Germany (scheduled to SWPA under Shipment #R6604-N)

1131st Engineer Combat Group

30 Mar 44 activated at Cp Chaffee Ark and departed the United States 9 Dec 44; landed in England 20 Dec 44; arrived in France 12 Apr 45 and entered Germany 14 Apr 45; returned to the United States 4 Sep 45 where inactivated at Ft Benning Ga on 30 Nov 45.

Campaigns: *Central Europe*
Aug 45 Loc: Speldorf Germany (scheduled to SWPA under Shipment #R4645-R)

1132nd Engineer Combat Group

30 Mar 44 activated at Cp Pickett Va and departed Boston P/E 23 Nov 44; landed in England 4 Dec 44 and France 25 Feb 45; crossed into Holland 10 Mar 45 and entered Germany 29 Mar 45; inactivated in France on 12 Nov 45.

Campaigns: *Rhineland, Central Europe*
Aug 45 Loc; Marseille France

1133rd Engineer Combat Group

30 Apr 44 activated at Cp Butner N.C. and departed the United States 16 Dec 44; arrived in England 21 Dec 44 and landed in Germany 12 Apr 45; sent to the Philippines 27 Aug 45 where inactivated on 25 Jan 46.

Campaigns: *Central Europe, Pacific Theater without inscription*
Aug 45 Loc: Shipment #R4502 at sea en route to the Philippines

1134th Engineer Combat Group

14 May 43 activated at Cp Maxey Tex and departed the United States on 27 Jun 44; arrived in England 3 Jul 44 and landed in France 6 Aug 44; crossed into Luxembourg 16 Mar 45 and entered Germany 6 Apr 45; arrived at Hampton Roads P/E 27 Oct 45 and inactivated at Cp Patrick Henry Va the same date.

Campaigns: *Normandy, Northern France, Rhineland, Ardennes-Alsace, Central Europe*
Aug 45 Loc: Nurnberg Germany

1135th Engineer Combat Group

14 May 43 activated at Cp Van Dorn Miss and departed United States on 26 Jul 44; arrived in England 1 Aug 44 and landed in France 19 Aug 44; crossed into Luxembourg 22 Dec 44 and entered Germany 26 Feb 45; arrived at New York P/E 21 Nov 45 and inactivated at Cp Kilmer N.J. 22 Nov 45.

Campaigns: *Northern France, Rhineland, Ardennes-Alsace, Central Europe*
Aug 45 Loc: Regensburg Germany

1136th Engineer Construction Group

1 May 43 activated at Cp White Oreg as the 1136th Engineer Combat Group and departed the United States on 1 Mar 44; arrived in New Guinea 24 Mar 44 where redesignated the 1136th Engineer Construction Group on 23 May 44; landed on Leyte Philippine Islands 22 Oct 44; inactivated in Japan on 31 Jan 46.

Campaigns: *New Guinea, Leyte, Luzon*
Aug 45 Loc: Luzon Philippine Islands

1137th Engineer Combat Group

25 Aug 43 activated at Cp Gruber Okla and departed the United States 24 Jul 44; arrived in England 30 Jul 44 and landed in France 19 Oct 44; crossed into Belgium 20 Dec 44 and into Luxembourg 31 Dec 44; entered Germany 13 Mar 45; arrived at Hampton Roads P/E 27 Oct 45 and inactivated at Cp Patrick Henry Va on 28 Oct 45.

Campaigns: *Northern France, Rhineland, Ardennes-Alsace, Central Europe*
Aug 45 Loc: Innstadt Austria

1138th Engineer Combat Group

15 May 43 activated at Cp Cooke Calif and departed the United States 21 Jun 44; arrived in Hawaii 27 Jun 44 and departed 12 Aug 44; landed on Angaur Palau Islands 17 Feb 44 and Ulithi Atoll on 23 Sep 44; arrived in New Caledonia 22 Jan 45 and landed in the Philippine Islands 17 May 45; inactivated in Japan on 18 Dec 45.

Campaigns: *Western Pacific, Leyte*
Aug 45 Loc: Leyte Philippine Islands

1139th Engineer Combat Group

25 Aug 43 activated at Cp Beale Calif; departed United States 2 Jul 44 and arrived in England 12 Jul 44; landed in France 6 Aug 44 and entered Germany 5 Mar 45; arrived at Boston P/E 26 Oct 45 and inactivated at Cp Myles Standish Mass 27 Oct 45.

Campaigns: *Northern France, Rhineland, Ardennes-Alsace, Central Europe*
Aug 45 Loc: Sulzbach Germany

1140th Engineer Combat Group

25 Aug 43 activated at Cp Breckinridge Ky; departed United States 10 Jun 44 and arrived in Hawaii 16 Jun 44; departed Hawaii 15 Sep 44 and assaulted Leyte Island Philippines 20 Oct 44 where inactivated 15 Feb 46.

Campaigns: *Leyte, Ryukyus*
Aug 45 Loc: Okinawa

1141st Engineer Combat Group

15 Oct 43 activated at Cp McCoy Wis; departed United States 30 Aug 44 and arrived in England 6 Sep 44; landed in France 26 Sep 44; crossed into Belgium 26 Oct 44 and Holland 10 Nov 44; entered Germany 28 Feb 45; arrived at Boston P/E 16 Nov 45 and inactivated at Cp Myles Standish Mass 17 Nov 45.

Campaigns: *Rhineland, Central Europe*
Aug 45 Loc: Lehrte France

526

1142nd Engineer Combat Group

15 Oct 43 activated at Cp Crowder Mo; departed United States 30 Aug 44 and arrived in England 6 Sep 44; landed in France 26 Sep 44; crossed into Belgium 9 Oct 44 and Holland 16 Nov 44; entered Germany 24 Dec 44; arrived at New York P/E 27 Nov 45 and inactivated at Cp Kilmer N.J. 29 Nov 45.

Campaigns: *Rhineland, Central Europe*
Aug 45 Loc: Bockenforde Germany

1143rd Engineer Combat Group

25 Oct 43 activated at Cp Joseph T. Robinson Ark; departed United States 11 Aug 44; arrived in England 22 Aug 44; landed in France 14 Sep 44; crossed into Belgium 15 Oct 44 and Holland 20 Oct 44; entered Germany 1 Mar 45 where inactivated 6 Oct 45.

Campaigns: *Northern France, Rhineland, Central Europe*
Aug 45 Loc: Vouziers France

1144th Engineer Combat Group

15 Nov 43 activated at Ft Devens Mass; departed United States 30 Oct 44 and arrived in England 10 Nov 44; landed in France 10 Feb 45 and entered Germany 28 Mar 45; arrived at Boston P/E 26 Nov 45 and inactivated at Cp Myles Standish Mass 27 Nov 45.

Campaigns: *Rhineland, Central Europe*
Aug 45 Loc: Goppingen Germany

1145th Engineer Combat Group

1 Nov 43 activated at Cp Cooke Calif; departed United States 30 Oct 44 and arrived in England 12 Nov 44; landed in France 24 Jan 45 and entered Germany 20 Mar 45 and inactivated there 8 May 46.

Campaigns: *Rhineland, Central Europe*
Aug 45 Loc: Goppingen Germany

1146th Engineer Combat Group

10 Nov 43 activated at Cp Swift Tex; departed United States 4 Sep 44 and arrived in England 15 Sep 44; landed in France 3 Oct 44; crossed into Holland 25 Oct 44 and entered Germany 1 Mar 45; arrived at Cp Myles Standish Mass 26 Nov 45 and inactivated there 27 Nov 45.

Campaigns: *Rhineland, Central Europe*
Aug 45 Loc: Gottingen Germany

1147th Engineer Combat Group

17 Dec 43 activated at Cp Gordon Ga; departed United States 30 Oct 44 and arrived in England 10 Nov 44; landed in France 27 Feb 45; crossed into Holland 6 Mar 45 and entered Germany 11 Mar 45; inactivated at Antwerp Belgium on 18 Sep 45.

Campaigns: *Rhineland, Central Europe*
Aug 45 Loc: Antwerp Belgium

1148th Engineer Combat Group

17 Dec 43 activated at Ft Jackson S.C.; departed United States 30 Oct 44 and arrived in England 12 Nov 44; landed in France 14 Feb 45 and entered Germany 2 Mar 45; arrived at New York P/E 27 Oct 45 and inactivated at Cp Kilmer N.J. 28 Oct 45.

Campaigns: *Rhineland, Central Europe*
Aug 45 Loc: Krefeld Germany

1149th Engineer Combat Group

17 Dec 43 activated at Cp Carson Colo; departed United States 4 Sep 44 and arrived in England 15 Sep 44; landed in France 4 Oct 44; crossed into Belgium 27 Oct 44 and Holland 6 Nov 44; entered Germany 6 Feb 45 where inactivated 12 Nov 45.

Campaigns: *Rhineland, Central Europe*
Aug 45 Loc: Ober Ingelheim Germany

1150th Engineer Combat Group

30 Dec 43 activated at Cp Shelby Miss; departed United States 30 Oct 44 and arrived in England 10 Nov 44; landed 15 Feb 45 in France; entered Germany 22 Mar 45; arrived at Hampton Roads P/E and inactivated at Cp Patrick Henry Va 6 Nov 45.

Campaigns: *Rhineland, Central Europe*
Aug 45 Loc: Ohringen Germany

1151st Engineer Combat Group

30 Dec 43 activated at Cp Van Dorn Miss; staged at Cp Shanks N.Y. 14 Oct 44 until departed New York P/E 3 Nov 44; arrived in England 9 Nov 44 and landed in France 1 Jan 45; entered Germany 16 Apr 45 where inactivated 27 Dec 46.

Campaigns: *Rhineland*
Aug 45 Loc: Bad Neuenahr Germany

1152nd Engineer Combat Group

20 Dec 43 activated at Ft Lewis Wash; departed United States 30 Oct 44 and arrived in England 10 Nov 44; landed in France 31 Dec 44 and entered Germany 20 Mar 45; arrived at New York P/E 29 Nov 45 and inactivated at Cp Shanks N.Y. 30 Nov 45.

Campaigns: *Rhineland, Ardennes-Alsace, Central Europe*
Aug 45 Loc: Gignac-la Nerthe France

1153rd Engineer Combat Group

17 Dec 43 activated at Cp Rucker Ala; departed United States 30 Oct 44; arrived in England 12 Nov 44; landed in France 5 Jan 45; crossed into Belgium 11 Jan 45; entered Germany 4 Feb 45; arrived at New York P/E 16 Nov 45 and inactivated at Cp Kilmer N.J. 18 Nov 45.

Campaigns: *Rhineland, Ardennes-Alsace, Central Europe*
Aug 45 Loc: Gournay Germany

1154th Engineer Combat Group

1 May 44 activated at Cp Pickett Va; departed New York P/E 26 Dec 44 and arrived in England 7 Jan 45; landed in France 17 Mar 45 and entered Germany 24 Mar 45; arrived at Cp Patrick Henry Va (Hampton Roads P/E) 27 Jul 45 and moved to Cp Polk La 31 Jul 45; relocated to Cp White Oreg 14 Dec 45; served at Cp Stoneman Calif 27 Mar–8 Apr 46; arrived at Ft Lewis Wash 13 Apr 46 where active through 1946.

Campaigns: *Rhineland, Central Europe*
Aug 45 Loc: Camp Polk Louisiana

1155th Engineer Combat Group

12 May 44 activated at Cp Shelby Miss; departed United States 3 Jan 45 and arrived in France 16 Jan 45; entered Germany 16 Apr 45; departed France and arrived in Philippines 29 Aug 45 where inactivated 25 Jan 46.

Campaigns: *Rhineland, Central Europe, Pacific Theater without inscription*
Aug 45 Loc: Shipment #R4645-N at sea en route to Philippines

1156th Engineer Combat Group

12 May 44 activated at Ft Riley Kans; departed United States 27 Feb 45 and arrived in France 11 Mar 45; entered Germany 6 Apr 45 where inactivated 13 Mar 46.

Campaigns: *Central Europe*
Aug 45 Loc: Fulda Germany (scheduled to SWPA under Shipment #R6604-TT)

1157th Engineer Combat Group

26 Jun 44 activated at Cp Gruber Okla; departed United States 3 Feb 45 and arrived in Scotland 11 Feb 45; arrived in England 13 Feb 45 and landed in France 24 Feb 45; entered Germany 7 Apr 45; departed Europe and arrived in Philippines 19 Aug 45, in passing through the Canal Zone 22–24 Jul 45, where inactivated 25 Jan 46.

Campaigns: *Central Europe, Pacific Theater without inscription*
Aug 45 Loc: Shipment #R6604-J at sea en route to Philippines

1158th Engineer Combat Group

26 Jun 44 activated at Cp Van Dorn Miss; staged at Cp Shanks 21 Dec 44 until departed New York P/E 3 Jan 45; arrived in France 16 Jan 45 and entered Germany 22 Apr 45; arrived at Hampton Roads P/E 2 Jul 45 and relocated to Ft Jackson S.C. 6 Jul 45 where inactivated 12 Oct 46.

Campaigns: *European Theater without inscription*
Aug 45 Loc: Ft Jackson South Carolina

1159th Engineer Combat Group

26 Jun 44 activated at Cp Rucker Ala; staged at Cp Myles Standish Mass 3 Jan 45 until departed Boston P/E 18 Jan 45; arrived in France 29 Jan 45 and entered Germany 12 Feb 45; arrived at Hampton Roads P/E 9 Jul 45 and relocated to Cp Gruber Okla 13 Jul 45 where inactivated 20 Feb 46.

Campaigns: *Rhineland, Central Europe*
Aug 45 Loc: Cp Gruber Oklahoma

1160th Engineer Combat Group

26 Jun 44 activated at Cp McCain Miss and staged at Cp Myles Standish Mass 13 Jan 45 until departed Boston P/E 18 Jan 45; landed in France 29 Jan 45 and crossed into Belgium 22 Feb 45; entered Germany 17 Mar 45 and arrived at New York P/E 15 Sep 45; inactivated at Ft Jackson, S.C. on 4 Dec 45.

Campaigns: *Rhineland, Central Europe*
Aug 45 Loc: Eisnach Germany (scheduled to SWPA under Shipment #R6604-L)

1161st Engineer Combat Group

15 Jul 44 activated at Cp Howze Texas and departed Seattle P/E 6 Jun 45; arrived in Hawaii on 12 Jun 45 and on Eniwetok 24 Jun 45; arrived at Ulithi Atoll 12 Jul 45 and landed on Okinawa 25 Jul 45; inactivated in Japan on 31 Jan 46.

Campaigns: *Ryukyus*
Aug 45 Loc: Okinawa

1162nd Engineer Combat Group

15 Jul 44 activated at Cp Bowie Tex and departed the United States on 15 Mar 45; arrived in France on 27 Mar 45 and returned to the United States 14 Sep 45; inactivated at Cp Breckinridge Ky on 23 Nov 45.

Campaigns: *European Theater without inscription*
Aug 45 Loc: Touziers France (scheduled to SWPA under Shipment #R6604-M)

1163rd Engineer Combat Group

15 Jul 44 activated at Cp Gordon Ga and departed the United States on 26 Jan 45; arrived in France 6 Feb 45 and entered Germany 24 Mar 45; returned to the United States 15 Sep 45 and inactivated at Cp Shelby Miss on 3 Dec 45.

Campaigns: *Central Europe*
Aug 45 Loc: Weimar Germany (scheduled to SWPA under Shipment #R6604-K)

1164th Engineer Combat Group

15 Jul 44 activated at Cp Breckinridge Ky and departed the United States on 12 Mar 45; arrived in the Philippine Islands 29 Mar 45 and inactivated in Japan on 31 May 46.

Campaigns: *Luzon*
Aug 45 Loc: Manila Philippine Islands

1165th Engineer Combat Group

16 May 44 redesignated from HHC, 34th Engineer Combat Regiment in Hawaii and landed on Saipan 18 Jul 44; arrived on Espiritu Santo on 16 Feb 45 and landed on Okinawa 9 Apr 45; inactivated in Korea on 6 Feb 46.

Campaigns: *Western Pacific, Ryukyus*
Aug 45 Loc: Okinawa

1166th Engineer Combat Group

15 Jul 44 activated at Cp Swift Tex; departed the United States 28 Apr 45 and arrived in Hawaii 6 May 45 which departed 14 May 45 and landed in Okinawa 15 Jun 45; inactivated in Japan 20 Feb 46.

Campaigns: *Ryukyus*
Aug 45 Loc: Okinawa

1167th Engineer Combat Group

15 Aug 44 activated at Cp Campbell Ky; departed the United States 15 Mar 45 and arrived in France 27 Mar 45; entered Germany 27 Mar 45; returned to the United States 9 Sep 45 and inactivated at Cp Bowie Tex 23 Nov 45.

Campaigns: *Central Europe*
Aug 45 Loc: Seckenheim Germany (scheduled to SWPA under Shipment #R4645-P)

1168th Engineer Combat Group

7 Dec 44 activated at Barberino Italy from the 4th AAA Group; returned to Boston P/E 22 Aug 45; arrived at Ft Campbell Ky 28 Aug 45 where inactivated 26 Nov 45.

Campaigns: *Rome-Arno, North Apennines, Po Valley*
Aug 45 Loc: Shipment #R0488-A en route to USA at sea (scheduled to SWPA)

1169th Engineer Combat Group

11 Jul 44 redesignated from HHC, 151st Engineer Combat Regiment at Ft Leonard Wood, Mo; staged at Cp Kilmer N.J. 20 Dec 44 until departed New York P/E 26 Dec 44; arrived in England 7 Jan 45 and landed in France 11 Apr 45; returned to New York P/E 5 Jul 45 and relocated to Cp Gruber Okla 9 Jul 45; arrived at Cp Cooke Calif 22 Aug 45 where inactivated 3 Nov 45.

Campaigns: *European Theater without inscription*
Aug 45 Loc: Cp Gruber Oklahoma

1171st Engineer Combat Group

15 Jan 44 redesignated from HHC, 20th Engineer Combat Regiment at Devizes England; assaulted Normandy France 6 Jun 44; crossed into Luxembourg 11 Sep 44 and Belgium 4 Oct 44; entered Germany 26 Oct 44 and Czechoslovakia 10 May 45; active in Germany through 1946.

Campaigns: *Normandy, Northern France, Rhineland, Ardennes-Alsace, Central Europe*
Aug 45 Loc: Klatovy Czechoslovakia

1172nd Engineer Combat Group

19 Sep 44 activated in France where remained until arrived at New York P/E 6 Mar 46; inactivated at Cp Kilmer N.J. 8 Mar 46.

Campaigns: *European Theater without inscription*
Aug 45 Loc: Epernay France

1173rd Engineer Combat Group

19 Sep 44 activated in France where inactivated 27 Jun 46.

Campaigns: *Northern France, Rhineland*
Aug 45 Loc: Epernay France

1174th Engineer Combat Group

19 Sep 44 activated in France where inactivated 27 Jun 46.

Campaigns: *European Theater without inscription*
Aug 45 Loc: Paris France

1175th Engineer Combat Group

31 Dec 44 activated in Marseille France from 106th AAA Group; entered Germany 26 Mar 45; arrived at Boston P/E 24 Oct 45 and inactivated at Cp Myles Standish Mass 25 Oct 45.

Campaigns: *Rhineland, Central Europe*
Aug 45 Loc: Herbrechtingen Germany

1176th Engineer Construction Group

21 Mar 44 redesignated from HHC, 47th Engineer General Service Regiment at Schofield Barracks Hawaii; departed Hawaii 23 Jun 44 and landed on Saipan 25 Jun 44; left Saipan 26 Mar 45 and landed on Okinawa 8 Apr 45; active in Korea through 1946.

Campaigns: *Western Pacific, Ryukyus*
Aug 45 Loc: Okinawa

1177th Engineer Construction Group

1 Apr 44 redesignated from HHC, 353rd Engineer General Service Regiment on New Caledonia; arrived at Guadalcanal 10 Apr 44; landed in the Philippines 11 Jun 45; inactivated 31 Jan 46.

Campaigns: *Luzon*
Aug 45 Loc: Manila Philippines

1178th Engineer Construction Group

22 Apr 44 activated at Sydney Australia with personnel from the 46th Engineer General Service Regiment; landed at Oro Bay New Guinea on 4 May 44 and Biak Island 11 Jul 44; arrived on Luzon Philippines 9 Jan 45 and inactivated in Japan on 31 Dec 45.

Campaigns: *New Guinea, Luzon*
Aug 45 Loc: Luzon Philippine Islands

1179th Engineer Construction Group

1 Aug 44 activated at Hollandia New Guinea from personnel of the 339th Engineer General Service Regiment; landed on Leyte Philippines 22 Oct 44 and transferred after the war to Japan where active through 1946.

Campaigns: *New Guinea, Leyte*
Aug 45 Loc: Tacloban Philippine Islands

1180th Engineer Construction Group

20 Jul 44 activated at Darwin Australia with personnel from the 340th Engineer General Service Regiment and landed at Hollandia New Guinea 29 Aug 44; assaulted Morotai Island 15 Sep 44 and arrived on Luzon Philippines 10 Jan 45; active in Japan on occupation duty through 1946.

Campaigns: *New Guinea, Luzon*
Aug 45 Loc: Luzon Philippine Islands

1181st Engineer Construction Group

15 Jul 44 activated at Schofield Barracks Hawaii and assigned to Tenth Army; landed on Okinawa 3 Apr 45 where inactivated on 20 May 46.

Campaigns: *Ryukyus*
Aug 45 Loc: Okinawa

1185th Engineer Combat Group

10 Oct 44 activated at Pozzouli Italy with personnel from the 591st Engineer Boat Regiment; landed in France on 20 Dec 44 and crossed into Germany 24 Mar 45 where redesignated as HHC, 591st Engineer Combat Group on 18 Apr 45.

Campaigns: *Ardennes-Alsace*

1186th Engineer Combat Group

2 Aug 44 activated at Ste Marie du Monte Normandy France with personnel from the 531st Engineer Shore Regiment; crossed into Holland 21 Nov 44 and into Belgium 29 Dec 44; returned to France 18 Jan 45 and entered Germany 21 Mar 45; arrived at New York P/E 16 Nov 45 and inactivated there on 18 Nov 45.

Campaigns: *Normandy, Northern France, Rhineland, Ardennes-Alsace, Central Europe*
Aug 45 Loc: Bad Frankenhausen Germany

1187th Engineer Construction Group

25 Aug 44 activated in India where inactivated 12 Jan 46.

Campaigns: *India-Burma*
Aug 45 Loc: Ledo India

1189th Engineer Base Depot Group

6 Aug 44 activated at Ft Leonard Wood Mo; relocated to Granite City Ill 17 Aug 44 and staged at Cp Stoneman Calif 9–20 Dec 44; departed San Francisco P/E 20 Dec 44; arrived Hollandia New Guinea 13 Jan 45; inactivated at Yokohama Japan 31 May 46.

Campaigns: *Pacific Theater without inscription*
Aug 45 Loc: Hollandia New Guinea

1190th Engineer Base Depot Group

15 Mar 44 activated at Cp Claiborne La; departed the United States 27 Sep 44 and arrived in England 3 Oct 44; landed in France and later transferred to Pacific; inactivated in Japan after 1946.

Campaigns: *Rhineland, Pacific Theater without inscription*

1191st Engineer Base Depot Group

1 May 44 activated on Guadalcanal with personnel of the 1305th Engineer General Service Regiment; arrived 28 Jul 45 in the Philippines; inactivated in Japan 31 May 46.

Campaigns: *Pacific Theater without inscription*
Aug 45 Loc: Manila Philippines

1192nd Engineer Base Depot Group

1 Dec 43 activated on New Caledonia at the South Pacific General Depot; inactivated there on 30 Jan 46.

Campaigns: *Pacific Theater without inscription*
Aug 45 Loc: New Caledonia

1193rd Engineer Base Depot Group

15 Nov 43 activated at Cp Claiborne La; departed the United States 3 May 44; arrived in England 15 May 44; landed in France 12 Jul 44; arrived back in the United States 27 Aug 45 and inactivated at Ft Leonard Wood Mo 10 Nov 45.

Campaigns: *Normandy, Northern France, Rhineland, Central Europe*

1194th Engineer Base Depot Group

15 Nov 43 activated at Cp Claiborne La; departed the United States 3 May 44 and arrived in England 15 May 44; landed in France 16 Aug 44 where inactivated 25 Jun 46.

Campaigns: *Rhineland*

1195th Engineer Base Depot Group

16 Aug 43 activated at Cp Claiborne La; departed the United States 9 Feb 44 and arrived in England 18 Feb 44; landed in France 19 Dec 44 and inactivated in Belgium 24 Aug 46.

Campaigns: *Rhineland*

1196th Engineer Base Depot Group

16 Aug 43 activated at Cp Claiborne La; departed the United States 11 Feb 44 and arrived in England 18 Feb 44; returned to the United States 22 Mar 46 and inactivated at New York P/E 23 Mar 46.

Campaigns: *European Theater without inscription*

1197th Engineer Base Depot Group

16 Aug 43 activated at Cp Claiborne La; departed the United States 11 Feb 44; arrived in England 18 Feb 44 and landed in France 16 Aug 44 where inactivated 19 Nov 46.

Campaigns: *Northern France, Rhineland, Ardennes-Alsace, Central Europe*

1198th Engineer Base Depot Group

15 Sep 43 activated at Cp Claiborne La; departed the United States 6 Apr 44; arrived in England 18 Apr 44; landed in France and inactivated in Belgium 8 Apr 46.

Campaigns: *Normandy, Northern France*

1199th Engineer Base Depot Group

15 Sep 43 activated at Cp Claiborne La; departed the United States 6 Apr 44; arrived in England 18 Apr 44; returned to the United States 11 Jul 45 and inactivated 5 Sep 46 at Granite City Engineer Depot.

Campaigns: *European Theater without inscription*
Aug 45 Loc: Ft Leonard Wood Missouri

1200th Engineer Base Depot Group

6 Aug 44 activated at Ft Leonard Wood Mo; relocated to Granite City Ill 17 Aug 44; staged at Cp Stoneman Calif 9 Dec 44 until departed San Francisco P/E 1 Jan 45; arrived at Finschhafen New Guinea 22 Jan 45; landed in the Philippines 19 Jun 45 where inactivated 10 Apr 46.

Campaigns: *Luzon*
Aug 45 Loc: La Union Philippines

1338th Engineer Combat Group

16 Sep 44 activated at Florence Italy with personnel of the 337th Engineer General Service Regiment; returned to the United States 19 Aug 45 and inactivated at Cp Swift Tex 24 Oct 45.

Campaigns: *Rome-Arno, North Apennines, Po Valley*
Aug 45 Loc: Shipment #R2666-B at sea en route to USA (sch to SWPA)

1347th Engineer Construction Group

19 Sep 44 activated in France where inactivated 1 Mar 46.

Campaigns: *European Theater without inscription*
Aug 45 Loc: Paris France (scheduled to SWPA under Shipment #R9850-C)

1348th Engineer Construction Group

19 Sep 44 activated in France where inactivated 25 Jun 46.

Campaigns: *European Theater without inscription*
Aug 45 Loc: Paris France (scheduled to SWPA under Shipment #R9850-D)

1350th Engineer Base Depot Group

19 Aug 44 activated at Cp Claiborne La; relocated to Granite City Ill 21 Sep 44; staged at Cp Stoneman Calif 9–17 Dec 44; departed San Francisco P/E 17 Dec 44; landed in Philippines 2 Jan 45; inactivated there 20 May 46.

Campaigns: *Leyte, Luzon*
Aug 45 Loc: Leyte Island Philippines

1378th Engineer Base Depot Group

30 Nov 44 activated in England and inactivated in Germany after 1946.

Campaigns: *European Theater without inscription*

1497th Engineer Port Construction and Repair Group

2 Dec 44 activated at Cp Gordon Johnston Fla and assigned to the Fourth Service Command; staged at Ft Lawton Wash 12 Apr 45 until departed Seattle P/E 17 Apr 45; arrived in Hawaii 23 Apr 45 and sent to Okinawa where inactivated on 20 May 46.

Campaigns: *Ryukyus*
Aug 45 Loc: Okinawa

1521st Engineer Construction Group

17 Dec 44 activated in Hawaii; departed 19 Jan 45 and landed on Saipan 6 Feb 45; inactivated there on 14 Feb 46.

Campaigns: *Western Pacific*
Aug 45 Loc: Saipan

1523rd Engineer Construction Group

15 Nov 44 activated at Cp Claiborne La; departed Boston P/E 19 Feb 45 and arrived in France 1 Mar 45; crossed into Belgium 15 Mar 45 and entered Germany 4 Apr 45; departed France 16 Jun 45 and arrived in the Philippine Islands on 20 Jul 45; inactivated in Japan on 31 Jan 46.

Campaigns: *Rhineland, Central Europe, Pacific Theater without inscription*
Aug 45 Loc: Manila Philippine Islands

1524th Engineer Construction Group

30 Nov 44 activated at Cp Claiborne La; departed New York P/E 15 Mar 45 and arrived in France 27 Mar 45; entered Germany 8 Apr 45 and departed France 16 Jun 45; arrived in the Philippines 20 Jul 45 where inactivated on 5 Apr 46.

Campaigns: *Central Europe, Pacific Theater without inscription*
Aug 45 Loc: Manila Philippine Islands

3188th Engineer Construction Group

12 Mar 45 redesignated from HHC, 176th Engineer General Service Regiment at Ft Belvoir Va where inactivated on 25 Oct 45.

5207th Engineer Service Group (Provisional)

13 Jul 44 activated at Oro Bay New Guinea with personnel of the 1007th Engineer Communications Zone Headquarters; landed in the Philippines 30 Apr 45 and discontinued in Japan after the war.

Campaigns: *New Guinea, Luzon*
Aug 45 Loc: Philippine Islands

5208th Engineer Service Group (Provisional)

13 Jul 44 activated at Milne Bay New Guinea with personnel of the 1004th Engineer Communications Zone Headquarters; arrived in the Philippine Islands 11 Jan 45 and discontinued in Japan after the war.

Campaigns: *New Guinea, Luzon*
Aug 45 Loc: Philippine Islands

5209th Engineer Service Group (Provisional)

13 Jul 44 activated at Milne Bay New Guinea with personnel of the 1003rd Engineer Communications Zone Headquarters; arrived in the Philippine Islands 11 Jan 45 and discontinued in Japan after the war.

Campaigns: *New Guinea, Leyte, Luzon*
Aug 45 Loc: Philippine Islands

5210th Engineer Service Group (Provisional)

13 Jul 44 activated at Hollandia New Guinea with personnel of the 1001st Engineer Communications Zone Headquarters; arrived in the Philippine Islands 7 Jun 45 and discontinued in Japan after the war.

Campaigns: *New Guinea*
Aug 45 Loc: Philippine Islands

5212th Engineer Service Group (Provisional)

13 Jul 44 activated at Brinkman's Plantation New Guinea with personnel of the 1002nd Engineer Communications Zone Headquarters; arrived in the Philippine Islands on 17 Jan 45 and discontinued in Japan after the war.

Campaigns: *New Guinea, Luzon*
Aug 45 Loc: Philippine Islands

5213th Engineer Service Group (Provisional)

13 Jul 44 activated in New Guinea and later sent to the Philippine Islands; discontinued in Japan after the war.

Campaigns: *New Guinea, Luzon*
Aug 45 Loc: Philippine Islands

5251st Engineer Base Depot Group (Provisional)

15 Jul 44 formed in New Guinea and later served in the Philippines.

Campaigns: *New Guinea, Luzon*

5252 Engineer Base Depot Group (Provisional)

15 Jul 44 formed in New Guinea and later served in the Philippines.

Campaigns: *New Guinea, Luzon*

5255th Engineer Pipeline Group (Provisional)

15 Jul 44 formed in New Guinea and later served in the Philippines.

Chapter 41

Engineer Regiments

Regiments:

1 Italian, 2 Italian, 3, 5, 11, 14, 18–21, 27, 28, 31, 34–52, 78, 79, 82, 91–98, 101–113, 115, 116, 118, 120, 121, 130–135, 146, 147, 151, 152, 175–177, 224, 226, 330–375, 377, 388–390, 392, 393, 398, 531–534, 540, 542–544, 591–594, 922–935, 1301–1327, 1329–1333, 1349, 1749, 2201, 2822

1st Italian Engineer General Service Regiment

10 Apr 44 activated at the Engineer Unit Training Center at Cp Sutton N.C. and moved to Pine Camp N.Y. 13 Jul 44; there disbanded on 5 Sep 44 and personnel transferred to the 134th–145th Italian Quartermaster Service Companies.

2nd Italian Engineer General Service Regiment

10 Apr 44 activated at the Engineer Unit Training Center at Cp Sutton N.C. and moved to Imperial Dam Calif on 17 Jul 44; assigned to the Yuma Branch of the Engineer Test Board at Yuma Ariz; discontinued at Cp Haan Calif on 12 Oct 45.

3rd Engineer Regiment (Combat)

1 Aug 40 activated at Schofield Bks Hawaii, built access road to aircraft warning station at Mt Kuala, and redesignated as 3rd Engineer Battalion in Hawaii 26 Sep 41.

5th Engineer Combat Regiment

Stationed at Ft Belvoir Va under II Corps; arrived at New York P/E 2 Sep 41 and departed 5 Sep 41; arrived in Iceland 16 Sep 41 and departed 19 Dec 43; arrived in England 22 Dec 43 where redesignated as HHC, 1128th Engineer Combat Group on 27 Dec 43; 1st and 2nd Bns redesignated 1277th and 1278th Engineer Combat Battalions, respectively.

Campaigns: *European Theater without inscription*

11th Engineer Combat Regiment

Stationed at Post of Corozal Canal Zone and improved Rio Hato AAF; arrived at Ft Clayton Canal Zone 13 Jan 40 to construct Quarry Heights command tunnel; there redesignated as the 11th Engineer Combat Battalion on 2 May 43.

Campaigns: *American Theater*

14th Engineer Regiment (Combat) (Philippine Scouts)

19 Apr 41 activated at Ft William McKinley Philippine Islands and surrendered to Japanese forces on Bataan 9 Apr 42.

Campaigns: *Philippine Islands*

18th Engineer Combat Regiment

21 Oct 39 activated at Ft Devens Mass and moved to Ft Benning Ga 30 Mar 40 and to Ft Logan Colo 2 Sep 40; staged at Vancouver Bks Wash 14 Feb 41 until departed Seattle P/E 5 May 42; arrived at Whitehorse Canada 13 Apr 42 and constructed Alaskan-Canadiana Highway to Duke River and White River; arrived at Skagway Alaska 16 Jan 43 and Adak Island 29 Mar 43 from Ft Greeley Alaska; arrived at Shemya 30 May 43; returned to Seattle P/E 30 Nov 44 and moved to Cp Bowie Tex 12 Dec 44 where broken up 8 Jan 45 and headquarters absorbed into 1081st Engr Maintenance Company; 1st and 2nd Bns redesignated 18th and 410th Engineer Combat Battalions, respectively.

Campaigns: *Aleutian Islands*

19th Engineer Combat Regiment

1 Jul 40 redesignated from 39th Engineer Regiment (General Service) at Cp Ord Calif; arrived in New York P/E 23 Jul 42 and departed 31 Aug 42; arrived in England 5 Sep 42; landed in North Africa 11 Nov 42; assaulted Sicily where completely ashore by 28 Jul 43; sent to Italy 18 Oct 43 where redesignated as HHC, 19th Engineer Combat Group 1 Mar 45. 1st and 2nd Bns redesignated 401st and 402nd Engineer Combat Battalions, respectively.

Campaigns: *Algeria–French Morocco, Tunisia, Sicily, Rome-Arno, North Apennines*

20th Engineer Combat Regiment

1 Jul 40 redesignated from 42nd Engineer Regiment (General Service) at Ft Benning Ga; transferred to Cp Blanding Fla 15 Jan 42; moved to Cp Kilmer N.J. 26 Jul 42; went to Cp Pickett Va 21 Sep 42; arrived at New York P/E and left 2 Nov 42; landed in North Africa 11 Nov 42; assaulted Sicily 10 Jul 43; arrived in England 27 Nov 43 where redesignated HHC, 1171st Engineer Combat Group 15 Jan 44. 1st and 2nd Bns redesignated 20th and 1340th Engineer Combat Battalions, respectively.

Campaigns: *Algeria–French Morocco, Tunisia, Sicily*

21st Engineer Aviation Regiment

20 Oct 39 activated as 21st Engineer Regiment (General Service) at Ft Benning Ga; redesignated 21st Engineer Regiment (Aviation) 4 Jun 40; transferred to Langley Field Va 17 Jun 40; moved to Richmond AAB Va 3 Aug 42 where used as parent unit for activation of new units; departed Hampton Roads P/E 27 Oct 42; landed in North Africa 7 Nov 42; arrived in Italy 6 Nov 43 where inactivated at Marcianisa Italy 13 Oct 45. 1st and 2nd Bns inactivated at Foggia Italy 30 Sep 45 and 3rd Bn inactivated in Italy 5 Oct 45.

Campaigns: *Algeria–French Morocco, Tunisia, Naples-Foggia, Rome-Arno*
Aug 45 Loc: Foggia Italy less 1st Bn at San Savero and 2nd Bn at Cerignola

27th Engineer Combat Regiment

28 Sep 42 activated at Cp Breckinridge Ky and assigned to III Army Corps; redesignated HHC, 1105th Engineer Combat Group there 15 Mar 43. 1st and 2nd Bns redesignated 27th and 208th Engineer Combat Battalions, respectively.

28th Engineer Regiment (Aviation)

1 Jul 40 activated at March Field Calif and assigned to GHQ Air Force; departed Seattle P/E 20 Aug 40 and arrived in Alaska 23 Aug 40 and moved to Annette Island Alaska 25 Sep 40 where disbanded on 1 Jul 41. Concurrently therewith the 802nd Engineer Battalion was constituted and activated.

31st Engineer Combat Regiment

29 Apr 42 redesignated from the 31st Engineer Battalion (Combat) at Ft Belvoir Va and designated as a "parent" unit on 27 May 42; there redesignated as HHC, 1114th Engineer Combat Group and assigned to the Engineer School on 22 Mar 43. 1st and 2nd Battalions redesignated 31st and 241st Engineer Combat Battalions, respectively.

34th Engineer Combat Regiment

17 Oct 41 activated in Hawaii concurrently with arrival of filler personnel and Company D invaded Kwajalein on 31 Jan 44; regiment headquarters redesignated in Hawaii as HHC, 1165th Engineer Combat Group on 16 May 44; 1st and 2nd Bns redesignated the 34th and 134th Engineer Combat Battalions, respectively.

Campaigns: *Central Pacific (Company D also entitled to Eastern Mandates)*

35th Engineer Combat Regiment

15 Jul 41 activated at Ft Snelling Minn and moved to Cp Joseph T. Robinson Ark on 14 Aug 41 and to Ft Ord Calif 23 Dec 41; arrived at Dawson Creek Canada on 14 Mar 42 and reached Ft Nelson 5 Apr 42; completed the southern road by 24 Sep 42 when met the 340th Engr Regt at Contact Creek and then built portion of Alaskan-Canadian Highway to Ft Simpson; arrived at Cp White Oreg 1 Sep 43 where redesignated as the HHC, 1122nd Engineer Combat Group on 25 Sep 43; 1st and 2nd Bns redesignated 35th and 145th Engineer Combat Battalions, respectively.

36th Engineer Combat Regiment

1 Jun 41 activated at Plattsburg Barracks N.Y. and moved to New York City 7–19 Jan 42 and returned to Plattsburg Bks; moved to Ft Bragg N.C. 13 Mar 42 and to Cp Bradford Va 28 Sep 42 and to Cp Pickett Va 8 Oct 42; staged at Cp Kilmer N.J. 14 Oct 42 until departed New York P/E 2 Nov 42; landed at Casablanca North Africa 11 Nov 42 and assaulted Licata Sicily 9 Jul 43 and Salerno Italy 10 Sep 43; assaulted Anzio Italy 22 Jan 44 and southern France on 15 Aug 44; redesignated as HHC, 36th Engineer Combat Group on 15 Feb 45 in France; 1st, 2nd, and 3rd Bns redesignated as 2826th, 2827th, and 2828th Engineer Combat Battalions, respectively.

Campaigns: *Algeria–Morocco, Tunisia, Sicily, Naples-Foggia, Anzio, Rome-Arno, Southern France, Rhineland, Ardennes-Alsace*

37th Engineer Combat Regiment

14 Jul 41 activated at Cp Bowie Tex under VIII Army Corps and moved to Cp Edwards Mass 20 May 42 under the Chief of Engineers; transferred to Marysville Calif less personnel and equipment on 16 Sep 42 and assigned to VII Corps; arrived at Cp Beale Calif 15 Oct 42 and served under II Armored Corps; there redesignated as HHC, 1106th Engineer Combat Group on 15 Mar 43; 1st and 2nd Bns redesignated 37th and 209th Engineer Combat Battalions, respectively.

38th Engineer General Service Regiment

28 May 41 activated at Ft Jackson S.C. as 38th Engineer Regiment (Combat); participated in Carolina Maneuvers Sep–Nov 41; arrived at Charleston P/E 3 Mar 42; arrived on Ascension Island 30 Mar 42; landed at Pointenoire West Africa 23 Aug 42; moved to Dakar Africa in increments 30 Dec 42–17 Feb 43; departed Africa 8 Dec 43 and redesignated Engineer General Service Regiment en route to England where arrived 4 Jan 44; completed landing in France 9 Jun 44 and assigned to Normandy Base Section; arrived at New York P/E 13 Mar 46 and inactivated at Cp Kilmer N.J. 14 Mar 46.

Campaigns: *Normandy, Northern France, American Theater without inscription*
Aug 45 Loc: Cauteleu France

39th Engineer Regiment (General Service)

1 Jun 40 activated at Cp Ord Calif where redesignated 19th Engineer Regiment (Combat) 1 Jul 40.

39th Engineer Combat Regiment

25 Apr 42 activated at Cp Bowie Tex and assigned to VIII Corps; participated in Louisiana Maneuvers Jul–Nov 42; arrived at Ft Dix N.J. 27 Dec 42 and departed New York P/E 13 Jan 43; landed at Oran North Africa 27 Jan 43; landed in Sicily 13 Jul 43 as part of I Armored Corps; landed in Italy 18 Oct 43 (first elements ashore 15 Sep 43) where redesignated HHC, 39th Engineer Combat Group 17 May 45. 1st and 2nd Bns redesignated 404th and 643rd Engineer Combat Battalions, respectively.

Campaigns: *Sicily, Naples-Foggia, Anzio, Rome-Arno, North Apennines*

40th Engineer Combat Regiment

15 May 42 activated at Cp Crowder Mo; departed United States 8 Jun 43; arrived in Oran North Africa 22 Jun 43; assaulted Scoglitti Sicily 10 Jul 43; landed in Italy 18 Oct 43; assaulted southern France 15 Aug 44 where redesignated HHC, 40th Engineer Combat Group 15 Feb 45. 1st, 2nd, and 3rd Bns redesignated 2829th, 2830th, and 2831st Engineer Combat Battalions, respectively.

Campaigns: *Sicily, Naples-Foggia, Rome-Arno, Southern France, Ardennes-Alsace*

41st Engineer General Service Regiment (Colored)

1 Aug 40 activated at Ft Bragg N.C.; participated in Carolina Maneuvers Aug–Dec 41; designated parent unit of 358th Engineer Regiment; arrived at Charleston P/E 27 May 42 and departed 28 May 42; arrived at Liberia Africa 16 Jun 42; transferred from Marshall Liberia 28 Feb 43 to Oran Algeria 27 Mar 43 where urgently needed for airdrome construction program in Algiers; landed in Italy; moved to Corsica 14 Dec 43; landed in France 12 Oct 44 and inactivated in Germany 31 Dec 46.

Campaigns: *Naples-Foggia, Rome-Arno, Southern France, Rhineland*
Aug 45 Loc: Les Mille France

42nd Engineer Regiment (General Service)

1 Jun 40 activated at Ft Benning Ga and redesignated there as the 20th Engineer Regiment (Combat) on 1 Jul 40.

42nd Engineer General Service Regiment

10 Feb 41 activated at Cp Shelby Miss and participated in Louisiana Mnvrs July-October 41; transferred to Cp Murray Wash 15 Jan 42; 1st Bn arrived at Juneau Alaska 28 Feb 42 and remainder of regiment departed Seattle P/E 2 Mar 42 and arrived at Juneau 7 Mar 42; 2nd Bn sent to Cordova south of Valdez; elements of regt engaged in construction of airstrip on Pribilof Islands Sep–14 Nov 42; transferred to Cp Earle Alaska where redesignated as the 42nd Engineer Construction Battalion on 25 May 44 and elements rendered surplus by this reorganization were disbanded.

Campaigns: *Aleutians*

43rd Engineer Regiment (General Service)

10 Feb 41 activated at Ft Snelling Minn and moved to Cp Joseph T. Robinson Ark 7 Mar 41 where participated in mnvrs at Boughton Ark August-October 41; arrived at New York P/E 18 Jan 42 and departed 23 Jan 42; arrived in Australia 26 Feb 42 and built Cp Seymour near Melbourne; 1st Bn sent to Northern Territories in mid-Mar 42; Cos D and F landed at Milne Bay New Guinea 8 Aug 42 and fought the Battle of Milne Bay 27 Aug–8 Sep 42; regiment flown to Dobodura New Guinea 25 Nov 42 and built the Oro Bay–Dobodura Road; arrived back in Australia on 3 Mar 44 where redesignated from Engineer General Service Regiment to Engineer Construction Battalion on 22 Apr 44.

Campaigns: *East Indies, Papua, New Guinea*

44th Engineer Regiment (General Service)

10 Jun 41 activated at Ft Belvoir Va and participated in Carolina Mnvrs September-December 41; inactivated at Ft Belvoir Va on 15 Dec 41.

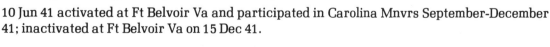
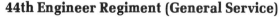

44th Engineer Combat Regiment

15 Jun 42 activated at Cp Crowder Mo and assigned to XI Corps and in Oct 42 designated "parent" unit for new engineer activations; participated in Tennessee Mnvrs Sep 42 and moved to Cp McCoy Wis on 12 Nov 42; there redesignated as HHC, 1109th Engineer Combat Group on 1 Apr 43; 1st and 2nd Bns redesignated 44th and 236th Engineer Combat Battalions, respectively.

45th Engineer General Service Regiment (Colored)

15 Jul 41 activated at Cp Blanding Fla and participated in Carolina Mnvrs October-December 41; arrived at Charleston P/E 26 May 42 and departed 28 May 42; arrived at Freetown Sierra Leone Africa 12 Jun 42 and departed 19 Jun 42; at Capetown Africa 1–4 Jul 42 only; landed at Karachi India 23 Jul 42 and assumed trucking details at Agra 5 Sep 42; moved to New Delhi and to Ledo India 10 Dec 42 for construction of Ledo Road; inactivated in India on 15 Jan 46.

Campaigns: *India-Burma*
Aug 45 Loc: Ledo India

46th Engineer General Service Regiment

14 Jul 41 activated at Cp Bowie Tex and participated in Louisiana Mnvrs September-October 41; moved to Indiantown Gap Mil Res Pa 17 Jan 42 and departed New York P/E 23 Jan 42; arrived in Australia 26 Feb 42 and moved to Woodstock on 13 Mar 42 to build airstrips in Townsville area of northern Queensland; Cos E and F arrived at Milne Bay and Merauke New Guinea 18 Jun 42 and 6 Aug 42 respectively; regt completed movement to New Guinea by 25 Nov 42 and worked at Port Moresby and then moved to Milne Bay; landed at Kiriwina Trobriand Islands 8 Jul 43 and returned to Australia 20 Jan 44; there redesignated the 46th Engineer Construction Battalion on 22 Apr 44.

Campaigns: *East Indies, Papua, New Guinea*

47th Engineer General Service Regiment

1 Aug 41 activated at Ft Ord Calif for shipment to Philippines; arrived at Oakland Sub-P/E 26 Dec 41 and departed 27 Dec 41; arrived in Hawaii 7 Jan 42 where remained due to loss of original destination; 1st Bn landed on Kwajalein 1 Feb 44 and built airfield on Eniwetok; regiment redesignated HHC, 1176th Engineer Construction Group in Hawaii on 21 Mar 44; 1st and 2nd Bns redesignated 47th and 1397th Engineer Construction Battalions, respectively.

Campaigns: *Pacific Theater without inscription*

48th Engineer Combat Regiment

25 Jul 42 activated at Cp Gruber Okla where redesignated as HHC, 1108th Engineer Combat Group on 15 Mar 43; 1st and 2nd Bns redesignated 48th and 235th Engineer Combat Battalions, respectively.

49th Engineer Combat Regiment

25 Aug 42 activated at Cp Carson Colo and redesignated as HHC, 1110th Engineer Combat Group there on 1 Apr 43; 1st and 2nd Bns redesignated 49th and 237th Engineer Combat Battalions, respectively.

50th Engineer Combat Regiment

1 Sep 42 activated at Cp White Oreg and moved to Ft Ord Calif 7 Jan 43 where 1st Bn redesignated 50th Engineer Combat Bn at Ojai Calif 21 Jan 43; remainder of regiment assaulted Attu Island 11 May 43 and was subjected to main Japanese counterattack of 29 May 43 in Chichaguf Valley; 2nd Bn landed on Kiska 15 Aug 43; relocated to Cp Earle Alaska and departed 10 Dec 44; arrived at Seattle P/E 20 Dec 44 and moved to Ft Riley Kans 26 Dec 44 where inactivated 1 Feb 45; 2nd Bn redesignated 205th Engineer Combat Battalion.

Campaigns: *Aleutian Islands*

51st Engineer Combat Regiment

13 Jun 42 activated at Cp Bowie Tex under VIII Corps and designated parent unit for new engineer activations in Oct 42; moved to Plattsburg Bks N.Y. 20 Oct 42 where redesignated HHC, 1111th Engineer Combat Group on 1 Apr 43; 1st and 2nd Bns redesignated 51st and 238th Engineer Combat Battalions, respectively.

52nd Engineer Combat Regiment

30 Nov 42 activated at Cp Butner N.C. under XII Corps where redesignated HHC, 1112th Engineer Combat Group on 1 Apr 43; 1st and 2nd Bns redesignated 52nd and 239th Engineer Combat Battalions, respectively.

78th Engineer Combat Regiment

Stationed at Ft Dupont Del with 1st Bn only active which transferred to Ft Buchanan Puerto Rico on 20 Oct 39; regimental HHC activated there on 28 Mar 42 but inactivated at Cp O'Reilly Puerto Rico 1 Sep 43; 1st Bn redesignated 78th Engineer Combat Battalion.

Campaigns: *American Theater without inscription*

79th Engineer Combat Regiment

10 Dec 42 activated at Cp Phillips Kans where redesignated HHC, 1113th Engineer Combat Group 1 Apr 43; 1st and 2nd Bns redesignated 79th and 240th Engineer Combat Battalions.

82nd Engineer Combat Regiment

25 Jan 43 activated at Cp Swift Tex where redesignated HHC, 1115th Engineer Combat Group 15 Mar 43; 1st and 2nd Bns redesignated 82nd and 291st Engineer Combat Battalions.

91st Engineer General Service Regiment (Colored)

6 Aug 42 redesignated from the 91st Engineer Battalion (Separate) in Australia and landed in New Guinea 19 Dec 42; landed on Biak Island 8 Oct 44 and transferred to the Philippine Islands 25 Aug 45 where inactivated at Manila on 20 Jan 46.

Campaigns: *Papua, New Guinea*
Aug 45 Loc: Biak Island

92nd Engineer General Service Regiment (Colored)

22 May 42 redesignated from 92nd Engineer Battalion (Separate) at Cp Forrest Tenn; arrived at New York P/E 22 Jun 42 and departed 1 Jul 42; arrived in Scotland 12 Jul 42 and England 14 Jul 42 and returned to Scotland 6 Feb 43; landed in North Africa on 15 Feb 43 and in Italy 17 Nov 43 where inactivated on 20 Apr 46.

Campaigns: *Naples-Foggia, Rome-Arno, North Apennines, Po Valley*
Aug 45 Loc: Sesto Italy

93rd Engineer General Service Regiment (Colored)

27 Mar 42 redesignated from 93rd Engineer Battalion (Separate) at Cp Livingston La; arrived at Seattle P/E 16 Apr 42 and departed 20 Apr 42; arrived at Carcross Canada on 7 May 42 under Northwest Service Command and engaged in construction on Alaskan-Canadian Highway where cleared trail east from Carcross toward Teslin River; arrived at Ft Randall Alaska 3 Jan 43 and returned to Seattle P/E on 3 Jul 44; moved immediately to Ft Lewis Wash where remained until 14 Mar 45; departed United States 24 Mar 45 and arrived at Calcutta India 10 May 45; departed India on 20 Oct 45 and arrived at New York P/E 16 Nov 45; inactivated at Cp Kilmer N.J. on 17 Nov 45.

Campaigns: *Aleutian Islands*
Aug 45 Loc: Kharagpur India less 1st Bn at Tergaon and 2nd Bn at Shamshernanar.

94th Engineer General Service Regiment (Colored)

1 May 42 redesignated from the 94th Engineer Battalion (Separate) at Ft Custer Mich and moved to Ft Dix N.J. 13 Jul 42; arrived and departed New York P/E 21 Mar 43; landed at Casablanca North Africa 29 Mar 43 and in Italy on 10 Oct 43; landed in southern France 18 Sep 44 and entered Germany 23 Apr 45; arrived at Boston P/E 21 Dec 45 and inactivated at Cp Myles Standish Mass on 22 Dec 45.

Campaigns: *Naples-Foggia, Rome-Arno, Rhineland, Central Europe*
Aug 45 Loc: Epinal France (scheduled to SWPA under Shipment #R9850-F)

95th Engineer General Service Regiment (Colored)

28 Feb 42 redesignated from the 95th Engineer Battalion (Separate) at Ft Belvoir Va and moved to Ft Bragg N.C. 6 Mar 42; arrived at Dawson Creek Canada 29 May 42 and constructed Alaskan-Canadian Highway between Ft St John and Ft Nelson; transferred to Cp Claiborne La 1 May 43 and staged at Cp Shanks N.Y. 8 Jul 43 until departed New York P/E 17 Jul 43; arrived in England 28 Jul 43 and landed in France 6 Jul 44; crossed into Belgium 6 Oct 44 and entered Germany 10 Mar 45; returned to New York P/E 12 Aug 45 and moved to Cp Claiborne La; arrived at Ft Lewis Wash 14 Apr 46 where inactivated on 16 Dec 46.

Campaigns: *Normandy, Northern France, Rhineland, Ardennes-Alsace, Central Europe*
Aug 45 Loc: Camp Claiborne Louisiana

96th Engineer General Service Regiment (Colored)

29 Jul 42 redesignated from the 96th Engineer Battalion (Separate) at Port Moresby New Guinea; departed Oro Bay New Guinea 20 Jul 44 and arrived at Maffin Bay New Guinea 26 Jul 44 where worked on the Mar airdrome at Sansapor; landed in the Philippine Islands on 22 Apr 45 where inactivated on 15 Feb 46.

Campaigns: *Papua, New Guinea, Leyte*
Aug 45 Loc: Cotabato Mindanao Philippine Islands

97th Engineer General Service Regiment (Colored)

22 Feb 42 redesignated from the 97th Engineer Battalion (Separate) at Elgin Field Fla and arrived at Seattle P/E 20 Apr 42; departed 22 Apr 42 and arrived at Valdez Alaska 29 Apr 42 at the southern terminus of the Richardson Highway; built pioneer road and constructed part of Alaskan-Canadian Highway from Slana in the Tanana River Valley and reached the Tanana River by 25 Aug 42; linked up with the 18th Engr Regt at Beaver Creek 25 Oct 42; returned to Seattle P/E 11 Sep 43 and moved to Cp Sutton N.C. 18 Sep 43; staged at Cp Stoneman Calif 29 Feb 44 until departed San Francisco P/E 10 Mar 44; arrived at Milne Bay New Guinea 24 Apr 44 and in April 1946 relocated to the Philippines; there redesignated the 97th Engineer General Service Battalion (Colored) on 30 Jun 46.

Campaigns: *New Guinea*
Aug 45 Loc: Finschhafen New Guinea

98th Engineer General Service Regiment (Colored)

22 May 42 redesignated from 98th Engineer Battalion (Separate) (Colored) at Cp Claiborne La; arrived at New York P/E 23 Jun 42 and departed 1 Jul 42; arrived in Scotland 13 Jul 42 and moved to Somerset England 15 Jul 42; landed in Algeria North Africa 15 Feb 43; transferred to Tunisia 3 Jun 43; landed in Italy 6 Dec 43 where remained until inactivated 25 Sep 45.

Campaigns: *Tunisia, Naples-Foggia, Rome-Arno, North Apennines*
Aug 45 Loc: Ardenza, Italy

101st Engineers (Combat)   Massachusetts National Guard

16 Jan 41 inducted into federal service as part of 26th Division at Cambridge Mass; moved to Cp Edwards Mass where Hqs, Hq & Sv Co and Cos D, E, and F redesignated 101st Engineer Combat Battalion 3 Feb 42; 1st Bn redesignated 1st Battalion, 134th Engineers; Hq 2nd Bn inactivated 12 Feb 42.

102nd Engineers (Combat)   New York National Guard

15 Oct 40 inducted into federal service as part of 27th Division at New York N.Y.; departed San Francisco P/E 10 Mar 42; arrived at Oahu Hawaii 15 Mar 42; relocated to Hilo Hawaii 18 Mar 42 where Hq redesignated Hq, 152nd Engineers 1 Sep 42; Hq & Sv Co, Cos A, B, and C redesignated 102nd Engineer Combat Battalion 23 Aug 42; Hq 1st Bn inactivated 23 Aug 42; 2nd Bn redesignated 2nd Bn, 152nd Engineers 23 Aug 42.

Campaigns: *Pacific Theater without inscription*

103rd Engineers (Combat)   Pennsylvania National Guard

17 Feb 41 inducted into federal service as part of 28th Division at Philadelphia Pa; relocated to Indiantown Gap Mil Res Pa where Hq, Hq & Sv Co, Cos A, B, and C redesignated 103rd Engineer Combat Battalion 4 Feb 42; Hq 1st Bn inactivated 4 Feb 42; 2nd Bn redesignated 180th Engineer Battalion (Heavy Ponton) per orders dated 7 Feb 42.

104th Engineers (Combat)   New Jersey National Guard

16 Sep 40 inducted into federal service as part of 44th Division at Teaneck N.J.; moved to Ft Dix N.J. and relocated to Cp Claiborne La 16 Jan 42 where Hq, Hq & Sv Co., Cos A, B, and C redesignated 104th Engineer Combat Battalion 20 Feb 42; Hq 1st Bn inactivated 16 Feb 42; 2nd Bn redesignated 1st Battalion, 175th Engineers.

105th Engineers (Combat)   North Carolina National Guard

16 Sep 40 inducted into federal service as part of 30th Division at Charlotte N.C. and moved to Ft Jackson S.C. where Hq, Hq & Sv Co, Cos C, D, and E redesignated 105th Engineer Combat Battalion 7 Feb 42; Hq 1st Bn redesignated 2nd Battalion, 175th Engineers per orders dated 7 Feb 42 (Cos A and B redesignated Cos D and E of 175th Engineers); Hq 2nd Bn inactivated; Co F redesignated Co F, 175th Engineers.

106th Engineers (Combat)   Mississippi National Guard

25 Nov 40 inducted into federal service as part of 31st Division at Jackson S.C. and moved to Cp Blanding Fla where Hq, Hq & Sv Co, Cos A, B, and C redesignated 106th Engineer Combat Battalion 10 Feb 42, Hq 1st Bn inactivated 26 Feb 42, and 2nd Bn redesignated 1st Battalion, 175th Engineers per orders dated 10 Feb 42.

107th Engineers (Combat)   Michigan National Guard

15 Oct 40 inducted into federal service as part of 32nd Division at Detroit Mich; moved to Cp Beauregard La; transferred to Cp Livingston 26 Jan 41; arrived at Ft Dix N.J. 4 Jan 42 where Hq, Hq & Sv Co, Hq 1st Bn, and Cos B, C, and E redesignated 107th Engineer Combat Battalion 16 Jan 42; Hq 2nd Bn and Cos A, D, and F redesignated 2nd Battalion, 131st Engineers per orders dated 16 Jan 42.

108th Engineers (Combat)   Illinois National Guard

5 Mar 41 inducted into federal service as part of 33rd Division at Chicago Ill and moved to Cp Forrest Tenn where Hq, Hq & Sv Co, Cos A, B, and C redesignated 108th Engineer Combat Battalion 12 Feb 42; Hq 1st Bn inactivated 21 Feb 42; 2nd Bn redesignated 181st Engineer Battalion (Heavy Ponton) per orders dated 12 Feb 42.

109th Engineers (Combat)   South Dakota National Guard

10 Feb 41 inducted into federal service as part of 34th Division at Rapid City S.D.; moved to Cp Claiborne La where Hq, Hq & Sv Co, Cos A, E, and F redesignated 109th Engineer Combat Battalion 1 Feb 42; 1st Bn redesignated 1st Battalion, 132nd Engineers 1 Feb 42; Hq 2nd Bn inactivated 30 Jan 42.

110th Engineers (Combat)   Missouri National Guard

30 Dec 40 inducted into federal service as part of 35th Division at Kansas City Mo; transferred to Cp Joseph T. Robinson Ark; moved to Cp San Luis Obispo Calif 17 Jan 42 where Hq, Hq & Sv Co, Cos A, B, and C redesignated 110th Engineer Combat Battalion 3 Feb 42; 1st Bn inactivated same date; 2nd Bn redesignated 2nd Battalion, 132nd Engineers per orders dtd 3 Feb 42.

111th Engineers (Combat)   Texas National Guard

25 Nov 40 inducted into federal service as part of 36th Division at Fort Worth Tex and moved to Cp Bowie Tex where Hq, Hq & Sv Co, Cos B, C, and E redesignated 111th Engineer Combat Battalion 31 Jan 42; Hq 1st Bn inactivated same date; 2nd Bn redesignated 2nd Battalion, 176th Engineers 31 Jan 42.

112th Engineer Combat Regiment   Ohio National Guard

15 Oct 40 inducted into federal service as part of 37th Division at Cleveland Ohio; moved to Cp Shelby Miss where redesignated (less 2nd Bn) as 112th Engineer Combat Battalion 16 Jan 42; 2nd Bn redesignated 191st Engineer Light Ponton Company. 112th Engineer Battalion sent to Ireland where it was expanded and redesignated 112th Engineers (Combat) (Corps) 1 Jun 42 with activation of new 2nd Bn added to regiment; relocated to Devizes England 12 Jan 43 where redesignated HHC, 1121st Engineer Combat Group; 1st and 2nd Bns redesignated 112th and 254th Engineer Combat Battalions, respectively, all effective 19 Aug 43.

Campaigns: *European Theater without inscription*

113th Engineers (Combat)   Indiana National Guard

17 Jan 41 inducted into federal service as part of 38th Division at Gary Ind and moved to Cp Shelby Miss where Hq, Hq & Sv Co, Cos A, B, and C redesignated 113th Engineer Combat Battalion 10 Feb 42; Hq 1st Bn inactivated same date; 2nd Bn redesignated 1st Battalion, 131st Engineers.

115th Engineers (Combat)   Utah National Guard

3 Mar 41 inducted into federal service as part of 40th Division at Salt Lake City Utah and moved to Cp San Luis Obispo Calif; transferred to Los Angeles Calif 9 Dec 41 where Hq, Hq & Sv Co, Cos A, B, and C redesignated 115th Engineer Combat Battalion 5 Feb 42; Hq 1st Bn inactivated 18 Feb 42; 2nd Bn redesignated 2nd Battalion, 133rd Engineers 5 Feb 42.

116th Engineers (Combat)   Idaho National Guard

16 Sep 40 inducted into federal service as part of 41st Division at Boise, Idaho and moved to Cp Murray Wash; relocated to Ft Lewis Wash 20 Mar 41 where Hq, Hq & Sv Co, Cos A, B, and C redesignated 116th Engineer Combat Battalion 14 Feb 42; Hq 1st Bn and Cos D, E, and F redesignated 1st Battalion, 133rd Engineers; Hq, 2nd Bn inactivated 14 Feb 42.

118th Engineers (Combat)   Rhode Island National Guard

24 Feb 41 inducted into federal service as part of 43rd Division at Providence R.I. and moved to Cp Blanding Fla where Hq, Hq & Sv Co, Cos B, C, and E redesignated 118th Engineer Combat Battalion 14 Feb 42 (Bn raised at Cp Shelby Miss, however); Hq 1st Bn inactivated 10 Feb 42; Hq 2nd Bn and Cos A, D, and F redesignated 2nd Battalion, 177th Engineers per orders dated 10 Feb 42.

120th Engineers (Combat)   New Mexico National Guard

16 Sep 40 inducted into federal service as part of 45th Division at Las Cruces N.M. and moved to Ft Sill Okla; transferred to Cp Barkeley Tex 23 Feb 41 where Hq, Hq & Sv Co, Cos D, E, and F redesignated 120th Engineer Combat Battalion 22 Feb 42; 1st Bn redesignated 1st Battalion, 176th Engineers 11 Feb 42; Hq 2nd Bn inactivated 22 Feb 42.

121st Engineers (Combat) **District of Columbia National Guard**

3 Feb 41 inducted into federal service as part of 29th Division at Washington D.C. and moved to Ft George G. Meade Md where Hq, Hq & Sv Co, Cos A, B, and C redesignated 121st Engineer Combat Battalion 28 Feb 42; Hq 1st Bn inactivated same date; 2nd Bn redesignated 2nd Battalion, 135th Engineers.

130th Engineers (Combat) **Puerto Rico National Guard**

15 Oct 40 inducted 1st Battalion as only element of regiment into federal service and moved to Cp Tortuguere P.R. 25 Oct 40; transferred to Ft Buchanan P.R. 9 Apr 41; moved to Caguas P.R. 26 Sep 41 and back to Ft Buchanan P.R. 10 Oct 41 where redesignated 130th Engineer Combat Battalion 24 May 43.

Campaigns: *American Theater without inscription*

131st Engineer Combat Regiment

12 Mar 42 activated at Cp Shelby Miss with Hq & Sv Co personnel derived from HHB, 150th Field Artillery; 1st Bn from 2nd Bn, 113th Engineers and 2nd Bn from 2nd Bn, 107th Engineers; participated in Louisiana Mnvrs Jul-Aug 42; left Cp Shelby Miss 1 Sep 42 and arrived at Ft Ord Calif 6 Sep 42; left San Francisco P/E 10 Oct 42 and arrived in New Caledonia 9 Nov 42; landed on Guadalcanal 12 Aug 43; landed on New Georgia Island 20 Aug 43; arrived back at Guadalcanal 27 Nov 43; landed on Bougainville 15 Dec 43 where redesignated HHC, 1129th Engineer Combat Group 15 May 44, 1st and 2nd Bns redesignated 131st and 1279th Engineer Combat Battalions, respectively.

Campaigns: *Northern Solomons*

132nd Engineer Combat Regiment

1 Feb 42 activated at Ft Dix, N.J. with 1st Bn from 1st Bn, 109th Engineers and 2nd Bn from 2nd Bn, 110th Engineers; moved to Ft Hancock N.J. 23 Mar 42; transferred to Framingham Mass 22 May 42 (less 2nd Bn which was moved to Ft Story Va 6 Jun 42 and back to Ft Hancock 1 Oct 42); regiment redesignated HHC, 1118th Engineer Combat Group in Framingham 5 Apr 43. 1st Bn redesignated 132nd Engineer Combat Battalion 5 May 43 and 2nd Bn redesignated 5 Mar 43 as 242nd Engineer Combat Battalion.

133rd Engineer Combat Regiment

16 Feb 42 activated at Ft Lewis Wash with Hq & Sv Co personnel derived from HHB, 146th Field Artillery; 1st Bn from 1st Bn, 116th Engineers and 2nd Bn from 2nd Bn, 115th Engineers; redesignated there as HHC, 1104th Engineer Combat Group 25 Mar 43. 1st Bn redesignated 133rd Engineer Combat Battalion 1 Feb 43 and 2nd Bn inactivated 25 Jan 43.

134th Engineers (Combat)

1st Battalion redesignated from 1st Battalion, 101st Engineers en route to Australia where it arrived 26 Feb 42 and was disbanded 17 Apr 42.

Campaigns: *Pacific Theater without inscription*

135th Engineers (Combat)

12 Mar 42 activated at Ft George G. Meade Md with personnel from HHB, 110th Field Artillery; 2nd Bn from 2nd Bn, 121st Engineers; arrived at New Orleans P/E 20 May 42 and departed 27 May 42; arrived at Ft Read Trinidad 19 Jun 42 where inactivated 31 May 43 and personnel transferred to 135th Engineer Combat Battalion.

Campaigns: *American Theater without inscription*

146th Engineer Combat Regiment

25 Jan 43 activated at Cp Swift Tex and assigned to Third Army where redesignated HHC, 1116th Engineer Combat Group 1 Apr 43. 1st and 2nd Bns redesignated 146th and 206th Engineer Combat Battalions, respectively.

147th Engineer Combat Regiment

29 Jan 43 activated at Cp Swift Tex and assigned to Third Army where redesignated HHC, 1117th Engineer Combat Group 1 Apr 43. 1st and 2nd Bns redesignated 147th and 207th Engineer Combat Battalions, respectively.

151st Engineers (Combat) Alabama National Guard

27 Jan 41 inducted into federal service at Huntsville Ala as a separate engineer regiment; transferred to Cp Shelby Miss 5 Feb 41; moved to Cp Claiborne La 14 Mar 41 and participated in Louisiana Mnvrs Aug-Sep 41 less 1st Bn which moved to Cp Murray Wash 8 Aug 41; 1st Bn left Seattle P/E 29 Aug 41 arriving at Dutch Harbor Alaska 2 Sep 41 and then moved to Kodiak Alaska; remainder of regiment arrived at Cp Murray Wash 30 Dec 41, departed Seattle P/E 20 Jan 42, and arrived at Cold Bay Alaska 29 Jan 42; moved to Amchitka Alaska 10 Feb 43; entire regiment arrived back at Ft Lawton Wash 10 Jun 44 and moved to Ft Leonard Wood Mo 19 Jun 44 where redesignated HHB, 1169th Engineer Combat Group 11 Jul 44. 1st and 2nd Bns redesignated 151st and 1343rd Engineer Combat Battalions, respectively.

Campaigns: *Aleutian Islands*

152nd Engineers (Combat)

1 Sep 42 activated at Hilo Hawaii with Hq from Hq 102nd Engineers; 2nd Bn from 2nd Bn, 102nd Engineers; regiment disbanded 23 Nov 42 and personnel transferred to 152nd Engineer Combat Battalion.

Campaigns: *Pacific Theater without inscription*

175th Engineer General Service Regiment

26 May 42 activated at Ft Jackson S.C. with personnel from HHB, 116th Field Artillery; 1st Bn from 2nd Bn, 104th Engineers and 2nd Bn from 1st Bn, 105th Engineers; moved to Ft Moultrie S.C. on 8 Jun 42 and to Cp Pickett Va 16 Sep 42; arrived at New York P/E 14 Oct 42 and departed 2 Nov 42; landed in North Africa 11 Nov 42 and in Sicily 1–4 Aug 43; arrived in Italy 16 Nov 43–22 Jan 44; arrived at Hampton roads P/E 29 Oct 45 and inactivated at Cp Patrick Henry Va on 29 Oct 45.

Campaigns: *Tunisia, Sicily, Naples-Foggia, Rome-Arno, North Apennines, Po Valley*
Aug 45 Loc: Pistoia Italy

176th Engineer General Service Regiment

10 Feb 42 activated at Cp Bowie Tex with 1st Bn from 1st Bn, 120th Engineers and 2nd Bn from 2nd Bn, 111th Engineers; moved to Ft Lewis Wash 22 May 42 and arrived at Seattle P/E where departed 17 Jun 42; arrived at Bethel Alaska 13 Jul 42 and stationed in central interior Alaska until 25 Nov 44; returned to Seattle P/E 2 Dec 44 and moved to Ft Belvoir Va 11 Dec 44; there regiment redesignated as 176th Engineer Construction Battalion on 12 Mar 45, less Co A which was redesignated HHC, 3188th Engineer Construction Group and Co C, which was redesignated 3187th Engr Base Equipment Company; certain other elements disbanded.

Campaigns: *Pacific Theater without inscription*

177th Engineer General Service Regiment

10 Feb 42 activated at Cp Claiborne La with 1st Bn from 1st Bn, 175th Engineers (originally 2nd Bn, 106th Engineers) and 2nd Bn from 2nd Bn, 118th Engineers; 1st Bn stationed at Cp Bowie and Cp Barkeley Tex and the 2nd Bn stationed at Cp Shelby Miss; regiment reassembled and arrived at New York City 14 Jul 42; transferred to Seattle P/E 5 Sep 42 and departed 2 Oct 42; arrived at Anchorage Alaska on 4 Oct 42; 2nd Bn deployed to Amchitka in Mar 43; remained in Alaska until 15 Nov 44 when disbanded; personnel used to fill new 177th Engineer Construction Battalion.

Campaigns: *Aleutian Islands*

224th Engineer General Service Regiment (Colored)

28 Mar 45 activated in Italy at Bottinuccio with personnel from the 366th Infantry Regiment (Colored) per GO 32 Hqs Fifth Army APO 464 dated 28 Mar 45; departed Naples Italy on 8 Jun 45 and arrived at Manila Philippine Islands on 15 Jul 45 where inactivated on 23 Dec 45.

Campaigns: *Po Valley, Pacific Theater without inscription*
Aug 45 Loc: Manila Philippine Islands

226th Engineer General Service Regiment (Colored)

28 Mar 45 activated in Italy at Bottinuccio with personnel from the 366th Infantry Regiment (Colored) per GO 32 Hqs Fifth Army APO 464 dated 28 Mar 45; departed Livorno Italy 20 Oct 45 and arrived at Hampton Roads P/E 9 Nov 45 and inactivated at Cp Patrick Henry Va on 7 Nov 45.

Campaigns: *Po Valley*
Aug 45 Loc: Loiano Italy (scheduled to SWPA under Shipment #R0570-J)

330th Engineer General Service Regiment

15 Apr 42 activated at Cp Claiborne La and arrived at Churchill Canada 31 Jul 42 where remained until 13 Nov 42; returned to Cp Claiborne La on 18 Nov 42 and arrived at Los Angeles Sub-P/E 8 Jan 43 and departed 20 Jan 43; arrived at Bombay India on 3 Mar 43 and elements reinforced the roadhead on the Ledo Road by late Apr 43; constructed airfields in Assam mid-43 and completely in Burma by 16 Oct 43; 1st Bn took lead breaking trail on Ledo Road 14 Nov 43; reached Singbwiyang Burma 27 Dec 43, engaged in combat at Tanai 3 Mar 44, and completed road to Myitkyina Burma by 10 Nov 44; inactivated in Burma on 25 Apr 46.

Campaigns: *Central Burma, India-Burma*
Aug 45 Loc: Myitkyina Burma, less 2nd Battalion at Ledo India

331st Engineer General Service Regiment

22 Apr 42 activated at Cp Claiborne La and staged at Cp Murray Wash 3 Sep 42 until departed Seattle P/E 30 Sep 42; arrived at Excursion Inlet Alaska 5 Oct 42 and moved to Yakutat Alaska 8 Sep 43 and to Seward Alaska 11 Sep 43 and finally to Adak Island on 19 Sep 43 where remained until disbanded on 15 Nov 44; 1st Bn had departed Edmonton Canada 2 May 44 and arrived at Cp Sutton N.C. 6 May 44 and later was redesignated the 1339th Engineer Construction Bn at Ft Lewis Wash 28 Aug 44.

Campaigns: *Pacific Theater without inscription*

332nd Engineer General Service Regiment

6 May 42 activated at Cp Claiborne La and arrived at New York P/E 23 Jul 42; departed 5 Aug 42 and arrived in England 17 Aug 42; landed in France 24 Jun 44 where engaged in construction of railroad lines, crossing into Belgium 13 Dec 44 and into Germany 29 Mar 45; inactivated in Germany on 28 Jan 47.

Campaigns: *Normandy, Northern France, Rhineland, Ardennes-Alsace, Central Europe*
Aug 45 Loc: Shringshausen Germany

333rd Engineer Special Service Regiment

12 May 42 activated at Cp Claiborne La and moved to the Quartermaster Depot at Toledo Ohio 23 Aug 42; transferred to Yuma Ariz 5 Dec 42 and returned to Cp Claiborne La 9 Aug 43; staged at Cp Shanks N.Y. 1 Oct 43 until departed New York P/E 8 Oct 43; arrived in England 18 Oct 43 and landed in France 30 Jun 44; entered Germany 22 Mar 45 where active through 1946.

Campaigns: *Normandy, Northern France*
Aug 45 Loc: Mourmelon-le-Grande France

334th Engineer Special Service Regiment

20 May 42 activated at Cp Claiborne La and arrived at New York P/E 23 Oct 42; departed 1 Nov 42 and arrived in Iraq 16 Dec 42 under the Persian Gulf Command; departed 29 Jan 45 and landed in Marseilles France 16 Feb 45; entered Germany 4 Apr 45 and inactivated in Belgium on 24 Aug 46.

Campaigns: *Rhineland, Central Europe*
Aug 45 Loc: Mannheim Germany

335th Engineer General Service Regiment

20 Jul 42 activated at Cp Gruber Okla and staged at Ft Dix N.J. 20 Mar 43 until departed New York P/E 2 Apr 43; arrived at Oran North Africa 13 Apr 43 and landed in Corsica 10 Jan 44; landed at St Tropez France on 23 Aug 44 and entered Germany 6 Apr 45; arrived at New York P/E 16 Mar 46 and inactivated there on 17 Mar 46.

Campaigns: *Naples-Foggia, Rome-Arno, Southern France, Rhineland, Central Europe*
Aug 45 Loc: Mannheim Germany

336th Engineer General Service Regiment

25 Jul 42 activated at Cp Rucker Ala where redesignated HHC, 1119th Engineer Combat Group on 7 Apr 43; 1st and 2nd Bns redesignated 336th and 234th Engineer Combat Battalions, respectively.

337th Engineer General Service Regiment

20 Jul 42 activated at Cp Swift Tex and moved to Cp Polk La 22 Jan 43; departed New York P/E 28 Apr 43 and arrived at Oran North Africa on 11 May 43; landed in Italy 21 Sep 43 and disbanded at Florence Italy on 16 Sep 44; personnel from 1st and 2nd Bns absorbed into 169th and 182nd Engineer Combat Battalions activated same date; and headquarters personnel placed in HHC, 1338th Engineer Combat Group.

Campaigns: *Naples-Foggia, Rome-Arno, North Apennines*

338th Engineer General Service Regiment

4 Sep 42 activated at Cp Atterbury Ind and moved to Cp Claiborne La 15 Nov 42; departed New York P/E 28 Apr 43 and arrived at Oran North Africa on 12 May 43; landed in Italy 8 Feb 44; arrived at Boston P/E 8 Nov 45 and inactivated at Cp Myles Standish Mass on 9 Nov 45.

Campaigns: *Rome-Arno, North Apennines*
Aug 45 Loc: Livorno Italy, less Co B at Torre Del Lago, 2nd Bn at Bolzano, Co D at San Giuliano, and Co E at Pisa

339th Engineer General Service Regiment

17 Aug 42 activated at Cp Butner N.C. and staged at Cp Stoneman Calif 3 Apr 43 until departed San Francisco P/E 10 Apr 43; arrived in Australia 1 May 43 and moved to Milne Bay New Guinea on 8 Jun 43; inactivated there 8 Aug 44 and absorbed into 339th Engineer Construction Battalion.

Campaigns: *New Guinea*

340th Engineer General Service Regiment

5 Mar 42 activated at Vancouver Barracks Wash and departed Seattle P/E 19 Apr 42; arrived at Skagway Alaska 22 Apr 42 and went by train to Carcross Canada and then sailed to Lake Teslin Yukon Territory on 10 Jun 42; started construction on Alaskan-Canadian Highway 18 Jun 42 and linked up with 35th Engr Regt at Contact Creek 24 Sep 42; built bridge across Nisutlin Bay; arrived at Whitehorse Canada on 10 Jan 43 and Cp Sutton N.C. 1 Sep 43; staged at Hathaway Wash 15 Feb 44 until departed Portland Sub-P/E 28 Feb 44; arrived in Australia 5 Apr 44 where redesignated the 340th Engineer Construction Battalion on 20 Jul 44.

Campaigns: *Pacific Theater without inscription*

341st Engineer General Service Regiment

10 Mar 42 activated at Ft Ord Calif and arrived at Dawson Creek Canada on 29 Apr 42; engaged in construction on Alaskan-Canadian Highway out of Ft St John; arrived at Cp Sutton N.C. on 5 Aug 43 and staged at Cp Shanks N.Y. 10 Oct 43 until departed New York P/E 21 Oct 43; arrived in England 2 Nov 43 and landed in France 26 Jun 44; crossed into Belgium 25 Sep 44 and entered Germany 12 Mar 45; returned to New York P/E 10 Sep 45 and moved to Cp Claiborne La and then to Ft Belvoir where inactivated on 22 Mar 46.

Campaigns: *Normandy, Northern France, Rhineland, Ardennes-Alsace, Central Europe*
Aug 45 Loc: Mehlen Germany (scheduled to SWPA under Shipment #R8485-G)

342nd Engineer General Service Regiment

15 Apr 42 activated at Cp Claiborne La and staged at Ft Dix N.J. 2 Jun 42 until departed New York P/E 1 Jul 42; arrived in England 12 Jul 42 and landed in France 12 Jun 44; crossed into Belgium 23 Dec 44 and returned to France 2 Jan 45; reentered Belgium on 9 Jan 45 and inactivated in France on 6 May 46.

Campaigns: *Normandy, Northern France, Rhineland, Ardennes-Alsace*
Aug 45 Loc: Liege Belgium

343rd Engineer General Service Regiment

22 Apr 42 activated at Cp Claiborne La and staged at Ft Dix N.J. 2 Jun 42 until departed New York P/E 1 Jul 42; arrived in England 20 Jul 42 and North Africa 6 Dec 42; arrived completely in Sicily by 4 Aug 43 and in Italy on 28 Sep 43; assaulted southern France 15 Aug 44; entered Germany 29 Mar 45 where active through 1946.

Campaigns: *Algeria–French Morocco, Tunisia, Sicily, Naples-Foggia, Anzio, Rome-Arno, Southern France, Rhineland, Ardennes-Alsace, Central Europe*

Aug 45 Loc: Ulm Germany

344th Engineer General Service Regiment

29 Apr 42 activated at Cp Claiborne La and departed New York P/E 1 Jul 42; arrived in England 12 Jul 42 and landed at Oran North Africa 1 Feb 43; landed in Italy 17 Nov 43 and assaulted southern France 15 Aug 44; entered Germany 22 Mar 45; arrived at New York P/E 29 Nov 45 where inactivated at Cp Shanks N.Y. on 30 Nov 45.

Campaigns: *Naples-Foggia, Rome-Arno, Southern France, Rhineland, Ardennes-Alsace, Central Europe*
Aug 45 Loc: Calais France

345th Engineer General Service Regiment

15 Jul 42 activated at Cp Crowder Mo; participated in Tennessee Mnvrs Sep-Nov 42; arrived at New York P/E 23 Jan 43 and departed 7 Feb 43; arrived at Casablanca Morocco 19 Feb 43; landed in Italy 3 Oct 43 where inactivated at Foggia 30 Jun 46.

Campaigns: *Algeria–French Morocco (1st Bn only), Naples-Foggia, Rome-Arno, North Apennines*
Aug 45 Loc: Livorno Italy less 1st Bn at Pisa, Co C at Pistoia, 2nd Bn at Secondigliano, Co E at Cecchignola, Co F at Civitavecchia

346th Engineer General Service Regiment

29 Apr 42 activated at Cp Claiborne La; arrived in New York P/E 22 Jul 42 and departed 5 Aug 42; arrived in England 18 Aug 42; landed in France 27 Jun 44; crossed into Belgium 11 Sep 44; entered Germany 11 Mar 45 where inactivated 31 Dec 46.

Campaigns: *Normandy, Northern France, Rhineland, Ardennes-Alsace, Central Europe*
Aug 45 Loc: Frankfurt Germany

347th Engineer General Service Regiment

6 May 42 activated at Cp Claiborne La; arrived in New York P/E 22 Jul 42 and departed 5 Aug 42; arrived in England 18 Aug 42; landed in France 27 Jun 44; crossed into Luxembourg 7 Feb 45; entered Germany 9 Apr 45 where inactivated 1 Jun 46.

Campaigns: *Normandy, Northern France, Rhineland, Ardennes-Alsace, Central Europe*
Aug 45 Loc: Feucht Germany

348th Engineer General Service Regiment

15 Jul 42 activated at Cp Crowder Mo; relocated to Desert Training Center Cp Young Calif 2 Nov 42 where redesignated HHC, 1120th Engineer Combat Group 15 Apr 43; 1st Bn redesignated 348th Engineer Combat Battalion same date, 2nd Bn had been redesignated 233rd Engineer Combat Battalion 25 Jan 43.

349th Engineer General Service Regiment

13 May 42 activated at Cp Claiborne La; arrived in New York P/E 27 Jul 42 and departed 5 Sep 42; arrived in Seattle P/E 10 Sep 42 and departed 21 Sep 42; arrived at Ft Mears Alaska 27 Sep 42; moved to Adak Alaska 3 Feb 43 and to Ft Glenn Alaska 28 Jun 44; arrived at Seattle P/E 6 Nov 44; transferred to Cp Claiborne La 14 Nov 44 where disbanded 12 Mar 45.

Campaigns: *Aleutian Islands*

350th Engineer General Service Regiment (Colored)

15 Jul 42 activated at Cp Shelby Miss and attached to Third Army; departed San Francisco P/E 28 Jan 43; arrived at Espiritu Santo 17 Feb 43; assigned to Service Command APO 708 and relocated to New Georgia Island 16 Jun 44; transferred to Hollandia New Guinea 13 Nov 44 where inactivated on 20 Jan 46.

Campaigns: *Northern Solomons, New Guinea (Bismarck Archipelago Co C and F only)*
Aug 45 Loc: Hollandia New Guinea

351st Engineer General Service Regiment

20 Aug 42 activated at Cp White Oreg; moved to Ft Lewis Wash 9 May 43; staged at Cp Kilmer N.J. 7–17 Jul 43; departed New York P/E 17 Jul 43; arrived in England 27 Jul 43; landed in France Aug 44; arrived at Cp Shanks N.Y. 12 Aug 45; relocated to Ft Lewis Wash 18 Aug 45 where inactivated 14 Dec 45 and absorbed into reorganization as 351st Engineer Construction Battalion.

Campaigns: *Northern France, Rhineland, Ardennes-Alsace*
Aug 45 Loc: En route to Ft Lewis Wash via train from Cp Shanks N.Y.

352nd Engineer General Service Regiment (Colored)

17 Apr 42 activated at Cp Gordon Ga; arrived and departed New York P/E 22 Sep 42; shipment cancelled and regiment transferred to Indiantown Gap Mil Res Pa 24 Sep 42; arrived at San Francisco P/E 4 Jan 43 and departed 13 Jan 43; arrived at Basra Iraq 22 Feb 43 and departed 1 Nov 44 for Ledo India; arrived in India 9 Nov 44 and departed Karachi India 21 Oct 45; arrived in New York P/E 9 Nov 45 and inactivated at Cp Kilmer N.J. 10 Nov 45.

Campaigns: *India-Burma*
Aug 45 Loc: Ledo India, less Cos B and C at Chabau India

353rd Engineer General Service Regiment

15 Aug 42 activated at Cp White Oreg; staged at Cp Stoneman Calif 8–22 May 43; departed San Francisco P/E 22 May 43; arrived in New Caledonia 13 Jun 43 where redesignated HHC, 1177th Engineer Construction Group 1 Apr 44; 1st Bn redesignated 353rd Engineer Construction Battalion and 2nd Bn redesignated 1393rd Engineer Construction Battalion.

Campaigns: *Pacific Theater without inscription*

354th Engineer General Service Regiment (Colored)

20 Sep 42 activated at Cp Maxey Tex; staged at Cp Shanks N.Y. 11 Jun–1 Jul 43; departed New York P/E 1 Jul 43; arrived in England 6 Jul 43; landed in France Aug 44; arrived in New York P/E 12 Aug 45; relocated to Ft Belvoir Va where inactivated 6 Nov 45.

Campaigns: *Northern France, Rhineland, Central Europe*
Aug 45 Loc: En route to Ft Belvoir Va via train from Cp Shanks N.Y.

355th Engineer General Service Regiment

1 Sep 42 activated at Cp White Oreg; transferred to Needles Calif 17 Dec 42; relocated to Ft Belvoir Va 9 Aug 43; staged at Cp Shanks N.Y. 14–21 Oct 43; departed New York P/E 21 Oct 43; arrived in England 3 Nov 43; landed in France 5 Jul 44; crossed into Belgium 1 Nov 44 and Holland 5 Mar 45; entered Germany 10 Mar 45 where inactivated 17 Jun 46.

Campaigns: *Normandy, Northern France, Rhineland, Ardennes-Alsace, Central Europe*
Aug 45 Loc: Monchengladback Germany (scheduled to SWPA under Shipment #R8485-E)

356th Engineer General Service Regiment (Colored)

20 Aug 42 activated at Cp Shelby Miss; moved to Desert Training Center Cp Young Calif 8 Feb 43; staged at Cp Shanks N.Y. 9–19 Sep 43; departed New York P/E 19 Sep 43; arrived in England 25 Sep 43; landed in France 3 Aug 44; arrived at Boston P/E 24 Jun 45; relocated to Ft Lewis Wash 26 Jun 45; departed San Francisco P/E 31 Aug 45; arrived in Hawaii 10 Sep 45 and departed 15 Sep 45; arrived back at San Francisco P/E 21 Sep 45 where inactivated 3 Oct 45.

Campaigns: *Normandy, Northern France*
Aug 45 Loc: Army Service Forces Training Center, Ft Lewis Wash

357th Engineer General Service Regiment (Colored)

25 Jun 42 activated at Cp Pickett Va; moved to Cp Claiborne La 19 Nov 42; departed New York P/E 28 Apr 43; arrived in Oran North Africa 11 May 43; landed in Italy 22 Jun 44 and departed Naples Italy 29 Aug 45; landed at Hampton Roads P/E 9 Sep 45 and inactivated at Cp Kilmer N.J. 24 Oct 45.

Campaigns: *Rome-Arno*
Aug 45 Loc: Aversa Italy, less 1st Bn at Gli Astroni, Co B at San Angelo, Co C at Bagnoli (entire regt to move to SWPA under Shipment #R0570-H)

358th Engineer General Service Regiment

10 Jan 43 activated at Cp Claiborne La; departed the United States 1 Jul 43 and arrived in Scotland 6 Jul 43 and England 8 Jul '43; landed in France 24 Aug 44 and crossed into Belgium 27 Nov 44 where remained until departed Europe for the United States; arrived at New York P/E 1 Jan 46 and inactivated there 2 Jan 46.

Campaigns: *Normandy, Northern France, Rhineland, Central Europe*
Aug 45 Loc: Antwerp Belgium (scheduled to SWPA under Shipment #R9850-G)

359th Engineer General Service Regiment

15 Feb 43 activated at Cp Claiborne La; departed the United States 1 Jul 43 and arrived in England 6 Jul 43; landed in France 7 Jul 44 and crossed into Belgium 30 Nov 44 where remained until departed Europe for the United States but scheduled shipment cancelled and regiment inactivated in France 15 Dec 46.

Campaigns: *Normandy, Northern France, Rhineland, Central Europe*
Aug 45 Loc: Charleville France

360th Engineer General Service Regiment

13 Aug 42 activated at Cp Claiborne La; departed the United States 24 Jun 43 and arrived in England 29 Jun 43; landed in France 4 Aug 44 and remained there until inactivated 6 May 46.

Campaigns: *Northern France, Rhineland*
Aug 45 Loc: Marseille France (scheduled to SWPA under Shipment #R9850-H)

361st Engineer Special Service Regiment

1 May 43 activated at Cp Claiborne La as Engineer General Service Regiment and redesignated Special Service 19 May 43; departed the United States 5 Oct 44 and arrived in England 13 Oct 44; landed in France 16 Oct 44; sent to the Philippines 25 Aug 45 after end of war in Europe and arrived there 26 Aug 45; inactivated in Japan 31 May 46.

Campaigns: *Rhineland*
Aug 45 Loc: Shipment #R5218-T en route to the Philippine Islands

362nd Engineer General Service Regiment (Colored)

20 May 42 activated at Cp Claiborne La; departed the United States 9 Jan 43 and arrived in New Caledonia 29 Jan 43; landed on Guadalcanal 29 May 44; moved into the Philippine Islands 6 Jul 45 where inactivated 23 Dec 45.

Campaigns: *Pacific Theater without inscription*
Aug 45 Loc: Manila Philippines

363rd Engineer Special Service Regiment

13 Aug 42 activated at Cp Claiborne La; departed the United States 30 Mar 43 and arrived at Basra Iraq 11 May 43 and stationed in Teheran Iran where inactivated 9 Jul 45.

364th Engineer General Service Regiment (Colored)

31 Aug 42 activated at Cp Swift Tex; transferred to Cp Claiborne La 19 Nov 42; staged at Cp Shank N.Y. 8–25 Jul 43; departed New York P/E 25 Jul 43 and arrived in England 30 Jul 43; landed in France 1 Jul 44; crossed into Belgium 28 Sep 44; sent back to France 18 Dec 44 and crossed into Belgium again 1 Jan 45; entered Germany 28 Feb 45; arrived at Boston P/E 4 Jul 45 and moved to Cp Claiborne La where inactivated 26 Oct 45.

Campaigns: *Normandy, Northern France, Rhineland, Ardennes-Alsace, Central Europe*
Aug 45 Loc: Cp Claiborne Louisiana

365th Engineer General Service Regiment (Colored)

20 Sep 42 activated at Cp Campbell Ky; participated in Tennessee Mnvrs Apr-Aug 43 at Lebanon; staged at Cp Shanks N.Y. 20 Sep–1 Oct 43; departed New York P/E 1 Oct 43 and arrived in England 9 Oct 43; landed in France 3 Jul 44; crossed into Belgium 1 Mar 45; entered Germany 10 Mar 45; arrived New York P/E 23 Jun 45; transferred to Ft Lewis Wash 30 Jun 45; arrived at Cp Stoneman Calif 26 Aug 45 and departed San Francisco P/E 30 Aug 45; arrived in Luzon Philippines 19 Sep 45 where inactivated 10 Dec 45.

Campaigns: *Normandy, Northern France, Rhineland, Central Europe*
Aug 45 Loc: Ft Lewis Washington (scheduled to SWPA under Shipment #0560-PP)

366th Engineer General Service Regiment (Colored)

29 Dec 42 activated at Cp Phillips Kans; participated in Tennessee Mnvrs Jun-Jul 43; moved to Cp Forrest Tenn 16 Aug 43; staged at Cp Shanks N.Y. 20 Sep–1 Oct 43; departed New York P/E 1 Oct 43 and arrived in England 9 Oct 43; landed in France 19 Aug 44; arrived New York P/E 27 Jun 45 and moved to Ft Lewis Wash 4 Jul 45; departed San Francisco P/E 31 Aug 45 and arrived in Hawaii 10 Sep 45; returned to San Francisco P/E 24 Sep 45 where inactivated 3 Oct 45.

Campaigns: *Northern France, Rhineland*
Aug 45 Loc: Ft Lewis Washington (scheduled to SWPA under Shipment #0560-RR)

367th Engineer Special Service Regiment

30 Jun 42 activated as personnel and facilities permitted on Hawaii; 1st Bn organized and departed Schofield Barracks Hawaii 3 Jun 43 and arrived on Canton Island 10 Jun 43 less Co B which arrived on Christmas Island 19 Jun 43; regiment disbanded less 1st Bn which was redesignated 1398th Engineer Construction Battalion 21 Mar 44.

Campaigns: *Pacific Theater without inscription*

368th Engineer General Service Regiment

25 May 43 activated at Cp Ellis Ill; departed New York P/E 21 Oct 43 and arrived in England 3 Nov 43; landed in France 25 Jul 44; crossed into Belgium 8 Mar 45 and into Holland 19 Mar 45; entered Germany 4 Apr 45; returned to the United States 10 Sep 45 and inactivated at Cp Claiborne La 24 Nov 45.

Campaigns: *Normandy, Northern France, Rhineland, Ardennes-Alsace, Central Europe*
Aug 45 Loc: Krefeld Germany (scheduled to SWPA under Shipment #R8485-F)

369th Engineer Special Service Regiment

20 Dec 42 activated at Cp Claiborne; transferred to San Bernardino Calif 8 May 43; moved to Cp Beale Calif 29 Nov 43; staged at Cp Stoneman Calif 28 Feb–6 Mar 44; departed San Francisco P/E 6 Mar 44 and arrived in Guadalcanal 23 Mar 44 where inactivated 1 May 44 and disbanded.

Campaigns: *Pacific Theater without inscription*

370th Engineer Special Service Regiment

1 Oct 42 activated as a personnel and facilities permitted on Hawaii; 1st Bn organized and attached to 1st Bn, 367th Engineer Special Service Regiment until 1 Jun 43 when attached to 47th Engineer Regiment (General Service); regiment disbanded less 1st Bn which was redesignated 1399th Engineer Construction Battalion 21 Mar 44.

Campaigns: *Pacific Theater without inscription*

371st Engineer General Service Regiment

25 May 43 activated at Cp Ellis Ill where redesignated 371st Engineer Construction Battalion 1 Feb 44.

372nd Engineer General Service Regiment

20 Dec 42 activated at Cp Claiborne La; departed the United States 14 Aug 43 and arrived in England 21 Aug 43; landed in France 9 Oct 44 and crossed into Germany 6 Apr 45; returned to the Unites States 2 Jul 45 and inactivated at Ft Belvoir Va 25 Oct 45.

Campaigns: *Rhineland, Ardennes-Alsace, Central Europe*
Aug 45 Loc: Ft Belvoir Va

373rd Engineer General Service Regiment

19 Apr 43 activated at Cp Claiborne La; departed Halifax 31 Oct 43 and arrived in England 7 Nov 43; landed in France 28 Aug 44; returned to the United States 10 Jul 45 and inactivated at Ft Belvoir Va 25 Oct 45.

Campaigns: *Rhineland, Ardennes-Alsace, Central Europe*
Aug 45 Loc: Ft Belvoir Va

374th Engineer General Service Regiment (Colored)

2 Aug 43 redesignated from 374th Engineer Battalion (Separate) (Colored) at Cp Hood Tex and assigned to Eighth Service Command; staged at Cp Shanks N.Y. 11–22 Jan 44; departed New York P/E 22 Jan 44 and arrived in England 28 Jan 44; landed in France 11 Jul 44; crossed into Belgium 14 Jan 45; entered Germany 4 Apr 45; arrived in the United States 30 Aug 45 and moved to Cp Claiborne La where inactivated 20 Nov 45.

Campaigns: *Normandy, Northern France, Rhineland, Ardennes-Alsace,Central Europe*
Aug 45 Loc: Liege Belgium (scheduled to SWPA under Shipment #R5218-H)

375th Engineer General Service Regiment (Colored)

2 Aug 43 redesignated from 375th Engineer Battalion (Separate) (Colored) at Ft Knox Ky; staged at Cp Shanks N.Y. 17–26 Nov 43; departed New York P/E 26 Nov 43; arrived in England 4 Dec 43; landed in France 3 Aug 44; crossed into Belgium 11 Sep 44; entered Germany 22 Jan 45; left France 25 Jul 45 and arrived in the Philippines 31 Aug 45 where inactivated 20 Jan 46.

Campaigns: *Northern France, Rhineland, Central Europe*
Aug 45 Loc: Shipment #R5218-J at sea en route to Manila Philippines

377th Engineer General Service Regiment (Colored)

2 Aug 43 redesignated from 377th Engineer Battalion (Separate) (Colored) at Ft Knox Ky and assigned to Fifth Service Command; staged at Cp Shanks N.Y. 17–23 Nov 43; departed New York P/E 23 Nov 43 and arrived in England 29 Nov 43; landed in France 28 Jul 44; departed Belgium 20 Dec 45 and arrived at Hampton Roads P/E 3 Jan 46 where inactivated at Cp Patrick Henry Va 3 Jan 46.

Campaigns: *Northern France, Rhineland*
Aug 45 Loc: Dijon France (scheduled to SWPA under Shipment #R8485-D)

388th Engineer General Service Regiment (Colored)

10 Jan 43 redesignated from 388th Engineer Battalion (Separate) (Colored) at Waterways Alberta Canada under Northwest Service Command; moved to Cp Sutton N.C. 12 Sep 43 under Fourth Service Command; staged at Cp Myles Standish Mass 17–23 Mar 44; departed Boston P/E 23 Mar 44; arrived in England 3 Apr 44; landed in France Jul 44; after end of hostilities in Europe moved to Manila Philippines 30 Aug 45 where inactivated 18 Dec 45.

Campaigns: *Normandy, Northern France, Pacific Theater without inscription*
Aug 45 Loc: Shipment #R5218-K at sea en route to Manila Philippines

389th Engineer General Service Regiment (Colored)

20 Aug 43 redesignated from 389th Engineer Battalion (Separate) (Colored) at Cp Young Calif and arrived at Cp Butner N.C. 26 Aug 43 under Fourth Service Command; staged at Cp Shanks N.Y. 6–23 Dec 43 and departed New York P/E 23 Dec 43 and arrived in England 29 Dec 43; landed in France 31 Jul 44; crossed into Belgium 13 Sep 44; returned to France 25 Sep–6 Dec 44; recrossed into Belgium 9 Dec 44; crossed into Luxembourg 26 Feb 45; entered Germany 2 Mar 45; departed France 21 Aug 45 and arrived at Boston P/E 31 Aug 45 and moved to Cp Claiborne La where inactivated 25 Nov 45.

Campaigns: *Northern France, Rhineland, Ardennes-Alsace, Central Europe*
Aug 45 Loc: Mainz Germany (scheduled to SWPA under Shipment #R5218-L)

390th Engineer General Service Regiment (Colored)

10 Aug 42 activated at Cp Claiborne La and staged at Cp Shanks N.Y. 28 May 43 until departed New York P/E 24 Jun 43; arrived in England 29 Jun 43 and landed in France on 27 Jun 44 where remained until returned to New York P/E 20 Dec 45; inactivated there on 22 Dec 45.

Campaigns: *Normandy, Northern France, Rhineland, Ardennes-Alsace*
Aug 45 Loc: Vorges France

392nd Engineer General Service Regiment (Colored)

10 Aug 42 activated at Cp Joseph T. Robinson Ark and moved to Cp Claiborne La 21 Nov 42; staged at Cp Shanks N.Y. 28 May 43 until departed New York P/E on 24 Jun 43; arrived in England 29 Jun 43 and landed in France during Jul 44; returned to New York P/E 12 Aug 45 and moved to Ft Belvoir Va 14 Aug 45 where inactivated on 25 Oct 45.

Campaigns: *Normandy, Northern France, Rhineland, Ardennes-Alsace, Central Europe*
Aug 45 Loc: Army Service Forces Training Center, Fort Belvoir Virginia

393rd Engineer General Service Regiment (Colored)

15 Feb 43 activated at Cp Claiborne La and arrived at Cp Joseph T. Robinson Ark 24 Jun 43; moved back to Cp Claiborne La on 2 Aug 43 and staged at Cp Patrick Henry Va 15 Jan 44 until departed Hampton Roads P/E 25 Jan 44; 2nd Bn arrived in England 8 Feb 44 with regimental headquarters and later landed in France after the war; 1st Bn arrived at Bombay India 28 Apr 44 and inactivated there 27 Dec 44 with personnel and equipment transferred into the 1007th Engineer Battalion; regiment (less 1st Bn) arrived at Boston P/E 29 Aug 45 and moved to Cp Claiborne La; transferred to Ft Belvoir Va 21 Nov 45 where inactivated on 7 Dec 45.

Campaigns: *India-Burma*
Aug 45 Loc: Le Mans France (scheduled to SWPA under Shipment #R5218-W)

398th Engineer General Service Regiment (Colored)

22 Mar 43 activated at Cp Claiborne La and staged at Cp Shanks N.Y. 20 Jul 43 until departed New York P/E 25 Jul 43; arrived in England 30 Jul 43 and landed in France 4 Aug 44; crossed into Luxembourg 23 Dec 44 and returned to France 24 Jan 45; returned to New York P/E 2 Aug 45 and moved to Cp Claiborne La; transferred to Ft Belvoir Va where inactivated on 7 Dec 45.

Campaigns: *Northern France, Rhineland, Ardennes-Alsace*
Aug 45 Loc: Cp Claiborne La

531st Engineer Shore Regiment

15 Jun 42 activated at Cp Edwards Mass; departed New York P/E 5 Aug 42 and arrived in England 17 Aug 42 and departed 22 Oct 42; assaulted Arzew Algeria North Africa 8 Nov 42; moved to Zeralda Algeria 13 Jun 43; assaulted Gela Sicily 10 Jul 43; returned to Damesne Algeria 26 Aug 43; assaulted Salerno Italy 9 Sep 43 and moved to Atripalda Italy 17 Oct 43 and Naples Italy 16 Nov 43; departed Italy 18 Nov 43 and arrived in England 12 Dec 43; assaulted Normandy France 6 Jun 44 where disbanded 2 Aug 44; personnel transferred to HHC, 1186th Engineer Combat Group and 3051st, 3052nd, and 3053rd Engineer Combat Battalions,

Campaigns: *Algeria–French Morocco, Sicily, Naples-Foggia, Normandy*

532nd Engineer Boat and Shore Regiment

20 Jun 42 activated at Cp Edwards Mass as Engineer Shore Regiment and redesignated Engineer Amphibian Regiment there 1 Oct 42; assigned to 2nd Engineer Amphibian Brigade and personnel from 3rd Bn transferred to 542nd Engineer Amphibian Regiment; switched 1st Bns with 592nd Engineer Amphibian Regiment; relocated to Tallahassee Fla 17 Oct 42 (Cp Carabelle); moved to Ft Ord Calif 10 Nov 42; arrived at San Francisco P/E 24 Jan 43 and departed 25 Jan 43; arrived in Australia 22 Jan 43 where redesignated Engineer Boat and Shore Regiment 10 May 43; Cos A and D assaulted Nassau Bay New Guinea 30 Jan 43; entire regiment ashore at Oro Bay New Guinea by 13 Aug 43; assaulted Hollandia New Guinea 22 Apr 44; Boat Bn assaulted Toem New Guinea 17 May 44; regiment assaulted Leyte Philippines 20 Oct 44; arrived at Seattle P/E 16 Dec 45; moved to Cp San Luis Obispo Calif until stationed at Ft Emory Calif 20 Jun 46 and then relocated to Ft Ord Calif 19 Dec 46.

Campaigns: *New Guinea, Leyte, Luzon, Southern Philippines*
Aug 45 Loc: Mindoro Philippines, less Cos A and F at Palawan, Co B at Batangas, Co C at Tacloban

533rd Engineer Boat and Shore Regiment

6 Aug 42 activated at Cp Edwards Mass as Engineer Shore Regiment and redesignated Engineer Amphibian Regiment there 9 Nov 42; 3rd Bn personnel transferred to 543rd Engineer Amphibian Regiment; switched 2nd Bn with 593rd Engineer Amphibian Regiment; relocated to Amphibious Training Center Cp Carrabelle Fla 15 Nov 42; arrived at Ft Ord Calif 27 Apr 43 where redesignated Engineer Boat and Shore Regiment 10 May 43; staged at Cp Stoneman Calif 2–22 Dec 43 and departed San Francisco P/E 22 Dec 43; arrived on Goodenough Island 12 Jan 44 and transferred to Cape Gloucester New Britain 20 Feb 44; moved to Finschhafen New Guinea 26 Jun 44; assaulted Lingayen Gulf Luzon Philippines 9 Jan 45 and Malabang Mindanao 17 Apr 45; inactivated in the Philippines 31 Dec 45.

Campaigns: *Bismarck Archipelago, Luzon, Southern Philippines*
Aug 45 Loc: Macajalar Bay Mindanao Philippines

534th Engineer Boat and Shore Regiment

1 Feb 43 activated at Ft Devens Mass as Engineer Amphibian Regiment and transferred to Cp Edwards Mass 9 Mar 43 under 4th Engineer Amphibian Brigade; redesignated Engineer Boat and Shore Regiment 10 May 43; moved to Cp Gordon Johnston Fla 20 Sep 43; staged at Cp Stoneman Calif 9–23 Apr 44; departed San Francisco P/E 23 Apr 44 and arrived at Milne Bay New Guinea 15 May 44; assaulted Morotai Island 15 Sep 44 (less Boat Bn); arrived in the Philippines 11 Jan 45; inactivated at Nagoya Japan 15 Apr 46.

Campaigns: *New Guinea, Luzon*
Aug 45 Loc: Luzon Philippines, less Boat Bn at Manila

540th Engineer Combat Regiment

11 Sep 42 activated at Cp Edwards Mass as Engineer Shore Regiment; 1st Bn transferred to Ft Bragg N.C. 12 Sep 42 and attached to 36th Engineer Combat Regiment followed by 2nd Bn on 16 Sep 42; regiment (less 2 Bns) moved to Bradford Va 28 Sep 42 where rejoined by other Bns; arrived at Cp Kilmer N.J. 14 Oct 42 and redesignated Engineer Combat Regiment 25 Oct 42 (3rd Bn inactivated at Cp Edwards Mass 3 Oct 42); departed Hampton Roads P/E and New York P/E 23 Oct 42 and assaulted North Africa 8 Nov 42; assaulted Licata Sicily 9 Jul 43; assaulted Salerno Italy 9 Sep 43; assaulted Anzio Italy 22 Jan 44; assaulted Southern France 15 Aug 44 and redesignated HHC, 540th Engineer Combat Group in France; 1st and 2nd Bns redesignated 2832nd and 2833rd Engineer Combat Battalions, respectively; all effective 15 Feb 45.

Campaigns: *Algeria–French Morocco, Sicily, Naples-Foggia, Rome-Arno, Anzio, Southern France, Ardennes-Alsace*

542nd Engineer Boat and Shore Regiment

1 Oct 42 activated at Cp Edwards Mass as Engineer Amphibian Regiment with personnel from 532nd and 592nd Engineer Regiments under 2nd Engineer Amphibian Brigade; moved to Ft Ord Calif 14 Nov 42; arrived at San Francisco P/E 28 Jan 43 and departed 29 Jan 43; arrived in Australia 28 Feb 43 where redesignated Engineer Boat and Shore Regiment 10 May 43; landed at Oro Bay New Guinea 16 Aug 43; det of Boat Bn assaulted Toem New Guinea 17 May 44; assaulted Leyte Philippines 20 Oct 44; det assaulted Biri Island 20 Feb 45; assaulted Cebu Island 20 Mar 45; assaulted Tanahmerah Bay 22 Apr 45; assaulted Macajalar Bay 10 May 45; arrived at Seattle P/E 3 Dec 45 and moved to Cp San Luis Obispo Calif 16 Dec 45; inactivated Ft Ord Calif 31 Dec 46.

Campaigns: *New Guinea, Leyte, Southern Philippines*
Aug 45 Loc: Cebu Philippines, less Co A at Tacloban, Cos C and D at Iloilo, Co E at Negros

543rd Engineer Boat and Shore Regiment

9 Nov 42 activated at Cp Edwards Mass as Amphibian Regiment with personnel from 533rd and 593rd Engineer Regiments; arrived at Cp Carrabelle Fla 19 Nov 42; arrived at Ft Ord Calif 21 Apr 43 where redesignated Engineer Boat and Shore Regiment 10 May 43; staged at Cp Stoneman Calif 10 Dec 43–5 Jan 44; departed San Francisco P/E 5 Jan 44 and arrived at Sansapor New Guinea 21 Jan 44; assaulted Noemfoor Island 2 Jul 44; assaulted Lingayen Gulf Luzon Philippines 9 Jan 45; assaulted Mindanao 10 Mar 45; assaulted Jolo Island 9 Apr 45; engaged in occupation duty in Japan 25 Sep–5 Dec 45; arrived at Portland Oreg 20 Dec 45 where inactivated 22 Dec 45.

Campaigns: *New Guinea, Bismarck Archipelago, Luzon, Southern Philippines*
Aug 45 Loc: Tacloban Philippines

544th Engineer Boat and Shore Regiment

1 Feb 43 activated at Ft Devens Mass as Amphibian Regiment; transferred to Cp Edwards Mass 31 Mar 43 where redesignated Engineer Boat and Shore Regiment 10 May 43; arrived at Cp Gordon Johnston Fla 4 Sep 43; staged at Cp Stoneman Calif 16–23 Apr 44; departed San Francisco P/E 23 Apr 44; landed at Milne Bay New Guinea 15 May 44; assaulted Morotai Island 15 Sep 44; transferred to Bougainville which departed 12 Dec 44 and landed in the Philippines 9 Jan 45; inactivated in Wakayama Japan 15 Apr 46.

Campaigns: *New Guinea, Northern Solomons, Luzon*
Aug 45 Loc: Manila Philippines

591st Engineer Boat Regiment

15 Jun 42 activated at Cp Edwards Mass; departed New York P/E 5 Aug 42 and arrived in England 17 Aug 42; departed England 2 Nov 42 and assaulted Oran 8 Nov 42; arrived in Italy 6 Dec 43 where inactivated 1 Nov 44 with assets to 1185th Engineer Group.

Campaigns: *Algeria–French Morocco, Tunisia, Naples-Foggia, Rome-Arno, North Apennines*

592nd Engineer Boat and Shore Regiment

20 Jun 42 activated at Cp Edwards Mass as Engineer Boat Regiment; redesignated Engineer Amphibian Regiment 1 Oct 42 and assigned to 2nd Engineer Amphibian Brigade; 3rd Bn personnel transferred to 542nd Engineer Amphibian Regiment; switched 1st Bns with 532nd Engineer Shore Regiment; transferred to Cp Carrabelle Fla 17 Oct 42; moved to Ft Ord Calif 12 Nov 42; arrived at San Francisco P/E 28 Jan 43 and departed 18 Feb 43; landed in Australia 8 Mar 43; landed in Oro Bay New Guinea 25 Oct 43; assaulted Los Negros Island 28 Feb 44; assaulted Leyte Island 20 Oct 44; elements assaulted Caballo Island 27 Mar 45, Legaspi 1 Apr 45, and El Fraile Island 13 Apr 45; inactivated in the Philippines 25 Jun 46.

Campaigns: *Bismarck Archipelago, Leyte, Luzon*
Aug 45 Loc: Batangas Philippines, less Co D at Manila

593rd Engineer Boat and Shore Regiment

6 Aug 42 activated at Cp Edwards Mass as Engineer Boat Regiment; transferred to Amphibious Training Center Cp Carrabelle Fla 1 Nov 42 where redesignated Amphibian Regiment 9 Nov 42; 3rd Bn transferred to 543rd Engineer Amphibian Regiment; switched 2nd Bns with 533rd Engineer Amphibian Regiment; arrived at Ft Ord Calif 22 Apr 43 where redesignated Engineer Boat and Shore Regiment 10 May 43; staged at Cp Stoneman Calif 12 Dec 43–10 Jan 44; departed San Francisco P/E 10 Jan 44; arrived on Goodenough Island 1 Feb 44; Boat Bn assaulted Talesea New Britain 6 Mar 44; regiment landed in New Guinea 26 Mar 44; assaulted Aitape New Guinea 22 Apr 44; Shore Bn assaulted Insoemar Island 18 May 44; regiment landed on Biak Island 22 Jun 44; assaulted Noemfoor New Guinea 2 Jul 44; assaulted Labuan Island 10 Jun 45; landed in the Philippines Jul 45; (Co B, Boat Bn assaulted Tarakan Island 1 May 45 and Co A, Boat Bn assaulted Balikpapan 1 Jul 45)) regiment arrived at Portland Sub P-E 20 Dec 45 where inactivated 22 Dec 45.

Campaigns: *Bismarck Archipelago, New Guinea, Luzon*
Aug 45 Loc: Biak Island, less Boat Bn at Morotai Island and Shore Bn at Batangas Philippines

594th Engineer Boat and Shore Regiment

1 Feb 43 activated at Ft Devens Mass as Engineer Amphibian Regiment; moved to Cp Edwards Mass 9 Apr 43; redesignated Engineer Boat and Shore Regiment 10 May 43; transferred to Cp Gordon Johnston Fla 9 Sep 43; staged at Cp Stoneman Calif 15 Apr–2 May 44; departed San Francisco P/E 2 May 44 and arrived in Milne Bay New Guinea 24 May 44; landed in the Philippines 9 Jan 45 and inactivated at Yokohama Japan 15 Apr 46.

Campaigns: *Bismarck Archipelago*
Aug 45 Loc: Manila Philippines

922nd Engineer Aviation Regiment

1 Aug 42 activated at Geiger Field Spokane Wash; 1st Bn redesignated 863rd Engr Avn Bn 1 Feb 43; 2nd Bn redesignated 1881st Eng Avn Bn 10 Apr 43; 3rd Bn redesignated 852nd Engr Avn Bn 1 Jan 43; regiment assigned to 2nd Engineer Aviation Unit Training Center; staged at Cp Myles Standish Mass 9–20 Aug 43; departed New York P/E 20 Aug 43; arrived in England 25 Aug 43 and assigned to Eighth Air Force; assigned to Ninth Air Force 7 Apr 44; landed in France 15 Jun 44; crossed into Belgium 14 Sep 44 and into Luxembourg 31 Jan 45; assigned to IX Engineer Command 20 Feb 45; entered Germany 9 Feb 45; arrived at Cp Patrick Henry Va and inactivated 5 Dec 45.

Campaigns: *Normandy, Northern France, Rhineland, Ardennes-Alsace, Central Europe*
Aug 45 Loc: Urberach Germany

923rd Engineer Aviation Regiment (Colored)

1 Aug 42 activated at Eglin Field Fla; 1st Bn redesignated 859th Engineer Avn Bn 1 Jan 43 and 2nd and 3rd Bns redesignated 1882nd and 1883rd Eng Avn Bns 15 Mar 43; staged at Cp Kilmer N.J. 5–14 Aug 43; departed New York P/E 14 Aug 43; arrived in England 21 Aug 43 and assigned to Eighth Air Force; assigned to Air Technical Service Command 17 Mar 44; landed in France 14 Sep 44; assigned to IX Engineer Command 12 Jun 45; inactivated in Germany 26 Nov 45.

Campaigns: *Northern France, Rhineland*
Aug 45 Loc: Eschborn Germany

924th Engineer Aviation Regiment

1 Oct 42 activated at Richmond AAB, Va; moved to Dow Field Bangor Maine 12 Apr 43; 1st, 2nd, and 3rd Bns redesignated 1905th, 1906th, and 1913th Engr Avn Bns 2 Jun 43; staged at Cp Shanks N.Y. 20–25 Jul 43; departed New York P/E 25 Jul 43 and arrived in England 30 Jul 43 where assigned to Eighth Air Force until 7 Apr 44 when assigned to Ninth Air Force; landed in France 8 Jul 44; crossed into Belgium 14 Sep 44; crossed into Holland 14 Mar 45 and entered Germany 26 Mar 45 where remained throughout 1946.

Campaigns: *Normandy, Northern France, Rhineland, Central Europe*
Aug 45 Loc: Warendorf Germany

925th Engineer Airborne Regiment (Provisional)

1 Nov 42 activated at Westover Field Mass and 871st–874th A/B Engr Avn Bns initially assigned; disbanded upon activation of the 1st Airborne Engineer Aviation Unit Training Center and personnel and equipment transferred to it; disbanded effective 1 Apr 43.

925th Engineer Aviation Regiment

20 Jun 43 activated at March Field Calif; staged at Cp Kilmer N.J. 4 Aug–20 Aug 43; departed New York P/E 20 Aug 43 and arrived in England 25 Aug 43; assigned to Ninth Air Force 26 Nov 43; landed in France 1 Jul 44; assigned to IX Engineer Command 20 Feb 45; entered Germany 20 Mar 45 where inactivated 29 Jun 46.

Campaigns: *Normandy, Northern France, Rhineland, Central Europe*
Aug 45 Loc: Allach Germany

926th Engineer Aviation Regiment (I)

14 Mar 43 activated at March Field Calif; personnel and equipment transferred to the 4th Engineer Aviation Unit Training Center and regiment disbanded 10 May 43.

926th Engineer Aviation Regiment (II)

20 Jun 43 activated at Richmond AAB Va; staged at Cp Shanks N.Y. 15 Aug 43; departed New York P/E 20 Aug 43 and arrived in England 25 Aug 43 and assigned to Ninth Air Force 28 Apr 44; landed in France Jul 44 and assigned to IX Engineer Command 13 Feb 45; arrived at New York P/E 1 Oct 45 and inactivated Cp Kilmer N.J. 2 Oct 45.

Campaigns: *Normandy, Northern France, Rhineland, Central Europe*
Aug 45 Loc: Furth Germany

927th Engineer Aviation Regiment (Colored) (I)

11 Mar 43 activated at MacDill Field Fla; personnel and equipment transferred to 3rd Engineer Aviation Unit Training Center; disbanded there 1 May 43.

927th Engineer Aviation Regiment (Colored) (II)

9 Dec 44 activated at MacDill Field Fla under Third Air Force; arrived on Guam Island 1 Mar 45; later inactivated 30 Jan 46 in Hawaii.

Campaigns: *Pacific Theater without inscription*
Aug 45 Loc: Guam Island, less det Hqs at Hickam Field Hawaii

928th Engineer Aviation Regiment

10 Apr 43 activated at Richmond AAB Va; staged at Cp Patrick Henry Va 24 Dec 43–3 Jan 44; departed Hampton Roads P/E 3 Jan 44; arrived in Azore Islands 18 Jan 44 and departed 25 Feb 45; arrived back at Hampton Roads P/E 10 Mar 45; relocated to Geiger Field Wash 21 Apr 45; moved to Ft Lawton Wash 7 Jul 45 and left 16 Jul 45; arrived in Okinawa 7 Sep 45 where inactivated 30 Jun 46.

Aug 45 Loc: Shipment #9055-E at sea en route to Okinawa from Seattle

929th Engineer Aviation Regiment (Colored)

10 Apr 43 activated at Davis-Monthan Field Az; staged at Cp Stoneman Calif 11–28 Jan 44; departed San Francisco P/E 28 Jan 44 and landed in Milne Bay New Guinea 18 Feb 44; landed in the Philippines 24 Nov 44 where redesignated 1931st Engineer Aviation Company 25 Mar 45.

Campaigns: *New Guinea, Leyte*

930th Engineer Aviation Regiment

10 Apr 43 activated at Gowen Field Boise Idaho; staged at Cp Patrick Henry Va 5–13 Dec 43; departed Hampton Roads P/E 13 Dec 43; arrived in India 13 Feb 44 where assigned to Tenth Air Force 7 Oct 44; assigned to India-Burma Air Service Command 5 Apr 45; moved to China in Apr 45; returned to India Dec 45 where inactivated 26 Dec 45.

Campaigns: *Central Burma, China Offensive*
Aug 45 Loc: Kunming China

931st Engineer Aviation Regiment

20 Jun 43 activated at Geiger Field Spokane Wash; staged at Cp Stoneman Calif 11–29 Jan 44; departed San Francisco P/E 29 Jan 44; arrived at Finschhafen New Guinea 27 Feb 44 and assigned to Fifth Air Force; landed on Morotai Island 15 Sep 44 where redesignated 931st Engineer Construction Group (Avn) 10 Oct 44.

Campaigns: *New Guinea, Bismarck Archipelago*

932nd Engineer Aviation Regiment (Special) (Colored)

1 Jul 43 activated at Eglin Field Fla and assigned to Army Air Forces Proving Ground Command; disbanded 1 Jan 44 and personnel and equipment absorbed into that command.

933rd Engineer Aviation Regiment

20 Aug 43 activated at Davis-Monthan Field Az and disbanded there 20 Dec 43; personnel were absorbed within the Second Air Force.

933rd Engineer Aviation Regiment

16 Jun 44 activated at Geiger Field Wash; staged at Ft Lawton Wash 24 Aug–2 Sep 44; departed Seattle P/E 2 Sep 44 and arrived in Hawaii 9 Sep 44; departed Hawaii 22 Dec 44 and arrived in Guam 24 Dec 44; departed Guam 14 Jun 45 and arrived in Okinawa 29 Jun 45 where inactivated 30 Jun 46.

Campaigns: *Western Pacific, Ryukyus*
Aug 45 Loc: Guam Island

934th Engineer Aviation Regiment

20 Aug 43 activated at Gowan Field Boise Idaho; arrived at Geiger Field Wash 1 Dec 43 where disbanded 20 Dec 43 and personnel and equipment absorbed within Second Air Force.

935th Engineer Aviation Regiment

14 Dec 44 activated at Geiger Field Wash; staged at Ft Lawton Wash 12–17 Apr 45; departed Seattle P/E 17 Apr 45 and arrived in Hawaii 23 Apr 45; arrived in Okinawa 25 May 45 where inactivated 15 Mar 46.

Campaigns: *Ryukyus*
Aug 45 Loc: Ie Shima Island

1301st Engineer General Service Regiment

25 Jun 43 activated at Cp Ellis Ill; departed the United States 24 Mar 44 and arrived in England 5 Apr 44; landed in France 6 Aug 44; crossed into Luxembourg 27 Feb 45; entered Germany 20 Mar 45; sent to the Philippine Islands where arrived 25 Aug 45; returned to the United States 25 Jan 46 and inactivated at Cp Anza Calif 26 Jan 46.

Campaigns: *Northern France, Ardennes-Alsace, Central Europe, Pacific Theater without inscription*
Aug 45 Loc: Shipment #R5218-M en route to the Philippines at sea

1302nd Engineer General Service Regiment

25 Jun 43 activated at Cp Claiborne La and assigned to Eighth Service Command; staged at Cp Shanks N.Y. 11–18 Jan 44; departed New York P/E 18 Jan 44; arrived in England 31 Jan 44 and did not land in France until 19 Mar 45; arrived at Cp Kilmer N.J. 29 Jan 46 where inactivated 30 Jan 46.

Aug 45 Loc: Yeovil England, less 1st Bn at Southampton, Cos A and F at Milton, Co B at Barry, Co C at Ashchurch (Regt sch to SWPA in Shipment #R8485-C)

1303rd Engineer General Service Regiment

15 Jul 43 activated at Cp Ellis Ill and assigned to Sixth Service Command; staged at Cp Myles Standish Mass 13–24 Mar 44; departed Boston P/E 24 Mar 44 and arrived in England 3 Apr 44; landed in France 23 Jul 44; crossed into Luxembourg 12 Dec 44; entered Germany 13 Mar 45; departed France 23 Jun 45 and arrived in the Philippines 27 Jul 45; inactivated at Tokyo Japan 31 Jan 46.

Campaigns: *Normandy, Northern France, Rhineland, Ardennes-Alsace, Central Europe, Pacific Theater without inscription*
Aug 45 Loc: Manila Philippines

1304th Engineer General Service Regiment

15 Jul 43 activated at Cp Claiborne La and assigned to Eighth Service Command; transferred to Cp Sutton N.C. 30 Jul 43 and assigned to Fourth Service Command; redesignated there as 1304th Engineer Construction Battalion 1 Feb 44.

1305th Engineer General Service Regiment

15 Jul 43 activated at Cp Claiborne La; transferred to Cp Sutton N.C. 30 Jul 43; staged at Cp Stoneman Calif 25 Mar–31 Mar 44; departed San Francisco P/E 31 Mar 44; arrived in Guadalcanal 20 Apr 44 where disbanded both battalions 1 May 44 and regiment redesignated 1305th Engineer Construction Battalion same date.

1306th Engineer General Service Regiment

25 Aug 43 activated at Cp Ellis Ill and assigned to Sixth Service Command; staged at Cp Shanks N.Y. 16–29 Mar 44; departed New York P/E 29 Mar 44 and arrived in England 9 Apr 44; landed in France 5 Aug 44; crossed into Belgium 26 Dec 44; crossed into Luxembourg 9 Mar 45; entered Germany 21 Mar 45; departed France 23 Jun 45 and arrived in the Philippines 27 Jul 45; inactivated at Tokyo Japan 31 May 46.

Campaigns: *Northern France, Rhineland, Ardennes-Alsace, Central Europe, Pacific Theater without inscription*
Aug 45 Loc: Manila Philippines

1307th Engineer General Service Regiment

25 Aug 43 activated at Cp Claiborne La and staged at Cp Stoneman Calif 10 Mar 44 until departed San Francisco P/E 16 Mar 44; arrived in Australia 2 Apr 44 and moved to Milne Bay New Guinea where redesignated 1307th Engineer Construction Battalion on 1 Nov 44.

Campaigns: *New Guinea*

1308th Engineer General Service Regiment

25 Aug 43 activated at Cp Sutton N.C. and assigned to the Fourth Service Command; staged at Cp Shanks N.Y. 4 May 44 until departed New York P/E 12 May 44; arrived in England on 23 May 44 and landed in France during August 44; sent to Ulithi Atoll 16 Aug 45 and to Okinawa 14 Sep 45; inactivated in Korea 16 May 46.

Campaigns: *Northern France, Rhineland, Ardennes-Alsace, Pacific Theater without inscription*
Aug 45 Loc: Shipment #R0598-H at sea between Eniwetok and Ulithi Atoll

1309th Engineer General Service Regiment

25 Aug 43 activated at Cp Ellis Ill and assigned to Sixth Service Command where redesignated the 1309th Engineer Construction Battalion on 20 Mar 44.

1310th Engineer General Service Regiment (Colored)

25 May 43 activated at Cp Claiborne La under the Eighth Service Command and staged at Cp Shanks N.Y. 8 Dec 43 until departed New York P/E 2 Jan 44; arrived in England on 8 Jan 44 and landed in France 24 Jul 44; arrived in the Philippines during August 45; arrived at Los Angeles P/E 22 Jan 46 and inactivated there on 23 Jan 46.

Campaigns: *Normandy, Northern France, Pacific Theater without inscription*
Aug 45 Loc: Shipment #R5218-N at sea en route to Philippines

1311th Engineer General Service Regiment (Colored)

25 May 43 activated at Cp Claiborne La and assigned to the Eighth Service Command; participated in the Tennessee Mnvrs Nov 43–Feb 44; staged at Cp Stoneman Calif 25 Apr 44 until departed San Francisco P/E 2 Jun 44; arrived at Finschhafen New Guinea on 23 Jun 44; sent to the Philippines in Aug 45 where inactivated on 28 Feb 46.

Campaigns: *New Guinea*
Aug 45 Loc: Manila Philippine Islands

1312th Engineer General Service Regiment (Colored)

25 Jun 43 activated at Cp Claiborne La and staged at Cp Stoneman Calif 11 Jan 44 until departed San Francisco P/E 20 Jan 44; arrived at Oro Bay New Guinea on 6 Feb 44 and landed in the Philippine Islands 18 Feb 45 where inactivated on 20 Jan 46.

Campaigns: *New Guinea, Luzon*
Aug 45 Loc: Luzon Philippine Islands, less 1st Bn at Oro Bay New Guinea

1313th Engineer General Service Regiment (Colored)

25 Jun 43 activated at Cp Claiborne La and assigned to Eighth Service Command; staged at Cp Myles Standish Mass 11–18 Jan 44; departed Boston P/E 18 Jan 44; arrived in England 29 Jan 44; landed in France 31 Aug 44; departed France 9 Aug 45 and arrived at Hampton roads P/E 20 Aug 45; moved to Cp Claiborne La 24 Aug 45 where inactivated 20 Nov 45.

Campaigns: *Northern France, Central Europe*
Aug 45 Loc: Shipment #R5218-P at sea en route to USA (sch to SWPA)

1314th Engineer General Service Regiment (Colored)

25 Jun 43 activated at Cp Claiborne La and assigned to Eighth Service Command; staged at Cp Shanks N.Y. 12–22 Jan 44; departed New York P/E 22 Jan 44 and arrived in England 28 Jan 44; landed in France 25 Aug 44 and arrived 1 Sep 45 in the Philippines after hostilities in Europe ended; left the Philippines 5 Jan 46 and arrived at Cp Stoneman Calif 25 Jan 46 where inactivated 27 Jan 46.

Campaigns: *Northern France, Rhineland, Pacific Theater without inscription*
Aug 45 Loc: Shipment #R5218-R

1315th Engineer General Service Regiment (Colored)

15 Jul 43 activated at Cp Claiborne La and assigned to Eighth Service Command; transferred to Cp Sutton N.C. 1 Aug 43; arrived at Great Smoky National Park near Ritter N.C. 16 Dec 43 and participated in Tennessee Mnvrs Jan-Feb 44; arrived back at Cp Sutton N.C. 29 Feb 44 where redesignated 1315th Engineer Construction Battalion 20 Mar 44.

1316th Engineer General Service Regiment (Colored)

15 Jul 43 activated at Cp Claiborne La and assigned to Eighth Service Command; transferred to Cp Sutton N.C. 1 Aug 43; moved to California-Arizona Maneuver Area 14 Jan 44; arrived at Ft Huachuca Az 30 Apr 44; staged at Ft Lawton Wash 3–7 Oct 44 and departed Seattle P/E 7 Oct 44; arrived at Oahu Hawaii 14 Oct 44 where disbanded 17 Dec 44.

Campaigns: *Pacific Theater without inscription*

1317th Engineer General Service Regiment (Colored)

25 Aug 43 activated at Cp Ellis Ill and assigned to Sixth Service Command; staged at Cp Shanks N.Y. 2–21 Mar 44; departed New York P/E 21 Mar 44 and arrived in England 27 Mar 44; landed in France 9 Feb 45 and crossed into Belgium 15 Feb 45; entered Germany 2 Apr 45; left France 7 Aug 45 and arrived at New York P/E 18 Aug 45; moved to Cp Claiborne La where inactivated 20 Nov 45.

Campaigns: *Rhineland, Central Europe*
Aug 45 Loc: Shipment #R5218-S en route to USA (sch to SWPA)

1318th Engineer General Service Regiment (Colored)

25 Aug 43 activated at Cp Butner N.C. under the Fourth Service Command; transferred to Cp Sutton N.C. 17 Jan 44 where redesignated 1318th Engineer Construction Battalion on 20 Mar 44; battalion reorganized and redesignated as 1318th Engineer General Service Regiment there 25 May 44; staged at Cp Shanks N.Y. 16 Oct 44 until departed New York P/E 30 Oct 44; arrived in England 10 Nov 44 and landed in France on 5 Mar 45; sent to Ulithi Atoll on 21 Aug 45; inactivated on Okinawa 30 Apr 46.

Campaigns: *Rhineland, Pacific Theater without inscription*
Aug 45 Loc: Shipment #R0146-K at sea approaching Eniwetok

1319th Engineer General Service Regiment (Colored)

25 Aug 43 activated at Cp Butner N.C. under the Fourth Service Command; transferred to Cp Sutton N.C. 17 Jan 44 where redesignated 1319th Engineer Construction Battalion on 20 Mar 44; battalion reorganized and redesignated 1319th Engineer General Service Regiment there 25 May 44; staged at Vancouver Barracks Wash 24 Oct 44 until departed Portland Sub-P/E 31 Oct 44; arrived in Hawaii 8 Nov 44 where disbanded 17 Dec 44.

Campaigns: *Pacific Theater without inscription*

1320th Engineer General Service Regiment (Colored)

16 Aug 43 activated at Cp Swift Tex under the Eighth Service Command and staged at Cp Stoneman Calif 10 Feb 44 until departed San Francisco P/E 15 Feb 44; arrived in Hawaii on 20 Feb 44 where disbanded on 17 Dec 44.

Campaigns: *Pacific Theater without inscription*

1321st Engineer General Service Regiment (Colored)

16 Aug 43 activated at Cp Sutton N.C. and participated in Tennessee Mnvrs Jan-Feb 44; returned to Cp Sutton N.C. 29 Feb 44 where redesignated 1321st Engineer Construction Battalion 20 Mar 44; battalion reorganized and redesignated 1321st Engineer General Service Regiment there 25 May 44; staged at Cp Myles Standish Mass 29 Sep 44 until departed Boston P/E 7 Oct 44; arrived in England 15 Oct 44 and landed in France 7 Dec 44; arrived on Ie Shima Island 12 Aug 45; served in Korea through the end of 1946.

Campaigns: *Rhineland, Pacific Theater without inscription*
Aug 45 Loc: Shipment #R5098-G at sea

1322 Engineer General Service Regiment (Colored)

16 Aug 43 activated at Cp Swift Tex under the Eighth Service Command and staged at Cp Stoneman Calif 5 Jan 44 until departed San Francisco P/E 8 Jan 44; arrived in Hawaii 16 Jan 44 and arrived in Palau Islands 3 Nov 44 less 1st Bn sent to Leyte Philippines 15 Nov 44; entire regiment arrived at Tinian on 27 Nov 45 where inactivated on 30 Jan 46.

Campaigns: *Western Pacific, Leyte*
Aug 45 Loc: Tinian Island, less 1st Bn at Leyte Philippine Islands

1323rd Engineer General Service Regiment (Colored)

25 Aug 43 activated at Cp Swift Tex and assigned to Eighth Service Command; staged at Cp Myles Standish Mass 13–23 Mar 44; departed Boston P/E 23 Mar 44; arrived in England 3 Apr 44; landed in France 7 Jul 44; entered Germany 1 Apr 45; departed France 17 Jul 45 and arrived in the Philippines 26 Aug 45 where inactivated 10 May 46.

Campaigns: *Normandy, Northern France, Rhineland, Ardennes-Alsace, Central Europe,*
  Pacific Theater without inscription
Aug 45 Loc: Shipment #R0102-C at sea en route to Batangas Philippines

1324th Engineer General Service Regiment (Colored)

25 May 44 redesignated from 1324th Engineer Construction Battalion at Cp Claiborne La; staged at Cp Shanks N.Y. 28 Oct–3 Nov 44; departed New York 3 Nov 44; arrived in France 13 Nov 44; departed Marseille France 14 Jul 45 and sent to Okinawa 15 Sep 45 where inactivated 20 Jan 46.

Campaigns: *Rhineland, Pacific Theater without inscription*
Aug 45 Loc: Shipment #R0146-D at sea en route to Okinawa

1325th Engineer General Service Regiment (Colored)

25 May 44 redesignated from 1325th Engineer Construction Battalion at Cp Claiborne La; staged at Cp Kilmer N.J. 6–22 Oct 44; departed New York P/E 22 Oct 44; arrived in England 2 Nov 44; landed in France 4 Jan 45; departed France 21 Jul 45 and landed in Hawaii 12 Aug 45; departed Hawaii 15 Aug 45 and arrived in Guam 27 Aug 45 where inactivated 20 Jun 46.

Campaigns: *Rhineland, Pacific Theater without inscription*
Aug 45 Loc: Oahu Hawaii unloading from Shipment #R0146-B

1326th Engineer General Service Regiment (Colored)

25 Mar 44 redesignated from 1326th Engineer Construction Battalion at Cp Claiborne La; staged at Cp Kilmer N.J. 2–19 Feb 45; departed New York P/E 19 Feb 45 and arrived at Le Havre France 1 Mar 45; departed France 10 Jul 45 and arrived in Okinawa 16 Aug 45 where inactivated 15 May 46.

Campaigns: *European Theater without inscription, Pacific Theater without inscription*
Aug 45 Loc: Shipment #R0146-L at sea

1327th Engineer General Service Regiment (Colored)

25 May 44 redesignated from 1327th Engineer Construction Battalion at Cp Claiborne La; HHC moved by air in echelons with one battalion from Miami Port of Aerial Embarkation commencing 3 Nov 44 while another battalion moved via sea from Los Angeles P/E; HHC and one battalion arrived at New Delhi India 13 Nov 44 while 2nd Battalion departed Los Angeles P/E 20 Dec 44 and arrived at Bombay India 23 Jan 45; regiment inactivated in India 15 Jan 46.

Campaigns: *Central Burma, India-Burma*
Aug 45 Loc: Calcutta India

1329th Engineer General Service Regiment (Colored)

25 May 44 redesignated from 1329th Engineer Construction Battalion at Cp Claiborne La; staged at Cp Shanks N.Y. 19–26 Dec 44; departed New York P/E 26 Dec 44 and arrived in England 7 Jan 45; departed England 22 Jun 45 and arrived at Manila Philippines 27 Jul 45; inactivated in Japan 30 Apr 46.

Campaigns: *European Theater without inscription, Pacific Theater without inscription*
Aug 45 Loc: Manila Philippines

1330th Engineer General Service Regiment (Colored)

25 May 44 redesignated from 1330th Engineer Construction Battalion at Cp Claiborne La; staged at Cp Shanks N.Y. 19–26 Dec 44; departed New York P/E 26 Dec 44 and arrived in England 7 Jan 45; landed in France 23 Mar 45 and departed 10 Jul 45; arrived in Okinawa 16 Aug 45 where inactivated 31 Mar 46.

Campaigns: *European Theater without inscription, Pacific Theater without inscription*
Aug 45 Loc: Shipment #R0146-G at sea

1331st Engineer General Service Regiment (Colored)

25 May 44 redesignated from 1331st Engineer Construction Battalion at Cp Claiborne La; staged at Cp Shanks N.Y. 19 Dec 44–11 Feb 45; departed New York P/E 11 Feb 45 and arrived in France 23 Feb 45; departed France 10 Jul 45 and arrived in Okinawa 16 Aug 45; inactivated in Japan 28 Mar 46.

Campaigns: *Rhineland, Pacific Theater without inscription*
Aug 45 Loc: Shipment #R0146-M at sea

1332nd Engineer General Service Regiment (Colored)

25 May 44 redesignated from 1332nd Engineer Construction Battalion at Cp Ellis Ill; staged at Cp Shanks N.Y. 18–26 Dec 44; departed New York P/E 26 Dec 44 and arrived in England 7 Jan 45; departed England 22 Jun 45 and arrived in the Philippines 27 Jul 45 where inactivated 15 Apr 46.

Campaigns: *European Theater without inscription, Western Pacific*
Aug 45 Loc: Hollandia New Guinea

1333rd Engineer General Service Regiment (Colored)

25 May 44 redesignated from 1333rd Engineer Construction Battalion at Cp Ellis Ill; departed New York P/E 11 Nov 44 and arrived in France 25 Nov 44; departed France 14 Jul 45 and arrived on Eniwetok Island 12 Aug 45 and moved to Ulithi Island 16 Aug 45; arrived in Okinawa 14 Sep 45 where inactivated 31 Mar 46.

Campaigns: *Rhineland, Pacific Theater without inscription*
Aug 45 Loc: In transit to Ulithi Atoll at sea

1349th Engineer General Service Regiment (Colored)

13 Aug 44 redesignated from 383rd Engineer Battalion (Separate) (Colored) in England; landed in France 13 Feb 45 and assigned to Normandy Base Section; inactivated in Germany 30 Nov 46.

Campaigns: *European Theater without inscription*
Aug 45 Loc: Le Havre France

1749th Engineer General Service Regiment (Colored)

30 Dec 44 activated at Ft Lewis Wash and assigned to Ninth Service Command; sent to Yakima Firing Center (Ft Lewis Sub Post) 1 Oct 45; inactivated at Ft Lewis 28 Nov 45.

2201st Engineer Aviation Regiment

17 Aug 45 activated at Kunming China per authority of AG 322 (30 Jul 45) OB-I-AFRPG-M from War Dept dated 7 Aug 45 (S) and assigned to XIV Air Force Engineer Command; departed China 1 Dec 45 and inactivated in India 27 Dec 45.

2822nd Engineer General Service Regiment (Colored)

26 Feb 45 activated at Ft Lewis Wash and assigned to Ninth Service Command; transferred to Sierra Ordnance Depot Calif 4 Jun 45; arrived back at Ft Lewis Wash 20 Jun 45 where disbanded 28 Sep 45.

Chapter 42

Engineer and Selected Transportation Battalions

Battalions:

1–13, 15–18, 20, 22–25, 27, 29–31, 33–35, 37, 42–44, 46–57, 60, 61, 63–65, 78–82, 84–98, 101–121, 124–127, 129–133, 135, 138, 139, 142, 145–161, 163–174, 176–188, 202–209, 215, 216, 220, 233–260, 263–266, 269–271, 275–329, 331, 336, 337, 339, 340, 348, 349, 353, 367, 369–371, 374–389, 401–405, 407–411, 487, 489, 515, 516, 551–558, 562–564, 599–607, 643, 648–657, 659, 660, 692, 711–730*, 732–735*, 737*, 740*, 741*, 743–746*, 748–750*, 752*, 753, 754*, 755*, 759*, 760, 762, 770*, 790*, 796, 801–886, 936–942, 1001–1004, 1006–1009, 1251–1300, 1304, 1305, 1307, 1309, 1315, 1318, 1319, 1321, 1324–1334, 1339–1346, 1393–1399, 1551, 1553, 1554, 1629, 1631, 1635–1637, 1684–1690, 1692–1700, 1759, 1760, 1777, 1778, 1800, 1862–1917, 1921–1924, 2755, 2756, 2759, 2803–2808, 2819, 2826–2834, 2912, 2913, 3051–3053, 3171 Provisional, 3189, 3190, 3230–3233, 5211 Provisional, 6486 Provisional, 6487 Privisional, 6495 Provisional, 6496 Provisional, Special Topographic, Aviation Topographic Training (Special)

*Converted or formed as Transportation Corps battalions (Railway)

⭐ EXAMPLE — HOW TO USE THIS TABLE

Unit Designation and Type	Date Formed and Location (Source of Unit)/Inactivation and Location	August 1945 Location

Overseas Wartime Locations followed by - **Campaign Key Numbers** and PE return to United States, if applicable or space allows
(notes and remarks in parenthesis)

27th Engineer Construction Bn	15 Mar 43 Cp Breckinridge Ky (1st Bn, 27th Engr Regt)/10 May 46 Japan	Manila Philippines

SFPE: 6 Jan 44   Goodenough I: 31 Jan 44   New Guinea: 21 Mar 44   Noemfoor I: 2 Jul 44   Philippines: 22 Oct 44 - **13,14,15**
(redes from Engr Combat Bn 1 Nov 44)

In this example, the 27th Engineer Construction Battalion was formed from the 1st Battalion of the 27th Engineer Regiment at Camp Breckinridge, Kentucky, on 15 Mar 1943. Earlier service of this unit can be tracked by looking up the service of the 27th Engineer Regiment in Chapter 41. The italicized notes show that the 27th Engineer Construction Battalion was initially the 27th Engineer Combat Battalion until converted on 1 November 1944. The 27th Engineer Combat Battalion *departed* San Francisco Port of Embarkation on 6 January 1944 and *arrived* at Goodenough Island on 31 January 1944. The battalion moved to New Guinea on 21 March 1944, to Noemfoor Island on 2 July 1944, and to the Philippines on 22 October 1944. There it was reorganized and redesignated as the 27th Engineer Construction Battalion on 1 November 1944 (per note). It participated in the Leyte, Luzon, and New Guinea campaigns of World War II. This information was derived by indexing the boldfaced campaign key numbers with Appendix I. The battalion was stationed at Manila in the Philippines during August 1945, and was inactivated in Japan on 10 May 1946.

BATTALION DESIGNATION AND TYPE	FORMED (SOURCE OF UNIT) / INACTIVATION *Active through 1946	AUGUST 1945 LOCATION
1st Engineer Combat Bn	12 Oct 39 Ft Dupont Del (1st Bn, 1st Engrs) / *	Frant Lazne Czechoslovakia

NYPE: 2 Aug 42   Scotland: 7 Aug 42   N.Africa: 8 Nov 42   Sicily: 10 Jul 43   England: 8 Nov 43
France-ETO: 6 Jun 44 - **23,25,26,30,32,34,36,38** *(1st Inf Div)*

2nd Engineer Combat Bn	16 Oct 39 Ft Logan Colo (1st Bn, 2nd Engrs)/*	Cp Swift Tex

NYPE: 8 Oct 43   England: 18 Oct 43   France-ETO: 7 Jun 44 - **25,26,30,32,34**   BPE: 19 Jul 45 *(2nd Inf Div)*

3rd Engineer Combat Bn	26 Sep 41 Schofield Bks Hawaii (3rd Engr Regt) / *	Davao Mindanao Philippines

Hawaii: 26 Sep 41   Australia: 8 Aug 43   Goodenough I: 15 Feb 44   New Guinea: 22 Apr 44   Philippines: 20 Oct 44 - **6,13,14,15,20** *(24th Inf Div)*

4th Engineer Combat Bn	1 Jun 40 Ft Benning Ga /19 Feb 46 Cp Butner N.C.	Cp Butner N.C.

NYPE: 18 Jan 44   England: 29 Jan 44   France-ETO: 6 Jun 44 - **25,26,30,32,34**   NYPE: 12 Jul 45 *(Engr Mtz Bn 9 Sep 42–1 Aug 43)*
(4th Inf Div)

5th Engineer Combat Bn	23 Jan 45 Malone Belgium (1278th Engr Comb Bn) / 26 Nov 45 NYPE	Frankenthal Germany

Belgium-ETO: 23 Jan 45 - **25,26,34**   NYPE: 25 Nov 45

6th Engineer Combat Bn	12 Oct 39 Ft Lawton Wash (1st Bn, 6th Engr Regt) / *	Bagabag Philippines

SFPE: 20 Sep 43   Hawaii: 26 Sep 43   New Guinea: 7 Feb 44   Philippines: 9 Jan 45 - **14,15** *(6th Inf Div)*

7th Engineer Combat Bn	16 Oct 39 Ft Logan Colo / 20 Sep 46 Cp Campbell Ky	Cp Campbell Ky

NYPE: 30 Apr 42   Iceland: 11 May 42   England: 9 Aug 43   France-ETO: 9 Jul 44 - **25,26,30,32,34**   BPE: 20 Jul 45 *(5th Inf Div)*

8th Engineer Combat Squadron	Active at Ft McIntosh Tex / *	Lucena Philippines

SFPE: 24 May 43   Australia: 18 Jun 43   New Guinea: 29 Dec 43   Los Negros: 28 Feb 44   Manus I: 15 Mar 44
Philippines: 20 Oct 44 - **3,13,14,15** *(1st Cav Div)*

9th Armored Engineer Bn	1 Nov 41 Ft Riley Kans /13 Oct 46 Cp Patrick Henry Va	Bayreuth Germany

NYPE: 20 Aug 44   England: 26 Aug 44   France-ETO: 6 Oct 44 - **25,26,34**   HRPE: 12 Oct 45 *(redes from Engr Sqdn 3 Jun 42)*
(9th Armd Div)

10th Engineer Combat Bn	13 Oct 39 Ft Lewis Wash (2nd Bn, 6th Engr Regt) / *	Salzburg Austria

HRPE: 27 Oct 42   N.Africa: 8 Nov 42   Sicily: 10 Jul 43   Italy: 18 Sep 43   France-ETO: 15 Aug 44 - **23,24,25,26,29,34,35,36,37,38**
NYPE: 4 Sep 46 *(3rd Inf Div)*

11th Engineer Combat Bn	1 Apr 43 Ft Clayton Canal Zone (11th Engr Regt) / 30 Nov 46 Austria	Gunzberg Germany

Panama: 1 Apr 43   SFPE: 10 Sep 43   BPE: 10 Nov 44   Scotland: 17 Nov 44   France-ETO: 31 Dec 44 - **25,26,34**

12th Engineer Combat Bn	1 Jul 40 Cp Jackson S.C. / 25 Oct 45 Ft Leonard Wood Mo	Ft Leonard Wood Mo

NYPE: 5 Dec 43   England: 15 Dec 43   France-ETO: 3 Jul 44 - **26,30,32,34**   HRPE: 13 Jul 45 *(Engr Mtz Bn 21 May 42–1 May 43) (8th Inf Div)*

13th Engineer Combat Bn	1 Jul 40 Cp Ord Calif / *	Okinawa

SFPE: 15 Apr 43   Attu I: 11 May 43   Hawaii: 17 Sep 43   Eniwetok: 25 Sep 44   Manus I: 3 Oct 44   Philippines: 20 Oct 44
Okinawa: 1 Apr 45 - **2,10,13,19** *(Engr Mtz Bn 21 May 42–1 May 43) (7th Inf Div)*

15th Engineer Combat Bn	1 Aug 40 Ft Bragg N.C. / 30 Nov 46 Germany	Hepberg Germany

NYPE: 12 Dec 42   N.Africa: 25 Dec 42   Sicily: 1 Aug 43   England: 28 Nov 43   France-ETO: 6 Jun 44 - **23,25,26,30,32,34,36,38**
(9th Inf Div)

16th Armored Engineer Bn	15 Jul 40 Ft Knox Ky /13 Apr 46 NYPE	Salzburg Austria

NYPE: 11 May 42   N.Ireland: 18 May 42   N.Africa: 21 Dec 42   Sicily: 10 Jul 43   Italy: 10 Nov 43 - **23,24,29,31,33,35,38** *(1st Armd Div)*

BATTALION DESIGNATION AND TYPE	FORMED (SOURCE OF UNIT)/INACTIVATION *Active through 1946	AUGUST 1945 LOCATION
17th Armored Engineer Bn	15 Jul 40 Ft Benning Ga / *	Baddeckemstadt Germany
NYPE: 12 Dec 42 N.Africa: 25 Dec 42 Sicily: 10 Jul 43 England: 25 Nov 43 France-ETO: 10 Jun 44 - **23,25,26,30,32,34,36** NYPE: 4 Feb 46 *(2nd Armd Div)*		
18th Engineer Combat Bn	8 Jan 45 Cp Bowie Tex (1st Bn, 18th Engr Regt) / 20 Feb 46 Ft Ord Calif	Blythe Calif
20th Engineer Combat Bn	15 Jan 44 Cornwall England (1st Bn, 20th Engr Regt) / 30 Mar 46 Germany	Susice Czechoslovakia
England: 15 Jan 44 France-ETO: 6 Jun 44 - **25,26,30,32,34**		
22nd Armored Engineer Bn	1 Oct 41 Ft Knox Ky /13 Oct 45 Cp Myles Standish Mass	Bad Tennstadt Germany
NYPE: 11 Feb 44 England: 23 Feb 44 France-ETO: 26 Jul 44 - **25,26,30,32,34** BPE: 12 Oct 45 *(5th Armd Div)*		
23rd Armored Engineer Bn	15 Apr 41 Cp Beauregard La /10 Nov 45 Germany	Arheiligen Germany
NYPE: 5 Sep 43 England: 15 Sep 43 France-ETO: 23 Jun 44 - **25,26,30,32,34** *(3rd Armd Div)*		
24th Armored Engineer Bn	15 Apr 41 Pine Camp N.Y. / 21 Apr 46 NYPE	Reideberg Germany
BPE: 29 Dec 43 England: 9 Jan 44 France-ETO: 13 Jul 44 - **25,26,30,32,34** NYPE: 20 Apr 46 *(4th Armd Div)*		
25th Armored Engineer Bn	15 Feb 42 Ft Knox Ky / 22 Sep 45 Cp Patrick Henry Va	Apolda Germany
NYPE: 11 Feb 44 England: 26 Feb 44 France-ETO: 19 Jul 44 - **25,26,30,32,34** HRPE: 22 Sep 45 *(6th Armd Div)*		
27th Engineer Bn (Combat)	9 Oct 39 Ft Dupont Del (2nd Bn, 1st Engrs) / 28 Mar 42 Ft Buchanan Puerto Rico	
NYPE: 12 Oct 39 Puerto Rico: 20 Oct 39		
27th Engineer Construction Bn	15 Mar 43 Cp Breckinridge Ky (1st Bn, 27th Engr Regt) /10 May 46 Japan	Manila Philippines
SFPE: 6 Jan 44 Goodenough I: 31 Jan 44 New Guinea: 21 Mar 44 Noemfoor I: 2 Jul 44 Philippines: 22 Oct 44 - **13,14,15** *(redes from Engr Combat Bn 1 Nov 44)*		
29th Engineer Base Topographic Bn	Active at Portland Oreg / *	Shipment #4815 unloading
SFPE: 6 Jul 45 Philippines: 29 Jul 45 - None *(Engr Bn [Topographic] [Army] P - 7 Nov 41 when redes Engr Topographic Bn [GHQ] until 20 Jun 44)*		
30th Engineer Base Topographic Bn	1 Sep 39 Portland Oreg / *	Schofield Barracks Hawaii
HRPE: 25 Nov 43 N.Africa: 4 Dec 43 BPE: 17 Nov 44 SPE: 1 Jan 45 Hawaii: 6 Jan 45 *(Engr Bn [Topographic] [Army] 1 Sep 39–15 Dec 41 when redes Engr Topographic Bn [GHQ] until 1 Nov 44 when redes Engr Base Topographic Bn)*		
31st Engineer Combat Bn (I)	15 Dec 41 Ft Belvoir Va/29 Apr 42 Ft Belvoir Va redes 31st Engr Regt	
31st Engineer Combat Bn (II)	22 Mar 43 Ft Belvoir Va (1st Bn, 31st Engr Regt) / 9 Mar 46 NYPE	Ruette Belgium
NYPE: 22 Oct 44 England: 2 Nov 44 France-ETO: 31 Dec 44 - **25,26,34** NYPE: 7 Mar 46		
33rd Armored Engineer Bn	2 Mar 42 Cp Polk La/11 Oct 45 NYPE	Gollma Germany
NYPE: 7 Jun 44 England: 13 Jun 44 France-ETO: 10 Aug 44 - **25,26,32,34** NYPE: 10 Oct 45 *(7th Armd Div)*		
34th Engineer Combat Bn	9 May 44 Hawaii (1st Bn, 34th Engr Regt) / *	Okinawa
Hawaii: 9 May 44 Saipan: 17 Jun 44 Espiritu Santo: 16 Feb 45 Tsugen Shima I: 10 Apr 45 - **6,19,21**		
35th Engineer Combat Bn	25 Sep 43 Cp White Oreg (1st Bn, 35th Engr Regt) /17 Sep 45 NYPE	Pausa Germany
NYPE: 2 Jul 44 England: 12 Jul 44 France-ETO: 7 Aug 44 - **25,26,32,34** NYPE: 15 Sep 45		
37th Engineer Combat Bn	18 Mar 43 Cp Beale Calif (1st Bn, 37th Engr Regt) / 2 Dec 45 NYPE	Einbeck Germany
BPE: 25 Oct 43 England: 1 Nov 43 France-ETO: 6 Jun 44 - **26,30,32,34** NYPE: 1 Dec 45		
42nd Engineer Construction Bn	25 May 44 Cp Earle Alaska (42nd Engr Regt) / *	Manila Philippines
Alaska: 25 May 44 SPE: 18 Jul 44 SFPE: 30 Mar 45 Philippines: 19 Apr 45 - **14**		
43rd Engineer Construction Bn	22 Apr 44 Australia (43rd Engr Regt) / *	Manila Philippines
Australia: 22 Apr 44 New Guinea: 8 Aug 44 Morotai I: 21 Sep 44 Philippines: 11 Jan 45 - **14,15**		
44th Engineer Combat Bn	1 Apr 43 Cp McCoy Wis (1st Bn, 44th Engr Regt) /14 Sep 45 Cp Patrick Henry Va	Krau Germany
NYPE: 23 Mar 44 England: 4 Apr 44 France-ETO: 6 Jul 44 - **25,26,30,32,34** HRPE: 14 Sep 45		
46th Engineer Construction Bn	22 Apr 44 Sydney Australia (46th Engr Regt) / *	Manila Philippines
Australia: 22 Apr 44 New Guinea: 4 May 44 Philippines: 20 Oct 44 - **13,14,15**		
47th Engineer Construction Bn	26 Apr 44 Hawaii (1st Bn, 47th Engr Regt) / 31 Dec 46 Okinawa	Okinawa
Hawaii: 26 Apr 44 Eniwetok I: 14 Jun 44 Saipan: 25 Jun 44 Okinawa: 11 May 45 - **10,19,21**		
48th Engineer Combat Bn	20 Apr 43 Cp Polk La (1st Bn, 48th Engr Regt) /19 Oct 45 Cp Patrick Henry Va	Eberbach Germany
NYPE: 21 Aug 43 N.Africa: 2 Sep 43 Italy: 10 Oct 43 France-ETO: 15 Aug 44 - **25,26,29,34,35,37** HRPE: 19 Oct 45		
49th Engineer Combat Bn	1 Apr 43 Cp Carson Colo (1st Bn, 49th Engr Regt)/27 Nov 45 NYPE	Eisleben Germany
HRPE: 13 Nov 43 N.Africa: 3 Dec 43 England: 20 Jan 44 France-ETO: 6 Jun 44 - **25,26,30,32,34** NYPE: 25 Nov 45		
50th Engineer Combat Bn	21 Jan 43 Ojai Calif (1st Bn, 50th Engr Regt) / 20 Feb 46 Korea	Okinawa
SFPE: 15 Apr 43 Attu I: 11 May 43 Hawaii: 2 Oct 43 Kwajalein: 2 Feb 44 Philippines: 20 Oct 44 Okinawa: 1 Apr 45 - **10,13,19**		

BATTALION DESIGNATION AND TYPE	FORMED (SOURCE OF UNIT) / INACTIVATION *Active through 1946	AUGUST 1945 LOCATION

51st Engineer Combat Bn
1 Apr 43 Plattsburgh Bks N.Y. (1st Bn, 51st Engr Regt) / 27 Oct 45 Cp Patrick   Biebelried Germany
HRPE: 12 Nov 43   N.Africa: 4 Dec 43   England: 20 Jan 44   France-ETO: 27 Jun 44 - **25,26,30,32,34**   HRPE: 27 Oct 45   Henry Va

52nd Engineer Combat Bn
1 Apr 43 Cp Butner N.C. (1st Bn, 52nd Engr Regt) /10 Mar 46 Japan   Cebu Philippines
SPE: 21 Jun 44   Hawaii: 27 Jun 44   Angaur I: 17 Sep 44   New Caledonia: 22 Jan 45   Philippines: 17 Mar 45 - **13,21**

53rd Armored Engineer Bn
1 Apr 42 Ft Knox Ky /12 Nov 45 Cp Kilmer N.J.   Norten Germany
NYPE: 7 Nov 44   England: 18 Nov 44   France-ETO: 7 Jan 45 - **25,26,34**   NYPE: 11 Nov 45 *(8th Armd Div)*

54th Engineer Combat Bn
Co B of 54th Engr Combat Bn activated 6 Jul 42 at Efate New Hebrides and redes there as 515th Engr Combat Co on 15 Jan 44, thus battalion never fully formed.

55th Armored Engineer Bn
15 Jul 42 Ft Benning Ga /13 Oct 45 Cp Patrick Henry Va   Garmisch-Partenkirchen
NYPE: 12 Sep 44   England: 23 Sep 44   France-ETO: 23 Sep 44 - **25,26,34**   HRPE: 13 Oct 45 *(10th Armd Div)*   Germany

56th Armored Engineer Bn
15 Aug 42 Cp Polk La / 31 Aug 45 Austria   Urfahr Austria
NYPE: 29 Sep 44   France-ETO: 9 Oct 44 - **25,26,34** *(11th Armd Div)*

57th Engineer Combat Bn
23 Apr 42 New Caledonia /10 Dec 45 Ft Lawton Wash   Cebu Philippines
New Caledonia: 23 Apr 42   Guadalcanal: 24 Nov 42   Fiji I: 29 Mar 43   Bougainville: 9 Jan 44   Philippines: 26 Jan 45 - **11,13,16,20**
(Americal Div)

60th Engineer Combat Bn
25 Jan 43 Cp San Luis Obispo Calif / 20 Nov 45 Cp Breckinridge Ky   Winnigen Germany
NYPE: 12 May 44   England: 25 May 44   France-ETO: 7 Jul 44 - **25,26,30,32,34** *(35th Inf Div)*

61st Engineer Combat Bn
25 Jan 43 Atlantic Beach Fla /18 Sep 45 Germany   Mulheim Germany
NYPE: 24 Mar 44   England: 4 Apr 44   France-ETO: 1 Jul 44 - **30,32,34**

63rd Engineer Combat Bn
1 Feb 43 Ft Lewis Wash / 29 Oct 45 Cp Chaffee Ark   Cp Chaffee Ark
BPE: 5 Sep 44   England: 15 Sep 44   France-ETO: 15 Sep 44 - **25,26,32,34**   NYPE: 20 Jul 45 *(44th Inf Div)*

64th Engineer Topographic Bn, Army
5 Apr 44 Schofield Bks Hawaii (64th Engr Co) / *   Guam
Hawaii: 5 Apr 44   Guam: 1 Apr 45

65th Engineer Combat Bn
1 Oct 41 Schofield Bks Hawaii / *   Bambam Philippines
Hawaii: 1 Oct 41   Guadalcanal: 29 Dec 42   New Georgia I: 7 Aug 43   Arundel I: 19 Sep 43   New Zealand: 10 Nov 43
New Caledonia: 13 Feb 44   Philippines: 11 Jan 45 - **6,11,14,16** *(25th Inf Div)*

78th Engineer Combat Bn
15 Oct 43 Cp O'Reilly Puerto Rico (1st Bn, 78th Engr Regt) /10 Apr 46 Japan   Manila Philippines
Puerto Rico: 15 Oct 43   NOPE: 21 Jul 44   SFPE: 5 Jun 45   Philippines: 10 Jul 45

79th Engineer Construction Bn
1 Apr 43 Cp Phillips Kans (1st Bn, 79th Engr Regt) / *   Canlubang Philippines
SFPE: 17 Jan 44   Goodenough I: 8 Feb 44   New Guinea: 22 Apr 44   Philippines: 13 Jan 45 - **14,15** *(redes fm Engr Combat Bn 23 Jun 44)*

80th Engineer Water Supply Bn
28 Jul 41 Cp Livingston La / 29 May 45 Cp Shelby Miss
LAPE: 30 Mar 43   Iraq-Iran: 11 May 43   HRPE: 13 Apr 45

81st Engineer Combat Bn
15 Mar 43 Ft Jackson S.C. / 2 Oct 45 Cp Kilmer N.J.   Bad Ems Germany
BPE: 10 Nov 44   England: 17 Nov 44   France-ETO: 6 Dec 44 - **25,26,32,34**   NYPE: 1 Oct 45 *(106th Inf Div)*

82nd Engineer Combat Bn
29 Mar 43 Cp Swift Tex / 21 Nov 45 NYPE   Detmold Germany
HRPE: 24 Nov 43   N.Africa: 12 Dec 43   England: 20 Jan 44   France-ETO: 17 Jun 44 - **26,30,32,34**   NYPE: 20 Nov 45

84th Army Engineer Camouflage Bn
4 Jun 41 Ft Belvoir Va /13 Nov 45 Cp Bowie Tex   Marseilles France sch to SWPA
NYPE: 2 Apr 43   N.Africa: 13 Apr 43   Italy: 16 Oct 43   France-ETO: 19 Sep 44 - **25,26,29,31,35,37**   HRPE: 2 Sep 45   under Shipment #R6604-GGG

85th Engineer Heavy Ponton Bn
4 Aug 41 Ft Belvoir Va /15 Nov 45 Cp Swift Tex   Cp Swift Tex
HRPE: 31 Mar 44   Italy: 9 Apr 44   France-ETO: 9 Sep 44 - **25,26,29,34,35,37**   BPE: 27 Sep 45

86th Engineer Heavy Ponton Bn
9 Jul 41 Ft Knox Ky / 2 Jan 46 NYPE   Strump Germany
NYPE: 13 Oct 43   England: 18 Oct 43   France-ETO: 5 Jul 44 - **25,26,30,32,34**   NYPE: 1 Jan 46

87th Engineer Heavy Ponton Bn
1 Aug 40 Ft Benning Ga /10 Jan 46 Cp Kilmer N.J.   Lambrichten Austria
NYPE: 11 Feb 44   England: 23 Feb 44   France-ETO: 24 Jul 44 - **25,26,32,34**   NYPE: 9 Jan 46

88th Engineer Heavy Ponton Bn
2 Jun 41 Cp Beauregard La / 23 Nov 45 Cp Bowie Tex   Calais France sch to SWPA
BPE: 24 Mar 44   England: 5 Apr 44   France-ETO: 22 Jul 44 - **25,26,30,32,34**   NYPE: 15 Sep 45   under Shipment #R6604-T

89th Engineer Heavy Ponton Bn
10 Jul 41 Ft Leonard Wood Mo /1 Jun 44 Cp Howze Tex
Dep Ft Leonard Wood Mo:29 May 42   Arrived Waterways Alberta Canada: 3 Jun 42   Dep Canada: 23 Jul 43
Arrived Ft Lewis Wash: 27 Jul 43 *(CANOL Project in Canada)*

90th Engineer Heavy Ponton Bn
1 Aug 41 Ft Lewis Wash /13 Jun 44 Cp Howze Tex
Dep Ft Lewis Wash: 28 May 42   Arrived Waterways Alberta Canada: 1 Jun 42   Dep Peace River Canada: 23 Sep 43
Arrived Ft Dupont Del: 27 Sep 43 *(CANOL Project in Canada)*

BATTALION DESIGNATION AND TYPE	FORMED (SOURCE OF UNIT)/INACTIVATION *Active through 1946	AUGUST 1945 LOCATION

91st Engineer Bn (Separate) (Cld)
NYPE: 4 Mar 42   Australia: 9 Apr 42

10 Feb 41 Cp Shelby Miss / 6 Aug 42 Australia redes 91st Engr Regt

92nd Engineer Bn (Separate) (Cld)

1 May 41 Ft Leonard Wood Mo / 22 May 42 Cp Forrest Tenn redes 92nd Engr Regt

93rd Engineer Bn (Separate) (Cld)

10 Feb 41 Cp Livingston La / 27 Mar 42 Cp Livingston La redes 93rd Engr Regt

94th Engineer Bn (Separate) (Cld)

12 Feb 41 Ft Custer Mich /1 May 42 Ft Custer Mich redes 94th Engr Regt

95th Engineer Bn (Separate) (Cld)

15 May 41 Ft Belvoir Va / 28 Feb 42 Ft Belvoir Va redes 95th Engr Regt

96th Engineer Bn (Separate) (Cld)
NYPE: 4 Mar 42   Australia: 9 Apr 42   New Guinea: 28 Apr 42 - **9**

1 Jun 41 Ft Bragg N.C. / 29 Jul 42 Port Moresby New Guinea redes 96th Engr Regt

97th Engineer Bn (Separate) (Cld)

1 Jun 41 Cp Blanding Fla / 22 Feb 42 Eglin Field Fla redes 97th Engr Regt

98th Engineer Bn (Separate) (Cld)

17 Aug 41 Cp Bowie Tex / 22 May 42 Cp Claiborne La redes 98th Engr Regt

101st Engineer Combat Bn
NYPE: 27 Aug 44   England: 7 Sep 44   France-ETO: 7 Sep 44 - **25,26,32,34**   HRPE: 1 Jan 46 *(26th Inf Div)*

3 Feb 42 Cp Edwards Mass (101st Engrs) /1 Jan 46 Cp Patrick Henry Va — Husinec Czechoslovakia

102nd Engineer Combat Bn
Hawaii: 23 Aug 42   Saipan: 17 Jun 44   Espiritu Santo: 9 Sep 44   Okinawa: 9 Apr 45 - **10,19,21** *(Co C also 5)*   SPE: 24 Dec 45
(27th Inf Div)

23 Aug 42 Hawaii (102nd Engrs)/31 Dec 45 Ft Lawton Wash — Okinawa

103rd Engineer Combat Bn
BPE: 8 Oct 43   England: 18 Oct 43   France-ETO: 20 Jul 44 - **25,26,30,32,34**   BPE: 2 Aug 45 *(28th Inf Div)*

4 Feb 42 Indiantown Gap Mill Res Pa (103rd Engrs) / 27 Oct 45 Cp Shelby Miss — Cp Shelby Miss

104th Engineer Combat Bn
SFPE: 10 Jul 43   Attu I: 22 Jul 43   Hawaii: 2 Oct 43   Eniwetok: 19 Feb 44   Philippines: 20 Oct 44   Okinawa: Unknown - **2,10,13,19**
SFPE: 6 Dec 45

20 Feb 42 Cp Claiborne La (104th Engrs) / 8 Dec 45 Cp Stoneman Calif — Okinawa

105th Engineer Combat Bn
BPE: 11 Feb 44   England: 23 Feb 44   France-ETO: 10 Jun 44 - **25,26,30,32,34**   NYPE: 21 Aug 45 *(30th Inf Div)*

7 Feb 42 Ft Jackson S.C. (105th Engrs) /16 Nov 45 Ft Jackson S.C. — Shipment #10390-P in England

106th Engineer Combat Bn
HRPE: 9 Feb 44   New Guinea: 17 Mar 44   Morotai I: 15 Sep 44   Philippines: 22 Apr 45 - **15,20,21**   SFPE: 21 Dec 45 *(31st Inf Div)*

10 Feb 42 Cp Blanding Fla (106th Engrs) / 21 Dec 45 Cp Stoneman Calif — Valencia Philippines

107th Engineer Combat Bn
NYPE: May 42   N.Ireland: May 42 *(relieved from 32nd Inf Div 27 Mar 42)*

16 Jan 42 Ft Dix N.J. (107th Engrs) /1 Jun 42 Northern Ireland

108th Engineer Combat Bn
SFPE: 6 Jul 43   Hawaii: 11 Jul 43   New Guinea: 11 May 44   Morotai I: 18 Dec 44   Philippines: 10 Feb 45 - **14,15** *(33rd Inf Div)*

12 Feb 42 Cp Forrest Tenn (108th Engrs) / 5 Feb 46 Japan — Baguio Philippines

109th Engineer Combat Bn
NYPE: 30 Apr 42   N.Ireland: 13 May 42   N.Africa: 3 Jan 43   Italy: 21 Sep 43 - **23,29,31,33,35,38**   HRPE: 3 Nov 45 *(34th Inf Div)*

1 Feb 42 Cp Claiborne La (109th Engrs) / 3 Nov 45 Cp Patrick Henry Va — Iseo Italy

110th Engineer Combat Bn
SFPE: 29 Jul 43   Adak I: 4 Aug 43   Hawaii: 2 Oct 43   Philippines: 20 Oct 44   Okinawa: 1 Apr 45 - **2,13,19**
(relieved from 35th Inf Div 27 Jan 43)

3 Feb 42 Cp San Luis Obispo Calif (110th Engrs) / 31 Jan 46 Korea — Okinawa

111th Engineer Combat Bn
NYPE: 2 Apr 43   N.Africa: 13 Apr 43   Italy: 9 Sep 43   France-ETO: 15 Aug 44 - **24,25,26,29,34,35,37**   BPE: 25 Dec 45 *(36th Inf Div)*

31 Jan 42 Cp Bowie Tex (111th Engrs) / 26 Dec 45 Cp Myles Standish Mass — Markt Oberdorf Austria

112th Engineer Bn (Combat)
NYPE: May 42   Ireland: May 42

16 Jan 42 Cp Shelby Miss (112th Engrs)/1 Jun 42 Northern Ireland redes
112th Engr Regt at Lough Foyle

112th Engineer Combat Bn
England: 19 Aug 43   France-ETO: 6 Jun 44 - **25,26,30,32,34**   NYPE: 25 Dec 45

19 Aug 43 Braunton England (1st Bn, 112th Engr Regt) / 27 Dec 45 NYPE — Dobrany Czechoslovakia

113th Engineer Combat Bn
NOPE: 3 Jan 44   Hawaii: 21 Jan 44   New Guinea: 23 Jul 44   Philippines: 14 Dec 44 - **13,14,15**   LAPE: 9 Sep 45 *(38th Inf Div)*

10 Feb 42 Cp Shelby Miss (113th Engrs) / 9 Sep 45 Cp Anza Calif — Manila Philippines

114th Engineer Combat Bn
SFPE: 22 Apr 42   Australia: 14 May 42   Goodenough I: 28 Oct 43   New Guinea: 8 Jan 44   Philippines: 14 Nov 44 - **13,14,15,17**
(32nd Inf Div)

4 Apr 42 Cp Edwards Mass / 28 Feb 46 Japan — Anabat Philippines

115th Engineer Combat Bn
SFPE: 4 Sep 42   Hawaii: 12 Sep 42   Guadalcanal: 31 Dec 43   New Britain I: 23 Apr 44   Philippines: 9 Jan 45 - **3,13,14,20**
SFPE: 5 Aug 46 *(40th Inf Div)*

5 Feb 42 Los Angeles Calif (115th Engrs) / 7 Apr 46 Cp Stoneman Calif — Negros Philippines

116th Engineer Combat Bn
SFPE: 22 Apr 42   Australia: 14 May 42   New Guinea: 15 Jan 43   Biak I: 24 May 44   Philippines: 28 Jan 45 - **14,15,17,20** *(41st Inf Div)*

14 Feb 42 Ft Lewis Wash (116th Engrs) / 31 Dec 45 Philippines — Zamboanga Philippines

BATTALION DESIGNATION AND TYPE	FORMED (SOURCE OF UNIT)/INACTIVATION *Active through 1946	AUGUST 1945 LOCATION

117th Engineer Combat Bn 10 Apr 42 Indiantown Gap Mil Res Pa /13 Dec 45 Cp Anza Calif   — San Jose Philippines
SFPE: 26 May 42   Fiji I: 10 Jun 42   Guadalcanal: 5 Apr 43   New Georgia I: 25 Jul 43   Bougainville: 28 Jul 43
Philippines: 9 Jan 45 - **14,16**   LAPE: 12 Dec 45 *(37th Inf Div)*

118th Engineer Combat Bn 14 Feb 42 Cp Shelby Miss (118th Engrs) / 26 Oct 45 Cp Stoneman Calif   — Cabanatuan Philippines
SFPE: 1 Oct 42   New Zealand: 30 Oct 42   New Caledonia: 6 Nov 42   Guadalcanal: 19 Feb 43   Russell I: 28 Feb 43
New Georgia I: 2 Jul 43   New Guinea: 23 Jul 44   Philippines: 9 Jan 45 - **11,14,15,16**   SFPE: 23 Oct 45 *(43rd Inf Div)*

119th Armored Engineer Bn 15 Sep 42 Cp Campbell Ky / 3 Dec 45 NYPE   — Heidenheim Germany
NYPE: 20 Sep 44   France-ETO: 1 Oct 44 - **25,26,34**   NYPE: 1 Dec 45 *(12th Armd Div)*

120th Engineer Combat Bn 22 Feb 42 Cp Barkeley Tex (120th Engrs) / 26 Nov 45 Cp Bowie Tex   — Munich Germany
HRPE: 8 Jun 43   N.Africa: 22 Jun 43   Sicily: 10 Jul 43   Italy: 10 Sep 43   France-ETO: 15 Aug 44 - **24,25,26,29,32,34,35,36,37**
BPE: 10 Sep 45 *(45th Inf Div)*

121st Engineer Combat Bn 28 Feb 42 Ft George G Meade Md (121st Engrs)/17 Jan 46 NYPE   — Osterholz Germany
NYPE: 5 Oct 42   England: 11 Oct 42   France-ETO: 6 Jun 44 - **26,30,32,34**   NYPE: 16 Jan 46 *(29th Inf Div)*

124th Armored Engineer Bn 15 Oct 42 Cp Beale Calif /12 Nov 45 Cp Cooke Calif   — Cp Cooke Calif
NYPE: 26 Jan 45   France-ETO: 6 Feb 45 - **26,34**   NYPE: 23 Jul 45 *(13th Armd Div)*

125th Armored Engineer Bn 15 Nov 42 Cp Chaffee Ark /19 Sep 45 Cp Myles Standish Mass   — Ampfling Germany
NYPE: 14 Oct 44   France-ETO: 28 Oct 44 - **25,26,34**   BPE: 17 Sep 45 *(14th Armd Div)*

126th Engineer Mountain Bn 14 Sep 42 Cp Carson Colo/21 Nov 45 Cp Carson Colo   — Shipment #22050-N unloading
HRPE: 6 Jan 45   Italy: 18 Jan 45 - **31,33**   HRPE: 11 Aug 45 *(Engr Light Combat Bn 15 Jul 43–6 Nov 44) (10th Mtn Div)*

127th Airborne Engineer Bn 25 Feb 43 Cp Mackall N.C. / *   — Okinawa *(arriving via air)*
SFPE: 3 May 44   New Guinea: 28 May 44   Philippines: 18 Nov 44   Okinawa: 12 Aug 45 - **13,14,15** *(11th A/B Div)*

129th Airborne Engineer Bn 13 Aug 43 Ft Bragg N.C. / 25 Feb 46 Ft Bragg N.C.   — Shipment #10580-S at sea
NYPE: 26 Jan 45   France-ETO: 6 Feb 45 - **25,26,34**   NYPE: 20 Aug 45 *(13th A/B Div)*

130th Engineer Combat Bn (Puerto Rican) 24 May 43 Ft Buchanan Puerto Rico (1st Bn, 130th Engr Regt) /15 Dec 45 Puerto   — Cp Swift Tex less Cos A, B, C at Cp Bowie Tex
Puerto Rico: 24 May 43   Panama Canal Zone: 27 Jul 43   NOPE: 12 Sep 44   NOPE: 6 Dec 45   Puerto Rico: 9 Dec 45   Rico

131st Engineer Combat Bn 15 May 44 Bougainville (1st Bn, 131st Engr Regt) / 25 Jan 46 Japan   — Manila Philippines
Bougainville: 15 May 44   Philippines: 9 Jan 45 - **14**

132nd Engineer Combat Bn 5 May 43 Framingham Mass (1st Bn, 132nd Engr Regt) / 31 Jan 46 Japan   — Ie Shima Island, Ryukyus
SPE: 28 Mar 44   Hawaii: 3 Apr 44   Guam: 21 Jul 44   Philippines: 23 Nov 44   Ie Shima I: 16 Apr 45 - **13,19,21**

133rd Engineer Combat Bn 1 Feb 43 Ft Lewis Wash (1st Bn, 133rd Engr Regt) /16 Apr 46 NYPE   — Urfohr Austria
NYPE: 8 Apr 44   England: 16 Apr 44   France-ETO: 13 Jul 44 - **25,26,30,32,34**   NYPE: 15 Apr 46

135th Engineer Combat Bn 1 Jun 43 Ft Read Trinidad (2nd Bn, 135th Engr Regt) /12 Dec 45 Cp Myles Stan-   — Reid Germany
Trinidad: 1 Jun 43   NOPE: 18 Aug 43   BPE: 26 Jun 44   Scotland: 5 Jul 44   England: 6 Jul 44   dish Mass
France-ETO: 9 Aug 44 - **25,26,32,34**   BPE: 11 Dec 45

138th Engineer Combat Bn 30 Mar 44 Ft Jackson S.C. / 31 Oct 45 Germany   — Katzenfurt Germany
NYPE: 10 Nov 44   England: 18 Nov 44   France-ETO: 3 Mar 45 - **26,34**

139th Airborne Engineer Bn 15 Apr 43 Cp Mackall N.C. /16 Sep 45 Cp Myles Standish Mass   — Duclair France
BPE: 17 Aug 44   England: 25 Aug 44   France-ETO: 24 Dec 44 - **25,26,34**   BPE: 15 Sep 45 *(17th A/B Div)*

142nd Engineer Combat Bn 14 Jul 43 Cp Gruber Okla / 29 Jun 46 Austria   — Bernau Germany
NYPE: 6 Jan 45   France-ETO: 18 Jan 45 - **26,34** *(42nd Inf Div)*

145th Engineer Combat Bn 25 Sep 43 Cp White Oreg (2nd Bn, 35th Engr Regt) / 8 Jan 46 Cp Patrick Henry Va   — Scheinfeld Germany
NYPE: 18 Apr 44   England: 26 Apr 44   France-ETO: 8 Jul 44 - **25,26,30,32,34**   HRPE: 8 Jan 46

146th Engineer Combat Bn 1 Apr 43 Cp Swift Tex (1st Bn, 146th Engr Regt) /18 Oct 45 Cp Shanks N.Y.   — Pilsen Czechoslovakia
BPE: 11 Oct 43   England: 17 Oct 43   France-ETO: 6 Jun 44 - **25,26,30,32,34**   NYPE: 17 Oct 45

147th Engineer Combat Bn 1 Apr 43 Cp Swift Tex (1st Bn, 147th Engr Regt) / 4 Mar 46 NYPE   — Bettinghausen Germany
NYPE: 8 Jan 44   England: 17 Jan 44   France-ETO: 6 Jun 44 - **26,30,32,34**   NYPE: 3 Mar 46

148th Engineer Combat Bn 22 Feb 43 Cp Shelby Miss / 6 Oct 45 France   — Mailly-le-Camp France
NYPE: 7 Oct 43   England: 18 Oct 43   France-ETO: 11 Jun 44 - **25,26,30,32,34**

149th Engineer Combat Bn 25 Feb 43 Cp McCain Miss /17 Dec 45 Cp Shanks N.Y.   — Brackel Germany
NYPE: 29 Dec 43   England: 10 Jan 44   France-ETO: 6 Jun 44 - **26,30,32,34**   NYPE: 15 Dec 45

150th Engineer Combat Bn 25 Feb 43 Ft Devens Mass / 29 Oct 45 NYPE   — Regensburg Germany
NYPE: 23 Dec 43   England: 29 Dec 43   France-ETO: 4 Jul 44 - **25,26,30,32,34**   NYPE: 28 Oct 45

BATTALION DESIGNATION AND TYPE	FORMED (SOURCE OF UNIT) / INACTIVATION	AUGUST 1945 LOCATION
150th Italian Engineer Utilities Bn	20 Apr 44 Cp Sutton N.C. /14 Sep 44 Cp Myles Standish Mass *(pers to 123rd–126th Italian QM Service Companies)*	
151st Engineer Combat Bn NYPE: 14 Oct 44 England: 25 Oct 44 France-ETO: 9 Jan 45 NYPE: 26 Dec 45	11 Jul 42 Ft Leonard Wood Mo (1st Bn, 151st Engr Regt) / 27 Dec 45 NYPE	Enghein-les-Bains Belgium
152nd Engineer Combat Bn Hawaii: 23 Nov 42 Makin I: 20 Nov 43 Hawaii: Feb 44 Saipan: 17 Jun 44 Espiritu Santo: 16 Feb 45 Okinawa: 9 Apr 45 - **19,21**	23 Nov 42 Kalaheo Hawaii (152nd Engr Regt) / 31 Jan 46 Japan	Okinawa
153rd Engineer Construction Bn SFPE: 31 Mar 44 New Guinea: 7 May 44 Philippines: 15 Nov 44 - **13,15** *(redes from Engr Combat Bn 25 May 44)*	1 Apr 43 Ft Lewis Wash / 31 May 46 Japan	Tacloban Philippines
154th Engineer Combat Bn SFPE: 21 Jun 44 Hawaii: 27 Jun 44 Guadalcanal: 24 Aug 44 Anguar I: 17 Sep 44 New Caledonia: 20 Feb 45 Philippines: 16 May 45 - **13,21**	15 Apr 43 Cp Cooke Calif / 23 Dec 45 Japan	Leyte Philippines
155th Engineer Combat Bn SFPE: 17 Jun 44 Hawaii: 25 Jun 44 Guadalcanal: 24 Aug 44 New Caledonia: 20 Feb 45 Philippines: 16 May 45 - **13,21**	15 Apr 43 Cp Cooke Calif /11 Mar 46 Japan	Leyte Philippines
156th Engineer Combat Bn	15 Apr 43 Cp Cooke Calif /1 May 44 Cp Ellis Ill	
157th Engineer Combat Bn NYPE: 27 Feb 44 England: 9 Mar 44 France-ETO: 25 Jun 44 - **25,26,30,32,34** BPE: 21 Dec 45	12 Apr 43 Cp Maxey Tex / 22 Dec 45 Cp Myles Standish Mass	Golling Austria
158th Engineer Combat Bn NYPE: 23 Mar 44 England: 4 Apr 44 France-ETO: 1 Aug 44 - **25,26,30,32,34**	12 Apr 43 Cp Maxey Tex /18 Sep 45 Germany	Allendorf Austria
159th Engineer Combat Bn NYPE: 27 Jun 44 England: 3 Jul 44 France-ETO: 22 Jul 44 - **25,26,30,32,34**	27 Apr 43 Ft George G Meade Md /18 Sep 45 Belgium	Antwerp Belgium
160th Engineer Combat Bn NYPE: 27 Jun 44 England: 3 Jul 44 France-ETO: 10 Aug 44 - **25,26,30,32,34** BPE: 26 Nov 45	27 Apr 43 Ft George G Meade Md / 27 Nov 45 Cp Myles Standish Mass	Redlin Germany
161st Airborne Engineer Bn *(relieved from 1st Cav Div 15 Mar 43; upon arrival of abn-qualified troops Co A was desig the Parachute Company 5 May 43)* *(assigned A/B Cmd 18 Oct 43) (redes from Engr Sqdn 1 May 43)*	15 Nov 42 Ft Bliss Tex as Engr Squadron / 22 Feb 45 Ft Knox Ky	
163rd Engineer Combat Bn NYPE: 27 Feb 44 England: 9 Mar 44 France-ETO: 27 Jun 44 - **25,26,30,32,34** NYPE: 6 Mar 46	5 May 43 Cp Van Dorn Miss/8 Mar 46 Cp Kilmer N.J.	Salzburg Austria
164th Engineer Combat Bn NYPE: 27 Feb 44 England: 9 Mar 44 France-ETO: 30 Jun 44 - **25,26,30,32,34** HRPE: 19 Oct 45	5 May 43 Cp Van Dorn Miss /19 Oct 45 Cp Patrick Henry Va	Eisenach Germany
165th Engineer Combat Bn NYPE: 27 Jun 44 England: 3 Jul 44 France-ETO: 27 Jul 44 - **25,26,32,34** NYPE: 19 Nov 45	5 May 43 Cp Van Dorn Miss / 20 Nov 45 Cp Kilmer N.J.	Salzburg Austria
166th Engineer Combat Bn NYPE: 27 Jun 44 England: 3 Jul 44 France-ETO: 7 Aug 44 - **25,26,32,34** NYPE: 30 Oct 45	15 May 43 Cp McCain Miss / 31 Oct 45 Cp Shanks N.Y.	Pfreimd Germany
167th Engineer Combat Bn NYPE: 28 Jun 44 England: 5 Jul 44 France-ETO: 5 Aug 44 - **25,26,32,34**	15 May 43 Cp McCain Miss /18 Sep 45 France	Mengeringhausen Germany
168th Engineer Combat Bn NYPE: 3 May 44 England: 15 May 44 France-ETO: 19 Jul 44 - **25,26,30,32,34** NYPE: 21 Nov 45	5 May 43 Cp Carson Colo / 22 Nov 45 Cp Kilmer N.J.	Breigelette Belgium
169th Engineer Combat Bn (I)	25 Jun 43 Cp Beale Calif /1 May 44 Cp Ellis Ill	
169th Engineer Combat Bn (II) Italy: 16 Sep 44 - **31,33** NYPE: 19 Aug 45	16 Sep 44 Florence Italy (1st Bn, 337th Engr Regt) /18 Feb 46 Ft Jackson S.C.	Shipment #R2666-C (sch to SWPA but returned to USA) at sea
170th Engineer Combat Bn SPE: 1 Aug 44 Hawaii: 7 Aug 44 Philippines: 20 Oct 44 Okinawa: 1 Apr 45 - **13,19**	25 Jun 43 Cp Beale Calif / 31 Mar 46 Japan	Okinawa
171st Engineer Combat Bn NYPE: 11 Aug 44 England: 22 Aug 44 France-ETO: 13 Sep 44 - **26,32,34** NYPE: 27 Dec 45	25 Jun 43 Cp Carson Colo / 28 Dec 45 Cp Kilmer N.J.	Arendsee Germany
172nd Engineer Combat Bn NYPE: 11 Aug 44 England: 22 Aug 44 France-ETO: 12 Sep 44 - **25,26,32,34** NYPE: 21 Mar 46	25 Jun 43 Cp Breckinridge Ky / 22 Mar 46 Cp Kilmer N.J.	Gladbeck Germany
173rd Engineer Combat Bn SPE: 1 Aug 44 Hawaii: 7 Aug 44 Philippines: 20 Oct 44 Okinawa: 1 Apr 45 - **13,19**	23 Jul 43 Cp Beale Calif /18 Feb 46 Korea	Okinawa
174th Engineer Combat Bn SPE: 1 Aug 44 Hawaii: 7 Aug 44 Philippines: 20 Oct 44 Okinawa: 1 Apr 45 - **13,19**	23 Jul 43 Cp Beale Calif / 24 Feb 46 Korea	Okinawa

BATTALION DESIGNATION AND TYPE	FORMED (SOURCE OF UNIT)/INACTIVATION *Active through 1946	AUGUST 1945 LOCATION

176th Engineer Combat Bn
SPE: 18 Jul 45   Okinawa: 12 Aug 45

12 Mar 45 Ft Belvoir Va (176th Engr Regt) / 24 Feb 46 Korea

Shipment #6092-F unloading from USS *Sarasota* (**APA.204**) at Naha Okinawa

177th Engineer Construction Bn

15 Nov 44 Ft Richardson Alaska (177th Engr Regt)/1 Nov 45 Alaska

Shemya Island less Co C at Amchitka Island Alaska

178th Engineer Combat Bn
NYPE: 11 Aug 44   England: 22 Aug 44   France-ETO: 28 Sep 44 - **25,26,32,34**   NYPE: 6 May 46

23 Jul 43 Cp Gruber Okla / 7 May 46 Cp Kilmer N.J.

Ober Dachstetten Germany

179th Engineer Combat Bn
NYPE: 2 Jul 44   England: 14 Jul 44   France-ETO: 9 Aug 44 - **25,26,32,34**   NYPE: 28 Oct 45

23 Jul 43 Ft Devens Mass / 29 Oct 45 NYPE

Vocklabruck Austria

180th Engineer Heavy Ponton Bn
NYPE: 11 Feb 44   England: 23 Feb 44   France-ETO: Aug 44 - **25,26,30,32,34**   BPE: 26 Nov 45

7 Feb 42 Philadelphia Pa (2nd Bn, 103rd Engrs) / 27 Nov 45 Cp Myles Standish Mass

Osterberg Germany

181st Engineer Heavy Ponton Bn
NYPE: 29 Dec 43 ·   England: 10 Jan 44   France-ETO: 9 Jul 44 - **25,26,30,32,34**

12 Feb 42 Cp Forrest Tenn (2nd Bn, 108th Engrs) / 5 Aug 45 Germany

182nd Engineer Combat Bn (I)

15 Oct 43 Cp Crowder Mo / 3 May 44 Cp Ellis Ill

182nd Engineer Combat Bn (II)
Italy: 16 Sep 44 - **31,33**   NYPE: 19 Aug 45

16 Sep 44 Florence Italy (2nd Bn, 337th Engr Regt) /19 Feb 46 Ft Jackson S.C.

Shipment #R2666-D (sch to SWPA but returned to USA) at sea

183rd Engineer Combat Bn (Cld)
BPE: 4 Oct 44   England: 12 Oct 44   France-ETO: Unknown - **25,26,30,32,34**

15 Oct 43 Cp McCain Miss /19 Jun 45 Germany

184th Engineer Combat Bn (Cld)
NYPE: 30 Oct 44   England: 10 Nov 44   France-ETO: 31 Dec 44 - **25,26,34**

15 Oct 43 Cp Maxey Tex /19 Jun 45 Germany

185th Engineer Combat Bn (I)

10 Nov 43 Ft Jackson S.C. / 1 May 44 Cp Ellis Ill

185th Engineer Combat Bn (II)
Italy: 25 Sep 44 - **31,33**   BPE: 22 Aug 45

25 Sep 44 Civitavecchi Italy (337th AAA S/L Bn) / *

Shipment #R0488-R (sch to SWPA but returned to USA) at sea

186th Engineer Combat Bn
SFPE: 17 Nov 44   New Guinea: 5 Dec 44   Philippines: 12 Jan 45 - **14,15**

5 Nov 43 Ft Jackson S.C. / 28 Feb 46 Japan

Luzon Philippines

187th Engineer Combat Bn
NYPE: 22 Oct 44   England: 2 Nov 44   France-ETO: 29 Dec 44 - **25,26,34**   NYPE: 25 Feb 46

15 Oct 43 Cp White Oreg / 26 Feb 46 Cp Kilmer N.J.

Bockenem Germany

188th Engineer Combat Bn
NYPE: 24 Jul 44   England: 31 Jul 44   France-ETO: Unknown - **26,32,34**   HRPE: 20 Oct 45

23 Jul 43 Ft Devens Mass / 20 Oct 45 Cp Patrick Henry Va

Stadtroda Germany

202nd Engineer Combat Bn
BPE: 11 Oct 43   England: 18 Oct 43   France-ETO: 14 Jul 44 - **25,26,30,32,34**   NYPE: 16 Nov 45

22 Feb 43 Cp Shelby Miss /18 Nov 45 Cp Kilmer N.J.

Le Havre France

203rd Engineer Combat Bn
NYPE: 2 Jan 44   England: 10 Jan 44   France-ETO: 7 Jun 44 - **25,26,30,32,34**

25 Feb 43 Cp McCain Miss / 6 Oct 45 France

Homberg Germany

204th Engineer Combat Bn
NYPE: 2 Jan 44   England: 8 Jan 44   France-ETO: 2 Jul 44 - **25,26,30,32,34**   NYPE: 26 Oct 45

25 Feb 43 Ft Devens Mass / 27 Oct 45 Cp Kilmer N.J.

Burglengenfeld Germany

205th Engineer Combat Bn

1 Feb 45 Ft Riley Kans (2nd Bn, 50th Engr Regt) / 23 Oct 45 Cp Gruber Okla

Cp Gruber Okla

206th Engineer Combat Bn
NYPE: 11 Oct 43   England: 18 Oct 43   France-ETO: 27 Jun 44 - **25,26,30,32,34**   NYPE: 27 Nov 45

1 Apr 43 Cp Swift Tex (2nd Bn, 146th Engr Regt) / 28 Nov 45 Cp Kilmer N.J.

Hess Lichfenau Germany

207th Engineer Combat Bn
NYPE: 3 Dec 43   England: 9 Dec 43   France-ETO: 17 Jun 44 - **25,26,30,32,34**

1 Apr 43 Cp Swift Tex (2nd Bn, 147th Engr Regt) / 25 Nov 45 Germany

Asbach Germany

208th Engineer Combat Bn
NYPE: 27 Feb 44   England: 20 Mar 44   France-ETO: 26 Jun 44 - **26,30,32,34**   NYPE: 20 Nov 45

13 Mar 43 Cp Breckinridge Ky (2nd Bn, 27th Engr Regt) / 2:. Nov 45 Cp Shanks N.Y.

Korbach Germany

209th Engineer Combat Bn
NYPE: 8 Sep 43   India: 12 Oct 43   Burma: 3 Nov 45 - **5,12**   NYPE: 26 Nov 45

18 Mar 43 Cp Beale Calif (2nd Bn, 37th Engr Regt)/27 Nov 44 NYPE

Ledo India less Co A at Myitkyina Burma

215th Engineer Service Bn
Iceland: 17 Dec 43   England: 20 Aug 45   NYPE: 31 Aug 45 *(redes Engr Service Bn 9 Feb 45 at Reykjavik Iceland)*

17 Dec 43 as Engr Composite Bn Iceland (Base Fire Brigade) / 31 Aug 45 NYPE

Aboard *Duchess of Bedford* en route from Iceland to England

216th Armored Engineer Bn
NYPE: 5 Feb 45   France-ETO: 17 Feb 45 - **26**   NYPE: 14 Oct 45 *(16th Armd Div)*

15 Jul 43 Cp Chaffee Ark /15 Oct 45 Cp Kilmer N.J.

Tachov Czechoslovakia

220th Armored Engineer Bn
BPE: 6 Feb 45   France-ETO: 17 Feb 45 - **26,34**   NYPE: 2 Aug 45 *(20th Armd Div)*

15 Mar 43 Cp Campbell Ky / 3 Apr 46 Cp Hood Tex

Cp Cooke Calif

BATTALION DESIGNATION AND TYPE	FORMED (SOURCE OF UNIT)/INACTIVATION *Active through 1946	AUGUST 1945 LOCATION

233rd Engineer Combat Bn — 25 Jan 43 Cp Pendleton Va (2nd Bn, 348th Engr Regt) /10 Dec 46 Philippines — Okinawa
SPE: 22 Mar 44   Hawaii: 29 Mar 44   Guam: 21 Jul 44   Philippines: 23 Nov 44   Yabaki Shima I: 26 Mar 45   Ie Shima I: 16 Apr 45 - **13,19,21**

234th Engineer Combat Bn — 7 Apr 43 Cp Rucker Ala (2nd Bn, 336th Engr Regt) / 27 Nov 45 Cp Shanks N.Y. — Sommesous France
NYPE: 21 Aug 43   England: 4 Sep 43   France-ETO: 7 Jun 44 - **26,30,32,34**   NYPE: 26 Nov 45

235th Engineer Combat Bn — 7 Apr 43 Cp Polk La (2nd Bn, 48th Engr Regt) / 31 May 46 Philippines — Porretta Italy sch to SWPA under Shipment #R2666-E
NYPE: 21 Aug 43   N.Africa: 2 Sep 43   Italy: 28 Oct 43 - **29,31,33,35**

236th Engineer Combat Bn — 1 Apr 43 Cp McCoy Wis (2nd Bn, 44th Engr Regt) / 2 Dec 45 NYPE — Ledo India
LAPE: 18 Nov 43   India: 26 Dec 44   Burma: 29 May 44   India: 9 Aug 44 - **5,12**   NYPE: 1 Dec 45

237th Engineer Combat Bn — 1 Apr 43 Cp Carson Colo (2nd Bn, 49th Engr Regt) / 28 Nov 45 NYPE — Helmsdorf Germany
HRPE: 14 Nov 43   N.Africa: 4 Dec 43   England: 20 Jan 44   France-ETO: 6 Jun 44 - **25,26,30,32,34**   NYPE: 26 Nov 45

238th Engineer Combat Bn — 1 Apr 43 Plattsburg Bks N.Y. (2nd Bn, 51st Engr Regt) / 31 Dec 45 Cp Kilmer N.J. — Eisleben Germany
HRPE: 13 Oct 43   N.Africa: 6 Nov 43   England: 21 Jan 44   France-ETO: 6 Jun 44 - **25,26,30,32,34**   NYPE: 30 Dec 45

239th Engineer Construction Bn — 1 Apr 43 Cp Butner N.C. (2nd Bn, 52nd Engr Regt) / 31 Jan 46 Cp Stoneman Calif — Macajalar Bay Philippines less Co A at Davao Mindanao
SFPE: 6 Jan 44   Goodenough I: 1 Feb 44   New Guinea: 22 Apr 44   Philippines: 29 Oct 44 - **13,15,20**   SFPE: 29 Jan 46
(redes from Engr Combat Bn per AG 322 [12 Apr 44] OB-I-SPMOU-M dtd 14 Apr 44 Confidential)

240th Engineer Construction Bn — 1 Apr 43 Cp Phillips Kans (2nd Bn, 79th Engr Regt) / * — Cotabato Philippines
SFPE: 17 Jan 44   New Guinea: 6 Feb 44   Goodenough I: 11 Feb 44   New Guinea: 21 Mar 44   Philippines: 20 Oct 44 - **13,14,15,20**
(redes from Engr Combat Bn 29 May 44)

241st Engineer Combat Bn — 22 Mar 43 Ft Belvoir Va (2nd Bn, 31st Engr Regt) / 31 Jan 46 Japan — Manila Philippines
SFPE: 27 Jun 45   Philippines: 29 Jul 45

242nd Engineer Combat Bn — 5 Mar 43 Ft Hancock N.J. (2nd Bn, 132nd Engr Regt) / 31 Jan 46 Japan — Ie Shima Island, Ryukyus
SPE: 28 Mar 44   Guam: 21 Jul 44   Philippines: 23 Nov 44   Keramo Retto I: 26 Mar 45   Ie Shima I: 16 Apr 45 - **13,19,21**

243rd Engineer Combat Bn — 15 Oct 43 Cp Breckinridge Ky / 27 Feb 46 Cp Kilmer N.J. — Schmollen Germany
NYPE: 22 Oct 44   England: 2 Nov 44   France-ETO: 20 Dec 44 - **25,26,34**   NYPE: 26 Feb 46

244th Engineer Combat Bn — 25 Oct 43 Cp Shelby Miss / 21 Jan 46 Cp Kilmer N.J. — Dahlemberg Germany
NYPE: 20 Oct 44   England: 10 Nov 44   France-ETO: 26 Dec 44 - **25,26,34**   NYPE: 20 Jan 46

245th Engineer Combat Bn — 25 Oct 43 Cp Shelby Miss /13 Mar 46 Cp Kilmer N.J. — Mattinghofen Germany
NYPE: 30 Oct 44   England: 10 Nov 44   France-ETO: 29 Dec 44 - **25,26,34**   NYPE: 12 Mar 46

246th Engineer Combat Bn — 1 Apr 43 Ft Lewis Wash / 28 Nov 45 NYPE — Schotten Germany
BPE: 18 Jan 44   England: 27 Jan 44   France-ETO: 12 Jun 44 - **26,30,32,34**   NYPE: 27 Nov 45

247th Engineer Combat Bn — 1 Apr 43 Ft Lewis Wash / 25 Oct 45 Cp Myles Standish Mass — Hirzenhain Germany
BPE: 18 Jan 44   England: 27 Jan 44   France-ETO: 12 Jun 44 - **26,30,32,34**   BPE: 24 Oct 45

248th Engineer Combat Bn — 5 May 43 Cp Bowie Tex / 24 Dec 45 Cp Kilmer N.J. — Bremen Germany
BPE: 28 Jun 44   England: 5 Jul 44   France-ETO: 27 Jul 44 - **25,26,30,32,34**   NYPE: 20 Dec 45

249th Engineer Combat Bn — 5 May 43 Cp Bowie Tex / 28 Nov 45 Cp Patrick Henry Va — Regensburg Germany
BPE: 3 Jul 44   England: 12 Jul 44   France-ETO: 19 Aug 44 - **25,26,32,34**   HRPE: 27 Nov 45

250th Engineer Combat Bn — 23 Jul 43 Cp McCoy Wis / 30 Nov 46 Germany — Olvenstadt Germany
NYPE: 27 Aug 44   England: 7 Sep 44   France-ETO: 26 Sep 44 - **26,34**

251st Engineer Combat Bn — 23 Jul 43 Cp McCoy Wis /19 Jan 46 Cp Kilmer N.J. — Schnde Germany
NYPE: 27 Aug 44   England: 7 Sep 44   France-ETO: 29 Sep 44 - **26,34**   NYPE: 18 Jan 46

252nd Engineer Combat Bn — 23 Jul 43 Cp Gruber Okla / * — Weende Germany
NYPE: 24 Aug 44   England: 1 Sep 44   France-ETO: 19 Sep 44 - **26,34**

253rd Engineer Combat Bn — 15 Oct 43 Cp Crowder Mo /10 Apr 46 NYPE — Ulm Germany
BPE: 31 Oct 44   England: 8 Nov 44   France-ETO: 26 Dec 44 - **25,26,34**   NYPE: 9 Apr 46

254th Engineer Combat Bn — 19 Aug 43 Braunton England (2nd Bn, 112th Engr Regt) / 22 Dec 45 Cp Myles Standish Mass — Stodten Germany
England: 19 Aug 43   France-ETO: 8 Jun 44 - **25,26,30,32,34**   BPE: 21 Dec 45

255th Engineer Combat Bn — 14 Jan 45 Malpensa Italy (354th AAA S/L Bn) /18 Feb 46 Cp Campbell Ky — Shipment #R0488-C (sch to SWPA but returned to USA)at sea
Italy: 14 Jan 45 - **31,33**   HRPE: 22 Aug 45

256th Engineer Combat Bn — 5 Nov 43 Cp Gordon Ga /15 May 46 Germany — Solach Germany
NYPE: 30 Oct 44   England: 12 Nov 44   France-ETO: 25 Dec 44 - **25,26,34**

257th Engineer Combat Bn — 5 Nov 43 Cp Gordon Ga /14 Mar 46 Cp Kilmer N.J. — Antwerp Belgium
NYPE: 30 Oct 44   England: 10 Nov 44   France-ETO: Dec 44 - **25,26,34**   NYPE: 13 Mar 46

BATTALION DESIGNATION AND TYPE	FORMED (SOURCE OF UNIT) / INACTIVATION	AUGUST 1945 LOCATION

258th Engineer Combat Bn
20 Nov 43 Cp Shelby Miss / 23 Mar 46 NYPE
NYPE: 22 Oct 44   England: 2 Nov 44   France-ETO: 29 Dec 44 - **26,34**   NYPE: 22 Mar 46
Korbecke Germany

259th Engineer Combat Bn
20 Nov 43 Cp Joseph T Robinson Ark / 20 Feb 46 Japan
Portland Sub-P/E: 30 Jul 45   Hawaii: 8 Aug 45
Oahu Hawaii

260th Engineer Combat Bn
10 Nov 43 Cp Swift Tex / 16 Apr 46 Germany
NYPE: 30 Oct 44   England: 10 Nov 44   France-ETO: 10 Jan 45 - **25,26,34**
Salzburg Austria

263rd Engineer Combat Bn
15 Jun 43 Cp Blanding Fla / 29 Sep 45 Cp Patrick Henry Va
NYPE: 5 Jan 45   France-ETO: 14 Jan 45 - **26,34**   HRPE: 29 Sep 45 *(63rd Inf Div)*
Weikersheim Germany

264th Engineer Combat Bn
30 Mar 44 Cp Pickett Va / 4 Dec 45 Cp Myles Standish Mass
NYPE: 3 Nov 44   England: 9 Nov 44   France-ETO: Unknown - **26,34**   BPE: 3 Dec 45
Peuerbach Austria

265th Engineer Combat Bn
16 Aug 43 Cp Shelby Miss / 31 Aug 45 Austria
NYPE: 10 Jan 45   France-ETO: 22 Jan 45 - **26,34** *(65th Inf Div)*
Linz Austria

266th Engineer Combat Bn
15 Apr 43 Cp Blanding Fla / 13 Nov 45 Cp Shanks N.Y.
NYPE: 1 Dec 44   England: 12 Dec 44   France-ETO: 28 Dec 44 - **32**   NYPE: 11 Nov 45 *(66th Inf Div)*
Villepail France

269th Engineer Combat Bn
15 May 43 Cp Shelby Miss / 16 Sep 45 NYPE
NYPE: 1 Dec 44   England: 12 Dec 44   France-ETO: 24 Jan 45 - **26,34**   NYPE: 14 Sep 45 *(69th Inf Div)*
Grossdeuben Germany

270th Engineer Combat Bn
15 Jun 43 Cp Adair Oreg / 15 Oct 45 Cp Patrick Henry Va
BPE: 8 Jan 45   France-ETO: 18 Jan 45 - **26,34**   HRPE: 15 Oct 45 *(70th Inf Div)*
Assmannhausen Germany

271st Engineer Combat Bn
15 Jul 43 Cp Carson Colo / 12 Mar 46 Cp Kilmer N.J.
NYPE: 26 Jan 45   France-ETO: 10 Feb 45 - **26,34**   NYPE: 11 Mar 46 *(Engr Light Combat Bn until 26 May 44) (71st Inf Div)*
Kremsmunster Austria

275th Engineer Combat Bn
15 Apr 43 Ft Leonard Wood Mo / 14 Nov 45 Cp Patrick Henry Va
NYPE: 14 Nov 44   England: 22 Nov 44   France-ETO: 14 Dec 44 - **25,26,34**   HRPE: 14 Nov 45 *(75th Inf Div)*
Werdohl Germany

276th Engineer Combat Bn
25 Oct 43 Cp Gruber Okla / 25 Dec 45 Cp Patrick Henry Va
NYPE: 30 Oct 44   England: 10 Nov 44   France-ETO: 25 Dec 44 - **26,34**   HRPE: 25 Dec 45
Weilburg Germany

277th Engineer Combat Bn
25 Oct 43 Cp Swift Tex / 25 Jun 46 France
NYPE: 22 Oct 44   England: 2 Nov 44   France-ETO: 26 Dec 44 - **25,26,34**
Boltenhagen Germany

278th Engineer Combat Bn
25 Oct 43 Cp Joseph T Robinson Ark / 10 Apr 46 NYPE
NYPE: 29 Sep 44   England: 9 Oct 44   France-ETO: 3 Dec 44 - **25,26,34**   NYPE: 9 Apr 46
Darmstadt Germany

279th Engineer Combat Bn
25 Oct 43 Cp Joseph T Robinson Ark / 31 Dec 45 Cp Kilmer N.J.
BPE: 22 Sep 44   England: 30 Sep 44   France-ETO: 2 Oct 44 - **26,34**   NYPE: 30 Dec 45
Gardelegen Germany

280th Engineer Combat Bn
15 Nov 43 Cp McCoy Wis / 23 Nov 45 Cp Myles Standish Mass
NYPE: 22 Oct 44   England: 2 Nov 44   France-ETO: 31 Dec 44 - **25,26,34**   BPE: 22 Nov 45
Ludinghausen Germany

281st Engineer Combat Bn
15 Nov 43 Ft Devens Mass / 3 May 46 Cp Kilmer N.J.
NYPE: 22 Oct 44   England: 2 Nov 44   France-ETO: 24 Dec 44 - **25,26,34**   NYPE: 2 May 46
Schwanenstadt Germany

282nd Engineer Combat Bn
15 Nov 43 Ft Devens Mass / 4 Apr 46 NYPE
NYPE: 22 Oct 44   England: 2 Nov 44   France-ETO: 24 Dec 44 - **25,26,34**   NYPE: 3 Apr 46
Eichendorf Germany

283rd Engineer Combat Bn
17 Dec 43 Cp Butner N.C. / 27 Feb 46 NYPE
NYPE: 22 Oct 44   England: 3 Nov 44   France-ETO: 25 Dec 44 - **26,32**   NYPE: 26 Feb 46
Frechen Germany

284th Engineer Combat Bn
17 Dec 43 Cp Breckinridge Ky / 27 Nov 45 Cp Myles Standish Mass
NYPE: 22 Oct 44   England: 2 Nov 44   France-ETO: 9 Jan 45 - **25,26,34**   BPE: 26 Nov 45
Nurnberg Germany

285th Engineer Combat Bn
17 Dec 43 Cp Crowder Mo / 19 Nov 45 Cp Patrick Henry Va
NYPE: 22 Oct 44   England: 2 Nov 44   France-ETO: 9 Jan 45 - **25,26,34**   HRPE: 19 Nov 45
Grofenau Germany

286th Engineer Combat Bn
17 Dec 43 Cp Carson Colo / 18 Feb 46 Cp Kilmer N.J.
NYPE: 22 Oct 44   England: 2 Nov 44   France-ETO: Jan 45 - **25,26,34**   NYPE: 17 Feb 46
Kornwestheim Germany

287th Engineer Combat Bn
17 Dec 43 Cp Rucker Ala / 27 Feb 46 Cp Kilmer N.J.
NYPE: 30 Oct 44   England: 12 Nov 44   France-ETO: 26 Dec 44 - **26,32,34**   NYPE: 26 Feb 46
Leuggreis Germany

288th Engineer Combat Bn
17 Dec 43 Cp Rucker Ala / 29 Nov 46 Germany
NYPE: 22 Oct 44   England: 2 Nov 44   France-ETO: 23 Feb 45 - **26,34**
Alsee Germany

289th Engineer Combat Bn
30 Dec 43 Cp Joseph T Robinson Ark / 18 Feb 46 Cp Kilmer N.J.
NYPE: 22 Oct 44   England: 1 Nov 44   France-ETO: 31 Dec 44 - **24,25,34**   NYPE: 18 Feb 46
Mosbach Germany

290th Engineer Combat Bn
30 Dec 43 Cp Shelby Miss / 31 Aug 46 Germany
NYPE: 22 Oct 44   England: 2 Nov 44   France-ETO: 31 Dec 44 - **25,26,34**
Boxberg Germany

BATTALION DESIGNATION AND TYPE	FORMED (SOURCE OF UNIT)/INACTIVATION *Active through 1946	AUGUST 1945 LOCATION

291st Engineer Combat Bn 29 Mar 43 Cp Swift Tex (2nd Bn, 52nd Engr Regt) / 20 Oct 45 Cp Patrick Henry Va — Bruckenau Germany
NYPE: 11 Oct 43   England: 18 Oct 43   France-ETO: 24 Jun 44 - **25,26,30,32,34**   HRPE: 20 Oct 45

292nd Engineer Combat Bn 5 Nov 43 Cp Butner N.C. / 2 Mar 46 Cp Kilmer N.J. — Mainz Germany
NYPE: 22 Oct 44   England: 2 Nov 44   France-ETO: 13 Dec 44 - **26,34**   NYPE: 2 Mar 46

293rd Engineer Combat Bn 18 Mar 43 Cp Gordon Ga / 27 Nov 45 Cp Myles Standish Mass — Oslo Norway
NYPE: 11 Feb 44   England: 23 Feb 44   France-ETO: 13 Jul 44 - **25,26,30,32,34**   BPE: 26 Nov 45

294th Engineer Combat Bn 18 Mar 43 Cp Gordon Ga /18 Nov 45 Cp Kilmer N.J. — Roblingen Ober Germany
NYPE: 18 Jan 44   England: 27 Jan 44   France-ETO: 7 Jun 44 - **25,26,30,34**   NYPE: 16 Nov 45

295th Engineer Combat Bn 3 Mar 43 Cp Shelby Miss /18 Nov 45 Cp Kilmer N.J. — Le Havre France
NYPE: 18 Jan 44   England: 27 Jan 44   France-ETO: 18 Jun 44 - **26,30,32,34**   NYPE: 16 Nov 45

296th Engineer Combat Bn 3 Mar 43 Cp Shelby Miss /17 Dec 45 Cp Shanks N.Y. — Bad Berka Germany
NYPE: 11 Oct 43   England: 18 Oct 43   France-ETO: 28 Jun 44 - **25,26,30,32,34**   NYPE: 14 Dec 45

297th Engineer Combat Bn 18 Mar 43 Cp Rucker Ala / 25 Oct 45 Cp Myles Standish Mass — Schochwitz Germany
NYPE: 18 Jan 44   England: 29 Jan 44   France-ETO: 8 Jun 44 - **25,26,30,32,34**   BPE: 24 Oct 45

298th Engineer Combat Bn 18 Mar 43 Cp Rucker Ala /18 Nov 45 Cp Kilmer N.J. — Alizay France
NYPE: 18 Jan 44   England: 28 Jan 44   France-ETO: 9 Jun 44 - **25,26,30,32,34**   NYPE: 16 Nov 45

299th Engineer Combat Bn 1 Mar 43 Cp White Oreg /18 Oct 45 Cp Shanks N.Y. — Bayreuth Germany
NYPE: 8 Apr 44   England: 17 Apr 44   France-ETO: 6 Jun 44 - **25,26,30,32,34**   NYPE: 17 Oct 45

300th Engineer Combat Bn 1 Mar 43 Cp White Oreg / 2 Nov 45 Cp Patrick Henry Va — Aschaffenburg Germany
NYPE: 3 Dec 43   England: 9 Dec 43   France-ETO: 17 Jun 44 - **25,26,30,32,34**   HRPE: 17 Oct 45

301st Engineer Combat Bn 15 Jun 42 Ft George G Meade Md/31 Aug 45 Germany — Grimmetschau Germany
BPE: 10 Dec 44   England: 20 Dec 44   France-ETO: 11 Jan 45 - **25,26,34** *(76th Inf Div)*

302nd Engineer Combat Bn 25 Mar 42 Ft Jackson S.C. /15 Mar 46 Japan — Cebu Philippines
SFPE: 24 Mar 44   Hawaii: 31 Mar 44   Guam: 21 Jul 44   Philippines: 23 Nov 44   Okinawa: 20 Apr 45 - **13,19,21** *(77th Inf Div)*

303rd Engineer Combat Bn 15 Aug 42 Cp Butner N.C. /15 Jun 46 Germany — Borken Germany
NYPE: 14 Oct 44   England: 25 Oct 44   France-ETO: 22 Nov 44 - **25,26,34** *(78th Inf Div)*

304th Engineer Combat Bn 15 Jun 42 Cp Pickett Va /11 Dec 45 Cp Kilmer N.J. — Ainsberg Germany
BPE: 6 Apr 44   England: 16 Apr 44   France-ETO: 16 Jun 44 - **25,26,30,32,34**   NYPE: 10 Dec 45 *(79th Inf Div)*

305th Engineer Combat Bn 15 Jul 42 Cp Forrest Tenn / 5 Jan 46 NYPE — Nurnberg Germany
NYPE: 1 Jul 44   England: 7 Jul 44   France-ETO: 6 Aug 44 - **25,26,32,34**   NYPE: 3 Jan 46 *(80th Inf Div)*

306th Engineer Combat Bn 15 Jun 42 Cp Rucker Ala / 20 Jan 46 Japan — Leyte Philippines
SFPE: 2 Jun 44   Hawaii: 11 Jun 44   Peleliu I: 15 Sep 44   New Caledonia: 6 Dec 44   Philippines: 16 May 45 - **13,21** *(81st Inf Div)*

307th Airborne Engineer Bn 25 Mar 42 Cp Claiborne La / * — Sissone France
NYPE: 28 Apr 43   N.Africa: 10 May 43   Sicily: 9 Jul 43   Italy: 13 Sep 43   N.Ireland: 9 Dec 43   England: 14 Feb 44   France: 6 Jun 44
England: 13 Jul 44   Holland-ETO: 17 Sep 44 - **24,25,26,29,30,34,35,36** *(Co C assaulted Anzio 22 Jan 44)*   NYPE: 3 Jan 46 *(82nd A/B Div)*

308th Engineer Combat Bn 15 Aug 42 Cp Atterbury Ind / 22 Mar 46 NYPE — Bad Harzburg Germany
NYPE: 8 Apr 44   England: 19 Apr 44   France-ETO: 24 Jun 44 - **25,26,30,32,34**   NYPE: 21 Mar 46 *(83rd Inf Div)*

309th Engineer Combat Bn 15 Oct 42 Cp Howze Tex / 24 Jan 46 NYPE — Gross Hilligsfeld Germany
NYPE: 20 Sep 44   France-ETO: 1 Oct 44 - **25,26,34**   NYPE: 23 Jan 46 *(84th Inf Div)*

310th Engineer Combat Bn 5 May 42 Cp Shelby Miss / 25 Cp Patrick Henry Va — Fagianeria Italy
HRPE: 24 Dec 43   N.Africa: 9 Jan 44   Italy: 29 Mar 44 - **31,33,35**   HRPE: 25 Aug 45 *(85th Inf Div)*

311th Engineer Combat Bn 15 Dec 42 Cp Howze Tex / 30 Dec 46 Philippines — Shipment #4520-P loading
BPE: 19 Feb 45   France-ETO: 1 Mar 45 - **26**   NYPE: 17 Jun 45   SFPE: 21 Aug 45   Philippines: 7 Sep 45 *(86th Inf Div)*

312th Engineer Combat Bn 15 Dec 42 Cp McCain Miss / 21 Sep 45 Ft Benning Ga — Ft Benning Ga
NYPE: 4 Nov 44   England: 12 Nov 44   France-ETO: 30 Nov 44 - **25,26,34**   NYPE: 13 Jul 45 *(87th Inf Div)*

313th Engineer Combat Bn 15 Jul 42 Cp Gruber Okla / * — Rezzato Italy
HRPE: 13 Nov 43   N.Africa: 4 Dec 43   Italy: 6 Feb 44 - **31,33,35** *(88th Inf Div)*

314th Engineer Combat Bn 15 Jul 42 Cp Carson Colo /19 Dec 45 NYPE — Mesnil-Esnard France
BPE: 10 Jan 45   France-ETO: 24 Jan 45 - **26,34**   NYPE: 17 Dec 45 *(89th Inf Div)*

315th Engineer Combat Bn 25 Mar 42 Cp Barkeley Tex / 22 Dec 45 Cp Patrick Henry Va — Weiden Germany
NYPE: 24 Mar 44   England: 9 Apr 44   France-ETO: 7 Jun 44 - **25,26,30,32,34**   HRPE: 22 Dec 45 *(90th Inf Div)*

BATTALION DESIGNATION AND TYPE	FORMED (SOURCE OF UNIT)/INACTIVATION *Active through 1946	AUGUST 1945 LOCATION
316th Engineer Combat Bn HRPE: 3 Apr 44 N.Africa: 21 Apr 44 Italy: 19 Jun 44 - **31,33,35** HRPE: 10 Sep 45 *(91st Inf Div)*	15 Aug 42 Cp White Oreg /17 Nov 45 Cp Rucker Ala	Mariano Del Friu Italy
317th Engineer Combat Bn (Cld) HRPE: 20 Sep 44 Italy: 4 Oct 44 - **31,33,35** NYPE: 26 Nov 45 *(92nd Inf Div)*	15 Oct 42 Ft McClellan Ala / 29 Nov 45 NYPE	Torre Del Lago Italy
318th Engineer Combat Bn (Cld) SFPE: 19 Feb 44 Guadalcanal: 5 Mar 44 Treasury I: 7 Jun 44 New Guinea: 4 Nov 44 Morotai I: 7 Apr 45 - **3,15,16,20** SFPE: 1 Feb 46 *(93rd Inf Div)*	17 Apr 42 Ft Huachuca Ariz / 3 Feb 46 Cp Stoneman Calif	Morotai Island less Co B at Zamboanga Philippines
319th Engineer Combat Bn NYPE: 6 Aug 44 England: 11 Aug 44 France-ETO: 14 Sep 44 - **25,26,32,34** NYPE: 6 Feb 46 *(94th Inf Div)*	15 Sep 42 Ft Custer Mich / 7 Feb 46 Cp Kilmer N.J.	Vohwinkel Germany
320th Engineer Combat Bn BPE: 10 Aug 44 England: 17 Aug 44 France-ETO: 12 Sep 44 - **25,26,32,34** BPE: 5 Jul 45 *(95th Inf Div)*	15 Jul 42 Cp Swift Tex / 8 Oct 45 Cp Shelby Mass	Cp Shelby Mass
321st Engineer Combat Bn SFPE: 26 Jul 44 Hawaii: 31 Jul 44 Philippines: 20 Oct 44 Okinawa: 1 Apr 45 Philippines: 31 Jul 45 - **13,19** LAPE: 2 Feb 46 *(96th Inf Div)*	15 Aug 42 Cp Adair Oreg / 3 Feb 46 Cp Anza Calif	Mindoro Philippines
322nd Engineer Combat Bn NYPE: 19 Feb 45 France-ETO: 1 Mar 45 - **26** NYPE: 12 Jun 45 SPE: 22 Aug 45 Philippines: 14 Sep 45 *(97th Inf Div)*	25 Feb 43 Cp Swift Tex / 31 Mar 46 Japan	Ft Bragg N.C.
323rd Engineer Combat Bn SPE: 17 Apr 44 Hawaii: 22 Apr 44 *(98th Inf Div)*	15 Sep 42 Cp Breckinridge Ky /16 Feb 46 Japan	Ft Hase Hawaii
324th Engineer Combat Bn BPE: 30 Sep 44 England: 9 Oct 44 France-ETO: 10 Nov 44 - **25,26,34** HRPE: 27 Sep 45 *(99th Inf Div)*	15 Nov 42 Cp Van Dorn Miss / 27 Sep 45 Cp Patrick Henry Va	Dettelbach Germany
325th Engineer Combat Bn NYPE: 6 Oct 44 France-ETO: 20 Oct 44 - **25,26,34** NYPE: 14 Jan 46 *(100th Inf Div)*	15 Nov 42 Ft Jackson S.C. /14 Jan 46 NYPE	Eislingen Germany
326th Airborne Engineer Bn NYPE: 5 Sep 43 England: 18 Oct 43 France: 6 Jun 44 England: 13 Jul 44 Holland-ETO: 17 Sep 44 - **25,26,30,34** *(101st A/B Div)*	15 Aug 42 Cp Claiborne La /30 Nov 45 Germany	Loffre France
327th Engineer Combat Bn NYPE: 12 Sep 44 England: 23 Sep 44 France-ETO: 23 Sep 44 - **25,26,34** NYPE: 20 Mar 46 *(102nd Inf Div)*	15 Sep 42 Cp Maxey Tex/21 Mar 46 Cp Kilmer N.J.	Neudiestendorf Germany
328th Engineer Combat Bn NYPE: 6 Oct 44 France-ETO: 20 Oct 44 - **25,26,34** NYPE: 18 Sep 45 *(103rd Inf Div)*	15 Nov 42 Cp Claiborne La / 20 Sep 45 NYPE	Zirl Austria
329th Engineer Combat Bn NYPE: 27 Aug 44 France-ETO: 7 Sep 44 - **26,32,34** NYPE: 3 Jul 45 *(104th Inf Div)*	15 Sep 42 Cp Adair Oreg /10 Dec 45 Cp San Luis Obispo Calif	Cp San Luis Obispo Calif
331st Engineer Construction Bn *(activated in lieu of 1337th Engr Combat Bn per AG 322 [24 Oct 44] OB-I-SPMOU-M dtd 27 Oct 44, Secret)*	15 Nov 44 Alaska (331st Engr Regt) / 9 Mar 46 Alaska	Adak Island Aleutians
336th Engineer Combat Bn NYPE: 23 Oct 43 England: 2 Nov 43 France-ETO: 6 Jun 44 - **26,30,32,34** BPE: 3 Dec 45	1 Apr 43 Cp Rucker Ala (1st Bn, 336th Engr Regt) / 4 Dec 45 Cp Myles Standish Mass	Ochtenburg Germany
337th Engineer Combat Bn Italy: 7 Dec 44 Philippines: 1 Aug 45 - **31,33** *(departed Italy for SWPA 20–30 Jul 45 under Shipment #R2666-F)*	7 Dec 44 Malpensa Italy (335th AAA S/L Bn) / 25 Jan 46 Philippines	Manila Philippines
339th Engineer Construction Bn New Guinea: 8 Aug 44 Philippines: 21 Oct 44 - **13,14,15**	8 Aug 44 Mariboe New Guinea (339th Engr Regt) /5 Nov 45 Philippines	Dagupan Philippines
340th Engineer Construction Bn Australia: 20 Jul 44 New Guinea: 26 Aug 44 Morotai I: 15 Sep 44 Philippines: 9 Jan 45 - **14,15**	20 Jul 44 Darwin Australia (340th Engr Regt) / *	Dagupan Philippines
348th Engineer Combat Bn Halifax Sub-P/E: 31 Oct 43 England: 7 Nov 43 France-ETO: 6 Jun 44 - **25,26,30,32,34** NYPE: 26 Feb 46	15 Apr 43 Cp Young Calif (1st Bn, 348th Engr Regt) / 27 Feb 46 Cp Kilmer N.J.	Waggum Germany
349th Engineer Construction Bn	15 Aug 45 Ft Lewis Wash /5 Dec 46 Ft Lewis Wash	Organizing at Ft Lewis Wash
353rd Engineer Construction Bn New Caledonia: 1 Apr 44 Russell I: 16 May 44 Espiritu Santo: 1 Dec 44 Philippines: 28 Jun 45 - **14**	1 Apr 44 New Caledonia (1st Bn, 353rd Engr Regt) / 30 Jun 46 Japan	Manila Philippines
367th Engineer Combat Bn France: 31 Dec 44 HRPE: 27 Oct 45 - **26,34**	31 Dec 44 St Victoret France (406th AAA Gun Bn) / 28 Oct 45 Cp Myles Standish Mass	Wasseralfingen Germany
369th Engineer Combat Bn France: 31 Dec 44 NYPE: 14 Nov 45 - **26,34**	31 Dec 44 Marignone France (215th AAA Gun Bn) /16 Nov 45 Cp Kilmer N.J.	Oberhausen Germany
370th Engineer Combat Bn France: 31 Dec 44 BPE: 13 Nov 45 - **26,34**	31 Dec 44 Gignac France (74th AAA Gun Bn) /14 Nov 45 Cp Myles Standish Mass	Ulm Germany

BATTALION DESIGNATION AND TYPE	FORMED (SOURCE OF UNIT)/INACTIVATION *Active through 1946	AUGUST 1945 LOCATION
371st Engineer Construction Bn NYPE: 13 May 44 England: 25 May 44 France-ETO: 8 Sep 44 - **25,26,32,34**	1 Feb 44 Cp Ellis Ill (371st Engr Regt) / 25 Jun 46 France	Rheydt Germany sch to SWPA under Shipment #R9850-J
374th Engineer Bn (Separate) (Cld)	15 May 42 Cp Gordon Ga / 2 Aug 43 Cp Hood Tex redes 374th Engr Regt	
375th Engineer Bn (Separate) (Cld)	15 Jun 42 Cp Sutton N.C. / 2 Aug 43 Ft Knox Ky redes 375th Engr Regt	
376th Engineer Bn (Separate) (Cld) HRPE: 23 Apr 43 N.Africa: 11 May 43 Italy: 29 Dec 43 France-ETO: 19 Sep 44 - **29,34,35,37** BPE: 23 Oct 45	25 Jun 42 Cp Polk La / 23 Oct 45 Cp Myles Standish Mass	Marignanc France
377th Engineer Bn (Separate) (Cld)	15 Jul 42 Cp Pickett Va / 2 Aug 43 Ft Knox Ky redes 377th Engr Regt	
378th Engineer Bn (Separate) (Cld) NYPE: 6 May 43 N.Africa: 12 May 43 France-ETO: 16 Aug 44 - **25,29,35,37**	20 Mar 42 Cp Shelby Miss / 10 Mar 45 France	
379th Engineer Bn (Separate) (Cld) HRPE: 10 Dec 43 Hawaii: 31 Dec 43	15 Jul 42 Cp Shelby Miss / 17 Dec 44 Hawaii	
380th Engineer Combat Bn SFPE: 27 Jun 45 Philippines: 29 Jul 45	30 Mar 44 Cp Pickett Va / 28 Feb 46 Japan	Shipment #2892-C unloading
381st Engineer Combat Bn NYPE: 30 Oct 44 England: 10 Nov 44 France-ETO: 8 Mar 45 - **26,34**	27 Mar 44 Cp Van Dorn Miss / 27 Feb 46 Cp Kilmer N.J.	Kirchberg Germany
382nd Engineer Construction Bn (Cld) SFPE: 27 Jul 43 India: 10 Sep 43 - **12** NYPE: 11 Nov 45 *(redes from Engr Bn [Sep] [Cld] 10 May 44)*	22 Sep 42 Ft Knox Ky / 12 Nov 45 Cp Kilmer N.J.	Ledo India
383rd Engineer Bn (Separate) (Cld) NYPE: 31 Aug 42 England: 5 Sep 42	6 Mar 42 Cp Shelby Miss / 13 Aug 44 England redes 1349th Engr Regt	
384th Engineer Bn (Separate) (Cld) NYPE: 2 Apr 43 N.Africa: 13 Apr 43 Italy: 3 Mar 44 France-ETO: 25 Sep 44 - **26,34,35** NYPE: 22 Nov 45	18 Apr 42 Ft Bragg N.C. / 24 Nov 45 NYPE	Rheingonheim Germany
385th Engineer Bn (Separate) (Cld) HRPE: 7 Feb 43 N.Africa: 21 Feb 43 Italy: 14 Feb 44 France-ETO: 22 Sep 44 - **26,34,35,38** BPE: 30 Oct 45	18 Apr 42 Cp Edwards Mass / 31 Oct 45 Cp Myles Standish Mass	Le Havre France
386th Engineer Bn (Separate) (Cld) HRPE: 6 May 43 N.Africa: 12 May 43 Italy: 10 Oct 43 - **29,35**	26 Mar 42 Ft Knox Ky / 25 Apr 45 Naples Italy	
387th Engineer Bn (Separate) (Cld) NYPE: 2 Apr 43 N.Africa: 13 Apr 43 Italy: 10 Sep 43 - **24,29,31,35** *(pers to 3rd Bn, 92nd Engr Regt)*	1 May 42 Ft George G Meade Md / 1 Feb 45 Sesto Italy	
388th Engineer Bn (Separate) (Cld) Departed Cp Claiborne La: 4 Jun 42 Arrived Norman NW Territory Canada: 15 Jun 42 *(direct movement) (Northwest Service Command)*	10 Jan 42 Cp Claiborne La / 10 Jan 43 Canada redes 388th Engr Regt	
389th Engineer Bn (Separate) (Cld) *(Desert Training Center)*	5 May 42 Cp Gordon Ga / 20 Aug 43 Cp Young Calif redes Engr Regt	
401st Engineer Water Supply Bn NYPE: 2 Nov 42 N.Africa: 11 Nov 42 Sicily: 13 Jul 43 Italy: 10 Nov 43 - **29,35,36** *(37 - Co B only)*	18 Apr 42 Plattsburg Bks N.Y. / 9 Oct 44 Naples Italy	
401st Engineer Combat Bn Italy: 1 Mar 45 - **31,33** HRPE: 24 Aug 45	1 Mar 45 Borgo di Basono Italy (1st Bn, 19th Engr Regt) / 6 Dec 45 Cp Polk La	Shipment #R0488-D (sch to SWPA but returned to USA) at sea
402nd Engineer Water Supply Bn NYPE: 11 Dec 42 N.Africa: 25 Dec 42 *(Co A and B inactiv 3 Aug 44)*	14 Mar 42 Cp Forrest Tenn / 1 Dec 44 North Africa	
402nd Engineer Combat Bn Italy: 1 Mar 45 - **31,33**	1 Mar 45 Filigare Italy *(2nd Bn, 19th Engr Regt)* / 30 Sep 45 Italy	Campeggio Italy
403rd Engineer Water Supply Bn NYPE: 29 Dec 43 England: 10 Jan 44	6 Aug 42 Cp Butner N.C. / 4 Mar 44 England	
404th Engineer Combat Bn Italy: 1 Mar 45 - **33** NYPE: 13 Oct 45	1 Mar 45 Pisa Italy (1st Bn, 39th Engr Regt) / 13 Oct 45 Cp Shanks N.Y.	Pisa Italy
405th Engineer Service Bn HRPE: 10 May 43 N.Africa: 2 Jun 43 Italy: 26 Nov 43 - **24,29,31,33,35** *(redes Engr Service Bn 18 May 45)*	20 Nov 42 Cp Breckinridge Ky as Engr Water Supply Bn / *	Verona Italy
407th Engineer Service Bn (Pipeline) Italy: 5 Dec 44 - **33**	5 Dec 44 Livorno Italy (1629th Engr Utilities Det) / 10 Nov 45 Italy	Livorno Italy

BATTALION DESIGNATION AND TYPE	FORMED (SOURCE OF UNIT)/INACTIVATION *Active through 1946	AUGUST 1945 LOCATION
408th Engineer Service Bn (Pipeline) France: 6 Jan 45 - **26,34** BPE: 20 Nov 45	6 Jan 45 (3rd Bn, 335th Engr Regt) / 21 Nov 45 Cp Myles Standish Mass	Sarrebourg France
409th Engineer Combat Bn Italy: 7 Dec 44 - **33**	7 Dec 44 Italy (354th AAA S/L Bn) /10 Jan 45 Italy	
410th Engineer Combat Bn	8 Jan 45 Cp Bowie Tex (2nd Bn, 18th Engr Regt) / *	Ft Belvoir Va
411th Engineer Special Shop Bn SFPE: 17 Jan 43 Australia: 30 Jan 43 New Guinea: 5 Jun 44 Philippines: 16 Dec 44 - **14,15** SFPE: 2 Feb 46 *(redes Engr Special Shop Bn 1 Nov 44 in New Guinea)*	17 Aug 42 Cp Edwards Mass as Engr Base Shop Bn / 4 Feb 46 Cp Stoneman Calif	Batangas Philippines
487th Engineer Water Supply Bn NYPE: 5 Nov 43 England: 17 Nov 43 France-ETO: 1 Jul 44 - **25,30,32,34**	10 Sep 42 Cp White Oreg / 5 May 45 Germany	
489th Engineer Water Supply Bn (Cld) SFPE: 11 Jan 44 Guadalcanal: 27 Jan 44 - *(16 - Co C only)*	31 Oct 42 Cp Maxey Tex / 21 Aug 44 Solomon Islands redes 1517th–1519th Engr Water Supply Cos	
515th Engineer Water Supply Bn	29 Jan 43 Cp Swift Tex / 26 Nov 43 Indio Calif	
516th Engineer Water Supply Bn	1 Mar 43 Cp White Oreg / 30 Nov 43 Ft Lewis Wash	
551st Engineer Heavy Ponton Bn BPE: 26 Jul 44 England: 1 Aug 44 France-ETO: 28 Aug 44 - **26,32,34** BPE: 12 Sep 45	15 May 42 Cp Gordon Ga / 27 Nov 45 Cp Breckinridge Ky	Munster Germany sch to SWPA under Shipment #R6604-R
552nd Engineer Heavy Ponton Bn NYPE: 29 Dec 43 England: 8 Jan 44 France-ETO: 28 Jul 44 - **25,26,32,34** *(30-Co A only)* NYPE: 1 Mar 46	15 May 42 Cp Gordon Ga /2 Mar 46 Cp Kilmer N.J.	Warburg Germany
553rd Engineer Heavy Ponton Bn BPE: 11 Feb 44 England: 23 Feb 44 France-ETO: 30 Jul 44 - **25,26,32,34**	25 Jan 43 Cp Swift Tex /1 Aug 45 Germany	
554th Engineer Heavy Ponton Bn BPE: 24 Jul 44 England: 30 Jul 44 France-ETO: 6 Sep 44 - **25,26,32,34** BPE: 1 Sep 45	25 Jan 43 Cp Swift Tex / 5 Nov 45 Cp Campbell Ky	Braunschweig Germany sch to SWPA under Shipment #R6604-S
555th Engineer Heavy Ponton Bn NYPE: 18 Feb 45 France-ETO: 16 Mar 45 - **26** HRPE: 14 Sep 45	1 May 43 Cp White Oreg /15 Nov 45 Cp Swift Tex	Hardheim Germany sch to SWPA under Shipment #R6604-P
556th Engineer Heavy Ponton Bn SFPE: 28 Apr 44 New Guinea: 20 May 44 Philippines: 24 Oct 44 - **13,14,15**	25 Jun 43 Cp Beale Calif /15 Dec 45 Philippines	Clark Field Philippines
557th Engineer Heavy Ponton Bn	23 Jul 43 Cp Breckinridge Ky /1 Jun 44 Cp Breckinridge Ky	
558th Engineer Heavy Ponton Bn SFPE: 18 Aug 45 Philippines: 12 Sep 45	26 Jun 44 Cp Gordon Ga / 5 Feb 46 Philippines	Shipment #2455-M loading at San Francisco Calif for Manila
562nd Engineer Boat Maintenance Bn Australia: 12 Jun 43 New Guinea: 6 Aug 43 Philippines: 25 Oct 44 - **3,15** SPE: 17 Dec 45	12 Jun 43 Cairns Australia (562nd Engr Co, 2nd Engr Special Bde) / *	Tacloban Philippines
563rd Engineer Boat Maintenance Bn SFPE: 7 Sep 43 New Guinea: 1 Oct 43 Biak I: 27 Sep 44 Philippines: 2 Aug 45 - **3,15** SFPE: 22 Dec 45	1 Jun 43 Ft Ord Calif (563rd Engr Co, 3rd Engr Spec Bde)/22 Dec 45 Cp Stoneman Calif	Luzon Philippines
564th Engineer Boat Maintenance Bn SFPE: 11 Jun 44 Australia: 28 Jun 44 New Guinea: 1 Jul 44 Philippines: 11 Jan 45 - **14,15**	1 Jun 43 Cp Edwards Mass (564th Engr Co, 4th Engr Spec Bde) /15 Apr 46 Japan	Manila Philippines
599th Engineer Topographic Bn	30 Mar 44 Cp McCoy Wis / 20 Jul 44 Cp McCoy Wis	
600th Engineer Service Bn Italy: 1 Aug 44 - **35** *(redes Engr Service Bn 13 Nov 44)*	1 Aug 44 Naples Italy as Engr Composite Bn / 25 Nov 45 Italy	Bari Italy
601st Engineer Camouflage Bn	1 Apr 42 Ft Ord Calif / 5 Feb 43 Cp Young Calif	
602nd Army Engineer Camouflage Bn NYPE: 8 Jan 44 England: 17 Jan 44 France-ETO: 9 Jul 44 - **25,26,30,32,34** NYPE: 1 Mar 46 *(redes Army Engr Camouflage Bn 19 Apr 45)*	28 Jan 43 Cp Butner N.C. as Engr Camouflage Bn / 2 Mar 46 Cp Kilmer N.J.	Germany
603rd Engineer Camouflage Bn, Special NYPE: 3 May 44 England: 15 May 44 France-ETO: 27 Jun 44 - **25,26,30,32,34** HRPE: 2 Jul 45	1 May 42 Ft George G Meade Md / 25 Sep 45 Pine Camp N.Y.	Pine Camp N.Y. under the 23rd Headquarters, Special Troops, Second Army
604th Army Engineer Camouflage Bn NYPE: 25 Oct 43 England: 7 Nov 43 France-ETO: 15 Aug 44 - **25,26,30,32,34** HRPE: 19 Nov 45 *(redes Army Engr Camouflage Bn 1 May 45)*	24 Sep 42 Cp Campbell Ky as Engr Camouflage Bn /19 Nov 45 Cp Patrick Henry Va	Paris France
605th Engineer Combat Bn BPE: 16 Apr 45 France-ETO: 28 Apr 45 BPE: Sep 45 *(redes Engr Combat Bn 10 Jul 44)*	5 Feb 43 Cp Young Calif as Engr Camouflage Bn /15 Dec 45 Cp Shelby Miss	Yvetot France sch to SWPA under Shipment #R6604-AAA
606th Army Engineer Camouflage Bn BPE: 18 Jan 45 France-ETO: 29 Jan 45 - **26,34** HRPE: 27 Jun 45 *(redes Army Engr Camouflage Bn 1 May 45)*	16 Apr 43 Cp Carson Colo as Engr Camouflage Bn /19 Feb 46 Cp Gruber Okla	Cp Shelby Miss

BATTALION DESIGNATION AND TYPE	FORMED (SOURCE OF UNIT) / INACTIVATION *Active through 1946	AUGUST 1945 LOCATION

607th Engineer Camouflage Bn
25 Jun 43 Cp Van Dorn Miss /10 Apr 44 Cp McCoy Wis

643rd Engineer Combat Bn
Italy: 1 Mar 45 - **33**   HRPE: 24 Aug 45
1 Mar 45 Monghidoro Italy (2nd Bn, 39th Engr Regt) /15 Nov 46 Cp Knox Ky
Shipment #R0488-E (sch to SWPA but returned to USA) at sea

648th Engineer Base Topographic Bn
SFPE: 26 May 42   Australia: 12 Jun 42 at Melbourne Base   Philippines: 7 Apr 45 - **14** (Engr Topographic Bn [Army] 15 Dec 41–1 Mar 43 when redes Engr Topographic Bn [GHQ] until 20 Jan 45 when redes Engr Base Topographic Bn) (Melbourne Base Map Plant)
15 Dec 41 Cp Claiborne La /10 Nov 45 Philippines
Manila Philippines

649th Engineer Topographic Bn (Army)
HRPE: 2 Apr 43   N.Africa: 13 Apr 43   Italy: Unknown   France-ETO: 19 Sep 44 - **25,26,29,34,37**   NYPE: 27 Nov 45
10 Dec 41 Ft Belvoir Va / 29 Nov 45 Cp Kilmer N.J.
Waiblingen Germany

650th Engineer Topographic Bn (Army)
SFPE: 31 Mar 44   New Guinea: 21 Apr 44   Philippines: 9 Jul 45 - **15**
20 Aug 42 Cp White Oreg /15 Nov 45 Japan
San Fernando Philippines

651st Engineer Topographic Bn (Army)
SPE: 22 Mar 44   Hawaii: 29 Mar 44
20 Sep 42 Cp Maxey Tex / 5 Apr 44 Hawaii

652nd Engineer Topographic Bn (Army)
NYPE: 21 Feb 44   England: 29 Feb 44   France-ETO: 16 Jul 44 - **25,26,30,32,34**   NYPE: 26 Dec 45
31 Oct 42 Cp Livingston La / 27 Dec 45 NYPE
Freising Germany

653rd Engineer Topographic Bn (Army)
NYPE: 7 Sep 44   India: 20 Oct 43 - **8,12**   NYPE: 21 Nov 45
15 Jun 42 Cp Claiborne La / 22 Nov 45 Cp Kilmer N.J.
New Delhi India less plat at Chinkiang China

654th Engineer Topographic Bn (Army)
NYPE: 10 Dec 43   England: 17 Dec 43   France-ETO: 26 Jun 44 - **25,26,30,32,34**
15 Jun 42 Ft Custer Mich /12 Mar 46 Germany
Bad Neuenahr Germany

655th Engineer Topographic Bn (Army)
NYPE: 9 Dec 44   England: 20 Dec 44   France-ETO: 31 Jan 45 - **26,34**
17 Dec 43 Cp McCoy Wis / 30 Nov 45 Germany
Munster Germany sch to SWPA under Shipment #R5009-D

656th Engineer Topographic Bn (Army)
NYPE: 11 Feb 45   France-ETO: 21 Feb 45   HRPE: 1 Jul 45
30 Mar 44 Cp McCoy Wis / *
Cp Swift Tex

657th Engineer Topographic Bn (Army)
NYPE: 18 Feb 45   England: 26 Feb 45   France-ETO: 14 Mar 45   Dep France: 21 Jul 45   Hawaii: 12 Aug 45
(Moved to Pacific Ocean Area from present overseas station [France] per WD 370.5 [12 May 45] OB-S-E-SPMOT-M dtd 13 May 45, Secret)
30 Mar 44 Cp McCoy Wis / *
Oahu Hawaii unloading from Shipment #R0051-B

659th Airborne Engineer Bn
30 Mar 44 Cp Pickett Va / 30 Jul 44 Cp Pickett Va redes 1291st Engr Combat Bn

659th Engineer Base Topographic Bn
NYPE: 7 Mar 45   France-ETO: 18 Mar 45   NYPE: 6 Jan 46
13 Nov 44 Ft Belvoir Va / 7 Jan 46 NYPE
Paris France

660th Engineer Base Topographic Bn
England: 8 Oct 43   France-ETO: 20 Oct 44 (Co C and Map Storage & Dist. Sec of Hqs activated 28 Aug 42 at Ft Belvoir Va, France left NYPE 8 Dec 42 and arrived England 13 Dec 42 and were thus already active) (redes Engr Base Topographic Bn 21 Aug 44)
8 Oct 43 Kew England as Engr Topographic Bn (Spec Engr Topo Bn) / 28 Jan 46
Paris France

692nd Engineer Special Shop Bn (Boat Cons)
NOPE: 10 Feb 44   New Guinea: 25 Feb 44   Philippines: 17 Jun 45 - **14,15**   LAPE: 25 Jan 46 (redes Engr Special Shop Bn 12 Aug 43)
15 May 43 Cp Edwards Mass as Engr Base Shop Bn / 27 Jan 46 Cp Anza Calif
Manila Philippines

711th Railway Operating Bn, TC
Dep ZI: 1 Nov 42   Iran: 16 Dec 42   Arrived ZI: 22 Aug 45 (redes from Engrs 16 Nov 42 to TC) (Assoc: None - was Training Battalion)
18 Jun 42 Ft Belvoir Va as Engr Bn / 20 Oct 45 Ft Benning Ga
Scheduled to Ft Benning Ga

712th Railway Operating Bn, TC
Dep ZI: 6 Apr 44   England: 16 Apr 44   France-ETO: 18 Aug 44 - **26,32,34**   NYPE: 9 Dec 45 (Assoc: Reading RR)
18 Oct 43 New Orleans La /11 Dec 45 Cp Kilmer N.J.
Frankfurt Germany

713th Railway Operating Bn, TC
Dep ZI: 7 Feb 43   N.Africa: 19 Feb 43   Italy: 6 Oct 43   France-ETO: 30 Aug 44 - **29,31,33,35** (redes from Engrs 16 Nov 42)
(Assoc: Atchinson, Topeka & Santa Fe RR)
25 Apr 42 Clovis N.Mex as Engr Bn / 6 Oct 45 Germany
Seckenheim Germany

714th Railway Operating Bn, TC
Dep ZI: 29 Mar 43   Alaska: 4 Apr 43   Canada: 13 May 43   Arrived ZI: 26 May 45 (redes from Engrs 16 Nov 42)
(Assoc: Chicago, St Paul, Minneapolis & Omaha RR)
31 Oct 42 Cp Claiborne La as Engr Bn / *
Cp Claiborne La

715th Railway Operating Bn, TC
Dep ZI: 28 Apr 43   N.Africa: 11 May 43   Italy: 11 Jan 44 - **29,31,33,35**   Arrived ZI: 19 Aug 45 (redes from Engrs 16 Nov 42)
(Assoc: Illinois Central RR)
31 Oct 42 Cp Claiborne La as Engr Bn /12 Dec 45 Cp Plauche La
At sea en route to New York P/E

716th Railway Operating Bn, TC
Dep ZI: 11 Aug 44   England: 22 Aug 44   France-ETO: 26 Aug 44 - **26,32,34**   NYPE: 26 Feb 46 (Assoc: Southern Pacific RR)
21 Dec 43 Ft Sam Houston Tex / 27 Feb 46 Cp Kilmer N.J.
Metz France

717th Railway Operating Bn, TC
Dep ZI: 12 May 44   England: 23 May 44   France-ETO: Aug 44   BPE: 11 Dec 45 (Assoc: Pennsylvania RR)
1 Dec 43 New Orleans La /12 Dec 45 Cp Myles Standish Mass
Aschurch England w/dets in ETO

718th Railway Operating Bn, TC
Dep ZI: 24 Jul 44   England: 31 Jul 44   France-ETO: Sep 44 - **25,26,32,34**   NYPE: 3 Dec 45
(Assoc: Cleveland, Cincinnati, Chicago & St Louis RR)
14 Dec 43 Ft Sam Houston Tex / 4 Dec 45 NYPE
Mainz Germany

BATTALION DESIGNATION AND TYPE	FORMED (SOURCE OF UNIT) / INACTIVATION	AUGUST 1945 LOCATION
719th Railway Operating Bn, TC Dep ZI: 28 Apr 43 N.Africa: 11 May 43 Italy: 6 Mar 44 - **29,31,33,35** Arrived ZI: 30 Aug 45 *(redes from Engrs 16 Nov 42)* *(Assoc: Texas & New Orleans RR)*	1 Sep 42 Cp Claiborne La as Engr Bn / 20 Nov 45 Cp Claiborne La	Livorno Italy
720th Railway Operating Bn, TC Dep ZI: 20 Jan 44 England: 9 Feb 44 France-ETO: Aug 44 - **26,30,32** NYPE: 5 Dec 45 *(Assoc: Chicago & Northwestern RR)*	26 Aug 43 New Orleans La / 7 Dec 45 Cp Kilmer N.J.	Rheydt Germany
721st Railway Operating Bn, TC Dep ZI: 10 Dec 43 India: 11 Jan 44 NYPE: 16 Nov 45 *(Assoc: New York Central RR)*	8 Apr 43 New Orleans La /17 Nov 45 Cp Kilmer N.J.	Calcutta India
722nd Railway Operating Bn, TC Dep ZI: 11 Aug 43 England: 22 Aug 44 France-ETO: 26 Aug 44 - **25,26,32,34** NYPE: 17 Jan 46 *(Assoc: Seaboard Air Line RR)*	14 Dec 43 Ft Sam Houston Tex /18 Jan 46 Cp Kilmer N.J.	Eisenach Germany
723rd Railway Operating Bn, TC Dep ZI: 11 Aug 43 England: 22 Aug 44 France-ETO: 27 Aug 44 - **26,32,34** NYPE: 2 Jan 46 *(Assoc. Union Pacific RR)*	21 Dec 43 Ft Sam Houston Tex / 3 Jan 46 Cp Kilmer N.J.	Chartes France
724th Railway Operating Bn, TC Dep ZI: 11 Aug 43 England: 22 Aug 44 France-ETO: 27 Aug 44 - **25,32** NYPE: 27 Jan 46 *(Assoc: Pennsylvania RR)*	28 Dec 43 Ft Sam Houston Tex / 28 Jan 46 Cp Kilmer N.J.	Compiegne France
725th Railway Operating Bn, TC Dep ZI: 10 Dec 43 India: 11 Jan 44 NYPE: 28 Oct 45 *(Assoc: Chicago, Rock Island & Pacific RR)*	17 Feb 43 New Orleans La / 29 Oct 45 Cp Kilmer N.J.	Lalmanir Hat India
726th Railway Operating Bn, TC Dep ZI: 10 Dec 43 India: 11 Jan 44 NYPE: 24 Nov 45 *(Assoc: Wabash RR)*	18 Jun 43 New Orleans La / 26 Nov 45 Cp Kilmer N.J.	Calcutta India
727th Railway Operating Bn, TC Dep ZI: 12 Dec 42 N.Africa: 25 Dec 42 Sicily: 11 Jul 43 Italy: Unknown France-ETO: 29 Sep 44 - **26,29,31,34,35,36,37,38** *(Assoc: Southern Railway)*	9 Apr 42 Cp Shelby Miss as Engr Bn / 6 Oct 45 Germany	Heidelberg Germany
728th Railway Operating Bn, TC Dep ZI: 5 Dec 43 England: 15 Dec 43 France-ETO: 26 Jul 44 - **26,30,32** NYPE: 22 Nov 45 *(Assoc: Louisville & Nashville RR)*	11 Jan 43 New Orleans La / 24 Nov 45 Cp Kilmer N.J.	Cherbourg France
729th Railway Operating Bn, TC Dep ZI: 9 Jul 43 England: 15 Jul 43 France-ETO: Aug 44 - **26,30,32** BPE: 17 Nov 45 *(Assoc: New York, New Haven & Hartford RR)*	11 Jan 43 New Orleans La /18 Nov 45 Cp Myles Standish Mass	Gifhorn Germany
730th Railway Operating Bn, TC Dep ZI: 7 Dec 42 Iraq-Iran: 14 Jan 43 Arrived ZI: 23 Jul 45 *(redes from Engrs 16 Nov 42) (Assoc: Pennsylvania RR)*	15 May 42 Ft Wayne Ind as Engr Bn/ 20 Oct 45 Cp Joseph T Robinson Ark	Cp Joseph T Robinson Ark
732nd Railway Operating Bn, TC Dep ZI: 20 Sep 44 France-ETO: 1 Oct 44 - **25,26,34** NYPE: 17 Feb 46 *(Assoc: Great Northern Railway)*	10 Feb 44 Ft Sam Houston Tex / 18 Feb 46 Cp Kilmer N.J.	Thionville France sch to SWPA under Shipment #R6604-JJJ
733rd Railway Operating Bn, TC Dep ZI: 16 Jun 44 England: 27 Jun 44 France-ETO: Aug 44 - **32,3** NYPE: 16 Dec 45 *(Assoc: Central RR of Georgia)*	23 Nov 43 New Orleans La /17 Dec 45 Cp Shanks N.Y.	Seckenheim Germany less Co A at Metz France
734th Railway Operating Bn, TC Dep ZI: 15 Nov 44 England: 27 Nov 44 France-ETO: 17 Dec 44 - **25,26,34** *(Assoc: Southern Pacific RR)*	22 Mar 44 Cp Plauche La /10 Feb 46 Germany	Maastricht Holland
735th Railway Operating Bn, TC Dep ZI: 20 Sep 44 France-ETO: 1 Oct 44 - **26,34** *(Assoc: Erie RR)*	3 Feb 44 Cp Plauche La /10 Feb 46 Germany	Munster Germany
737th Railway Operating Bn, TC Dep ZI: 14 Feb 45 New Guinea: 8 Mar 45 Philippines: 26 Mar 45 - **14** *(Assoc: New York Central RR)*	30 Sep 44 Ft Francis E Warren Wyo/10 Apr 46 Korea	Clark Field Philippines
740th Railway Operating Bn, TC Dep ZI: 18 Jul 44 England:9 Jul 44 France-ETO: 16 Aug 44 - **25,26,32,34** NYPE: 2 Jan 46 *(Assoc: Chesapeake & Ohio RR)*	14 Dec 43 New Orleans La / 4 Jan 46 Cp Kilmer N.J.	Bad Godesberg Germany
741st Railway Operating Bn, TC Dep ZI: 20 Sep 44 England: 1 Oct 44 France-ETO: 22 Oct 44 - **25,26,34** *(Assoc: Gulf, Mobile & Ohio RR)*	10 Feb 44 Ft Sam Houston Tex /10 Feb 46 Germany	Liege Belgium
743rd Railway Operating Bn, TC Dep ZI: 20 Sep 44 France-ETO: 1 Oct 44 - **26,34** NYPE: 9 Feb 46 *(Assoc: Illinois Central RR)*	27 Jan 44 Cp Plauche La /10 Feb 46 Cp Kilmer N.J.	Munster Germany
744th Railway Operating Bn, TC Dep ZI: 11 Aug 44 England: 22 Aug 44 France-ETO: Unknown - **25,32,34** NYPE: 11 Jan 46 *(Assoc: Chicago, Milwaukee, St Paul & Pacific RR)*	21 Dec 43 Ft Sam Houston Tex /12 Jan 46 Cp Kilmer N.J.	Charleroi Belgium
745th Railway Operating Bn, TC Dep ZI: 10 Dec 43 India: 11 Jan 44 NYPE: 28 Oct 45 *(Assoc: Chicago, Burlington & Quincy RR)*	12 May 43 New Orleans La / 29 Oct 45 Cp Kilmer N.J.	Jorhat India
746th Railway Operating Bn, TC Dep ZI: 26 Dec 44 England: 7 Jan 45 France-ETO: 25 Jan 45 - **26** *(Assoc: Missouri, Kansas & Texas RR)*	27 Apr 44 Cp Plauche La /10 Feb 46 Germany	Fulda Germany
748th Railway Operating Bn, TC Dep ZI: 10 Dec 43 India: 11 Jan 44 NYPE: 24 Nov 45 *(Assoc: Texas & Pacific Railway)*	12 May 43 New Orleans La / 26 Nov 45 Cp Kilmer N.J.	Chabua India
749th Railway Operating Bn, TC Dep ZI: 14 Feb 45 New Guinea: 5 Mar 45 Philippines: Unknown India: Unknown - **14** *(Assoc: New York, New Haven & Hartford RR)*	20 Jun 44 Cp Plauche La /31 May 46 Korea	Chabua India

BATTALION DESIGNATION AND TYPE	FORMED (SOURCE OF UNIT)/INACTIVATION *Active through 1946	AUGUST 1945 LOCATION

750th Railway Operating Bn, TC
13 Mar 44 Cp Plauche La/10 Feb 46 Germany
Dep ZI: 27 Oct 44   France-ETO: 6 Nov 44 - **26,34** (Assoc: St Louis–San Francisco Railway)
Wurzburg Germany

752nd Railway Operating Bn, TC
27 Apr 44 Cp Plauche La/1; Feb 46 Germany
Dep ZI: 26 Dec 44   England: 7 Jan 45   France-ETO: 25 Jan 45 - **26,34** (Assoc: Boston & Maine RR)
Namur Belgium

753rd Engineer Railway Shop Bn (Steam)
15 Apr 42 Bucyrus Ohio/16 Nov 42 Cp Willard Ohio redes TC Railway Shop Bn

754th Railway Operating Bn, TC
15 Oct 42 Cp Claiborne La as Engr Bn/25 Jul 45 Tehran Iran
Dep ZI: 13 Jan 43   Iraq-Iran: 22 Feb 43 (redes from Engrs 16 Nov 42) (Assoc: Southern Pacific RR)

755th Railway Operating Bn, TC
30 Oct 42 Cp Claiborne La as Engr Bn/1 Jan 46 Cp Patrick Henry Va
Dep ZI: 2 Dec 43   England: 12 Dec 43   France-ETO: Unknown - **32**   HRPE: 1 Jan 46 (redes from Engrs 16 Nov 42)
(Assoc: Norfolk & Western Railway)

759th Railway Operating Bn, TC
1 Sep 42 Cp Claiborne La as Engr Bn / 26 Nov 45 Cp Kilmer N.J.
Dep ZI: 28 Apr 43   N.Africa: 11 May 43   Italy: Unknown   France-ETO: 15 Oct 44 - **26,29,34,35,37**   NYPE: 23 Nov 45
(redes from Engrs 16 Nov 42) (Missouri Pacific RR)
Erlangen Germany

760th Engineer Railway Shop Bn (Diesel)
15 Jun 42 Cp Claiborne /16 Nov 42 Cp Patrick Henry Va redes TC Railway Shop Bn

762nd Engineer Railway Shop Bn (Diesel)
15 Oct 42 Cp Claiborne La /16 Nov 42 Cp Claiborne La redes TC Railway Shop Bn

770th Railway Operating Bn, TC
9 Aug 42 Cp William C Reid N.Mex / 8 Nov 46 Korea
SFPE: 23 Aug 45   Philippines: 26 Sep 45
Cp Anza Calif

796th Engineer Forestry Bn
25 Jun 43 Cp Claiborne La/20 Oct 45 Ft Lewis Wash
NYPE: 26 Jul 44   England: 6 Aug 44   France-ETO: 25 Aug 44 - **25,26,34**   BPE: 27 Aug 45
Shipment #10897-AAA
loading at Le Havre France

801st Engineer Aviation Bn
1 Feb 43 Davis-Monthan Field Ariz / 23 May 46 Okinawa
HRPE: 3 Jan 44   Azores I: 18 Jan 44   HRPE: 10 Mar 45   SPE: 16 Jul 45   Hawaii: 23 Jul 45   Okinawa: 7 Sep 45
Shipment #9055-F at sea
en route to Okinawa

802nd Engineer Aviation Bn
1 Jul 41 Ft Glenn Alaska /*
Alaska: 1 Jul 41   SPE: 27 Jun 44   SPE: 13 Feb 45   Hawaii: 20 Feb 45   Okinawa: 2 Apr 45 - **2,19**
Okinawa

803rd Engineer Bn, Aviation (Separate)
8 Jul 41 Westover Field Mass / 9 Apr 42 Bataan Philippines
SFPE: 4 Oct 41   Philippines: 26 Oct 41 - **18** (surrendered to Japanese forces)

804th Engineer Aviation Bn
21 Jul 41 Schofield Bks Hawaii /13 Nov 45 Cp Stoneman Calif
Hawaii: 21 Jul 41   Baker I: 1 Sep 43   Makin I: 22 Nov 43   Saipan: 20 Jun 44 - **6,21**   SFPE: 10 Nov 45
Saipan less det at Schofield Bks Hawaii

805th Engineer Aviation Bn
28 Jun 41 Albrook Field Canal Zone / 4 Jan 46 Ft Lawton Wash
Panama: 28 Jun 41   NYPE: 7 Apr 43   SFPE: 16 Dec 43   Hawaii: 20 Dec 43   Saipan: 30 Jun 44   Ie Shima I: 1 Jun 45 - **6,21**   SPE: 31 Dec 45
Ie Shima Island, Ryukyus

806th Engineer Aviation Bn
14 Feb 42 Puerto Rico (806th Engr Co) /15 Mar 46 Okinawa
Puerto Rico: 14 Feb 42   NOPE: 20 Apr 43   Portland Sub-P/E: 26 Apr 44   Hawaii: 3 May 44   Saipan: 31 Jul 44   Ie Shima I: 1 Jun 45
Okinawa: 2 Jun 45 - **19,21**
Okinawa

807th Engineer Aviation Bn
14 Feb 42 Ft Glenn Alaska (807th Engr Co) / 7 Jan 46 Vancouver Bks Wash
Alaska: 14 Feb 42   Adak I: 31 Aug 42   SPE: 6 Jul 44   SPE: 1 Jul 45   Hawaii: 9 Feb 45   Okinawa: 4 May 45 - **2,19**   SPE: 4 Jan 46
Okinawa

808th Engineer Aviation Bn
15 Sep 41 March Field Calif /*
SFPE: 12 Jan 42   Australia: 1 Feb 42   New Guinea: 26 Jul 42   Biak I: 28 Feb 44   Philippines: 22 Oct 44 - **9,13,14,15,17**
Batangas Philippines

809th Engineer Aviation Bn
5 Dec 41 Westover Field Mass /15 Sep 45 Italy
NYPE: 1 Jul 42   England: 15 Jul 42   N.Africa: 11 Nov 42   Sicily: 14 Jul 43   Italy: 20 Oct 43
France-ETO: 16 Aug 44 - **23,29,31,34,35,36,37,38**
Grosseto Italy

810th Engineer Aviation Bn (Cld)
26 Jun 41 MacDill Field Fla /*
NYPE: 23 Jan 42   Australia: 27 Feb 42   New Caledonia: 12 Mar 42   Guadalcanal: 15 Jun 43   Biak I: 1 Aug 44   Philippines: 15 Jan 45 - **14**
Manila Philippines

811th Engineer Aviation Bn (Cld)
1 Dec 41 Langley Field Va /*
NYPE: 17 Jan 42   New Caledonia: 26 Feb 42   Guadalcanal: 1 Apr 44   Hawaii: 2 Oct 44   Iwo Jima: 22 Apr 45 - **1**
(attached Americal Div 24 May 42–1 May 43)
Iwo Jima

812th Engineer Aviation Bn (Cld)
15 Dec 41 MacDill Field Fla / 26 Sep 45 Italy
Dep ZI: 22 Jul 42   Kenya Africa: 29 Jul 42   Egypt Africa: 7 Feb 43   Libya Africa: 25 Mar 43   Algeria Africa: 28 Sep 43
Sicily: 8 Nov 43   Corsica: 11 Jan 44   Italy: 12 May 45 - **29,35**
Borgo Corsica less Co C at Chisonaccia Corsica

813th Engineer Aviation Bn
15 Dec 41 McChord Field Wash / 7 Jan 46 Cp Stoneman Calif
SPE: 1 May 42   Alaska: 8 May 42   SPE: 10 Dec 44   SPE: 25 Apr 45   Hawaii: 5 May 45   Guam: 13 Jun 45   Okinawa: 5 Jul 45 - **2**
SFPE: 5 Jan 46
Okinawa

814th Engineer Aviation Bn
15 Jan 42 March Field Calif /15 Sep 45 Italy
NYPE: 1 Jul 42   England: 12 Jul 42   N.Africa: 11 Nov 42   Sicily: 20 Jul 43   Italy: 27 Oct 43 - **23,29,35,36,38**
Foggia Italy less Co A and B at Celone and Co C at Salsola

BATTALION DESIGNATION AND TYPE	FORMED (SOURCE OF UNIT) / INACTIVATION *Active through 1946	AUGUST 1945 LOCATION

815th Engineer Aviation Bn   21 Jan 42 Jackson Army Airbase Miss / 22 Sep 45 Geiger Field Wash
NYPE: 3 Jun 42   England: 9 Jun 42   N.Africa: 8 Nov 42   Sicily: 10 Aug 43   Italy: 28 Sep 43 - **23,24,29,31,35,36,38**   BPE: 25 May 45

Geiger Field Wash

816th Engineer Aviation Bn   15 Feb 42 Langley Field Va / 20 Nov 45 Germany
NYPE: 5 Aug 42   England: 17 Aug 42   France-ETO: 9 Jun 44 - **26,30,32,34**

Schleissheim Germany

817th Engineer Aviation Bn   15 Feb 42 Langley Field Va /15 Sep 45 Italy
NYPE: 1 Jul 42   England: 12 Jul 42   N.Africa: 21 Nov 42   Italy: 9 Sep 43   Corsica: 16 Mar 44   Italy: 21 Jun 44   Corsica: 15 Jul 44
France-ETO: 20 Aug 44   Italy: 11 Oct 44 - **29,31,33,35,37,38**

Sesto Italy less Cos A, B, C at
Perestola Italy

818th Engineer Aviation Bn   10 Mar 42 Savannah Ga / 29 Nov 45 Cp Shanks N.Y.
NYPE: 1 Jul 42   England: 20 Jul 42   France-ETO: 30 Jun 44 - **25,26,30,32,34**   NYPE: 28 Nov 45

Cassel France

819th Engineer Aviation Bn   15 Mar 42 Tucson Ariz / 8 Dec 45 Cp Patrick Henry Va
NYPE: 30 Jun 42   England: 14 Jul 42   France-ETO: 12 Jun 44 - **26,30,32,34**   HRPE: 8 Dec 45

Giebelstadt Germany

820th Engineer Aviation Bn   15 Mar 42 Tucson Ariz / 20 Nov 45 Germany
NYPE: 5 Aug 42   England: 14 Aug 42   France-ETO: 8 Jun 44 - **26,30,32,34**

Knuthagen Germany

821st Engineer Aviation Bn   15 Mar 42 Tucson Ariz / 20 Dec 45 Cp Stoneman Calif
SFPE: 22 Jun 42   Fiji I: 9 Jul 42   Russell I: 15 Jan 44   Admiralty I: 24 Apr 44   Philippines: 24 Oct 44 - **3,13,14**   SFPE: 17 Dec 45

Manila Philippines

822nd Engineer Aviation Bn (Cld)   15 Feb 42 Langley Field Va / *
SFPE: 19 Oct 42   Espiritu Santo: 20 Nov 42   New Guinea: 23 May 44   Philippines: 15 Nov 44   Okinawa: 26 Jun 45 - **13,15,19**

Okinawa

823rd Engineer Aviation Bn (Cld)   15 Feb 42 Langley Field Va / 22 Feb 46 India
Charleston Sub-P/E: 28 May 42   India: 23 Jul 42   Burma: 27 Feb 43 - **5,12**

Myitkyina Burma

824th Engineer Bn, Aviation (Separate)   21 Apr 42 Iceland /1 Jul 44 Iceland redes 1923rd Engr Composite Bn, Aviation

825th Engineer Aviation Bn   21 Apr 42 Greenland / 27 Dec 45 NYPE
Greenland: 21 Apr 42   BPE: 20 Jun 42   NYPE: 19 Aug 42   England: 31 Aug 42   France-ETO: 1 Jul 44 - **26,30,32,34**   NYPE: 24 Dec 45

Gablingen Germany

826th Engineer Aviation Bn   17 Jun 42 Ft George Wright Wash / 20 Nov 45 Germany
NYPE: 19 Aug 42   England: 31 Aug 42   France-ETO: 12 Jun 44 - **26,30,32,34**

Frankfurt Germany

827th Engineer Aviation Bn (Cld)   8 Apr 42 Savannah Ga / 20 Nov 45 England
NYPE: 7 Dec 42   England: 16 Dec 42

Mere Village England sch to
SWPA under Shipment #R;542-AAA

828th Engineer Aviation Bn (Cld)   15 Apr 42 Will Rogers Field Okla / 5 Dec 45 Ft Lewis Wash
SFPE: 19 Oct 42   New Hebrides: 12 Nov 42   Guadalcanal: 12 Aug 43   New Georgia I: 4 Sep 43   Biak I: 10 Aug 44
Philippines: 13 Jan 45 - **14,15,16**   SPE: 4 Dec 45

Clark Field Philippines

829th Engineer Aviation Bn (Cld)   14 Apr 42 Dale Mabry Field Fla /12 Dec 45 Cp Myles Standish Mass
NYPE: 18 Aug 42   England: 1 Sep 42   France-ETO: 25 Nov 44 - **34**   BPE: 11 Dec 45

Orly France

830th Engineer Aviation Bn   1 Apr 42 Gowen Field Idaho / 20 Nov 45 Germany
NYPE: 18 Aug 42   England: 1 Sep 42   France-ETO: 3 Jul 44 - **26,30,32,34**

Kitzingen Germany

831st Engineer Aviation Bn   10 May 42 Fresno Calif / *
NYPE: 5 Aug 42   England: 18 Aug 42   France-ETO: 18 Sep 44 - **26**

Ansbach Germany

832nd Engineer Aviation Bn   1 Apr 42 El Paso Tex /10 Dec 45 Cp Patrick Henry Va
NYPE: 19 Aug 42   England: 31 Aug 42   France-ETO: 1 Jul 44 - **26,30,32,34**   HRPE: 10 Dec 45

Giebelstadt Germany

833rd Engineer Aviation Bn   1 May 42 McChord Field Wash / 20 Nov 45 Germany
NYPE: 5 Aug 42   England: 18 Aug 42   France-ETO: 30 Jun 44 - **26,30,32,34**

Lechfeld Germany

834th Engineer Aviation Bn   14 Apr 42 Westover Field Mass / 24 Dec 45 Cp Myles Standish Mass
NYPE: 5 Aug 42   England: 17 Aug 42   France-ETO: 7 Jun 44 - **26,30,32,34**   BPE: 23 Dec 45

Furth Germany

835th Engineer Aviation Bn   16 Apr 42 Langley Field Va / 7 Nov 45 Geiger Field Wash
SFPE: 16 Feb 43   Egypt Africa: 29 Mar 43   Libya Africa: 1 Jul 43   Algeria-Africa: 15 Oct 43   Italy: 8 Dec 43 - **29,35**   HRPE: 9 Sep 45
(Sch to SWPA under Shipment #R0411-E)

Termoli Italy less Co A at
Ramitelli, Co B at Pomigliano,
and Co C at Lesina Italy

836th Engineer Aviation Bn   15 Jul 42 Hammer Field Calif / 31 Aug 46 Japan
SFPE: 31 Jul 43   Australia: 18 Aug 45   New Guinea: 31 Aug 43   Los Negros I: 30 Mar 44   Wadke I: 18 May 44   Morotai I: 21 Sep 44
Philippines: 9 Jan 45 - **3,14,15**

Manila Philippines

837th Engineer Aviation Bn (Cld)   10 Jul 42 Greenville S.C. / *
NYPE: 7 Feb 43   Bermuda: 15 Feb 43   N.Africa: 18 Mar 43   Italy: 14 Sep 44   France-ETO: 19 Apr 45 - **31**

Istres France sch to SWPA
under Shipment #R0542-BBB

838th Engineer Aviation Bn (Cld)   8 Jul 42 MacDill Field Fla / *
NYPE: 7 Feb 43   N.Africa: 15 Feb 43   Italy: 29 Sep 44 - **31**   NYPE: 10 Nov 45 *(sch to SWPA under Shipment #R0411-G)*

Pisa Italy less Cos A and C at
Rosignano and Co B at Grosseto

BATTALION DESIGNATION AND TYPE	FORMED (SOURCE OF UNIT)/INACTIVATION * Active through 1946	AUGUST 1945 LOCATION

839th Engineer Aviation Bn (Cld) 1 Oct 42 Will Rogers Field Okla / *
SFPE: 28 Aug 43   Australia: 23 Sep 43   New Guinea: 5 Dec 43   Philippines: 19 Nov 44 - **13,15**

Tacloban Philippines

840th Engineer Aviation Bn 1 Sep 42 Bradley Field Conn / 20 Nov 45 Germany
NYPE: 10 May 43   England: 18 May 43   France-ETO: 9 Jul 44 - **26,30,32,34**

Kaufbeuren Germany

841st Engineer Aviation Bn 1 Sep 42 Hunter Field Ga / 21 Dec 45 Cp Stoneman Calif
SFPE: 25 Sep 43   Australia: 9 Oct 43   Goodenough I: 23 Nov 43   New Britain I: 17 Jan 44   New Guinea: 22 May 44
Morotai I: 16 Sep 44   Philippines: 11 Jan 45 - **3,14,15**   SFPE: 18 Dec 45

Manila Philippines

842nd Engineer Aviation Bn 1 Sep 42 Ft George Wright Wash /10 Jan 46 Ft Lawton Wash
SFPE: 26 Feb 43   Australia: 23 Mar 43   New Guinea: 21 Apr 43   Goodenough I: 31 Aug 43   Philippines: 29 Nov 44
Okinawa: 26 Jun 45 - **3,13,15,19**   SPE: 7 Jan 46

Okinawa

843rd Engineer Aviation Bn 4 Sep 42 McChord Field Wash / 20 Nov 45 Germany
NYPE: 23 May 43   England: 1 Jun 43   France-ETO: Unknown - **26,30,32**

Munich Germany

844th Engineer Aviation Bn 1 Oct 42 March Field Calif / 20 Nov 45 England
NYPE: 24 Jun 43   England: 29 Jun 43

Bassingbourne England sch to SWPA under Shipment #R0542-CCC

845th Engineer Aviation Bn 1 Nov 42 Geiger Field Wash / 7 Nov 45 Geiger Field Wash
NYPE: 7 Feb 43   N.Africa: 19 Feb 43   Italy: 15 Oct 43   Corsica: 16 Feb 44   France-ETO: 19 Aug 44   Italy: 11 Oct 44 - **29,31,33,35,37**
HRPE: 9 Sep 45

Mondolfo Italy less Co B at Fano and Co C at Cattolica sch to SWPA under Shipment #R0411-F

846th Engineer Aviation Bn 1 Nov 42 Geiger Field Wash / 20 Nov 45 Germany
NYPE: 6 Jan 43   England: 13 Jan 43   France-ETO: 14 Jul 44 - **26,30,32,34**

Bremen Germany

847th Engineer Aviation Bn (Cld) 1 Oct 42 MacDill Field Fla / 25 Dec 45 Cp Kilmer N.J.
NYPE: 24 Jun 43   England: 29 Jun 43   France-ETO: 22 Oct 44 - **34**   NYPE: 22 Dec 45

Eschborn Germany sch to SWPA under Shipment #R0542-DDD

848th Engineer Aviation Bn (Cld) 1 Nov 42 Greenville Army Airbase N.C. / 24 Oct 45 Cp Kilmer N.J.
NYPE: 10 Jul 43   India: 12 Aug 43   NYPE: 23 Oct 45

Chabua India

849th Engineer Aviation Bn (Cld) 1 Nov 42 MacDill Field Fla / 26 Nov 45 NYPE
NYPE: 10 Jul 43   India: 12 Aug 43 - **12**   NYPE: 25 Nov 45

Ledo India

850th Engineer Aviation Bn 1 Oct 42 Westover Field Mass / *
NYPE: 10 May 43   England: 18 May 43   France-ETO: 22 Jun 44 - **26,30,32,34**

Hessdorf Germany

851st Engineer Aviation Bn 30 Oct 42 Geiger Field Wash / 20 Nov 45 Germany
NYPE: 24 Jun 43   England: 29 Jun 43   France-ETO: Unknown - **26,34**

Fritzlar Germany sch to SWPA under Shipment #R0542-EEE

852nd Engineer Aviation Bn 1 Jan 43 Gieger Field Wash (3rd Bn, 922nd Engr Regt) / 20 Nov 45 Germany
NYPE: 5 May 43   England: 11 May 43   France-ETO: 15 Jul 44 - **26,30,32,34**

Munster Germany

853rd Engineer Aviation Bn 1 Jan 43 Dyersburg Army Airbase Tenn / 4 Jan 46 NYPE
HRPE: 3 Oct 43   N.Africa: 23 Oct 43   India: 1 Feb 44   NYPE: 3 Jan 46

Chabua India

854th Engineer Aviation Bn 1 Jan 43 March Field Calif /15 Mar 46 Okinawa
SFPE: 1 Dec 43   Hawaii: 11 Dec 43   Kwajalein: 2 Feb 44   Guam: 7 Oct 44   Ie Shima: 24 Jun 45   Okinawa: 25 Jun 45 - **10,19,21**

Okinawa

855th Engineer Aviation Bn (Cld) 1 Jan 43 March Field Calif / 31 Dec 45 Cp Stoneman Calif
SFPE: 28 Oct 43   Australia: 7 Dec 43   New Guinea: 3 Feb 44   Philippines: Unknown - **14,15**   SFPE: 26 Dec 45

Manila Philippines

856th Engineer Aviation Bn (Cld) 1 Jan 43 March Field Calif / 22 Dec 45 Cp Stoneman Calif
SFPE: 31 Jul 43   Australia: 18 Aug 43   New Guinea: 1 Sep 43   Kiriwina I: 7 Sep 43   Goodenough I: 29 Nov 43   Biak I: 25 Sep 44
Philippines: 7 Jun 45 - **14,15**   SFPE: 18 Dec 45

Manila Philippines

857th Engineer Aviation Bn (Cld) 15 Nov 42 Eglin Field Fla /15 Aug 46 Philippines
SFPE: 26 Feb 43   Australia: 23 Mar 43   New Guinea: 8 Apr 43   Philippines: 19 Nov 44 - **13,14,15**

Manila Philippines

858th Engineer Aviation Bn (Cld) 1 Jan 43 Avon Park Fla /13 Dec 45 Ft Lewis Wash
HRPE: 3 Oct 43   N.Africa: 23 Oct 43   India: 27 Dec 43   China: 23 May 45 - **12**   SPE: 12 Dec 45

Siakwan China less det at Kinming China

859th Engineer Aviation Bn (Cld) 1 Jan 43 Eglin Field Fla / 20 Nov 45 Germany
NYPE: 5 May 43   England: 11 May 43   France-ETO: 9 Nov 44 - **34**

Eschborn Germany sch to SWPA under Shipment #R0542-FFF

860th Engineer Aviation Bn 1 Jan 43 March Field Calif / 30 Jun 46 Japan
SFPE: 23 Oct 43   Australia: 13 Nov 43   New Guinea: 7 Dec 43   Biak I: 8 Jun 44   Philippines: 19 Nov 44 - **13,14,15**

Mindoro Philippines

861st Engineer Aviation Bn 1 Jan 43 Richmond Army Airbase Va / 20 Nov 45 England
NYPE: 5 May 43   England: 11 May 43

Stansted England sch to SWPA under Shipment #R0542-GGG

862nd Engineer Aviation Bn 1 Feb 43 Richmond Army Airbase Va / *
NYPE: 23 May 43   England: 1 Jun 43   France-ETO: 6 Aug 44 - **26,32,34**

Ober Pfaffenhofen Germany

BATTALION DESIGNATION AND TYPE	FORMED (SOURCE OF UNIT)/INACTIVATION *Active through 1946	AUGUST 1945 LOCATION

863rd Engineer Aviation Bn — 1 Feb 43 Geiger Field Wash (1st Bn, 922nd Engr Regt) /15 Jun 46 Philippines
SFPE: 7 May 43   Australia: 22 May 43   New Guinea: 5 Aug 43   Biak I: 8 Jun 44   Philippines: 21 Dec 44 - **13,14,15**
Manila Philippines

864th Engineer Aviation Bn — 1 Jan 43 Geiger Field Wash / 30 Jun 46 Japan
SFPE: 13 Aug 43   Australia: 1 Sep 43   New Guinea: 17 Sep 43   New Britain I: 10 Jan 44   Biak I: 30 May 44
Philippines: 13 Jan 45 - **3,14,15**
San Fernando Philippines

865th Engineer Aviation Bn — 1 Feb 43 Davis-Montham Field Ariz / *
SFPE: 23 Oct 43   Australia: 13 Nov 43   New Guinea: 7 Dec 43   Philippines: 24 Oct 44 - **13,15,20**
Macajalar Bay Philippines

866th Engineer Aviation Bn — 1 Feb 43 Geiger Field Wash /17 Jun 46 Philippines
SFPE: 22 Apr 44   New Guinea: 13 May 44   Philippines: 19 Nov 44 - **13,14,15**
Manila Philippines

867th Engineer Aviation Bn (Cld) — 3 Jan 43 Eglin Field Fla /15 Jun 46 Philippines
NOPE: 26 Jan 44   New Guinea: 25 Feb 44   Philippines: 28 Nov 44 - **13,14,15**
Batangas Philippines

868th Engineer Aviation Bn (Cld) — 15 Jan 43 MacDill Field Fla/31 Dec 45 Cp Stoneman Calif
SFPE: 27 Oct 43   Australia: 13 Nov 43   New Guinea: 18 Dec 43   Philippines: 24 Jul 45 - **15**   SFPE: 17 Dec 45
Clark Field Philippines less Co A at Nadzab New Guinea

869th Engineer Aviation Bn (Cld) — 15 Jan 43 MacDill Field Fla / 22 Jun 46 Philippines
SFPE: 10 Mar 44   New Guinea: 3 Apr 44   Philippines: 20 Mar 45 - **14,15**
Manila Philippines

870th Engineer Aviation Bn (Cld) — 1 Feb 43 Dale Mabry Field Fla / 30 Dec 46 Guam
SFPE: 31 Jul 43   Australia: 18 Aug 43   New Guinea: 31 Aug 43   Philippines: 17 Feb 45   Japan: 25 Nov 45   Guam: 28 Jan 46 - **13,14,15**
Clark Field Philippines

871st Engineer Aviation Bn — 1 Sep 42 Westover Field Mass as A/B Engr Avn Bn /15 May 46 Japan
SFPE: 1 May 43   Australia: 26 May 43   New Guinea: 5 Jun 43   Biak I: 8 Jul 44   Philippines: 28 Feb 45 - **14,15**
(redes Engr Avn Bn 21 Dec 44)
Clark Field Philippines

872nd Engineer Aviation Bn — 14 Oct 42 Westover Field Mass as A/B Engr Avn Bn / 30 Jun 46 Japan
SFPE: 24 May 43   Australia: 14 Jun 43   New Guinea: 7 Jul 43   Philippines: 14 Nov 44   Okinawa: 14 Jun 45 - **13,15,19**
(redes Engr Avn Bn 21 Dec 44)
Okinawa

873rd Engineer Aviation Bn — 14 Oct 42 Westover Field Mass as A/B Engr Avn Bn /1 Feb 46 Japan
SFPE: 8 Jun 43   New Caledonia: 20 Jun 43   Guadalcanal: 12 Aug 43   New Guinea: 29 Sep 44   Philippines: 19 Nov 44
Okinawa: 27 Jun 45 - **13,15,19,20** *(redes Engr Engr Avn Bn 21 Dec 44)*
Zamboanga Phillipines

874th Engineer Aviation Bn — 15 Nov 42 Cp Claiborne La as A/B Engr Avn Bn / 2 Dec 45 Philippines
SFPE: 28 Jan 44   New Guinea: 18 Feb 44   Philippines: Unknown - **14,15** *(redes Engr Avn Bn 21 Dec 44)*
Manila Philippines

875th Airborne Engineer Aviation Bn — 15 Nov 42 Cp Claiborne La / 21 Dec 44 New Guinea
SFPE: 6 Nov 43   Australia: 21 Nov 43   New Guinea: 4 May 44 - **15**

876th Airborne Engineer Aviation Bn — 15 Nov 42 Cp Claiborne La / 4 Oct 45 Cp Myles Standish Mass
NYPE: 25 Jul 43   England: 30 Jul 43   France-ETO: 1 Jul 44 - **26,30,32,34**   BPE: 3 Oct 45
Aumont France

877th Airborne Engineer Aviation Bn — 1 Jan 43 Westover Field Mass / 4 Oct 45 Cp Myles Standish Mass
NYPE: 27 Feb 44   England: 6 Mar 44   France-ETO: 8 Jul 44 - **30,32**   BPE: 3 Oct 45
Lippstadt Germany

878th Airborne Engineer Aviation Bn — 1 Feb 43 Westover Field Mass/4 Oct 45 Cp Myles Standish Mass
NYPE: 27 Feb 44   England: 8 Mar 44   France-ETO: 4 Aug 44 - **34**   BPE: 3 Oct 45
Nancy France

879th Airborne Engineer Aviation Bn — 1 Mar 43 Westover Field Mass / 2 Jan 46 NYPE
HRPE: 14 Dec 43   India: 13 Feb 44   Burma: 17 May 44 - **5,8,12**   NYPE: 1 Jan 46
Myitkyina Burma less Co A at Lashio and Co B at Bahe Burma

880th Airborne Engineer Aviation Bn — 1 Mar 43 Westover Field Mass / 21 Dec 44 New Guinea
SFPE: 21 Mar 44   New Guinea: 11 Apr 44 - **15**

881st Airborne Engineer Aviation Bn — 1 Mar 43 Westover Field Mass /19 Feb 44 Richmond Army Airbase Va

882nd Airborne Engineer Aviation Bn — 1 May 43 Bradley Field Conn /15 Jan 45 New Guinea
SFPE: 22 Apr 44   New Guinea: 15 May 44 - **13,15**

883rd Airborne Engineer Aviation Bn — 1 May 43 Bradley Field Conn / 25 Mar 44 Richmond Army Airbase Va *(1st Air Force)*

884th Airborne Engineer Aviation Bn — 1 Jun 43 Bradley Field Conn/21 Mar 44 Richmond Army Airbase Va

885th Airborne Engineer Aviation Bn — 1 Jun 43 Bradley Field Conn / 3 Jan 44 Richmond Army Airbase Va

886th Airborne Engineer Aviation Bn — 1 Aug 43 Bradley Field Conn / 25 Dec 43 Bradley Field Conn

936th Engineer Aviation Camouflage Bn — 1 Aug 42 Richmond Army Airbase Va / 2 Feb 44 Walterboro Army Airbase S.C.

937th Engineer Aviation Camouflage Bn — 1 Sep 42 Fresno Calif /13 Nov 45 Cp Patrick Henry Va
NYPE: 27 Feb 44   England: 6 Mar 44   France-ETO: 27 Jun 44 - **25,30,32,34**   HRPE: 13 Nov 45
Urcel France

BATTALION DESIGNATION AND TYPE	FORMED (SOURCE OF UNIT)/INACTIVATION *Active through 1946	AUGUST 1945 LOCATION
938th Engineer Aviation Camouflage Bn	1 Jan 43 Hammer Field Calif /11 Feb 44 March Field Calif	
939th Engineer Aviation Camouflage Bn	1 Feb 43 Richmond Army Airbase Va / 29 Feb 44 Richmond Army Airbase Va	
940th Engineer Aviation Camouflage Bn	1 Mar 43 Davis-Monthan Field Ariz /10 Feb 44 Colorado Springs Colo	
941st Engineer Aviation Topographic Bn Italy: 1 Apr 44 - **31,35** HRPE: 26 Oct 45	1 Apr 44 San Severo Italy (see remarks) / 26 Oct 45 Cp Patrick Henry Va *(pers and equip from 951st, 953rd, 954th, and 956th Engr Topographic Cos)*	Firenze Italy less Co A at Bari sch to SWPA under Shipment #R0411-A
942nd Engineer Aviation Topographic Bn France-ETO: 10 Aug 44 - **25,34**	10 Aug 44 France (942nd Engr Topographic Co) / 20 Nov 45 France	Le Bourget France
1001st Engineer Forestry Bn BPE: 19 Feb 45 France-ETO: 1 Mar 45 - **26,34** NYPE: 7 Apr 46	19 Aug 44 Cp Claiborne La / 9 Apr 46 NYPE	Manoy France sch to SWPA under Shipment #R9850-E
1002nd Engineer Forestry Bn New Guinea: 10 Oct 44 Philippines: 11 Feb 45 - **13,14**	10 Oct 44 Finschhafen New Guinea /15 May 46 Philippines	Tacloban Philippines
1003rd Engineer Service Bn (Pipeline) France: 13 Jan 45 NYPE: 6 Oct 45 *(assigned 1499th Engr Petroleum Production Depot)*	13 Jan 45 Paris France / 8 Oct 45 Cp Shanks N.Y.	Marseille France
1004th Engineer Service Bn (Pipeline) France: 13 Jan 45 - **34** *(assigned 1499th Engr Petroleum Production Depot)*	13 Jan 45 Paris France / 25 Feb 46 Holland	Maastricht Holland
1006th Engineer Refinery Bn *(Santa Anita Ordnance Tng Center)*	1 Mar 44 Santa Anita Calif /11 Sep 44 Pomona Calif	
1006th Engineer Service Bn (Pipeline) France: 13 Jan 45 *(assigned 1499th Engr Petroleum Production Depot)*	13 Jan 45 Paris France/6 Oct 45 France	Paris France
1007th Engr Special Service Bn (Barge Cons) India: 14 Dec 44 - **5,12** NYPE: 10 Jan 46	14 Dec 44 Ledo India (1st Bn, 393rd Engr Regt)/11 Jan 46 NYPE	Ledo India less Co C at Calcutta India
1008th Engineer Refinery Bn *(1st Engr Petroleum Production Depot)*	1 Mar 44 Santa Anita Calif /11 Sep 44 Pomona Calif	
1008th Engineer Power Plant Bn France: 10 Feb 45	10 Feb 45 Argenteuil France /19 Nov 45 France	Paris France sch to SWPA under Shipment #R9850-K
1009th Engineer Oil Field Bn *(1st Engr Petroleum Production Depot)*	1 Mar 44 Santa Anita Calif /11 Sep 44 Pomona Calif	
1251st Engineer Combat Bn Dep ZI: 22 Oct 44 England: 1 Nov 44 France-ETO: 31 Dec 44 - **26,34** NYPE: 17 Mar 46	30 Dec 43 Cp Swift Tex /18 Mar 46 Cp Kilmer N.J.	Udem Germany
1252nd Engineer Combat Bn Dep ZI: 22 Oct 44 England: 2 Nov 44 France-ETO: 1 Jan 45 - **25,26,34** Arrived ZI: 4 Sep 45	30 Dec 43 Cp Swift Tex /10 Dec 45 Cp Polk La	Rotenburg Germany sch to SWPA under Shipment #R6604-CCC
1253rd Engineer Combat Bn Dep ZI: 22 Oct 44 England: 2 Nov 44 France-ETO: 15 Mar 45 - **26,34**	15 Dec 43 Cp Cooke Calif /17 Dec 46 France	Vierson Germany sch to SWPA under Shipment #R6604-DDD
1254th Engineer Combat Bn Dep ZI: 22 Oct 44 England: 2 Nov 44 France-ETO: 26 Feb 45 - **26,34** NYPE: 7 Mar 46	15 Dec 43 Cp Cooke Calif / 9 Mar 46 Cp Kilmer N.J.	Coutaqinville France
1255th Engineer Combat Bn Dep ZI: 22 Oct 44 England: 1 Nov 44 France-ETO: 30 Dec 44 - **25,26,34** NYPE: 28 Feb 46	17 Feb 44 Ft Jackson S.C. /1 Mar 46 Cp Kilmer N.J.	Gotha Germany
1256th Engineer Combat Bn Dep ZI: 22 Oct 44 England: 3 Nov 44 France-ETO: 6 Mar 45 - **26,34** BPE: 26 Nov 45	21 Feb 44 Cp McCain Miss / 27 Nov 45 Cp Myles Standish Mass	Karl Germany sch to SWPA under Shipment #R6604-EEE
1257th Engineer Combat Bn Dep ZI: 22 Oct 44 England: 2 Nov 44 France-ETO: 1 Jan 45 - **26,34** NYPE: 28 Feb 46	21 Feb 44 Cp Bowie Tex /1 Mar 46 Cp Kilmer N.J.	Wollendorf Germany
1258th Engineer Combat Bn Dep ZI: 22 Oct 44 England: 1 Nov 44 France-ETO: 8 Jan 45 - **25,26,34**	21 Feb 44 Cp Swift Tex / 29 Nov 46 Germany	Regensburg Germany
1259th Engineer Combat Bn NYPE: 24 Apr 45 France-ETO: 6 May 45 BPE: 4 Sep 45	10 Feb 44 Cp Pickett Va / *	Vyetot France sch to SWPA under Shipment #R6604-BBB
1260th Engineer Combat Bn Dep ZI: 3 Nov 44 France-ETO: 13 Nov 44 - **25,26,34** NYPE: 3 Apr 46	10 Feb 44 Cp Pickett Va / 4 Apr 46 Cp Kilmer N.J.	Dungelbeck Germany
1261st Engineer Combat Bn Dep ZI: 10 Nov 44 England: 17 Nov 44 France-ETO: 15 Apr 45 - **26**	17 Feb 44 Cp Gordon Ga / 6 Sep 45 Germany	Le Havre France

BATTALION DESIGNATION AND TYPE	FORMED (SOURCE OF UNIT)/INACTIVATION *Active through 1946	AUGUST 1945 LOCATION
1262nd Engineer Combat Bn Dep ZI: 30 Oct 44 England: 10 Nov 44 France-ETO: 9 Jan 45 - **26,34**	17 Feb 44 Cp Shelby Miss / 25 Jun 46 France	Litchenfels Germany
1263rd Engineer Combat Bn Dep ZI: 30 Oct 44 England: 10 Nov 44 France-ETO: 26 Feb 45 - **26,34** NYPE: 15 Apr 46	17 Feb 44 Cp McCoy Wis /16 Apr 46 Cp Kilmer N.J.	Lustheide Germany
1264th Engineer Combat Bn Dep ZI: 22 Oct 44 England: 1 Nov 44 France-ETO: 30 Dec 44 - **26,34**	21 Feb 44 Cp Bowie Tex / *	Eisenach Germany
1265th Engineer Combat Bn Dep ZI: 15 Nov 44 England: 27 Nov 44 France-ETO: 18 Mar 45 - **26,34**	27 Mar 44 Cp Van Dorn Miss / *	Korbach Germany
1266th Engineer Combat Bn Dep ZI: 4 Dec 44 England: 12 Dec 44 France-ETO: 18 Mar 45 - **26** Arrived ZI: 27 Aug 45	27 Mar 44 Cp Bowie Tex / 8 Nov 45 Cp Gruber Okla	Shipment #RR4645-YY (sch to SWPA but returned to USA) at sea
1267th Engineer Combat Bn Dep ZI: 9 Dec 44 England: 20 Dec 44 France-ETO: 11 Apr 45 Shipment #R0102-MM Philippines: 27 Jul 45 LAPE: 25 Jan 46	27 Mar 44 Cp Maxey Tex / 26 Jan 46 Cp Anza Calif	Manila Philippines
1268th Engineer Combat Bn Dep ZI: 9 Dec 44 England: 20 Dec 44 France-ETO: 15 Apr 45 - **26** Shipment #R0102-LL Philippines: 14 Aug 45	27 Mar 44 Cp Maxey Tex / 25 Jan 46 Philippines	Shipment #R0102-LL unloading
1269th Engineer Combat Bn Dep ZI: 27 Oct 44 France-ETO: 6 Nov 44 - **26,34** NYPE: 1 Mar 46	30 Mar 44 Cp Chaffee Ark / 2 Mar 46 Cp Kilmer N.J.	Augsburg Germany
1270th Engineer Combat Bn Dep ZI: 22 Oct 44 England: 1 Nov 44 France-ETO: 22 Mar 45 - **26,34** Arrived ZI: 14 Sep 45	30 Mar 44 Cp Chaffee Ark / 27 Nov 45 Ft Benning Ga	Bad Nauheim Germany sch to SWPA under Shipment #R6604-FFF
1271st Engineer Combat Bn Dep ZI: 27 Oct 44 France-ETO: 6 Nov 44 - **25,26,34** BPE: 4 Dec 45	20 Apr 44 Cp Breckinridge Ky / 5 Dec 45 Cp Myles Standish Mass	Inst Austria
1272nd Engineer Combat Bn Dep ZI: 10 Nov 44 Scotland: 17 Nov 44	20 Apr 44 Cp Carson Colo/18 Jan 45 Scotland	
1273rd Engineer Combat Bn Dep ZI: 15 Nov 44 England: 27 Nov 44	20 Apr 44 Cp Chaffee Ark / 20 Apr 45 England	
1274th Engineer Combat Bn Dep ZI: 15 Nov 44 England: 27 Nov 44	20 Apr 44 Cp Chaffee Ark / 20 Apr 45 England	
1275th Engineer Combat Bn Dep ZI: 2 Dec 44 France-ETO: 12 Dec 44 Shipment #R4645-AA Philippines: Aug 45 LAPE: 26 Jan 46	20 Apr 44 Cp Gruber Okla / 27 Jan 46 Cp Anza Calif	Manila Philippines
1276th Engineer Combat Bn Iceland: 6 Dec 43 England: 25 Aug 44 France-ETO: 25 Sep 44 - **26,34**	6 Dec 43 Iceland (1st Bn, 5th Engr Regt) /18 Sep 45 France	Epernay France
1277th Engineer Combat Bn England: 27 Dec 43 France-ETO: 15 Jul 44 - **25,26,30,32,34** NYPE: 10 Feb 46	27 Dec 43 Painswick Park England (5th Engr Regt) /11 Feb 46 Cp Kilmer N.J.	Alteumarkt Germany
1278th Engineer Combat Bn England: 27 Dec 43 France-ETO: 26 Jun 44 - **30,32**	27 Dec 43 Painswick Park England (2nd Bn, 5th Engr Regt) / 23 Jan 45 Belgium redes 5th Engr Combat Bn	
1279th Engineer Combat Bn Bougainville: 15 May 44 New Britain I: 26 Nov 44 Philippines: 9 Jan 45 - **14**	15 May 44 Bougainville (2nd Bn, 131st Engr Regt) /17 Jan 46 Japan	Manila Philippines
1280th Engineer Combat Bn Dep ZI: 9 Dec 44 England: 20 Dec 44 France-ETO: 16 Apr 45 - **26** Arrived ZI: 10 Sep 45	20 Apr 44 Cp Gruber Okla / 27 Nov 45 Cp Breckinridge Ky	Yvetot France sch to SWPA under Shipment #R6604-E
1281st Engineer Combat Bn Dep ZI: 9 Dec 44 England: 20 Dec 44 France-ETO: 20 Apr 45 Philippines: 26 Aug 45	3 Apr 44 Cp McCain Miss / 31 Jan 46 Philippines	Shipment #R4645-Y
1282nd Engineer Combat Bn Dep ZI: 9 Dec 44 England: 20 Dec 44 France-ETO: 20 Apr 45 Philippines: 26 Aug 45	3 Apr 44 Cp Van Dorn Miss /15 May 46 Philippines	Shipment R4645-W
1283rd Engineer Combat Bn Dep ZI: 3 Jan 45 France-ETO: 16 Jan 45	30 Apr 44 Cp Pickett Va /16 Jan 45 France	
1284th Engineer Combat Bn Dep ZI: 9 Dec 44 England: 20 Dec 44 France-ETO: 15 Apr 45 - **26** (**14** - *Co A only*) Shipment #R0102-NN Philippines: 20 Aug 45	3 Apr 44 Cp Swift Tex/5 Feb 46 Philippines	Shipment #R0102-NN at sea less Co A already in Philippines
1285th Engineer Combat Bn Dep ZI: 9 Dec 44 England: 20 Dec 44 France-ETO: 15 Apr 45 - **26** Arrived ZI: 24 Aug 45	3 Apr 44 Cp Howze Tex / 29 Jan 46 Cp Bowie Tex	Shipment #R4645-T (sch to SWPA but returned to USA) at sea
1286th Engineer Combat Bn Dep ZI: 4 Dec 44 England: 12 Dec 44 France-ETO: 9 Apr 45 Arrived ZI: 20 Aug 45	12 May 44 Cp Rucker Ala / 5 Nov 45 Cp Campbell Ky	Shipment #R4645-DD (sch to SWPA but returned to USA) at sea
1287th Engineer Combat Bn Dep ZI: 3 Jan 45 France-ETO: 16 Jan 45	12 May 44 Cp Rucker Ala /14 Feb 45 France	

BATTALION DESIGNATION AND TYPE	FORMED (SOURCE OF UNIT) / INACTIVATION *Active through 1946	AUGUST 1945 LOCATION
1288th Engineer Combat Bn Dep ZI: 4 Dec 44 England: 12 Dec 44 France-ETO: 11 Apr 45 - **26** Arrived ZI: 20 Aug 45	10 May 44 Cp Van Dorn Miss / 31 Jan 46 Cp Swift Tex	Shipment #R4645-CC (sch to SWPA but returned to USA) at sea
1289th Engineer Combat Bn Dep ZI: 9 Dec 44 England: 20 Dec 44 France-ETO: 15 Apr 45 - **26** Shipment #R4645-E Philippines: 27 Aug 45	10 May 44 Cp Maxey Tex / 21 Mar 46 Philippines	Shipment #R4645-E at sea
1290th Engineer Combat Bn NYPE: 4 Dec 44 England: 12 Dec 44 France-ETO: 16 Apr 45 NYPE: 24 Aug 45	10 May 44 Cp Joseph T Robinson Ark / *	Shipment #R4645-BB (sch to SWPA but returned to USA) at sea
1291st Engineer Combat Bn Dep ZI: 3 Jan 45 France-ETO: 15 Jan 45	30 Jul 44 Cp Pickett Va (659th A/B Engr Bn) / 14 Feb 45 France	
1292nd Engineer Combat Bn SFPE: 28 Jun 45 Philippines: 1 Aug 45	15 Aug 44 Ft Leonard Wood Mo / 31 Jan 46 Philippines	Shipment #2892-E unloading
1293rd Engineer Combat Bn	26 Jun 44 Cp Breckinridge Ky / 18 Oct 45 Ft Belvoir Va	Ft Belvoir Va
1294th Engineer Combat Bn SFPE: 28 Jun 45 Philippines: 1 Aug 45	26 Jun 44 Ft Jackson S.C. / 20 Jan 46 Philippines	Shipment #2892-D unloading
1295th Engineer Combat Bn	26 Jun 44 Ft Riley Kans / 10 Jan 45 Ft Riley Kans	
1296th Engineer Combat Bn SFPE: 2 Jul 45 Philippines: 27 Jul 45	15 Jul 44 Ft Riley Kans / 28 Feb 46 Philippines	Manila Philippines
1297th Engineer Combat Bn	26 Jun 44 Ft Riley Kans / 10 Jan 45 Ft Riley Kans	
1298th Engineer Combat Bn SFPE: 30 Jul 45 Hawaii: 8 Aug 45 Philippines: 27 Sep 45	26 Jun 44 Cp Rucker Ala / 31 Jan 46 Japan	Shipment #0486-A in Hawaii
1299th Engineer Combat Bn SFPE: 20 Jun 45 Philippines: 13 Jul 45	26 Jun 44 Cp Bowie Tex / 28 Feb 46 Japan	Manila Philippines
1300th Engineer Combat Bn	26 Jun 44 Cp Bowie Tex / 10 Jan 45 Cp Bowie Tex	
1304th Engineer Construction Bn Dep ZI: 29 Jun 44 India: 7 Aug 44 Burma: 1 Nov 44 - **5,8,12**	1 Feb 44 Cp Sutton N.C. (1304th Engr Regt) / 25 Apr 46 India	Myitkyina Burma less Co C at Kweiyang China
1305th Engineer Construction Bn Guadalcanal: 1 May 44 Okinawa: Aug 45	1 May 44 Guadalcanal (1305th Engr Regt) / 1 Feb 46 Korea	Okinawa
1307th Engineer Construction Bn New Guinea: 1 Nov 44 Philippines: 30 Apr 45 - **14,15** SFPE: 20 Jan 46	1 Nov 44 New Guinea (1307th Engr Regt) / 22 Jan 46 Cp Stoneman Calif	Batangas Philippines
1309th Engineer Construction Bn	20 Mar 44 Cp Ellis Ill (1309th Engr Regt) / 1 Maya 44 Cp Ellis Ill	
1315th Engineer Construction Bn (Cld) SFPE: 28 Oct 44 Biak I: 19 Nov 44 Philippines: 12 Aug 45 - **14,15**	20 Mar 44 Cp Sutton N.C. (1315th Engr Regt) / *	Manila Philippines (arriving)
1318th Engineer Construction Bn (Cld)	20 Mar 44 Cp Sutton N.C. (1318th Engr Regt) / 25 May 44 Cp Sutton N.C. redes 1318th Engr Regt	
1319th Engineer Construction Bn (Cld)	20 Mar 44 Cp Sutton N.C. (1319th Engr Regt) / 25 May 44 Cp Sutton N.C. redes 1319th Engr Regt	
1321st Engineer Construction Bn (Cld)	20 Mar 44 Cp Sutton N.C. (1321st Engr Regt) / 25 May 44 Cp Sutton N.C. redes 1321st Engr Regt	
1324th Engineer Construction Bn (Cld)	16 Feb 44 Cp Claiborne La / 25 May 44 Cp Claiborne La redes 1324th Engr Regt	
1325th Engineer Construction Bn (Cld)	16 Feb 44 Cp Claiborne La / 25 May 44 Cp Claiborne La redes 1325th Engr Regt	
1326th Engineer Construction Bn (Cld)	21 Feb 44 Cp Claiborne La / 25 May 44 Cp Claiborne La redes 1326th Engr Regt	
1327th Engineer Construction Bn (Cld)	21 Feb 44 Cp Claiborne La / 25 May 44 Cp Claiborne La redes 1327th Engr Regt	
1328th Engineer Construction Bn (Cld) NYPE: 26 Dec 44 England: 7 Jan 45 France-ETO: 2 Apr 45 - **26** NYPE: 18 Aug 45	1 Mar 44 Cp Claiborne La / 20 Nov 45 Cp Claiborne La	Shipment #R5218-Y (sch to SWPA but returned to USA) at sea
1329th Engineer Construction Bn (Cld)	15 Mar 44 Cp Claiborne La / 25 May 44 Cp Claiborne La redes 1329th Engr Regt	
1330th Engineer Construction Bn (Cld)	15 Mar 44 Cp Claiborne La / 25 May 44 Cp Claiborne La redes 1330th Engr Regt	
1331st Engineer Construction Bn (Cld)	25 Mar 44 Cp Claiborne La / 25 May 44 Cp Claiborne La redes 1331st Engr Regt	
1332nd Engineer Construction Bn (Cld)	15 Mar 44 Cp Ellis Ill / 25 May 44 Cp Ellis Ill redes 1332nd Engr Regt	

BATTALION DESIGNATION AND TYPE	FORMED (SOURCE OF UNIT)/INACTIVATION *Active through 1946	AUGUST 1945 LOCATION

1333rd Engineer Construction Bn (Cld)
15 Mar 44 Cp Ellis Ill / 25 May 44 Cp Ellis Ill redes 1333rd Engr Regt

1334th Engineer Construction Bn (Cld)
1 Jun 44 Naples Italy (6486th Engr Bn) / 25 Apr 45 Italy
Italy: 1 Jun 44 - **31,35**

1339th Engineer Construction Bn
28 Aug 44 Ft Lewis Wash (1st Bn, 331st Engr Regt) / 21 Jan 46 Cp Anza Calif
Shipment #R0146-DD at sea
BPE: 14 Apr 45   France-ETO: 1 May 45   Dep France: 9 Jul 45   Okinawa: 2 Sep 45   LAPE: 21 Jan 46
aboard USS *Admiral H.T.Mayo* **(AP.125)**

1340th Engineer Combat Bn
15 Jan 44 Carclew England (2nd Bn, 20th Engr Regt / 2 Jan 46 NYPE
Perezow Czechoslovakia
England: 15 Jan 44   France-ETO: 6 Jun 44 - **25,26,30,34**   NYPE: 1 Jan 46

1341st Engineer Combat Bn
26 Apr 44 Schofield Bks Hawaii (2nd Bn, 34th Engr Regt) /13 Apr 46 Korea
Okinawa
Hawaii: 16 May 44   Kwajalein Atoll: 1 Feb 44   Saipan: 20 Jun 44   Tinian I: 24 Jul 44   Espiritu Santo: 16 Feb 45
Okinawa: 9 Apr 45 - **19,21**

1342nd Engineer Service Bn
13 Jun 44 Ft Richardson Alaska as Engr Composite Bn / 30 Apr 46 Adak Island
Adak I Aleutians Alaska
(Engr Composite Bn until 10 Apr 45)

1343rd Engineer Combat Bn
11 Jul 44 Ft Leonard Wood Mo (2nd Bn, 151st Engr Regt) / 26 Jan 46 NYPE
Suippes France
NYPE: 14 Oct 44   England: 25 Oct 44   France-ETO: 9 Jan 45 - **34**   NYPE: 15 Jan 46

1344th Engineer Combat Bn
26 Jun 44 Cp Howze Tex / 20 Feb 46 Japan
Okinawa
SFPE: 27 Jun 45   Okinawa: 4 Jul 45 -**19**

1345th Engineer Combat Bn
26 Jun 44 Cp Van Dorn Miss / 15 Feb 46 Okinawa
Okinawa
SFPE: 6 Jun 45   Hawaii: 18 Jun 45   Okinawa: Jul 45

1346th Engineer Combat Bn
26 Jun 42 Cp McCain Miss / 28 Feb 46 Japan
Okinawa
SFPE: 6 Jun 45   Eniwetok I: 19 Jun 45   Ulithi Atoll: 12 Jul 45   Okinawa: 24 Jul 45

1393rd Engineer Construction Bn
1 Apr 44 New Caledonia (2nd Bn, 353rd Engr Regt) /28 Feb 46 Japan
Manila Philippines
New Caledonia: 1 Apr 44   Guadalcanal: 7 Apr 44   Philippines: 24 May 45 - **14**

1394th Engineer Construction Bn
1 May 44 Guadalcanal (369th Engr Regt) / 31 Jan 46 Cp Stoneman Calif
Cebu Philippines
Guadalcanal: 1 May 44   Philippines: 16 May 45 - **13**   SFPE: 29 Jan 46

1395th Engineer Construction Bn
1 May 44 Guadalcanal (1305th Engr Regt) /1 Feb 46 Korea
Okinawa
Guadalcanal: 1 May 44   Espiritu Santo: 25 May 44   New Caledonia: 4 Sep 44   Okinawa: 1 May 45 - **19**

1396th Engineer Service Bn
1 May 44 Cp Ellis Ill as Engr Composite Bn / 28 Feb 46 Philippines
Oro Bay New Guinea
NOPE: 22 Aug 44   New Guinea: 2 Oct 44   Philippines: Unknown - **14** *(Engr Composite Bn until 10 Nov 44)*

1397th Engineer Construction Bn
26 Apr 44 Schofield Bks Hawaii (2nd Bn, 47th Engr Regt) / 20 Feb 46 Okinawa
Okinawa
Hawaii: 26 Apr 44   Saipan: 5 Jul 44   Okinawa: Apr 45 - **19,21**

1398th Engineer Construction Bn
21 Mar 44 Aiea Staging Area Hawaii (1st Bn, 367th Engr Regt) /20 Feb 46 Okinawa   Okinawa
Hawaii: 21 Mar 44   Saipan: 15 Jul 44   Okinawa: 6 Apr 45 - **19,21**

1399th Engineer Construction Bn (Nisei)
21 Mar 44 Schofield Bks Hawaii (1st Bn, 370th Engr Regt) / 31 May 46 Hawaii
Schofield Barracks Hawaii
(21 - Det of Co C only).

1551st Engineer Heavy Ponton Bn
26 Jun 44 Cp Swift Tex /15 Jan 45 Cp Swift Tex

1553rd Engineer Heavy Ponton Bn (Cld)
5 Jun 44 Algeria (6495th Engr Bn Prov) /12 Dec 45 NYPE
Hardeim Germany sch to SWPA
N.Africa: 5 Jun 44   Italy: 15 Jul 44   France-ETO: 13 Sep 44 - **26,34,35,37**   NYPE: 11 Dec 45
under Shipment #R6901-LLL

1554th Engineer Heavy Ponton Bn (Cld)
5 Jun 44 Algeria (6496th Engr Bn Prov) / 23 Oct 45 Cp Gruber Okla
Cp Gruber Okla
N.Africa: 5 Jun 44   Italy: 15 Jul 44 - **31,33,35**   HRPE: 31 Jul 45

1629th Engineer Construction Bn
2 Jan 45 Ft Lewis Wash / 20 Sep 46 Japan
Manila Philippines
SFPE: 26 Apr 45   Philippines: 12 Jun 45 - **14**

1631st Engineer Construction Bn
15 Jan 45 Ft Lewis Wash/20 May 46 Okinawa
Okinawa
SPE: 27 May 45   Hawaii: 4 Jun 45   Okinawa: Jul 45

1635th Engineer Construction Bn
29 Jan 45 Ft Lewis Wash/15 Mar 46 Okinawa
Okinawa
SPE: 4 Jun 45   Hawaii: 11 Jun 45   Okinawa: Jul 45

1636th Engineer Construction Bn
20 Nov 44 Ft Lewis Wash / 28 Feb 46 Japan
Manila Philippines
Dep ZI: 31 Mar 45   France-ETO: 12 Apr 45 - **26**   Philippines: 20 Jul 45

1637th Engineer Construction Bn
20 Nov 44 Ft Lewis Wash / 28 Feb 46 Philippines
Shipment #5218-AA loading
Dep ZI: 15 Mar 45   France-ETO: 27 Mar 45 - **26**   Philippines: 11 Sep 45

1684th Engineer Combat Bn
26 Jun 44 Cp Swift Tex /19 Oct 45 Cp Callan Calif
Cp Swift Tex sch to SWPA
(left Cp Swift Tex 18 Aug 45 and was at SPE Ft Lawton Wash 22–31 Aug 45 but then relocated to Cp Callan Calif 3 Sep 45)
under Shipment #2188-D

BATTALION DESIGNATION AND TYPE	FORMED (SOURCE OF UNIT) / INACTIVATION *Active through 1946	AUGUST 1945 LOCATION
1685th Engineer Combat Bn SPE: 6 Jun 45 Hawaii: 15 Jun 45 Okinawa: 24 Jul 45	26 Jun 44 Cp McCain Miss / 28 Feb 46 Japan	Okinawa
1686th Engineer Combat Bn	15 Aug 44 Ft Leonard Wood Mo / 18 Sep 44 Ft Leonard Wood Mo	
1687th Engineer Combat Bn	15 Aug 44 Cp Bowie Tex / 15 Nov 45 Cp San Luis Obispo Calif	Cp San Luis Obispo Calif
1688th Engineer Combat Bn SPE: 30 Jul 45 Hawaii: 8 Aug 45 Philippines: 27 Sep 45	15 Aug 44 Cp Bowie Tex / 31 Jan 46 Japan	Shipment #2188-D at Hawaii
1689th Engineer Combat Bn SFPE: 15 Jun 45 Philippines: 9 Jul 45	16 Aug 44 Cp Gruber Okla / 31 May 46 Japan	Manila Philippines
1690th Engineer Combat Bn	15 Aug 44 Cp Gruber Okla / 2 Oct 44 Cp Gruber Okla	
1692nd Engineer Combat Bn (Cld) SFPE: 19 Jun 45 Philippines: 15 Jul 45	3 Aug 44 Cp Livingston La / 15 Dec 46 Japan	Manila Philippines
1693rd Engineer Combat Bn (Cld) *(left Cp Shelby Miss 15 Aug 45, arrived Ft Lawton Wash 19 Aug 45 and was at SPE and Portland Sub-P/E 19 Aug–4 Sep 45, but then relocated to Ft Ord Calif 6 Sep 45)*	31 Jul 44 Cp Rucker Ala / 17 Nov 45 Ft Ord Calif	Co Shelby Miss sch to SWPA under Shipment #0486-B
1694th Engineer Combat Bn (Cld) LAPE: 22 Jul 45 Philippines: 17 Aug 45	31 Jul 44 Cp Rucker Ala / 5 Feb 46 Philippines	Shipment #2209-A at sea aboard **SS** *Cape Victory*
1695th Engineer Combat Bn (Cld) NYPE: 22 Oct 44 England: 2 Nov 44 France-ETO: Unknown - **26,34**	15 Mar 44 Cp Pickett Va / 19 Jun 45 Germany	
1696th Engineer Combat Bn (Cld) NYPE: 9 Dec 44 England: 20 Dec 44 France-ETO: 6 Mar 45 - **26,34** HRPE: 14 Sep 45	19 Mar 44 Cp Swift Tex (933rd FA Bn) / *	Darmstadt Germany sch to SWPA under Shipment #R6604-Y
1697th Engineer Combat Bn (Cld) NYPE: 30 Oct 44 England: 10 Nov 44 France-ETO: 4 Mar 45 - **26,34**	19 Mar 44 Cp Van Dorn Miss (353rd FA Bn) / 29 Nov 46 Germany	Bad Durkheim Germany
1698th Engineer Combat Bn (Cld) NYPE: 30 Oct 44 England: 10 Nov 44 France-ETO: 3 Mar 45 - **26,34**	20 Mar 44 Cp Gordon Ga (931st FA Bn) / 25 Sep 45 Germany	Mailly France
1699th Engineer Combat Bn (Cld) NYPE: 30 Oct 44 England: 10 Nov 44 France-ETO: 9 Jan 45 - **26,34**	1 May 44 Cp Butner N.C. (930th FA Bn) / 19 Jun 45 Germany	
1700th Engineer Combat Bn (Cld) NYPE: 4 Dec 44 England: 12 Dec 44 France-ETO: Unknown - **26,34**	13 Mar 44 Ft Jackson S.C. / 19 Jun 45 Germany	
1759th Engineer Special Shop Bn (Boat Cons) New Guinea: 15 Nov 44 Philippines: 12 May 45 - **14**	15 Nov 44 Milne Bay New Guinea (1307th Engr Regt) / 20 Jan 46 Philippines	Batangas Philippines
1760th Engineer Special Shop Bn (Boat Cons) New Guinea: 15 Nov 44 Philippines: 12 Jul 45	15 Nov 44 Milne Bay New Guinea (411th Engr Bn) / 20 Jan 46 Philippines	Batangas Philippines
1777th Engineer Construction Bn BPE: 16 Apr 45 France-ETO: 28 Apr 45 Dep France: 16 Jun 45 on Shipment #R0598-J Philippines: 20 Jul 45	4 Dec 44 Ft Lewis Wash / 31 Aug 46 Japan	Manila Philippines
1778th Engineer Construction Bn SPE: 26 Jun 45 Okinawa: 5 Aug 45	18 Dec 44 Ft Lewis Wash / 10 Jun 46 Korea	Shipment #4496-M unloading
1800th Engineer General Service Bn	1 Mar 44 Ft Leonard Wood Mo / 2 Jul 45 Cp Shelby Miss	
1862nd Engineer Aviation Bn (Cld) SPE: 27 May 45 Hawaii: 3 Jun 45 Guam: 19 Jun 45	28 Nov 44 Gulfport Army Airbase Miss / 30 Jan 46 Guam	Guam
1863rd Engineer Aviation Bn (Cld) SPE: 17 May 45 Hawaii: 26 May 45 Guam: 21 Jun 45 Saipan: 6 Nov 45	28 Nov 44 Gulfport Army Airbase Miss / 12 Mar 46 Saipan	Guam
1864th Engineer Aviation Bn (Cld) SPE: 12 Jun 45 Hawaii: 18 Jun 45 Guam: 10 Jul 45	1 Dec 44 Drew Field Fla / 17 Jun 46 Oahu Hawaii	Guam
1865th Engineer Aviation Bn (Cld) SFPE: 26 Jun 45 Philippines: 20 Jul 45	19 Jan 45 Avon Park Army Airfield Fla / 29 Apr 46 Philippines	Manila Philippines
1866th Engineer Aviation Bn (Cld) SFPE: 26 Jun 45 Philippines: 20 Jul 45	15 Jan 45 Columbia Army Airbase S.C. / 15 Jun 46 Philippines	Manila Philippines
1867th Engineer Aviation Bn (Cld) SFPE: 15 Jun 45 Philippines: 10 Jul 45	20 Jan 45 Key Field Miss / 15 Jun 46 Philippines	Manila Philippines
1868th Engineer Aviation Bn (Cld) SPE: 27 Jun 45 Guam: 15 Jul 45	18 Jan 45 Greenville Army Airbase S.C. / 31 May 46 Guam	Guam

BATTALION DESIGNATION AND TYPE	FORMED (SOURCE OF UNIT / INACTIVATION *Active through 1946	AUGUST 1945 LOCATION
1869th Engineer Aviation Bn (Cld) SPE: 27 Jun 45 Guam: 15 Jul 45	16 Jan 45 Dale Mabry Field Fla /12 Mar 46 Guam	Guam
1870th Engineer Aviation Bn (Cld) SPE: 24 Jul 45 Hawaii: 30 Jul 45 Okinawa: Aug 45	15 Jan 45 Drew Field Fla / 31 May 46 Okinawa	Shipment #9858-C
1871st Engineer Aviation Bn (Cld) SFPE: 11 Dec 43 Australia: 29 Dec 43 New Guinea: 3 Jan 44 Philippines: 19 Nov 44 - **13,14,15**	1 Feb 43 Greenville Army Airbase S.C. /15 Jun 46 Philippines	Manila Philippines
1872nd Engineer Aviation Bn (Cld) SFPE: 28 Jan 44 New Guinea: 18 Feb 44 Philippines: 20 Jun 45 - **14,15**	1 Mar 43 Davis-Monthan Field Calif /10 May 46 Japan	Manila Philippines
1873rd Engineer Aviation Bn (Cld) SFPE: 24 Apr 44 New Guinea: 14 May 44 Okinawa: Unknown - **15,19** SPE: 7 Jan 46	1 Mar 43 Davis-Monthan Field Calif /10 Jan 46 Ft Lawton Wash	Ie Shima Island, Ryukyus
1874th Engineer Aviation Bn SFPE: 21 Dec 43 Australia: 17 Jan 44 New Guinea: 21 Jan 44 Noemfoor I: 2 Jul 44 Philippines: 12 Nov 44 - **13,14,15,20**	1 Mar 43 McChord Field Wash / 30 Jun 46 Japan	Cotabato Philippines
1875th Engineer Aviation Bn HRPE: 14 Dec 43 N.Africa: 21 Dec 43 India: 13 Feb 44 Burma: Unknown - **5,12** NYPE: 1 Jan 46	1 Mar 43 McChord Field Wash / 2 Jan 46 NYPE	Dudhkundi India
1876th Engineer Aviation Bn SFPE: 22 Mar 44 New Guinea: 10 Apr 44 Morotai I: 16 Sep 44 Philippines: 15 Jan 45 - **14,15**	1 Mar 43 March Field Calif /17 Jun 46 Philippines	Bagabag Philippines
1877th Engineer Aviation Bn HRPE: 16 Dec 43 N.Africa: 25 Dec 43 India: 13 Feb 44 Burma: 2 Oct 44 - **5,12** NYPE: 3 Jan 46	1 Mar 43 Venice Fla / 4 Jan 46 NYPE	Nampanmao Burma less Co A at Mogaung Burma
1878th Engineer Aviation Bn SFPE: 16 Dec 43 Hawaii: 20 Dec 43 Saipan: 25 Jul 44 Okinawa: 8 May 45 - **19,21**	1 Mar 43 Richmond Army Airbase Va / 24 Feb 46 Korea	Okinawa
1879th Engineer Aviation Bn SFPE: 20 Jan 44 New Guinea: 8 Feb 44 Philippines: 21 Dec 44 - **3,13,14,15** SFPE: 13 Dec 45	1 Mar 43 Geiger Field Wash /15 Dec 45 Cp Stoneman Calif	Manila Philippines
1880th Engineer Aviation Bn HRPE: 26 Mar 44 N.Africa: 9 Apr 44 India: 12 May 44 Burma: 9 Nov 44 China: 12 Jun 45 - **5,12** NYPE: 19 Dec 45	1 Mar 43 Geiger Field Wash / 20 Dec 45 Cp Kilmer N.J.	Chanyi China
1881st Engineer Aviation Bn SFPE: 21 Jun 43 Australia: 6 Jul 43 New Guinea: 28 Aug 43 Philippines: 22 Oct 44 - **13,14,15**	10 Apr 43 Geiger Field Wash (2nd Bn, 922nd Engr Regt) /15 Jun 46 Philippines	Manila Philippines
1882nd Engineer Aviation Bn (Cld) (I)	15 Mar 43 Eglin Field Fla (2nd Bn, 923 Engr Regt) / 20 Dec 43 Eglin Field Fla	
1882nd Engineer Aviation Bn (Cld) (II) SPE: 16 Apr 45 Hawaii: 23 Apr 45 Saipan: 19 May 45	15 Oct 44 Greenville Army Airbase S.C. / 31 May 46 Okinawa	Saipan
1883rd Engineer Aviation Bn (Cld) NYPE: 10 Jul 43 India: 12 Aug 43 - **5,12** NYPE: 9 Nov 45	15 Mar 43 Eglin Field Fla /10 Nov 45 NYPE	Ledo India
1884th Engineer Aviation Bn SPE: 9 Jul 44 Hawaii: 15 Jul 44 Anguar I: 17 Sep 44 Guam: 17 Dec 44 Okinawa: 4 Jul 45 - **19,21**	1 Apr 43 Geiger Field Wash / 21 Mar 46 Okinawa	Okinawa
1885th Engineer Aviation Bn SPE: 8 Jun 44 Hawaii: 17 Jun 44 Guam: 25 Aug 44 Okinawa: 29 Jun 45 - **19,21**	1 Apr 43 March Field Calif / 31 May 46 Okinawa	Okinawa
1886th Engineer Aviation Bn SPE: 21 Sep 44 Hawaii: 28 Sep 44 Guam: 11 Dec 44 Okinawa: Unknown - **21**	1 Apr 43 March Field Calif / 17 Jun 46 Okinawa	Okinawa
1887th Engineer Aviation Bn (Cld) SPE: 15 May 44 Hawaii: 22 May 44 Angaur I: 17 Sep 44 Guam: 15 Mar 45 - **21**	1 Apr 43 March Field Calif / 30 Jan 46 Guam	Guam
1888th Engineer Aviation Bn (Cld) LAPE: 27 Feb 44 India: 31 Mar 44 Burma: Unknown - **5,12** NYPE: 3 Jan 46	1 Apr 43 MacDill Field Fla / 4 Jan 46 NYPE	Myitkyina Burma
1889th Engineer Aviation Bn (Cld) SPE: 21 May 44 Hawaii: 28 May 44 Guam: 25 Aug 44 Okinawa: 14 Jul 45 - **21**	1 Apr 43 Davis-Monthan Field Calif / 28 Feb 46 Okinawa	Okinawa
1890th Engineer Aviation Bn (Cld) (I)	1 May 43 March Field Calif / 20 Dec 43 March Field Calif	
1890th Engineer Aviation Bn (Cld) (II)	1 Aug 45 Tinian Island (890th Engr Co) /30 Jan 46 Tinian Island	Tinian less Co B on Kwajalein
1891st Engineer Aviation Bn LAPE: 30 Aug 44 India: 7 Oct 44 Burma: 8 Nov 44 China: 11 Apr 45 - **5,7,8**	1 May 43 Geiger Field Wash / 20 Dec 45 India	Mengtze China
1892nd Engineer Aviation Bn SFPE: 26 Oct 44 New Guinea: 13 Nov 44 Ie Shima I: 22 Jun 45 - **15,19**	1 May 43 Gowen Field Idaho/17 Jun 46 Okinawa	Ie Shima Island, Ryukyus
1893rd Engineer Aviation Bn	1 May 43 Gowen Field Idaho / 20 Dec 43 Gowen Field Idaho	

BATTALION DESIGNATION AND TYPE	FORMED (SOURCE OF UNIT) / INACTIVATION *Active through 1946	AUGUST 1945 LOCATION
1894th Engineer Aviation Bn (Cld) SPE: 15 May 44 Hawaii: 22 May 44 Saipan: 10 Aug 44 Okinawa: 24 Jul 45 - **21**	1 Apr 43 MacDill Field Fla /15 Mar 46 Okinawa	Okinawa
1895th Engineer Aviation Bn (Cld) SPE: 10 Jun 44 Hawaii: 16 Jun 44 Guam: 4 Nov 44 - **21**	1 May 43 Greenville Army Airbase S.C. / 30 Jan 46 Guam	Guam
1896th Engineer Aviation Bn SFPE: 12 Mar 44 Australia: 20 Mar 44 New Guinea: 5 Apr 44 Biak I: 12 Aug 44 Philippines: 13 Jan 45 - **14,15**	1 May 43 Richmond Army Airbase Va /10 May 46 Japan	Manila Philippines
1897th Engineer Aviation Bn SFPE: 10 Mar 44 Australia: 2 Apr 44 New Guinea: 11 Apr 44 Philippines: 24 Oct 44 Okinawa: Unknown - **13,15,19,20**	1 May 43 Richmond Army Airbase Va /1 Feb 46 Japan	Okinawa
1898th Engineer Aviation Bn (Cld) HRPE: 12 Feb 44 Italy: 7 Mar 44 - **29,35** NYPE: 11 Nov 46 *(sch to SWPA under Shipment #R0411-H in Aug 45 but never sent)*	1 Jun 43 Eglin Field Fla / *	Pantamella Italy less Co A at Venosa & Co C at Spinnazzola
1899th Engineer Aviation Bn (Cld) SPE: 29 Sep 44 Hawaii: 8 Oct 44 Guam: 11 Dec 44 - **21**	1 Jun 43 MacDill Field Fla / 29 Jul 46 Guam	Guam
1900th Engineer Aviation Bn	1 Jun 43 March Field Calif / 20 Dec 43 March Field Calif	
1901st Engineer Aviation Bn (I)	1 Jun 43 March Field Calif / 20 Dec 43 March Field Calif	
1901st Engineer Aviation Bn (II) SPE: 13 Feb 45 Hawaii: 20 Feb 45 Okinawa: 2 Apr 45 - **19**	9 Jul 44 Geiger Field Wash / 30 Jun 46 ZKorea	Okinawa
1902nd Engineer Aviation Bn (I)	1 Jun 43 Geiger Field Wash / 20 Dec 43 Geiger Field Wash	
1902nd Engineer Aviation Bn (II) SPE: 26 Feb 45 Hawaii: 9 Mar 45 Ie Shima I: 21 Apr 45 - **19**	9 Jul 44 Geiger Field Wash/17 Jun 46 Okinawa	Ie Shima Island, Ryukyus
1903rd Engineer Aviation Bn (I)	1 Jun 43 Geiger Field Wash / 20 Dec 43 Geiger Field Wash	
1903rd Engineer Aviation Bn (II) SPE: 26 Feb 45 Hawaii: 9 Mar 45 Ie Shima I: 18 Apr 45 - **19**	9 Jul 44 Geiger Field Wash /16 May 46 Okinawa	Ie Shima Island, Ryukyus
1904th Engineer Aviation Bn	1 Jun 43 Geiger Field Wash / 20 Dec 43 Geiger Field Wash	
1905th Engineer Aviation Bn NYPE: 8 Sep 43 India: 12 Oct 43 - **5,12** NYPE: 3 Jan 46	2 Jun 43 Dow Field Maine (1st Bn, 924th Engr Regt) / 4 Jan 46 NYPE	Ledo India
1906th Engineer Aviation Bn NOPE: 26 Jan 44 New Guinea: 25 Feb 44 Wadke I: 15 Oct 44 Philippines: 12 Nov 44 Okinawa: 14 Jun 45 - **13,15,19**	2 Jun 43 Dow Field Maine (2nd Bn, 924th Engr Regt) / 28 Feb 46 Philippines	Okinawa
1907th Engineer Aviation Bn	1 Sep 43 Richmond Army Airbase Va / 25 Dec 43 Richmond Army Airbase Va	
1908th Engineer Aviation Bn (Cld) SPE: 10 Mar 45 Hawaii: 18 Mar 45 Saipan: 24 Apr 45 Okinawa: 12 Aug 45	15 Oct 44 Greenville Army Airbase S.C. / 17 Jun 46 Okinawa	Shipment #98721 unloading
1909th Engineer Aviation Bn (Cld) (I)	1 Jul 43 March Field Calif / 20 Dec 43 March Field Calif	
1909th Engineer Aviation Bn (Cld) (II) SPE: 16 Apr 45 Hawaii: 23 Apr 45 Saipan: 19 Jun 45 Okinawa: Aug 45	20 Oct 44 Dale Mabry Field Fla/17 Jun 46 Okinawa	Okinawa
1910th Engineer Aviation Bn	1 Jul 43 Geiger Field Wash / 20 Dec 43 Geiger Field Wash	
1911th Engineer Aviation Bn	1 Jul 43 Geiger Field Wash / 20 Dec 43 Geiger Field Wash	
1912th Engineer Aviation Bn	1 Aug 43 March Field Calif / 31 Mar 44 March Field Calif	
1913th Engineer Aviation Bn Dep ZI: 13 Aug 43 Australia: 1 Sep 43 New Guinea: 18 Sep 43 New Britian I: 1 Jan 44 Philippines: 24 Dec 44 - **3,13,14,15** SPE: 4 Dec 45	2 Jun 43 Dow Field Maine (3rd Bn, 924th Engr Regt) / 5 Dec 45 Ft Lewis Wash	Clark Field Philippines
1914th Engineer Aviation Bn Dep ZI: 20 May 45 Hawaii: 27 May 45 Okinawa: Jul 45	1 Aug 43 Gowen Field Idaho /17 Jun 46 Okinawa	Okinawa
1915th Engineer Aviation Bn Dep ZI: 27 Apr 45 Hawaii: 6 May 45 Okinawa: Jul 45	1 Aug 43 Geiger Field Wash / 28 Feb 46 Okinawa	Okinawa
1916th Engineer Aviation Bn (Cld)	1 Aug 43 MacDill Field Fla /1 May 44 MacDill Field Fla	
1917th Engineer Aviation Bn (Cld)	1 Aug 43 March Field Calif / 20 Dec 43 March Field Calif	
1921st Engineer Aviation Bn	1 Sep 43 Westover Field Mass /19 Feb 44 Richmond Army Airbase Va	
1922nd Engineer Aviation Bn	1 Sep 43 Westover Field Mass / 27 Dec 43 Westover Field Mass	

BATTALION DESIGNATION AND TYPE	FORMED (SOURCE OF UNIT) / INACTIVATION	AUGUST 1945 LOCATION
1923rd Engineer Aviation Utilities Bn *(redes Engr Aviation Utilities Bn on 20 Jan 45)*	1 Jul 44 Iceland as Engr Composite Bn, Avn (824th Engr Bn) / 25 Aug 45 Iceland	Massey Iceland
1924th Engineer Aviation Bn Dep ZI: 3 May 45 Hawaii: 10 May 45 Guam: 25 May 45 Okinawa: Jul 45	9 Jul 44 Geiger Field Wash / 17 Jun 46 Okinawa	Okinawa
2755th Engineer Combat Bn Italy: 10 Oct 44 France-ETO: 20 Dec 44 - **25,26,34** NYPE: 1 Jan 46	10 Oct 44 Qualiano Italy (1st Bn, 591st Engr Regt) / 2 Jan 46 Cp Kilmer N.J.	St Martin Czechoslovakia
2756th Engineer Combat Bn Italy: 10 Oct 44 France-ETO: 20 Dec 44 - **25,26,34**	10 Oct 44 Qualiano Italy (2nd Bn, 591st Engr Regt) / 25 Jun 46 France	St Martin Czechoslovakia
2759th Engineer Combat Bn Italy: 10 Oct 44 France-ETO: 20 Dec 44 - **25,26,34** NYPE: 7 Jan 46	10 Oct 44 Qualiano Italy (3rd Bn, 591st Engr Regt) / 8 Jan 46 Cp Kilmer N.J.	St Martin Czechoslovakia
2803rd Engineer General Service Bn (Cld) Hawaii: 17 Dec 44 Saipan: 8 Feb 45 - **21**	17 Dec 44 Aiea Staging Area Hawaii (1st Bn, 1316th Engr Regt) / 30 Jan 46 Saipan	Saipan
2804th Engineer General Service Bn (Cld) Hawaii: 17 Dec 44 Saipan: 1 Feb 45 - **21**	17 Dec 44 Hawaii / 19 Dec 45 Saipan	Saipan
2805th Engineer General Service Bn (Cld) Hawaii: 17 Dec 44 Saipan: 7 Feb 45 - **21**	17 Dec 44 Schofield Bks Hawaii (1st Bn, 1320th Engr Regt) / 30 Jan 46 Saipan	Saipan
2806th Engineer General Service Bn (Cld) Hawaii: 17 Dec 44 Saipan: 2 Feb 45 - **21**	17 Dec 44 Aiea Staging Area Hawaii (2nd Bn, 1316th Engr Regt) / *	Saipan
2807th Engineer General Service Bn (Cld) Hawaii: 17 Dec 44 Saipan: 6 Feb 45 - **21**	17 Dec 44 Schofield Bks Hawaii (3rd Bn, 1320th Engr Regt) / 29 Nov 45 Guam	Saipan
2808th Engineer General Service Bn (Cld) Italy: 25 Apr 45 HRPE: 14 Jun 45	25 Apr 45 Livorno Italy (1334th Engr Cons Bn) / 16 Nov 45 Ft Lewis Wash	Ft Lewis Wash
2819th Engineer Service Bn (Pipeline) France: 14 Feb 45 *(Seine Petroleum Depot)*	14 Feb 45 France / 25 Feb 46 France	Bagnoles France
2826th Engineer Combat Bn France-ETO: 15 Feb 45 - **26** NYPE: 19 Dec 45	15 Feb 45 Baccarat France (1st Bn, 36th Engr Regt) / 21 Dec 45 NYPE	Kemathen Germany
2827th Engineer Combat Bn France-ETO: 15 Feb 45 - **26** NYPE: 23 Feb 46	15 Feb 45 Heming France (2nd Bn, 36th Engr Regt) / 25 Feb 46 NYPE	Kempfenhausen Germany
2828th Engineer Combat Bn France-ETO: 15 Feb 45 - **26,34**	15 Feb 45 Val-et-Chatillon France (3rd Bn, 36th Engr Regt) / 15 Jun 46 Germany	Mittenwald Germany
2829th Engineer Combat Bn France-ETO: 15 Feb 45 - **26,34** NYPE: 13 Nov 45	15 Feb 45 Tannmuhl France (1st Bn, 40th Engr Regt) / 14 Nov 45 Cp Shanks N.Y.	Fleitsbach Germany
2830th Engineer Combat Bn France-ETO: 15 Feb 45 - **26,34** BPE: 20 Nov 45	15 Feb 45 Romanswiller France (2nd Bn, 40th Engr Regt) / 21 Feb 45 Cp Myles Standish Mass	Prein Germany
2831st Engineer Combat Bn France-ETO: 15 Feb 45 - **26,34** BPE: 15 Oct 45	15 Feb 45 Wasselonne France (3rd Bn, 40th Engr Regt) / 16 Oct 45 Cp Myles Standish Mass	Rosenheim Germany
2832nd Engineer Combat Bn France-ETO: 15 Feb 45 - **26,34** NYPE: 13 Nov 45	15 Feb 45 Lutzelbourg France (1st Bn, 540th Engr Regt) / 15 Nov 45 Cp Kilmer N.J.	Grafelfing Germany
2833rd Engineer Combat Bn France-ETO: 15 Feb 45 - **26,34** NYPE: 26 Nov 45	15 Feb 45 Phalsbourg France (2nd Bn, 540th Engr Regt) / 27 Nov 45 Cp Kilmer N.J.	Landsberg Germany
2834th Engineer Service (Pipeline) France: 14 Feb 45 *(personnel not received until 9 Mar 45)*	14 Feb 45 Chartes France / 25 Feb 46 France	St Merme France
2912th Engineer Service Bn (Depot)	10 May 45 Schofield Bks Hawaii (595th Engr Base Depot) / 22 Apr 46 Hawaii	Schofield Barracks Hawaii
2913th Engineer Service Bn (Depot)	10 May 45 Ft Shafter Hawaii (Prov Engr Shop Bn) / 22 Apr 46 Hawaii	Schofield Barracks Hawaii
3051st Engineer Combat Bn France-ETO: 2 Aug 44 - **26,30,32,34**	2 Aug 44 St Marie du Mont France (1st Bn, 531st Engr Regt) / 6 Sep 45 Germany	Gournay France
3052nd Engineer Combat Bn France-ETO: 2 Aug 44 - **26,30,32,34**	2 Aug 44 St Marie du Mont France (2nd Bn, 531st Engr Regt) / 6 Sep 45 France	Gournay France
3053rd Engineer Combat Bn France-ETO: 2 Aug 44 - **26,30,32,34**	2 Aug 44 St Martin de Varreville France (3rd Bn, 531st Engr Regt) / 6 Sep 45 Germany	Gournay France

BATTALION DESIGNATION AND TYPE	FORMED (SOURCE OF UNIT) / INACTIVATION	AUGUST 1945 LOCATION
3171st Engineer Fire Fighting Bn, Prov	21 May 45 Ft Lewis Wash / 12 Oct 45 Ft Douglas Utah	Ft Douglas Utah
3189th Engineer Service Bn	15 May 45 Ft Belvoir Va / 21 Nov 45 Ft Lewis Wash	Ft Lewis Wash sch to SWPA under Shipment #2201-A
3190th Engineer Service Bn Hawaii: 28 Jun 45 - None	28 Jun 45 Schofield Bks Hawaii (1339th Engr Cons Bn) / 26 Jun 46 Hawaii	Ft Shafter Hawaii less 1st Water Distill Plat on Iwo Jima
3230th Engineer Service Bn	4 Aug 45 Epernay France / 19 Nov 46 France	Paris France
3231st Engineer Service Bn	4 Aug 45 Epernay France / 6 Oct 45 France	Paris France
3232nd Engineer Service Bn	4 Aug 45 Epernay France / 6 Oct 45 France	Paris France
3233rd Engineer Service Bn (Engr School)	4 Aug 45 Epernay France (1261st Engr Bn) / 27 Jun 46 France	Paris France

5211th Engineer Steel Hull Assembly Bn, Prov 11 Sep 43 Jungara Australia (Co E, 411th Engr Bn) / 18 Jul 44 New Guinea
Australia: 11 Sep 43   New Guinea: 25 Oct 43 - **15** *(built 950 Landing Craft, Medium)*

6486th Engineer Construction Bn, Prov (Cld) 29 Mar 44 Algeria N.Africa / 1 Jun 44 Italy redes 1334th Engr Combat Bn
N.Africa: 29 Mar 44   Italy: Apr 44 - **35**

6487th Engineer Construction Bn, Prov (Cld) 31 Mar 44 Algeria N.Africa (28th Cav Regt) / 6 Jun 44 Aversa Italy redes 134th
N.Africa: 31 Mar 44   Italy: 26 Apr 44 - **35**   Quartermaster Bn (Mobile) (Cld)

6495th Engineer Heavy Ponton Bn, Prov (Cld) 23 Mar 44 Algeria N.Africa (4th Cav Brigade) / 5 Jun 44 N.Africa redes 1553rd
N.Africa: 31 Mar 44   Engr Heavy Ponton Bn (Cld)

6496th Engineer Heavy Ponton Bn, Prov (Cld) 29 Mar 44 Algeria N.Africa (162nd Engr Sqdn) / 5 Jun 44 Mostaganem N.Africa
N.Africa: 29 Mar 44   redes 1554th Engr Heavy Ponton Bn

7057th Engineer Separate Bn (Italian)
Formed in N.Africa on 3 Nov 43 and sent to Italy 13 Jan 45. 7076th, 7086th, 7096th, and 7204th Engr Sep Bns (Italian) also formed. As there were all completely staffed and manned by expatriated Italian prisoners from North African POW enclosures, they are not considered part of the U.S. Army forces for this book.

Engineer Aviation Topographic Training Bn 20 Oct 42 Colorado Springs Colo / 1 May 44 Will Rogers Field Okla

Engineer Special Topographic Bn 15 May 43 Lancaster Pa / 8 Oct 43 England redes 660th Engr Base Topographic Bn
NYPE: 4 Aug 43   England: 11 Aug 43

*Active through 1946.

Appendixes and Sources

✪ Appendix I. Campaign Key Codes

CAMPAIGN KEY CODES — PACIFIC

1	Air Offensive Japan	17 Apr 42–2 Sep 45
2	Aleutian Islands	3 Jun 42–24 Aug 43
3	Bismarck Archipelago	15 Dec 43–27 Nov 44
4	Burma 1942	7 Dec 41–26 May 42
5	Central Burma	29 Jan 45–15 Jul 45
6	Central Pacific	7 Dec 41–6 Dec 43
7	China Defensive	4 Jul 42–4 May 45
8	China Offensive	5 May 45–2 Sep 45
9	East Indies	1 Jan 42–22 Jul 42
10	Eastern Mandates	31 Jan 44–14 Jun 44
11	Guadalcanal	7 Aug 42–21 Feb 43
12	India-Burma	2 Apr 42–28 Jan 43
13	Leyte	17 Oct 44–1 Jul 45
14	Luzon	15 Dec 44–4 Jul 45
15	New Guinea	24 Jan 43–31 Dec 44
16	Northern Solomons	22 Feb 43–21 Nov 44
17	Papua	23 Jul 42–23 Jan 43
18	Philippine Islands	7 Dec 41–10 May 42
19	Ryukyus	26 Mar 45–2 Jul 45
20	Southern Philippines	27 Feb 45–4 Jul 45
21	Western Pacific	15 Jun 44–2 Sep 45

CAMPAIGN KEY CODES — EUROPE - AFRICA

22	Air Offensive Europe	4 Jul 42–5 Jun 44
23	Algeria–French Morocco	8 Nov 42–11 Nov 42
24	Anzio	22 Jan 44–24 May 44
25	Ardennes-Alsace	16 Dec 44–25 Jan 45
26	Central Europe	22 Mar 45–11 May 45
27	Egypt-Libya	11 Jun 42–12 Feb 43
28*	Ground Combat, EAME Theater	11 May 42–8 May 45
29	Naples-Foggia	9 Sep 43–21 Jan 44
30	Normandy	6 Jun 44–24 Jul 44
31	North Apennines	10 Sep 44–4 Apr 45
32	Northern France	25 Jul 44–14 Sep 44
33	Po Valley	5 Apr 45–8 May 45
34	Rhineland	15 Sep 44–21 Mar 45
35	Rome-Arno	22 Jan 44–9 Sep 44
36	Sicily	9 Jul 43–17 Aug 43
37	Southern France	15 Aug 44–14 Sep 44
38	Tunisia	17 Nov 42–13 May 43

*Officially the campaign extended from 7 Dec 41 to 2 Sep 45, but the above time frames are used for entries so labeled in this book, unless otherwise indicated.

✪ Appendix II. Abbreviations Used in Text

General note: All abbreviations in this Order of Battle deliberately conform to World War II usage and do not necessarily coincide with modern military parlance.

A - Assault Credit, Austria

AA - Antiaircraft

AAA - Antiaircraft Artillery

AAB - Army Air Base

AAF - Army Air Field or Force

A/B - Airborne

AG - Adjutant General Orders

AGF - Army Garrison Force

Amph - Amphibious or Amphibian

APO - Army Post Office

Armd - Armored

Assoc - Associated with (railway)

AT - Antitank

ATF - Army Task Force

Att - Attached

Avn - Aviation

AW - Automatic Weapons

A-Wpns - Automatic Weapons

Bde - Brigade

BG - Brigadier General

Bks - Barracks

Bn - Battalion

BPE - Boston Port of Embarkation

Br - British

Btry - Battery

C - Czechoslovakia

CA - Coast Artillery

Cav - Cavalry

Chem - Chemical

Cld - Colored (Negro)

Co - Company

Comb - Combat

Comd - Command

Constab - Constabulary

Cons - Construction

Cp - Camp

CZ - Canal Zone in Panama

D - Drawn

Dep - Departed

Desig - Designated

Det - Detachment

Disb - Disbanded

Div - Division

DTC - Desert Training Center

Dtd - Dated

EDC - Eastern Defense Command

Elmts - Elements

Engr - Engineer

EPD - Earliest Practical Date

EOW - End of World War II in August 1945

ETO - European Theater of Operations

F - Force, France

FA - Field Artillery

Ft - Fort

G - Germany

GHQ - General Headquarters

GO - General Order

Gp - Group

Haw - Hawaii

HD - Harbor Defenses

H-D - Horse-Drawn

HHB - Headquarters & Headquarters Battery

HHC - Headquarters & Headquarters Company

HHD - Headquarters & Headquarters Detachment

HHT - Headquarters & Headquarters Troop

How - Howitzer

HRPE - Hampton Roads of Embarkation

I - Island(s), Italy

Inactiv - Inactivated

Inf - Infantry

LA - Low Altitude

LAPE - Los Angeles Port of Embarkation

LI - Long Island

Lt - Light

Ltr - Letter Orders

M. - Mount

Mecz - Mechanized

MG - Major General

Mnvr - Maneuver

Mtn - Mountain

MTO - Mediterranean Theater of Operations

Mtz - Motorized

NATO - North African Theater of Operations

NG - National Guard, New Guinea

Nondiv - Nondivisional (separate)

NOPE - New Orleans Port of Embarkation

NYPE - New York Port of Embarkation

OSS - Office of Strategic Services

P - Active before 8 Sep 39 or at that location before 8 Sep 39

PE - Port of Embarkation

PI - Philippine Islands

Pk - Pack

Plat - Platoon

POW - Prisoner of War

PR - Puerto Rico

Prcht - Parachute

Prov - Provisional

PS - Philippine Scouts

QM - Quartermaster

Rcn - Reconnaissance

Redes - Redesignated

Regt - Regiment

RR - Railroad

R & S Cmd - Replacement & School Command

Ry - Railway

S - Secret

Sch - Scheduled

SDC - Southern Defense Command

Sep - Separate

SFPE - San Francisco Port of Embarkation

S/L - Searchlight

Sqdn - Squadron

S-P - Self-Propelled

SPE - Seattle Port of Embarkation

Spec - Special

Spt - Support

SWPA - Southwest Pacific Area

Svc - Service

T - Towed

TC - Transportation Corps

TD - Tank Destroyer

TF - Task Force

T/O - Table of Organization

Topo - Topographic

Trac-D - Tractor-Drawn

Transp - Transportable

Trk-D - Truck-Drawn

Trp - Troop

USA - United States of America

WNRC - Washington National Records Center

ZI - Zone of Interior (continental USA)

✪ Appendix III. Army Ground Forces Installations

Installation	Location	Activity	Acreage*	Troop Capacity* Officer	Enlisted
Abbott, Camp	Bend, Oreg	Engineer Replacement Training Center	17,635	482	6,141
Aberdeen Proving Grounds	Aberdeen, Md	Replacement Training Center and Proving Grounds	72,962	2,348	24,189
Adair, Camp	Corvallis, Oreg	Division camp	57,159	2,133	37,081
Allen, Fort Ethan	Essex Junction, Vt	Field Artillery camp (declared inactive 20 Mar 44)	13,531	200	5,050
Anza, Camp	Arlington, Calif	Staging area for Los Angeles Port of Embarkation	1,241	—	9,678
Ashland, Camp	Ashland, Nebr	National Guard tent camp	878	—	2,400
Atterbury, Camp	Columbus, Ind	Division training camp	40,513	2,243	41,916
Barkeley, Camp	Abilene, Tex	Armored Division camp and Medical Replacement Training Center	69,879	3,192	54,493
Beale, Camp	Marysville, Calif	Division camp	86,364	2,107	35,228
Beauregard, Camp	Alexandria, La	Military Reservation	8,872	106	4,913

Installation	Location	Activity	Acreage*	Troop Capacity* Officer	Enlisted
Beltsville Outpost	Beltsville, Md	Ground Forces Training area	144	—	1,700
Belvoir, Fort	Alexandria, Va	Engineer School and Replacement Training Center	9,146	2,183	21,954
Belvoir, Fort Training Area	Shenandoah Nat'l Park	Shenandoah National Park Training area	183,312	20	257
Benning, Fort	Columbus, Ga	Ground Forces Training Center and Infantry School	197,159	3,970	94,873
Bethany Beach AAA Station	Bethany Beach, Del	Antiaircraft Training Station	120	33	779
Blanding, Camp	Starke, Fla	Infantry Replacement Training Center	152,672	2,157	58,570
Bliss, Fort	El Paso, Texas	Antiaircraft Replacement Training Center	618,343	1,559	47,604
Boise Barracks	Boise City, Idaho	Training Center (declared surplus 17 Mar 44)	6,885	—	1,480
Bonneville, Camp	Vancouver Wash	Range used in connection with Vancouver Barracks, Wash	3,019	—	—
Bouse, Camp	Phoenix, Ariz	Training area	352,300	—	—
Bowie, Camp	Brownwood, Tex	Armored Division camp	116,264	2,237	43,247
Brady, Fort	Rexford, Mich	Military Reservation (declared surplus 5 Apr 44)	7,843	325	4,477
Bragg, Fort	Fayetteville, N.C.	Field Artillery Replacement Training Center	129,422	4,311	76,175
Breckinridge, Camp	Morganfield, Ky	Infantry Division camp	36,070	2,031	42,092
Brown, Fort	Brownsville, Tex	Cavalry Post	2,966	47	1,253
Butner, Camp	Durham, N.C.	Division camp	40,344	2,403	41,700
Callan, Camp	San Diego, Calif	Antiaircraft Replacement Training Center	3,782	426	9,926
Campbell, Camp	Hopkinsville, Ky	Armored Division camp	102,414	2,422	45,198
Carlisle Barracks	Carlisle, Pa	Medical Field Service Training School	1,390	164	3,332
Carrabelle, Camp *See Camp Gordon Johnston*					
Carson, Camp	Colorado Springs, Colo	Division Camp	68,355	2,707	44,240
Cat Island War Dog Center	Gulfport, Miss	War Dog Reception and Training Center (surplus 15 Jun 44)	22,898	15	248
Catoctin Training Center	Thurmont, Md	Strategic Services Training Camp	9,638	20	400
Chaffee, Camp	Fort Smith, Ark	Armored Division camp	75,028	2,491	41,330
Chopawamsic Training Center	Chopawamsic, Va	Strategic Services Training Camp	198,553	84	433
Chrysler Tank School	Center Line, Mich	Training Center	11	20	380
Claiborne, Camp	Alexandria, La	Engineer Unit Training Center and Infantry Division camp	29,363	6,665	57,002
Clark, Fort	Brackettville, Tex	Cavalry Post (declared surplus 2 Jun 44)	31,937	588	8,129
Cooke, Camp	Oceano, Calif	Division camp	88,803	2,346	35,288
Cotuit Training Area	Cotuit, Mass	Engineer Amphibious Training area	798	—	—
Croft, Camp	Spartanburg, S.C.	Infantry Replacement Training Center	19,403	864	20,431
Crowder, Camp	Neosho, Mo	Signal Corps Training Center	43,007	1,988	40,642

Installation	Location	Activity	Acreage*	Troop Capacity* Officer	Troop Capacity* Enlisted
Custer, Fort	Battle Creek, Mich	Military Police Replacement Training Center	16,005	1,279	27,553
Davis, Camp	Wilmington, N.C.	Antiaircraft Artillery School and Training Center	35,518	1,978	35,327
Dawson, Camp	Kingwood, W.Va	National Guard camp (reactivated 10 Jun 44)	200	—	—
Daytona Beach WAC Training Center	Daytona Beach, Fla	Women's Army Corps Replacement Training center	421	249	6,886
Desert Training Center	Indio, Calif	Maneuver Area	781,452	—	—
Des Moines, Fort	Des Moines, Iowa	Women's Army Corps Replacement Training Center	896	170	7,845
Devens, Fort	Ayer, Mass	Military Reservation	11,796	2,066	33,232
Dix, Fort	Wrightstown, N.J.	Training and Pre-staging Center	28,344	1,825	51,598
Dodge, Camp	Des Moines, Iowa	Basic Training Center	2,686	91	1,844
Dugway Proving Ground	Tooele, Utah	Chemical Warfare Service Proving Ground	218,880	86	776
Edison, Camp	Sea Girt, N.J.	Signal Corps Unit Training Center	168	166	3,389
Edwards, Camp	Falmouth, Mass	Antiaircraft Artillery Training Center	21,322	1,945	34,108
Ellis, Camp	Table Grove, Ill	Army Service Forces Training Center	17,503	1,795	24,654
Erie Proving Ground	Lacarne, Ohio	Ordnance Testing Ground	1,459	178	1,540
Eustis, Fort	Lee Hall, Va	Antiaircraft Artillery Replacement Training Center	8,098	815	17,266
Fannin, Camp	Tyler, Tex	Infantry Replacement Training Center	14,075	1,616	18,768
Fisher, Fort	Wilmington, N.C.	Antiaircraft Artillery Firing Point	1,224	404	6.078
Forrest, Camp	Tullahoma, Tenn	Infantry Division camp	73,124	1,886	32,368
Front Royal Quartermaster Depot	Front Royal, Va	War Dog Training Center	4,168	21	720
Gordon, Camp	Augusta, Ga	Division camp	55,708	2,171	43,055
Grant, Camp	Rockford, Ill	Medical Replacement Unit Training Center	3,349	453	20,836
Gruber, Fort	Braggs, Okla	Division camp	65,447	1,882	42,986
Guernsey Maneuver Area	Guernsey, Wyo	Bivouac Maneuver Area used by Ft Francis E. Warren, Wyo	4,500	—	—
Haan, Camp	Riverside, Calif	Antiaircraft Artillery Training Center	8,975	2,463	35,584
Hale, Camp	Pando, Colo	Infantry Division Camp and Mountain Training Center	247,243	915	16,298
Harrison, Fort Benjamin	Indianapolis, Ind	Finance Replacement Training Center	2,823	736	13,632
Harrison, Fort William Henry	Helena, Mont	Ground Forces Training Area (declared inactive 28 Feb 44)	11,737	122	2,892
Henry, Camp Patrick	Oriana, Va	Staging area for Hampton Roads Port of Embarkation	1,649	1,621	22,916
Hill, A. P. Military Reservation	Fredericksburg, Va	Maneuver area	77,332	74	858
Hood, Camp	Temple, Tex	Infantry and Tank Destroyer Replacement Training Center	158,706	6,007	82,610

Installation	Location	Activity	Acreage*	Troop Capacity* Officer	Troop Capacity* Enlisted
Houston, Fort Sam	San Antonio, Tex	Military Reservation incl. Leon Springs Military Reservation	23,592	719	25,825
Howze, Camp	Gainesville, Tex	Division camp	59,850	1,882	39,010
Huachuca, Fort	Tombstone, Ariz	Military Reservation	71,253	1,251	24,437
Hulen, Camp	Palacios, Tex	Antiaircraft Artillery Training camp	21,607	1,049	10,487
Hunter-Liggett Military Reservation	Jolon, Calif	Military Reservation	274,877	51	1,345
Indiantown Gap Military Reservation	Indiantown Gap, Pa	Training Center	17,065	1,440	25,562
Irwin, Camp	Barstow, Calif	Antiaircraft Artillery Training Center	638,720	—	8,930
Jackson, Fort	Columbia, S.C.	Infantry Training Center	58,653	5,907	72,817
Jefferson Barracks	Barnhart, Mo	Range	1,518	16	1,500
Johnston, Camp Gordon	Carrabelle, Fla	Army Service Forces Training Center (named 30 Jan 43 from Cp Carrabelle)	153,702	1,416	24,198
Kilmer, Camp	Stelton, N.J.	Staging area for New York Port of Embarkation	1,815	2,074	35,386
Kingston Demolition Range	Harriman, Tenn	Engineer Demolition Range	55,098	—	—
Knox, Fort	Louisville, Ky	Armored Replacement Training Center and School	107,148	3,489	57,048
Kohler, Camp	Sacramento, Calif	Western Signal Corps Training Center	3,563	347	8,742
Los Alamos Demolition Range	Los Alamos, N.M.	Demolition Range and atomic laboratory	71,413	—	—
Leavenworth, Fort	Leavenworth, Kans	Command and General Staff School	6,011	2,644	9,844
Lee, Camp	Petersburg, Va	Army Service Forces Replacement Training Center	7,534	2,143	38,427
Lewis, Fort	Tacoma, Wash	Army Ground Forces Training camp	90,870	3,542	63,727
Lincoln, Fort	Bismarck, N.D.	Military Reservation	1,156	—	—
Livingston, Camp	Alexandria, La	Army Ground Forces Training Station	47,967	2,092	42,831
Lockett, Camp	Campo, Calif	Cavalry Training Camp	7,581	260	3,340
Logan, Fort	Denver, Colo	Military Post	1,933	176	6,797
Mackall, Camp	Hoffman, N.C.	Airborne Center	61,971	2,640	27,006
Madison Barracks	Sackets Harbor, N.J.	Military Reservation (surplus on 4 Feb 44)	122	45	2,057
Maxey, Camp	Paris, Tex	Division camp	36,683	2,022	42,515
McCain, Camp	Grenada, Miss	Division camp	42,243	2,779	39,341
McClellan, Fort	Anniston, Ala	Infantry Replacement Training Center	42,286	2,170	42,126
McCoy, Camp	Sparta, Wis	Division camp	60,284	2,485	39,921
McIntosh, Fort	Laredo, Tex	Cavalry Post	209	55	1,392
McPherson, Fort	Atlanta, Ga	Reception and Reclassification Center	371	335	5,917
McQuaide, Camp	Watsonville, Calif	Coast Artillery Replacement Training Center	863	234	5,428

Installation	Location	Activity	Acreage*	Troop Capacity* Officer	Enlisted
Meade, Fort	Sturgis, S.D.	Ground Forces Training Center (surplus on 24 Mar 44)	13,638	85	2,006
Meade, Fort George G.	Baltimore, Md	Army Ground Forces Replacement Center	18,048	2,019	35,131
Millard, Camp	Bucyrus, Ohio	Military Railway Unit Training Center	106	82	36
Mississippi Ordnance Plant	Jackson, Miss	Ordnance Unit Training Center	9,135	523	7,104
Missoula, Fort	Missoula, Mont	Military Reservation	7,390	—	—
Monmouth, Fort	Red Bank, N.J.	Signal Corps Laboratory and Camp Cole; Eastern Signal Corps Ctr	1,713	1,559	19,786
Monroe, Fort	Suffolk, Va	Coast Artillery School	584	333	6,335
Monterey, Presidio of	Monterey, Calif	Reception Center	406	288	5,364
Murphy, Camp	Stuart, Fla	Signal Corps Technical School	11,535	854	5,962
Myer, Fort	Washington, D.C.	Military Reservation	608	179	4,779
New Cumberland Reception Center	New Cumberland, Pa	Army Service Forces Reception Center	98	147	3,563
Niagara, Fort	Youngstown, N.Y.	Army Service Forces Training Center	288	633	3,986
Niantic, Camp	Niantic, Conn	Army Service Forces Training Center (inactive 17 Apr 44)	1,820	32	905
Oglethorpe, Fort	Chattanooga, Tenn	Women's Army Corps Training Center	2,742	382	13,293
Ontario, Fort	Oswego, N.Y.	Pre-Basic Training Station (inactive 21 Feb 44)	205	114	2,282
Ord, Fort	Monterey, Calif	Landing Vehicle Board and Army Ground Forces Training Area	28,690	—	51,253
Peason Ridge Artillery Range	Vernon Parish, La	Artillery Range	33,431	—	—
Pendleton, Camp	Wallaceton, Va	Dover Range Combat Training Area	4,900	346	6,856
Phillips, Camp	Salina, Kans	Division camp	44,078	1,920	36,104
Pickett, Camp	Blackstone, Va	Division camp	45,867	2,363	41,552
Pine Camp	Watertown, N.Y.	Armored Division camp	99,816	1,434	21,998
Plattsburg Barracks	Plattsburg, N.Y.	Military Reservation (surplus 28 Jan 44)	728	—	—
Polk, Camp	Leesville, La	Armored Division camp	95,406	2,477	40,790
Pontchartrain, Camp	New Orleans, La	Engineer Fire Fighting School	104	34	1,500
Quantico Military Reservation	Quantico, Va	Training Center	8,000	28	612
Reynolds, Camp	Greenville, Pa	Army Service Forces Replacement Depot	2,440	2,596	23,732
Riley, Fort	Junction City, Kans	Cavalry Replacement Training Center and School	54,183	3,078	32,907
Rimini, Camp	Helena, Mont	Quartermaster War Dog Reception and Training Center	160	20	200
Ringgold, Fort	Rio Grande City, Tex	Cavalry Post (surplus 15 May 44)	758	25	829
Ritchie, Camp	Cascade, Md	Military Intelligence Training Center	639	515	3,199
Roberts, Camp	San Miguel, Calif	Infantry and Field Artillery Replacement Training Center	44,379	1,612	34,181

Installation	Location	Activity	Acreage*	Troop Capacity* Officer	Enlisted
Robinson, Camp Joseph T.	Little Rock, Ark	Infantry Replacement Training Center	42,124	2,596	44,077
Rucker, Camp	Ozark, Ala	Division camp	58,999	3,280	39,461
Russell, Fort D. A.	Marfa, Tex	Cavalry Training Center	2,675	92	2,300
San Carlos War Dog Training Center	San Carlos, Calif	War Dog Training Center	54	29	233
San Francisco, Presidio of	San Francisco, Calif	Military Reservation	1,442	220	5,501
San Luis Obispo, Camp	San Luis Obispo, Calif	Infantry Division camp	15,433	1,523	19,383
Santa Anita, Camp	Arcadia, Calif	Ordnance Training Center	1,705	524	15,323
Savage, Camp	Merriam, Minn	Military Intelligence Language School	136	200	1,291
Seeley, Camp	El Centro, Calif	Ordnance Desert Proving Ground	8,950	20	482
Shanks, Camp	Orangeburg, N.Y.	Staging area for New York Port of Embarkation	2,009	2,545	46,367
Shelby, Camp	Hattiesburg, Miss	Division camp	83,561	3,999	84,058
Shenango Personnel Repl. Depot	Greenville, Pa	Army Service Forces Replacement Depot	2,440	—	26,668
Sheridan, Fort	Highwood, Ill	Military Post	729	692	12,313
Sherman, Camp	Chillicothe, Ohio	Military Reservation	3,417	—	—
Sibert, Camp	Attalia, Ala	Chemical Warfare Replacement Training Center	37,394	1,299	22,738
Sill, Fort	Lawton, Okla	Field Artillery School and Replacement Training Center	70,303	2,335	49,467
Snelling, Fort	St. Paul, Minn	Army Service Forces Reception Center	2,222	133	6,765
Standish, Camp Myles	Boston, Mass	Staging area for Boston Port of Embarkation	1,485	1,298	23,100
Stewart, Camp	Hinesville, Ga	Antiaircraft Artillery Replacement Training Center	277,497	2,705	37,267
Stoneman, Camp	Pittsburg, Calif	Staging area for San Francisco Port of Embarkation	3,242	2,604	35,607
Sutton, Camp	Monroe, N.C.	Engineer Replacement Training Center incl. Pageland Range, S.C.	9,549	289	22,784
Swift, Camp	Bastrop, Tex	Division camp	52,950	2,552	46,658
Toccoa, Camp	Toccoa, Ga	Basic Training Center (surplus 15 Feb 44)	17,530	564	4,320
Totten, Fort	Bayside, L.I., N.Y.	Antiaircraft Artillery Camp	146	136	2,452
Tyson, Camp	Paris, Tenn	Barrage Balloon Training Center	7,014	772	12,543
U.S. Military Academy	West Point, N.Y.	United States Army Cadet Corps	14,615	—	2,353
Upton, Camp	Long Island, N.Y.	Reception Station	6,736	331	12,311
Van Dorn, Camp	Centreville, Miss	Division camp	40,092	2,173	36,926
Vancouver Barracks	Vancouver, Wash	Staging area for Seattle Port of Embarkation	3,019	250	7,295
Vint Hills Farm School	Warrenton, Va	Signal Corps Training Center	2,045	128	1,705
Wallace, Camp	Hitchcock, Tex	Replacement Training Center (surplus 13 Apr 44, transferred to U.S. Navy)	4,917	—	13,262
Warren, Fort Francis E.	Cheyenne, Wyo	Army Service Forces Training Center	94,874	665	16,518
Washington, Fort	Fort Washington, Md	Adjutant General's School	347	362	2,526

Installation	Location	Activity	Acreage*	Troop Capacity* Officer	Enlisted
Washington & Lee University	Lexington, Va	Army Service Forces Spec. & Morale Service School	20	800	200
Wellfleet, Camp	Mashpee, Mass	Antiaircraft Artillery Firing Point and School	1,948	64	1,052
West Point Military Reservation	West Point, Va	Strategic Services Training camp	73	—	—
West Virginia Training Area	Elkins, W.Va	Monongahela Impact Area	9,470	—	—
Wheeler, Camp	Macon, Ga	Infantry Replacement Training Center	11,934	1,290	24,440
White, Camp	Medford, Oreg	Division camp	49,638	1,884	35,557
Williams, Camp	Jordan Narrows, Utah	National Guard Camp (inactive 18 Jan 44)	23,180	—	1,160
Williams, Camp	Camp Douglas, Wis	Military Reservation	1,928	—	4,465
Williston, Camp	Boulder City, Nev	Military Police Training Camp (surplus 11 Mar 44)	100	—	1,035
Wolters, Camp	Mineral Wells, Tex	Infantry Replacement Training Center	20,532	1,067	24,081
Wood, Camp Charles	Eatontown, N.J.	Signal Corps Unit Training Center	672	24	3,622
Wood, Fort Leonard	Rolla, Mo	Engineer Replacement Training Center and Division camp	72,168	2,352	43,800
Wyoming National Guard Camp	Guernsey, Wyo	Ft Warren Maneuver Area	14,829	—	2,000
Yakima Artillery Range	Yakima, Wash	Field Artillery Firing Center	107,125	120	5,880
Young, Camp	Indio, Calif	Hqs, Desert Training Center	106,860	—	—

*Data as of June 1944

✪ Appendix IV. Proposed (Ghost) and Deception (Phantom) Divisions

Ghost divisions were those planned for activation but dropped by the War Department during 1943 because of mounting personnel requirements for service units, overhead, and the Army Air Force B-29 bomber program:

15th Airborne Division	191, 192, 545 Inf Regts	459 Prcht, 678 Glider, 679 Glider FA Bns
61st Infantry Division	247, 248, 249 Inf Regts	716, 855, 856, 857 FA Bns
62nd Infantry Division	250, 251, 252 Inf Regts	717, 858, 859, 860 FA Bns
67th Infantry Division	265, 266, 267 Inf Regts	722, 873, 874, 875 FA Bns
68th Infantry Division	268, 269, 270 Inf Regts	723, 876, 877, 878 FA Bns
72nd Infantry Division	280, 281, 282 Inf Regts	727, 888, 889, 890 FA Bns
73rd Infantry Division	283, 284, 285 Inf Regts	728, 891, 892, 893 FA Bns
74th Infantry Division	286, 287, 288 Inf Regts	729, 894, 895, 896 FA Bns
105th Infantry Division	419, 420, 421 Inf Regts	585, 586, 587, 588 FA Bns
107th Infantry Division	308, 312, 316 Inf Regts	Unknown FA composition

Phantom divisions were those created to deceive German forces during Operation Fortitude in June-August 1944, which was a deliberate attempt to convince their high command that additional Allied divisions would land at Pas de Calais. Patches were approved, but subdivisional components remained a complete fiction:

6th Airborne Division	22nd Infantry Division	108th Infantry Division
9th Airborne Division	46th Infantry Division	119th Infantry Division
11th Infantry Division	48th Infantry Division	130th Infantry Division
14th Infantry Division	50th Infantry Division	135th Airborne Division
17th Infantry Division	55th Infantry Division	141st Infantry Division
18th Airborne Division	59th Infantry Division	157th Infantry Division
21st Airborne Division		

Sources

The author gathered the material for this book from the original unit records of World War II. The materials the author relied on included the unit after action reports, periodic histories, operational reports, daily staff journals, combat reports, training files, official documents and orders, and other historical records of concerned units which are now kept in the custody of the National Archives of the United States.

Army requirements for historical reporting during World War II were premised on Army Regulations 345-105 (Historical Records and Histories of Organizations) and 210-10 (Post Diaries). Reports were also submitted in compliance with periodic instructions from higher headquarters. War Department Circular 287 (Historical Manuscripts—Review and Disposition) was issued 20 September 1945. General supervision over the preservation and processing of the source material connected with the war was exercised by the Historical Branch G-2, established in the Military Intelligence Division of the War Department General Staff in 1943. It also had responsibility for the preparation of publication of operational monographs, administrative histories, and theater and campaign histories. On the unit level appointed historical officers or interested commanders prepared their historical summaries based on official documents such as staff journals and orders or extracts, minutes of staff conferences, interviews with participants, or internal memorandums and records such as maps and overlays. In most headquarters the author found significant historical material under the following file numbers: 391.1, 320.2, 322, 333.1, 337, 352, and 353.

The records of subordinate SHAEF commands, 1943–45, were extremely helpful. These consist of general correspondence and other records of the 1st Allied Airborne Army and the 6th and 21st Army Groups (21st on microfilm), 1944–45, and the 12th Army Group, 1943–45.

The records of Allied Force Headquarters (AFHQ), 1942 on (in WNRC), were used as well. The AFHQ was established on September 12, 1942, as an Allied command to plan and direct ground, air, and naval operations and military government activities in the North African Theater of Operations (renamed the Mediterranean Theater of Operations in November 1944). Its records, most of which are microfilm copies (in WNRC) of records in the British Cabinet Office, London, include general records consisting of correspondence and other records of the Command Group and of General Staff Sections G-2 to G-5 (G-5 partly on microfilm), 1942–47, and of Special Staff sections, boards, committees, commissions, and other organizations, 1942–46 (partly on microfilm). Also included are records of subordinate commands, comprising correspondence and other records (partly on microfilm) of the 15th Army Group and the 5th Army.

The records of General Headquarters, Southwest Pacific Area (SWPA), 1941 on, were used. General Headquarters, SWPA, established at Melbourne, Australia, on April 18, 1942, had operational control over all Allied ground, air, and sea forces in the area, including the U.S. Army units that had been in Australia since 1941. It was in integrated, combined headquarters, with staff officers drawn from the air, ground, and naval services of the United States, Australia, the United Kingdom, and the Netherlands. In February 1943 a subordinate element, later designated the Far East Command, was established under General Headquarters, SWPA, to supervise Army training and administrative activities not closely related to the tactical and strategic direction of the war in the Southwest Pacific. The records consist of directives, plans, intelligence summaries, correspondence, and propaganda pamphlets of the Psychological Warfare Branch, General Headquarters, SWPA, relating to operations in the Southwest Pacific, 1941–45. Also historical monographs, indexes, intelligence summaries, operation reports, staff studies, directives, SCAP summations, and related documents collected for a history of operations in the SWPA and the Far East Command (known as the MacArthur Histories), 1942 on (in WNRC).

The records of Headquarters, Army Ground Forces (AGF), 1942 on, were consulted. General records of the Adjutant General's Section consist of general decimal files, 1942 on; unit movement orders, 1942–45, with related correspondence; and personnel movement orders, 1943–45. Also included are Classification and Replacement Division statistical reports, 1942–46, and Machine Records Division statistical tabulations and strength reports and Personnel Division records, 1942–46. There are correspondence and reference files of the Office of the Commanding General and journals of the Office of the Chief of Staff, 1940–45. Records of the General Staff consist of G-1 correspondence, 1945 on; records of the Control, Enlisted, and Officers' Divisions, 1946 on; the Women's Army Corps Division, 1943 on, and the Miscellaneous Division, 1942 on. G-2 records include correspondence, 1942 on, and intelligence reports, 1943–46. G-3 records consist of Training Group directives, 1942–43, and Replacement Training Branch, Maneuvers, and Special Project files from 1942 on.

Where units duly submitted meaningful historical reports which were then properly processed and preserved, no major problems were presented in recording vital data into this work. However, contradictory sources and absence of historical reporting (either completely or for certain periods) was encountered frequently. In such cases the author relied on other original sources, such as higher unit historical reports if available, or the types of documents illustrated and explained by the following examples.

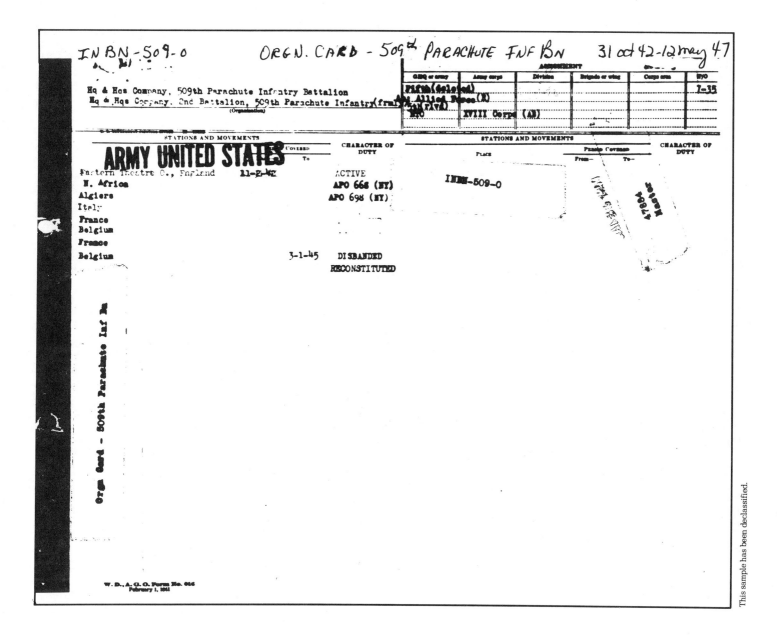

Example 1a. Typical Army Organizational Card, War Department Form used during 1941–1945
(Front side)

The Adjutant General's Office entered certain critical unit data on army organizational cards during World War II. These included assignments, status, and stations, as well as full unit titles.

While organizational cards are very useful, caution must be exercised as these are secondary sources which derive input from a variety of transmissions (Example 1b). Transcription errors and data problems sometimes arise. For example, official orders activating a unit as a result of War Department authorization were often issued in advance of actual unit formation, and such orders are generally the basis of card authority. Thus, the 1125th Armored Field Artillery Battalion is officially cited as being activated in North Africa because its activation orders were issued in anticipation of its formation there. However, it was actually in Naples, Italy, on its official activation date.

This organizational card on the 509th Parachute Infantry Battalion highlights another common problem. Since unit lineage is not necessarily concerned with unit movement or assignment details, information on change of station and subordination is very sparse.

HISTORICAL DATA

2nd Battalion, 509th Prcht Inf is constituted and will be activated effective Oct. 31, 1942 in Australia with the personnel and equipment of 2nd Battalion, 503rd Prcht Inf - per AG 320.2 (10-16-42) OB-I-GN-M, dated 10-22-42. (S)

Ltr above is amended to show effective date of be November 2, 1942, instead of October 31, 1942; ltr also states unit will be activated in the European Theater of Operations - per AG 320.2 (11-3 42) OB-I-B-M, dated November 8, 1942 (S).

2nd Bn, 509th Prcht Inf reported in N. Africa - per AG 370.5/3 MGC dated 12-14-42. (S)

2nd Bn, 509th Prcht Inf reported in Algiers - per U.S. Army Postal Service of APO's and locations. (S)

GO #3, this Hqs. dated Jan 11, 1943 is rescinded and the 2nd Bn, 509th Prcht Inf is assigned to the Fifth Army - per GO #6 from Hqs Fifth Army, APO #464, dated Jan. 15, 1943.

2nd Bn, 509th Prcht Inf is deleted from assignment to Fifth Army and reassigned to the Allied Force - per 3d Ind. from Hqs. Fifth Army APO #464 (AG 322.1) dated March 1, 1943.

Effective 10 December 1943, 2d Bn, 509th Prcht Inf is redesignated 509th Prcht Inf Battalion; unit will continue to be organized under T/O 7-35 (2-17-42). Concurrently with the redesignation, 509th Prcht Inf is disbanded - per AG 322 (23 Nov 43) OB-I-GNGCT-M dated Nov. 25, 1943. (S) Assigned Fifth Army - per X #3 from Hq Fifth Army dt 12-10-43. (S)

509th Prcht Inf Bn reported in Italy - per station list NATO dated Nov. 11, 1943. (S)

509th Prcht Inf Bn participated in The Tunisian Campaign during the period 17 November 1942 to 13 May 1943 per Operations Report, Hq. North African Theater of Operations AG 200.6/263, P-O dated 23 December 1943. (S) Also see ltr, Hq NTOUSA, AG 200.6,

10 509th Prcht Inf Bn participated in the Algeria & French Morocco Campaign during the period 8 Nov 1942 to 11 Nov 1942 - per Operations Report, Hq. NATO dated 23 December 1943 as amended 17 Dec 1943 and 20 March 1944. (S) *

509th Prcht Inf Bn is cited for outstanding performance of duty in action on 29 February 1944 in Italy - per WD GO No 53 dated 29 June 1944

509th Prcht Inf Bn now in or enroute to France is relieved from assignment to 5th Army and assigned to ETO effective 1 Nov 44 - per AG 370.5/530 C-O from Hqs. NATO. USA. APO 534 dated 29 October 1944 (S).

509th Prcht Inf Bn will be disbanded at the earliest practicable date at ETO. Personnel rendered surplus by this action will be absorbed within the replacement system & reflected in future requisiteons - per AG 322 (29 Nov 44) OB-I-GNGCT-M dtd 1 Dec 44 (S)

509th Prcht Inf Bn has received battle participation awards for the North Africa, Tunisian, Naples-Foggia, Rome-Arno, Southern France and the German Campaigns - per GO #53 Hqs., 101st Airborne Div., APO 472 dated 14 December 1944 (S).

509th Prcht Inf Bn is relieved from assignment to Sixth Army Op. and assigned to the XVIII Corps (AB) effective 22 Nov 1944 - per Hqs., ETO, APO 887 dated 4 December 1944 (S).

509th Prcht Inf Bn is reported located in Belgium - per Change #2 to MDS #13, Hqs., ETO, APO 887 dated 6 January 1945 (S)

509th Prcht Inf Bn is reported located in France - per Change #6 to MDS #14, Hqs., ETO, APO 887 dated 24 January 1945 (S)

509th Prcht Inf Bn is reported located in Belgium - per Change #7 to MDS #14, Hqs., ETO, APO 887 dated 25 January 1945 (S).

509th Prcht Inf Bn is disbanded effective 1 March 1945 - per Radio from Hq. ETO, Paris, France dated 3 March 1945 CM-IN-4140 (4 Mar 45)(S) not filed.

* See ltr, Hq NTOUSA, AG 200.6, 10 Nov 44 (S).

509th Prcht Inf. Bn. is entitled to battle credits for participation in the NAPLES-FOGGIA CAMPAIGN, 9 Sep 43 to 21 Jan 44; ROME-ARNO CAMPAIGN, 22 Jan 44 to (Final date to be announced later). *

509th Prcht Inf. Bn is entitled to battle credits for participation in the SOUTHERN FRANCE CAMPAIGN, 15 Aug 44 to 14 Sep 44. See ltr, Hq NATOUSA, AG 200.6, 18 Oct 44 (S). Also MDC #37 dtd 16 October 1945.

509th Parachute Inf Regt, 2nd Bn. is designated by theater commander as having participated in an amphibious or airborne assault landing in North Africa (airborne 8 to 15 Nov 42 - per GO#70 from War Dept dated 30 Aug 45.

509th Parcht Inf Regt is entitled to battle credits for participation in the Ardennes Central 16 December 1944 to 5 January 1945 - per WD GO #114 dtd 7 December 1945.

Example 1b. Typical Army Organization Card, War Department Form used during 1941–1945.
(Reverse side)

The historical data section of the organizational card relates all authorizations for information posted on the front side. These sources included messages from commanding headquarters, general orders, movement orders, and station lists. Actual unit journals and historical reports were rarely consulted, as they were normally unavailable when the Adjutant General'a Office was composing the cards.

$\underline{S} \underline{E} \underline{C} \underline{R} \underline{E} \underline{T}$

CHECKED BY #4
HISTORICAL
SECTION

HEADQUARTERS
356th AAA SL Bn (Sem)   GHM/hsb
APO 709

31 March 1944

Subject: Historical Data.

To   : Commanding General, Headquarters USAFISPA, APO 502.
         (Thru: CG, 68th AAA Brigade).

1. Historical Data - 1 January 1944 to 31 March 1944.
    a. Original unit.
        (1). 504th CA (AA), 3rd Battalion.
        (2). 1 July 1942
        (3). Camp Hulen, Texas.
        (4). All members of organization transferred from other units.

    b. Changes in organization.
        (1). Reorganized 25 March 1944 under T/O 44-135 dated 28
              December 1943.

    c. Strength, commissioned and enlisted.
        (1). 1 January 1944.
              (a). Commissioned Officers   30
                    Enlisted Men   823
        (2). Net increase each month
              (a). January
                    Commissioned Officers   0
                    Enlisted Men   0
              (b). February
                    Commissioned Officers   0
                    Enlisted Men   0
              (c) *March
                    Commissioned Officers   1
                    Enlisted Men   81
        (3). Net decrease each month
              (a). January
                    Commissioned Officers   0
                    Enlisted Men   4
              (b). February
                    Commissioned Officers   1
                    Enlisted Men   12

- 1 -
$\underline{S} \underline{E} \underline{C} \underline{R} \underline{E} \underline{T}$

30 MAi 1944

1709-601

This sample has been declassified.

Example 2a. Typical Unit Historical Data Report during World War II
(Page One)

Periodic Unit Historical Data Reports were issued on a monthly, quarterly, or yearly basis by the unit historical officer and submitted through regular channels up the chain of command. They were also known as Unit After Action Reports.

S E C R E T

      (c). March
          Commissioned Officers   0
          Enlisted Men   0

d. Stations (permanent or temporary) of unit or parts thereof:
    (1). Date of arrival at each station.
        (a). None
    (2). Date of departure from each station.
        (a). None

e. Marches
    (1). None

f. Campaigns
    (1). None

g. Battles
    (1). None

h. Commanding Officer in important engagements.
    (1). None

i. Losses in action; Officers and Men.
    (1). None

j. Former and present members who have distinguished themselves
    in action.
    (1). None

k. Photographs of personnel, important news or events.
    (1). None.

    * 1 Officer and 90 Enlisted Men transferred this organization 1 March 1944
per paragraph 7, General Order Number 20, Headquarters 68th AAA Brigade, dated
20 February 1944. Designated as 1st Platoon, Battery C.

                      G. H. MUNDT
              Lt Col, 356th AAA SL Bn (Sem)
                      Commanding

- 2 -
S E C R E T

Example 2b. Typical Unit Historical Data Report during World War II
(Page Two)

While Periodic Unit Historical Data Reports varied greatly in quality and length, they represent the bulk of prepared historical documentation by units serving in World War II.

S E C R E T

Headquarters Alaska Defense Command
OFFICE OF THE COMMANDING GENERAL
Fort Richardson, Alaska.

```
:::::::::::::::::::::::
:    S E C R E T     :
:Auth: CG, ADC       :
:Initials            :
:Date: 4-17-42       :
:::::::::::::::::::::::
```

GENERAL ORDERS)
              :
NUMBER   34)

April 17, 1942

E X T R A C T

I. CONSTITUTION, ACTIVATION & REDESIGNATION OF COAST
ARTILLERY UNITS - A. A.

1. Having been constituted by WD Ltr. AG 320.2 (3-6-42) MR-M-C
dated March 8, 1942, the following elements of the 420th CA Bn. (Comp) (AA) are
activated in Alaska, effective 17 April, 1942, at present stations of units of
the 205th CA (AA):

Hq & Hq Btry; 1st and 2nd Platoons, Battery A;
Batteries B, C, D, E.

2. Personnel and equipment of the 205th CA (AA) are transferred to
elements of 420th CA Bn (Comp) (AA) as indicated in following tabulation:

FROM 205th CA (AA)	TO 420th CA Bn (Comp) (AA)	STATION
Det., Hq & Hq Btry.	Hq & Hq Btry.	Ft Raymond
1st Plat., Btry A	1st Plat., Btry A	Ft Raymond
2nd Plat., Btry A	2nd Plat., Btry A	Ft Raymond
Battery C	Battery C	Ft Raymond
Battery D	Battery B	Ft Ray
Battery E	Battery E	Ft Raymond
Battery H	Battery D	Ft Ray

3. Concurrently with activation of 420th CA. Bn (Comp) AA the units
of the 205th CA (AA) are transferred less personnel and equipment to permanent
station at Camp Haan, California.

4. Final and initial rosters, original and duplicate, on WD AGO
Form 309 with report of changes will be forwarded to Machine Records Unit, Ft.
Lewis, Washington.

5. Newly activated units retain present allottments grades and
ratings now authorized 205th CA (AA) under Ltr AG 221 (1-18-42) EA-A, Jan 21,
42 Subject: "Allottments Grades & Ratings and Auth Strength to Tactical Units
(less Air Corps and Services with Air Corps). T/O will be furnished upon receipt.

By command of Major General BUCKNER:

ELWYN D. POST,
Lieut. Colonel, General Staff Corps,
Chief of Staff.

OFFICIAL:

L. E. SCHICK,
Lt. Col., Adjutant General's Department,
Adjutant General.

DISTRIBUTION:
(See other side)

S E C R E T

Example 3. Typical Army General Orders

General Orders issued by higher echelon headquarters contain valuable information on units under their jurisdiction. In this instance, the authority for a newly created unit gives particulars regarding its assets, personnel, composition, and location.

~~C O N F I D E N T I A L~~

HEADQUARTERS FIFTH ARMY
A.P.O. #464,U.S. ARMY

3 December 1944

GENERAL ORDERS)
          :   E X T R A C T
NUMBER   180)

IV. <u>DISBANDMENT AND INACTIVATION OF CERTAIN AAA UNITS.</u>

    1. a. The following units are disbanded and/or inacitivated at the places shown, effective 9 December 1944, and the records thereof will be disposed of as outlined in MTOUSA Circular 79, cs.

Unit	Action	Place
Hq & Hq Btry, 4th AAA Gp	Disbanded	Vic. BARBERINO, Italy

    b. Personnel and equipment rendered surplus by above action will be utilized to the greatest extent practicable in the activation of Hq & Hq Co, 1168th Engr C Gp and the 337th and 409th Engr C Bns, respectively.

    2. a. No enlisted man will be reduced in grade as a result of this action.

    b. Personnel not utilized in the activation of units in par 1 b above, and who cannot be absorbed in other units under control of the Commanding General, Fifth Army, will be transferred to the 8th Replacement Depot.

    3. All equipment not utilized in the activation of units in par 1 b above, will be turned in to the appropriate Army Supply Service. Copies of signed "Tally-Ins" will be furnished to this headquarters.

    4. a. A final roster will be prepaird and forwarded by each unit in accordance with AR 345-900, as amended by Changes No. 4.

    b. The Appropriate data will be entered in the morning report of each unit in accordance with Section III, AR 345-400, as modified by letter Headquarters MTOUSA, AG 330.33/430 A-0, 26 September 1944, subject: "Morning Report".

    5. Authority: Letter Headquarters, MTOUSA, AG 322/088-0, 13 November 1944, Subject: "Activation, Inactivation, Disbandment and Reorganization of Units in the Mediterranean Theater of Operations".

INCL #2   C O N F I D E N T I A L

Example 4. Typical Extract of Army General Orders

During World War II, unit records often contained certified copies of extracts from higher headquarters General Orders, citing only that portion applicable to their own status. In this example, a unit was ordered disbanded and the locality, date, authority, and disposition are all covered in detail.

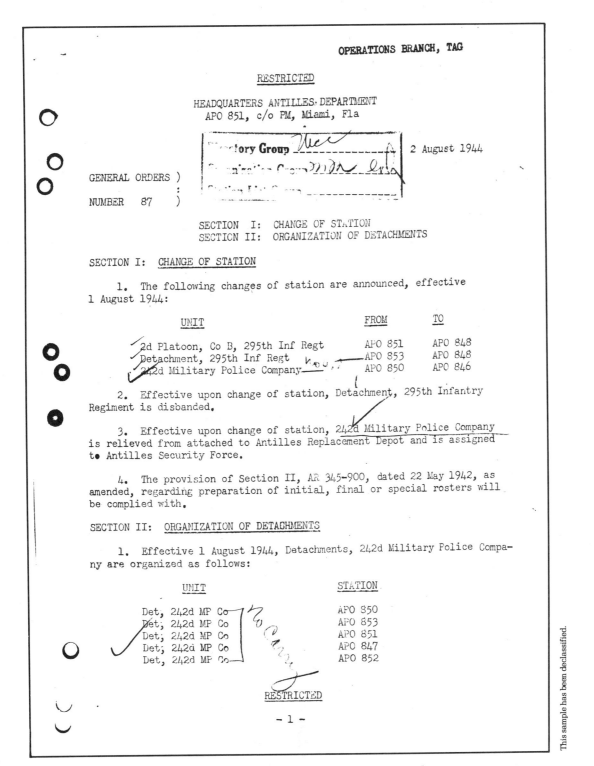

Example 5. Typical Command General Orders

This General Order contains both movement and organizational data but has cited Army Post Office (APO) addresses as a security precaution. While changes in station are ordered *effective* 1 August 1944, the actual move would have transpired either before or after that date.

In such a case, the researcher must reference APO location lists to track such movement. APO locations were mailing addresses representing close proximity rather than an absolute statement of unit physical location at that site. APOs were often highly mobile. However, in this instance Miami APO 853 was at Camp O'Reilly, Puerto Rico, from 21 July 1942 until 29 June 1946, while Miami APO 848 was only at Ponce Air Base, Puerto Rico. Chances are quite good that the APO in these orders actually correspond to the unit stations in these orders at the time.

612

R-E-S-T-R-I-C-T-E-D

3rd BN

CO

EXEC

Adjutant

S-2

S-3

MTO

HEADQUARTERS
371st Antiaircraft Artillery Searchlight Battalion

Portsmouth, Va.
May 24, 1943

GENERAL ORDERS)
NUMBER   1)

1. **Activation of the 371st AAA Searchlight Battalion.**—Pursuant to authority contained in GO #17 Hq AAAC, EDC, Fort Totten, N. Y. dated May 20, 1943, the activation of the 371st AAA Searchlight Battalion, in accordance with T/O 44-135, February 17, 1943, (less Battery C), as of May 24, 1943, with station at Portsmouth, Virginia, and assignment to the 48th CA Brigade (AA), Norfolk, Virginia, is announced.

2. **Assumption of Command.**—The undersigned hereby assumes command of the 371st AAA Searchlight Battalion.

3. **Appointment of Staff.**—The following appointments to the staff, this headquarters, are announced:

a. Executive Officer—MAJOR WILLIAM S HEATH 0341774, 371st AAA Searchlight Battalion.

b. Adjutant (S-1)—2ND LT LEONARD J WEINER 01049692, 371st AAA Searchlight Battalion.

c. Intelligence Officer (S-2)—1ST LT WILLIAM J RUPPEL 01041892, 371st AAA Searchlight Battalion.

d. Plans and Training Officer (S-3)—1ST LT CARL H RIETSCHEL 01042408, 371st AAA Searchlight Battalion.

e. Supply Officer (S-4)—WOJG LOUIS BOBROWSKY W2111548, 371st AAA Searchlight Battalion

4. **Redesignation of Units.**—By authority of above mentioned letter:

a. Headquarters and Headquarters Battery, Third Battalion 67th Coast Artillery Regiment (AA), is hereby redesignated Headquarters and Headquarters Battery, 371st AAA Searchlight Battalion.

b. Battery I, 67th Coast Artillery Regiment (AA), is hereby redesignated Battery A, 371st AAA Searchlight Battalion.

c. Battery K, 67th Coast Artillery Regiment (AA), is hereby redesignated Battery B, 371st AAA Searchlight Battalion.

d. 3rd Battalion 67th Coast Artillery Regiment (AA) Medical Section, is hereby redesignated 371st AAA Searchlight Battalion Medical Detachment.

R-E-S-T-R-I-C-T-E-D
- 1 -

This sample has been declassified.

Example 6. Typical Unit General Orders

Unit General Orders were issued in sequence by year and, in many cases, contain the most detailed available record of unit structure and other order of battle essentials.

```
                    C O N F I D E N T I A L

                         HEADQUARTERS                    AG
      CAMP HULEN ANTIAIRCRAFT ARTILLERY TRAINING CENTER
                        CAMP HULEN TEXAS
                                              3 November 1943
SPECIAL ORDERS)
            :            E X T R A C T
NUMBER    268 )         X           X              X

         1.   The 356th AAA SL Bn (Sem), (less Btry B), P by rail o/a
     5 Nov 43 to Cp Stoneman, Calif, for Shipment No. 5956-A. This is a
     PERMANENT change of station.

            1st Rail Serial:
               Train Comdr:  CAPT RALPH A GANNON 0297730 CAC
               Train QM   :  2nd Lt FRED A DAY 01046764  CAC

            2nd Rail Serial:
               Train Comdr:  CAPT TOM V BARRON 0409541  CAC
               Train QM   :  1ST LT MOORMAN E. GREEN 01049180 CAC

     The 356th AAA SL Bn (Sem), (less Btry B), is placed on a garrison rat
     status for the period of the journey and two-thirds of one rat plus
     25% for emergency purposes.  Train Quartermasters of each serial will
     make accounting of their stewardship and any ret of funds in connection
     with this travel to the QMC, Cp Stoneman, Calif.  TC will furnish nec
     rail T.  TDN FD 1-5200 P 433-01,02,03,04,05,07,08 A 0425-24. Auth: WD
     Ltr 6 Aug 43, file WD 370.5 (5 Aug 43) OB-S-E-M, subj: "Movement Orders,
     Shipment No. 5956" and 1st Ind Hq AAC, 7 Aug 43, file AAC 370.5/ KR-1-
     GNSTO (6 Aug 43 ) and TWX, Hq AA Comd, 30 Oct 43.

              X              X              S

         By command of Brigadier General ALLEN:


                                        R. H. KRAVEN,
                                        Major, AGD,
                                        Adjutant General.

     OFFICIAL:
              /s/ R H Kraven
              /t/ R. H. KRAVEN,
                  Major, AGD,
                  Adjutant General.
     DISTRIBUTION:
     CO, 356th Bn               100     Rail Trans Of, Cp Hulen, Tex   3
     CG, AA Comd                  3     CO, Cp Stoneman, Calif         3
     Finance Off, Cp Hulen, Tex   3
     CO, Cp Hulen, Tex            3

                    C O N F I D E N T I A L

     I certify that this is a true copy.
                                        R. M. SIMON
                                        1st Lt., 356th AAA SL Bn (Sem)
                                        Adjutant
```

Example 7. Typical Extract of Special Orders

Special Orders, such as these movement orders, contain valuable data pertinent to changes of station. This example is a certified extract issued to the unit which relayed authority, shipment assignment number, travel destination, and mode of transport (See also Example 8).

SECRET

IGF – It being impracticable for the Govt to furn cooking facilities for rat	TPC – Travel by privately owned conveyance is authorized if desired
TCT – The Transportation Corps will furn the necessary transportation	IMT – It has been determined impracticable for meals to be furn on meal tickets in this case
TDN – The Travel directed is necessary in the military service	WP – Will proceed

HEADQUARTERS
ANTIAIRCRAFT ARTILLERY TRAINING CENTER   /cgd
CAMP STEWART, GEORGIA.

February 15, 1943

SPECIAL ORDERS)
                    :   EXTRACT
NO.........46)

.Auth CG AAATC...
.Initials. ......
.Date.2.-15.-43

    1. Following orgns this sta WP by Rail T to Ft Dix, NJ to arrive on dates indicated. This movement constitutes a PERMANENT change of sta.

TO ARRIVE ON 21 FEB 1943
Hq and Hq Btry 106th AA AW Gp – 5698-O
360th CA SL Bn (AA) (less 1 SL Btry) 5698-S

TO ARRIVE ON 22 FEB 1943
637th CA Bn (AA)(AA)(H) – 5698-R
215th CA Bn (AA) – 5698-P
(Amended par. 7, S.O. 48 dated 17 Feb. 43

    The CO 106th AA AW Gp will advise the CO Ft Dix, NJ in advance as to the scheduled arrival time of the movement as prescribed in Sec II WD Cir 33 Jan 30, 1943.

    Field rat will be issued units to include last meal prior to departure. Garrison rat will furn the movements while enroute to destination for a period of two (2) days increased by fifty per cent (50%) as prescribed in Sec III Cir 415 WD 21 Dec 1942.

    Organizational and individual equipment will be taken as prescribed in Ltr WD AGO (File 370.5 (1-26-43) OB-S-E-M)Sub "Movement Orders, Shipment 5698" 27 Jan 1943.

    Freight sec of Shipment 5698-O-R-P will be shipped to the PORT TRANS O HR P of E Newport News, Va.

    Freight sec of Shipment 5698-S will be shipped to the PORT TRANS O NY P of E Brooklyn, NY.

    TCT TDN FD 33 P 433-01 02 03 04 65 07 08 A 0425-23.
(Auth: Ltr WD AGO (File WD 370.5 (1-26-43)OB-S-E-M) Sub "Movement orders, Shipment 5698" 27 Jan 1943 and Ltr Hq NYPE Brooklyn, NY (File SPTAA 370.5-OPP(TMO) Sub "Amendment No 1 to Movement Orders, Shipment 5698" 9 Feb 1943)

By Comd of Brig Gen METZGER:

B C KIRKAHAM
Capt AGD
Adj Gen

OFFICIAL:

B C KIRKAHI
Capt AGD
Adj Gen

SECRET

No. 4

Example 8. Typical Amendment of Special Orders

This amended Special Orders extract directs final movement to a Port of Embarkation, giving authority, destination and administrative details, and a new shipment assignment number. All orders were subject to further amendment, which require the researcher to carefully survey all files.

```
        S-E-C-R-E-T                    .ECRET Auth:  C.G.:
                                       :Guadalcanal Is Comd:
   I-M-M-E-D-I-A-T-E  A-C-T-I-O-N      :2 Feb. 45  9??? IBT:

            HEADQUARTERS
       GUADALCANAL ISLAND COMMAND           IBT:LGC:jls.
     c/o Postmaster, San Francisco
            California                    2 February 1945.


AG 400

SUBJECT:  Supplies for AVID - Shipping Order No. 311.

TO     :  Port Superintendent, Guadalcanal.

          In compliance with 290655, 300710 and 310404 January dispatches from
COMGENSOPACBACOM, it is desired that you load the following aboard the SS JAMES
B. BONHAM and SS SEA CAT:


     For 356th AAA Searchlight Battalion:
     (Chestnut Exchange)

          2 Officers
          20 Enlisted Men
                             (GA-9)
          General Cargo                 23722 cu.ft.     396.0 tons
          Vehicles                      28562 sq.ft.    1149.0 tons

     For 356th AAA Searchlight Battalion:
     (Call Above Orgn., thru Chestnut Exchange)

          27 Officers
          757 Enlisted Men
                             (GA-10)
          General Cargo                  9151 cu.ft.      91.1 tons
          Vehicles                        114 sq.ft.       2.5 tons

     For OSSO-CWS V-LLH783: (To be transhipped if necessary)
     (Call Lt. Biron, CWS, Port Section)

          360 bxs. Grenade, Smoke,
                   Colored.      (BO-19)   576 cu.ft.      10.5 tons


NOTE:  SS JAMES B. BONHAM, after completion above, will proceed to BRED
       for loading as indicated below, then to TRIM for further routing
       to AVID.  Vessel must arrive TRIM not later than 14 February 1945:

     To be loaded at BRED:

          For Hq & Hq Btry., 13th AAA Group:

               11 Officers
               54 Enlisted Men

               General Cargo            5302 cu.ft.      54.0 tons
               17 Vehicles (2 heavy lifts)  1291 sq.ft.   32.0 tons
                    S-E-C-R-E-T
                       - I -
```

Example 9. Typical Frontline Shipping Order

Unit movement data can also be found in field orders under shipping instructions. Details of vessels, loading particulars, and affected units are given in such instrument. However, coded destinations were often used as a security measure.

```
IG Form No. 10 (NYP/E, 3-13-43)
                 C O N F I D E N T I A L

              DATA SHEET  --  Non-Divisional Units

Staged at  CAMP SHANKS        Data as of    APRIL 43
                                          (date)
Shipment No.  6920 P          Units _____

Home Station CAMP STEWART, GA. Date of Arrival in SA  4 APRIL 43
                                                    (date)
Reference:
"Preparation for Overseas Movement", February 1, 1943 and amendments
thereto.  Paragraph numbers in parenthesis refer to this document.
If answer to question is "No", explain deficiencies in a correspond-
ing numbered and lettered paragraph under comments.
```

1. Personnel:
   a. Have deficiencies noted at home station been corrected?
      (par 16)   (Yes)   No
   b. Has personnel not to accompany unit been cleared?
      (par 16h (13)   (Yes)   No
   c. Have shortages in personnel been filled?(Par 16g(6) (Yes) No
2. Administrative:
   a. Has processing of all records been completed?
      (par 6e and 6f)   (Yes) No
   b. Has proper disposition been made of AWOLs records?
      (par 6e (6))   (Yes) No
   c. Have records to be shipped been packed?(Par 9a (2) (Yes) No
   d. Are service records prepared to accompany troops?
      (Par 6e (5)   (Yes) No
   e. (1) Has unit been paid to end of last month?   (Yes) No
      (2) Has unit received a partial payment for current
          month? PAYMENT   CONTEMPLATED   Yes (No)
   f. Are all men provided with pay cards?(Par 6e(7)(a) (Yes) No
   g. Are all matters relative to allotments, insurance,
      etc, completed? (par 6e)   (Yes) No
   h. Has all presonnel been informed of provisions of
      AW28? (Par 6a   (Yes) No
3. Supplies and Equipment:
   a. Have deficiencies noted at home station been
      corrected?(par 16)   (Yes) No
   b. Has "showdown" inspection been completed?
      (Par 16g (5)   (Yes) No
   c. Have all shortages been filled? (Par 16g(6)   (Yes) No
   d. Is unit equipped in accordance with T/BA or other
      proper table? (Par 16g(5)   (Yes) No
   e. Has all surplus property been turned in?
      (Par 16h (10)   (Yes) No
   f. Has "Final Status of Equipment Report" been
      completed? (Par 16g (8)   (Yes) No
   g. Are barrack bags properly marked? (Par 13a(1)   (Yes) No
   h. Have identifying markings been eliminated?
      (Par 5b (2)   (Yes) No
   i. Has unit equipment been properly packed and marked
      (Par 13)   (Yes) No
   j. Have combustibles been eliminated from individual
      baggage and unit equipment?   (Yes) No
                  C O N F I D E N T I A L
                          -1-

Example 10. Typical Port of Embarkation Checklist

Port inspection data sheets were used to check critical preparation requirements prior to overseas deployment. These are most useful for staging area arrivals and shipment assignment numbers. Note that in this case everything had been processed except the troops' pay, but that never delayed shipments.

U.S. SECRET EQUALS BRITISH MOST SECRET

SECRET

57

AP 443 RAS/jgw

HEADQUARTERS
NORTH AFRICAN THEATER OF OPERATIONS
UNITED STATES ARMY
APO 534

:::::::::::::::::::::
:   S E C R E T   :
: Auth: CG NATOUSA :
: Initials: *[illegible]* :
: 9 September 1944 :
:::::::::::::::::::::

AG 370.5/024 C-O

9 September 1944

SUBJECT: Attachment of Units.

TO   : General Officer Commanding, 52d Antiaircraft Brigade.

1. Effective 0001B hours, 10 September 1944, the following units are relieved from an operational antiaircraft role and from attachment to 52d Antiaircraft Brigade for operations.

> Hq & Hq Battery, 4th AAA Group
> 335th AAA Searchlight Battalion
> 354th AAA Searchlight Battalion
> 355th AAA Searchlight Battalion
> 360th AAA Searchlight Battalion

2. Concurrently with the above action the units listed will be concentrated
by battalions in the general vicinity of Foggia, Italy, and will commence rigor-
ous training as prescribed in our cable FX 90640, dated 1 September 1944. A
44 hour training week will be maintained.

By command of Lieutenant General DEVERS:

R. A. STUKEY,
1st Lt., AGD,
Asst Adjutant General.

DISTRIBUTION:

1 - G-1
3 - G-3
3 - G-4
3 - Tn(A)
10 - CG, SOS NATOUSA
5 - GOC, 52d AA Bde
2 - ea unit listed
2 - CG, AAF/MTO
2 - CG, PBS
2 - GOC, No. 2 District
1 - 60th MRU and 21st MRU
4 - AA & CD
4 - AG Personnel
2 - AG Stats
2 - AG Postal
2 - AG Records
1 - AG Org
1 - AG M & D

U.S. SECRET EQUALS BRITISH MOST SECRET SECRET

Example 11. Typical Theater of Operations Command Letter

Command letters directed such things as attachments and subordination of units. In this case it also directs a time frame for movement to a specific locality in Italy.

SECRET

Unit	Combat Experience		Specialized Training in NATO			Specialized Training in U.S. prior to arrival in NATO		REMARKS (See Below)
	Campaign	Approx. Dates	Type	Place	Dates	Type	Dates	
355th CA Slt Bn	None	None	Night Fighter Searchlight Defense System	Chateaudun du Rhumel, Algeria, N.A	28 March- 12 July 1943	Tactical defense of West Coast (Night Fighter Searchlight Defense.	1 May-21 December 1942	
			AA Harbor Defense	Bizerte- Ferryville Area, Tunisia, N.A.	19 August 1943 to present date.			

REMARKS.
The organization has not participated in a recognized campaign, but has undergone enemy bombing activity while in the Staging Area at Bizerte, North Africa, 13 July-19 August 1943. This organization engaged and illuminated enemy aircraft on the night of 6 September 1943, while in defense of the Bizerte-Ferryville harbor area.

Component parts of this command trained as batteries of the First Provisional Searchlight Battalion from August 1941 to May 1942. The First Provisional Searchlight Battalion was the first organization trained in the Night Fighter Searchlight System. On 1 May 1942, the 355th Coast Artillery Searchlight Battalion was formed. The training continued while the Battalion was in active defense of Los Angeles and San Diego, California. The organization was an integral part of the AA defense of the Air Bases near Telergma-Chateaudun du Rhumel, Algeria, North Africa, from 28 March to 12 July 1943. From 19 August to present date, the Battalion has continued its training, occupying positions in and around Bizerte and Ferryville, operating in the port defense of these areas, under the tactical command of the 52nd AA Brigade (Br.).

SECRET

Example 12. Typical Unit Training Report

Periodic Unit Training Reports can contain a wealth of historical data. This report records all movements of a coast artillery battalion, its previous history, as well as some stateside duty and combat operational details.

HV
3—7752

SECRET

WAR DEPARTMENT

THE ADJUTANT GENERAL'S OFFICE

WASHINGTON

AR/h1

IN REPLY
REFER TO   AG 320.2 (8-6-42)MR

~~August 6, 1942.~~

SECRET

Auth .... TAG........

Initials: RMC _____

Date: __AUG 6 1942_____

SUBJECT: Activation and Transfer of Unit.

To: Commanding Officer,
           57th Coast Artillery Regiment,
           APO 958,
              c/o Postmaster,
                San Francisco, Calif.

It is desired that the date of activation of the 3d Battalion, 57th Coast Artillery Regiment, authorized by letter AG 320.2 (1-7-41)M(Ret)M-C, dated January 13, 1941, and the dates of departure and arrival in connection with the movement of Battery G from HD of Chesapeake Bay, Va. to Camp Pendleton, Va., be reported to this office by indorsement hereon.

By order of the Secretary of War:

Adjutant General.

320.2 (8-6-42)   1st Ind.

HQ.57TH C.A., APO 957, October 5, 1942. TO: The Adjutant General, Washington, D.C.

In compliance with basic communication, following information is submitted:

a. The 3d Bn., 57th C.A. was activated effective June 15, 1941. (See cy GO #6, this Hq, 6-11-41)

b. Btry G 57th C.A. was activated at Camp Pendleton, Va. on April 12, 1941, pursuant to verbal orders of the C.G., HD of Chesapeake Bay. (See cy GO #4, this Hq., 4-12-41.)

c. The permanent station of the 57th C.A. was changed from Ft. Monroe, Va. to Camp Pendleton, Virginia Beach, Va., effective February 20, 1941. (See cy GO #5 Hq HD of CB, Ft. Monroe, Va., 2-18-41)

3 Incls:
#1-Cy GO #6, Hq 57th CA, 6-11-41 (in dup.)
#2-Cy GO #4, Hq 57th CA, 4-12-41 (in dup.)
#3-Cy GO #5, Hq HD of CB, 2-18-42 (in dup.)

BEN E. CORDELL,
Colonel, 57th C.A.,
Commanding

85 A G O
OCT 15 1942
Rec'd Back
OR-- -7

Hist. Sec.	
Org. Sec.	
Stat. Sec.	

SECRET

Example 13. Typical War Department Request for Information

War Department letters, filed by area and branch of service, were issued seeking precise information required at the Adjutant General level. These could provide details either missing in unit records or lost as a result of historical nonreporting.

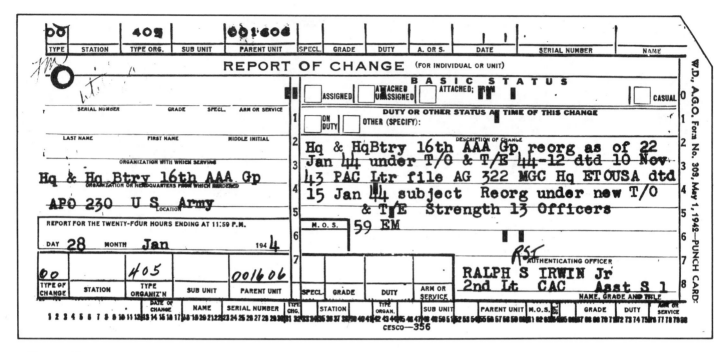

Front side

Reserve side

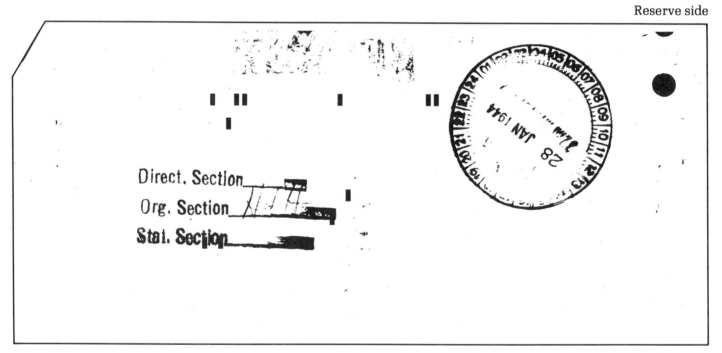

This sample has been declassified.

Example 14. Typical Report of Change Input Card of World War II

Report of Change cards were used to program Machine Records Unit compilations, and contain crucial historical information not always available in the resulting listings.

Addendum

Genealogy of Divisions of the U.S. Army in World War II

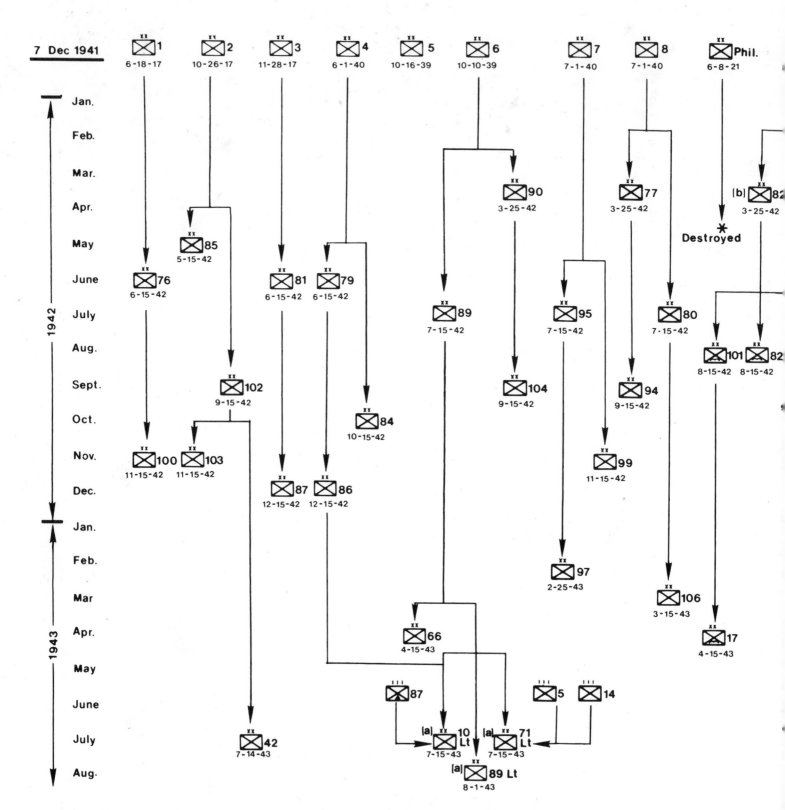

(a) The 10th Light Division was converted to the 10th Mountain Division 11-6-44, and the 71st and 89th Light Divisions were converted to Infantry Divisions on 5-26-44 and 6-15-44, respectively.

(b) The 82nd Infantry Division was split 8-15-42 and, with the addition of parachute elements, formed the 82nd and 101st Airborne Divisions.

(c) The 88th Infantry Division, plus parachute elements, formed the 17th Airborne Division.

(d) The 2nd Cavalry Division (white, except for the colored 4th Cavalry Brigade) was inactivated on 8-15-42, with the white troops being absorbed into the 83rd Infantry Division and 9th Armored Division. The 4th Cavalry Brigade became part of the 2nd Cavalry Division (Colored) on its activation 2-25-43.

(e) The 1st and 2nd Armored Division were formed from the 7th Cavalry Brigade; the 3rd and 4th Armored Divisions were formed from the 2nd and 1st Armored Divisions, respectively; and the 5th Armored Division was formed from the 4th Armored Division, all prior to 1942.

(f) These National Guard Divisions were mobilized 1940–1941, and thus directly inducted into federal service from their home states.

(g) Both 24th and 25th Infantry Divisions were formed from the assets of the Hawaiian Division which had been organized on 3-1-21.

Chart © Shelby L. Stanton